Short Story Criticism

Guide to Gale Literary Criticism Series

When you need to review criticism of literary works, these are the Gale series to use:

If the author's death date is:	You should turn to:
After Dec. 31, 1959 (or author is still living)	**Contemporary Literary Criticism** for example: Jorge Luis Borges, Anthony Burgess, William Faulkner, Mary Gordon, Ernest Hemingway, Iris Murdoch
1900 through 1959	**Twentieth-Century Literary Criticism** for example: Willa Cather, F. Scott Fitzgerald, Henry James, Mark Twain, Virginia Woolf
1800 through 1899	**Nineteenth-Century Literature Criticism** for example: Fedor Dostoevski, Nathaniel Hawthorne, George Sand, William Wordsworth
1400 through 1799	**Literature Criticism From 1400 to 1800** (excluding Shakespeare) for example: Anne Bradstreet, Daniel Defoe, Alexander Pope, Francois Rabelais, Jonathan Swift, Phillis Wheatley **Shakespearean Criticism** Shakespeare's plays and poetry
Antiquity through 1399	**Classical and Medieval Literature Criticism** for example: Dante, Homer, Plato, Sophocles, Vergil, the Beowulf Poet

Gale also publishes related criticism series:

Children's Literature Review

This series covers authors of all eras who have written for the preschool through high school audience.

Short Story Criticism

This series covers the major short fiction writers of all nationalities and periods of literary history.

ISSN 0895-9439

Volume 6

Short Story Criticism

Excerpts from Criticism of the
Works of Short Fiction Writers

Thomas Votteler
Editor

Shannon J. Young
Associate Editor

Gale Research Inc. • *DETROIT* • *NEW YORK* • *LONDON*

Since this page cannot legibly accommodate all the copyright
notices, the Acknowledgments constitute
an extension of the copyright page.

Copyright © 1990 Gale Research Inc.
835 Penobscot Bldg.
Detroit, MI 48226-4094

Library of Congress Catalog Card Number 88-641014
ISBN 0-8103-2555-1
ISSN 0895-9439

Printed in the United States of America

Published simultaneously in the United Kingdom
by Gale Research International Limited
(An affiliated company of Gale Research Inc.)

10 9 8 7 6 5 4 3 2

Contents

Preface

S*hort Story Criticism (SSC)* presents significant passages from criticism of the world's greatest short story writers and provides supplementary biographical and bibliographical materials to guide the interested reader to a greater understanding of the authors of short fiction. This series was developed in response to suggestions from librarians serving high school, college, and public library patrons, who had noted a considerable number of requests for critical material on short story writers. Although major short story writers are covered in such Gale literary criticism series as *Contemporary Literary Criticism (CLC), Twentieth-Century Literary Criticism (TCLC), Nineteenth-Century Literature Criticism (NCLC),* and *Literature Criticism from 1400 to 1800 (LC),* librarians perceived the need for a series devoted solely to writers of the short story genre.

Scope of the Work

SSC is designed to serve as an introduction to major short story writers of all eras and nationalities. For example, the present volume includes commentary on F. Scott Fitzgerald, who, while best known for his novel *The Great Gatsby,* also chronicled in his short fiction the prosperity, excess, and subsequent disillusionment of the Jazz Age; Hans Christian Andersen, nineteenth-century Danish author of countless beloved and classic fairy tales; and Edith Wharton, American novelist of manners, whose novella *Ethan Frome* is a standard text for students of American literature. Since these authors have inspired a great deal of relevant critical material, *SSC* is necessarily selective, and the editors have chosen the most important published criticism to aid readers and students in their research.

Ten to fifteen authors are included in each volume, and each entry presents a historical survey of the critical response to that author's work. The length of an entry is intended to reflect the amount of critical attention the author has received from critics writing in English and from foreign critics in translation. Critical articles and books that have not been translated into English are excluded. Every attempt has been made to identify and include excerpts from the most significant essays on each author's work. In order to provide these important critical pieces, the editors will sometimes reprint essays that have appeared in previous volumes of Gale's Literary Criticism Series. Such duplication, however, never exceeds twenty percent of an *SSC* volume.

Organization of the Book

An *SSC* author entry consists of the following elements:

- The **author heading** cites the author's full name, followed by birth and death dates. The unbracketed portion of the name denotes the form under which the author most commonly wrote. If the author wrote consistently under a pseudonym, the pseudonym will be listed in the author heading and the real name given in parentheses on the first line of the biographical and critical introduction.

- The **biographical and critical introduction** contains background information designed to introduce a reader to the author and the critical debates surrounding his or her work. Parenthetical material following the introduction provides references to other biographical and critical series published by Gale, including *CLC, TCLC, NCLC,* and *LC, Children's Literature Review, Contemporary Authors, Dictionary of Literary Biography,* and *Something about the Author.*

- A **portrait of the author** is included when available. Many entries also contain illustrations of materials pertinent to an author's career, including holographs of manuscript pages, title pages, dust jackets, letters, or representations of important people, places, and events in the author's life.

- The list of **principal works** is chronological by date of first publication and lists the most important works by the author. The first section comprises short story collections, novellas, and novella collections. The second section gives information on other major works by the author. For foreign authors, the editors have provided original foreign-language publication information and have selected what are considered the best and most complete English-language editions of their works.

- **Criticism** is arranged chronologically in each author entry to provide a useful perspective on changes in critical evaluation over the years. All short story, novella, and collection titles by the author featured in the entry are printed in boldface type to enable a reader to ascertain without difficulty the works discussed. Also for purposes of easier identification, the critic's name and the publication date of the essay are given at the beginning of each piece of criticism. Unsigned criticism is preceded by the title of the journal in which it appeared.

- Critical essays are prefaced with **explanatory notes** as an additional aid to students and readers using *SSC*. The explanatory notes provide several types of useful information, including: the reputation of a critic, the importance of a work of criticism, and the specific type of criticism (biographical, psychoanalytic, structuralist, etc.).

- A complete **bibliographical citation,** designed to help the interested reader locate the original essay or book, follows each piece of criticism.

- The **further reading list** appearing at the end of each author entry suggests additional materials on the author. In some cases it includes essays for which the editors could not obtain reprint rights.

New Features

Beginning with this volume, *SSC* contains two additional features designed to enhance the reader's understanding of short fiction writers and their works:

- Each *SSC* entry now includes, when available, **comments by the author** that illuminate his or her own works or the short story genre in general. These statements are set within boxes to distinguish them from the criticism.

- A **select bibliography of general sources on short fiction** is included as an appendix. Updated and amended with each new *SSC* volume, this listing of materials for further research provides readers with a selection of the best available general studies of the short story genre.

Other Features

A **cumulative author index** lists all the authors who have appeared in *SSC, CLC, TCLC, NCLC, LC,* and *Classical and Medieval Literature Criticism (CMLC),* as well as cross-references to the Gale series *Children's Literature Review, Authors in the News, Contemporary Authors, Contemporary Authors Autobiography Series, Dictionary of Literary Biography, Something about the Author, Something about the Author Autobiography Series,* and *Yesterday's Authors of Books for Children.* Users will welcome this cumulated index as a useful tool for locating an author within the Literary Criticism Series.

A **cumulative nationality index** lists all authors featured in *SSC* by nationality, followed by the number of the *SSC* volume in which their entry appears.

A **cumulative title index** lists in alphabetical order all short story, novella, and collection titles contained in the *SSC* series. Titles of short story collections, separately published novellas, and novella collections are printed in italics, while titles of individual short stories are printed in roman type with quotation marks. Each title is followed by the author's name and the corresponding volume and page numbers where commentary on the work may be located. English-language translations of original foreign-language titles are cross-referenced to the foreign titles so that all references to discussion of a work are combined in one listing.

A Note to the Reader

When writing papers, students who quote directly from any volume in the Literary Criticism Series may use the following general forms to footnote reprinted criticism. The first example pertains to material drawn from periodicals, the second to material reprinted from books:

[1]Henry James, Jr., "Honoré de Balzac," *The Galaxy* 20 (December 1875), 814-36; excerpted and reprinted in *Short Story Criticism,* Vol. 5, ed. Thomas Votteler (Detroit: Gale Research, 1990), pp. 8-11.

[2]F. R. Leavis, *D. H. Lawrence: Novelist* (Alfred A. Knopf, 1956); excerpted and reprinted in *Short Story Criticism,* Vol. 4, ed. Thomas Votteler (Detroit: Gale Research, 1990), pp. 202-06.

Suggestions Are Welcome

Readers who wish to suggest authors to appear in future volumes, or who have other suggestions, are invited to contact the editors, either by letter or by calling Gale's toll-free number: 1-800-347-GALE.

Acknowledgments

The editors wish to thank the copyright holders of the excerpted criticism included in this volume, the permissions managers of many book and magazine publishing companies for assisting us in securing reprint rights, and Anthony Bogucki for assistance with copyright research. We are also grateful to the staffs of the Detroit Public Library, the Library of Congress, the University of Detroit Library, Wayne State University Purdy/Kresge Library Complex, and the University of Michigan Libraries for making their resources available to us. Following is a list of the copyright holders who have granted us permission to reprint material in this volume of *SSC*. Every effort has been made to trace copyright, but if omissions have been made, please let us know.

COPYRIGHTED EXCERPTS IN *SSC*, VOLUME 6, WERE REPRINTED FROM THE FOLLOWING PERIODICALS:

American Literary Realism 1870-1910, v. 15, 1982. Copyright © 1982 by the Department of English, The University of Texas at Arlington. Reprinted by permission of the publisher. v. 21, Fall, 1988. Copyright © 1988 by McFarland & Company, Inc., Publishers, Jefferson, NC 28640. Reprinted by permission of the publisher.—*American Literature,* v. XXXIV, November, 1962. Copyright © 1962 Duke University Press, Durham, NC. Reprinted with permission of the publisher. v. 27, November, 1955. Copyright © 1955, renewed 1983, by Duke University Press, Durham, NC. Reprinted with permission of the publisher.—*American Quarterly,* v. XVI, Winter, 1964 for "The Art and Satire of Twain's 'Jumping Frog' Story" by Sidney J. Krause. Copyright 1964, American Studies Association. Reprinted by permission of the publisher and the author.—*Black American Literature Association,* v. 14, Fall, 1980 for "Old John in Harlem: The Urban Folktales of Langston Hughes" by Susan L. Blake; v. 15, Fall, 1981 for "Narrative Technique and Theory in 'The Ways of White Folks'" by David Michael Nifong. Copyright © 1980, 1981 Indiana State University. Both reprinted by permission of Indiana State University and the respective authors.—*Book World—The Washington Post,* October 22, 1972. © 1972, *The Washington Post.* Reprinted by permission of the publisher.—*The Canadian Review of American Studies,* v. VIII, Fall, 1977. © Canadian Review of American Studies 1977. Reprinted by permission of the publisher.—*CLA Journal,* v. XI, September, 1967; v. XI, June, 1968; v. XXVII, March, 1984. Copyright, 1967, 1968, 1984 by The College Language Association. All used by permission of The College Language Association.—*Colby Library Journal,* Series IX, December, 1971; Series XVII, March, 1981; Series XVIII, 1982. All reprinted by permission of the publisher.—*College English,* v. 25, November, 1963 for "Fitzgerald's 'Babylon Revisited'" by Seymour L. Gross. Copyright © 1963 by the National Council of Teachers of English. Reprinted by permission of the publisher and the author.—*Counterpoint,* 1964. Copyright 1964 by Rand McNally.—*Criticism,* v. XII, Spring, 1970 for "Edith Wharton's Ghost Stories" by Margaret B. McDowell. Copyright, 1970, Wayne State University Press. Reprinted by permission of the publisher and the author.—*The Denver Quarterly,* v. 17, Winter, 1983. Copyright © 1983 by the University of Denver. Reprinted by permission of the publisher.—*Early American Literature,* v. IX, Winter, 1975 for "A Modern Version of Edward Taylor" by Karl Keller. Copyrighted, 1975, by the University of Massachusetts. Reprinted by permission of the publisher and the author.—*Eire-Ireland,* v. XVIII, Spring, 1983 for "The Sage Who Deep in Central Nature Delves: Liam O'Flaherty's Short Stories" by Richard J. Thompson; v. XXIII, Summer, 1988 for "Introduction to the Present State of Criticism of Liam O'Flaherty's Collection of Short Stories: 'Dúil'" by William Daniels. Copyright © 1983, 1988 Irish American Cultural Institute, 2115 Summit Ave., No. 5026, St. Paul, MN 55105. Both reprinted by permission of the publisher and the respective authors.—*English Journal,* v. XXIV, October, 1935 for "Mark the Double Twain" by Theodore Dreiser. Copyright 1935 by the author. Reprinted by permission of The Dreiser Trust.—*English Literature in Transition: 1880-1920,* v. 30, 1987 for "'A Story of the Days to Come' and 'News from Nowhere': H. G. Wells as a Writer of Anti-Utopian Fiction" by Robert M. Philmus. Copyright © 1987 *English Literature in Transition, 1880-1920.* Reprinted by permission of the publisher.—*English Studies,* Netherlands, v. 55, October, 1974.© 1974 by Swets & Zeitlinger B.V. Reprinted by permission of the publisher.—*ESQ,* v. 19, 4th Quarter, 1973. Reprinted by permission of the publisher.—*Extrapolation,* v. 18, May, 1977. Copyright 1977 by Thomas D. and Alice S. Clareson. Reprinted by permission of the publisher.—*The Explicator,* v. 45, Winter, 1987; v. 46, Winter, 1988. Copyright 1987, 1988 by Helen Dwight Reid Educational Foundation. Both reprinted by permission of the Helen Dwight Reid Educational Foundation, published by Heldref Publications, 4000 Albemarle Street, N.W., Washington, DC 20016.—*Fitzgerald/Hemingway Annual: 1973,* 1974 for "Pat Hobby: Anti-Hero" by Thomas E. Daniels; 1974 for "Guilt and Retribution in 'Babylon Revisited'" by David Toor. Copyright © 1974 by Gale Research Inc. Both reprinted by permission of the respective authors.—*Freedomways,* v. 8, Spring, 1968. Copyright © 1968 by Freedomways Associates, Inc. Reprinted by permission of the *Freedomways.*—*The Hudson Review,* v. XXX, Spring, 1977. Copyright © 1977 by The Hudson Review, Inc. Reprinted by permission of the publisher.—*Illinois Quarterly,* v. 40, Spring, 1978 for "Appearance and Reality in Mark Twain's 'Which Was the Dream?', 'The Great Dark', and 'Which Was It?'" by Richard Tuerk. Copyright, Illinois State University, 1978. Reprinted by permission of the publisher and the author.—*The International Fiction Review,* v. 14, Winter, 1987. © copyright 1987 International Fiction Association. Reprinted by permission of the publisher.—*The Journal of Narrative Technique,* v. 17, Winter, 1987. Copyright© 1987 by *The Journal of Narrative Technique.* Reprinted by permission of the publisher.—*Kansas*

COPYRIGHTED EXCERPTS IN *SSC,* VOLUME 6, WERE REPRINTED FROM THE FOLLOWING BOOKS:

Authors to Be Featured in *SSC*, Volumes 7 and 8

Raymond Carver, 1938-1988. (American short story writer, poet, and editor)—Credited with helping to revive the popularity of short stories in the United States, Carver wrote minimalistic tales that often focus on working-class protagonists struggling to survive outside mainstream society. Collected in such books as *Will You Please Be Quiet, Please, What We Talk about When We Talk about Love, Cathedral,* and *Where I'm Calling From*, Carver's realistic stories are frequently infused with elements drawn from his own difficult life.

Stephen Crane, 1871-1900. (American novelist, short story writer, poet, and journalist)—Crane was one of America's foremost realistic writers whose works mark the beginning of modern American Naturalism. Although he is perhaps best remembered for his Civil War novel *The Red Badge of Courage,* Crane's often-anthologized short stories "The Open Boat," "The Blue Hotel," and "The Bride Comes to Yellow Sky" are considered among the most skillfully crafted stories in American literature.

Isak Dinesen, 1885-1962. (Danish short story writer, autobiographer, novelist, and translator)—One of Denmark's most widely acclaimed modern writers, Dinesen is perhaps best known for her novel *Out of Africa,* and for her short fiction collections *Seven Gothic Tales* and *Winter's Tales.*

Hermann Hesse, 1877-1962. (German novelist, short story writer, poet, and essayist)—Internationally revered for his novels *Demian, Steppenwolf,* and *Siddhartha,* Hesse also wrote a considerable body of short fiction, much of which has been collected in his *Stories of Five Decades.*

Henry James, 1843-1916. (American novelist, short story writer, essayist, biographer, autobiographer, and dramatist)—James is considered one of the greatest novelists in the English language for, among other reasons, his development of the point of view technique and his leadership in the advancement of realism in American literature. In his stories and novellas, including "The Beast in the Jungle," *The Aspern Papers*, "The Lesson of the Master," and *The Turn of the Screw*, James successfully applies techniques and explores themes similar to those of his longer fiction.

Katherine Mansfield, 1888-1923. (New Zealand short story writer, critic, and poet)—During her brief career, Mansfield helped shape the modern short story form with her poetic, highly descriptive tales that emphasize mood over plot. Although she lived in London for most of her adult life, such acclaimed stories as "Prelude" and "A Doll's House" are set in her native New Zealand and evoke vivid images of her childhood.

Grace Paley, b. 1922. (American short story writer and essayist)—Critically acclaimed for her fiction collections *The Little Disturbances of Man, Enormous Changes at the Last Minute,* and *Later the Same Day*, Paley creates seriocomic stories noted for their authentic portrayals of working-class New Yorkers.

Virginia Woolf, 1882-1941. (English novelist, critic, essayist, short story writer, diarist, and biographer)—Best known for her stream-of-consciousness novels *Mrs. Dalloway* and *To the Lighthouse,* Woolf also published several collections of short stories, including *The Mark on the Wall, Monday or Tuesday,* and *The Haunted House, and Other Stories*. In these works, as in her novels, Woolf experiments with narrative perspectives and perceptions of reality.

Additional Authors to Appear in Future Volumes

Agnon, Shmuel Yosef
  1888-1970
Aiken, Conrad 1889-1973
Aldiss, Brian 1925-
Aleichem, Sholom 1859-1916
Asimov, Isaac 1920-
Atherton, Gertrude 1857-1948
Babel, Isaac 1894-1941?
Baldwin, James 1924-1987
Barth, John 1930-
Beattie, Ann 1947-
Beerbohm, Max 1872-1956
Bellow, Saul 1915-
Benét, Stephen Vincent
  1898-1943
Bierce, Ambrose 1842-1914?
Boccaccio, Giovanni 1313?-1375
Böll, Heinrich 1917-1985
Brentano, Clemens 1778-1842
Caldwell, Erskine 1903-
Calisher, Hortense 1911-
Camus, Albert 1913-1960
Carter, Angela 1940-
Carver, Raymond 1938-1988
Cassill, R. V. 1919-
Cervantes 1547-1616
Chandler, Raymond 1888-1959
Chaucer, Geoffrey 1345-1400
Chopin, Kate 1851-1904
Conrad, Joseph 1857-1924
Coover, Robert 1932-
Cortázar, Julio 1914-1984
Crane, Stephen 1871-1900
Dahl, Roald 1916-
Dante Alighieri 1265-1321
Davenport, Guy 1927-
de la Mare, Walter 1873-1956
Dick, Philip K. 1928-1982
Disch, Thomas M. 1940-
Doyle, Arthur Conan 1859-1930
Elkin, Stanley 1930-
Ellison, Harlan 1934-

Fast, Howard 1914-
Flaubert, Gustave 1821-1880
Forster, E. M. 1879-1970
France, Anatole (ps. of Anatole-
  François Thibault) 1844-1924
Friedman, Bruce J. 1930-
Gaines, Ernest J. 1933-
Galsworthy, John 1867-1933
García-Márquez, Gabriel 1928-
Gardner, John 1933-1982
Garland, Hamlin 1860-1940
Gass, William H. 1924-
Gide, André 1869-1951
Gilchrist, Ellen 1935-
Golding, William 1911-
Gordimer, Nadine 1923-
Gordon, Caroline 1895-1981
Grau, Shirley Ann 1929-
Greene, Graham 1904-
Grimm, Jakob Ludwig
  1785-1863
Grimm, Wilhelm Karl
  1786-1859
Hammett, Dashiell 1894-1961
Harris, Joel Chandler
  1848-1908
Harte, Bret 1836-1902
Heinlein, Robert A. 1907-
Hoffmann, E. T. A. 1776-1822
Jackson, Shirley 1919-1965
James, Henry 1843-1916
James, M. R. 1862-1936
Jhabvala, Ruth Prawer 1927-
King, Stephen 1947-
Knowles, John 1926-1979
Lardner, Ring 1885-1933
Laurence, Margaret 1926-1987
LeFanu, Joseph Sheridan
  1814-1873
LeGuin, Ursula K. 1929-
Machado de Assis, Joaquim
  Maria 1839-1908

Malamud, Bernard 1914-1986
Mansfield, Katherine 1888-1923
Masters, Edgar Lee 1869?-1950
McCullers, Carson 1917-1967
Maugham, W. Somerset
  1874-1965
Mérimée, Prosper 1803-1870
O'Brien, Edna 1936-
O'Faolain, Sean 1900-
Olsen, Tillie 1913-
Ozick, Cynthia 1928-
Pasternak, Boris 1890-1960
Pavese, Cesare 1908-1950
Perelman, S. J. 1904-1976
Pritchett, V. S. 1900-
Robbe-Grillet, Alain 1922-
Roth, Philip 1933-
Saki (ps. of H. H. Munro)
  1870-1916
Saroyan, William 1908-1981
Schwartz, Delmore 1913-1966
Scott, Sir Walter 1771-1832
Solzhenitsyn, Alexander 1918-
Spark, Muriel 1918-
Stafford, Jean 1915-1979
Stead, Christina 1902-1983
Stein, Gertrude 1874-1946
Steinbeck, John 1902-1983
Stevenson, Robert Louis
  1850-1894
Sturgeon, Theodore 1918-1985
Tagore, Rabindranath
  1861-1941
Taylor, Peter 1917-
Thackeray, William Makepeace
  1811-1863
Tolstoy, Leo 1828-1910
Turgenev, Ivan 1818-1883
Updike, John 1932-
Vonnegut, Kurt, Jr. 1922-
West, Nathanael 1904-1940
White, E. B. 1899-1986
Zola, Émile 1840-1902

Hans Christian Andersen

1805-1875

(Also wrote under the pseudonym Villiam Christian Walter.) Danish fairy tale writer, poet, short story writer, novelist, travel writer, autobiographer, and dramatist.

Andersen is perhaps the foremost writer of fairy tales in world literature. Known for such stories as "The Little Mermaid," "The Steadfast Tin Soldier," and "The Ugly Duckling," he expanded the scope of the fairy tale genre by creating original stories drawn from a wealth of folklore and personal experience that reveal his boundless imagination. Andersen utilized the simple premise and structure of the fairy tale to transform his ideas about human nature into allegories that are written in a conversational language children can understand and enjoy. "I seize an idea for older people," he wrote, "and then tell it to the young ones, while remembering that father and mother are listening and must have something to think about." Many critics believe that Andersen's genius lay in his ability to see nature, events, people, and objects with childlike curiosity and imagination, and to infuse his subjects with traits never before attributed to them. His plants and animals, for example, represent innocence and simplicity, while such inanimate objects as the red shoes from "The Red Shoes," become symbols of greed, pride, and envy. A master craftsman, Andersen has created a body of literature that continues to be loved by readers of all ages throughout the world.

Andersen's childhood experiences greatly influenced his literary perspective and are reflected in his fairy tales. He was born in Odense, Denmark, to a poor shoemaker and his superstitious, uneducated wife. His father, a religious man who had hoped for a more fulfilling career, encouraged his son to aspire to a better life by telling him glamorous stories about the theater and opera and by sending him to school at an early age. The elder Andersen also encouraged his son's vivid imagination; he read to the boy from the comedies of Ludvig Holberg, *The Arabian Nights,* and the fairy tales of Jean de La Fontaine, and built him a puppet theater. Andersen was a shy child, and instead of playing with other children, he wrote puppet dramas and designed costumes for his characters. In 1819, three years after his father's death, Andersen moved to Copenhagen to pursue an acting career. As a young boy without references, he was denied admittance to the Royal Theater and was rejected by Copenhagen's opera company. However, Jonas Collin, a director of the Royal Theater, was impressed by the promise Andersen showed as a writer. Collin took Andersen into his home, sent him to grammar school, and supported him until he passed the entrance exams to the University of Copenhagen. He was Andersen's confidant, critic, and friend, and Andersen remained closely connected with the Collin family throughout his life.

Andersen's initial works were inspired by William Shakespeare and Sir Walter Scott; his pseudonym at that time, Villiam Christian Walter, was adopted in homage to the two writers. Although his first works were virtually ignored, Andersen won recognition in 1829 for *Fodreise fra Holmens Canal til østpynten af Amager i aarene,* the chronicle of an imaginary journey through Copenhagen. He traveled to Ger-

many in 1831 and then to Italy in 1833. During his stay in Italy, Andersen began his *Eventyr, fortalte for børn* (*Fairy Tales Told for Children*), tales that would later be recognized as among his most significant works. By 1835, when his *Eventyr,* or "Wonder Stories," was published, Andersen was well-known in Denmark for his travel books, plays, and a novel, *Improvisatoren* (*The Improvisatore: or, Life in Italy*). Early critical reception of *Eventyr* was generally negative, and at first, Andersen agreed with his detractors, calling his tales *smaating,* or trifles. However, he soon realized that these short works were the perfect outlet for his messages to the world and continued to write stories in this vein. Andersen also discovered that his tales commanded his greatest audience and could bring him the international fame he craved. His popularity increased in Europe and America, and he traveled extensively throughout Germany, Holland, and England. Andersen was unpopular in Denmark, however, and it was not until his health began to fail that he was acknowledged by his native country as its most universally popular and prominent author.

Andersen's fairy tales fall into two general categories: twelve adaptations of traditional Danish folktales and one hundred forty-four original creations. In his adaptations, Andersen frequently integrated plots from more than one source. "The

Tinder Box," for example, is based on a combination of an old Danish tale, "The Spirit of the Candle," and an episode from the *Arabian Nights*. Andersen himself divided his original tales into two distinct classes: *eventyr* and *historier*. The *eventyr* are fairy tales in which a supernatural element contributes to the outcome of the narrative. "The Little Mermaid," for example, is set in a kingdom beneath the sea and tells the story of a mermaid who drinks a magical potion brewed by a sea-witch in hopes that she will be metamorphosed into a human. Andersen's *historier* are stories that do not employ a supernatural element. Frequently, the *historier* starkly portray poverty and suffering, leaving readers disturbed when good is not necessarily rewarded at a story's conclusion. The *historier* also often reveal their author's strongly moralistic and religious attitudes: Andersen had a childlike faith in God and perceived death as a reward for a difficult life. This perception is perhaps most vividly portrayed in "The Little Match Girl," a grim story in which an impoverished child dies from exposure on Christmas Eve when no one will buy her matches. The child is finally freed from her suffering when her deceased grandmother arrives to lead her to heaven. Although many of Andersen's *historier* and fairy tales end unhappily, most critics concur that his underlying attitude in his stories is positive. Andersen often offers an optimistic approach to otherwise distressing situations and invests many of his tales with a mischievous sense of humor. Of all his stories, Andersen's semi-autobiographical sketches are considered his most enduring. Stories like "The Little Mermaid," "The Nightingale," and "The Steadfast Tin Soldier" reflect in part Andersen's own unrequited love affairs in varying degrees of melancholy and satire. "The Ugly Duckling," the story of a homely cygnet who becomes the most beautiful of all swans, is probably Andersen's best-loved and most popular work of this type. Just as the snubbed cygnet becomes a beautiful swan, so Andersen became the pride of Denmark and its international literary representative.

In general, Andersen's works have been consistently well received. Georg Brandes, one of the first prominent critics to recognize Andersen's literary significance, especially commended Andersen's use of conversational language, which he claimed distinguished the author from other children's writers and prevented his stories from becoming outdated. Later, such Danish critics as Elias Bredsdorff and Erik Haugaard praised the uncluttered structure of Andersen's tales. Some twentieth-century commentators have considered Andersen's work maudlin and overly disturbing for small children. Nevertheless, he is usually recognized as a consummate story teller who distilled his vision of humanity into a simple format that has proved universally popular. His fairy tales remain the enduring favorites of children and adults throughout the world. Edmund Gosse wrote, "It will probably be centuries before Europe sees again a man in whom the same qualities of imagination are blended."

(For further information on Andersen's life and career, see *Nineteenth-Century Literature Criticism*, Vol. 7; *Children's Literature Review*, Vol. 6; and *Yesterday's Authors of Books for Children*, Vol. 1.)

PRINCIPAL WORKS

SHORT FICTION

Eventyr, fortalte for børn. 2 vols.   1835-44
   [*Fairy Tales Told for Children*, 1845]

Billedbog uden billeder   1840
   [*A Picture-Book without Pictures*, 1847]
En digters bazar   (poetry, short stories, and travel essays)
   1842
   [*A Poet's Bazaar*, 1846]
Samlede voerker. 15 vols.   (fairy tales, short stories, travel essays, novels, and poetry)   1876-80
Eventyr og historier. 5 vols.   1894-1900
The Complete Andersen. 6 vols.   1942-48
Hans Christian Andersen's Fairy Tales   1950

OTHER MAJOR WORKS

Ungdoms-Forsøg [as Villiam Christian Walter]   (novel)
   1822
Fodreise fra Holmens Canal til østpynten af Amager i aarene 1828 og 1829   (travel sketch)   1829
Improvisatoren   (novel)   1835
   [*The Improvisatore: or, Life in Italy*, 1845]
Kun en spillemand   (novel)   1837
   [*Only a Fiddler!*, 1845]
De to baronesser   (novel)   1838
   [*The Two Baronesses*, 1848]
Mulatten [from a story by Fanny Reybaud]   (drama)   1840
I Sverrig   (travel sketches)   1851
   [*Pictures of Sweden*, 1851]
At voere eller ikker voere   (novel)   1857
   [*To Be or Not To Be*, 1857]
Mit livs eventyr   (autobiography)   1859
   [*The Story of My Life*, 1871]
I Spanien   (travel sketches)   1863
   [*In Spain*, 1864]
Lykke-Peer   (novel)   1870
   [*Lucky Peer*, 1871]

GEORG BRANDES   (essay date 1869)

[*An esteemed Danish literary critic and biographer, Brandes was the first prominent scholar to write extensively on Andersen. According to Elias Bredsdorff, Brandes was "the first scholar altogether who realised that Andersen's tales gave him an important and unique place in world literature and who saw that the tales themselves merited serious critical discussion." In the following excerpt from an essay that is recognized as significant in Andersen scholarship, Brandes favorably assesses Andersen's tales, admiring in particular his ability to write as a child might think and speak.*]

To replace the accepted written language with the free, unrestrained language of familiar conversation, to exchange the more rigid form of expression of grown people for such as a child uses and understands, becomes the true goal of the author as soon as he embraces the resolution to tell nursery stories for children. He has the bold intention to employ oral speech in a printed work, he will not write but speak, and he will gladly write as a school-child writes, if he can thus avoid speaking as a book speaks. The written word is poor and insufficient, the oral has a host of allies in the expression of the mouth that imitates the object to which the discourse relates, in the movement of the hand that describes it, in the length or shortness of the tone of the voice, in its sharp or gentle, grave or droll character, in the entire play of the features, and in the whole bearing. The nearer to a state of nature the being addressed, the greater aids to comprehension are these auxiliaries. Whoever tells a story to a child, involuntarily accompanies the narrative with many gestures and grimaces, for the child sees the story quite as much as it hears it, paying heed, almost in the same way as the dog, rather to the tender or irritated intonation, than to whether the words express friendliness or wrath. Whoever, therefore, addresses himself in writing to a child must have at his command the changeful cadence, the sudden pauses, the descriptive gesticulations, the awe-inspiring mien, the smile which betrays the happy turn of affairs, the jest, the caress, and the appeal to rouse the flagging attention—all these he must endeavor to weave into his diction, and as he cannot directly sing, paint, or dance the occurrences to the child, he must imprison within his prose the song, the picture, and the pantomimic movements, that they may lie there like forces in bonds, and rise up in their might as soon as the book is opened. In the first place, no circumlocution; everything must be spoken fresh from the lips of the narrator, aye, more than spoken, growled, buzzed, and blown as from a trumpet: "There came a soldier marching along the high-road—*one, two! one, two!*" "And the carved trumpeters blew, 'Trateratra! there is the little boy! Trateratra!'"— "Listen how it is drumming on the burdock-leaves, 'rum-dum-dum! rum-dum-dum!' said the Father Snail." At one time he begins, as in **"The Daisy,"** with a "Now you shall hear!" which at once arrests the attention; and again he jests after the fashion of a child: "So the soldier cut the witch's head off. There she lay!" We can hear the laughter of the child that follows this brief, not very sympathetic, yet extremely clear presentation of the destruction of an imposter. Often he breaks into a sentimental tone, as for instance: "The sun shone on the Flax, and the rainclouds moistened it, and this was just as good for it as it is for little children when they are washed, and afterward get a kiss from their mother; they became much prettier, and so did the Flax." That at this passage a pause should be made in the narrative, in order to give the child the kiss mentioned in the text, is something to which every mother will agree, and which seems to be a matter of course; the kiss is really given in the book. This regard for the young reader may be carried still farther, inasmuch as the poet, by virtue of his ready sympathy, so wholly identifies himself with the child and enters so fully into the sphere of its conceptions, into its mode of contemplation, indeed, into the range of its purely bodily vision, that a sentence like the following may readily flow from his pen: "The biggest leaf here in the country is certainly the burdock-leaf. Put one in front of your waist, and it is just like an apron, and if you lay it upon your head, it is almost as good as an umbrella, for it is quite remarkably large." These are words which a child, and every child, can understand.

Happy, indeed, is Andersen! What author has such a public as he? What is, in comparison, the success of a man of science, especially of one who writes within a limited territory for a public that neither reads nor values him, and who is read by four or five—rivals and opponents! A poet is, generally speaking, more favorably situated; but although it is a piece of good fortune to be read by men, and although it is an enviable lot to know that the leaves of our books are turned by dainty fingers which have employed silken threads as bookmarks, nevertheless no one can boast of so fresh and eager a circle of readers as Andersen is sure of finding. His stories are numbered among the books which we have deciphered syllable by syllable, and which we still read to-day. There are some among them whose letters even now, seem to us larger, whose words appear to have more value than all others, because we first made their acquaintance letter by letter and word by

word. And what a delight it must have been for Andersen to see in his dreams this swarm of children's faces by the thousands about his lamp, this throng of blooming, rosy-cheeked little curly-pates, as in the clouds of a Catholic altar-piece, flaxen-haired Danish boys, tender English babies, black-eyed Hindoo maidens,—rich and poor, spelling, reading, listening, in all lands, in all tongues, now healthy and merry, weary from sport, now sickly, pale, with transparent skin, after one of the numberless illnesses with which the children of this earth are visited,—and to see them eagerly stretch forth this confusion of white and swarthy little hands after each new leaf that is ready! Such devout believers, such an attentive, such an indefatigable public, none other has. None other either has such a reverend one, for even old age is not so reverend and sacred as childhood. (pp. 2-5)

[It] is only needful to study the imagination of the audience, in order to become acquainted with that of the author. The starting-point for this art is the child's play that makes everything out of everything; in conformity with this, the sportive mood of the artist transforms playthings into natural creations, into supernatural beings, into heroes, and, *vice versa,* uses everything natural and everything supernatural—heroes, sprites, and fairies—for playthings, that is to say, for artistic means which through each artistic combination are remodelled and freshly stamped. The nerve and sinew of the art is the imagination of the child, which invests everything with a soul, and endows everything with personality; thus, a piece of household furniture is as readily animated with life as a plant, a flower as well as a bird or a cat, and the animal in the same manner as the doll, the portrait, the cloud, the sunbeam, the wind, and the seasons. Even the leap-frog, made of the breastbone of a goose, becomes thus for the child a living whole, a thinking being endowed with a will. The prototype of such poesy is the dream of a child, in which the childish conceptions shift more rapidly and with still bolder transformations than in play; therefore, the poet (as in **"Little Ida's Flowers," "Ole Shut Eye," "Little Tuk," "The Elder-Tree Mother"**) likes to seek refuge in dreams as in an arsenal; therefore, it is, when he busies his fancy with childish dreams, such as fill and trouble the mind of childhood, there often come to his his wittiest inspirations, as, for instance, when little Hjalmar hears in his dream the lamentation of the crooked letters that had tumbled down in his copy-book: " 'See, this is how you should hold yourselves,' said the Copy. 'Look, sloping in this way, with a powerful swing!' 'Oh, we should be very glad to do that,' replied Hjalmar's letters, 'but we cannot; we are too weakly.' 'Then you must take medicine,' said Ole Shut Eye. 'Oh no,' cried they; and they immediately stood up so gracefully that it was beautiful to behold." This is the way a child dreams, and this is the way a poet depicts to us the dream of a child. The soul of this poetry, however, is neither the dream nor the play; it is a peculiar, ever-childlike, yet at the same time a more than childlike faculty, not only for putting one thing in the place of another (thus, for making constant exchange, or for causing one thing to live in another, thus for animating all things), but also a faculty for being swiftly and readily reminded by one thing of another, for regaining one thing in another, for generalizing, for moulding an image into a symbol, for exalting a dream into a myth, and through an artistic process, for transforming single fictitious traits into a focus for the whole of life. Such a fancy does not penetrate far into the innermost recesses of things; it occupies itself with trifles; it sees ugly faults, not great ones; it strikes, but not deeply; it wounds, but not dangerously; it flutters around like a winged butterfly from spot to spot, lingering about the most dissimilar places, and, like a wise insect, it spins its delicate web from many starting-points, until it is united in one complete whole. What it produces is neither a picture of the soul nor a direct human representation; but it is a work that with all its artitic perfection was already indicated by the unlovely and confusing arabesques in **"The Foot Journey to Amager."** Now while the nursery story, through its contents, reminds us of the ancient myths (**"The Elder-Tree Mother," "The Snow Queen"**), of the folk-lore tale, on whose foundation it constructs itself at times, of proverbs and fables of antiquity, indeed, sometimes of the parables of the New Testament (the buckwheat is punished as well as the fig-tree); while it is continually united by an idea, it may, so far as its form is concerned, be compared with the fantastic Pompeian decorative paintings, in which peculiarly conventional plants, animated flowers, doves, peacocks, and human forms are entwined together and blend into one another. A form that for any one else would be a circuitous route to the goal, a hindrance and a disguise, becomes for Andersen a mask behind which alone he feels truly free, truly happy and secure. His child-like genius, like the well-known child forms of antiquity, plays with the mask, elicits laughter, awakens delight and terror. Thus the nursery story's mode of expression, which with all its frankness is masked, becomes the natural, indeed, the classic cadence of his voice, that but very rarely becomes overstrained or out of tune. The only disturbing occurrence is that now and then a draught of whey is obtained instead of the pure milk of the nursery story, that the tone occasionally becomes too sentimental and sickly sweet (**"Poor John," "The Poor Bird," "Poor Thumbling"**), which, however, is rarely the case in materials taken from folk-lore tales, as **"The Tinder-Box," "Little Claus and Big Claus,"** etc., where the naïve joviality, freshness, and roughness of the narrative, which announces crimes and murders without the slightest sympathetic or tearful phrase, stand Andersen in good stead, and invest his figures with increased sturdiness. Less classic, on the other hand, is the tone of the lyric effusions interwoven with some of the nursery stories, in which the poet, in a stirring, pathetic prose gives a bird's-eye view of some great period of history (**"The Thorny Path of Honor," "The Swan's Nest"**). In these stories there seems to me to be a certain wild flight of fancy, a certain forced inspiration in the prevailing tone, wholly disproportionate to the not very significant thought of the contents; for thought and diction are like a pair of lovers. Thought may be somewhat larger, somewhat loftier, than diction, even as the man is taller than the woman; in the opposite case there is something unlovely in the relation. With the few exceptions just indicated, the narrative style of Andersen's nursery stories is a model of its kind. (pp. 5-8)

[What] is there in plants, in animals, in the child, so attractive to Andersen? He loves the child because his affectionate heart draws him to the little ones, the weak and helpless ones to whom it is allowable to speak with compassion, with tender sympathy, and because when he devotes such sentiments to a hero,—as in *Only a Fiddler,*—he is derided for it, . . . but when he dedicates them to a child, he finds the natural resting-place for his mood. It is owing to his genuine democratic feeling for the lowly and neglected that Andersen, himself a child of the people, continually introduces into his nursery stories (as Dickens, in his novels), forms from the poorer classes of society, "simple folk," yet endowed with the true nobility of the soul. As examples of this may be mentioned the washerwoman in **"Little Tuk"** and in **"Good-for-Nothing,"** the old maid in **"From a Window in Vartou,"** the

watchman and his wife in **"The Old Street-Lamp,"** the poor apprentice boy in **"Under the Willow-Tree,"** and the poor tutor in **"Everything in its Right Place."** The poor are as defenseless as the child. Furthermore, Andersen loves the child, because he is able to portray it, not so much in the direct psychologic way of the romance,—he is by no means a direct psychologist,—as indirectly, by transporting himself with a bound into the child's world, and he acts as though no other course were possible. Rarely, therefore, has charge been more unjust than that of Kierkegaard when he accused Andersen of being unable to depict children; but when Kierkegaard, who, moreover, as a literary critic combines extraordinary merits with great lacks (especially in point of historic survey), takes occasion, in making this criticism, to remark that in Andersen's romances the child is always described "through another," what he says is true. It is no longer true, however, the moment Andersen, in the nursery story, puts himself in the place of the child and ceases to recognize "another." He seldom introduces the child into his nursery stories as taking part in the action and conversation. He does it most frequently in the charming little collection *A Picture-Book without Pictures,* where more than anywhere else he permits the child to speak with the entire simplicity of its nature. In such brief, naïve child-utterances as those cited in it there is much pleasure and entertainment. Every one can recall anecdotes of a similar character. I remember once taking a little girl to a place of amusement, in order to hear the Tyrolese Alpine singers. She listened very attentively to their songs. Afterward, when we were walking in the garden in front of the pavilion, we met some of the singers in their costumes. The little maiden clung timidly to me, and asked in astonishment: "Are they allowed to go about free?" Andersen has no equal in the narration of anecdotes of this kind. In his nursery stories we find sundry illustrations of the fact, as in the charming words of the child in **"The Old House,"** when it gives the man the pewter soldiers that he might not be "so very, very lonely," and a few kind answers in **"Little Ida's Flowers."** Yet his child forms are comparatively rare. The most noteworthy ones are little Hjalmar, little Tuk, Kay and Gerda, the unhappy, vain Karen in **"The Red Shoes,"** a dismal but well-written story, the little girl with the matches and the little girl in **"A Great Sorrow,"** finally Ib and Christine, the children in **"Under the Willow-Tree."** Besides these real children there are some ideal ones, the little fairy-like Thumbling and the little wild robber-maiden, undoubtedly Andersen's freshest child creation, the masterly portrayal of whose wild nature forms a most felicitous contrast to the many good, fair-haired and tame children of fiction. We see her before us as she really is, fantastic and true, her and her reindeer, whose neck she "tickles every evening with her sharp knife." (pp. 23-5)

[Sympathy] with child-nature led to sympathy with the animal which is doubly a child, and to sympathy with the plants, the clouds, the winds, which are doubly nature. What attracts Andersen to the impersonal being is the impersonal element in his own nature, what leads him to the wholly unconscious is merely the direct consequence of his sympathy. The child, young though it may be, is born old; each child is a whole generation older than its father, a civilization of ages has stamped its inherited impress on the little four-year-old child of the metropolis. How many conflicts, how many endeavors, how many sorrows have refined the countenance of such a child, making the features sensitive and precocious! It is different with animals. Look at the swan, the hen, the cat! They eat, sleep, live, and dream undisturbed, as in ages gone by. The child already begins to display evil instincts. We, who are seeking what is unconscious, what is naïve, are glad to descend the ladder that leads to the regions where there is no more guilt, no more crime, where responsibility, repentance, restless striving and passion cease, where nothing of an evil nature exists except through a substitution of which we are but partially conscious, and which therefore, robs our sympathy of half its sting. An author like Andersen, who has so great a repugnance to beholding what is cruel and coarse in its nakedness, who is so deeply impressed by anything of the kind that he dare not relate it, but recoils a hundred times in his works from some wanton or outrageous deed with the maidenly expression, "We cannot bear to think of it!" Such an author feels content and at home in a world where everything that appears like egotism, violence, coarseness, vileness, and persecution, can only be called so in a figurative way. It is highly characteristic that almost all the animals which appear in Andersen's nursery stories are tame animals, domestic animals. This is, in the first place, a symptom of the same gentle and idyllic tendency which results in making almost all Andersen's children so well-behaved. It is, furthermore, a proof of his fidelity to nature, in consequence of which he is so reluctant to describe anything, with which he is not thoroughly familiar. It is finally an interesting phenomenon with reference to the use he makes of the animals, for domestic animals are no longer the pure product of nature; they remind us, through ideal association, of much that is human; and, moreover, through long intercourse with humanity and long education they have acquired something human, which in a high degree supports and furthers the effort to personify them. These cats and hens, these ducks and turkeys, these storks and swans, these mice and that unmentionable insect "with maiden's blood in its body," offer many props to the nursery story. They hold direct intercourse with human beings; all that they lack is articulate speech, and there are human beings with articulate speech who are unworthy of it, and do not deserve their speech. Let us, therefore, give the animals the power of speech, and harbor them in our midst.

On the almost exclusive limitation to the domestic animal, a double characteristic of this nursery story depends. First of all, the significant result that Andersen's animals, whatever else they may be, are never beastly, never brutal. Their sole faults are that they are stupid, shallow, and old-fogyish. Andersen does not depict the animal in the human being, but the human in the animal. In the second place, there is a certain freshness of tone about them, a certain fulness of feeling, certain strong and bold, enthusiastic, and vigorous outbursts which are never found in the quarters of the domestic animal. Many beautiful, many humorous and entertaining things are spoken of in these stories, but a companion piece to the fable of the wolf and the dog—the wolf who observed the traces of the chain on the neck of the dog and preferred his own freedom to the protection afforded the house dog—will not be found in them. The wild nightingale, in whom poetry is personified, is a tame and loyal bird. "I have seen tears in the Emperor's eyes; that is the real treasure to me," it says. "An emperor's tears have a peculiar power!" Take even the swan, that noble, royal bird in the masterly story, **"The Ugly Duckling,"** which for the sake of its cat and its hen alone cannot be sufficiently admired,—how does it end? Alas! as a domestic animal. This is one of the points where it becomes difficult to pardon the great author. O poet! we feel tempted to exclaim, since it was in your power to grasp such a thought, to conceive and execute such a poem, how could you, with your inspiration, your pride, have the heart to permit the swan to end thus! Let him die if needs must be! That would be tragic

Portrait of Jonas Collin, Andersen's benefactor, confidant, critic, and friend.

and great. Let him spread his wings and impetuously soar through the air, rejoicing in his beauty and his strength! let him sink down on the bosom of some solitary and beautiful forest lake! That is free and delightful. Anything would be better than this conclusion: "Into the garden came little children, who threw bread and corn into the water. And they ran to their father and mother, and bread and cake were thrown into the water; and they all said, 'The new one is the most beautiful of all! so young and handsome!' and the old swans bowed their heads before him." Let them bow, but let us not forget that there is something which is worth more than the recognition of all the old swans and geese and ducks, worth more than receiving bread-crumbs and cake as a garden bird,—the power of silently gliding over the waters, and free flight!

Andersen prefers the bird to the four-footed animal. More birds than mammals find place with him; for the bird is gentler than the four-footed beast, is nearer to the plant. The nightingale is his emblem, the swan his ideal, the stork his declared favorite. It is natural that the stork, that remarkable bird which brings children into the world,—the stork, that droll, long-legged, wandering, beloved, yearningly expected and joyfully greeted bird, should become his idolized symbol and frontispiece.

Yet plants are preferred by him to birds. Of all organic beings, plants are those which appear most frequently in the nursery story. For in the vegetable world alone are peace and harmony found to reign. Plants, too, resemble a child, but a child who is perpetually asleep. There is no unrest in this domain, no action, no sorrow, and no care. Here life is a calm, regular growth, and death but a painless fading away. Here the easily excited, lively poetic sympathy suffers less than anywhere else. Here there is nothing to jar and assail the delicate nerves of the poet. Here he is at home; here he paints his Arabian Nights' Entertainments beneath a burdock leaf. Every grade of emotion may be experienced in the realm of plants,—melancholy at the sight of the felled trunk, fulness of strength at the sight of the swelling buds, anxiety at the fragrance of the strong jasmine. Many thoughts may flit through our brain as we follow the history of the development of the flax, or the brief honor of the fir-tree on Christmas evening; but we feel as absolutely free as though we were dealing with comedy, for the image is so fleeting that it vanishes the moment we attempt to render it permanent. Sympathy and agitation gently touch our minds, but they do not ruffle us, they neither rouse nor oppress us. . . . Nowhere has the poet with greater delicacy invested plants with speech than in **"The Fir-Tree," "Little Ida's Flowers,"** and in **"The Snow Queen."** In the last named story, every flower tells its own tale. Let us listen to what the Tiger-lily says: "Hearest thou not the drum? Bum! bum! those are the only two tones. Always bum! bum! Hark to the plaintive song of the old woman! to the call of the priests! The Hindoo woman in her long robe stands upon the funeral pile; the flames rise around her and her dead husband, but the Hindoo woman thinks on the living one in the surrounding circle; on him whose eyes burn hotter than the flames; on him, the fire of whose eyes pierces her heart more than the flames which soon will burn her body to ashes. Can the heart's flame die in the flame of the funeral pile?"— "I do not understand that at all," said little Gerda.—"That is my story," said the Tiger-lily.

Yet a step farther, and the fancy of the poet appropriates all inanimate objects, colonizes and annexes everything, large and small, an old house and an old clothes-press (**"The Shepherdess and the Chimney Sweep"**), the top and the ball, the darning needle and the false collar, and the great dough men with bitter almonds for their hearts. After it has grasped the physiognomy of the inanimate, his fancy identifies itself with the formless all, sails with the moon across the sky, whistles and tells stories like the wind, looks on the snow, on sleep, night, death, and the dream as persons. (pp. 25-30)

The most marked trait in Andersen's mode of viewing life, is that which gives the ascendency to the heart, and this trait is genuinely Danish. Full of feeling itself, this method of contemplation takes every opportunity to exalt the beauty and significance of the emotions. It overleaps the will (the whole destiny of the Flax, in the story of its life, comes from without), does combat with the critique of the pure reason as with something pernicious, the work of the Devil, the witch's mirror, replaces pedantic science with the most admirable and witty side-thrusts (**"The Bell," "A Leaf From the Sky"**), describes the senses as a tempter, or passes them over as unmentionable things, pursues and denounces hardheartedness, glorifies and commends goodness of heart, violently dethrones coarseness and narrowness, exalts innocence and decorum, and thus "puts everything in its right place." The key-note of its earnestness is the ethic-religious feeling coupled with the hatred felt by geniality for narrowness, and its humorous satire is capricious, calm, in thorough harmony with the idyllic spirit of the poet. Its satire has only the sting of a gnat, but it stings in the tenderest places. (pp. 33-4)

The romance is a species of poetic creation which demands of the mind that would accomplish anything remarkable in it, not only imagination and sentiment, but the keen understanding, and the cool, calm power of observation of the man of the world; that is the reason why it is not altogether suited to Andersen, although it is not wholly remote from his talent. In the entire scenery, the background of nature, the picturesque effect of the costumes, he is successful; but where psychological insight is concerned, traces of his weakness may be detected. He will take part for and against his characters; his men are not manly enough, his women not sufficiently feminine. I know no poet whose mind is more devoid of sexual distinctions, whose talent is less of a nature to betray a defined sex, than Andersen's. Therefore his strength lies in portraying children, in whom the conscious sense of sex is not yet prominent. The whole secret lies in the fact that he is exclusively what he is,—not a man of learning, not a thinker, not a standard-bearer, not a champion, as many of our great writers have been, but simply a poet. A poet is a man who is at the same time a woman. Andersen sees most forcibly in man and in woman that which is elementary, that which is common to humanity, rather than that which is peculiar and interesting. I have not forgotten how well he has described the deep feeling of a mother in **"The Story of a Mother,"** or how tenderly he has told the story of the spiritual life of a woman in **"The Little Sea-Maid."** I simply recognize the fact that what he has represented is not the complicated spiritual conditions of life and of romance, but the element of life; he rings changes on single, pure tones, which amid the confused harmonies and disharmonies of life, appear neither so pure nor so distinct as in his books. Upon entering into the service of the nursery story all sentiments undergo a process of simplification, purification, and transformation. The character of man is farthest removed from the comprehension of the poet of childhood, and I can only recall a single passage in his stories in which a delicate psychological characteristic of a feminine soul may be encountered, and even this appears so innocently that we feel inclined to ask if it did not write itself. It occurs in the story of the new porcelain figures, **"The Shepherdess and the Chimney-Sweep."** (pp. 36-7)

A more profound, more mercilessly true, more self-evident analysis of a certain kind of feminine enthusiasm and its energy when it undertakes to act boldly without regard to consequences, and without looking backwards, can be found, I think, in the works of no other Danish writer. What delicacy of presentation: the momentary resolute enthusiasm, the heroic conquering of the first horror, the endurance, bravery, firmness, until the moment which requires courage, when the firmness is shattered, and the yearning for the little table under the looking-glass is awakened. Many a voluminous romance would have been exalted by such a page, and we find in it a compensation for the fact that Andersen is no master in the province of the romance. (pp. 37-8)

Andersen somewhere remarks, that he has made attempts in pretty much every radiation of the nursery story. This remark is striking and good. His nursery stories form a complete whole, a web with manifold radiations, that seems to address the beholder in the words of the spider's web in *Aladdin,* "See how the threads can become entwined in the delicate net!" If it will not seem too much like bringing the dust of the schoolroom into the parlor, I should like to call the reader's attention to a celebrated scientific work in Adolf Zeising's *Æsthetic Investigations,* in which can be found a complete series of æsthetic contrasts, in all their different phases (the beautiful, the comic, the tragic, the humorous, the touching, etc.), arranged in one great star, just as Andersen has planned in respect to his nursery stories.

The form of fancy and the method of narration in the nursery story admit the treatment of the most heterogeneous materials in the most varied tones. Within its province may be found sublime narratives, as **"The Bell"**; profound and wise stories, as **"The Shadow"**; fantastically bizarre, as **"The Elfin Mound"**; merry, almost wanton ones, as **"The Swineherd,"** or **"The Leap Frog"**; humorous ones, as **"The Princess on the Pea," "Good Humor," "The False Collar," "The Lovers"**; also stories with a tinge of melancholy, as **"The Constant Tin Soldier"**; deeply pathetic poetic creations, as **"The Story of a Mother"**; oppressively dismal, as **"The Red Shoes"**; touching fancies, as **"The Little Sea-Maid"**; and those of mingled dignity and playfulness, as **"The Snow Queen."** Here we encounter an anecdote like **"A Great Sorrow,"** which resembles a smile through tears, and an inspiration like **"The Muse of the Coming Age,"** in which we feel the pinion strokes of history, the heart-throbs and pulse-beats of the active, stirring life of the present, as violent as in a fever, and yet as healthy as in a happy moment of enthusiastic inspiration. In short, we find everything that lies between the epigram and the hymn.

Is there, then, a boundary line which limits the nursery story, a law which binds it? If so, where does it lie? The law of the nursery story lies in the nature of the nursery story, and its nature is dependent on that of poetry. If, at the first moment, it would seem that nothing is prohibited a species of poetic creation which can permit a princess to feel a pea through twenty mattresses and twenty eider-down beds, it is but a semblance. The nursery story, which unites unbridled freedom of invention with the restraint its central idea impresses upon it, must steer between two rocks: between the luxuriance of style that lacks ideas, and dry allegory; it must strike the medium course between too great fulness and too great meagreness. This, Andersen most frequently succeeds in doing, and yet not always. Those of his stories that are based on materials derived from folk-lore, as **"The Flying Trunk,"** or those which may be classed with the fairy-tale proper, as **"Thumbling,"** do not attract grown people as they do children, because the story in such instances conceals no thought. In his **"Garden of Paradise"** everything preceding the entrance to the garden is masterly, but the Fairy of Paradise herself seems to me to be invested with little, if any, beauty or charm. The opposite extreme is when we see the barren intention, the dry precept, through the web of poetic creation; this fault, as might be expected in our reflecting and conscious age, is one of more frequent occurrence. We feel it keenly because the nursery story is the realm of the unconscious. Not only are unconscious beings and objects the leaders of speech in it, but what triumphs and is glorified in the nursery story is this very element of unconsciousness. And the nursery story is right; for the unconscious element is our capital and the source of our strength. The reason why the travelling companion could receive aid from the dead man, was because he had entirely forgotten that he had formerly helped this same dead man, and even simple Hans gains the princess and half the kingdom, because with all his folly he is so exceedingly naïve. Even stupidity has its genial side and its good luck; with the poor intermediate beings, the Nureddin natures alone, the nursery story knows not what to do.

Let us consider some instances of sins against the unconscious. In the beautiful story of **"The Snow Queen"** a most disturbing influence is exercised by the scene where the Snow Queen requests little Kay to make figures with the ice puzzle for the understanding, and he is unable to represent the word "Eternity." There is also clumsy and unpoetic bluntness in **"The Neighboring Families"** whenever the sparrow's family mention the rose by the abstract, and for a sparrow rather unnatural, term, "the beautiful." It would have been understood, without this hint, that the roses were the representatives of the beautiful in the narrative, and in encountering this abstract word in the nursery story we recoil as though we had come into contact with a slimy frog.

This tendency to allegory in narratives for children appears most frequently, as might be expected, in the form of instruction and moralizing; in some of the nursery stories, as in **"The Buckwheat,"** the pedagogic element plays an exaggerated rôle. In others, as **"The Flax,"** we feel too strongly at the conclusion—as in Jean Paul—the tendency to exhibit, in season and out of season, the doctrine of immortality. Toward the end of the latter story a few little, somewhat "insipid beings" are created who announce that the song is never done. In some cases finally the tendency is more personal. A whole series of stories (**"The Duckling," "The Nightingale," "The Neighboring Families," "The Daisy," "The Snail and The Rose-Tree," "Pen and Inkstand," "The Old Street Lamp"**) allude to the poet's life and the poet's lot, and in single cases we see traces—a rare exception with Andersen—of invention being dragged in forcibly in order to bring out the tendency. What sense and what conformity to nature is there, for instance, in the fact that the street lamp can only let others see the beautiful and symbolic sights that had been interwoven with its experience when it is provided with a wax candle, and that its faculties are useless when provided with an ordinary light? It is quite incomprehensible until we conceive it to be an allegory on a poet's supposed need of prosperity in order to accomplish anything. "And so genius must run after cupboard lore!" wrote Kierkegaard on the occasion of the appearance of *Only a Fiddler*. Still more infelicitous is the scene where the street lamp, in its melted-down condition, in its other life, finds its way to a poet and thus fulfils its destiny. So strongly as this the tendency has rarely shown itself.

The first duty of the nursery story is to be poetic, its second to preserve the marvellous element. Therefore, it is first of all necessary that the order of the legendary world be sacred to it. What in the language of legendary lore is regarded as a fixed rule, must be respected by the nursery story, however unimportant it may be in relation to the laws and rules of the real world. Thus it is quite inappropriate for the nursery story, as in Andersen's **"The Dryad,"** to part its heroine from her tree, to let her make a symbolic journey to Paris, to go to the "bal Mabille," etc., for it is not more impossible for all the kings of the earth to place the smallest leaf on a nettle than it is for legendary lore to tear a dryad away from its tree. But in the second place, it lies in the nature of the nursery story form that its outline can frame nothing that, in order to obtain its poetic rights, requires a profound psychological description, an earnest development, such as would be adapted either to the nature of the drama or the romance. A woman like Marie Grubbe, a sketch of whose interesting life Andersen gives us in the story of **"Chicken-Grethe,"** is too much of a character for it to be possible for the author of the nursery story to describe or interpret; when he attempts to do so, we feel a disproportion between the object and the form. There is less occasion, however, to marvel at these few blemishes than at the fact that they so very rarely occur. I have only called attention to them because it is interesting to become acquainted with the boundary lines by observing how they have been overstepped, and because it seemed to me more important to ascertain how the Pegasus of the nursery story, notwithstanding all its freedom to race and fly through the circle, has its firm tether in the centre. (pp. 41-5)

[Andersen] has the genuine gift for creating supernatural beings, in modern times so rare. How deeply symbolical and how natural it is, for instance, that the little sea-maid, when her fish-tail shrivelled up and became "the prettiest pair of white feet a little girl could have," should feel as though she were treading on pointed needles and sharp knives at every step she took! How many poor women tread on sharp knives at every step they take, in order to be near him whom they love, and are yet far from being the most unhappy of women!

What a splendidly drawn band is that multitude of sprites in **"The Snow Queen,"** what a superb symbol the witches' mirror, and how thoroughly the author has comprehended this queen herself, who, sitting in the midst of the desert snow field, had imbibed all its cold beauty! This woman is to a certain degree related to Night, one of Andersen's peculiarly characteristic creations. It is not Thorwaldsen's mild, sleep-bringing night, not Carstens' venerable, motherly night; it is black, gloomy, sleepless, and awful night. "Out in the snow sat a woman in long black garments, and she said, 'Death has been with you in your room; I saw him hasten away with your child; he strides faster than the wind, and never brings back what he has taken away.' 'Only tell me which way he has gone,' said the mother. 'Tell me the way, and I will find him.' 'I know him,' said the woman in the black garments; 'but before I tell you, you must sing me all the songs that you have sung to your child. I love those songs; I have heard them before. I am Night, and I saw your tears when you sang them.' 'I will sing them all, all!' said the mother. 'But do not detain me, that I may overtake him, and find my child.' But Night sat dumb and still. Then the mother wrung her hands, and sang, and wept. And there were many songs, but yet more tears." Then the mother journeys onward, weeps out her eyes in order that for this price she may be borne to the opposite shore, and in the great hot-house of Death gives her long black hair to an old gray-haired woman in exchange for the old woman's white hair.

We meet with a countless multitude of fanciful creations, little elf-like divinities, such as Ole Shut-Eye (the sandman), or the goblins with the red caps, and the northern dryad, the Elder-Tree Mother. We feel Andersen's strength when we compare it with the weakness of the contemporary Danish poets in this respect. (pp. 47-8)

One story I have reserved until the end; I will now search for it, for it is, as it were, the crown of Andersen's work. It is the story of **"The Bell,"** in which the poet of naïveté and nature has reached the pinnacle of his poetic muse. We have seen his talent for describing in a natural way that which is superhuman, and that which is below the human. In this story he stands face to face with nature herself. It treats of the invisible bell which the children, who had just been confirmed, went out into the wood to seek—young people in whose breasts yearning for the invisible, alluring, and wondrous voices of nature was still fresh. The king of the country had "vowed that he who could discover whence the sounds proceeded should have the title of 'Universal Bell-ringer,' even if it were not really a bell. Many persons now went to the wood, for the sake of getting the place, but one only returned with a sort

of explanation; for nobody went far enough; that one not farther than the others. However, he said that the sound proceeded from a very large owl, in a hollow tree; a sort of learned owl, that continually knocked its head against the branches. . . . So now he got the place of 'Universal Bell-ringer,' and wrote yearly a short treatise 'on the Owl'; but everybody was just as wise as before." The children who had been confirmed go out this year also, and "they hold each other by the hand; for, as yet, they had none of them any high office." But soon they begin to grow weary, one by one, and some of them return to town, one for one reason, another on another pretext. An entire class of them linger by a small bell in an idyllic little house, without considering, as the few constant ones, that so small a bell could not possibly cause so enticing a play of tones, but that it must give "very different tones from those that could move a human breast in such a manner"; and with the small hope, their small yearning, they betake themselves to rest near their small discovery, the small bell, the small idyllic joy. I fancy the reader must have met some of these children after they were grown up. Finally but two remain, a king's son and a poor little boy in wooden shoes, and "with so short a jacket that one could see what long wrists he had." On the way they parted; for one wished to seek the bell on the right, the other on the left. The king's son sought the bell in the road that lay "on the side where the heart is placed"; the poor boy sought it in the opposite direction. We follow the king's son, and we read admiringly of the mystic splendor with which the poet has invested the region, in altering and exchanging the natural coloring of the flowers. "But on he went, without being disheartened, deeper and deeper into the wood, where the most wonderful flowers were growing. There stood white lilies with blood-red stamens; sky-blue tulips, which shone as they moved in the winds; and the apple-trees, the apples of which looked exactly like large soap-bubbles: so only think how the trees must have sparkled in the sunshine!" The sun goes down; the king's son begins to fear that he will be surprised by night; he climbs upon a rock in order to see the sun once more before it disappears in the horizon. (pp. 51-2)

Genius is the wealthy king's son, its attentive follower the poor boy; but art and science, although they may have parted on their way, meet in their enthusiasm, and their devotion to the divine, universal soul of nature. (p. 53)

*Georg Brandes, "Hans Christian Andersen (1869),"
in his* Creative Spirits of the Nineteenth Century, *translated by Rasmus B. Anderson, Thomas Y. Crowell Company, 1923, pp. 1-54.*

EDMUND GOSSE (essay date 1875)

[*A distinguished English literary historian, critic, and biographer, Gosse wrote extensively on seventeenth- and eighteenth-century English literature. He is also credited with introducing the works of Norwegian dramatist Henrik Ibsen and other Scandinavian writers to English readers. In the following excerpt from an essay originally published in the* Academy *in 1875, Gosse praises Andersen's natural style.*]

Among all [Andersen's] multitudinous writings, it is of course his so-called Fairy Tales, his *Eventyr,* that show most distinctly his extraordinary genius. No modern poet's work has been so widely disseminated throughout the world as these stories of Andersen's. They affect the Hindoo no less directly than the Teutonic mind; they are equally familiar to children all over the civilised world. It is the simple earnestness, humour, and tenderness that pervades them, their perfect yet not over-subtle dramatic insight, their democratic sympathy with all things in adverse and humble circumstances, and their exquisite freshness of invention that characterise them most, and set them on so lofty a height above the best of other modern stories for children. The style in which they are composed is one never before used in writing; it is the lax, irregular, direct language of children that Andersen employs, and it is instructive to notice how admirably he has gone over his earlier writings and weeded out every phrase that savours of pedantry or contains a word that a child cannot learn to understand. When he first wrote these stories he was under the influence of the German writer Musaeus, and from 1830 to about 1835 he was engaged in gradually freeing himself from this exotic manner, and in bringing down his style to that perfection of simplicity which is its great adornment. (pp. 222-23)

> *Edmund Gosse, "Four Danish Poets," in his* Northern Studies, *Walter Scott, 1890, pp. 198-240.*

HORACE E. SCUDDER (essay date 1875)

[*Scudder was Andersen's first American champion. Although the Danish writer's tales sold well in the United States, he never received any monetary compensation for them until Scudder intervened. As the editor of* Riverside Monthly Magazine for Young People, *Scudder negotiated a contract between Andersen and* Riverside's *publishers, Hurd and Houghton. Their agreement specified that Andersen's stories would be sent in advance of their publication in Europe, and several of the later tales were published in America before they were published in Denmark. Scudder and Andersen carried on an amicable professional correspondence for many years, though they never met. Scudder also translated several of Andersen's fairy tales as well as his autobiography,* The Story of My Life. *In the following excerpt, Scudder discusses Andersen's contribution to the fairy tale genre, noting that Andersen wrote in a style that "feeds and stimulates the imagination of children."*]

It is customary to speak of Andersen's best known short stories as fairy tales; wonder-stories is in some respects a more exact description, but the name has hardly a native sound. Andersen himself classed his stories under the two heads of *historier* and *eventyr;* the historier corresponds well enough with its English mate, being the history of human action, or, since it is a short history, the story; the eventyr, more nearly allied perhaps to the German *abenteuer* than to the English *adventure,* presumes an element of strangeness causing wonder, while it does not necessarily demand the machinery of the supernatural. When we speak of fairy tales, we have before our minds the existence, for artistic purposes, of a spiritual world peopled with beings that exercise themselves in human affairs, and are endowed in the main with human attributes, though possessed of certain ethereal advantages, and generally under orders from some superior power, often dimly understood as fate; the Italians, indeed, call the fairy *fata*. In a rough way we include under the title of fairies all the terrible and grotesque shapes as well, and this world of spiritual beings is made to consist of giants, ogres, brownies, pixies, nisses, gnomes, elves, and whatever other creatures have found in it a local habitation and name. The fairy itself is generally represented as very diminutive, the result, apparently, of an attempted compromise between the imagination and the senses, by which the existence of fairies for certain purposes is conceded on condition they shall be made so small that the senses may be excused from recognizing them.

The belief in fairies gave rise to the genuine fairy tale, which is now an acknowledged classic, and the gradual elimination of this belief from the civilized mind has been attended with some awkwardness. These creations of fancy—if we must so dismiss them—had secured a somewhat positive recognition in literature before it was finally discovered that they came out of the unseen and therefore could have no life. (pp. 598-99)

It may be accepted as a foregone conclusion that with a disbelief in fairies the genuine fairy tale has died, and that it is better to content ourselves with those stories which sprang from actual belief, telling them over to successive generations of children, than to seek to extend the literature by any ingenuity of modern skepticism. There they are, the fairy tales without authorship, as imperishable as nursery ditties; scholarly collections of them may be made, but they will have their true preservation, not as specimens in a museum of literary curiosities, but as children's toys. Like the sleeping princess in the wood, the fairy tale may be hedged about with bristling notes and thickets of commentaries, but the child will pass straight to the beauty, and awaken for his own delight the old charmed life.

It is worth noting, then, that just when historical criticism, under the impulse of the Grimms, was ordering and accounting for these fragile creations,—a sure mark that they were ceasing to exist as living forms in literature,—Hans Christian Andersen should have come forward as master in a new order of stories, which may be regarded as the true literary successor to the old order of fairy tales, answering the demands of a spirit which rejects the pale ghost of the scientific or moral or jocular or pedantic fairy tale. Andersen, indeed, has invented fairy tales purely such, and has given form and enduring substance to traditional stories current in Scandinavia; but it is not upon such work that his real fame rests, and it is certain that while he will be mentioned in the biographical dictionaries as the writer of novels, poems, romances, dramas, sketches of travel, and an autobiography, he will be known and read as the author of certain short stories, of which the charm at first glance seems to be in the sudden discovery of life and humor in what are ordinarily regarded as inanimate objects, or what are somewhat compassionately called dumb animals. When we have read and studied the stories further, and perceived their ingenuity and wit and human philosophy, we can after all give no better account of their charm than just this, that they disclose the possible or fancied parallel to human life carried on by what our senses tell us has no life, or our reason assures us has no rational power.

The life which Andersen sets before us is in fact a dramatic representation upon an imaginary stage, with puppets that are not pulled by strings, but have their own muscular and nervous economy. The life which he displays is not a travesty of human life, it is human life repeated in miniature under conditions which give a charming and unexpected variety. By some transmigration, souls have passed into tin-soldiers, balls, tops, beetles, money-pigs, coins, shoes, leap-frogs, matches, and even such attenuated individualities as darning-needles; and when, informing these apparently dead or stupid bodies, they begin to make manifestations, it is always in perfect consistency with the ordinary conditions of the bodies they occupy, though the several objects become by this endowment of souls suddenly expanded in their capacity. Perhaps in nothing is Andersen's delicacy of artistic feeling better shown than in the manner in which he deals with his animated creations when they are brought into direct relations with human beings. The absurdity which the bald understanding perceives is dexterously suppressed by a reduction of all the factors to one common term. For example, in his story of **"The Leap-Frog,"** he tells how a flea, a grasshopper and a leap-frog once wanted to see which could jump highest, and invited the whole world "and everybody else besides who chose to come," to see the performance. The king promised to give his daughter to the one who jumped the highest, for it was stale fun when there was no prize to jump for. The flea and the grasshopper came forward in turn and put in their claims; the leap-frog also appeared, but was silent. The flea jumped so high that nobody could see where he went to, so they all asserted that he had not jumped at all; the grasshopper jumped in the king's face, and was set down as an ill-mannered thing; the leap-frog, after reflection, leaped into the lap of the princess, and thereupon the king said, "There is nothing above my daughter; therefore to bound up to her is the highest jump that can be made: but for this, one must possess understanding, and the leap-frog has shown that he has understanding. He is brave and intellectual." "And so," the story declares, "he won the princess." The barren absurdity of a leap-frog marrying a princess is perhaps the first thing that strikes the impartial reader of this abstract, and there is very likely something offensive to him in the notion; but in the story itself this absurdity is so delightfully veiled by the succession of happy turns in the characterization of the three jumpers, as well as of the old king, the house-dog, and the old councilor "who had had three orders given him to make him hold his tongue," that the final impression upon the mind is that of a harmonizing of all the characters, and the king, princess, and councilor can scarcely be distinguished in kind from the flea, grasshopper, leap-frog, and house-dog. After that, the marriage of the leap-frog and princess is quite a matter of course.

The use of speaking animals in story was no discovery of Andersen's, and yet in the distinction between his wonder-story and the well-known fable lies an explanation of the charm which attaches to his work. The end of every fable is *hæc fabula docet,* and it was for this palpable end that the fable was created. The lion, the fox, the mouse, the dog, are in a very limited way true to the accepted nature of the animals which they represent, and their intercourse with each other is governed by the ordinary rules of animal life, but the actions and words are distinctly illustrative of some morality. The fable is an animated proverb. The animals are made to act and speak in accordance with some intended lesson, and have this for the reason of their being. The lesson is first; the characters, created afterward, are, for purposes of the teacher, disguised as animals; very little of the animal appears, but very much of the lesson. The art which invented the fable was a modest handmaid to morality. In Andersen's stories, however, the spring is not in the didactic but in the imaginative. He sees the beetle in the imperial stable stretching out his thin legs to be shod with golden shoes like the emperor's favorite horse, and the personality of the beetle-determines the movement of the story throughout; egotism, pride at being proud, jealousy, and unbounded self-conceit are the furniture of this beetle's soul, and his adventures one by one disclose his character. Is there a lesson in all this? Precisely as there is a lesson in any picture of human life where the same traits are sketched. The beetle, after all his adventures, some of them ignominious but none expelling his self-conceit, finds himself again in the emperor's stable, having solved the problem why the emperor's horse had golden shoes. "They were given to

the horse on my account," he says, and adds, "the world is not so bad after all, but one must know how to take things as they come." There is in this and other of Andersen's stories a singular shrewdness, as of a very keen observer of life, singular because at first blush the author seems to be a sentimentalist. The satires, like **"The Emperor's New Clothes"** and **"The Swiftest Runners,"** mark this characteristic of shrewd observation very cleverly. Perhaps, after all, we are stating most simply the distinction between his story and the fable when we say that humor is a prominent element in the one and absent in the other; and to say that there is humor is to say that there is real life.

It is frequently said that Andersen's stories accomplish their purpose of amusing children by being childish, yet it is impossible for a mature person to read them without detecting repeatedly the marks of experience. There is a subtle undercurrent of wisdom that has nothing to do with childishness, and the child who is entertained returns to the same story afterward to find a deeper significance than it was possible for him to apprehend at the first reading. The forms and the incident are in consonance with childish experience, but the spirit which moves through the story comes from a mind that has seen and felt the analogue of the story in some broader or coarser form. The story of **"The Ugly Duckling,"** is an inimitable presentation of Andersen's own tearful and finally triumphant life; yet no child who reads the story has its sympa-

A 1935 English illustration to "The Emperor's New Clothes."

thy for a moment withdrawn from the duckling and transferred to a human being. Andersen's nice sense of artistic limitations saves him from making the older thought obtrude itself upon the notice of children, and his power of placing himself at the same angle of vision with children is remarkably shown in one instance, where, in **"Little Klaus and Big Klaus,"** death is treated as a mere incident in the story, a surprise but not a terror.

Now that Andersen has told his stories, it seems an easy thing to do, and we have plenty of stories written for children that attempt the same thing, sometimes also with moderate success; for Andersen's discovery was after all but the simple application to literature of a faculty which has always been exercised. The likeness that things inanimate have to things animate is constantly forced upon us; it remained for Andersen to pursue the comparison further, and, letting types loose from their antitypes, to give them independent existence. The result has been a surprise in literature and a genuine addition to literary forms. It is possible to follow in his steps, now that he has shown us the way, but it is no less evident that the success which he attained was due not merely to his happy discovery of a latent property, but to the nice feeling and strict obedience to laws of art with which he made use of his discovery. Andersen's genius enabled him to see the soul in a darning-needle, and he perceived also the limitations of the life he was to portray, so that while he was often on the edge of absurdity he did not lose his balance. Especially is it to be noted that these stories, which we regard as giving an opportunity for invention when the series of old-fashioned fairy tales had been closed, show clearly the coming in of that temper in novel-writing which is eager to describe things as they are. Within the narrow limits of his miniature story, Andersen moves us by the same impulse as the modern novelist who depends for his material upon what he has actually seen and heard, and for his inspiration upon the power to penetrate the heart of things; so that the old fairy tale finds its successor in this new realistic wonder-story, just as the old romance gives place to the new novel. In both, as in the corresponding development of poetry and painting, is found a deeper sense of life and a finer perception of the intrinsic value of common forms. (pp. 599-602)

> Horace E. Scudder, "Andersen's Short Stories," in
> The Atlantic Monthly, *Vol. XXXVI, No. CCXVII,*
> *November, 1875, pp. 598-602.*

HJALMAR HJORTH BOYESEN   (essay date 1895)

[*Boyesen was a Norwegian-born American novelist, poet, and educator. His critical studies include* Goethe and Schiller *(1879) and* Essays on Scandinavian Literature *from which the following excerpt is taken. Here Boyesen offers an appreciative assessment of the diversity of philosophical and narrative perspectives in Andersen's fairy tales, admiring as well the author's manipulation of plot and denouement.*]

Hans Christian Andersen was a unique figure in Danish literature, and a solitary phenomenon in the literature of the world. Superficial critics have compared him with the Brothers Grimm; they might with equal propriety have compared him with Voltaire or with the man in the moon. Jacob and Wilhelm Grimm were scientific collectors of folk-lore, and rendered as faithfully as possible the simple language of the peasants from whose lips they gathered their stories. It was the ethnological and philological value of the fairy-tale which stimulated their zeal; its poetic value was of quite secondary

significance. With Andersen the case was exactly the reverse. He was as innocent of scientific intention as the hen who finds a diamond on a dunghill is of mineralogy. It was the poetic phase alone of the fairy-tale which attracted him; and what is more, he saw poetic possibilities where no one before him had ever discovered them. By the alchemy of genius (which seems so perfectly simple until you try it yourself) he transformed the common neglected nonsense of the nursery into rare poetic treasure. Boots, who kills the ogre and marries the princess—the typical lover in fiction from the remotest Aryan antiquity down to the present time—appears in Andersen in a hundred disguises, not with the rudimentary features of the old story, but modernized, individualized, and carrying on his shield an unobtrusive little moral. In **"Jack the Dullard"** he comes nearest to his primitive prototype, and no visible effort is made to refine him. In **"The Most Extraordinary Thing"** he is the vehicle of a piece of social satire, and narrowly escapes the lot which the Fates seem especially to have prepared for inventors, viz., to make the fortune of some unscrupulous clown while they themselves die in poverty. In **"The Porter's Son"** he is an aspiring artist, full of the fire of genius, and he wins his princess by conquering that many-headed ogre with which every self-made man has to battle—the world's envy, and malice, and contempt for a lowly origin. It is easy to multiply examples, but these may suffice.

In another species of fairy-tale, which Andersen may be said to have invented, incident seems to be secondary to the moral purpose, which is yet so artfully hidden that it requires a certain maturity of intellect to detect it. In this field Andersen has done his noblest work and earned his immortality. Who can read that marvellous little tale, **"The Ugly Duckling,"** without perceiving that it is a subtle, most exquisite revenge the poet is taking upon the humdrum Philistine world, which despised and humiliated him, before he lifted his wings and flew away with the swans, who knew him as their brother? And yet, as a child, I remember reading this tale with ever fresh delight, though I never for a moment suspected its moral. The hens and the ducks and the geese were all so vividly individualized, and the incidents were so familiar to my own experience, that I demanded nothing more for my entertainment. Likewise in **"The Goloshes of Fortune"** there is a wealth of amusing adventures, all within the reach of a child's comprehension, which more than suffices to fascinate the reader who fails to penetrate beneath the surface. The delightful satire, which is especially applicable to Danish society, is undoubtedly lost to nine out of ten of the author's foreign readers, but so prodigal is he both of humorous and pathetic meaning, that every one is charmed with what he finds, without suspecting how much he has missed. **"The Little Mermaid"** belongs to the same order of stories, though the pathos here predominates, and the resemblance to De la Motte Fouqué's "Undine" is rather too striking. But the gem of the whole collection, I am inclined to think, is **"The Emperor's New Clothes,"** which in subtlety of intention and universality of application rises above age and nationality. Respect for the world's opinion and the tyranny of fashion have never been satirized with more exquisite humor than in the figure of the emperor who walks through the streets of his capital in *robe de nuit,* followed by a procession of courtiers, who all go into ecstasies over the splendor of his attire.

It was not only in the choice of his theme that Andersen was original. He also created his style, though he borrowed much of it from the nursery. "It was perfectly wonderful," "You would scarcely have believed it," "One would have supposed that there was something the matter in the poultry-yard, but there was nothing at all the matter"—such beginnings are not what we expect to meet in dignified literature. They lack the conventional style and deportment. No one but Andersen has ever dared to employ them. As Dr. Brandes has said in his charming essay on Andersen [see excerpt dated 1869], no one has ever attempted, before him, to transfer the vivid mimicry and gesticulation which accompany a nursery tale to the printed page. If you tell a child about a horse, you don't say that it neighed, but you imitate the sound; and the child's laughter or fascinated attention compensates you for your loss of dignity. The more successfully you crow, roar, grunt, and mew, the more vividly you call up the image and demeanor of the animal you wish to represent, and the more impressed is your juvenile audience. Now, Andersen does all these things in print: a truly wonderful feat. Every variation in the pitch of the voice—I am almost tempted to say every change of expression in the story-teller's features—is contained in the text. He does not write his story, he tells it; and all the children of the whole wide world sit about him and listen with eager, wide-eyed wonder to his marvellous improvisations. (pp. 155-59)

We all have a dim recollection of how the world looked from the nursery window; but no book has preserved so vivid and accurate a negative of that marvellous panorama as Andersen's **Wonder Tales for Children,** the first collection of which appeared in 1835. All the jumbled, distorted proportions of things (like the reflection of a landscape in a crystal ball) is capitally reproduced. The fantastically personifying fancy of childhood, where does it have more delightful play? The radiance of an enchanted fairy realm that bursts like an iridescent soap-bubble at the touch of the finger of reason, where does it linger in more alluring beauty than in **"Ole Lukōie" ("The Sandman"), "The Little Mermaid,"** or **"The Ice-Maiden"**? There is a bloom, an indefinable, dewy freshness about the grass, the flowers, the very light, and the children's sweet faces. And so vivid—so marvellously vivid—as it all is. (p. 171)

[The tale **"The Sandman"**] strikes me as having the very movement and all the delicious whimsicality of a schoolboy's troubled dream. It has the delectable absurdity of the dream's inverted logic. You feel with what beautiful zest it was written; how childishly the author himself relished it. The illusion is therefore perfect. The big child who played with his puppet theatre until after he was grown up is quite visible in every line. He is as much absorbed in the story as any of his hearers. He is all in the game with the intense engrossment of a lad I knew, who, while playing Robinson Crusoe, ate snails with relish for oysters.

Throughout the first series of **Wonder Tales** there is a capital air of make-believe, which imposes upon you most delightfully, and makes you accept the most incredible doings, as you accept them in a dream, as the most natural thing in the world. In the later series, where the didactic tale becomes more frequent (**"The Pine Tree," "The Wind's Tale," "The Buckwheat"**), there is an occasional forced note. The storyteller becomes a benevolent, moralizing uncle, who takes the child upon his knee, in order to instruct while entertaining it. But he is no more in the game. A cloying sweetness of tone, such as sentimental people often adopt toward children, spoils more than one of the fables; and when occasionally he ventures upon a love-story (**"The Rose-Elf," "The Old Bachelor's Nightcap," "The Porter's Son"**), he is apt to be as unin-

tentionally amusing as he is in telling his own love episode in *The Fairy-Tale of My Life.* However, no man can unite the advantages of adult age and childhood, and we all feel that there is something incongruous in a child's talking of love. (pp. 173-74)

[Andersen's life was] as marvellous as any of his tales. A gleam of light from the wonderland in which he dwelt seems to have fallen upon his cradle and to have illuminated his whole career. It was certainly in this illumination that he himself saw it, as the opening sentence of his autobiography proves: "My life is a lovely fairy-tale, happy and full of incidents."

The softness, the sweetness, the juvenile innocence of Danish romanticism found their happiest expression in him; but also the superficiality, the lack of steel in the will, the lyrical vagueness and irresponsibility. If he did not invent a new lit-

---

In the volume which I first published, [*Eventyr fortalte for børn*], I had, like Musäus, but in my own manner, related old stories, which I had heard as a child. The tone in which they still sounded in my ears seemed a very natural one to me, but I knew very well that the learned critics would censure the style of talk, so, to quiet them I called them *Wonder Stories told for Children,* although my intention was that they should be for both young and old. . . .

I had written my narrative down upon paper, exactly in the language, and with the expressions in which I had myself related them, by word of mouth, to the little ones, and I had arrived at the conviction that people of different ages were equally amused with them. The children made themselves merry for the most part over what might be called the actors; older people, on the contrary, were interested in the deeper meaning. The stories furnished reading for children and grown people, and that assuredly is a difficult task for those who will write children's stories. They met with open doors and open hearts in Denmark; everybody read them. . . .

A refreshing sunshine streamed into my heart; I felt courage and joy, and was filled with a living desire of still more and more developing my powers in this direction,—of studying more thoroughly this class of writing, and of observing still more attentively the rich wells of nature out of which I must create it. If attention be paid to the order in which my stories are written, it certainly will be seen that there is in them a gradual progression, a clearer working out of the idea, a greater discretion in the use of agency, and, if I may so speak, a more healthy tone and a more natural freshness may be perceived.

As one step by step toils up a steep hill, I had at home climbed upward, and now beheld myself recognized and honored, appointed a distinct place in the literature of my country.

Hans Christian Andersen, in an excerpt from his autobiography Mits livs eventyr (The Story of My Life.)

erary form he at all events enriched and dignified an old one, and revealed in it a world of unsuspected beauty. He was great in little things, and little in great things. He had a heart of gold, a silver tongue, and the spine of a mollusk. Like a flaw in a diamond, a curious plebeian streak cut straight across his nature. With all his virtues he lacked that higher self-esteem which we call nobility. (pp. 177-78)

> *Hjalmar Hjorth Boyesen, "Hans Christian Andersen," in his* Essays on Scandinavian Literature, *Charles Scribner's Sons, 1895, pp. 155-78.*

ROBERT LYND   (essay date 1922)

[*Lynd was an Irish journalist and author who served as literary editor of the* London News Chronicle *and contributed regularly to the* New Statesman and Nation *under the pseudonym "Y. Y." Primarily an essayist, Lynd cultivated the imaginative, whimsical conversational style of English essayist Charles Lamb. In the following excerpt from an essay originally published in 1922, Lynd explores the moral content and realistic denouements of Andersen's fairy tales.*]

Hans Andersen, indeed, was in many respects more nearly akin to the writers of tracts and moral tales than to the folklorists. He was a teller of fairy-tales. But he domesticated the fairy-tale and gave it a townsman's home. In his hands it was no longer a courtier, as it had been in the time of Louis XIV, or a wanderer among cottages, as it has been at all times. There was never a teller of fairy-tales to whom kings and queens mattered less. He could make use of royal families in the most charming way, as in those little satires, **"The Princess and the Pea"** and **"The Emperor's New Clothes."** But his imagination hankered after the lives of children such as he himself had been. He loved the poor, the ill treated, and the miserable, and to illuminate their lives with all sorts of fancies. His miracles happen preferably to those who live in poor men's houses. His cinder-girl seldom marries a prince: if she marries at all it is usually some honest fellow who will have to work for his living. In Hans Andersen, however, it is the exception rather than the rule to marry and live happily ever afterwards. The best that even Hans the cripple [in **"The Cripple"**] has to look forward to is being a schoolmaster. There was never an author who took fewer pains to give happy endings to his stories. (p. 156)

[In] his fairy-tales Hans Andersen has always appealed to men and women as strongly as to children. We hear occasionally of children who cannot be reconciled to him because of his incurable habit of pathos. A child can read a fairy-tale like "The Sleeping Beauty" as if it were playing among toys, but it cannot read **"The Marsh King's Daughter"** without enacting in its own soul the pathetic adventures of the frog-girl; it cannot read **"The Snow Queen"** without enduring all the sorrows of Gerda as she travels in search of her lost friend; it cannot read **"The Little Mermaid"** without feeling as if the knives were piercing its feet just as the mermaid felt when she got her wish to become a human being so that she might possess a soul. Even in **"The Wild Swans,"** though Lisa's eleven brothers are all restored to humanity from the shapes into which their wicked stepmother had put them, it is only after a series of harrowing incidents; and Lisa herself has to be rescued from being burned as a witch. Hans Andersen is surely the least gay of all writers for children. He does not invent exquisite confectionery for the nursery such as Charles Perrault, having heard a nurse telling the stories to his little son, gave the world in "Cinderella" and "Bluebeard." To read sto-

ries like these is to enter into a game of make-believe, no more to be taken seriously than a charade. The Chinese lanterns of a happy ending seem to illuminate them all the way through. But Hans Andersen does not invite you to a charade. He invites you to put yourself in the place of the little match-girl who is frozen to death in the snow on New Year's Eve after burning her matches and pretending that she is enjoying all the delights of Christmas. He is more like a child's Dickens than a successor of the ladies and gentlemen who wrote fairy-tales in the age of Louis XIV and Louis XV. He is like Dickens, indeed, not only in his genius for compassion, but in his abounding inventiveness, his grotesque detail, and his humour. He is never so recklessly cheerful as Dickens with the cheerfulness that suggests eating and drinking. He makes us smile rather than laugh aloud with his comedy. But how delightful is the fun at the end of **"Soup on a Sausage Peg"** when the Mouse King learns that the only way in which the soup can be made is by stirring a pot of boiling water with his own tail! And what child does not love in all its bones the cunning in **"Little Claus and Big Claus,"** when Big Claus is tricked into killing his horses, murdering his grandmother, and finally allowing himself to be tied in a sack and thrown into the river?

But Hans Andersen was too urgent a moralist to be content to write stories so immorally amusing as this. He was as anxious as a preacher or a parent or Dickens to see children becoming Christians, and he used the fairy-tale continually as a means of teaching and warning them. In one story he makes the storks decide to punish an ugly boy who had been cruel to them. 'There is a little dead child in the pond, one that has dreamed itself to death; we will bring that for him. Then he will cry because we have brought him a little dead brother.' That is certainly rather harsh. **"The Girl Who trod on the Loaf "** is equally severe. As a result of her cruelty in tearing flies' wings off and her wastefulness in using a good loaf as a stepping-stone, she sinks down through the mud into hell, where she is tormented with flies that crawl over her eyes and, having had their wings pulled out, cannot fly away. Hans Andersen, however, like Ibsen in *Peer Gynt,* believes in redemption through the love of others, and even the girl who trod on the loaf is ultimately saved. 'Love begets life' runs like a text through **"The Marsh King's Daughter."** His stories as a whole are an imaginative representation of that gospel—a gospel that so easily becomes mush and platitude in ordinary hands. But Andersen's genius as a narrator, as a grotesque inventor of incident and comic detail, saves his gospel from commonness. He may write a parable about a darning-needle, but he succeeds in making his darning-needle alive, like a dog or a schoolboy. He endows everything he sees—china shepherdesses, tin soldiers, mice, and flowers—with the similitude of life, action, and conversation. He can make the inhabitants of one's mantelpiece capable of epic adventures, and has a greater sense of possibilities in a pair of tongs or a door-knocker than most of us have in men and women. His is a creator of a thousand fancies. He loves imagining elves no higher than a mouse's knee, and mice going on their travels leaning on sausage-skewers as pilgrims' staves, and little Thumbelina, whose cradle was 'a neat polished walnut-shell . . . blue violet-leaves were her mattresses, with a rose-leaf for a coverlet.' His fancy never becomes lyrical or sweeps us off our feet, like Shakespeare's in *A Midsummer Night's Dream.* But there was nothing else like it in the fairy-tale literature of the nineteenth century. And his pages are full of the poetry of flights of birds. More than anything else one thinks of Hans Andersen as a lonely child watching a flight of swans or storks till it is lost to view, silent and full of wonder and sadness. Edmund Gosse, in *Two Visits to Denmark,* a book in which everything is interesting except the title, describes a visit which he paid to Hans Andersen at Copenhagen in his old age, when 'he took me out into the balcony and bade me notice the long caravan of ships going by in the Sound below—"they are like a flock of wild swans," he said.' The image might have occurred to any one, but it is specially interesting as coming from the mouth of Hans Andersen, because it seems to express so much of his vision of the world. He was, above all men of his century, the magician of the flock of wild swans. (pp. 158-60)

Robert Lynd, "Hans Andersen," in his Essays on
Life and Literature, *J. M. Dent & Sons Ltd., 1951,
pp. 155-60.*

MARGERY WILLIAMS BIANCO   (essay date 1927)

[*Bianco was a British novelist, translator, and author of children's books. In the excerpt below, which originally appeared in the* Horn Book Magazine *in 1927, she illuminates Andersen's perception of reality and presentation of humanity in his fairy tales.*]

It would be interesting to know, supposing certain writers for children of an earlier time were confronted with the general mass of children's literature today, what their impression would be. Of a very considerable expansion, I think, in one sense and a quite marked restriction in another. In an age in which child culture has become a wide and earnest preoccupation there is, side by side with a desire to give the child from the earliest moment every possible opportunity of free development, a definite conspiracy—in fiction at least—to shield him from everything that we consider of an unchildish or non-happy nature. The desire is a quite natural one. The child's life must be gay, must be happy. Open all the windows to the sun, and nothing but the sun. But does it never strike us that in a room filled entirely with sunlight, even sunlight itself may in the end lose its most essential quality?

It is rather a shock to realize that, judged by this standard of imperative cheerfulness, and of what we consider fitted for a child's mind, more than one-half of Hans Andersen's priceless stories might never have passed a publisher's reader. "What?" he might say. "The Fir Tree burn up? Impossible! The little Match Girl can't die; she must be adopted by some really nice family, and the morocco ball should certainly not end in the gutter!"

For nearly all of these stories are sad, and some are more than just sad. Who, for instance, would take the responsibility of including today, in a child's volume, such tales as **"Anne Lisbeth," "She Was Good for Nothing,"** or even **"Ib and Christine"** or **"The Marsh King's Daughter"**? It is true that in nearly all modern editions of Andersen there is considerable selection, but in the earlier editions that the children of my generation were brought up on there was no such attempt. At nine years old I remember reading **"Anne Lisbeth"** as eagerly as **"The Little Fir Tree"** or **"Soup on a Sausage-Peg,"** and the actual impression that remained was only of a very real and enduring beauty.

In very few of Andersen's stories is there any deliberate effort to choose the bright side of things, or even to ensure a happy ending, unless it occurs naturally. With that he was not in the least concerned, and he was not always concerned with the story itself; many of his best tales are just pictorial impressions. What then is the secret of his appeal to children? I think it is that he was, most essentially, a poet, and that the poet's and the child's mind are a great deal closer than many of us suppose.

He wrote of the world about him and of the things in it, as colored by his own vision. He didn't choose those things; they were there, and he saw no reason to exclude or disguise them. In this world as he saw it there were drunken old washerwomen, mothers who abandoned their children, dark ruinous houses with neglected and unhappy old people living in them; there were ingratitude, poverty and death, hypocrisy and a great deal of foolish talk, which none than he knew better how to satirize. But there were also faith, charity and humour, love and happy, respected old age; there were enchanted forests, trees that dreamed and birds and beasts who talked, and there was at times, if only for his eyes, a great and shining spiritual light that fell on all these things alike and made one as beautiful as another.

"You must not look at it from the sorrowful side," says the little boy. "To me it all appears remarkably pretty. . . ."

This is not priggishness; still less is it the conventional optimism which, by insisting so much on the "happy ending," also postulates a possible unhappy ending. To Andersen all endings were happy; they were as they should be. Old people die, but would you have them go on living forever? Wicked Inge is punished for her pride, but her soul, after long suffering, turns into the little bird that "flew straight into the sun"; the little Match Girl starved, but she had the vision of eternal life, and the happiest moment of the little Fir Tree is when it bursts into deathless flame.

He had the child mind, which does not conceive of sadness as does the older mind. It is all relative. He was not sorry for this sort of thing at all. What he was really sorry for were the stupid people, the mean and the snobbish and the little-minded, who are blind to beauty though it walks beside them and who can never see life—or death—as the real adventure that it is; the huckster and the Emperor and the Portuguese duck. These he satirizes again and again, but his satire is always kindly; it could not be otherwise.

There has been no writer for children with such amazing range and variety as Andersen. "Tell me a story!" cries the little boy in the **"Elder Tree Mother."** And the stories begin to come out of the teapot. Each is different from the next; each is as spontaneous as though it were the only story he really wanted to write. He gave of his best unsparingly, and to choose among them were an almost hopeless task.

Everything in his world is animate, has personality and expression; the old street-lamp, the china ornaments, the toys, the poker and the darning-needle, no less than the daisy, the farmyard fowl and the family of snails. This is truly a child's world as a child might conceive it. Everything has its own philosophy, everything moves and acts in its proper way. The soul of the flower is as real as the soul of the poet. The old cupboard creaks; it has a voice and wants to tell us something. Listen, and you will hear the knives and forks chattering in the table drawer. No sooner are the family abed than the tulips and hyacinths jump out of their flowerpots and begin to dance. Everything has a story to tell. And before us, turning those magic pages, there arises surely the most wonderful tapestry that any single human mind has conceived.

I remember a print, seen in childhood, of a well-known poet surrounded by all the creations of his genius. Enormous, indeed, would be the canvas that could contain all the figures to which Hans Andersen gave being and life.

The story of **"Waldemar Daa and His Daughters"** produces very much the same atmosphere as *Wuthering Heights* or Balzac's *Quest of the Absolute;* against a majestic background of storm and ruin the characters move inexorably to their doom. It has the feeling of some old romantic landscape, blackened with age. Here in a few pages is the tragic story of a whole generation. In **"The Marsh King's Daughter,"** with its rare fantasy and rarer spiritual beauty, is a great conception, but no greater in degree than **"Anne Lisbeth," "The Angel"** or **"The Child in the Grave."** Even the humblest things take somehow an element of greatness; he gave nobility to whatever he touched. And if there is one motif that stands out more than any other in his writing, that recurs again and again, it is that expressed most clearly in the words of the angel to the child:

> The good and the beautiful shall not be forgotten;
> it shall live on in legend and in song.
>
> (pp. 58-62)

Margery Williams Bianco, "The Stories of Hans Andersen," in Writing and Criticism: A Book for Margery Bianco, *edited by Anne Carroll Moore and Bertha Mahony Miller, The Horn Book, Inc., 1951, pp. 58-62.*

HELGE TOPSÖE-JENSEN AND PAUL V. RUBOW (essay date 1930)

[*Topsöe-Jensen spent much of his career analyzing the accuracy of Andersen's memoirs and the contents of his letters. Elias Bredsdorff called Topsöe-Jensen's studies of Andersen "among the pillars of contemporary Andersen research." Rubow published* H. C. Andersen Eventyr (*1927;* Hans Andersen's Fairy Tales), *a scholarly discussion of the literary genres in Andersen's fairy tales that is considered an important forerunner of later works in the field. In the following excerpt, the critics favorably assess Andersen's short story collection* A Picture-Book without Pictures.]

[Andersen's] art was distinctly an art of moods, born of momentary inspiration. Many of his best fairy tales were, as he tells us in **"The Bell,"** lying dormant in his mind "like a seed that only needed a breath, a sunbeam, a drop of wormwood, in order to blossom." But this did not prevent him from laboring with his manuscripts. He went over them again and again, with all the care of a skilled craftsman, until he had attained a finish that was at once perfect art and pure nature. (p. 205)

[*A Picture-Book without Pictures*] is the finest expression of Andersen's romanticism—a romanticism more akin to the French in the 1830's than to the German in the beginning of the century. The romantic element is not merely present in the setting which gathers all the various pictures within the single frame of a moonlight mood; it is in the principle of contrasts on which the whole is built and which is the very essence of romance. Contrast is the effective law that has guided the juxtaposition of the pictures—from the exotic, brilliant overture with the Hindu maid seeking to know the fate of her beloved, down to the simple and homely nursery scene in the last picture, **"The Child's Evening Prayer."** Therefore the picture book is made as motley and changing as possible; the

most distant in time and space alternates with the near and familiar; the agony of death lies close to the impulsive joy of the child; tragedy is followed by comedy. And the element of contrast is present also in the individual pictures. Typical are the picture of the light woman in whom love of pleasure is contrasted with death, the misery of the present with the innocence of childhood; or the child of the proletariat, who on the day of the Revolution dies on the throne of France wrapped in imperial purple; or the quiet old maid who in her coffin is carried on a mad ride behind runaway horses; or the strangest one of all in its unsolved contradictions, the next to the last picture, that of the prisoner who is carried away, no one knows where, and leaves behind him on the prison wall a scribbled bit of melody, no one knows what.

A Picture-Book without Pictures brings us to the threshold of the *Fairy Tales.* Both have in common the important rôle played by the narrator with his constant marginal notes. This is a characteristic of Andersen's literary method so significant that it may perhaps contain the clue to why he was never quite at home either in the purely subjective lyric or in the purely objective drama. Both necessarily presuppose the absence of any narrator, any mediator between the subject matter and the audience. On the other hand, the presence of the narrator is a fundamental requisite of the fairy tale, and it was the harmony between the author's mentality and this special form of composition that gave his fairy tales their immediate success and lasting world fame.

Truth and *beauty*—that was the watchword of Hans Christian Andersen's authorship as he himself conceived it when he was at the peak of his powers. Reality is a fairy tale of which we know only a small part; truth alone is eternal.

Andersen broke definitely with the romanticism that had its face turned toward the past. He was a believer in the future and could be moved to enthusiasm by the fairy tale of reality, whether it came through the music of Wagner or through the progress of scientific achievement. New inventions give new impulses, and he drew not only on feeling and imagination, but also on intellect. "He expounds eternal truth, and therein lies greatness and romance."

He felt that the great creative writer must necessarily turn against all forms of imitation in literary art. In literature, as in the conception of life, the future must break with the past. Terseness, clarity, richness—these should be the characteristics of the literature of the future. But as human character is the one fixed quantity in a shifting world, and the content of living literature is the emotions of the human heart, so its essence must always be the same, even though the external form changes.

Andersen felt that in his fairy tales he was working for the literature of the future. In **"The Gardener and the Family,"** one of the stories which he especially recommends to the notice of his listeners, he has in a few words defined his position in the world of letters. He writes: "What no other gardener had thought of planting in the flower garden, he set in the kind of soil that each should have, and in shade or in sunshine as every kind required. He tended it in love, and it grew in magnificence." (pp. 208-10)

Helge Topsöe-Jensen and Paul V. Rubow, "Hans Christian Andersen the Writer," in The American-Scandinavian Review, *Vol. XVIII, No. 4, April, 1930, pp. 205-12.*

PAUL ROSENFELD (essay date 1938)

[*In the following excerpt, Rosenfeld characterizes Andersen's fairy tales and ranks him with Shakespeare as one of only two modern "historical myth-makers."*]

[Andersen's] stories rivalled those which, elaborated by entire peoples, have come to us down the ages.

Fairy tales such as those which underpin a few of Andersen's and were rivalled by his original tales of crowned birds, dreaming fir-trees, and constant nightingales, are but the detritus of the great nature myths. That, at least, is the opinion of so eminent an authority as Max Müller. Like the blocks from which they have become detached in the course of centuries, they symbolize, with representations of the actions of living beings, particularly human beings, or imaginary extra-human creatures—eloquent animals and things behaving like men—the operations of natural forces and the psyche's nameless powers. And only twice in modern times have individuals, from out their own imaginations, produced nature myths with the magic and the vitality of those which have come to us down the ages, and thus in single lifetimes paralleled the long careers of races. One of these individuals was, as we have said, the grotesque daddy-long-legs. The poetry, wit, and exquisite freshness of the detail in his fairy stories make half of those in the collections of the brothers Grimm seem wooden. The other historical myth-maker was Shakespeare. His infinitely glamorous nature myth is *A Midsummer Night's Dream.*

In what manner Andersen's deepest wisdom, his personal experience of the profound powers of the psyche, their life, struggles, and goals of release and perfection, and also his acute social criticism, transformed itself into original and humorous mythological symbols couched in the language of the people, we do not know: any more than we know how Shakespeare came to compose his fairy comedy. We do not, for instance, know whether Andersen found his images in dreams or in waking fantasies. We merely surmise his stories were not allegories; or even fables—though they have their archly didactic side. They possess all the earmarks of direct poetic experience: the inimitable force and freshness of ideas not mentally worked up and not quite susceptible of rational analysis. Quantities of the details too have this unfathomable poetic quality: for example, the famous picture of the stork "tiptoeing on his red legs, jabbering Egyptian, a language his mother had taught him." This alone is certain, that by an infallible instinct their author took these gay and melancholy, brilliant and deeply moving little tales directly to one of their predestined audiences. Long before he wrote them down, Andersen recounted them to children—his friends' and acquaintances'—with appropriate gestures and grimaces which enchanted his hearers and later became the rhetoric of his narratives. The child, of course, is much closer to the pan-psychic, marvelous world of sentient darning-needles and tops and of reasoning field mice than is the rationalistic adult. And the stories, as has been said, contain all that satisfies the child. They convey the feeling of life, the sense of the familiar, and portray human relations, in especial those of adults and children. They are filled with surprises, with sense-impressions, with beauty, wonder, mystery, magic, adventure, action, success, humor, and poetic justice. They are rhythmic and repetitive, and sincerely emotive despite their occasional sentimentalities, and full of appeal to the imagination. Besides, children have this in common with the embodiments of the human psyche which figure in these immortal tales under the names Thumbelina and the little mermaid, the soldier and the sister of the swan-fraternity: the determination of growth and the persuasion that "ripeness is all."

And Andersen had intense sympathy for these little manikins; he gracefully adjusted his tales to their understandings, and represented the natural world from their angle of vision. "To the water's edge," he says in a characteristic passage, "the bank was covered with great wild rhubarb leaves so high that little children could stand upright under the biggest of them." No wonder no author has ever had a greater audience of children. None ever has placed better material within their grasp. But while he addressed children, he very subtly and poetically expressed mature experience. The humbug of society, the self-interest which controls judgment, the cowardice and fear of acting otherwise than the world which keeps men from speaking the truth—wherever has it more lightly and deftly been expressed than in **"The Emperor's New Clothes"**? The deadliness of rationalism and mechanistic science, the life-be-stowal of all which holds us in bondage to nature—where more succinctly than in **"The Nightingale"**? The fact that what happens in life doesn't matter quite so much as the way in which we accept what happens—where has it been put less pedantically than in **"The Steadfast Tin Soldier"**? Or the truths that grandeur alone recognizes grandeur, and that ugly ducklings become swans only through struggle with the world and by doing something for themselves,—where have they been put more penetratingly than in the most enchanting of all his enchanting tales?

Indeed . . . we cannot help wondering whether any story-teller other than Andersen ever has represented equally significant material in compasses as diminutive as theirs. We cannot help finding even their interpretations of human nature more acceptable than those in most naturalistic novels. Andersen archly comprehends its inexplicable incoherency, as where, in **"Big Claus and Little Claus,"** he lets the bully who has the small man in a bag and is about to kill him, think, as he passes a church and hears singing within it, that "it might be a good thing to go in and hear a little hymn before going any further." Above all, through his myths we again feel the struggles, deaths, and births of the basic forces of the human soul: their self-expenditure in fruitless yearning, their travail to free themselves from the webs of circumstance; their ability to endure endless winter and to transform and spiritualize themselves and reawaken from subterranean slumbers and fly and sing. And to do so is to grasp anew the mystery, wonder, and meaning of life. (pp. 10-11)

Paul Rosenfeld, "The Ugly Duckling," in The Saturday Review of Literature, *Vol. XVIII, No. 3, May 14, 1938, pp. 10-11.*

PAUL V. RUBOW (essay date 1947)

[*In the following excerpt, Rubow studies Andersen's depictions of his native Denmark in his fairy tales and discusses aspects of the author's craftsmanship.*]

To most of us, Hans Andersen (1805-1875) is the typical Danish writer. That may be a mistake, for others have as much of the native blood in their veins. But he was happy enough to live and write in an age when feeling for the national features in landscape and character was developed as never before. Denmark had been discovered, and the great writers and poets from the first decades of the century had revealed the thousand secrets of the language. Especially from the

German strip cartoon of "The Steadfast Tin Soldier."

poets he had learned to describe and impart the visible world by suggestion. He wove into his novels, poems, and fairy tales—a whole picture of his country. At first his conception of nature was rather ordinary. But after his travels in France and Italy he used his own eyes, and later he got to know his own country very well. He describes in a way which is never partial all strata of society and many different types of men: the fashionable world which attracted him without blinding him (for after all he was a writer of fairy tales), the scholar, the artist, the young officer, the clerk, the watchman in the street, the little girl selling matches, the prisoner in his cell. He knows the countryside too, as well as the town. You will find Fyen, the island of his childhood, in such tales as **"The Travelling Companion"** and **"The Buckwheat,"** Zealand in his tales from manor houses such as **"The Ugly Duckling"** and **"The Happy Family"**; and Jutland, which he discovered as early as the 'thirties and which during the 'fifties became the main country, in **"A Story from the Dunes"** and **"The Bishop of Borglum."** Instead of the empty landscape of the traditional fairy tales he inserted the real countryside with sun and wind, the indigenous nature and climate: 'It was lovely in the country—it was summer! The wheat was yellow, the oats were green, the hay was stacked in the green meadows, and the stork went strutting about . . . ' Instead of the roses, lilies, and fig-trees of the popular fairy tales we have a complete Danish flora including pease-blossom, burdock, and many weeds. The poet knew the secret of each flower as he shows in such tales as **"The Snow Queen,"** where the orange lily, the convolvulus, the hyacinth, the buttercup, and the white narcissus in turn tell their dreams. Andersen is a specialist in the seasons. **"The Snow Queen"** is like a whole mythus of the birth and death of the year, and of the intervention in human destiny by an animated nature. Each month has its own description: in January 'the panes are pasted with snow, and it falls in heaps from the roofs'; in March the moss shines fresh on the trunks of the trees; in July the evening sky gleams like gold and the moon is up between dusk and dawn; in October the King of the Year paints from his big colour-pot. (pp. 92-3)

A very important feature in [Andersen's] tales is the narrator. Andersen took over this anonymous character from the popular tale. He is an intermediary between the reader and the experience. In some of the shorter tales his presence is felt everywhere, in others he hangs back discreetly. But in all cases it is he who gives to the tale its definite form. Without him Andersen's art would be too subjective for the small genre. In the first tales, like **"The Goloshes of Fortune,"** he is an actor who is very much alive. Note, for instance, the beginning of this tale where the two fairies talk together in the anteroom of a Copenhagen home, giving us the theme of the story, then the quick changing of scene when, almost unprepared, we are put back three hundred years in time, then again Copenhagen interiors, interrupted by an animal fable, and in the next moment an Italian scene. In conclusion the life and death of the theme are discreetly touched upon. But in the tales from the 'forties, Andersen's great time, these living mimics are replaced by the tragic and the comic masks. On a small scale he now produces the great art. The many sentimental asides, the playful, satirical tricks from his first period are now gone. He realized his ideal and created in his tales a universal poetry. He condensed the stuff of tragedy into a nut-shell and wrote **"The Story of a Mother"** and **"The Little Match Girl."** He wrote tales that are comedies in miniature such as **"The Top and the Ball," "The Shepherdess and the Chimney-Sweep."** On the same scale he wrote such sto-

ries of life as **"The Ugly Duckling"** and **"The Fir Tree."** Already in his first period he had been able to re-cast the burlesque heroic poem in the vest-pocket size of **"The Steadfast Tin Soldier."** It was his ambition to translate all the beautiful, but heavy poetry of the world into a form that was short, rich, and clear. He tackled the greatest subjects when he dared to write about the closed book of fate, about pity, ambition, and even about love, of which he knew little.

Later, in another and larger group of tales and stories, the narrator shows another face. Late in the 'fifties, he disguises himself as a divinely inspired bard. Like Ossian on the heath, he lets the elements sound in his work without mediating. He has sung **"The Wind Tells of Valdemar Daae and His Daughters,"** this wonderful tragedy of fate in prose (it is called prose), the most original work of fiction in our literature. He also wrote **"The Last Dream of the Old Oak"** that tells about his unstilled longing for love and about the fettered strength of his soul.

But most of the stories in his great collection are the popular tales. Starting from the two types of popular tales we can divide Andersen's work into two similar main types.

In one group he simply re-tells the tales which tradition has brought him, often in a language closely related to the popular one. These are tales such as **"The Tinder-Box," "Little Claus and Big Claus," "The Princess and the Pea," "The Swineherd," "What Father Does,"** and **"The Emperor's New Clothes"**—that is to say some of the best known and beloved of all. It holds good of all these tales that Andersen sticks to humorous models. They are old rogue's stories. He has renewed them in a style close to the original. He retains all essential features down to the component of popular formulas. Before he became a writer of tales he had written comical stories in the manner of the medieval *fabliaus* and of La Fontaine and the Danish poets Wessel and Baggesen.

Another group consists of the serious tales: **"The Little Mermaid," "The Travelling Companion," "The Snow Queen,"** and others. Here Andersen uses his models quite freely or works entirely on his own. The point is that the serious popular tales have roots in a mystical conception of the world and use an apparatus of magic requisites which he could not lightly transfer into his own poetry. Here he describes a milieu, dresses up the real or fantastic figures and animates the supernatural elements that had in the course of time lost their original meaning.

He knew this job. That, in a certain sense, is his secret. He was a primitive soul to whom the surrounding world was alive. Andersen was not an orthodox Protestant; as a religious man he was a rationalist. But that is of no import. At the bottom of the world which Science described to him lay, according to his holy conviction, the *fairy tale*. To him dead things were alive.

Hans Andersen is the greatest illusionist of literature. This is due to his kinship with the child's mind, his faculty of daydreaming. Happy are those who are able to see motives in everything. One sometimes sees a child getting bored with his toy and going to another child who is playing with another. The first child takes away the second one's toy. Then the second child will take two sticks and play with them. The first child will look to see what he is doing and does not understand it. He lacks the gift of illusion, and that cannot be borrowed. Early childhood is the proper age of illusion. Boyhood is more one-sided, boys early acquire a certain maidenlike hardness and narrowness. Youth means a sort of revenge for the productive mind. This age has a passion for tragedy. Manhood again is poor in imagination and vegetative meditation. Poets often dry up in the real working years of life—unless (like Kierkegaard or Andersen) they 'escape when they are going to be men'. The old, when they are not completely withered in the struggle of life, become poetic again and play with their tools, arbitrary remembrance replacing imagination.

In Hans Andersen there was something of a youth, an aunt, and a child. He has the spiritual intensity and power of imagination of early childhood. He has the child's gift of imitation. His tales are full of mimics, of limitated gestures and speeches, including an immense store of animal sounds. Another childish feature is his impetuosity. He is said to have been hysterical as children sometimes are. And he was a great dreamer and visionary in the manner of little folks. He lets his scholar ask the Shadow who has been in the Anteroom of Poetry: 'Did all the gods of antiquity walk through the great halls? Did the old heroes fight there? Did sweet children play there and tell you their dreams?'

However, dreams alone do not suffice. I have mentioned that Andersen's tales build on the popular tales. It is even certain that the book of tales would never have been created had he not from the start retained a humble attitude towards the popular art of story-telling. His heroes and heroines can be followed back to the primitive tales that were once the common property of all European peoples. The child-hero, whom Andersen first introduced in his novels, but only made something of in his tales, is an inheritance from the brave prince or the innocent Cinderella of the popular tales. The child-hero in the serious tales has morals and right on his side in Andersen's version as with the old story-tellers. But in the merry tales the hero is a rogue, even though sometimes a sympathetic rogue like Little Claus.

Andersen's enchanted world is also anchored in the popular tales. The world of the old tales is magic and ceremonial. Its characters are stiff like dolls, the plot is like a formula. The people live up to their definition: the good by their goodness, the cunning by their artfulness, the stupid by their stupidity. They are known by their deeds. The hero is one with his action. The three lives of three brothers are told in perfectly parallel terms. The characters and the plot are reiterated from one tale to another. After overcoming various obstacles the hero wins the princess, who is often bewitched or ill, the old king gladly gives half his kingdom away, the stepmother persecutes her stepdaughter, and so on. The characters behave in a similar way under similar circumstances. When the princess carries a secret she pretends to be dumb. When a man has lost his wife, he marries for his daughter's sake a widow who is wicked and has a daughter who is also wicked, and the two wicked women chase away the real daughter. When a man is in distress an unknown person appears to help him, but demands as a reward that which his wife carries under her girdle; the man thinks it is the keys, while in reality it is the child. When two young lovers die, two red roses grow on their graves, and on the grave of a virgin grows a pale lily.

All this is found in Hans Andersen's tales as well. But he uses the supernatural with caution. In **"The Travelling Companion"** or **"The Wild Swans"** he still sticks to tradition. John gets three feathers from the swan's wing and a small bottle. He puts a big tub of water by the bridal bed, and when the princess comes to the bed he pushes her into the water and

dips her three times, having thrown the feathers and the contents of the bottle into it; then she is transformed. Elisa throws eleven shirts over the swans and eleven beautiful princes stand before her. But in his later tales the supernatural is balanced against the profoundly human. In **"The Story of a Mother"** the Night and the Lake and the Thorn-Bush are personifications that extend beyond the real world—but the mother's love is a natural force stronger than they. Andersen also favoured a form of conclusion like that of **"The Little Match Girl"** or **"A Story from the Dunes"**: the great ecstasy of release from mortal misery precedes the moment of death and is followed by a description of the immensity and inclemency of the surrounding world.

I have tried to give glimpses into Hans Andersen's workshop. It is a curious shop, for Andersen is in a way the hero of all his tales, just as he is in another sense the narrator of all of them. Yet it is not a purely subjective and arbitrary world he creates. As he has inherited strong traditions from the story-tellers of the past, so he employs a technique that must force from us a deep admiration. Looking closer at his work we find that his small poetic creations are actually very complicated. There is a firmness of form, even though it is wound about with the vines of imagination. It is a very national work, but a work that has its roots in an international kind of literature. Behind the picture of nineteenth century Denmark there is a huge rock-like pre-world. This is the reason why Andersen has been able to conquer the whole globe from his native country. His tales contain palaces built by imagination—but built on rock. He has revived the lost age, the childhood we no longer remember. His poetic book of tales, first and foremost to Danes, but then to the whole world, is the key of a wonderland whose enchanted tracts look like those of the real world—only they are richer. (pp. 94-8)

> *Paul V. Rubow, "Hans Andersen and His Fairy Tales," in* Life and Letters and the London Mercury, *Vol. 53, April-June, 1947, pp. 92-8.*

W. H. AUDEN (essay date 1952)

[*Auden was a major twentieth-century literary figure. His early poetry and criticism are informed by the psychological and political theories of Sigmund Freud and Karl Marx; his later work is heavily influenced by his conversion to Christianity. Among his best-known critical works are* The Enchafed Flood; or, The Romantic Iconography of the Sea (1950), The Dyer's Hand, and Other Essays (1962), *and* Forewords and Afterwords (1973). *In the following excerpt from his introduction to* Tales of Grimm and Andersen (1952) *reprinted in* Forewords and Afterwords, *Auden contrasts fairy tales by Andersen with those by the Brothers Grimm.*]

Hans Andersen, so far as I know, was the first man to take the fairy tale as a literary form and invent new ones deliberately. Some of his stories are, like those of Perrault, a reworking of folk material—**"The Wild Swans,"** for example, is based on two stories in the Grimm collection, "The Six Swans," and "The Twelve Brothers"—but his best tales, like **"The Snow Queen,"** or **"The Hardy Tin Soldier,"** or **"The Ice Maiden"** are not only new in material but as unmistakably Andersen's as if they were modern novels.

Compared with the Grimm tales, they have the virtues and the defects of a conscious literary art. To begin with, they tend to be parables rather than myths.

Little Kay was blue with cold—nay almost black—

but he did not know it, for the Snow Queen had kissed away the icy shiverings, and his heart was little better than a lump of ice. He went about dragging some sharp flat pieces of ice which he placed in all sorts of patterns, trying to make something out of them, just as when we at home have little tablets of wood, with which we make patterns and call them a 'Chinese puzzle."

Kay's patterns were most ingenious, because they were the 'Ice Puzzles of Reason.' In his eyes they were excellent and of the greatest importance: this was because of the grain of glass still in his eye. He made many patterns forming words, but he never could find the right way to place them for one particular word, a word he was most anxious to make. It was 'Eternity.' The Snow Queen had said to him that if he could find out this word he should be his own master, and she would give him the whole world and a new pair of skates. But he could not discover it.

Such a passage could never occur in a folk tale. Firstly, because the human situation with which it is concerned is an historical one created by Descartes, Newton, and their successors, and, secondly, because no folk tale would analyze its own symbols and explain that the game with the ice-splinters was the game of reason. Further, the promised reward, "the whole world and a new pair of skates" has not only a surprise and a subtlety of which the folk tale is incapable, but, also a uniqueness by which one can identify its author.

It is rarely possible, therefore, to retell an Andersen story in other words than his; after the tough and cheerful adventurers of the folk tales, one may be irritated with the Sensitive-Plantishness and rather namby-pamby Christianity of some of Andersen's heroes, but one puts up with them for the sake of the wit and sharpness of his social observation and the interest of his minor characters. One remembers the old lady with the painted flowers in her hat and the robber's daughter in **"The Snow Queen"** as individuals in a way that one fails to remember any of the hundreds of witches and young girls in the folk tales. The difference may be most clearly seen by a comparison of stories about inanimate objects.

Soon . . . they came to a little brook, and, as there was no bridge or foot-plank, they did not know how they were to get over it. The straw hit on a good idea, and said: 'I will lay myself straight across, and then you can walk over on me as a bridge.' The straw therefore stretched itself from one bank to the other, and the coal, who was of an impetuous disposition, tripped quite boldly onto the newly built bridge. But when she had reached the middle, and heard the water rushing beneath her, she was, after all, afraid, and stood still, and ventured no further. The straw, however, began to burn, broke in two pieces, and fell into the stream. The coal slipped after her, hissed when she got into the water, and breathed her last. The bean, who had prudently stayed behind on the shore, could not but laugh at the event, was unable to stop, and laughed so heartily that she burst. It would have been all over with her, likewise, if, by good fortune, a tailor who was traveling in search of work, had not sat down to rest by the brook. As he had a compassionate heart, he pulled out his needle and thread and sewed her together. The bean thanked him most prettily but, as the tailor used black thread, all beans since then have a black seam.

So Grimm. The fantasy is built upon a factual question. "Why do beans have a black seam?" The characterization of the straw, the coal, and the bean does not extend beyond the minimum required by their respective physical qualities. The whole interest lies in the incidents.

Andersen's story, **"The Darning Needle,"** on the other hand, presupposes no question about its protagonist.

The darning needle kept her proud behavior and did not lose her good humor. And things of many kinds swam over her, chips and straws and pieces of old newspapers.

'Only look how they sail!' said the darning needle. 'They don't know what is under them! . . . See, there goes a chip thinking of nothing in the world but of himself—of a chip! There's a straw going by now. How he turns! how he twirls about! Don't think only of yourself, you might easily run up against a stone. There swims a bit of newspaper. What's written upon it has long been forgotten, and yet it gives itself airs. I sit quietly and patiently here. I know who I am and I shall remain what I am.'

One day something lay close beside her that glittered splendidly; then the darning needle believed that it was a diamond; but it was a bit of broken bottle; and because it shone, the darning needle spoke to it, introducing herself as a breastpin.

'I suppose you are a diamond?' she observed.

'Why, yes, something of that kind.'

And then each believed the other to be a very valuable thing; and they began speaking about the world, and how very conceited it was.

'I have been in a lady's box,' said the darning needle, 'and this lady was a cook. She had five fingers on each hand, and I never saw anything so conceited as those five fingers. And yet they were only there that they might take me out of the box and put me back into it.'

'Were they of good birth?' asked the bit of bottle.

'No, indeed, but very haughty. . . . There was nothing but bragging among them, and therefore I went away.'

'And now we sit here and glitter!' said the bit of bottle.

Here the action is subordinate to the actors, providing them with a suitable occasion to display their characters which are individual, i.e., one can easily imagine another Darning Needle and another Bit of Bottle who would say quite different things. Inanimate objects are not being treated anthropomorphically, as in Grimm; on the contrary, human beings have been transmuted into inanimate objects in order that they may be judged without prejudice, with the same objective vision that Swift tries for through changes of size. The difference is one that distinguishes all primitive literature, primitive, that is, in attitude, not in technique, from modern.

In the folk tale, as in the Greek epic and tragedy, situation and character are hardly separable; a man reveals what he is in what he does, or what happens to him is a revelation of what he is. In modern literature, what a man is includes all the possibilities of what he may become, so that what he actually does is never a complete revelation. The defect of primitive literature is the defect of primitive man, a fatalistic lack of hope which is akin to a lack of imagination. The danger for modern literature and modern man is paralysis of action through excess of imagination, an imprisonment in the void of infinite possibilities. That is why, maybe, contemporary novelists seem to have their greatest difficulties with their plots, for we, their characters, find it so much easier to stop to think than to go into action with the consequence, all too often, that, more apathetic than any primitive hero, we wait helplessly for something, usually terrible, to be done to us. (pp. 204-07)

> *W. H. Auden, "Grimm and Andersen," in his* Forewords and Afterwords, *edited by Edward Mendelson, Random House, Inc., 1973, pp. 198-208.*

FREDRIK BÖÖK (essay date 1955)

[*Böök is a Swedish literary critic and biographer. In the following excerpt from a translation of his 1955 critical biography of Andersen, Böök discusses religious, philosophical, and social issues treated by Andersen, focusing in particular on the tale "Everything in Its Right Place."*]

No one denies that Hans Christian Andersen was a brilliant artist; but if we wish to take him and his fairy tales seriously, we must ask what sort of wisdom it is he preaches.

At first glance it seems to be anything but deep. Life is a beautiful fairy tale, and there is a loving God Who arranges everything for the best. Andersen takes the practical proof of this teaching from his own life story; the hopeful dream was realized as if through a miracle.

This is the basic type of all his fairy tales: that they treat of fortune's chosen darling. It can scarcely have escaped the author that not all the children of men maintain a magical alliance with the Almighty: on the contrary, some of them lead an unhappy life, in want and poverty, frustrated and betrayed in their fondest desires. Andersen does not close his eyes to any of these unfortunates, and he has a consolation for them, for the little match girl frozen to death, for the withered cripple in the cellar beside a metropolitan street: the joys of Heaven, bliss in the arms of God. Even the little mermaid, apparently excluded, will reach this goal by a detour. Thus the books always balance; we all become favorites like the ugly duckling, although some of us do not attain happiness save through that second sandman, the one who is called "Death." "Fantasos" could be a common name for both the sandman-figures, and when, still in the class room, Andersen wrote his first finished poem, it dealt with the two sandmen, and with the child who falls into happy sleep beneath Fantasos' magic wand.

Religion, a firm belief in an eternal bliss, is thus the foundation of the fairy tales and their optimism. However, Andersen was by no means an orthodox Christian. He resembled the picture he had given of his poor father, a seeker, a brooder, a doubter. Now and then he glorified the faith, the mystery of Christ, and the authority of the Bible, but it was more an expression of his longing than of his conviction. (pp. 208-09)

In essence, a belief in immortality was a moral postulate for both Andersen and Rydberg. Andersen once had a conversation with Oehlenschläger, in the course of which the latter, no doubt half in jest, said that Andersen was not content with all he could get on earth—to top it all off, he wanted to be immortal too. Andersen replied that he would become furious with God if He did not grant eternity to all those people who had never known a single joy in all their wretched days on earth. In the novel *To Be or Not To Be* from 1857, Esther, the heroine, develops a similar line of thought. "We perceive disharmonies," she says, "we see an unjust distribution of life's goods, we witness gifts cast away, and the triumph of evil, stupidity, vice, power—the triumph of Caligula. It is unthinkable, it cannot be true! Our sums here on earth will never come out even, unless we add to them the number: *an eternal life.*"

Noting such expressions of opinion, one could assume, it seems, that Andersen surely no more distorted the metaphysical urge for eternity, religious idealism, into an argument for the preservation of earthly injustice than Viktor Rydberg did. Marx has said that religion is the opium of people; but Charles Kingsley, a Christian idealist and also a contemporary of Andersen's, has given the matter an equally caustic formulation: "The Bible has become a mere police handbook, a dose of opium to make the beasts of burden patient beneath their loads." Did Andersen write his fine fairy tales so that they might be used in the same spirit? Did he have the sandman's magic lantern enchant sick children so that they would forget their pain—or forget to seek a cure for it? In principle, the two matters are very different; in practice the boundary between them often becomes blurred. Morphine is a boon for suffering humanity—a fact which, one guesses, neither Marx nor Lenin would dare dispute—but it is not a panacea; it has no use in the science of hygiene, nor can it prevent sickness; the man who tries to make it the basis of therapeutics is a charlatan, a spirit akin to those men who make an idyllic falsification of religion. Was Andersen one of their number? They were legion in that age, and one must ask oneself whether Andersen's moral and intellectual independence was sufficient to enable him to see through their sophisms. This is no vain question, for in the final analysis it concerns the content of truth in Andersen's fairy tales.

The request for a vote of confidence was made in all due order by the critical representative of the new generation, the realistic age—by Georg Brandes, who in 1869, to the very great pleasure of the old poet, wrote an excellent treatise on Andersen's fairy tales [see excerpt dated 1869]. Georg Brandes' admiration is provided with a number of question marks and reservations; he criticizes, among other things, H. C. Andersen's preference for tame and submissive domestic animals—even the nightingale, which is supposed to symbolize poetry, is a docile bird with monarchistic tendencies, and the ugly duckling ends in a castle park, where it swims around as a prisoner and is fed with cakes and crumbs from the table of the rich. "How can your enthusiasm, your pride allow you to let the swan end in this way?" Brandes cries pathetically. Let it die, tragically and magnificently, let it fly away unfettered through the air, rejoicing at its beauty and its strength, let it sink into the depths of a lonely forest lake—but spare it the approval of old swans and ducks, spare it the cakes and the crumbs!

This is indeed a very elegantly formulated criticism of Andersen's social attitudes, and no one can deny that Brandes put his finger on a sore spot. But at the same time one has a strong feeling that we no longer could formulate the accusation as Brandes did. It cannot be considered a failing on the ugly duckling's part, on the part of poetic genius, if it is too humble, if it shows too little arrogance at its strength and its beauty, if it remains among men and joins their community instead of mirroring its fascinating and tragic ego in a wilderness lake. In Brandes one detects the ghost of Romantic individualism from the nineteenth century's beginning, or else it is a sign of the superman who would appear at the century's close; it does not harm Andersen in our eyes if he fails to be demonic or autocratic. On the contrary: Brandes' enthusiasm for the wild, freedom-loving wolf seems to us to be a rather empty pose.

No, we should like to express our criticism in a different way. Has the ugly duckling, once he has succeeded in entering the paradise of the swans, forgotten his brothers in misery, all the other starved, mistreated, and hapless creatures? Did he lament only at his own misfortune, his own sufferings, did life's injustice merely consist in all the hardships he had to undergo himself, was he merely another of the world's many sentimental complainers? In this case Kierkegaard would have been right in his contemptuous criticism of *Only a Fiddler,* even though the philosopher himself was all too entangled in the prejudices of his time to find the correct perspective. Was Andersen, in other words, actually the incurable egoist, the literary hustler blinded by vanity, whom Carsten Hauch happened—quite by accident—to portray? Does the fairy tales' optimism, their free play of humor, simply mean that, after the poet himself is in the clear, his heart no longer bleeds so readily? And, that the sandman with his magic wand (or Fantasos with his morphine-filled needle) may take charge of the other victims?

If this had really been true in Andersen's case, then we still should not have the right to condemn him too severely, for this was the typical moral attitude of the nineteenth century's *bourgeoisie,* and one cannot require miracles of perspicacity or tolerance from Andersen. He was a child of the age of aesthetic idealism, his intellectual energy was concentrated on the theater, art, literature, poetry; and the refinement, the mastery, he and his kindred spirits achieved was dearly purchased at the cost of one-sidedness, passivity, blindness. The world's center was the stage and the parquet of the Royal Theater at Copenhagen. Quaking, Fru Heiberg spoke of the hyena of politics, and Andersen himself said on one occasion: "At the time when politics played no role whatsoever among us, our public life was the theater, the day's and the evening's most important subject of conversation." The prerequisite condition for this attitude was that patriarchal despotism, the noblest virtues of which were incorporated in old Jonas Collin—can one be surprised that Andersen remained unpolitical, and that he received his bread from the King's hand, as the swans did from the master of the castle? Failing that hand, he would have perished.

Of this remarkable systematic one-sidedness, which, seen from a sociological standpoint, is indissolubly connected with an exaggeratedly rich flowering of religious, aesthetic, and moral ideologies, many traces are quite naturally to be found in Andersen. (pp. 210-14)

But there were a number of points at which Andersen succeeded in freeing himself from prevalent catchwords. He distinguished himself from the vast majority of his Romantic fellow poets by never believing in the "good old days"—the great teller of fairy tales had no patience for that fairy tale. To a certain extent, this attitude of his perhaps was inspired by his intimate friendship with H. C. Ørsted, the liberal scientist; Ørsted's influence can easily be discerned in **"The Galoshes of Fortune,"** in which Andersen settles his accounts

with Romanticism's enthusiasm for the middle ages. However, in the final analysis Andersen needed neither ingenious philsophical arguments nor learned historical comparisons in order to become conscious of these reactionary sophistries. Like all other genuinely poor people, he had made the necessary studies in his own self and his relatives; he knew the truth about the good old days at first hand, just as he knew the poetry of the stagecoach. Conservative panegyrics about the happiness and harmony of the past, about the healthy satisfaction of the spirit which more than outweighs its concomitant, an apparent poverty of the flesh, have stemmed, of course—directly or indirectly, consciously or unconsciously—from those privileged circles standing to profit by the idyl. If one allows members of the proletariat (or anyone else who has come to grips with the good old days) to bear witness, then the story has a different flavor. However well things went for H. C. Andersen, he was never ashamed of his origins; he never went back on his childhood memories or his family's experiences.

Thus there is no doubt at all where Andersen's deepest sympathies lie: with the unpropertied, the oppressed, and the cowed, with the people—the withered cripple in a back street, the beggar girl, the drunken laundress and her boy in his broken-billed cap. To be sure, he did not demand reforms or pose problems or incite to revolution; but although he stayed quite clear of politics, his fairy tales perhaps exerted a psychological influence nonetheless, an influence which then extended itself into the sphere of action: they had a chastening, a softening, a disturbing effect upon their readers. Edvard Lehmann attested to this fact when he wrote:

> Remember that the ***Fairy Tales*** were the first book we read as children, and that their gentleness toward the unfortunate became part of our initial concept of life. We heard about starving and freezing, about being mocked and crushed, and we heard the story from someone who knew whereof he spoke, from a poet who could make human existence itself speak through his words. And reality itself: for every detail is taken from reality, from the cap's broken bill to the grieving heart.

This is the influence Andersen had in Denmark, and not in Denmark alone; this is the influence he had on one generation, and on many. One thinks of the nightingale's promise to the sick emperor: that he would bring him news of happy men and of those who suffer, of the poor fisherman and the cottager's roof—that he would report whatever is otherwise kept hidden from the court and the throne. It is a program, of course, which Andersen did not realize; but the nightingale's words cannot be dismissed as exaggerations, either: attempts in this direction are to be found more than once in Andersen's works.

Andersen's social attitudes become most readily apparent in the strange tale he published in 1853 under the title **"Everything in Its Right Place."** It must have been written just previous to its publication, and it shows that Andersen by no means let the revolutionary year of 1848 slip past him without a thought, a conclusion to which one might very well come after reading *The Fairy Tale of My Life.* The tale deals with the life of several generations on one of those Danish estates where Andersen, visiting as a respected and honored guest, got along so splendidly. His reception there did not keep him from making certain observations, and the more one studies them, the more respect one gets for the sense of reality the teller of fairy tales possessed. There were many contemporary historians and social philosophers who had ever so much more obscure ideas on the subject.

He tells about the old days—he begins more than a hundred years before the time of writing down the story—when the estate's masters, loving the hunt, fill the castle with their horses and their dogs and their merriment. One of the young gentlemen, overwhelmed by high spirits, pushes a poor goosegirl down into the mud of the moat, from which she is saved by a traveling peddler, who has likewise had a taste of the nobility's jests. "Everything in its right place!" was the cry as the girl was shoved into the mud, and "Everything in its right place!" the peddler repeats as he pulls her out, and plants in the earth a willow branch which the girl, reaching out, had broken off in her mortal terror. Years pass, the willow shoot grows up into a tree, the mighty squire, become a beggar, has to leave house and lands, and his successor in the castle is the peddler, grown wealthy through trade and wedded to the erstwhile goosegirl. Card games disappear and Bibles take their places; piety, industry, and thrift flourish, just like the willow beside the moat—a new dynasty has been founded. But the years continue their course, and when one has come to Andersen's own days, a blue-blooded family once again dwells in the castle: the descendants of the peddler and the goosegirl—the young barons practice with their bows and arrows, using the old family portraits of their ancestors, which have landed in the rubbish heap, as their targets. The young barons' tutor is a pastor's son, a youth filled with the thoughts of his times; taking a branch from the old willow tree, the ancestral tree, he has carved himself a flute. A great festival at the castle includes a concert, and the fine gentlemen tease the tutor, trying to force him to play a solo on his rustic instrument. At last he accedes; but it turns out that he has carved a magic flute—its wood has come from the mysterious ancestral tree whose motto is: "Everything in its right place!" The first tone from the flute resembles a locomotive's whistle, and it passes over all the land like a storm wind: the old baron flies down to the groom's cottage beside the stables, and the pastor's son finds himself sitting at the high table beside the young baroness, the daughter of the house. An ancient count from the country's oldest family is allowed to keep his place for "the flute was fair, and that's the way people are supposed to be"; but the witty gentleman lands on his head in the chicken house; the family of a rich wholesaler, out riding behind their four fine steeds, are blown out of their coach and can not even stand on the footman's dickey; two rich peasants, grown too big for their own fields, are blown down into the muddy ditch. It was a dangerous flute, H. C. Andersen concludes, but happily it went back into the owner's pocket—that is where one gets the expression "to change one's tune," he adds with a quizzical glint in his eye.

The revolution of 1848 had been broken off after the overture; the flute had been put back into the owner's pocket. Andersen had gone through approximately the same experiences as the goblin did in the grocer's house—that tale is also from 1853. During the night of tempest and fire the goblin's heart beat in warm sympathy with the student, and he wrapped his dearest treasure, the Holy Scripture, in his red goblin's cap; but when the holocaust was past, he continued his friendship with the grocer—"And that was quite human! We others also go to the grocer—for our porridge's sake." The self-ironization is subtle and witty, but **"Everything in Its Right Place"** offers a deeper perspective. The transition from a feudal order of society to the bourgeois-capitalistic era is brilliantly symbolized in the story of the old Danish estate, and

in it Andersen has taken as critical and as just a view of the middle class as of the nobility. He had not sworn an oath of allegiance to either side. (pp. 215-20)

One cannot mistake the fact: the injustice and brutality of the previous age pursued Andersen like a nightmare. Moreover, it must be remembered that neither the self-centered egoist nor the querulous sentimentalist is giving voice to his resentments here, for it is highly unlikely that Andersen ever endured severe corporal punishment, even as a small boy in school. Instead, he has become a spokesman for the experiences, sufferings, and thoughts of society's lower strata, the strata to which he belonged.

There is nothing which would indicate that H. C. Andersen ever forgot his origins, however high he climbed on the social ladder. On the contrary: one gets the impression that these feelings of human solidarity were best able to assert themselves in Andersen's old age, after his passionate ambition, surfeited with prey, had finally begun to doze a little. In 1867, on the way home from Paris, he stopped at Odense; a festival, bringing all classes of the town's society together, was being held to welcome a battalion which had just been transferred to the capital of Fyn; and the soldiers were greeted with songs and flying colors. Attending the celebration, Andersen told a friend about another visit he had once paid to the Odense riding school, where the ceremonies were concluded: as a little boy he had been there to see a soldier run the gauntlet. "How bright and beautiful our time is in comparison with those old days I knew," he burst out. His own father had been a soldier; as a schoolboy he had been present at that popular amusement, the public execution—it is not surprising that he could give such a vivid description of the moments leading up to the soldier's near execution in **"The Tinderbox."** (p. 222)

If one assembles all these testimonies, one is inclined to declare Andersen innocent of the charge that he got along much too well with Copenhagen's patriciate and Denmark's nobility, at courts and in castles. It may be that the swan bowed his neck in greeting; he also lifted his head in pride. It may be that he took his bread from his masters' hands; he had earned it honestly, and no one need begrudge him the crumbs. All the gratitude and friendship he felt for his benefactors—and primarily for the noble, the incomparable Jonas Collin—is accurately mirrored in the fairy tales. He had not forgotten the shadows of the past, and he kept his glance toward the future.

"Only a Fiddler" was the title he once gave to his hero and to himself. But the instrument he played on was, to be sure, not a doomsday trump, designed to make walls come tumbling down, nor a warlike bugle, for firing soldiers' hearts; his instrument always retained, perhaps, something of the rustic willow-flute's idyllic and pastoral tone—but "the flute was fair, and that's the way people are supposed to be." It played a melody which tried to put everything in its right place. (p. 223)

Fredrik Böök, in his Hans Christian Andersen: A Biography, *translated by George C. Schoolfield, University of Oklahoma Press, 1962, pp. 208-33.*

ISABELLE JAN (essay date 1969)

[*In the following excerpt from a translation of her book* On Children's Literature, *originally published in 1969, Jan con-*

Self-caricature of Andersen.

siders Andersen's perceptions of life, childhood, maturity, and
death as expressed in his fairy tales and through his method
of storytelling.]

From the very beginning Hans Andersen was more than a
mere anthologist. He used the folk tale as a loose framework
for his early stories but often exploded its conventions, especially its stock of endings. The folk tale never follows life's
unpredictable, fanciful and irreversible pattern; it corrects,
compensates and inevitably contrives reassuring endings.
Hans Andersen's tales, on the other hand, never try to reassure; they offer no outlet to desire, no concessions to wishful
thinking, and do not redress the balance of life. He does not
lead his heroes to their destination but leaves them to wander
as best they can towards a goal they may never reach. In a
fairy story the peasant-prince as in Grimm's "King Thrush-
beard" or the outcast brother as in "Ivan the Ninny" may finally marry the princess; but Hans Andersen's swineherd refuses to do so.

> And with that he went into his Kingdom, shut
> the door and bolted it; but she could stand out-
> side if she cared to and sing:
>
> > Ach du lieber Augustin
> > Alles ist Voek, Voek, Voek!

The tune ends on a note that echoes in the imagination with
the sadness of a future beyond human control. Thus **"The**

Swineherd" is an anti-story where real time, fluid and unpredictable, takes the place of mythical time and this is the poet's
first step towards the conquest of reality.

From then on Hans Andersen tried, in one tale after another,
to distinguish between the folk tale and the story and to establish their different forms: **"Little Ida's Flowers," "The Snow
Queen, a folk tale in seven parts," "The Wind tells the Story
of Valdemar Daa and his Daughters," "Willie Winkie," "The
Elder Mother."** His whole output may be seen as an exercise
in the art of the narrative, in the various ways of telling a
story. He invites the reader to share the exercise and participate in the story. In a single tale we find different paces in the
narrative and different depths of imagination. (pp. 47-8)

In folk tales the hero sets out 'to seek his fortune'; the goal
is never more definite than that and in Andersen's early stories the wanderers are aimless, too: 'Hi, there, my friend,
where are you off to?' 'Out into the wide world. . . . ' But
the meaning of these wanderings gradually emerges: the bird,
the leaf and the story-teller himself are in search of a story;
they set out 'into the wide world' to look for stories. Tales are
to be found in the most unexpected places, in the heart of a
rose or in the eye of a needle and when they are recognized,
they transform the most commonplace objects into something magical. . . . How can we recognize a story? What is
the gift that makes mere talk fall into place and become a
story? How does a story with its characters and its pattern
emerge from a jumble of words or ideas suggested by the
wind, a leaf, a bird, perhaps something mentioned idly by a
child, or by the story-teller himself? The answer is a sudden
flash of perception about the nature of an object. The thing
itself will not necessarily take first place in the story—the teapot, the tin soldier, the rose or the pea—it is more likely simply to be the thing that sparks off the story-teller's imagination, setting the creative mechanism in motion—the flowers
on the balcony in **"The Shadow,"** the window-boxes on the
roof in **"The Snow Queen."** Simply to see the thing is not always enough to give birth to a story, sometimes it must be
touched as well; 'Mother says that everything you look at becomes a fairy tale and that everything you touch turns into
a story' says the little sick boy to his old neighbour in **"Elm-
Tree Mother."** Here the sensuous nature of inspiration is emphasized by the mention of 'touch'. Hans Andersen was not
given to abstract visions. He was not obsessed by strange
imaginary worlds like Blake or Poe, nor did he see things in
a haze, emerging from mists or artistically blurred: he saw
them clearly, and to make doubly sure of their real existence
he went right up to them and touched them. A man becomes
a poet when seeing things in their total reality, as though he
had been short-sighted and had put on a pair of spectacles for
the first time: 'I see everything so clearly, I feel so bright and
intelligent,' says the clerk turned poet under the spell of the
"Goloshes of Fortune." It is not sufficient to see things from
far, you must go as close as you can. That is the reason why
so many tales begin with a gesture such as knocking at a door
or opening a window which expresses a desire to go further,
to penetrate more deeply. . . . (pp. 49-50)

To enter is to try to reach what is most hidden in all things
and all beings, to get to know them so intimately that one becomes almost a part of them. . . . (p. 50)

Things and people, however ordinary and humble they are,
have a secret which has nothing to do with their outward appearance, but which beckons and calls to us, and this gives
them a kind of vibration which attracts the viewer's attention.

The viewer is the child, discovering his familiar surroundings, looking and *perceiving,* not conditioned by moral and social conventions, but in terms of the emotional relationships he spontaneously creates around him. In this respect some of the games Andersen's children play are very revealing, as when they make use of a specific object without resorting to fancy or to notions picked up in books. . . . (p. 51)

This closeness of observation, this appreciation of the object from a child's-eye view is the second step towards the conquest of reality. For Hans Andersen what the world around him had to offer was not a store of conventional ideas; living people or inanimate objects affect us, certainly, in terms of the past, but this past is not so much 'history' as the story of each particular person or thing. Hans Andersen's memories are always of a particular kind: they are not primarily concerned with historical or legendary events. Unlike the Scandinavian story-teller Selma Lagerlof, whose inspiration is entirely derived from the legends of her native land, Hans Andersen does not set out to evoke an image of Denmark—except in one or two stories, and these are not his best works. In fact, even if the tales are set in a specific place and describe traditional objects, actions and customs in detail, this is never done to provide local colour. The places—countryside or town—and their inhabitants are described for their own sake—nothing more. Hans Andersen was undoubtedly a national writer, but not a folklorist. He had no particular veneration for the past—in fact he sometimes made fun of historical yearnings and staunchly supported the present day. In **"The Goloshes of Fortune,"** the councillor's heart 'was full of thankfulness for the happy reality of our own time' when he realized that he had awakened from his medieval nightmare. Memories are everywhere because to be is to have been, and everything in the world—living creatures and inanimate objects—remembers. Creatures and things represent nothing but themselves, however, and the past survives in the present so that a man can relive his childhood experiences whenever he pleases; all he has to do is be on the alert for signs. When a young man finds his tin soldier in the sand he does not recognize it, but he recalls a fragment of his past and for a moment the child he was lives again in him (**"The Old House"**). Past and present merge in each of us and time is continuous.

Hans Andersen was convinced that childhood never ends. It is not a specific experience in which the human being is confined for a given time, more or less in limbo until he finally starts to live. There was no such break for Hans Andersen between one state and the other; he rejected the need for initiation rites, and saw childhood, forever present and vigorous, continuing to develop for the whole of life. As winter contains all the seeds and the promise of spring, memory preserves childhood intact in the grown man. Thus, in **"The Snow Queen"**—the parable of Andersen's dearest beliefs—Kay and Gerda, hand in hand, after a long winter find the rose-trees blossoming on the roof in front of the window and their little stools side by side, just as before; the only thing that has changed, in fact, is themselves: they are both grown up; 'There they sat, the two of them, grown up and yet children—children at heart. And it was summertime, warm, delicious summertime' and the Grandmother was reading these words: 'Except ye become as little children, ye shall not enter into the Kingdom of Heaven. . . .'

To be aware of the continuity of time, one must be on the look-out for certain signs. There are favourable moments and also certain messages and unexpected messengers which must

be perceived. Space is peopled with organisms, invisible and unimaginable to those who will not see, but they are there, connecting creatures to creation so that the infinity of existence may be perceived. There is the angel—who has nothing in common with the angels of the 'baby Jesus' cult of Christian mythology—and the elves, and the 'daughters of the air', and those particles of light commonly known as sparks; there are, also, other less perceptible messengers: 'And more delicate even than the flame, quite invisible to the human eye, there hovered tiny beings, just as many as there had been blossoms on the flax. . . . But the little invisible beings each of them said: "No, no, the song is never over. That is what is so lovely about the whole thing. I know this and that's luckiest of them all".'

These mediating beings are therefore related to the elements air and fire. . . . The little mermaid, prisoner of an earthly love, physically and spiritually tortured, regains her freedom and plenitude of being, not by returning to the sea, but by dissolving into air and rising to the sun, because air and fire are the elements of combustion, which ensures life—and the continuity of life.

In spite of this, people die a great deal in Hans Andersen's fairy tales. His partiality for the macabre is as notorious as his unhappy endings which are so traumatic for small children. His characters die, and often more than once in the same tale. For instance the flax undergoes the pangs of death for the first time when it turns from plant into linen; then again when it is made into paper; and lastly when, as a bit of wastepaper, it is thrown into the fire. If death is an end, can this really be death? Not that we find in Hans Andersen's tales any consoling notions of an after-life. No, it is death itself which is seen as a renewal. He forces the reader to ask himself whether death is, in fact, irreversible and final; to wonder how it occurs and what visions accompany it. At the moment of death, the two basic elements air and fire—those life-giving principles which form the very texture of Hans Andersen's thought—are once again present; death comes like a revelation, a sudden flash, an ascent towards the light. This is the symbol contained in the story of **"The Little Match-Seller"** for whom death is the place where 'it became brighter than broad daylight'. But other characters, too, experience this splendour at the moment of vanishing: the Tin Soldier, melting in the fire with his love, the Dancer:

> . . . when the maid cleaned out the ashes next morning, she found him in the shape of a little tin heart; but all that was left of the dancer was her spangle, and that was burnt black as coal.

The little mermaid 'had no feeling of death. She saw the bright sun. . . .' Death is sometimes not even mentioned because it has become synonymous with this luminosity, as in **"The Snow Queen"**: 'Grannie was sitting there in God's clear sunshine'. This is not rhetoric. The image represents a deeply felt, definite idea. For Hans Andersen physical death is this combustion which ensures the continuity of the species and the permanence of life. Through death the living become light and merge into the universe. . . . This cannot be seen as an orthodox adherence to the Christian faith in the immortality of the soul and in a life to come. It is rather—and quite simply—a negation of physical death: the Phoenix rising from its ashes, the bird of folk poetry whose voice 'cannot die' and the flaming paper says: 'the song is never over. That is what is so lovely about the whole thing!' For, in fact, nothing dies, not even what seems most vulnerable and transitory—

childhood. There are not two distinct worlds, one for grown-ups and one for children, just as life and death are not distinct; there is only a perpetual renewal. Hans Andersen, the poet of continuity and fusion, was the meeting-place of two worlds: in him childhood and manhood merged. (pp. 51-5)

*Isabelle Jan, "Hans Christian Andersen or Reality,"
in her* On Children's Literature, *edited by Catherine
Storr, Allen Lane, 1973, pp. 45-55.*

MARVIN MUDRICK   (essay date 1977)

[*In the following excerpt, Mudrick challenges critics who favorably compare Andersen to Dickens and asserts that the Danish writer's original tales are sentimental "Victorian trash."*]

Andersen is less interested in truth than in high-mindedness and justice. **"The Swineherd"** is one of his better tales—an adaptation, and his adaptations are usually simpler and livelier than his inventions—it's about a prince wooing a beautiful (what else?) and spoiled (who cares?) princess; so far so good, until Andersen reverses the original happy ending and sees to it that the prince casts her off because the princess quite forgivably prefers a couple of charming gadgets to God's precious little creatures (a rose and a nightingale): " 'I have come to despise you,' said the prince"; vindictively abandons her in a pouring rain out in the middle of nowhere; "entered his own kingdom and locked the door behind him." Andersen seems to think he does justice to the beauty of women by pretending that what gives so much pleasure has no special privileges. But Perrault, one of Andersen's predecessors, knows just what sort of acknowledgment a true prince owes to a beautiful princess (in "Ricky of the Tuft"): "Beauty is so great an advantage that everything else can be disregarded; and I do not see that the possessor of it can have anything much to grieve about." Moreover the Grimm brothers, doting on the beautiful and spoiled princess of "The Frog-King," don't let some silly promises she has made to the frog get in the way of her amphibicidal revulsion when he demands that she take him to bed with her:

> "I'm tired, I want to sleep as much as you do: pick me up, or I'll tell your father." Then she really got angry, picked him up, and threw him against the wall with all her might: "Now you can go to sleep if you like, you nasty frog!"

> But when he fell he wasn't a frog but a prince . . .

and of course they live happily ever after. In the world's wish-books virtue is its own reward but beauty takes the cake. Who—certainly not Chaucer!—would ever think of punishing zesty and beautiful Alisoun of *The Miller's Tale* for cuckolding her old husband, humiliating one of her suitors, having a wonderful time herself, and generally making the world a wilder place for anybody who lays his eyes or hands on her?

Andersen persuades himself that fairy tales aren't fiction (articulate fears and wishes, reasonable dreams) but lessons, as for instance: nature is better than art (for towering oaks from teeny acorns grow), feeling is better than thinking, ignorance is better than learning, children are better than grownups ("I can't give her any more power than she already has! Don't you understand how great it is? . . . it is in her heart, for she is a sweet and innocent child"), funerals are better than weddings, mothers are better than people—

> The poor mother kissed the dead child and then

kissed the rose, before she placed it on the young girl's breast, as if she hoped that the freshness of a rose and a mother's kiss could make the girl's heart beat again.

> The petals of the rose shook with happiness. It was as if the whole rose swelled and grew. "I have become more than a rose, for, like a child, I have received a mother's kiss. I have been blessed and will travel into the unknown realm, dreaming on the dead girl's breast. Truly, I am the happiest of us all."

—(when there are no swelling roses available, Andersen rhymes his pubescent girls with tumescent pearls: "The girl said, ' . . . I feel within my closed hand the glow of the jewel. I can feel it pulse and swell . . . ' "), as a matter of fact though God is good ("To Him alone belongs all honor") people are no damn good ("the trash, the cheap tinsel that mankind considered beautiful"), ugly is gorgeous, poor is rich, ad infinitum and caveat emptor. Whoever has read only the few most often reprinted stories (chiefly adaptations) of Andersen's wouldn't guess that most of his hundred and fifty-six are nondenominational tracts, homilies, exempla, with the mixture of mush ("who can distinguish between raindrops and tears of happiness?"), bluff, archness, and spite characteristic of such productions, though usually Andersen's make a not necessarily laudable effort to disguise themselves as fairy tales.

Some of the best-known tales—e.g. **"The Little Mermaid," "The Snow Queen," "The Ice-Maiden"**—don't even observe the blessed folk convention of brevity; they have their moments (especially **"The Ice-Maiden,"** in which the fine realistic account of a courtship doesn't deserve to be juxtaposed and confused with the claptrap supernaturalism) but they tend to trail off into mazes of fancy, sentiment, Victorian trash and tinsel: Andersen and Dickens were mutual admirers, and much of Andersen reads like the worst of Dickens: **"The Little Match Girl," "Grief," "The Dead Child," "She Was No Good."** When Andersen is doing an adaptation of a highly vertebrate folk tale that resists invention and pathos and coy asides—as for example **"The Emperor's New Clothes," "The Tinderbox," "The Princess and the Pea," "Little Claus and Big Claus," "What Father Does Is Always Right"**—he can be economical and entertaining, and give evidence of the great storyteller's conscience and sense of pace and rhythm. On his own though he has too many options, his detail is often distracting and irresponsible, the sort that passes itself off in the abominable deserts of children's literature as "imaginative": "He did not ride away on a horse: no, he mounted an ostrich, for that could run faster. But as soon as he saw the wild swans he picked out the strongest among them and rode on that instead, for he liked a change" (**"The Philosopher's Stone"**).

The best of the world's fairy tales have a symmetry and a cutting edge that are quite beyond even the best of Andersen. (pp. 133-35)

Marvin Mudrick, "The Ugly Duck," in The Hudson Review, *Vol. XXX, No. 1, Spring, 1977, pp. 131-37.*

ROGER SALE   (essay date 1978)

[*Sale is an American essayist, editor, and academic. In the following excerpt, he discerns flaws in Andersen's fairy tales, con-*

cluding that Andersen's understanding and representation of a child's world were frequently clouded by "false rhetoric."]

Hans Christian Andersen wrote what he called fairy tales, what were accepted by his audience as fairy tales, but which show on almost every page how much a break had been made, with the oral as well as the written tradition. The voice of Andersen is the voice of a teller, but Andersen was a writer, a writer of the Romantic period, and so he tries to put his personal stamp on his tales, even the ancient ones he only retold, and he always considered himself his own major resource, his own necessary and sufficient inspiration. Many of his openings reveal this all too clearly:

> The Emperor of China is a Chinese, as of course you know, and the people he has about him are Chinese too.

[**"The Nightingale"**]

Not just a joke, but a bad one; and if not that, pretty vividness:

> Far out at sea the water is as blue as the bluest cornflower, and as clear as the clearest glass; but it is very deep, deeper than any anchor cable can fathom.

[**"The Little Mermaid"**]

And, if not vividness, remarks about storytelling:

> Listen! Now we are going to begin. When the story has ended, we shall know a lot more than we do now.

[**"The Snow Queen"**]

He aims satiric shafts, he points his morals and adorns his tales. Of all the major reputations among authors of children's literature, Andersen's is much the hardest to understand or justify. Yet for precisely these reasons he is useful here, as a way to mark the transition from fairy tales to later children's literature, because what is wrong with his work is, almost without exception, what is wrong with all inferior children's literature and what mars even some of the masterpieces. Since children's literature is written by adults and "for" children, authors of children's books can be strongly tempted to make the central relation be between the teller and the audience rather than the teller and the tale. The older authors of fairy tales . . . know their audience very well, but never alter anything in the tale to suit or please the audience; their respect for their materials is too great. But when children's literature was invented, the adults who wrote the tales often started contemplating the children who were to hear and read them, and they tended to get lost, because they became involved in what was essentially a false rhetoric. "The Emperor of China is a Chinese" is such a silly thing to say that it must express an essentially patronizing attitude toward the audience. The teller has an idea of a child in his head, he acts as though he knows "what children like" or "how children think," and the moment he does that his language becomes false. The tellers of fairy tales before this never thought their audience was any different from themselves, never thought of themselves as authors forced to conceive a relation to an audience. But after childhood was invented, adults inevitably began thinking about what language, what stance or tone, what materials were appropriate for children, and so we get something like the large and often subtle machinery of the Pooh books in which A. A. Milne guides his son toward an acceptance of the loss of early childhood. Even in many books which idealize children, the im-

plicit rhetoric insists it is better to be an adult, and thereby be able to do this idealizing, than it is to be a child, who doesn't know any better than not to know that his or hers is the ideal time of life. Of course, anyone who writes a book for children will make some adjustments, but when the writer is really concerned with the tale and not the audience, the adjustments are easily made, since they will concern themselves with a simplification of vocabulary and the avoidance of prolonged abstract argument and discourse.

Andersen had certain initial advantages as a teller of fairy tales. . . . He was an only child, smaller and slighter than the others in his school, and his response to feeling an ugly duckling was to create his own small worlds, with dolls, puppets, songs, and retold stories; he became famous in Odense as a gifted lad who gave charming performances. The results of these beginnings can be seen in his lifelong love of the theatre, in his continual stance as a performer, in his love of pathos, in his evocations of the outcast who longs to be different or in a different place. Clearly, too, this early success failed to satisfy for very long. He hated Odense, for all it gave him the setting and imagery for many of his tales, and he was in Copenhagen before he was fifteen, trying to be an actor. All his apparent advantages, then, were something he wanted to exploit, to use as food for his inventiveness, his powers of mimicry, his theatricality, his desire not to be an ugly duckling. He wanted to be latter-day, to be famous as a writer and actor, but his shyness and sense of personal inadequacy kept throwing him back on his origins, on his loneliness, on his incurably provincial sense that life was better where the lights were brighter.

So Andersen is the soldier as well as the cobbler's boy in **"The Tinder Box,"** he is the little mermaid, the mole in **"Thumbelina,"** the steadfast tin soldier. Women could only admire and pity him, and their rejection in turn intensified his sense of himself as an outcast, with pathos and spurts of satiric revenge his only weapons. His stories of the figures he made out of himself gained him fame greater than any Danish writer, before or since, has achieved, and during the last thirty years of his life he could travel anywhere he wished, meet anyone he chose, and be adored. But a writer who uses personal unhappiness as an exploitable resource is artistically as well as humanly engaged in civil war, since what succeeds is also what makes miserable. Especially in his earlier years Andersen was stubborn in his belief in his talent, but there was always something compulsive about this belief, because it was designed to take him away from who and where he had been as much as to take him any place he wished to go. The result was, on the one hand, great creative energies. He wrote many plays, novels, poems, and travel books in addition to the fairy tales for which he is still known, and the complete tales make a volume of half a million words. But on the other hand he wrote quickly, even slapdash, and counted on his assumed talent to carry him through. The result is not just a good deal of inconsequential work, but many stories whose confusions and contradictions reveal his civil war, often in embarrassing ways.

"The Little Mermaid," for instance, is one of Andersen's most popular tales, which means its pathos has found a responsive echo in many who feel they are little mermaids. But it really is a chaotic, desperate piece of work, very much out of touch with itself. "You are to keep your gliding motion, no dancer will be as able to move as gracefully," the sea-witch tells the mermaid who wants to become a human being, "but at every step it will feel you are treading on a sharp-edged knife." Andersen, himself willing to suffer great pain to be near the woman he loved, apparently never saw the trouble he entailed the moment he made the mermaid want to become a human being and established conditions for her transformation. D'Aulnoy and many other writers of fairy tales have characters willing to suffer for the sake of their beloved. In most of these cases, a transformation is involved, one that assumes the natural state of the lover is human, and the unnatural state is the green snake, the white deer, or the ram. In **"The Little Mermaid,"** Andersen is driven to making the mermaid naturally inferior to the prince as a way of expressing his own sense of his social or sexual inferiority. If she is going to step "up" to the prince's class, she must no longer be a mermaid. To complicate the issue still further, since Andersen was also resentful of those who rejected him, he makes all the mermaids beautiful and the beloved prince a dense and careless man, so that one cannot imagine where the "natural" inferiority of the mermaid lies, and it seems like lunacy to suffer as she does in order to be able to dance before the prince.

All these difficulties would tear away at the story even if the prince finally were to love the mermaid, but Andersen felt driven, in addition, to have the prince reject her as Andersen himself had been. Since he could find no way to describe the appearance or the behavior of the mermaids so as to make them seem inferior to human beings, Andersen posited that mermaids have no immortal souls. He cannot say what this means, however, since the mermaids seem to lack nothing possessed by human beings except legs. The sea-witch tells the mermaid she can have a soul if a mortal will love her, which reduces "soul" to a romantic and sexual prize; worse, the mermaid has vastly more of something like a soul than does the prince. Then, since Andersen partly wants to revenge himself against the prince for rejecting the mermaid, he has the mermaid's sisters tell her she can become a mermaid again if she will kill the prince, which makes the mermaid's love into even more of an unnatural passion than it is before this. Finally, since of course the mermaid will not kill the prince, Andersen must invent a trapdoor to escape from these impossible tangles, and so he invents the daughters of the air, who "have no immortal soul either, but they can gain one by their good deeds." But the trapdoor refuses to open, since Andersen cannot imagine why daughters of the air, any more than mermaids, should have to work for immortal souls, while human beings have them as part of their birthright. Indeed, the whole question of an immortal soul is much trickier in a story like this than Andersen realizes, and it illustrates the great good sense of earlier oral and written tellers of fairy tales in leaving out all explicit religion. To make socially inferior into sexually inferior, and to make sexually inferior into naturally inferior, is bad enough, but to make naturally inferior into religiously inferior is sheer desperation. The original longings which created the story are, I think, the reason for its continued popularity; all the snobberies and reverse snobberies that follow seem just to be ignored, at least by people I know who claim the story as one of their favorites—and they invariably first read it early in adolescence.

"Thumbelina" has the same kind of difficulty, though the surface of the story is much more clear and calm. Thumbelina, born tiny, on the pistil of a tulip, is captured by a toad who takes her away so she can be married to the toad's ugly son. Andersen must have known many stories in which such a kidnapping was threatened or achieved by giants, ogres, and dwarves. But the toads here, though indeed ugly, are not the least wicked or brutal, so that when Andersen says "She did not want to live with the horrid toad, neither did she want the toad's ugly son for a husband," he is once again confusing difference and inferiority. The toad isn't nasty at all, just a toad. James Thurber has a fable about a crow and a Baltimore oriole which employs this same situation, but Thurber's aims are far different from Andersen's. Thurber's crow may be a fool for falling in love with a Baltimore oriole, but the pretty oriole is no prize either. Andersen, though, can't avoid sanctioning Thumbelina's distaste for toads by implying that toads should stay in their place and know better than to want Thumbelina. Indeed, the same thing happens a second time when a field mouse rescues Thumbelina from the oncoming winter and very pleasantly thinks she would make a good mate for her friend the mole, who is prosperous and has a shiny dark coat. Thumbelina understandably does not care for this idea, especially since she doesn't want to live underground and prefers sunshine and song. But Andersen persists in blaming the field mouse and the mole for being a field mouse and a mole, ground and underground animals: "For their neighbor, the tiresome mole in the black velvet coat, had proposed to her"; "But she was not at all happy, for she did not care one bit for the tiresome mole." It is as though Andersen never asked what the implications were of his projecting his own feelings of being rejected onto the animal world. Stranger still is a little story called **"Sweethearts,"** which makes a class matter between a top and a ball, so both the top who wants and the ball who rejects are figures of mere silliness. Andersen was always improvising, outfitting objects and animals with his own feelings, and so seldom stopped to respect the nature of his characters.

Fortunately, some of Andersen's stories are more impersonal and therefore much better than **"The Little Mermaid"** or **"Thumbelina."** **"The Snow Queen"** is riddled with faults, but it shows what Andersen could do well, which was something that older tellers and writers of fairy tales had not tried to do. By the time he wrote **"The Snow Queen,"** a long, loose narrative in seven stories, he had done a lot of traveling, and everyone he met in Germany, France, England, and Italy knew he was a Dane, a man from a little-known northern country. In this tale he seems to be asking what it means to be from such a country, considered not as a place where Andersen had suffered, and not as a society, but as a climate. He opens with some little devils that go everywhere with their looking glass, "reducing the reflection of anything good and beautiful to almost nothing, while what was no good or was ugly stood out well and grew even worse." The devils take their mirror too high in the heavens, and it breaks, but that only means that its pieces, when they fall to earth, can become lodged in the eyes and hearts of people: "A few people even got a splinter of it into their hearts, and that was terrible indeed, for then their hearts became exactly like a lump of ice." Andersen knew all about ice, and when, one summer day, a bit of the glass strikes a boy named Kay in the heart, and another lodges in his eye, Andersen knows this lump of iciness can have little effect in the summertime. Come winter, though, Kay starts trying to act more grown-up; he ridicules the childish delights of his friend Gerda, and then he begins to offer clever parodies of his grandmother and to insist that a snowflake under a magnifying glass is better than one that just falls to the ground, and much better than a rose's petals.

One day Kay goes out into the square with his sled, and soon a big sleigh comes along and the driver ties up Kay's sled and carries it out of the village: "All of a sudden they flew to one side, the big sleigh stopped, and the person who was drawing it stood up. The fur coat and cap were made entirely of snow. It was a woman, tall and slender, and glittering white. It was the Snow Queen." She kisses Kay, and:

> Kay looked at her. She was so beautiful. He could not imagine a brighter or more lovely face. She didn't seem to be all ice now, as she did when she sat outside the window and beckoned to him. In his eyes she was perfect. He was not at all frightened; he told her he could do mental arithmetic even with fractions; that he knew the areas of all the countries, and the answer to "What is their population?" And she went on smiling. Then he began to suspect that he did not know so much after all. Bewildered he gazed into space. She flew away with him, flew high up onto the black cloud, while the storm howled and roared—it sounded very much like old folk tunes. They flew over woods and lakes, over sea and land; below them the cold icy wind went whistling, wolves howled, black screaming crows flew low over the glistening snow, but over it all shone the moon, large and clear, and on that Kay gazed during the long, long winter's night. By day he slept at the feet of the Snow Queen.

We have seen nothing like this before; it is grand, atmospheric writing about nature, seeking effects the teller of "The Juniper Tree" would not have needed or understood. Andersen here is finding something new for a fairy tale to do. This abduction is thrilling as well as frightening, because Andersen has pondered what it means to be a snow *queen* as well as a *snow* queen. Unlike the devils, the Snow Queen is a natural force, and therefore powerful, and to be queen of such a force is to be beautiful and perfect, so that all Kay's homage to her, his fractions and facts, is not enough. By introducing the little devils, by having them make Kay susceptible with the glass caught in his heart and eye, Andersen frees the Snow Queen of any suggestion that she is demonic or malicious; she is really only claiming her own.

Just as the author of *Beowulf*, of an earlier time but a similar latitude, knew that what lay outside the meadhalls was named Grendel, and that what lived in the meres was Grendel's mother, so Andersen knows that even in a city snow and cold can grip and dominate, finding the victims of the imps and claiming for them a particularly northern fate. But the Snow Queen must take Kay out of Denmark, because spring and summer return there, and up to Lapland, her home. Gerda, the child who didn't want to be grown up, sets out to find him. She visits an old wizard woman who is kind to her but wants to keep Gerda for herself, which makes her like the Snow Queen except her dominion is a flower garden, not a sleigh, and that makes all the difference. Gerda keeps asking the flowers where Kay is, and they all give lovely irrelevant answers, lovely because each tells a fairy tale, irrelevant because they know nothing of Kay, and Gerda can barely understand them. That all things are bright and beautiful does not connect them, or make them know each other—the world is too large and various for that, especially in the warmer months.

But as autumn comes, Gerda sets out again, and meets a crow who tells her about a princess who has announced she will marry any young man who can come and talk to her as though he were at home. Most young men became so nervous at trying that they failed, but one lad finally appeared and said to the palace guards, "It must be boring standing on the stairs; I'm going inside." That is exactly how Kay sounded after the glass pierced his heart and eye, so Gerda goes to the palace, is sneaked in by the crow's sweetheart, only to discover the prince is not Kay. Very nice he is, as is the princess, and they listen to Gerda's tale and offer to outfit her trip north. "How good they are, human beings and animals," Gerda thinks as she tries to overcome her disappointment, and to remember that everyone she has met on her journey has been as helpful as he or she could be. So it is with the rough robber band that captures Gerda, where a woman wants to kill her but her perky daughter gets her mother drunk so Gerda can escape; so too with the Lapp woman and the Finn woman and the reindeer who guide and take her to the Snow Queen's palace. The story is long because it must be, in order to show the world, when it is not dominated by the Snow Queen, is not paradise but the world, multiple, varied, usually helpful to a distressed girl if it doesn't have to go far out of its way to do so. Gerda, seen by herself, is an awfully passive, pallid heroine, but Andersen, though he praises her highly, only offers sweetness and innocence as her virtues, and he does not pretend they light up the sky.

In the Snow Queen's palace all is cold, ordered, and dazzling; Kay drags about pieces of ice, makes shapes and words, because the Snow Queen has told him "you shall be your own master, and I will give you the whole world, and a new pair of skates" if you can spell the word "eternity." But he cannot, and it is winter now, so the Snow Queen is off in more southern regions; Kay "looked at the pieces of ice and thought and thought for all he was worth." This is satire, of course, derived from Andersen's dislike of the math and spelling taught in schools, but here it is decently muted, and the point Andersen makes is not entirely irrelevant. At least as good, surely, to have the Snow Queen set Kay the task of spelling "eternity" as it is to have Winnie-the-Pooh hunt for a backson because Christopher Robin doesn't quite know how to spell "back soon."

Then, at the climax:

> She walked into the big empty hall, caught sight of Kay, and knew him at once, and flew towards him and flung her arms around his neck, held him tight and shouted: "Kay! darling little Kay! At last I've found you!"
>
> But there he sat quite still, and stiff and cold. Then Gerda shed hot tears, which fell on his breasts, and penetrated right into his heart. They thawed the lump of ice, and dissolved the splinter of glass that was lodged in it. He looked at her, and she sang:
>
> As roses bloom in the valley sweet, So the Christ child there ye shall truly meet.
>
> Kay burst into tears. He cried and cried so hard that his tears washed the tiny chip of glass out of his eyes. Now he knew her and exclaimed for joy.

The Savior makes a much better appearance here than the immortal soul does in **"The Little Mermaid."** Salvation is in the world, not in eternity, and we can know this by knowing the roses in the valley, which fade and are not perfect. Roses have no place in the Snow Queen's palace, no more than do hot tears and hymns, and it is Gerda's "heroism" that her persistence has allowed her to do so much with the little she has, and it is the glory of the world that it has, this way and that way, shown her the way.

The symbols and actions all work in **"The Snow Queen"** because Andersen has asked what it means to be captured by the queen of the snow, and what power can rescue what she has captured. Gerda is no Beowulf or Siegfried, and the Snow Queen cannot be killed, and it takes all the power of the spring and summer, all the determination of Gerda, plus a prince, a princess, a crow, reindeer, and two women who live up north just to release the lad with the glass in his eye and heart. Someone who lived much south of Denmark might not need to know all this, and someone who lived much north of Denmark might not be able to. But, knowing what he knows, and, for once, trusting what he knows, Andersen can release his story from the personal bondage that ties up so much of his other work. To be sure, there are the nips and barks of the satire, the idealization of the child for her innocence only, the lengthy clumsiness of the stories of Gerda's journey, and we can see that it is always unfortunate that Andersen was a *writer* in ways earlier tellers of tales did not have to be, and in ways that Tchaikovsky and the great choreographers and dancers did not have to be either. (pp. 63-73)

It is often said of Andersen, and of many later successful storytellers for children, that they never grew up themselves and so could better speak to the young. There is perhaps truth in this, but most of the conclusions one might want to draw from this idea seem false. In Andersen's case it is demonstrable that what retarded his maturing as a person handicapped him as an author, and all his defects, by comparison with the earlier authors of fairy tales, seem the result of an inability to be calm, confident, transparently anonymous, a partaker in a tradition older than he, and wiser. (p. 73)

> *Roger Sale, "Written Tales: Perrault to Andersen," in his* Fairy Tales and After: From Snow White to E. B. White, *Cambridge, Mass.: Harvard University Press, 1978, pp. 49-75.*

BO GRØNBECH   (essay date 1980)

[*Grønbech is a well-known Danish essayist and academic who has written extensively on Andersen. In the following excerpt from his critical biography of Andersen, Grønbech surveys Andersen's fairy tales and short stories.*]

[Andersen's] achievement was twofold: first, he put into print spoken language with all its inconsistencies of logic and syntax; second, he removed all those words and expressions, particularly the abstract ones, that only adults used. How thoroughly he carried this out is made apparent by comparing "The Ghost" (1829) with its reworked version entitled **"The Traveling Companion"** (1835). (pp. 89-90)

Andersen had begun by retelling tales that he had heard in his childhood on Funen: **"The Tinder Box," "Little Klaus,"** and **"The Princess on the Pea"**; but the fourth one, **"Little Ida's Flowers,"** which concluded the first volume, was more or less an original story. Soon he was inventing more than retelling. **"The Traveling Companion," "The Wild Swans,"** and **"The Swineherd"** are folktales, while **"The Naughty Boy"** was an idea he got from a short poem written by the classic Greek lyricist Anacreon. **"The Emperor's New Clothes"** is an old Spanish story, **"The Rose Elf"** reproduces an Italian folksong, while **"The Flying Trunk"** has its motif from *The Arabian Nights*. Of the 156 tales printed in his collected works Andersen claims that only nine are retellings: **"The Tinder Box," "Little Klaus," "The Princess on the Pea," "The Traveling Companion," "The Wild Swans," "The Gar-**

den of Eden," "The Swineherd," "Simple Simon,"** and **"What Father Does is Always Right."** The remainder are his own inventions.

No matter the origin of the tales, Andersen's young audience was delighted. The concrete, direct narrative was brilliantly adapted to their range of comprehension; children have always enjoyed folktales, and the other stories are equally simple in plot and theme and take place among persons and in settings that children know—or did in those days.

Andersen was long in realizing the value of his fairy tales, and for a number of years regarded them as sideline compositions. But their unparalleled success finally helped change his mind. They were read and admired not only in Denmark but in other countries, and by an increasing number of adults. (p. 91)

[Andersen wrote] for both the children and the adults. This was two-level composition in Andersenian terms: the language and the fairy tale setting he kept, but the thoughts behind them were for the listening parents. This creative process was, however, not completely new. Tales as early as **"The Little Mermaid"** and **"The Goloshes of Fortune"** were not primarily intended for children, and in the children's tales "a little something for the thoughts" was scattered about that could scarcely be comprehended by children. However, after 1843 Andersen deliberately aimed at an adult audience. Children certainly enjoy both **"The Snow Queen"** and **"The Nightingale"** as well as many others, but they can hardly plumb the depths of these stories; while tales such as **"The Bell," "The Story of a Mother,"** or **"The Shadow"** are just not understood by young listeners. The simple, pseudochildish narrative style is no more than an intriguing disguise, a refined naiveté permitting irony or seriousness to have a stronger hold.

Andersen had gradually developed this original form of telling tales, and reached perfection in the years following 1843. All his masterpieces—such as **"The Sweethearts," "The Ugly Duckling," "The Fir Tree," "The Little Match Girl," "The Shirt Collar,"** and so on—came into being during this period. In 1849 his entire production to date of fairy tales was published in a large, collected edition: a tribute to the artistic capacity of the not yet forty-five-year-old writer.

Yet he was not finished with the tales. In 1852 he published two more collections, though with a new title. He now called them *Stories*—he needed a more comprehensive title and he had his reasons. The two collections did contain more fairytalelike descriptions, such as **"The Goblin at the Grocer's"** and **"It's Perfectly True,"** but there was much more as well: **"The Story of the Year"** is a long, lyrical nature painting; **"A Good Temper"** is a cheerful causerie; **"Heartbreak"** and **"She was No Good"** are situations and fates from real life; **"In a Thousand Years' Time"** presents a futuristic vision; and **"Beneath the Willow-Tree"** is a short story. Moreover, Andersen had earlier tried his hand at reporting and lyrical pictures. *Picture Book without Pictures* (1839) is comprised of a number of scenes and experiences from both near and far, pathetic, touching, humorous, ironic—brief tales told by the moon to the lonely young artist up in his garret. It was to creative writing in this genre that Andersen returned in 1852, and during the last twenty years of his life he wrote many similar descriptions in addition to a number of narratives of the sort we would nowadays call short stories. (pp. 92-3)

[Andersen] came from the common people. To him their

world was not something that needed to be learned; it was his own world and had been so since birth. So the luggage that the youth from Odense had with him was something that other poets of the day did not, and could not, have: a new literary form, the fairytale, or perhaps better, the fairy short story. Moreover, he was bringing something of greater importance, a new world, one of quite different people, natural laws, and even morals from those the bourgeoisie of Copenhagen was used to. Andersen was able to plant a new tree in the garden of Danish literature, a tree with strange blossoms and wonderfully fresh fragrance.

What did Andersen do to the folktale? He changed it; he had to. After all, he had to tell the tale to well-reared Copenhagen children, so much retouching was necessary. In a note to **"The Swineherd"** Andersen says that it could not with "decency" be retold in the manner he had heard it as a child, for it was not for delicate ears. There were other reasons why he had to change them. The way they were told among the common people would not satisfy cultivated literary taste. (pp. 95-6)

If Andersen was to have any hope of his writings being accepted within the world of literature, in short, if he wanted to create a Danish *Kunstmärchen,* then he had to meet these requirements. He did so from the very first tales, in part, perhaps, because he had an adult audience in mind from the very beginning, and, possibly because he realized the need to write for an educated public. . . .

"The Tinder Box," the first of his retellings, is a literary pearl. (p. 96)

This story follows the usual pattern of the folk fairy tale: the brave young hero comes through many trials and finally wins the princess and the kingdom. But what a difference there is from the haphazard form of the folktale! In Andersen's version the plot is intensified as much as possible. Events follow each other in quick succession. There are no unnecessary words. There is no beating about the bush when the witch tackles the soldier about fetching the tinderbox nor when she refuses to tell him what she will do with the strange object: the matter is settled immediately. No sooner have the dogs dispatched the king and queen and court than the wedding takes place. However, the greatest difference lies somewhere else. The folktale does not make much out of setting or characters, while in Andersen the story is full of details that bring people and situations closer and make them more familiar: the king and queen drink tea at breakfast, the soldier smokes a pipe, and the witch's grandmother can forget things. Moreover, the persons are distinct individuals with traits we all recognize. An additional attraction lies in the incredibly short space within which the characterization is drawn. A stroke and the character is alive. The soldier's friends are very fond of him when he is rich, but they cannot manage all the stairs when he is poor and is living in an attic. When the queen hears of the nighttime visit her comment, "That's a pretty tale, if you like!" is enough for us to recognize her, as too is the king's, "I won't be tossed," when the dogs are hurling the courtiers to their deaths.

As for the soldier himself: when he hears that there is a pretty princess at the castle he immediately asks, "Where is she to be seen?" But alas she is not to be seen, for she is locked up. "I'd like to see her!" thought the soldier but, "of course, he could not possibly get leave to." To indicate more in so short a space would be impossible: a brave soldier, both inquisitive

and fond of women, and bored to boot, who does not seem likely to be stopped by something being forbidden or by there being a copper castle with walls and towers between him and the object of his wishes. That inserted "of course" speaks wonders. When he finally sees the princess she really does look so lovely that he simply cannot resist kissing her, for "he was a soldier all over."

Probably only adults take in the subtlety of these details or understand the perspective in the brief comment that one of the *old* ladies-in-waiting was told to sit up after the first night adventure "to see if it was a real dream or something quite different." Do children notice that it is the king and queen, the old lady-in-waiting, and all the officers who sally forth in the morning to see where the princess has been? That was not kind to the army!

"The Traveling Companion" is also one of the first retellings. (pp. 97-8)

This story is written specifically for children, as is made clear by the somewhat sentimental compassion that the narrator shows toward the characters and the occasional use of child's language ("Ugh, how fierce it looked"). The psychology, too, in several places is as simple as in the folktale ("the wicked men," "the good John") and is how children normally accept it. But the description of the settings certainly exceeds the narrow framework of the folktale. The description of the ogre's palace in the mountain is a wealth of original and imaginative details—and there is great charm about the presentation of the ogre's courtiers who "were so grand and genteel; though anyone with eyes in his head soon saw what they were. They were nothing but broomsticks with cabbages for heads that the ogre had bewitched into life and dressed in embroidered robes. But it didn't make any difference for they were only for show"—An amusing aside about the demands court life makes on people.

Moreover, several of the situations possess such animation that they become familiar and real. The wicked princess causes her old father such sorrows that he can scarcely eat, "and anyhow the gingernuts were too hard for him." The king had once and for all said that he would never have anything whatever to do with her suitors, yet he is so full of concern when the new suitor presents himself that he "began to cry so hard that he dropped both scepter and orb on the floor and had to wipe away his tears with his dressing gown. . . . Poor old king!"

Indeed, even the ogre in his mountain responds in a reasonable manner, at least, it is reasonable from his own special viewpoint. When the wicked princess tells him that while she was flying out to the mountain she was whipped so terribly by the hailstorm, he replies, "Yes, one can have too much of a good thing"—a quite natural response for, after all, an ogre is a form of inverted human for whom the most vile of weathers would be the most pleasant. (pp. 98-9)

The retelling of old tales was, however, only a starting point for Andersen. With his imagination he could invent in the same style and had at his fingertips the requirements of the genre and the possibilities of the settings.

Folklore figures from legends and tales were often little more than names; but Andersen endowed them with individual features and thus gave them fresh life. A suitable example is found in **"The Hill of the Elves."** (p. 99)

This is a fantastic party in the realm of the supernatural, and yet it is described in such human terms that the reader practically feels at home. Although Andersen has introduced the whole gamut of the denizens of folklore, as well as the animals of the forest, the happenings at the Elf king's court closely resemble those of an ordinary family: an old respectable housekeeper; daughters to be married off; and bickering over who is to be invited to the banquet. The Elf king only puts in an appearance on the most ceremonious of occasions and, when the guests arrive, is anxious to be seen wearing his gold crown—polished with finest slate-pencil—while standing in the moonlight. The old grey-bearded troll from Dovre is a picture of an elderly Norwegian gentleman, jovial and open; while his two cocksure sons have much in common with another type of Norwegian who in Andersen's day was attracting some rather unflattering attention. The Death-horse is so sensitive that the toe-spinning dance of the Elf girls makes him giddy, and he is compelled to leave the table. Those inquisitive creatures, the lizard and earthworm, are not unlike humans, since the most interesting thing for them is to observe and discuss the goings-on of fashionable people. They look down on each other and distrust each other with typical human pettiness. (pp. 100-01)

No matter which category of tale Andersen is telling the style is completely his own. Part of its originality lies in the reader's constant awareness of the narrator's presence in the middle of the listening audience. He narrates and explains, claims his audience's attention, even exchanges words with them, and along with them enjoys the story he is telling. At times he speaks as if he was a man who had experienced everything himself and perhaps even knows about the real facts of the matter and the innermost thoughts of the characters; at other times he argues with his audience as to how the phenomena in the narrative are to be understood.

The unquenchable vivacity of the style is also due to Andersen's living intensely in the situations and events he is describing. At the beginning of **"The Ugly Duckling"** the whole description exudes the warmth of the pleasure he derived from the summer: "It was so lovely in the country! It was summer!" At the very moment of narrating he seems to see and experience that wonderful landscape.

There is even more: he assimilates to his characters and makes their thoughts his own. They slip imperceptibly into the narration as indirect speech or *style indirect libre* (i.e., the account reflects the wording of the person in question). When the soldier in **"The Tinderbox"** is at the bottom of the tree recovering the tinderbox for the witch and the money for himself, he has to go into three rooms, each of which contains a dog sitting on the money, each dog being larger than the one before. In the third room, so the witch had told him, the dog has eyes as big as the Round Tower in Copenhagen. When he gets there, "Oh, but it was horrible! The dog in there really did have eyes as big as the Round Tower" (the soldier's thoughts). When our brave soldier has spent all of his money and has to live in a tiny attic room, "none of his friends ever came to see him for there were so many stairs to climb" (his friends' explanation). Then when he was rich again and had changed back to fine rooms "all his friends remembered him again at once and were tremendously fond of him" (friends' words to soldier).

In part one of **"Heartbreak"** the good widow puts her pug dog down and he "began growling. After all, he had gone with her for enjoyment and the sake of his health and so they

had no right to put him on the floor" (the pug dog's thoughts).

Occasionally the narrative moves without warning from the thoughts of one character to those of the next. When the nightingale has won favor with the emperor of China by her singing Andersen writes, "Now she was to remain at court and have her own cage, with leave to go out for two walks in the daytime and one at night. Twelve attendants were to accompany her, each holding tightly to a silk ribbon fastened to her leg. There was absolutely no fun in a walk like that." The word "leave" shows that this is the court's view of the matter, while the last sentence must be the nightingale's opinion.

Not only the thoughts and feelings of the individual characters are brought out but also those of the people who are attending or might be attending the events. In **"The Top and the Ball,"** when the top has jumped too high and disappeared, we are told: "They looked and looked, even down in the basement, but he was not to be found. Wherever had he got to?" This question is obviously posed by the searcher, but it might equally well be asked by any person present, even the reader of the tale. After the artificial nightingale has been repaired, though alas not very satisfactorily, the learned master of music "made a little speech full of the most difficult words, declaring that the bird was just as good as ever—and so of course it was just as good as ever." To whom is it just as good as ever? This must be the courtiers and the whole foolish mass of blindly obedient people, all those who heard the master of music's declaration. **"The Nightingale"** ends with the emperor, having survived the crisis of his illness, rising in the morning to greet his servants who are coming "to attend their dead emperor. Yes, there they stood, and the emperor exclaims, 'Good morning!'" That outburst, "Yes, there they stood," could clearly come quite naturally from anybody witnessing this grotesque scene, including, of course, the principal character, the emperor. Actually, it could also come naturally from the narrator and his readers.

There are, in fact, many instances where it is just not possible to differentiate between the thoughts and feelings of the principal characters, those of other characters present, and those of the narrator. They all blend into one living consistent picture. On the dung-beetle's wanderings in the world he is caught in a rain storm and looks for shelter; he catches sight of something white; it was some linen laid out to bleach. "He came up to it and crept into a fold of the soaking fabric"—this is the narrator's objective information—"Of course, this could not be compared with lying in the warm dung in the stable"—here we have slipped over to the beetle's point of view—"but there was nothing better to be had here"—this could well be expressing the beetle's dissatisfaction with his lodging place, but could also be the narrator's objective comment—"so he stayed where he was for a whole day and night, and the rain stayed too"—once more we are back with the narrator's observations.

Like this, life sways backward and forward in the narrative. The narrator stays in the background or steps forward depending on the circumstances. But the continuity of the narration is never broken. Even the author's reasoning asides grow organically from the situation as, for example, at the conclusion of **"The Shirt Collar"** or **"The Naughty Boy."**

The mastery with which Andersen controls this sensitive suggestive style is clearly shown in the great philosophical fairy

Andersen at Frijsenborg Manor, 1865.

and poetry and become one with the universal spiritual forces that give life to nature.

This story stands a little apart from the other fairy tales because the mysterious bell is not something tangible: it is an abstract symbol of the romantic experience of nature as a spiritual force. Nevertheless, the narrative radiates human nature. The writer is present in every line, he lives in the situations and characters, his sensitive temperament is there in the immense pathos as well as in the subtle irony. There is imposing strength and beauty in the final picture of sea and sunset with the prince and the poor boy watching from the high rocks. The ecstatic mood possesses extra strength when contrasted with the description of city life at the beginning of the tale. There can be no doubt as to Andersen's attitude toward the inhabitants, young and old, of the city, but his criticism rarely comes to the surface. One or two insignificant expressions give rise to a suspicion that the citizens' search for the mysterious bell is not so very serious: they are only out to enjoy themselves. Of the ostentatiously appointed Universal Bell Ringer there is the laconic remark that every year he wrote a little essay, "but no one was any wiser than before." Then there is the confirmation! "The parson had spoken with a fine sincerity"—and then in four lines comes the respectable nonsense said on such occasions. The eloquence of the account is such that the reader can actually see everybody nodding approval at the parson's words while being borne along by the sentiments. Andersen holds back his skepticism for the empty phrases and only records what is said. The explanations of the three children as to why they cannot join the search are expressed in such differentiated language that three different voices can be made out. The first one is from a girl for whom a ball-dress was at least as important as the sacred occasion: she "had to go home to try on her ball-dress, for it was on account of this dress and this ball that she had been confirmed this time, otherwise she would not have come." The second is "a poor boy who had borrowed his confirmation suit and shoes from the landlord's son, and he had to return them not a minute later than he had promised." The third one "said that he never went to strange places without his parents and that having always been a good boy he would go on being one, even after being confirmed. And that's not a thing to jeer at," adds the narrator to the unsuspecting reader—and then observes, "—but that's just what they all did." Reality is harsher than people's good intentions.

Andersen was able to switch from narrative to general reflections, from gravity to fun, from poetry to commonplace triviality with an adroitness and elegance that no other Danish writer has been able to approach. His command of his mother tongue was perfect. He knew precisely how colored a word to use in a lyrical or pathetic description, and he was familiar with all the secrets of those small adverbs that abound in the Danish language and hint at the speaker's opinion or reveal his mood. Andersen understood where to place them in ambush; with a single word or two he could bring a character alive or unveil it in all its meanness.

Andersen's narrative style contains many secrets, but only some can be discovered. The Chinese master of music in **"The Nightingale"** wrote twenty-five volumes full of the most difficult Chinese words to explain the mechanism of the artificial bird. This was not possible with the real nightingale. (pp. 116-20)

Andersen was not a philosopher; he was unable to present a complete world picture or a consistent view of life. He was

tale **"The Bell."** At the close of day, in the narrow streets of the city—begins the tale—people often hear a strange sound like the ringing of a distant church bell. The sound seems to come from the depths of the mysterious wood, and people are curious and ask each other what it might be. Eventually, some people do go looking for it, but they soon grow tired, give up their search, and make do with a pleasant day in the woods. One of them claims, however, that he has found an explanation, incidentally not a very convincing one. He is rewarded with the appointment of Universal Bell Ringer, and every year he writes a little essay on the strange phenomenon. One Confirmation Sunday the boys and girls who have just been confirmed have a desire to find the unknown bell; three of them, however, are prevented by some reason or other from joining in the search. The rest depart but do not go far enough. All but one stop off on the way, the one who continues is a prince. He makes his way through the wild wood and finally just before sunset climbs upon some rocks, from which place he can see stretching before him the ocean rolling its long waves in toward the shore. While he is standing caught in the beauty of the evening, one of the three who had been prevented from joining the search comes toward him from another path. This poor boy has had to return the confirmation clothes that he had borrowed. They take each other by the hand and there in the midst of magnificent nature they hear right above their heads the great invisible bell of nature a creative writer, not a thinker; in other words, his immediate feelings toward life's phenomena were more powerful than his deliberations about them. But still—sometimes it did happen, mostly in works produced after 1850, that a tale was constructed around a general idea or a didactic thesis that was to be demonstrated through the course of events. This is true of **"The Red Shoes,"** for example, which tells about a poor little girl who loses her parents and then is taken into a fine, wealthy home. She is given good clothes and a pair of fine red shoes and she is so taken up with them that she cannot think of anything else, not even at her confirmation in the church. Her vanity takes the upper hand, she disregards the old lady, her benefactor, who is ill and dying, and goes to a ball with the red shoes. But then her punishment falls. A strange old soldier (we are not told who he is) bewitches the shoes so that they dance off with her; she cannot control them nor can she get them off. Night and day she dances off until finally, in desperation, she begs the executioner to cut her feet off. But even that does not stop her vanity; she wants to show herself in the church but has to turn back because she sees the red shoes dancing in front of her. Finally, she humbles herself and goes into service at a vicarage. She does not dare to go to church, but one Sunday when the hymns waft over to her, her heart breaks and she finds peace in death.

It is rare for an Andersen tale to be so clearly moralizing. In practically all of his other tales the interest is in the events, which are unfolding freely with their own inherent logic. An admonition or two sometimes closes the story, but they have no influence on the action. In **"The Red Shoes"** things are different. All events, including the supernatural, appear to be directed to showing the reprehensible vanity of the girl and the misery it brings with it. There is no inner coherence in the events beyond that required by the moral demonstration. Naturally it is a personal matter whether you regard the events as reasonably coherent. But to the present writer the events in **"The Red Shoes"** lack cohesion and justification. For example, who is the old soldier? Is he the Devil (as one modern critic believes)? Or is he a representative of Providence who is to bring the girl back from her delusion? Why does his face appear above the treetops in the forest at night?

A comparison with the tale **"The Buckwheat"** is illuminating. In this tale a thunderstorm moves across a cornfield; all the corn bends before the storm; only the buckwheat holds its head stiff and therefore is singed by lightning (as can, in fact, happen). Its unbending arrogance has been punished, as is said at the end. But this concluding moral observation does not determine the events, for the storm crosses the landscape as it needs must do by nature, and with natural consequences. The moral is only the writer's reflection afterward. In **"The Red Shoes"** the moral idea is demonstrated throughout the story. The explanation of this display of moral zeal, so unusual in Andersen's works, is presumably that he is judging himself. In part the story rests on a recollection from his own confirmation. For the solemn occasion he had been given new boots, but with dismay and remorse he realized that he was more taken up with them than with the religious ceremony. He never forgot this episode.

Of course, Andersen was absorbed in the problems of his time, particularly those that an artist had to face: his position in the bourgeois society and the contrast between genuine art and the lack of understanding of it shown by the public at large. Andersen wrote about this in **"The Swineherd," "The Nightingale,"** and **"The Goblin at the Grocer's,"** among oth-

ers, but always in such a manner that the events had their own independent life.

A more fundamental problem that engaged him throughout his life was this: Why do some people have a happy existence while others undeservedly have to suffer sorrow and misery? His solution was that given to him by his childhood Christianity: the account had to be squared in another life. "The fairy tale has its harmonic dissolution here on earth; reality most often places it beyond this life into time and eternity," is how he expressed it in **"The Thorny Path of Honor"**; but he also gave this idea an artistic form several times after 1850, particularly in the two long tales **"A Story from the Dunes"** and **"The Philosophers' Stone,"** both written in 1859. (pp. 120-22)

Few of Andersen's tales are built around a clearly defined idea. Nevertheless, the tales as a whole do express a universal wisdom of life. In the multiplicity of events in his tales Andersen has put down thoughts about mankind, the world, and life in general, thoughts that have grown out of the extensive experiences and adventures of his own life.

First, Andersen makes no bones about which kind of person is worthy of respect and which is not. Those who accept the gifts life offers with gratitude are always depicted with sympathy. The person with a warm heart or the one who throws himself into life with a cheerful spirit and pays no heed to formalities will eventually defeat the scheming rationalist. The loving Gerda rescues her friend Kay from the Snow Queen's palace of cold intellect; the cheerful, singing nightingale is stronger than Death at the emperor's bedside; Simple Simon (in the tale with the same title) wins the princess. On the other hand, the self-satisfied philistine who is only interested in his own affairs and nothing more, who arrogantly judges all and sundry from his own limited experience, and who is always willing to strut in borrowed plumage (like the Beetle and the Shirt Collar), is mercilessly exposed in the fairy tales to laughter, whether directly or indirectly does not matter, for the intention is always plain. The narrow-mindedness of the philistine was an abomination to Andersen.

Second, the fairy tales contain quite precise ideas about the universe and the evaluation of its phenomena. These are far from always being explicitly expressed. Yet it is striking that no form of common universe exists for the characters of the tales. Each group of creatures lives within its own surroundings which for the individuals of that group is *the world:* they are unaware of what lies beyond. Nor is there any uniform opinion about existence concerning what is better or worse. Just as great a difference exists among the humans. The little girl with the matches has few thoughts in common with the princess on the pea; children and adults live in separate worlds.

Even the same surroundings and the same events can look fundamentally different. In the great fairy story set in Switzerland, **"The Ice Maiden,"** the characters appear on three levels: (1) the Ice Maiden and the other sinister spirits of nature who rule the great icy wastes of the glaciers, for whom humans are ridiculous insignificant creatures who in their arrogance believe that they can control the forces of nature; (2) Rudy, the young chamois hunter, his sweetheart, and their families; and (3) the domestic animals which, so to speak, see the humans from a lower level and who, by the way, think that humans are strange, illogical creations. Time upon time these three completely different views of life come into conflict; the most charming occasion being brought out in the little scene where the kitchen cat relates what it has heard the rats say about happiness. Happiness to them was to eat tallow candles and to have their bellies filled with putrified pork; while Rudy and his sweetheart had said that the greatest of happinesses was understanding each other. "Whom should we believe, the rats or the sweethearts?" is the cat's question.

The answer to this reasonable question must be that both are right, in their own ways, since the appearance of the world and its objects depends on the eyes that are doing the looking, and we humans, who are often mutually in disagreement, have no grounds on which we can claim that our view of the world is the only correct one. In the fairy tales there are countless other creatures that have other opinions and whose words have as much weight as those of the humans. This point can be seen at the conclusion of **"The Marsh King's Daughter"** which, like **"The Ice Maiden,"** also contains three levels: the trolls, the humans, and finally the stork family; the storks watch and comment on the events from their point of view. While it is the fate of the human characters that makes up the main theme of the tale, it is the storks' comments that conclude the story. The final words in **"Heartbreak,"** a tale described earlier, state directly that what might seem unimportant to adults might be of extreme importance to children. When the pea pod in **"Five Peas from one Pod"** gradually turns yellow, the five peas that are inside say that the whole world is turning yellow, "and they had a perfect right to say so," adds the narrator. Different beings must inevitably have different thoughts and opinions about the world, and they have a right to have them, the small and insignificant just as much as the great. When judgment is passed in the fairy tales it is only passed on those who believe they have a monopoly of the truth: they are handled roughly.

Now to the third point: What thoughts about life as a whole are to be found in the fairy tales? Is life good or evil, just or unjust? Has it anything to offer us pitiful humans, or should we turn our backs on it?

At a first glance the tales provide self-contradictory answers to these questions. Andersen's works can both affirm the highest of expectations and shatter all illusions. Comfort can be found, for instance, in **"The Traveling Companion"** and **"The Wild Swans,"** where the pious and good principal characters go through much hardship but nevertheless are finally happy—and, naturally, in **"The Ugly Duckling,"** an inspired symbol of Andersen's own life where the most important moods, events, and, in part, characters from his strange career have been recast in other dimensions and thereby made universal in an impressive hymn of praise to life. Many of the other fairy tales contain similar reassuring thoughts: everything will take up its rightful place, the good will not be forgotten, arrogance and wickedness will suffer defeat, and, if not at once, it is because the Lord has time to wait.

But far more fairy tales depict quite a different course of events. Nearly all the short stories are about people for whom things have gone badly in life and who finally are left with their frustrated hopes, alone and disappointed—if, that is, they do not find freedom and reconciliation in death.

The bitter pessimism revealed here lay deep in Andersen's mind and is also to be felt in some of the shorter fairy tales, though nowhere so movingly as in **"The Story of a Mother."** One cold winter's night Death fetches a little, sick child, and the desperate mother runs out into the darkness to overtake

him. She meets Night, comes to a crossroads where there is a thorn bush all frosted over, and then reaches a lake that she must cross; at each place she has to sacrifice something of herself in order to find out which way she has to go. When she finally gets to Death's great greenhouse, Death has not yet arrived and when he does he cannot, and will not, surrender the child.

A harrowing story, a monument to mother-love as well as to the mercilessness of existence. In form it is a fairy tale; mythological beings such as Death appear; natural phenomena, Night, the Thorn Bush, the Lake, are personified; the mother's sorrow makes her travel even faster than Death, for in the world of the fairy tale the soul is stronger than the body. But **"The Story of a Mother"** is far from being a folktale. The subject is handled with supreme imagination and brilliant mastery. We are also far from the noncommittal pleasure of **"The Tinderbox"** or the elegant irony in **"The Shirt Collar"** or the optimism of **"The Ugly Duckling."** **"The Story of a Mother"** speaks with relentless earnestness; Night, Thornbush, Lake, and Death, all show a heartrending remorselessness toward the poor mother. For all her sacrifices she gains nothing save an awareness that perhaps it would be even worse for the child to be brought back to life. Without a strong faith in the Providence of God the reader of this terrifying story will be horror-stricken by the meaninglessness of life.

Matters are no better in **"The Shadow,"** which tells of a learned man whose shadow leaves him and, after a number of years, returns for a visit. The shadow has blackmailed his way to great riches and now has the desire to go to a health resort, mainly because his beard will not grow and something must be done about it. Will the learned man go with him? Well, things had been going badly for the scholar, and the shadow is willing to pay his expenses on the simple condition that they exchange roles: that the learned man should recognize the shadow as a person and act as his shadow. He hesitantly accepts. At the spa the man and his shadow meet a princess who is taking the waters to cure her disturbingly oversharp sight.

She falls in love with the elegant, prosperous shadow who, to all appearances, is a person, and who moreover explains to her that the gentleman accompanying him is his dressed-up shadow. The shadow and the princess become engaged, and when the learned man, who is scandalized at the engagement, tries to disclose the shadow's identity he is thrown into prison and put to death. The wedding then takes place.

There are a few fairy-tale features in the story. The shadow liberates himself from his master and begins his own existence; that it is possible to have a disturbing disease of being able to see too well is quite natural; and that a rich, eccentric gentleman dresses up his shadow as a person is no more out of the ordinary than taking the waters in order to get his beard to grow. But these points are only markers along the way in a shocking drama about a respectable, well-meaning, study-bound scholar who becomes the powerless slave of his own shadow, his former servant and companion who, without disdaining any means no matter how low, climbs up the social ladder to achieve his ambition. The two characters are painfully true to life; the same can be said of the princess who, although she is clever, is not clever enough to see through a swindler, even though he is but a shadow she could very nearly see right through, as it is said with deadly irony about her when her amorous glance rested upon him. The bitter philosophy of the tale is that there are wise people who want to do good, but their wisdom and goodness do not help them—and there are ruthless people who do just what they want and emerge victorious. There are no redeeming features. "Such is the world and like this it will always be," says the shadow.

For those people afraid of the pitilessness of existence and the infamy of mankind there is no comfort to be found in this macabre tale.

But even though existence, in the fairy tales as well as in reality, can be brutal and unjust, and sorrows more frequent than pleasures, the reader is left in no doubt that life is worth living. One must take things as they come. Sorrows are heavy, but if we accept them as part of the pattern of life they can also bring us blessings (as shown in **"The Last Pearl"**). Everything depends on oneself. With open eyes and receptive mind it is possible to discover that existence is rich and beautiful, full of events, both big and small; that the world contains a multitude of people and other beings, each with his own individuality, all so different that we need never be bored if we will just look and listen. For the hearse driver in **"A Good Temper"** life is a great and cheerful theater, and when the young copying clerk in **"The Goloshes of Fortune"** and the young aspiring poet in **"Something to Write About"** have their eyes and ears opened stories buzz about them. All the flowers in **"The Snow Queen"** tell their stories to little Gerda, who has an open mind.

It is possible to experience something interesting or enjoyable from even the smallest of things, anything that people do not usually find interesting. An old, discarded street lamp becomes the joy of the watchman's family in their little living room in the cellar; a pea flower invokes the will and the courage to live in a young sick girl in the attic; and a ray of sunshine can be a sermon about the gospel of life. Situations where nothing particular happens can contain both beauty and poetry for those who can see and hear. However, it is not everybody who can. The little fir tree in the fairy tale of the same name is so preoccupied with growing up and being big that it has no time for the sunshine, and the fresh air, or for its many fellow trees both pine and fir, or for the village children chattering so gaily together while they gather berries. But, come to that, the fir tree never understood how to live. (pp. 125-30)

The fairy tales emphasize the gospel of an open mind and immediate emotion; they speak the case for the small, overlooked creatures, and they let it be understood that existence is richer and greater than our limiting notions of good and evil, so rich as never to be exhausted.

It is plain that such a philosophy has spoken to many hearts and given much comfort to many people. It will also appeal to modern readers. But by reading the tales carefully and by drawing conclusions from what is told, the reader will be more disquieted than comforted. Even the portraits of the philistines are enough to frighten the reader: Was it not only in those days that people were like that, or are there many of that type today? Are you yourself so narrowminded? Do you dress up in borrowed plumage like so many of the philistines in the fairy tales? Do fine phrases also pour from our lips? Are we slaves of catchwords, slogans, and other simplifications of reality?

A chill runs down your spine when you see the gulf separating the characters, including the human ones, in the tales. Are people really so different? Can we not somehow become

homogeneous? Are not our democratic ideals valid? Are those not due to one-eyed idealists' rejection of an inescapable reality? The fairy tales are one great rejection of any uniformalization of life and any comformalization of people. Was Andersen, as a writer, more realistic than we are?

Furthermore, is the great physical universe that we are brought up to believe in, the ultimate truth? Is it possible that things are not dead and that natural forces are not impersonal? Our knowledge of physics says one thing while the artist in Andersen claims another. Should we believe the physicist or the artist? The fairy tales say that if you live intensely with your immediate surroundings they will come to life for you, and then the great mechanism loses all interest. Does the modern reader accept such a viewpoint?

Finally, the fairy-tales' message about the riches of life: Do we understand how to accept its gifts both large and small? Are we just as open as the writer and many of his characters? Or do we go through life deaf and blind, unable to respond to the little experiences that it has to offer us? Do we have a superficial and rash relationship to our surroundings?

The fairy-tales are not a harmless and innocent reading. If you know how to read, they leave your soul disturbed. Andersen's worldly wisdom, his knowledge of people and life was far beyond the normal man's. (pp. 130-31)

> *Bo Grønbech, in his* Hans Christian Andersen, *Twayne Publishers, 1980, 171 p.*

JOHN GRIFFITH (essay date 1984)

[*In the following excerpt, Griffith illuminates Andersen's handling of love and sexuality in his fairy tales.*]

[Andersen] wrote love-stories by the dozen—**"The Little Mermaid," "Thumbelina," "The Steadfast Tin Soldier," "The Shepherdess and the Chimney Sweep," "The Sweethearts"** and **"The Bog King's Daughter"** are perhaps the most famous. Through them all runs one story, the basic Andersen fantasy. The central character is small, frail, more likely to be female than male—above all, *delicate,* an embodiment of that innocence which is harmlessness, that purity which is incapacity for lust. He/she is usually incapable of ordinary motion, physically unsuited to pursuit and consummation: the tin soldier has only one leg, the mermaid has no legs at all, Thumbelina is carried from place to place as if she were crippled. Andersen's imagination is much taken with *statues* as the emblem of chaste erotic feeling: the tin soldier and his ballerina are inanimate figurines, the shepherdess and the chimney sweep are made of porcelain, the little mermaid falls in love with a marble statue before she ever sees the prince in the flesh. (It is fitting that Copenhagen has immortalized the little mermaid herself as a statue.) In another story, **"Psyche,"** the hero creates a statue of the girl he loves, the pristine symbol of his devotion. The girl herself rejects him.

Andersen's ideal lovers are often rejected. A few of the folktales he retold—such as **"The Tinderbox"**—end with the hero married and living happily ever after; but the stories he made up himself do not. Usually something prevents marriage—rejection, misunderstanding, snobbery, fate. At the end of **"The Bog King's Daughter,"** the heroine steps out onto a balcony on her wedding night and just disappears. Andersen doesn't care very much if love is satisfied in this world, since the conclusion his fantasy really works toward is splendid, mystical death—the launching out of the soul into the infinite, leaving troublesome flesh behind. "It is lovely to fly from love to love, from earth into heaven," says Andersen, describing the death of the hero in **"The Ice Maiden."** "A string snapped, a mournful tone was heard. Death's kiss of ice was victorious against corruption." Similarly, the little mermaid leaves her body behind and becomes a daughter of the air. The tin soldier and the ballerina die together in flames, he melting into a tin heart and she reduced to a bright spangle. The shepherdess and the chimney sweep "loved each other until they broke." Thumbelina dons white wings and flies away with her fairy-lover, who is "almost transparent, as if he were made of glass." The bog king's daughter becomes "one single beautiful ray of light, that shot upward to God."

Physical sensuality in these stories tends to be pictured as grasping, slimy, and disgusting. Thumbelina is coaxed, abducted, clutched at by a toad and her son, a fat black mole, and an ugly insect before she flies away to the fairy-king; the shepherdess is pursued by a satyr who had "a long beard, . . . little horns sticking out of his forehead and the legs of a goat." The princess in **"The Bog King's Daughter"** is shudderingly embraced by an "ancient king; a mummy, black as pitch, glittering like the black slugs that creep in the forest." Frequently the physical ordeal Andersen's lovers must go through in pursuit of transcendent love is a descent into dark, close, filthy places—the tin soldier floats down a gutter into a sewer and is swallowed by a fish; the shepherdess and the chimney sweep have to creep up and down a chimney flue; the ball and the top met in a garbage bin where "all kinds of things were lying: gravel, a cabbage stalk, dirt, dust, and lots of leaves that had fallen down from the gutter."

Andersen's sharpest vision of sensual horror is in **"The Little Mermaid."** There the heroine, smitten with love for a human prince, sets out to find what she must do to make him love her in return. The grotesque ordeal Andersen contrives for her is a direct fantasy-enactment of the idea that, in order to be a wife, a girl must submit to rape. She must "divide her tail," and the experience is an excruciating one. She has to travel down to a terrible forest in the deepest part of the ocean, through polyps "like snakes with hundreds of heads," with "long slimy arms, and they had fingers as supple as worms" that reach out to grab her as she "held both her hands folded tightly across her breast" and hurries past.

> At last she came to a great, slimy open place in the middle of the forest. Big fat eels played in the mud, showing their ugly yellow stomachs. . . . Here the witch . . . sat letting a big ugly toad eat out of her mouth, as human beings sometimes let a canary eat sugar candy out of theirs. The ugly eels she called her little chickens, and held them close to her spongy chest.

The witch tells her that if the prince is to love her, she must lose her tail with a sensation of having her body pierced by a sword. "The little mermaid drank the potion, and it felt as if a sword were piercing her body. She fainted and lay as though she were dead."

Nowhere else in classic children's literature is there so terrified a vision of sex, seen through the eyes of innocence. The scene in **"The Ice Maiden"** where Rudy accepts death as his lover is calm by comparison:

> He threw his arms around her and looked into her marvelous clear eyes for a second. Only for a second! And how is one to describe, to tell in words, what he saw in that fraction of a moment? What was it that overpowered him—a ghost? Or was it a bit of life that exists in death? Had he been lifted upward or had he been plunged into a deep, death-filled world of ice?

When she kisses him, "the eternal coldness penetrated his backbone and touched his forehead." Here, as elsewhere, Andersen compresses into one scene the contradictory ideas that death is erotic, and that one can escape eroticism by dying. Something of that same paradox is present in another Andersen story, **"The Garden of Eden,"** which posits sex as original sin. A young prince falls from innocence by kissing the lips of a beautiful naked woman, and death is both the reward and punishment for his action.

> A fearful clap of thunder was heard, deeper, more frightening than any ever heard before. The fairy vanished and the garden of Eden sank into the earth: deep, deep down. The prince saw it disappear into the dark night like a far distant star. He felt a deathly coldness touch his limbs; his eyes closed, and he fell down as though he were dead.

This troubled view of sex is important even in Andersen stories which are not explicitly about erotic subjects, for it explains his obsession with innocence in many forms. *Innocence* is the watchword in Andersen's fantasies. No virtue rates so high with him as child-like purity, by which he means freedom from adult desire, ambition, and thought. He found inspiration of a sort in folk-tales, because they often begin with heroes who are simple, humble and childlike. But he had to change the folk-tale pattern in order to bring out his personal fantasies. The traditional folk-tale shows its protagonist's growth and happiness directly; he gets money, love and power—as for instance in Andersen's own re-telling of **"The Tinderbox,"** in which a soldier seizes a princess, kills her father, and ascends to the throne; or **"Little Claus and Big Claus,"** in which an underdog-hero kills his rival and gets rich. The stories that Andersen made up himself turn this pattern inside out. Like folk-tale heroes, Andersen's start poor—but his stories demonstrate that the poor in spirit are blessed. Like them, Andersen's heroes hurl themselves into life—but discover that they would do better to die and be with God. In an Andersen story, it is better to be the peasant girl who can hear the nightingale than the chamberlain who cannot (**"The Nightingale"**); better to be little Gerda, who trusts and believes and wants to stay at home, than Kay, who "gets a piece of the Devil's glass in his eye" and questions and criticizes and explores (**"The Snow Queen"**).

In story after story, Andersen makes fun of and punishes people who care about money and power and artifice and prestige and critical judgment; he celebrates the humble and long-suffering and credulous and sentimental. His attitude belongs partly to Christian asceticism, and partly to nineteenth-century Romantic primitivism, sentimentalism, and anti-intellectualism, and no doubt takes many of its forms and phrases from those philosophies. But for Andersen personally the value of innocence is closely tied to his nightmarish view of sex, a fact which is easily discernible in several of his most famous stories. For him, to be innocent is, first and foremost, to expunge or repress one's sexual urges.

One especially graphic case in point here is his tale **"The Red Shoes,"** a story Andersen found to be a particular favorite in the Puritan strongholds of Scotland, Holland, and the United States. Read in the loosest, most abstract terms, the story is a parable on the idea that pride goeth before a fall: a pretty girl, preoccupied with beauty and finery, shows her vanity, is punished for it, and learns her lesson. But given the concrete details of Andersen's personal fantasy, the story vibrates with sexual panic, celebrating innocence that is won through the repression of sexuality.

Andersen records that **"The Red Shoes"** was inspired by a memory from his youth: "In *The Fairy Tale of My Life,* I have told how I received for my confirmation my first pair of boots; and how they squeaked as I walked up the aisle of the church; this pleased me no end, for I felt that now the whole congregation must know that my boots are new. But at the same time my conscience bothered me terribly, for I was aware that I was thinking as much about my new boots as I was about our Lord." Out of that bothersome conscience came Andersen's story, with the new boots transformed to red shoes, and Andersen, the boy wearing them, transformed to a pretty girl named Karen.

What Andersen consciously thinks of as an emblem of pride and vanity, he unconsciously imbues with sexual significance in a number of ways. First, he gives his heroine the name of his scandalous half-sister, the one who disappeared into the red-light districts of Copenhagen and later embarrassed her brother by turning up with a common-law husband. Shoe and foot-symbolism tends to be sexual in many uses—the Old Testament and other folk-literatures often say "feet" as a euphemism for sexual organs, and foot-fetishism is a common neurotic device for expressing forbidden interest in the genitals. That **"The Red Shoes"** emanates from Andersen's memory of a ritual of puberty, and of his flaunting the new boots he had for that occasion, also helps to place it psychologically. Andersen emphasizes the sexual quality by making Karen's shoes red, the traditional color of unruly passion, and by making them dancing shoes, with a power to catch her up and carry her away against her conscious will: "Once she had begun, her feet would not stop. It was as if the shoes had taken command of them . . . her will was not her own." Giving herself over to their excitement, she faces the debility Andersen associated with sexual excess: "You shall dance in your red shoes until you become pale and thin. Dance till the skin on your face turns yellow and clings to your bones as if you were a skeleton."

She must first acquire the red shoes against her mother's wishes; it is a man who sets them doing their fearful, orgiastic dancing, an old soldier with "a marvelously long beard that was red with touches of white in it." When he touches them, they begin dancing.

The shoes "grow fast" to Karen's feet and will not come off—they are part of her body. The only way she can purge their evil is to cut off the offending members. "Do not cut off my head," she begs the executioner, "for then I would not be able to repent. But cut off my feet!" He does as she asks, and she becomes like Andersen's other acceptable lovers: crippled. For a time thoughts of the lost sexuality still linger—she sees the red shoes dancing before her when she tries to go to church. Finally, in an agony of contrition and self-reproach, she wins God's mercy, and He sends His sunshine: "The sunshine filled Karen's heart till it so swelled with peace and happiness that it broke. Her soul flew on a sunbeam up to God; and up there no one asked her about the red shoes."

"The Red Shoes" is a harrowing, gothic little tale, to be sure, and that may help to explain its popularity. Actually, it doesn't succeed very well in advancing the dry moral idea that we should be humble and love God better than ourselves. What the solid events of the story convey is rather the idea that there is something we are tempted to do with our feet, but old ladies and ministers and angels don't want us to do it. If we refuse to listen to their warnings, a leering old man will touch our feet and set them working and we won't be able to stop. Then we'll be glad to have the grown-ups chop them off, and to be allowed to die and go to God. I suppose there is more than one way to say what that fantasy means; but any description which fails to account for the evocative image of the red-bearded man touching the girl's feet and setting them dancing uncontrollably has hardly done it justice.

Andersen himself was aware—at least partly—of the psychological links between his inhibited sexuality and his artistic creativity, his wish for fame as an artist, and his longing for death. The story **"Psyche"** shows clearly that he believed that his pursuit of ideal beauty and immortality through art and religion sprang from sexual longings that he could not allow himself to fulfill.

"Psyche" is the story of a young artist, poor and unknown, who strives for perfection in his art, but cannot produce anything that satisfies him. His worldly friends tell him he is too much the dreamer: "You have not tasted life. You ought to take a big healthy swallow and enjoy it." They invite him to join them in their orgies and he is excited—"his blood ran swiftly through his body, his imagination was strong." But he cannot bring himself to go with them—he feels "within himself a purity, a sense of piety" that stops him, and turns him toward working in clay and marble instead, as a superior alternative to physical lust. "What he wanted to describe [in his sculpture] was how his heart sought and sensed infinity, but how was he to do it?"

The answer is that he sees a girl, just in passing, and falls in love. At first he makes no attempt to approach her; he turns his attention to a mental image he has of her, as she becomes "alive in his mind." He sets to work on a statue of her, made from marble he has to dig out from heaps of "broken glass," "discarded vegetables," "the tops of fennel and the rotten leaves of artichokes." With these materials—a fantasy-image snatched from a passing glimpse of a beautiful girl, and white marble extracted from the filth of ordinary life—the artist constructs an image of perfect beauty.

He wants to believe that he now has what his friends have—only better. "Now I know what life is," he rejoices. "It is love! It is to be able to appreciate loveliness and to delight in beauty. And what my friends call 'life' is nothing but empty vanity, bubbles from the fermentation of the dregs, instead of the pure wine, drunk at the altar to consecrate life." But despite this brave speech, he finds that his feelings for the statue are rooted in those "dregs" of erotic passion. He desires not just the idea of beauty, but the girl herself. "Soon both God and his tears were forgotten; instead he thought of his Psyche, who stood before him, looking as if she had been cut out of snow and blushing in the light of the dawn. He was going to see her: the living, breathing girl who stepped so lightly, as if she walked on air, the girl whose innocent words were music."

His attempt to make love to the girl is a disaster. "He grabbed her hand and kissed it, and he thought it was softer than a rose petal and yet it inflamed him. He was so excited, so aroused, that he hardly knew what he was saying; words gushed out of his mouth and he could no more control their flow than the crater can stop the volcano from vomiting burning lava. He told her how much he loved her." Contemptuously she spurns him.

His lust aroused, the young artist yields to his friends' coaxing and spends a riotous night with some beautiful peasant girls. Andersen's metaphors convey the sexual excitement, release, and disappointment he feels: "The flower of life . . . bloomed, bent its head, and withered. A strange, horrible smell of corruption blended itself with the odor of roses, it lamed his mind and blinded his sight. The fireworks of sensuality were over and darkness came." Sickened with guilt, he buries the beautiful statue, enters a monastery, and begins a lifelong struggle to suppress the "unclean, evil thoughts" that spring up inside. "He punished his body, but the evil did not come from the surface but from deep within him." He dies at last, his body and bones rot away, and the centuries pass over the unmarked grave of the statue which his love inspired him to make. At last, workmen digging a grave in a convent unearth the statue. No one knows the name of its creator. "But his gain, his profit from his struggle, and his search, the glory that proved the godliness within him, his Psyche, will never die. It will live beyond the name of its creator. His spark still shines here on earth and is admired, appreciated, and loved."

What Andersen says in this elaborate parable is that the erotic hunger which other men feed with "a big healthy swallow of life"—"not only the bread, but the baker woman"—has for him been diverted to a hunger for ideal beauty and fame and spirituality. But he can find no satisfaction in these ideals; he goes to his grave cursing "the strange flames that seemed to set his body on fire." The statue he has made is beautiful, perfect, and his own, a product of his imagination inspired by passion. But there is no primary gratification to be had from it—only highly theoretical pleasure in the hope that this embodied fantasy would constitute a "gain, his profit from his struggle and his search, the glory that proved the godliness within him."

Andersen's stories are like the artist's statue—minded from the "dregs" and "filth" of ordinary life, with energy that might otherwise have been spent in sensual revels. Their substance is the stuff of desire, the drive for love and power; but the art that shapes them is self-doubt and anxiety and troubled conscience. So they become in the end monuments to chastity and innocence, a marble statue in a nun's grave: no abiding satisfaction to their creator, but still something to be admired by others, "his spark that still shines here on earth and is admired, appreciated, and loved." Thus, finally, and

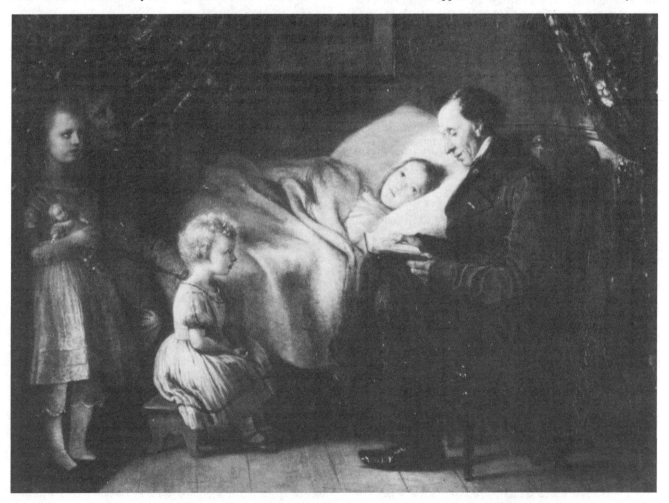

Painting by Jerichau-Baumannsborn of Andersen reading aloud to the children of his friend Madame Baumann.

39

by a most circuitous route, is the desire for love and eminence to be fulfilled, for Andersen. (pp. 82-8)

John Griffith, "Personal Fantasy in Andersen's Fairy Tales," in Kansas Quarterly, *Vol. 16, No. 3, Summer, 1984, pp. 81-8.*

CELIA CATLETT ANDERSON (essay date 1986)

[*In the following excerpt, Anderson disputes claims that Andersen's short stories are not suitable reading material for children.*]

Hans Christian Andersen's fairy tales have sometimes been described as too adult or too pessimistic for children. For example, May Hill Arbuthnot in her classic *Children and Books,* although praising Andersen as an allegorist, notes that "because of the double meaning, the adult themes, and the sadness of many of these stories, the whole collection is usually not popular with children." P. L. Travers found a "devitalizing element" of nostalgia in the tales. Bruno Bettelheim has commented that the conclusions of some of Andersen's stories are discouraging in that "they do not convey the feeling of consolation characteristic of fairy tales," and Jack Zipes accuses Andersen of teaching lessons in servility to the young. Andersen's tales continue, however to be published, read, discussed, and used as a basis for children's theater, and the most popular of them have an undeniable appeal for children. Furthermore, the most popular tales, such as **"The Ugly Duckling," "The Little Mermaid," "The Steadfast Tin Soldier," "The Little Fir Tree,"** and **"The Nightingale,"** include for the most part, those stories that were original with Andersen. His view of the world, then, the problems he poses and the solutions he offers must touch some nerve in us; there must be something more to them than simple pessimism, more than a servile call to compromise.

Andersen does indeed often deliberately undercut the facile happy ending that is the trademark of fairy tales, but are his many characters who fail to win a reward defeated in spirit? I would argue that they are not. Take the one that may be, perhaps, saddest of all his protagonists, the little fir tree (or pine tree as Erik Haugaard translates it). The tree fails to appreciate its youth in the forest, is bewildered and frightened during its one glorious evening as a baubled Christmas tree, is exiled to an attic, and there is unable to hold an audience of mice who want to hear stories of "bacon or candle stumps," not of "How Humpty-dumpty Fell Down the Stairs but Won the Princess Anyway." Hauled out into the spring sunlight, the pine tree is forced to recognize that it is a dead thing among the green renewal of the season and achieves its one brief moment of wisdom: "If I only could have been happy while I had a chance to be." Finally the poor tree is burned, sighing its sap away in shots, and "Every time the tree sighed, it thought of a summer day in the forest, or a winter night when the stars are brightest, and it remembered Christmas Eve and Humpty-dumpty: the only fairy tale it had ever heard and knew how to tell. Then it became ashes." The tree dies unfulfilled, yes, but in one sense undefeated. It never loses its vision of the possibility of beauty in the world. Like King Lear, the tree is ennobled by wisdom that comes too late.

When we read this tale to our son, then eight years old, he had tears in his eyes and commented that it was the saddest story he had ever heard. Initially, I judged this as a negative reaction, a rejection of the story, but I was wrong. He re-

turned to the story again and again. Like the small boy who rips the golden star from the tree's branch and pins it to his chest, our son took something shining from the story and, for all I know, wears it to this day.

Of course not all of Andersen's tales end sadly. Even considering only those stories that are not simply retellings of old folktales (and therefore with conventional conclusions), we can find several types of endings. There are some which express religious optimism, and some which reward the hero or heroine with acceptance and love. Stories in the first group are rather self-consciously overlaid with Christianity and conclude optimistically. To mention only one of these, consider **"The Old Oak Tree's Last Dream,"** a story quite different in tone and message from **"The Pine Tree."** The oak lives three hundred and sixty-five years, many of them as a landmark for sailors. It pities the mayflies and flowers for their short existences, but learns in a death dream of ascension into a joyous heaven that "Nothing has been forgotten, not the tiniest flower or the smallest bird." The story concludes

> The tree itself lay stretched out on the snow-covered beach. From the ship came the sound of sailors singing a carol about the joyful season, when Christ was born to save mankind and give us eternal life. The sailors were singing of the same dream, the beautiful dream that the old oak tree had dreamed Christmas Eve: the last night of its life.

At least for the believer, this conclusion is more encouraging than that which gives the pine tree only ashes of regret.

Another class of stories in Andersen does include more tangible rewards. In these, the protagonists win acceptance by remaining true to their natures and persisting in some quest or duty. **"The Ugly Duckling"** comes immediately to mind, but perhaps **"The Nightingale"** is an even better example. In that tale, the small bird is as plain and dull in plumage at the end as at the beginning, but its ability to remain natural, to sing a spontaneous, honest song finally wins it the respect of the emperor who has been saved by the power of its singing and now realizes the false choice he made in earlier preferring the bejewelled, mechanical bird who can sing only one song. Of all Andersen's stories, this may be the one in which the triumph of spirit over matter is most simply and directly presented.

Love is the ultimate form of acceptance, and the tale **"The Snow Queen"** most fully elaborates this theme. Bettelheim concedes that this tale belongs among the tales that console. An allegory of reason versus love, **"The Snow Queen"** is, like all allegories, explicitly symbolic, and this very explicitness makes the story a good choice for analysis.

The childhood paradise of Gerda and Kai is blighted by Kai's growing away from Gerda into a cynical stage of adolescence (symbolized by the splinters of the mirror of reason that have entered his eyes and heart and by the numbing kisses of the Snow Queen who kidnaps him). Gerda, like the sister in Andersen's retold folktale **"The Wild Swans,"** endures much suffering before she is able to restore Kai to his natural state as a warm-hearted, loving person. The story is a classic example of what Marie-Louise von Franz describes as the projection of anima—the suffering, brave woman as a projection of the man's problem with his feminine side. In this case the identification is very appropriately used since Gerda, in bringing about the union of intellect and emotion, is indeed a Sophia-like figure.

The story is one of Andersen's most successful blendings of Christian and folk elements. It contains not only many magical creatures (the Snow Queen herself, a talking raven, and a Finnish white witch), but also a hymn in place of the usual incantation, angels formed from the breath of prayers, and a wise old grandmother who knows both the language of ravens and that of the Bible. After Gerda, through her persistence, reaches the ice castle and frees Kai with her warm tears, the two retrace her steps and finally arrive back at the old grandmother's apartment. Andersen tells us that "as they stepped through the doorway they realized that they had grown: they were no longer children." But the grandmother is reading "Whosoever shall not receive the Kingdom of Heaven as a little child shall not enter therein." Kai and Gerda understand the lesson and "There they sat, the two of them grownups; and yet in their hearts children; and it was summer: a warm glorious summer day!" In choosing that particular text from the New Testament, Andersen voices a central theme shared by Christian theologians and writers for children. For the child, and for all of us, the test of spirit is to grow into intellectual wisdom without losing the capacity for emotion, for love.

Certainly this is a central theme with Andersen himself. Elizabeth Cook holds that "two of his strongest themes are the plight of the outsider, and the primacy of Love over Reason." We see these ideas combined in two tales where the endings are unhappy and love must be its own reward. In both **"The Little Mermaid"** and **"The Steadfast Tin Soldier"** the main characters persist and suffer and do not win. These stories, along with **"The Pine Tree," "The Little Match Girl,"** and that very complex Andersen tale **"The Shadow,"** are probably most responsible for the author's reputation for pessimism. The mermaid *is* promised eternal life at the last minute, but in this story the Christian promise is not as successfully woven into the plot as it is in some others (the tale always seems to me to end with the mermaid's dissolution into foam). Are these stories, then, about the defeat of the spirit? As I said earlier, I think not. Neither the mermaid nor the tin soldier turn aside from their goal, nor do they become bitter or vengeful. Through many trials they continue to be humane and loving. Many of Andersen's heroes and heroines, though they suffer greatly, remain true to their ideals. If not rewarded, neither are they defeated. And the true triumph of the spirit, after all, consists not in winning the prince or princess, the kingdom or riches, or even immortality, but in being worthy of the winning.

Much that is written for and about children springs from the premise that the young need the hope and encouragement provided by the success of the hero in the stories presented to them, and that they cannot cope with models of failure. This may be true for certain ages and types, but it is in many cases a condescending and even dishonest attitude. Hope can help develop a child, but false hope can absolutely devastate. Hans Christian Andersen knew that when Humpty-dumpty fell, he didn't win the princess anyway and that a storyteller who claims he did is a liar and, further, that an innocent, like the foolish pine tree, who believes the lie will reap much unhappiness.

The child who comes to Andersen for spiritual sustenance will learn that we must both test our dreams and be tested by them and that in this world some bright dreams have gray awakenings. Will this harm or strengthen a child? I think it strengthened our own children, that our son drank courage,

not despair, from the tears he shed over the story of the pine tree. In Andersen's tale **"The Pixy and the Grocer"** the pixy peeks through the keyhole and sees the turbulent visions that the poor student enjoys while sitting under the magic tree of poetry. Before such splendor, the pixy "experienced greatness. . . . He cried without knowing why he cried, but found that in those tears happiness was hidden." So art redeems us; as Tolkien put it so well in his famous essay on children and fairy stories, "It is one of the lessons of fairy stories (if we can speak of the lessons of things that do not lecture) that on callow, lumpish, and selfish youth peril, sorrow, and the shadow of death can bestow dignity and even sometimes wisdom." Hans Christian Andersen gives us in his stories "peril, sorrow, and the shadow of death" but also "dignity" and "wisdom." (pp. 122-26)

Celia Catlett Anderson, "Andersen's Heroes and Heroines: Relinquishing the Reward," in Triumphs of the Spirit in Children's Literature, *edited by Francelia Butler and Richard Rotert, Library Professional Publications, 1986, pp. 122-26.*

FURTHER READING

Andersen, Hans Christian. *The Complete Andersen: All of the 168 Stories by Hans Christian Andersen.* Edited and translated by Jean Hersholt. 6 vols. New York: Heritage Press, 1942.
    Valuable collection of Andersen's fairy tales. Hersholt provides detailed notes and an extensive chronological bibliography.

Bennett, James O'Donnell. "Hans Andersen's Fairy Tales." In his *Much Loved Books: Best Sellers of the Ages,* pp. 291-96. New York: Boni and Liveright, 1927.
    Charming account of the similarities between Andersen's personal life and his fairy tale "The Ugly Duckling."

Bredsdorff, Elias. *Hans Christian Andersen: The Story of His Life and Work, 1805-75.* New York: Charles Scribner's Sons, 1975, 376 p.
    Authoritative, well-organized biography that offers criticism of Andersen's stories as well.

Hersholt, Jean, and Westergaard, Waldemar, eds. *The Andersen-Scudder Letters.* Berkeley and Los Angeles: University of California Press, 1949, 181 p.
    Andersen's correspondence with his American editor, Horace E. Scudder.

Knapton, Shirley. "Hans Andersen: An Appreciation." *The Bookman,* London XXV, No. 147 (December 1903): 121-28.
    Considers the messages that Andersen conveyed in his fairy tales and personal actions predominantly positive.

Lederer, Wolfgang. *The Kiss of the Snow Queen: Hans Christian Andersen and Man's Redemption by Woman.* Berkeley: University of California Press, 1986, 262 p.
    Considers the fairy tale "The Snow Queen" particularly revealing in psychoanalyzing Andersen's life and personality.

Mishler, William. "H. C. Andersen's 'Tin Soldier' in a Freudian Perspective." *Scandinavian Studies* 50, No. 4 (Autumn 1978): 389-95.
    Provides a Freudian interpretation of "The Steadfast Tin Soldier" and notes that Andersen implemented a style of romance that resembles the Freudian concept of wish-fulfillment.

"Hans Christian Andersen: The Story of His Life and His Fairy

Tales." *The New York Times,* Hans Christian Andersen Special Supplement (2 April 1905): 1-4.
>   Entertaining biographical account commemorating the hundredth anniversary of Andersen's birth.

Robb, Nesca A. "Hans Andersen." In her *Four in Exile,* pp. 120-53. London: Hutchinson & Co., 1948.
>   Analyzes contrasting elements in Andersen's tales.

Spink, Reginald. *Hans Christian Andersen and His World.* London: Thames and Hudson, 1972, 128 p.
>   Excellent biographical source. Spink consulted numerous Andersen scholars in the compilation of this work.

Stirling, Monica. *The Wild Swan: The Life and Times of Hans Christian Andersen.* New York: Harcourt, Brace & World, 1965, 383 p.
>   Well-written biography.

Toksvig, Signe. *The Life of Hans Christian Andersen.* New York: Harcourt, Brace and Co., 1934, 289 p.
>   Personal approach to Andersen. Toksvig's biography emphasizes Andersen's emotional growth throughout his career.

F(rancis) Scott (Key) Fitzgerald

1896-1940

American novelist, short story writer, essayist, scriptwriter, and dramatist.

Renowned for his classic novel *The Great Gatsby,* Fitzgerald is considered one of the most influential novelists and short story writers of the twentieth century. He was the spokesman for the Jazz Age, America's decade of prosperity, excess, and abandon, which began soon after the end of World War I and concluded with the 1929 stock market crash. As such, in his novels and stories, Fitzgerald examined an entire generation's search for the elusive American dream of wealth and happiness. Among his most widely read stories, "Babylon Revisited," "The Diamond as Big as the Ritz," "The Rich Boy," "Crazy Sunday," and "Winter Dreams" were often derived from Fitzgerald's own experiences and portray the consequences of his generation's adherence to false values. The glamour and insouciance of many of Fitzgerald's writings reveal only one side of a writer whose second and final decade of work characterized a life marred by alcoholism and financial difficulties, troubled by personal tragedy, and frustrated by lack of inspiration.

Born in St. Paul, Minnesota, the son of well-to-do midwestern parents, Fitzgerald was a precocious child with an early interest in writing plays and poetry. As a young man he emulated the rich, youthful, and beautiful, a social group with whom he maintained a lifelong love-hate relationship. Following two years in an eastern preparatory school, he enrolled in 1913 at Princeton University. His first stories appeared in *Nassau Lit,* Princeton's literary magazine, which was edited by his friend and fellow student Edmund Wilson. Leaving Princeton for the army during World War I, Fitzgerald spent his weekends in camp writing the earliest draft of his first novel, *This Side of Paradise.* The acceptance of this work for publication by Charles Scribner's Sons in 1919 and the ensuing popular and financial success it achieved enabled Fitzgerald to marry Zelda Sayre, a socially prominent young woman he had met and courted during his army days. Zelda significantly affected her husband's life and career. During the 1920s she was Fitzgerald's private literary consultant and editor, while publicly she matched Fitzgerald's extravagant tastes and passion in living for the moment.

While continuing to illuminate the manners of the Roaring Twenties, Fitzgerald's second and third novels, as well as the story collections published between novels, evidenced a growing awareness of the shallowness and brutal insensitivity that are sometimes accoutrements of American society. These weaknesses and America's lost ideals are movingly described in Fitzgerald's strongest and most famous work, *The Great Gatsby.* Although it gained the respect of many prominent American writers and is now considered a classic, *The Great Gatsby* was not a popular success and marked the beginning of the author's decline in popularity. Another commercial disappointment, *Tender Is the Night* reflected the disillusionment and strain caused by the Great Depression and Zelda's gradual deterioration from schizophrenia and eventual breakdown. These events scarred Fitzgerald, contributing to a deep, self-reproaching despair that brought his career to

a near standstill during the mid-1930s. Fitzgerald described his tribulations in detail in the three confessional "Crack-Up" essays of 1936, which brilliantly evoke his pain and suffering. Trying to start anew, he became a motion picture scriptwriter and began *The Last Tycoon,* a novel based on his Hollywood experiences, which remained unfinished when Fitzgerald died in late 1940.

Fitzgerald's short stories have often been dismissed as slick, commercial productions intended to capitalize on the successes of his novels. The author's own disparaging remarks regarding his stories have also helped lend discredit to their status as works of literature. Yet, since the 1960s critics have come to regard many of Fitzgerald's short pieces as works that reflect themes characteristic of his most significant writings while experimenting with new techniques and subjects. In "The Rich Boy," for example, which was written around 1920, Fitzgerald makes what has become perhaps his most famous statement regarding one of his typical themes: "Let me tell you about the very rich. They are different from you and me." Using a prominent narrator in this story, as in *The Great Gatsby,* Fitzgerald offers what Sergio Perosa termed "a kind of parable on the isolation and impotence of the very rich." Protagonist Anson Hunter comes from a background of unlimited wealth and privilige. From this milieu he has developed a sense of superiority and aloofness, a need for dominance, and a contempt for commonplace life—attitudes that result in alienation from those who would love him and separation from happiness. Instead of a means to fulfill his dreams, wealth has become for Anson an obstacle to self-realization. Another early tale, "Winter Dreams," relies, like many of Fitzgerald's writings, on his recollections of childhood. In this story a young boy's longing for the "glittering things" of life guide his actions over the years until he realizes as a successful and wealthy adult that the greatest value of dreams resides in dreaming and striving, not in fulfillment.

The somewhat innocuous warnings in these pieces turn somber and complex in "May Day." A tragic and sordid tale that many critics have interpreted as a remarkable evocation of the imminent collapse of the Jazz Age, "May Day" focuses on the intersecting lives of three young protagonists—wealthy Phillip Dean; Dean's penniless former Yale roommate, Gordon Sterrett; and shallow, pretty Edith Bradin—during the events of May 1, 1919, in New York. Suggesting the rich stores of meaning in this tale, Anthony J. Mazzella noted the significance of the title as simultaneously a day commemorating the working classes, a spring festival celebrating the advent of life through the crowning of a May Queen and a dance around a maypole, and a distress signal. The title assumes irony, according to Mazzella, when, in the story workers fight against each other, the dance is portrayed as a riot around a building, the crowning of the queen as an attack on Edith, and the advent of life as suicide and death. In "Absolution" Fitzgerald deviates from his usual subject matter and treats the crises in faith among an aging Roman Catholic priest and a young boy who comes to the priest for confession. A reworking of a discarded opening section to *The Great Gatsby*, "Absolution" establishes a dichotomy between the Church, which is associated in the story with repression, denial, and fear, and life, which is characterized by warmth, glamour, and sensuality.

In "Babylon Revisited," overwhelmingly Fitzgerald's most frequently anthologized and analyzed short story, the author returns to and expands upon characteristic themes. Set against the backdrop of expatriate Europe during the 1930s, this story focuses on Charlie Wales, wealthy playboy of 1920s Paris whose excesses contributed at least in part to the death of his wife and subsequent removal of his daughter to the custodianship of his bitter and resentful sister-in-law, Marion. He has now returned to Paris, having put aside his careless ways and re-established himself as a responsible member of society, to reclaim his daughter. Marion's suspicions of Charlie's insincerity are apparently confirmed, however, when two acquaintances from his halcyon days emerge to momentarily divert his attention, and as a result, Marion will not relinquish the child. The story ends as Charlie resolves to return and try again to regain his daughter, believing that "they couldn't make him pay forever." Seymour L. Gross observed: "Though 'Babylon Revisited' is centrally an exploration of the waste inherent in the quest for the gorgeous life, it is not thereby a paean to Main Street." Gross suggests that Marion's presence in the tale indicates Fitzgerald's uneasiness with ascribing the middle classes sole guardianship of value and worth.

In a 1920 interview Fitzgerald called himself "a professed literary thief, hot after the best methods of every writer in my generation." He considered Edmund Wilson his "intellectual conscience," and during the first half of his career Fitzgerald looked to his former editor for advice and discipline. Ernest Hemingway was Fitzgerald's "artistic conscience," a friend and competitor who often rebuked Fitzgerald for writing slick, but financially successful, magazine stories. At the time of his death, Fitzgerald was virtually forgotten and unread. But a growing Fitzgerald revival, begun in the 1950s, has led to the publication of numerous volumes of stories, letters, and notebooks. Since that time, critics have universally praised Fitzgerald's mastery of style and technique that renders even his most trivial efforts entertaining and well-executed. In his best stories, like his novels, Fitzgerald displays what Kenneth G. Johnston termed an "ability to perceive the reality behind the glittering carnival, the face behind the mask." He is regarded as a profound and sensitive artist, as well as the unmatched voice of the Jazz Age.

(For further information on Fitzgerald's life and career, see *Twentieth-Century Literary Criticism,* Vols. 1, 6, 14, 28; *Contemporary Authors,* Vol. 110; *Dictionary of Literary Biography,* Vols. 4, 9; *Dictionary of Literary Biography Yearbook: 1980;* and *Dictionary of Literary Biography: Documentary Series,* Vol. 1.)

PRINCIPAL WORKS

SHORT FICTION

Flappers and Philosophers 1920
Tales of the Jazz Age 1922
All the Sad Young Men 1926
Taps at Reveille 1935
The Stories of F. Scott Fitzgerald 1951
Afternoon of an Author: A Selection of Uncollected Stories and Essays 1957
Six Tales of the Jazz Age, and Other Stories 1960
The Pat Hobby Stories 1962
The Apprentice Fiction of F. Scott Fitzgerald: 1909-1917 1965
Babylon Revisited, and Other Stories 1971
The Basil and Josephine Stories 1973
Bits of Paradise: Twenty-One Uncollected Stories by F. Scott and Zelda Fitzgerald 1973
The Price Was High: The Last Uncollected Stories of F. Scott Fitzgerald 1979

OTHER MAJOR WORKS

This Side of Paradise (novel) 1920
The Beautiful and Damned (novel) 1922
The Vegetable (drama) 1923
The Great Gatsby (novel) 1925
Tender Is the Night (novel) 1934
The Last Tycoon (novel) 1941
The Crack-Up (essays, notebooks, letters, miscellany) 1945
The Letters of F. Scott Fitzgerald (letters) 1963
Dear Scott/Dear Max: The Fitzgerald-Perkins Correspondence (letters) 1971
As Ever Scott Fitz—Letters between F. Scott Fitzgerald and His Literary Agent Harold Ober (letters) 1972
The Notebooks of F. Scott Fitzgerald (notebooks) 1978
The Correspondence of F. Scott Fitzgerald (letters) 1980
Poems, 1911-1940 (poetry) 1981

H. L. MENCKEN (essay date 1920)

[*Mencken was one of the most influential social and literary critics in the United States from the eve of World War I until the early years of the Great Depression. As coeditor of* Smart Set *magazine, he published several of Fitzgerald's short stories. In the following excerpt from a review of* Flappers and Philosophers *that originally appeared in* Smart Set, *Mencken notes a fluctuation in quality among Fitzgerald's fiction.*]

F. Scott Fitzgerald, in **Flappers and Philosophers,** offers a sandwich made up of two thick and tasteless chunks of *Kriegsbrod* with a couple of excellent sardines between. In brief, a collection that shows both the very good and the very bad. The best story in it, I think, is **"Benediction,"** which, when it was first printed in *The Smart Set,* brought down the maledictions of the Jesuits and came near getting the magazine barred from the Knights of Columbus camp-libraries. Rereading it, I can see no reason why any intelligent Catholic should object to it in the slightest. It is a well-written story, a story with an air to it, and it is also a story that rings true. I commend it to the rev. clergy; they will enjoy it. From **"Benediction"** the leap to **"The Offshore Pirate"** and other such confections is like the leap from the peaks of Darien to the slums of Colon. Here is thin and obvious stuff, cheap stuff—in brief, atrociously bad stuff. Fitzgerald is curiously ambidextrous. Will he proceed via the first part of *This Side of Paradise* to the cold groves of beautiful letters, or will he proceed via **"Head and Shoulders"** into the sunshine that warms Robert W. Chambers and Harold MacGrath? Let us wait and see.

> *H. L. Mencken, in an excerpt from* F. Scott Fitzgerald: The Critical Reception, *edited by Jackson R. Bryer, Burt Franklin & Co., Inc., 1978, p. 48.*

SAN FRANCISCO CHRONICLE (essay date 1921)

[*In the following excerpt, the anonymous reviewer characterizes* Flappers and Philosophers *as a collection of admirable, polished magazine stories that are "not meant to be taken very seriously."*]

Flappers and Philosophers marks the conversion of F. Scott Fitzgerald's undisciplined and turbid genius of *This Side of Paradise* into a bridled and clarified talent. *This Side of Paradise* was an irritating book because, while much of it was false, there was in it a sincere effort after beauty of expression. Its analysis of adolescence may have been as lurid and abnormal as adolescence itself sometimes is; but the attempt to see daylight through the jungle, however tortuous the path, commanded respect.

Flappers and Philosophers, though concerned with some of the same sort of people, is a collection of well-made short stories, in which the author is careful to avoid threadbare solutions, and in which the interest depends almost altogether on the skill with which the game plot is played. To be sure, Fitzgerald is still presenting American youth in a fashion which makes them look like futurist posters come to life.

His attitude has the supreme advantage of being free at once from supercilious ridicule and from the deadly seriousness which makes "a Sophoclean tragedy out of a cut finger." One may, however, confess to a very scant acquaintance with the little daughters of the rich and at the same time doubt whether they are so very different from the ordinary run of folks as Fitzgerald makes out. Even millionaires, after all, are peo-ple. Fitzgerald is inclined to sympathize with the hardness and frankness and scorn of subterfuge which he predicates of modern youth; but when the repartee of his debutantes consists for the most part in telling everyone within hearing to "shut up," in the fashion of the Queen's "off with his head," one is inclined to doubt whether mere disagreeable rudeness and crude selfishness is the sole characteristic of the wit of the young people with sufficiently large incomes to come within Fitzgerald's purlieu.

However, the stories in **Flappers and Philosophers** are not meant to be taken very seriously. They range from the fantasia of **"The Off Shore Pirate"** to the entirely credible **"Dalyrimple Goes Wrong,"** and **"Benediction."** In the latter story, the sentimental-moralistic ending was so ready to the author's hand that one can almost see the sardonic grin with which he turned to the psychologically more credible, and therefore in fiction more unusual, denouement. Almost all of these tales are creditable magazine fiction, with well-carpentered themes. But despite their highly polished surface, they are the work of an artisan rather than an artist—though of an artisan who cannot quite forget that he was once an artist, albeit a very imperfect one. (pp. 51-2)

> *"Youth Insurgent," in* F. Scott Fitzgerald: The Critical Reception, *edited by Jackson R. Bryer, Burt Franklin & Co., Inc., 1978, pp. 51-2.*

HILDEGARDE HAWTHORNE (essay date 1922)

[*In the following excerpt, Hawthorne offers an enthusiastic review of* Tales of the Jazz Age.]

There is plenty of variety in . . . [**Tales of the Jazz Age**], more than in the **Flappers and Philosophers,** which preceded it. Some of the stories are tragic, like **"May Day,"** which is tragic in a bitter and sordid way, and **"The Lees of Happiness,"** which is tragic after the Greek fashion, because the fates were unkind and the human beings helpless in their grasp.

One, which Fitzgerald likes the least of all, is tremendously amusing, arrant fooling that it is. It is called **"The Camel's Back,"** and the author hastens to tell us that it is no symbolic camel whose story is to be told, but a real one—or resembling reality, at least. There are other bits of fooling, too, such as **"Jemima, the Mountain Girl,"** a skit on the red-blooded story which begins: "It was night in the mountains of Kentucky. Wild hills rose on all sides. Swift mountain streams flowed rapidly up and down the mountains" . . . and so on. Funny enough, but it is hardly worth while to put such trifles into a book. They give too much the effect of samples, as though the author were saying, "See, here is my lightest side. I do this well and if you want it you can have it; but, on the other hand, here is a piece of imagination, here one of fantasy, here straight comedy . . . 'a story in each mood and manner, and every one of them good, in fact, but producing on the reader an impression of odds and ends that is unfortunate. The book is more like a magazine than a collection of stories by one man, arranged by an editor to suit all tastes and meant to be thrown away after reading.

But Fitzgerald when he is good, when he is writing a good story, is much too good for throwing away. His **"O Russett Witch"** is a beautiful piece of work, where fancy runs hand in hand with perception and understanding, giving the tale a hint of magic that does not remove it from reality. It is in the group under the heading "Fantasies" with that other story, **"The Diamond as Big as the Ritz,"** which is, as Fitzgerald calls it, an extravaganza, but which is also true stuff, life and people living it.

These stories are announced as being in the writer's second manner. They certainly show a development in his art, a new turn. His flapper stories, he says, are finished with. They were the best of their kind, but they could have used only a small part of Fitzgerald's talent. A great deal of him remains untouched as yet, and this "second manner" is surely the outcropping of a rich vein that may hold much wealth.

The book as it stands is amusing, interesting and well done, but it is filled besides with all sorts of hints, promise and portents that make it exciting beyond its actual content. There are flashes of wings and sounds of trumpets mingled with the tramp of feet and casual laughter, and though it is, as to its performance, a finished thing, each piece polished and fit for showing, yet there is also the effect of a glimpse into a workshop where tools are about and many matters afoot. Assuredly this makes for additional interest. On laying the book down the dominant thought is: "What will this man do next? He's at something, something we want very much to see."

> Hildegarde Hawthorne, in a review of "Tales of the Jazz Age," in The New York Times Book Review, October 29, 1922, p. 12.

WILLIAM ROSE BENÉT   (essay date 1926)

[*Benét was an American poet, editor, and novelist. Among his works are the* Oxford Anthology of American Literature *(1938), which he edited in collaboration with Norman Holmes Pearson, and his Pulitzer Prize-winning autobiographical novel in verse,* The Dust Which Is God *(1941). In the excerpt below from a review of* All the Sad Young Men, *Benét admires Fitzgerald's ability to turn out marketable short fiction but feels that his work is inspired by "the pressure of living conditions rather than the demand of the spirit."*]

What is one to expect [from **All the Sad Young Men**]? Well, if one has any acquaintance with the problem of "living by one's pen" in America, with the present status of the magazine short story, with the relationship that ordinary periodical publication bears to what a writer is actually capable of achieving in fiction, one is a proven fool if expectation be set too high. Mr. Fitzgerald determined to "make a living by writing." He has made it. And in spite of all the compromises to which one must come with the Market, he has succeeded in producing at least one book, *The Great Gatsby,* that is undeniable achievement. Meanwhile, here, in **All the Sad Young Men** (Mr. Fitzgerald is always fortunate with his titles) is evidence of his almost uncanny facility for magazine writing.

"The Rich Boy" leads off. It was over-advertised in *The Red Book,* even as, in our opinion, Julian Street's "Mr. Bisbee's Princess" was overadvertised. It isn't bad, in spots. Mr. Fitzgerald draws a recognizable type. He refuses to tie a machine-made plot to his character sketch. But such a character, being essentially empty, yields little that seems salient. We found too little pith, after all, in this study of a stuffed shirt. It is sincere, but it failed to touch our emotions.

"Winter Dreams" is better. It is youthful in conception, but it achieves a sharper irony than that in **"The Rich Boy."** **"The Baby Party"** is simply an entertaining little magazine story. And then we come to **"Absolution."**

Despite the shadow of Sherwood Anderson in the background, **"Absolution"** is almost first-rate. Three-quarters of it, at least, are masterly. Then the author falters. He doesn't know quite what to do with his absorbing juxtaposition of Father Schwartz and Rudolph Miller; and while he doesn't exactly throw his story away, he seems to us to fall back on Anderson. For all that, this tale is memorable.

And right after it fox-trots **"Rags Martin-Jones,"** with a revival of the Jazz Age type of thing. Lively O. Henry, at that. A brilliant bit of bunk. Then **"The Adjuster,"** a "significant" magazine story, that is yet a shade better than most "significant" magazine stories. It has a peculiar pathos one remembers. **"Hot and Cold Blood"** and **"The Sensible Thing"** are lesser work. **"Gretchen's Forty Winks"** furnished us much amusement. That is the lot.

A young writer who is earning his living at literature must work fast and put his books close together. Mr. Fitzgerald has elected so to live. His ingenuity at evolving marketable ideas is extraordinary. But one naturally feels, behind most of the writing in this book, the pressure of living conditions rather than the demand of the spirit. As a writer of short stories the author more displays his astonishing facility than the compulsions of his true nature. He is keeping his hand in and paying the rent. And the performance is energetic with a certain gallantry. But now that he has written *The Great Gatsby* we are, perhaps, exorbitant in our demands.

> William Rose Benét, "Art's Bread and Butter," in The Saturday Review of Literature, Vol. II, No. 36, April 3, 1926, p. 682.

EDITH H. WALTON   (essay date 1935)

[*In the following excerpt from a review of* Taps at Reveille, *Walton praises Fitzgerald's stylistic abilities while echoing a common grievance among critics that Fitzgerald's work does not reflect his talent.*]

The characteristic seal of [Fitzgerald's] brilliance stamps [**Taps at Reveille**], but it is a brilliance which splutters off too frequently into mere razzle-dazzle. One wishes for more evidence that he has changed and matured since the days of **Flappers and Philosophers** and **Tales of the Jazz Age**.

Most in key with those earlier books are the three stories grouped under the heading, "Josephine." With a kind of deadly accuracy, Mr. Fitzgerald describes a specimen of the predatory young who makes [Booth] Tarkington's Lola Platt seem like a milk-and-water baby. Josephine is sixteen—beautiful, ruthless and fickle. Whether or not he is earmarked as somebody else's property she goes out and gets her man with an appalling directness. Proms and tea-dances are her natural habitat, and she takes a certain pride in being considered fast. She dates—more, perhaps, than Mr. Fitzgerald realizes—but her wiles and adventures are undeniably comic.

Better, and poignant as well as amusing, is the longer sequence of stories which deals with a pre-war boy in his middle teens. Though his method is different from Booth Tarkington's, Mr. Fitzgerald approaches at times the same startling veracity. Basil Duke Lee is a bright, sensitive, likable boy, constantly betrayed by a fatal tendency to brag and boss. He knows his failing, especially after the minor hell of his first year at boarding school, but again and again he is impelled to ruin an initial good impression. Two of the Basil stories—

"He Thinks He's Wonderful" and **"The Perfect Life"**—are small masterpieces of humor and perception, and Mr. Fitzgerald is always miraculously adept at describing adolescent love affairs and adolescent swagger.

A full half of *Taps at Reveille* is given over to these tales of youth. The remaining stories vary greatly in mood and merit. **"Crazy Sunday,"** which has Hollywood for a setting, is clever but contrived; **"Majesty,"** for all its irony, has a strangely hollow ring; **"One Interne"** is entertaining, but gets nowhere and has no real characterization. Even **"The Last of the Belles,"** with its undertone of regret for youth and bright gayety, fails to make a point which one can regard as valid. Far better is **"A Short Trip Home,"** a ghost story which yet can be considered as definitely realistic.

Three of the stories point toward directions which Mr. Fitzgerald might profitably take. **"A Trip to Chancellorsville,"** in which a trainload of light ladies is catapulted unawares into the realities of the Civil War, is restrained irony at its best. **"Family in the Wind,"** the story of a Southern town ravaged by tornadoes and of a drink-ridden doctor who stumbles on salvation, strikes a new and healthy note. **"Babylon Revisited,"** which seems oddly linked in spirit to Mr. Fitzgerald's latest novel, *Tender Is the Night,* is probably the most mature and substantial story in the book. A rueful, though incompleted, farewell to the jazz age, its setting is Paris and its tone one of anguish for past follies.

It has become a dreadful commonplace to say that Mr. Fitzgerald's material is rarely worthy of his talents. Unfortunately, however, the platitude represents truth. Scott Fitzgerald's mastery of style—swift, sure, polished, firm—is so complete that even his most trivial efforts are dignified by his technical competence. All his writing has a glamourous gloss upon it; it is always entertaining; it is always beautifully executed.

Only when one seeks to discover what he has really said, what his stories really amount to, is one conscious of a certain emptiness. *Taps at Reveille* will bore no one, and offend no trained intelligence, but when one remembers how fine a writer Mr. Fitzgerald could still be, it simply is not good enough.

Edith H. Walton, "Scott Fitzgerald's Tales," in The New York Times Book Review, *March 31, 1935, p. 7.*

SERGIO PEROSA (essay date 1961)

[*An Italian editor, translator, and critic, Perosa has contributed significantly to the understanding of English and American literature in Italy. In the following excerpt from his book* L'arte di F. Scott Fitzgerald *(1961;* The Art of F. Scott Fitzgerald, *1965), Perosa characterizes Fitzgerald's stories written after the completion of* The Great Gatsby *as works in which the author dealt with mature themes and introduced new subjects and techniques that he later developed in his novel* Tender Is the Night.]

From the long time lapse between the publication of *The Great Gatsby* (1925) and the publication of *Tender Is the Night* (1934), one might infer that Fitzgerald's creative vein had exhausted itself. In fact, this was a period of silence and artistic impotence only superficially. The author's creative powers did show signs of weariness and fatigue, and there were plenty of objective reasons to account for it: his wife's illness and her eventual hospitalization with its disastrous consequences for his tranquility of mind and his literary ac-

tivities, his own sense of instability and bewilderment after the ruinous collapse of the "Golden Twenties," his psychological strain and poor health, his increasing financial obligations. His favorite subject matter, now that the boom was over, lost all its interest, and, for that matter, he had exhausted it artistically. The writer had to find new sources of inspiration in the painful experiences of those sad years, and consequently to renew and vary the formal and technical patterns through which he was to express himself. In this difficult and exacting task Fitzgerald wavered for a while and lost his momentum, frequently taking refuge among the specters of the past for sentimental and, more often, purely economic reasons. But he did continue to search for new subjects and to experiment with new techniques, working with stubborn dedication and unflagging commitment to his craft. At the end of nine long years he was to show that he had found a new, elusive artistic reality.

Fitzgerald began working on a new novel as soon as he had finished *Gatsby,* and he also wrote a great number of stories during the next few years. At least some of them, dealing with motives later developed in the novel, redeem his frequent concessions to the economic muse and his unfortunate harking back to the past. The signs of renewal become apparent after 1930, when the ghost of the past has been exorcised in "Echoes of the Jazz Age"; but even earlier, in the stories where the suggestions of the past are still predominant, one can perceive at times the partial apprehension of maturer themes.

In **"The Rich Boy"** and **"The Last of the Belles"** Fitzgerald's creative power seems clearly on the wane, and yet he has taken a different attitude toward themes that were already familiar to him. **"The Rich Boy"** codifies, as it were, the poetic and moral feeling with which the author up to that time had considered the very rich. It is, in fact, a kind of parable on the isolation and impotence of the very rich, which is embodied in the pathetic story of Anson Hunter. His unlimited wealth has given Hunter a sense of superiority and aloofness (that "came to him when he realized the half-grudging American deference that was paid to him in the Connecticut village"), a desire for predominance and a vague contempt for everyday life ("he disclaimed to struggle with other boys for precedence—he expected it to be given him freely"), and an excessive indulgence for his own faults. When he grows up this attitude results in complete isolation from his fellow creatures and ends by compromising his sentimental love for Paula, who might have given him a happy domestic life. Wealth separates him from happiness; instead of fulfilling his dreams, it becomes an obstacle for his self-realization. For him, as for Gatsby and for his predecessors, the awakening comes too late. The link of this story with previous handlings of the same motive is evident, and yet it lacks the quality of dramatic development and inevitability of situation. In spite of Fitzgerald's statement ("there are no types, no plurals"), he wanted, here, to represent the plight of a whole social class. . . . (pp. 83-4)

But owing to this general formulation, **"The Rich Boy"** becomes a kind of essayistic comment rather than a story; it suffers from a lack of dramatic intensity, and it has none of those poetic moments that enlivened an earlier story on the same topic, **"The Diamond as Big as the Ritz."** The method of presentation, moreover, is rather clumsy in **"The Rich Boy"**: the writer begins with an initial "portrait" of Hunter, which determines and conditions the subsequent development of the story, as in Fitzgerald's early fiction, while the use of a "narrator" involved in the story is not completely controlled. The narrator deals openly here with the events of the story and intrudes with superfluous observations and explicit comments, so that finally he destroys the structural unity that he should actually give the story.

"The Last of the Belles" takes up again the motive of the flapper, and here too the principle of the "narrator" is technically imperfect. The interest of the writer is almost exclusively directed upon him in the first and third sections of the story, resulting in a lack of structural harmony. Furthermore, the narrator participates too openly in the action, and he colors it with a kind of elegiac sentimentalism which contrasts with the unusual course taken by the events. The "last of the belles," Ailie, who at the beginning of the story has so much in common with Gloria and Daisy, differs radically from them in that she accepts reality in the end. She is brought to give in before the requirements of life and her emotional feelings by marrying her modest suitor. This means renouncing, after a whirling, brilliant life, the frivolous ideals of a flapper, and it is already a clear indication of the break-up of a sentimental world of selfish pleasure. And the crisis which has brought her to refuse the false values of the flappers shows that the writer was becoming aware of a new reality, more common and domestic, less brilliant and glamorous, that was confronting him. (p. 85)

The last of the belles *is* gone—and this is the important aspect of the story, almost a new departure in Fitzgerald's fiction. The flappers give way under the pressure of everyday life; and "aesthetes" and college "philosophers" discover in their adventures the signs of an unfamiliar, unexpected experience of gloomy suffering. In **"A Short Trip Home,"** a student from Yale wins the love of his girl, Ellen, only after having gone through a nightmarish experience and after having rescued her from the evil influence of an actual ghost ("He was dead. He was dead as hell—he had been dead all along") who had been pursuing her. The heedless, superficial world of the college youngsters betrays the hidden presence of evil; more than the apparition that had frightened Amory, the ghost that throws its dark shadow over the whole story recalls the devilish figure that haunted Miriam in *The Marble Faun* of Hawthorne. And this fact is significant. If the obsession with evil of the great nineteenth-century novelist is echoed in the supposed singer of the Jazz Age, it is only because Fitzgerald has turned to his own bitter experience for inspiration, because he has started to reconsider his fictional material. And he deals with this new experience with technical skill, making a child the narrator and allowing him, as a "controlling center," to discover the evil influence that has haunted Ellen. The story is seen through the eyes of Ellen's little brother, who gradually discovers corruption, as had been the case with Maisie in James's novel.

The actual presence of evil in our lives also plays a preponderant part in **"One Interne,"** which deals with the same theme on a more realistic level. There is only a reference to a possible happy ending here, and the young protagonist can hope for the love of his girl only when she has freed herself from an obscure relationship with a thirty-five year old doctor (the ghost in the preceding story was the same age). In this case, however, Doctor Durfee does not hide under his mask an incorporeal being or a mysterious incarnation, nor is he a new Rappacini. But his disquieting figure hides a dubious soul and suggests that mysterious and wicked element which seems to be inherent in life. It is the girl, Thea, rather than the youth, Bill, who has to disengage herself from his influence; but for both of them life is a source of apprehension and pain.

That love triumphs is no longer important, and if it can bear such a burden of anxiety, it is so because the writer has surrendered himself to the evidence of facts and recognized the obsessive presence of evil. One must add that the story remains a literary exercise, lacking a precise informing idea, and that Fitzgerald was trying to organize more material than was possible without including a "center of interest." But in these stories there is already a clear reflection of Fitzgerald's own experience of suffering as he followed his wife from one clinic to another, and of his foreboding fear of disaster. We can therefore acknowledge the fact that his fiction was developing in the direction of *Tender Is the Night*.

"The Bridal Party," once more, is a variation on the theme of *Gatsby*. Like many of his predecessors, the protagonist, Michael, who is hopelessly poor, is deserted by his flapper Caroline. But the novelty of this story, as in **"The Last of the Belles,"** lies in the conclusion. Even though Michael becomes suddenly rich (this time more easily than ever, through an inheritance), Caroline ends by marrying her fiancé Hamilton, who finds himself without a cent on the eve of the wedding. She reaffirms her faith in the man who is strong and sure of himself, despising Michael's weakness, which cannot be changed by money. Her responsible choice shows that new values must now be taken into account and, in some ways, foreshadows Nicole's choice in *Tender Is the Night*. Her "realistic" decision, moreover, leads Michael to reconsider his position and free himself from illusions and regrets—a first step, as we know from *This Side of Paradise,* toward maturity: "The ceremonial function [Caroline's marriage], with its pomp and its revelry, had stood for a sort of initiation into a life where even his regret could not follow them."

We are undoubtedly confronted with new "germs" and suggestions; but sometimes, as Fitzgerald himself warns us, "a ghostly rumble among the drums, an asthmatic whisper in the trombones" swing him back into the past. Out of this return is born a compact series of stories, woven around two fixed characters, Basil and Josephine, who are the posthumous incarnations of "philosopher" and "flapper." The nine stories about Basil Lee and the five about Josephine represent almost a short novel, although Fitzgerald refused to have them published in collected form. They hark back to distant events of his own childhood, with the same intention of tracing the crucial phases of the "education" of the two characters that inspired *This Side of Paradise*. Young Basil must pass through the "conquest of the successive worlds of school, college and New York"; Josephine has her first experiences as flapper even before the word itself was coined. These stories have been taken as a clear indication of Fitzgerald's waning power and of his decline as a writer, and it must be admitted that his "reversion" is rather childish and naive, after the long stretch of road he had covered. And yet even these stories have their significance and place in Fitzgerald's fiction if they are interpreted as the author's turning toward what must have appeared to him as an oasis of freshness in the midst of his utter dejection. They have been described as "escapist" stories, and Fitzgerald was undoubtedly driven by a desire to escape his plight and to take shelter in the uncorrupted world of childhood. But he brought with him into that shelter the awareness of the bitter lesson he had learned. The childhood and adolescence to which Fitzgerald turned his attention are no longer seen as a longed-for Eden which had been lost; they are seen "through a glass darkly"—filtered, as it were, through his present suffering. They are no longer a world of simple innocence or repose, but rather they offer as a whole a panorama where his conscience brings to the surface the hidden presence of evil and disillusionment.

As Arthur Mizener has rightly remarked, [in his introduction to *Afternoon of an Author* (1957)], in these stories Fitzgerald "combined the innocence of complete involvement with an almost scientific coolness of observation." He was involved emotionally in the world of his youth, and he conveyed the sense of his intense participation; at the same time he was able to evoke the past from the point of view of the present and judge it in the light of his new awareness. This double perspective results in an odd kind of irony and detachment, and it has something typically Jamesian about it. The second level—the ironic judgment—is suggested rather than fully realized, but Fitzgerald was able all the same to reconcile it with a kind of intimacy; and in this aspect is laid the significance and the aesthetic value of these stories. His intimacy does not prevent him from a recognition that the principle of evil is already active in the idyll of youth; boys and girls act out of malice or spite, and the suffering that they cause may in itself become a maturing experience. Moreover, these stories are deeply rooted in a definite social context. With both Basil and Josephine the scene of the various episodes is usually a small provincial town, an unfashionable prep school, outside the fringes of the great universities or of the big cities in the East. And it is a setting bristling with motives and fictional possibilities, sketched with precision, which by its nature makes the adventures of the two youngsters, otherwise unbelievable, rather plausible. They become representative, in other words, of an experience that is typically American, or better still typically Middle Western.

With this premise, a few remarks on the single stories will be sufficient to illustrate the mechanics of the various situations and to make them familiar to the reader. **"The Scandal Detectives,"** the first in the series about Basil, tells of a boy's prank: envious of the charm and self-assurance of Hubert Blair, the "beau" of these stories, Basil and a friend take their revenge on him by sending him anonymous threats and frightening him in the dark. Hubert is made fun of because he takes the threats seriously and then enlarges fantastically upon his supposed danger, while in fact the ambuscade has miscarried in a comic way. An element of real interest is provided by the antagonism between Basil and Hubert: a small town dandy on one side and on the other the sensitive, intelligent youth, who usually gains his victory over Basil, in spite of Basil's imaginary triumphs. This motive will reappear in the following stories; here it is interwoven with a subtle notation of the suspicious atmosphere of the small town, embodied in the ridiculous figure of Hubert's father, whose satiric portrait gives some substance to the thinness of the plot. At such an early stage of his "education" Basil is somehow brought to recognize that he is conceited and to renounce his ambition of becoming a "gentleman burglar" like Arsène Lupin. In the next episode, **"A Night at the Fair,"** by succeeding in wearing long pants for the first time and by refusing to have anything to do with the girls picked up at the fair, Basil stands out from the rest of his friends. He remains "faithful" to Gladys—the good girl, both rich and proper—even if Gladys too lets him down in the end. His disappointments follow one upon the other in **"The Freshest Boy"** and **"He Thinks He's Wonderful"**; either at

Scott and Zelda Fitzgerald, February 1921.

prep school or back home, Basil is unpopular, and he ruins his chances of social success through his arrogance, his presumption, and his false self-assurance. In the second of these stories the prospect of a pleasant vacation is ruined by his endless and absurd talks ("he had undone the behavior of three days in half an hour"), and he has learned a painful lesson. In the first, which might be considered the central story in the Basil group, he gives a demonstration of courage and seriousness by remaining in his school when he could have escaped his unpopularity by going to Europe. He has learned that the has to find out and avoid the reasons for his unpopularity and "that life for everybody was a struggle, sometimes magnificent from a distance, but always difficult." Through his stubborn resistance he wins back the respect of his fellow students, and his final achievement is to be called by his own name, and no longer by nicknames.

Two more partial victories are won by Basil in **"The Captured Shadow"** and in **"The Perfect Life."** In the first Basil succeeds in producing his play, though he has to lower himself to a compromise with Hubert and then fight his opposition. The play is a success all the same, and Basil is even brought to recognize the absurdity and uselessness of all his schemes: he begins to see things in their true perspective and in their actual value. In the second story he is initiated into a life of "perfect morality," and he runs the risk of becoming an insuf-

ferable "prig," but he succeeds at the very end in making himself socially useful to others by preventing an ill-advised elopement. Once the many obstacles of prep school and small town are overcome, Basil is confronted with the greater obstacles of college and big city. In **"Forging Ahead"** Basil is forced to find sufficient means to go to Yale ("the faraway East, that he had loved with a vast nostalgia since he had first read books about great cities"). He has to submit himself to humiliations and compromises, work hard with his own hands until a mechanical solution releases him from his burden when the financial fortunes of his family are suddenly restored. His efforts have shown that he has reached a certain maturity, and he can again be "faithful" to his girl. And in the last episode, **"Basil and Cleopatra,"** he takes a further step in his education by renouncing the obsessive ideal of a sentimental love. Here the war of the sexes becomes the chief element of the story, but at the edge of manhood and on his way to college, Basil turns his back on the world of youthful emotion and enters a new, virile world, free from his many prejudices and weaknesses. Acquiring popularity among his companions, he can now rely on his psychological balance and pass judgment on the weakness of his rival, resist the lure of a new sentimental involvement, and turn to the future. . . .
(pp. 86-90)

His "education" is still incomplete, of course, but he has achieved a better awareness of life than Amory did, and he has gone through a series of painful trials that will prevent him, as it were, from following the steps of his predecessor at college. His emotional freshness, his very simplemindedness carry in them a touch of a greater engagement: it is hardly believable that he will repeat the mistakes of Amory, assume the mask of the "aesthete," strike an "egotistical" attitude. In the supposed limbo of infancy and adolescence, Basil has already discovered the secret flaw of falsehood and conflict and has become aware that life, at any stage, is a painful struggle.

It is not so for Josephine. In her group of stories, starting from a beginning in many ways similar to that of Basil, she is born and remains a "flapper" to the very end. She does not go through a real progress of "education"; although she may come in the end to her own form of self-recognition, it is a less keenly felt and suffered one, and less conclusive than Basil's. She does not build her own future, and she plays a disturbing part only in the game of existence or in the war of the sexes. This lack of development in her character is partly due to the writer's intent, but it is for the most part imposed upon him by the very situation in which he had to place Josephine. To trace the line of Basil's development it was sufficient for him to rely on his own childhood memories and to represent his own process of growth. To give shape and substance to Josephine, he had to exert all his imaginative power to project an objectively realized character. Fitzgerald succeeded in making Josephine representative, by conferring on her some of the typical characteristics of the American girl—such as her need to dominate men, to feel herself all-important and to show off her emotional and social power—and by projecting her figure on a small-town background that would permit her to play that role and exercise her influence. But just because Josephine *is* representative, there is no warmth of feeling in her character and no sympathetic participation in her adventures on the part of the author. Moreover, her portrait is drawn with a mildly satirical intention, and these satirical features prevent the proper development of an

"education." Fitzgerald's objective perception of her shortcomings and of her basic wickedness allows him a greater detachment of vision, but insisting on the fatuous and egotistical sides of her character, he was driven to give us a rather static portrait.

It is not without significance that he abandoned Josephine much earlier than Basil and that he brought her to a "conversion" that is both dubious and doubtful. In **"First Blood,"** sixteen-year-old Josephine succeeds in drawing the attention of her sister's fiancé, Anthony, on herself, and when Anthony pledges his undying love she immediately loses all her interest in him. Almost the same trick is played in **"A Nice Quiet Place"** on Sonny Dorrance, a rich boy who is for a while ensnared by Josephine's "speedy" attitude, and only when Josephine has become **"A Woman with a Past,"** in the third episode, after having been expelled from school, is she brought to the sudden realization that personal conquests cannot be based on the sacrifices of others. For the first time she has tried to attract a man and failed, and her attempt to break an engagement this time comes to nothing. She is left therefore with the simple truth of her own statement that "one couldn't go on forever kissing comparative strangers behind closed doors." The flapper seems to have learned her lesson, but one can easily imagine that after a while she will continue in her disturbing career. This is in fact what happens in the fourth, uncollected story—**"A Snobbish Story."** To emphasize her change in the direction of seriousness Josephine becomes involved again with an older man, this time married. Her defiance of Chicago society, however, remains the typical gesture of protest of a flapper who has *not* grown up; and even if she is brought to **"Emotional Bankruptcy"** in the fifth story (also uncollected), we are still left with the suspicion that she will not mature further than that. Her "youthful cockiness" is lost when she realizes that her love affairs are like "a game played with technical mastery, but with the fire and enthusiasm gone"; but she is still looking for a man who is a leader and "with lots of experience," and *her* final "education" resembles Amory's. She seems to accept the wisdom of experience, but she is in fact left with a *tabula rasa*:

> She was very tired and lay face downward on the couch with that awful, awful realization that all the old things are true; one cannot both spend and have. The love of her life had come by, and looking in her empty basket, she had found not a flower left for him—not one. After a while, she wept.
>
> "Oh, what have I done to myself?" she wailed. "What have I done?"

She has done nothing that we did not expect of a flapper, and, if she knows herself, that is not all: this premature vamp will continue in the illusion of both spending and having. Slave as she is of herself, Josephine will substantially remain what she has always been, whereas Basil did suffer a kind of "education."

There is more bitterness here, perhaps, than regret. If the past has been recaptured, it shows that the principle of evil and conflict is present everywhere, even in the golden years of youth and adolescence. Confronted with this discovery, the writer seems to withdraw in dismay, and it is again significant that his best care is devoted to Basil, who can still be saved. In this sense, the variety of motives and the consistent development of the education theme contributes to a better artistic achievement in the Basil stories than in the Josephine group. There is more love for and concern with Basil, while Fitzgerald seems to bear Josephine a grudge. And there is a greater chance for fictional development in dealing with a character who is painfully attaining his own integrity and finding his right way in the world. The sequence stops, however, before any real conclusion is reached, and the value of this experiment should not therefore be overestimated. At the same time it must not be overlooked or brushed aside in haste, as has been quite often the tendency. Fitzgerald's *recherche du temps perdu* does not land him in *le temps retrouvé,* and there is no reason why we should expect it. The various adventures of his youths do not attain the same profound significance of moral initiation as do the adventures of Nick in Hemingway's *In Our Time.* Nevertheless, Fitzgerald's return to the past has proved, if nothing else, the impossibility of any evasion from the present and has shown that suffering is already present in the supposed lost Eden of childhood. It is just the same, then, or probably better, to confront the present without looking back, to find in the foreboding experience of those years the reasons for survival or possibly the way to salvation.

The present was poor in consolations but rich in warnings: Fitzgerald was well aware of it, and this was already a new beginning for his maturer fiction. Glamorous New York, upset by the crisis of 1929, was now "a lost city"; Ring Lardner had died without fulfilling his expectations. And as adolescence was already far in the past, only "echoes" were left of the Golden Twenties. In his essay "Echoes of the Jazz Age," Fitzgerald evoked that world with nostalgia and a sense of participation; but he described its collapse, too, in a kind of pitiless post mortem, and his analysis became lucid in the extreme, cold and unimpassioned, almost scientific, when he had to record the disastrous consequences of the past euphoria. The present was different, tragic and tormented. . . . (pp. 90-3)

There is no palliative for this reality, no possibility of escape, except perhaps the staunch resistance of personal integrity: and this seems to be the conclusion reached by Fitzgerald when he has succeeded in exorcising the past. The new reality that confronts him now is no longer marked by the motives of love and money, of dream and youthful illusion; even its legendary possibilities have vanished. And if the heart rebels for its own reasons, the mind must listen to and obey its reasons as well. Faced with the collapse of his former world, the author can be less involved or assume an attitude of detachment, but his lucid analysis allows him a fresh start. Turning to the present and to everyday life, availing himself of his own private experiences of suffering—his two stays in Hollywood, his life as an expatriate and his self-deception, his efforts to preserve his integrity as a man and as an artist in spite of his wife's illness, and so on—he was to find new and richer material for his fiction, both for the stories and for the novel which was under way at the time. (p. 94)

In **"Outside the Cabinet-Maker's,"** the protagonist reaffirms his personal integrity in a quiet and domestic way. In this beautiful little sketch, which shows what delicacy of feeling and bareness of style Fitzgerald could attain, there is practically no action: the sketch catches a glimpse of a father with his daughter, attached to each other by boundless love and affection, in a moment of intimacy and expectation. He buys her a doll's house and almost identifies himself for a while with her fanciful expectation. We are reminded for a single moment of Dick Diver with his children—for a single moment because any external intrusion would shatter the perfect balance of this sketch. There is a hint of impending tragedy

in the story, and no more; perhaps Fitzgerald wanted to imagine an oasis of rest in the whirlwind of life, to project an illusion of safety, which would redeem the utter dejection of his mood. Everything here, however, is suggested, rather than made explicit, with an unmatched delicacy of touch. And as Arthur Mizener has remarked:

> **"Outside the Cabinet-Maker's"** is, both in substance and technique, a wholly mature story. Only a writer who had seen that the significant values of experience exist in all experience could have said so much with material so magnificently homely and familiar; only a writer who had known and could remember what it felt like to see and had completely accepted the blindness of middle age could have presented that little girl's murderous innocence without romantic irony; only a writer with the most delicate sense of how meaning inheres in events could have kept his story so unpretentious; only a writer whose dramatic sense was a function of his understanding could have managed the ending of this story without leaving an impression of technical trickiness.

When panic has spread, however, and violence has been loosed, one's integrity becomes a laborious conquest—when it is not actually lost. In **"Two Wrongs"** and in **"Babylon Revisited"** we have two examples of this further development of the theme. The principle of the "transference of vitality" (which will become the central motive of *Tender Is the Night*) permits in **"Two Wrongs"** the affirmation of a personal integrity, but only at the expense of the parallel sacrifice of another. Bill McChesney, a successful producer at the beginning, comes to Europe where his integrity is shattered by the contact with an elusive reality that he is unable to control. His wife builds up her character on his gradual degradation. Bill lets himself be swallowed by a questionable environment—as Dick will do in the novel—with its pseudo-aristocratic Europeans and expatriate Americans, utterly neglecting his wife Emmy, ruining his health and his reputation, while Emmy, in New York, becomes a successful ballet dancer. In her husband's dissipation Emmy finds the spur to a life of liberty and self-affirmation. When she is told that Bill cannot recover his health, she chooses to follow her own destiny as a dancer: if she has suffered a "wrong" from Bill, Bill will now suffer one from her. But this is not owing to the law of compensation on which Emerson had theorized so enthusiastically; here we are faced with the mysterious motive of the dissipation of energy which is accompanied by the parallel birth of new forms of vitality. The motive of the "transference of vitality" is clearly foreshadowed here: reality has reasons that are sometimes cruel, and the writer's task is to record them in their objective display. No enthusiasms or severe judgments are introduced into the story—only a kind of mature understanding pervades every detail. That is the burden and the lesson of experience, and the lesson is none the less bitter if, as in **"Babylon Revisited,"** the conclusion is less pessimistic. Here the protagonist, Charlie, succeeds in reacquiring his lost integrity, but he has a penalty to pay and sacrifices to make before his ordeal is over.

In **"Babylon Revisited"** the tragedy of the Golden Twenties reaches its highest artistic realization. Convinced that the "snow of twenty-nine wasn't real snow," Charlie is forced to realize how real it was and how much of his life and of his world has been swept away by the whirlwind. A playboy during the Twenties, to the extent of becoming at least partly responsible for his wife's death, Charlie has returned to a ghostly Paris (the Babylon of the past) after the tragedy has canceled every trace of the boom, to try to get his daughter Honoria from his sister-in-law, Marion, who has been her custodian. Having tirelessly rebuilt a position for himself, Charlie would now like to have his own home, but he is looked upon with suspicion and mistrust and thwarted in his attempt to get Honoria back. In an ashgray Paris, no longer full of light and excitement, he is faced with Marion's belief that he has not mended his ways and that he might begin drinking again, and when an unfortunate misunderstanding seems to confirm her suspicions she refuses to give up the girl.

Marion is also driven by a kind of personal resentment for his past happiness and wealth, when she could hardly provide for her own family, and from this point of view her refusal is both selfish and cruel. Cruel in particular, because Charlie's redemption has been fully paid for, as we can see by watching him with his daughter in Paris—no longer in bars and bistros but in the boulevards and respectable cafes. But against Marion's ruthless opposition, Charlie emerges a new, vigorous man. The past is not completely dead, and in the crucial point of the story it rises through the ghostlike figures of Charlie's former acquaintances to demand new victims. After this bitter trick of fate, he is about to begin drinking again, to lose hope and abandon himself to a darker, deeper dissipation. And yet, he finds strength enough in himself to resist the temptation and cling more than ever to his hope of regaining Honoria. He is resolved to have her back, and when he leaves the bar without accepting another drink, we know that he can go back to his task and sooner or later succeed in his attempt. "He would come back some day; they couldn't make him pay forever . . . he wanted the child, and nothing was much good now, beside the fact." His long sacrifice will continue until his penalty has been fully paid, but he has acquired a new form of integrity and the sense of human values. His catharsis has been made possible, and the collapse of the Golden Twenties has not destroyed everything. On the ashes of that world at least one is left who in his struggle for a noble aim finds it possible to reassert his own personality and to discover the sense of his human condition.

The story is developed with complete economy of means, without any concession to easy writing or to elaborate devices, and it achieves a perfect structural balance and tightness. A few brief hints are sufficient to evoke the past, which hangs heavily and menacingly over the whole of the story. A few scenes illustrate Charlie's situation, and the crucial point is reached almost immediately, without undue haste or omissions. The climax of the story has all the force and the absurdity of an inescapable tragic knot, and when the tragedy leans toward a possible happy solution the figure of Honoria acquires a symbolic light of redemption and eventual salvation. Like Pearl in *The Scarlet Letter,* or, better still, like Maisie in *What Maisie Knew,* Honoria stands between the contrasting parties, between wickedness and purity of intentions, malice and self-denial, and she is entrusted with all hopes of salvation for her elders. (pp. 95-8)

In **"Crazy Sunday,"** set in Hollywood, the protagonist succeeds once more in preserving his integrity, although on a human level that is less suffered and painful. But he seems to be the last one to win his battle; after him the forces of dissolution will get the upper hand. Invited among important people and in the midst of a complex game of interests, a young scriptwriter, Coles, attracts the sympathy of an actress married to a producer. Although unfaithful himself, the producer

is extremely jealous of his wife Stella, and Coles must keep a fine balance between the demands of both to avoid ruining his career. There could be a mechanical solution, when the actress throws herself into the arms of Coles at the news of her husband's death in an airplane accident. It could be the final big scene of a popular film, and it did happen in life, but Coles resists his first impulse to stay, and even though he is in love with Stella he goes away. There is a clear hint that he might return, but in the crucial moment he has had enough strength to refuse an equivocal involvement and to assert his honesty of feeling. By refusing an easy solution he seems to escape evil and possible ruin, but he is the last character in our sequence who succeeds in doing so. The others who remain to be examined—before coming to *Tender Is the Night*—prefigure Dick Diver's final surrender.

"Crazy Sunday" is not as good as the previous stories because Fitzgerald has not clarified his attitude toward his characters. The exact relationships between them are not properly explained, their motivations are obscure, and their merits and defects are not clearly indicated. There is also a structural disharmony between the first part of the story, which is rather humorous, and the second part; moreover the device of the airplane accident to remove the producer from the scene is an easy and mechanical solution, a kind of *deus ex machina* to get things in motion again. And yet several motives and several situations that will reappear in the novel that follows are already brought together in this story. Just as Dick loves his wife but is attracted to Rosemary, so Stella loves her husband but would like to find a solution for her troubles with Coles. Coles has the same feeling as Rosemary of being a "pawn" in a cruel game (and we should note here that in the first draft of the novel Rosemary was to be a young Hollywood technician). If Nicole, suffering from a father complex, is inferior to and dependent on Dick, here it is the producer who suffers from a mother complex, which makes him dependent on Stella. And so on. We are confronted with significant analogies, both for the inherent similarity of some motives, and for the similar way in which they are brought together and handled. (pp. 99-100)

The Jazz Age has given way to an age of crisis and uncertainty. Human integrity is the victim of deep lacerations, eaten by the worm of inner evil, of personal weaknesses, of restlessness. The theme of "education" must be turned over—in the new reality, only motives of deterioration and personal ruin are fit material for artistic elaboration. The naturalistic writers had already been aware of this at the end of the nineteenth century; in the Thirties, a whole group of "engaged" writers was becoming aware of it, from Farrell to Caldwell, from Dos Passos to Steinbeck.

Fitzgerald, too, had come to realize it from personal experience and from his acute sense of the times. In those long years between *The Great Gatsby* and *Tender Is the Night* he had discovered or created a new, exacting subject matter. The germs and the first shapeless trials are clearly to be found in the stories; in the novel that followed they found their elaborate and laborious consecration. (p. 101)

Sergio Perosa, in his The Art of F. Scott Fitzgerald, *translated by Charles Matz and Sergio Perosa, The University of Michigan Press, 1965, 239 p.*

SEYMOUR L. GROSS (essay date 1963)

[*Gross is an American critic and scholar who has written extensively on the fiction of Nathaniel Hawthorne and who served as coeditor of the* Viking Portable American Literature Survey *(1962). In the following excerpt, Gross portrays protaganist Charlie Wales from "Babylon Revisited" as an undeserving victim of his own inescapable past.*]

The action of **"Babylon Revisited"** begins and ends in the Ritz bar. This structural maneuver is absolutely right, for the bar is one of the story's chief symbols of the relentless impingement of the past on the present, though it is not until the end of the story after Charlie's defeat, that it clearly takes on this signification. Indeed, ironically enough, Charlie's initial appearance at the Ritz seems to imply precisely the opposite: the apparent separation of the past from the concerns, needs, and desires of the present. The very fact that Charlie can return to the hub of a life which had cost him his wife and his child does not at all indicate, as the story's most recent commentator has it, that the old way of life "still appeals to him," but rather demonstrates the extent and depth of his self-mastery and the confidence he feels in his belief that his wildly squandered yesterdays are over and done with, that there is no tab left for him to have to pick up.

The opening scene's primary function is to show how divorced Charlie feels from the blurred life of several years ago. His questions to the bartender about cronies from the past are mechanically curious but fundamentally uninterested. The news that "Mr. Campbell [is] a pretty sick man" and that Claude Fessenden cheated the bar of thirty thousand francs and is now "all bloated up" evokes no comment. The pricks to memory of "familiar names from the long list of a year and a half ago" strike no responsive chord. Charlie feels out of place and "polite" in the bar that, in the time of wine and roses, he had felt he had "owned." "It had gone back into France," he thinks. When he goes through the remembered ritual of placing his foot firmly on the bar rail and turning to survey the room, only a single pair of indifferent eyes "fluttered up from a newspaper in the corner." Charlie's dissociation from his past is capped by the brief bit of dialogue with which the scene ends:

> "Here for long, Mr. Wales?"
>
> "I'm here for four or five days to see my little girl."
>
> "Oh-h! You have a little girl?"

In the Babylon who "saith in her heart [I] shall see no sorrow," there can be neither children nor the risk of their loss. The figures there float rootlessly free of human ties and responsibilities, having sprung full-born from their skyrocketing blue chips and capacity for dissipation. The adults are the only children. "We *did* have such good times that crazy spring [Lorraine wistfully recalls in the letter to Charlie], like the night you and I stole the butcher's tricycle, and the time we tried to call on the president and you had the old derby rim and the wire cane." But Charlie Wales's return to Paris is an attempted return to fatherhood, an attempt to lay the ghost of his past childishness through the recovery of his lost child, Honoria. "Oh-h! You have a little girl?" is a bitterly reasonable question for one whose life had been nothing more than a "catering to vice and waste . . . on an utterly childish scale." After all, children have no children.

The tragedy is that Charlie no longer deserves such a question. There is in us a desire to find the present Charlie some-

how deserving of his wretched fate—which is what perhaps accounts for Professor Harrison's reading—for it is easier to live with a belief in reasonable justice. But Fitzgerald does not allow us this luxury. Throughout the story he ironically stresses the splendid achievement of Charlie's reform. His sensitivity, poised intelligence, and quiet power over himself *should* be enough to get his daughter back. That moral renovation may not be enough is the injustice that lies at the center of the story.

Charlie's recovery of "character"—"the eternally valuable element"—which was implied in the opening scene in his being unafraid to confront the old life, is made explicit as he leaves the bar. Walking the street, he feels, all at once, "the sudden provincial quality of the left bank." But Charlie is not a prig: his selfmastery is too final to need the subtly corrupt support of the moral outrage of a libertine turned puritan. He can still be moved by the "pink majesty" of the Place de la Concord and "the blue hour spread over the magnificent façade" of the Avenue de l'Opera; he can even afford to indulge in the fantasy of imagining that "the cab horns, playing endlessly the first few bars of *Le Plus que Lent,* were the trumpets of the Second Empire." Paris is not, after all, Babylon. Only the Left Bank, which in the "crazy years" had seemed the epitome of romantic possibility, strikes him with "its sudden provincialism." Brentano's, cheap restaurants (in which he had never eaten), such as Duval's, with its "trim little bourgeois hedge," had never been "spoiled," because they had never been touched, by the crowd of three years ago who had made "months into days." Babylon, Charlie thinks sadly, had been an American creation.

The following scene with Marion and Lincoln Peters, Charlie's sister-in-law and her husband, who had been given custody of Honoria when Charlie's wife, Helen, was dying and he himself was broke and in a sanitarium for alcoholism, is the symbolic obverse of the opening scene at the Ritz bar, which had depicted the repudiated past. Here the "warm and comfortably American room," the intimate movements of children, "the cheer of six o'clock" as dinner is being prepared, and Honoria (in Charlie's mind) at the center of the bustle, represent the future which Charlie anticipates with excruciating need. The contrasts between the two scenes are extensive. The mechanical exchange in the bar has become the sincerely interested conversation between Charlie and Lincoln Peters; the "single bored voice in the once-clamorous women's room" has changed into "the eager smacks of the fire and sounds of French activity in the kitchen"; the shrill group of homosexuals ("strident queens") has been replaced by a family. Honoria's ecstatic shriek of welcome—"oh, daddy, daddy, daddy, daddy, dads, dads, dads!"—is the answer to the barman's surprised question.

Yet for all the obvious contrasts between the two scenes, there is also present an ominous similarity—a similarity which functions as the first of many symbolic foreshowings of Charlie's failure to redeem his daughter (and thus himself) from the carnival years. In both scenes Charlie is fundamentally isolated from the radical quality of the life going on around him: in the bar because of his maturity, in the home because of his position as a suppliant. Despite Honoria's presence (with its infinite promise), it is Marion Peters' hostility which dominates the scene, making Charlie's heart sit "up rigidly in his body." Although it is not until Part III that we come fully to understand why Marion has set herself against Charlie's future, her animosity, interposing itself as it does between father and daughter, so serves to consign Charlie's presence to the periphery of the room that the final effect of the scene is the disturbing implication that Charlie's proximity to the symbols of the life he hopes for is as deceptive as was his proximity in the opening scene to the symbols of the life he left behind him. It is significant that Honoria never speaks again in the scene after her cry of joy and that the last bit of dialogue is Marion's frigid reply to Charlie's statement that he takes but one drink a day—"I hope you keep to it."

The parallelism between the two scenes is reinforced by the similarity of Charlie's response to both the bar and the Peters' home: relief at being able to get away and a desire to roam the streets alone to see Paris "with clearer and more judicious eyes than those of other days." His second view is more severely contemptuous, the result, no doubt, of his recent contact with Honoria. Montmartre, "where he had parted with so many hours and so much money," stripped of its alcoholic haze, reveals itself as cheap, meretriciously exuberant, and corrupt. As he watches the prowling prostitutes, devouring cafes, and "bleak and sinister cheap hotels," he "suddenly realized the meaning of the word 'dissipate'—to dissipate into thin air; to make nothing out of something." Then follows what is perhaps Fitzgerald's most profound insight into the nature of Babylon, Jazz Age style: "In the little hours of the night every move from place to place was an enormous human jump, an increase of paying for the privilege of slower and slower motion."

On the literal level, the sentence describes early morning bar-hopping: greater and greater expenditures of cash for the "privilege" of more and more uncertain physical movement. But the passage reaches out to larger significances. The impulse towards the enlargement of experience which lies behind the spree manifests itself in the *little* hours of the night (which Fitzgerald elsewhere described as "the dark night of the soul")—"little" not only in the sense of early, but also in the ironic sense of compressed and constricted. The "enormous human jump" required of the drunk in moving from place to place, for whom physical space is constantly hostile, enlarges to an understanding of the expense of spirit which the movement entails. Not only is money being spent ("an increase of paying"), but the human quality is being spent, used up, too. The desire to make the sun run by filling each moment so full of gaiety and abandon that time will seem to stand still succeeds only in so weighting down the figures that they can manage only the contrived movements of an artificially slowed-down motion picture. Life, not time, has stopped.

Part II opens deceptively. The "fine fall day," Charlie's euphoria, and lunch with Honoria at the only restaurant Charlie can think of "not reminiscent of . . . long luncheons that began at two and ended in a blurred and vague twilight," seem to promise, structurally, that the happier of the alternatives symbolically offered in Part I will occur. This scene—the only extended contact between father and daughter—is particularly poignant because in dramatizing a glimpse of the future Charlie yearns for, Fitzgerald make us *feel* (and not merely abstractly acknowledge) the absolute rightness of Charlie's desire to be reunited with his daughter. Though Charlie knows that he needs his daughter back in order to give shape and direction to his renascence, to redeem his lost honor, and, in a sense, to recover something of his wife "escaped to a grave in Vermont," he is aware of the danger in the very intensity of his need. He knows how perilously easy

it would be to make Honoria into a smothered surrogate for all that he has irremediably lost. For example, when Honoria "tranquilly" agrees that she won't always love her daddy best, but will someday "grow up and meet somebody her own age and go marry him and forget [she] ever had a daddy," Charlie is not upset. The conversation between father and daughter is tender and loving and wholly free of sinister psychiatric pressures, dramatic proof of Charlie's ability to act in terms of his understanding as it is articulated in Part IV:

> The present was the thing—work to do and someone to love. But not to love too much, for he knew the injury that a father can do to a daughter . . . by attaching [her] too closely: afterward, out in the world, the child would seek in the marriage partner the same blind tenderness and, failing probably to find it, turn against love and life.

Hawthorne once observed that every crime we commit destroys more Edens than our own. In focusing on Charlie's need it is easy to miss Honoria's. Though Fitzgerald does not cheapen the scene by sentimentalizing the unsatisfactoriness of Honoria's present life, it is clear that Honoria likes neither Marion nor Marion's daughter, though she is too well-bred and sensitive to engage in spiteful recriminations that could only serve to deepen her father's unhappiness. Her sudden "Daddy, I want to come and live with you," though unaccompanied by Dickensian emotional fanfare, is an eloquent plea that broadens the base of the tragedy, much as does the silent presence of the children at the end of the *Oedipus*. This encounter will painfully remind us, when Charlie's undeserved defeat is at the center of our response, of Honoria's loss as well.

The past and future, which were structurally separated in Part I (though the past was made to impinge symbolically upon the future) are narratively intersected in Part II. Duncan Schaeffer and Lorraine Quarles—"Sudden ghosts out of the past"—intrude themselves upon the promise of tomorrow. They are *ghosts* not only because they will eventually haunt Charlie to defeat, but also because they are disembodied, dislocated spirits inhabiting a world which exists only in their self-conscious strivings. Lorraine's "This your little girl?" (which echoes the bartender's question) announces her exclusion from reality; similarly, when Charlie tries to stop the banal bantering about his being sober by indicating Honoria with his head, both Lorraine and Duncan can only laugh. The innocent pleasure of father and daughter attending the vaudeville at the Empire becomes, in Lorraine's "There! That's what I want to do. . . . I want to see some clowns and acrobats and jugglers," an obscene activity, a Babylonian revel of ruinous irresponsibility and desperate hilarity. But they are ghosts in yet another sense, for Lorraine and Duncan are the anonymous figures in slow motion in the passage already quoted. Doomed as they are to being out of time, where gestures pass through all the essential realities, they can only drift, "trite, blurred, worn away," in search of some vampiristic contact with those who inhabit the real world. "They liked him," Charlie thinks, "because he was serious . . . because he was stronger than they were, because they wanted to draw a certain sustenance from his strength." He has located their essential weakness; but he has miscalculated their power to destroy. Human blood cannot make vampires normally human; but vampires destroy what is human in achieving temporary sustenance.

The intrusion of the ghosts from Charlie's past accounts,

symbolically, for the tableau with which Part II ends. Charlie does not accompany his daughter into the Peters's house. He waits, instead, "in the dark street until she appeared all warm and glowing, in the window above, and kissed her fingers out into the night." The distance between the shadowed father and radiant daughter, which the kiss can only symbolically but not actually traverse, is the measure of their inevitable separation. Honoria, framed in the window, has become, the passage seems to imply, a portrait—something that was once livingly available but is now only accessible as a memory in a gallery of remembrances of things past. The tableau, moreover, looks back to the terminal passage of Part I, in which Charlie eludes the "encouraging stare" of a streetwalker, though he buys her supper and gives her a twenty-franc note (as he is later to buy Honoria lunch and give her a doll), and forward to the terminal passage of Part III, when Charlie in a half-dream tries to talk to his dead wife, who "was in a swing in a white dress, and swinging faster and faster all the time, so that at the end he could not hear clearly all that she said." These structural juxtapositions indicate that although Charlie has wilfully removed himself from the sterility of his past, as represented by the prostitute, he is nevertheless actually closer to her than he is to the distanced Honoria or receding Helen. He is offered the physical presence of a non-wife, non-mother, but only the "portrait" of his child and the "ghost" of his wife.

In Part III Marion becomes a significant actor in the drama. Having dressed herself in a black dress "that just faintly suggested mourning," as if already prepared to preside over the death of Charlie's hopes, Marion sets herself squarely against her brother-in-law's dream of the future. Although she has obviously convinced herself that she is motivated solely by a concern for Honoria's welfare and duty to her dead sister, it soon becomes apparent that her hard stance is not morally unequivocal. In Marion we see a subtly corrupt desire for self-justification masking itself in the virtues of duty and responsibility. Marion, because she had never really loved her sister, jealously resented her sister's materially superior marriage. Lincoln, though a wholly decent person, has never been capable of making much money; even in the boom time he "never got ahead enough to carry anything but [his] insurance." Indeed, although Charlie has had recently to start over again from scratch, he is already making twice as much money as Lincoln. Marion's response to this "injustice" has been to take psychological refuge in the cliché that the rich are never happy; she has submerged her envy in "a curious disbelief in her sister's happiness." Marion's hostility did not originate, as Lincoln believes, in the Babylonian days—"Marion felt there was some kind of injustice in . . . you not even working toward the end, and getting richer and richer"—but long before that. The party years merely aggravated—and seemed to give justification for—an already existing mean condition of mind. Marion's vindication came in "the shock of one terrible night" when Helen was locked out in a snowstorm and barely escaped pneumonia. Convinced, because she wanted to be, that this was "one of many scenes from her sister's martyrdom," Marion's repressed envy was able to flower forth as self-righteous "hatred" for Charlie. The death of Helen (which Marion falsely insists on blaming Charlie for) and Charlie's own crack-up affirmed once and for all the superiority of her own married life. Her "investment" has paid off in the legal guardianship of Honoria; and the power to beat Charlie with this moral triumph is what she has instead of a materially lavish life.

Marion, however, is not merely an interesting piece of psychological portraiture, for she complicates what might otherwise have been an unqualified commitment to the life of the "solid citizen." Though **"Babylon Revisited"** is centrally an exploration of the waste inherent in the quest for the gorgeous life, it is not thereby a paean to Main Street. It is clear that Charlie's "plans, vistas, futures for Honoria and himself " are organized around what we have come to call middle-class values and virtues—home, responsible job, hard work, the respect of the community. But it is also clear—as Marion's presence in the story indicates—that the achievement of worth is not to be found in the middle class automatically. Every mode of life is shadowed by its own kind of treachery and means of self-aggrandizement. Marion, no less than Lorraine and Duncan, "needs" Charlie, in her case as a "tangible villain." It is therefore both ironic and apt that although Marion is revolted by people like Lorraine and Duncan—they "make her really physically sick"—she will, in Part IV, unwittingly ally herself with them to destroy Charlie. She too has set herself against Charlie's attempt to extricate himself from his past: "from the night you did that terrible thing [Charlie's accidental locking out of his wife in the snow] you haven't really existed for me." Indeed, without Marion, Lorraine and Duncan are without effect. How fully she has committed herself to keeping Charlie from escaping into the future is revealed when, after being forced to acklnowledge that Charlie "had somehow arrived at control over the situation" and that Lincoln will not help her keep Honoria from her father, she responds with hysterical viciousness, "I think if she were my child I'd rather see her—" and retreats to her bed with a neurasthenic headache.

In Part IV, which ironically opens with Charlie's ecstatic feeling that the "door of the world was open again," Charlie is to feel the full weight of his history. As if duplicating the ultimate movement of the entire section, Charlie's happiness fades suddenly into the sad memory of all the plans he and Helen had made that would never materialize. Though he turns away from the past—"The present was the thing"—the arrival of a letter from Lorraine, nostalgically recalling the "good times that crazy spring," reinforces the mounting sense of an unreasonably vengeful past. It will turn out to be of no avail that Charlie can dismiss the thought of a "trite, blurred, worn away" Lorraine to "think of Sundays spent with [Honoria] . . . and knowing she was there in his house at night, drawing her breath in the darkness."

For at the very threshold of Charlie's new life, the "ghosts from the past" drift up the corridors of time. Fitzgerald's paragraph describing their emergence is appropriately eerie. First, like an annunciation of doom, the long peal of the bell; then the voices in the corridor coming closer, "which developed under the light into Duncan Schaeffer and Lorraine Quarles." Drunk, incoherent, irresponsible, the world of Babylon has shattered the world of "people together by a fire." In a brilliant symbolic gesture, Charlie, horrified, moves closer to them, "as if to force them backward down the corridor." That it is Charlie's own past that he is trying to force backward into time is amply demonstrated by the fact that Lorraine and Duncan are specifically identified with the figures in the "little hours of the night" passage: "Still in slow motion, with blurred, angry faces, with uncertain feet, they retired along the corridor."

But Charlie's power is finally useless: the door of the world opens to both the past and the future. Charlie is now more isolated than he had ever been before. Marion stands rigidly with an arm encircling each of her children and Lincoln is "swinging Honoria back and forth like a pendulum from side to side." The implications of this tableau are totally devastating. The past has set the pendulum of the future in motion; time will serve only to take Honoria further away from him; "the tangible, visible child" will swing away into dimmer and dimmer memory, like Helen in the dream in Part III, who was "swinging faster and faster all the time, so that in the end he could not hear clearly all that she said." All that is left for Charlie to do is to return alone down the corridor, turning to say a final goodbye—"Good night, sweetheart. . . . Good night, dear children."

The story ends in the Ritz bar, where Charlie furiously goes to find Lorraine and Duncan. But he soon realizes that "there was nothing he could do." The return to the bar, as well as the first appearance of Paul, the head barman, "who in the latter days of the bull market had come to work in his custom-built car," symbolizes Charlie's bondage to a world which he mistakenly supposed could be cast off completely. Charlie does not change in the course of **"Babylon Revisited"**; his undeserved defeat does not become an occasion for either self-pity or self-indulgence; in the bar he neither talks of his loss nor takes more than the one drink a day he has allowed himself.

The idea of **"The Ice Palace"** (Saturday Evening Post, May 22d), grew out of a conversation with a girl out in St. Paul, Minnesota, my home. We were riding home from a moving picture show late one November night.

"Here comes winter," she said, as a scattering of confetti-like snow blew along the street.

I thought immediately of the winters I had known there, their bleakness and dreariness and seemingly infinite length, and then we began talking about life in Sweden.

"I wonder," I said casually, "if the Swedes aren't melancholy on account of the cold—if this climate doesn't make people rather hard and chill—" and then I stopped, for I had scented a story.

I played with the idea for two weeks without writing a line. I felt I could work out a tale about some person or group of persons of Anglo-Saxon birth living for generations in a very cold climate. I already had one atmosphere detail—the first wisps of snow weaving like advance-guard ghosts up the street.

At the end of two weeks I was in Montgomery, Alabama, and while out walking with a girl I wandered into a graveyard. She told me I could never understand how she felt about the Confederate graves, and I told her I understood so well that I could put it on paper. Next day on my way back to St. Paul it came to me that it was all one story—the contrast between Alabama and Minnesota.

F. Scott Fitzgerald, in an extract from a letter that was published in the Fitzgerald/Hemingway Annual *in 1972.*

But his substantial endowments have not been enough. Though he thinks that he will "come back someday; they couldn't make him pay forever," the whole movement of the story makes it bitterly clear that they can. When he asks the waiter "What do I owe you?" the answer the story supplies is "your hopes and dreams."

A part of Charlie's life had stopped in the little hours of some night when if you didn't want something to be real, "you just paid some money." Looking back, Charlie now realizes how utterly he "lost everything [he] wanted in the boom"; and Fitzgerald, in the final sentence of the story, crushes any lingering hopes by indicating that there is nothing left for Charlie to do but turn for comfort to the dead, for whom time has also stopped. "He was absolutely sure Helen wouldn't have wanted him to be so alone." (pp. 129-35)

Seymour L. Gross, "Fitzgerald's 'Babylon Revisited'," in *College English, Vol. 25, No. 2, November, 1963, pp. 128-35.*

KENNETH EBLE (essay date 1963)

[*Eble is an American critic, editor, and educator. His many publications include* The Profane Comedy: Higher Education in the Sixties *(1962) and* F. Scott Fitzgerald *(1963; revised edition, 1977). In the following excerpt from the latter work, Eble provides an overview of Fitzgerald's short fiction.*]

The early professional stories of Fitzgerald, those written shortly before and after *This Side of Paradise* was published, are collected in **Flappers and Philosophers** and **Tales of the Jazz Age.** Neither collection is as good as **Taps at Reveille**—Fitzgerald's last collection of short stories—and **Tales of the Jazz Age** suffers badly from the inclusion of some early writing which might better have remained in the *Nassau Lit,* where it first appeared. Together, **Flappers and Philosophers,** published September 10, 1920, five months after *This Side of Paradise,* **Tales of the Jazz Age,** published March 26, 1922, contain all but two of the stories Fitzgerald published in magazines in 1920 and 1921.

These two uncollected stories are **"Myra Meets His Family,"** which appeared in the *Post* (March 20, 1920), and **"The Smilers,"** in the *Smart Set* (June, 1920). **"Myra"** was written and rejected during those first frustrating months in New York. Though accepted after being revised, its omission from **Flappers and Philosophers** is for obvious reasons: **"The Offshore Pirate,"** which was included, uses the same device. The device was to be used a third time and most successfully in **"Rags Martin-Jones and the Pr-nce of W-les"**; varied slightly, it did service in a fourth story, **"Flight and Pursuit"** (1932).

The device obviously appealed to Fitzgerald's theatrical nature: in an otherwise realistic story, the hero stages an elaborate fantasy complete in all its details and convincing to both the reader and the heroine of the story. In **"Myra Meets His Family,"** the Fitzgerald woman, bored with men to the point of seeking a mate, fixes upon a young, wealthy, desirable chap, Knowleton Whiting, who is somewhat suspicious of her motives but blinded by her charms. The fantasy is the "family" Knowleton creates to test Myra's motives. It includes a run-down suburban estate, two hired actors, two dozen dogs, and a portrait of a Chinese ancestor. The trickster tricked, with which the story concludes, is Myra's way of revenge. Having discovered the plot and having secured Knowleton's apologies, she offers to marry him anyway. The marriage she arranges is as phony as Knowleton's "family," and she slips off the honeymoon train leaving him to discover his mistake somewhere past Buffalo. The closing line—"Tell the driver the Biltmore, Walter"—typifies the "flapper" story by which Fitzgerald won his dubious but imperishable reputation as "Chronicler of the Jazz Age."

The second was also a previously rejected story called **"The Smilers"** when it was published in *Smart Set*. The story is what Fitzgerald called a "plant" and is mercifully both short and buried deep in the magazine. The idea, however, relates to the serious concern Fitzgerald felt for truth as against appearances. The narrator begins by declaring himself against the smile which falsifies true feelings, and then the story shows through the main character how the world's sorrows lie in wait for the smilers and the misanthropes alike. In 1922, Fitzgerald expressed somewhat similar distaste for "the smilers" as part of an article "What I Think and Feel at Twenty-Five" in the *American Magazine*. Still later, in 1925, he wrote a popular story about a mild-mannered cashier who tires of affecting politeness in the face of the world's rudeness and becomes momentarily famous as a "pusher-in-the-face," the title of the story. The idea, however, does not save either story from being a mere working out of a contrivance. It should be observed that **"May Day,"** in the very next issue of *Smart Set,* showed Fitzgerald at his best.

Among the stories collected in *Flappers and Philosophers*, **"The Ice Palace"** is clearly the best and, in its way, as good a story as Fitzgerald ever wrote. It was the last to be written in the burst of energy which followed the acceptance of *This Side of Paradise*. Of the nine stories produced during that period, **"Dalyrimple Goes Wrong," "Benediction," "The Cut-Glass Bowl," "Head and Shoulders,"** and **"The Ice Palace"** appeared in *Flappers and Philosophers*. **"The Ice Palace,"** as Fitzgerald observed in "Early Success," was written with the professional's knack of making use of experience almost as it was going on. In an interview during these early years, Fitzgerald said the story grew out of two experiences. The one was a conversation with a St. Paul girl. " 'Here comes winter,' she said, as a scattering of confetti-like snow blew along the street. I thought immediately of the winters I had known there, their bleakness and dreariness and seemingly endless length. . . ." The other was with Zelda Sayre when he went to visit her in Montgomery shortly after his novel had been accepted. "She told me I would never understand how she felt about the Confederate graves, and I told her I understood so well that I could put it on paper. Next day on my way back to St. Paul it came to me that it was all one story. . . ." The success of the story is in those observations: like all the best of Fitzgerald's work, **"The Ice Palace"** is created out of an intensely felt past, not only from recent moments of great emotional impact but from long-held feelings that go back into his youth.

The foremost characteristic of Fitzgerald's developing craft in this story is his use of the two contrasting settings to unify and intensify the story. Scene, milieu, and characters are blended so successfully that the reader finds himself not only engaged in the story but in the larger clash between two cultures, temperaments, and histories. By comparison with the use of setting and its relation to character and action in the Eleanor episode of *This Side of Paradise*, **"The Ice Palace"** is a great advance.

For all the contrast between North and South, Fitzgerald does not lose touch with the reality of the individual cities—

St. Paul and Tarleton, Georgia—he is describing. In Sally Carrol Happer, he creates one of his most convincing young girls, individualizing her through a muted Southern accent which seems always to find the words precisely appropriate to her character. A tightly plotted story, it uses the right incidents to illuminate character and has an inevitability that even a somewhat forced climax does not mar. Finally, the story is a long one that hangs tightly together. The languorous scenes in Georgia make it end where it began: the opening sentence, "The sunlight dripped over the house like golden paint over an art jar," is exactly paralleled by the first sentence of the closing section, "The wealth of golden sunlight poured a quite enervating yet oddly comforting heat over the house. . . ." The story ends with Sally Carrol and the best bit of dialogue in the story:

> "What you doin?"
> "Eatin' green peach. 'Spect to die any minute."

Perhaps the reason **"The Ice Palace"** is so successful is that Fitzgerald not only infused the story with the tensions that separated him from Zelda Sayre yet held him to her but also with the warring strains in his own background: the potato-famine Irish and the Maryland gentleman ancestry; the provincial and the Princetonian; poverty, cold, and control against richness, ripeness, and passion.

Of the other stories in *Flappers and Philosophers,* only **"The Cut-Glass Bowl"** attempts a literary device somewhat similar

Dust jacket to Fitzgerald's first short story collection.

to the large contrasts in cultures in **"The Ice Palace."** Like **"Benediction,"** it is a serious story, but longer and more ambitious. The setting is St. Paul; the principal characters are Evelyn Piper and her husband, Harold. The story takes place over twenty-five years during which time Harold's business declines and the Pipers' marriage degenerates into a "colorless antagonism." Its climactic events are melodramatic, and all are related to the cut-glass bowl. Evelyn was given the bowl as a wedding present from a disappointed suitor because she, too, was "hard, beautiful, empty, and easy to see through." Evelyn's first (and only) affair is discovered when the other man reveals his presence by accidentally bumping into the bowl. Harold's drunkenness is similarly dramatized. The daughter, Julie, cuts her hand on the bowl and has to have it amputated. The letter telling of the son's death in the war gets misplaced in the bowl. Finally, Evelyn carries the bowl from the house, smashes it to earth, and falls upon it. In outline, such a story's faults appear clearly enough, and the Fitzgerald style and perception are not quite able to outweigh these defects. In addition, the story suffers from a habit which Fitzgerald had to discipline himself to overcome: the tendency to put himself into the characters and to urge their feelings rather than to disclose them through carefully chosen and precisely described actions.

"Benediction," as serious in its intent as it is slight in its effect, is a greatly changed version of **"The Ordeal,"** which was published in the *Nassau Lit* (1915). The original story tried hard to dramatize convincingly the spiritual struggles of a boy of twenty about to take religious vows. At the moment of taking his vows, the boy is confronted with an immaterial yet powerful evil that has a way of turning up in other Fitzgerald stories. "Some evil presence," Fitzgerald wrote, "was in the chapel, on the very altar of God. . . . The eternity and infinity of all good seemed crushed, washed away in an eternity and infinity of evil."

Though the supernatural recurs fitfully in Fitzgerald's later work, very few of the stories and none of the novels after *This Side of Paradise* make explicit use of his Catholicism. The debate within him seems to have been written out (if not permanently stilled) in Amory's questionings in the novel. "The gaudy, ritualistic, paradoxical Catholicism whose prophet was Chesterton, whose claquers were such reformed rakes of literature as Huysmans and Bourget, whose American sponsor was Ralph Adams Cram, with his adulation of thirteenth-century cathedrals—a Catholicism which Amory found convenient and ready-made, without priest or sacrament or sacrifice" was unable to arouse even strong denial once this phase was over. Mention of it seldom appears in his notes or in any consequential way in his writings. At his death, his books were proscribed by the Church, and he was not permitted burial in hallowed ground. How little he knew of or felt for the religious life may explain the essential weakness of **"Benediction."** However, the moral concern and the sense of evil to be found in all his serious work my be important consequences of his youthful religious interest.

The other stories in *Flappers and Philosophers* are entertaining ones in which Fitzgerald indulges in his fondness for involved plots and ironic twists and relies upon characters close to himself and his experiences. **"Bernice Bobs Her Hair"** was the first story, he observed in "Early Success," to provoke a large number of letters. "For a shy man," he added, "it was nice to be somebody except oneself again: to be 'the Author' as one had been 'the Lieutenant.' Of course one wasn't really

an author any more than one had been an army officer, but nobody seemed to guess behind the false face." One of Fitzgerald's great strengths in his early work is the projection of this feeling into his fiction: the world in which his characters live is both real and fantastic, a bright, exciting world with no aggrieved past and no wearying future. Such an attitude does not create "serious" fiction, and Fitzgerald's "serious" stories here and to a certain extent later are less successful than his "light" ones. When, as in **"The Ice Palace,"** he could retain the manner of his light stories and still invest the characters and events with seriousness, he was moving in the direction of his best work. As he developed his craft, the abandon with which Fitzgerald created the rich imaginative details of the light story became the detachment which made it possible for him to become serious without becoming either sententious or wooden.

The contrast between **"Bernice Bobs Her Hair,"** and **"The Four Fists"** may add to what has just been said. In 1920, a story could hardly have been better designed to elicit public response than the Bernice story. Its characters are the college set; its setting the comfortable middle class; its plot that of the ugly duckling. The effect of the story depends upon how much the reader is willing to let himself become engaged in the transformation of Beatrice from the unattractive cousin to the girl who bobs her hair. Its success is in the accuracy with which Fitzgerald captured the world of the moment and made it seem not necessarily important but terribly attractive. That attractiveness is only in part traceable to the story; in large part it is in the writing, in the way things are said, the way they are described. The story is not a great one; even by comparison with similar stories, it is rather obviously contrived. But, in not pretending to greatness, it pleases in that we get more than we had a right to expect.

"The Four Fists" is quite the opposite. It, too, is a story created out of a conventional, carefully contrived design, but the over-all intent is serious. It creates a young male protagonist, not unlike Basil in **"The Freshest Boy,"** and shows the effects of four physical blows upon his character. One blow was for snobbishness; the second, for personal unpleasantness; another, for selfishness; and the last, for immorality. Character and situation are about as well created as they are in **"Bernice Bobs Her Hair,"** but the reader, expecting more, gets much less. The story differs from the former one chiefly in that Fitzgerald was caught up in Bernice's world and in her emotions in a way he was not in those of Samuel Meredith in **"The Four Fists."** The reader feels the essential truth of the one—trivial as that truth may be—and the essential falsity of the other—profound as the sought truth may have been. It is testimony to Fitzgerald's awareness as a writer that **"The Four Fists"** irritated him almost as soon as he finished it and even after it had been widely praised. He wrote Maxwell Perkins: "Not that it is any cheaper than **'The Off-Shore Pirate'** because it isn't, simply because it's a plant, a moral tale and utterly lacks vitality." (pp. 54-60)

Tales of the Jazz Age is a more varied collection of short stories than *Flappers and Philosophers*; it is also a more interesting one because of its bearing upon Fitzgerald's development as a writer; but, perhaps because he needed stories to pad out the volume, it is a very uneven collection. **"May Day," "The Diamond as Big as the Ritz,"** and **"The Jelly-Bean"** belong among his best stories. **"Tarquin of Cheapside," "Mr. Icky,"** and **"Jemina"** are undergraduate sketches, and **"The Lees of Happiness"** is weak in its pretensions to seriousness.

In the original edition, the table of contents of *Tales of the Jazz Age* included Fitzgerald's offhand comments about each of the stories. **"The Camel's Back,"** according to his note, was the story he liked least, though it was the easiest to write and gave him the most amusement. **"The Diamond as Big as the Ritz"** was the favorite story of a well-known critic, but Fitzgerald claimed to prefer **"The Off-Shore Pirate."** (In a letter written six months earlier he put this story among his cheap stories.) **"O Russet Witch!"** was written just after completing the first draft of *The Beautiful and Damned* when he was "somewhat carried away by the feeling that there was no ordered scheme to which he must conform." **"The Lees of Happiness,"** he said, "will be accused perhaps of being a mere piece of sentimentality." The three short pieces were dismissed as ephemera. Except for the expressed liking for **"The Off-Shore Pirate,"** his comments seem to be both candid and discerning.

"My Last Flappers" is the title given to the first four stories in the book: **"The Jelly-Bean," "The Camel's Back," "Porcelain and Pink,"** and **"May Day."** **"The Jelly-Bean"** is an excellent story, a kind of Southern version of **"Winter Dreams,"** cut off at the point where the provincial poor boy has met the ineffable rich girl and before he goes on to success. The boy is "the Jelly-Bean," Jim Powell; the girl is Nancy Lamar, who "had a mouth like a remembered kiss." Jim is a precisely sketched member of the lower middle class, an unambitious mechanic living over a garage when the story begins. Characteristically, however, his family was a good Southern one in days past, and at the end, he is planning to buy up a piece of land with the small inheritance he has received. Fitzgerald need not have provided his central character with such an ancestry, for the story concentrates on the feelings of an attractive, intelligent boy, in a tolerant small town, who discovers what being on the wrong side of the tracks means.

The story is in Fitzgerald's best casual manner. By this time, his stories frequently begin with a kind of address to the reader—a display piece whereby the author catches the reader's attention by revealing his personality in relation to some aspect of the story. The device could have been borrowed from a number of contemporary writers: Ring Lardner was using it more deftly than anyone else in the popular magazines of the time. In this story, the display piece is about the term "jelly-bean," "the name throughout the undissolved Confederacy for one who spends his life conjugating the verb *to idle* in the first person singular—I am idling, I have idled, I will idle."

Most of Fitzgerald's stories are oblivious to the world of menial, dull, deadly work which runs beneath the world his golden girls occupy. And yet, like the image of green Princeton set down amidst festering swamps and industrial blight, Fitzgerald's light, gay, middle- and upper-class world is from time to time juxtaposed with the world of vice, poverty, and boredom. **"The Jelly-Bean"** is set against the background of both worlds. Though the dark South does not explicitly appear in the story, it hovers at the edge. . . . (pp. 75-6)

Gordon Sterrett's situation in **"May Day"** is more intense than that of Jim Powell in **"The Jelly-Bean,"** but it is the same kind. Both, having been exposed to a world beyond their own, must try to come to terms with that vision. **"May Day,"** ending as it does in Gordon Sterrett's suicide, is the starkest of Fitzgerald's early stories. In its episodic character and its seriousness it evinces the faults of the two novels, but the skill Fitzgerald displays in marshaling large scenes, in keeping background and continuing action nicely balanced, and in tying the disparate elements of the story closely together is admirable. Though his characters from the lower depths—Carrol Key and Gus Rose—are as much from literature as from life, they are used effectively. For all the contrived relationship between Edith Bradin, the Fitzgerald girl, and her brother Henry, the young idealist who works on a Socialist newspaper, the atmosphere of the May Day riots is powerfully created.

For a writer not used to depicting violence, the mob's attack on the *New York Trumpet,* Key's fall from the window, Gordon's suicide, are all done with restraint without losing impact. In the end, we might quarrel about the character of Gordon Sterrett, the young provincial artist with the vision of debutante beauty clouding his eyes and his mind. Readers of Fitzgerald's earlier fiction are likely to find him fitting a standard pattern, though his appearance in this story arouses more response than one might expect. His suicide comes as a shock; like Judge Brack in *Hedda Gabler,* the reader attuned to Fitzgerald's conventional characters is likely to say, "People don't *do* such things."

What passes muster in **"May Day"** does not get by in **"The Lees of Happiness."** Fitzgerald said the story came to him in an irresistible form, crying to be written. It is a short story, as Fitzgerald's stories go, and yet it covers some dozen years in the lives of four principal characters. As Fitzgerald seemed aware in the introductory note, the story is pure melodrama. A young writer, like Fitzgerald, marries a young girl, like Zelda Sayre. At the peak of his early success, he develops a brain tumor which dooms his wife, Roxanne, to caring for him during his vegetable existence for eleven years. Running parallel to these events is the unsuccessful marriage of a close fiend, Harry, to a girl, Kitty, who, for all her physical charms, turns out to be dirty, lazy, and expensive. Kitty leaves Harry, and they are divorced shortly after the principal character suffers the brain tumor. After the writer's death, Harry and Roxanne both reflect upon the cruelties life has inflicted, but neither is willing to try to find happiness again with the other. Fitzgerald's usual perceptiveness is in this story mere sententiousness, found in passages like, "To these two, life had come quickly and gone, leaving not bitterness but pity, not disillusion, but only passion." Where the story has any strength at all, it is in observations about the young writer's work: "here were passably amusing stories, a bit out of date now, but doubtless the sort that would then have whiled away a dreary half hour in a dental office"; in such incidental details as Kitty's uncleanliness and Roxanne's inept attempts to help her; and in such farcical touches as nailing the bride's biscuits in a frieze around the kitchen. But even these minor amusements do not save the story from being the kind that deserves to remain in *The Chicago Tribune,* where it first appeared.

The fantasies in *Tales of the Jazz Age* are skillfully done, and **"The Diamond as Big as the Ritz"** is likely to remain as an outstanding story among modern stories of its kind. Of **"O Russet Witch!,"** on the other hand, we never know whether it intends to be a fantasy or a realistic story, to be serious or merely diverting. Its theme is the transience of youth and the passing of youthful desires. Its moral fits a collection of stories about the Jazz Age. The central character, now a grandfather, "had angered Providence by resisting too many temptations. There was nothing left but heaven, where he would meet only those who, like him, had wasted earth." **"Benjamin Button"** plays upon the same idea; its plot was created from a remark of Mark Twain that it was a pity that the best part of life came at the beginning and the worst at the end. To accommodate this idea, Fitzgerald has Benjamin Button born to his Baltimore parents at the age (*Benjamin's* age) of seventy. His life marches from there to infancy, and the story is not so remarkable in its telling as in the fact that Fitzgerald stuck to it all the way through. It was the kind of story which provoked a response Fitzgerald printed in the table of contents: "Sir—I have read the story 'Benjamin Button' in *Collier's* and I wish to say that as a short story writer you would make a good lunatic. . . ."

"Tarquin of Cheapside" tells how Shakespeare wrote "The Rape of Lucrece." The setting is sixteenth-century London, and the central character, a friend of Shakespeare, hides him from a brother bent on avenging his sister's defilement. Stated thus bluntly, the story may have justified Maxwell Perkins' wish to keep it out of the collection because he thought the story morally offensive. The handling of the situation, however, makes Perkins seem unduly prissy in that respect and unduly tolerant in respect to its literary offensiveness.

"The Diamond as Big as the Ritz" has become one of Fitzgerald's most celebrated stories, partly because of its merit and partly because it is so useful for discussing Fitzgerald's attitude toward money and American materialism. Putting aside the second point for a moment, let us look at the story. The situation is brilliantly set forth. A sketchy background using a variety of obvious thematic names—the Ungers from Hades, St. Midas' school, Percy Washington—brings the story to the thesis statement, delivered by Percy, "That's nothing at all. My father has a diamond bigger than the Ritz-Carlton Hotel." There is, despite considerable Fitzgerald foolery, more serious satire in the story than in the other fantasies. The forbidding village of Fish with the twelve men who "sucked a lean milk from the almost literally bare rock," is one vision of the barren materialistic world Fitzgerald saw beneath the very surface of the American life that his stories most often described. The kingdom of Braddock Washington, with his rococo motion-picture chateau, his unmatchable wealth, and his slaves is the vision of Heaven that the undernourished American imagination most often envisions. The climax of the story is the attack upon Washington's kingdom and his attempt to bribe God—"God had his price, of course." But God refuses the bribe; the dream ends with the young man, John Unger, escaping from the mountains with Kismine and Jasmine, Braddock Washington's two daughters. The wealth of John Unger's dreams has escaped him, and he ends with second-best—the sentimental romance of the beautiful and empty-headed girl, "with one dress and a penniless fiancé." At the end, we arrive very close to the Fitzgerald of *The Great Gatsby.* Gatsby had to be "about his Father's business, the service of a vast, vulgar, and meretricious beauty." In the course of that novel, Fitzgerald explores thoroughly not only the cheapness and tawdriness of Gatsby's desires, but the essential greatness of Gatsby's vision, of any vision which proves superior to the objects it fastens upon.

In **"The Diamond as Big as the Ritz,"** Fitzgerald's perception is neither so broad nor so unified as it was to become in the novel. What the story does most successfully is to assert some fundamental beliefs that Fitzgerald had already hinted at in other stories: that poverty is dull, degrading, and terrifying, and irremediable by pious homilies about the blessed poor; that money is no more the root of all evil than is the absence of it; that evil has a way of pushing in on everyone, rich or poor; that the rich probably have a better chance of getting something from life before it gets them than the poor; and that youth is the most precious form of wealth and even that is somewhat non-negotiable without the fact of or the illusion of wealth and beauty. There is a good deal of brimstone to be found in **"The Diamond as Big as the Ritz,"** despite the hero's final assertion: "Your father is dead. Why should he go to Hades? You have it confused with another place that was abolished long ago."

The end of **"The Diamond as Big as the Ritz"** may seem to back away from the harsher implications of the story into a conventional boy and girl ending. But such a conclusion tends to gloss over the fact that, throughout the story, the romance and the satire are tightly interwoven, the one providing the surface which teases the imagination, the other suggesting the depths beneath. A recent critic has argued that the sentimentality of the romantic ending is played off against that of the dream images which precede it. The emotional extravagance of the dream is comparable to the emotional cheapness of the romance; "they are both equally the products of the same sensibility." (pp. 77-81)

[Fitzgerald's stories of the years 1926 to 1934] include the two groups of Basil and Josephine stories, a large number of stories contrived from familiar Fitzgerald characters and situations, some drawing on current experiences, a number of retrospective ones, and a few like **"A Short Trip Home"** and **"Family in the Wind"** that are somewhat uncharacteristic of Fitzgerald's magazine fiction. At least two—**"Babylon Revisited"** and **"Crazy Sunday"**—are commonly included among Fitzgerald's best stories. The best of them went into *Taps at Reveille,* making that collection the richest of his short-story collections. A number of others were included in Malcolm Cowley's edition, *The Stories of F. Scott Fitzgerald,* and in Arthur Mizener's edition, *Afternoon of an Author.* (p. 115)

Of the stories in *Taps at Reveille* which drew upon personal experiences, **"Two Wrongs"** is the most revealing. Its central actions relate closely to the drunkenness, belligerence, and subsequent guilt of Fitzgerald's life in 1928 and 1929 and to Zelda Fitzgerald's dancing. The hero, Bill McChesney, is a producer rather than a writer—a kind of grown-up Basil Duke Lee—who is still capable of saving a play when the actors threaten to walk out. Almost everything of Fitzgerald's early success is in this story, as are Fitzgerald's later feelings that the late 1920's marked his decline. McChesney is a markedly dual character: on one hand he is "a fresh-faced Irishman exuding aggressiveness and self-confidence"; on the other, "the quietly superior, sensitive one, the patron of the arts, modeled on the intellectuals of the Theatre Guild." Emmy, McChesney's wife, is a Southern girl who decides to become a ballet dancer at twenty-eight. Three years after their marriage and after the husband's two flops and a period of increased drinking, McChesney becomes somewhat mildly attracted to Lady Sybil Combrinck. In a climax which exposes most of Fitzgerald's feelings of insecurity and guilt, McChesney crashes Lady Sybil's party and is thrown out. While he goes on to get blind drunk, Emmy has had to arrive at the hospital alone, falls in getting out of the taxi, and delivers a stillborn child. It is after she recovers that she begins to dance.

Despite the melodramatic climax, the story exposes many of Fitzgerald's deep feelings: his real and imagined abuse of Zelda and her abuse of him, his feeling of decline both in popularity and personal strength, his attitude toward his excessive drinking, and his still intense feelings for rank and position. The marital relationship, as it is described in the concluding section of the story, anticipates that of the Divers in *Tender Is the Night*. As Emmy increases in vitality, McChesney declines. He comes "to lean, in a way, on her fine health and vitality," the author comments. When she receives an offer to dance at the Metropolitan, McChesney insists that she take the opportunity. He leaves for the West feeling that the trip is, for him, a definite finish. "He realized perfectly that he had brought all this on himself and that there was some law of compensation involved."

There is nothing new here in Fitzgerald's using the events and feelings of his own life soon after they had taken place, nor in his turning to melodrama and contrivance to enhance the story. There is, however, something moving about the preciseness of the description and about the feeling of helplessness which pervades the story—"an almost comfortable sensation of being in the hands of something bigger than himself." The reader with a knowledge of Fitzgerald's life may find the story too uncomfortably close to reality to be enjoyed.

"The Bridal Party," written shortly after **"Two Wrongs,"** also uses a recently experienced event for its plot. Arthur Mizener ascribes its central situation to the wedding of Powell Fowler in Paris in the summer of 1930, but he attributes the feeling to Fitzgerald's deepest reactions to his own marriage. The situation dramatized in the story is very close to the central one to which Fitzgerald returned again and again. The rich young man about to be married learns he has lost every cent; but without a moment's hesitation he goes through with every expensive detail of the elaborate wedding. As it turns out, such bravado so confounds adverse Fortune that, ten minutes before the wedding, he is offered a salary of $50,000 a year. This triumph is set against the failure of the other central character, a man too poor, too afraid, too futile to win the girl in the first place, and now come too late into an inheritance of a quarter of a million dollars. Despite his ineffectual attempts to break into the wedding plans, he is forced to admire the superior brashness of his successful rival. Though many Fitzgerald stories create similar figures involved in similar actions, few disclose these two contrasting images—the failure who hesitates, the successful man who always pushes on—as clearly as they are presented here.

"The Rough Crossing," like **"One Trip Abroad,"** is a story about a couple like the Fitzgeralds in Europe during the late 1920's. The first, written a year and a half before the other, is a less ambitious, less successful story; it is little more than the reflection of the jealousies aroused in both the Fitzgeralds by their being attractive to and attracted by other people. The central character is the playwright, Adrian Smith, who, on a trip abroad, is drawn to a young girl half his age. The jealousy of his wife Eva and her own flirtation motivate the action. The storm, during which Eva gets drunk and mistakenly thinks Adrian is with the young girl, is a way of emphasizing the chaos that seems close to the surface of both the main characters' lives. The boat arrives in Europe, the young girl has forgotten that she ever kissed Adrian, and the Smiths ostensibly pick up life at a less stormy level.

"One Trip Abroad," written in 1930, is a more ambitious story and one directly connected with *Tender Is the Night*. Like *Tender Is the Night*, the story is centrally concerned with the gradual decay in Europe of a handsome American couple of good breeding and sufficient wealth to be idle. The

structure of the story poses the central couple, Nicole and Nelson Kelly, against an older couple, the Mileses, at the beginning, and against another young couple, who appear at both the beginning and the end. In these couples, the Kellys see themselves as they will become and as they actually are.

As in all the successive versions of *Tender Is the Night*, the corruption of innocence is a central theme. Almost all the important parts of the final version of the novel are in **"One Trip Abroad"**: the ease and grace and brilliance of the Kellys; the glittering surface of their lives which conceals the growing emptiness within; the cynicism and waste in Oscar Dane (Abe North in the novel); the steady drinking amidst the international set; the violence into which the Kellys occasionally erupt; the tentative affairs which both have; the repeated unsuccessful attempts to start over; and the Lake Geneva of the ending—"the dreary one of sanatoriums and rest homes."

The unexplainable decline of the Kellys is set forth with just the right air of vague, meaningless terror. In great part, the effect comes from the background scenes: the beginning, in Africa with the air black with locusts; the ending, against the Alps in Switzerland, "a country where very few things begin, but many things end." The reason for the Kellys' decline is made even less explicit than Dick Diver's decline in the novel. Their movement away from "the music and the far away lights," like the Fitzgeralds' loss of youth and joy, ends in a question neither can answer: "Why did we lose peace and love and health, one after the other?" Perhaps at the heart of it is the moral answer Fitzgerald casually introduces into the story: "There is some wise advice in the catechism about avoiding the occasions of sin." With its posing of an essentially moral question, its fine shadings, and its deliberate balancing of characters, the story is strongly reminiscent of Henry James. Among its other virtues, the story serves to remind the reader how much continuity Fitzgerald's writing has with the past.

Though Hollywood furnished all or part of the material for four stories, only two found their way into collections. The first, **"Magnetism,"** derived from Fitzgerald's six weeks' experience in 1927. A carefully plotted story, it makes use of Fitzgerald's general experiences rather than specific personal ones. The hero possesses what Fitzgerald claimed was the "top thing" and what he himself did not have: great animal magnetism. George Hannaford, a highly successful though limited Hollywood star, has gained his eminence by being magnetic to those who attend the movies as well as to the women he actually meets. The running quarrel between him and his wife Kay, provoked by her jealousy and her own flirtations, is much of the story. The events include the attempted suicide of a script girl who has been in love with George. In the final scene, his animality is still drawing women to him, and he, unable to understand or deal with his mysterious power, prepares to go barracuda fishing.

A more celebrated story of Hollywood is **"Crazy Sunday,"** which transcribes an actual experience during Fitzgerald's second stay there in the late months of 1931. The story is a revealing one in its central idea—the man who makes a fool of himself before people who count. Dwight Taylor, in his recent book, *Joy Ride*, tells the story which Fitzgerald turned into fiction. He and Fitzgerald were invited to a party given by Irving Thalberg and Norma Shearer. Thalberg later became the model for Monroe Stahr in *The Last Tycoon*. The only two writers invited, both were determined to keep Fitzgerald sober and not damage his already fragile reputation.

Fitzgerald got drunk, insulted Robert Montgomery, and then insisted on singing a song—"a kind of song," Taylor writes, "which might have seemed amusing if one were very drunk and still in one's freshman year at college." No one laughed; indeed, Jack Gilbert and Lupe Velez, "the most liberal members of the herd," hissed. Later, while Fitzgerald was castigating himself for the fiasco, Norma Shearer sent him a telegram: "Dear Scott: I think you were the nicest person at my party." He was fired, Taylor says, the next Saturday.

The story reproduces these events with great fidelity. The song is changed to a take-off on a Jewish producer, the embarrassed writer sends a note of apology, and he receives a telegram in return like the one cited. This central incident is expanded into a longer story by creating a brief love affair between the writer and the producer's wife which plays itself out after the party. Dwight Taylor was understandably vexed to find that Joel Coles, the drunken writer, bears Taylor's parentage (he was the son of actress Laurette Taylor), and by such a transference, Taylor became the man who made a fool of himself and Fitzgerald the writer who tried to save him. But the fictional background for Joel Coles does not disguise the fact that his emotional reactions are precisely those of Fitzgerald. So is the mixture of opportunism, conscience, guilt, and moralizing which are central to Coles's character. No perceptive reader of Fitzgerald's fiction is likely to mistake him for anyone else. (pp. 122-26)

Two stories that I have called uncharacteristic of Fitzgerald's short fiction are **"Family in the Wind"** and **"A Short Trip Home."** In the first, Fitzgerald uses a series of 1932 tornadoes in Alabama to create background for a story whose value, to quote Arthur Mizener, "is a result of his attempt to adjust to the wreckage of his own career and his present condition." Aside from its bearing upon his personal plight (the central character is a skilled surgeon ruined by drink), the story shows Fitzgerald's ability to use people, settings, and even events somewhat distant from him in a convincing, significant way. The description of the country people, the dialogue between members of the Janney family, and the two tornadoes striking the town and countryside are all done well. The story is surprisingly good in capturing the feeling of the depression of the 1930's—a subject common enough in the writing of the time but not so in Fitzgerald's work.

Unfortunately, the story ends in a wash of sentimentality. A little girl is left an orphan by the storm, and Dr. Janney appears to draw a lesson from her experience. "Daddy stood over me," she tells the doctor, "and I stood over kitty." He starts for Montgomery at the end of the story, intending to resume practice. We cannot be quite sure he will succeed; he is still drawing courage from the bottle on his hip as he starts off, but he vows to put it aside in order to assume responsibility for the little orphan girl.

"A Short Trip Home" is better fiction, if only because it creates such a fine sense of mystery and such a curious aura of evil. Though Fitzgerald was obviously fond of fantasy and though he mixes realism and fantasy in other works, this story is a most perplexing mixture. That same comfortable world of Fitzgerald's earlier fiction is in this story inexplicably charged with evil. The evil is embodied in a creature—an incubus, perhaps—who fixes upon Ellen Baker, the eighteen-year-old Fitzgerald girl full of "that sure, clear confidence that at about eighteen begins to deepen and sing in attractive American girls." The creature's physical form is that of "a hard thin-faced man of about thirty-five." (pp. 127-28)

In the first part of the story, the man is the kind who "hangs around," who hits with brass knuckles, who engages in any shady practice the world offers him. He is, in short, a very real sinister man whom Ellen has met on the train. In the second part, he has become a "thing," a presence lurking outside the door of Ellen's compartment on the train taking them to the East. When he confronts the narrator, he is both human and fantastic—a punk who threatens the narrator with a gun but also a presence who was "getting around my abhorrence." A long struggle ensues between the narrator and "the thing"; the prize is the girl in the compartment. At its conclusion, the narrator wins, for the man is dead. "A small round hole like a larger picture nail leaves when it's pulled from a plaster wall" is in his forehead. In a few seconds, he falls to the floor. "There was something extended on the bench also—something too faint for a man, too heavy for a shadow. Even as I perceived it, it faded off and away." Ellen, inside the compartment, now sleeps peacefully; "what had possessed her had gone out of her."

The third part of the story follows the narrator's attempt to find out something about the man. An informant says his name was Joe Varland; he worked the trains; he lived off girls traveling alone. He was shot, so the man says, in a row in a station in Pittsburgh. Ellen and the narrator meet again before the story closes, but they never mention the incident.

The story is confused, but whether deliberately or carelessly is hard to say. We have to assume that Joe Varland is a corporeal being in the first part of the story; he is given explicit existence in the third part; and he is both that and a projection of the narrator's imagination in the second. But that alone does not answer for the malevolence of the man, for his sinking as the train approaches Pittsburgh, for the bullet hole in his forehead, and for his physical disappearance after he dies. This leaves a rather large burden to be carried by a genuine psychic experience on the part of the narrator which is not only general and pervasive but particular and accurate as to detail. Not much more can be done to explain the central peculiarity, but some conjectures may be made about why the story takes this form.

The story was written during those years of re-exploring the past, of thinking again about both Ginevra King and Zelda Sayre. Thus the pull is strong to explain the duality Fitzgerald saw in both women and which, fairly or not, he saw rather steadily as bountiful innocence joined with almost malignant knowingness. His own duality accented what he saw in them. Beyond that, and in all the girls he portrays, beauty is somehow entwined with evil. For at the center of Ellen's beauty lurks an evil, a corruption which threatens her self as well as those around her. Finally, Zelda's increasing obsessions help to explain the intensity with which Fitzgerald wrote this story of a woman literally possessed.

The narrator's role is one of trying to protect the girl, but of being unable to enlist her feelings or to gain her concurrence in his attempt to save her. He is not really the lover but the almost-lover, a familiar role for a Fitzgerald narrator to play. Above all other fears when in the presence of Joe Varland is the narrator's fear of being an agent, if not an accomplice. "Suddenly I realized that from a while back I had stopped hating him, stopped feeling violently alien to him. . . ." The fear aroused at this point is that of weakening or loss of will—one certainly uppermost of Fitzgerald's anxieties during the period he was writing this story. Beneath the story's climactic struggle is the silent one waged inside both Scott and Zelda when her obsession aroused his "New England conscience raised in Minnesota" to look at his own self in which will had been persistently draining away. Ultimately, the story may rest on Fitzgerald's intensely moral view in which evil is active and dominant over a will which is weak or passive. Whatever the weaknesses in the story because of its uneasy mixture of realism and fantasy, it cuts deep into the inner battle that Fitzgerald was waging then and throughout the rest of his life.

The inner conflicts and the outward circumstances of Fitzgerald's personal decline in the 1920's are matched with the decline of the Jazz Age itself in **"Babylon Revisited"**; in fact, it may become a period piece, so closely is it tied to that time. The story is of Charlie Wales, thirty-three, handsome, Irish, who has lived a Babylonian life during the 1920's, has reformed, and has returned to Paris to visit his daughter Honoria. The conflict is between Wales and his past; specifically it is between Wales and Marion Peters, a tight-lipped, mean-spirited woman, almost the only one of that type in Fitzgerald's fiction. Marion is the sister of Wale's deceased wife Helen, whose death is connected with a boozy quarrel in which Wales locked her out of the house in the snow. Though she recovered from pneumonia at that time and died later of heart trouble, Wales's guilt remains and Marion is unwilling to give him custody of his child.

The story is a celebrated one, with a famous line, "the snow of twenty-nine wasn't real snow. If you didn't want it to be snow, you just paid some money." It creates a nice contrast between Marion and her husband—"they were not dull people, but they were very much in the grip of life and circumstances"—and the freer spirit of Charles Wales. It is notable too for its creation of the great love and longing which exists between Wales and his daughter: "He wanted his child, and nothing was much good now, beside that fact. He wasn't young any more, with a lot of nice thoughts and dreams to have by himself. He was absolutely sure Helen wouldn't have wanted him to be so alone." (pp. 128-30)

> *Kenneth Eble, in his* F. Scott Fitzgerald, *revised edition, Twayne Publishers, 1977, 187 p.*

ROY R. MALE (essay date 1965)

[*Male is an American educator, critic, and editor whose works include* Hawthorne's Tragic Vision *(1957) and* Enter Mysterious Stranger *(1979). In the following excerpt, Male characterizes "Babylon Revisited" as the story of an "exile's return," placing it in the context of other similarly structured stories in American literature.*]

F. Scott Fitzgerald's **"Babylon Revisited,"** although widely reprinted, has not produced many commentaries. . . . [Mainly], I suppose, because its meaning is clear. It has some symbols, but they are not mysterious; some ambiguity, but it is not hidden; considerable irony, but it is readily discernible. It strikes us, in short, as an example of the really excellent story that is widely read and reread, usually with considerable appreciation and understanding. This paper asks, in effect, whether it is possible to write profitably about a story that everybody already understands, or nearly understands.

My basic assumption is not particularly startling, but it does run counter to that of the extreme formalists (now perhaps nearly extinct), who used to maintain that criticism and teaching of a short story should be rigorously limited to an examination of the text. "Stay inside the story," they said, as if one story is of no help in understanding another, as if the time spirit supplies nothing to shape an author's fiction, as if his life tells us nothing about his art. No, I would maintain that we should place a story in as many contexts as possible. I limit myself here to the three just mentioned: generic, historical, and biographical, paying particular attention to the first because it is the least familiar. (p. 270)

Having jettisoned the whole idea of genres somewhere in the nineteenth century, we lack descriptive terms to define fictions in any fundamental and illuminating way. The major exceptions to this generalization are terms like picaresque novel, *Bildungsroman, Künstlerroman,* and Lionel Trilling's description of the story of the Young Man from the Provinces. These terms define stories either according to the situation of the hero or according to the action imitated; they have the great advantage of being easily recognizable; and I think that their defining principle can be extended. It is not that every story can or should be classified in this way; but if we do find a group of stories imitating the same basic action, we are being critically and pedagogically provincial if we ignore their interrelationship.

From this point of view, **"Babylon Revisited"** belongs with a number of stories in which the protagonist returns after a prolonged absence, either to his home or to some substitute for it. This category we may call the story of the Exile's Return, and in American fiction it would include (among others) Washington Irving's "Rip Van Winkle," Nathaniel Hawthorne's "Ethan Brand," Hamlin Garland's "The Return of a Private," Henry James's "The Jolly Corner," Ernest Hemingway's "Soldier's Home," Theodore Dreiser's "The Old Neighborhood," Lionel Trilling's *The Middle of the Journey,* and Frederick Buechner's "The Tiger." Behind these American stories, of course, are such prototypes as Ulysses returning to Penelope, Plato's myth of the cave, the Biblical account of the return of the prodigal son, and Dante's return from his vision of hell, purgatory, and paradise.

The advantages of placing stories together in this way are obvious: first, certain conventions and common themes emerge clearly, aiding explication of each individual story; and second, once the similarities are established, differences in execution or technique are more clearly discernible. As Henry James said, in a somewhat different connection, "our aim is to get the correspondences and equivalents that make differences mean something."

Certain themes are inherent in the basic situation of a man returning after a long absence. In fiction as in life, the most obvious and the most poignant is the mutability theme or, more specifically, the sense of permanence and change. Although some aspects of the setting seem unchanged, their apparent permanence simply emphasizes the fundamental law of life, that all things pass. Thus we have in these stories something like the *ubi sunt* formula in poetry. Rip Van Winkle asks, "Where's Nicholas Vedder? Where's Brom Dutcher? Where's Van Bummel, the schoolmaster?" Gone, all of them gone. Even Vedder's wooden tombstone, Rip learns, is "rotten and gone." This, of course, is where Fitzgerald's story begins. "Where's Mr. Campbell?" "And George Hardt?" "And where is the Snow Bird?" "What's become of Claude Fessenden?" All gone, some of them "rotten and gone." In the Babylonian Ritz Bar only the "strident queens" remain; "they go on forever."

The hero may ask about the men, his former friends, but the essential motivation for his return is always a reunion with some form of the feminine principle. She may be a person: the faithful wife as in "The Return of a Private," the daughter as in "Rip Van Winkle" and **"Babylon Revisited,"** the stable and intimate friend Alice Staverton in "The Jolly Corner." Or it may be more abstract and symbolic: the "mother earth" invoked and then rejected by Ethan Brand, the "girls" that bother Krebs in "Soldier's Home," or the alma mater as in "The Tiger." Thomas Wolfe, whose fiction flowed forth from the archetypal pattern of departure and return, described the impulse this way: "By the 'earth again' I mean simply the everlasting earth, a home, a place for the heart to come to, and earthly mortal love, the love of a woman, who, it seems to me, belongs to the earth and is a force opposed to that other great force that makes men wander, that makes them search, that makes them lonely, and that makes them both hate and love their loneliness."

As anyone who has returned home after a long absence will testify, the experience often has a dreamlike quality, a curious mixture of pain and pleasure as one feels his identity dissolving into two selves, past and present, private and public. (pp. 271-72)

This aspect of the exile's return is central, of course, in "The Jolly Corner," where Spencer Brydon hunts down his alter ego, the self he missed becoming when he left America, " 'the American fate' with which he never has come to terms." And

Fitzgerald's inscription to H.L. Mencken in a copy of Flappers and Philosophers.

this theme of split identity recurs, as we shall see, in **"Babylon Revisited,"** where the basic question about Charlie is whether he is indeed "the old Wales," as his former friends call him, or the new.

A final theme given in the situation of the returning exile is that of freedom and responsibility. The mere fact that he has been gone suggests the possibility of egotism and escapism. Rip, we recall, was dodging not merely his wife "but all the obligations of maturity: occupation, domestic and financial responsibility, a political position, duty to his country in time of war." This is the major issue in Trilling's short novel, *The Middle of the Journey*. The protagonist, John Laskell, has returned midway in the journey of life from an inferno of pain, a nearly fatal illness. His image on the cover of the Anchor paperback might stand for all the modern exiles, returning not "home"—Laskell's hot bachelor apartment in New York—but to friends in the country. He is "the stranger, the outlander, the foreigner from New York," and in his weakened condition he is overwhelmed by irrational terror when no one meets the train. One is reminded of Randall Jarrell's poem "On the Railway Platform" and its lines: "What we leave we leave forever: / Time has no travellers. And journeys end in / No destinations we meant." That no one met the train, it turns out, was the fault of his friends' handy man, Duck Caldwell. Later, while conversing with his friends, Laskell quickly decides to "drop the whole matter of fault and blame," but this, of course, is precisely what Trilling does not do. The book's complex though somewhat abstract plot, culminating in the death of Caldwell's daughter (who has heart trouble), turns on the question of involvement, responsibility, and guilt. So, too, in **"Babylon Revisited,"** we find Charlie Wales maintaining that he is now a responsible person but denying responsibility for his wife's death. " 'Helen died of heart trouble,' " he says. " 'Yes, heart trouble,' " Marion retorts, "as if the phrase had another meaning for her."

So much for the important themes these stories have in common. They are equally notable, of course, for their differences of technique. In a full-length study one might profitably observe in some detail what we will here summarize in a paragraph: the movement toward dramatization, immediacy, and restricted point of view in the modern stories as contrasted with the pictorialism, detachment, and omniscient point of view in "Rip Van Winkle," "Ethan Brand," and "The Return of a Private"; Fitzgerald's skillful transitions in this story, particularly the way he whisks Charlie out of the Ritz Bar in the first scene, as compared with Dreiser's lumbering shifts of scene in "The Old Neighborhood"; and the way in which Fitzgerald's dialogue is both realistic in tone and radiant with meaning, compared with the gritty, often trivial speech of Garland's story or the rather melodramatic rhetoric of "Ethan Brand."

To grasp some of the reasons why Fitzgerald's story came off so well, we need to see it as a product of his life and times. William Rose Benét, reviewing Fitzgerald's best novel in *The Saturday Review of Literature* (May 9, 1925), wrote, "*The Great Gatsby* reveals thoroughly matured craftsmanship. It has high occasions of felicitous, almost magic phrase. And most of all, it is out of the mirage. For the first time Fitzgerald surveys the Babylonian captivity of this era unblinded by the bright lights." In this review, which Fitzgerald quite probably read, we have important clues to the success of **"Babylon Revisited,"** written five years later. It suggests, in the first place, why he gave the story its title, avoiding the more obvious "Paris Revisited," with its narrowing of connotations. Fitzgerald was writing about the end of an era, not just some changes in a corner of tourist France.

We do not need the description of Charlie Wales—"He was good to look at. The Irish mobility of his face was sobered by a deep wrinkle between his eyes"—to know that he is close to Scott Fitzgerald. In 1930 his wife was not in a grave in Vermont, but she was in a sanitarium; his daughter, though not living with his sister-in-law, was attending school in Paris. But even though the story clearly flows from emotional autobiography, it also has the perspective that Malcolm Cowley summed up in his memorable remark about Fitzgerald's work: "It was as if all of his novels described a big dance to which he had taken . . . the prettiest girl . . . and as if at the same time he stood outside the ballroom, a little Midwestern boy with his nose to the glass, wondering how much the tickets cost and who paid for the music." This double vision of actor and spectator, with the mature spectator no longer a gawky outsider but a judge, informs all of Fitzgerald's best work, and in this story it allows him to view Charlie Wales with both sympathy and ironic detachment.

Benét's remark about Fitzgerald's "almost magic" phrasing also provides a clue to the all-important relation between art, spending, and morality in this story. When Charlie says of the old times, "We were a sort of royalty, almost infallible, with a sort of magic around us," we see the precise appeal of the rich, or at least of the spenders, for Fitzgerald. He not only wrote about how he lived; he also saw life in the high style as allied to, though not identical with, writing. It was a spending of one's resources to gain release from the rigid grip of time, space, and circumstance. "The snow of twenty-nine wasn't real snow. If you didn't want it to be snow, you just paid some money." The spenders juggled time and space as the novelist does, making "months into days," shrinking and magnifying dimensions at will. "In the little hours of the night, every move from place to place was an enormous human jump, an increase of paying for the privilege of slower and slower motion." The squandering of unearned money called forth "effort and ingenuity" and imagination; it permitted or demanded the playing of roles, wearing the old derby rim and carrying the wire cane.

The basic conflict of the story, then, is not just between Charlie and Marion; it is between Charlie Wales (who presumably takes his last name from the prince who was the epitome of the goodtime Charlies in the twenties) and "Mr. Charles J. Wales of Prague," sound businessman and moralist, between the regally imaginative but destructive past and the dull, bourgeois but solid present. As Charlie now sees it, the old time spent did bring about transformations, but they were all morally destructive. To "dissipate" was to perform a magic disappearing act, "to make nothing out of something." It was all, he now realizes, on an "utterly childish scale," like the pedalling of Lorraine on a tricycle all over Paris between the small hours and dawn.

With our natural sympathy for the Charlie who at the end sees that he lost everything he wanted in the boom, we are likely to think that he wants only the honorable part of the past, that he would like to disengage himself from the rest of it, that, as he tells Marion, he *has* radically changed. But Fitzgerald is not at all sentimental on this point; he insists upon the reader's seeing more clearly than Charlie does. For the trouble with Charlie is that he *still* wants both worlds. The harsh fact is that if he had not stopped in the Ritz Bar in the

first place, had not tried to get in touch with Duncan Schaefer, he would have won back his daughter. Fitzgerald has him commit this fatal act in the very beginning of the story; it comes back to haunt him inexorably in the "ghosts" of Dunc and Lorraine.

The two sides of Charlie are clearly revealed, of course, in the luncheon scene with Honoria. " 'Now, how about vegetables?' " he asks. " 'Oughtn't you to have some vegetables?' " This is Charlie trying to prove to himself and Honoria that he is the ordinary or garden variety of father. But he gently mocks this role by formally introducing himself as Charles J. Wales of Prague and is delighted when she quickly responds, imaginatively accepting the role of an adult woman. The game is short, however, because it rapidly evokes too many parallels with the destructive aspects of playing at life:

> "Married or single?"
> "No, not married. Single."
> He indicated the doll. "But I see you have a child, madame."
> Unwilling to disinherit it, she took it to her heart and thought quickly.
> "Yes, I've been married, but I'm not married now. My husband is dead."
> He went on quickly, "And the child's name?"
> "Simone. That's after my best friend at school."

It is probably significant that it is Honoria who brings the conversation back to reality with this reference to school, because in this whole scene she is educating her father. She approves his suggestion that they go to the vaudeville but frowns on his approval of unlimited spending at the toy store. She is polite but cool to Lorraine, who makes clear the link between the tarnished magic of the old times and the world of childhood. " 'There,' " she says, " 'That's what I want to do . . . I want to see some clowns and acrobats and jugglers.' "

The acrobats, the imagery of the vaudeville, remind us, finally, that this is a story of suspension between two worlds. Charlie's dream of his wife concludes with this vision: "she was in a swing in a white dress, and swinging faster all the time, so that at the end he could not hear clearly all that she said." Fitzgerald continues this image in the climactic scene when the drunken Lorraine and Dunc invade the Peters' apartment. After they leave, Lincoln is "still swinging Honoria back and forth like a pendulum from side to side." Up to this point Charlie has virtually convinced even Marion that his feet are "planted on the earth now," but actually, as we have seen, he is caught between two worlds. Fitzgerald has arranged their representatives with a symmetry reminiscent of James. On the one hand is the pale blonde, Lorraine, with her escort Duncan Schaeffer; on the other, Marion, clothed in a "black dress that just faintly suggested mourning," with her husband, Lincoln, who appropriately works in a bank. Charlie is indebted to both of the women: to Marion for taking care of Honoria; to Lorraine, as she unpleasantly reminds him, for playing the game. " 'I remember once,' " she says, " 'when you hammered on my door at four A.M. I was enough of a good sport to give you a drink.' " Fitzgerald does not need to force the association, for the reader, along with Marion, silently balances the equation: Lorraine let him in at four A.M.; he locked his wife out in the snowstorm.

And so here is Charlie at the end, back at the Ritz Bar, the place where his old friend Claude Fessenden had run up a bill of thirty thousand francs, until Paul finally told him he "had to pay." Half-heartedly thinking he will send Honoria some things, lots of things, tomorrow, asking the waiter how much he owes him, Charlie is left with his remembrances of time spent and his determination to "come back some day; they couldn't make him pay forever." But he knows and we know that they can and he will. The prodigal has returned, but his effort to "conciliate something," to redress the balance, has failed, and he remains an exile. (pp. 273-77)

Roy R. Male, " 'Babylon Revisited': A Story of the Exile's Return," in Studies in Short Fiction, *Vol. II, No. 3, Spring, 1965, pp. 270-77.*

CLINTON S. BURHANS, JR.   (essay date 1969)

[*In the following excerpt, Burhans explores the value of "Winter Dreams" both in its relationship to* The Great Gatsby *and in its reflection of themes that characterize much of Fitzgerald's most significant writing.*]

Fitzgerald once described **"Winter Dreams"** as "a sort of first draft of the Gatsby idea," and it seems too bad that he did. In discussing the story, writers on Fitzgerald have apparently accepted his comment as a First Principle, with results that often seem unjust appraisals of the story itself as well as inaccurate understandings of its relationship to *The Great Gatsby.* On both counts, therefore, **"Winter Dreams"** is well worth careful study. (p. 401)

Son of a middle-class storekeeper and of a mother with a peasant background, Dexter dreams of better things. He caddies in an upper-class country club, and all summer long his mind fills with images of wealth and position and privilege. These images become the substance of his winter dreams: "October filled him with hope which November raised to a sort of ecstatic triumph, and in this mood the fleeting brilliant impressions of the summer at Sherry Island were ready grist to his mill." Now, there is nothing either Platonic or idealistic about Dexter's dreams. Taken separately or together, they simply add up to a way of life that seems to him obviously richer, both literally and figuratively, than his own; that is to say, Dexter Green has a clear-eyed perception and a hard-headed understanding that, all else being equal, it is better to be wealthy than to be poor, better to have money than not to have it, better to have a great deal of money than only a little.

Consequently, Dexter dreams not of some ineffable gaudiness, some intangible perfection, some eternal beauty, but rather of what in his young experience seems the best this world can offer—wealth and position and privilege and the infinite possibilities they promise. . . . His dreams are no reflections of transcendental urgings, no gleams in the wake of immortal longings. They are highly specific images of personal superiority—of golf championships and fancy driving before admiring crowds, of expensive clothes and luxury cars, of excellence in everything his life may touch. He reaches out for the best simply because it is the best, because the best is clearly more worth having than second or third best. Unlike so many other Fitzgerald heroes, therefore, no tension or conflict exists between Dexter's dreams and either their particular embodiments or the means he employs in pursuing them.

Ambitious, intelligent, hard-headed, pragmatic, and hard-working, Dexter builds his life on the blueprint of his winter dreams. He attends one of the best universities in the East instead of the less expensive state university not from snobbishness but because he is fully aware that the Eastern degree will open doors for him that the state university degree never could and that it will give him a background and manners to help him function more successfully within those doors. And so it proves: with the help of his degree, he borrows enough money to buy into a small laundry that he rapidly expands and then sells, taking his money to New York, where he becomes a successful financier. In the midst of this growing success, however, he becomes entangled with Judy Jones, who turns out to be one of "the mysterious denials and prohibitions in which life indulges."

Dexter first meets Judy when he is fourteen and she is eleven and "beautifully ugly as little girls are apt to be who are destined after a few years to be inexpressibly lovely and bring no end of misery to a great number of men." There is "a general ungodliness" in her smile and "in the almost passionate quality of her eyes." Dexter is "treated to that absurd smile, that preposterous smile—the memory of which at least a dozen men were to carry into middle age"; and suddenly, surprising even himself, he quits his job rather than caddy for her. "As so frequently would be the case in the future, Dexter was unconsciously dictated to by his winter dreams." Intense, full of vitality, beautiful, and imperious, Judy Jones becomes for Dexter without his realizing it one of the "glittering things" that form the stuff of his dreams; and he is therefore unable to accept a relationship in which he is inferior to her.

Nine years later, in the process of achieving his first success, Dexter meets Judy again and falls completely in love with her. Twenty now, she has become "arrestingly beautiful . . . a continual impression of flux, of intense life, of passionate vitality. . . . " She makes "men conscious to the highest degree of her physical loveliness," and her "exquisite excitability" is irresistible. "Her deficiencies were knit up with a passionate energy that transcended and justified them." Kissing her for the first time, Dexter waits "breathless for the experiment, facing the unpredictable compound that would form mysteriously from the elements of their lips. Then he saw— she communicated her excitement to him, lavishly, deeply, with kisses that were not a promise but a fulfillment." Before long, Dexter realizes "that he had wanted Judy Jones ever since he was a proud, desirous little boy," and he surrenders "a part of himself to the most direct and unprincipled personality with which he had ever come in contact."

At first, there are "mornings when she was fresh as a dream," but soon Dexter becomes just another in the long line of those who have loved Judy only to lose her. Men are playthings for Judy, passing tributes to her beauty and desirability, and she wearies of them as soon as they become hers. She brings Dexter "ecstatic happiness and intolerable agony of spirit" until finally "it occurred to him that he could not have Judy Jones." In time, he meets and becomes engaged to Irene Scheerer; but Judy, finding her discarded toy in the hands of someone else, reclaims it, only to throw it away again a month later. Dexter had not hesitated to break his engagement to Irene; he "was at bottom hard-minded. . . . Nor, when he had seen that it was no use, that he did not possess in himself the power to move fundamentally or to hold Judy Jones, did he bear any malice toward her. He loved her, and he would love her until the day he was too old for loving—but he could not have her. So he tasted the deep pain that is reserved only for the strong, just as he had tasted for a little while the deep happiness."

In loving Judy Jones as well as in his responses to losing her, Dexter is once again "unconsciously dictated to by his winter dreams." The most beautiful and desirable girl in his world, she is one of the "glittering things" he has dreamed of having; and when he accepts the fact that she is beyond his grasp, he continues to love her and no one else. In loving her, he had "reached out for the best," and nothing less will do.

The end of the story occurs seven years later. Now a wealthy Wall Street financier, Dexter has realized all his winter dreams except Judy, and he has neither seen her nor heard much about her during those years. A business visitor from Detroit mentions that the wife of his best friend had come from Dexter's home town, and Dexter learns what has become of Judy Jones. When she had first come to Detroit, Devlin remarks, she had been " 'pretty' "; now she is " 'fading' " but " 'all right.' " She is " 'awfully nice,' " and people are " 'sorry for her' "; she is " 'a little too old' " for her husband, who drinks and is unfaithful to her. She loves him nevertheless and " 'stays at home with her kids' "; and " 'when he's particularly outrageous she forgives him.' " Dexter's visitor " 'likes' " her but can't understand how his friend " 'could fall madly in love with her.' " Most damning of all, even " 'the women like her.' " Dexter is stricken by this new incomprehensible image of Judy; and after Devlin leaves, he lies on his office lounge and cries. . . . (pp. 401-04)

Men like Dexter Green do not cry easily; his tears and the language explaining them therefore point either to melodrama or to a complex significance. The difficulty lies in understanding precisely what Dexter has lost and whether its loss justifies the prostration of so strong and hard-minded a man. It seems clear that he is not mourning a new loss of Judy herself, the final extinction of lingering hopes; he had long ago accepted as irrevocable the fact that he could never have her. Nor has he lost the ability to feel deeply, at least not in any general sense: Fitzgerald makes it clear that Dexter has lost only the single and specific ability to respond deeply to images of Judy and of their moments together; and he is certainly able to feel deeply the loss of this response. Similarly, he is not crying over the loss of any illusions of eternal youth or beauty. Given his character, the nature of his dreams, and the history of his striving to achieve them, Dexter is simply not the kind of man to have such illusions. And in the unlikely event that he could somehow entertain them, he is even less the kind of man to weep over the loss of abstractions. Hardly more plausible are the views that he is shocked by a sudden awareness of the destructiveness of time or of the impossibility of repeating the past. Again, it seems unlikely that this man, especially at thirty-two, could have missed the reality of time and the finality of the past.

What is it, then, that Devlin's description of Mrs. Lud Simms has destroyed in Dexter Green? To begin with, Devlin has taken from Dexter's image of Judy the same things he would have lost if he had married her and seen her suddenly "fade away before his eyes": the specific features and qualities that comprised her unparalleled beauty and desirability, her appeal to him as one of the "glittering things," one of the "best." These had been the basis of his love for her—not her reflection of eternal youth or beauty but their physical and perishable realities. Once before, in turning from Judy to Irene Scheerer, he had found almost unendurable the loss of these tangible and emotional qualities: "fire and loveliness

were gone, the magic of nights and the wonder of the varying hours and seasons . . . slender lips, down-turning, dropping to his lips and bearing him up into a heaven of eyes. . . . The thing was deep in him. He was too strong and alive for it to die lightly." At first glance, *thing* may seem a strange and imprecise word for Dexter's profound and encompassing love, but it is more consistent and apt than it might appear. His love for Judy is no more Platonic than his other winter dreams; it is sensuous and emotional, and "thing" suggests this tangible reality as well as the nature of what he has lost. Moreover, Fitzgerald's conscious use of the term for these purposes is reflected in his repetition of it nine times in the final passage of the story.

Paradoxically, in finally giving up all hope of Judy and in going to New York, Dexter is able to have her in a way he never could had they married. With the real Judy out of his life, the girl he had dreamed of having can remain alive in his imagination, unchanging in the images of her youthful beauty and desirability. More importantly, these images keep alive in Dexter the "thing" they had originally so deeply stirred in him—his love for Judy and his dream of having her. It is all this that Devlin kills in Dexter by forcing on him a new and intolerable image of Judy.

In Devlin's description of her as Mrs. Lud Simms, Fitzgerald carefully strips away every feature and every quality of the Judy Jones Dexter had known and still loves in his images of her. His " 'great beauty' " becomes an ordinarily pretty woman; the unique and imperious paragon courted by worshippers becomes a conventional and submissively put-upon housewife; the queen of his love and dreams becomes a rather mousy commoner he could not conceivably love. No wonder Dexter is devastated. Having accepted the loss of the real Judy Jones, he had thought himself safe from further hurt; now, with every word of Devlin's, he finds himself not only losing her again but what is worse losing the ability to go on loving her.

As long as Dexter knows little or nothing new about Judy, she can stay alive and immediate in his imagination; thus, the real past continues unchanged as the imaginative present. Responding to these images of Judy Jones, Dexter can continue to love her as he had in the beginning, when the dream of having this "glittering thing" and the striving for her could still be part of that love. But Devlin destroys the time-suspending equation. When he tells Dexter what has happened to Judy, when he forces him to imagine her as the older and fading Mrs. Lud Simms, then the young and vibrant girl Dexter had loved disappears into the wax museum of the irredeemable past. The real present supplants the imaginative present and forces the past to become only the past.

For Dexter, "the dream was gone"; when he tries to recall his images of the earlier Judy, they come to him not as a continuing present but as a completed past, as "things . . . no longer in the world," things that "had existed and . . . existed no longer." Now they are only memories of a girl he had known and loved who has unaccountably become Mrs. Lud Simms, and they no longer have the power to stir his love or his dreams. "He did not care about mouth and eyes and moving hands. He wanted to care, and he could not care." Dexter wants desperately to care because these images have been the source of his love for Judy Jones and the means of keeping it alive. The end of their power to stir him is therefore the end of that love, and his tears are a bitter mourning for a second and this time total loss of Judy Jones. " 'Long ago,' he said, 'long ago, there was something in me, but now that thing is gone. . . . That thing will come back no more.' "

Dexter cries with good reason, then, but he has even more reason to cry. When his images of Judy Jones no longer create an imaginative present, he loses not only his ability to go on loving her but also something else equally and perhaps even more shattering. Gone, too, is a part of himself also deeply associated with and still alive in these images: the fragile moment in time when youth and his winter dreams were making his life richer and sweeter than it would ever be again.

Fitzgerald makes it clear that the story centers on this moment in time and its significance. The story is not Dexter's "biography . . . although things creep into it which have nothing to do with those dreams he had when he was young." Specifically, Fitzgerald writes, "the part of his story that concerns us goes back to the days when he was making his first big success." These are the years between twenty-three and twenty-five, the years just after college and just before New York. "When he was only twenty-three . . . there were already people who liked to say: 'Now *there's* a boy—'." Already Dexter is making a large amount of money and receiving guest cards to the Sherry Island Golf Club, where he had been a caddy and had indulged his winter dreams. At twenty-four he finds "himself increasingly in a position to do as he wished," and at twenty-five he is "beginning to be master of his own time" as "the young and already fabulously successful Dexter Green. . . . "

This progress towards making his winter dreams come true is not, however, unqualified. Almost from the beginning, disillusion casts strange shadows on Dexter's bright successes. He had dreamed of being a golf champion and defeating Mr. T. A. Hedrick "in a marvellous match played a hundred times over the fairways of his imagination"; now, as a guest playing in a foursome on the real fairways of the Sherry Island Golf Club, Dexter is "impressed by the tremendous superiority he felt toward Mr. T. A. Hedrick, who was a bore and not even a good golfer any more." A year later, "he joined two clubs in the city and lived at one of them. . . . He could have gone out socially as much as he liked—he was an eligible young man, now, and popular with the down-town fathers . . . But he had no social aspirations and rather despised the dancing men who were always on tap for Thursday or Saturday parties and who filled in at dinners with the younger married set." The farther he moves into the world of his winter dreams, the more he is disillusioned with it.

Significantly, and again reflecting Fitzgerald's central concern with the relationship between reality and the imagination, the only one of Dexter's winter dreams with which he is not ultimately disillusioned is the only one he cannot have in the real world and time—Judy Jones. After quitting his job rather than caddy for her, he doesn't see her again until she plays through his foursome on the afternoon when he is a guest at the Sherry Island Golf Club. That evening they meet again and Fitzgerald carefully creates a scene in which Judy becomes identified with this particular moment in Dexter's life. "There was a fish jumping and a star shining and the lights around the lake were gleaming." Lying on a raft, Dexter is listening to a piano across the lake playing a popular song, a song he had heard "at a prom once when he could not afford the luxury of proms, and he had stood outside the gymnasium and listened. The sound of the tune precipitated in him a sort of ecstasy and it was with that ecstasy he viewed what happened to him now. It was a mood of intense appreci-

ation, a sense that, for once, he was magnificently attune to life and that everything about him was radiating a brightness and a glamour he might never know again."

For Dexter, the melody drifting over the water fuses the past and the present, the years of struggle just behind and the fulfillment just beginning. This is the magic moment when dreaming and striving reach out to grasp realization, the time of rapture before the fullness of achievement brings its seemingly inevitable disillusion. Suddenly, a motor-boat appears beside the raft, "drowning out the hot tinkle of the piano in the drone of its spray," and Judy Jones becomes part of this moment in which Dexter is "magnificently attune to life" as he will never be again. She asks him to take her surf-boarding; and highlighting her association with Dexter's "mood of intense appreciation," Fitzgerald repeats the line with which he had begun the scene. As Dexter joins Judy in the boat, "there was a fish jumping and a star shining and the lights around the lake were gleaming." When she invites him to dinner on the following night, "his heart turned over like the fly-wheel of the boat, and, for the second time, her casual whim gave a new direction to his life."

This is the night Dexter realizes he is in love with Judy, and her identification with his sense of being "magnificently attune to life" deepens. " 'Who are you, anyhow?' " she asks him. " 'I'm nobody,' he announced. 'My career is largely a matter of futures.' " He is " 'probably making more money than any man of my age in the Northwest' "; and with all the "glittering things" shining just ahead of him, Dexter realizes that he has wanted Judy since boyhood. She "communicated her excitement to him," and her youthful beauty thus becomes both a part of his dreams as well as the embodiment of his "intense appreciation" of life at the beginning of their fulfillment.

As the next two years bring him increasing success and his first disillusion with its products, Dexter's love for Judy remains constant. "No disillusion as to the world in which she had grown up could cure his illusion as to her desirability." Not even her roller-coaster inconstancy can diminish his love for her or disillusion him with her. In Judy, he continues to find the excitement and anticipation that had made the striving for his winter dreams and the threshold of their fulfillment somehow better than their realization was proving to be. When he first loses her and becomes engaged to Irene, he wonders "that so soon, with so little done, so much of ecstasy had gone from him." And when Judy returns to him, "all mysterious happenings, all fresh and quickening hopes, had gone away with her, come back with her now." In finally giving up all hope of having her, Dexter is thereafter safe from being disillusioned with Judy and thus can keep imaginatively alive the excitement and anticipation she represents for him not only in herself but also in her identification with his youthful winter dreams.

Against this background, Dexter's tears are even more comprehensible. At thirty-two, he finds that all his winter dreams, except for Judy Jones, have come true, and there are "no barriers too high for him." But the world he has won has lost the brightness it had had in his dreams; realizing them has cost him the illusions that were their most precious dimension. Now, having long ago accepted the loss of Judy and with his illusions gone, he thinks he has "nothing else to lose" and is therefore "invulnerable at last." Devlin's detailed picture of Judy as Mrs. Simms strips away this last illusion.

Because Judy Jones and his love for her had become so close-ly associated with the untarnished richness of his youthful winter dreams, the imaginative present in which she remains alive for Dexter also preserves that youthful richness. When Devlin destroys this imaginative present, Dexter finally and forever loses not only Judy and his love for her but also his ability to keep alive in his imagination the best part of his youth and its winter dreams. He has "gone away and he could never go back any more." Devlin has wrought a kind of death in Dexter's imagination, and "even the grief he could have borne was left behind in the country of illusion, of youth, of the richness of life, where his winter dreams had flourished." Dexter's tears are justifiably for himself, then: he has lost even more than his love for Judy Jones. In realizing his winter dreams, he has discovered that their greatest value was in the dreaming; and now he has lost the only way left to preserve that priceless capacity.

In this complex and moving conclusion, **"Winter Dreams"** becomes a story with many values. In itself, it is an interesting and often profound treatment of the ironic winner-take-nothing theme, the story of a man who gets nearly everything he wants at the cost of nearly everything that made it worth wanting. In its relationship to Fitzgerald's other writing, **"Winter Dreams"** makes a valuable prologue to *The Great Gatsby* and reflects several of the themes that characterize Fitzgerald's view of the human condition. (pp. 405-11)

Beyond its useful relationship to Fitzgerald's masterpiece, **"Winter Dreams"** is also valuable in its early reflection of the themes that characterize most of his significant writing. The dream-and-disillusion motif in the story appears in varying forms and degrees from its intermittent emergence in *This Side of Paradise* to its central exploration in *The Last Tycoon*; it is Fitzgerald's major theme. Dexter Green's painful recog-nition that the richest part of dreams is not their fulfillment but the dreaming of and striving for them appears implicitly or explicitly in many other works; related to this theme and even more important in Fitzgerald's thought and art is the central stress of the story on the power and value of imagina-tive life and time. Taken together, these themes reflect the es-sentially tragic vision of the human condition working at the core of Fitzgerald's serious writing: his increasing concern with man as a creature whose imagination creates dreams and goals his nature and circumstances combine to doom. For any reader, then, **"Winter Dreams"** can be a fertile and challenging story; for a student of Fitzgerald, its careful anal-ysis is a rewarding necessity. (p. 412)

Clinton S. Burhans, Jr., " 'Magnificently Attune to Life': The Value of 'Winter Dreams',' " in Studies in Short Fiction, *Vol. VI, No. 4, Summer, 1969, pp. 401-12.*

THOMAS E. DANIELS (essay date 1973)

[*In the following excerpt, Daniels views the series of Pat Hobby stories as a significant indicator of Fitzgerald's evolving literary concerns.*]

Fitzgerald's Pat Hobby Stories represent a collection of his writing and thought during the last couple of years of his life which probably have not received the attention due them. They well indicate the direction his fiction was to take during the last phase of his career and interestingly they forecast that which a good deal of modern American literature would fol-low in the next two decades. There are definitely in Pat

Hobby character traits which would appear in *The Last Ty-coon*. Particularly noticeable is the similarity between Pat Hobby and Wylie White, the writer·in *The Last Tycoon*. In fact, most of Fitzgerald's characterizations of writers in his later life are rather bitter portraits of men who though ex-tremely sensitive and extremely articulate cannot "cope" with the system simply because they are better than most men who surround them. Pat Hobby is not the sensitive, articulate failure that many of the other writers are but he is similar in other respects, and the writers in the Hobby series who are enjoying varying degrees of success are never successful in ul-timate terms (which to Fitzgerald's mind at this point in his career would certainly include economic success) and are often similar to Pat in their degree of alcoholic dissipation, if not in his economic straits.

The Hobby series was written during 1939 and 1940. All the stories were submitted to Arnold Gingrich of *Esquire*. There is no doubt but that their specific purpose was to make money to help pay the bills, but, as Gingrich argues, certainly all of Fitzgerald's work was written for the same purpose. Though he attempted to distinguish between his good work and his "hack" material, I feel that he had a difficult time doing so, and indeed some of the so-called "hack work" is superior in quality to the novels, which were supposedly the "serious" material.

There is in the Hobby stories good evidence of the evolution of Fitzgerald's thought from the stance of the young man to the middle-aged man. In fact, I think we see a significant shift from his authorial stance in *This Side of Paradise*, or perhaps better in *The Great Gatsby*, to Pat Hobby or Monroe Stahr. Nick Carraway is not portrayed as the "new rich" or the "old rich," more as the representative of certain values which emerged from his particular type of background, perhaps the old lower upper-class. We see in Nick the positive values, as opposed to the negative and destructive values held by the characters with money.

Between the writing of *The Great Gatsby* and *The Last Ty-coon*, then, we see a definite shift on Fitzgerald's part. Mon-roe Stahr, the man who went from "rags to riches" is the hero of the work, from the beginning through Fitzgerald's notes for the completion of the book. He was to have been finally corrupted by the Brady world with which he had to deal, but it was to have been an "aware" destruction unlike the totally naive and ignorant demise of Jay Gatsby.

Similarly, the entire series of the Pat Hobby stories exhalt the "Tycoons" in the industry, who generally are the men who "know," even opposed to Pat Hobby who like many other writers is sympathetically portrayed but is generally the in-competent fool who lives for alcohol, dreams of his past in silent pictures when he "almost" made it, and an eternal "gate pass" which will bring him into contact with the men in command who dole out the weeks at $250 on which he sur-vives. All of the "Tycoons" of the industry are intelligent, perceptive men who though they are fully aware of Pat's in-competence and complete degeneracy nevertheless keep him around and even pay him. All of the stories indicate Fitzger-ald's shift in attitude in this regard, but perhaps two, **"No Harm Trying"** and **"Pat Hobby's Christmas Wish"** best ex-emplify it.

"No Harm Trying" begins with the usual portrait of Pat doing nothing though—"If I could get out of Santa Anita, . . . I could maybe get an idea about nags." Mr.

LeVigne, who is one of the moguls at the studio, calls him. The "job" LeVigne offers him is no job at all. The purpose of the paycheck of $250 a week is to provide one of Pat's ex-wives with hospital care—she attempted suicide, but failed. She was at one time a script girl for the studio. LeVigne is then portrayed as a very humane and generous person while Pat grumbles because he has to give up $150 a week for the care of his ex-wife, though he is not required to do anything for the money. In the best tradition of the anti-hero, he was upset by the arrangement: "He did not mind not *earning* his salary, but not getting it was another matter."

With his righteous indignation providing the spur, Pat decides to collect all the people he knows who are on the lot and who are on salary but not working and put together a film. He discovers a call boy, Eric, who wants to be a writer, and who is quite good with ideas; he cons his ex-wife, Estelle, into helping Eric with the script; he convinces Harmon Shaver, an eastern representative for money interests in the studio to back the project; he finds Lizzette Starheim to star in it, Dutch Waggoner will direct it, and Jeff Manfred will supervise it.

When the project is defiantly presented to LeVigne he informs the company gathered that Miss Starheim has not been able to learn enough English to even be considered for a role in a picture; Dutch Waggoner is on drugs; Jeff Manfred is absolutely talentless and is only on the payroll because his wife's cousin had enough influence to place him there; and Pat Hobby is a drunk and a liar. LeVigne, by visiting Estelle, discovered the script was written by Estelle and Eric and not by Pat, and he finally convinces Pat that the studio is right and Pat's plan for the movie is foolish. LeVigne also gives Pat another month at two-fifty, simply because he likes to have him around.

The important element here is that LeVigne comes through as the intelligent, perceptive, humane person. It's Pat and his cronies who are the fools, both to themselves and to the world. They are all cripples in one way or another, and are masquerading as competent people. The studio, represented by LeVigne, is willing to put up with them, even pay them, primarily because of humanitarian inclinations on the part of its executives—certainly a shift from the Warrens or the Buchanans of Fitzgerald's earlier work.

In **"Pat Hobby's Christmas Wish"** similar character traits emerge, though Pat is the only character who is the same. The story is very simply a blackmail attempt on the part of Pat and Helen Kagle. He has been doing his usual hack script work, and rather than giving his secretary a present he fires her the day before Christmas. She is replaced by Helen Kagle who was the former secretary, and girlfriend, of Mr. Harry Gooddorf, one of the studio executives. Miss Kagle has just been sent "back to the department" because she reminds Harry that "he was getting on." She indicates to Pat that she, though still in love with Gooddorf, has some "information" that could ruin him. Given Pat's predatory nature, and his belief that "deals" always make the man, Pat decides to find out the information and use it for his and Helen's benefit—he even suggests the possibility of their marriage.

The point at which Pat decides to confront Gooddorf is one of the most effective ironies of the series. On his way to the executive's office he remembers that "back in the brief period when he had headed a scenario department Pat had conceived a plan to put a dictaphone in every writer's office. Thus

their loyalty to the studio executives could be checked several times a day.

"The idea had been laughed at. But later, when he had been 'reduced back to a writer,' he often wondered if his plan was secretly followed." With this fear in mind, then, he decides not to mention any details while in Harry's office, but in a bar in which Helen is waiting.

The "information" which Helen had was a note that Harry Gooddorf had written years before when she was his secretary. . . . The note indicates that Gooddorf had murdered William Desmond Taylor, and indeed Taylor had been murdered and no one had been convicted of the crime; since Gooddorf had thrown Helen over she decides to get even.

Harry plays the game with them for awhile thinking that perhaps the 1 February 1921 date that Pat mentioned while in Harry's office was a reference to the night Harry and Helen first fell in love—and waits while Pat demands to be made a producer, and other things while drinking "three large whiskeys." Then Harry informs the group that he and his friends in the industry had decided to quiet things down a bit and Taylor wouldn't so they let him "hang" himself. The note is an admission on Gooddorf's part that "they"—the other tycoons of the industry and himself—were guilty of Taylor's financial demise by "giving him 'too much rope;' " however, they had nothing to do with his physical murder. "Some rat shot him" is the only explanation Fitzgerald gives for the real murder. The money group in 1921 again is portrayed as a collection of perceptive men who tried to keep Taylor from self-destruction, and Pat and Helen had completely misconstrued the letter. Gooddorf gives Pat a Christmas wish, however, that he will say nothing and forget the incident.

As in **"No Harm Trying"** Fitzgerald again characterizes the tycoon as the good guy while Hobby and his friends, though likeable as blundering rogues, are not to be taken seriously. They are ill-informed misfits who try every scheme possible to make the big time, but they are generally talentless and ambitionless and therefore fail—though they are always saved from total self-destruction by the "big" men in the industry.

Not only is there the interesting shift in Fitzgerald's thought related to the Tycoon of Hollywood as opposed to his earlier more hyper-critical stand towards such people, but we also see Fitzgerald moving in the direction of the so-called anti-hero. Pat Hobby is the sort of "likeable rogue" that has been in literature for a long time, and who has become quite prevalent in modern fiction—especially the rogue with the generally ironic stance towards himself and society. Fitzgerald's portrait of Pat Hobby is strikingly objective compared to many of his earlier characters, and a good deal of his success in the portrayal is his ability to present Hobby in such a way that he is neither authorially condemned nor approved.

In one of the most effective stories in the group, **"A Patriotic Short,"** Fitzgerald weaves together all the major characteristics of Hobby which are developed throughout the series. Pat is again employed by the studio for "—one week at two-fifty—" to do a touch-up job on a script. The script has to do with a post-civil war scene in which President McKinley is awarding a commission to Fitzhugh Lee, a nephew of Robert E. Lee, and Pat is constantly reminded of the days a decade earlier when he was invited to lunch at the studio with a party of executives and the President of the United States, who was visiting Hollywood at the time. He dredges up memories of his swimming pool and his past successes, which Fitzgerald very effectively contrasts with Pat's present plight. In fact, this story is one of the most effective in the entire series for a number of reasons. The weaving of Hobby's past with his present situation is better done here than in any of the other stories, though the contrast is through them all, and there is perhaps a significant bit of perception on Pat's part when he changes the script right at the point when McKinley is giving the commission to Lee, and Pat has Lee tell him, *"Mr. President, you can take your commission and go straight to hell."*

Pat's realization that the "promise" of America has not been fulfilled for him, and perhaps even his realization that the promise the United States made to the South was not fulfilled is stated quite effectively here. The ending of the story also helps a great deal in eliciting the sympathy necessary for an anti-hero. The symbols in the story, the swimming pool he once had (though it leaked a bit, it was nevertheless a swimming pool), the luncheon with the President back when, and the contrasting symbol of his being generally ignored by a group of important personages who are escorting a new female star down the hallway, are all very nicely woven into the general fabric of the story in much the same way Fitzgerald was capable of injecting symbolic import into prosaic action in his better-known material.

"A Patriotic Short" is one of the few stories of this particular series in which Fitzgerald allows Hobby any self-perception, or gives him any action which indicates Hobby realizes his plight. It is, therefore, quite important to the series since we see for once a Pat Hobby who, though worthless and degenerate in all ways, perhaps begins to understand that so also is the organization and the civilization which has victimized him. There is a very similar construction that Fitzgerald worked on in *The Last Tycoon* when Monroe Stahr is also to conclude that his fall was not due to the plotting of Brady, but to the entire fragmentation of the American Corporation, and therefore the sort of individual which he himself was has no place left in the system. Pat, though a much different type of character in many ways, comes to a similar realization in this particular story, which enhances the story and the entire series.

One of the tightest and most effective stories of the group is **"Two Old-Timers."** Pat is portrayed very sympathetically in this story. He and another "has-been" of Hollywood, Phil Macedon, "collided" in their automobiles early one morning. Macedon, a former star, had saved enough money to retire on his "hacienda" in the San Fernando Valley, "with the same purposes in life as Man o' War"; Pat had not been as fortunate, or provident, and Fitzgerald very effectively and concisely sets Pat's economic plight by stating simply that "the accident found him driving a 1933 car which had lately become the property of the North Hollywood Finance and Loan Co." Sergeant Gaspar, of the local police department, finds both "drunks" in a belligerent frame of mind primarily because Macedon refuses to acknowledge that he and Pat are old acquaintances.

Pat, as expected, is the more truculent of the two and is put in a cell to wait for the Captain's return. Most of the story takes place with Pat in the cell while Sergeant Gaspar tells Macedon what an excellent actor he was and how well Macedon had "explained" World War I to the people who had not been through it by his role in a picture titled *The Final Push.* Pat, who is within hearing distance of this conversation, tries to jolt Macedon's memory concerning their former relation-

ship by interjecting into this discussion the details of what had really happened when the great "shell hole" scene of the movie was shot. Pat explains that the director, Bill Corker, knew that Macedon was "the toughest ham in Hollywood to get anything natural out of"—so he devised a scheme to do so. Macedon, primarily concerned about the fit of his uniform, was unexpectedly pushed into a hole, then while he tried to claw his way out Corker had cameras on him. Finally, Macedon gave up and cried. Of course Macedon is not happy about Pat's revealing to the Sergeant the reality of the making of the movie and refuses still to acknowledge he knew Pat. When the Captain arrives at the police station both Pat and Macedon are taken to the hospital for the drunk test. Macedon is held for bail while Pat is let go—though he has no place to go since he has been evicted from his room.

Sympathy is elicited for Pat when Sergeant Gaspar offers to lend him a couple of bucks for a room, and then finally believes Pat's story about his earlier relationship with Macedon. All the feeling built for Pat is built by the action of the story; none is attempted through authorial intervention. Sergeant Gaspar's final realization that Pat is telling the truth is most significant in that the reader is given to understand that, though Pat is a "has-been," at least he is honest about the past. He does not, like Macedon, attempt to live a past that never existed, and at least in this story he is perfectly candid about his current situation—which is something less than admirable. He also understands that movies are movies and that Macedon's acting is only Hollywood type of acting. Pat is aware of, and more importantly admits to, the phoniness of making movies, which makes him more admirable than Macedon. He is also far more sympathetic because he has not benefitted from Hollywood even in crass economic terms, which enhances his stance as the likeable rogue.

The Pat Hobby stories are better as individual units than as a series. When presented as a series there is too much repetition of character, setting, and devices Fitzgerald found necessary to tie the stories together. Arnold Gingrich, in his introduction to the volume, argues that " . . . while it would be unfair to try to judge this book as a novel, it would be less than fair to consider it as anything but a full-length portrait." It is not a "full-length portrait" in the sense that it totally develops the character, and it appears that Fitzgerald intended each individual story as an entity in itself by his obvious attempt to include in each story all the background material necessary for an understanding of each story—therefore the repetition. (pp. 131-38)

Many of the stories do survive very well, though it is quite apparent in most cases they were hurried in composition. Gingrich does point out that Fitzgerald was concerned enough with them beyond their monetary value, however, that he revised most of them after submitting them to *Esquire.*

Perhaps the major significance of the collected stories is Fitzgerald's ability here to create a character quite different from what he had done in the past, and then to present Hobby in a very objective way. His portrait of a rogue who is likeable and worthless is most effective, and indeed is exactly what Fitzgerald had in mind in the series. Also, there is the portrayal of Hollywood and the movie industry which interested him very much, and which he was to develop in greater detail in *The Last Tycoon.* The stories may be seen as apprentice work for the novel, but in many instances I feel they are much more important than mere warm-up exercises. They deserve more serious consideration than they have received in the past in any attempted understanding of the last phase of Fitzgerald's work. (pp. 138-39)

Thomas E. Daniels, "Pat Hobby: Anti-Hero," in Fitzgerald/Hemingway Annual: 1973, *1974, pp. 131-39.*

DAVID TOOR (essay date 1973)

[*In the following excerpt, Toor interprets "Babylon Revisited" as "a story about self destruction."*]

Roy R. Male's perceptive article on **"Babylon Revisited"** goes far in clearing up many of the unresolved problems that have recently been discussed in relation to the story [see excerpt dated 1965]. Male has pointed out, as James Harrison had shown in an earlier note, that Charlie Wales is in a sense responsible for the appearance of Duncan and Lorraine at the Peters' house at precisely the wrong moment. Male has further called into serious question the general interpretation of the story, most specifically Seymour Gross' contention that Charlie has been renovated and that the punishment he suffers is brought upon him from external sources [see excerpt dated 1963]. Gross says: "That moral renovation may not be enough is the injustice that lies at the center of the story." Both Male and Harrison point out that had Charlie not given the bartender the Peters' address at the opening of the story, Duncan and Lorraine would not have shown up there and given Marion Peters a real reason to refuse to return Honoria to Charlie.

Gross' further statement, "Nor is there anything here of that troubled ambivalence which characterizes our response to that fantastic ambiguity, Jay Gatsby," seems quite wrong, because it is precisely in the troubled ambivalence of Charlie Wales that the meaning of the story is found. But Charlie's ambivalence is not the result of the fact that, as Male argues, "his is a story of suspension between two worlds," although to a great extent the story is structured on the contrasts between the past, as represented by Lorraine and Duncan, and the present, in the persons of Marion and Lincoln, but in a deeper awareness of Charlie's own guilt and his inability to work it out. It is in a kind of personal psychological morality that the meaning of the story is found.

It is convenient for Charlie to blame the errors of his past for the pains of his present—and future. But Fitzgerald's world is not a world of external retribution—you are not made to pay for what you've done—not at least by a God, or in Hemingway's words, "what we have instead of God," a code, or even by a deterministic fate. The payment is self-punishment, and the ironically disastrous result of such punishment is the intensification of the feelings of guilt. There is no explanation, only the further degeneration of the mind—neurotic reinforcement of behavior that leads eventually to total insanity or a form of suicide.

Charlie Wales is not torn between the poles of two opposing worlds so much as he is torn by his own inner sense of guilt and his inability to expiate it. He is not morally renovated, only sicker and less able to cope with the guilt. In one part of him he wants his Honoria (honor) back, but in the deeper man, the guilt-ridden one, he knows he doesn't deserve her. He has exiled himself to a dream world free of past responsibilities—Prague—where he creates the fresh image of himself as a successful businessman. Of course the image cannot

hold, and his distorted view of the real world leads him into delusion and jealousy: "He wondered if he couldn't do something to get Lincoln out of his rut at the bank." What kind of rut is Lincoln really in? A warm homelife that Charlie envies, children who love him, a neurotic wife, yes, but a reasonable contentment.

There are many hints through the story which point to these conclusions, and one of the most significant may be viewed as flaws in the technique of the tale. Fitzgerald chose a third-person limited point of view to tell the story, and the lapses, few as they are, are telling. All of the lapses—the shifts from limited to omniscient—are concerned with the Peters. The three most important ones directly involve Marion:

> She had built up all her fear of life into one wall and faced it toward him.

> Marion shuddered suddenly; part of her saw that Charlie's feet were planted on the earth now, and her own maternal feeling recognized the naturalness of his desire; but she had lived for a long time with a prejudice—a prejudice founded on a curious disbelief in her sister's happiness, and which, in the shock of one terrible night, had turned to hatred for him. It had all happened at a point in her life where the discouragement of ill health and adverse circumstances made it necessary for her to believe in tangible villainy and a tangible villain.

> Then, in the flatness that followed her outburst, she saw him plainly and she knew he had somehow arrived at control over the situation. Glancing at her husband, she found no help from him, and as abruptly as if it were a matter of no importance, she threw up the sponge.

In a way these passages are indeed flaws. Certainly a craftsman like Henry James, whose meanings so much depend on careful control of point of view, would not have allowed them to pass. But Fitzgerald, as much a conscious artist as he was, as in the excellent handling of such matters in *The Great Gatsby,* for instance, did let them pass because, I think, perhaps he might have been too involved in the problems of this tale, as he was not in *Gatsby.* There is the possibility that these few passages can be read as consistent with a limited third-person point of view and that these were indeed Charlie's reactions to the situation.

But what these flaws may represent is Charlie's attempt to somehow put himself in a position to account for the (subconscious) terrors that were plaguing him on this return to Babylon. All three of these cited passages are explanations of the sources of Marion's hostility and her resignation in the face of Charlie's apparent renovation. Charlie is convinced that Marion has seen that he is a changed man. But it becomes more and more clear as we examine the story that he himself was by no means convinced.

Aside from the early action of leaving the Peters' address for Duncan Schaeffer at the bar—and Charlie's subsequent denial of any knowledge of how Duncan could have found it out—we need examine in some detail what Charlie does and says through the story to understand just how completely he is caught between the psychologically necessary self-delusion that he is somehow blameless and changed, and the deeper recognition of his own guilt.

Charlie's pose, once again, is that of the reformed alcoholic, allowing himself one drink a day to prove to himself he

A cover from 1922 of H.L. Mencken's Smart Set *magazine, in which several of Fitzgerald's early stories were first published.*

doesn't need it. " 'I'm going slow these days,' " he tells Alix at the beginning. " 'I've stuck to it for over a year and a half now.' " The reassurance seems to ring true—it has been a long time. But in the way that he tells himself he can face and beat alcohol, he hasn't allowed himself to try to face and beat the deeper problems. He lives in Prague, adding to Alix, " 'They don't know about me down there.' " The dream world of escape, a foreign land where maybe Charlie too, doesn't know about himself. He is cooling it—going slow these days—even the taxi horns play the opening bars of *Le Plus que Lent.*

The Peters' home reminds Charlie of what he has lost. It "was warm and comfortably American." He responds inwardly to the intimacy and comfort of the children in the house, but his outward reaction, while holding his daughter close to him, is to boast to the Peters about how well he himself is doing. He has more money than he'd ever had before. But he cuts it off when he sees "a faint restiveness in Lincoln's eye." His defensive opening had been wrong, he sees, but still he persists. He boasts also about the past: " 'We were a sort of royalty, almost infallible, with a sort of magic around us.' " And twice in three lines he repeats, " 'I take one drink every afternoon. . . .' "

In one way Charlie is ready to admit to himself—and others—that he has a large burden of blame to carry, but too

often this admission is qualified with either a denial, a shifting, or a sharing of the blame. As he looks at his daughter he silently hopes that she doesn't "combine the traits of both [Charlie and Helen] that had brought them to disaster." In his lyrical reminiscences of the past in Paris, especially about the money squandered, he tries to convince and justify himself: "But it hadn't been given for nothing." Hadn't it? The next passage is really quite confused, and although it sounds meaningful, in reality it is a pastiche of attempted self-justification and escape from responsibility:

> It had been given, even the most wildly squandered sum, as an offering to destiny that he might not remember the things most worth remembering, the things that now he would always remember—his child taken from his control, his wife escaped to a grave in Vermont.

He thinks about Honoria being "taken from his control," not that "he had lost the right to her control." His wife has not "died," but has "escaped." The last part of the sentence essentially contradicts and yet reinforces the first part.

His encounters with Duncan and Lorraine demonstrate much the same kind of ineffectual self-justification: "As always, he felt Lorraine's passionate, provocative attraction, but his own rhythm was different now." After they leave the restaurant where he had been dining with Honoria, Charlie tries to separate himself from Duncan and Lorraine:

> They liked him because he was functioning, because he was serious; they wanted to see him, because he was stronger than they were now, because they wanted to draw a certain sustenance from his strength.

How do we understand this in terms of his later desire to get "Lincoln out of his rut at the bank?" We can't because of Charlie's inability to admit consciously the distorted state of his mind. Once again, it is not a conflict between the past and present, between Charlie Wales and Charles J. Wales of Prague, but between Charlie and his guilt. Charles J. Wales does not really exist, except in Charlie's limited perception.

Back at the Peters' on the evening of that first encounter with these spectres from the past, he proposes that he take Honoria back with him to Prague. He again boasts about his position and how well he is prepared to care for the girl, but he knows what he is in for—and in a way he is demanding to be punished, but he will put on an act for the Peters: "If he modulated his inevitable resentment to the chastened attitude of the reformed sinner, he might win his point in the end." But Charlie doesn't really know what his point is.

Marion, hurt and ill herself, pushes him to further self-justification: " 'You know I never did drink heavily until I gave up business and came over here with nothing to do. Then Helen and I began to run around with—' ". He is cut short, but he can't help but bring Helen into it. When Marion blames him for being in a sanitarium while Helen was dying, "He had no answer." Marion pushed him further. "Charlie gripped the sides of the chair. This was more difficult than he expected; he wanted to launch out into a long expostulation and explanation, but he only said: 'The night I locked her out—' ".

When Marion asks him why he hadn't thought about what he had done before, and the damage he had caused to Honoria and himself, he again refuses to admit to the full blame. . . . His guilt at the damage he'd done to Helen is further reflected in the fear of what his daughter might learn about him: "sooner or later it would come out, in a word here, a shake of the head there, and some of that distrust would be irrevocably implanted in Honoria."

Marion hits Charlie hardest when she verbalizes the real and deepest source of Charlie's guilt: " 'How much you were responsible for Helen's death, I don't know. It's something you'll have to square with your own conscience.' " And this is just what Charlie can't do. "An electric current of agony surged through him. . . ." But his only outward response, after Lincoln's attempt to defend him, is, " 'Helen died of heart trouble.' " There is no other answer Charlie can give, for to admit consciously, even for an instant that he might really have been to blame for Helen's death might permit him to face his guilt and thus enable him to start the cleansing process that might lead back towards balance.

In the reverie of Helen that follows the bitter scene ending with Marion's agreeing to return Honoria, we find evidence of his inability to admit to his blame. "The image of Helen haunted him. Helen whom he had loved so until they had senselessly begun to abuse each other's love, tear it into shreds." He excuses himself again for the events of the night he had locked her out. "When he arrived home alone he turned the key in the lock in wild anger. How could he know she would arrive an hour later alone, that there would be a snowstorm in which she wandered about in slippers, too confused to find a taxi?" The final scene of the vision of Helen that night is again part of his ambivalent attempt and refusal to find expiation. Helen seems to comfort him with tenderness and forgiveness, except that as she swings faster and faster the forgiveness is not complete: "at the end he could not hear clearly all that she said," leaving him to delude himself into half-believing the closing words of the story about Helen forgiving him.

The remaining two sections of the story, IV and V, reinforce what has gone before. Further self-delusions of himself as cured, even a garbled version of how best to raise a daughter:

> The present was the thing—work to do, and someone to love. But not to love too much, for he knew the injury that a father can do to a daughter or a mother to a son by attaching them too closely: afterward, out in the world, the child would seek in the marriage partner the same blind tenderness and, failing probably to find it, turn against love and life.

This is just the kind of distortion that Charlie's mind would drive him to. Certainly there is a base in Freudian psychology for what he says, but only in his conscious rationalization of "not to love too much," can Charlie make sense out of his own inability to love fully and completely. He is too warped to see that the only love worth having or giving is one without reservations and limits. (pp. 155-61)

The ghastly scene [when Duncan and Lorraine barge in] at the Peters ends with Charlie getting what he was begging for subconsciously all along—Marion's rejection of his plea for Honoria. Before Charlie leaves he lies—consciously or not—to Lincoln: " 'I wish you'd explain to her [Marion] I never dreamed these people would come here. I'm just as sore as you are.' "

Charlie cannot make amends, cannot "conciliate something," as he puts it, and the story ends on a note of almost total despair. It is not by accident that his thoughts turn back to money and his imagination of the power of money. He reflects that "the snow of twenty-nine wasn't real snow. If you didn't want it to be snow, you just paid some money." Charlie hasn't been able to deal in love, but he has been able to handle money and the things money can produce. He still isn't convinced that the two are not equal, nor can he admit to himself the possibility that the main source of his troubles was his inability to love and that his present guilt feelings stem directly from that source. So he will turn back to the new old ways and instead of dealing with people, deal with things. "There wasn't much he could do now except send Honoria some things; he would send her a lot of things tomorrow. He thought rather angrily that this was just money—he had given so many people money. . . ." And that's all he had given.

In the tormented inner world of Charlie Wales, the world where God could not exist and therefore not punish, and where the individual retains, if not a sense of sin, at least a sense of guilt, we find the real conflict. **"Babylon Revisited"** is not a story about the inability of the world to forgive and forget, or even about a man drawn back to the past and therefore unable to come to terms with the present. It is a story about self destruction, about the human mind's ability to delude itself into thinking that what it does is based on logic and reason. The story ends with only the promise of emptiness to come in Charlie's life; it ends with the lie that may lead Charlie to destruction: "He was absolutely sure Helen wouldn't have wanted him to be so alone." (p. 162)

David Toor, "Guilt and Retribution in 'Babylon Revisited'," in Fitzgerald/Hemingway Annual: 1973, 1974, pp. 155-64.

ANTHONY J. MAZZELLA   (essay date 1977)

[In the following excerpt, Mazzella analyzes "May Day" in terms of form and content, describing the story as "an early work of surprising complexity, structured on the careful modulation of opposites."]

["May Day"] was published originally in 1920 in *The Smart Set* when Fitzgerald was twenty-three, five years before the publication of *The Great Gatsby*. Considering that its themes belong to Fitzgerald's late period as well, it should also be noted that **"May Day"** was first published twenty years before his death. It, thus, turns out to be an early work of surprising complexity, structured on the careful modulation of opposites, of integration and disintegration. It is also a moving expression of order struggling against approaching chaos. In its carefully revised version for *Tales of the Jazz Age* (1922), the lives of several central characters—young, wealthy Philip Dean; penniless and dissipated Gordon Sterrett, his former Yale roommate; and shallow, pretty, narcissistic Edith Bradin—intersect in the story's eleven sections with the lives of returning soldiers, mob forces, social dilettantes. May Day itself links various lives and various events: a trivial fraternity dance at Delmonico's; the soldiers Gus Rose and Carroll Key whose entanglement in a mob ends with Key's accidental death plunge from the window of a newspaper office run by radical editor Henry Bradin, Edith's brother; the pre-dawn drunken spree of Philip Dean and Peter Himmel enacting a charade of "Mr. In" and "Mr. Out," desperately trying to encompass a lifetime in an evening; and finally the suicide of Gordon Sterrett after awakening to find himself married to Jewel Hudson, lower class and impossible. The story, when examined closely, reveals in the young Fitzgerald a sophisticated and highly controlled writer, one quite unlike the novice usually depicted as antedating *The Great Gatsby.*

The content of **"May Day"** is chaos and destruction, but the story's form reverses the direction of the content, giving the reader attuned to form a sense of order and stability. It is this disparity between form and content that produces the story's tension. **"May Day"**'s title, structure, tone, incident word, even section numbers, together demonstrate Fitzgerald's command of detail in developing this paradox. These elements of form go counter to the madness that is the story's content. Opposites paradoxically link. And Fitzgerald has created a sense of triumph-in-despair through the "assertiveness" of the form running counter to the defeatism of its content.

The title, for example, is a paradox, specifying numerous opposites when related to the story. First, it denotes the day (May 1, 1919) when most of the random incidents occur—largely incidents involving violence and death. Next, besides denoting the date of occurrence, the title has several suggestive connotations which, because they are both apt and capable of wide application, create a sense of life where the events in the story create an opposite effect: a sense of defeat, despair, the abyss. May Day, of course, commemorates the working class, but in the story we have confusion in the working class. There, the Socialists supporting the workers are attacked by the soldiers of that same working class. As Henry Bradin observes to his sister, " 'The human race has come a long way . . . but most of us are throw-backs; the soldiers don't know what they want, or what they hate, or what they like. They're used to acting in large bodies, and they seem to have to make demonstrations. So it happens to be against us. There've been riots all over the city to-night. It's May Day, you know.' " Thus, elements of the same class are working against each other; supposed allies become enemies, similarities become opposites, and the day of commemoration becomes the night of death and destruction. But May Day connotes more than a commemoration—in the story, a commemoration gone awry. It connotes the celebration of a spring festival, crowning a May Queen, dancing around a May pole, the advent of new life; but in the story we encounter the reverse: the dance around a May pole is a mob assault on a building, the crowning of a May Queen is Edith Bradin facing a retinue of attackers and consoling her brother whose leg has just been broken by the men he calls " 'the fools,' " and the advent of new life is the death of Carroll Key and the suicide of Gordon Sterrett. Finally, **"May Day,"** from the French *m'aidez,* means 'help me'; it is the familiar distress call, what all the beleaguered characters in the story itself are crying out without ever expressing the words but which a kind of nameless chorus in the prologue does utter: " 'May Heaven help me.' " The title, therefore, names a day, signals an event, makes a plea. The title's amplitude, thus, in not only referring to the time of the story but also in giving connotations of commemoration, celebration, and help, offers a richness that counterbalances the defeatism of the plot and produces a tension of opposites which, as we shall see, is sustained throughout the work.

If we examine the prologue to the story, for instance, we discover another paradox, this time largely in a tone that is opposed to that of the rest of the work, and in a form that ap-

pears nowhere else in the story. The form is that of the fairy tale; the tone, that of pained as well as mocking exaggeration. The fairy tale form is suggested by the passive voice of the narrator ("There had been a war fought and won. . . . " "Never had there been such splendor. . . . " "So gaily and noisily were the peace and prosperity impending hymned by the scribes and poets of the conquering people. . . . "), the use of archaisms ("scribes" above), the generality of reference ("in the great city"), the artificiality of language and the central object of at least one well-known fairy tale—the slipper (" 'Alas! I have no more slippers! and alas! I have no more trinkets! May Heaven help me, for I know not what I shall do!' "). The tone of mocking and pained exaggeration is suggested by the depiction of a postwar scene of unbridled consumption that is loud in its clamor and unheeding in its conduct so that the voice that says 'help me' goes unheard. This placement of the title's connotation of pleading in the context of febrile and foolish exhortation reinforces the note of pained exaggeration. The thematic oppositions that the rest of the work presents to the fairy-tale form and exaggerated tone are realistic form and serious tone.

Whereas the prologue dealt in generalities, the first section deals in specifics: "nine o'clock on the morning of the first of May, 1919, . . . at the Biltmore Hotel." The obvious opposites of the general and the specific are carried one step further with the immediately subsequent introduction of Gordon Sterrett and Philip Dean. When we are introduced to these two men, we meet first a man "dressed in a well-cut, shabby suit [who] was small, slender, and darkly handsome; his eyes were framed above with unusually long eyelashes and below with the blue semicircle of ill health" and then a man who "was blond, ruddy, and rugged under his thin pajamas [about whom] radiated fitness and bodily comfort." Clearly, we are introduced to a pair of opposites again. Were we to have these two apart from the context of the prologue, they would appear merely as foils to one another. But after the title opposites of denotation-connotation and the prologue-story opposites of form and tone, encountering still another pair of opposites places the reader in the position of being moved in one direction while still advancing as the story progresses. The very structure of the work, then, has a pulsating movement, a step in one direction followed by a step in an opposite direction.

If this principle of structure—the pulsation of opposites—is examined against the story's eleven sections, the tight organic nature of the work as a whole is evident. While the story appears disorienting because the plot advances in different directions, each section is really closely linked through subtle formal devices. The first section, for example, ends with the "have" (Dean) and the "have-not" (Sterrett) hating each other, and with the juxtaposition of exterior wealth (Dean's "thick silk shirts . . . impressive neckties and soft woollen socks") and interior destruction (Sterrett's "unnatural glow which colored his face like a low, incessant fever"); and the second section opens with a descriptive passage that embodies these last-named opposites but in an entirely different setting: "Working-girls, in pairs and groups and swarms, . . . stood in front of the jewelry stores and picked out their engagement rings, and their wedding rings and their platinum wrist watches [exterior wealth], and then drifted on to inspect the feather fans and opera cloaks; meanwhile digesting the sandwiches and sundaes they had eaten for lunch [in a very literal sense, interior destruction]."

The second section ends with a pair of men (Sterrett and Dean), one of whom is to die violently; the third section opens with a pair of men (Carroll Key and Gus Rose), one of whom is also to die violently. (Their names, in addition, are also paradoxes: the feminine sounds of Carroll and Rose, but belonging to men rather than women.) Section III ends with Rose and Key using metaphorical language to describe the heat in a storeroom at Delmonico's (" 'It's hot in here, ain't it?' . . . 'Hot as hell.' "); and section IV opens with a variation on that metaphor and with a different character. Instead of heat as infernal we have heat as choler ("She [Edith Bradin] was still quite angry"). Section IV ends with the defeat of Sterrett as he mistakenly believes Edith Bradin is sincere in loving him; section V begins with the defeat of Peter Himmel who is snubbed by the same Edith Bradin. Moreover, Himmel, another of the world's rejected, is linked with Rose and Key here, and with Dean in section X; thus, while we have a series of formal links, these links in content do not in fact link as in harmony but end as in dissolution. These structural links paradoxically do not link but disengage.

By now, half-way through the story, a rhythm of simultaneous gain and loss is clearly evident; i.e., the structure metaphorically moves in a forward direction (with its various formal links), but that forward direction is checked by plot reversals that move in an opposite direction. Stated in different terms, the form's complexity may be seen as a positive factor while the story's plot may be seen as a negative one, the resultant antiphony contributing to the story's tension. (pp. 379-83)

The pulsating rhythm that we have seen throughout the story's form paradoxically gives the story's deadly content a sense of life. It is almost as if the pulsating structure were an analog for the human heartbeat in this story of death, where seemingly disparate but actually related incidents and brutal events culminate in paired climaxes of death—those of Key and Sterrett. These two characters die violently; and, in a similar way, the story's structure with its pulsing rhythm appears to end violently as well because the pulsation of Sterrett's heart and the pulsation of the story's structure both cease simultaneously. One feels a sense of futility in the story's content but at the same time one has to marvel at Fitzgerald's technique: a story about death told in a method that bespeaks life.

Perhaps more remarkable, given the outlines of Fitzgerald's entire career—the charmingly egocentric bravado of *This Side of Paradise* (1920), the bittersweet, self-indulgent despair of **"Winter Dreams"** (1922), the enormous capacity for hope that refuses to acknowledge either the seedy in *The Great Gatsby* (1925) or the destroying ego in **"The Rich Boy"** (1926), the self-deluding romanticism that is likely to withstand the conspiracies of fate in **"Babylon Revisited"** (1931), the vampiric exchange of health and sanity in *Tender Is the Night* (1934), the anti-martyr honesty of "The Crack-Up" (1937)—perhaps in the face of these what is more remarkable about **"May Day"** is that in its concerns it anticipates the entire career, as if Fitzgerald sensed his inevitability and was writing a paradigm of that future. For while several of the characters in **"May Day"** are destroyed or self-destroying in the content, the form—the very being of the story—denies that destruction. Life may reward its privileged few and defeat its hapless many, but art is better than life because it is invulnerable to it. Life may wreck but art is unconquerable. And while the person will die, the art cannot since by its very nature it is born of life *not* to be its subject. This appears to be what Fitzgerald was saying—doing—in the whole of **"May Day."** (pp. 384-85)

Anthony J. Mazzella, "The Tension of Opposites in Fitzgerald's 'May Day'," in Studies in Short Fiction, *Vol. 14, No. 4, Fall, 1977, pp. 379-85.*

ROBERT K. MARTIN   (essay date 1978)

[*Martin is an American-born educator and critic living in Canada. In the following essay, he interprets "May Day" as an exploration of changing relationships between individuals and groups and examines the clash between past fantasy and present reality.*]

Fitzgerald's prologue to **"May Day"** suggests that one is to see the threads of the narrative as part of a single strand, or even to see that they are the same thread, viewed differently: "there were many adventures that happened in the great city, and, of these, several—or perhaps one—are here set down." But despite this invitation, critics have not been able to see the identity of theme—the crisis of the male-bonding relationship. Return from war, like graduation from college, was potentially frightening for Fitzgerald's characters, as they lost their sense of comradeship and found themselves suddenly alone.

In the first section of the story, Fitzgerald emphasizes carefully that the encounter is between two very attractive young men: Gordon is "small, slender, and darkly handsome . . . with unusually long eyelashes" and Philip is "blond, ruddy, and rugged under his thin pajamas." The scene is then eroticized. Philip goes off to take a shower as soon as Gordon arrives, then emerges from the bathroom, apparently nude, "polishing his body." He continues to display himself to Gordon, then "survey[s] his shining self complacently in the mirror" and finally, about half a page later, "drap[es] himself reluctantly in fresh underwear."

The erotic basis of their competitive relationship is clear. Philip is aware of his superiority, both financial and sexual, over Gordon. He uses his display of his body as an element of sadistic control, an assertion of power. Gordon, who has failed in his career and failed in his romantic life, undergoes a ritual enactment of Philip's superior virility. The theme becomes crucial to the story, as Gordon is increasingly tormented by his own sense of failure until he commits suicide. Fitzgerald used the erotic relationship between two men as a foundation for sexual humiliation, and he apparently recognized that the competition for a woman in the world of the fraternity dance is a rivalry acted out primarily between the two men, in sexual-political terms, with the woman remaining quite distant, at best the anticipated reward. The Gordon-Philip relationship hovers on the boundary of love and hatred. "For an instant before they turned to go their eyes met and in that instant each found something that made him lower his own glance quickly. For in that instance they quite suddenly and definitely hated each other."

It is also important to note the narcissism of the scene, with Philip's elaborate emphasis on his own body, which is turned into an object, to be polished and to shine. Edith's regard for her body is similarly eroticized: "She dropped her arms to her sides until they were faintly touching the sleek sheath that covered and suggested her figure. She had never felt her own softness so much nor so enjoyed the whiteness of her own arms." The masturbatory vision of Philip and Edith is essential to Fitzgerald's creation of a work in which men and women inhabit quite separate worlds, and in which the pressures to break down the boundaries between them can be destructive.

The street scene in New York emphasizes the group identities. "Working-girls" loiter "in pairs and groups and swarms." Philip and Gordon meet "a group of their former classmates" and have "a highball all around." Later they lunch "together *en masse.*" Meanwhile the soldiers find they hold no interest for the city unless they are "nicely massed into pretty formations." With that introduction we are led into the world of Key and Rose, two pathetic figures, detritus of society, who at the same time form a comic couple in the manner of Laurel and Hardy or Mutt and Jeff. They have been cast up, like driftwood as Fitzgerald suggests, after the war and have lost their sense of meaning which they had once found in relating to authority as obedient soldiers and in relating to the other soldiers in the male community of the war.

They briefly find their meaning again as they lead the attack on Edith's brother's newspaper. Key and Rose come to the head of the group and have their moment of "glory" in leading the mob. Fitzgerald sees this as a continuation of their military nature—he explains through the voice of Henry: "The soldiers don't know what they want, or what they hate, or what they like. They're used to acting in large bodies, and they seem to have to make demonstrations."

The real source of the soldiers' violence lies in their aimlessness, in their sense of loss, and in their need for reinforcement through others. Much the same can be said of Fitzgerald's Yale men. They seem happiest when drinking together with other Yale men, or, like Philip, when alone with their bodies. When the loss of innocence, or in this case, the loss of Yale, forces them into another world, they seek consolation in their old "buddies."

Gordon has gone beyond the imaginary line. He has become involved with a woman, and not a débutante likely to be seen at the Gamma Psi dance at Delmonico's. She is "over-rouged" with "soft, pulpy lips." She is far too much life, and too little dream. When Gordon awakens to find that he is married to Jewel, this realization comes as a part of his recognition of "the sense of life close beside him." Faced with the inevitability of his shabby life he prefers to retreat one last time, by firing "a cartridge into his head just behind the temple."

Gordon's journey towards death had begun some time before, as he confesses to Edith: "I was always queer—little bit different from other boys. All right in college, but now it's all wrong. Things have been snapping inside me for four months like little hooks on a dress, and it's about to come off when a few more hooks go. I'm very gradually going loony." It is impossible to know whether Fitzgerald intended us to take "queer" in its sense as homosexual, but it seems likely, given his frequent reference to homosexual characters—the priest in **"Absolution"** is but the most obvious of many. And in terms of **"May Day"** itself it is certainly tempting to suggest that Fitzgerald was treating, albeit covertly and perhaps unconsciously, the problems faced by the repressed homosexual when he is forced to leave a place of relative happiness and security, such as the military or a men's college, and to take up a place in a heterosexual world which he fears. Gordon's reaction against the physical nature of Jewel seems to me

Fitzgerald's way of expressing Gordon's repulsion at the thought of a woman (not unlike Hamlet's reaction, which also includes a repulsion against make-up on Gertrude). "All right in college, but now it's all wrong." The crisis for such a man comes when he is forced to play a sexual role which repels him, but for which he has no terms of reference and no real alternatives.

The alternatives, such as they are, are suggested by the deaths of Key and Gordon, and by the antics of "Mr. In and Mr. Out," otherwise the most mysterious element of the story. Another comic male couple, they are so interchangeable that they put on "In" and "Out" signs, become Mr. In and Mr. Out, and go "arm in arm," "with their arms interlocked" to a series of champagne breakfasts. They deny all reality and when they ascend the elevator "skyward" they announce to the elevator man:

> "Have another floor put on," said Mr. Out.
>
> "Higher," said Mr. In.
>
> "Heaven," said Mr. Out.

We see the horror of their indifference, as their frivolity is juxtaposed to the deaths and violence of the rest of the story. But we also see that escape from reality can take many forms. These "drinking buddies" are striving against all odds to prevent the vanishing of the dream world in which they live, a world in which all the nice young men are handsome and dance forever at Yale proms with women who will never have "pulpy lips" or wear too much rouge, but instead be what Fitzgerald ecstatically called Edith, "a complete, infinitely delicate, quite perfect thing of beauty, flowing in an even line from a complex coiffure to two small slim feet." (pp. 99-101)

> *Robert K. Martin, "Sexual and Group Relationship in 'May Day': Fear and Longing," in* Studies in Short Fiction, *Vol. 15, No. 1, Winter, 1978, pp. 99-101.*

KENNETH G. JOHNSTON   (essay date 1978)

[*In the following excerpt, Johnston questions narrator Joel Coles's ability in "Crazy Sunday" to distinguish between appearance and reality and asserts that the key to understanding the story is its point of view.*]

"Crazy Sunday," which was first published in the *American Mercury* in 1932, is yet another variation of the Cinderella tale. The cast includes a beautiful actress with golden hair; a motion-picture director whose " 'magical' " touch has " 'brought that little gamin alive and made her a sort of masterpiece' "; and a handsome young man who falls in love with the little gamin, a former bit player. In the climactic scene, a clock strikes "in trumpet notes. *Nine—ten—eleven—twelve—*". The central focus of Fitzgerald's story, however, is not on the Cinderella character, but rather on a Hollywood script writer who, as the story opens, has just been invited to a "top-drawer" party at "Cinderella's" lavish home in Beverly Hills. (p. 214)

The key to **"Crazy Sunday"** is its point of view. Joel Coles provides the focus of narration, but at the very outset his trustworthiness—that is, his ability to distinguish between appearance and reality—is called into question: the son of a successful actress, "Joel had spent his childhood between London and New York trying to separate the real from the unreal, or at least to keep one guess ahead." As a grown man, he is still trying, but without much success; herein lies the major source of dramatic irony which pervades **"Crazy Sunday."** By using an unreliable narrator, who is also the central character, Fitzgerald invites one to look behind and beyond Joel's explanations and perceptions, while at the same time permitting the reader to participate in, even to enjoy, at first hand the excitement and glamour of several Hollywood parties. . . . In **"Crazy Sunday"** Fitzgerald has his eye on Joel Coles. It is Joel's blunted and uncertain perception which is responsible for the inconsistent portrayal of character, the blurred relationships and motivations, and the "structural disharmony." These "shortcomings" reflect flaws in his own character and, thus, they eventually lead one to the thematic center of the story.

Sunday, according to Joel, is different from the other days of the week. For a few blessed hours, he tells us, the sets and sequences, "the ceaseless compromise," "the clash and strain of many personalities," "the struggles of rival ingenuities," are left behind. But as the story unfolds, it becomes clear to the reader that Sunday is remarkably like the other days at the studio.

"Crazy Sunday" begins with a Sunday afternoon "tea" at the home of Miles Calman, the director. It is a gathering of important figures and personalities from the motion picture world: writers, actors, actresses, and money men. The Calman mansion provides an appropriate setting: the "house was built for great emotional moments—there was an air of listening, as if the far silences of its vistas hid an audience, but this afternoon it was thronged, as though people had been bidden rather than asked." It is on this stage that Joel Coles, an ambitious film writer, plans to advance his career by playing the role of "a young man of promise." He even rehearses his part:

> "I won't take anything to drink," he assured himself. Calman was audibly tired of rummies, and thought it was a pity the industry could not get along without them.
>
> Joel agreed that writers drank too much—he did himself, but he wouldn't this afternoon. He wished Miles would be within hearing when the cocktails were passed to hear his succinct, unobtrusive, "No, thank you."

Stella Walker Calman does not move on to her other guests after she speaks to Joel. "She lingered." He pays tribute to her youthful beauty: " 'Well, you look about sixteen! Where's your kiddy car?' " Stella is visibly pleased. A recent mother, the beautiful actress apparently needs to be reassured about her charm. " 'After a pretty woman has had her first child . . . ,' " Joel tells her, " 'she's got to have some new man's unqualified devotion to prove to herself she hasn't lost anything.' " Nonetheless, Joel is flattered by her attentions. "She presented several people to Joel *as if* he were important" (italics mine). When she slips a drink into his hand, his abstemious intentions are compromised. "Reassuring himself that Miles was at the other side of the room, Joel drank the cocktail." Their conversation is "interrupted at the exact moment Joel would have chosen." Thus far, Joel is satisfied with the script.

With the party nearly over, Joel, who by now is quite drunk, decides to perform at center stage. But his performance, a burlesque based upon the cultural limitations of an independent producer, is by his own admission " 'a flop.' " It ends

in the midst of a confused silence. He feels the undercurrent of derision; he hears the great screen lover shout " 'Boo! Boo!' " It is "the resentment of the professional toward the amateur, of the community toward the stranger, the thumbs-down of the clan." He has "made a fool of himself " before an important group of the picture world, "upon whose favor depended his career." But Stella Walker whose radiant smile never vanished throughout the ordeal, thanks him "as if he had been an unparalleled success." He bows "rather drunkenly" and makes his exit.

The next day Joel awakens to "a broken and ruined world." He sends the Calmans a note of apology, slinks about the studio like a malefactor, finds a gloomy consolation in staring at some other misfits in the studio restaurant—"the sad, lovely Siamese twins, the mean dwarfs, the proud giant from the circus picture." Although he vows never again to make another social appearance in Hollywood, a telegram from Stella the following morning ends his permanent retirement: " 'You were one of the most agreeable people at our party. Expect you at my sister June's buffet supper next Sunday.' "

The second crazy Sunday is filled with "the clash and strain of many personalities." Miles and Stella arrive, tense and angry, having quarreled fiercely most of the afternoon. Stella has just learned of her husband's affair with her best friend, Eva Goebel. Quivering with shock and emotion, Stella turns to Joel, whose eyes are filled with "unstinted admiration." She sits down "vehemently on the arm of Joel's chair," as though to retaliate for the girl perched "on the arm of Miles's chair." Joel is struck by Stella's natural beauty: he notices "that the mass of her hair was made up of some strands of red gold and some of pale gold, so that it could not be dyed, and that she had on no make-up. She was that good-looking—" When the spectacle of a new girl "hovering" over her husband becomes unbearable, Stella leads Joel into a bedroom, and seated at either end of a big bed, they continue to talk. Miles sticks his head in the room, but Stella goes on talking to Joel as if her husband were not there. Impatiently, Miles suggests that, since his wife had so much to say to Joel, he return home with them.

The scene now shifts back to the theater-like Calman home, where it occurs to Joel that Stella's tears and anger are simply part of a performance. . . . As if to confirm his suspicions, a short time later while Joel and Miles are discussing pictures, Stella comes "suddenly back into the conversation as if they'd never discussed her personal affairs." She is incensed because old Beltzer tried to change her husband's picture and stands "hovering protectively over Miles, her eyes flashing with indignation in his behalf." It is at this moment that "Joel realized that he was in love with her." What he does not seem to realize is that Stella is deeply in love with her husband and that she has been using Joel, once again, in an effort to rekindle Miles's love and affection. Her displays of grief and jealousy during the afternoon and evening were real, not playacting.

The third and final crazy Sunday brings the story into sharp thematic focus. But first there is a Saturday night prelude, which blends illusion and reality. "Self-conscious in his silk hat against the unemployment"—a reminder of the economic reality, the depression—Joel waits outside the Hollywood Theatre. When Stella and her friends arrive in their smart limousines, he learns that Miles has flown east for the Notre Dame football game after all. During the performance of the play, Joel "turned and looked at [Stella] and she looked back

at him, smiling and meeting his eyes for as long as he wanted." Between acts, she suggests that afterwards they go to her
house and " 'talk.' " She expresses doubt that her husband
has actually gone to South Bend, suspects that the telegram
from there is not authentic. " 'Supposing he was here watching everything I do,' " she wonders. Later, after saying goodnight to the others, they drive along a boulevard under a full
moon which is "only a prop." "If Miles had trained a camera
on them," an angry Joel thinks, "he felt no obligations toward Miles." When they arrive at the house, Stella finds another telegram, this one from Chicago. " 'You see,' she said,
throwing the slip back on the table, 'he could easily have
faked that.' "

Joel now suspects that he is being used as a " 'pawn in a spite
game' " that Stella is playing against her husband. A remark
by Miles earlier in the week apparently planted the seed of
suspicion: " 'I can't tell what Stella might do just out of
spite,' " he said. Joel vaguely senses that he is caught up in
a struggle between rival ingenuities, but when confronted,
Stella refuses to confirm or to deny it. Evasively, she offers
him a drink instead. Undeterred, Joel declares his "love,"
then spends the next half hour trying to seduce her. (One recalls that Joel had posed as a man of honor just a few days
before. " 'I've never made any passes whatsoever at Stella,' "
he told Miles on Wednesday. " ' . . . . You can trust me absolutely.' " When she rebuffs him, he feels "faintly relieved"
that an entanglement has been avoided, a curious response
for a rejected lover. Actually he is not in love with Stella Calman, the attractive wife and mother; rather he is fascinated
by Stella Walker, the beautiful rose-gold actress blown full
of life by his imagination. As usual, he is having difficulty in
separating his true emotions from the false. As he prepares
to take his leave, somewhat hurt by Stella's readiness to have
him go, the phone rings—and the clock strikes.

Twelve o'clock ushers in another crazy Sunday and signals,
for the reader at least, a return to reality. The voice on the
phone reads from a telegram reporting a plane crash west of
Kansas City. Miles Calman is dead, and Stella Calman desperately needs someone to lean on in her hour of need. Stella,
however, refuses to believe the first, and Joel is unable to recognize the reality of the second. She pleads with him to stay
and not to call anyone; frantically, she is trying to deny the
reality of her husband's death by sustaining the *illusion* of a
romantic triangle. She is not a cheap tramp trying to lure him
to her bed. She is " 'frightened' " and " 'alone.' " Even when
others start to arrive, when the door-bell begins to ring and
automobiles are pulling up in front of the door, she begs him
to stay. Now she really needs the affection and friendship
which she earlier exploited to make her husband jealous. She
is still the beautiful golden girl, despite the death of the man
whose "magical" touch had made her a screen star. Hers is
a natural beauty which is not dependent on hair dyes, or fa-
cial make-up, or camera angles, or talented directors. Beautifully gowned as ever, she stands before Joel, but he sees only
a ragged little gamin. His perception of "reality" leads Joel
right back into the illusory world of the fairy tale—and the
film studio: the director has left the set, but the actress, refusing to acknowledge that the scene is over, continues to emote
on the empty stage. Joel has never quite believed in actresses'
grief, and now when a lovely young woman appeals to him
from the depths of her loss and sorrow, he is not convinced
that her need is real. Promising to come back " 'if you need
me,' " he stalks off the "set" praising the man whom, only
moments before, he fully intended to betray. He abandons the

one person who, just two short weeks ago, stood by him in
his hour of need when he was suffering through his drunken
embarrassment and sober disgrace. Thus, once again, and on
the very same stage, Joel plays the fool. On that ironic note,
the story concludes.

Fitzgerald once explained in an essay on his craft that if he
were to avoid false starts he had to "start out with an emotion—one that's close to me and that I can understand." Certainly, he had played the fool many times himself and had
blurred, and sometimes crossed over, the line between illusion and reality. During his first Hollywood sojourn in 1927,
for instance, one madcap night he "made the Hollywood
skies literally rain down money in silver puddles." According
to Aaron Latham, Scott obtained a hundred dollars in coins
from the desk clerk; he then threw handfuls of silver up
against the windows of the Ambassador Hotel, shouting,
" 'It's money, it's money, it's money! It's free!' " Just four
years later he returned to Hollywood to work in films because, as he admitted, "he needed the money badly." Little
wonder then that Fitzgerald would remark, " 'Sometimes I
don't know whether I'm real or whether I'm a character in
one of my own novels.' "

Fitzgerald's special gift as a writer was his ability to perceive
the reality behind the glittering carnival, the face behind the
mask. But occasionally he must have wondered if the time
would ever come when he would no longer be able to separate
the real from the unreal, "to detect where the milk is watered
and the sugar is sanded, the rhinestone passed for diamond
and the stucco for stone." Clearly, that day has arrived for
Joel Coles in **"Crazy Sunday."** Although alcohol is a contributing factor, Joel's inability to distinguish between appearance and reality is primarily the result of having lived and
worked too long in a world of make-believe. When he comes
face to face with genuine, shattering grief, he fails to recognize or to respond to it. The situation is no more real to him
than a scene from a film script or a page from a fairy tale. (pp.
215-20)

> *Kenneth G. Johnston, "Fitzgerald's 'Crazy Sunday':*
> *Cinderella in Hollywood," in* Literature/Film
> Quarterly, *Vol. VI, No. 3, Summer, 1978, pp. 214-*
> *21.*

JOHN GERY (essay date 1980)

[*In the following essay, Gery describes "The Curious Case of
Benjamin Button" as a satire of the Gilded Age, which by its
use of irony also comments on the role of the alienated individual in society.*]

F. Scott Fitzgerald's **"The Curious Case of Benjamin Button"**—the tale of a man born at the age of seventy who grows
younger each year—belongs in the tradition of "Rip Van
Winkle," in that its protagonist finds himself, by a quirk,
chronologically at odds with the society in which he lives.
But the consequence of Benjamin's fate is not, as we might
expect, his alienation from that society. Unlike his more existential counterparts (for example, Gregor Samsa in "Metamorphosis"), Benjamin succeeds handsomely at his life despite his obvious handicap. Why? Whereas the tendency of
the alienated character is to turn inward, to examine his own
peculiarity of nature, Fitzgerald's character turns outward in
an effort to adapt to his society. Not only does this create the
satiric structure of the story, as is generally noted, it also establishes its primary irony: Benjamin, rather than opposing

the mores of his world, in fact more exactly than any other character in the story adheres to and lives by those mores. This irony, evident in both the narrative and the historical setting, raises the story above the level of mild satire to that of an American fable.

"As long ago as 1860, it was the proper thing to be born at home," the story begins, so that Fitzgerald describes Benjamin's birth in a hospital as an "anachronism," because his parents, "the Roger Buttons" from a fashionable Baltimore family, are "fifty years ahead of style." Benjamin, on the other hand, begins his life as an old man full of reason and common sense. Despite Roger Button's vain attempts to dress his son in a child's clothing and to confine him to a nursery, Benjamin manages to enjoy smoking Havana cigars and reading the *Encyclopaedia Britannica,* activities he shares, appropriately, with his distinguished grandfather. And even though the Button's doctor quits the family for fear of ruining his reputation, though Roger Button wishes "passionately that his son was black" instead of wrinkled and white-haired, and though the newspapers learn to dub Benjamin "The Mystery Man of Maryland"—Benjamin himself, we are told, takes life as he finds it. As he grows younger, his achievements mount up proportionally. When Yale refuses to grant him admission because he looks too old and he is laughed out of New Haven, it marks "the biggest mistake that Yale College . . . ever made." When he courts the twenty-year-old Hildegarde Moncrief (who considers him a "mellow" fifty), the two find themselves "marvelously in accord on all the questions of the day." During the Golden Age of capitalism, he turns the family hardware concern into a thriving business, receives a medal for heroism at San Juan Hill in 1898, perfects all the fashionable dance steps at the turn of the century, and scores seven touchdowns and fourteen field goals *against* Yale as he stars for the 1910 Harvard football team—all the while to the aggravation of his normally aging contemporaries.

In short, Benjamin depicts *ideally* the appropriate age for an American male to be, as the author imagines him, between 1860 and 1930. (Characteristic of Fitzgerald's writing, all dates in the story are carefully documented.) Introducing the story when it first appeared, Fitzgerald claims it was "inspired by a remark of Mark Twain's to the effect that it was a pity that the best part of life came at the beginning and the worst part at the end." Benjamin's life ends in a crib, surrounded by "soft mumblings and murmurings," without regrets, memories, or even thoughts, since he has become a helpless infant. Is the author suggesting perhaps, in keeping with the earlier phases of Benjamin's adaptability, that a model for the American of the Twenties is found in the carefree and careless lifestyle of the child? Even Benjamin's son, the "efficient" Roscoe who, like his grandfather, grossly attempts to hide his infant father from the public view, ultimately is portrayed as more "curious and perverse" than Benjamin. He is afraid to spend more than half an hour thinking about Benjamin, for fear that it will drive him mad.

What Fitzgerald's story conveys, then, in addition to its sometimes prolonged satiric view of the Gilded Age, is the underlying American social ideal of the unique power of individualism, even if that individualism assumes a grotesque manifestation. If **"The Curious Case of Benjamin Button"** implies that it is wrong to shun the extraordinary individual because he threatens the social conventions, more significantly it expresses the innate superiority of the "curious and per-

verse" manner and affirms that, in the final analysis of an era such as the Gilded Age, it is precisely the curious individual who shapes history itself—in spite of and because of his alienation from it. This Romantic ideal, which we later find deeply embedded and compounded in Fitzgeraldian characters like Jay Gatsby and Monroe Stahr, determines the role of Benjamin Button less as the victim of a petty society than as that man *lucky* enough to be born out of step with his time. And though Fitzgerald's tale may treat history as fantastically as it does its central character, it speaks from the core of the American consciousness. (pp. 495-97)

> *John Gery, "The Curious Grace of Benjamin Button," in* Studies in Short Fiction, *Vol. 17, No. 4, Fall, 1980, pp. 495-97.*

WILLIAM J. BRONDELL   (essay date 1982)

[*In the following excerpt, Brondell analyzes what he views as Fitzgerald's adaptation of a conventional five-act dramatic model in "Absolution," "The Freshest Boy," and "Babylon Revisited." According to Brondell, these stories display Fitzgerald's development of a dual structure: a dramatic superstructure of five parts that develops cause-and-effect relationships in the action, and a substructure that fluctuates from story to story and traces the hero's psychological state.*]

In a letter to Harold Ober, his agent, F. Scott Fitzgerald distinguished between two types of short stories: those that are "conceived like novels, which require a special emotion, a special experience," and present "something new, not in form, but substance"; and those "pattern stories" in which stock characters behave in a typical fashion and achieve a predictable ending, thus fulfilling, rather than challenging the reader's expectations. About this latter kind, Fitzgerald parenthetically remarked, "It'd be better for me if I could do pattern stories, but the pencil just goes dead on me."

In the forty-odd years since the publication of his last magazine story, careful readers of Fitzgerald have noticed that, despite his disclaimer, his pencil had often "gone dead" on him; that the larger portion of his short fiction exhibits a small amount of innovation in either form or substance. Clearly he could "do pattern stories," and did. In the same letter he says, "I wish I could think of a line of stories like the Josephine or Basil ones which could go faster & pay $3000." Two of the stories in the Basil and Josephine series, **"The Freshest Boy"** and **"A Nice Quiet Place,"** along with twelve more of his short stories, are noted as much for form as for their substance; all are ostensibly structured according to a conventional Five-Act dramatic model. They generally reflect the time-honored Freytag structural pattern of Exposition, Rising Action, Crisis or Climax, Falling Action, and Resolution or Denouement; but they are much freer in movement and not bound to a strict correspondence between their sections and the Freytag divisions. Fitzgerald usually spends a great deal more time and a greater number of sections on the rising action of his stories, often waiting until late in the fourth or fifth section before bringing the conflict to a climax. After that critical moment, when either the hero's fortunes or personality changes directions, the story races through the falling action and denouement.

In most of these stories, the hero or heroine reaches a psychological or moral nadir, or discovers a significant truth near the end of the fourth section. The last section then commonly resolves the plot by the use of a *dues ex machina,* a surprise, a trick reversal, or a further ironic discovery. Yet, although most of the plots, and the structures that advance the plots, seem contrived and artificial, nearly all of them exhibit a kind of logic or an appropriate motivation. Seldom does the protagonist step too far beyond the limits of probability and perform an action or say a word inappropriate to his or her character.

Judicious readers consign most of these five-act stories to a lower place in his canon; Fitzgerald himself recognized the weakness of five of them: " . . . Each story contains some special fault—sentimentality, faulty construction, confusing change of pace—or else was too obviously made for the trade." Even though they inhabit the lower regions, Mathew Bruccoli gives them a fitting and reasoned epitaph: "Even his weak stories are redeemed by glimpses of what can be conveniently called 'the Fitzgerald touch'—wit, sharp observations, dazzling descriptions, or the felt emotion. . . . Above all, Fitzgerald's style shines through: the colors and rhythms of his prose."

Three of the Five-Act stories **"Absolution," "The Freshest Boy,"** and **"Babylon Revisited,"** which on the surface follow the predictable and contrived pattern of the others, are another matter altogether. They exhibit that "special emotion" and "special experience" that characterize his best efforts in the novels, and they admirably realize Fitzgerald's "conception" in both form and substance. (pp. 95-6)

In [Fitzgerald's] best Five-Act stories, there are two discrete motions that flow along at their own pace and in their own direction yet in close harmony: an external movement of the central action; and an internal rhythm of the hero. To manage these motions, which support and fulfill each other, Fitzgerald has created two structures: a dramatic superstructure of five parts which develops the cause-and-effect relationships in the action; and a deep structure, whose phases vary from story to story, which traces the hero's psychological state as he responds to the action. The superstructure certifies the dramatic probability of the action; the deep structure verifies the psychological probability of the hero's response. In addition, just as Fitzgerald has indicated the pattern of the superstructure by dividing the movement of the action into five sections, he has suggested the pattern of the deep structure by providing a metaphor which informs the hero's psychological motion. In these three stories, the structural metaphor appears at a critical moment, just before the climax; and not only does it signal the impending crisis, it also resonates throughout the story's deep structure to motivate and to clarify the true nature of the crisis. (pp. 96-7)

The superstructure created by Fitzgerald to carry the action of **"Absolution"** seems at first to deserve the criticism directed at it. In his study of this short story John Higgins avers that despite the story's standing "among Fitzgerald's major achievement in the genre," the balance of the story is diminished somewhat by a major structural flaw: a "split character focus" in the story. Such an opinion is logical if it grows out of a conviction that Rudolph is more than a general prototype of Gatsby—that he *becomes* Jimmy Gatz and then Jay Gatsby himself. If this view of the necessary connection between **"Absolution"** and *The Great Gatsby* controls an analysis of the structure, then Father Schwartz, who *must* be the antagonist in the conflict, receives too much attention. As a result, the importance of Rudolph's role as the protagonist is lessened. Undeniably, the framing sections set in the priest's rectory do focus on Schwartz, and the remainder of

the plot does focus on Rudolph. With his eye on the *coda* that closes the story, Higgins concludes, "The last paragraph, which describes the sensuous Swede girls and echoes the opening scene, diverts the reader's attention from Rudolph to the priest." Therefore the story is flawed in its structure. A careful examination of the structural metaphor of **"Absolution"** suggests that indeed there is a shift in focus, but that shift is not a flaw nor a weakness but a virtue and a strength.

The structural metaphor in **"Absolution"** appears in the Latin phrase which serves as a headnote to Section V: *"Sagitta Volante in Dei."* Fitzgerald excerpted the phrase from Psalm 90 in the Vulgate, and in the process, metathesized the last word of the phrase from *"die"* to *"Dei."* There is no certain way of knowing whether the metathesis was deliberate or accidental, for all of the extant versions of the story exhibit the same transformation. From what is known of Fitzgerald's casual attention to the rules of spelling, and especially his habit of writing "etc." as "ect.," it seems reasonable to assume that the error was accidental. If the assumption is correct, then the phrase should be translated, "Arrows flying by day," rather than "Arrows flying to God." Moreover, some twenty years after the composition of **"Absolution"** Fitzgerald repeats the phrase, correctly, in "Sleeping and Waking": *"Scuto circumdabit te veritas eius: non timebis a timore nocturno, a sagitta volante in die, a negotio perambulante in tenebris"* ("His faith will surround you as a shield; you will not fear the terror of the night, nor the arrows flying by day, nor the trouble moving about in the darkness"). The extended quotation from the essay suggests that Fitzgerald knew the Psalm in its entirety, and selected the middle verses to fit his particular needs at the time of composition. In "Sleeping and Waking" the quotation is used to describe a "sinister, ever widening interval" between the "first sweet sleep of night," and the last deep sleep of the morning.

The headnote then seems to apply immediately to Father Schwartz: of all the characters in the story, he is the most likely to know the phrase. Psalm 90 frequently appears in the breviary from which, according to ecclesiastical law, he must read daily, and it has a prominent place in the Compline service for Sundays. Moreover, the "sinister" and fearful aspects of the quotation are reflected in both the first and last sections of the story, where the priest, a depressed and frightened creature, is brought to the edge of madness by the assault of the "heat and sweat and life" of the world.

In Section I Father Schwartz's senses are under continuing attack by the world outside his rectory windows. He hears the "shrill laughter" of the Swedish girls; he sees the "yellow lights" and "gleaming" nickel taps in the drugstore; he smells the sweet "cheap toilet soap" that floats upward "like incense toward the summer moon." Under such a constant barrage of the noises and smells and sights of the daylight world, he tries to escape: often by a prayer for darkness to come to quiet the laughter; sometimes, when he is caught out in the open between the church and his rectory, by a detour around the lights and the smell of soap emanating from the drugstore. But there is no escape; he is trapped in his room with the world outside full of heat and life and terror. Even his thoughts are imprisoned in "grotesque labyrinths" from which there is no escape from "the unavoidable sun." By the end of the first two paragraphs of the story, Father Schwartz has "reached the point where the mind runs down like an old clock."

When he comes into focus again in Section V, the priest's de-

Zelda and Frances Scott (Scottie) Fitzgerald, who was born October 26, 1921.

pressive condition seems not to have undergone any great obvious change during Rudolph's confession. The same "cold watery eyes" are fixed upon the same carpet pattern of lifeless figures of "flat bloomless vines and the pale echoes of flowers"—echoing, ironically, the outside world with its ripening and wind-blown wheat, golden in the afternoon sun. Yet he seems to be in the manic phase of his psychosis, for he begins to hallucinate and to watch his rosary beads change into evil snakes and crawl about on the green felt of his table. He struggles out of his hallucination and startles Rudolph with a peculiar non-sequitur that in some ways is an image of the Communion of Saints: "When a lot of people get together in the best places things go glimmering." (pp. 97-8)

Later in the fifth section, with his eyes "dried out and hot," signifying an increasingly desperate deterioration in his condition, Father Schwartz envisions a seductive yet pernicious world. It is an amusement park filled with the sights, sounds, and smells of life. He says, "You'll see a big wheel made of lights turning in the air. . . . " There will be the sounds of a "band playing somewhere," and the "smell of peanuts." But the priest warns Rudolph, "Don't get up close, because if you do you'll only feel the heat and the sweat and the life." This admonition has already been given to Rudolph in another form during the boy's first confession in Section II: "Don't you know, my child, that you should avoid the occasions of sin as well as the sin itself?" There can be no clearer statement of the priest's fear of life than this. To him, all the world is an occasion of sin. Thus, in his scrupulous and fearful world, the laughter of the Swedish girls, and the gleaming

nickel taps of the soda fountain, and the sweet incense of the soap are the "arrows flying by day" into the very heart of Father Schwartz. The Ferris wheel and the band and the peanuts become the "terrors of the night."

Certainly there are enough associations between Father Schwartz and the headnote to clarify his psychological state; but the metaphor can also be seen as an index of Rudolph's interior life. Not that the boy is another example of the fear of life, for his personality and actions described in the early sections put him in direct conflict with the priest. But even though the two are in conflict and, on some levels, obvious foils for each other, by the end of Section IV they have come into a condition of psychological and spiritual parity.

The fundamental nature of this parity is only suggested in Section I. Father Schwartz's state of depression and the fears that have caused it are already at a critical stage before Rudolph is ushered into the room. They are immediately locked together by their eyes: the priest, with his "cold watery eyes," stares into Rudolph's "enormous, staccato eyes, lit with gleaming points of cobalt light." The contrast is as obvious as the connection. The two disparate characters are more firmly joined when the priest, on the margin of a breakdown from his terrors, sees that the boy is in a similar "state of abject fear." Rudolph intimates the cause of his fear when he confesses "in a despairing whisper" that he has committed a "terrible sin": a sin worse than impurity, worse than murder. Despite their obvious differences in age, experience, and knowledge; despite the symbolic contrast between the gloomy Father Schwartz, whose very name in German means "darkness," and the beautiful boy who sits in the patch of sunlight, the two protagonists of the story converge on several levels. The priest is afraid of life; and Rudolph is fearful of the consequences of his undescribed "terrible sin"; the priest is isolated from God, unable to achieve a "mystical union with our Lord"; and the boy in his sinning has turned away from God. Yet, although they converge in this section, they have not merged in their parity. The priest's psychological and spiritual state is almost terminal, whereas the state of Rudolph's soul is only implied. It is the function of the middle sections to fulfill the implications.

The middle flashback sections (II-IV), wherein Rudolph comes into prime focus, describe his inevitable fall from a state of grace to mortal sin. The central action of each section is Rudolph's proud and sinful rebellion against a figure of authority, against a father. The rebellion always takes place in the home of the particular father against whom Rudolph rebels, and it is always followed by an imaginative attempt to escape, not the guilt, but the consequences of the rebellion. These escape attempts, and the fear that prompts them, lead inexorably to another graver sinful act. The moral tangle continues until Rudolph commits a sacrilegious communion near the end of Section IV. (pp. 98-100)

[In] Section IV, [Rudolph's] moral state and his psychological condition grow critical. Forced to attend confession again, he lies to spite his father, and in so doing steps a bit deeper into sin. His initial response is one of "maudlin exultation." But as the time to take communion approaches, he feels that "there was no reason why God should not stop his heart." The next paragraph shows his growing fear not only of death, but of death by execution. As he kneels at the communion rail waiting for the host, "a cold sweat broke out on his forehead . . . and with gathering nausea Rudolph felt his heart valves weakening." Just before he receives the host, he bows his head, not in adoration but in fearful expectation of the worst; and in that position, he "waited for the blow." The last image of Section IV suggests the completeness of Rudolph's isolation from God, and from everyone else. As the other communicants leave the communion rail they are "alone with God." But Rudolph "was alone with himself, drenched with perspiration and deep in mortal sin." In that state he feels like a fallen angel walking back to his pew on his "cloven hoofs."

The nature of his "terrible sin" and his "abject fear" is now certain. His fears and his spiritual condition are now on a par with Father Schwartz's. The two troubled souls, priest and boy, Father and son, are brought together by their fears. The Father fears life and the boy fears death. Both seek help and protection from each other; both require absolution. At the moment of the climax their association is more of a sterile symbiosis, wherein two dissimilar souls feed off each other, yet derive little spiritual benefit from their union. It is Rudolph's eyes like "blue stones" and lashes that spray out "like flower petals" that remind the priest of the arrows that fly by day and push him into his spiral toward unconsciousness; it is the priest's mad visions and his subsequent collapse that send Rudolph fleeing from the Church. They have come together seeking forgiveness, but have been denied.

Despite this convergence, which fulfills the implications of the structural metaphor, their fears are not sufficient motivation for the action that follows. The essential action of the climax to which these kindred souls have been brought concerns the necessary elements in the Sacrament of Penance: confession, contrition, absolution—and a sin. But clearly, fear is not a sin. Father Schwartz's avoidance of the "heat and sweat" of life is not *sui generis* a sinful act. And even though his imagination has turned him into a devil, Rudolph has confessed his lies and sacrileges to the priest, and has even calmed down. Thus it is not fear that causes their exchange of roles and eventual separation; it is their sin. The headnote suggests the nature of their sin: they both exhibit signs of an imperfect faith; one which denies the dual nature of Christ.

The essential thrust of Psalm 90 is that the man who trusts in God, who *"habitat in adjutorio Altissimus"* ("he dwells in the shelter of the Almighty"), will receive several benefits as a result of his faith. These benefits, suggested in a series of metaphors in the first thirteen verses of the Psalm, promise protection, defense, and refuge from all the world's enmity. In the last three verses, God himself speaks and promises to protect, deliver and glorify the believer: *"Quoniam in me speravit, liberabo eum; protegam eum, quoniam cognovit me"* ("Because he has hoped in me, I will free him; I will protect him, because he has known my name"). Of special significance to the climax of **"Absolution"** is God's vow, *"Clamabit ad me, et ego exaudiam eum; cum ipso sum in tribulatione"* ("He calls out to me, and I will hear him; I will be with him in his tribulation").

By the end of the first paragraph of Section V, it is clear that Rudolph has called upon the Lord. He has confessed his sin, and has grown less fearful; he even feels a sense of security in "God's shelter" because the representative of God is with him: "He knew that as long as he was in the room with this priest God would not stop his heart." As it turns out, this faith is imperfect, for God's representative is too much concerned with his own problems to help Rudolph. At the end of the story, Rudolph is left alone with only his imagination

as a refuge against the spiritual death he fears, and he runs "in panic" away from the rectory, the bogus shelter of God.

Father Schwartz also calls upon the Lord in Section V. Soon after his vision of the amusement park, and after the "horror" of his realization "entered suddenly at the open window," the priest "collapsed precipitously down on his knees." In at least the position, if not the attitude of prayer and supplication, he cries out, "Oh my God!" This may be a cry of despair; but it could also be a call for help. His words are identical to the first three words of the *Confiteor;* and they are the same words that Basil recited "meaninglessly" after his first confession. Like Rudolph's, his act of contrition, his call to the Lord in time of grave peril, may very well not be answered—it may be voiced too late in a life characterized by an imperfect faith.

Earlier, in an attempt to "fix" Rudolph's guilt and absolve him, Father Schwartz says, "Apostasy implies an absolute damnation only on the supposition of a previous perfect faith." Undeniably, the critical problem in the spiritual lives of both protagonists is that neither one can be supposed to have a perfect faith. The two fundamental dogmas of the Catholic faith which both profess are the Trinity, which proves the divinity of Christ, and the Incarnation, which accomplishes His humanity. As Aquinas states, *"Duo nobis credenda proponuntur: occultum Divinitas . . . et mysterium humanitatis Christi"* ("Two things are proposed for believing: the secret of the Divinity and the mystery of the humanity of Christ"). Instead of dwelling in the shelter of the Almighty, and of believing in His mercy and His humanity, Father Schwartz has retreated to his dark and dingy room, crossed the street to avoid the sweet smells, and turned his eyes away from the sights of a world filled with warmth and love. In emphasizing the justice and vengeance of God the Father because of his fear, he has denied the mercy and humanity of the Son of God, the Christ he has vowed to serve.

Rudolph, whose instruction in the faith of his fathers has been in the hands of Father Schwartz, exhibits the same kind of exaggerated insistence on the vengeance of God. It is clear throughout the scenes dealing with his confessions and his sins that he has misunderstood the true nature of the Sacrament of Penance and the real meaning of Absolution. In Section V, after he hears the priest's description of the amusement park, he mistakenly feels that "there was something ineffably gorgeous somewhere that had nothing to do with God." In essence, he has denied the omnipresence of God, and thus in a sense, the divinity of God. Obviously, Father Schwartz has failed twice to give Rudolph the proper instruction in the faith; he has not fulfilled his duty as a pastor, to lead men to a perfect faith.

Thus the deep structure informed by the headnote has carried two protagonists to an unbearably tense moment in their spiritual and psychological development. Their imperfect faith cannot protect them from each other nor from the debilitating effects of their fears. They can only call out to the wrong God, as does Rudolph, or call out too late, as does Father Schwartz. The ultimate condition of their souls is not certain, but is certainly suggested in the story's last paragraph.

The coda implies in its imagery the futility and waste in a life controlled by an imperfect faith. The crisis in faith of both heroes, identical in design and equal in psychological intensity, has arrived at the turning point in the confinement of the priest's room: a dingy, haunted, stale and lifeless box. But outside, the "hot fertile life" goes on as indifferent to the fearful world of Father Schwartz as it is to the imaginative, almost Byronic world of Rudolph. In its warmth and life, and in its fluid and natural movement, the coda is a remarkable comment on the constricted and barren scene of two souls who, because of the imperfect faith, failed to find the refuge and comfort they sought. (pp. 100-02)

Unlike **"Absolution," "The Freshest Boy"** moves easily and naturally through its Five-Act superstructure. The introductory section, or the exposition, clearly indicates the protagonist, his special romantic personality, and his impending conflicts. Sections II and III move the protagonist down the vortex of unpopularity and isolation until at the end of Section III, he is alone in his room, rejected by his school masters and classmates, and in the deepest despondency of his young life. The climactic Section IV traces his journey to New York, where he considers fleeing his difficulties at St. Regis school, and then moves to his epiphany wherein he discovers an important truth about life and gets "wise" to himself. After his discovery Basil decides against flight and makes his first unselfish motion toward another human being. Section V, the denouement, quickly describes his attempts to act according to his new-found wisdom, and ends with a reward for his endeavors. There are no hitches, no breaks, and no delays in Basil's fall and rise. There is a clear line of motivation and a careful and trenchant system of correspondences that result in a tight unity in the superstructure. This unity can be seen in Section IV as Fitzgerald develops an ironic analogy between the world of romantic illusions and reality.

In this climactic section, Basil really attends two three-act plays: the romantic musical comedy, "The Quaker Girl," which traces the separation and reunion of two lovers; and the real-life drama which describes the union and separation of Ted Fay and his love, the heroine of "The Quaker Girl." (p. 103)

Fitzgerald states immediately prior to Act I of the cited comedy that the "program itself had a curious sacredness—a prototype of the thing itself." As the program is the prototype of the play, the play is an ironic prototype of the Ted Fay-Jerry relationship. And the play can also be seen as a prototype of the story. In a sense, as Basil discovers the truth about life after watching the two three-act plays, the reader discovers the truth about Basil, after watching him move through the three acts of his life at St. Regis.

Somewhat like an overture, which provides a preview of the major songs to be heard later in the play, and even more like a program that lists the cast and generally describes the structure of the play, the expository section forshadows the significant action of the story to follow. It is a self-contained unit of three interrelated movements: it begins with a daydream and ends with a daydream; sandwiched in between the two dreams is a real-world struggle between two young boys, opposite in character, feelings, and knowledge. The first dream characterizes Basil's romantic hopes; the interlude suggests the problem that dashes these hopes; and the final dream of athletic glory foreshadows Basil's victory over his problems.

The action of the first daydream takes place in a Broadway restaurant filled with a "brilliant and mysterious group of society people," especially a girl with "dark hair and dark tragic eyes" who wears French perfume. In the guise of the mysterious Shadow, Basil enters the room with gun in hand, glances around, announces his identity, and, "like a flash, turns and goes into the night." Basil's dream then dissolves

into the reality of Lewis Crum, Basil's companion on the train ride to St. Regis. It is Lewis who establishes the central conflict of the story, the struggle between Basil's "freshness" and the rest of the boarding school world. After some argument started over Basil's boast of playing football for St. Regis, Lewis prophesies, "You wait! They'll take all that freshness out of you." Basil escapes from Lewis's "dismal presence" by reentering the dream world. However, the setting for this final dream of Act I is the playing field at St. Regis. Basil is called from the bench with two minutes to play and his team down by three points. "Lee!" his coach calls, "It all depends on you now." As his signal is called by the quarterback, Basil awakens, and, anxious for the glory he is sure to come, he says, "I wish we'd get there before tomorrow." All three of these episodes, the two dreams and the real world interlude, will reappear in an altered, significant, but ironic form in the action that follows.

The setting and actions and characters of the first act of "The Quaker Girl" now begin to reverberate through Sections II and III of the story. There is no more appropriate setting for the "freshest boy" from the Midwest than a "village green," especially when his ignorance of the ways of boarding school, and his annoying personality are so aptly portrayed in Section II. (pp. 104-05)

Section II is a long and realistic description of Basil's difficulties at school and his descent into loneliness. As he searches for companions to travel with him to New York, he meets rejection at every turn. (p. 105)

The separation and sadness of the play's first act are reflected in an even more melodramatic fashion in Section III. Unable to find even one student to accompany him, Basil returns disconsolately to his room. He spends his time trying to choose his favorite pin-up from a package of eight Harrison Fisher photographs. After some listless deliberation, his eyes are finally drawn to "Babette, a dark little violet-eyed beauty," who seems more romantic and mysterious than all the others. While Basil sobs into his pillow, and flails away at those who have rejected him, Treadway enters the room and begins to pack his belongings. When questioned, Treadway announces, "I'm moving in with Wales," takes a last look about the room's "new barrenness," and leaves. This last blow, the loss of his roommate to his arch enemy, evokes a mournful, "Poor little Babette! Poor little Babette!" All alone at the nadir of his life, he seeks the comfort and companionship of a glossy reproduction of a coquettish French girl, whose eyes and hair and romantic nature are remarkably like the dark-haired girl of the opening daydream. The high spirits and romantic hopes embodied in the first section are now in ruins at the end of the third.

Act II of the musical comedy continues to be an analogue of Basil's life in Section IV. The heroine of the play has left the village and has come to New York, to the "Foyer of the Hotel Astor." She has become an overnight sensation, and because of her unsophisticated background, she is caught up in a kind of life style very different from and more exciting than her former way of life. Entranced by her new life and her stardom, she spurns her village lover, and "dances wildly" with her new lover. But at the end of the act, the romantic strains of her theme song, so "poignant and aching," signal a forthcoming change in the direction of her life as they catch her again "like a leaf helpless in the wind" and carry her into—Act III. Similarly, Basil has escaped the "dismal and dreary round of school," and traveled to New York. He also finds himself in the foyer, or on the threshold, of a new, liberating experience. His mother's letter affords him a real opportunity to escape from school and flee to Europe: "Almost strangling with happiness," he turns his back on school, crying out, " 'No more St. Regis!' " Now Doctor Bacon and Mr. Rooney and Brick Wales and Fat Gaspar are only "impotent shadows in the stationary world that he was sliding away from, sliding past, waving his hand." But after his epiphany, wherein he loses his "freshness" and "gets wise" to himself, he realizes that he will not go to Europe, but will return to school—in Section V.

Basil now is in the final act of his life's story at St. Regis; and Act III of "The Quaker Girl" is an equivalent figure of that story. The program is now fulfilled: the heroine and her lover are quickly reunited on the roof garden (the city's echo of a village green); they sing "one lovely plaintive duet"; and only the passage of time is necessary to realize the "promise of felicity" in the anachronistic "bright tropical sky." In the corresponding last section of the story, Basil returns to school, armed with new knowledge and with a renewed commitment to his three-act dream of "the conquest of the successive worlds of school, college and New York." He makes "numberless new starts" and fails. But buoyed up by his recollections of the trip to New York, he survives the winter of his discontent. Eventually he is reunited with Fat Gaspar and the others; even the masters and the small boys who were first to move away from him now move closer. His new life at school has not been as felicitous as the musical promised, but one February afternoon, "a great thing happened"; which ironically recalls both Act III of the play and Section I of the story.

This "great thing" is nothing more than a "poor makeshift" of a nickname bestowed on him by his enemy, Brick Wales. It is a "poor makeshift" because Wales is "unconscious that he had done anything in particular." But to Basil it is a signal of his acceptance and the proof that he is finally reunited with all of those from whom he has been separated. The calling out of his nick-name, "Lee-y!" a name which "could scarcely be pronounced," is a far cry from a "lovely plaintive duet"; but it is better than "Bossy." The irony expands even further when the final dream of Section I is recalled. Before Basil's "play" begins, he dreams of being called ("Lee!") by his coach to rescue the varsity football team from defeat in the big game of the year. As his "comedy" comes to its conclusion, Basil is playing second-string basketball during a scrimmage and is called ("Lee-y!") by Brick Wales, who only wants the ball himself—and Basil makes a "poor pass." To a boy whose fictional life has moved in five sections, but whose romantic interior life has been divided according to the three acts of a musical comedy, Basil's response is indeed "overly dramatic," but eminently "plausible" and well-motivated. The motivation is further enhanced by a final correspondence. Basil takes his unpronounceable nickname "to bed with him that night," and holds it close "happily to the last" as he falls "easily to sleep." In the last scene of Section III he has also gone to bed with a name; but "Babette" was the name he had for comfort in his loneliest hours. Thus Sections I, III, and V are tied together: the imagined glory of I has yielded to the despair of III and has been ironically fulfilled in V.

In **"The Freshest Boy,"** Fitzgerald has cleverly created two structures to describe Basil's progress through his first year of school: a superstructure which defines the external action

of Basil's getting "wise to himself"; and a deeper structure which clarifies the boy's interior life—a life so moved by imagination and romance that Basil does not clearly "understand all he has heard." Basil's romantic response to the "poor makeshift" world of reality suggests that he has grown in knowledge, but not in wisdom. But of course, **"The Freshest Boy"** is only the first act in Basil's three-act comedy of "school, college and New York."

"Babylon Revisited" has deservedly received more critical attention and praise than any other Fitzgerald short story, with most commentators expressing admiration for its flawless blend of a tight, balanced structure and a significant theme. (pp. 106-07)

Even though some disagree with Seymour Gross's interpretation of the ultimate meaning of the story, his reading of **"Babylon Revisited"** remains the most judicious and detailed appraisal of the relationships between the structure and the theme—so detailed that the following examination of the deep structure and the structural metaphor will be but a fine-tuning of his argument and a moderation of his gloomy interpretation. (p. 108)

As in **"The Freshest Boy,"** the structural metaphor in **"Babylon Revisited,"** to be found immediately prior to the climax, informs both the superstructure and the deep structure. At the end of Section III, after Marion has agreed to relinquish her custody of Honoria, Charlie returns to his rooms in an "exultant" state of mind. But immediately, he discovers that he cannot sleep, because the "image of Helen haunted him." He begins to review their stormy relationship, and especially the particulars of the night when he, in a pique of jealous anger, locked her out in the snow. He then recalls the aftermath and all its horrors, the superficial "reconciliation," and the eventual death of his wife—"martyrdom," as Marion would have it. The memories are so strong and become so real that Charlie imagines that Helen talks to him. She reassures him that she also wants him to have custody of Honoria, and she praises him for his reformation. Then she says a "lot of other things—friendly things—but she was in a swing in a white dress, and swinging faster and faster all the time, so that at the end he could not hear clearly all that she said." This image of Helen in the swing emanates throughout the story's superstructure. Just as the dream of his dead wife in a white dress (suggestive of the innocent past of long ago) swings into his mind to restrain his "exultation," so the sins of the past, in the shape and form of Lorraine and Duncan, will appear in Section IV to dash his hopes for the custody of Honoria. Similarly, the action of the swing reflects the pacing of the action in the climactic section: its faster and faster movement implies the quick arrival and departure of Lorraine and Duncan, Marion's abrupt change of heart, and the sudden reversal of Charlie's fortunes.

The metaphor with its back and forth motion not only serves to describe and motivate the climax, but also marks the progress of the action which precedes and follows the climax. From the beginning to the end, the plot is characterized by a series of alternating currents from the past to the present. . . . Clearly, every contact with the past seems to dampen Charlie's spirits or to cloud his expectations, or to defeat his hopes. Just as clearly, the swing functions as a metaphor of the intrusion of the past and reinforces the theme of man's inability to escape the consequences of his past behavior. Furthermore, because of its insistent continual motion, the metaphor seems to suggest that as long as Charlie's life continues, he will, like Sisyphus, almost reach the moment of joy; but something out of the past will turn him away. (pp. 108-09)

According to the physics of swinging, there is a state of near-equivalence between the terminus of the forward motion and the terminus of the rearward motion. But if the swing must rely on its own momentum, the laws of gravity demand that the terminus of the succeeding motion be lower than the terminus of the preceding motion. There is a similiar "balance" in the heights and depths of Charlie's emotional responses to the actions that elicit these responses. In a sense, the physical laws that control the swing are transformed into the metaphysical and ethical laws that govern Charlie's feelings. Thus for every action in the plot, there is Charlie's less-than-equal reaction—and never any overreaction. Unlike the reactions of every other character in the story, Charlie's are always under control. He may not be able to control the events of his life, but he can and does control his reactions. As he states in Section III while justifying his daily drink, "It's a sort of stunt I set myself. It keeps the matter in proportion."

Throughout the difficult inquisition in Section III, Charlie consciously restrains his natural desires to match the venom of Marion's accusations. "Keep your temper," he tells himself after discovering that he "would take a beating." When Marion recalls the morning after he had locked his wife out in the snow, Charlie "wanted to launch out into a long expostulation," but he doesn't. Later, he becomes "increasingly alarmed" because he feared for Honoria if she remained in the "atmosphere" of Marion's hostility. But "he pulled his temper down out of his face and shut it up inside him. . . . " Near the end of Section III, Marion, eaten up by her prejudice against him and her inescapable memories of her sister's death, cries out, "How much you were responsible for Helen's death I don't know." Even in this desperate moment, as he feels a "current of agony" surge through him, he "hung on to himself" and restrained his emotions—he kept "the matter in proportion." Even Marion realizes the extent of his mastery over himself: "She saw him plainly and she knew he had somehow arrived at control over the situation." In essence, by restraining his reactions, Charlie makes Marion's actions seem all the more out of control. Thus, by being more controlled and reasonable, Charlie proves his reformation and achieves a victory over Marion. For every swing of Marion's argument, Charlie swings back with a controlled response. (pp. 109-10)

It is this moderation and control that characterizes Charlie's response to the devastating swing of the past that squashes his hopes for reunion with Honoria. The climax brings into clear focus the essential nature of his "character," and his mastery over his emotions. After Lorraine and Duncan materialize, Charlie's attempts to control the situation prove fruitless. At first he was "astounded," then "anxious and at a loss." Later he approaches them "as if to force them backward down the corridor," back into the past. But the momentum of their untimely visit can't be stopped; and in their swinging, they figuratively knock him out of the way: Marion changes her mind and therefore Charlie's future. His last lines in the section show the completeness of his self-control. They are peculiarly measured and restrained, not at all the farewell speech of a man who feels that he has lost everything he has ever wanted. His farewell to his daughter, "Good night, sweetheart," echoes Horatio's farewell to Hamlet; but Charlie broadens his farewell in order to lessen the possible tragic overtones: "Trying to make his voice more tender, trying to conciliate something, 'Good night, dear children.' " Undeniably, the action of the climax proves that even a man of strong character cannot control the actions and feelings of others, nor the strange, almost accidental swing of fortune; but, Charlie's reactions prove that a man who has mastery over his emotions and can control himself has a sense of integrity and honor that cannot be made hostage to the quirks of fate and the meanness of others.

In the first three sections of the story, Charlie's tactics of control and his measured responses to the actions of others accomplished their purpose. As Marion realized in Section III, Charlie is in control of the situation, and is on the point of reclaiming his daughter and redeeming his honor. But as the events of the climax show, Charlie's tactics are not enough. But by this time, his self-control is no longer just a tactic; it is clearly a habitual ethical strategy based on a strong belief in the "eternally valuable element," character. By the end of the story, he realizes that "there was nothing he could do" about the remote and recent past, nor about the future: he is neither a pessimist nor an optimist, but a realist. From the beginning, he has known that he wanted Honoria, and in Section III, "He was sure now that Lincoln Peters wanted him to have his child." Looking back on his experience he also realizes that Marion has yielded before, and may very well yield again. Finally, as he sits in the Ritz bar considering his victories and defeats, he becomes "absolutely sure Helen wouldn't have wanted him to be so alone." All of his experiences during the last few days in Paris suggest to him that it is only a matter of time, perhaps Lincoln's "six months," before the swing of the past will have lost its momentum.

A large measure of the success of **"Absolution," "The Freshest Boy,"** and **"Babylon Revisited"** depends on Fitzgerald's ability to portray accurately and convincingly the inner life of the characters who inhabit the stories. He has drawn, as it were, a believable picture of souls in motion. To control this motion, he has created a deep structure which traces the characters' most profound thoughts and emotions; and in these stories, he has provided a map, the structural metaphor, so that the reader may follow the motion of these souls. Using this map, the careful reader will be able to discover and feel that "special emotion" and "special experience" that is at the heart of the stories and at the center of Fitzgerald's art. (pp. 110-11)

William J. Brondell, "Structural Metaphors in Fitzgerald's Short Fiction," in Kansas Quarterly, *Vol. 14, No. 2, Spring, 1982, pp. 95-112.*

PETER WOLFE (essay date 1982)

[*Wolfe is an American educator who has published books on Iris Murdoch, Rebecca West, John Fowles, Jean Rhys, and others. In the following excerpt, taken from* The Short Stories of F. Scott Fitzgerald: New Approaches in Criticism, *a collection of twenty-two original essays by various critics covering many aspects of Fitzgerald's short fiction, Wolfe presents "The Rich Boy" as "a parable of escapist psychology" in which Fitzgerald dramatizes the effects of a privileged life on his protagonist, Anson Hunter.*]

The third paragraph of **"The Rich Boy"** (1926) begins with Fitzgerald's most famous pronouncement: "Let me tell you about the very rich. They are different from you and me." Through the career of the story's main character, Anson

Hunter of New York City, Fitzgerald spells out the difference that both charmed and bedeviled him throughout his adult life: the rich believe that the prizes they possess and enjoy early are theirs by right. No process of logic has convinced Anson Hunter of his superiority. Privilege has accompanied him from the start; he has never doubted his claim to it, nor will he let it go away. But what does it consist of? And what price must he pay for it?

A rarely challenged truism of our consumer-industrial urban state decrees that riches buy happiness. To accept this nostrum is to invite its corollary. If the rich man basks in happiness, then the rich boy is twice blessed; for he can enjoy the privileges that money brings without having to justify himself. He can make his own rules. Because the middle-class virtue of moral consistency doesn't apply to him, he can carouse all night, go home for a cold shower and a change of clothes, and then teach Sunday school with stony-jawed piety. Time has given him opportunities to develop his foibles and eccentricities. No wonder Paula Legendre, the only woman Hunter ever loved, thinks of him as a dual personality. Wearing the stripes of the dissolute and the conservative, he alternates recklessness and control.

At a deeper level, his princely code rules out adult actions like getting married or even acting decently and responsibly in personal relationships. Hunter's life is a calculated smash-and-grab raid on the hearts of others. In his younger and more vulnerable years, he had everything he wanted. Freed from the middle-class urge to get ahead, he now summons all the force of his forceful personality to keep and even build on his advantage. The effort entails denying the reality of other persons as independent centers of significance. After his military discharge removes the barrier of distance between him and Paula, he doesn't know how to act with her, his confusion stemming from a need to protect himself. His preference for conducting intimacies through the mail rather than in person conveys his fear of commitment. The first-hand and the immediate threaten him. Only a boy, he hasn't learned to share. He deems it safer to pine for someone he can't have than to work at a relationship with somebody available and at hand. As can be expected, Paula's value for him increases as she moves away from him. By stages, their broken romance, her marriage, and finally her death enrich the rosy hues of an attachment whose main ingredient consists of apartness rather than union. Maintaining his identity as rich young prince always wins his first priority. Thus every stage of his adult life (we know him from ages twenty-one to thirty) shows Hunter displaying photographs taken at an earlier time and living emotionally through them.

Hugging a reconstructed, idealized past denies his truest self in other ways, too. In what is perhaps a legacy from his favorite writer Keats, the Fitzgerald of **"The Rich Boy"** believes that a romantic relationship can attain a flame-tip of psychic intensity, during which the emotion-charged lovers both see that the moment has come for a declaration of mutual commitment. Fitzgerald also believes that if the moment isn't seized and shared, it will probably vanish forever. Anson Hunter attains this sort of romantic crescendo with Dolly Karger in Port Washington, Long Island, when a glimpse at Paula Legendre's picture cools his ardor and sends him from Dolly's bedroom with a nasty remark. (A more vibrant example of the crescendo, or shared epiphany, occurred a few years earlier when he visited Paula in Florida, presumably to propose marriage.) Looking at Paula's picture while embrac-

ing Dolly gives him the courage to do what he has wanted to do all along. His conduct with both women reflects both the impudence and the arrogance of power. The interlude with Paula also shows that a calculating lover is no lover at all. His need for her, great as it is, falls short of his need to sustain his princely self-image. Shrinking from a marriage proposal he knows will be accepted, he tries instead to impose a less binding tie:

> They embraced recklessly, passionately. . . . Then Paula drew back her face to let his lips say what she wanted to hear—she could feel the words forming as they kissed again. . . . Again she broke away, listening, but as he pulled her close once more she realized that he said nothing. . . . Humbly, obediently, her emotions yielded to him and the tears streamed down her face, but her heart kept on crying: "Ask me—oh, Anson, dearest, ask me!"
> "Paula. . . . *Paula!*"
> The words wrung her heart like hands, and Anson, feeling her tremble, knew that emotion was enough. He need say no more, commit their destinies to no practical enigma. . . .
> He had forgotten that Paula too was worn away inside with the strain of three years. Her mood passed forever in the night.

As her passing mood shows, Paula won't play by his rules. Like Dolly after her, she recovers from her setback, outgrows him, and marries another man when Hunter squanders their moment of deep physical and psychic communion. That she has already outpaced him shows in the moral gamble she took for his sake: Paula risked losing Lowell Thayer, her future husband, who was playing bridge with her and Hunter at the time she left the table without excusing herself to join Hunter for a walk on the moonlit beach. Such spontaneity and moral courage discomfits Hunter, with his meager powers of commitment. Predictably, he goes back to New York the very next morning.

This haste typifies him. If the American South represents softness and drowsy, easygoing charm for Fitzgerald, then Hunter has the energy, aggressiveness, and determination of the practical-minded industrial North. No brooding isolato he. Even though responsibility and authority are thrust upon him by the accident of being the eldest of six children whose millionaire parents both die before he is thirty, he warms to the challenge. His set ideas about right and wrong banish any pangs of self-doubt. These ideas he applies to others as strictly as to himself. When Dolly Karger tries to end her romance with him, ironically at the same time he wants to break with *her*, he refuses to walk away. His sense of superiority must not be tampered with; she must suffer for presuming to control the romance, even for sparing him the trouble of instigating an action agreeable to him. Paula, too, has felt the weight of his cold, strong will. In her last meeting with him, seven years after their romantic heyday, she explains, "I was infatuated with you, Anson—you could make me do anything you liked. But we wouldn't have been happy."

She argues well. His fear of impulse and commitment shows frontier energy fighting itself in the age of the closed frontier. Hunter mixes memory and desire with strong lashings of money, social rank, and vanity. Yet every exercise of his powerful will diminishes him rather than confirming his preeminence. An excellent example of the slamming recoil caused by his bullying comes after his discovery of his aunt's love affair. Hunter, it is seen here, lives at a great moral distance

Dust jacket of Fitzgerald's third short story collection.

from himself. So alien is he to emotion that when he sees it, he crushes it; perhaps sexual commitment in any form, even that of others, threatens him so much that he must stamp it out. Of little import to him is the fact that in the process of stepping between his uncle's wife and her lover, he wrecks a few lives—including his own. Invoking the creed of family honor, he breaks up the affair. (His aunt's first response to the moral lecture he gives her, "Edna stood up, leaving her crab-flake cocktail untasted," has the same perfection of detail as Tom and Daisy Buchanan's conspiratorial supper of cold chicken and ale the night of Myrtle Wilson's death in *Gatsby*.) But his meddling creates other, unexpected changes. Edna's lover kills himself, and Anson stops receiving invitations to his uncle's home.

The act he performed in the name of solidarity has proved, ironically, divisive. Another irony inheres in the timing of his self-righteous act, which comes at a stage of his life when he most needs the security and warmth represented by the family. Modifying Gatsby's belief that the past can be relived is his conviction that it can be prolonged. **"The Rich Boy"** tallies the high cost of trying to maintain the status quo. Though he lives amid fast change, Hunter won't alter the basic realities governing his life. Leaning on his tie with Yale, he helps his former classmates find jobs, women to date and marry, and places to live. But playing the busybody with ex-classmates helps him no more than it did with Edna. Like his women, his college friends outgrow their dependence on him—moving to the suburbs, becoming absorbed by their

new marriages, and sometimes going to Hollywood to write for the movies. At thirty, he is trapped by a past he can never revive. The sight of a new desk clerk at the Plaza makes him wince; so remote is the past he constantly invokes that the exchange of a phone number he dials in order to beat back loneliness no longer exists. The atavistic associations called up by his last name hearken to primitive cultures in a manner befitting his persistence in dredging up the past.

What this modern caveman proves is that Eden lies beyond recovery, especially by money or power. He misreads and mistreats the past throughout. His strongest link to a living past, namely the family, he forfeits by trying to control Edna (whose name and harmless affair both recall Eden, together with the idea of self-renewal through sexual love). Fitzgerald believes in the value of family, money, and even power. But he also believes this value to be instrumental rather than absolute: Nick Carraway's solid midwestern family strengthens him for the ordeal of coping in a fast-moving, competitive society, but it doesn't ensure his success. Any virtue prolonged or extended to the point where it rules people loses its value, like southern Georgia's drowsy charm in **"The Ice Palace"** (1920) and, more hauntingly, Braddock Washington's stupendous castle in **"The Diamond as Big as the Ritz"** (1922). Wealth must be shared rather than hoarded. Characters less favored by birth than Anson Hunter have put this lesson to work in the Fitzgerald canon. Dexter Green, for instance, amasses money and status to impress his *princesse lointaine*, Judy Jones, in **"Winter Dreams"** (1922), just as Gatsby believes that winning a fortune, however dishonestly, will also win him Daisy's love. The Midwesterners Gatsby and Green surpass the New York blueblood Hunter in their purity of motive; however wrongheaded their methods, they want to marry and serve the women they love. Their goal is one of sharing. Hunter, on the other hand, wants a chorus of admirers, and he wants them at a safe distance; he uses his money to boost his ego. Since the reassurances he buys count more to him than those who reassure him, he is really buying what he fears most and wants least—loneliness.

Self-distrust runs high with him, as befits a hunter whose arrows usually miss their mark. Both his love for Paula Legendre and his later elevation of her to near-legendary grandeur take root in self-distrust, perhaps even self-dislike. If love is to have a place in his life, let it be safe and tame rather than stormy. Thus his courtship of serious, gentle Paula has a solemn, nervous tone he has substituted for passion. Yet Paula's choice of passion over safety puts her beyond his control during their last meeting. His final words to her, four successive yesses, show that while he has remained a boy, she has grown into a woman—another sign of which is her heavy pregnancy. Overmatched, he can only agree and consent. Yet this biddable boy once came close to marrying Paula. His choice of Dolly Karger as a major romantic involvement—the only one Fitzgerald dramatizes after Paula—shows how much Paula frightened him. So well does he know what excites him in a woman that, in Dolly, he deliberately selects one who falls short of those things. And she fails to meet his standards of human decency and dignity more vividly than he himself does. His female mirror-image, Dolly resembles Anson Hunter as strikingly as Paula, who comes from a more prominent family, differs from him. Whereas Paula is repelled by his hard drinking, Dolly hopes to profit from it. This "gypsy of the unattainable" also yearns for the men she can't have rather than trying to build a relationship with one within reach. So close is she in spirit and purpose to Hunter that they write each other identical letters at precisely the same time on the same subject—the wisdom of ending their relationship. His similarity to her disturbs as well as comforts Hunter. Angered that she should presume to take charge of her relationship with him, he concocts an elaborate scheme to punish her. His inability to revise the scheme in the face of change—the sudden romantic glow he ignites with her—spells out his rigidness. Both he and Dolly suffer from his failure to cope with change and chance. As the episode with Edna showed, the crime of resisting his mental concepts carries stiff penalties for all. (pp. 241-46)

[Hunter's] story reaches us through the narration of a contemporary, a fellow New Yorker and Ivy Leaguer who did not attend Yale. The nameless narrator has known Hunter for about eight years, i.e., during the time of the recorded action. That he is also with him at the end indicates that the men are well enough acquainted to sail together on an ocean cruise. The fellow passengers team well artistically: Hunter needs an audience to play to, and the narrator is content to stand back. If bullying, badgering Hunter resembles Tom Buchanan, the self-effacing narrator recalls Nick Carraway's quiet stability. His lack of a name reflects his willingness to let life happen to him instead of imposing himself. Only in Part I, the prologue, does he state opinions about Hunter. And even here, he is providing a moral context for what will happen rather than judging. Nor does he complain at the end, when Hunter deserts him aboard ship to spend time with the girl in the red tam. This likeable, trustworthy man makes

good company as well as providing a good foil to the bully whose tale he tells. First, his well-bred reticence tones down the hectic pace created by Hunter's anxiety. Next, his long personal tie with Hunter fends off dryness and cold. It is material that he holds the stage alone in the story's first part, only mentioning Hunter by name in the next-to-last sentence. Besides wanting his moment of glory, he also knows that he must grab it quickly. Once introduced, Hunter will dominate. The burden of the story consists of the rich boy's need to extend and solidify his self-importance. In the last section, though, the narrator comes forth as more of a person than a device or disembodied voice. A well-to-do man and not a rich boy, he feels lucky that he hasn't been tempted as Hunter has; the blessings that came to Hunter at birth have blocked the latter's growth. On the other hand, the narrator reacts to Hunter personally as well as socially; as he said in his opening monologue, Hunter is more of an individual than a type. And his personal behavior has given the narrator plenty to resent. Hunter forgets about the narrator for years at a stretch; he only phones him on the Saturday he happens upon Paula Legendre Hagerty because, for once, he has nothing to do and nobody to be with. Hunter discards him aboard the *Paris* the first day out in favor of the girl in the red tam, having already made sure that she is traveling alone.

In view of these slights, why aren't the tone and the thesis of **"The Rich Boy"** both bitter? First, the narrator sees Hunter as a victim. The depression Hunter has suffered in recent months and his sharp attraction to the girl in the red tam, even though Paula died only three days before, both show his helpless addiction to female approval. His job is an incidental in his life. Were he able to certify his self-being through the world of work and men, he'd not have needed the European vacation his colleagues forced upon him. Also tempering the narrator's harsh judgment of Hunter is the suspicion that love can kill: Paula dies delivering the baby of the only man she ever loved, and the middle-aged passion of Edna and Cary Sloane has created a contagion of physical and moral death. The narrator has seen this wreckage. Presumably lacking a rich private life of his own (and a career as well, judging from his ability to leave New York for three to six months in order to go to Europe with Hunter?), he won't censure Hunter directly for shrinking from the dangers of love. Better half a life than none. If this tame, bystanderish behavior indicates a different half from that of the predatory Hunter, it infers no moral superiority. And the narrator knows it. He has also reached the age—i.e., thirty—where he cannot lie to himself. Failing to live at full stretch, he can't attack Hunter. Besides, the rich boy has always gladdened the hearts he shatters. Nor was the shattering permanent, Paula and Dolly both benefiting from his negative example to marry other men. The narrator has probably never made such an impact upon a woman.

No drab factual report, **"The Rich Boy"** resembles a moral parable channeled through the media of escapist psychology and urban social history. The passage of years creates changes in the lives of various privileged New Yorkers, during which time Hunter fights change and growth. The absence of a concluding judgment of his immaturity, a function of the narrator's restraint and moral malaise, promotes narrative economy. It also reflects artistic self-confidence. Fitzgerald revealed Anson Hunter and his biographer so well that he didn't need to explain them. (pp. 247-49)

Peter Wolfe, "Faces in a Dream: Innocence Perpetu-

ated in 'The Rich Boy'," in The Short Stories of F.
Scott Fitzgerald: New Approaches in Criticism, *edited by Jackson R. Bryer, the University of Wisconsin Press, 1982, pp. 241-49.*

GERALD PIKE (essay date 1986)

[*In the following excerpt, Pike delineates four distinct authorial voices used by Fitzgerald in the story "Winter Dreams."*]

In **"Winter Dreams,"** Fitzgerald experiments with distinct shifts in authorial voice, occasionally with less than felicitous effect, but always with a sense that the voice should match the texture of the thing described. I count four authorial voices in the story, but two dominate. The first of these uses the richly romantic prose style which many readers associate with Fitzgerald, the style for which he is either applauded or condemned: a selection of ornate terms so mutually dependent that to alter one is to alter all.

Although discussing *This Side of Paradise,* Brian Way [in his *F. Scott Fitzgerald and the Art of Social Fiction*] makes some observations regarding Fitzgerald's poetic sense that apply to **"Winter Dreams"** as well. He says that Fitzgerald "is preoccupied—particularly in the first part of this novel—with finding ways in which the language of fiction can take on the dimension of poetry." Way also points out that Fitzgerald was raised on his father's editions of Poe and Byron, and that later he favored the poetry of Keats, Swinburne, and Rupert Brooke, and the prose of Pater, Wilde, and Compton Mackenzie: "For all these writers except Keats and Byron, poetry tends to be a self-validating ecstasy rather than a way of saying something. It is not so much a mode of communication as a state of mind. . . . "

This poetic voice primarily depicts Dexter Green's character and point-of-view. We first see him skiing across the snowbound fairways of the golf course where "winter shut down like the white lid of a box . . . in enforced fallowness, haunted by ragged sparrows." And later his reverie, his winter dream, surfaces: "October filled him with hope which November raised to a sort of ecstatic triumph, and in this mood the fleeting brilliant impressions of the summer at Sherry Island were ready grist to his mill."

This language expresses an emotional investment in the thing described that verges on the autobiographical and renders moot the usual distinctions drawn between first and third-person narration. Similarly, Judy Jones is first described as one of her infatuated suitors might, assuming—of course—that he happened to be blessed with Fitzgerald's eloquence:

> The girl who had done this [made Dexter quit his caddying job] was eleven—beautifully ugly as little girls are apt to be who are destined after a few years to be inexpressibly lovely and bring no end of misery to a great number of men. The spark, however, was perceptible. There was a general ungodliness in the way her lips twisted down at the corners when she smiled, and in the—Heaven help us!—in the almost passionate quality of her eyes.

The "Heaven help us!"—aside from its comic reference to this temptress' mere eleven years—indicates an authorial voice as vulnerable to the object of its composition as any first-person narrator would be. The next time we see her (years later), Judy Jones is again on the golf course and again observed by Dexter. What was ungodly in an eleven-year-old

has blossomed in a twenty-year-old beauty and is depicted in appropriately florid style:

> The color of her cheeks was centered like the color of a picture—it was not a "high" color, but a sort of fluctuating and feverish warmth, so shaded that it seemed at any moment it would recede and disappear. This color and the mobility of her mouth gave a continual impression of flux, of intense life, of passionate vitality—balanced only partially by the sad luxury of her eyes.

This voice works through the first four sections of the story to describe the exteriors of characters and situations; it *shows* things. In counterpoint, a second voice, generally more sober and stylistically conventional, gives editorial comment on action. This voice, from the American naturalistic tradition, *tells* us things about Dexter.

When Judy Jones intrudes so deeply into his winter dreams that Dexter's self-esteem insists that he quit his job as caddy, the "enormity of his decision frightened him. . . . As so frequently would be the case in the future, Dexter was unconsciously dictated to by his winter dreams." Later, this lean, objective voice summarizes Dexter's financial success: "He made money. It was rather amazing." And before Judy Jones—now a young woman—appears on the golf course, Dexter observes the caddies who trail along with his foursome "trying to catch a gleam or gesture that would remind him of himself, that would lessen the gap which lay between his present and his past."

So far, Fitzgerald is in control. When he wants to show youthful infatuation reaching for that fine sparkling jewel just beyond the outstretched fingers, he uses a style at once excessive and selective, like the condition he wants to capture. But when he needs naturalistic objectivity—in a sense, the adult's view of life—the voice becomes neutral and rational. When Dexter looks at things, the first voice dominates; when we look at Dexter, we hear the second.

After his second encounter with Judy Jones, a descriptive passage clearly presents both of these voices in extreme contrast:

> Later in the afternoon the sun went down with a riotous swirl of gold and varying blues and scarlets, and left the dry, rustling night of Western summer. Dexter watched from the veranda of the Golf Club, watched the even overlap of the waters in the little wind, silver molasses under the harvest-moon. Then the moon held a finger to her lips and the lake became a clear pool, pale and quiet. Dexter put on his bathing-suit and swam out to the farthest raft, where he stretched dripping on the wet canvas of the springboard.

The first portion of this passage stretches even Fitzgerald's capacity for purple prose, but it works because the authorial voice simply translates a young man's love-soaked vision. When attention shifts to the man and away from what he sees, as in the last sentence of the passage above, the voice switches to a restrained and objective tone.

Fitzgerald, it seems safe to say, consciously chooses these first two voices to illustrate the paradox of his own world-view, his "cynical idealism" as he depicted it through Amory Blaine two years before **"Winter Dreams."** Cynicism and idealism nearly converge in Fitzgerald, but his desire for romantic abandon outreaches his capacity for detached, disillusioned observation; and though we hear the voice of each in **"Winter Dreams,"** the gap between the two creates certain obvious problems with point-of-view that he attempts to patch up with a third voice which imposes itself on the story like an uninvited pedant.

This voice, instructing us how to read the story, is first heard at the beginning of the second section, immediately following a particularly resonant description of Dexter:

> He wanted not association with glittering things and glittering people—he wanted the glittering things themselves. Often he reached out for the best without knowing why he wanted it—and sometimes he ran up against the mysterious denials and prohibitions in which life indulges. It is with one of those denials and not with his career as a whole that this story deals.

With this last sentence, Fitzgerald—seeing potential confusion—steps into the text and simply inserts a rhetorical shim, a type of footnote, rather than solving the problem at its source, which might require an entire restructuring of point-of-view.

The second instance of this editorial voice, like the first, involves Dexter's motivation, his internal self:

> He wanted to take Judy Jones with him. No disillusion as to the world in which she had grown up could cure his illusion as to her desirability. Remember that—for only in the light of it can what he did for her be understood.

This behavioral analysis again verges on the naturalistic, and Fitzgerald delivers it, as Dreiser or Anderson might, in a neutral style, universal in fit and scope. But it also reveals a distinctly inappropriate authorial insecurity: Fitzgerald fears his protagonist's development is insufficient to carry the weight of the author's tendency toward social analysis; thus, we are told what we might be better shown.

The final instance of this imperative voice comes at the beginning of the sixth (and last) section of the story and explains Fitzgerald's sudden invocation of the War:

> He was one of those young thousands who greeted the war with a certain amount of relief, welcoming the liberation from webs of tangled emotion. This story is not his biography, remember, although things creep into it which have nothing to do with those dreams he had when he was young.

Here the "thing" that creeps into the story is that upheaval which reshaped his generation's world-view and subsequently propelled it into maturity. Fitzgerald needs the War as an ultimate initiation device, undeniable and universally recognized. Dexter enters the War "with a certain amount of relief " because he thinks he has finally freed himself from Judy Jones' will. Fitzgerald uses the imperative voice, then, by way of apology for shoving Dexter through the War, an awkwardness necessitated by the need for a fully mature Dexter.

The War divides Dexter's past innocence from his present dull maturity at the end of the story, just as the transitional paragraph—with its authorial "footnote"—divides the main text of the story from the closing sixth section.

This last section employs a fourth voice, more stylistically reserved than the first, to show a mature protagonist's observations; and it suits a more deadened, reserved character—one compromised by age. The pain is no less poignant, but the terms by which he perceives it are more utilitarian and stripped of stylistic glitter, as seen in the penultimate paragraph of the story:

> For the first time in years the tears were streaming down his face. But they were for himself now. He did not care about mouth and eyes and moving hands. He wanted to care, and he could not care. For he had gone away and he could never go back any more. The gates were closed, the sun was gone down, and there was no beauty but the gray beauty of steel that withstands all time.

Such extreme emotion would have been expressed in the most extravagant terms had it occurred in any of the preceding five sections. Here, in a work predating Fitzgerald's association with or even knowledge of Hemingway, a distinctly lean and muscular style dominates, utilizing omission as much as commission in its tip-of-the-iceberg approach. Such lines as "He did not care, and he could not care"—very much of the style upon which Hemingway based his career—illustrate an important step in Fitzgerald's artistic evolution: first into the tight control of *Gatsby* and later in the more poetic *Tender Is the Night.* (pp. 315-19)

Observing Fitzgerald struggling with these four voices early on in his career invites a view of **"Winter Dreams"** as a stylistic turning point, a smaller world in which the writer's difficulties with novels reveal themselves, sometimes with the overt and vital confusion of the youth he describes. The first voice stylistically mirrors the protagonist's inflated point-of-view, an effect traditionally limited to first-person narration. The second voice offers naturalistic objectivity. The imperative third voice is an apologist for structural inadequacies. And the fourth voice, over which he labored extensively, repeats the function of the first but in a style appropriate to a mature protagonist. Because the four voices are discrete and their union is not seamless, readers may fault Fitzgerald.

The flaws are visible because he departs from the cover offered by convention, searching for new approaches to old stylistic devices. When he struggles, it is an honest struggle and one which spans his career as he attempts to bring poetry to prose and reshape what he considered his true artistic medium: the novel. (p. 320)

> *Gerald Pike, "Four Voices in 'Winter Dreams',"* in Studies in Short Fiction, *Vol. 23, No. 3, Summer, 1986, pp. 315-20.*

LELAND S. PERSON, JR.   (essay date 1986)

[*In the following excerpt, Person characterizes the story "O Russet Witch!" as a fantasy through which Fitzgerald reveals his attitudes toward women and art.*]

One of Fitzgerald's lesser-known stories, **"O Russet Witch!"** (1921) seems to epitomize the female character dualism that Leslie Fiedler [in his *Love and Death in the American Novel*] and others view as endemic to American male writing—women polarized into Fair Lady and Dark, goddess and bitch—for in the character of Caroline (or Alicia Dare) Fitzgerald represents a woman with two identities, at least in the mind of the hero, Merlin Grainger. As Caroline, the woman is a wish-fulfilling projection of Merlin's imagination, but as Alicia Dare, the notorious dancer and mistress, she fulfills a different need: Merlin's "romantic yearning for a beautiful and perverse woman." This sort of opposition, of course, has long been identified with the American romance, so it is not surprising that **"O Russet Witch!"** should be a product (along with **"The Diamond as Big as the Ritz"** and **"The Curious Case of Benjamin Button"**) of Fitzgerald's desire to write fantasy. Indeed, my contention in this essay is that Fitzgerald used Merlin Grainger's experience with the fabulous Caroline to explore the connection between his art and his relationship to women. Predicated on a series of oppositions that reflect a radically divided personality, the story reveals Fitzgerald's fears about the dangers of male-female relationships and the self-destructive power of his art. (p. 443)

With its "serpentine embroidery," its perpetual smell of musk, and its posters of "breathless exotic intent," Merlin Grainger's Moonlight Quill bookshop recalls one of Poe's dream chambers, while the name of the store suggests the sort of "neutral territory" Hawthorne preferred for his art—a space which liberates images from the "haunted mind" yet allows some measure of control. Specifically, the store specializes in illicit books, for the windows are "always full of something that passed the literary censors with little to spare; volumes with covers of deep orange which offer their titles on little white squares." Yet in the midst of this atmosphere of the "radical" and the "dark," Merlin Grainger remains deeply repressed. His secret passion is going home to Caroline, the mysterious woman on whose apartment he spies each night: "She was like a ghost in that she never existed until evening. She sprang into life when the lights went on in her apartment at about six, and she disappeared, at the latest, about midnight." Caroline even derives her name (and much of her meaning) from her association with the literature which Merlin sells; he calls her Caroline because "there was a picture that looked like her on the jacket of a book of that name down at the Moonlight Quill."

When she actually appears at the bookshop, however, Caroline seems more the product of a nightmare than of a dream. From the safe vantage point of Merlin's apartment she can be abstracted from reality and endowed with the "sort of features you thought belonged to your first love," but in the flesh she threatens that perfected image. Her appearance on a dark afternoon, for example, suggests the "end of the world" and the collapse of buildings (as of dreams) "like card houses." Robert Sklar has argued [see Further Reading list] that **"O Russet Witch!"** is a story about "the need for fantasy to give color to drab lives, and also about fantasy's inevitable disruptive effects on stolid middle-class respectability," but it seems to me that Fitzgerald goes further in exploring the anarchic, disordering power of fantasy itself. From the beginning, for example, Caroline violates the bounds of aesthetic as well as social form. Her voice "rich and full of sorcery," she hurls book after book at the ceiling, where they lodge as "bulging rectangles" in the crimson chandelier—magnified and glowing, it seems clear, in order to emphasize their lurid and irresistible meaning for Merlin's boggled imagination. That is, Caroline's presence forces Merlin to acknowledge his hitherto repressed fascination with erotic art. Although Caroline appears destructive, her behavior is so wildly contagious for Merlin that he feels possessed. Finding himself also throwing books at the ceiling, he is astonished that words seem "for the first time in his life to run at him shrieking to be used, gathering themselves into carefully arranged squads and platoons, and being presented to him by punctilious adjutants of paragraphs." Caroline, in brief, inspires a "perfect orgy of energy" that causes all formality to dissolve into irrational, yet spontaneously creative, formlessness. Amidst a tremendous noise of "smashing and ripping and tearing," she and Merlin throw books in "all directions, until sometimes three or four were in the air at once, smashing against shelves, cracking the glass of pictures on the walls, falling in bruised and torn heaps upon the floor."

At once creative and destructive, such an "orgy" reflects deep ambivalence toward art and creativity. The martial imagery and the destruction of books and pictures, coupled with the spontaneous streaming forth of language into the conscious mind, suggest the attraction and the danger Fitzgerald identified with surrender to irrational impulses. For Merlin is overwhelmed by the internal forces Caroline has evoked. He is in the position of "Monarch Thought" in Roderick Usher's poem, "The Haunted Palace"—beset on all sides by a "hideous throng" of "evil things" that originate in the "palace" of the mind itself. Caroline only provokes their eruption, and it is only when she disappears that Merlin's lapse into irrationality ends.

Although he tries to detain her, in order to "extract for another moment that dazzling essence of light he drew from her presence," Merlin quickly regains his composure and sets about "restoring the shop to its former condition," So frightening a transformation has Caroline inspired that Merlin feels compelled to cling to conventionality for the rest of his life. Indeed, within a year of Caroline's "catastrophic" visit to the bookshop, he seems to have aged excessively. His appearance is that of a "deserted garden," devoid of the wild energy Caroline had inspired, and to consummate his choice of a conventional life, he proposes to his stenographer, Olive Masters—her name suggesting his desire to commit himself to a woman who will keep his life carefully controlled.

Like Hawthorne's Kenyon or Hollingsworth, who choose domestic lives of retreat with household saints, Merlin can think of "nothing more fun than rising in the world with Olive. There would be a cottage in a suburb, a cottage painted blue, just one class below the sort of cottages that are of white stucco with a green roof." Richard Lehan sees in this choice the "dread Fitzgerald attached to marriage and domestic life." Lehan has a point, because Fitzgerald emphasizes the internal conflict which Merlin's choice provokes. He continues to embody that conflict in Caroline, who appears mysteriously at the restaurant where Merlin has just proposed, as if evoked by the repression Merlin's proposal signals. Merlin in effect has split his mental image of woman in two, but his own mind (or at least his creator's) resists the process and works to force the two images together. Whereas his prospective married life will be marked by the "dead routine of dead generations" and he and Olive will become the "sort of people for whom life was ordered," the "wicked" Caroline displays such erotic energy as she dances upon a table that she nearly causes a riot. As a symbol of disorder and the eruption of creative zeal, Caroline poses a serious threat to Merlin, yet even as Olive drags him from the restaurant (fulfilling her promise as "master"), he is plainly "fascinated."

Eight years later, when Merlin sees her again, Caroline has grown even more powerful. By repressing them, Merlin has provoked those forces within himself which Caroline represents to become more volatile, and the riotous scene on Fifth Avenue proceeds like some horrible nightmare. Although "breathless to watch her," he is still careful to keep his distance. Again associated with some subversive force which is both "stupendous" and "terrible," Caroline radiates such an attractive charge that within minutes she is the center of a huge swarm of men: "men of all ages who could not possibly have known Caroline jostled over and melted into the circle of ever-increasing diameter, until the lady in lavender was the centre of a vast impromptu auditorium." So powerful is the magic circle that she superintends that, like some mysterious black hole in space, she herself virtually disappears from view; she is identifiable only by the effect she has on the objects on the circumference of her circle.

Radiating outward in contagious waves of emotion, the circle churns into a frenzy. Whereas in the bookshop Caroline's effect had been limited to art, now she seems to have unleashed all the subversive political and social forces which were surfacing in the Twenties: "A quarter mile down the block a half-frantic policeman called his precinct; on the same corner a frightened civilian crashed in the glass of a fire-alarm and sent in a wild paean for all the fire-engines of the city; up in an apartment high in one of the tall buildings a hysterical old maid telephoned in turn for the prohibition enforcement agent, the special deputies on Bolshevism, and the maternity ward of Bellevue Hospital." As he had been at the restaurant, Merlin is both dazzled and frightened by Caroline's behavior, so transfixed that, once again, Olive must lead him away. A kind of final opportunity for Merlin, the scene of the traffic jam climaxes Caroline's meaning for his imagination. When he fails here to deal with the feelings she inspires, he effectively surrenders the possibility of doing so forever. Like other American heroes, he has been suspended between two powerful forces represented by two women, and the safe, conventional Olive has finally "mastered" him. The rest of **"O Russet Witch!"** describes the accelerated process of aging which overtakes Merlin—and his ultimate disillusionment. Whereas the Moonlight Quill once served as a repository for illicit literature (and for his own repressed desires), Merlin now becomes an automaton at his job and feels oppressed by a purely mechanical need to obtain an "accurate inventory of a thousand authors whom he could never have understood and had certainly never read." When he chooses Olive over Caroline (a choice clearly different from the one Fitzgerald had made), imagination and a love of art both die out of him.

Thus, when Caroline next appears in the bookshop some thirty years later, she is, appropriately, a ghost of her former self. Her features, like her power over Merlin's imagination, are "in decay," and her voice is "no more than the echo of a forgotten dream." Whereas she once was "dazzling and light," in old age she has become even more abstract: an objective correlative for Merlin's need to invest part of himself in a vessel where it cannot be corrupted by time. " 'Olive's arms were closing about me,' " he confesses to her, " 'and you warned me to be free and keep my measure of youth and irresponsibility.' " And as he recalls the magnificent "beauty and power" she radiated on Fifth Avenue, he admits that she "became personified" even to Olive: " 'she feared you. For weeks I wanted to slip out of the house at dark and forget the stuffiness of life with music and cocktails and a girl to make me young.' " As an indication of the price he has paid for his failure to cultivate his potential relationship with Caroline, however, Merlin must finally admit that at this point in his life he "no longer knew how."

Brian Higgins sees in **"O Russet Witch!"** the first appearance of the "central paradox that Fitzgerald . . . sees in the romantic attitude toward life: that while the romantic may waste his life living an illusion, pursuing an unattainable

The Fitzgeralds on the Riviera, 1929.

dream, the very dream and even its impossibility of fulfillment make his life emotionally richer and more exciting." Sklar, on the other hand, rejects this view, arguing that Merlin had no chance to attain Alicia Dare and thus no real chance to incorporate the imaginative power she symbolized. I think the story is more ambiguous than either Higgins or Sklar allows. However fascinated he is by Caroline, Merlin regards her behavior as dangerously subversive and thus resists imaginative identification with her. Yet in resisting the possibility of a relationship with Caroline at every opportunity—thereby resisting the forces within himself that Caroline evokes—Merlin clearly causes potentially creative forces within himself to wither and die. Indeed, his state of mind at the end of the story is represented through the telling image of his brain as "suddenly fatigued and still." He becomes a "death's head," a man "too old now even for memories." If anything, then, **"O Russet Witch!"** offers a fascinating example of the dangers Fitzgerald associated with women and with art. It demonstrates his inability early in his career to reconcile his divided feelings about the sources and effects of his art. (pp. 444-48)

Leland S. Person, Jr., "Fitzgerald's 'O Russet Witch!': Dangerous Women, Dangerous Art," in Studies in Short Fiction, *Vol. 23, No. 4, Fall, 1986, pp. 443-48.*

SANFORD PINSKER (essay date 1987)

[*Pinsker is an American poet and critic whose books include* The Schlemiel as Metaphor (1971), Still Life, and Other Poems (1975), *and* The American Novel in the 1960s (1978). *In the following excerpt, Pinsker cites "The Baby Party" as an example of Fitzgerald's ability to juxtapose in his fiction "the Romantic Dream and a foreboding sense of doom about that Dream."]*

F. Scott Fitzgerald's **"The Baby Party"** appeared originally in the February 1925 issue of *Heart's International* and was reprinted in his collection, ***All the Sad Young Men*** (1926). In many respects, it is emblematic of the larger conditions that dogged the composition of, and the critical attention to, Fitzgerald's short fiction. Arthur Mizener [see Further Reading list] reminds us that the story was written in a single, all-night session and with the exception of a handful of one-sentence judgments by reviewers (interestingly enough, equally divided between those who liked the story and those who didn't, those who found it humorous and those who responded to its tragic overtones), nothing remotely resembling a sustained critical analysis exists.

"The Baby Party" exploits its satiric premise—namely, an exhibition of thoroughly "modern" baby-adults for the edification of adult-babies—but frames this central tale with psychic distress of a deeper, more serious sort. For Edith Andros, the baby party is an exercise in narcissistic investment, a chance to match her "proud and jealous heart" against the competition. As she remarks, more accurately than she realizes, "It'll be funny. Ede's going to be all dressed up in her new pink dress. . . . " For "grown-up Edith," the baby party is a serious business, one that requires careful orchestration and, above all, good timing:

> The baby party began at half past four, but Edith Andros, calculating shrewdly that the new dress would stand out more sensationally against vestments already rumpled, planned the arrival of herself and little Ede for five.

It is hardly surprising that mother and daughter share the same name or that the baby party itself is portrayed as a thinly disguised narcissistic war. Snarls hide just beneath the nervous, decorous smiles, and this is doubly true for Mrs. Markey:

> "Little Ede looks perfectly darling," said Mrs. Markey, smiling and moistening her lips in a way that Edith found particularly repulsive. "So *grown-up*—I can't *believe* it!"

Edith Andros is more than willing to "hold forth" on behalf of little Ede; after all, the "real business of the afternoon . . . lay in relating the recent accomplishments and insouciances of her child." All of which is to say, nothing brings out repressed hostility better than a party—unless, of course, it's a baby party.

Such is the limited premise of what might have been simply one more limited Fitzgerald short story, an amusing enough diversion, but magazine fare of the second water nonetheless. Nobody was quicker to deprecate Fitzgerald's efforts on behalf of *Heart's International* or *The Saturday Evening Post* than Fitzgerald himself. The difference in **"The Baby Party"** is John Andros. Unlike "grown-up Edith," his narcissism strikes richer chords. Not only do his sensibilities frame the story, but the double-plotting that pits his fisticuffs with Bill Markey against the bedlam created by little Ede and Billy Markey is more intricate, more tightly structured, than Fitzgerald is usually given credit for being. Consider, for example, an innocent detail in the story's opening paragraphs. John Andros "found solace in the thought of life continuing through his child," but "having paid . . . homage" to the

idea of little Ede, her actual presence is filled with annoyances:

> After ten minutes the very vitality of the child irritated him; he was inclined to lose his temper when things were broken, and one Sunday afternoon when he had disrupted a bridge game by permanently hiding up the ace of spades, he had made a scene that had reduced his wife to tears.

"The Baby Party," I would submit, is a death-haunted story, one that revolves not only around versions of the family romance (" . . . his feeling about his little girl was qualified. She had interrupted his rather intense love-affair with his wife, and she was the reason for their living in a suburban town.") but also around John Andros' increasing intimations of mortality. After his comic battle royal—in which he "defends" a variety of honors (his wife's? his daughter's? his own?)—"grown-up Edith's" unconscious once again speaks volumes "I'm going to get the doctor," she said insistently. "You may be hurt internally." Or even more to the death-ridden point: "I'm certainly glad we have beefsteak in the house for tomorrow's dinner. . . . Do you know I came within an ace of ordering veal?"

For Edith, the Markeys remain what they have always been—namely, *common*. She clings to the notion that social veneer is Everything, and that it runs thick. By contrast, John Andros has learned otherwise, in something akin to what, in a Joyce story, we might call an epiphany. To be sure, his confrontation with Bill Markey is a mirror image of his daughter's tussle with Billy Markey—regressive, foolish, an escalation of molehills into kings of the mountain—but it is also elemental and, in that sense, psychologically decisive. No doubt Leslie Fiedler could wax eloquent about the male-bonding it authenticates ("It was no perfunctory hand-shake: John Andros's arm went around Markey's shoulder, and he patted him softly on the back for a little while."), but I am more concerned with Andros *redux*, as he reestablishes control of a domestic situation that has gradually slipped from his thirty-eight-year-old grasp:

> "I did beat him," he announced. "At least, I beat him as much as he beat me. And there isn't going to be any next time. Don't you go calling people common any more. If you get in any trouble, you just take your coat and go home. Understand?"
> "Yes, dear," she said meekly.

Dispatching "grown-up Edith" is, however, much easier than coming to terms with his complicated feelings about little Ede. In the opening lines of the story, little Ede is, primarily, an object—something he considers abstractly ("a definite piece of youth") and wonders at. She is a mirror of his mortality, and his narcissistic impulses are vaguely unsettling. After he catalogs her physicality, "John was content that the nurse should take her away." Like other children in Fitzgerald's fiction, little Ede is most conspicuous in her absence. One does not need a thick biography to feel Fitzgerald's pathos and guilt about Scottie at work. In **"The Baby Party,"** however, John Andros gives full vent to his maternal instincts: "he reached over into the bed, and picking up his daughter, blankets and all, sat down in the rocking chair holding her tightly in his arms." However much we may feel that Fitzgerald's insistence on masculine dominance is embarrassingly out of touch with our ethos—we applaud aspects of his scuffle with Bill Markey and cheer, despite ourselves, when he yanks Edith up short—the final notes are subtle, muted and much more evocative than one might expect in a *Heart's International* saga:

> John Andros knew at length what it was he had fought for so savagely that evening. He had it now, he possessed it forever, and for some time he sat there rocking very slowly to and fro in the darkness.

Fitzgerald's special genius has always been an ability to arrange the Romantic Dream and a foreboding sense of doom about that Dream into an equipoise—and to do this, always, by incorporating both aspects within himself. **"The Baby Party"** is a small, but rich, example of exactly this. (pp. 52-5)

> Sanford Pinsker, "Fitzgerald's 'The Baby Party'," in The Explicator, *Vol. 45, No. 2, Winter, 1987, pp. 52-5.*

> I have asked a lot of my emotions—one hundred and twenty stories. The price was high, right up with Kipling, because there was one little drop of something—not blood, not a tear, not my seed, but me more intimately than these, in every story, it was the extra I had. Now it has gone and I am just like you now.
>
> *F. Scott Fitzgerald from "Our April Letter," "The Notebooks" in* The Crack-Up *(1945).*

HELGE NORMANN NILSEN   (essay date 1987)

[*In the following excerpt, Nilsen characterizes Fitzgerald's story "The Rich Boy" as a damning portrait of "a certain type of American upper-class man" whose inflated self-image contributes to his inability to love.*]

In **"The Rich Boy"** Fitzgerald gives us an unsparing portrait of the essential shallowness of a certain type of American upper-class man, the millionaire Anson Hunter. He is a second generation rich boy who lacks some of the more important virtues of his father, the Gilded Age entrepreneur who combined his accumulation of wealth with a Puritan morality which, however narrowminded, did involve a sense of responsibility to something greater than the individual self.

The story is about the failure of love on Anson's part, his inability to respond to the genuine devotion that his fiancée Paula Legendre gives him. His selfish and undeveloped personality is to blame, and Fitzgerald persistently underlines Anson's easy self-confidence and suggests, with subtle irony, that it is out of proportion to any actual quality or accomplishment in the man. Though charming and affable, he is self-indulgent, drinks too much, and seems to have no intellectual or artistic interests whatever. He becomes a successful businessman, but his personality develops and matures little, if at all. This is the basic criticism of his hero that the author conveys, indirectly, by having his anonymous narrator observe Anson's life and comment on it in an affectionate as well as detached manner. The ironic and even judgmental view of Anson is thus expressed by the implicit author rather than the narrator.

At the same time, Anson Hunter is also seen as a victim of his own circumstances, even though he was born into a rich

family. To be rich means to run the risk of being damaged, though in a different and less drastic way than is the case among the poor. Even as a child Anson is made to feel the difference between himself and the other children in the village where the family has a summer house:

> Anson's first sense of his superiority came to him when he realized the half-grudging American deference that was paid to him in the Connecticut village. The parents of the boys he played with always inquired after his father and mother, and were vaguely excited when their own children were asked to the Hunter's house. He accepted this as the natural state of things, and a sort of impatience with all groups of which he was not the centre—in money, in position, in authority—remained with him for the rest of his life. He disdained to struggle with other boys for precedence—he expected it to be given him freely, and when it wasn't he withdrew into his family.

The result of this sense of superiority is to impair Anson's growth as a complete human being. To speak of victimization may seem out of place with regard to Anson Hunter, rich and popular as he is, but his stunted development is to be deplored because he is endowed with the potential for something greater and better than what he finally settles for. His siblings are clearly more ordinary than himself, and he is equipped with leadership qualities and perhaps also an ability to love a woman which never get much chance to flourish. (p. 41)

"The Rich Boy" is primarily about the failure of personal relations, and the essence of this failure is the abortive romance between Paula and Anson. The sensitive description of their relationship shows the superior awareness of the woman in a manner which is in close accordance with some current feminist thought and its claim that women have an intuitive understanding of the meaning of love which many men lack. Paula is rich, like Anson, yet somehow she has preserved a capacity for love which he never really understands or is capable of reacting to on an equal basis. He realizes that "on his side much was insincere" in their relationship, and he is even said to despise the "emotional simplicity" of her feelings for him. At the same time, and in spite of himself, he is drawn to her sincerity and the "enormous seriousness" of what is called their "dialogue."

With a part of himself, Anson is aware of what Paula has to offer him and what is at stake, but he values neither her nor his own feelings highly enough to grant love the central place it might have occupied in their lives. In the course of their courtship, he squanders his own emotional potential and rejects, without understanding it, Paula's love for him. The relation to her is the only thing that could have "saved" Anson from his superficiality and made it possible to develop other and more deeply human qualities in him, but the arrogance behind his relaxed self-confidence precludes any such change. Failing to see any need for adjustment in himself, he makes real interaction and communication with Paula impossible, and she is not the sort of person who is willing to submit her will and wishes totally to those of a future husband. Thus, after their first argument, when Anson has been drunk at a dinner party, he apologizes to Paula and her mother but shows no real remorse and makes no promises. Consequently, as it is stated, "the psychological moment had passed forever." In other words, the chances of establishing a genuine dialogue, a process of give and take, are lost.

Anson and Paula then go their separate ways, he to become an established businessman and popular bachelor, she to get married and remarried and have three children. They meet again after a lapse of several years, and this encounter demonstrates that Anson still does not fathom what has happened to either of them. Paula makes it clear that her love for him had stayed with her for a long time in spite of her other men. She tells Anson, woundingly but with understandable bitterness, that she now has found love for the first time, with her second husband, but then she dies in the attempt to bring this man's child into the world. Thus her short life comes to a tragic end at least partly due to Anson Hunter's failure to live up to her sincere expectations.

Their final dialogue is revealing:

> "I was infatuated with you, Anson—you could make me do anything you liked. But we wouldn't have been happy. I'm not smart enough for you. I don't like things to be complicated like you do." She paused. "You'll never settle down," she said.
>
> The phrase struck at him from behind—it was an accusation that of all accusations he had never merited.
>
> "I could settle down if women were different," he said, "If I didn't understand so much about them, if women didn't spoil you for other women, if they had only a little pride. If I could go to sleep for a while and wake up into a home that was really mine—why, that's what I'm made for, Paula, that's what women have seen in me and liked in me. It's only that I can't get through the preliminaries any more."

Because of Anson's immaturity, their love could not develop beyond the stage of infatuation, although Paula had been aware of the power of her emotions and had been willing to do anything for him. Anson likes the idea of marriage and claims that he is made for the role of husband and head of the home, but he is not ready to make the emotional effort that is required, or, as he puts it, get on with the preliminaries. Without seeming to be aware of it, he reveals his spiritual laziness in his wish that he might go to sleep and wake up in a home of his own without having to work for it in any sense. This laziness is Anson Hunter's great misfortune, and though he is never made to understand himself clearly, his underlying feelings of despair and loss emerge on two occasions. When Paula becomes engaged to her first husband, he breaks down and cries, even in public, several times, and after their last meeting he suffers from "depression" and "intense nervousness" and goes to Europe on a three months' vacation.

When Paula dies, his depression seems to lift as he sets out on his voyage, suggesting that her ceasing to function as a reminder to him of his weakness makes him capable of forgetting it and resuming his old role as a charming but superficial ladies' man. On the ship he returns to this role and becomes involved with a girl wearing a red tam-o-shanter. He likes and needs women, but only to "spend their brightest, freshest, rarest hours to nurse and protect that superiority he cherished in his heart." Anson remains a child, emotionally speaking, attractive but unreliable, and ultimately egocentric in a manner which probably will spoil his chances of achieving the happy marriage he seems to want. The suggestion is that he will always need new, admiring women to affirm the sense of superiority that has become the essence of his identity. Through the figure of Anson Hunter, Fitzgerald has deliv-

ered a damaging blow against the American rich and their frequently inflated image of themselves as the leaders of their nation. (pp. 42-3)

> *Helge Normann Nilsen, "A Failure to Love: A Note on F. Scott Fitzgerald's 'The Rich Boy',"* in The International Fiction Review, *Vol. 14, No. 1, Winter, 1987, pp. 40-3.*

ROBERT ROULSTON (essay date 1988)

[*In the following excerpt, Roulston characterizes "May Day" as a work in which Fitzgerald combines elements of his early* Saturday Evening Post *stories with those published in H. L. Mencken's* Smart Set.]

Many of the flaws of **"May Day"** result from its being a combination of incongruous elements. Part traditional fiction and part avant-garde, it combines plot devices characteristic of Fitzgerald's early *Saturday Evening Post* stories with themes of the less popular pieces that appeared in *The Smart Set*. It also juxtaposes naturalism and satire. It has some of the breadth of the novel it was originally to have been and the concentration of the successful short story. It is alternately funny and sad, ludicrous and disturbing—a discordant piece that captures the silliness and pathos, the banality and vitality of the Jazz Age, whose opening it heralds and dramatizes. As in a Charles Ives symphony, where hymn tunes collide with passages from Beethoven, the effect is simultaneously crude and stimulating. Faults become inseparable from virtues, and the lack of synthesis is part of the message.

Fitzgerald should not have been surprised when *The Saturday Evening Post* rejected **"May Day."** Few stories would seem less likely to have appealed to the magazine's morally conservative, probusiness editor, George Horace Lorimer. After all, it opens with a parody of the Bible and ends with a suicide. In between are riots, debauchery, a sordid liaison, and a monstrous marriage. One character gets his leg broken; another is shoved from a window to his death. Throughout nearly everyone is intoxicated, as Fitzgerald offers mordant comments on rich and poor, reactionaries and radicals.

Such fare was patently closer to the tastes of H. L. Mencken, the iconoclastic editor of *The Smart Set*, who published the story in July 1920 after it had been spurned by editors of all the large-circulation magazines. Yet in certain respects **"May Day"** is closer to the six Fitzgerald stories the *Post* published in 1920 than to most of his other works that appeared in *The Smart Set*. Not only is it more plotted than *The Smart Set* pieces usually are, but the narrative pivots about the central device of the *Post* stories, the mismatched couple—a congenial subject, no doubt, because of Fitzgerald's difficulties at the time with Zelda. Sometimes the obstacle—as in **"Myra Meets His Family," "Head and Shoulders,"** and **"The Offshore Pirate"**—is a disparity in wealth or social status. In **"The Camel's Back"** the impediment is temperamental incompatibility. In **"The Ice Palace"** different regional backgrounds divide the pair. In the sixth *Post* story, **"Bernice Bobs Her Hair,"** the heroine's small-town provinciality brings her into conflict with both male and female members of the country-club set in a large midwestern city.

In **"May Day,"** therefore, Gordon Sterrett, trapped in a relationship with a proletarian Circe, Jewel Hudson, has the kind of problem that confronts the heroes of the early *Post* fiction. So, too, does Peter Himmel, who escorts Gordon's old flame,

Edith Bradin, to a fraternity dance at Delmonico's Restaurant in New York, only to be rebuffed by her before he sets off on a binge with another Yale man, Phil Dean. The rejection and the subsequent bacchanalian capers are reminiscent of events in **"The Camel's Back."**

In many of the early *Post* stories, however, the plots are so farcical or improbable that Fitzgerald can resolve narrative dilemmas in them through a sequence of ever more absurd twists leading to preposterous and usually comic culminations. (pp. 207-08)

In **"May Day"** all the story lines end unhappily. Gordon Sterrett, blackmailed by his vulgar mistress, wakes from a drunken stupor to find himself married to her. He then shoots himself. Peter Himmel and his drinking partner, Phil Dean, climax their debauch by soaring pointlessly in an elevator to the top of the Biltmore Hotel wearing In and Out signs stolen from the cloakroom of Delmonico's. In a third narrative line, two recently discharged veterans, Gus Rose and Carrol Key, crash a party at Delmonico's, where Key's brother is a waiter, and later join a mob in an attack on a socialist newspaper edited by Edith Bradin's brother, Henry. Key gets shoved to his death, and Gus breaks Henry Bradin's leg.

The unhappy endings in **"May Day,"** however, are as contrived as the happy ones in the early *Post* stories. Too many characters happen to be at the right place at the right times, and Sterrett's collapse and destruction occur too precipitously. His compromising letters to Jewel Hudson are an implausible device to put him in her power; furthermore, his marriage to her is as unbelievable as anything in **"The Offshore Pirate."** Where did they get a marriage license so quickly? Who would have officiated while the groom was so inebriated he could barely stand erect? Where did Sterrett's pistol come from? Would a young man just three years out of Yale and from a good family be in such desperate straits? It is also unlikely that Peter Himmel would be dating the very girl Sterrett has been pining for, that she in turn would be the sister of the editor whose office is attacked by Gus and Carrol, whose brother works at Delmonico's—and so forth, as the coincidences mount as high as the Biltmore where just about everyone shows up including Gus, who, for no discernible reason, is there exactly when Edith comes in and recognizes him as the man who has broken her brother's leg.

So many improbabilities would devastate an entire novel by Theodore Dreiser or Frank Norris. **"May Day,"** on the other hand, not merely survives them; it flourishes in part because of them. While not exactly a fantasy, Fitzgerald's story is phantasmagoric with a nightmarish, drunken hallucinatory quality that can accommodate barely credible events. In this regard, as in others, it more resembles *Post* farces like **"The Camel's Back"** and **"Heads and Shoulders"** than it does naturalistic fiction, resonances of Dreiser and Norris notwithstanding.

Too much has been made of such resonances. Lehan, in particular, believes that the influence of Norris is a major cause of the melodrama and implausibility of both **"May Day"** and *The Beautiful and Damned.* But an important difference exists between the story and Fitzgerald's novel. *The Beautiful and Damned,* like Norris's *McTeague* and *Vandover and the Brute,* writhes along from episode to episode, the main structural principle being the protagonist's downward trajectory. All three books abound in extraneous incidents and descriptions. In **"May Day"** Gordon Sterrett may plunge like Van-

dover, but Sterrett is no mere naturalistic hero, just as the story as a whole is no Norris-like boa constrictor bulging with indigestible prey. Although some of the themes of **"May Day"** savor of Norris and of Norris's advocate, H. L. Mencken, the overplotted narrative suggests Fitzgerald's recent *Post* stories.

Unlike Lorimer of the *Post,* Mencken preferred loosely structured fiction. In fact, five years later, in defending *The Great Gatsby* against Mencken's charge that the novel is hardly more than an anecdote, Fitzgerald contended that he had written the book as a protest against the formless works Mencken liked.

Although Mencken's influence is undoubtedly present in **"May Day,"** it should not be overestimated. Many Menckenesque features of the story—flippancy, scoffing at authority, admiration for superior people, contempt for incompetent lower orders, and disdain for plutocrats—abound in undergraduate stories Fitzgerald had written when, as he himself stated, Mencken had been "little more than a name." To be sure, throughout his career Fitzgerald would acquire ideas and techniques second-hand from conversations, book reviews, and imitative works. And even before 1920 Mencken had been so famous that Fitzgerald must have had some inkling of what Mencken had been advocating.

But whether as a result of direct influence or of a fortuitous convergence of sensibilities, **"May Day"** does reveal certain clear affinities with Mencken. James W. Tuttleton may be correct in perceiving Mencken's impact upon the style. Certainly the "hyperbole, the high-flown rhetoric and the archaisms" Tuttleton cites savor of the master. Even more redolent of Mencken are the flippant asides, as when Fitzgerald describes Edith Bradin's dreamy state after prolonged dancing as "equivalent to a noble soul after several long highballs." Fitzgerald here is indulging in the kind of Prohibition bashing that led Mencken to propose to "abolish all the sorrows of the world by the simple device of getting and keeping the whole human race gently stewed" ("Portrait of an Ideal World").

Even more characteristic of Mencken is Fitzgerald's barb about Henry Bradin, the socialist editor, having come to New York "to pour the latest cures for incurable evils into the columns of a radical newspaper." Fitzgerald's thrust at socialism resembles Mencken's assault on Thorstein Veblen's critique of capitalism as a "wraith of balderdash" ("Professor Veblen"). Furthermore, Fitzgerald's description of that pair of *Untermenschen,* Gus Rose and Carrol Key—the one "swart and bandy-legged," the other with a "long, chinless face . . . dull, watery eyes . . . without a suggestion of either ancestral worth or native resourcefulness"—are like Mencken's jibes at "the weak and the botched" and disdain for the "simian gabble of the crossways" he encountered in Dayton, Tennessee, while covering the Scopes trial for *The Baltimore Sun* ("In Memoriam: W. J. B.").

Despite scattered Menckenseque touches, however, the dialogue, syntax, and even the tone of **"May Day"** are not substantially different from their equivalents in Fitzgerald's *Post* fiction of 1920. One finds the same briskness and brashness, fondness for brittle ironic banter, and bursts of colorful rhetoric. A stylistic difference, however, between **"May Day"** and, say, **"The Ice Palace"** or even the frivolous **"The Offshore Pirate"** is that whereas in these *Post* stories Fitzgerald permitted himself passages of unabashed lyricism, in **"May**

Day" the cynicism is relentless. Thus he defaces with a sneer the most beautiful passage in the story, the marvelous evocation of morning light coming through the window of Child's Restaurant: "Dawn had come up in Columbus Circle, magical breathless dawn, silhouetting the great statue of the immortal Christopher, and mingling in a curious and uncanny manner with the fading yellow electric light inside." Robert Sklar is right: Fitzgerald has robbed the passage of "romantic wonder" with his daub of irony.

Yet Fitzgerald's reluctance to evoke "romantic awe" in such a story is understandable. He would later envelop Jay Gatsby and Dick Diver in shimmering prose because he wanted to invest them with glamour. In **"May Day,"** on the other hand, he deflates not just buffoons like Gus Rose and Peter Himmel but precisely the sort of characters he exalts elsewhere. Thus Edith Bradin, a potential Daisy Fay, is a narcissist whose language is "made up of the current expressions, bits of journalese and college slang strung together into an intrinsic whole, careless, faintly provocative, delicately sentimental." She is also given to admiring her own face and figure and telling herself that she smells sweet and is "made for love." Sterrett, a failed artist, stumbles about in a perpetual alcoholic fog, with blood-streaked eyes and trembling hands—more contemptible than pathetic as he wallows in self-pity. Lest any reader confer undue respect upon Edith's idealistic brother, Fitzgerald deflates him with the denigratory comments previously cited and underscores his disdain by adding that Edith, "less fatuously" than Henry Bradin, wants to cure Sterrett rather than the "incurable evils" of society.

More striking even than the wedding of Menckenesque sarcasm with *Saturday Evening Post* material is Fitzgerald's blend in **"May Day"** of traditional narrative methods with innovative ones. James R. Miller, Jr., too readily accepts Fitzgerald's claim that he had no model for the technique of the story. Miller is right, however, in noting how the technique anticipates what John Dos Passos would later do and in observing that Fitzgerald would not employ this approach again. In 1920, however, the use of parallel stories loosely connected, yet in some measure autonomous, was hardly unprecedented. Elizabethan dramatists frequently resorted to such plots, and like Fitzgerald they would intermix comedy with tragedy.

A search, however, for an earlier practitioner of this kind of storytelling need not extend back beyond the nineteenth century. There, right in the heart of Victorian England, loomed Charles Dickens, his novels bursting with plots, subplots, and parallel plots—all with melodrama cheek and jowl with low comedy. Dickens' contemporary, Thackeray, whose influence on *Gatsby* Fitzgerald acknowledged, was also given to multiple plots. So was Leo Tolstoy, whose twin crisscrossed story lines in *Anna Karenina* foreshadow the contrasting fates of Sterrett and Dean. Similarly, the concluding part of Dreiser's *Sister Carrie* shifts back and forth between Carrie ascending toward stardom on the stage and Hurstwood, her lover, sinking lower until he commits suicide in a flophouse. In short, **"May Day"** looks back to Dickens, Thackeray, Tolstoy, and Dreiser as much as it looks forward to Dos Passos. In one important sense, in fact, it is closer to nineteenth-century fiction than to most serious twentieth-century writing. Fitzgerald binds together his narrative strands with unlikely encounters between characters in a manner reminiscent of Dickens but that would have been alien to Joyce, Hemingway, or Faulkner.

Yet **"May Day"** seems modern in a way that the *Post* stories and even *The Great Gatsby* and *Tender Is the Night* do not. Much of that avant-garde aura comes from the pacing of the story more than from the structure. In 1920—and indeed long afterwards—modernity meant angularity, jaggedness, disconnectedness. It meant the dissonance of Stravinsky, the distortions of Picasso, the fragmentation of Joyce and Eliot. In *This Side of Paradise* Fitzgerald made some gestures toward this type of sensibility by altering his narrative method from section to section much as Joyce had done in *A Portrait of the Artist as a Young Man* and would soon do on an even grander scale in *Ulysses.* But like most great modernists Joyce used rigorously applied methods to give new forms to his apparent chaos. Fitzgerald, however, in *This Side of Paradise* arbitrarily switches from prose to poetry and from dialogue to narrative, tossing in undergraduate pieces here and afterthoughts there. The result is a modernistic manner without the innovative substance of Joyce and Eliot. Fitzgerald, in truth, was never a radical in aesthetics any more than in politics. When he rebelled, he was likely to produce what Edmund Wilson perceived in *This Side of Paradise* as "a gesture of indefinite revolt" rather than a sustained assault on authority and convention.

A similar gesture pervades **"May Day."** The cynical asides, the mocking preface, and the fragmented narrative do not obliterate the conservatism that was always a part of Fitzgerald's character. Just as Gordon Sterrett and Edith Bradin look back nostalgically on their own prewar days, so Fitzgerald reaches back to traditional forms of fiction. The story is less an experiment in form than a speeded-up version of a nineteenth-century novel with multiple plots, chance encounters, theatrical climaxes, and tidy denouements. The effect, however, of forcing into a few pages what Dickens would have put in hundreds is that of a motion picture film run at high speed. All is jerky, ludicrous, and surreal. **"May Day,"** then, becomes a frenzied film clip of the birth of the Jazz Age. Its disparate elements, juxtaposed so daringly, do not coalesce and should not, because underlying both the action and the language are two irreconcilable emotions—disgust and élan. Perhaps only a story that should not be taken altogether seriously could adequately capture simultaneously this incongruous pair of attitudes that, in their very incompatibility, seem to capture the *Zeitgeist* of the early 1920s. Fitzgerald, of course, was already becoming the self-proclaimed bard of that *Zeitgeist* and was well upon his way toward viewing himself as both its exemplar and its victim.

Much of the disgust, hence, is self-disgust of the sort that made Fitzgerald exclaim in 1921 to Maxwell Perkins: "I'm sick of the flabby semi-intellectual softness in which I flounder with my generation." Even in that outburst, however, he viewed his own weakness as symptomatic of a larger malaise. In **"May Day"** he directs his disgust at nearly every target in sight. The largest target is the central event of the story, the May Day riots of 1919, which he would recall a decade later with rancor.

> When the police rode down the demobilized country boys gaping at the orators in Madison Square, it was the sort of measure bound to alienate the more intelligent young men from the prevailing order. We didn't remember anything about the Bill of Rights until Mencken began plugging it, but we did know that such tyranny belonged to the jittery little countries of South Europe. ("Echoes of the Jazz Age")

But, if the brunt of Fitzgerald's disgust here would seem to fall upon the authorities and their minions, in **"May Day"** hardly any group escapes it. Wealthy Phil Dean is a profligate and a cad. Plebians Gus Rose and Carrol Key are subhuman. One of the two major female characters is a low-class temptress; the other is a shallow upper-class flirt. The socialists are naive fools; the Ivy League graduates are self-centered debauchees. Waiters, like Carrol Key's brother, are sycophants. History, embodied in the statue of Columbus, is derided; the future is a pointless ride up an elevator to a nonexistent floor as Dean and Himmel scream "higher" to the operator after reaching the top. And through all the folly and selfishness flows a ceaseless stream of alcohol. Sterrett's suicidal alcoholism, of course, is a lurid enlargement of Fitzgerald's own growing drinking problems, just as Dean's and Himmel's drunken prank with the In and Out signs from Delmonico's is a fictionalized version of one of Fitzgerald's binges with a fellow Princetonian, Porter Gillespie.

Indeed, Fitzgerald imposed some of his own less attractive qualities on various characters in **"May Day."** Sterrett shares not just his creator's weakness for liquor but also his self-pity. And just as Sterrett berates himself for failing to become an artist, so Fitzgerald complained constantly about the hackwork that kept him from writing serious fiction. Dean's vanity about his shirts and ties resembles Fitzgerald's sartorial snobbery. Even the lowly Carrol Key is akin to Fitzgerald in more than one way. Key's last name suggests that, like Francis Scott Key Fitzgerald, he is descended from the author of "The Star Spangled Banner." The first name also links him to the Maryland aristocracy to which Fitzgerald's father belonged. If the Fitzgeralds of Minnesota had not declined through "generations of degeneration" like Key's forebears, they were certainly less splendid than their Tidewater ancestors had been.

Yet despite the disgust directed at patricians and paupers, past and future, humanity and himself, Fitzgerald does not make **"May Day"** an orgy of nihilism. Perhaps he does not because Mencken had taught him to laugh at the world more than to rage at it. The Baltimore burgher was too much the sybarite to demolish the pleasant things in life to get at the bad ones. Similarly, for all his pessimism, the young man who wrote **"May Day"** had too much zest for living to surrender to the despair warranted by some of the events he depicts. **"May Day,"** in fact, captures the *carpe diem* exuberance Ernest Hemingway was to depict on a grander scale in *The Sun Also Rises.* Thus the anguished Sterrett, like the melancholy Robert Cohn, seems a colossal party-pooper. His troubles are real enough but are largely self-induced, and nothing in his demeanor or conduct is very prepossessing. He bawls and complains and reels about with rolling, bloodshot eyes. No doubt his college friend, Phil Dean, is being a bounder by refusing him the three hundred dollars Sterrett needs to meet Jewel Hudson's demand. Yet Sterrett is "bankrupt morally as well as financially", Jewel would certainly repeat her blackmail, and Sterrett appears incorrigible. Thus, under the circumstances, Dean's behavior is not unreasonable. He has come to New York for a holiday, and Sterrett is spoiling his fun. Like the botched Carrol Key, Sterrett is symptomatic of those "incurable evils" only foolish idealists like Henry Bradin worry about.

And so, in the bizarre carnival atmosphere of **"May Day,"** Sterrett's chamber of horrors is counterbalanced by the crazy-house revelry of the irresponsible Phil Dean and his equally irresponsible cohort, Peter Himmel. Sterrett's alcoholic nightmare is antithetical to the "warm glow" Himmel experiences after his third highball when he feels as though he were "floating on his back in pleasant water." Looking at the crowd on the street, Dean and Sterrett have opposite responses to the "display of humanity at its frothiest and gaudiest." To Dean the struggle is "significant, young, cheerful"; to Gordon it is "dismal, meaningless, endless." As Sterrett's already low fortunes decline even farther, Himmel and Dean soar to a manic state where everything becomes hilarious, and the wildest caprice seems feasible. Why not wear cloakroom signs? Why not threaten bodily harm to a waiter at Child's? Why not toss hash at the customers? Why not have liquor with breakfast? And why stop riding up an elevator even after reaching the top floor of the Biltmore?

Fitzgerald, to be sure, was no more a Dean or Himmel than he was a Sterrett, albeit pieces of himself went into all three characters, just as other pieces went into Key or even into the radical Henry Bradin. (After all, Amory Blaine, the hero of the largely autobiographical *This Side of Paradise,* claims to be a socialist.) Yet in at least one respect Dean and Himmel are closer than the other characters to the heart of **"May Day."** Their irresponsibility is perfectly attuned to the giddy pace, the capricious grafting together of genres, and the flippant comments throughout. Sterrett or Bradin could never have written **"May Day."** A talented Himmel or Dean just might have.

The sensibility that pervades Fitzgerald's later works, however, is remote from Himmel's. By the mid-1920s, when much of his own *joie de vivre* had waned, Fitzgerald would adopt the more somber point of view of Nick Carraway for *The Great Gatsby.* At the end of the decade Charles Wales, disgusted by his own and his friends' dissipation, would provide the focal point of **"Babylon Revisited,"** Fitzgerald's sad epilogue to the Jazz Age. In the prologue to that era, **"May Day,"** however, youth cavorts, and wet blankets are thrown aside with more sneers than tears. (pp. 208-14)

> *Robert Roulston, "Fitzgerald's 'May Day': The Uses of Irresponsibility," in* Modern Fiction Studies, *Vol. 34, No. 2, Summer, 1988, pp. 207-15.*

HERBIE BUTTERFIELD (essay date 1989)

[*In the following excerpt from* Scott Fitzgerald: The Promises of Life, *a collection of original criticism on various aspects of Fitzgerald's career, Butterfield surveys what he regards as Fitzgerald's ten best short stories from the 1920s.*]

Many of [Fitzgerald's stories] are slight, hasty, or formulaic stuff, but a few must rank with the finest of American short stories; and precisely ten I have found to stand out, to represent his best work in the genre from that decade, and as a group to take their place alongside *The Great Gatsby* and *Tender is the Night* as the third peak of his literary achievement.

Like the two great novels, these stories together chart the course of that decade, as Fitzgerald, both a deeply involved participant and a highly judgemental observer, experienced it. Indeed, one of the earliest, **"May Day",** is set on the very day that Fitzgerald singled out as the symbolic beginning of the era, 'when the police rode down the demobilized country boys gaping at the orators in Madison Square', which 'was the sort of measure bound to alienate the more intelligent young from the prevailing order'; while the last to be written, **"Babylon Revisited"**, has as its imaginative fulcrum that financial crash in which the age so 'spectacularly' died. In kind they range from fantasies, reminiscent both of Poe's Arabesques and Hawthorne's allegories (**"The Diamond as Big as the Ritz"**) to Joycean epiphanies (**"Absolution"**) to Jamesian nouvelles (**"The Rich Boy"**); in verbal texture from an early tendency to decorative excess to the limpid economy of **"Babylon Revisited"**, and in setting from the Middle West where he grew up, to the deep South where he did his army training and courted Zelda, to New York where he found fame, to Paris and fashionable Europe, where he spent and lost more than just his hard-earned money. As for the basic matter of the stories, it may all be discovered and contained in a brief biographical resumé: he was a lapsed Roman Catholic (**"Absolution"**), whose lineage on his Virginian father's side predisposed him to be youthfully entranced by the legend of the old sleepy time down South (**"The Ice Palace"**, **"The Last of the Belles"**); but whose entrepreneurial heritage on his McQuillan mother's side stirred him to be fascinated, albeit critically so, by the world of the rich (**"May Day"**, **"The Diamond as Big as the Ritz"**, **"Winter Dreams"**, **"The Rich Boy"**); and whose own professional success brought him at least a writer's measure of those riches, enough certainly for him to succumb to the characteristic ills, of conduct and spirit, that beset the rich (**"The Rough Crossing"**, **"One Trip Abroad"**, **"Babylon Revisited"**). But the ten stories are of course more than chronicles of a time or episodes from an autobiography; they are, at their best, small masterpieces of art and imagination, and they make a critique, all the more searing for its being founded in sympathy, of a nation and its dominant assumptions, its yearnings and aspirations, its prevailing ideology.

"The Ice Palace", written when Fitzgerald was 23 and published in May 1920, pivots upon the perception of extreme and ultimately irresolvable differences, of which the original and fundamental is that between the American South and the North. The idea for the story was apparently Zelda's, but its power, remarkable despite the too artificial symmetry of its design, must derive from its enactment of the profound division within Fitzgerald himself, at once a child of the 'energetic' North and of the 'lazy' South, which imaginatively he favoured. The Southern town here is Tarleton, Georgia—Zelda's Montgomery, Alabama, presumably, as much as anywhere else; the Northern city is coldly anonymous, but a version surely of St. Paul, Minnesota. The emblem of the South is the girl, 19-year-old Sally Carrol Happer, wholly identified with the South but attracted by 'a sort of energy' within her to the North, whose embodiment is her fiancé, Harry Bellamy. The South is all somnolence, elegance, memory, and melancholy. When we meet Sally Carrol she is gazing down 'sleepily . . . with a pleased and pleasant langour', in this town that is a 'languid paradise of dreamy skies and firefly evenings and noisy niggery street fairs', a place of 'drowsy picturesqueness', inhabited by 'gracious, soft-voiced girls, who were brought up on memories instead of money'. Facing backwards into the past, Sally Carrol has as 'one of her favourite haunts, the cemetry'; but her haunting there is not altogether morbid and Gothic, it being also to establish a temporal continuum, a flow of past into present, a bond between the dead and the living. 'Even when I cry I'm happy here, and I get a sort of strength from it.' For this is a world (idyllic, of course, not actual) of connections, of organic relationships, where 'over the trees and shacks and muddy rivers, flowed the heat, never hostile, only comforting, like a great warm

nourishing bosom for the infant earth. 'Down from his Northern city', Harry enters abruptly, 'tall, broad, and brisk'. Not for him mellow reverie or musing retrospect. 'Are you mournful by nature, Harry?' 'Not I.'

If it's summer in the South, according to the story's pattern of oppositions it must be winter in the North, when Sally Carrol travels there in the Pullman, with the cold creeping in everywhere, and outside the prospect of "a solitary farmhouse . . . ugly and bleak and lone in the white waste'. The differences are multiple and pervasive. . . . Where the South is courtly, feminine, and, in Sally Carrol's word, 'feline', the North is Bourgeois, 'a man's country', and 'canine'. The culmination of Sally Carrol's increasingly disenchanted Northern experience is the visit to the ice palace, an immense, fantastical construction out of blocks of ice, both a triumph of architectural engineering, whose proportions Harry tediously enumerates, and a symbol, in its very nature, of all that is ephemeral. When its blaze of electric lights goes out, Sally Carrol is left, confused, lost, likely to freeze to death, and terrified. Her terror, however, seems to be less of simply dying, than of dying here, 'frozen, heart, body, and soul', unable to be returned, earth to earth, in a place, such as her warm Southern cemetery, where flesh and soil more readily mingle.

Rescued, in her delirium she screams only: 'I want to get out of here! I'm going back home'; and we last see her in a brief tableau, again gazing sleepily at a Southern boy coming in his 'ancient Ford' to take her swimming in water 'warm as a kettla steam', under a sky whose 'wealth of golden sunlight poured a quite enervating yet oddly comforting heat'. She has recoiled from, rejected, the North; and, in addition to its climate and location, the North is, effectively and essentially, the culture of industrial capitalism, characterized by qualities cold rather than warm, by power rather than affection, efficiency rather than sentiment, severance rather than connectedness, ephemerality rather than continuity, the ice palace where 'all tears freeze' rather than the cemetery where 'even when I cry I'm happy.'

With its series of coincidentally overlapping stories, **"May Day"**, which was written soon after **"The Ice Palace"**, seems to belong to an indeterminate genre; in its length and number of viewpoints it is more than a short story, yet not quite a short novel, nor formally James's 'beautiful and blessed nouvelle'. It is the most naturalistic of his shorter works, evidence of the fact that he had by this time read and admired Dreiser and Frank Norris. The events of the story begin exactly 'at nine o'clock on the morning of the first of May, 1919', to conclude barely twenty-four hours later, yet the story proper is preceded by an introduction that has the character and is in the generalized time of the folk-tale or parable: the contemporary events we are to witness are but the latest shapes of ancient injustice and recurrent wrong.

The principal elements that are drawn together in this neatly co-ordinated story are the recently demobilized soldiery, the socialist opposition, the unfortunate and impoverished, and of course the rich. The soldiers are typically illiterate, drunken, spasmodically violent, and mindlessly mobbish. They are portrayed, if not with sympathy, at least with pity for their poverty and hunger, despised and discarded as they are, 'finding the great city thoroughly fed up with soldiers unless they were nicely massed into pretty uniforms under the weight of a pack and rifle'. And it must be on Fitzgerald's part in some sort of act of solidarity with their plight, as some expression of moral allegiance, that he gives to one of them his own family name of Key, 'a name hinting that in his veins, however thinly diluted by generations of degeneration, ran blood of some potentiality'. Key dies in a ludicrous accident, falling from a window while smashing up the offices of a socialist paper, which is edited by Henry Bradin, the idealist who seeks 'the latest cures for incurable evils', and whose legs are broken in the same fracas. We have come upon Bradin via his sister Edith, very much a socialite rather than a socialist, the former flame of Gordon Sterrett, a Yale graduate, full of artistic talent and promise, but down on his luck and now entangled in a relationship that is all unromantic reality, complicated, squalid, and touched by blackmail. Gordon needs money, desperately, and for a loan seeks out his college-friend, Philip Dean, who for this story represents the rich man, here unredeemed by any splendour of imagination, merely complacent, hard-hearted, meanly calculating, grossly self-indulgent, and self-righteously reproving:

> 'You seem to be sort of bankrupt—morally as well
> as financially. . . . There's a regular aura about
> you that I don't understand. It's a sort of evil.'
> 'It's an air of worry and poverty and sleepless
> nights', said Gordon, rather defiantly.

But his is a small ration of defiance, and the story ends with this soft and sensitive man's suicide, while the boorish, overweening Philip cavorts in a drunken oblivion. The socialist, a marginal figure at best, is in hospital, broken by those he would strengthen; the cast-off warrior is dead, and the failed artist and foolish lover too. Only the rich survive intact, gambolling and gallivanting on May Day. In its connections, implicit and explicit, in its perception of a wholly interlocking society, **"May Day"** is very much a political story, but also a very pessimistic one. 'The events of 1919', observed Fitzgerald many years later, 'left us cynical rather than revolutionary'.

The rich in **"May Day",** gathered at the Yale Club and Delmonico's are rich by inheritance; and their riches are simply what they have grown up accustomed to and have never been for them the fabulous stuff of dreams. There is no magic in **"May Day",** as there will be magic in *The Great Gatsby,* for instance. Nor is there magic in the quintessentially entitled **"The Rich Boy",** though its opening section contains the famous sentences, which Hemingway thought he lampooned: 'Let me tell you about the very rich. They are different from you and me.' Written and published some five years after **"May Day", "The Rich Boy",** which traces Anson Hunter's early life until the age of 29, is more truly a nouvelle than the earlier work. It is also a study, not one of Fitzgerald's fables; but a singular study, not a sociology: 'There are no types, no plurals. There is a rich boy, and this is his and not his brother's story.' Even so, we know that this rich boy's is an exemplary tale. (pp. 94-9)

There is nothing especially vicious about Anson, and early on at least he is capable of love and tears. But gradually his wealth chills and hardens and shrinks him, until he is at best letting others do the living for him (taking 'a vicarious pleasure in happy marriages'), and at worst casually destroying trust ('Dolly Karger, lying awake and staring at the ceiling, never again believed in anything at all') and purposefully creating the circumstances that drive another man to suicide, for his part in which human disaster he 'never blamed himself'. He fends off any self-questioning, comes to let nothing touch him deeply, fully reach him. At 29 he is something of a

beached shell, dry, deserted, around New York society displaced by arrivistes, indeed a hollow man in a waste land; but, as he sails world-wearily for a summer in Europe he still has charm and desire enough for a mildly revivifying shipboard romance. . . . **"The Rich Boy"** is less pathetic and less catastrophic than many of Fitzgerald's tales of life amongst the rich, but it is in many respects bleaker and morally more devastating, with its last glimpse of a superior young man, trying to shore up the walls within which he may continue to immure himself in a numbed and sterile solipsism.

According to Hawthorne's differentiation of the Novel from the Romance, **"May Day"** and **"The Rich Boy"** in their social and psychological realism belong, their lack of length apart, within the order of the Novel. In contrast, **"The Diamond as Big as the Ritz",** which had been written in the Autumn of 1921, is entirely a Romance, or a Fantasy as Fitzgerald himself categorized it for its inclusion in *Tales of the Jazz Age;* from which it should not be inferred that its principal intent is anything other than symbolically to uncover the hidden, dangerous, and altogether real power in the hands of the very rich, those who hold the world's purse-strings.

John T. Unger comes from 'a small town on the Mississippi', Hades, not to be 'confused with another place that was abolished long ago', Twain's world surely, of boosters and suckers and hoaxers and con-men and Tall-Tale-tellers. Sent back East to St. Midas's School to learn a knowledge of priorities, he befriends Percy Washington, whose father is simply 'by far

Photograph by Carl Van Vechten of Fitzgerald shortly before he went to Hollywood in 1937.

the richest man in the world', and is invited to spend a holiday with him at his home 'in the West'. Out there in the Montana Rockies there is revealed to him what is indeed a religious vision for one who 'has the earnest worship of and respect for riches as the first article of [his] creed'. The Washington estate, an uncharted El Dorado in a mountain stronghold, is a paradise of infinite riches, and the home a fabulous castle 'in a sort of floating fairyland', a dream of oriental magnificence translated to the occident, which Fitzgerald delineates in a tour de force of exotic description and extravagant detail.

The source of this immeasurable wealth is the mountain itself, 'literally nothing else but solid diamond . . . bigger than the Ritz-Carlton hotel', which Percy's grandfather, FitzNorman Washington, had stumbled upon by accident. The Washingtons and their experience are to be taken as archetypally American. They are descended from the first national hero and president, and also, so that catholics may not feel excluded from the heritage, from the Roman Catholic founder of Maryland, Lord Baltimore. The fortune stems from sheer chance, as in many a gold and oil strike. The smooth running of affairs requires an ignorant, complaisant, and uncritical work-force (here a line of black slaves who do not realize that the Civil War is over). And the place is the West, whither vast wealth progressively, boundlessly, moves. Bribery, general corruption, all manner of falsification, misapplication of science, and murder have been amongst the methods by which FitzNorman and his son Braddock have preserved their riches, the secret of the amount of those riches and their origins, and ultimately their control of the world economy. For Braddock Washington now is not just the richest man in the world but its absolute monarch, even if unknown to his subjects, the 'Emporer of Diamonds, king and priest of the age of gold'. When finally the world breaks through and threatens his kingdom, it is 'not in suppliance, but in pride' that, 'magnificently mad', he addresses God as an equal, offering Him a bribe to turn back time, unable to believe that anything in the Universe, even its creator, is beyond price. But God, with 'a mutter of dull, menacing thunder, . . . refused to accept the bribe'. Whereupon, with dynamite, not yet nuclear weapons, Braddock Washington blows up his world, leaving John T. Unger (in the company of Braddock's two daughters, whose sentimental sideshow has rightly not detained us) to 'escape to tell thee', like Ishmael escaping from that other world-destroying megalomaniac. Fabulously opulent as William Randolph Hearst, fabulously secretive as Howard Hughes, Braddock Washington, with his wealth and his power, is no figure of fantasy.

The Great Gatsby partakes of both the romance of **"The Diamond as Big as the Ritz"** and the realism of **'The Rich Boy'**, but its closest affinity is with **"Winter Dreams"**, which is in important respects the seed-bed of the novel. For Jimmy Gatz, not yet Jay Gatsby, digging clams on the shore of Lake Superior, read Dexter Green, caddying on the golf-course in Black Bear; for Daisy Buchanan, read Judy Jones, whose voice (like Daisy's 'full of money'), whose smile, and not least whose tantrums, at the age of mere 11, enthrall Dexter, himself 'not yet fourteen', so that abruptly he changes the shape of his young life, 'unconsciously dictated to by his winter dreams'. The girl, with her style born of money, composes an image of another world, beyond present reach, beyond hope of immediate entry, but not beyond dream and aspiration. So over the next few years, Dexter acquires first a preliminary

social undercoat at 'a famous university in the East', and then, almost effortlessly, 'he made money. It was amazing.'

Now he meets Judy again, if not as her equal, at least self-confident in the knowledge that he is 'the rough, strong stuff from which [the rich, her kind] eternally sprang'; poetical rough stuff, though, enchanted by 'the sound of a piano over a stretch of water', and of course enchanted by Judy, a spoiled child, playful and fanciful, 'entertained only by the gratification of her desires and by the direct exercise of her own charm'. In their intermittent involvement that follows, blown hot and cold at Judy's whim, they hurt others and they hurt themselves, twisting in 'webs of tangled emotions'. He comes to know 'deep happiness', and he comes to know 'deep pain', for their romance is as marvellous as their relationship is impossible. Then she ends it. Seven years later he hears of her again, a faded beauty now, by no means wretched, but married, as Daisy will be, to a man who 'drinks and runs around'. Her ordinary, slightly sad, slightly shabby fortune rings a death-knell for him; it signals the loss of a certain kind of vision, of a sense of possibility, of a glow around the edge of things. 'Even the grief he could have borne was left behind in the country of illusion, of youth, of the richness of life, where his winter dreams had flourished.' A tale eventually of disenchantment and disillusionment, **"Winter Dreams"** is nevertheless as affecting as it is precisely because of the conviction with which Fitzgerald casts the earlier spell of enchantment and conducts the play of illusion, a hint of the triumph to come.

"Absolution" also has a connection with *The Great Gatsby*, being a reworking of a discarded opening to the novel. Of all Fitzgerald's works, it is the one most concentrated upon Roman Catholicism, although it would seem to be less closely autobiographical than many of his other stories. It is a tale of release, of escape from a markedly puritanical version of the faith, and of entry into the life of the world. To one side is the church, requiring denial of appetite and desire, and dominating through fear; to the other is the world, warm and natural and sensual by day, bright and artificial and glamorous by night. In the middle, as he feels it, is Rudolph Miller, 'a beautiful, intense little boy of eleven', who has already felt 'a strange, romantic excitement' on overhearing 'immodest things' spoken of between a boy and a girl, yet who, fumbling in the confessional and inadvertently telling a lie, is still gripped by a terror of God's supernatural power. The priest to whom he confesses, in this small town in the prairie heartlands, is Father Schwartz, who from 'cold, watery eyes' shed cold tears, 'because the afternoons were warm and long, and he was unable to attain a complete mystical union with our Lord'. And there is Rudolph's father, Carl, a dim, drab man, but a zealous all-American catholic, whose 'two bonds with the colourful life were his faith in the Roman Catholic Church and his mystical worship of the Empire Builder, James J. Hill', and who beats his son with 'savage ferocity' to force him to go to Communion, when the son, unbeknown to the father, is in a state of sin. But the heavens do not fall, God does not pitch him into hell-fire; and Rudolph, carrying his mortal sin quite lightly, returns to make one last confession to Father Schwartz. And there before his eyes, the old priest, cracking under the strain of years of repressed longings and 'unclean thoughts' and self-thwarting, goes frighteningly, blatheringly mad, chattering to the little boy of crowds and parties and amusement parks, full of 'the heat and the sweat and the life', and the 'glitter' and, many times, the 'glimmering' of things—all the light and movement of the world, of which his faith has deprived him. As he collapses, in nervous exhaustion and hysterical laughter, bringing down his faith with him, Rudolph runs from the priest's house, runs from the church, into the arms of the world, ready for its romance and sensuous magic, having discovered that 'there was something ineffably gorgeous that had nothing to do with God.' Heaven will be a different place from now on, more worldly, more American, though no less heavenly and no more tangible; and Rudolph may begin to dream of golden girls and fairy riches, and metamorphose into Jay Gatsby.

If in **"Absolution"** Fitzgerald, in the guise of Rudolph Miller, walks away from the Roman Catholic Church, of which his mother in particular was a devout member, so in **"The Last of the Belles"** he bids farewell to the South, emptying his heart of the mystique that his father had inculcated in him. Written in November 1928, by which time relations between Scott and Zelda were deteriorating, it may also reflect the fact that by now his own Southern Belle appeared very much as a real person rather than a romantic ideal. Apart from **"The Rich Boy"**, whose narrator is peripheral and spectatorial, it is the only one of these ten stories to be told in the first person by one who is very much a participant.

It is set, like **"The Ice Palace"**, in Tarleton, Georgia, at the time of the First World War, and features again, though here as a secondary character, Sally Carrol Happer. On centre stage is her friend, the last of the belles, Ailee Calhoun, her 'lovely name' an echoing symbol of the old ante-bellum South, as she in herself is symbolic, 'the Southern type in all its purity', with 'notes in her voice that ordered slaves around, that withered Yankee captains'.

But already she has one foot in the real, modern world, where she overdoes her make-up, putting 'too much fever-coloured rouge on her face'; she is transmogrifying herself into the contemporary form of the flirt, or more specifically the flapper. With the officers' training camp nearby, she is surrounded by suitors, though, properly, sentimentally dynastic, she will marry only a man who 'measures up' to 'her brother who had died in his senior year at Yale'. One suitor, to her barely disguised thrill, kills himself in unrequited love of her; another, a Harvard man who might well 'measure up', seems to be leading the field, until the arrival in camp of Lieutenant Earl Schoen from New Bedford. Schoen certainly does not 'measure up'; promoted from the ranks, he does not come 'out of any background at all', and Ailee immediately spots him as a street-car conductor. Yet he is 'as fine a physical specimen as I have ever seen', and in his uniform, 'high-tempered and commanding'. He is as sexually alluring as, for Ailee, he is socially, sportively tantalizing, and, taking him off another girl, she begins an affair with him that belongs to the genre of wartime, or holiday, romance. Inevitably, after the war, out of uniform, dressed now according to his vulgar individuality, he appears to Ailee quite impossible. ' "Well, that's the end of it", he said moodily'; and on the train back North turned his attention to another girl, another 'jane'. And there for the time being the story ends, with Ailee, having played the wrong cards, bereft of all her suitors. There is a sequel, six years later, when the narrator, Andy, returns nostalgically to Tarleton and, meeting Ailee, thinks he discovers he has always been 'deeply and incurably in love with her'. But she is pledged now to a fellow-Southerner, in whom, unlike in a Northerner, she can feel secure, about whom she cannot be mistaken. Making one last visit to the site of the training camp, of which not a vestige remains, Andy shakes off the Southern spell:

> All I could be sure of was this place that had once been so full of life and effort was gone, as if it had never existed, and that in another month Ailee would be gone, and the South would be empty for me for ever.

"The Last of the Belles" is Fitzgerald's latest improvization on his major theme of disenchantment, of awakening in sour dawns from sweet dreams.

After this story of loss, with its diminuendo closure, Fitzgerald a few months later wrote **"The Rough Crossing"**, all tumult and crescendo, with a hesitant and pointedly unresolving coda. It is set on a transatlantic liner sailing from New York to Le Havre and meeting in mid-ocean with a hurricane, and it begins with a marvellous evocation of departure, the confusion, the excitement, the awe, 'when the past, the continent, is behind you; the future is that glowing mouth in the side of the ship'. Into that glowing mouth pass, with their children and their children's nurse, Adrian and Eva Smith, specifically a successful young playwright and his wife, but generally Adam and Eve Everyman we are surely invited to infer. The ship in which they sail will become a ship of fools, and the voyage, at the extremity of the storm's delirium, something of a dance of death. Personal emotion and the impersonal elements pace each other through the story, skilfully plotted on parallel courses. For Adrian Smith, somewhat jaded with wealth and fame, there will be, as the storm rises and exhilarates his blood, a hectic, restorative 'affaire' with a young girl whose 'youth seemed to flow into him, bearing him up into a delicate romantic ecstasy that transcended passion'. For Eva, untranscendently and comprehensively seasick, yet with enough awareness of things to be also comprehensively infuriated, there will be a different kind of ecstasy, a midnight drama of the self, as she ranges the ship in a fever of alcohol and jealousy. Eventually, climactically, at the height of the hurricane, she and Adrian, embodiments of nervous excess and emotional indulgence, are flung into one another's arms by wind and wave, and clinging together for the sake of their lives manage—this time—just—to survive. Meanwhile, as above deck the rich have disported themselves or plaintively suffered their bouts of seasickness, below the ship's doctor and nurse have all the time been trying and at length failing to save the life of a young steward. Coming upon him taken ill in her cabin, Eva, absorbed in her own mild biliousness, had groaned, ' "It made me sick to look at him. I wish he'd die" ', although she does have grace enough later to regret these words. His funeral, even in the midst of the hurricane, is conducted with due order and dignity. It is a British ship, and the funeral was all 'very British and sad'. **"The Rough Crossing"** is a story in the best tradition of American self-criticism and self-admonition, as it extends back through James to Cooper: these rich making such a distasteful, disorderly and undignified show of themselves are also, exclusively, these Americans. It is in all a thoroughly ominous story, permeated by a sense of engulfing disasters, individual and communal, to come.

The two remaining stories of my group of ten were both written in 1930, after the Wall Street Crash of the preceding October and at a time when the Fitzgeralds' marriage, now of ten years' duration, was about as steady and as promising as the national economy. Over the past few years, which they had spent mainly in France—in Paris and on the Riviera—

Scott's drinking had become increasingly uncontrolled, and Zelda's nervous health, also under alcoholic pressure, had finally collapsed in April 1930, when she entered a clinic in Switzerland with a severe breakdown. Together with the portentous **"The Rough Crossing"**, the stories of this time reflect, literally or symbolically, the experiences both of the Fitzgeralds personally and of the American nation, experiences which Fitzgerald felt to be significantly entwined.

If **"Winter Dreams"** was a jotting for *The Great Gatsby*, **"One Trip Abroad"** is even more clearly a sketch for *Tender is the Night*. The story's Nelson Kelly will emerge, fully portrayed, as Dick Diver; his wife is already forenamed Nicole. A rich young American couple, they are making their way around the old world, North Africa first, where they 'survive a plague' of locusts, as they may not in their travels survive a less natural, more social plague. It is here that they first come across another young couple, Mr. and Mrs. Liddell Miles, personifications of blasé aloofness and posturing world-weariness, opining that 'every place is the same. The only thing that matters is who's there.' In Sorrento they dabble in the arts, drink too much, and offend the English. (Where Fitzgerald's Americans are subtly and importantly discriminated, his English are caricatures: the unlikely figure of a cockney airman, and a choleric general and his choleric wife.) By Monte Carlo Nicole is being lightly reproved by a well-wisher for wasting her time with 'that crowd of drunks you run with'. . . . In Paris they descend further into pathos and ridicule when, as representative Americans, they are spectacularly bamboozled, publically taken for a ride, 'ripped off' as we would now say, by a sophisticated Europe, in the masquerading shape of a Count. And everywhere they go, mysteriously they catch a glimpse of the Mileses. At length, alcoholically and nervously deranged, they seek refuge in Switzerland, pitiably self-questioning: 'Why did we lose peace and love and health, one after the other?' So it seems have the Mileses, for they too are here, he looking 'weak and self-indulgent', she with 'eyes, intelligent enough, but with no peace in them'. One wild night, as the storm is lifting, Nelson and Nicole wander out into the garden of their hotel, where a late flash of lightning draws from Nicole 'a sharp, terrified cry'. For in that moment of illumination, of piercing insight, she sees in the garden the Mileses yet again and knows them, in all their spiritual sickness and vacancy, to be their döppelgangers: 'They're us! They're us! Don't you see?' It is a powerful and entirely convincing effect, and for Fitzgerald in the writing painfully and unflinchingly self-revealing.

In the last month of that year of breakdown and disintegration, Fitzgerald wrote **"Babylon Revisited"**, an exceptionally, exquisitely poignant story, told with a fine simplicity of means, his best story I think. It is Fitzgerald's definitive review both of his and Zelda's expatriate years and of the American 1920s and their collapse. Charlie Wales, now working in Prague, returns to Paris after eighteen months' absence—long, long ago, it feels, in part because so much has changed, and in part because Fitzgerald's sense of past time is always long-focused and essentially nostalgic. The American era, the American occupation is over. . . . Those royal days had been lavish and extravagant—and ephemeral. . . . Now he wishes to reassert something more austere and traditional; perhaps the true republican America: 'He believed in character; he wanted to jump back a whole generation and trust in character again as the eternally valuable element.'

Charlie Wales is here back in Paris, hoping to be reunited

with his 9-year-old daughter Honoria. Her mother, Helen, has died amidst the alcoholic delirium of the age of royalty, and Honoria lives now under the legal guardianship of Helen's sister, Marion Peters, who with a cold, level hatred blames Charlie for Helen's death and for most other things too. But Charlie has worked hard on himself, rigorously controlled his drinking, and set his heart, for Helen's sake too and in her memory, on making a home with and for Honoria. It begins to seem that his quest will be successful and that even a reluctant Marion may be agreeable, until Nemesis falls upon him from a great height in the shape of two drunken friends from the past who invade the Peters's house, sickening and shocking Marion, and reconfirming her in her opinion of Charlie. Defeated by these circumstances and now again rebuffed by Marion, he must pay for and be seen to pay for the human damage of the careless years. It is a moral matter, Fitzgerald knows, before and after it is financial. It was not in the crash that Charlie Wales had lost. No,

'I lost everything in the boom.'

'Selling short.'

'Something like that.'

Yet, for all the further sentence of loneliness, he is newly resolute and by that resolve self-confident. 'He would come back some day; they couldn't make him pay forever. . . . He wanted his child, and nothing was much good now, beside that fact.' It is a sad ending, of course, but a far less depressing ending than those to all the other stories we have read about the lives of the American rich, for it ends with an understanding of and a commitment to, not romance, but love.

These stories that have opened, followed and closed a peculiarly compact decade ensure Fitzgerald's place amongst the foremost American practitioners of the genre of the short story. At the same time, since they do not offer in their formal shapes and characters the very highest level of aesthetic satisfaction, they do not put him quite in the company of the outstanding masters of the form amongst his immediate predecessors and contemporaries, whom I take to be, in the English language, James, Kipling, Conrad, Joyce, Lawrence and Hemingway. Only **"Babylon Revisited"**, in its emotional concentration and in its rare fusion of intensity and reticence, is a story to rank with the very few and finest.

Nevertheless, not having read some of these stories before and not having read others for some time, I have been surprised to discover how good these ten are. The voice is at once awed (in the tradition of wonder and enthusiasm) and ironic (in the tradition of discrimination and judgement); and the style is at once sumptuous and melancholy, and always marvellously cadenced, as if his adored Keats had been translated through time and space and literary form to ode in story the American 1920s. And as for their substance, what a highly charged and well founded critique they provide of the world of the rich, or of the adventures of the capitalist economy, flourishing and floundering by turns, setting up and incidentally casting off its human elements. (It is a critique conducted, it seems to me, from midway between the wistfully patrician standpoint of John Peale Bishop and the panoramic Marxism, incipient in the late 1920s, of Fitzgerald's other closest literary friend at Princeton, Edmund Wilson.) The critique is all the more telling because it is regularly also a self-criticism, or stems from a self-criticism, oblique but severe; and in being of such a kind it is thereby able to demonstrate all the more effectively the attraction and allure of that money-making, money-mesmerized ethos. (pp. 100-10)

> *Herbie Butterfield, " 'All Very Rich and Sad': A Decade of Fitzgerald Short Stories," in* Scott Fitzgerald: The Promises of Life, *edited by A. Robert Lee, London: Vision Press, 1989, pp. 94-112.*

FURTHER READING

Allen, Joan M. *Candles and Carnival Lights: The Catholic Sensibility of F. Scott Fitzgerald,* pp. 93-101. New York: New York University Press, 1978.
Focuses on symbolism and religious themes in Fitzgerald's story "Absolution."

Arnold, Aerol. "Why Structure in Fiction: A Note to Social Scientists." *American Quarterly* X, No. 3 (Fall 1958): 325-37.
Discussion of the importance of structure to meaning and understanding in fiction. Arnold devotes a brief section to an analysis of what he considers the flawed narrator in Fitzgerald's story "The Rich Boy."

Atkinson, Jennifer McCabe. "Lost and Unpublished Stories by F. Scott Fitzgerald." *Fitzgerald/Hemingway Annual 1971* (1971): 32-63.
Catalogues and provides synopses for a number of Fitzgerald's previously unpublished stories.

Bewley, Marius. *The Eccentric Design,* pp. 259-87. New York: Columbia University Press, 1963.
Treats "The Diamond as Big as the Ritz" as a prologue to *The Great Gatsby,* stating that in this story "Fitzgerald's attitude to wealth as a constituent part of the American dream is most clearly revealed."

Bryer, Jackson R., and Kuehl, John. Introduction to *The Basil and Josephine Stories,* by F. Scott Fitzgerald. Edited by Jackson R. Bryer and John Kuehl, pp. vii-xxix. New York: Charles Scribner's Sons, 1973.
Chronicles composition and publication history of these stories and provides an appreciative critical overview.

Cass, Colin S. "Fitzgerald's Second Thoughts about 'May Day': A Collation and Study." *Fitzgerald/Hemingway Annual 1970* (1970): 69-95.
Compares the originally published *Smart Set* version of "May Day" with the revised version, included two years later in *Tales of the Jazz Age,* to illuminate the development of Fitzgerald's literary talent.

Casty, Alan. " 'I and It' in the Stories of F. Scott Fitzgerald." *Studies in Short Fiction* IX, No. 1 (Winter 1972): 47-58.
Expounds upon the assertion that Fitzgerald's "inability to choose, define, and become a self" is a central and abiding theme in the author's short fiction.

Cowley, Malcolm. Introduction to *The Stories of F. Scott Fitzgerald,* by F. Scott Fitzgerald, pp. vii-xxv. New York: Charles Scribner's Sons, 1951.
Poignant portrait of Fitzgerald amid the social and literary milieu of America during the 1920s and 1930s—"one decade with its long aftermath."

Crosland, Andrew. "Sources for Fitzgerald's 'The Curious Case of Benjamin Button'." *Fitzgerald Hemingway Annual 1979* (1979): 135-39.
Investigates the genesis of this story, extrapolating from Fitz-

gerald's own acknowledgment of debt to Mark Twain and Samuel Butler.

Daniels, Thomas E. "The Text of 'Winter Dreams'." *Fitzgerald/Hemingway Annual 1977* (1977): 77-100.
Proposes the superiority of the English over the American versions of Fitzgerald's short stories, focusing on "Winter Dreams."

———. "Toward a Definitive Edition of F. Scott Fitzgerald's Short Stories." *The Papers of the Bibliographical Society of America* 71, No. 3 (1977): 295-310.
Recounts the confusion surrounding the many extant versions of Fitzgerald's short stories.

Drake, Constance. "Josephine and Emotional Bankruptcy." *Fitzgerald/Hemingway Annual 1969* (1969): 5-13.
Examines the theme of emotional bankruptcy in Fitzgerald's Josephine stories.

Elstein, Rochelle S. "Fitzgerald's Josephine Stories: The End of the Romantic Illusion." *American Literature* 51, No. 1 (March 1979): 69-83.
Traces the psychological and emotional collapse of the protagonist of the Josephine stories.

Fulkerson, Tahita N. "Ibsen in 'The Ice Palace'." *Fitzgerald/Hemingway Annual 1979* (1979): 169-71.
Assertion of Fitzgerald's debt in "The Ice Palace" to Norwegian dramatist Henrik Ibsen

Gallo, Rose Adrienne. *F. Scott Fitzgerald.* New York: Frederick Ungar Publishing Co., 1978, 166 p.
Biographical and critical study. Includes a chapter on Fitzgerald's short fiction.

Gruber, Michael Paul. "Fitzgerald's 'May Day': A Prelude to Triumph." *Essays in Literature* 2, No. 1 (1973): 20-35.
Characterizes "May Day" as "the first important work in [Fitzgerald's] canon of fiction" and as "a prelude to the author's later masterpieces."

Hagemann, E. R. "For the Record: Should Scott Fitzgerald Be Absolved for the Sins of 'Absolution'." *Journal of Modern Literature* 12, No. 1 (March 1985): 169-74.
Details incidents of "loose diction, violated point of view, flawed characterization, and even faulty grammar" in Fitzgerald's "Absolution."

Higgins, John A. *F. Scott Fitzgerald: A Study of the Stories.* New York: St. John's University Press, 1971, 212 p.
Detailed analysis of Fitzgerald's short stories, designed to "familiarize the interested reader with their nature and to evaluate them as art" and to study "their relationship to the novels."

Katz, Joseph. "The Narrator and 'The Rich Boy'." *Fitzgerald Newsletter* No. 32 (Winter 1966): 208-10.
Disputes the common identification of Fitzgerald with the narrator of "The Rich Boy," characterizing this story as an example of Fitzgerald's "concern with the technique of point of view."

Kuehl, John. Introduction to *The Apprentice Fiction of F. Scott Fitzgerald: 1909-1917,* by F. Scott Fitzgerald, pp. 3-16. New Brunswick, N.J.: Rutgers University Press, 1965.
Surveys Fitzgerald's earliest stories and dramas, emphasizing in the essay's second half prefigurations of the *femme fatale,* a character type that Kuehl maintains dominated the author's later work.

———. "A la Joyce: The Sisters Fitzgerald's Absolution." *James Joyce Quarterly* 2, No. 1 (Fall 1964): 2-6.
Traces influences of Joyce's story "The Sisters" in Fitzgerald's "Absolution."

LaHurd, Ryan. " 'Absolution': *Gatsby*'s Forgotten Front Door." *College Literature* III, No. 2 (Spring 1976): 113-23.
    Discusses "Absolution" as a prologue to *The Great Gatsby.*

Le Vot, André. *F. Scott Fitzgerald.* Translated by William Byron. Doubleday & Co.: Garden City, N. Y., 1983, 393 p.
    Biography from a European perspective, claiming Fitzgerald as a kindred spirit of French writers.

Lehan, Richard D. *F. Scott Fitzgerald and the Craft of Fiction.* Carbondale and Edwardsville: Southern Illinois University Press, 1966, 206 p.
    Study of Fitzgerald and the Romantic tradition, with critical treatment of *The Pat Hobby Stories* and several other works.

Mizener, Arthur. *The Far Side of Paradise: A Biography of F. Scott Fitzgerald.* Boston: Houghton Mifflin Co., Riverside Press, 1951, 362 p.
    First significant Fitzgerald biography.

Murphy, Garry N., and Slattery, William C. "The Flawed Text of 'Babylon Revisited': A Challenge to Editors, a Warning to Readers." *Studies in Short Fiction* 18, No. 3 (Summer 1981): 315-18.
    Argues for the publication of a revised, authorized version of "Babylon Revisited" that corrects what the critics see as "a monumental editorial error."

Murphy, Patrick D. "Illumination and Affection in the Parallel Plots of 'The Rich Boy' and 'The Beast in the Jungle'." *Papers on Language and Literature* 22, No. 4 (Fall 1986): 406-16.
    Compares aspects of Fitzgerald's "The Rich Boy" and Henry James's "The Beast in the Jungle."

Perlis, Alan. "The Narrative Is All: A Study of F. Scott Fitzgerald's 'May Day.' " *Western Humanities Review* XXXIII, No. 1 (Winter 1979): 65-72.
    Focuses on Fitzgerald's narrative techniques and point of view in "May Day."

Piper, Henry Dan. *F. Scott Fitzgerald: A Critical Portrait.* New York: Holt, Rinehart and Winston, 1965, 334 p.
    Analytical portrait of Fitzgerald's literary life. Includes several chapters on his short fiction.

Prigozy, Ruth. "The Unpublished Stories: Fitzgerald in His Final Stage." *Twentieth Century Literature* 20, No. 2 (April 1974): 69-90.
    Appraises Fitzgerald's unpublished short stories, valuing them chiefly for the insight they lend to the author's "developing style in the last years of his life."

Rees, John O. "Fitzgerald's Pat Hobby Stories." *The Colorado Quarterly* XXIII, No. 4 (Spring 1975): 553-62.
    Surveys the Pat Hobby Stories.

Roulston, Robert. "Rummaging through F. Scott Fitzgerald's 'Trash': Early Stories in *The Saturday Evening Post.*" *Journal of Popular Culture* 21, No. 4 (Spring 1988): 151-63.
    Argues that Fitzgerald's early stories contain elements of his best works.

Sklar, Robert. *F. Scott Fitzgerald: The Last Laocoön.* New York: Oxford University Press, 1967, 376 p.
    Often-discussed biographical and critical study with many passing references to the short fiction.

Staley, Thomas F. "Time and Structure in Fitzgerald's 'Babylon Revisited'." *Modern Fiction Studies* X, No. 4 (Winter 1964-65): 386-88.
    Examines the unity of time past and present in "Babylon Revisited."

Stanley, Linda C. *The Foreign Critical Reputation of F. Scott Fitzgerald: An Analysis and Annotated Bibliography.* Westport, Conn.: Greenwood Press, 1980, 276 p.
    Exhaustive treatment of criticism on Fitzgerald published outside the United States, including information on his short fiction.

Taylor, Dwight. "Scott Fitzgerald in Hollywood." *Harper's Magazine* 218, No. 1306 (March 1959): 67-71.
    According to Taylor: "An account of the crazy gin-soaked Sunday in Malibu when Fitzgerald looked like a fool—until he made it into one of his best short stories."

Twitchell, James B. " 'Babylon Revisited': Chronology and Characters." *Fitzgerald/Hemingway Annual 1978* (1978): 155-60.
    Briefly studies the chronology of events in "Babylon Revisited" to demonstrate that protagonist Charlie Wales's reformation is sincere.

Way, Brian. *F. Scott Fitzgerald and the Art of Social Fiction.* pp. 72-97. New York: St. Martin's Press, 1980.
    Overview of what Way considers Fitzgerald's best short stories.

West, James L. W. III, and Inge, J. Barclay. "F. Scott Fitzgerald's Revision of 'The Rich Boy'." *Proof* 5 (1977): 127-46.
    Examines the composition and revision of "The Rich Boy" as revealed in three separate texts.

White, William. "Two Versions of F. Scott Fitzgerald's 'Babylon Revisited': A Textual and Bibliographical Study." *The Papers of the Bibliographical Society of America* 60, No. 4 (1966): 439-52.
    Provides a bibliographic history and comparison of the two extant published versions of "Babylon Revisited."

Wycherley, H. Alan. "Fitzgerald Revisited." *Texas Studies in Literature and Language* VII, No. 2 (Summer 1966): 277-83.
    Paints a harsh portrait of Fitzgerald as "a writer pathetically limited in the artist's ability to control his materials, to advance beyond the limitations of his own—and his wife's or his first love's—personality, and to refuse to bow to the demands of the 'buck.' "

(James) Langston Hughes

1902-1967

American poet, short story writer, novelist, dramatist, autobiographer, editor, translator, and author of children's books.

A prolific author in many genres, Hughes was a seminal figure of the Harlem Renaissance, a period during the 1920s of unprecedented artistic and intellectual achievement among black Americans. His 1926 article "The Negro Artist and the Racial Mountain" was widely acclaimed as the literary manifesto of this movement, and such poems as "The Negro Speaks of Rivers" and "Montage of a Dream Deferred" earned him the epithet "Poet Laureate of Harlem." In his poems and prose, Hughes often employed structures and rhythms derived from blues and jazz music, and he is considered one of the first black Americans to use colloquial language in his writings. Hughes gained his largest audience among both black and white readers with his Simple tales. Initially published as a series of newspaper sketches, these short pieces of dialogue between an urban, working-class man named Jesse B. Semple, or Simple, and his intellectual, middle-class friend are highly regarded for Simple's sardonically humorous and penetrating statements about race and for his authentic reflection of the attitudes and circumstances of many black Americans.

Hughes was born in Joplin, Missouri. Following the separation of his parents when he was a young boy, he lived with his maternal grandmother in Lawrence, Kansas. Hughes recalled that through stories his grandmother told him, he gained a deep sense of pride for his black heritage, as well as a determination to fight for the opportunity to live freely. He wrote in his autobiography, *The Big Sea*: "Through my grandmother's stories always life moved, moved heroically toward an end. Nobody cried in my grandmother's stories. They worked, or schemed, or fought. . . . Something about my grandmother's stories (without her ever having said so) taught me the uselessness of crying about anything." After the death of his grandmother when he was twelve years old, Hughes was reunited with his mother in Lincoln, Illinois. Hughes subsequently moved to Cleveland, Ohio, where, as a student at Central High School, he wrote his first short story. Hughes's relationship with his father was problematic, as the elder Hughes spent little time with his son and had small regard for Hughes's endeavors. Arthur P. Davis suggests that the rejection Hughes received from his father emerges as the tragic mulatto theme in several works, including his short stories "African Morning" and "Father and Son." In 1921 Hughes published poems and prose pieces in *Crisis,* a magazine of black culture sponsored by the National Association for the Advancement of Colored People (NAACP), and enrolled at Columbia University in New York City. While in New York, Hughes made frequent visits to Harlem, where he immersed himself in the jazz clubs and music halls that flourished during the early Harlem Renaissance—experiences that profoundly affected his literary style and themes.

In the summer of 1923, working as a crewman on an ocean freighter, Hughes journeyed to Africa, Holland, and Paris. Upon his return to the United States in 1925, Hughes lived in Washington, D.C. Working as a busboy at the Wardam

Park Hotel, he attracted the attention of poet Vachel Lindsay by leaving three poems on Lindsay's table. The next day reporters and photographers eagerly greeted Hughes at work to hear more from this newly discovered "busboy poet." Shortly thereafter, with the help of critic and art patron Carl Van Vechten, Hughes published his first book, *The Weary Blues,* a collection of poems that reflect the frenzied atmosphere of the Harlem nightclubs, as well as a distinctive sense of racial pride. During the late 1920s, Hughes published his first short stories in the *Messenger,* a small magazine that featured black writers. These stories, which are mainly based upon Hughes's experiences as a sailor along the West African coast, are characterized by themes of lost youth and innocence amid exotic settings. In 1927 he contributed to *Fire!!,* a short-lived publication that he helped establish with Wallace Thurman, Zora Neale Hurston, and five other writers as an outlet for young black artists. Also during the late 1920s, Hughes met Mrs. R. Osgood Mason, an elderly white widow who served as both his literary patron and friend. Strongly committed to developing the talents of young black artists, Mason supported Hughes while he wrote his first novel, *Not without Laughter.* Following this book's publication in 1930, however, Hughes and Mason suffered a dramatic and bitter break in their relationship. Hughes later reconstructed these events in his story "The Blues I'm Playing."

In 1932 Hughes traveled to Moscow with other black Americans on an unsuccessful filmmaking venture that nevertheless proved instrumental to his short story writing. While working as a journalist in Moscow, a friend loaned Hughes a copy of D. H. Lawrence's short story collection *The Lovely Lady*. After reading the title story, Hughes was struck by the similarities between Lawrence's main character and Mrs. Mason, his former Park Avenue patron. Overwhelmed by what he felt as the power of Lawrence's stories, Hughes began writing short fiction of his own. By 1933, when he returned to the United States, Hughes had sold three stories and had begun compiling his first collection, *The Ways of White Folks*. Between 1933 and 1935, Hughes wrote the majority of his short stories, and in 1943 the first of his Simple tales appeared in the black-owned *Chicago Defender* newspaper. During his middle and late career, Hughes continued to write in a variety of genres and increasingly served as an editor and advocate of African-American literature until his death at age sixty-five.

Hughes's stories in *The Ways of White Folks* differ from his earlier pieces published in the *Messenger*. His subjects shifted in focus from romantic tales in an African setting to satiric stories that portray disillusionment with white patronage. "The Blues I'm Playing," for instance, is an autobiographical story about Oceola, a young artist who rejects her patron when the patron attempts to control her life and art. According to Robert Bone, " 'The Blues I'm Playing' is at once an arraignment of Western Culture and an affirmation of Negro folk forms. The classical and jazz idioms, which compete for Oceola's loyalty, give dramatic substance to the theme of cultural dualism which is basic to the Harlem Renaissance." Noted for drawing upon the rhythms and structures of blues music in his poetry, Hughes incorporated elements of the blues in his short fiction as well. In many stories Hughes combined pathos and irony in the blues tradition to fictionalize experiences of black Americans. His satire in "The Blues," "Slave on a Block," and "Poor Little Black Fellow" is aimed not only at white patronage but also at black intellectuals of the New Negro movement who advocated an elite black population fully assimilated into white culture. Hughes was one of the first writers to reject this elitism and celebrate ordinary black people and culture in his works.

Hughes's second collection, *Laughing to Keep from Crying*, did not appear until 1952, though most of the stories were written in 1934 and 1935. Whereas in his first collection Hughes depicted characters striving for independence, in this volume he celebrates characters acting as rebel heroes. Although race is a constant theme in Hughes's writings, critics note his ability to write about essentially racial themes while delineating the personal circumstances of each main character in this volume. In one lyrical story, "On the Way Home," Hughes relates a man's grief over the death of his mother without specifying the race of his characters. In another story from this volume, "The Big Meeting," Hughes draws upon the oral traditions of African-American religion and folklore to treat the theme of black lynchings by white racists.

Among his short fiction, Hughes will probably be best remembered for the Simple tales. These short pieces that center upon conversations between Jesse B. Semple and a narrator identified as Boyd first appeared in 1943 in the black-owned *Chicago Defender* newspaper. With the creation of Jesse B. Semple, or Simple, as he is most often called, Hughes reached a large black audience for the first time. When the columns

were serialized into five collections during the 1950s and 1960s, these tales reached racially diverse mainstream audiences as well. Early reviews were generally positive, stressing the humorous dialogue between Simple and the narrator. Personifying Simple as a "black Everyman" because he represented the typical urban African-American, critics also noted that beneath the humor in these stories lies a serious examination of problems regarding race and racism in the United States. Recent commentators have emphasized the intricate social attitudes Hughes expressed in these tales.

One of Hughes's prevalent themes in these works is Simple's insistent discussion of race issues. The narrator, acting as a perfect foil to Simple's common-sense wisdom, voices opinions of the black bourgeoisie and intellectuals who see many positive reasons to conform to the standards of white Americans. More subtly, Boyd also voices opinions of white liberals who would like to see blacks assimilated into mainstream culture but who ignore African-American cultural and ethical values. Critics have noted that in this way Simple served as an early proponent of *négritude*, a movement popularized in the 1960s that sought to raise consciousness and pride in African heritage. Analysis of the Simple tales has largely focused on the fact that these pieces were among the first popular works to address racial issues for both black and white readers. Critics praise Hughes's vision in these stories and extol his ability to satirically convey the complexities and injustices of ordinary life.

Hughes's career, which spanned over forty years, is regarded as one of the most influential of the Harlem Renaissance. Because his writing focused on race relations and the plight of oppressed people, he was labeled a protest writer early in his life. In response, Hughes stated: "That designation has probably grown out of the fact that I write about what I know best, and being a Negro in this country is tied up with difficulties that cause one to protest naturally. I am writing about human beings and situations that I know and experience, and therefore it is only incidentally protest—protest in that it grows out of a live situation." Hughes's appeal to mainstream reading audiences has at times drawn the ire of those who condemn the use of ordinary black characters and colloquial dialects as literary devices. Toward the end of his life, Hughes did not share the popular appeal of the more militant writers who began to emerge in the late 1960s. Nevertheless, critics commonly agree that Hughes holds a prominent place in American literature and among writers of short fiction. Arthur P. Davis stated: "His short stories form a world of fiction built with truth and a special love—a little civilization shaped by high purpose and steadfast integrity."

(For further information on Hughes's life and career, see *Contemporary Literary Criticism*, Vols. 1, 5, 10, 15, 35, 44; *Contemporary Authors*, Vols. 1-4, rev. ed., 25-28, rev. ed. [obituary]; *Contemporary Authors New Revision Series*, Vol. 1; *Something about the Author*, Vols. 4, 33; and *Dictionary of Literary Biography*, Vols. 4, 7, 48, 51. See also the "Harlem Renaissance" entry in *Twentieth-Century Literary Criticism*, Vol. 26.)

PRINCIPAL WORKS

SHORT FICTION

The Ways of White Folks   1934
Simple Speaks His Mind   1950

E. C. HOLMES (essay date 1934)

[*In the following excerpt, Holmes views the stories in* The Ways of White Folks *from a sociological perspective.*]

Langston Hughes' development has been steady, sure and positive. His works from 1926 to 1931 are links in this evolution. Save for occasional retrogressions (*Dream Keeper, Dear Lovely Death, Popo and Fifina*) which are allowable in the development of the sincere fellow-traveller, Hughes' career has been brilliant and straightforward. His work, it is true, has not always possessed the anti-bourgeois note so evident in his work from 1931 to 1934. Nevertheless, it was reasonable to believe that Hughes would go further in the only direction in which an artist should go, than any of his colleagues of the "New Negro Renaissance."

Langston Hughes, was in 1926, an integral part of that unhealthy "New Negro" tradition. He shared the beliefs in the new theories of bourgeois estheticism as much as Countee Cullen, Jean Toomer and Claude McKay. Even so, the poems in "Weary Blues" signified the arrival of a remarkable poetic genius. And in "Not Without Laughter," he had broken almost definitely with the "Harlem Tradition." Today, with the publication of *The Ways of White Folks,* Hughes has travelled much further, nearer his goal of true revolutionary liter-

ature. It must be remembered that there had to be a good deal of excision, a complete denial of bourgeois traditions and parlor radicalism before he could write *Scottsboro Limited,* "*Columbia,*" *Good Morning, Revolution* and **The Ways of White Folks.**

Since it is difficult to review these fourteen stories in any but a laudatory fashion, it should not be incorrect to analyze the entire content as well as the author. First, Hughes has shown that he has mastered the objective short story form. These stories are as nearly perfect as one could desire. They are not unlike the stories of Pauteileimon Romanov, and of Romanov's master, Tchekov. The resemblance extends to the superb irony, the simplicity and the splendid craftsmanship.

Every word seems to be weighed, tested, burnished and carefully inserted. There is such economy of structure, the stories are told so ably, that one experiences the feelings of having read what might have been a novel. There is in this book a sense of ease, but yet vivid writing. These stories remain indelibly on the mind. You live them. They constitute special experiences for you. These properties belong to great art.

Eight years ago, Hughes, in defending Negro Art, wrote, "If white people are pleased, we are glad. If they are not, it does not matter. We know we are beautiful. And ugly too." Now, he writes of these same white people. Now, his approach is a class approach. Now, he does not mean all white folks, but as Berry says "some white folks." Hughes, realizing the struggles in existence between two classes, conceives of those white people who in their control, circumscribe and influence the lives of the Negro masses. He writes of Negroes in relation to white people who are part of their very existence. This is so for Hughes because all men stand in relation to each other as parts of a social whole. He is interested in Negro and white class psychology, in their class differentiations. He uses working class themes, showing the intensity of the exploitation of share-croppers, bookkeeper, domestic and laborer.

When read together, these stories present a rather tightly knit pattern. Taken together, they show an indictment against the decadence of capitalistic society. When read singly, such stories as **"A Good Job Gone," "Little Dog," "One Christmas Eve,"** etc., may evoke the remarks that they are good as stories go, but that they are not examples of bourgeois realism or of revolutionary literature. Such criticism is specious, of course, when these stories are taken together. For, one of the largest effects gained in the body of the book is in the use of irony and satire, concealed and open. Also, his ability to generalize is characteristic of his anti-bourgeois outlook. This characteristic enables him to apply his scalpel to Negroes and whites alike.

In **"Father and Son,"** the most powerfully absorbing story in the volume, the author states his belief in the knowledge that the union of white and black workers will be the single force which will smash American Capitalism. . . . That is why Hughes' art is social. Call it propaganda if you like. He has succeeded, nevertheless, in overcoming his former schematism and abstractness. He has succeeded in depicting social relations in a realism of the highest order.

All the stories are excellent. There are, of course, some which stand out as being more powerful, such as **"Red Headed Baby," "Father and Son," "Cora Unashamed," "Home,"** and **"Rejuvenation Through Joy."**

The thing which makes this volume one of the most outstanding contributions to American literature is the fact that Hughes understands the people about whom he writes. He understands their relations—exploiting and exploited—to each other. He knows what the solution of these problems of a capitalist society will be. No longer will he attempt to solve any problems, art, racial or personal, within the framework of capitalism. He knows that if he is to write in such a society, he must portray life as he sees it. He must come to terms with the life of his time. Above all, he must point the way out. In this volume, Hughes justifies his experiment and his use of the short story form finds a most felicitious outlet for his talent. (pp. 283-84)

> *E. C. Holmes, in a review of "The Ways of White Folks," in* Opportunity, *Vol. XII, No. 9, September, 1934, pp. 283-84.*

LEON DENNEN (essay date 1934)

[*In the following excerpt from a review of* The Ways of White Folks, *Dennen acknowledges Hughes's technical abilities but faults him for displaying limited scope and characterization and for pursuing uninspired subject matter.*]

Those who have followed Langston Hughes' literary work for the last few years will be somewhat disappointed in [*The Ways of White Folks*]. . . .

There is no doubt that the author of this volume is one of the more talented among the younger American writers. He is, however, more than that. He is also known as one of the outstanding revolutionary interpreters of Negro life in America. And yet, there is very little that is revolutionary about *The Ways of White Folks.* (p. 50)

Truth in our days, to repeat a much repeated phrase, is revolutionary. But to depict the truth of our present-day life is not a simple matter. To depict the truth one must have a thorough understanding of the conflicting forces in our society, and, what is more, one must have a broad vision. But Langston Hughes' vision, at least exemplified by this collection of stories, is, unfortunately, very limited.

Take, for instance, the story of **"Cora Unashamed."** Cora Jenkins, a Negro woman, was one of the last of the citizens of the little miserable town of Melton. She worked for the Studevants. The Studevants were rich white people. They treated Cora as an inferior, as a dog. Cora stood it. She had to stand it or go jobless. . . . The woman's life was gray and uneventful except once when she fell in love with a white Wobbly, [the epithet given to members of the revolutionary Industrial Workers of the World labor union], who happened to pass through the town. The union was a short one. The Wobbly disappeared. Cora gave birth to a little girl. She called her Josephine, after Joe, the Wobbly. Cora did not go anywhere to have the child. Nor tried to hide. She was "humble and unashamed before the fact of the child." It was quite different with the Studevant's youngest daughter who was also going to have an illegitimate child. The girl wanted the child. Not so the Studevant family. It was a blot upon their life of fake respectability. The mother preferred the daughter's death to an illegitimate grandchild. The girl was forced to have an abortion. She died. Cora was indignant. The Studevant's criminal stupidity amazed her. Cora was unashamed.

I have given the gist of **"Cora Unashamed"** somewhat at

length not only because it is the most powerful story in the volume but also it gives us a clue to the Hughes' other stories.

Langston Hughes is a superb story teller. His style is lyrical and swift-moving except when he labors hard to achieve a jazz effect. Also, his characters are real and alive. They suffer, however, from one weakness: they never think; they just feel.

Cora is elemental. She is naive, simple and static, like "a tree—once rooted she stood, in spite of storms and strife." All Negro characters in *The Ways of White Folks*—whether they are artists or workers—are elemental, naive, simple and static.

Is that the truth? Perhaps. Only it is a limited truth. Certainly it is no longer symbolic of all the Negroes in America. Although Langston Hughes is supposed to be a revolutionary writer, the drama of the rising revolutionary consciousness of the Negro masses in America has altogether escaped him.

Cora's story, the author will say, is dramatic. True enough. But is the story of the thinking and fighting Negroes any less dramatic? (p. 51)

And if it was the author's intention to depict primarily the relation between whites and Negroes, why should he have limited himself to elemental Negroes and diseased, sophisticated or queer and sex-starved white rich ladies?

What about the relation between white and black workers? What about the relation between Negro and white sharecroppers fighting hand in hand in the South? (p. 52)

> *Leon Dennen, "Negroes and Whites," in* Partisan Review, *Vol. I, No. 5, November-December, 1934, pp. 50-2.*

WILLIAM GARDNER SMITH (essay date 1950)

[*An American journalist, novelist, and editor, Smith was noted for his protest novels* Last of the Conquerors (1949) *and* South Street (1954). *In the following review of* Simple Speaks His Mind, *Smith emphasizes the humor in the character of Jesse B. Semple.*]

Langston Hughes knows and loves the people of Harlem, and others like them throughout the nation. He knows that though they do not speak with eloquence, theirs is the most profound understanding of what race prejudice means. Consequently he has created their symbol [in Jesse B. Semple], a Negro Joe Doakes, to say what all of them have on their mind. Forty-four of these dialogues, which appeared originally in the Chicago *Defender*, the *New Republic* and *Phylon*, comprise *Simple Speaks His Mind.*

Because most of these columns were written for a Negro audience, they are uninhibited, intimate, to the point. The white reader gets a rare insight into the private conversations of Negroes. Dominating the conversations, of course, is Simple, whose irresistible tongue wanders incisively over such topics as the Harlem riots, lynchings, Jackie Robinson's appearance before the House Un-American Activities Committee, The Law, why Simple can't hope to be President, the relative treatment accorded dogs and Negroes, and Simple's family life. We also come to know his friends: Hughes, who invariably comes off second-best in arguments with the hero; Joyce, his wonderful girl; his landlady; and Zarita, the *femme fatale.*

Simple makes such priceless understatements as, "White

folks is the cause of a lot of inconveniences in my life." Comes World War III, he wants to reverse the usual process and "see some Negro generals pinning medals on white men." In one of his moments of cynicism, Simple wishes the Lord would smite all white folks down, with one exception: "I hope he lets Mrs. Roosevelt alone."

The best dialogues are those in which Hughes, as the supercilious straight man, disagrees with the things Simple has to say. In some of the others, we feel the cards have been stacked against us—even though we know the things discussed are true.

Unfortunately, segregation begets a degree of "segregated" humor. There are hilarious passages in this book which no white American will be able fully to appreciate. But to people who would like an idea of what the ordinary Negro thinks about the world in general, without frills and without pretension, the book will be a revelation.

> *William Gardner Smith, "Simple's Dialogues," in*
> The New Republic, *Vol. 123, No. 10, September 4,*
> *1950, p. 20.*

The Negro artist works against an undertow of sharp criticism and misunderstanding from his own group and unintentional bribes from the whites. "O, be respectable, write about nice people, show how good we are," say the Negroes. "Be stereotyped, don't go too far, don't shatter our illusions about you, don't amuse us too seriously. We will pay you," say the whites. . . .

But in spite of the Nordicized Negro intelligentsia and the desires of some white editors we have an honest American Negro literature already with us.

[To] my mind, it is the duty of the younger Negro artist, if he accepts any duties at all from outsiders, to change through the force of his art that old whispering "I want to be white," hidden in the aspirations of his people, to "Why should I want to be white? I am a Negro—and beautiful!" . . .

We younger Negro artists who create now intend to express our individual dark-skinned selves without fear or shame. If white people are pleased we are glad. If they are not, it doesn't matter. We know we are beautiful. And ugly too. The tom-tom cries and the tom-tom laughs. If colored people are pleased we are glad. If they are not, their displeasure doesn't matter either. We build our temples for tomorrow, strong as we know how, and we stand on top of the mountain, free within ourselves.

> *Langston Hughes, from his essay "The*
> *Negro Artist and the Racial Mountain,"*
> *1926.*

G. LEWIS CHANDLER   (essay date 1951)

[*In the following excerpt from a review of* Simple Speaks His Mind, *Chandler praises Hughes for writing an entertaining yet socially significant work.*]

Divided into four parts ("Summer Time"; "Winter Time"; "Hard Times"; "Any Time"), **Simple Speaks His Mind**—

beginning as a weekly series in the Chicago *Defender*—is a book of short-stories photographing the mind and chronicling the droll experiences of a semi-literate Harlemite, Simple, who confides in or talks back to his creator (Hughes) in much the same way as does Charlie McCarthy to Edgar Bergen. But Charlie is white and is an aristocrat. Simple is colored and is proletariat. This makes the vast difference between the two in what they see, feel, and say. Simple is completely race conscious, sex conscious, and bread conscious. Suffering from the impact of such consciousnesses, he makes articulate what the average Negro experiences, mentally and physically, in a segregated society struggling for integration. The capacity to feel as a Negro and to think and talk as a man makes Simple more than a marionette. He is a live character who, though not a capital debater, takes a definite stand on many issues within the areas of sex, security, and race relations. In the matter of sex, he stands firm for male supremacy; he is genuinely indifferent to his wife (Isabel), completely loves Joyce (his girl friend), thoroughly disrespects Zarita, with whom he drinks away his money and time. Again, he has not had much economic security, though he has drudged hard to earn so little. . . . However, if Simple is anything, he is a thoroughgoing race man. He hates prejudice; he hates segregation; he hates the white man. But he loves Mrs. Roosevelt, and the Brooklyn Dodgers—because Jackie Robinson plays for them. . . . Simple is indeed a character—a Hughesian character: ignorant and wise; selfish and magnanimous—a roustabout and angel; a coward and hero; an hypochondriac and idealist.

But the significance of this book does not lie wholly in the character and reflections of Simple. It lies also in Hughes' characteristic skill in treating the serious humorously, in deftly handling dialogue (he matches Hemingway here), in selecting and compressing material germane to mood, character, and action—in achieving unity out of diversity. In short, if you read **Simple Speaks His Mind** for sheer entertainment, you will not be disappointed. If you read it, however, for esthetic and civic implications, you will be challenged. (pp. 94-5)

> *G. Lewis Chandler, "For Your Recreation and Reflection," in* PHYLON: The Atlanta University Review of Race and Culture, *Vol. XII, No. 1, first quarter (Spring, 1951), pp. 94-5.*

BUCKLIN MOON   (essay date 1952)

[*Moon is an American editor and author of such books as* Brother (*1943*), Primer for White Folks (*1945*), *and* The Darker: The High Cost of Prejudice (*1947*). *In the excerpt below, he offers a favorable review of* Laughing to Keep from Crying.]

Laughing to Keep from Crying, which contains pieces dating from as far back as the Twenties, is a short book, but it is a highly successful one.

In these twenty-odd stories, almost all of them concerned with minority groups, there is little special pleading, as such, and no attempt to show only the best in the people about whom Hughes is writing. What the reader senses, however, if he happens to be a human being, is that the worst of them are caught between their environment and our inhumanity to a point where it got to be more than they could handle. It is this quality, I think, which makes every story (with the possible exception of **"One Friday Morning,"** which seems overly familiar because of similar stories which followed it) become amazingly fresh and free from the stereotype, and the self-consciousness of too much of our protest writing.

It could be said, I suppose, that these are not the best short stories that Langston Hughes ever wrote, but the best of them are very good, indeed. **"Professor"** is a highly successful story. It tells of the feelings of a Negro from the faculty of a small colored college in the South who is going to dinner at the home of a prominent Midwestern philanthropist where he will have to sing for his supper because of the job he needs and knows he will get only if he Uncle Toms a little.

The story concludes:

> As the car sped him back toward town, Dr. Brown sat under its soft fur rug among the deep cushions and thought how with six thousand dollars a year earned by dancing properly to the tune of Jim Crow education, he could carry his whole family to South America for a summer where they wouldn't need to feel like Negroes.

Almost as effective, though the irony is directed in another direction, is **"Trouble With the Angels,"** in which a young singer on the road with a successful Broadway Negro folk musical tries to get the rest of the cast to go on strike when they hit a theatre in Washington where Negroes are turned down at the box office—only to find "God" suddenly acting as a strikebreaker.

Some of the shorter vignettes come alive with a sudden flash of imagery, or the poet's fine ear for the spoken word and the patterns of sound. Though less than two pages long, **"Rouge High,"** the bitterly fatalistic story of two Harlem prostitutes, seems to hang in the air long afterward, like a song you want to forget but cannot.

Other stories are less successful; they seem a little dated, almost archaic, because in the meantime our racial thinking has subtly changed. None the less, each is the work of a "writer" in the finest sense of the word; for here is underwriting and an economy of words that put to shame many a writer who has said less in an overblown novel than is often said here in less than a dozen pages.

> *Bucklin Moon, "Laughter, Tears and the Blues," in* The New York Times Book Review, *March 23, 1952, p. 4.*

JOHN W. PARKER (essay date 1952)

[*In the excerpt below, Parker acknowledges a sense of pessimism in* Laughing to Keep from Crying *yet praises Hughes for his technique and theme.*]

[**Laughing to Keep from Crying**] is written against the background of the color and feel of Negro America and of the author's own travels across the world; and while it employs the Harlem scene as a point of departure, it sets about to explore the ebb and flow of life in the Negro ghetto in such widely separated points as Manhattan and Pasadena, Mexico City and Havana, Hong Kong and Africa. It is predicated upon the assumption that minority-majority problems are no unique American creations; they are part and parcel of a pathological social phenomenon that embraces points throughout the world where people of color are concentrated.

A total of twenty-four stories of fairly even quality makes up the collection. One of them discloses the flavor of Bohemian primitivism of the Mid-twenties; another deals with a "big meeting" down South where sinners "remain to pray," but where white people came sightseeing; and yet another brings into focus the escapades of a mixblooded Harlem fop, whose total conduct left much to be desired. **"One Friday Morning"** is a study of the operation of color prejudice in the case of Nancy Lee Johnson, Negro prize-winning painter in a northern high school, who had to go home with a "strange emptiness" in lieu of a first prize. And in the story **"Professor,"** the Negro intellectual loses face. . . . [In **"Saratoga Rain"**] one finds two broken parcels of humanity resorting to illicit love as a means of escape from themselves and from the totality of their social milieu. To each other they whisper, "We will never be angels with wings."

These interrelated stories turn primarily upon theme rather than upon character; taken together, they range from the bootleg era of the Roaring Twenties to the present. The author has managed a spontaneity as well as an intensity and a charm that all but assure reader interest. That one finds in this volume what is perhaps a conscious blending of humor of characterization and of situation is a tribute to Hughes' creative genius in an area of Negro literature hitherto largely neglected. Everywhere the laughing comes as a means of comic relief; it prevents crying eternally.

Despite the fact that segments of his subject matter go back to the early Twenties, it is hard to see how in a period of growing social awareness Mr. Hughes' new book is almost totally lacking in perspective for the Negro people. A sort of a consistent vanity of vanities, it points up disillusionment and loss of faith. The roads lead nowhere; nothing amounts to anything; and almost nobody is too much concerned. The implications in some of the stories are that the Negro's conduct—passing, raising cane, saying, "Yes, Sir," and looking down dead-end streets—is not so much his own responsibility as that of the social order of which he is a part. Nor does one find sufficient evidence that the white man is either aware of or concerned about the Negro's reaction to his plight. This note of unwavering pessimism leaves one wondering when he remembers the author's firm faith in our tomorrows.

This weakness, however, in no sense negates the basic force of this significant book. To his task, Langston Hughes has brought an intimate and a sympathetic knowledge of his subject matter and of the technique and province of the short story. *Laughing to Keep from Crying,* illuminating as it does the "Negro theme" in American literature (aspects of which yet remain largely unexplored), is an eloquent plea for social awareness and social justice for minorities in America and throughout the world. (pp. 257-58)

> *John W. Parker, "Literature of the Negro Ghetto," in* PHYLON: The Atlanta University Review of Race and Culture, *Vol. XII, No. 3, 1952, pp. 257-58.*

ABNER BERRY (essay date 1953)

[*In the following excerpted review of* Simple Takes a Wife, *Berry discusses the significance of Simple as a representative of average black Harlemites.*]

Among the 66,000 furnished room dwellers who live in Harlem between the two rivers from 110th Street, on the south, to just beyond the Polo Grounds, on the north, is one Jesse B. Semple—called "Simple," for short, by his friends. We don't know Simple's exact address, but it appears from his salty comments on landladies, bars, upper class Negroes and patronizing whites that he lives in the "valley," in "Deep Harlem," east of Seventh Avenue in the 130's.

Simple and his neighbors, refugees from the sterner racism of the South, understand and denounce the jimcrow nuances of New York City with a fierce race consciousness. This rooming house set, whose addresses denote the place where they bathe, sleep and change clothes, and for whom their favorite tavern must serve as a living room, furnish the characters and the action in Langston Hughes' *Simple Takes a Wife.* (pp. 55-6)

In Simple, Hughes has found the perfect protagonist for the thousands of racial battles that are fought in conversations in every ghetto throughout the United States. It is a warm and human story of distant relatives arriving unexpectedly and sharing the cubicle of a room until they can get a foot on the ladder of New York life. We share the problems of a young couple falling in love, marrying and rearing their first child in their own one-room home. But we sense the quality of laughing at heartbreak, or being able to "escape" through the humor derived from commonplace situations, of bitterness which evades frustration. For Simple, the composite of Harlem's common man, is not defeated nor dejected, even though the road ahead is not clearly marked.

On one thing Simple is irrevocably determined: to be free from jim crow and to avenge the many insults the South has handed him and his people. He dreams one night he was a bird and wishes on awaking he could make the dream true for a while. Among the things he would like to do as a bird is to "just fly *over* the South, stopping only long enough to spread my tail feathers and show my contempt." And musing on the racist "blood theories," Simple twits their proponents:

> Why is Negro blood so much more powerful than any other kind of blood in the world? If a man has Irish blood in him, people will say, 'He's *part* Irish.' If he has a little Jewish blood, they'll say, 'He's *half* Jewish.' But if he has just a small bit of colored blood in him, Bam!—'*He's a Negro!*' . . . Now, that is what I do not understand—why one drop is so powerful. . . .

I suspect it is the author who steers Simple away from more basic political topics, keeping the discussions on the level of "race talk." For there was a much wider topical range in Hughes' first volume about Simple—*Simple Speaks His Mind.* Whereas in the first book, Simple had some sharp observations to make on the Un-American Activities Committee, he now limits his discussion of Congress to the absence of Negroes. And it should be remembered that Hughes, since the appearance of *Simple Speaks His Mind,* has been a "guest" of Sen. Joseph McCarthy.

It is also notable that Hughes before McCarthy did not fare nearly as well as did Simple before the Un-Americans, for Simple really "told off " that "old Georgia chairman" with some biting comments on jimcrow. Simple still has bite in discussing jimcrow, but he "talks at the big gate," out of earshot of the oppressors, to his anonymous friend. However, Simple remains a healthy representative of Negro ghetto dwellers continuing in every way they know to struggle for first class American citizenship.

I hope that in future stories, Hughes will let us see and hear Simple (who is a poorly-paid worker) in his relationships with other workers and his employers. So far we have only seen him after work, relaxing over a beer, discussing his and other Negroes' problems, within the relationship of Negro to Negro. Hughes should give us more of Simple's sides. . . . (pp. 57-8)

The present volume exhibits an artistic weakness: Hughes combines the reporter's eye, the novelist's ear, but misses the third dimension of the ghetto scene as reflected in the real characters of whom Simple is a composite. One feels that Simple and those around him can do little more than complain, futilely, of the oppressive jimcrow conditions under which they live. Despite the charm and the many nuggets of wisdom in this panorama of Harlem, the reader can conclude that Simple and his friends will remain as they are indefinitely.

It would be a mistake to say that this makes *Simple Takes a Wife* poor or insubstantial reading. On the contrary, with all of his weaknesses, Hughes has given us a vivid picture of Negro life and its richness, a picture which is sharply opposed to the "arty" degeneracy of writers like Richard Wright and Ralph Ellison. For even though he is held under wraps by the author, Simple is a healthy, probing, salty young Negro, a pleasant relief from Ellison's *Invisible Man* and Wright's fascistic killer in *The Outsider.* Simple may not show us the way to the future, but he certainly gives us a seldom seen and delightful picture of today. (p. 58)

> *Abner Berry, "Not So Simple," in* Masses & Mainstream, *Vol. 6, No. 9, September, 1953, pp. 55-8.*

ARTHUR P. DAVIS (essay date 1954)

[*An American author and scholar of black American literature, Davis has contributed numerous articles, short stories, and book reviews to magazines, anthologies, and professional journals. He has also coedited* The Negro Caravan (*1941*) *and* Cavalcade: Negro American Writers from 1760 to the Present (*1971*). *In the following excerpt, Davis explores both the comic and tragic dimensions of Hughes's character Jesse B. Semple.*]

In his companion-works, *Simple Speaks his Mind* (1950) and *Simple Takes a Wife* (1953), Langston Hughes has given us one of the freshest and most fascinating Negro characters in American fiction. Mr. Jesse B. Semple, or Simple for short, is an uneducated Harlem man-about-town who speaks a delightful brand of English and who, from his stool at Paddy's Bar, comments both wisely and hilariously on many things, but principally on women and race. An unusual character in several respects, Simple's most appealing trait is that he is a Negro comic figure at whom Negroes themselves can laugh without being ashamed. Simple is so human, so believable, and so much like each of us that we are drawn to him in spite of ourselves. We laugh with Simple rather than at him; and our laughter is therapeutic because it tends to make us aware of our own cliché-thinking on the race question, a shortcoming which we all evidence at one time or another. (p. 21)

Accepting Simple for what he is, Hughes makes effective use of the contrast in viewpoint between Simple's segment of society and his own. He has made Simple the very highly articulate spokesman of the untrained-worker group and himself the voice of the educated Negro liberal. The merit of this arrangement is that the two attitudes tend to complement each other. Simple generally exemplifies the directness and single-mindedness of the untrained Negro and Hughes the sophisti-

Hughes, "the busboy poet," working at the Wardam Park Hotel in Washington, D.C., after his encounter with Vachel Lindsay.

point with certainty to the cause of all his troubles: "I have been caught in some kind of riffle ever since I been black." When Hughes remonstrates with him and accuses him of always bringing up the race question, Simple's answer is that a black man does not have to bring up the race question; it is always present. "I look in the mirror in the morning to shave—and what do I see? Me." Brushing aside all fancy and sophisticated extenuations and commentary, Simple has brought the issue home to himself. A black face in our color-conscious world is the problem. Simple and every other Negro knows that.

It is this going to the heart of racial matters that amuses and intrigues us. Simple may be biased, but he is always realistic. For example, he and Hughes are discussing that much-discussed topic, race relations, one evening, and the latter insists that inter-marriage is not and should not be an important consideration in such relations. Simple ridicules the highfalutin' argument and as usual puts his finger on the real issue: "But if races are ever going to relate," he asserts ungrammatically, "they must also mate, and then you will have race relations." Again, as humorous and literal-minded as Simple's answer is, it makes sense. Or let us take Simple's discussion with his well-meaning downtown white friends concerning the progress Negroes have made (a typical topic of well-meaning whites): "Them white folks," Simple informs us, "are always telling me, 'Isn't it wonderful the progress that's been made amongst your people. Look at Dr. Bunche.' All I say is Look at Me!"

Simple's comment is excellent social criticism. (pp. 22-3)

The squeamish reader may be unfavorably impressed when he finds that Simple is anti-white. As a working man living in a society in which a black face means an inferior position, Simple naturally and understandably has anti-white feelings, but one soon discovers that these feelings are neither morbid nor bitter, are not very deep, and as a matter of fact are not even consistent. But when you hear Simple holding forth from the stool at Paddy's Bar, he sounds like a rabid racist. In such cases, Simple is doing what most Negroes do on occasion; he exaggerates his anti-white feelings for the sake of the argument. For example, Hughes and Simple are discussing the "second coming" of Christ (they had read about a lecture being given on the subject), and Simple naturally added a racial angle to the debate. Christ, he maintained loudly and belligerently, should come back and "smite down" all of the white folks for the way they treated Negroes. "You don't mean all white folks, do you?" Hughes asked. "No," said Simple. "I hope he lets Mrs. Roosevelt alone." In this one short sentence Simple has expressed much of the inconsistency which characterizes the American Negro's anti-white tendencies. It would take volumes of sociology to explain all of the nuances of irritation and concession and extenuating circumstances which make up this attitude, but Simple has put it all into one humorous statement.

Simple is guilty of another inconsistency in his racial thinking. Although he tends to blame all of his troubles on being colored, yet he refuses to use race as an excuse for shoddiness on the part of Negroes. Therefore when he goes into a Harlem restaurant and gets bad service or into a 125th Street dime store and finds an impolite and inefficient Negro girl clerking he is vitriolic in his denunciation. In this respect Simple is typical not only of his class but of all decent, self-respecting Negroes. The severest criticism of Negro misconduct comes not from Negro-haters but from Negroes themselves, a fact

cated tolerance and broadmindedness of the black intellectual. The clash and interplay of these attitudes furnish much of the humor in Simple, but they also serve a deeper purpose; they point up and accentuate the two-level type of thinking which segregation tends to produce in all Negroes. And as we read these dialogues, we often find ourselves giving lip-service to the sophisticated Hughes side of the debate while our hearts share Simple's cruder but more realistic attitude. It is this "double" approach that appeals to the Negro reader because . . . the Negro in our country has to live a dual life—as a Negro and as an American.

But enough of this analysis of Langston Hughes' approach. Let us turn now to Simple himself. Our first impression of Mr. Jesse B. is that however unpredictable he may be in other things he is thoroughly consistent in one respect: first, last, and always, he is a "race man"—a fourteen carat, one hundred percent, dyed-in-the-wool race man. No professional Negro leader, no Harlem orator, no follower of Marcus Garvey is more concerned about the fate and well-being of the black brother than Simple. Morning, noon, and night and seven days a week, Simple thinks and talks and gripes about being colored. Whatever happens to him, if it is bad, Simple can trace to some remote origin in race. "No matter what a man does, sick or well," he tells us, "something is always liable to happen especially if you are colored." He constantly reminds us that "a dark man shall see dark days"; and he can often overlooked by whites. Simple's attitude stems from an awareness that the Negro group, unlike any other group in America, is often judged by each individual act; he is therefore always alert to any act that will stigmatize the race. His position is summed up in a very forthright declaration: "When my race does wrong, I say, No. But when they do right, I give 'em credit." And Simple is big enough to be objective about himself on this score. One day he and another "cat" were about to mix it up in a 125th Street store when an old Negro lady said to them: "Now, sons, sons, you-all are acting just like Negroes." Simple immediately regained control of himself. "That made me ashamed," he confesses ruefully, "so I cut out." (pp. 23-4)

The American Negro's propensity to laugh at as well as to criticize himself is nowhere better exemplified than in Simple; and this laughter usually has its source in certain "racial" characteristics and features which distinguish the Negro from whites. For example, the gradations of color among American Negroes is a perennial source of such laughter, and Hughes in his delineation of Simple has drawn heavily upon this reservoir of folk humor. Simple's description of himself is in this vein: "I am a light black," he tells us. "When I were a child, Mama said I were a chocolate, also my hair was straight. But that was my Indian blood." When a mild doubt is raised concerning Simple's redskin genealogy, he becomes almost indignant: "Anybody can look at me and tell I am part Indian." Knowing Simple's color and knowing also the thousands of real-life Simples who, in all seriousness, make such claims, we can appreciate the humor of such remarks, but it is almost impossible to explain that humor to an outsider. For one reason, it is a very grim sort of humor because underneath the fun is the harsh reality that color is all-important in America. Though they laugh at themselves for doing it, the Simples unconsciously seek any mythical alliance that will alleviate in some measure the full social and economic stigma of blackness. For instance, when Simple's girl friend Joyce takes him to the photographer's, she requests that Simple's portrait be made "a little lighter than natural." There is, of course, an extra charge for this service, but both Joyce and Simple know that "color" comes high in a world where "white is right." Humor of this sort has many tragic overtones; it is essentially defensive; it is the Negro laughing first at his own "differences" in order to remove the sting of outside ridicule.

Another aspect of Simple's racial humor is his language. The jive talk of ghetto Negroes, it seems to me, has its origin in social ostracism. Set apart from the whole community, the black segment tends to flaunt its exclusion by a kind of "inside" vocabulary—a vocabulary known only to the initiate. Mastery of this peculiar speech serves oftentimes as a badge of belonging, consequently when the uneducated migrant comes to a community like Harlem, he acquires the new speech pattern not only for purposes of communication but also as a sign of his having made the grade up North.

Simple impresses me as being typical in this respect. Like most Harlemites, he was born in the South, in his case, Virginia. He, therefore, has a twofold speech background—his native Southern and his acquired Harlem. His language, reflecting the conflict and the adjustment between the two, is made of good old-fashioned Southern idiom and Harlem jive talk. For example, when Simple says, "I am tired of trickeration. Also I have had too many hypes laid down on me. Now I am hep," he is blending both traditions. The first sentence

is pure Southern; the rest pure Harlemese. But Simple's language is typical in yet another respect. The uneducated Negro is inclined to avoid usual words just because they sound too natural. Simple has this attitude towards "was" and "were." Why do you use "was" and "were" both in the same way, he is asked. His answer is a lesson in applied linguistics: "Because sometimes I were and sometimes I was, . . . I was at Niagara Falls and I were at the Grand Canyon. . . . " For Simple "was" denotes the immediate past and "were" the remote. This is Simple's explanation, but the real reason as we know is that Simple likes the sound of "were"; it is much more "proper" than plain old everyday "was" which any "downhome" boy could use. (pp. 25-6)

Simple's love of the black ghetto shines through every comment he makes. "Harlem," he boasts, "has got everything from A to Z. Here, like the song says, 'I have found my true love.' " Simple likes Harlem because it is "so full of Negroes." He feels the protection that black faces give from a predominantly white world, a world which is too often hostile. Simple works downtown, but he plays uptown. Harlem therefore means for him release from harsh and unpleasant duties; it means a chance to climb a bar stool or to ring a doorbell and say, "Baby, here I am." He loves Harlem because there are no time clocks or bosses to think about—just joy, relaxation and his girl friend. And although he does not state it bluntly, Simple loves Harlem because to him it is the only place in New York where a black man can find sanctuary; elsewhere in New York he is an alien. It is this sense of finding refuge that underlies much of his comment on the black city. "I will take Harlem for mine," he says emphatically. "At least if trouble comes, I will have my own window to shoot from." When Langston Hughes reminds him that most of the houses in Harlem are owned by whites, Simple is not disturbed: "I might not own 'em, but I live in 'em! It would take an atom bomb to get me out."

Even in his wildest dreaming, Simple cannot stay away from Harlem. Indulging his fancy one evening at Paddy's, Simple imagines himself a bird (black bird of course) flying away in the wild blue yonder following Jackie Robinson as the team moves from place to place. But as Simple envisioned himself flying over New York, he found that the pull of Harlem was too strong: "I fell in on Lenox Avenue like a fish falls back in the pool when it gets off the hook." In short, even in his dream world of escape, Simple can conceive of no place better than Harlem. But Simple knows that Harlem and New York can be a challenge to the peasant coming up from the South. All of them do not make it, he tells us. They come and they go. (pp. 26-7)

Simple is actually a displaced person as far as his native region is concerned. This accounts for his love of Harlem and for the fierce protective instinct that makes the Simples of Harlem such tragic characters deep down. As a matter of record, Simple in spite of his good nature and his ebulliency leads a very narrow and lonely existence. From Monday to Saturday he works downtown in an alien world. His real life uptown lies between his drab Third-Floor-Rear room and Paddy's Bar, with trips, of course, to see Joyce, his girl friend. This is his whole limited life. He has no friends—as he tells us—only barroom acquaintances. When he asks Hughes to be his best man at the June wedding, he confesses the real loneliness of his existence: "I likes to be rowdy myself, but don't like to run with rowdies. Why is that? I like to drink, but I don't like drunks. I don't have the education to mingle myself with educated folks. . . . So who are my buddies? You—and a couple of bartenders." (pp. 27-8)

In this light Simple is no longer a comic character but a black Pagliacci. Underneath all of his gaiety and humor there is the basic tragedy of the urban Negro and his circumscribed life. As such Simple becomes a symbol of all the limited and proscribed figures of all the black ghettos in America. The Simples talk gaily and laugh loudly, but they are really laughing to keep from crying.

Simple, however, like every other great fictional character is a complex and many-sided figure, and I do not wish to stress his tragic aspect to the exclusion of the more obvious one. Whatever else he may be, Simple is also exceptionally funny; and his greatness as a comic character lies, as I have said, in his averageness and typicalness. The Negro reader finds in him all of the slightly mixed-up racial thinking, all of the "twofold loyalties," and all of the laughable inconsistencies which the segregation pattern produces in us. The pressure of jim crow living is so uniform that even though Simple is an uneducated worker his responses to this pressure ring true for all classes. In this sense, Simple is the American Negro. If you want to understand the black brother, learn to know Simple. (p. 28)

> Arthur P. Davis, "Jesse B. Semple: Negro Ameri-
> can," in PHYLON: The Atlanta University Re-
> view of Race and Culture, *Vol. XV, No. 1, first
> quarter (Spring, 1954), pp. 21-8.*

ARTHUR P. DAVIS (essay date 1955)

[*In the excerpt below, Davis analyzes the tragic mulatto theme
in the short story "African Morning."*]

[For] over a quarter of a century, Hughes has been concerned with [the tragic mulatto] theme; returning to it again and again, he has presented the thesis in four different genres, in treatments varying in length from a twelve-line poem to a full-length Broadway play.

Before discussing [one of] Mr. Hughes' several presentations of the theme, however, let us understand the term "tragic mulatto." As commonly used in American fiction and drama, it denotes a light-colored, mixed-blood character (possessing in most cases a white father and a colored mother), who suffers because of difficulties arising from his bi-racial background. In our literature there are, of course, valid and convincing portrayals of this type; but as it is a character which easily lends itself to sensational exaggeration and distortion, there are also many stereotypes of the tragic mulatto to be found. . . . Whether any given character is a true flesh and blood portrait or a stereotype depends, of course, upon the knowledge, the skill, and the integrity of the artist; and this is true whether the author be Negro or white. But it would not be unfair to state that though both are guilty, the white writer tends to use the stereotype more often than the Negro.

Regardless of the approach, however—valid portrayal or stereotype—the tragic mulatto, because of our racial situation, has been popular with the American writer from the very beginnings of our literature. In fiction and in drama, we have a long line of tragic mixed-blood characters, extending from Cooper's Cora Munro (*Last of the Mohicans*) and Boucicault's Zoe (*The Octoroon*) down to the present day creations of William Faulkner and Fannie Hurst. Considering its popu-

larity, we are not surprised that Langston Hughes has made use of the theme, but we are intrigued by the persistency with which he has clung to it over the years.

Why then has Hughes been so deeply concerned with the tragic mulatto? Has he given us a deeper and more realistic analysis of the mixed-blood character? Are his central figures different from the stereotypes created by other writers? Or, does Hughes, perhaps unconsciously, employ the theme of the tragic mulatto to express vicariously and symbolically some basic inner conflict in his own personality? (pp. 195-96)

[The tragic mulatto theme] is found in **"African Morning,"** a short story appearing in *Laughing to Keep from Crying* (1952). The scene of this little sketch is laid in the delta country of the River Niger. The story depicts a day in the life of Maurai, a lonely, twelve-year-old, half-white, half-native boy, the only mixed-blood person in his seaport village. Son of the English local bank president and his native mistress, Maurai had been reared inside the European enclosure in the home of his father. Having lost his mother, Maurai had been rejected by her people and left with his father's new African mistress. He was also rejected by his father who tolerated him, used him for running errands, but who wasted no love or affection on the little half-caste child. For example, when white visitors came, the father made Maurai eat in the kitchen with the black mistress.

When the story opens we find Maurai changing from his native to European dress in order to go on an errand for his father. (Note that even in dress he has no fixed world.) Going to the bank, he walked into his father's office where whites were counting gold. "Wait outside, Maurai," said his father sharply, covering the gold with his hands. Natives were not allowed to possess gold; it was the white man's jealously-guarded prerogative to do so, and because of this proscription gold became a symbol of the whites' power and control. "Maybe that's why the black people hate me," Maurai mused, "because I am the color of gold." (Langston Hughes here and elsewhere uses "yellow" as a symbol for the degradation and unhappiness which supposedly come from mixed-blood situations.)

After delivering his father's message to a sea captain, Maurai is taken for a native "guide boy" by one of the white sailors; but as soon as he reaches the docks he is taunted and beaten by the native black boys and the black women because of his color and his European clothes. He runs to the jungle with the sound of their "yellow bastard" ringing in his ears. In a jungle lagoon, he finds solace for both bruised body and lacerated spirit. Maurai was not afraid of the jungle or of the crocodiles or snakes that could be in the lagoon. Maurai was afraid of only three things: "white people and black people—and gold." As he floated in the pool, he began to pity himself and his sad lot: "Suppose I were to stay here forever," he thought, "in the dark at the bottom of the pool." But Maurai was only twelve, and these morbid thoughts soon passed. He got out of the pool, dressed, and returned to his home inside the European enclosure. As lonely as his present existence was, he realized that it would be much worse when his father returned to England, "leaving him in Africa where nobody wanted him."

Artistically, **"African Morning"** ranks with [Hughes's opera libretto] *"The Barrier."* Probably because of its African background, it seems more convincing than the other versions of the tragic mulatto theme. It is also more touching because it concerns a defenseless child. All in all **"African Morning"** is a restrained, finished, and effectively-written sketch. Possessing none of the sensationalism of the Mulatto-trio, it nevertheless tells once more the same basic story—that of a mixed-blood boy, hungry for recognition, being rejected by a father.

On the surface, Langston Hughes' tragic mulattoes do not seem to be essentially different from the stereotypes of other writers. Their violence, as in the case of Bert, [in *"Mulatto"*] their loneliness, their divided loyalty, their frustrations, their maladjustments, and their tendency to destroy themselves—all of these characteristics, typical of the stereotype, are found (or suggested) in Hughes' central figures. But there are at least two vital differences in the latter's approach. In the first place, many—not all—but many white writers state or imply that the effect of mixed blood per se has something to do with the mulatto's supposedly confused personality; note, for example, the following passage from Paul Green's *In Abraham's Bosom:*

Bud:	White and black make bad mixtry.
Lije:	Do dat. (Thumping his chest) Nigger down heah. (Thumping his head) White mens up here. Heart say do one thing, head say 'nudder. Bad, bad.

As a Negro, Hughes is never guilty of this kind of nonsense. Knowing, as do all intelligent persons, that heredity works along individual rather than racial patterns, he has avoided this aspect of the stereotype, and that in itself is a difference of some importance.

The outstanding contribution, however, which Hughes has made in his delineation of the tragic mulatto, it seems to me, is to point out that at bottom the problem of the mixed-blood character is basically a personal problem. Bert and Maurai, for example, would have been satisfied just to have the recognition of their respective fathers. They were apparently not interested in the larger sociological aspects of divided inheritance. They were not trying to create racial issues. They wanted two very simple but fundamental things: a home and a father. In short, Hughes reduces his tragic mulatto problem to a father and son conflict, and for him the single all-important and transcending issue is rejection—personal rejection on the part of the father.

I am convinced that Langston Hughes felt very keenly on this whole matter of rejection, and I believe that a most revealing postscript to this discussion of father-son relationships may be found in his autobiography, *The Big Sea* (1940). In this work there is a chapter entitled simply "Father," in which Hughes has accounted for, it seems to me, several of the attitudes he portrays in his tragic mulattoes.

Coming from a split home, Langston Hughes did not get to know his father until he was seventeen, the latter having moved to Mexico after the family break-up. During all of his early years of frequent removals and hand-to-mouth living with his mother and other relatives, Hughes came to look upon his father, living "permanently" in Mexico, as the "one stable factor" in his life. "He at least stayed put," and to the young Langston this was an impressive achievement. Although his mother had told him that the senior Hughes was a "devil on wheels," he did not believe her. On the contrary, he created in his mind a heroic image of his father, picturing him as a "strong bronze cowboy in a big Mexican hat," living free in a country where there was no race prejudice.

And then at seventeen, Hughes met his father and went to live with him in Mexico. Disillusionment came quickly, followed by a reaction far more serious. He found that the elder Hughes was neither kind nor understanding. "As weeks went by," he writes, "I could think of less and less to say to my father. His whole way of living was so different from mine. . . . " For the first time, the boy began to understand why his mother had left her husband; he wondered why she had married him in the first place; and most important of all he wondered why they had chosen to have him. "Now at seventeen," Langston Hughes tells us, "I began to be very sorry for myself. . . . I began to wish that I had never been born—not under such circumstances."

And then this unhappy, seventeen-year-old boy, like Maurai in **"African Morning,"** contemplated suicide: "One day, when there was no one in the house but me," he writes, "I put the pistol to my head and held it there, loaded, a long time, and wondered if I would be any happier if I were to pull the trigger."

Subsequently, during a spell of serious illness, Langston Hughes' dislike of his father crystallized into something dangerously approaching fixation. "And when I thought of my father," he tells us, "I got sicker and sicker. I hated my father."

That last short sentence helps to explain for me Hughes' persistent concern with the tragic mulatto theme. In his handling of the theme he has found an opportunity to write out of his system, as it were, the deep feelings of disappointment and resentment that he himself felt as a "rejected" son. (pp. 201-04)

> *Arthur P. Davis, "The Tragic Mulatto Theme in Six Works of Langston Hughes," in* PHYLON: The Atlanta University Review of Race and Culture, *Vol. XVI, No. 2, second quarter (June, 1955), pp. 195-204.*

JAMES A. EMANUEL   (essay date 1961)

[*An American poet and scholar of black American literature, Emanuel has written numerous essays on Hughes and other black writers. He is the author of* Langston Hughes (1967), *a critical biography, and a coeditor of* Negro Symphony: Negro Literature in America (1968), *an influential anthology of black American writing. His own poetry, collected in several volumes that include* The Treehouse, and Other Poems (1968), Panther Man (1970), *and* The Broken Bowl (1983), *reflects Hughes's influence. In the following excerpt, Emanuel analyzes the importance of "Mary Winosky," Hughes's first short story, as an indicator of his more mature stylistic and thematic techniques.*]

"Bodies in the Moonlight" is the engaging title of a story found on pages 105-106 of *The Messenger* of April, 1927. . . .

The magazine, edited by George S. Schuyler and Wallace Thurman, placed beneath the title three italicized lines that should already be of importance to literary historians: *"The first short story by the author of 'The / Weary Blues' and 'Fine Clothes / to the Jew.' "* (p. 267)

[Yet], **"Bodies in the Moonlight,"** which was published when Hughes was twenty-five, is not his first short story. Almost ten years before, he wrote what must be considered his first story, **"Mary Winosky."**

"Mary Winosky" was first seen by the English teacher at Central High School in Cleveland, Ohio, to whom young Hughes turned it in to fulfill a class assignment. Since then, according to a statement Hughes made to me January 28, 1961, no one has read the story. "Mary Winosky" has left no printed trail. The manuscript, like the author's other literary papers, is destined to come to rest in Yale University's James Weldon Johnson Collection, where Curator Donald Gallup will keep it available along with other voluminous material on and by Hughes. (pp. 267-68)

The story is an imaginative development of a newspaper item: "Mary Winosky, who scrubbed floors and picked rags, died and left $8,000." Hughes' brief narrative illuminates crucial events in her life—her arrival as an immigrant, her job-seeking, her romance, and her end, all reflected in dull colors to a reader with a sensitive mind by the two-line report in the newspaper.

The importance of "Mary Winosky" lies chiefly in its forecast of talent and technique. The young student's use of a framework for his story provides the first example. The newspaper lines make up the second and the penultimate passages of the tale, framing the story in both content and tone. This technique is seen again in "Burutu Moon" in 1925 (a sketch in *The Crisis* which some might argue approximates a short story and therefore also precedes "Bodies in the Moonlight"); in "Red-Headed Baby" in 1934; in "Why, You Reckon?," "Professor," "Powder-White Faces" and "Rouge High" in 1952.

The tone thus set early in the story by the laconic newspaper lines is indicative of Hughes' later style. In the often-praised "Cora Unashamed" (1934), which the author told me in January, 1961 is one of his favorite stories, the relatively early line, "Cora was humble and shameless before the fact of the child," begins a refrain that gives both emotional and intellectual force to the story. In "Poor Little Black Fellow" (1934) the fifth sentence contains the words "poor little black Arnie," which recur again and again until they vibrate in the reader's ear with appropriate, ironic offensiveness. In "Trouble with the Angels" (1952) the second sentence offers "the Negro actor who played God," a line on which is strung a variety of episodes all salted with the same critical tone.

Once the tone is set in "Mary Winosky," the young writer is skillful in maintaining it. In the second paragraph he calls Mary's life a "dull tragedy," "A drab-colored life of floors to scrub and rags to pick. . . ." Mary's dull, suppressed life is reflected in a narrative having only eighteen words of dialogue, all spoken in four terse sentences by a scrubwoman who tells Mary how to make a living: " 'I scrub,' said the woman. 'Easy work. Just scrubbing from ten in the night till two in the morning. Good pay.' " The reader's view of Mary's life is full, yet narrow, filled with "filthy tenements, squalid, stifling," "streets ugly and crowded," "miles of marble halls" to be cleaned, and "hands red from . . . lye and scrubwater."

The image of those rough, clumsy hands is sharpened by contrasts pictorially explicit in the gentle atmosphere in which Hughes first lets the reader become aware of Mary's hands removed from steam iron, dishwater, or scrub brush. Unfeminine and coarse, they are made to contrast with balmy springtime, moon and stars, and Mary's white Sunday dress as she walks through the park watching lovers. Other contrasts are aptly used. The brightly expectant Winosky family arrives in New York only to find "the skies blurred with a gray smoke, so different from the blue heavens they had known." Birdsongs, in their absence, are echoed against "the heavy rumble of the elevated all day long and in the night its intermittent roar." Mary, solid of build and dull of features, "was not slim and pretty and deft of movement like her younger sister, so it was hard for Mary to find a job." However, Mary does find a lover, a ditch digger; here again, for contrast, at least the name of his occupation is a semantic blot on the sweet lightness of spring.

Mary's life as scrubwoman and junk dealer is hard. More telling and kinesthetic is Hughes' adjective, "heavy." This word is used in several places to enhance the somber tone of the narrative. The "heavy rumble of the elevated" has been mentioned. More to the point is "the heavy grayness of early morning" in which the tired scrubwomen come home. After Mary, as a wife, is left alone, each year finds her "a little older, a little more stoop-shouldered, loneliness resting a little heavier on her simple heart." And before the final act of her life, "A heaviness pressed upon her heart."

This strumming of a predominant chord throughout the story is often characteristic of Hughes' later work. In "Little Dog" (1934), another commonly praised story and a favorite of the author's, one finds recurrent images exactly suitable to the poignant sense of impossibility that invades an aging spinster who has unwittingly fallen in love with her Negro janitor. He moves through the tale "surrounded by children," with "kids all around him," with "his house full of children." In "Spanish Blood" (1952) the short-lived craze for Harlem's smooth-dancing Valerio is steadily underscored by the cautious refrain that "it was well his mama kept her job in the Chinese laundry. . . ." In "Home" (1934), a much-praised story involving the lynching of a fine young musician, the air of sadness and illness pervades the story with clinging intensity, largely through the wise use of repetition.

Other traits evident in "Mary Winosky" can be traced in Hughes' maturer stories. A rather vivid portrait of the young ditch digger, Andrew Czarnac, is presented: "He had a curled moustache and flashing black eyes and he wore a red bandanna hankerchief [*sic*] inside his collar on hot days." In "Slice Him Down" (1952), a tale which Hughes favors, the author depicts two characters somewhat like Andrew in economic and class status—Sling and Terry, "who rode the rods by way of entry" into Reno in the 1930's. Readying themselves to meet their girl friends, Terry "tapped on down the street" in a cocked derby, brown and white oxfords, and borrowed honey-brown tie; and Sling appeared on the cold streets in a "sky-blue suit with wide shoulders . . . key chain just a-swinging, shining, and swinging." Both, for warmth, had first donned a variety of "sweaters, sweat-shirts, and other warm but unsightly garments."

Such vividness in his stories of the Thirties is probably to be expected of a poet turned short-story writer. One might also expect sentimentality. It seems noteworthy that Hughes' earliest story, as well as characteristic later ones, is almost wholly free of this trait. A writer's sentimentality can be judged by his rejecting of opportunities for the indulgence of that bent. Hughes turns down a number of such invitations in "Mary Winosky": Mary's failures to find a job, her longing for love in the spring, her falling in love with Andrew ("He began to like Mary and Mary liked him."), their honeymoon ("They celebrated . . . by a whole day at Coney Island."), Andrew's desertion ("One day he went away without saying goodbuy [*sic*] and he did not come back."), and Mary Winosky's death.

A sixteen-year-old writer could be forgiven for dispersing a mist of sentiment over the death of his heroine, but Hughes controls himself. Mary simply "gave a little moan and sank down among the rags. . . . She uttered a soft low cry and lay still." This is somewhat Browningesque, but one sees the dry puffs of dust and the rust of old scrap metal in which her dreary life has been spent.

Many similar examples can be found in Hughes' later stories. In **"Cora Unashamed"** the unfortunate Jessie, thin and pale after her trip to Kansas City with her mother, whispers to Cora, "The baby's gone." A sentimental scene could easily have followed, but Hughes disposes of it in twenty-six words not at all sentimental. On two occasions when tears fall in the stories—at the end of **"Big Meeting"** and **"Trouble with the Angels,"** both in *Laughing to Keep from Crying*—they bring to mind, not weakly folded hands, but balled fists.

A different and more felicitous poetic tendency appears in **"Mary Winosky,"** skill in shaping figurative language to the emotional needs of the story. The immigrant Winosky family meets in America, not sweet flowers and cool, green trees and fields, but "hard, hot surfaces." Hughes' high school teacher wrote "good" in the margin near the line, "Then one day Fortune smiled a wry smile at Mary and offered her a job." The personification is common, but the word "wry" is perfect for the whole grim meaning. Again, the spring stars are aided by a "love moon," a term which suitably brings together ancient influences and couples on park benches as Mary walks by. And "the dull swish-swash of Mary's scrub brush" never quite leaves the story once it catches the reader's ear.

A poet-to-be would seem to have an affinity for other things besides sentiment and figures of speech, among them springtime. Absorbing the conventional uses of spring, Hughes employs it here and elsewhere to suggest youth, opportunity on the wing, and a number of other positive, natural values. The story **"Mary Winosky"** apparently opens in the spring, just as it closes—enveloped, then, in hope and the death of hope. Mary becomes lonely in the spring, donning her white dress and finding a lover. After having been deserted, she finds her solitude acute in the spring, and seems to grow older and more stoop-shouldered especially during that fresh season. It is in the spring that Mary's life ends, the same turn of the year that brought her to America, and to the arms of Andrew.

The uses of spring in other stories by Hughes would fill a lengthy paper. Several, as in **"Mary Winosky,"** are initial settings. Stories that open in the spring include **"Father and Son"** (1934), the powerful tale of a lynching, related to Hughes' play *"Mulatto"* and the opera *"The Barrier"*; and **"One Friday Morning"** (1952), the story of a school girl whose prize for art is rescinded because she is colored. In the story of the Studevants' unashamed maid, Cora remembers "her own Spring, twenty years ago" and feels that onrushing sympathy for Jessie which brings the story to an unforgettable climax.

Several other points about **"Mary Winosky"** should be pursued at length. It must suffice here, however, merely to mention them: the narrative style, which contrasts interestingly with that of **"Mother and Child"** (1934), which has no exposition by the author whatsoever; the use of sentence fragments, which are later abundant in stories like **"Red-Headed Baby,"** another Hughes favorite; the treatment of family life

and of death, significantly carried forward in stories like **"On the Way Home"** (1952) and **"Home,"** respectively.

"Mary Winosky," then, is important to literary history, not because it deserves exhaustive analysis for its own sake, but because it is of chronological value in the canon of a writer in whom much of the world has taken a long interest. It is important, further, because it reveals a germinating talent for high competence in a genre that has become typically American. It is important because it shows how early in life Hughes disclosed a tendency that has remained an admirable characteristic of his wide-ranging literary works: that of seeing the world in ordinary, individual human sorrow and joy—in this case, as in others, be it noted, "nonracial." (pp. 268-72)

> James A. Emanuel, "Langston Hughes' First Short Story: 'Mary Winosky'," in PHYLON: The Atlanta University Review of Race and Culture, Vol. XXII, No. 3, third quarter (Fall, 1961), pp. 267-72.

WATERS E. TURPIN (essay date 1967)

[*An American novelist, dramatist, and editor, Turpin was perhaps best known for his historical novels* Those Low Grounds (1937) *and* O Canaan! (1939), *which trace heroic black American characters from the time of the American Revolution to the Depression era. In the excerpt below, Turpin presents* "Slave on the Block" *as an example of Hughes's successful use of satire.*]

Langston Hughes's **"Slave on the Block"** is a penetrating, satirical portraiture of arty, "liberal" whites, represented by Michael and Anne Carraway in this short story. Ostensibly it is the story of a young Negro migrated to New Jersey from the deep South, who has come to retrieve the belongings of his Aunt Emma, lately deceased in the employ of the Carraways, residents of Greenwich Village. However, the story becomes a vehicle for the author to reveal certain absurdities in the behavior of white employers toward their Negro domestics, and at the same time pungently scathe the stereotypes of Negroes held by certain strata of white America, particularly phony liberals. The ironic twist of the narrative is that the Carraways lose their domestics by the very tactics and attitudes with which they had hoped to retain them.

The first . . . paragraphs of **"Slave on the Block"** set the tone and prepare the way for what is to happen:

> They were people who went in for Negroes—Michael and Anne—the Carraways. But not in the social-service, philanthropic sort of way, no. They saw no use in helping a race that was already too charming and naive and lovely for words. Leave them unspoiled and just enjoy them, Michael and Anne felt. So they went in for the Art of Negroes—the dancing that had such jungle life about it, the songs that were so simple and fervent, the poetry that was so direct, so real. They never tried to influence that art, they only bought it and raved over it, and copied it. For they were artists, too.
>
> (pp. 64-5)

> They were acquainted with lots of Negroes, too—but somehow the Negroes didn't seem to like them very much. Maybe the Carraways gushed over them too soon. Or maybe they looked a little like poor white folks, although they were really quite well off. . . . As much as they loved Negroes, Negroes didn't seem to love Michael and Anne. But they were blessed with a wonderful colored

cook and maid—until she took sick and died in her room in their basement. . . .

And the place of their maid's abode and death tells the reader something very pertinent about Michael and Anne.

Into these circumstances comes young Luther, "as black as all the Negroes they'd ever known put together." Anne describes Luther: "He *is* the jungle. . . . " Michael describes him as "He's 'I Couldn't Hear Nobody Pray. . . .' " Each adheres to the terms of the Carraway art interest —Anne's in painting, Michael's in music. And Hughes, no doubt at this point, was having a chuckling good time all by himself.

Luther becomes a combination houseboy, model for Anne, and purveyor of Negro music for Michael. They inform him that they "loved your aunt so much. She was the best cook we ever had."

The redoubtable foil of the Carraways, however, is Mattie, their fortyish but still sexually active replacement for Luther's lately mourned aunt. She proceeds to enlighten the young man about the ways of his new environment, downtown and uptown, and especially her favorite Harlem haunts. Soon they are sleeping together, to the momentary shock of the Carraways but without their disapproval. "It's so simple and natural for Negroes to make love," is Anne's blithe comment. And when Luther, as a result of his nocturnal forays to Harlem night-spots with Mattie, culminating in carnal calisthenics during the wee hours, poses somnolently for Anne, she decides to do a painting of him, entitled "The Sleeping Negro." Following this, she asks him to pose in the half-nude for her painting dubbed "The Boy on the Block," with a New Orleans slave auction background. Michael, not to be outdone by his wife,

> . . . went to the piano and began to play something that sounded like "Deep River" in the jaws of a dog, but . . . said it was a modern slave plaint, 1850 in terms of 1933. Vieux Carre remembered on 135th Street. Slavery in the Cotton Club.

As a consequence of these contretemps, the servant-master-mistress relationships in the Carraway establishment becomes strained, if not dissipated, since the "boy" from the South no longer is the likeable, "child-like creature he first appeared to be by Carraway standards. He takes all sorts of liberties, strolling about in the half-nude, availing himself of Carraway potables and cigaretts. The breaking point is reached upon the appearance of Michael's Kansas City mother—the apotheosis of Philip Wiley's "Mom," who, after an affront by Luther, gets her son to dismiss both servants summarily. Mattie's reaction to this is Hughes' final thrust at the phony white type he is satirizing:

> "Yes, we'll go," boomed Mattie from the doorway, who had come up from below, fat and belligerent. "We've stood enough foolery from you white folks! Yes, we'll go. Come on, Luther."
> What could she mean, "stood enough?" What had they done to them, Anne and Michael wondered. They had tried to be kind. "Oh!"
> "Sneaking around knocking on our door at night," Mattie went on. "Yes, we'll go. Pay us! Pay us!"
> So she remembered the time they had come for Luther at night. That was it.

And to complete the Carraway's bouleversement, Luther

hands the roses he has gathered from the small garden he had nurtured to Anne, saying:

> "Good-bye. . . . You fix the vases."
> He handed her his armful of roses, glanced impudently at old Mrs. Carraway and grinned—grinned that wide, beautiful white-toothed grin that made Anne say when she first saw him, "He looks like the jungle." Grinned and disappeared in the dark hall, with no shirt on his back.
> "Oh," moaned Anne distressfully, "my 'Boy on the Block'!"
> "Huh!" snorted Mrs. Carraway.

In his **"Slave on the Block,"** it is obvious that Hughes is having a gleeful time stilettoing his satirical prey. Yet, the ring of truth chimes from the piece. He has caught with eye and ear the totality of his subject. At the same time we can see here the piercing of the stereotype image which still haunts the white mind in many quarters. (pp. 65-6)

Waters E. Turpin, "Four Short Fiction Writers of the Harlem Renaissance—Their Legacy of Achievement," in CLA Journal, Vol. XI, No. 1, September, 1967, pp. 59-72.

The circumstances of my beginning to write were curious. Shortly after I moved into the New Moscow Hotel, I met there Marie Seaton from London. . . . [She] had with her a paper-bound copy of D. H. Lawrence's short stories, *The Lovely Lady* which she lent me. I had never read anything of Lawrence's before, and was particularly taken with the title story, and with "The Rocking Horse Winner." Both tales made my hair stand on end. The possessive, terrifying elderly woman in "The Lovely Lady" seemed in some ways so much like my former Park Avenue patron that I could hardly bear to read the story, yet I could not put the book down, although it brought cold sweat and goose-pimples to my body. A night or two after I had read the Lawrence stories, I sat down to write an *Izvestia* article on Tashkent when, instead, I began to write a short story. I had been saying to myself all day, "If D. H. Lawrence can write such psychologically powerful accounts of folks in England, that send shivers up and down my spine, maybe I could write stories like his about folks in America. I wonder."

It had never occurred to me to try to write short stories before, other than the enforced compositions of college English. But in wondering, I began to think about some of the people in my own life, and some of the tales I had heard from others, that affected me in the same hair-raising manner as did the characters and situations in D. H. Lawrence's two stories concerning possessive people like the lovely lady and neglective people like the parents of the "Rocking Horse Winner." . . .

I sent my first three stories from Russia to an agent in New York, and by the time I got back to America he had sold all three, one to *The American Mercury,* one to *Scribner's Fiction Parade,* and one to *Esquire.* The money came in handy. And once started, I wrote almost nothing but short stories.

Langston Hughes, from his autobiography I Wonder as I Wander.

JAMES A. EMANUEL (essay date 1968)

[*In the following excerpt, Emanuel provides a general overview of Hughes's short stories.*]

Justly esteemed for his versatility and competence as a writer, especially as a poet and humorist, Langston Hughes deserves close study as the author of sixty-six published short stories. (p. 170)

The ninety-odd reviews of *The Ways of White Folks* and the less numerous brief critical notices of his other collections of stories record as their main consensus that Hughes's style is natural, humorous, restrained and yet powerful. The naturalness is largely found in his characters' talk, which merges incident, personality, and racial history into recurrent patterns. The dialogue is particularly true to facts of race, which authentically control cadences, accents, and ductile phrases. The realism and pathos in much of his work are not adequately recognized in published commentary; nor is his characteristic irony—a point of view that Negro reviewers have best understood. At least twenty-five other typical traits of the stories, including their linguistic play, lyrical exuberance, juxtapositions, and repartee, have been relatively unnoticed. Their rhythm even, not to mention their tension and imagery, has barely been subjected to analysis. Hughes's interspersed songs and Chekhovian endings, which suggest both racial history and modern impasses in social progress, enhance his virtues of style.

The comprehensiveness of his stories has been generally admitted, although not usually detailed. Using settings as different as Harlem and Hong Kong, Havana and Africa, Hollywood and the Midwest, Alabama and New England, and in the main limiting himself to ordinary Negroes, Hughes reflects all the crucial factual realities and psychological depths of Negro experience, especially in urban communities. The variety of themes, images, and symbols through which he mounts this large picture can be indicated by a few statistical and analytical references. Of his forty-odd distinct themes, his main theme is racial prejudice (the focus of thirty-eight stories); his much less intense thematic purposes are to present usually delinquent fathers, affection-seeking women, interracial love, the faddish misconceptions of Negroes by whites, religion and morality, the life of the artist, and jealousy. His images, classifiable into sixteen general types, are most vivid when he is treating nature, physical violence, and weariness. His symbols, usefully introduced in at least seventeen different varieties, into material approached with uncluttered directness, most effectively employ crosses, Negro voices and laughter, snow, coal, and steel.

Hughes's skill in plotting and in creating character demands some comment. The easy and lively movement of **"A Good Job Gone"** exemplifies what Sherwood Anderson meant in calling him a "natural story teller." Hughes's plots are never complicated, and flashbacks are usually handled with grace. Some of his plots are mere gossamer, as in the sketches that he calls his "prose-poems"; some are rather mechanical, like that of **"One Friday Morning,"** which he judges his most "contrived" story; and some are skillfully unified, like that of **"Little Dog."** Some tales invite the risibilities in the manner of sure-fire anecdotes, like **"Tain't So."** Only in such uncollected narratives as **"Saved from the Dogs"** does the usual interest lag.

Not ordinarily concerned with fully rounding his characters, Hughes intimately develops only ten (Cora Jenkins of **"Cora Unashamed,"** Mr. Lloyd of **"A Good Job Gone,"** Oceola Jones of **"The Blues I'm Playing,"** Clara Briggs of **"Little Dog,"** Colonel Norwood and Bert of **"Father and Son,"** Carl Anderson of **"On the Way Home,"** and Professor Brown, Charlie Lee, and Flora Belle Yates in three other stories); and some details of appearance, activities, background, and range of emotion and attitude are missing even in these portraits. Characterization is Hughes's primary technical consideration, however: he said conversationally in 1961, "I do not analyze what goes into the story from the standpoint of emotion, but in terms of whoever I am writing about." Racially, his characters are rather well balanced, despite a few claims to the contrary. One Negro newspaper review of *The Ways of White Folks* asserts that "Hughes's characters are no Uncle Toms"; but old Sam in **"Father and Son,"** complete with multiple *yes, sah's,* chattering teeth, popping eyes, and moaning, justifiably fits the mold—and more are stationed in Colonel Norwood's kitchen. And the pompous Dr. Jenkins in **"The Negro in the Drawing Room"** impressively qualifies. It is true, however, that Hughes almost never subjects Negroes to his own ridicule; and he never attributes any unmitigated felonious activity to them.

Regarding his characterization of whites, which has been usually termed compassionate, even "generous," the author clarified his view in a letter to me in 1961:

> I feel as sorry for them as I do for the Negroes usually involved in hurtful . . . situations. Through at least one (maybe *only* one) white character in each story, I try to indicate that 'they are human, too.' The young girl in 'Cora Unashamed,' the artist in 'Slave on the Block,' the white woman in the red hat in 'Home,' the rich lover in 'A Good Job Gone' helping the boy through college, the sailor all shook up about his 'Red-Headed Baby,' the parents-by-adoption in 'Poor Little Black Fellow,' the white kids in 'Berry,' the plantation owner in 'Father and Son' who wants to love his son, but there's the barrier of color between them. What I try to indicate is that circumstances and conditioning make it very hard for whites, in interracial relationships, each to his 'own self to be true.'

Hughes's sense of personal identification with specific characters in **"Slave on the Block," "Father and Son," "On the Way Home,"** and five other stories, explained in the same letter, increases the importance of characterization to his reshaping of experience into fiction.

Hughes's demonstrable sympathetic characterization of whites stands in revealing conjunction with the bitterness observed by about one-fifth of the reviewers of the 1934 collection and by a somewhat smaller percentage of those commenting upon *Laughing to Keep from Crying* in 1952. This bitterness, emphasized in a *Phylon* review by the perceptive John W. Parker in 1952 as "unwavering pessimism," is generalized by another Negro critic, Blyden Jackson, in 1960 in *CLA Journal,* as the impoverishing "ogre" of the ghetto-ridden substance of Negro fiction. The fact that it coexists, in the not unusual case of Hughes, with restraint of style—a characteristic attributed to *The Ways of White Folks* almost as often as bitterness—should invite psychologically oriented critics to explore ways in which Negro writings illuminate the creative process itself.

The nature of the bitterness in Hughes's stories throws light upon his art, his wisdom, and his realism. In the forty-one narratives in his first two collections, only two characters have personalities substantially weighted with bitterness: Bert in **"Father and Son"** and Charlie Lee in **"Powder-White Faces."** Both kill because of it. The bitterness in four other characters is modified: Johnny Logan, in **"Trouble with the Angels,"** gives in, only at the end, to a bitterness that is bound to subside into resignation; the bitterness of Bill, in **"Sailor Ashore,"** and of little Maurai, in **"African Morning,"** is too dispirited to merit the name, and is evanescent. The bitterness of the Columbia University-trained secretary, in **"The Negro in the Drawing Room,"** means less to him than his stewardship of the papers of an important man, and is merely occasional stimulation for his sense of virtue.

There remains only the bitterness of circumstance. Into this tight corner is pushed the meaning of what commentators have felt with a clarity often sharper than their powers of explanation. It is here that one understands how fully Hughes has accomplished what he stated as his purpose: "to explain and illuminate the Negro condition in America." The bitterness spreads throughout that condition, not as a definable mood of Negroes in the stories (and Hughes knows that the healthy mind cannot long sustain pure bitterness, however rational that attitude might be), but as a stern, incessant truth suffused through the countenance of factual life.

Ugly truth, when recorded by Negro authors, usually raises the blanket indictment of "protest writing," the persistent balderdash which Hughes disposes of in a reply to Rochelle Girson for one of her "This Week's Personality" features in *The Saturday Review* after the publication of *Laughing to Keep from Crying:*

> I have . . . often been termed a propaganda or a protest writer. . . . That designation has probably grown out of the fact that I write about what i know best, and being a Negro in this country is tied up with difficulties that cause one to protest naturally. I am writing about human beings and situations that I know and experience, and therefore it is only incidentally protest—protest in that it grows out of a live situation.

Some of Hughes's narrative sketches in his books about Jesse B. Semple that qualify as short stories (**"A Dog Named Trilby,"** a few pieces on Cousin Minnie, **"Banquet in Honor,"** and **"A Veteran Falls"**) ably combine social protest with humor, artistic restraint, and the bright accumulations of energetic wordplay for which Simple is famous.

A nighttime and pre-dawn writer who composed his average first draft in three days and his second and third drafts in an additional day or more, Hughes has reflected in his short stories his entire purpose as a writer. Early in his career, he knew what he wanted to accomplish in his art: to interpret "the beauty of his own people," a beauty, he wrote in 1926 in *The Nation,* that they were taught either not to see or not to take pride in. He sought to portray their "soul-world." Above the weaknesses of his stories (didacticism, dialogue from unseen "white folks" and other voices, and too many exclamations and parentheses) rise his humanity, his faithful and artistic presentation of both racial and national truth—his successful mediation, that is, between the beauties and the terrors of life around him.

One becomes alive to the vigor and delicacy, the fun and somber meaning, in Hughes's short stories only by reading them attentively. But it would be helpful to read or reread his best works mindful of certain themes, technical excellences, or so-cial insights. **"Slave on the Block,"** available in *The Langston Hughes Reader* (1958), for example, a simple though vivid tale, reveals the lack of respect, and even human communication, between Negroes and those whites whose interest in them is only modishly superficial. **"Poor Little Black Fellow,"** found in *The Ways of White Folks,* satirizes religious, rather than social cant in race relations, treating corrosive varieties of self-deceit with a subtle complexity—although its consistent point is merely that Negroes, even little ones, want only to be treated like everyone else.

Hughes's best stories include four that portray racial violence, but his more comprehensive revelation of prejudices is woven, for the most part, into eleven other tales of uneven quality. Among the eleven, **"Professor,"** which is in *Something in Common, and Other Stories,* excels in its use of irony and ambiguity, and in its solid but artful attack on discrimination in education; **"Powder-White Faces"** and **"Sailor Ashore,"** reprinted in the same collection, deserve close reading too, the former for its meditative picture of the chaos that prejudice can swell in a Negro's mind, the latter for its exploration of a uniquely baneful government-tolerated prejudice, that suffered by military men.

Among the four well-written stories containing racial violence (all except **"Home"** reprinted in *Something in Common*), two employ religious themes and events. **"On the Road"** is a story perfectly conceived as both fantasy and reality, and poetically executed, using intense patterns of wintry images to join Christ and a black hobo in a brief adventure against systemized, prejudiced religion. **"Big Meeting,"** less artistically ingenious than **"On the Road"** but richer in racial meaning, pursues the theme of Negro identification with Christ more emotionally and picturesquely, using a green-coated, big revival preacher whose timing and histrionics are masterful. **"Home,"** published in *The Ways of White Folks,* ends with a savagery that tends to obscure the profound interplay between life and art which thematically deepens the action; the sensitive, gifted little Negro violinist who finds the world too "rotten" for his survival, is a doomed purveyor of beauty into the midst of European decay and hometown American racism. In **"Father and Son,"** Hughes works at a number of themes (psychopathic Southern violence, sexual exploitation of Negro women, Negro miseducation, and religious abuses) and uses effective symbols and striking arrays of atmospheric images; but the title itself underscores his strongest theme: the climactic encounters of steel will and frustrated love between a white father and his mulatto son.

One of Hughes's best stories, **"The Blues I'm Playing"** (collected in *The Ways of White Folks*), addresses itself not only to the Harlem "cult" of the Negro in the Twenties, but to the exploration of American Negritude as conceived by Hughes in that decade. Although this story, like **"Home,"** written in the same month, September, 1933, closely pictures the conflict between life and art, the blues-playing heroine represents life more so than art precisely because she is so much of a Negro, so close to the roots of art—the blues—in her own racial community experience. The last few pages of the story, almost chart-like in their clarity, support Negritude as an insistence upon the black artist's preservation of personal and racial integrity.

Two of Hughes's top stories, **"A Good Job Gone"** and **"Little Dog,"** both available in *Something in Common,* cross the color line on the wings of interracial love. The former fast-moving tale, in which a "sugar-brown" with a suppressed hatred of bigots drives a promiscuous rich white man insane, remains as popular as the "hugging and kissing" with which Harlem's updated Luani of the Jungles works her charms. **"Little Dog"** is distinguished by Hughes's adept characterization of a lonely white spinster who falls in love with a "big and brown and kind looking" Negro janitor; the formidable task of presenting a wasted life without minimizing its integrity or ridiculing its belated humanity is handled admirably. **"Red-Headed Baby,"** reprinted in *The Langston Hughes Reader,* tells of a white sailor's carelessly destructive amours; it is unique for its ably used stream-of-consciousness passages, not attempted again, however, until twenty-eight years later, in **"Blessed Assurance."**

Two essentially nonracial stories, **"Cora Unashamed"** and **"On the Way Home,"** are among Hughes's best narratives. The former, twice published the same year, in *The Ways of White Folks* and *Best Short Stories of 1934,* shows the ignoble defeat of both parental and carnal love; its tragedy is moderated only by the earth-rooted strength of a Negro maid whose simple thoughts ("And there ain't no reason why you can't marry, neither—you both white") free her of all but natural impulses. **"On the Way Home,"** reprinted in *Something in Common,* suggestively employing various images of wine and water, understandingly describes a young man's ambivalent responses to his mother's death; trapped in both guilty exhilarations and anguish, the dutiful son—who is never racially identified—struggles to be reborn.

Traveling throughout the world, Langston Hughes was always a man of the people, equally at home eating camel sausage in an Asian desert or tasting strawberries in a Park Avenue penthouse. He once said that he had lived much of his life in basements and attics. Metaphorically, his realism and his humanity derive from this fact. Moving figuratively through the basements of the world, where life is thickest and where common people struggle to make their way, he remained close to his vast public. At the same time, writing in attics like the one he occupied in Harlem for twenty years, he rose to the long perspective that enabled him to shine a humanizing, beautifying, but still truthful light on what he saw. His short stories form a world of fiction built with truth and a special love—a little civilization shaped by high purpose and steadfast integrity. (pp. 172-78)

James A. Emanuel, "The Short Fiction of Langston Hughes," in Freedomways, *Vol. 8, No. 2, Spring, 1968, pp. 170-78.*

JAMES A. EMANUEL (essay date 1968)

[*In the excerpt below, Emanuel explores Hughes's experimentation with interior monologue in order to reveal different levels of meaning in the stories "Red-Headed Baby" and "Blessed Assurance."*]

Technical experimentation in Hughes's short fiction . . . becomes inseparable from personal style as the reader grows accustomed to Hughes's interspersed songs, parenthetical tableaus, and recurrent, racially significant images. Some unusual passages, however, are clearly experimental. Chief among them are his uses of interior monologue, limited to **"Red-Headed Baby"** and **"Blessed Assurance."** The rarity of stream-of-consciousness writing in Hughes's fiction rouses speculation about the occurrence of it even in those two stories, published twenty-eight years apart. A brief inspection of the contexts in which these passages of interior monologue

appear may throw light on the problem of craftsmanship which they were meant to resolve. (p. 336)

[**"Red-Headed Baby"**] recounts the brief visit of a red-headed sailor, Clarence, from his tramp steamer to the hut of Betsy, the Florida Negro girl he had enjoyed for a price three years earlier. While drinking with Betsy and her mother, the sailor is surprised by the appearance of what he calls "a damn runt of a red-headed baby," a deaf mute named Clarence, he soon discovers. Angered by the stares of the child, the sailor violently departs.

After the midpoint of this story, told almost completely through the fragmented thoughts of the predatory white sailor, Clarence takes on his lap the girl who three years before was a church-going teetotaler, but who now drinks liquor "strong enough to knock a mule down." He thinks:

> Soft heavy hips. Hot and browner than the moon— good licker. Drinking it down in little nigger house Florida coast palm fronds scratching roof hum mosquitoes night bugs flies ain't loud enough to keep a man named Clarence girl named Betsy old woman named Auntie from talking and drinking in a little nigger house on Florida coast dead warm night with the licker browner and more fiery than the moon.

Near the end of the story, the sailor, thoroughly startled by the features of the child ("over two years old," says Betsy's mother, "and can't even say, 'Da!' "), vigorously insists on the baby's removal from the room:

> A red-headed baby. Moonlight-gone baby. No kind of yellow-white bow-legged goggled-eyed County Fair baseball baby. Get him the hell out of here pulling at my legs looking like me at me like me at myself like me red-headed as me.

The third and final passage, on the last page of the story, reveals the sailor's thoughts as he stumbles out of the shack:

> Knocking over glasses by the oil lamp on the table where the night flies flutter where skeleton houses left over from boom sand in the road and no lights in the nigger section across the railroad's knocking over glasses at edge of town where a moon-colored girl's got a red-headed baby deaf as a post like the dolls you wham at three shots for a quarter in the County Fair half full of licker and can't hit nothing.

In this story—a favorite of Hughes's—why does the author forsake standard exposition in these three passages? He is expert with dialogue, whether it is spoken by one of the Negro characters ("That chile near 'bout worries de soul-case out o' me. Besty spiles him, that's why") or by the sailor ("Hey! Take your hands off my legs, you lousy little bastard!"). And expository sentence fragments elsewhere effectively convey the careless but sentient rush of the sailor's movements. The probable answer credits Hughes with an artistic deliberation that has seldom been recognized, linked with a humanity that, on the contrary, is widely acknowledged. Hughes must get inside the mind of Clarence, now slightly muddled with liquor but nevertheless—and perhaps for that very reason— keenly aware on a nonverbal level of its meandering fusions of personal and racial responses. The knowledge that he is white and that he is a father—and that he momentarily is both these things under the wrong conditions and in the face of the wrong consequences—unsettles him with a shock that defines a predicament of twentieth-century white America.

En route to Moscow in 1932 with a group of amateur filmmakers to begin work on a movie about American race relations. Hughes is standing in the middle row, third from the right.

Hughes catches all the meaning, none of which would be as effective if rendered in coherent, rational prose. In the first passage, one senses the rough comforts of a sailor ashore: voluptuousness; brown skin turned into brown liquor; humming sounds that ward off a "scratching" world and unite three people with names instead of races in a carousal subconsciously ritualistic with its "Auntie" and "nigger" setting. The disruptive truth appears and controls the second passage, which appropriately begins with hints of ambivalent paternal pride and masculine sternness. In the middle of that natural response obtrudes awareness of race ("looking like me at me like me"), which is the signal for racial unreason and its stylistic counterpart, syntactical incoherence. That incoherence properly dominates the final passage. One should estimate Hughes's feeling for the sailor—as a father, not as a white man—in the complex of sensations and ideas blurred in the paragraph: blind, almost fearful, escape; perception of economic and political injustice; and guilt-ridden violence accentuated by a sense of failure (the failure of bawdy virility fathering only a "baby deaf as a post," a "baseball baby" whose rollicking sire in his sexual life "can't hit nothing"). Asked whether the stream-of-consciousness style was deliberately chosen as a necessary effect in **"Red-Headed Baby,"** Hughes wrote to me in July, 1961, "Yes—like what goes through the characters' minds in the room." (pp. 336-38)

The six-page story [**"Blessed Assurance"**] concentrates on the Spring Concert of the Tried Stone Baptist Church, where the protagonist-father's anguish over his son Delmar's occasional femininity culminates. When Dr. Manley Jaxon, Minister of Music, who has written an anthem for the concert and assigned the female lead to "Delly," faints and falls off his organ stool as the boy hits a sweet high note, the father's "I'll be damned" concedes his moment of worst despair.

As in **"Red-Headed Baby,"** three passages of interior monologue detail the protagonist's crucial bewilderment. The first one offers a glimpse of the thoughts of John, the father, when his seventeen-year-old son chooses spectacles with exaggerated rims: " 'At least he didn't get rhinestone rims,' thought John half-thought didn't think felt faint and aloud said nothing." The second passage pictures John wondering about Delmar after the boy starts to grow a beard in imitation of certain beatniks he has seen in Greenwich Village:

> "God, don't let him put an earring in his ear like some," John prayed. He wondered vaguely with a sick feeling in his stomach should he think it through then then think it through right then through should he try then and think it through should without blacking through think blacking out then and there think it through?

Instead of thinking it through, John ponders Delmar's remark that he would like to study at the Sorbonne in Paris—not at Morgan, the Negro university that is his own alma mater. After the embarrassment at the Spring Concert, John wonders about the Sorbonne: "Does it have dormitories, a campus? In Paris he had heard they didn't care about such things. Care about such what things didn't care about what?"

Again, why does Hughes not employ standard exposition? Dealing this time with a Negro father and son whose race is essentially irrelevant to their dilemma—rather than with a white sailor whose race exacerbates his predicament—the author must again illuminate a perversion of feeling by reaching psychological depths where the whirl of things remembered and feared constitute a disorder frightfully coherent to the unsteady mind but resistant to the shaping powers of traditional syntax. John's thinking and not thinking—that is, his thinking about his son and half-thinking or not thinking about himself—are captured in the first passage with an economy not available to ordinary prose. In the second passage, interior monologue makes almost kaleidoscopic the changing patterns of the father's unstated past failures and his present weakness—the patterns of causation and time, as modified by doubts about the laws of heredity, being strictly controlled by the juxtapositions "then then" and "then and there." In the third passage, the knuckle-rapping self-administered by the father sharply opposes consciousness and conscience in this man struggling to be honest with himself. That struggle, according to a letter that Hughes wrote to me on September 19, 1961, represents to the author the plight of "one afraid to fully face realities." (And the dilemma of Clarence in **"Red-Headed Baby,"** the same letter indicates, is meant to show that white people "are human, too.") (pp. 338-40)

> James A. Emanuel, "The Literary Experiments of Langston Hughes," in CLA *Journal, Vol. XI, No. 4, June, 1968, pp. 335-44.*

JULIAN C. CAREY   (essay date 1971)

[*In the following excerpt, Carey portrays the character Jesse B. Semple as a prototypical black American.*]

Born in Virginia, the initial port of debarkation in America for the black man, instructed by Aunt Lucy to carry himself "right and 'sociate with peoples what's decent and be a good boy," told by his grandmother "to hitch [his] wagon to a star," Jesse B. Semple matured and moved his bohunkas to Harlem, along the way being "underfed, underpaid, undernourished, and everything but undertaken." He suffers from more maladies than most people endure in a lifetime, having been "born with the measles" which preceded "smallpox, chickenpox, whooping cough, croup, appendicitis, athlete's foot, tonsillitas, arthritis, backache, mumps, and a strain." But as Simple reminds his audience, "Daddy-o, I'm still here!" and this, perhaps, is what Langston Hughes wanted when, in 1943, Jesse B. Semple first appeared in the Chicago *Defender,* a Negro weekly. Simple simply endures. The uncultured Harlemite endures being fired, jim crowed, insulted, eliminated, called black, black-jacked, caught in raids, false arrested, third degreed, caught with another man's wife, and near about lynched. If Simple is, then, as Arthur Davis suggests, "Like the overwhelming majority of Harlemites, . . . a plain, garden variety of untrained but honest and hard-working peasant from the South who has found a new and freer home in the north," he is not an entirely burlesque fig-

ure, being the prototype for a mass of black Americans. (p. 158)

He remains black, despite the temptations put forth by [his fiancee], Joyce, who is influenced by that culture fiend, Mrs. Sadie Maxwell-Reeves, a resident of Sugar Hill, and by the antagonistic "I," a foil parroting the attitudes of the black bourgeoisie. Simple, the protagonist, although sometimes staggered by their demands and logic, recovers and remains steadfast to his conception of *négritude.* He does not, as Davis asserts, think that his blackness is "the cause of all his troubles [see excerpt dated 1954]. On the contrary, Simple not only accepts his identity, but he also affirms his pride in black men when he states, "I am race conscious . . . and I ain't ashamed of my race." The cause, then, is not Jess B. Simple; it is, instead, white, racist America. Davis's thoughts, furthermore, are dated when he remarks, "a black face in our color-conscious world is the problem. Simple and every other Negro knows that." Again, and this is what Simple expresses, the problem is white—not black. . . .

[He] does not go to the movies because he sees "nothing but white folks on the screen." That reader who may have been, according to Davis, "unfavorably impressed when he finds that Simple is anti-white," should no longer be squeamish. Simple is not anti-white—he is pro-black. (p. 159)

Simple's greatest challenge to his *négritude* comes from his friend and bourgeois foil, "I." An articulate, sophisticated, educated Negro liberal, the antagonist questions Simple's militancy and simple solutions to his problem. Simple, for example, is amazed that "white folks is scared to come to Harlem," when it is he who should be afraid of them. . . . "I" reminds him that he sounds just like a Negro nationalist, "someone who wants Negroes to be on top." Simple replies, "when everybody else keeps me on the bottom, I don't see why I shouldn't want to be on top. I will, too, someday." The antagonist asks Simple to have an open mind about white people, to separate the good ones from the bad, to which he replies, "I have near about lost my mind worrying with them. . . . In fact, they have hurt my soul." "I" then reminds him that white people "blasted each other down with V-bombs during the war." However equally distributed the white man's brutality, "to be shot down is bad for the body," says Simple, "but to be Jim Crowed is worse for the spirit."

Simple, however, is not entirely antagonistic to white people. He would just like for them to experience and endure his life; he wants to "share and share alike." He believes that if the "good white friends" that "I" mentions would share a hot old half-baggage jim crow train car with him or use a "COLORED" toilet in a Southern town, they would stop resolving and start solving.

There is yet another conflict involving his *négritude* that Simple has with "I," and it is an intellectual one. Being educated and "observing life for literary purposes," "I" finds fault with Simple's verse when the latter expresses himself poetically. It would seem that the antagonist is trying to make a poet out of a Negro, but Simple would just as soon remain a Negro poet. (p. 160)

Simple's continued efforts to glorify the black race and his unceasing struggles to show that white is not right do not always find a receptive audience. But when Simple discovers an old man who shares his philosophy, he is ecstatic. The elderly gentlemen, being belatedly honored at a dinner, has "always played the race game straight and has never writ no Amos and Andy books nor no songs like 'That's Why Darkies Are Born' nor painted no kinky-headed pictures." Simple hears the "Honorable Dr. So-and-So-and-So" ridicule the complaisant attitude of his audience when it comes to supporting and encouraging *négritude.*. . . . (p. 161)

Working daily in a white world, Simple endures such shallow statements as, "Isn't it wonderful the progress that's been made amongst your people. Look at Dr. Bunche!" Jim crowed in the South and tokened in the North, he has but one retreat, Harlem. He loves Harlem because "it's so full of Negroes," because even if the houses are not his, the sidewalk is, and because he elected, by his own vote, black Congressmen. Simple will defend his sanctuary. He will break store front windows of the whites that remind him of his enslavement; Harlem will be his fortress from which he will have his "own window to shoot from"; he is certain that even an atom bomb could not harm Harlemites because, "if Negroes can survive folks in Mississippi . . . we can survive anything." Harlem, then, is that "Game Preserve for Negroes" that Simple seeks, where "nobody can jump on [him] and beat [him], neither lynch [him] nor Jim Crow [him] everyday." But this refuge is also a prison from which Simple dreams of rocketing "so far away from this color line in the U.S.A. till it wouldn't be funny" or becoming a plain old ugly bird that caws and soars way up into the blue where heaven is, and the smell of the earth does not go, neither the noise of juke boxes nor radios, television or record shops." Simple's Harlem is a paradox.

If, as other critics suggest, Semple is the universal black man in the street, the average and typical Afro-American, the cause of his (their) problems is not his lack of cultural awareness or his misdirected efforts to champion his *négritude:* "White folks is the cause of a lot of inconveniences in my life." White America has tried to give him a false sense of culture and to replace his black pride with a desire to be white. In both instances, Jesse B. Semple, the prototype for black Americans, has repulsed white America's efforts. (pp. 162-63)

If Langston Hughes's character has any shortcoming it is that while Simple is laughing to keep from crying, most of his readers are only laughing—laughing and failing to recognize the tragic ethos that Simple symbolizes. His efforts to acknowledge the cultural, social, and political assets of *négritude* are challenged by lovers, friends, states, and institutions. Nevertheless, he perseveres, he endures. He refuses to believe that Negroes are "misbred, misread, and mislead." He is not sophisticated enough to diagnose the racist psyche, but he does know that he is not the problem. Simple is not made for defeat. He is just simple, and in his simplicity and compassion and bufoonery he exposes his soul, truly hurt by a racist country; he illustrates, sometimes too humorously, the reason he is lonesome inside himself. He knows he is equal; what he wants is to be treated equal. He prays a prayer that we learn to do right, that we learn to get along together because he "ain't nothing but a man, a working man, and a colored man at that." (p. 163)

Julian C. Carey, "Jesse B. Semple Revisited and Revised," in PHYLON: The Atlanta University Review of Race and Culture, *Vol. XXXII, No. 2, second quarter (Summer, 1971), pp. 158-63.*

ROBERT BONE (essay date 1975)

[*An American critic and educator, Bone is the author of the informative critical histories* The Negro Novel in America *(1958) and* Down Home: Origins of the Afro-American Short Story *(1975). A student of Afro-American, English, and American literature, with a special interest in Shakespeare, Bone has said of himself: "A white man and critic of black literature, I try to demonstrate by the quality of my work that scholarship is not the same thing as identity." In the excerpt below from* Down Home, *which was originally published in 1975, Bone traces Hughes's career through four major phases by interweaving aspects of Hughes's personal life with analyses of his short fiction.*]

The impulse toward the picaresque, as the two volumes of his autobiography attest, was strong in Langston Hughes. His quest for experience took him to Africa, Europe, and the Caribbean in his twenties, and through Moscow to Soviet Asia and the Far East in his early thirties. These years of vagabondage are reflected in his poems, plays, and stories. Yet still more basic to his art was the bardic impulse that tied him to the Negro folk experience and led him at the age of forty to settle down in Harlem. For it was Hughes' ambition from the first to play the role of bard, singing the joys and sorrows of his people, and establishing himself, in his own phrase, as the Shakespeare of Harlem.

The performance of this bardic role required of him that he curb his impulse toward sophistication and remain in close rapport with his folk origins. To this end, he donned the Mask of Simplicity that is the hallmark of pastoral. An early poem called "Disillusion" contains the central metaphor of his career:

> I would be simple again
> Simple and clean
> Like the earth,
> Like the air.

Hughes loved to pretend to less sophistication than in fact he possessed. Hence the famous Hughes persona, Jess' B. Semple. The Simple sketches, which first appeared in the *Chicago Defender* in 1943, and were subsequently published in several volumes, attest to the persistence of the pastoral mode throughout his long career. Their form, consisting of a dialogue between a shrewd countryman (transplanted in this case to the streets of Harlem) and his urbane interlocutor, derives from the *Eclogues* of Virgil. By splitting his consciousness in two, the artist gains access to the folk wisdom of his race without relinquishing the insights of sophistication and urbanity. (pp. 239-40)

Pastoral, whose source is disillusionment with courtly life, contains within itself the seeds of satire. The higher the degree of alienation from the life-style of courtiers and kings, the greater the tendency toward satire. Langston Hughes is essentially a satirist, at least in the short-story form. His first book of stories, *The Ways of White Folks,* might well have been subtitled "In Dispraise of Courtly Life." The pride and pretentiousness, arrogance and hypocrisy, boorishness and inhumanity of white folks are the targets of his caustic prose. The genius of Langston Hughes, which is a gift for comedy and satire, is thus displayed within the broad outlines of the pastoral tradition.

Within the context of its times, however, *The Ways of White Folks* functioned as antipastoral. The early, or ascending phase of the Harlem Renaissance was dominated by the myth of primitivism. Hughes himself, during what may be described as the undergraduate phase of his career, conformed substantially to the requirements of the myth. The late, or declining phase of the Renaissance, however, was increasingly antagonistic to the stereotype of the Negro as primitive. Finely turned as always to the climate of the times, Hughes joined forces with such authors as Wallace Thurman and Sterling Brown to discredit the myth and challenge its pastoral assumptions. (pp. 240-41)

Since Hughes wrote steadily from 1925 or 1926 until his death in 1967, it is essential to establish an overview of his career. We cannot expect tidy compartments in the case of an author who is so prolific, but allowing for some overlap we may discern four distinct phases. Hughes' early period (1926 to 1934) encompasses his first four books: *The Weary Blues* (1926), *Fine Clothes to the Jew* (1927), *Not Without Laughter* (1930), and *The Ways of White Folks* (1934). Roughly co-extensive with the Harlem Renaissance, this period is dominated by the vogue of the Negro and the myth of primitivism. Hughes establishes himself as a romantic poet and a satirist—a not uncommon breed if we bear in mind the Byron of *Childe Harold* and *Don Juan.*

His second, or fellow-traveling, period (1930 to 1939), overlaps with his late Renaissance phase. As early as 1930-1931, Hughes was a frequent contributor to the *New Masses.* In 1932 he published a verse pamphlet in defense of the Scottsboro boys, [nine young black men who were accused in Alabama of raping two white women in 1931], and was promptly rewarded with a trip to Russia. From 1935 to 1937 he placed several stories in such Party-oriented journals as *Anvil, Fight Against War and Fascism,* and *New Theater.* The climax of his proletarian phase came in 1938 with the staging of an historical pageant, *Don't You Want to Be Free?,* and the publication of a verse pamphlet, *A New Song.* Both display the revolutionary sloganeering characteristic of the times. (pp. 245-46)

The Big Sea marks the onset of Hughes' mature phase (1940 to 1955). The book appeared when he was thirty-eight: both parents were dead, and he was able to confront his filial emotions. Liberated from the past by the act of composing an autobiography, Hughes proceeded to accomplish his mature work. This includes, above all, the creation of Simple, who first appeared in the *Chicago Defender* columns of 1943, and Alberta K. Johnson, his female counterpart in *One Way Ticket* (1949). (p. 246)

I Wonder As I Wander (1956) marks the beginning of Hughes' decline. Inferior to *The Big Sea,* this rambling and evasive work betrays the author's inability to cope in retrospect with his fellow-traveling phase. Symptomatic of Hughes' waning imaginative power is a corresponding increase in his editorial activities. In the last decade of his life, he is more enterprising as an editor, anthologist, or folklorist than as a creative writer. Increasingly he repeats himself, or simply reprints old material. Among the books of Hughes' decline are *Tambourines to Glory* (1958), **Something in Common** (1963), and *The Panther and the Lash* (1967). These books are distinctly inferior, in their respective genres, to earlier achievements.

It is against this background that we must seek to comprehend Hughes' career as a short-story writer. After a brief experimental period in 1927-1928, he turned to serious professional work in 1933. During that year he wrote fourteen sto-

ries, all of which were published in **The Ways of White Folks.** Retaining this momentum, in 1934 he wrote eleven more, most of which were collected some years later in *Laughing to Keep from Crying.* From 1935 to 1939 there was a tapering off (only five stories), as he turned from fiction to drama. A year at Hollow Hills Farm in 1941 produced a cluster of four stories. In 1943 the first Simple sketch appeared, and from that date until his death in 1967 Hughes wrote only seven tales.

The point is that Hughes never remotely matched the productivity of 1933 and 1934. More than half of his stories, and nearly all of his best stories, were written in a period of two years, marked by an exclusive concentration on the short-story form. Apart from a flurry of activity in 1941, he never made a sustained effort in the genre again. He published two collections, to be sure, in 1952 and 1963, but these publication dates are misleading, since both volumes draw substantially on stories written in the 1930's. In point of fact, most of Hughes' significant production in the short-story form falls within the chronological limits of the Harlem Renaissance.

Hughes' first published stories appeared in the *Messenger,* a little magazine of the Harlem Renaissance edited by Wallace Thurman and George Schuyler. **"Bodies in the Moonlight," "The Young Glory of Him,"** and **"The Little Virgin"** (April, June, and November 1927) reflect the author's personal experience as a mess boy in 1923 on the S.S. *Malone.* Together with **"Luani of the Jungle"** (*Harlem,* November 1928), these tales comprise what James Emanuel has called the West Illana Series. Their common setting is a freighter, the *West Illana,* making various ports of call along the West Coast of Africa.

These early tales are lushly romantic: their dominating image is a tropic moon. They express an adolescent eroticism not quite certain of its object, but focusing tentatively on dusky maidens with names like Nunuma or Luani. Imitative of Joseph Conrad and Eugene O'Neill, they reflect the atavistic yearnings and primitivistic posturings of the postwar generation. Yet they sound a deeper note which reveals the central thrust of Hughes' career. This is the outreach toward experience, and its inevitable price, the loss of innocence. In one way or another, these stories are concerned with the wound or trauma or symbolic scar which marks the rite of passage from the innocence of childhood to the bittersweet enchantments of adult sexuality.

When Hughes returned to short fiction after a lapse of several years, it was not to write romantic idyls, but caustic satires. What had happened in the interval? A clue is provided by his account of the winter of 1933, when he was stranded in a Moscow hotel. After reading a copy of D. H. Lawrence's *The Lovely Lady,* he remarks: "I had never read anything of Lawrence's before, and was particularly taken with the title story, and with 'The Rocking Horse Winner.' Both tales made my hair stand on end. The possessive, terrifying elderly woman in 'The Lovely Lady' seemed in some ways so much like my former Park Avenue patron that I could hardly bear to read the story. . . . "

The Park Avenue dowager that Hughes will never name was Mrs. R. Osgood Mason. The widow of a prominent physician, she thought of herself as godmother of the New Negro movement, and adopted several of its luminaries as her protégés. Hughes had met her when he was an undergraduate at

Lincoln, and she not only offered to support him during the summers of 1928 and 1929, when he was working on his first novel, but provided him with a year of economic freedom following his graduation. Her emotional support was equally important to the young author. It is not too much to say that Mrs. Mason became a surrogate parent, supplying Hughes with the love and admiration and affectionate concern that he had never known as a child.

The breach in their relationship was shattering in its effect on Hughes. It precipitated what can only be described as a nervous breakdown. As he recounts the story of this crisis in *The Big Sea,* he cites three factors that contributed to their estrangement. First was Mrs. Mason's demand for constant productivity, which interfered with his desire to rest between projects. He was enjoined, in short, to "hurry up." Second was the painful contrast between his patron's wealth and the growing misery of the Great Depression. This was a goad to Hughes' social conscience, filling him with guilt for accepting her largesse. Third was her conception of the Negro as a primitive, which she attempted to impose on her protégé:

"She wanted me to be primitive and know and feel the intuitions of the primitive. But, unfortunately, I did not feel the rhythms of the primitive surging through me, and so I could not live and write as though I did. I was only an American Negro—who had loved the surface of Africa and the rhythms of Africa—but I was not Africa. I was Chicago and Kansas City and Broadway and Harlem. . . . " This passage from Hughes' autobiography tends to minimize his collaboration with the myth of primitivism, and place the responsibility for it outside the self. But the disillusionment is genuine enough, and from it sprang his caustic antipastoral, *The Ways of White Folks.*

The breach with Mrs. Mason brought about a psychosomatic illness reminiscent of a boyhood episode in Mexico. Hughes himself is well aware of this connection when recounting matters in *The Big Sea.* Through a series of allusions to his father, he invites us to perceive the two events as manifestations of a single psychological reality. What we have, in short, is the reenactment of a primal drama, in which his patron is assigned the father's role. Nor is there anything mysterious about this drama. Hughes resented his father's domineering ways almost as much as he coveted his love. The result was a deep emotional conflict, in which a strong desire for independence clashed with infantile dependency needs.

Transpose this conflict to the cultural plane, and we touch a sensitive nerve of the Harlem Renaissance. For an end to white paternalism was one of the things that the Renaissance was all about. Hughes' literary manifesto, ["The Negro Artist and the Racial Mountain"], in the *Nation* was nothing if not a declaration of independence. Yet paradoxically, it was promulgated by a writer who depended on a series of white patrons for his daily bread. The stark reality of the New Negro movement was that Hughes and his contemporaries were dependent in many ways on white patrons, impresarios, editors, agents, critics, and ordinary members of the reading public. It was an agonizing dilemma, which neither Hughes nor the generation of which he was a leading spokesman was able to resolve.

The Ways of White Folks was at bottom an attempt to come to grips with this dilemma. Hughes' solution was to strike a satirical stance toward his former patron and the world that she represents. In this way, he was able to preserve an essential dignity and self-respect, even while living rent-free in Noel Sullivan's cottage at Carmel. His experience with Mrs. Mason had left him in a satirical frame of mind. He was more than ready for a caustic treatment of white folks, rich folks, or pompous and pretentious folks of any hue. This turn to satire, moreover, involved a momentary shift from poetry to prose. For a brief period, the short-story form became the growing edge of his career.

The unmasking of hypocrisy became his central theme. The emotional source of this impulse was of course his father, who made a show of fatherly concern which in fact he didn't feel. By a process of transference, Hughes attributed the sins of his delinquent father to the patrons of the Harlem Renaissance. They too, he had come to feel, were lacking in a genuine commitment to the cause that they espoused. This is the burden of several stories in *The Ways of White Folks.* (pp. 246-51)

Eleven of [this book's] . . . fourteen tales are satires, and the rest contain satiric elements. The book was born in a sense of personal affront. Wounded by his former patron, Hughes lashes back at white paternalism in all its forms. His objects of attack include delinquent parents, domineering patrons, unscrupulous employers, and self-appointed missionaries in whatever guise. In the caustic language of H. L. Mencken (it is no accident that two of these stories first appeared in the *American Mercury*), Hughes excoriates the guile and mendacity, self-deception and equivocation, insincerity and sanctimoniousness, sham, humbug, and sheer fakery of white America in all its dealings with the black minority.

The author's personal pique is obvious enough, and to lift the curse of his vindictiveness toward Mrs. Mason, Hughes assumes a mask of genial humor. His comic muse is most apparent in such light satires as **"Slave on the Block," "A Good Job Gone,"** and **"Rejuvenation Through Joy."** Hughes is a gifted humorist, but it would be an error to construe this gift in narrow literary terms. Rather it constitutes a lusty adaptation to his life circumstances. Nourished by the boundless absurdities of American racism, this humor is, by the author's own account, a matter of "laughing to keep from crying." But "laughing to keep from hating" may be closer to the mark. In any case, a humor of diverse tonalities is an essential feature of Hughes' satiric mask.

Irony . . . is the satirist's linguistic mode. Hughes is a resourceful ironist whose verbal indirections often saturate his tales. Among his favorite rhetorical devices are ironic understatement (to intensify, while seeming to diminish, the satirical attack); ironic inversion (to apportion praise or blame by indirection); ironic reversal (to add an element of shock or surprise to the attack); and ironic repetition or refrain (to create a cumulative tension that is finally discharged against the satiric victim). These are but a few of the devices by which Hughes is able to control his anger and simulate the coolness and detachment of effective satire.

Two standards of morality are juxtaposed in Hughes' satiric fiction: a white and Negro code. This division is the basis of the bipartite structure of his tales. He begins with the arraignment of a white society which constantly betrays its own professed ideals. But at some point a Negro character is introduced who embodies a different and more authentic moral code. This character—whether maid-of-all-work, kitchen boy, janitor, or jazz musician—provides the low norm by which the conduct of the whites is judged and found wanting.

For the whites, despite their wealth and power, are failures as human beings, while the blacks, despite their poverty and vulnerability, are tough and resourceful and certain to survive.

Hughes' achievement as a satirist is clearly of a high order. Yet literary men may fruitfully debate the degree of consistency with which he attains his top form. In [his critical biography *Langston Hughes*], critic James Emanuel compiles a list of the author's twelve best stories. Eight of the twelve titles were selected from *The Ways of White Folks.* I cannot concur in this generous estimate of Hughes' first collection. I find only four stories—**"Cora Unashamed," "The Blues I'm Playing," "Little Dog,"** and **"Red-Headed Baby"**—to be vintage Hughes. (pp. 252-54)

"Cora Unashamed" is one of Hughes' most bitter, as well as most successful satires. Written in Moscow, it was published in the *American Mercury* of September 1933, and chosen by Edward O'brien as one of the best short stories of the year. It is the lead story in *The Ways of White Folks,* where it serves to establish the book's basic operational mode: satire of the low norm with close affinities to pastoral. Cora is the first of several Negro servants who provide Hughes with a base from which to satirize their white employers. Simple, natural, and unpretentious, these folk Negroes are forerunners of Jess' B. Semple and his signifying ways.

Cora is employed by the Studevants as maid-of-all-work in a small Midwestern town. Lonely and isolated (hers is the only black family in town), she has an illegitimate child, who dies in infancy of whooping cough. All of her maternal love is thus transferred to Jessie Studevant, a "backward" child born at the same time as her own daughter. At the age of nineteen, Jessie is impregnated by a high-school classmate of "unacceptable" social stock. Mrs. Studevant rushes her daughter off to Kansas City "for an Easter shopping trip." Jessie dies as a result of the abortion, and at her funeral the outraged and bereaved Cora speaks the truth, scandalizing the entire community.

The Studevants, who in effect have murdered their own daughter, are the targets of Hughes' most devastating satire. They are guilty, at bottom, of a spiritual crime: a false and artificial isolation, both socially and morally, from the human community. Obsessed with their own purity, they fail to respond to their daughter's predicament with love, yielding instead to a ruthless puritanic impulse to expel evil from their midst. Hypocrisy compounds the sin of pride and issues forth in tragedy. Hughes' satiric portrait of the Studevants constitutes a blistering attack on Middle America, and a crushing indictment of the value-system and life-style of the white middle class.

Beyond its power as a satire, **"Cora Unashamed"** affords a crucial insight into Hughes' career, whose inner dialectic manifests itself in the clash of pastoral and antipastoral. Among the elements of pastoral are Cora's simplicity; her natural (or unashamed) attitude toward pregnancy and childbirth; and the way of life that she adopts at the story's end: "Now she and Ma live from the little garden they raise. . . ." Among the antipastoral elements are the opening description of Melton, a rural seat of no charm whatsoever; Cora's rebellious and even blasphemous moods, which make a mockery of pastoral humility; and her disruption of the idyllic funeral service, which opens with a hymn, "He Feedeth His Flocks Like a Shepherd."

The interplay of genre and counter-genre is best revealed in a refrain concerning "green fields and sweet meadows" which appears three times in the course of the tale. The first occasion is the summer night when Cora gives herself to a white lover; the second, the burial of her child, when she curses God; the third, the pregnancy of Jessie, which revives her memory of love as well as loss. These passages reflect three successive spiritual states: an initial period of youthful innocence and happiness; a time of disillusionment, when hopes are buried and the heart becomes embittered; and a retrospective phase of complicated double vision, when both attitudes are simultaneously present in the mind.

This dialectic of the soul, which constitutes the irreducible core of Hughes' art, derives in form and spirit from the blues. For the complex vision of the blues, even as it balances the claims of hope and disillusionment, absorbs both attitudes in a higher synthesis. The blues, as Richard Kostelanetz has remarked [in his "The Politics of Passing: The fiction of James Weldon Johnson"], is a "tightly organized lyric form in which the singer narrates the reasons for his sadness, usually attributed to his failure to attain the ideal role he conceives for himself." The blues are born, in short, out of the inexorable tension of dream and actuality. By mediating poetically between the two, the form itself makes possible a bittersweet and retrospective triumph over pain.

The centerpiece of the collection is **"The Blues I'm Playing."** This story is a fictional account of Hughes' relationship with Mrs. Mason. The black heroine, Oceola Jones, is a gifted young pianist equally at home in the jazz or classical tradition. Her white antagonist, Mrs. Dora Ellsworth, is a rich and aging patron of the arts. The plot traces the successive stages of their relationship: discovery and sponsorship; increasing efforts to dominate not only the musical career, but the private life of her protégée; a crisis following the girl's announcement of her impending marriage; and eventual estrangement, after a painful, parting interview.

The dramatic conflict centers on the girl's stubborn effort to preserve her black identity in the face of her patron's determined onslaught. Mrs. Ellsworth looks on Oceola as a kind of refractory material that resists cultivation or refinement. She is in short a missionary. Mrs. Ellsworth embodies that Faustian urge toward total possession of another human being which informs so much of the short fiction of Edgar Allan Poe. This is the urge responsible for slavery and other forms of European empire. Oceola fights with all her strength to fend it off, and to establish her life on an independent footing.

"The Blues I'm Playing" is at once an arraignment of Western culture and an affirmation of Negro folk forms. The classical and jazz idioms, which compete for Oceola's loyalty, give dramatic substance to the theme of cultural dualism which is basic to the Harlem Renaissance. In the sexual sphere, conflicting codes divide the two women. Oceola has a lover she is helping through medical school, and whom she ultimately marries. Mrs. Ellsworth hopes that she will learn to sublimate her sexual desires through art. An irreconcilable conflict thus unfolds between the Platonist and transcendental values of the patron (symbolized by her aspiration toward the stars) and the earthy, down-home folk morality of her protégée.

A sublimated sexuality implies a disembodied art. Through Mrs. Ellsworth, Hughes is satirizing the otherworldly strain in Western art. He decries the separation of art from life, and the transcendental impulse to resolve all human contradictions in the vastness of eternity. Through Oceola's music, on the other hand, Hughes defines his own esthetic. Hers is an art grounded in folk sources, steeped in sensuality, and based on the life-affirming rhythms of the blues. It is a music close to dance, full of movement and expression, vibrant with the joy and pain of living. The blues is an art of paradox and ambiguity, and it is through this form that Langston Hughes has chosen to express his complex sense of life.

In the end, Hughes resorts to a satiric image. The final scene takes place in Mrs. Ellsworth's music room, whose decor is dominated by a row of Persian vases filled with white lilies. As Oceola entertains her patron for the last time, she breaks into a jazz rhythm that shakes the long-stemmed flowers in their rootlessness and artificial isolation. . . . (pp. 254-57)

"Little Dog" is a prime example of the blues-oriented art of Langston Hughes. It is the story of an old maid who withholds herself from life, and who buys a dog to fill the void at the center of her being. Through her pet she becomes acquainted with, and sexually attracted to, a black janitor who brings the dog his nightly meal of meat and bones. Torn by conflicts over sex and race which she scarcely understands, she moves away in terror of her own emotions. The story is evocative of Sherwood Anderson in its theme of loneliness and lost potential. A delicate tale, it is suffused with a deep compassion which springs perhaps from the author's boyhood loneliness.

"Little Dog" may not seem at first glance to be a satire. But once we notice that Miss Briggs is employed as a bookkeeper, everything falls into place. That vocation, which is not without emotional significance for Hughes, is emblematic of the value system of his father. Business efficiency at the expense of human warmth, an excessively routinized existence, false pride of caste or class, a petty-bourgeois narrowness of soul: these are the targets of Hughes' satire. Miss Briggs, who embodies a sterile way of life, is the butt of a withering irony. The result is a tonality peculiar to the blues.

Pathos and irony mingle here in equal proportions. The point is that Hughes might have focused entirely on the pathetic

Hughes in the mid-1950s at a neighborhood bar that resembles the meeting place for Simple and Boyd as depicted in the Simple sketches.

aspects of the spinster's situation. Or he might have made her the victim of an unalloyed satire. Instead he combines both perspectives into the double vision of the blues. This tragicomic vision prevents the tale from lapsing into sentimentality. At the same time, it requires of us an expansiveness of mind and heart. For the blues specializes in the reconciliation of opposites. It will not permit us to simplify our vision to the detriment of our humanity.

"Red-Headed Baby" is at once the most caustic and the most compelling of Hughes' satires. Written under great compression, it achieves a depth and resonance unmatched in the Hughes canon. The story is concerned with a white sailor on shore leave in a Florida coastal town. He revisits a mulatto girl whom he deflowered several years ago, but their present revels are interrupted by a red-headed baby who is bowlegged, dwarfish, deaf, and dumb. The sailor denies the obvious reality and flees from the situation. Knowledge of paternity is half-refused by his conscious mind, and yet his sudden obsession with paying for his drinks bears witness to the surge of guilt that engulfs him.

The mode of presentation is satiric monologue, consisting of the sailor's stream of consciousness. An unusual technique for Hughes, its effectiveness in this story has been ably demonstrated by James Emanuel [see second excerpt dated 1968]. Suffice it to observe that the interior monologue serves to individuate the sailor, and thus increase audience identification. Dramatic ironies do the rest, of which one or two examples must suffice. The sailor, longing in his vanity to be distinguished from the girl's casual lovers, is singled out from the rest in a fashion that destroys him morally. He calls his son a "runt," but he is the real runt, who suffers from a stunted or retarded spiritual growth.

The story is a study in damnation. In the opening paragraph, words like *dead* and *hell* and *damned* convey the sailor's spiritual state. Like the houses of the town, abandoned after the collapse of the Florida real estate boom, his soul is "halfbuilt," and "never will be finished." It is symbolic of his incapacity for growth that he should sire a retarded child. And a Negro child at that! To be damned, after all, is to be cast into outer darkness: "No street lights out here. There never is where niggers live." But above all, damnation consists of the conviction that only other men are damned. To preserve this flattering illusion, a scapegoat is essential. And that is precisely the fate of the red-headed baby.

The story culminates in a powerful epiphany: "Betsy's redheaded child stands in the door looking like one of those goggly-eyed dolls you hit with a ball at the County Fair." In that obscene American rite of exorcism, all comers are offered three shots for a quarter at their own evil impulses, projected outward and made visibly assailable. The psycho-dynamics of racial prejudice are here exposed. Like the sailor piling the sins of his youth on the head of his unacknowledged son, white Americans have for generations been tossing baseballs at goggly-eyed dolls. Step right up, ladies and gentlemen: hit the nigger and win a cigar.

During the winter of 1934-1935, Hughes found himself stranded in Mexico City. He had come by train from Reno, Nevada, after learning of his father's death, only to discover on arrival that he was disinherited. Making the best of a bad situation, he remained in Mexico for several months, until he could make enough money from his writing to afford a return ticket. And being Langston Hughes, which is to say a true *afi-*

cionado of the blues, he managed to enjoy himself in spite of his adversity.

Recounting the episode in his autobiography, [*I Wonder As I Wander*], Hughes recalls that "For me it was a delightful winter. I have an affinity for Latin Americans, and the Spanish language I have always loved. One of the first things I did when I got to Mexico City was to get a tutor . . . and begin to read *Don Quixote* in the original, a great reading experience that possibly helped me to develop many years later in my own books a character called Simple."

Such were the beginnings of Hughes' faith in the impossible dream. To him it meant primarily the dream of racial equality and confraternity so often desecrated by his white compatriots. (pp. 258-60)

Faith in the invincibility of the dream, no matter how it might be battered in the realm of actuality, was a vital part of the black folk-tradition. Hughes captured this dimension of the folk spirit when he wrote, in a poem called "The Negro Mother," that "God put a dream like steel in my soul." In his bardic role, Hughes wished to honor and commemorate above all else the endurance and tenacity and sheer stamina of black people in the face of white oppression. It was their fidelity to the impossible dream that inspired his mature work and sustained him through his most productive years.

Hughes did not come all at once to his mature vision. The deaths of both parents in the 1930's, and the composition of *The Big Sea* in 1939, prepared the way. The end of his proletarian digression (roughly 1930 to 1939) was likewise a prerequisite to his artistic growth. Relieved of these burdens and preoccupations, his talents reached fruition in the 1940's and early 1950's. The stages of his maturation may be traced in the short fiction written from 1934 to 1952, and collected for the most part in his second book of stories, *Laughing to Keep from Crying.*

In 1933 and 1934, Hughes focused his attention more or less exclusively on the short-story form. Of the stories written during this period, about half were included in *The Ways of White Folks,* while the rest, published at the time in various periodicals, eventually formed the nucleus of *Laughing to Keep from Crying.* The stories written in 1933 were retrospective in nature, looking backward to the 1920's and the heyday of the Harlem Renaissance. The tales composed in 1934 and early 1935, however, were addressed to the issues of the Great Depression, and reflected the politics of Hughes' Marxist phase. (p. 261)

In the fall of [1934], Hughes spent several weeks in Reno, Nevada, where he observed the hardships and sufferings of jobless and rejected men, crossing and recrossing the country in search of work. It must be recalled that from 1929 to 1934 he had been sheltered from the worst effects of the Depression, either by his various patrons or his extended visit to the Soviet Union. What he saw in Reno must have come as something of a shock. Apparently it served to crystallize his Marxist leanings, for among the stories written or revised in Reno are several of his most militant and class-conscious tales.

Eight of Hughes' stories, written from 1934 to 1939, are direct expressions of his revolutionary politics. What is involved from a literary point of view is the creation of a new kind of hero. In *The Ways of White Folks,* heroes were content to establish their psychological or cultural independence of the white world. Now they move from independence to de-

fiance of white power. The new hero may be defined in negative as well as positive terms, and this leads to two distinct types of stories. Some stories seek to discredit the servile or Uncle Tom or renegade black—the class-collaborationist or traitor to his people—while others celebrate the rebellious worker, union organizer, political activist, or incipient revolutionary.

Four of the eight Marxist tales are anti-Uncle Tom. The archetypal figure is the old man of **"Little Old Spy"**—the former pimp now employed in counterrevolutionary work by one of Cuba's reactionary governments. The metaphor appears again in **"Fine Accommodations,"** where a Southern Negro educator of accommodationist persuasion is compared in the closing passage to a pimp. **"Professor,"** a companion piece, depicts a black sociologist who sells out to the white power structure. In **"Trouble with the Angels,"** a famous Negro actor playing God in *The Green Pastures* tries to break a strike instigated by the cast to prevent the show from playing to Jim Crow audiences.

These anti-Uncle Tom stories are of course satires. The author's satirical barbs, which formerly were aimed at the ways of white folks, are now directed toward counterrevolutionary elements within the black community. These satires, in short, are intended as a goad. Their implicit norm, which formerly consisted of folk values, now derives from a political ideology, and more precisely from a revolutionary code of appropriately militant attitude or conduct. Often this implicit norm is defined ironically through the derogatory, "red-baiting" remarks of unsympathetic characters. The net result is to heighten or intensify the satirical attack upon the Uncle Tom.

Four of the Marxist tales celebrate the rebel hero. **"The Sailor and the Steward"** is a pure party-liner, in which a Cuban sailor learns that individual resistance is not as effective as collective bargaining. **"Gumption"** is the story of an unemployed family whose members combat racial discrimination in the WPA. **"Tain't So"** depicts a Negro woman faith healer who cures a white Southern lady of her psychosomatic ailments by the simple expedient of contradicting her assertions. **"On the Road"** is the best of Hughes' Marxist fables. Set in Reno, the story is concerned with a Negro vagrant who tries to destroy a church that has refused him sanctuary in a snowstorm.

Hughes' Marxist tales have an historical importance that transcends their intrinsic worth, for they represent a link between the writings of the Harlem Renaissance and those of the next generation. Their theme of insubordination (or servility turned inside out) is essentially New Negro, but the older concept has been extended to include a new class consciousness. Hughes' satirical attacks on Uncle Tom and his celebration of the rebel hero anticipate Richard Wright's more famous dramatizations of the theme in *Uncle Tom's Children* (1938). Such an observation is not intended to detract from Wright's originality, but rather to stress the continuities of the Afro-American short story.

Even at his most class-conscious, Hughes did not abandon his bardic role. While the surface waves of his art were flowing in a fashionable proletarian direction, the deeper currents were concerned, as always, with the celebration of ethnicity. Throughout his Marxist phase, to change the figure, he was never so intoxicated on red wine as to lose his grasp on black reality. The proof of his sobriety consists of six tales, written from 1934 to 1941, which stress the theme of black identity. These are cautionary tales, in the sense that they constitute a warning to his black readers not to cut their ethnic ties.

These ethnic tales, like their Marxist counterparts, display a negative and positive polarity. At the negative pole, they condemn any loosening of ethnic ties, and especially any denial of one's blackness that is based on a false assumption of superiority. Such negative attacks are again satirical: their target is the racial renegade. They are anti-assimilationist, anti-dicky, or anti-cosmopolitan in thrust. At the positive pole we find stories that affirm the group tradition, prescribe survival tactics, promote fraternal ties, and celebrate communal rituals.

Three of these ethnic tales are satires. **"Spanish Blood"** depicts a Harlem youth of mixed Puerto Rican and Afro-American parentage who attempts to repudiate his blackness only to have it thrust upon him by some white gangsters. **"Slice Him Down"** explores the anti-dicky theme: two black buddies who arrive in Reno on the same boxcar get involved in a carving contest over a "hinckty hussy" who holds herself aloof from the common herd. **"Who's Passing for Who?"** is a satirical attack on the cosmopolitan pretensions of the Harlem Renaissance. Viewing retrospectively the follies of his youth, Hughes deplores the shallow assimilationism of the black intelligentsia.

Three stories take a more affirmative view of what it means to be black. **"Why, You Reckon?"** tests the outlaw code of Brer Rabbit against the crisis of the Great Depression, and finds it still a meaningful guide to black survival. **"Sailor Ashore"** is a tribute to the survival value of the dream. Reflecting Hughes' mature phase, and especially his reading of Cervantes, this tale argues the necessity of having an ideal to live by, even in the most desperate of circumstances. **"Big Meeting,"** one of Hughes' best stories, is a celebration of revivalist religion, and an eloquent defense of its survival value to the black community.

On the formal plane, what can be observed at this stage of Hughes' career is a shift from satire to celebration. Whether writing as revolutionist or bard, in the political or ethnic vein, Hughes is groping toward more affirmative literary modes. Satire persists, but no longer suffices; its objects change, but even that is not enough. Holding the Uncle Tom or racial renegade up to scorn gives way at some point to a more affirmative stance. The satirist, after all, is precise and overt in his antipathies, but vague and indirect in his sympathies. Hughes' desire to be an advocate, proponent, or celebrant thus bursts the seams of the satirical mode.

Hughes was discovering, in short, the basic contradiction between the roles of satirist and bard. While one attacks the enemy without or within, the other strengthens the defenses of the soul. Put another way, his idealistic strain was coming to the fore. His incorrigible optimism, and his stubborn faith in the impossible dream, would not permit him to persist in the jaundiced vision of the satirist. For satire deals with human imperfection, with the limitations of actuality, with the inevitable gap between the actual and the ideal. But Hughes had learned from Cervantes a grudging respect for Perfection, for the limitless and finally invincible power of the dream.

Hughes' second book of stories is something of a catchall, which gathers up the output of nearly two decades. It is necessarily lacking the thematic unity, tightness of design, and

consistency of style of **The Ways of White Folks,** whose fourteen stories were completed in about a year. Despite its diffuseness, however, the book contains some of Hughes' finest work. James Emanuel ranks four of the tales from this collection among the author's best: **"Professor," "On the Road," "Big Meeting,"** and **"On the Way Home."** I would concur, except in the case of **"Professor,"** which strikes me as too didactic (that is, too explicit and direct) for good satire.

"On the Road" is at bottom an attempt to record certain changes in black consciousness, induced by the desperate circumstances of the Great Depression. The resulting state of mind may be described as prerevolutionary. It is a transitional state in which a black protagonist abandons his former docility and moves in the direction of political revolt. This shift in consciousness necessitates the exorcism or extrusion of certain traits associated with the Christian deity. Before the black man can hope to defend himself against oppression, he must cease to identify with the long-suffering, patiently enduring, dutiful Christ-figure. The Negro's version of Christianity, in short, must be expanded to include the concept of social justice.

The hero of the tale is Sergeant, a Negro vagrant who arrives in Reno in the midst of a snowstorm. Seeking refuge at a parsonage, he is rebuffed by the white minister and directed to a Relief Shelter, where he has already been denied admission on the grounds of race. Half-crazed with hunger and fatigue, he breaks down the doors of the adjoining church. When two policemen try to arrest him, he resists, and is severely beaten. Hallucinating, he imagines that, like Samson, he has pulled the temple down. Surrealistically, a stone Christ descends from the cross and accompanies him to a hobo jungle. When Sergeant awakens in the morning he finds himself in jail, shaking the bars and threatening to break down the door of his cell.

Insofar as the story is a satire, its target is the institutional church, whose moral blindness prevents it from responding with compassion to the plight of the unemployed. The focus of the tale, however, is on Sergeant and his inner transformation. No hero at the outset, he hopes only to accommodate his elemental human needs. Deprived of even these, he grows desperate, violates the law, and emerges in the end as a potential revolutionary. In the course of his rebellion, he takes on the stature of an epic hero. (pp. 262-67)

The story is superbly crafted. On the macro-level (structure), realism and fantasy are smoothly joined. Through the device of hallucination, induced by a policeman's club, Hughes prepares us deftly for a supernatural visitation. A dialogue with Christ is a risky business, but he brings it off by means of a terse understatement. On the micro-level (language), the imagery imparts a rich texture to the prose. Images of white-on-black (snowfall at night, or white flakes on a dark skin) sustain the story's racial overtones. Images of light and darkness provide objective correlatives for the moral qualities of vision or blindness. Images of stone are emblematic of an obdurate society and petrified religion.

"Big Meeting" is a moving tribute to the survival value of black religion. The tale depicts a Southern revival meeting as it moves through the successive stages of testimonials, sermon, and invitation to the mourners' bench. The proceedings are observed from an adjoining wood by a double audience: a group of white adults and a pair of Negro youths, all of whom have come to be amused. The teen-age boys, whose mothers are participating in the service, are symbolically positioned between the cynicism of the whites and the religious fervor of their parents. In effect, Hughes invites the younger generation to rise above its skepticism and achieve a sympathetic understanding of its folk tradition.

His strategy consists of disclosing the psychological content of black religion. The worshipers who rise to testify recount their troubles, both personal and racial, and close with the refrain, "But I'm goin' on!" This determination to endure is sustained by the hope of a better future, celebrated in their songs of "de Hallelulian side." The ritual itself, with its rhythmic hand-clapping, body-swaying, and "dancing before the Lord" evokes the ancient African religion and serves to fortify the black identity. The sermon, with its powerful metaphors of slavery and oppression, drawn from Old and New Testament alike, endows their lives with emotional significance and helps them to cope on the interior plane with their oppressed condition.

Much of the story's meaning is conveyed through the impact of events on the double audience. The whites, who have come to enjoy the singing, protect themselves with cynical remarks from the serious implications of the service. At the climax of the sermon they depart with a vague disquiet in their hearts. Meanwhile, under the pressure of the white presence, the boys undergo a drastic change of attitude. Half amused at first, they become increasingly resentful of the white folks' mocking comments. Placed on the defensive, they are forced to vindicate their parents' values. In the end, if not brought to the mourners' bench, they have at least been deeply moved, and thereby reconciled to their religious heritage.

A word should be said about the sermon that comprises half of **"Big Meeting."** Closely attuned to folk forms, Hughes draws on the emotional power, imaginative vigor, and picturesque language of the folk sermon to carry the main burden of his tale. His masterful representation of the black preacher's oratorical skill bears witness once again to his commitment to the oral tradition. Especially effective is his portrayal of the Crucifixion as a lynching. Unlike the early story **"Home,"** where he attempts a realistic treatment, here Hughes succeeds in *ritualizing* the lynching theme. Through indirection he gains in power and intensity, and by stressing the divine analogy generates an irony which contains the otherwise intolerable pain.

The last of Hughes' top-notch stories, and the only one to be written after 1935, is **"On the Way Home."** Begun at Hollow Hills Farm in 1941 and published in *Story Magazine* (May/June 1946), this tale is unique in the Hughes canon for its lack of racial specificity. Since the story is intensely lyrical, depicting the emotions of a man on the occasion of his mother's death, racial designation hardly seems germane. Theme alone, however, does not account for Hughes' departure from his usual ethnicity. We must bear in mind that he had lost his own mother only three years before the story was composed. Like Dunbar, when his subject was too personal for comfort, he "neutralized" it by assuming in effect a white mask.

Carl Anderson is an office worker who has moved to Chicago from his hometown of Sommerville. Lonely, sexually repressed, and something of a mama's boy, he returns once a month to enjoy the old-fashioned pleasures of popcorn and cider with his mother. As the story opens, he receives a telegram informing him that she is gravely ill. A virtual teetotal-er, he buys a bottle of wine to fortify himself against disaster, gets drunk, misses his bus, and fails to reach his mother's side before the end. More upset than ever, he rushes to a nearby bar, where a prostitute attempts to entice him to her room. Her frequent reference to "home" destroys his composure, and overcome by grief and remorse he succumbs to a fit of sobbing.

The theme of this story is the indivisibility of freedom and responsibility. Carl looks forward avidly to the new era of sexual freedom that his mother's death will make possible. But he is not prepared to forswear those infantile dependency needs that she has so unstintingly supplied. He wants to grow and to resist growth at the same time. Carl's panic at his impending expulsion from the Garden is the focus of the tale. Like many men, he covets freedom in the abstract, even as he shrinks from its concrete burdens and responsibilities. At the climax of the story, he takes refuge from his fears in drunkenness and passivity, entrusting himself to the false security of a tub of warm water.

James Emanuel perceives the story as a myth of rebirth and renewal: "It is a story . . . of a man whom death brings painfully into the world a second time, in a rebirth made necessary by a superfluity of maternal love." I see it rather as the story of a man's escape from freedom. Carl is barred from manhood by his infantile emotions. An incipient alcoholic, he is far more likely to substitute one form of dependency for another than to achieve a genuine rebirth or liberation. This interpretation would seem to be substantiated by Emanuel's interview with Hughes, in which the author says, "I've known two or three people who in the presence of death go to pieces in a drunken way and think they're having a good time."

If *Laughing to Keep from Crying* represents a falling off from *The Ways of White Folks,* Hughes' third collection carries this decline to the point of mediocrity. *Something in Common* contains thirty-seven prose pieces, of which nine are mere sketches. Of the twenty-eight stories that remain, twenty are reprints from the first two collections, while only eight are assembled for the first time. Several of the last-mentioned, moreover, were written in 1934-1935, but not included in *Laughing to Keep from Crying.* It is hard to avoid the suspicion that Hughes resorted to his file of rejected stories to pad out the volume.

Of the eight "new" stories, two [**"Gumption"** and **"Fine Accommodations"**] have been discussed in the context of the author's Marxist phase. As for the remaining six, written from 1944 to 1961, they are uniformly thin and anemic. They are based perhaps on a promising idea, but lacking in a robust development. Instead they display the clever plots and trick endings of the O. Henry tradition. Several of these tales are essentially refurbishings of old material. One or two, like **"Rock, Church,"** are amusing, but lacking in the high seriousness of Hughes' most trenchant comedy. A faltering of the imagination, in short, is everywhere in evidence.

The truth is that *Something in Common* was a commercial rather than imaginative venture. To reissue stories long out of print was, for the aging author, a sort of deferred-income plan. As for the more recent tales, the most that can be said is that they display the weary competence of a jaded professional. From any author who tries to make a living by his craft we must expect a certain amount of inferior work. What matters, however, when the threshing and winnowing is done, is the body of enduring work that remains. In the case of Langston Hughes, no one who has taken the measure of his best work would wish to deny him a secure place in the annals of the Afro-American short story. (pp. 267-71)

Robert Bone, "Langston Hughes," in his Down Home: Origins of the Afro-American Short Story, *Columbia University Press, 1988, pp. 239-71.*

PETER BRUCK (essay date 1977)

[*In the following excerpt, Bruck provides a socio-literary and historical perspective on Hughes's short fiction.*]

Langston Hughes (1902-1967), according to many critics "poet laureate of Harlem" and "Dean of American Negro Writers," began his literary career by winning a poetry contest sponsored by the black magazine *Opportunity* in 1925. "The Weary Blues" was noted by Carl Van Vechten, through whose sponsorship Hughes was able to get his first contract with the noted publisher Alfred Knopf. Van Vechten, who acted as a main ambassadorial advisor and patron of black literature to white publishing firms during the 1920's, not only paved the way for Hughes' literary career but also became the "chief architect of his early success." Just as with [Paul Laurence] Dunbar and [Charles Waddell] Chesnutt, white patronage played a decisive role in the literary emergence of Langston Hughes. The omnipresence of the white patron with his significant socio-literary influence on the black author was a discovery that the young Hughes was still to make; his gradual and painstaking emancipation from the grip of such white patrons was to become the major concern of his early phase and to play a dominant theme in his short fiction.

Starting to publish in the midst of the 1920's meant for Langston Hughes to be intrinsically involved in a debate over the function, theme, and aesthetic form of black literature. The problem became even more urgent when the 'Harlem Renaissance' period began and, at the same time, the widely acclaimed emergence of the "New Negro" confronted the black writer with the task of defining his role as a literary artist. In order to foster a critical discussion of these questions, the leading black magazine *The Crisis* organized a symposium, "The Negro in Art: How Shall He Be Portrayed?," throughout the March-November issues of 1926. Prior to this, Alain Locke, "father of the 'New Negro' and the so-called Harlem Renaissance," had attempted to define the cultural stance of the 'New Negro' in the following manner:

> He [the New Negro] now becomes a conscious contributor and lays aside the status of a beneficiary and ward for that of a collaborator and participant in American civilization. The great social gain in this is the releasing of our talented group from the arid fields of controversy and debate to the productive fields of creative expression. The especially cultural recognition they win should in turn prove the key to that revaluation of the Negro which must precede or accompany any considerable further betterment of race relationships.

Locke, who clearly pursued [W. E. B.] DuBois' philosophy of a "talented tenth," aspired to an attitude of cultural elitism that envisioned art and culture to be a bridge across the racial barrier; hence his calling for a "carefully maintained contact between the enlightened minorities of both race groups." This philosophy of culture undoubtedly presented a challenge to all those young black writers who were primarily concerned with expressing the new feeling of ethnic identity and racial pride. One of those willing to face this challenge was the young Langston Hughes who, on June 23, 1926, published an essay [in the *Nation*] that may not only be viewed as an indirect reply to Locke but also became known as the first significant black literary manifesto.

The importance of the "Negro Artist and the Racial Mountain" for the evolution of black literature cannot be overstressed. In the words of Charles S. Johnson, former editor of *Opportunity,* none other than Hughes with this essay "so completely symbolized the new emancipation of the Negro mind."

In outlining his stance as a black writer, Hughes placed particular emphasis on racial pride and ethnic identity:

> To my mind, it is the duty of the younger Negro artists . . . to change through the force of his art that old whispering, "I want to be white," hidden in the aspirations of his people, to "Why should I want to be white? I am a Negro and beautiful."

Hughes' emphasis on blackness, which anticipated the present-day discussion of the possibilities of a black aesthetic, clearly signalled the renunciation of the well-known problem of "racial" vs. "universal" art. Instead Hughes turned to depicting the ordinary black American. . . . His extensive reliance on folk forms and rhythms and his application of oral folk culture to poetry highlight his innovating efforts and mark the beginning of the "reconciliation of formal black poets to their folk roots and grass roots audience." One of the most popular results of his preoccupations in terms of narrative fiction were the "Simple folk tales" that first appeared in the black weekly *Chicago Defender* in November 1942. (pp. 71-3)

From a socio-literary point of view, the Simple tales marked Hughes' first success in gaining a genuine black audience. In the late 1920's, however, this goal still proved utopian. . . . Whereas the bulk of his poetry is usually associated with the Harlem Renaissance, . . . [Hughes's] career as a short story writer did not begin before the wane of this epoch. Although his first stories, all reflecting the author's experiences as a seaman on a voyage along the West coast of Africa, were already published in Harlem's literary magazine *The Messenger* in 1927, it took another six years before Hughes really devoted himself to writing short fiction. From the spring of 1932 to the fall of 1933 he visited the Soviet Union and the Far East. It was during his stay in Moscow that he had a decisive reading experience [having read D. H. Lawrence's collection *The Lovely Lady*] which prompted him to devote himself to the short story. . . . The years to come were to see amazing results from this literary initiation. Between 1933 and 1934 he devoted himself exclusively to this genre. (pp. 73-4)

[*The Ways of White Folks,*] which received rather favorable reviews, presents, thematically, a close examination of black-white relationships. Mostly satirical in tone, the stories try to unmask several manifestations of the Harlem Renaissance. Specifically, the theme of white patronage, as displayed in **"Slave on the Block," "Poor Little Black Fellow,"** and **"The Blues I'm Playing,"** is used to demonstrate the dishonesty of whites and the absurd notion of their paternalistic philanthropy. In this context, it is of particular socio-literary interest to note that Hughes' fictional treatment of the incipient dissociation from white predominance caused him no setback in magazine publication. Instead, his new literary efforts soon found their way into leading periodicals. Whereas Hughes' poetry was usually printed in such black journals as *Opportunity* and *The Crisis* (he had complained in 1929 that "magazines used very few stories with Negro themes, since Negro themes were considered exotic, in a class with Chinese or East Indian features), four out of his five stories written in Moscow were now accepted and published by such noted periodicals as *The American Mercury, Scribner's Magazine* and *Esquire.* This major breakthrough provided him with a nation-wide, non-parochial platform, allowing him to escape from his predicament, and opened up the opportunity of gaining a primarily white reading audience.

The reading of Lawrence's *The Lovely Lady* not only prompted Hughes to concentrate on the short story but also persuaded him to use the story's protagonist Pauline Attenborough as a model for the creation of Dora Ellsworth, the fictional representative of his former white Park Avenue patroness. **"The Blues I'm Playing,"** written after his return from the Soviet Union and first published in the May 1934 issue of *Scribner's Magazine,* was thus subject to an interesting combination of influence.

The impact of Lawrence's story becomes apparent when one compares the opening description of both women. Lawrence describes Pauline Attenborough as a women who "could still sometimes be mistaken . . . for thirty. She really was a wonderfully preserved woman, of perfect *chic. . . .* She would be an exquisite skeleton and her skull would be an exquisite skull." The narrator's mocking emphasis on her appearance, which she can change through a "mysterious little wire" of "will," exposes her artificiality. As a collector of art, Pauline is herself a "self-made object d'art." Dora Ellsworth is introduced in a similar way. Hughes' description, however, is more mocking and obviously aims at unmasking his character's self-deception from the very beginning. Hence one common denominator of both figures seems to be hypocrisy:

> Poor dear lady, she had no children of her own. Her husband was dead. And she had no interest in life now save art, and the young people who created art. She was very rich, and it gave her pleasure to share her richness with beauty. Except that she was sometimes confused as to where beauty lay. . . . She once turned down a garlic-smelling soprano-singing girl, who, a few years later, had all the critics in New York at her feet.

This passage reveals several central aspects of the narrative texture. The focus of interest, which is on Mrs. Ellsworth throughout the story, suggests that Hughes is primarily concerned with depicting the ignorance of the white philanthropist. This intention is underlined by authorial comments which, although sometimes quite devastating, are seldom strongly aggressive. Instead, Hughes pities his white character, thereby producing the particular reading process of **"The Blues I'm Playing."** By undermining the cultural status of his protagonist and exposing the absurdity of her judgements, Hughes creates in the reader's imagination the illusion of witnessing the forthcoming degradation of so-called superior white culture.

Satire hence sets the emotional tone throughout the story. Its function, autobiographically, is to unveil the devastating influence that Hughes' former patroness had on his creative impulses: "She wanted me to be primitive and know and feel the intuitions of the primitive. But, unfortunately, I did not feel the rhythms of the primitive surging through me, and so I

could not live and write as though I did." On the cultural level, this conflict was representative of a whole range of dilemmas that had emerged during the Harlem Renaissance. The black writers' "search back to a national past," their literary journey of ethnic self-discovery, marked the beginning of a declaration of cultural independence, whose paradigm may be seen in Hughes' literary manifesto "The Negro Artist and the Racial Mountain." Satire as employed in **"The Blues I'm Playing"** signals the end of white paternalism, thereby demystifying the 'cult of the primitive Black' that many whites took for granted during the 1920's.

This historical conflict is reflected in the antagonistic relationship of Dora Ellsworth and her black protegée, the pianist Oceola Jones. Both women represent opposing points of view; [according to Robert Bone in his *Down Home*], this structural contrast manifests a clash between "two standards of morality," between a "white and a Negro code" [see excerpt dated 1975]. The conflict itself evolves throughout five stages, each dramatizing their incompatible positions: the financial sponsorship is followed by increasing efforts on part of Mrs. Ellsworth to dominate the private life of her protegée; Oceola's return to Harlem and the announcement of her engagement to a black medical student cause a severe crisis and finally lead to a dissolving of their relationship.

The mocking irony with which the narrator emphasizes Mrs. Ellsworth's ignorance prevails through all these scenes. Her ignorance of art and artists is even excelled by her total lack of insight into black life and, in particular, Harlem: "Before going to bed, Mrs. Ellsworth told her housekeeper to order a book called 'Nigger Heaven' . . . , and also anything else . . . about Harlem." Here Hughes tries not merely to unmask the fakery of white patronage; he also scores Carl Van Vechten's *Nigger Heaven.* This novel, published at the height of the Harlem Renaissance in 1926, served as a kind of guide-book to Harlem for many white readers and was mostly rejected by blacks. DuBois' review [in the *Crisis,* 1926] perhaps sums up best the black reaction of that time: " 'Nigger Heaven' is a blow in the face. It is an affront to the hospitality of black folk. . . . It is a caricature. It is worse than untruth because it is a mass of half-truths." Although Hughes' own criticism of *Nigger Heaven* and Van Vechten [in his autobiography, *The Big Sea*] was rather friendly, the satirical connotation of the passage quoted above seems to suggest that by 1934 Hughes felt free enough do denounce Van Vechten's patronage in the same way as he did that of his former Park Avenue patroness.

Moreover, the same passage reveals another important feature of Mrs. Ellsworth's personality. Her reliance on books instead of personal experience, her preference for a substitute for reality, demonstrates that she is unable to differentiate between substance and appearance. This failure is particularly emphasized in the scene where she drives Oceola to her Harlem home:

> Mrs. Ellsworth had to ask could she come in. "I live on the fifth floor," said Oceola, and there isn't any elevator," "It doesn't matter, dear," said the white woman, for she meant to see the inside of this girl's life, elevator or no elevator.

Devoid of any emotional and psychological perception, she mistakes the exterior for the interior, form for being, and thereby reduces life to a mere artefact. This attitude is equally apparent in her conception of art. Having substituted art for life, Mrs. Ellsworth, like Pauline Attenborough, becomes a self-made *objet d'art;* her stress merely on the refining, cultivating, and sublimating function of art not only separates art from life, but also deprives it of its vitality and reduces it to a dead object.

Mrs. Ellsworth's attitudes contrast with Oceola's character and music. Having grown up in the musical tradition of the black church, Oceola's life is firmly rooted in jazz and the blues. Her music, which derives its strength from her cultural identity, distinctly sets her apart from Dora Ellsworth, who conceives of art as essentially classical. The evolving conflict thus centers around the clash of two antagonistic modes of life. In contrast to her patroness' understanding of music, Oceola has kept an original sense of it, one that "demanded movement and expression, dancing and living to go with it." As an initial, spontaneous expression of black life and experience, the blues is devoid of "classical runs or fancy falsities." Rather, it becomes, as Ralph Ellison once remarked, a form of individual therapy:

> The blues is an impulse to keep the painful details and episodes of a brutal experience alive in one's aching consciousness, to finger its jagged grain, and to transcend it, not by consolation of philosophy but by squeezing from it a near-tragic, near-comic lyricism. As a form, the blues is an autobiographical chronicle of personal catastrophe expressed lyrically.

Oceola's music hence becomes not only an assertion and definition of her identity; it also links her, culturally, to that chain of black folklore tradition, which, as Ellison has pointed out, "announced the Negro's willingness to trust this own experience, his own sensibilities as to the definition of reality, rather than allow his masters to define these crucial matters for him." Oceola's "sheer love of jazz", her hatred of "most artists, . . . and the word art in French or English," gives voice to an attitude which considers music a manifestation of an experienced reality, thus merging both art and life. Her contempt for a philosophy that separates these two arises out of her primal emphasis on the affirmative and virile nature of music. . . .

The "bipàrtite structure" of this story, emphasizing two opposing ethnic codes and philosophies of art, is also equally apparent in the different geographical settings of the various scenes. From the very beginning of their relationship, the Park Avenue patroness tries to alienate Oceola from Harlem: "I must get her out of Harlem at once. I believe it's worse than Chinatown." Her efforts finally result in Oceola's moving to Greenwich Village, and then for two years' study to Paris. The effects of her training in classical music are not, however, as sublimating as Mrs. Ellsworth had hoped. Returning from Paris, Oceola is determined more firmly than ever not to give up the black musical tradition. This is especially shown in her decision to move back to Harlem: "I've been away from my own people so long, I want to live right in the middle of them again." This symbolic rediscovery of her heritage, induced by a stay in Paris, is one of the earliest black reiterations of the Jamesian pattern. For it is in Europe that Oceola, to paraphrase a title of one of James Baldwin's essays, makes the discovery of what it means to be black.

The different settings hence express metaphorically the various stages of their relationship. The symbolic confrontation of Harlem with Greenwich Village and Paris ultimately demonstrates that the conflict is again dramatized on a personal as well as cultural plane. Her return to Harlem signals the attempt to preserve her black cultural identity. Significantly enough, it is only after she has accepted her lover's proposal that Oceola at a concert in a Harlem church suddenly lives up to her own musical intentions by "not sticking to the classical items listed on the program," for now she is able to "insert one of her own variations on the spirituals."

The inevitable separation of Oceola and Mrs. Ellsworth takes place one evening in the patroness' apartment, where Oceola had come to play for the last time "with the techniques for which Mrs. Ellsworth had paid." Again, the conflict is described in the contrasting images that are representative of the two different cultural spheres. Dora Ellsworth's position is almost entirely linked with exquisite, though lifeless antique objects, evoking the impression of her emotional sterility and deadness. These objects, acting as objective correlatives of her emotional state, cannot be reconciled with life. The vital, life-promising nature of Oceola's music, which grew "into an earth-throbbing rhythm that shook the lilies in the Persian vases of Mrs. Ellsworth's music room," ultimately exposes her limited point of view and suggests the final triumph, as it were, of black over white culture.

Because of her limited point of view, Dora Ellsworth remains unchanged. Even though she is dressed at the end in the same black velvet that Oceola used to wear, [James A.] Emanuel's reading this as "a symbolic fusion of herself and her protegée" seems to be an unwarranted conjecture. Rather, the story's ending calls for a reading [as Bone states] which views the two unreconciled positions as a re-emphasis of "the theme of cultural dualism which is basic to the Harlem Renaissance" and Hughes' position therein.

Oceola's self-conscious revolt against her patroness, which has strong autobiographical parallels, underlines historically the black's incipient ethnic assertion, his pride in his race and the rediscovery of his cultural heritage. Within this cultural context, **"The Blues I'm Playing"** may be considered a twofold satire. One of its objectives, of course, is to unmask the hypocrisy of white patronage. In addition to this, the philosophy of black cultural elitism and the 'New Negro' seems to be equally under attack. By refuting the 'high culture' of the Renaissance champions, Hughes satirizes through his fictional character those attempts to bridge the gap between the two races by means of art. For this must, as he demonstrates through Oceola, inevitably lead to servility and a loss of black identity. In contrast to Emanuel's general dictum that "Hughes as a writer cannot be explained by references to the Harlem Renaissance," this particular short story echoes, both on the autobiographical and cultural plane, historical problems that were firmly rooted in this period; thus Hughes' delineation of Oceola may ultimately be conceived as a fictional representation of his own literary manifesto and the story as a satirical reaction to the Harlem Renaissance.

Within the bulk of Hughes' sixty-six published short stories, **"The Blues I'm Playing"** holds a unique position. In keeping with Emanuel, who classified Hughes' short fiction thematically, this story turns out to be his only genuine artist story. It marks one of Hughes' outstanding achievements in this genre and established him as a serious writer of satirical short fiction. Most stories in the collection *The Ways of White Folk* are retrospective, looking back to the 1920's and trying to unveil many of the manifestations of the Harlem Renaissance. The date of publication, however, suggests a further significance. For the year 1934 signals the end of Hughes' early phase. (pp. 74-80)

Despite favorable reviews, the first issue of *The Ways of White Folk* sold only 2500 copies. This meagre success may be accounted for not only by the fact that Hughes had not yet gained, as he was to do later with his "Simple Tales," a genuine black reading audience; the commercial failure also seems to demonstrate that with the end of the Harlem Renaissance the potential white audience no longer shared a larger enthusiasm in black literary products. From a historical and socio-literary perspective, however, the stories of *The Ways of White Folk* caused a major breakthrough in paving the way for a racially unrestricted audience. By re-examining the black-white relationships of the 1920's and by unmasking the falseness of the enthusiasm of whites for the 'New Negro,' [Donald C. Dickinson states that] Hughes "clarified for the Negro audience their own strength and dignity and . . . supplied the white audience with an explanation of how the Negro feels and what he wants." Six years after the publication of this collection, Richard Wright, in a review of Hughes' autobiography *The Big Sea,* perhaps summed up the importance of the early works of Hughes best. In his eyes, Hughes, on account of his extensive publications, had served as a "cultural ambassador for the case of the blacks." (pp. 80-1)

> Peter Bruck, "Langston Hughes: 'The Blues I'm Playing' (1934)," in The Black American Short Story in the 20th Century: A Collection of Critical Essays, *edited by Peter Bruck, B. R. Grüner Publishing Co., 1977, pp. 71-84.*

SUSAN L. BLAKE   (essay date 1980)

[*In the following excerpt, Blake compares the Simple stories to the John-and-Old-Marster cycle, a series of traditional oral folktales that center around a black slave and his white master.*]

"If you want to know about my life," says Simple in the story that introduces him to readers of *Simple Speaks His Mind* and *The Best of Simple,* "don't look at my face, don't look at my hands. Look at my feet and see if you can tell how long I been standing on them." In the well-known catalogue of things Simple's feet have done—the miles they've walked; the lines they've stood in; the shoes, summer sandals, loafers, tennis shoes, and socks they've worn out; and the corns and bunions they've grown—Langston Hughes characterizes Jesse B. Semple, Harlem roomer, as the personification of the accumulated black experience. But what is especially significant about Simple is that he not only acknowledges his past, but uses it to shape his present. (p. 100)

In creating the Simple stories, Hughes has done the same thing with the black folk tradition that his character does with black history—made it live and work in the present. It is easily recognized that Hughes has a relationship to the folk tradition. . . . But Simple is more than vaguely "folk," and Hughes's relationship to the folk tradition is direct and dynamic. Simple is the migrant descendant of John the militant slave of black folklore, and the fictional editorials that Hughes wrote for the *Chicago Defender* from 1943 to 1966 function as real folktales in the political storytelling tradition of the John-and-Old-Marster cycle. Not only do they follow the pattern of the John tales in characterization and conflict, not only do they include traditional motifs, they also recreate on the editorial page of a newspaper the dramatic relationship between storyteller and audience that characterizes an oral storytelling situation.

The principal difference between folk and self-conscious literature is in the relationship between the work and the audience. Generally speaking, self-conscious literature, usually written, isolates the experience of individuals; is addressed to individuals, who may or may not share either personal or social experience with either the author or the characters; and is experienced by the individual as an individual. Folk literature, usually oral, isolates the experience of a socially-defined group; is addressed to all members of the group; and is experienced by a group, even if it consists of only two members, as a group. The self-conscious artist tells a story to suit himself, and the audience takes it or leaves it. The folk storyteller chooses and adapts a traditional text according to the occasion and the audience. The folk audience, therefore, participates in the storytelling and, in a sense, is also part of the story told. The story is told by, to, and for the people it is about; it is part of their lives as they are part of it. The Simple stories close the gap between story and audience created by the medium of print in several ways. They, too, adapt traditional material—from black folklore, the Bible, U.S. history, and popular culture. They, too, are occasional, as they deal with current events and social conditions. Their consistent subject, race, is the one experience that unites and defines the folk group to which they are addressed. Their principal character is an avid reader of the very publication in which the audience encounters him. Their story-within-a-story structure creates a dialogue between characters and audience. And their purpose is to function in the social conflict in which both characters and audience are engaged.

The typical Simple story is narrated by [Simple's bar-buddy] Boyd, who reports an encounter with Simple in which Simple has narrated an experience of his own. Each story contains two conflicts—one expressed in Simple's confrontation with an outside antagonist, the other in the conversation with Boyd in which he narrates it. Both conflicts are based on the consequences of race, which Simple defines in this exchange:

> "The social scientists say there is no difference between colored and white," I said. "You are advancing a very unscientific theory."
> "Do I look like Van Johnson?" asked Simple.
> "No, but otherwise—"
> "It's the *otherwise* that gets it," said Simple. "There is no difference between me and Van Johnson, except otherwise. I am black and he is white, I am Harlem and he is in Beverly Hills, I am broke and he is rich, I am known from here around the corner, and he is known from Hollywood around the world. There is as much difference between Van Johnson and me as there is between day and night. And don't tell me day and night is the same. If you do, I will think you have lost your mind."

The otherwise that Simple is talking about—the social, political, and economic disparity between blacks and whites—generates other disparities: between Christianity and racism, legislation and application, "race leaders" and black folks, "say-ola" and "do-ola," *ought* and *is,* the American Dream and the American Dilemma. These in turn produce the psychological disparity, the twoness that Du Bois classically defined, between being black and being American. In general, the story Simple narrates addresses the social disparity; his dialogue with Boyd addresses the psychological. The dual structure of the stories makes Simple both actor and storyteller; it makes Boyd actor, teller, and audience. It enables Hughes to explore all the implications of American race discrimination and to bring them home to the audience that experiences them.

In the inside story, Simple follows the model of John, the insubordinate slave in the cycle of folktales about the perpetual contest between John and Old Marster. John is Old Marster's favorite slave, his foreman, his valet, his confidant, his fortune-teller, his alter ego. When Old Marster throws a party, John plays the fiddle; when he gambles with his neighbors, he bets on John; when he goes on a trip, he leaves John in charge. John is as close to Old Marster as a slave can be, but he is still a slave. He spends his life trying to close the gap between himself and Old Marster, between slavery and manhood. In the words of Julius Lester, John does "as much living and as little slaving" as he can.

He does so by effectually swapping places with Old Marster. At every opportunity, he puts himself in Old Marster's shoes: throws a party in the big house when Old Marster takes a trip, appropriates Old Marster's hams and chickens, "borrows" his clothes and his best horse, copies his manners, kisses his wife, and generally assumes the prerogatives of manhood that Old Marster takes for granted. He also shows Old Marster what it is like to go barefoot. When Old Marster and Old Miss sneak back from their trip in ragged disguise to spy on his party, John sends them to the kitchen like white trash. When Old Marster sends John out at night to guard his cornfield from a bear, John ends up holding the gun while Old Marster plays ring-around-the-rosy with the bear.

John is neither big nor strong, and he is more than clever. He is a political analyst. When he wins a round with Old Marster, his victory is the result of an objective understanding of the political and psychological principles of slavery that enables him to turn those principles back upon the institution. In one version of a popular tale called "The Fight," for example, John bluffs his opponent into forfeiting a fight on which Old Marster has staked his entire plantation by slapping Old Miss across the face. Since John has saved the plantation, Old Marster is reduced to diffidence when he inquires why John has violated the rock-bottom rules of slavery. When John explains, "Jim knowed if I slapped a white woman I'd a killed him, so he run," there is nothing further Old Marster can say. Even when John himself loses, the tale contains the analysis of slavery that represents the teller's and audience's intellectual control over their situation. Whether he wins or loses, John is the personification of this control.

Simple, the character in his own stories, like John, has the circumstances of a slave and the psychology of a free man. Although he works for a wage instead of for life, it's a subsistence wage, as evidenced by his chronic inability to save the One Hundred and Thirty-Three Dollars and Thirty-Four Cents to pay for his share of his divorce from Isabel so he can marry Joyce. Although he doesn't need a pass to leave Harlem, as John needs a pass to leave the plantation, Simple knows that there are barber shops, beaches, and bars outside Harlem where he would be unwelcome or in danger. Although his antagonists are as various as newspaper reporters, hotel clerks, Emily Post, and Governor Faubus, they all represent institutions of a society that excludes him, just as Old Marster represents slavery. But just as John refuses to behave like a slave, Simple refuses to be restricted by race: "What makes you think I'm colored?" he demands when told a fac-

tory is not taking on any "colored boys." "They done took such words off of jobs in New York State by law."

As a storyteller, Simple points out the same kinds of disparities that concerned the tellers of John tales. First, there are the practical disparities between life uptown and life downtown. The folk storyteller points out that John sees chicken on Old Marster's table and fat bacon on his own. Simple observes that Joyce buys her groceries downtown because "everything is two-three-four cents a pound higher in Harlem"; that he could get a hotel room if he asked for it in Spanish, but not if he asked for it in English; that white folks Jim Crow and lynch him "anytime they want to," but "suppose I was to Jim Crow and lynch white folks, where would I be?" Second, there is the disparity between stated and practiced values. Two of the themes that Simple returns to most frequently are also common themes in folk literature: the difference between Christian doctrine and Christians' doings, and the reversed status of people and animals when the people are black. In **"Cracker Prayer,"** a variant of a traditional type of satiric prayer of which there is an example in Hurston's folklore collection *Mules and Men,* Simple impersonates a pious bigot who prays to the "Great Lord God, Jehovah, Father . . . to straighten out this world and put Nigras back in their places." In **"Golden Gate,"** he dreams a dream based on the traditional tale of The Colored Man Barred From Heaven, in which he arrives at the gate of Heaven and finds "Old Governor of Mississippi, Alabama, or Georgia, or wherever he is from," telling him to go around the back. Black folklore compares the lot of the black man, often disadvantageously, to that of the mule. Simple does the same thing with dogs. "Even a black dog gets along better than me," says Simple. "White folks socialize with dogs—yet they don't socialize with me." The army "Jim Crows me, but it don't Jim Crow dogs." In slavery days, Simple recalls, "a good bloodhound was worth more than a good Negro, because a bloodhound were trained to keep the Negroes in line." And dogs are still, he observes, more carefully counted than Negroes, better fed, sometimes even better clothed.

As an actor, Simple, like John, endeavors to resolve the disparities he has pointed out. His most common method is the folktale expedient of swapping places. (pp. 100-02)

Just as John not only seats himself at the head of Old Marster's table, but uses the opportunity to treat Old Marster as Old Marster has treated him, Simple insists not simply on integration, but on "reintegration"—"Meaning by that, what?" asks his white boss. "That you be integrated with *me,*" replies Simple, "not me with you." . . .

The circumstance that makes Simple act as John acts is the same one that makes Simple experience what John experiences. Slavery and Jim Crow are both manifestations of the idea that race determines place. The society dictates the theme of swapping places by creating places. . . . What Simple really wants is not for top and bottom to be inverted but for there to be no top or bottom, no "place," to swap:

> "Anyhow," said Simple, "if we lived back in fairy tale days and a good fairy was to come walking up to me and offer me three wishes, the very first thing I would wish would be:
>
> THAT ALL WHITE FOLKS WAS BLACK
>
> then nobody would have to bother with white blood and black blood any more."

But Simple does not live back in fairy-tale days, so he tries to combat racism by showing how unfair it would look if the tables were turned. The principle of swapping places is literally the principle of revolution. But the elimination of places is equally revolutionary. Hughes's purpose in Simple's stories is to make revolution look simple.

To the extent that inside and outside plots can be separated, the inside plot of a Simple story is addressed to the problem of Jim Crow and the outside plot to the people who suffer from it. The narrator of the Simple stories, identified in the later stories as Boyd (though "Boyd" in the earlier stories is the name of another roomer in Simple's house), is both the immediate audience of Simple's narrative—and, thus, a stand-in for the newspaper audience—and one of Simple's antagonists. For although Simple and Boyd are both black, and in full agreement on what *should* be, they disagree about what *is*. Because Boyd views reality in terms of American ideals and Simple views it in terms of black experience, their friendly disagreements focus on the psychological disparity between being black and being American.

Boyd talks American. He is a romantic, an idealist, one of the two hundred ninety-nine out of a thousand people, as George Bernard Shaw figured it, who recognize the conventional organization of society as a failure but, being in a minority, conform to it nevertheless and try to convince themselves that it is just and right. Simple talks black. He is Shaw's realist, the one man in a thousand "strong enough to face the truth the idealists are shirking." The truth he faces and Boyd shirks is the importance of race. Though Boyd is black, rooms in Harlem, listens to Simple nightly, seeks the evidence of race discrimination all around him, he keeps trying to believe that what ought to be is. . . .

Boyd considers Simple's race-consciousness provincial, chauvinistic, and un-American. He repeatedly encourages Simple to "take the long view," "extend a friendly hand," get to know more white people, try some foreign foods. But Simple insists on his Americanness as much as his blackness. . . . To Boyd, as to the hotel clerks and employers Simple encounters, "Negro" and "American" are mutually exclusive; "American" identity is an achievement upon which "Negro" identity may be put aside. To Simple, they are mutually necessary. America is not American *unless* it has room for him, "black as I can be," "without one plea." From Simple's point of view, Boyd's is not American at all, but white. Though Boyd voices the ideals of freedom, he represents the influence of racist conventions in his interpretation of them. The repartee between Simple and Boyd puts a contemporary conflict of attitudes into the context of the historical conflict between John and Old Marster. Through Boyd, Hughes shows that to deny the reality of racial oppression is actually to support it. (p. 103)

Folktales could not free the slaves who told them, but they could keep the slaves from being tricked into believing they were meant to be slaves; the tales could keep the distinction between living and slaving clear. The Simple stories do the same for the distinction between American ideals and black reality. The principle of the Simple stories is that the way to overcome race discrimination is to confront it, and they keep their audience confronted not only with the principle of confrontation but also with the evidence of discrimination. In the words of Ellison's definition of the blues, they keep alive the painful details and episodes of black experience and tran-

scend them—keep them alive in order to transcend them—just as Simple remembers his past in order to free his future.

The similarity between Simple's conflict and John's makes the Simple stories resemble folktales, but the active engagement in the audience's social and psychological experience makes them to be to an urban newspaper-reading folk what the John tales must have been to a rural storytelling folk: a communal affirmation of the group's own sense of reality. Like the folk storyteller, Hughes speaks of and to the group. . . .

Implicitly in the Simple stories, Hughes has redefined the notion of black folk tradition. Most of the writers who consciously used black folk materials in the first half of the twentieth century located "the folk tradition" in the South, in the past, in a pastoral landscape. They either employed it—as did Toomer, Hurston, O'Neill in *The Emperor Jones,* Heyward in *Porgy*—or rejected it, as did Wright, as a retreat from the social complexities of modern life into either pastoral simplicity or the individual psyche. But Hughes's definition of black folk tradition is dynamic. Limited by no time, place, or landscape, it is simply the continuity of black experience—an experience that is "folk" in that it is collective and a "tradition" in that it defines the past, dominates the present, and makes demands on the future.

Hughes asks his audience to recognize their place in this tradition and use it as Simple uses the history stored up in his feet. The force and purpose of his writing is to project his understanding of the folk tradition out among the folk, to bind black people together in a real community, united by their recognition of common experience into a force to control it. Modestly, like a relay runner, Langston Hughes picks up the folk tradition and carries it on toward the goal of social change in the real world. (p. 104)

Susan L. Blake, "Old John in Harlem: The Urban Folktales of Langston Hughes," in Black American Literature Forum, *Vol. 14, No. 3, Fall, 1980, pp. 100-04.*

DAVID MICHAEL NIFONG   (essay date 1981)

[*In the following excerpt, Nifong examines seven stories from* The Ways of White Folks *to illustrate the importance of point of view as a narrative technique in Hughes's short fiction.*]

[**The Ways of White Folks**] serves two important purposes for the critic of Black American literature. First, it offers stories which deal truthfully, ironically, and (often-times) humorously with "some nuance of the race relation." Second, the collection offers a unique opportunity for the study of numerous different narrative points of view in a single volume. While the first purpose has intrigued readers for years, the second has been ignored. A close reading of the collection reveals the effectiveness of Hughes' conscious or subconscious experimentation with narrative perspective, and a review of formalistic critical theory further illuminates these techniques. . . .

The close interrelationship between form and content of poetry has been widely discussed by the formalist critics, and it is only natural that the critical concepts which they developed should be carried into the study of fiction. As the formalistic critical theories have been applied to works of fiction, there has been born a renewed awareness of technique

Hughes with friend and art patron Carl Van Vechten photographed by Richard Avedon, 2/16/63, New York City. Through his patronage Van Vechten was largely responsible for popularizing African-American art and literature during the Harlem Renaissance.

and of the importance which narrative point of view plays in shaping a work of fiction.

Mark Schorer is one of the most influential spokesmen of the formalist movement, and his essay "Technique as Discovery" is one of the central essays in modern criticism of the novel because, [according to Robert Murray Davis]

> it states most explicitly and emphatically the formalist attitude toward fiction, in which the unit is the word, the embodiment the technique, and the result an aesthetic whole that is valid on its own terms.

The far-reaching effects of Schorer's essay, written in 1948, can be seen in the writings of Robert Scholes, Robert Kellogg, Norman Friedman, John E. Tilford, and Wayne C. Booth. These men acknowledge the importance of Schorer's concepts and base their theories on his premise that technique and subject matter are inseparable and that technique is something more crucial than mere embellishment. . . .

Schorer's widely quoted definition states that

> Technique is the means by which the writer's experience, which is his subject matter, compels him to attend to it; technique is the only means he has of

discovering, exploring, developing his subject, of conveying its meaning, and finally, of evaluating it.

Furthermore, when applying the term "technique" to fiction, Schorer uses the term to signify two fundamentals of writing. First, technique refers to the manner in which language is used to express the experience which the author wishes to relate; second, technique refers to the use of point of view "not only as a mode of dramatic delineation, but more particularly of thematic definition." (p. 93)

In *The Ways of White Folks* one discovers that Langston Hughes experiments with seven points of view and meets with varying degrees of success.

The first-person narrator appears in three stories in *The Ways of White Folks,* yet each is slightly different. **"A Good Job Gone,"** a story about a wealthy white man who goes crazy after his black mistress leaves him, is related as an historic monologue from the point of view of the black houseboy who finds himself without a job after Mr. Lloyd's breakdown. Scholes and Kellogg point out that there is a quite useful distinction between the first person speaker in empirical narrative and the first person speakers of fictional narrative. By the "telling" of this story, Hughes limits the reader to information which the protagonist shares. Everything appears through this unnamed protagonist's eyes, and the only picture of the protagonist available to the reader is a mirror's reflection. One must also realize that the entire story is written in the historic past. By reporting what has already happened, the narrator further selects and limits what the reader perceives. This retrospective point of view also gives the story a folk tale quality, especially when one realizes by the last sentences ("Say boy, gimme a smoke will you? I hate to talk about it.") that the story has been presented orally and "overheard" by the reader. As John Tilford explains, by telling the story from the "inside"—that is, having one of the characters tell it—there is a certain tone, focus, conviction, meaning, and flavor of style which could not be retained if the story were told in the third person.

The short sketch entitled **"Passing"** is also written in the first person but is in the form of a letter. Jack, the son of a black mother and a white father, writes to thank his mother for pretending she did not know him when he and his white fiancée passed her on the street. The narrative focus is so limited in the epistolary form that it is questionable as to whether **"Passing"** can be called a short story. The characterization, setting, and plot are so tied up in the implied author's choice of words that, as a traditional short story, it simply does not suffice. Jack finds it necessary to tell his mother details of which she would not need to be reminded unless she were senile and blind. For instance, he writes that his brother Charlie is "darker than you, even, Ma," and recalls the generosity of his white father who "did buy you a house and send all us kinds through school." In case she has forgotten where he went to college, Jack adds, "I'm glad I finished college in Pittsburgh before he died." The structural irony of the piece is its sole redeeming quality. Jack has already passed but has not yet severed his last tie to the black community—his relationship with his mother. The only thing which still holds them together is their correspondence through letters. In what Scholes and Kellogg term "empirical narration" through an autobiographical confessor, Jack lets his mother know that it was not the presence of his white girl friend that kept him from speaking to her, but that it was the whole concept of "crossing the color line." Early in the letter he states, "If I hadn't had the girl with me, Ma, we might have talked," and later he writes, "But I don't mind being 'white,' Ma." The pitiful closing of the letter pleads: "Even if we can't meet often, we can write, can't we, Ma?" Jack, who has definitely constructed his whole world and has determined his own future, knows that he and his mother can no longer write, that when he betrayed his heritage by passing his mother on the street he had completed the passing process and could now refer to himself as white—without the quotation marks.

Hughes creates a most effective story by combining the first-person point of view with a poetic internal monologue in **"Red-Headed Baby."** This powerfully written piece, about a white sailor who returns to the house of his black lover and finds himself face to face with his three-year-old, red-headed, deaf and dumb son, would easily fit between the covers of Jean Toomer's *Cane*. Poetry and fiction are successfully fused as Hughes allows his creativity full reign. One observes the futile life of Clarence, a poor white sailor whose existence is nothing but "Mosquitoes, sand, niggers." The stagnation of Clarence's life is made quite obvious through the restlessness of the narrative style. Short choppy sentences show a man wanting to run but with no place to go except back to Betsy. . . . This stream-of-consciousness technique is reminiscent of "Penelope" in [James Joyce's] *Ulysses,* a book with

which Hughes probably became familiar in Paris even before it was allowed into the United States. Clarence's complete rejection of his son, and his need to prostitute the evening by paying for his drinks, brings this excellent story to a conclusion of complete pathos.

Perhaps the most difficult point of view to incorporate in one's writing is that of the omniscient narrator. Scholes and Kellogg deny the availability of omniscience as a method for the modern writer. Since omniscience includes the god-like attribute of omnipresence, [Scholes and Kellogg state that]

> a narrator in fiction is imbedded in a time-bound artifact. He does not "know" simultaneously but consecutively. He is not everywhere at once but now here, now there, now looking into this mind or that, now moving to other vantage points.

The range of the story is wide open since the narrator is often compelled to tell the reader everything about every character in every situation. The closest which Hughes comes to this approach in *The Ways of White Folks* is in the lengthy story entitled **"Father and Son."** The plot of this tale revolves around the homecoming of Bert, the twenty-year-old son of Cora, a black housekeeper, and Colonel Norwood, a white plantation owner. The conflict arises when Bert refuses to be a "white folks' nigger" and expects to be treated like the well-educated man he is. Bert's pride and his father's obstinacy lead to patricide, Cora's mental breakdown, Bert's suicide, and the lynching of both Bert's dead body and the live body of his brother Willie—the perfect "white folks' nigger."

The narrator does not exploit his omniscient capabilities but allows the reader to see behind the different characters at certain times. Therefore, one is able to see that Colonel Norwood is eagerly awaiting his son's return even though his actions around the other characters would never indicate this. The narrator, in the third paragraph, states: "Colonel Norwood never would have admitted, *even to himself,* that he was standing in his door-way waiting for his half-Negro son to come home. But in truth that is what he was doing" (my italics). One quickly sees that the narrator is separated from Norwood and is capable of observing the Colonel's mental state and motives when the Colonel cannot even do this himself. The narrator obviously has power. In section five he begins to set the tone of Bert's rebellion:

> There are people (you've probably noted it also) who have the unconscious faculty of making the world spin around themselves, throb and expand, contract and go dizzy. Then, when they are gone away, you feel sick and lonesome and meaningless.

Here the narrator foreshadows the forthcoming trouble caused by Bert's refusal to be a "white folks' nigger." Through the use of the parenthetical expression, the narrator steps out of the boundaries of the story and directly addresses the reader. Hughes enjoys making these parenthetical "asides," and there are 73 in the book. The ultimate result of the omniscient narrator in this story is the full characterization of Bert, Cora, and Colonel Norwood. Since the point of view is not limited to any one of these main characters, each is able to be developed to an extent not possible with any other narrative perspective.

The simple third-person point of view is used in the majority of the selections in *The Ways of White Folks.* Hughes adds variety to this common narrative approach by giving the implied author or narrator a definite skin color. The reader readily understands that he is viewing the characters and situations through racial eyes, and this understanding adds an extra depth to the stories. **"Berry"** is a rather short sketch about the mistreatment of a young black man who works at a summer camp where crippled children receive care which is far inferior to what their middle-class white parents have paid for. Milberry, or Berry as the children call him, is uneducated but possesses "plenty of mother wit and lots of intuition about people and places." His insightfulness allows him to see through the scam of the children's home, but since jobs are scarce, Berry puts up with the inept white staff until he is mercilessly dismissed. The first sentence of the story ironically reveals the race of the narrator: "When the boy arrived on the four o'clock train, lo and behold, he turned out to be colored!" From this point, the narration proceeds in a matter-of-fact fashion, commenting on the characters and their relationships with this one black employee. The narrator realizes that Milberry is being overworked, but "Still he did everything and didn't look mad—jobs were hard to get, and he had been hungry too long in town. . . . " The reader is forced to respond with anger when he sees the injustice performed against Milberry. As Booth points out, the implied author can be more or less distant from other characters and can be inferred as approving of actions almost completely while the reader, as chief "reflector," definitely disapproves of the social injustices. Thus, the one good character of the story—a young man who shows love to the crippled children—is sent away without pay. Thereby, the world of the indifferent white narrator triumphs over the helpless black man.

In **"Little Dog,"** Hughes follows the Jamesean technique of further developing the third-person narrator into a central intelligence. In what Friedman terms "selective omniscience," the reader is limited to the mind of only one of the characters. "Instead, therefore, of being allowed a composite of viewing angles, he is at the fixed center." Here, the narrator focuses on the thoughts and actions of Miss Clara Briggs, a forty-five-year-old white spinster who fantasizes about the black janitor who brings meat and bones to her little white dog. The reader is not limited to the shadowing of Miss Briggs' actions by an outsider, but is able to get inside her mind. One sees a lonely, introverted lady who tries to share her life with her little white dog but who runs when she is faced with the possibility of sharing her life with her big black janitor. The strangely sexual imagery of this black man nightly bringing his meat to the lady is fully exploited by the narrator and is reflected in Miss Briggs' mind:

> When the Negro really knocked on the door with the meat, she was trembling so that she could not go to the kitchen to get it. "Oh, Flips," she said, "I'm so hungry." She meant to say "*You're* so hungry." So she repeated it. "You're so hungry! Heh, Flipsy, dog?"
> And from the way the little dog barked, he must have been hungry. He loved meat.

Through the use of the central intelligence, one is fully acquainted with the strange thoughts and actions of Miss Clara Briggs. [Tilford describes this point of view as] "The result is unity of focus, intensity, strong identification of the reader with one character, and a certain esthetic distance not possible in first person narration."

One final point of view is found in **"Mother and Child,"** a story about the birth of a black baby to a white family and the resulting turmoil in the small Ohio town. The baby's fa-

ther, Douglass Carter, a twenty-six-year-old black farmer, refuses to run as the black community advises; the resolute Carter stays in Boyd's Center waiting for his lover's husband to turn out both baby and mother. In this story Hughes employs the effaced narrator in a dramatic dialogue. Having eliminated the author and the narrator, Hughes is now ready to dispose of mental states altogether. A story with an effaced narrator, as Friedman suggests, is

> in effect a stage play cast into the typographical mold of fiction. But there is some difference: fiction is meant to be read, drama to be seen and heard, and there will be a corresponding difference in scope, range, fluidity, and subtlety.

This technique (also used by Hemingway in "The Killers") would seemingly be difficult to incorporate since all of the story's vital information must be presented in the conversation of the characters without the aid of Shavian stage directions. However, the technique works exceptionally well in this particular story since the characters involved in the dialogue are a bunch of old ladies who doubtlessly like nothing better than spreading the latest gossip. An outside narrator probably couldn't get a word in edgewise! When the ladies are finally called to order by Madam President, the irony of the story is made apparent:

> "The March meeting of the Salvation Rock Ladies Missionary Society for the Rescue o' the African Heathen is hereby called to order. . . . Sister Burns, raise a hymn. . . . Will you-all ladies *please* be quiet? What are you talking 'bout back there anyhow?"

Amidst the singing, the Sisters realize that there are heathens in need of rescue much closer than Africa. Once again, the narrative technique works for Langston Hughes in this interesting dramatic sketch.

Thus, as one studies narrative technique and applies the theories to a given work of art, he discovers the vast, controlling importance of point of view. . . . As one reads *The Ways of White Folks,* it is easy to enjoy the well-developed plots and the masterful character studies, but when the reader takes a closer look to analyze just what it is that makes this collection of short stories good, he discovers Hughes' excellent use of point of view. Whether he is creating the self-centered narrator of **"A Good Job Gone"** or the all-seeing narrator of **"Father and Son,"** Hughes carefully molds the narrator to fulfill the function of shaping experience into art. The result is an exceptional assortment of narrative perspectives which do not appear as superfluous embellishment but prove to be integral parts of the aesthetic whole. (pp. 94-6)

> *David Michael Nifong, "Narrative Technique and Theory in 'The Ways of White Folks'," in* Black American Literature Forum, *Vol. 15, No. 3, Fall, 1981, pp. 93-6.*

STEVEN C. TRACY (essay date 1984)

[*In the following excerpt, Tracy focuses on the Jesse B. Semple character in the story "Jazz, Jive and Jam" to portray the cultural situation of blacks in American society.*]

By now most critics of Langston Hughes have recognized the brilliance of his comic creation Jesse B. Semple—Simple. Although Simple is a sharply delineated individual, he has often been called a Negro Everyman because of the vitality with which he recognizes the centrality of cultural identity. Hughes has not made Simple a common man for common man's sake: for Hughes he is the natural, unpretentious man representative of a racial pride that suggests an alternative approach to the racial difficulties haunting an America which doesn't embrace as much as it sucks up alternative cultures. This problem of cultural individuality and racial disharmony is confronted by Hughes in his "Simple" stories, and most effectively in **"Jazz, Jive and Jam,"** the humor of which clearly hinges on the subject of retaining African-American cultural individuality in the face of the standards of the "high" culture of dominant whites—a "high" culture supported not only by whites, but also by some African-American confidence men who attempt to sell African-Americans on this "high" culture.

It has been a characteristic of man to habitually express confidence in the features and attitudes of "high" culture. In America, during the first two hundred years of its infancy—and some say even today—those characteristics which testified to the attainment of Western social, cultural, and ethical ideals . . . were absent in America. . . . The residual was "the Great American Joke," which Louis D. Rubin, Jr., identifies as

> the fact that in a popular democracy the customary and characteristic institutions that have traditionally embodied cultural, social, and ethical values are missing from the scene, and yet the values themselves, and the attitudes that derive from and serve to maintain them, remain very much part of the national experience.

This dichotomy can be expressed by the incongruity between American cultural, social, and ethical ideals and the mundane realities of existence in an emergent, heterogeneous human society; it is a major source of the doubts about whether American democracy can succeed. Built into the American experience, and American humor, then, is the tension between the ideal and the real. . . . (pp. 239-40)

This same tension is intensified in the African-American experience, because those social, cultural, and ethical ideals were simply never attainable for African-Americans. The benefits of American democratic society and Western civilization were for the man, not the animal; the free man, not the slave. Part of the problem was American society's inability to understand the culture, traditions, and institutions of the African society it confronted. Consequently, society assumed that either no civilization or culture, or a vastly inferior primitive one, existed. As a result, the Africans brought to this country became slaves—not only socially and intellectually, but culturally—to the established values of a culture that denied the validity of these Africans' existence except within the confines of a new definition of where they fit into the conquering culture. Therefore, Africans became redefined within American culture as savages without State, sovereignty, court, loyalty, aristocracy, church, clergy, army, and all other forms of "high" civilization. American culture also evolved over the years a new character for them, as portrayed in minstrel shows. . . . (pp. 240-41)

This happy, shuffling, darky stereotype, accepted and delighted in by white Americans, and the devaluation of African-American culture are part of the basis for what Hughes was trying to combat in much of his work. Hughes knew that, in fact, social, intellectual, and cultural values did exist in Africa, traditions as old or older than those of Western civiliza-

tion, and with just as much validity. Therefore the white American concept of African-Americans reflects the ignorance and sickness of American culture, criticizing the cultural values which, when embraced by African-Americans, is tantamount to a betrayal of pride in their own culture. Thus, when Booker T. Washington exhorted Negroes to work patiently within the system, he was selling a white American product, not an African one, advocating implicitly a cultural capitulation.

Langston Hughes was, however, a "New Negro," part of the Harlem Renaissance movement that investigated African ties, affirmed African beauty, and elevated the cultural harvest of the "lowdown" folks—the blues, jazz, oral sermons, and folk tales that provide potent links to Africa—to a level that began to assert the importance that had been denied both the creator and creation. Throughout Hughes's work there is an affirmation of African-Americanism, both in style and content. Very often to understand his work one must know blues and jazz in particular. One must meet Hughes on his own ground, as African-Americans have had to meet whites on theirs.

This was naturally a very serious subject, one that had been dealt with seriously by many African-American authors, Hughes among them. Hughes, however, recognized the importance of humor in African-American cultural identity:

> There is so much richness in Negro humor, so much beauty in black dreams, so much dignity in our struggle, and so much universality in our problems, in us—in each living human being of color—that I do not understand the tendency today that some Negro artists have of seeking to run away from themselves, of running away from us, of being afraid to sing our songs, paint our own pictures, write about ourselves.

Hughes did not run away from humor; he was not afraid to laugh. Instead he went about creating a realistic comic figure with which his audience could identify: Jesse B. Semple, a native of Harlem, Negro capital of America. In dialect the name blurs into an exhortation to "just be simple," a role into which many African-Americans were forced by circumstance, albeit often ironically and for self-preservation, given America's racial situation. Under those circumstances, simple is complex, and so is Simple.

He is not a member of the "upwardly mobile" African-American middle and upper class; he is not the kind to embrace white culture and values to "get ahead." He is the common man, the unpretentious, the irrepressible, full of mother wit, complaining "the people's" complaints, telling their stories, jokes, and tall tales: the representative of those that "are the soul of the race and most deserve to be expressed in black art." His most common complaint is the pervasive racism that has cautioned him to be just simple—that is, to be simple in the stereotypical sense, not to be himself. His wife Joyce, who has adopted an "upwardly mobile" middle-class attitude toward Simple's behavior, exhorts, "Jess Semple . . . don't be simple," when he characteristically undercuts very easily one of her "intellectual" arguments. But the name "Joyce" itself is not far from "Jess," or "just" either; indeed, she indicates the ever-present African-American middle-class attitudes that present real problems for Afro-Americans. In the use of the word "simple" there is a complex dichotomy that creates a taut tightrope of tension for those still struggling to define their "natural" mannerisms and activities. Jess embodies a relaxed naturalness, a confidence, that becomes for Joyce unnatural in its seeming simplicity; it is Jess' self-assurance and pride that transcends Joyce's intellectuality and makes her appear to be simple—which indeed she is—Joyce Semple, his "other half," his alter ego, the straining pretensions to which he is married, for better or for worse. And he must certainly come to terms with her attitudes. Clearly this punning on his name indicates the position of the African-American. White society will tell the African-American who and what to be, all within the context and confines of the white power structure. Simple recognizes this, and he plays on it. He recognizes the disparity between the real and ideal: "What is and what ought to be is two different things"; he recognizes the gap between African-Americans and white Americans: "He were white and did not know I was making a joke"; he is vigilant: "It is best to keep one eye open . . . even when you are asleep." (pp. 241-44)

Researchers have spent some time trying to locate Hughes's attitudes in the Simple stories: some see Hughes's attitudes in the narrator called "Boyd" . . . who is a rationalist-intellectual; others locate Hughes's attitudes in Simple's attitudes. Onwuchekwa Jemie probably comes closest to relating the three to each other: "Simple speaks for Boyd about as often as he speaks for Hughes and the black masses, which is most of the time. . . . Boyd is Hughes's alter-ego, but so is Simple; Hughes's identity embraces them both." This can be easily demonstrated by consideration of the narration itself in **"Jazz, Jive and Jam."**

The story itself is a creation of the artist, Hughes, narrated by Boyd, who recounts a narrative of Simple's concerning a disagreement between Simple and Joyce. At the outset of the story Boyd is the first-person narrator, and Simple, when identified as speaker, is referred to by his proper name: " 'It being Negro History Week,' said Simple." As the story progresses, Simple takes over the narration, presenting the dialogue between Joyce and himself, which had taken place earlier. However, there are points within Simple's narrative when the language seems to be shifting from Simple's words to those of another narrator. For example, when Joyce argues with Simple about his drinking, Simple narrates,

> "She answers me back, 'How come your gullet has
> got to be so wet?' "

and this sounds very much like a natural first-person narrative. However, shortly after this exchange, Simple's presentation of Joyce's words sounds much less natural, much less like he would narrate it, as if the narration was shifting elsewhere, even as he spoke:

> " 'Married to you for three years, I can read your
> mind,' said Joyce."

This "said Joyce" at the end of the narration of her words does not sound natural; it sounds much more like a detached observer presenting the words, much the way Boyd did in the beginning of the story. Shifts of this nature occur several times within the story, identifying Boyd in one sense with Joyce's point of view, while in another sense, since he hangs out in the bars of the "lowdown folks," he is identified with Simple. What the narrative shift does, then, is indicate the relationship among the three characters. Hughes seems to be using the three to represent alternative impulses within his own mind: the artist creator using his rational observer-commentator describing the alternate impulses to retain ethnic identity (Simple) and adopt white values to achieve social

and economic stability in the white world. It is in itself a delineation of the crisis of the African-American intellectual, often trained away from his cultural heritage, who needs to merge his intellectuality with the attitudes of the lowdown folks. Therefore, Hughes often allows Simple to get the best of the "more intellectual" people around him in order to indicate the importance of Simple's attitudes to African-American identity. Simple is serious about his ideas; it is his style that is humorous, the subtle way he challenges preconceptions and pretensions, the way he states complex things so simply, the way he outsmarts the more intelligent people around him. He is a variation on the "wise fool" motif, with a deceptive naivete that gulls other characters and readers who disagree with him into a false sense of security, whereupon he turns their "sophistication" and "intelligence" back on them. Simple is African-American soul and pride, triumphing under the pressure of a sophistication and intelligence that seems to be taking the African out of the African-American.

"Jazz, Jive and Jam" is the final story in the collection *Simple Stakes a Claim,* so placed because of its centrality and importance in highlighting the incongruity between the seeming ideal all-inclusiveness of American society and the African-American experience. It expresses very clearly the difficulties that minority cultures experience in retaining ethnic identity when faced with American culture and values. The "jazz, jive and jam" of the title represents an alternative method for solving the racial problems of America—on African-American terms—and this method is replicated in the artistry of the story itself. Simple's complaints in the story are based on his wife Joyce's insistence on dragging him to boring lectures dealing with integration—lectures that Simple finds an affront to his own values. Simple's method of ridiculing the opposition and exposing their pretensions depends on his African-American speech patterns and inventive signifying, which subtly pick apart the elaborately constructed arguments simply and methodically. The phrase "jazz, jive and jam" derives from various phrases attributed to Dr. Conboy, the chief "villain" of this story. As the story opens, the "intellectual" Boyd misinterprets Simple's wordplay as a mispronunciation: he corrects Simple's calling Conboy a "hysterian" rather than a historian. Simple makes clear his intent—asserts his own intelligence and ability—by repeating "hysterian" as originally pronounced. The pun introduces from the outset Simple's opposition to the pretentious intellectuals like Dr. Conboy and the inability of an even less pretentious intellectual like Boyd to understand and appreciate fully Simple's ability. The intellectual's pretentiousness often gives Simple the advantage of being able to outwit him without the intellectual's knowing it, since Simple, according to the intellectual, doesn't have the knowledge of "high" culture that would allow him to communicate on equal terms with an intellectual.

The doctor's name—Conboy—in the story is significant, in that it places him in the tradition of the confidence man who is selling trust in his product. We see the confidenceman tradition at work in John Smith's writings, in the tracts that promised great wealth and abundance for the grabbing in the New World, in practical Ben Franklin's rules for diligence and success in America. These cons obviously worked on the consciousness of the white settlers in America, and worked more desperately and frustratingly so on African-Americans who accepted the givens of the con man without recognizing that one extra rule of the game that even more assuredly precluded success—the rule that you don't really even have to play by the rules with African-Americans at all, that even if African-Americans "win," they lose because that is the rule. To Hughes, Dr. Conboy is working a con, selling confidence in the fact that he is a doctor, which therefore gives him the authority to espouse the attitudes and values of white society for the growing black middle class. In terms of his affirmation of white values, he is what would be termed a "good boy," hence the name Conboy. Part of Conboy's con is to undermine Simple's point of view. Simple relates that "he laid our Negro race low;" he later comments that Conboy "tore us down good." Conboy berates the colored race for being "misbred, misread and misled," wasting their time "jazz-shaking" instead of "time-taking and money-making." These words form the basis for much of Simple's wordplay, particularly with the concepts of high and low, which Simple clearly thinks are inverted in Conboy's viewpoint. "That high-speaking doctor done tore my spirits down," moans Simple, who sees "the higher things in life" as "high flown gab, gaff and gas," spouted by what he derisively terms orators. "Gab, gaff, and gas" is clearly a play on Conboy's "misbred, misread and misled," mocking Conboy's speech tactics in order to demonstrate the prentiousness of the "high" and the destructiveness of lying low. Both are in opposition to Simple's honesty and simplicity, and he clearly doesn't envy the Dr. Conboys of the world their position: "Thank God I did not have to set up there like you with the delegation."

Joyce, who claims to have been pursuing "culture" since her childhood, supports the historian's emphasis on values that emphasize "high" culture, the Protestant work ethic, and the American dream of home ownership, de-emphasizing the "jazz" elements of African-American culture. She identifies Simple—a "jazz shaker"—and his appetite for alcohol with animal behavior: he wets his "gullet" at a "licker trough" drinking himself "to the dogs." Implicit in her attitude is an association between Simple and primitive, animal savages. His attitudes, his whole life, is related to the primitive, as opposed to the outlook of the sophisticated intelligentsia.

Joyce, who is pursuing the values of the sophisticated intelligentsia like Conboy, takes over the lecturing from Dr. Conboy in her discussions with Simple. The authorities that Joyce invokes as being representative of the values of her movement are very revealing. She considers Conboy smart because he quotes Aristotle, whose thought, more than anyone else, determined the content and direction of Western civilization, and who along with Socrates (also named by Joyce) and Plato laid the philosophical foundations of Western culture. Simple replies, "Who were Harry Stottle?" While the "educated" reader's impulse may well be to ridicule Simple for his unfamiliarity with Aristotle and the mispronunciation of his name, Hughes uses this unfamiliarity with this central Western authority to undercut the importance of one of the great Western minds in the context of the African-American experience. In Simple's experience, Booker T. Washington, a man concerned with racial problems in America, is more immediate, more important. Hughes's reference to Aristotle here has a further dimension. Aristotle has been viewed as having a crucial role in the development of racial (and racist) attitudes. In *Politics* he discusses the character of citizens of his ideal state and generalizes those characteristics from racially biased postulates to a racially biased conclusion:

> The Greek race combines the high spirit of the northern races with the intelligence of the eastern. Hence it alone combines freedom with good gov-

ernment, and if it could be formed into one state, would be able to govern the world. The most perfect combination of intelligence with spirit is the best possible character for the citizens of the state.

Indeed, he was criticized for his failure to adopt his pupil Alexander's ideas on racial intermixing, and in *On Colonization* he counsels Alexander to deal with the Hellenes and the Orientals differently: with the former as a king and the latter as a master. Additionally, Aristotle expresses the ethics of the Greek upper class in a slave society, claiming that some men are by nature free, some by nature slaves or living possessions who are not actually citizens of the ideal state. As Ashley Montagu points out, Aristotle developed the necessary theoretical justifications for slavery when the institution came under criticism, but the justification "consists of nothing but the most ill-founded rationalizations, and shows Aristotle . . . at his weakest." Therefore Hughes's use of Aristotle in the story as a philosopher less important for Simple than Booker T. Washington has obvious reference to Aristotle's racial ideas and acceptance of the concept of natural slavery and natural aristocracy, all of which have correlates in American society.

In the same way, Simple will have none of the pretensions of lineage or royalty. When Joyce proceeds to lecture on the black and "comely" Sheba, Simple reduces the reference to a punning sexual joke: "I wonder would she come to me?" To Joyce the fact that royalty is attracted to a black woman gives the woman added significance; to Simple the accident of high birth is a coincidence, not an achievement, and he refuses to accede to royalty:

> "He was a king," said Joyce.
> "And I am Jesse B. Semple," I said.

There is, however, a further dimension to the humor here. Joyce's reference to "Sheba" is inaccurate in that it was Makeda, the Queen of Sheba, not a person named Sheba, who visited Solomon, and the visit, recounted in I Kings, II Chronicles, and the Song of Solomon, seems to have had more to do with business and trade negotiations than romance, although one story relates that Solomon tricked the virtuous Makeda into coupling with him (which, incidentally, adds to the appropriateness of Simple's comment concerning her). Joyce's choice of "Sheba" as an example was not necessarily the wisest one, since the Ethiopian rulers' chronicle, the Kebar Negast, describes Makeda's "conversion" from the sun worshipping of her people to the worship of the God of Israel because of the great wisdom of Solomon—in effect deserting her cultural values. At any rate, Joyce might have done better to emphasize Makeda's achievements as a great ruler and tactician rather than focusing on her outward beauty. (pp. 244-51)

Simple is not just interested, however, in exposing this opposition. He knows what he likes, that what he feels is important, and that what he feels will succeed. He feels that Conboy and Joyce are "misbred, misread and misled," and he suggests replacing "gab, gaff and gas" with his own trebling-phrased program: jazz, jive and jam. In order to solve racial problems, in order to bring people together, Simple seeks to approach the problem with African-American culture as a basis. All three words are traceable etymologically to Africa, and all three have significant meaning in the African-American community. Jazz is an African-American creation, a cultural medium; jive is the message and the vocabulary of the African-American, employed to name Simple's program and evident in much of Simple's language; the jam is the creative interaction of the muscians/participants, allowing each soloist his time to preach: the jazz and jive crystallize in the jam session.

Simple proposes a gathering that includes several different styles of jazz—his authorities: Harlem "intellectual" composer-pianist Duke Ellington and his band; Count Basie's swinging Kansas City-style band; vibraphonist and one-time member of the integrated Benny Goodman band Lionel Hampton; and female singer Pearl Bailey. The utilization of different jazz artists and styles recognizes the importance of different approaches to jazz, just as Hughes has presented viewpoints of several African-Americans in the story in order to give all a chance to express themselves. The difference is that in the story, only Simple identifies with the jazz artists fully—only Simple is jamming with the jazz musicians—and, therefore, Simple's viewpoint clearly wins out over the others.

Once he starts creating within his idiom, when he begins discussing jazz, Simple excels. He turns a woman's complaint against her man in Lil Green's "Why Don't You Do Right?" into a racial joke aimed at the white audience in attendance, which would have come of course to hear the African-American musicians play: "Then play 'Why Don't You Do Right?' which could be addressed to white folks. They could pat their feet to that." The comment implies that such an important message addressed explicitly to whites asking "Why don't you do right?" would not be understood or heeded unless it was expressed in a boring (to Simple) speech. White Americans would, in effect, concentrate on one aspect, the jazz (the medium), totally missing the jive (message), as Joyce concentrated on the Queen of Sheba's beauty rather than her cultural betrayal.

The white American's inability to grasp the importance of African-American culture and its traditions and messages—the inability of the dominant culture to accept cultural differences unchauvinistically—cinches Simple's triumph over his opposition. Simple's Great African-American Joke is that in an ethnic group and minority culture that is supposedly lacking in the characteristics of "high" civilization—which is itself a culture that is presumably lacking those things as well—he understands better than the leaders of the culture, better than middle-class African-Americans running away from themselves, that so much is left. (pp. 251-53)

"Jazz, Jive and Jam" advocates collective involvement to solve racial problems, through the creative interaction of leaders (purveyors of culture, the jammers who at their best allow each other room for free improvisation and work at interacting to support each others' expression) and the integrated participation of followers. In this "inverted" world where the "lowdown folks" are now on high, Simple can't refuse to return to his wordplay. This time, though, as the band plays "How High the Moon," the high is really high for Simple—a simple unpretentious man striving for identity. However, Joyce's attitude is a major obstacle to putting Simple's ideas into actual practice. With her rejection of pure African-American culture, Joyce reduces Simple to a musical and racial stereotype: "Joyce just thought I was high."

Langston Hughes understood that the Simples of the world are not crazy or "high." He understood that the African-American intellectual needs to recognize the beauty of the "common man," needs to retain and nurture his ethnic and

cultural identity, and that the "common man" needs to accept that identity as well. He understood that white Americans need to recognize and value African-Americans' cultural, social, and ethical ideals. Simple understands them. And until others do, that is his joke. (p. 253)

Steven C. Tracy, "Simple's Great African-American Joke," in CLA Journal, *Vol. XXVII, No. 3, March, 1984, pp. 239-53.*

FURTHER READING

Anderson, Sherwood. "Paying for Old Sins." *The Nation* CXXXIX, No. 3601 (11 July 1934): 49-50.
    Review of *The Ways of White Folks* in which Anderson commends Hughes for his portrayal of black characters but criticizes him for depicting white characters as caricatures.

Bonsky, Phillip. "Humor and Hope." *Mainstream* 11, No. 1 (January 1958): 53-7.
    Positive review of *Simple Stakes a Claim* in which Bonsky focuses on Hughes's use of humor as an effective means to convey racial issues.

Bontemps, Arna. "Black and Bubbling." *The Saturday Review* XXXV, No. 14 (5 April 1952): 17.
    Laudatory review of *Laughing to Keep from Crying* by Hughes's longtime friend.

Dandridge, Rita B. "The Black Woman as a Freedom Fighter in Langston Hughes' *Simple's Uncle Sam.*" *CLA Journal* XVIII, No. 2 (December 1974): 273-83.
    Compares three women in *Simple's Uncle Sam*—Joyce, Lynn Clarisse, and Minnie—to the historical figures Booker T. Washington, Martin Luther King, Jr., and Malcolm X to show their similarities as advocates of black liberation.

Dickinson, Donald C. *A Bio-Bibliography of Langston Hughes: 1902-1967.* Hamden, Conn.: Archon Books, 1972, 273 p.
    Provides extensive information on Hughes's life and works.

Emanuel, James A. *Langston Hughes.* New York: Twayne Publishers, 1967, 192 p.
    Considered the first critical biography to avoid a sociological interpretation of Hughes's writing and to focus on serious literary analyses.

Gomes, Emmanuel. "The Crackerbox Tradition and the Race Problem in Lowell's *The Biglow Papers* and Hughes's Sketches of Simple." *CLA Journal* XXVII, No. 3 (March 1984): 254-69.
    Examines similarities and differences between the social and political satire of James Russell Lowell's *The Biglow Papers,* a collection of serialized letters that revolve around New England characters in the mid-1800s, and Hughes's Simple sketches.

Hart, Robert C. "Black-White Literary Relations in the Harlem Renaissance." *American Literature* XLIV, No. 4 (January 1973): 612-28.
    Studies relations between black and white literary figures of the 1920s, emphasizing the influence of white patrons on black writers. Hart examines Carl Van Vechten's influence on Hughes's career.

Kinnamon, Keneth. "The Man Who Created 'Simple'." *The Nation* 205, No. 19 (4 December 1967): 599-601.
    Overview of Hughes's literary career and legacy.

Klotman, Phyllis R. "Jesse B. Semple and the Narrative Art of

Langston Hughes." *The Journal of Narrative Technique* 3, No. 1 (January 1973): 66-75.

Analyzes four narrative techniques that make the Simple tales appealing to both black and white audiences.

Koprince, Susan. "Moon Imagery in *The Ways of White Folks.*" *The Langston Hughes Review* I, No. 1 (Spring 1982): 14-17.

Examines Hughes's use of the moon as a symbol of idealism and disillusionment in *The Ways of White Folks.*

Moses, Wilson Jeremiah. "More Stately Mansion: New Negro Movements and Langston Hughes' Literary Theory." *The Langston Hughes Review* IV, No. 1 (Spring 1985): 40-6.

Discusses Hughes within the context of the New Negro movement.

O'Daniel, Therman B., ed. *Langston Hughes: Black Genius—A Critical Evaluation.* New York: William Morrow & Co., 1971, 245 p.

Collection of thirteen critical essays on Hughes and a selected bibliography.

Presley, James. "The American Dream of Langston Hughes." *Southwest Review* XLVIII, No. 4 (Autumn 1963): 380-86.

Discusses both Hughes's belief in and disillusionment with the American Dream for black people as it is portrayed in his writings.

———. "The Birth of Jesse B. Semple." *Southwest Review* LVIII, No. 3 (Summer 1973): 219-25.

Provides background to the creation of Jesse B. Semple as he first appeared in Hughes's column in the *Chicago Defender.*

Rampersad, Arnold. *The Life of Langston Hughes.* 2 vols. New York: Oxford University Press, 1986-1988.

Well-received literary biography.

Redding, J. Saunders. "Emergence of the New Negro." In his *To Make a Poet Black.* 1939. Reprint, pp. 93-125. New York: Cornell University Press, 1988.

Considered the first scholar-critic of African-American literature, Redding provides an analysis of the New Negro during the Harlem Renaissance and characterizes Hughes as "the most prolific and the most representative of the new Negroes."

Van Vechten, Carl. "In the Heart of Harlem." *The New York Times Book Review* LVIII, No. 22 (31 May 1953): 5, 13.

Praises Hughes for humor and authenticity in a review of *Simple Takes a Wife.*

Williams, Melvin G. "Langston Hughes's Jesse B. Semple: A Black Walter Mitty." *Negro American Literature Forum* 10, No. 2 (Summer 1976): 66-9.

Draws a parallel between Simple and Walter Mitty—two characters who fantasize in order to defeat their humiliators.

(Theodora) Sarah Orne Jewett

1849-1909

(Also wrote the under pseudonyms A. C. Eliot, Alice Eliot, and Sarah O. Sweet) American short story writer, novelist, and poet.

Regarded as a premier writer of American regional, or local color fiction, Jewett is best known for her short stories about provincial life in New England during the late nineteenth century. Her works are often discussed in conjunction with those of other contemporary local colorists, including Harriet Beecher Stowe, Rose Terry Cooke, and Mary E. Wilkins Freeman, and she is regarded as an important contributor to the development of the local color movement. Critics concur that Jewett's finest stories are from *The Country of the Pointed Firs,* a loosely woven tapestry of character sketches about the inhabitants of a small Maine coastal village. Assigning her a distinct place in American literature, Edmund Gosse stated: "Jewett is one of the best literary artists amongst the American writers of short stories. Her composition is simple, yet full of force, while the pictures she paints of village life are inspired by a deep-felt sympathy with the common people."

Jewett was born in the rural port community of South Berwick, Maine, and was the daughter of a wealthy and respected physician. As a child she often accompanied her father on his daily rounds to patients' homes where she met many of the New England characters she later recalled in her fiction. Jewett's youth was for the most part uneventful, secure, and happy. Her father tutored her in literature and local history, encouraging her to read from his extensive library. Among the many works Jewett read during her childhood was Stowe's *The Pearl of Orr's Island* (1862), a novel often cited as a forerunner of the local color movement in American fiction. Set along the coastline of Maine, Stowe's novel led Jewett to realize that her own people and countryside were worthy literary material. Jewett was further inspired when tourism began to flourish in the region. As she explained: "The way they [the city boarders] misconstrued the country people and made game of their peculiarities fired me with indignation. I was determined to teach the world that country people were not the awkward, ignorant set those people seemed to think. I wanted the world to know their grand simple lives; and, so far as I had a mission when I first began to write, I think that was it."

Jewett began publishing short stories in 1867 under the pseudonyms A. C. Eliot, Alice Eliot, and Sarah O. Sweet. Her first notable success came just prior to her twentieth birthday when William Dean Howells accepted the short story "Mr. Bruce" for publication in the *Atlantic Monthly.* Guided by Howells's suggestions as well as by her own understanding of life in New England, Jewett subsequently produced a number of successful local color stories for the *Atlantic;* at Howells's behest, she revised and collected these stories in 1877 in her first book, *Deephaven.* The success of *Deephaven* gained Jewett many literary admirers, and her close association with the *Atlantic Monthly* brought her frequently into contact with its editor, James T. Fields, and his wife Annie, an esteemed philanthropist and literary hostess. Jewett was

readily welcomed into the circle of eminent writers and editors who frequented the Fields's Charles Street salon in Boston. Following the deaths of Jewett's father in 1878 and James Fields in 1881, Jewett and Annie Fields cultivated what became a lifelong friendship. They traveled extensively, making several trips to Europe, during which Jewett met Alfred Tennyson, Matthew Arnold, Henry James, Christina Rossetti, and Rudyard Kipling. Although she thrived on such encounters, Jewett invariably returned to South Berwick every summer to write, believing her travels enabled her to focus more clearly on the unique aspects of her home community. In 1902 Jewett seriously injured her spine in a carriage accident. As writing was not, in her own words, "a bread and butter affair," she never returned to work. Jewett spent her remaining years in leisure, visiting and corresponding with friends. She died of a stroke in 1909.

In her fiction, Jewett considered plot and action secondary to the mood or atmosphere of a story. According to Martha Hale Shackford: "There is nothing spectacular nor very tense in her presentments of life; she shows people living simple, normal, average lives, and the tissue of their existence is not external event but slow pondering of life, and still slower exchange of comment about it." Jewett's aim was toward naturalism and she followed Gustave Flaubert's exhortation to "write of ordinary life as one writes history." Her writings about New England captured the history of its people—Yankee widows and spinsters, farmers, fishermen, and aging seamen. Growing up, Jewett listened to many tales of antebellum Maine when Berwick had flourished as a seaport. She rewrote stories she had heard from retired sea captains, including her grandfather, capturing the personalities of the original storytellers in such characters as Captain Littlepage. Jewett depicted changes in the deteriorating maritime communities with compassion, and scholars concur that the influence on her of this type of limited, nonindustrial society cannot be overestimated. Most of her stories focus upon the elderly, predominantly female population amid which she grew up and only occasionally include male personas. Her knowledge of men in general was limited, and few of her male characters are considered realistic. However, critics have praised Jewett's portraits of women. Many of her female characters are self-reliant, optimistic, and versatile; few are married. In her stories, Jewett frequently focuses upon oddities in her characters' perceptions of life. For example, in "The Queen's Twin" she comments with subtle humor on the power of the human imagination: because Abbey Martin was born on the same day as Queen Victoria, she considers herself a psychic twin to the queen and establishes a shrine in honor of her royal sister. While such tales are recognized chiefly for their humor, critics also praise the pathos and gentleness with which Jewett relates idiosyncracies of her characters.

The role of nature in Jewett's stories is significant. The natural environment never simply serves as isolated background but is integrated into the action and is often subtly evoked by characters who speak in dialect of "ellum trees" and "rosbry bushes." Critics find Jewett's most important examination of the relationship between humanity and nature in "A White Heron," a story in which a nine-year-old girl must choose between love of nature, represented by a white heron, and human love, symbolized by the approval of an urban ornithologist who wants to capture the bird. As Josephine Donovan has explained: " 'A White Heron' resolves the conflict between urban and rural by affirming the values of country life and rejecting the evils of the industrial city . . . , while at the same time acknowledging the limitations of the country world and recognizing the excitement and opportunity for growth the city represents."

Jewett continued her exploration of conflicts inherent in rural New England life in *The Country of the Pointed Firs,* a collection that reflects the major tendencies within her fiction and is regarded as her finest local color writing. Jewett achieves unity in *Pointed Firs* through her use of a single narrator—a writer from the city who visits a fictional coastal village, Dunnett Landing, and recounts her observations of the region and its inhabitants. As with the bulk of Jewett's stories, setting and character are emphasized over plot and action. Thematic conflicts that are prominent throughout Jewett's works—"female versus male" and "country versus city" (with their attending subthemes "tradition versus progress" and "pastoral versus industrial")—are here repeated and refined. Central to the collection is the narrator's landlady, Almira Todd, an herbalist who appears at times to have almost supernatural powers and whose association and identification with the local landscape is complete. Considered Jewett's most memo-

rable and representative character, Almira Todd successfully joins nature and society, embracing both with equal fervor and understanding.

Although popular interest in Jewett's stories has waned, her stature among New England local colorists is well acknowledged, and her works continue to be read, studied, and criticized in conjunction with these writers. In particular, feminist scholars of the 1970s have contributed many valuable assessments of Jewett's short stories, focusing upon her portrayal of the role of women in nineteenth-century American society. Jewett's chief contribution to American literature is considered to reside primarily in the vibrancy with which she depicted the disappearing culture of maritime New England. John Eldridge Frost concluded that Jewett brought the local color sketch "to a degree of perfection that has not been excelled. The quality of her style, especially in *The Country of the Pointed Firs,* gives her high rank among the prose writers of America."

(For further information on Jewett's life and career, see *Twentieth-Century Literary Criticism,* Vols. 1, 22; *Contemporary Authors,* Vols. 108, 127; *Something about the Author,* Vol. 15; and *Dictionary of Literary Biography,* Vols. 12, 74.)

PRINCIPAL WORKS

SHORT FICTION

Deephaven   1877
Play Days: A Book of Stories for Children   1878
Old Friends and New   1879
Country By-Ways   1881
The Mate of the Daylight, and Friends Ashore   1884
A White Heron, and Other Stories   1886
The King of Folly Island, and Other People   1888
Strangers and Wayfarers   1890
Tales of New England   1890
A Native of Winby, and Other Tales   1893
The Life of Nancy   1895
The Country of the Pointed Firs   1896; also published as *The Country of the Pointed Firs* [enlarged edition], 1910
The Queen's Twin, and Other Stories   1899
Stories and Tales. 7 vols.   (novel and short stories)   1910
The Uncollected Short Stories of Sarah Orne Jewett   1971

OTHER MAJOR WORKS

A Country Doctor   (novel)   1884
A Marsh Island   (novel)   1885
Betty Leicester: A Story for Girls   (juvenile fiction)   1890
Betty Leicester's English Xmas   (juvenile fiction)   1894; also published as *Betty Leicester's Christmas,* 1899
The Tory Lover   (novel)   1901
Verses   (poetry)   1916
Sarah Orne Jewett Letters   (letters)   1967

WILLIAM DEAN HOWELLS   (essay date 1877)

[*Howells was the chief progenitor of American Realism and the most influential American literary critic of the late nineteenth century. Through Realism, he sought to disperse the "conventional acceptations by which men live on easy terms with them-*

selves" that they might "examine the grounds of their social and moral opinions." According to Howells, to accomplish this, the writer must record detailed impressions of everyday life, endow characters with true-to-life motives, and avoid authorial comment in the narrative. An admirer of Jewett's New England idylls, Howells became her friend and literary advisor and was among the first to publish her short stories. In the following excerpt, Howells offers an appreciative review of Deephaven.]*

The gentle reader of [the *Atlantic*] cannot fail to have liked, for their very fresh and delicate quality, certain sketches of an old New England sea-port, which have from time to time appeared here during the last four years. The first was **"Shore House,"** and then there came **"Deephaven Cronies"** and **"Deephaven Excursions."** These sketches, with many more studies of the same sort of life, as finely and faithfully done, are now collected into a pretty little book called ***Deephaven,*** which must, we think, find favor with all who appreciate the simple treatment of the near-at-hand quaint and picturesque. No doubt some particular sea-port sat for Deephaven, but the picture is true to a whole class of old shore towns, in any one of which you might confidently look to find the Deephaven types. It is supposed that two young girls—whose young-girlhood charmingly perfumes the thought and observation of the whole book—are spending the summer at Deephaven, Miss Denis, the narrator, being the guest of her adored ideal, Miss Kate Lancaster, whose people have an ancestral house there; but their sojourn is only used as a background on which to paint the local life: the three or four aristocratic families, severally dwindled to three or four old maiden ladies; the numbers of ancient sea-captains cast ashore by the decaying traffic; the queer sailor and fisher folk; the widow and old-wife gossips of the place, and some of the people of the neighboring country. These are all touched with a hand that holds itself far from every trick of exaggeration, and that subtly delights in the very tint and form of reality; we could not express too strongly the sense of conscientious fidelity which the art of the book gives, while over the whole is cast a light of the sweetest and gentlest humor, and of a sympathy as tender as it is intelligent. **"Danny"** is one of the best of the sketches; and another is **"The Circus at Denby,"** which perhaps shows better than any other the play of the author's observation and fancy, with its glancing lights of fun and pathos. A sombre and touching study is that of the sad, simple life so compassionately depicted in **"In Shadow,"** after which the reader must turn to the brisk vigor and quaintness of **"Mrs. Bonny."** Bits of New England landscape and characteristic marine effects scattered throughout these studies of life vividly localize them, and the talk of the people is rendered with a delicious fidelity.

In fact, Miss Jewett here gives proof of such powers of observation and characterization as we hope will some day be turned to the advantage of all of us in fiction. Meanwhile we are very glad of these studies, so refined, so simple, so exquisitely imbued with a true feeling for the ideal within the real.

William Dean Howells, in an originally unsigned review of "Deephaven," in The Atlantic Monthly, *Vol. XXXIX, No. CCXXXVI, June, 1877, p. 759.*

EDWARD M. CHAPMAN   (essay date 1913)

[*Chapman was an American author and cleric. In the following excerpt originally published in the* Yale Review *in 1913,*

he admires Jewett's portrayal of the people, landscapes, and seasons of New England.]

[Jewett] was of New England ancestry, birth, and training. Her home was in a New England village and she always kept it there. The "atmosphere" of her books was the atmosphere she breathed. Her "types" were not so much the result of study and abstraction from observed subjects as the transcription of direct appeals which the life of her neighbors made to her own heart. Born thus through contact of life with life, they not only embody various human qualities, but they really possess souls. The reader can rarely speak of them as "quaint" or "bleak" or anything else that merely accords with literary convention. They are too personal to submit themselves to easy definition; so human, indeed, as generally to be humane.

This intimacy with her material—an intimacy that sometimes approaches identity in the Wordsworthian manner—is shown at once as the reader looks out through Miss Jewett's eyes upon the face of the country. She never bores us with mere description for description's sake; nor does she seem to care very much about imparting information concerning New Hampshire hamlets and the coast of Maine. Least of all does she deem it necessary to catalogue beast, bird, and flower in its appropriate season. These things are all there. New Hampshire hillsides and Maine islands with their appropriate flora and fauna are as clear to see as though one had lived among them; but the grace of Miss Jewett's art appears in the fact that her references to them come to the reader almost as reminders of past experience. Instead of bald description, she chooses the gentler way of reminiscence. In *A Marsh Island,* for instance, she shows us the icebound "salt-meadows" after a fashion at once so realistic and yet incidental that any man who has carried a gun over them in winter finds himself wondering that a woman, however sturdy a walker, could possibly have come to know them so intimately. But Miss Jewett's happy gifts enabled her so to catch the spirit of a world like this as to bring back old and veritable experiences of winter, not so much by description as by implication. Nor can any one look upon these same scenes with her under the oppression of an August sun without a sense of dog-day languor, teased by the buzzing of insects. It was on such an afternoon that, in the tale called **"Marsh Rosemary,"** Ann Floyd's tragedy began as Jerry Lane walked down the long road across the marshes, while the air quivered and flickered with the heat, the tide inlets exhaled their muddy odors, and the big green-headed flies basked securely on the back of his Sunday waistcoat.

Who that knows New England has not seen it all—seen it, some of us think, at its debilitating and sultry worst,—this lean, sinewy, virile, and generally wholesome land aping the tropics? Who cannot remember too, when they are pointed out, the elements of beauty so often overlooked by languid dog-day eyes? The dark brown pods of the "blackgrass," the soft pussy clover of the highway side, the bronze gold of the "red-salt," the green of the lesser sedges, and the mingled green and scarlet of the "mutton-sass," are all there for the yellow butterflies to flutter over; and there too is the Marsh Rosemary. Few seem to know this brave and cheerful little plant of the marshes and almost none have sung it. It stands sturdily upright amid the lassitudes of August bearing upon its tree-like stems a cloud of lavender flowers; and in late October under the pelting of a great storm, it may be seen just as sturdy as in summer and almost as cheerful, not only by contrast with the low estate of its neighbors, but because after its petals have gone the little whitish grey residuum of each flower preserves the spray-like appearance of the plant and almost persuades the onlooker that it is still in bloom. Now Miss Jewett is sometimes charged with taking too sentimental a view of New England life and character. In her recently published letters there appears a tendency to overwork the adjective "dear," and it is said that love for the land of her birth reacting upon a thoroughly feminine nature, left her with a keener vision for the pathetic than for the really tragic elements in the world about her. It may be admitted that she loved best the peaceful pastures and quiet weather of hum-drum and half-humorous prosperity; yet the fact remains that she could not only picture the rigor of January and the lan-guor of August as relentlessly as Mr. Hardy, but she could quite as readily introduce Humanity hand in hand with Trou-ble—and poignant trouble too.

To illustrate this we have only to recur to her Marsh Rose-mary and the chapter in a woman's life which it symbolizes. Ann Floyd was brave, honest, independent, kindly, and in outward aspect perhaps a little hard. To her, busy despite the heat upon that August afternoon, came Jerry Lane, an old ac-qaintance, shiftless, self-confident, and scheming. She was lonely; he good-natured and with as many tales as Othello,

> Of moving accidents by flood and field.

Her hungry heart was at last too much for her judgment and she took him for better, for worse; for better, as it seemed at first, and then for worse, as the old shiftlessness came back. Finally, after long dependence upon her, he drifted off to sea again. Upon his going, Ann grew old as though an autumn frost had fallen upon her suddenly; so that when, instead of his promised return, news came that the *Susan Barnes* was lost, her elderly widowed estate seemed almost as natural to herself as to her neighbors. Yet in a sense her life was richer and more useful than ever. Still a little grim of aspect, the in-nate kindness of her heart flowed out in a hundred channels of friendly and neighborly service. Then, after some interval, it was revealed to her that her ne'er-do-well had deserted his schooner before the wreck and was living with another woman in the Provinces. The shock was overwhelming, but there was no hysteria; only a grim resolve to go to Schediac and expose the man's faithlessness. She went and found his residence, but before knocking looked in by the early evening lamplight to see him, care-free as ever, sitting with wife and child in a comfortable home. The sight of the other woman, young, innocent, and competent, strangely touched Ann Floyd's heart. She could not wreck the happiness of inno-cence even for the sake of punishing a wrong-doer. As well as she could see through her tears and the rain that fell in sympathy with them, her path lay back to her home and her old work again. She followed it and the story leaves her in her own house resolutely though tearfully putting cup and saucer upon the table for her solitary meal—Ann Floyd, tailoress, once more.

"Who can laugh at my Marsh Rosemary," asks Miss Jewett, "or who can cry for that matter? The grey primness of the plant is made up from a hundred colors if you look close enough to find them. This Marsh Rosemary stands in her own place, and holds her . . . tiny blossoms towards the same sun that the pink lotus blooms for, and the white rose." The note of tragedy here is as clearly sounded and as nobly restrained as in the close of George Gissing's *The Nether World;* while Miss Jewett's vision of her Marsh Rosemary is

that of Wordsworth singing "The Primrose of the Rock" or "The Small Celandine."

She shows a like intimate acquaintance with the fickleness of the New England spring, whose promises are so certainly and repeatedly contradicted by recurrent cold. The Connecticut saying that the frogs must be frozen up three times before spring can be finally trusted, was very likely unknown to her, though her knowledge was so wide and unaffected that any word spoken out of native experience might seem at home upon her pages. She never grieves over the baffling variety of our weather or rails at its frequent harshness. Frances Thompson's whimsical complaint about "the snivel of our ca-tarrhal May and the worthless I O U which a sharping En-glish spring annually presents to its confiding creditors" finds no echo from this candid friend of New England. She knew, however, that there is little lushness or softness in spring's ad-vent, and the April night in **"Miss Tempy's Watchers"** when Sarah Ann Binson and Mrs. Crowe care for that good woman's home and person preparatory to her funeral, is per-fect in its kind. It was upon the whole a quiet night, and yet "the spring wind whistled in the window crack, now and then, and buffeted the little house in a gusty way that had a sort of companionable effect." No one but a true child of New England could have written that sentence. The "literary per-son," however sympathetic, would have called the whistling in the window "eerie" and told us of the wind's "moaning" as it sighed about the house. Not so Miss Jewett. She knew April winds well enough to read June's promise in them, and even when they whispered around a house of mourning at midnight, their message was only half sad, because they blew the fire within into a brighter flame and heartened those who watched beside it into speaking of Miss Tempy Dent's good deeds to man and nature alike. (pp. 55-8)

A deal of New England's best efficiency is suggested by the gift of this lonely woman to "sense" things, to see the point, to nurse a reluctant quince tree into blooming, and then, when it has borne its "apernful" of quinces, most austere of fruits, to extract their last atom of goodness and preserve it—for others rather than herself.

I have dealt thus at length with Miss Jewett's treatment of the revolving year for two reasons. Weather plays so large a part in New England life; there is so much of it to the square mile that a genuine love of weather for its own sake is needful to any sympathetic acquaintance with the face of the country. This Miss Jewett felt in high degree. Then too, this weather, largely interpreted, has played no inconsiderable part in the development of New England character. It has represented an ever present condition—generally a hard condition—which must needs be patiently endured or ingeniously turned to account. This also she has realized and made much of; in-deed she has gone so far as to develop an almost mystic sense for the symbolic nature of the seasons. Her characters may come upon the scene, hand in hand with trouble, like Mr. Hardy's, or humorously rejoicing in modest success. But whether pinched by the cold of winter and poverty like the two gently bred sisters in **"The Town Poor,"** or lying dead in the lonely April night like Miss Tempy, these creatures of her brain seem to rule their fate and to retain the mastery of their souls. So in general the occasional tragedy and the fre-quent comedy of these New England tales are normal and wholesome, because, whatever the philosophers may say, men live and act in them as though their wills were free. This makes the poignancy of **"The Failure of David Berry"** endurable; it adds a note of grace to the dominant idea of **"The Queen's Twin"**; and it fills such farce as **"The Courting of Sister Wisby"** full of honest laughter.

It remains to say something of Miss Jewett's acquaintance with what Mr. Hardy calls "The Custom of the Country." In her later books, notably ***The Country of the Pointed Firs,*** she pictures the Maine coast, the Maine summer, and the people of the islands and harbor towns. Again her eye is keen for the characteristics of the weather. She notes the beauty of such August days as at once complete the summer and suggest autumn. "There was something shining in the air, and a kind of lustre on the water and the pasture grass—a northern look that except at this moment of the year, one must go far to seek."

What child of New England does not remember that "northern look," in no sense bleak or forbidding, but the aspect of a country, cool, ripe, and clean, stripped of the lushness of June, yet far from the bareness of winter? It is in this book too that she brings us into closest intimacy with two people who exactly correspond to such a setting—Mrs. Blackett of the Island, and her middle-aged son, William. They are mother and brother to Mrs. Todd, who serves Miss Jewett in the Dunnet Landing stories as the chorus did the Greek dramatists, with her comment upon life's passing show and her ready philosophy. William and his mother are among the great figures of New England fiction in their delicacy and fidelity. They are unskilled in the ways of the world and their simplicity follows the pleasant path between the fields of humor and pathos with frequent though rarely forced excursions into both. It is, however, a simplicity that enhances rather than compromises their native dignity and purity of soul. Every true country minister or doctor in New England knows their type and counts the knowledge a chief reward of his profession. William is tall, lean, bronzed, and of that reticent shyness which often characterizes men of fine quality who do all their work alone and some of it in peril of their lives. At heart the mother is like him, but brisk, cheerful, and frank in manner; while beneath the surface there are great depths of reverence, tenderness, and such an experience of life's realities as makes knowledge of the ways of the world quite a negligible thing. No reader who knows the New England coast and has had natural access to its homes will forget the chapter in which mother and son sing together for their two visitors.

Such glimpses as she gives us of the Blacketts on their island and such a memorial as President Eliot provided for a Maine friend and neighbor in his essay on John Gilley, are the better worth preserving because the day of the old-time farmer-fisherman is passing. The influx of summer visitors, the failure of some fisheries and the changed character of others, the advent of truck and dairy farming, and the influences exerted by increased facilities of communication and travel, have doubtless done much to raise the general standard of comfort; they probably have improved the average of intelligence, and possibly have bettered rural morals; but it is also true that the rare, fine, William Blackett type has retired before them. He will live long in the memory of any who may have seen him in the flesh, and longer yet in ***The Country of the Pointed Firs.*** So true is Miss Jewett to New England manners and customs in such tales as these that even the occasional note of exaggeration is likely to put the critic to confusion by unexpectedly justifying itself. Most discriminating readers have probably thought 'Lijah Tilley, the old farmer-fisherman who

solaced his widowed estate by knitting, and habitually referred to his late wife as "poor dear," to be rather sadly overdrawn. " 'Lijah's worthy enough," says Mrs. Todd. "I do esteem 'Lijah, but he's a ploddin' man." "So do I esteem him," comments the critical reader; "but the knitting needles and the 'poor dear' are not quite in character"; when, lo, the recent publication of Miss Jewett's letters shows this knitting and mourning widower to have been a man of veritable flesh and blood. Her insight was so keen and her touch so sure that this type of sketch represents her real *métier* and she rarely departed from it without loss of distinction. Indeed when she brought a character to Boston for a visit, as in **"The Life of Nancy,"** the story at once took on too "improving" a complexion to represent her best work. The Irish tales were well enough in their way and their dialect was managed with rather notable skill, but they might have been written by another than Miss Jewett. Her novels are of course little more than a series of sketches strung upon the slenderest thread of plot, and there are occasional passages in them which in their treatment of the village folk barely escape sounding the fatal note of patronage. This note was, however, quite foreign to her best work and only comes in here and there when for the moment she is betrayed by literary convention.

On the contrary, **"The Hiltons' Holiday,"** a tale which merely recounts the visit of a poor man with his two little girls to the neighboring county town, is perfect in its kind. Its adventure is the least imaginable. The anxious wife and mother cleans and dresses her children, sees them sedately seated in the farm wagon with their father and watches them drive off. They depart, arrive, return;—and that is all there is to it; yet each trivial incident by the way is told with such truth to human nature in general and to New England's best human nature in particular that their author writes herself down $\pi o\iota\eta\tau\eta\delta$—creator. She breathes upon these humble folk and they become living souls. On their way up the town street they stop that the children may see the home of a prominent and highly respected citizen who had been a schoolmate of John Hilton's mother. As they linger, Judge Masterson comes out of his gate, recognizes the father, greets him with grave politeness and a reminiscence of old days, speaks cordially to the children, and goes his way. John Hilton is a sturdy, independent son of the soil who will do obeisance to no man's wealth or presumption; but his deference to eminent learning and the honor of an upright judge is as real as his delight in the great man's personal greeting. "Now," he says to the wondering girls, "you have seen one of the first gentlemen of the country. It was worth comin' twice as far."

This self-respect which is so genuine as to permit in turn unfeigned respect for all honorable men and things, not only characterizes Miss Jewett's men and women of the better type, but marks her own work. Her treatment of the Deephaven congregation—the eminent respectability of the Widow Ware and Miss Experience Hull, the old sea captains bronzed by sun and spindrift, the minister so often choosing his illustrations from the sea, and always praying for those who go down to it in ships—is touched with a fine reverence. She sees the humor in it all but perceives beneath it the greater qualities of constancy, courage, and faith that give character to a people.

Perhaps this is nowhere better illustrated than in **"An Only Son,"** which for more reasons than I have space to enumerate seems to me to be one of her greatest stories. Its hero is a New England Deacon. Now the Deacon may be taken as the crux of those who attempt New England tales, and rarely is the writer found who can compass him. It is the fashion to make him hypocritical, sour, puritanical, or in some other way either absurd or ridiculous. The mere smart writer, learned in literary convention but ignorant of the custom of the country, does not stop to consider that the New Englander, whatever else he may be, is rarely fool enough to choose from among the men whom he has known all his life either a simpleton, a hypocrite, or a curmudgeon to officiate in the church.

The particular Deacon who figures in **"An Only Son"** is selectman as well as church officer, and a farmer too in a small and not especially thrifty way. The meeting with his two colleagues on a midsummer day, the slow progress of business, the final decision by the Board to pay a town note, and all the rest of it, are perfectly told, down to the patient waiting of the three old horses for their respective masters, and the Deacon's plodding homeward in the dust, the money to make the payment in his pocket. He has one son whose soul is so wrapped up in machinery that the farm work suffers, and a bit of broken fence by the wayside reminded the father of this neglect so that he reached home rather heavy-hearted. He put the town money under his pillow, not unnoticed as it happened by the boy, and as afternoon came on found himself alone, the niece who kept his house having meanwhile gone to spend the night at a distant family reunion, while the son had disappeared in the direction of the town. Then the note of half petty sadness which has so far characterized the story deepens into that of genuine tragedy as the father discovers that the money is gone. It is in her treatment of this old and lonely man's experience under the shadow of his boy's disgrace that Miss Jewett shows her greatness as a revealer of the heart's secrets. The Deacon's impatience has vanished; the note of pettiness is silent; and instead appear the deep convictions of a heart that would have chosen death rather than dishonor, and the self-reproach of an irritable but sincere man reviewing the past and perceiving too late how he might have shown more sympathy and patience toward the son who is to bring his grey hairs with sorrow to the grave. His evening chores, done with meticulous care, and the old man's attempt to prolong them because they deaden thought, become solemn episodes in a soul's tragedy. The contrast that Browning suggested in "An Epistle" between the anxiety of Lazarus over his son's chance word as compared with his calm anticipation of the coming of the Roman armies is illustrated here by plain New England daylight.

There is no need to follow the story through; to tell how the Deacon made solemn pilgrimage to an old friend and raised the money needed to make good the defalcation; nor how his housekeeper, returning full of the gossip of adventure, found his wallet exactly where she had put it, when in her housewifely zeal to leave him with clean bed clothes, she had discovered and cared for it; nor how the boy himself came back from town half apologetic for his negligence and excusing it a little by the shyly imparted news that his long-brooded-over invention had at last found commercial acceptance and financial backing. The lifting of this incubus, like its imposition, was borne quietly so far as outward signs went; but the heart responded with a gladness which sent the old man out to the family burying ground to lift up his prayer of thanksgiving and penitence beside the grave of the boy's mother, and then brought him back to confer cheerfully with the boy himself— about painting the farmhouse blinds. Altogether it is a memorable picture of New England character. Its humor, in which the story abounds, its seriousness, its reserve, its overanxiety

and too quick premonition of evil, are all true to the elder custom of the country.

Like Jane Austen, Sarah Orne Jewett was at her best when thus painting her "two inches square of ivory." She exercised, too, an artist's privilege in choosing subjects that seemed to her worth painting. There is no realistic setting forth of rustic squalor, though degeneracy exists in New England hamlets as in most rural communities. There is nothing either of the grim fatalism which Mr. Hardy has done so much to popularize and which must finally prove to be the element in his work most vulnerable to the tooth of time. But judged by his perhaps involuntary canons, such a story as this with its delineation of New England's summer face, of people who have wrought their lives into its life, and of the established habits of a countryside will go far toward placing Miss Jewett in the front rank of those who have portrayed their native land. Buttressed by its sister tales it makes that place secure. (pp. 58-63)

Edward M. Chapman, "The New England of Sarah Orne Jewett," in Appreciation of Sarah Orne Jewett: 29 Interpretive Essays, *edited by Richard Cary, Colby College Press, 1973, pp. 52-63.*

PERRY D. WESTBROOK (essay date 1951)

[*Westbrook is an American biographer and academic. In the following excerpt from his critical study* Acres of Flint: Sarah Orne Jewett and Her Contemporaries *originally published in 1951, he comments on two stories from* The King of Folly Island, and Other People, *discerning elements of tragedy not evident in Jewett's more popular short story collections.*]

Jewett at the age of eight years.

Jewett was not an incurable Pollyanna, despite her Victorian—or should we say merely human—tendency to overlook things that she did not wish to see. Although she could rarely refrain from romanticizing her recluses and neurotics, she sometimes rather grudgingly recognized the futility of their lives and, less often, the tragedy of them, particularly where other people involved were being made unhappy. Examples of this will not be found, however, in her best-known books, *Deephaven* and *The Country of the Pointed Firs.* One must turn to a volume composed apparently in a less optimistic frame of mind when Jewett was between forty and fifty years old, *The King of Folly Island and Other People.* Two stories from this volume illustrate their author at her most realistic if not her most artistic.

The title piece is the story of an inhabitant of the fictitious John's Island, twelve miles off the Maine coast, who becomes disgruntled with the meanness of his neighbors and buys the even more remote Folly Island with the purpose of living there in complete isolation. Here he moves with his wife and daughter, swearing never to set foot on any other man's land again. He fulfills his vow. He manages to build a comfortable house and clear an adequate farm; he sets trawls and takes his catch to market, doing his business from his boat at the wharf. One shares with Jewett an admiration for the man's self-sufficiency and steadfastness. We are not surprised to find

> an air of distinction and dignity about this King of Folly Island, and uncommon directness and independence. He was the son and heir of the old Vikings who had sailed that stormy coast and discovered its harborage and its vines five hundred years before Columbus. . . .

But as the story proceeds the King is seen in a slightly less favorable light. For him the life on Folly Island has been rewarding; he has lived up to his vow and gained recognition for doing so, and he has known the satisfaction of wresting out of nature single-handedly a life for himself and his family. But for his wife and daughter the experience has been death. More isolated than he, since in his fishing and business transactions he has human contact, the mother dies early and is laid away in a corner of the fields. The daughter, who minds the loneliness less because she has known nothing else, becomes ill of consumption. But her father, who had driven off and ducked in the water the only suitor she ever had, would sacrifice his daughter to the sanctity of his vow by refusing to take her to a more healthful climate. Here Jewett perceives, but does not utilize, the rudiments of true tragedy—the essentially noble man or woman marred by a fatal flaw in character. "This man, who should be armed and defended by his common-sense, was yet made weak by some prejudice or superstition. What could have warped him in this strange way?" she asks. Because she couldn't or wouldn't probe more deeply for an answer in her own question, **"The King of Folly Island"** falls short of greatness.

Another story in the same volume, **"The Landscape Chambers,"** puts a similar question. Jewett, who tells the story in the first person, has been riding far into the country. Because of the unexpected lameness of her horse she is forced to put up in a ramshackle Colonial mansion inhabited by an equally dilapidated man and his daughter. The man is kind and expert in his care of the lame horse, and the rider remains for several nights in the home. Gradually the dreary drama being performed by these two forlorn actors reveals itself. The man

is not only a miser, but a monomaniac, convinced, like some character in Hawthorne, that he is living under an ancestral curse. Quite correctly Jewett finds the pitiable part of the story to be the daughter's misery as an enforced participant of her father's madness.

The mood of these stories, it will be seen, is very different from that of the sketches of eccentrics in *The Country of the Pointed Firs.* Yet the frequently made criticism that Jewett cannot write tragedy remains just. The necessary psychological insight is always lacking; we are never brought face to face with the agony of these warped minds. Another, perhaps more serious lack is the absence of any great issues in her stories of this type. What she does achieve is largely through atmosphere, and at times this achievement is so great as to approach the mood, if not the profundity and significance, of tragedy. In *The King of Folly Island* a single scene not only sets the atmosphere of dreary isolation but also sounds the solemn, sombre note that is the essence of all tragic writing. The sick girl is standing on the shore with a spyglass watching a "floating funeral" set out from a neighboring island. There was

> the coffin with its black pall in a boat rowed by four men, who had pushed out a little way from the shore, and other boats near it. From the low, gray house near the water came a little group of women stepping down across the rough beach and getting into their boats; then all fell into a rude sort of orderliness, the hearse-boat going first, and the procession went away across the wide bay toward the main-land.

It is such description as this, to be found in even her weakest stories, that lifts Sarah Orne Jewett's writings above the commonplace. One of her chief claims to reputation is her skill in atmosphere. (pp. 68-70)

> *Perry D. Westbrook, "Self-Reliance and Solitude: The Country Folk of Sarah Orne Jewett and Helen Hunt Jackson," in his* Acres of Flint: Sarah Orne Jewett and Her Contemporaries, *revised edition, The Scarecrow Press, 1981, pp. 59-70.*

MARGARET FARRAND THORP   (essay date 1966)

[*Thorp was an American journalist and critic. In the following excerpt, she discusses prominent characteristics and techniques in Jewett's short stories.*]

Deephaven does not have a plot in the usual sense of the term. It is a series of impressions of a little Maine coastal town and its inhabitants, as they are received by two lively girls in their early twenties who decide to spend the summer there because one of them has at her disposal the house of a great aunt who has recently died. Miss Brandon was so much respected in Deephaven that everyone welcomes her niece as an old friend. It seems to the young people that the society and way of life of the town are just what they were fifty years ago when it ceased to be an important seaport, but they find this a good way of life, full of interest and devoted to high standards.

The niece's friend, who tells the story, describes first **"The Brandon House"** (which resembles in many ways the Jewett house in Berwick), its furnishings, its treasures, its memories. Then she gives accounts of the various kinds of people she and her friend come to know in the town: **"My Lady Brandon and the Widow Jim," "Deephaven Society," "The Captains."**

The sketches present individuals of different types and the girls' relations with them. We listen to their conversation and hear the stories they tell, ranging from the history of their neighbors to adventures at sea to tales of second sight. There are Miss Brandon's aristocratic friends; there are old sailors—each must be addressed as Captain; there are fishermen; there are housewives of various degrees of social importance. The men are full of wisdom and salty talk, but they tend to blur a little into one another. The women are more distinctive. There is the lady of the old school, Miss Honora. There is the Widow Jim who has "an uncommon facility of speech" but has endured, courageously, hard years with a drunken husband and is known as "a willin' woman," always respected. There is Mrs. Bonny who comes down from the hills in the summertime riding on her rough-coated old horse with bags and baskets of "rosbries" tied to the saddle. There is old Miss Chauncey, her mind so dim that she thinks herself still rich and elegant as she lives in her denuded, neglected old house, sustained by the charity of her neighbors. There is Mrs. Kew, the lighthouse keeper's wife, with a fine original gift of wit and speech.

There are lively accounts, too, of **"Cunner-Fishing,"** of sailing and cross-country walking, of going to church, attending a lecture, driving to **"The Circus at Denby"** where the girls hear an illuminating conversation between the Kentucky Giantess and the lighthouse keeper's wife, who had gone to school together.

There seems to be no particular order in the telling of events or in the presentation of characters—that was an art Miss Jewett learned much later—but the young women's enthusiasm for their new friends and new experiences is refreshing and contagious. The tempo and tone of the town become very clear.

The device by which she held these people and events together Miss Jewett was to use again and again. It bears some resemblance, though it is less subtle, to Henry James's central intelligence. A visitor—usually a woman—from Boston or some other part of the outside world comes to Maine and settles for a time in Deephaven, or Grafton, or Dunnet Landing. She meets the most interesting inhabitants of the village, learns their histories, and often makes them into friends. She delights in the old houses she visits and is captivated by the beauty of the austere fields, woods, and sea, so that she presents both narrative and background.

In **Deephaven,** unfortunately, the actual narrator, who is fairly self-effacing, is concerned not only to tell her stories but to make us love her companion, Kate, and admire the way in which she endears herself to different types of people. This puts, from time to time, more emphasis on the double central intelligence than is good for it, but the device of an observer slightly detached but interested is admirable. The weakness is that this central intelligence cannot really function alone; too many of the episodes to be related occurred long before her arrival. It becomes necessary to add an assistant intelligence, an older relative or some longtime resident of the community who knows all the history and legend and can impart them to an eager newcomer.

As a variant on the summer visitor Miss Jewett liked to send back to Maine someone who had roots there but had not lived in the state for a long time. Important among these is the **"Native of Winby,"** now senator from Kansota, who makes

a surprise visit to his old school and then to an elderly widow whom he might once have married.

Nineteen years later, when she was writing **The Country of the Pointed Firs** (1896), Miss Jewett was using her visitor device with real skill. The intelligence there is a woman from Boston who has settled in Dunnet Landing as a quiet place to write during the summer. Her response to the people and the stories she encounters is swift and warm but this is not insisted on, as it is in **Deephaven;** it is only implied, so that she does not intrude upon the tale she is telling. Involvement and detachment are beautifully balanced. The assistant narrator, the local herbwoman, is the most interesting of all the narrator assistants, one of the best characters, in fact, Miss Jewett ever drew.

Another literary instrument for which she was to be much admired Miss Jewett used first in **Deephaven:** her accurate and effective employment of Maine speech. Her ear and her memory had been recording it unconsciously ever since she was a little girl and when she came to reproduce it on the printed page she devised a simple method of presenting it to the reader without the cumbersome misspellings so frequently resorted to by the local colorists, even sometimes by a writer as accomplished as Harriet Beecher Stowe.

Miss Jewett's chief tool is the apostrophe, to indicate a dropped final *g* (goin'), or a blurred *a* (same's I always do), or the pronunciation of a word like v'y'ge. She uses it, too, to indicate the shortened vowel sound so characteristic of Maine: co't, bo't, flo't. In addition to this she has a rich knowledge of characteristic words and phrases, some of them very old: "They beseeched me after supper till I let 'em go"; "bespoke"; "master hard"; "master pretty"; "a power of china"; "I'd rather tough it out alone"; "There she goes now, do let's pray her by"; "It allays creeps me cold all over"; "You're gettin' to be as lean as a meetin'-house fly."

One is impressed often by the subtle variations her dialect presents, differences in education and culture, between the young and the very old, between men and women. Sometimes Miss Jewett remarks on the relative social position of two characters she is presenting and this distinction within democracy is reflected by differences in speech.

In the handful of Irish stories the language is not nearly so convincing. Miss Jewett had heard the brogue all her life, chiefly from family servants, but she did not think in it or even, apparently, take an interest in it. As she sets it down it seems correct enough but contrived, not overheard. She records it with a fair amount of restraint but it seems always a little thicker than it ought to be, as though the personages were moving on a stage, not along a country road.

With the occasional French-Canadian characters at whom she tried her hand she is very timid. The Canadians were beginning to come across the border into Maine but not yet to settle, simply to make some money and go home, so that they were not a real part of state life. Of French-Canadian villages Miss Jewett knew something, for she made several trips to Quebec and observed with all her good curiosity the St. Laurent countryside and community life so different from the American. But she did not know it, of course, and what she writes is tentative and generalized. In **"Little French Mary,"** a very slight sketch of a six-year-old daughter of French-Canadians whose pretty affectionate ways charm the old men who sit about the post-office stove in a Maine village, the child has French manners and features but she speaks scarcely two sentences. In **"Mère Pochette,"** set in a French-Canadian village, there is very little dialogue though a good deal of direct report of the dominant character's thinking. The phraseology falls too often into the tiresome form of English translation of the French idiom: "She will be incapable . . . to bring up an infant of no gifts." The story is an uninteresting one, anyway, of a grandmother who finally repents her mistake in breaking up a true love affair.

These dialects never became a serious problem, for Miss Jewett wrote only a few stories about the Irish and the Canadians. What mattered in **Deephaven** and in the later stories was the Maine speech, and her use of that, as I have said, delighted both her readers and the editors who were interested in her literary development. The three particularly concerned to help her were Horace Scudder, at that time editor of the *Riverside,* Howells, the novelist-editor, and Thomas Bailey Aldrich, poet, story writer, and editor of the *Atlantic,* who gave her all the guidance and assistance they could. She asked them many questions and listened with respect to their advice though she did not always follow it. She was quite accurately aware of her own abilities and limitations. One of the points on which she differed with her advisers most strongly was the matter of plot. They urged her to enlarge her sketches to something more nearly resembling the currently popular magazine story and she knew that at that kind of invention she had no skill at all. "I have no dramatic talent," she wrote to Scudder in 1873. "It seems to me I can furnish the theater, and show you the actors and the scenery, but there never is any play." When she tried to make a "play" the result was either sentimental or melodramatic. She contrived sudden inheritances, unfaithful lovers, missing young men who return suddenly rich, wayward daughters who come home to die. There are even thieves and drunkards.

Yet sometimes a preposterous situation produces a convincing story. In **"A Lost Lover"** all the town of Longfield knows that Miss Horatia had a lover who was lost at sea. The young cousin who comes to visit her one summer is full of curiosity about the romance but Miss Horatia is thoroughly reserved and only a few facts are to be gleaned from Melissa, the devoted family servant. The affair, if it was a real love affair, took place very rapidly many years before when Miss Horatia was on a visit to Salem. The young man went off to sea and his ship was never heard from again.

One morning during the young cousin's visit a tramp comes by asking for food. While he eats he talks freely with Miss Horatia about himself, his bad luck, shipwrecks, craving for drink, and general discouragement. He does not recognize her but she gradually becomes aware who he is. When he leaves she faints, but tells her cousin it is the heat. "God forgive him," she says to herself and takes up her lonely life again.

"The Lost Lover" is an exception. The components of a Jewett story are usually much simpler. The incidents evolve perhaps from two characters in conversation or from a character in relation to an old house or a community. A typical plot is **"Miss Tempy's Watchers"** in which two elderly women keep the traditional guard, the night before the funeral, over the body of a mutual friend. They install themselves in the kitchen, work at their knitting, and talk about Miss Tempy to whom both of them had been devoted. The circumstances make them speak more openly than they normally would. Nothing happens, but from the conversation emerge three definite and interesting New England characters and some il-

luminating information on the qualities of generosity and "closeness."

This construction from everyday materials makes the Jewett stories seem more durable than the in many ways comparable tales of Mary E. Wilkins Freeman and Rose Terry Cooke. The plots these writers contrive are ingeniously interesting or amusing, but the joints of their manufacture are too often evident. They are made; they do not grow. Miss Jewett's plots seem inevitable, not something she has invented but something she has seen or overheard or been told of by a friend. It is because she had to manufacture the plots of her Irish and French-Canadian stories that they lack the authenticity of her tales of Maine. (pp. 18-24)

> *Margaret Farrand Thorp, in her* Sarah Orne Jewett, *University of Minnesota Press, Minneapolis, 1966, 48 p.*

RICHARD CARY (essay date 1971)

[*An American biographer, editor, and academic, Cary has written several critical studies of Jewett and has edited collections of her short stories and letters. In the following excerpt from an essay originally published in the* Colby Library Quarterly *in 1971, he surveys Jewett's short fiction, focusing on her character portrayals and literary technique in stories from* The Uncollected Short Stories of Sarah Orne Jewett (1971).]

With complete intrepidity, it may be stated that no fewer than seventeen of the forty-four stories in **The Uncollected Short Stories** are up to Miss Jewett's optimum level. To take the bull by the horns, they are: **"Stolen Pleasures," "A Guest at Home," "Miss Manning's Minister," "A Garden Story," "The Growtown 'Bugle,' " "Mrs. Parkins's Christmas Eve," "An Every-Day Girl," "A Change of Heart," "The Gray Mills of Farley," "The Parshley Celebration," "A Landlocked Sailor," "The Foreigner," "A Born Farmer," "The Honey Tree," "Sister Peacham's Turn," "The Lost Turkey," "A Spring Sunday."** Leaving aside inevitable differences of opinion, these stories represent Miss Jewett in her finer vein of psychological sympathy, nativist perception, and developed suppleness of style. The intimacy of her knowledge about people and places which radiates in these stories lodges them in the sturdiest tradition of regional writing, while her profound insight into human motivation invests them with universality. She had marked regard for the significance of the ordinary and educed from its daily iterations extraordinary fables of the world. The house to house trek of little Debby Gaines in **"An Empty Purse"** is an unheralded mission of Christ *redivivus.*

The first short story Miss Jewett published is **"Jenny Garrow's Lovers"** in *The Flag of Our Union,* January 18, 1868, under the pen name of A. C. Eliot. Long misidentified as "Lucy Garron's Lovers" and sometimes confused with the first story she wrote at fourteen—an unfinished romp called **"Philip and Margie"**—it was left unmentioned by F. O. Matthiessen (*Sarah Orne Jewett,* 1929) in his account of her beginnings as a writer, most likely because he was unaware of its existence. In light of her subsequent development, Miss Jewett's own silence about **"Jenny"** may be construed as a desire to forget that this youthful indiscretion did irrevocably exist. Staged in unfamiliar England, caparisoned with lords and ladies, awash with incident, it is a far cry from the line she adopts and perfects later. The plot proceeds by a series of melodramatic spasms, quite in keeping with the frenetic talk and doomful mood. Every person except the female narrator is papier maché. Margery Blake, precursor of the Jewett persona who reappears in different masks in so many of her stories, usurps the opening. She pleads inexperience at the craft of writing, grumbles generally at the queer caboodle of authors, then shrugs off the whole matter somewhat petulantly, somewhat defensively, perhaps a necessary camouflage for the scared neophyte launching her first literary vessel. Margery also interjects herself and her sentiments gratuitously throughout the action, capping all with the final line, "How do you like my story?" Although Thackeray's reduction to puppetry at the close of *Vanity Fair* tempts comparison, there is less of his classical detachment here than sheer adolescent egoism. It rings frivolous after such adversity. Sarah Orne Jewett had a lot to unlearn.

"The Girl With the Cannon Dresses" came out in *Riverside Magazine,* August 1870. In the interval since **"Jenny Garrow's Lovers"** Miss Jewett had published **"Mr. Bruce"** and **"The Shipwrecked Buttons,"** neither relevant to her ultimate accomplishment. The first is a transparent pseudo-high-comedy hoax in a city setting; the second, strictly for junior consumption. Thus, **"The Girl With the Cannon Dresses"** is in point of time the first of Miss Jewett's stories to adumbrate her future course, a distinction improperly accorded the *Deephaven* sketches, which did not begin to emerge until three years later. **"Dresses"** is the first of her six publications to bear her own name. It abounds in strong autobiographical parallels: the narrator Alice Channing (rhythm from Sarah Jewett, appellative from Alice Eliot) is sickly; has a mother, sister, and father (though not a doctor); lives in a sea-oriented town; at 18 reverts to little-girl ways; is fascinated by nature lore; and is cognizant of a reciprocal father-daughter partiality.

In this story Miss Jewett introduces most of the local-color elements that she gradually masters during the next quarter-century and brings to a crest in *The Country of the Pointed Firs* (1896). There is the major theme of conflict between town and country, and Miss Jewett's roseate dream of reconciling the two; there is the unblinking appreciation of nature's physical beauty and spiritual beneficence; the discovery of country virtues by city visitors; the self-assured, ascendant female and the taciturn, acquiescent male; the quizzical child with immense aboriginal potentials; the lackadaisical plot; the resistance to time and change in an idyllic backwater; the concurrent surrender to incursive modernity; the forfeiture of unrealized individuality to social conformity. Dulcidora Bunt is the forerunner of a train of preternaturally wise moppets who grow by stages into Polly Finch, Esther Hight, and the nonpareil Almira Todd, or in the more desolate trend of Joanna Todd, Ann Floyd, and the Dulham sisters. **"Dresses"** lacks the specificity of nature detail which Miss Jewett limns so tellingly later, and a residue of the melodramatic stains the first encounter of Alice and Dulcy. Nevertheless, some of the underbrush has been cleared away and the route to Miss Jewett's cardinal competency becomes visible.

Her next expeditions into the heart of nature's liaison with man are **"The Shore House"** (1873), pilot of the *Deephaven* sketches, and **"Miss Sydney's Flowers"** (1874), which she duly collected. Sometime in the 1880s (exact date undetermined), and possibly before those two, Miss Jewett published **"Stolen Pleasures,"** transitional in style and innovative in point of view. Melodrama still haunts the tone and Miss Jewett displays rather raw bias in her contrast of the Stinces, un-

savory towners, and Johnny Weber, country boy working in a machine shop. But increasing strength is perceivable in the characterization. Johnny's wife, vacillating between the catchpenny glamor of the Stinces and allegiance to her husband's homelier values, creates a shifting fulcrum upon which the unequal city-country conflict turns. Johnny's mother, an archetypal figure of earth, counsels him with grave, indisputable sapience. In the face of her disillusionment with the Stinces' slick, city-bred morals and her exposure to "dear, old-fashioned, simple country life" in Vermont, it does not surprise that Johnny's wife elects to return to the upland farm of his birth. The silver poplar in Johnny's backyard certifies the spirit of nature persisting within him despite the drabness deepening around him. In Part II Miss Jewett swerves without warning for a single paragraph only into the immediate present tense, obliterating all distance between protagonist and reader. The effect is peculiarly disturbing, as of a screen ripped swiftly aside, the reader catapulted headlong into proceedings abruptly magnified and palpitant, stark light laying bare the privacy of one's own dread: "Hallo, there is a folded piece of white paper pinned to the table cloth." This device of sudden cinematic closeup she utilizes again with unfailing shock, most notably in **"A White Heron."**

Miss Jewett's conviction that a mystic affinity exists between man and nature expresses itself in a sustained language of analogy in **"An Every-Day Girl"** (1892). Young John Abbott congratulates Mary Fleming on how pretty her pear trees (herself) look; the boarder Davis, presumed to be fond of Mary, bends down a blossoming branch and holds it to his face; John tells Mary she should see the beautiful flowering cherry trees (himself) at his place; when she has difficulty tying up the grapevine, he deftly trims the vine and mends the trellis (he is part of the resolution of her dilemma); when Mary returns home after the fire she sees first two flourishing green pear trees (herself and John); and after their marriage plans are sealed, the pears begin to brown (achieved maturity).

This story is in other respects a staunch and versatile exhibit of Miss Jewett's special art. It exemplifies the chromatic richness and restrained rhythms of parochial speech, without the excess of eye-catching vernacular that doomed most of the local-color movement to quick oblivion. Aunt Hannah is another of Miss Jewett's sure-footed natives who draw sustenance directly from the soil, tangibly humorous, intuitively understanding, prudent, and prophetic. Through her resounds the canticle of Yankee caution: don't overreach. Mary Fleming, on her way to becoming Aunt Hannah, picks up the theme and carries it a step farther to Yankee self-reliance: chart your own course and solve your own problems. She lays the track for her irresolute father, who recaptures his verve, sells his house in the "crowded country village" and goes "back up country." The flashes of flora and fauna, consummately spaced, serenely disciplined, signally apt, leave no room to doubt Miss Jewett's stand in the contention of country versus city.

The touch of nature that makes the whole world kin operates under differing circumstances in three other stories. In **"A Spring Sunday"** (1904), Alonzo and Mary Ann Hallet undergo rejuvenation through a retrospective visit to their early home place some distance from the small city they have lived in for twenty years. Typically prim New Englanders, they steal away like young truants, retrace experiences of long ago, and are refreshed to new appreciation of each other. Miss Jewett reinforces her belief in the enduring quality of love by allying it to the cycle of seasons. In the autumn of their years the Hallets rediscover the green days of the soul, renew the loveliness of their beginnings, and glimpse the promise of more autumns and more springs, more springs.

Aging Sally Martin in **"A Change of Heart"** (1896) overcomes her long term of recalcitrance and voluntarily returns to her lover. Two admirable people are brought to natural fruition by a turn in the psychic season. After the protracted freeze of winter (between them), love thaws out their congealed self-pride. External nature coincides with human nature: change of season, change of heart. Miss Jewett pointedly closes with the observation that "Somehow, their happiness seemed all the lovelier because it had come at last in the spring."

Nature in more tangible form is brought to bear upon the maturation of young Johnny Hopper in **"The Honey Tree"** (1901). Unabashedly selfish about his lucky find, he wants to restrict gifts of the honey to only a favored few. His father gently implants the lesson of solidity and joy in community. "You're goin' to be just like other folks when you grow up," he tells the lad. Although it costs Johnny most of the honey, he concurs. Tradition, a tree that grows and ages and gives off good substance, is safe in Johnny's hands. There will be no generation gap. This story is in the forefront of local-color writing, one of Miss Jewett's most sagacious realistic-idealistic presentations of people, place, preoccupations, peculiarities—the uniqueness, the unanimity of country folk. She raises the taking-out of the honey to the plane of ritual. Grandma Prime is memorable portraiture in the round; the introductory chorale in Simmon's store a gem of creative reportage.

As in **"Stolen Pleasures,"** **"An Every-Day Girl,"** and **"A Change of Heart,"** Miss Jewett depends upon the transforming benignity of nature in **"A Garden Story"** (1886) to accentuate the division between country and city. Brisk, industrious, independent Ann Dunning personifies her beloved garden, thus the country in general; puny Peggy McAllister, the Scottish orphan, epitomizes the city and becomes the channel through which the two worlds communicate. Peggy nourishes the seedlings which Ann forthrightly tells her to uproot. What to Ann are merely pestiferous weeds represent beauty and vitality in the hospital wards. The little child leads her to unsuspected insights: "Think of all those folks in Boston being so pleased just to have the leavings." Love of nature effloresces into love of people. In a narrower sense Miss Jewett is giving body to her oft-repeated dictum from Plato that "the best thing one can do for the people of a State is to make them acquainted with each other." Country prevails here, hands down, for even the least of its properties has much to bestow upon the deprived city. However, country learns selflessness and gains broader awareness of human needs by extension of its severely constricted circle. Ann Dunning is fundamentally the largest beneficiary.

Less stress upon the influence of nature is present in **"A Guest at Home"** (1882). Annie Hollis is a wholesome, self-reliant New England girl on the style of Polly Finch. She shuttles between her uncle's luxurious New York home and her father's old farmhouse. She enjoys the advantages of education and refinement in the city, yet yearns to be a help and comfort to her loving, indigent family in the country. In the end she accepts a kind of comfortable compromise. Miss Jewett stands astride the relative values of country-city here, with just the slightest list toward country because it is Annie's original source. Until the explicit preachment of the final paragraphs, this story rates among the best in Miss Jewett's catalogue. It has lithesome style, satisfying content, slender story line, strength and warmth in depiction of place, people, and family ties. Aunt Harriet is a template of all Miss Jewett's ailing, whining spinsters; Mr. Hollis of her silent, sacrificial, steadfast *patresfamilias*.

The establishment of a new box factory in the village strews accumulating blight upon the old inhabitants in **"A Visit Next Door"** (1884). The Grangers and their next-door neighbors the Filmores drift farther and farther apart, their separation symbolized by the hedge of Norway spruces which they stop clipping. Miss Jewett's remedy for this deteriorating situation is ingenious and amusing, effective in restoring the former relationship. The theme, unfortunately, outruns the story. Miss Jewett disseminates a basketful of platitudes to endorse her thesis that resumption of country ways in a growingly urban society revives the goodness in people. **"A Financial Failure"** (1890) restates more strenuously the preferability of country over city. Bank and farm are cast in head to head opposition. Jonas Dyer suffers psychic dislodgement when he leaves the land for a junior clerkship, but all is set to rights by auspiciously named Love Hayland when they marry "in planting time" and retreat to the farm. The title of this story would be misleading without its subtitle "The Story of a New England Wooing," yet Miss Jewett's treatment of young love is as stiff as brocade, only conventional interchanges conventionally observed. Between prevailing Victorian rectitudes and Miss Jewett's own maiden constraints, the two youngsters never have a chance to come alive.

In the last of her stories about country pitted against city— **"A Born Farmer"** (1901)—Miss Jewett places the odds at three to one in favor of the former. Jacob Gaines, who is empowered by a legacy to sell his chattel and move his family to Boston, has lingering regrets about quitting the old gray farmhouse, regrets which never die despite his success in business. His wife and daughter similarly miss "the starlit sky and the dim familiar shapes of the old Maine hills" and are overjoyed when he suggests they return. Only his son Jake orients to the city. Perhaps one had to be brashly young and independent and masculine to confute Miss Jewett's dire warning that "it is a serious thing to pull up a human plant by the roots, and start it again with even the least delay in unsuitable soil." Especially the city.

One other facet of the country-city dialectic that engrossed Miss Jewett's attention in her stories, collected and uncollected, is the return-of-the-native theme. It crops up in crude semblance in her very first effusion, **"Jenny Garrow's Lovers."** Will Tyler departs his home town and returns years later, in the accepted pattern. Miss Jewett makes this no occasion for a canvas of values as she does, for instance, in a **"A Guest at Home."** Annie Hollis at first hates the thought of having to go back to her paternal home and the dullness thereof after three years of New York City and its opportunities to pursue her "naturally refined" artistic propensity. When she does, however, the elemental pull of family affection and the therapy of plain country routines reassert the tenacity of original roots.

The experience of Hannah Dalton in **"A Pinch of Salt"** (1897) is forged of the same metal, without the irony, of

Horatia Dane's in **"A Lost Lover."** The young swains of these now mature spinsters plunged years ago into the larger world to take its measure and make their fortune. Depravity exacts such toll of Horatia's hero that he incorrigibly fails to recognize her on his return, an earnest of urbanite wickedness. On the other side, John Brayton demonstrates the umbilical nature of the ancestral terrain and the constancy of rural love. He comes back prosperous and instantly amends the aridity of lost years. Miss Jewett's trappings of local folklore and natty coincidence elicit less of sentimentality, more of heartwarming advocacy for dear Miss Dalton from the reader. **"Told in the Tavern"** (1894) traces the same stripe, shuns the softer touch.

In a spiritual sense, Miss Prudence Fellows of **"The Growtown 'Bugle' "** (1888) belongs to this breed of returned native. Although she never travels outside of Simmsby, Massachusetts, her essential self, along with her investments, shifts to Growtown, Kansas. When little Lizzie Peck dies of lung fever, Prudence is whipped back to reconsideration of her own native heath. Miss Jewett unrelentingly pounds out the truisms that riches are not all gold and love thy neighbor, compensating by tempered, seamless unfoldment of narrative, now at the apex of her craftsmanship.

Miss Jewett's fiction abounds with self-sufficient, self-reliant New England women, speckled products of the Protestant ethic, Emersonian optimism, and indestructible heredity. Mrs. Kew, Nan Prince, Hannah West, Ann Ball, Betsey Lane, and Almira Todd spring foremost to mind. The world may often be too much with them but they face it down indomitably. None is in pronounced degree the duplicate of another, so it would be imprecise to label them a type. Their counterparts recur with expected variegation in these assembled stories, affidavits of Miss Jewett's lasting infatuation with their kind. Among the younger set, Mary Fleming in **"An Every-Day Girl"** and Annie Hollis in **"A Guest at Home"** roundly qualify for this category, as of the older group do Ann Dunning in **"A Garden Story"** and Prudence Fellows in **"The Growtown 'Bugle.' "**

Four other females of radically different status—two spinsters, a widow, a maid newly out of college—exercise self-reliance and are agreeably recompensed. Narcissa Manning (**"Miss Manning's Minister,"** 1883), fifty, stout and sentimental, is the least forceful of the four, persuading time to trot to her tune rather than grabbing it by the forelock. Having aged in the service of her father's, then her mother's illnesses, she lives alone in the home they have left her, habitbound and at peace with herself. When the congregation quibbles about the upkeep of their paralyzed minister, an affable, skeptical bachelor in his forties, she volunteers to nurse him in her house gratis. The upshot is that they marry and he provides a permanent outlet for her benevolent energies. Here too Miss Jewett interposes her doctrinal motif of the concordance between man and nature. In the first scene four lilac bushes, described as "elderly" to befit the superannuated romance, are sighted in front of Miss Manning's house, significantly in spring. When the reverend comes back to claim her in a later spring, the lilacs are shown in full bloom. The avid seeker of autobiographical hieroglyphs may read this story as an ambivalent fantasy of Miss Jewett's own hope for release from single blessedness. At the threshold of 34, with no record of male affiliations, she was in rare position to empathize with Narcissa Manning.

The second spinster is not one to leave matters to their own

management. Lydia Bent is neat, reticent, and quietly invincible. When *her* minister drifts into imminent danger of losing his parishioners, she does some determined soliciting and happily turns the tide. **"The First Sunday in June"** (1897) mounts some excellent woodcuts of the retiring generation in a small town, of a befuddled pastor slowly losing his hold on reality, of a meeting-house full of smiling faces, sun shining on mahogany pulpit—nature's sign of moral approval. Quintessentially a religious story for a religious magazine, the action is dull and curiously unmoving. Yet the image of Miss Lydia walking softly and purposefully from door to door remains fixed on the eye. To the minister she proffers the miracle of Lazarus; for the congregation she sparks a Christian renaissance.

The widow is cut from quite disparate cloth. Lydia Parkins, "a saving woman" who had married a saving man, is now a confirmed skinflint, even to the point of refusing to contribute toward *her* minister's Christmas present. Her ingrained egocentricity, punctured by momentary fear, becomes responsive to the necessities and incentives of other people's lives. The unaccustomed radiance of traditional family festivals at Yuletide induces an epiphany, after which she takes an irresistible and irretraceable "upward step" in charity and good-neighborliness. In **"Mrs. Parkins's Christmas Eve"** (1890-1891) Miss Jewett's main concern is to fashion an apologue of Christ's redemptive influence. She succeeds in this handily, and by way of increment offers one of her most incisive etchings of a dried-up New England niggard and a series of scenes drawn with marvelous economy of realistic projection.

Lizzie Harris is a young, spunky Radcliffe graduate who sets her mind on a goal of attainment and attains it. She vows to make a go of her blind father's tavern in the hinterland, applying the utmost of her intelligence, industry, and amicability to the task. **"A Stage Tavern"** (1900) starts with what seems a Cinderella gambit and ends with a May-November marriage, the whole pervaded by an aura of happy fiction. Lizzie impresses herself upon the reader as the very model of the healthy, hopeful, sensible, personable, zealous New England country girl, sister to Hawthorne's Phoebe Pyncheon. Miss Jewett's depicture of the hospitality accorded General Norton on his first visit to the tavern puts to shame the famous Southern variety. What Miss Jewett sees as common denominators in the self-reliance of her widely diversified individuals are innate acumen from a chain of canny forebears, physical and moral hardiness acquired from long association with the soil, agility to learn from circumstance and turn it to good purpose for themselves and others. (pp. 265-73)

Matthiessen says intemperately that "Without style Sarah Jewett's material would be too slight to attract a second glance" [see Further Reading list]. Miss Jewett makes no pretensions of profundity. Her effective voice is muted-lyric, not oracular-epic. She avows that "you must write to the human heart," which she consistently does in the manner of Mark Twain in his best chapters on boyhood on the Mississippi, staying well within his outer boundaries of romance and realism. She sees as indubitably as did Thoreau the transcendental ligature between man and nature, and a century before "the quality of life" became an ecological shibboleth she deprecates the toxic effect of urbanization on physical landscape and human psyche. Like Whitman, she perceives the likelihood of encountering saintliness in "an every-day girl" or the farmer down the lane. No avid feminist, she nevertheless broaches liberation of women from the deadening coils of domesticity. In *A Country Doctor* (1884) she prematurely pointed to the medical profession as an outlet. In these stories she promotes schoolteaching to a mystique; a goodly quota of her heroines accepts—or rejects—that road as the way out. War she appraises on the scale of the engaged individual. No prodigious field maneuvers, no spillage of gore, no flags flapping in parade, only the private anguish of a trapped spirit and his perfunctory annihilation.

In a time when all of these issues are under attack of stridulous rhetoric from factions on every side, the poised optimism of Miss Jewett's views constitutes a reaffirmation. Spring, she assures, will be around again after long frost—it is immanent in the law of the universe and the nature of man. Only the naive will regard this as naivete. (p. 282)

Richard Cary, "The Uncollected Short Stories of Sarah Orne Jewett," in Appreciation of Sarah Orne Jewett: 29 Interpretive Essays, *edited by Richard Cary, Colby College Press, 1973, pp. 264-83.*

JOHN B. HUMMA (essay date 1973)

[*Humma is an American essayist and academic. In the excerpt below, he disputes Richard Cary's critical conclusion that Jewett's story "The Courting of Sister Wisby" lacks a cohesive dramatic center.*]

"The Courting of Sister Wisby" is a deceptively simple story that has not received the critical consideration it deserves. Although it is among Sarah Orne Jewett's better known stories (though not so well known as **"The Dulham Ladies"** and **"A White Heron"**), almost nothing has appeared about **"Sister Wisby."** The longest analysis, for instance, is Richard Cary's, which runs for a scant page and a half [see Further Reading list]. Cary asserts that the story, or "sketch-anecdote," as he calls it, suffers from "extraneous framework and lack of dramatic spark." According to Cary, Miss Jewett is on a "holiday *al fresco,* noting weather, flora and fauna with pictorial adroitness as she hops fences and heads over pasture and hill." She meets her old friend, the elderly Mrs. Goodsoe, a fine character portrait, who spins some reminiscences as they cut mulleins. "When the essential tale has been told, Miss Jewett resumes her stroll, impressing a familiar cyclical design upon the afternoon's outing." Cary does remark on Mrs. Goodsoe's independent New England virtues and her affinity with nature, but his essential point is made: the story lacks a cohesive dramatic center.

If Cary's analysis is correct, if there is nothing more to the story than what he finds, then I believe **"Sister Wisby"** deserves the critical oblivion to which it has been consigned. But I think that Cary is a victim of the *appearance* of artlessness of the story. **"Sister Wisby"** is not the loosely knit "sketch-anecdote" that it seems. The framework is not "extraneous," but rather artistically tight; there is a sustained, *internal* spark; the flora and fauna are subtly, but cohesively, integrated into the story as are the fences the narrator jumps and the pastures she climbs; finally, the two stories that Mrs. Goodsoe tells (as well as many of her most offhand remarks) are directly related and subservient to the central theme—the narrator's unfolding vision of the continuity of life amidst suffering and death—that knits the several parts of the story into an artistically coherent whole.

At the beginning of the story, the narrator, who may or may not be Miss Jewett—Cary says she is—but who at least em-

bodies, we would probably agree, a consciousness similar to Miss Jewett's, feels the call of an "increasing temptation" to visit a "far-away pasture" on the slope of a high hill. Although she cannot conceive of what she wants from the pasture, or it from her, she is on "the farther side of as many as three fences" before she stops to think about "where [she] is going or why." We have then, metaphorically, a woman not old but approaching middle age (Miss Jewett was thirty-seven when the story appeared) considering her life and what lies ahead. The day's adventure represents a mounting toward a certain kind of understanding: specifically a mystical comprehension of the principles of life and death and the inseparable cyclical nature of the two. As she mounts higher, the narrator observes repeated signs of these principles, or forces, at work. Her "education" is carried still further by her warm encounter with Mrs. Goodsoe in the far pasture. Progressively, as their two human natures blend in fellowship, she comes to perceive the continuity and knit of all human existence. When at last the two people retire out of the sun and into the shade just prior to Mrs. Goodsoe's reminiscence of Eliza Wisby, her knowledge, as we shall see, moves to its completion. The success of Miss Jewett's story resides in the fact that the narrator's musings are never direct or explicit; the reader rather infers the meaning of her experience by way of symbol and implication.

The day is a perfect late summer's day, with a breath of autumn in the air that hints, significantly, at something ominous. "Every living thing grows suddenly cheerful and strong; it is only when you catch sight of a horror-stricken little maple in swamp soil—a little maple that has second sight and fore-knowledge of coming disaster to her race—only then does a distrust of autumn's friendliness dim your joyful satisfaction." Furthermore, the narrator observes that the sun is "slightly veiled." These are only the first of several reminders that the narrator encounters on her excursion of the approaching season of death. (pp. 85-7)

The farther the narrator advances upon the slope, the "more and more enticing" the higher pasture land becomes. In these wild fields she feels as if she is in direct communication with Nature and asks us now "to share the winter provision which I harvested that day." This request is a clue. Nature has a message, though an indirect one, to impart, and it follows that we should be alert since we shall come by our provision as indirectly as she does by hers.

At last she comes to a mossy old fence—the fourth—which stands as the "last barrier" between her and the pasture (between her and the fulfillment of her quest) "which had sent an invisible messenger earlier in the day." Someone has arrived before her, "dear old Mrs. Goodsoe, the friend of my childhood and fond dependence of my maturer years." As such, Mrs. Goodsoe ("Good Soul," as Cary suggests) serves as the teacher, or spiritual exemplar, of the narrator. A confirmed herbalist, she is getting her mulleins in, just as one, in the autumn of his life, might make preparations for the last assizes. The narrator offers her a hand. As they work, Mrs. Goodsoe discourses upon the general evils of progress, condemning doctors, the telegraph, and " 'livin' on wheels." Through their conversation, Miss Jewett underlines the passing of time and the changes that time works; but she wishes mainly to point up the fact that, in spite of the technological advances Mrs. Goodsoe denigrates, there has been no *real* change. As Mrs. Goodsoe says, "There was as big thoughts then as there is now." The continuity is unbroken.

Mrs. Goodsoe is drawn into two reminiscences of her past, each illustrating the way life goes on, sometimes cheerfully, other times not, in the face of privation, sudden tragedy, and death. She first tells about Jim Heron, the fiddling Irishman, who consoled the widow Foss after the death of her three small children by scarlet fever had sunk her into a catatonic trance. Her neighbors had feared that unless she could be brought to a good purgative cry she would suffer permanent damage to her reason: "By an' by Jim Heron come stealin' right out o' the shadows an' set down on the doorsteps, an' 'twas what the whole neighborhood felt for that mother all spoke in the notes." The music works the desired effect, and the widow Foss is brought around. Jim Heron's violin, in its ability to evoke both merriment ("How he would twirl off them jigs and dance tunes") and suffering, embodies the joy and woe which form for Miss Jewett the woven structure of our lives.

The courtship of Sister Wisby is the subject of the second tale. The couple has retired from the sun into the shade of a pine woods. The move has symbolic significance, dramatizing the turn—the mystical comprehension of which will comprise a portion of the narrator's "winter provision"—that Nature's cycle is about to take. But more importantly the shade may also signify what we might call an umbrella of fellowship: it is here that the friends eat the two peaches the narrator has brought with her, the significance of which act Miss Jewett will soon make clear. Like the first tale, this one about Sister Wisby is, if essentially comic, not without meaning for the narrator. The wooer is one Deacon Brimblecom: "The way he come a-courtin' o' Sister Wisby was this: she went a-courtin' o' him." Their protracted "trial" marriage, which later culminates in their actual one, commits the couple to heavy ridicule and numerous practical jokes, which they can only endure. In addition, Lizy and the deacon are subjected to the eccentricities and failings of one another, and these are considerable: the deacon, for instance, must reckon with the "streak that wa'n't just right somewheres in Lizy's wits" as well as with her "fractious" moods in "thundery weather"; Lizy, on her part, must reckon with the deacon's inveterate shiftlessness. Yet both in the end succeed in accommodating themselves to their unlikely circumstances; and their marriage, for all its trials, is an enduring one. One can argue, of course, that this anecdote, like the previous one, is no more than marginally related to Miss Jewett's principal concerns in the story. Nevertheless, Miss Jewett did choose to entitle her story after one of them, and her reason for doing so is essentially this: both anecdotes render concretely the bearing-up of human beings under difficulties and stresses of middling to great magnitude and their persevering through them to positive conclusions.

The tale of Sister Wisby's courtship concludes Mrs. Goodsoe's reminiscences; but it does not quite conclude Miss Jewett's story. Mrs. Goodsoe remarks, "There, they're all gone now; seems to me sometimes, when I get thinkin', *as if I'd lived a thousand years!* [my italics]" In a serious frame of mind, she goes on to say that when the time comes she would like to be "laid right out in the pasture ground" by some old graves in the lower field—in the vicinity, that is, of those portents our narrator had earlier witnessed. It is appropriate that the story concludes with the narrator's and Mrs. Goodsoe's descent from the hill: the narrator has attained her vision—symbolized or allegorized by the stages of her ascent—and now she returns to the "world" to live out her fulfillment. Similarly, it is appropriate that Mrs. Goodsoe is to be buried

in the *lower* field: here she will be close to the flux, the continuity, of human existence and to Nature, her maker and destroyer (Mrs. Goodsoe, after all, at one point is described as being "made out of the old-fashioned country dust," and there are several instances, as Cary points out, of her tendency to dissolve into the natural setting).

The narrator accompanies Mrs. Goodsoe down the slope to Mrs. Goodsoe's house. Mrs. Goodsoe has kept the pair of peach stones, symbolic of resurrection, or rebirth, with the intention of planting them in her yard: "It only takes four years for a peach pit to come to bearing, an' I guess I'm good for four years, 'thout I meet with some accident." She tells the narrator to return to see the peach trees in four years, "after I get 'em well growin'." and the narrative ends. The stones, it need hardly be said, are central in the story. They represent more than rebirth; they represent as well community, or fellowship. Though casually introduced, they have played an essential part in the communion of two human beings. And their role is not finished. They will serve to splice that fellowship, to insure its endurance beyond the afternoon, beyond even the day of Mrs. Goodsoe's death.

For fellowship, as Miss Jewett sees it, is a continuous thing. The unobtrusive way she uses *apparently* trivial and unrelated details to dramatize this aspect of her theme is the highest form of art. For instance, after the two women eat the peaches, the narrator, poking about in the ground, extracts "a long fine root, bright yellow to the eye and a wholesome bitter to the taste": goldthread. Mrs. Goodsoe says, "Now, I want to know why you should a bit it, and took away all the taste o' your nice peach? I was just thinkin' what a han'some entertainment we've had. I've got so I 'sociate certain things with certain folks, and goldthread was somethin' Lizy Wisby couldn't keep house without, no ways whatever. I believe she took so much it kind o' puckered her disposition." The herb is rightly called. It is the thread, the natural fact, that subtly connects by process of association the past existence of Eliza Wisby to the present existences of Mrs. Goodsoe and the narrator. And since the lives of Eliza Wisby and the others contained their shares of woe, it is beautifully *right* that the taste of the herb is bitter: the lesson that we must endure pain may not be pleasant, but it is, in the long view, "wholesome" in the same sense that the wormwood of Cliff Klingenhagen is.

We have observed the way Miss Jewett throughout has reinforced her theme by studding her story with allusions to age and the passing of time. For instance, in addition to Mrs. Goodsoe's comments about progress, she makes reference at one point to "Methusalahs" and at another point to her running on "like a clock that's onset her striking hand"; and at the end we hear her remark that she feels as if she has lived a thousand years. In the early paragraphs of the story, as we have seen, the narrator faces one reminder after another that the season of death—and Death itself—is approaching. Significantly, Mrs. Goodsoe's reminiscences are about people who are now all dead; as the only one left, with about four years remaining to her, she is, so to speak, "the last man among the bobolinks."

But Miss Jewett's story is not about death so much as it is about the persistence and continuity of life. At the beginning the narrator, observing the signs all about her, laments that "the world must fade again, that the best of her budding and bloom was only a preparation for another spring-time, for an awakening beyond the coming winter's sleep;" but this fading is, after all, in the way of preparation for that reawakening. Winter embraces not just death, and summer not just life. They blend, and each points to the advent of the other: "In midwinter there is always a day when one has the first foretaste of spring; in late August there is a morning when the air is for the first time autumn-like." Similarly, though the actors in Mrs. Goodsoe's reminiscences are dead, life goes on, the cycle perpetuates itself. Even the afternoon on the slope with Mrs. Goodsoe will be reborn, resurrected in the sprouting of the peach trees from the commemorative stones. Finally, there is continuity in the fact that, even though Jim Heron and the widow Foss and Lizy Wisby and Ezra Brimblecom have passed away, the stories of their lives live on, not only in the reminiscences of Mrs. Goodsoe, but also in **"The Courting of Sister Wisby"** itself, which perpetuate, like the stones, the subtle thread of fellowship between present and past, between the living and the dead. (pp. 87-91)

> John B. Humma, "The Art and Meaning of Sarah Orne Jewett's 'The Courting of Sister Wisby'," in Studies in Short Fiction, *Vol. X, No. 1, Winter, 1973, pp. 85-91.*

MICHAEL W. VELLA (essay date 1973)

[In the following excerpt, Vella offers an interpretation of The Country of the Pointed Firs, relating the narrator's role and vision to Jewett's understanding of and identification with the life and literary traditions of New England.]

Perhaps the most familiar praise given Sarah Orne Jewett's **The Country of the Pointed Firs** is Willa Cather's remark that the three books of American literature which would "have the possibility of a long, long life" would be *The Scarlet Letter, The Adventures of Huckleberry Finn,* and **The Country of the Pointed Firs.** More recent Jewett critics have better articulated what it is that makes her novel a success comparable to *The Scarlet Letter* or *Huckleberry Finn;* most frequently focusing upon its style and technique, they have consistently and justifiably analyzed them in terms of their pictorial qualities. Jewett's descriptions of Dunnet Landing do have a static, two-dimensional quality not unlike that of a painting. But the novel's picturesqueness, which critics usually have described in terms drawn from art criticism, is an aesthetic quality more important than ornamentation. In **The Country of the Pointed Firs** pictorial style reinforces the novel's theme while it functions architectonically; and it suggests the novel's place in American literary history.

We might better understand the nature of Jewett's literary achievement if we briefly consider **Pointed Firs** as a nexus of tradition and the individual talent, a unique combination of Sarah Orne Jewett's individual vision and a moment in American literary history when she benefitted from two rich veins of literary tradition. For on the one hand, imbued with the realities of South Berwick, Maine, Sarah Orne Jewett had an attitude toward nature which was significantly of New England, an attitude characterized by her ability to perceive the natural order as inherently symbolic; this ability belongs to the tradition which Charles Feidelson has shown to extend back through Emerson's *Nature* to Jonathan Edwards' *Images or Shadows of Divine Things* and to form the core of New England literature. At the same time, as an individual talent writing in the last decades of the nineteenth century, Miss Jewett shared with the realists and local colorists a preoccupation with verisimilitude and a predilection for the careful recording of the observed and localized experience. In a letter of advice to a literary novice Miss Jewett wrote that the writer should express "a simple helpful way of looking at life and speaking the truth about it . . . in what we are pleased to call its everyday aspects." But behind this statement, which implies a "realistic" orientation, Miss Jewett also believed that creativity issued from "a divine, mystical springhead." She was convinced, as Richard Cary points out, that "the great messages and discoveries of literature come to us—they *write us,* and we do not control them in a certain sense," an idea which hardly suggests a realistic bias. Such an artistic sensibility, then, would naturally express its perception of significant meaning on a deeply symbolic level.

In **The Country of the Pointed Firs** Miss Jewett uses an unobtrusive narrator to present a symbolic representation of a vision of universal human nature placed within the transcendental framework of natural landscape as cosmos and of village community as history. During her summer visit the narrator learns to perceive within the flux of nature and history something transcendental and permanent within mortal man, something which serves for her as an intimation of immortality.

Emerson's remark in "The Poet" that "every thing in nature answers to a moral power, if any phenomenon remains brute and dark, it is that the corresponding faculty in the observer is not yet active," can perhaps best lead us into a consideration of the narrator of **Pointed Firs.** She arrives at Dunnet Landing with her "corresponding faculty" sensitive but unexposed; through her summer stay there she gradually activates her corresponding faculty so that "every thing in nature answers to a moral power." Thus, the coherence of vision attained in the novel is a function of the central narrator; for the extent to which a unity of vision is reached through simile, allusion, and descriptive detail bordering on the inherently metaphoric is the extent to which the narrator employs her corresponding faculty to understand the meaningfulness of Dunnet Landing life. In terms of intellectual currents in the late nineteenth century, the narrator sees this meaningfulness as a kind of primitivism sired by evolutionism, in which man contains within him a more primordial human nature. For the narrator of **Pointed Firs** this static, unchanging core of human nature is the resource of stoical and fortitudinous reserves against the onslaughts of time and mortality. What precipitates her vision of such a fundamental, primitive identity between all men is her awareness of death.

It is significant that the narrator's stay at Dunnet Landing is of one summer; she, herself in middle age, has the spring of youth behind her, and the winter of old age before her. Though death is not imminent for her, she is manifestly aware of its proximity. From the schoolhouse where she writes, "feeling like a besieged miser of time," she sees almost immediately upon her arrival the funeral procession of Mrs. Begg. (pp. 275-76)

Though death is present in the novel, it is not totally negative, but rather a fact of existence beside which life can become profoundly meaningful. For the narrator the most regenerative resource in the face of mortality is what can be known symbolically through her corresponding faculty's attentiveness to natural facts. She becomes increasingly aware of this potential source of knowledge through Mrs. Todd.

The most important aspect of Mrs. Todd is her herbalism, a form of medicine predicated upon the existence of a natural, all-inclusive harmony between man and nature. The characterization of Mrs. Todd given us by the narrator connotes her arcane, natural wisdom: Mrs. Todd is referred to in various places in the novel as a sybil, an oracle, a caryatide, a rustic philosopher and an enchantress. Her knowledge of herbs extends beyond natural medicine; it approaches "an understanding with the primal forces of nature." Mrs. Todd's herbalism, within the context envisioned by the narrator, is an index of her natural wisdom. Charmed by the scents of the garden, the narrator tells us that to her the herbs suggest a secret, primitive knowledge to which Mrs. Todd has access under her homely, provincial practices:

> At one side of this herb plot were other growths of a rustic pharmacopoeia, great treasures and rarities among the commoner herbs. There were some strange and pungent odors that roused a dim sense and remembrance of something in the forgotten past. Some of these might once have belonged to sacred and mystic rites, and have had some occult knowledge handed with them down the centuries; but now they pertained only to the humble compounds brewed at intervals with molasses or vinegar or spirits in a small caldron on Mrs. Todd's kitchen stove.

The odor of the herbs becomes a motif suggesting enchantment; the narrator says "I do not know what herb of the night it was that used sometimes to send out a penetrating odor late in the evening, after the dew had fallen, and the moon was high, and the cool air came up from the sea. Then Mrs. Todd would feel she must talk to somebody, and I was only too glad to listen. We both fell under the spell." The scent of the herbs, described on significant occasions throughout the novel, suggests this "spell" and the mystic, arcane wisdom of Mrs. Todd and her beneficent, enchanting influence over the narrator.

As the narrator increasingly shares this natural wisdom with Mrs. Todd, the two move into a "deeper intimacy" and the narrator finds herself exposed to a different way of seeing Dunnet Landing. The herbs' connotation of primitive, natural wisdom, the motif of the scent-induced spell, the periodical "wisdom-giving stroll" with Mrs. Todd, each serves to enable the narrator to exercise her corresponding faculty within the contexts of a harmony between man and nature, the same harmony upon which Mrs. Todd's magical herbalism is based. The narrator has, as a consequence, a subtle apprehension of a kind of primitive transcendence over death.

The narrator's description of Mrs. Todd standing in the middle of a braided rug suggests how the narrator sees Dunnet Landing in the wisdom which radiates out from Mrs. Todd, much as the scents exude from her herbs: "She stood in the centre of a braided rug, and its rings of black and gray seemed to circle about her feet in the dim light. Her height and massiveness in the low room gave her the look of a huge sybil, while the strange fragrance of the mysterious herb blew in from the little garden."

The narrator's habit of seeing various natives of Dunnet Landing in correspondence with various plants is not simply a quaint literary technique; it is an essential part of the vision she has gained in her summer stay with Mrs. Todd. To the narrator the sick girl who calls at Mrs. Todd's door is like a white windflower; Captain Littlepage seems to her like the wind-bent trees of the coastline and a medicinal herb growing in Mrs. Todd's garden. To Mrs. Todd, Sarah Tilley appears

like a flower, and folks in general are like the Dunnet schoolyard's tansy which grows better for the wear it receives under the children's feet. That these correspondences are sometimes those of Mrs. Todd, and sometimes those of the narrator, evidences the extent to which the latter picks up Mrs. Todd's way of seeing people as integral parts of nature, much as her herbs are. The fullest symbol in this respect, connoted by the symbolic texture of the work, is the pointed firs themselves as they stand perched on the edge of a sea infinitely larger than the small world of Dunnet Landing. As Mrs. Todd and the narrator look toward the outer islands the trees are anthropomorphized by the military metaphor: "We were standing where there was a fine view of the harbor and its long stretches of shore all covered by the great army of the pointed firs, darkly cloaked and standing as if they waited to embark. As we looked far seaward among the outer islands, the trees seemed to march seaward still, going steadily over the heights and down to the water's edge." The view of the pointed firs as almost human is akin to the view of the inhabitants of Dunnet Landing as if they were plants. The correspondence works both ways, and the narrator's vision of the pines about to embark seaward suggests her understanding of the mortality of all the natives of Dunnet Landing as they stand poised in life before the infinite expanse of death.

If there is an apex in *Pointed Firs,* it occurs when Mrs. Todd and the narrator visit Mrs. Blackett on Green Island. Before their visit they stare out at Green Island: "It had been growing gray and cloudy, . . . and a shadow had fallen on the darkening shore. Suddenly, . . . a gleam of golden sunshine struck the outer islands, and one of them shone out clear in the light, and revealed itself in a compelling way to our eyes. . . . The sunburst upon that outermost island made it seem like a sudden revelation of the world beyond this which some believe to be so near." The island which "reveals itself " in the light is Green Island, whose name suggests regeneration; and which, since Green Island is the home of Mrs. Todd's mother, is a symbol of the narrator's regenerative movement back to the "source." What the narrator comes to learn of the power to know immortality within life, through a kind of primitivistic communion between men immersed in nature, she learns on this island.

There, when William takes the narrator for a walk to an advantageous position where the "prospect" is magnificent, she is first exposed to a kind of immediate, primordial communication which can take place within nature, when man is in nature so comprehensively as to be as the plants, animals, and stones. Their immediate sharing of nature forms a bond of communication which escapes verbal expression. After they return to Mrs. Blackett's home, and after the mother and son entertain the narrator with singing, Mrs. Blackett shows the narrator into the master bedroom and she is made to sit in the old lady's rocking chair; the narrator says, "Here was the real home, the heart of the old house on Green Island! I sat in the rocking-chair, and felt that it was a place of peace, the little brown bedroom, and the quiet outlook upon field and sea and sky. I looked up, and we understood each other without speaking." Like Mrs. Todd's herbalism, non-verbal communication is so dependent upon the community's immersion in nature that it cannot occur in more complex environments such as the city. There such immediacy is lost in garish commercialism and patent-leather sophistication. Reverend Dimmick, for example, is city-bred; according to Mrs. Todd he has "a great use of words" but he knows "no remedies." In contrast are the fishermen of the landing: "There was an alliance and understanding between them so close that it was apparently speechless. They gave much time to watching one another's boats go out or come in; they lent a ready hand at tending one another's lobster traps in rough weather; they helped to clean the fish, or to sliver porgies for the trawls, as if they were in close partnership."

About two such fishermen the narrator says, "Arguments and opinions were unknown to the conversation of these ancient friends; you would as soon have expected to hear small talk in a company of elephants as to hear [them] . . . and their two mates waste breath in any form of trivial gossip." Only the essentials are communicated by these men as they work within the exigencies of nature; this is not simply a characterization of the typical laconic New Englander but is an aspect of the primitive sharing of felt reality by men: "As you came to know them you wondered more and more that they should talk at all. Speech seemed to be a light and elegant accomplishment, and their unexpected acquaintance with its arts made them of new value to the listener. You felt almost as if a landmark pine should suddenly address you in regard to the weather."

In Dunnet Landing the sights of animals, trees, plants, sea, and the scents of herb, salt-breeze, and flower become immediate forms of expression for a community well aware of its place within the large panoply of nature. This kind of primitive, non-verbal communication happens because the inhabitants are aware of their fundamental one-ness as they live according to nature's exigencies, not the least of which is death. At the core of this community of shared existence, below the level of articulated thought, is man's ability to "speak," without words, from the well-spring of his universal human nature; but what makes the narrator aware of this type of communication are her acquisition of vision and her increasing valuation of the contours of nature—the former given her through her intimate relationship with Mrs. Todd, and the latter given her on Green Island and by the people of Dunnet Landing. Through the power of her corresponding faculty she sees more and more the unity of interpersonal life at Dunnet Landing, enclosed as it is within nature; and most importantly for her, this unity is transcendental.

Parallel to the pattern of comparisons between plants and the natives of Dunnet Landing is a pattern of historical correspondences between these inhabitants and historical figures. Mrs. Begg is compared to the Countess of Carberry, and the narrator suggests that history repeats itself. Mrs. Todd appears at one point like Antigone. The narrator says that because of Mrs. Todd's wisdom "She might belong to any age." She sees something "mediaeval" in the behavior of Joanna Todd. Each of these correspondences is more than the gratuitous projection of an educated narrator onto a provincial. For as much as the narrator sees characters in terms of herbs, she sees each of them individually as "renewal of some historic soul." These correspondences expand the significance of Dunnet Landing life beyond the narrow confines of a provincial village; but, more importantly, they evidence the narrator's ability to see man comprehensively within history much as she sees man comprehensively within nature. Her corresponding faculty, attuned to the bonds of nature and history, enables her to see that fundamental human core which all men share regardless of the place or age in which they live. She muses, "In the life of each of us, I said to myself, there is a place remote and islanded, and given to endless regret or secret happiness; we are the unaccompanied hermit and re-

cluse of an hour or a day; we understand our fellows of the cell to whatever age of history they may belong."

There are other means, too, by which this kind of historical extension suggests a kind of transcendence which intimates immortality. According to the narrator, as individuals "we always keep the same hearts, though our outer framework fails and shows the touch of time," but collectively, what remains the same in all men is something which can only be perceived symbolically and is difficult to express in words. When Mrs. Blackett and Mrs. Todd visit their neighbors on the way to the Bowden reunion, the narrator shares with them "one revelation after another . . . of the constant interest and intercourse that had linked the far island and these scattered farms into a golden chain of love and dependence." The intense intimacy of community life at Dunnet Landing impresses her as she moves toward the reunion, and she broadens her understanding of human nature beyond these individuals to mankind in general. The Bowden house symbolizes the extension of family; just as "a man's house is really but his larger body, and expresses in a way his nature and character," so the Bowden house, worn by "five generations of sailors and farmers and soldiers," stands before the reunion a symbol of the microcosmic family of man at Dunnet Landing. The intensity of the narrator's recognition of the significance of the Bowden festivities is clear. . . . (pp. 276-80)

The celebration at the Bowdens' is a quasi-ritual which expresses the shared brotherhood and the transcendental communion of life at Dunnet Landing. Both this brotherhood and communion are under that life's simple surface and homely routine; but on occasions such as the Bowden reunion such brotherhood and communion break out in an "enthusiasm" definitely religious in its implications. As the celebrants arrive they strike the narrator as "old illustrations of the Pilgrim's Progress," and indeed the reunion is a secularized religious revival. As the crowd moves to the selected grove of trees in a long procession, the narrator recognizes a kind of immortality. . . . (p. 280)

Here, the Dunnet Landing natives, who follow the courses of their lives within the largeness of nature, come together in a ritual in which their human identity is shared in the clan or tribe, as well as with all men throughout history. Here again are the suggestion of vegetation and the symbolic meanings behind the herbs represented in the "green branches" and in the sacred grove. On the level of the natural surface this is a simple countryside gathering before the long winter sets in; but on the metaphoric or symbolic level, what is taking place is a non-verbal, ritualized ceremony, reminiscent of ancient vegetation rites, in which the narrator perceives her own sacramental unity with all men. Perhaps herself transfigured, she reaches a state of transcendent awareness through all that she has experienced during her summer at Dunnet Landing; armed with the transcendental vision which is the fulfillment of Emerson's *Nature,* she recognizes through her corresponding faculty the radical identity of all men. She understands her self in terms of her primal human nature as it is enveloped in nature and history; and as her self dissolves into these, egoless and perhaps mystically, she understands whatever it is of immortality that can be understood in this life. **The Country of the Pointed Firs,** beginning with Mrs. Begg's funeral procession, closes with the procession at the Bowden reunion to the sacred grove.

If there can be a denouement in a novel whose "plot" exists

chiefly as metaphoric meaning, then the last chapter of *Pointed Firs,* in which the narrator leaves Mrs. Todd and Dunnet Landing, is such a denouement. Her description of the landscape at the close of the summer season evidences the lucidity of perception which she has attained by her summer residence. Time is slipping out of her hands as "unwillingly as a miser spends his coins," and she says, "I wished to have one of my first weeks back again, with those long hours when nothing happened except the growth of herbs and the course of the sun. . . . I felt hurried and full of pleasant engagements, and the days flew by like a handful of flowers flung to the sea wind." First arriving at Dunnet Landing sensitive but unattuned to life, she has since been initiated: "Once I had not even known where to go for a walk; now there were many delightful things to be done and done again." But she is not simply nostalgic; she is fully aware of the qualifications life holds with its bounties. Especially there is the qualification of death. As she watches Mrs. Todd for the last time, the prose suggests mortality faced with lucidity: "At last I lost sight of her as she slowly crossed an open space on one of the higher points of land, and disappeared again behind a dark clump of juniper and pointed firs." Of their separation she says simply, "So we die before our own eyes; so we see some chapters of our lives come to their natural end." Thus the novel ends as the ship carries the narrator away from Dunnet Landing, with the note of such "ends" which in experience always suggest mortality, but also with a quiet affirmation which the narrator has learned, along with Mrs. Todd and others of the Landing, to put into her life.

Each of the strands of meaning which I have attempted to trace through the novel points to a transcendent human reality recognized by the narrator through her stay at Dunnet Landing. Since this is a reality which remains fundamentally unaltered by time, the static, pictorial quality of the prose in *Pointed Firs,* which previous critics have pointed out, reinforces this dimension of meaning. The narrator's summer has been one of vision; she has seen into her unalterable primal unity with all men in nature and history. In this regard the novel itself becomes a symbol for the understanding which Sarah Orne Jewett attained through an intimate identification with New England life and New England literary tradition.

Sarah Orne Jewett's *The Country of the Pointed Firs* is the product of a sensibility poised at a moment in literary history offering the advantages of contemporaneity with realist and local colorist writers along with immersion in the rich New England tradition of such works as *Nature, A Week on the Concord and Merrimack Rivers,* and *Walden.* With the attention of the realist and the vision of the Transcendentalist, Jewett manages to create in *Pointed Firs* a symbolic novel which fulfills the Emersonian dictum that "words are signs of natural facts," and that "particular natural facts are symbols of particular spiritual facts." *The Country of the Pointed Firs* becomes in this context a novel whose descriptive details are nearly as inherently symbolic as those of *Walden,* and whose literary technique carries it beyond the category of local color. (pp. 280-81)

Michael W. Vella, "Sarah Orne Jewett: A Reading of 'The Country of the Pointed Firs'," in *ESQ, Vol. 19, No. 4, 4th quarter, 1973, pp. 275-82.*

JOSEPHINE DONOVAN (essay date 1980)

[*Donovan is an American biographer and critic whose works explore women in literature and women writers from a feminist perspective. According to Donovan: "In much of Western literature the moral being of women has been denied or repressed. Feminist literary criticism points this out and looks for works (often by women) in which women characters seek to achieve fullness of being." In the following excerpt from her critical study* Sarah Orne Jewett, *Donovan explicates several of Jewett's stories, including pieces from the early collections* Deephaven, Play Days, *and* Old Friends and New.]

On 13 July 1872, Sarah Orne Jewett took note in her diary of a criticism by Charles Lamb that a book could be too "preachy" and full of literal scripture, but that no book could have "too much of silent scripture" in it. She resolved not to write "parsonish" stories herself, but to retain a level of moral meaning, of "silent scripture," in her work.

During her first decade of publishing—up to about 1880—Jewett put forth nearly forty stories, most of which were collected into three books: *Deephaven* (1877), *Play Days* (1878) and *Old Friends and New* (1879). In many of these stories the scriptural element is not so silent as one might perhaps wish. However, the moral messages that Jewett attempted to convey are themselves an interesting documentation of social attitudes in Victorian America. They reveal some of the tensions that she was experiencing as a writer and as a woman, tensions that she would have to resolve before she could move into a mature sense of her own fictional vision. By the end of the decade she had made significant progress to this end.

Front cover of Jewett's first book, Deephaven.

Jewett's first published story is quite uncharacteristic of her later work. **"Jenny Garrow's Lovers"** (*The Flag of Our Union* 18 January 1868, *Uncollected Stories* 1971) was indeed written by "A. C. Eliot." It is a romantic melodrama set in rural England, a region Jewett only knew from her own reading of romantic novels. The plot concerns two brothers, Will and Dick, who compete in courtship for the heroine, Jenny Garrow. One night Will disappears. Dick is unjustly accused and convicted of Will's murder. He is sent to prison. Jenny in the meantime dies of the plague. Will finally returns five years later to explain that he had left town and gone to sea after Jenny rejected him. Dick is then released, and they both eventually die unmarried.

Perhaps Jewett exhausted her interest in plot in her first story, for there are more dramatic episodes in it—three deaths, a plague, imprisonment, and several broken hearts—than in almost any of her subsequent works. However, we may note that already in this story Jewett's style is tight and spare and surprisingly polished for a novice. And already Jewett has begun experimenting with narrative technique. The story is narrated in the first person by an elderly woman, Margery Blake, who had known Jenny Garrow in her youth; the episodes described had occurred forty years earlier. This was a device Jewett was to use often. Ironically, the narrator apologizes in an opening address to the reader for her lack of narrative skill.

"Mr. Bruce" (*Atlantic Monthly* December 1869, *Old Friends and New* 1879), also by "A. C. Eliot," is quite different. The setting is one its author knew well, the upper-middle-class Boston domestic scene, and its central theme of role playing or masquerading is one that fascinated Jewett throughout the early years of her literary production.

Again we find a self-conscious concern with narrative structure. The opening section of the story is narrated by Aunt Mary, a "maiden lady," to her twenty-year-old niece Elly (probably a Jewett persona), about another maiden lady friend of hers, Miss Margaret Tarrant of Boston. Miss Tarrant, who "possesses the art of telling a story capitally," picks up the narrative line and tells a tale, set twenty to thirty years earlier, about her older sister Kitty and how she met her husband, Mr. Bruce. The central episode is a dinner party where, as a lark, Kitty had volunteered to help out by acting as a servant girl at the table. She even assumed an Irish brogue for the occasion, as most of the Boston working class was in those days Irish. This was all unbeknownst to Mr. Bruce, who later met Kitty in her real role as fashionable Brahmin debutante, much to his surprise and Kitty's amusement.

Like many of Jewett's early stories, this one gives us insights into the lives and attitudes of leisure class adolescent females of the period. (pp. 19-21)

[**"The Best China Saucer"** (*The Independent* 25 July 1872)] is the first of many stories in which an archaic sense of class consciousness is evident. Usually, however, Jewett expresses compassion for the poor and urges upon the wealthy a sense of obligation. The story also reflects another of Jewett's basic moral principles, however: that one can better one's situation or at least make it tolerable with the right attitude and a goodly amount of effort. This characteristically American or Emersonian optimism recurs in much of her early writing. (pp. 23-4)

Deephaven was Jewett's first major work. It is the most highly regarded of her early compositions; it has been reprinted

many times (as recently as 1966) and continues to be the subject of critical commentary. Although flawed, it remains of considerable historical and literary value. It is not, however, as strong a work as *Old Friends and New,* Jewett's other major collection of the seventies. Jewett's standards in several of the *Old Friends and New* stories—especially **"Miss Sydney's Flowers," "A Lost Lover," "A Late Supper"** and **"A Bit of Shore Life"**—were extremely high.

Nevertheless, *Deephaven* remains of great interest for several reasons. First, it continues to develop several of the themes that appear in *Play Days* and investigates new issues that were to become important in Jewett's subsequent works. Second, the structural problems in the work are indicative of conflicting viewpoints toward her subject matter and her art that existed within Jewett herself and that needed to be resolved. Third, it describes extensively and realistically the seacoast region that was to become Jewett's favorite locale. If only for its extraordinary veracity of detail *Deephaven* still deserves to be read. In this regard it has the value of charming and well-edited oral history. Nineteenth-century daily life comes alive in this work as it does in few others.

Because of its extraordinary sense of verisimilitude, there has been considerable speculation as to where *Deephaven* is really set. Its setting seems to resemble York, Maine, a coastal town about ten miles from South Berwick. Especially suggestive is the author's reference to the "cliffs and pebble beaches, the long sands and the short sands," terrain characteristic of York. However, in her preface to the second edition of *Deephaven* (1893), Jewett insisted that it was a "fictitious village which still exists only in the mind." This was a position she was to take in regard to all her fiction.

This analysis of *Deephaven* proceeds more or less in order of composition. Like most of Jewett's fiction, these sketches were first published in magazine form and later collected. Unlike most of her other collections (with the notable exception of *The Country of the Pointed Firs*), Jewett attempted in revising these sketches for book publication to fuse them together into a form that would approach the coherence and design of a novel. This attempt was not entirely successful. These sketches do not form a continuous pattern: rather, they remain isolated units only loosely and roughly connected. The main reason for this is that they were written at different times and only later patched together into a continuous fabric. By contrast, *The Country of the Pointed Firs, Deephaven*'s more mature structural analogue, seems to have been composed in reverse order: first written all of a piece and then later divided for serial presentation.

The work's other major structural problem stems from Jewett's attempt to use the relationship between the two young women as the central unifying device. The only continuity in the work (other than the geographic unity forced by the location) is provided by the continuing presence through all the sketches of the two friends, Kate Lancaster and Helen Denis. The latter is the narrator and a Jewett persona.

For the most part these protagonists remain outsiders to the events and characters of the sketches. They do not participate in the action or the world of the text, nor is their relationship with one another integrated into that world. Indeed, the sentimentality of their liaison and their adolescent enthusiasm clash with the mood of their somber environment.

There is, however, one important connection between the girls and the environment: they learn from it. Their surroundings provide several important educational experiences for them that are especially related to their growth into adult women. (pp. 30-2)

By the end of the work the girls express an escapist wish, to "copy the Ladies of Llangollen and remove ourselves from society and its distractions." The Ladies of Llangollen, Lady Eleanor Butler and Miss Sarah Ponsonby, were a celebrated lesbian couple of the late eighteenth and early nineteenth centuries who lived much of their life together in a Welsh rural retreat. Here perhaps most clearly we see that the escapist theme that recurs in Jewett's work (the desire to remain in a state of perpetual childhood or to retreat into some woodland haven) probably reflects a desire not to have to conform to the role demands that "adulthood" required in Victorian America.

Consequently, *Deephaven* is in reality made up of two separate texts that do not fit together well. One is the romantic/escapist story of the girls' relationship, and the other is the description of a nineteenth-century New England port village that is suffering an economic decline. Thus, *Deephaven* remains an inconsistent work that reflects its author's conflicting aims. On the one hand, she wished to create a work that would memorialize a valued personal relationship. This is demonstrated by the biographical evidence presented in Chapter I and also by Jewett's own secretive dedication of the 1877 edition: to her parents "and also to all my other friends, whose names I say to myself lovingly, though I do not write them here." On the other hand, she was motivated by a desire to preserve in fiction the beloved regional locale that was fast giving way to the modern world.

This conflict was resolved in Jewett's later work by simply removing personal matters like Helen's and Kate's relationship from her fiction. (pp. 32-3)

The first two sketches in *Deephaven,* "Kate Lancaster's Plan" and "The Brandon House and the Lighthouse," were originally published as "The Shore House" (*Atlantic Monthly* September 1873). The story opens in Boston when Kate Lancaster proposes to her friend Helen Denis that they spend the summer in Deephaven at the beach home of her recently deceased aunt, Katherine Brandon. This agreed, the two proceed by rail and by stagecoach to their destination. In the coach they meet their first local "character," Mrs. Kew, who has lived with her husband, the lighthouse keeper, in the lighthouse for seventeen years. (It seems likely that this is the still much photographed Nubble Light on Cape Neddick, Maine.) Mrs. Kew speaks in "downeast' " dialect, as do all the characters in the work except the girls.

After getting settled in the Brandon House, which from its description strongly resembles Jewett's own house in South Berwick, the two go to visit the Kews in the lighthouse. While there, some tourists stop by and mistake the girls for natives. Kate plays the part of tour guide, another example of the masquerade theme. Ironically, one of the tourists takes pity on her, seeing Kate's lighthouse life as one of loneliness and poverty, and suggests that she move to the city where she could obtain a well-paid position such as department store saleswoman (a job she, the tourist, holds). This is a comically ironic reversal of the usual Jewett situation, with in this case the outsider being mistaken for the insider and the wealthy person for the poor. It betrays once again Jewett's concern about, or at least interest in, these social roles and the "masquerades" they require. (pp. 34-5)

The next two sketches, **"Deephaven Society"** and **"The Captains"** were originally published, together with **"Danny,"** **"The Circus at Denby"** and **"Last Days in Deephaven"** as **"Deephaven Cronies"** (*Atlantic Monthly* September 1875). Perhaps the best description of the town is to be found in **"Deephaven Society."** We learn that it "is utterly out of fashion. It never recovered from the effects of the embargo of 1807, and a sand bar has been steadily filling in the mouth of the harbor." In this sketch, too, we find the girls' sense of themselves as cultured "outsiders" at perhaps its most pronounced. "There was a great deal of sea lingo in use; indeed we learned a great deal ourselves . . . and used it afterward to the great amusement of our friends."

"The Captains" introduces a series of retired sea captains and mates who relate their stories to the girls. Especially interesting in this sketch is Captain Lant's story of a psychic phenomenon: how his stepfather had once dreamed of his nephew being hung, which he later found out had happened on the other side of the world on the very same day as the dream. The central figure of the next sketch, **"Danny,"** is a sailor who relates a touching and pathetic story about his long-term relationship with a cat he had once rescued. **"Captain Sands,"** which follows **"Danny"** in *Deephaven* but which had not been published previously, introduces a character who is the protagonist of a later sketch, **"Cunner-Fishing."**

"The Circus at Denby" is one of the most interesting sketches in the book. Helen and Kate accompany Mrs. Kew to the circus, which has set up its tents in a nearby town. On the way they pass by red-bearded, consumptive Mr. Craper (a figure out of Dostoevsky) and his five children. They too are going to the circus, despite his obvious ill health. The circus turns out to be somewhat disillusioning; it is shabby and the animals look uncomfortable. The central figure of the sketch is "the Kentucky giantess," the fat lady in the side show. It happens that Mrs. Kew had known the woman in her youth. Her story is another tale of an incompetent, drunk husband. She has turned to her current profession as a means of supporting herself. "She used to be real ambitious," Mrs. Kew comments dismally on their way home. Once again the girls are presented with a grim example of the fate of a married woman.

That evening the two girls go to a free lecture on the **"Elements of True Manhood."** The main point of the lecture—that young men should exercise their duties and responsibilities as citizens and voters—is largely lost on the audience, which is composed of three old men, four women, two adolescent girls, four children, and "the sexton, a deaf little old man with a wooden leg." Women of course were not considered citizens and did not have the right to vote until the twentieth century.

"Cunner-Fishing" delves further into the question of psychic phenomena. Captain Sands tells the girls of four separate occurrences he knows in which people have anticipated or learned of events through extrasensory perception. Kate and Helen reflect upon how country people seem to be more in tune with their spiritualistic instincts than city dwellers. "They believe in dreams, and they have a kind of fetichism, and believe so heartily in supernatural causes." Helen speaks of having a certain reverence for this side of their lives: "They live so much nearer to nature than [city] people. . . . I wonder if they are unconsciously awed by the strength and purpose in the world about them, and the mysterious creative power which is at work with them on their familiar farms."

In their simple life they take their instincts for truths, and perhaps they are not always so far wrong as we imagine. Because they are so instinctive and unreasoning, they may have a more complete sympathy with Nature.

Kate remarks that "the more one lives out of doors the more personality there seems to be in what we call inanimate things." Captain Sands had suggested that our psychic powers are really in an embryonic state; he had drawn an analogy to a tadpole's legs, which are useless "faculties" until it becomes a frog. So too, he speculated, our psychic faculties may in some future state find their use.

The last three sketches, **"Mrs. Bonny," "In Shadow,"** and **"Miss Chauncey"** were originally published together as **"Deephaven Excursions"** (*Atlantic Monthly* September 1876). Mrs. Bonny is one of Jewett's great characters. A tobacco-smoking country woman who wears men's clothes and boots, several layers of aprons, a tight cap and "steel-bowed" spectacles, she is an original, uncontaminated by the civilized world. Kate and Helen visit her in her mountain home which is filled with "a flock of hens and one turkey."

> Living there in the lonely clearing, deep in the woods and far from any neighbor, she knew all the herbs and trees and the harmless wild creatures who lived among them, by heart; and she had an amazing store of tradition and superstition.

Mrs. Bonny is an archetypal Jewett figure, the single woman who is in tune with nature and who has an extensive knowledge of herbal and natural lore. While presented in a somewhat comic vein here, she prefigures Jewett's monumental women, particularly Almira Todd of *The Country of the Pointed Firs*.

"In Shadow" presents a darker side of life, again the world of rural poverty. Here the characters are a poverty-stricken couple who die during the summer, between the girls' two visits to their home, leaving their children as orphans to be farmed out to unwilling relatives (the alternative being that nefarious nineteenth-century institution, the "poorhouse"). These people are not "shif'less"; they simply had bad luck. As one neighbor remarked, " 'twas against wind and tide with 'em all the time."

The two girls' responses to this example of inexplicable misery and suffering differ. Kate gleans a Christian moral, but Helen meditates, "I wonder how we can help being conscious in the midst of our comforts and pleasures, of the lives which are being starved to death in more ways than one." This comment is probably a fair expression of Jewett's own developing attitude toward her rural environment; it is one of compassion.

"Miss Chauncey" describes another life that faded from an early promise to an impoverished end. The central figure is an aristocratic old woman from a distinguished but mad family (one of her brothers had committed suicide, another had gone insane). She lost her own bearings at one point, was institutionalized for a while and then returned home to find that all her belongings had been sold. She lived for years in an empty house, half crazy, dreaming of the past. The girls visit her several times and then learn, after leaving Deephaven, that Miss Chauncey had died while revisiting her house, unbeknownst to anyone, in the dead of winter. *Deephaven* thus follows the cycle of the year, beginning in a season of promise, early summer, and ending in winter. (pp. 36-40)

Miss Sydney, one of Jewett's "maiden lady" figures [in **"Miss Sydney's Flowers"** (*The Independent* 16 July 1874; *Old Friends and New,* 1879)], is the last in a distinguished old family line. Her home is the last of its kind standing. "One by one the quiet, aristocratic old street had seen its residences give place to shops and warehouses. . . ." Once again we see quality and uniqueness giving way to industrialization and mass production, a perennial Jewett lament. As the story opens, Miss Sydney's environment is about to be even more abused, as a new commercial street is being put in behind it. At first Miss Sydney resents the intrusion the bustling traffic brings into her quiet space. However, even these miserable new circumstances have their positive side: it turns out that the crowds of people passing by are attracted to the beautiful flowers growing in her greenhouse, an event that tends to break into the isolation of this lonely spinster who had heretofore kept "selfishly" to herself. It forces her back into human society.

A parallel plot is developed in the second part of the story. Here we see the underside of life again, the world of urban poverty. Mrs. Marley, a candy saleswoman, has earned barely enough to support herself and her lame sister Polly. Her candy stand had been located where the winter winds had harshly aggravated her rheumatism. With the advent of the new avenue that goes by Miss Sydney's, however, Mrs. Marley is able to relocate to a position that makes business much brisker and the task much pleasanter, as it is well sheltered from the winds. The location is in front of Miss Sydney's, beside the greenhouse. The sister, Polly, is another example of the Jewett character who makes do with meager pleasures (she cares for a crippled pigeon on her window ledge, for example.)

At first Miss Sydney resents the commercial enterprise Mrs. Marley has brought to her corner. Eventually, however, she takes pity on the woman, invites her in, learns of her dire situation, and offers the sisters substantial financial help. Miss Sydney learns to be unselfish and charitable late in life, and the moral of the story is that the "seeds of kindness and charity and helpfulness began to show themselves above the ground in the almost empty garden of her heart." Although it is openly moralistic, this story succeeds even for the modern reader; it approaches the power and pathos of a Tolstoy moral tale. (pp. 41-2)

Josephine Donovan, in her Sarah Orne Jewett, *Frederick Ungar Publishing Co., 1980, 165 p.*

CHARLES W. MAYER (essay date 1981)

[*In the excerpt below, Mayer examines Jewett's short story "The Only Rose" and compares her literary style with that of D. H. Lawrence.*]

Having pictured a New England in decline, Sarah Orne Jewett is usually seen as the guardian of a past culture who is intellectually and emotionally dependent on memories and uneasy in a contemporary world of time and change. She is described eloquently as presiding over a community's "flush of dying" or being bent on a "quest for permanence" to be found in the country life of former days. Recently she has been explained as a writer in conflict who created unresolved tensions between the attractions of an unchanging past and the necessity for growth and change or, similarly, between the "lost life of childhood" and an aggressive adult world. Such approaches, invaluable when showing how a sense of the past

The young writer of these Deephaven sketches was possessed by a dark fear that townspeople and country people would never understand one another, or learn to profit by their new relationship. She may have had the unconscious desire to make some sort of explanation to those who still expected to find the caricatured Yankee of fiction, striped trousers, bell-crowned hat, and all, driving his steady horses along the shady roads. It seemed not altogether reasonable when timid ladies mistook a selectman for a tramp, because he happened to be crossing a field in his shirt sleeves. At the same time, she was sensible of grave wrong and misunderstanding when these same timid ladies were regarded with suspicion, and their kindnesses were believed to come from pride and patronage. There is a noble saying of Plato that the best thing that can be done for the people of a state is to make them acquainted with one another. It was, happily, in the writer's childhood that Mrs. Stowe had written of those who dwelt along the wooded sea-coast and by the decaying, shipless harbors of Maine. The first chapters of *The Pearl of Orr's Island* gave the young author of **Deephaven** to see with new eyes, and to follow eagerly the old shore paths from one gray, weather-beaten house to another where Genius pointed her the way. . . .

The writer frankly confesses that the greater part of any value which these sketches may possess is in their youthfulness. There are sentences which make her feel as if she were the grandmother of the author of **Deephaven** and her heroines, those "two young ladies of virtue and honour, bearing an inviolable friendship for each other," as two others, less fortunate, are described in the preface to *Clarissa Harlowe*. She begs her readers to smile with her over those sentences as they are found not seldom along the pages, and so the callow wings of what thought itself to be wisdom and the childish soul of sentiment will still be happy and untroubled.

In a curious personal sense the author repeats her attempt to explain the past and the present to each other. This little book will remind some of those friends who read it first of

light that lit the olden days;

but there are kind eyes, unknown then, that are very dear now, and to these the pages will be new.

Sarah Orne Jewett in her preface to an 1893 edition of Deephaven.

to that book when nearly all of her finest stories were written. It is illustrated best, perhaps, by **"The Only Rose"** (1894), one of the last things published in that culminating decade. (p. 26)

"The Only Rose" is an admired story, but little or nothing has been done to define its art or its relationship to the other works of Jewett's maturity. With its strong conflict, rich interpenetration of character and action, and sustained tension ending in a moment of illuminating significance, it remains one of the most modern of her stories. Although the form is not typical of her highly pictorial, undramatic art, the theme captures accurately and vividly the vision I have been describing in the other works.

The story is in two sections. In the first, a well-to-do widow is arranging the flowers of early spring into bouquets of "absolute impartiality" for the graves of her three dead husbands. A single red rose blooms in the window, but Mrs. Bickford cannot decide which of the bouquets deserves it most. Disregarding the comment of a friendly neighbor, ". . . they're all in a better world now" and "can't feel such little things or take note o' slights same's we can," she is racked by indecision: to her last husband she owes "recognition" because he found her poor and left her comfortable; to her second husband, Mr. Wallis, she owes "amends" for disapproving of his foolish inventions that kept them in poverty; to her first husband, Albert, whom she married for love when both were little more than children, she feels neither indebted nor forgiving. In the second part Mrs. Bickford sets out on a visit to her sister's attended by her favorite nephew, the burying grounds being along the way; but still unable to decide about the rose, the poor woman has lost all spirit for the holiday. Learning, however, that John is engaged to be married to his childhood sweetheart, she becomes excited and at the cemetery lets her impetuous nephew carry the flowers to the grave, thus giving the rose up to "fate." John returns, the red rose "gay in his buttonhole." When he says, "I can give it to Lizzie," Mrs. Bickford laughingly accepts this verdict. The resolution of the conflict is expressed in her final words: "My first husband was just such a tall, straight young man as you be. . . . The flower he first give me was a rose."

On one level this deceptively simple tale develops a conflict of conscience through the protagonist's efforts to weigh and determine her moral debts to departed spouses. Yet the isolated, retarded pattern of her daily life reveals a deeper tension between the fretful intellect that looks to the dead past for answers and spontaneous feelings that open the valves of the heart and enable memory to illumine and enrich life instead of tormenting and confusing it. Supporting this view is Jewett's quite subtle use of Mrs. Bickford's house to suggest that, within it, life is arrested or flowing meagerly, cut off from the springs of vitality—passionate feelings—and guarding its owner from the natural rhythms of life outside.

The opening passages read very like some of D. H. Lawrence's in conveying through natural details a sense of isolation and suspension. Mrs. Bickford's large house stands alone just where the village ends, "looking down the road with all its windows." Behind these windows sits the old lady, her flower pots still on the ledge, although it is already early summer and others have put theirs out long ago. The flowers suggest a mechanical, though dutiful activity: "They rarely undertook to bloom, but had most courageously maintained life in spite of their owner's unsympathetic but conscientious care." Later we see that her housework is performed scrupu-

was crucial to the success of her regional pictures, seldom make allowances for her highly developed sense of the destructive or debilitating powers of the past over those who live for it or in it and are unable, as a result, to live vitally in the present. Nor do they always recognize how surely she knew that, although the past is dead, the memory of it is not, and may enrich life by helping us to seal the bond between generations and make commitments of the heart. This vision of the past, dependent on Jewett's appreciation of the act of living, is important in *The Country of the Pointed Firs* (1896) and in the chapters added after her death. The same vision, too, is very evident in the decade of achievement leading up lously but dully, without joy or pleasure. By degrees Mrs. Bickford emerges as a lonely, complaining, careworn, not unkindly woman, given to fits of silence, though always glad to be entertained or "taken off her own hands." She is reflective but seems to lack the inner resources that might nourish and sustain her, as her opposite number, the gay, sympathetic Abby Pendexter, seems to suspect. The house, the proof of her escape from poverty into comfort and safety, binds her to the past and gives her a prickly compunction to honor that past. For instance, she complains of the care her house costs her, while seeming to be jealously conscious of her right to it. It protects but troubles her. Nature, on the other hand, attracts and threatens. Mildly hypochondriacal, Mrs. Bickford won't have a garden because she must avoid the morning sun and because flowers in a close room give her a headache. Her fear of the sun is belied by the rolled-up curtains that always make her kitchen a "blaze of light." And her objection to flowers in the house quite ignores the possibility of enjoying them uncut. It is clear that she is afraid of nature because it is associated with intense passion suppressed throughout the long years of her two loveless marriages.

Through the motives of her central character Jewett has created an interesting association between conscience and comfort. Mrs. Bickford, in her security and ease, can forgive one husband who made her life hard and feel grateful to another who brought about her present state. By dwelling obsessively on the past, however, she has translated these feelings into stiff moral obligations that have little to do with reality: "I never done right by him," she says of the man whose rickety contrivances never worked right, except once when he succeeded in making a self-perpetuating butter churn even though the cow they depended on was completely dry. The other man, the saintly Bickford himself, was both enervated and boring and seems like Wallis to have taken as much as he gave in marriage: he "done everything by rule an' measure. . . . he was a very dignified appearing man; he used 'most always to sleep in the evenin's, Mr. Bickford did."

The falseness of Mrs. Bickford's position is revealed when she can give no convincing reason for wanting to pick the rose and cause herself such trouble in the first place. Something deeper than the carping mind makes her do it, of course. Her rose is a red one, the symbol of passionate love, and though she has not yet consciously thought of it, a rose was the first flower given her long ago by Albert, who, hearty and vigorous, was so different from a punctilious Bickford or a feckless Wallis. Of Albert she says, "I thought the world was done for me when he died." After subjecting her other husbands to the dissecting intellect, she thinks, "And then there was Albert," stopping because the reasoning mind or the moral conscience can take her no further. Although spontaneous feelings interfere repeatedly with the habitual processes of rumination, superficial reason is still dominant at the end of the first section when the romantic Abby is told by Mrs. Bickford that she is better off having failed to win the man she loved, for "a single woman's got her liberty."

The sureness with which Jewett has developed her character's inner struggle allows the recognition scene to unfold with perfect naturalness and credibility. In the carriage with her nephew, Mrs. Bickford at first continues to be alienated from nature, having a "contracted and assailed feeling out of doors"; but soon she feels the reassuring companionship of youth—the young son of her other sister is her favorite in that family—and begins to feel easy and "protected." Presently

she learns of John's love affair and is roused into a "comfortable self-forgetfulness." Thus, by bringing her away from the house, youth has brought her out of morbid imprisonment in the past, and now the news of love brings her back to nature: "I know who I do hope's got the right one," she murmurs when John disappears with the flowers. Moments later, when she sees the rose in his lapel, she has come, finally, to the human bond: "She thought of Albert, and the next moment tears came into her old eyes. John was a lover, too." The fretful self is quieted by the knowledge of the heart that love is always now, whether its name is Albert or John, and by a heightened sense of the continuity of life from one generation to the next, a feeling vital to old folks in so much of Jewett's fiction.

As at the start, there is something Lawrencian about Mrs. Bickford's illumination. Does it matter that her visit is a carefully planned event orchestrated by her sister's family for eliciting a formal blessing from a woman of property with no child of her own? The memory of love has been pushing itself into her consciousness—possibly for a very long time. Now it comes flooding forth, allowing her to escape the tyranny of a narrow reason in which the instinctive dictates of the heart have been ignored. Late in her life Jewett wrote to her young friend, Willa Cather, about a writer's conscience: "You must find your own quiet centre of life, and write from that to the world. . . ." She was thinking of the writer's rather solitary lot but added, "in short, you must write to the human heart. . . . And to write and work on this level, we must live on it. . . ." So it was that Jewett associated her own quiet centre—and that of her characters as well—not with some nostalgic vision of the past or uninvolved view of the passing scene but with a full commitment of the heart to the human life that flowed around her. (pp. 30-3)

Charles W. Mayer, "'The Only Rose': A Central Jewett Story," in Colby Library Quarterly, *Vol. XVII, No. 1, March, 1981, pp. 26-33.*

GEORGE HELD (essay date 1982)

[*In the following excerpt, which was originally published in the* Colby Library Quarterly *in 1982, Held examines moral conclusions drawn by Jewett through her juxtaposition of an experienced urban ornithologist and an innocent country girl in her story "A White Heron."*]

Though **"A White Heron"** has been among Sarah Orne Jewett's most admired stories since its publication in 1886, its richness and strength may appear even greater today in the light of a feminist perspective. This tale of nine-year-old Sylvia's encounter with a young male ornithologist, reverberates with meaning for such issues as the socialization of girls, the balance of power between the sexes, and the need for a woman to be true to her nature. In the heroine's conflict over revealing the heron to the young man, the story also concerns the need for mankind to resist the erosion of our integrity with the natural world.

Jewett herself claimed to "love" this fiction, though she despaired that it was too romantic to appeal to many readers in an age of literary realism. In fact an earlier story, **"The Shore House,"** had drawn praise from the champion of realism, William Dean Howells, who had "urged her to do more, for he thought that she had found her true bent in realism." Thus after having written the romantic **"A White Heron,"** Jewett refrained from trying to publish it in a magazine, as was her practice, and instead withheld it to appear first as the title story of a new collection of her work. Her reasons for this strategy she explained in a letter to her dearest friend, Annie Fields: "Mr. Howells thinks that this age frowns upon the romantic, that it is no use to write romance any more; but dear me, how much of it there is left in every-day life after all. It must be the fault of the writers that such writing is dull, but what shall I do with my **"White Heron"** now she is written? She isn't a very good magazine story, but I love her, and I mean to keep her for the beginning of my next book. . . .

Despite its admitted romanticism, **"A White Heron"** reflects some of the tough-minded independence that Sarah Jewett had developed from childhood and displayed particularly in the years following her father's death. The story dates from the end of that transitional period in her life when she was transferring her deepest human affection from her deceased father to Annie Fields, widow of the publisher James T. Fields. (p. 58)

Jewett was set apart by nature to be a writer and to be the companion of first her father and then another woman. In the three or four years prior to writing **"A White Heron,"** then, she had secured her union with Annie Fields, had paid homage to her late father, and had openly declared, for anyone willing to read *A Country Doctor* plainly, her independence from matrimony.

It was against this background that Jewett wrote **"A White Heron."** As its main character she chose a nine-year-old girl very like herself at that age and equally like little Nan Prince, of *A Country Doctor*, though children are rare in her fiction, which mainly concerns old people. "This lonely country child" Jewett named Sylvia, in reference to the girl's affinity for the forest. Like little Sarah and little Nan, "this little woods-girl" is at home among the trees and animal life of the "New England wilderness." Describing herself as a child, Jewett once wrote Whittier that in "the country out of which I grew, . . . every bush and tree seem like my cousins." And Annie Fields called her friend "a true lover of nature and . . . one accustomed to tender communings with woods and streams, with the garden and the bright air." In a similar vein, Dr. Leslie says of Nan Prince that "she has grown up as naturally as a plant grows, not having been clipped back or forced in any unnatural direction." Sylvia, then, clearly descends from Jewett and the autobiographical Nan Prince.

Also like Nan, Sylvia, through family misfortune, has come to live with her grandmother; Nan, based more explicitly on Sarah Jewett, soon proceeds to live with a doctor, her guardian Dr. Leslie. But for Sylvia it's crucial that she be isolate on her grandmother's farm, with no males about, because the conflict in this story occurs with the sudden, unexpected arrival of the ornithologist. The farmhouse is "lonely" and Sylvia's only "companion" is a prankish milch cow: "a plodding, dilatory, provoking creature in her behavior, but a valued companion for all that." Thus with an economy of detail that F. O. Matthiessen found new to her work in *A White Heron and Other Stories* [see Further Reading list], Jewett establishes the aloneness of her heroine.

Though alone—"the child had no playmates"—Sylvia is not lonesome; indeed she is incomparably happier in the country than she was during the first eight years of her life, spent "in a crowded manufacturing town." Released in the environs of the farm, Sylvia seems almost mythically at home: "there

never was such a child for straying about out-of-doors since the world was made!" thinks her grandmother. And "as for Sylvia herself, it seemed as if she never had been alive at all before she came to live at the farm." The key to her vivacity is that she is utterly in harmony with nature. As her grandmother tells the ornithologist, "There ain't a foot o' ground she don't know her way over, and the wild creatur's counts her one o' themselves."

The town-country antithesis indicated by the contrast between Sylvia's earlier life in "the noisy town" and her previous year on the "beautiful" farm introduces part of the underlying dialectic of this story. Its next increment appears in the ornithologist, whose presence Sylvia first becomes aware of through his whistle: "suddenly this little woods-girl is horror-stricken to hear a clear whistle not very far away. Not a bird's whistle, which would have a sort of friendliness, but a boy's whistle, determined, and somewhat aggressive." Jewett underscores the intrusion of this foreign sound into Sylvia's world by shifting, in these two sentences, into the present tense, a device she will use significantly twice more in the story. The comparison between a bird's whistle and a boy's helps to emphasize the antithesis between the forest creatures with whom Sylvia is friendly and "the great red-faced boy who used to chase and frighten her" in her hometown, about whom she has been thinking uneasily just before she hears the whistle. Thus when Jewett first introduces the ornithologist himself, she labels him "the enemy" and Sylvia responds "trembling," "alarmed," "awed." There seems, then, to be something threatening in his very "boyness" that makes Sylvia fearful and that perhaps psychologically predisposes her to reject him in the climax. Her awe of the ornithologist may in part be caused by his being the first grown-up boy she has seen in her woodland isolation. When he first appears to the girl she is practically unable to speak, and "she did not dare to look boldly at the tall young man, who carried a gun over his shoulder . . ." A gun, to paraphrase Freud, is sometimes only a gun, but in **"A White Heron"** the ornithologist's weapon may be a symbolic as well as a real threat. Later, her initial fear of him having abated, "Sylvia would have liked him vastly better without his gun . . . ," for whether deadly weapon or symbolic phallus, his hunting piece makes her uncomfortable.

No description of "the tall young man" or his dress is given; he is simply identified by the accoutrements of his profession, a gun and a game-bag heavy with the birds he has killed and collected. Mainly, the ornithologist is characterized by his voice. Toward Sylvia, whom he hails as "little girl," he adopts the superior tone of one older, more cosmopolitan, and maler, but he also speaks to her "kindly" and "gallantly," trying to calm her fears and win her assistance. By the time he has supped, the recipient of the grandmother's hospitality, the young man and his hosts have become "new-made friends." Yet we sense exploitation in the relationship: in exchange for supper and lodging, the guest provides merely the entertainment of a stranger to the isolated and his charm, while all the time plotting to use his hosts in his quest to collect the white heron.

That Jewett sees the ornithologist as an outsider inimical to the farmstead is illustrated by Mrs. Tilley the grandmother's reference to her son Dan, who "was a great hand to go gunning," but who hunted only for food. By contrast, her guest goes gunning in the interest of an abstraction, the science of ornithology, and of his egoistic desire to complete his bird collection. He self-importantly tells Mrs. Tilley, "I am making a collection of birds myself. I have been at it ever since I was a boy." Then in response to her question whether he cages them, he says, "Oh, no, they're stuffed and preserved, dozens and dozens of them, . . . and I have shot or snared every one myself." His pride in his expertise allies him with those characters in Hawthorne who have sacrificed warm humanity on the chill altar of science; but Jewett's ornithologist is less evil than banal, for his cheery egoism reflects the optimism of the nineteenth-century despoilers of nature who deforested the woods where she grew up. (pp. 59-62)

During the ornithologist's conversation with his aged hostess, he listens insensitively yet selectively: he "did not notice [the] hint of family sorrows [in Mrs. Tilley's discourse] in his eager interest in something else," but he grasps alertly the useful information that Sylvia knows all about birds. And at this point he brings up a white heron he has spotted and pursued to the vicinity of the farm. He calls the bird a little white heron, a species unknown to that area. In ornithological fact, such a bird was never more than a casual visitor as far north as southern Maine. It is usually known as the snowy egret, but also as the little white egret and the snowy heron, among several other names. Around the time Jewett wrote her story the snowy egret was being extirpated to fill the need of the millinery industry. By 1900 it was almost extinct, and in 1913 it was completely protected by the federal government. Thus its rareness may have prompted Jewett to select the little white heron for her story in order to give her bird unusual value. In addition, she depicts the creature as odd: the ornithologist describes it as "a queer tall bird," and Sylvia instantly knows it as "that strange white bird." Strangeness and whiteness in a wild creature recall Moby Dick. Does Jewett hope to probe the skies with her bird as Melville tries to sound the depths with his whale? On her decidedly smaller scale, **"A White Heron"** does involve a hunt that focuses on a white prey valuable for both material and symbolic reasons and that causes a conflict in values between its pursuers such as we find in *Moby Dick or, The White Whale.* Of course, the ornithologist is no Ahab, Sylvia no Starbuck; but saving the white heron is the rough equivalent of Starbuck's humane policy's winning out in *Moby Dick.*

In order to induce Sylvia to lead him to the sought-after bird, the ornithologist offers a reward of ten dollars. In the moral and dialectical scheme of the story, this offer amounts to a bribe of the poor by the rich, the seduction of good by evil. Its impact on the girl is so great that "no amount of thought, that night, could decide how many wished-for treasures the ten dollars, so lightly spoken of, could buy." By offering to pay for a favor that would otherwise be done as but a gesture of country hospitality, the ornithologist introduces into a subsistence economy the instrumentality of money. Perhaps no other element of his determination to secure the heron as a specimen more bespeaks his alien presence at the farm and suggests the possibility of corruption from without than his proffer of the ten dollars. Thus at the climax Sylvia, dearly tempted to please the young man, reasons, "He can make them rich with money; he has promised it, and they are poor now." Despite his attractive qualities, there is something insidious about his attempt to bribe the girl in effect to betray her world. Yes, he represents the broader, more cosmopolitan world beyond the New England wilderness, the man of science and technique, and the rich, in contradistinction to the poor but homely people on the farmstead. But he also suggests a sort of blithe Satan tempting a naïve Eve to eat of the

fruit of the Tree of Knowledge. From this point of view the Maine woods parallels the Garden of Eden, and the early label of "the enemy" for the ornithologist becomes recognizable as a traditional term for Satan.

It should also be noted that the introduction of money into the story has the effect of interfering with Sylvia's instinctive harmony with the natural world. As the ornithologist tells of his quest for the heron, the girl has been watching a hop-toad and disguising her recognition of the white bird he has referred to. But after the ten dollars has been mentioned, "Sylvia still watched the toad, not divining, *as she might have done at some calmer time,* that the creature wishes to get to its hole under the doorstep, and was much hindered by the unusual spectators at that hour in the evening" (my emphasis). Her mind on the "treasures" his money could buy, she loses her usual sympathy for the wild.

The next day, however, Sylvia is tempted less by the young sportsman's money than by his masculine appeal. Though he "hovered about the woods" like the bird of prey he speculates may have chased the heron out of its home region, Sylvia finds him "friendly," "most kind and sympathetic." In a gesture with possible phallic significance, "he gave her a jack-knife, which she thought as great a treasure as if she were a desert-islander," though the gift also has the aspect of a trinket for the natives. Despite her discomfort over his gun and the birds he brings down with it, "Sylvia still watched the young man with loving admiration. She had never seen anybody so charming and delightful; the woman's heart, asleep in the child, was vaguely thrilled by a dream of love." If this romantic response seems a strange turn for a story about a nine-year-old to take, it nevertheless has a certain psychological validity. Though originally frightened by her association of the ornithologist with the town boy, Sylvy now sees only the superficial charm and attractiveness of the young sportsman; he also impresses her with his knowledge of birds, though this is not so great as to lead him to perceive that they should be preserved, not collected. Moreover, many a nine-year-old girl feels attracted to or develops a crush on an older boy or a man, especially one who might drop unique from the sky like our ornithologist *ex machina.* If the young girl has no one to warn her of the possible consequent dangers, she is quite liable to go on, as Sylvia does, in a kind of thrall to him. At this point Jewett's alliterative style enhances the romantic aura of the situation: "Some premonition of that great power [love] stirred and swayed these young foresters who traversed the solemn woodlands with soft-footed silent care"—a twenty-one word sentence containing twelve sibilants, including six initial *s*'s.

True to the roles that age and gender have assigned them, the young man leads the way and the girl follows. In other words, even though she knows these woods better than he, expertise leads instinct, male leads female. Nevertheless, Sylvia's feelings are ambivalent: "She grieved because the longed-for white heron was elusive, but she did not lead the guest, she only followed, and there was no such thing as speaking first." In this sentence Jewett implies that if the girl would, she could take the lead; she could speak up and say she's seen the heron and will show the way to it. But her socialization as a girl, ironically, saves her from revealing the bird and therefore betraying her world to this intruder. For if Sylvia were a boy or if the element of romantic attraction were eliminated, she could quite readily speak up and take the lead.

Given the situation as it is, however, Sylvia feels extraordinary tension: "The sound of her own unquestioned voice would have terrified her—it was hard enough to answer yes or no when there was need of that." The tone has now, within the space of a few sentences, shifted from sensuously romantic to threateningly gothic. What does "her own unquestioned voice" mean? That she has not been asked a question that would allow her to voice a response? Or that she herself daren't make a sound without questioning her motivation? In any case, this sentence depicts a girl in peril. This is also the climax of the first part of the story, which ends a sentence later in a tone of pastoral serenity as Sylvy and the sportsman drive home the cow together, and the "pleasure" that she felt the previous evening over listening to the thrushes is replaced by the "pleasure" of coming "to the place where she heard the whistle and was afraid only the night before." A day's outing has thus brought the girl closer in sympathy to the young man than to the natural world.

Part 2 of **"A White Heron"** relates Sylvia's quest for the sought-after bird and focuses on a giant pine tree, "the last of its generation" to remain standing in the wake of the wood-choppers. No doubt the tree is based on Jewett's memory of a childhood favorite of hers that did not survive the lumbermen, and about which she wrote to Annie Fields, "Alas, when I went to see my beloved big pitch-pine tree that I loved best of all the wild trees that lived in Berwick, I found only the broad stump of it beside the spring, and the top boughs of it scattered far and wide. It was a real affliction. . . ." The "excitement" that Sylvia felt while walking behind the ornithologist the previous day has been superseded by "a new excitement" as she thinks of climbing the tree to enable her to "see all the world, and easily discover whence the white heron flew, and mark the place, and find the hidden nest."

At this point in the story the narrator formulates its crux: "Alas, if the great wave of human interest which flooded for the first time this dull life should sweep away the satisfactions of an existence heart to heart with nature and the dumb life of the forest!" This didactic rendering of the threat to Sylvia's innocence is both condescending and supererogatory. To call the girl's romantic excitement over the young sportsman a "great wave of human interest" generalizes and diminishes what has earlier been "a dream of love"; to speak of her "dull little life" unnecessarily belittles the charming, if not charmed, existence that has earlier been characterized as making Sylvia feel "as if she had never been alive at all before she came to live at the farm." Still, this authorial intrusion does express nicely the substance of Sylvia's quiet strength: living "heart to heart with nature." It is this wholly integrated existence that the ornithologist, and all that he represents, ultimately threatens. We have seen how the lure of his money put Sylvia out of sympathy with the hop-toad. Now, as she climbs the great pine tree at dawn, she disturbs a bird in its nest, and a red squirrel scolds her; she has become a "harmless housebreaker" to the very creatures among whom she'd walked at the beginning of the story "as if she were a part of the gray shadows and the moving leaves" of the forest. But the "little birds and beasts" were then "in the great boughs overhead," and Sylvia was on the ground. Once she is aloft in the pine tree, "the sharp dry twigs caught and held her and scratched her like angry talons, the pitch made her little fingers clumsy and stiff," as though nature itself sought to keep her from succeeding in her project and thereby breaching their heart-to-heart relationship.

The higher Sylvia climbs, however, the more her harmony with nature seems restored. Jewett personifies the great tree as in a fairy tale: "The old pine tree must have loved his new dependent," supporting and lifting her along the way to his summit. Purified in the heights she has reached, Sylvia becomes metaphorically at one with the universe: her face is "like a pale star," and she feels "as if she . . . could go flying among the clouds" with a pair of hawks. Despite the wonder of the view from atop the tree, the girl resolutely wants to discover the white heron's nest: "was this wonderful sight and pageant of the world the only reward for having climbed to such a giddy height?" Would she who has lived so contentedly in the natural world have thought about a "reward" previous to the ornithologist's offer of ten dollars? At this point the narrator shifts into the imperative mood and the present tense, pointing out to Sylvia the white heron rising in flight from a dead hemlock far below, directing her to remain motionless and unconscious lest she reveal herself and deflect the bird from reaching the perch he assumes on a pine bough close to her. "Well satisfied" by knowing the secret of the heron's nesting place, Sylvia painfully "makes her perilous way down again" filled with thoughts of the ornithologist's response to her news of the bird's location.

The present tense works well to create a sense of immediacy and heighten the drama of Sylvia's discovery. In contrast, back at the farm her grandmother and the guest awake in the past tense, removed in time, place, and sense of wonder from the girl's experience. But as she enters their presence, with the young man determined that she tell what she knows of the heron, Jewett once more shifts into the present tense: "Here she comes now, paler than ever, and her worn old frock is torn and tattered, and smeared with pine pitch." "Paler," she approximates the whiteness of the heron, while the pitiful condition of her frock emphasizes her poverty and her need of the ten dollars; "smeared with pine pitch," she wears the shameful sign of her enterprise to find the bird but also the badge of her identity as a "dependent" of the tree. The shift in tense here increases the suspense at the climactic moment, "the splendid moment [that] has come to speak of the dead hemlock-tree . . .". In this instant Sylvia balances the desire to earn the ten dollars and to please the attractive stranger against her unspoken fidelity to nature. As Jewett formulates it, "Has she been nine years growing, and now, when the great world for the first time puts out a hand to her, must she thrust it aside for a bird's sake?" But how can "the great world" that the ornithologist represents compensate her for the world that she has seen from atop the pine tree, a world in which she recalls having achieved a union, with the white heron as it "came flying through the golden air and . . . *they* watched the sea and the morning *together*" (my emphasis)? Her heart stirred for a bird, "Sylvia cannot speak; she cannot tell the heron's secret and give its life away."

Most readers will find that **"A White Heron"** would better end here. They will regret the didactic final paragraph, with its apostrophes, its needless question, and its mixed tone. But it also contains some pertinent material. In its first sentence Jewett addresses Sylvia as "Dear loyalty" and rather satirically suggests that, had things been otherwise with the guest, "she could have served and followed him and loved him as a dog loves." Though Sylvia has earlier followed the ornithologist in the woods, Jewett's principled opposition to such subservience, as expressed in *A Country Doctor,* makes it clear that no heroine of hers could be allowed such a fate. The final paragraph also contains this vivid picture of the fate that would have awaited the white heron had Sylvia revealed its nest to the collector: "the sharp report of his gun and the piteous sight of thrushes and sparrows dropping silent to the ground, their songs hushed and their pretty feathers stained and wet with blood."

As the story concludes, all woodland and summertime secrets are, like the heron's, safe with "this lonely country child." For in the end the heron's life has become the equivalent of the girl's life, at least of her existence heart to heart with nature. In addition, the heron signifies the solemnity and beauty of the natural world that human beings relinquish at the cost of impoverishing their existence. For Sylvia, to surrender the bird would be to surrender her integrity with the natural world as well as with herself, since the heron has come to represent anything precious that a girl might yield for the sake of a man, but only at her peril. Resistant to masculine allure, and the offer of monetary profit, Sylvia, can grow into a woman like Nan Prince or Sarah Jewett, a woman committed to values that will allow her to be her natural self and lead a life heart to heart with her own nature. (pp. 62-7)

> George Held, "Heart to Heart with Nature: Ways of Looking at 'A White Heron'," in Critical Essays on Sarah Orne Jewett, edited by Gwen L. Nagel, G. K. Hall & Co., 1984, pp. 58-68.

MARJORIE PRYSE (essay date 1982)

[*In the following excerpt from an essay originally published in the journal* American Literary Realism *in 1982, Pryse identifies "foreigners" and "foreign" experiences in Jewett's story "The Foreigner," comparing the tale with Henry James's "The Turn of the Screw" and determining whether it should be viewed as a ghost story.*]

Like *Pointed Firs* itself and many of Jewett's stories, **"The Foreigner"** appears to rely heavily on setting. However, from the opening paragraphs, particularly for the reader who approaches the story apart from *Pointed Firs,* the apparent setting serves immediately to bring out the inner anxieties of the women present. The story opens as "The first cold northeasterly storm of the season was blowing hard outside" and Mrs. Todd arrives to pay the narrator a visit. For the narrator, the storm possesses significance even before Mrs. Todd enters her room: "I could hear that the sea was already stirred to its dark depths, and the great rollers were coming in heavily against the shore. One might well believe that Summer was coming to a sad end that night. . . . It seemed as if there must be danger offshore among the outer islands."

For Mrs. Todd, the storm evokes fears which may appear initially unrelated to her actual story about "the foreigner." She tells the narrator, " 'I know nothing ain't ever happened out to Green Island since the world began, but I always do worry about mother in these great gales.' " She dwells on imagined dangers: tidal waves, an accident to her brother William's boat, that the August storm might have caught them unprepared. As she and the narrator sit before the fire, "we could feel the small wooden house rock and hear it creak as if it were a ship at sea." The two women might be the wives of seagoing men from the days when Dunnet Landing was an active port, except that neither woman is worried about a man. Both join in worrying about "mother" out on Green Island.

The narrator sympathizes with the "families of sailors and coastwise adventurers by sea." They "must always be worrying about somebody, this side of the world or the other. There was hardly one of Mrs. Todd's elder acquaintances, men or women, who had not at some time or other made a sea voyage, and there was often no news until the voyagers themselves came back to bring it." Some women, Mrs. Todd comments, go to sleep in order to forget, " 'but 't ain't my way.' " Her way is to sit and worry, preferably not alone. The narrator's initial function, for Mrs. Todd, seems not that of mere listener to the story the older woman eventually relates, but rather that of an intimate who can share Mrs. Todd's anxieties.

" 'You have never told me any ghost stories,' " says our narrator by way of suggestion, and as **"The Foreigner"** unfolds, it is easy to disregard the storm as merely an introduction to what does seem to be a ghost story. Like the narrative frame of James's "The Turn of the Screw," the opening section of **"The Foreigner"** appears to set the stage for the tale; yet this tale comments on the narrative frame itself in much more subtle ways than does James's novella. **"The Foreigner"** is no mere ghost story.

As is the case with many of Jewett's stories and sketches, a story within a story creates the narrative design and a visit provides the narrative occasion for **"The Foreigner."** Both of these elements in the work remain apparent throughout. At no point does our narrator move directly into the story Mrs. Todd tells; at every point she allows Mrs. Todd to tell her own story. The effects are several. For one, the device makes Mrs. Todd herself as much the focus of the story as the story she tells. Second, both that story and our narrator's experience with Mrs. Todd are clearly mediated, even translated, for the reader by means of the narrative within a narrative. And finally, because our narrator is conspicuously present throughout the telling, the story creates a Jamesian "personal, direct impression" in the reader by portraying the impression Mrs. Todd herself makes on the narrator. For some readers unaccustomed to Jewett's method, the result may be an apparent loss of suspense. Most of us, after all, may have been trained by Henry James in the art of telling a good ghost story. For James, the ghosts in "The Turn of the Screw" must make their own direct impressions on their readers/hearers. For Jewett, the final appearance of the ghost is anticlimactic; the story dramatizes not the appearance of the ghost but rather Mrs. Todd's attempt to translate the experience of being "foreign" for her listener, our narrator.

Both Mrs. Todd and the narrator are trying to understand an experience which has been "foreign" to them. In Mrs. Todd's case, both her character and her listener are foreign. She becomes an interpreter for her listener, who is a guest in her house and at Dunnet Landing. For our narrator, the reader is also a foreigner; in creating the world of Dunnet Landing by means of local speech rhythms and details of weather, history, and topography (all in self-conscious use of the stylistic conventions of "local color" writing), our narrator becomes Mrs. Todd's interpreter for her own "listener"— the reader. In a sense, the impulse to "translate" or to "interpret" life for listeners and readers explains the realist's intention, as Howells implied when he wrote that a writer's business "is to make you understand the real world through his [or her] faithful effigy of it." But the unexamined question which runs through Jewett's work involves the nature of the world itself which Jewett's "effigies" portray. In this particular story, the nature of foreign experience is the central concern. What is "foreign" about Mrs. Todd? What does the narrator need to "translate" about her in order for the reader to understand her?

There is, of course, the experience she had with Mrs. Tolland, the main character in Mrs. Todd's own narrative. Mrs. Tolland was herself a foreigner, alienated from the community of women in Dunnet Landing by religion (she was Catholic) and cultural heritage (she was French). Her manners and customs differed from theirs—she felt alone in the meeting house and danced in the vestry; she was isolated for her strangeness. She was hard to feel close to; she died of solitude and grief just a few months after hearing the news that her husband had died at sea. But she has given Mrs. Todd more than the money she eventually left her: she has shown Mrs. Todd a great deal about herbs, plants, and cooking. Hearing about Mrs. Tolland therefore helps our narrator understand Mrs. Todd better. Some of this understanding seems superficial—she knows why Mrs. Todd makes good omelettes. But some of it goes deeper—Mrs. Todd herself is different from the other women in the community. At her mother's urging she initially befriended Mrs. Tolland, even though she remained aware of their distance. " 'I never gave her a kiss till the day she laid in her coffin and it came to my heart there wa'n't no one else to do it.' "

Mrs. Todd thinks that she has gained from Mrs. Tolland a knowledge of death. She describes sitting with Mrs. Tolland in the last moments of her life, when " 'All of a sudden she set right up in bed with her eyes wide open. . . . And she reached out both arms toward the door, an' I looked the way she was lookin', an' I see some one was standin' there against the dark.' " This is the moment in which **"The Foreigner"** becomes a ghost story. At first Mrs. Todd was uncertain: " 'I felt dreadful cold and my head begun to swim. . . .' " But she carried on: " 'I did try to act calm, an' I laid Mis' Tolland down on her pillow, an' I was a-shakin' as I done it.' " But Mrs. Tolland was consoled: " 'You saw her, didn't you?' she says to me, speakin' perfectly reasonable. ' 'T is my mother,' she says again. . . .' " Mrs. Todd's uncertainty passed and she, too, felt relieved: " 'I felt calm then, an' lifted to somethin' different as I never was since.' " Mrs. Tolland opened her eyes in the moment of death and asked Mrs. Todd a second time, " 'You saw her, didn't you?' " And Mrs. Todd tells how she said, " 'Yes, dear, I did; you ain't never goin' to feel strange and lonesome no more.' "

What is unexpected for the reader, and probably for the narrator as well, about Mrs. Todd's response to seeing Mrs. Tolland's mother is that no one is frightened. We know that the narrator initially expected to be frightened—she states, at the beginning of **"The Foreigner,"** that after she had suggested to Mrs. Todd that she tell a ghost story, "I was instantly filled with reluctance to have this suggestion followed. . . . I was really afraid that she was going to tell me something that would haunt my thoughts on every dark stormy night as long as I lived." In the moment of Mrs. Tolland's death, the James reader might feel most strongly the apparent anticlimax—the ghost, when it finally does arrive, does not appall. Rather, the appearance of the ghost allows Mrs. Todd to console her dying friend: " 'you ain't never goin' to feel strange and lonesome no more.' " Death, the one experience to which all living narrators and readers feel foreign, is stripped of its strangeness and its lonesomeness.

Mrs. Todd, then, becomes a figure very much like the speaker in Emily Dickinson's poem "Just lost, when I was saved!"—

someone who has caught a glimpse of death and returns to tell about it. The real foreigner now seems to be not Mrs. Tolland but her mother—the ghost. But the experience of having seen the ghost makes Mrs. Todd an equal foreigner. Her story is about the glimpse she once had of another world, and as she translates that glimpse, she sits knitting, and the storm rages. We have moved back into the narrative frame. She expresses her opinion that " 'You know plain enough there's somethin' beyond this world; the doors stand wide open. There's somethin' of us that must still live on; we've got to join both worlds together an' live in one but for the other. The doctor said that to me one day, an' I never could forget it. . . .' " In the process of telling her ghost story, ghost stories have ceased to create anxiety. In relating the sense of calm she felt when Mrs. Tolland's mother appeared to her daughter, she calms those other anxieties with which the story opened, and as the weather returns to normal ("the sea still roared, but the high wind had done blowing"), Mrs. Todd's worry about her own mother has implicitly calmed: " 'Yes, there goes the boat; they'll find it rough at sea, but the storm's all over.' "

For the narrator, Mrs. Todd is like someone who has journeyed to another world and come back to tell the story. Making a "sea voyage" takes on the resonance of exploring "this side of the world or the other," like those "sailors and coastwise adventurers by sea" whose families the narrator had sympathized with earlier; and this is precisely what Mrs. Todd has done by the time she finishes her narrative: she has described the time *she* explored "the other" side of the world in the moment in which she saw the "foreigner," the ghost of Mrs. Tolland's mother. Again like those "adventures by sea," about whom "there was often no news until the voyagers themselves came back to bring it," Mrs. Todd has told the circumstances of Mrs. Tolland's death "to but very few." The effect is that she has "come back" from a voyage bringing news.

What is ultimately "foreign" for the reader about this story may be that Mrs. Todd's "sea voyage" has no real ship, and that her "news" is so well disguised as ghost story that we miss its greater import. Her "ship" and the "news" with which she returns are intertwined. It is her anxieties, her fears and her memories, which are tossed about as she and the narrator sit indoors while the season's first "nor'easter" rages outside. In earlier nineteenth-century American fiction, we are accustomed to seeing real battles with the elements (in *Moby Dick,* for example) as metaphors for experience; in **"The Foreigner,"** Mrs. Todd's experience seems at first to be only a metaphoric "sea voyage"—yet it is as real a battle as women in her circumstances can have. It is a story about a woman's anxieties and the way she tries to calm them; it concerns Mrs. Todd's inner life in more detail than even the sketches in *The Country of the Pointed Firs;* and it illustrates the way in which Mrs. Todd tries to "join both worlds together an' live in one but for the other." It is too easy to identify one of those "worlds" as the world of men and of action and the other as the world of the women who stay home knitting while the men enact the "real" battles. Rather, **"The Foreigner"** suggests that while the women's experience of the storm may have nothing to do with the immediate effects of battling it (they sit indoors knitting), the real storm for the women is the one anxiety creates. And the real anxiety for women is not that of being cut off from the physical elements but of feeling separated from that "other world" where "mother" resides, and therefore where it is not necessary to feel "strange an' lonesome."

Eased anxiety and a sense of being "at home" rather than being "at sea," for both Mrs. Tolland and Mrs. Todd, are the result of becoming reunited with their mothers. What initially seems "foreign" about the story becomes quite commonplace indeed, very much an effigy of real life: the story is about the anxiety Mrs. Todd feels at being separated from her mother; she is "at sea" until the storm passes. While Mrs. Tolland lived, Mrs. Todd's mother served to unite the younger women; in the moment of her death, her own mother appears to unite the two friends. Mrs. Todd is left with her memory of the moment in which Mrs. Tolland's mother eased her daughter's way into that most foreign of human experiences, death—and, therefore, telling Mrs. Tolland's story brings her into close contact with her own mother, in spite of the danger she feels on her mother's behalf from the "great gales."

The story which our narrator "composes" (in the Howellsian sense) involves the juxtaposition of the dead Mrs. Tolland and her mother, and the living Mrs. Todd and *her* mother; but the pattern comes to include the narrator as well. By her very presence as a "foreigner," a summer visitor, in Dunnet Landing, she is either trying to escape urban turmoil or, more accurately, to find inner peace. Her presence there suggests that she, too, feels cut off from that "other world." At the beginning of the story, then, it is the narrator who appears as Jewett's foreigner. Mrs. Todd is her friend but also her hostess; when the older woman enters the narrator's room, she becomes her "guest" as well. Despite the "harmony" of their "fellowship," a conventional and formal distance separates the two women—until Mrs. Todd tells her story. Mrs. Todd's description of the woman she came to feel close sympathy with (Mrs. Tolland) parallels the unspoken experience of the narrator, who is encountering the inner life of a woman she has become acquainted with, and encountering it directly and deeply for the first time. In the Jamesian sense, then, our narrator comes to have a "personal, direct impression" of Mrs. Todd's "other world," her inner life.

By implication, telling the story about Mrs. Todd allows the narrator to become reunited with her own inner life, just as Mrs. Todd has had a consoling experience of the "other world" and has "come back" to tell about it. Just as the narrator stated at the beginning when she became aware of Mrs. Todd's worries about her mother, by the story's end she has also "thought as [she] had never thought before of such anxieties." Yet in thinking about them, and particularly by telling her story, she is also able to ease them. Mrs. Todd's story, far from telling her "something that would haunt [her] thoughts on every dark stormy night," gives her something to mitigate those thoughts. For Mrs. Todd, in her stance not simply as storyteller but as the older woman and a "sea-goer," becomes a figure of the narrator's mother. More is at stake than the relationship between storyteller and listener; and by extension, more is also at stake between the story's narrator and her own reader, if that reader happens to be female. Women sit together around the home fire on a stormy night not merely to entertain each other, as they ostensibly do in James's "The Turn of the Screw," but to teach each other, to pass down from mother to daughter the ability to "live in one world but for the other." (pp. 90-6)

Mrs. Todd understands that much as the lives of women, like the lives of men, may furnish metaphors for vision, she is not

a separatist and Dunnet Landing, though populated by many women alone, is no mere sisterhood. In describing the " 'old part of the buryin' ground' " to Jewett's narrator, Mrs. Todd remarks, " 'All their women folks lies there; the sea's got most o' the men.' " Those great foreign experiences of death and human anxiety in the face of the unknown know no gender. It is significant that Mrs. Todd's closing advice to the narrator ("we've got to join both worlds together") comes not out of her own experience but from one of the " 'old doctor's books.' " This may be the only moment in **"The Foreigner"** which assumes prior knowledge of *The Country of the Pointed Firs,* for the doctor is a familiar figure for the readers of that novel: he is Mrs. Todd's rival. He with his medicines and the herbalist with her lore have learned to work together to heal the sick and comfort the lonely in Dunnet Landing. In creating a fictional world which, though not devoid of men, seems unconcerned with relationships between men and women, Jewett lends even greater significance to Mrs. Todd's advice. "We've got to join both worlds together"—the world of men at sea and women, at home but equally "at sea"—in order to comprehend fully not just New England regional literature but the entire canon of American fiction. Literary critics have a lot to learn from those women writers (like Harriet Beecher Stowe, Mary E. Wilkins Freeman, Rose Terry Cooke, Alice Brown, and others including Jewett) whom they have for so long described as "limited in scope." Mrs. Todd's mother, speaking through her own daughter's narrative, offers the best advice of all to readers both male and female who would re-examine the work of our women writers with the goal of understanding more than the male half of the American experience:

> " 'What consequence is my supper?' says she to me; mother can be very stern,—'or your comfort or mine, beside letting a foreign person an' a stranger feel so desolate; she's done the best a woman could do in her lonesome place, and she asks nothing of anybody except a little common kindness. Think if 't was you in a foreign land!' "

Let us provision the house of American criticism, like Captain Tolland, as if our women were going to put to sea the same as our men. Only then will the inner lives of women cease to be foreign, and women themselves cease to be foreigners. (pp. 97-8)

> *Marjorie Pryse, "Women 'at Sea': Feminist Realism in Sarah Orne Jewett's 'The Foreigner',"* in Critical Essays on Sarah Orne Jewett, *edited by Gwen L. Nagel, G. K. Hall & Co., 1984, pp. 89-98.*

MICHAEL HOLSTEIN   (essay date 1988)

[*Holstein is a lecturer at the Chinese University of Hong Kong. In the following excerpt, he examines women as healers and educators in* The Country of the Pointed Firs, *citing specific cases that reflect general patterns in the development of Jewett's characters.*]

Crucial to an understanding of *The Country of the Pointed Firs* is an appreciation of the narrator Sarah Orne Jewett presents. Unlike Jewett, who was a native of Maine and needed no introduction to the inhabitants of a small coastal town, Jewett's narrator comes as a summer visitor. She is a *näif* in the tradition of other protagonists of travel literature whose initial impressions of a quaint people are gradually disabused. This narrator is further particularized as a writer facing a di-

Jewett in the front doorway of her house at South Berwick.

lemma: whether to disengage herself from society in order to write about it objectively, obeying "the voice of conscience" that urges her to isolate herself in order to write, or to participate in the life of the community, an obligation that chides her when, in order to write, she finally does excuse herself with "unkind words of withdrawal." Although the explicit stories Jewett tells concern the inhabitants of a mythical New England town, Dunnet Landing, a secondary narrative records the process of the narrator's finding a stance adequate to her subject and her needs as a writer. At issue are the competing claims of artistic and social responsibility, questions of whether she should stand in her material or outside of it, and ultimately, the choice between solipsism and social meliorism.

The narrator solves her dilemma by adopting the role of a writer-healer, a role she perfects at the elbow of Almira Todd, her landlady, business associate, and friend, under whom she serves a summer apprenticeship. Mrs. Todd is an herbalist, but from the beginning she seems to possess skills and insight essential to a writer. . . . Mrs. Todd is, among other things, a good story teller who, as she dispenses herbs, manages words ably and knows nature and human nature well enough to weave a good plot into her prescriptions. She has important lessons for the narrator. The education of the narrator in her vocation, especially as it is supervised by the healer and parallels the healer's role, is the theme that brings together the many episodes that would otherwise diffuse into anecdotes and sketches.

The starting point for both healer and narrator is the general deterioration of the people of the region. The narrator depicts the grim toll taken on the population of Dunnet Landing by the depressed economy and demographic shift in the latter part of the nineteenth century. As a result of blockade during the Civil War, as well as rising tariffs, by the conclusion of the century New England shipping was at a standstill, its condition poignantly captured at the end of the book when the narrator casts a retrospective glance at Dunnet Landing and "the tall masts of its disabled schooners." Fishing grounds were no longer as prolific as in the past, so that fishermen had to work harder to bring in less. The decline of the region was further aggravated by the deaths of its mariners at sea, fatalities during the Civil War, and, later, the migrations westward towards the cheap, fertile land of the middle west and the plains states. Small farms on windswept, rocky land were no longer profitable once they had to compete with mechanized farming. The narrator passes abandoned houses on farms being reclaimed by the forest. Over the town hangs a brooding sense of mortality. Few unqualified young and healthy inhabitants appear in the book. The world of Dunnet Landing is old, weary, empty, impoverished, sick, and in its steep decline. Its inhabitants are synecdoches for the region: they represent the fact of mortality. As Mrs. Todd remarks, "the time o' sickness and failin' has got to come to all."

Although both the travelogue and sketch suggest themselves as shaping *Pointed Firs,* another kind of narrative at work here, one Jewett learned accompanying her father on his medical practice, is the case history. The "case histories" of *Pointed Firs* are the closely observed, detailed accounts the narrator keeps of people she meets, usually in the company of Mrs. Todd making her rounds. In her many visits to her neighbors, she tells the stories of those who endure serious physical or psychological sufferings. Her method is that of an interviewer. She listens closely, queries gently, and puts herself in sympathetic proximity to the inner lives of the people she visits. Then she writes the record, a blend of what she witnessed and the meaning she finds in the experience.

That meaning is usually, but not always, the successful struggle of the inhabitants against deterioration. Out of her case histories, themselves part of a social history (Jewett's realism), the narrator weaves a therapeutic plot (Jewett's idealism). There is a constant interplay in the book between the specific case and a general pattern of inner trial and affirmation. Individual lives are primary material for the resiliance that belongs to the species. The narrator generalizes from settings, incidents, and characters so often because generalizations insist on the vigor of the human spirit in a sea of troubles. In random meetings, she portrays a collective struggle against environment, old age, disease, personal loss, and economic decline. Indeed, the seeming randomness of episodes guarantees the universality of her theme, for wherever she goes she encounters people resisting their fate. Her motive is to assemble records of those who have succumbed to their trials as well as of those who have triumphed over them and have set an example for others. Common to the life stories of the characters is the thread of self-healing achieved through solitude, duty, and rituals of the everyday, the significant routines of ordinary life that offer examples of discipline and direction to the apprentice writer.

Thus, in individual case histories the narrator finds admirable composure in those who face the "burden of years," especially in Mrs. Blackett and Mrs. Todd, about whom she remarks, "I hoped in my heart that I might be like them as I lived on into age, and then smiled to think that I too was no longer very young. So we always keep the same hearts, though our outer framework fails and shows the touch of time." To face the inevitable facts of the human condition while having enough heart left to offer a writer's remedies is a major project of *Pointed Firs.* From the accounts of individuals the narrator generalizes about the spiritual resilience within this New England community. If there is rural decline, there is also the strength of Jewett's characters, not only sickness and aging but the determined conservation of health; not only provinciality, but an elemental rootedness in tradition, in the land and in the sea; not only reclusiveness, but solitudes as deliberately chosen as monastic vocations. The narrator comes to Dunnet Landing to record the daily lives of its inhabitants and to discover the spiritual resources still available to the community. Warner Berthoff has remarked [in his essay "The Art of Jewett's *Pointed Firs*" published in *Women Writers of the Short Story* (1980)] on the "fight for life" in Jewett's work: "In a society without future the woman's instinct to carry on the life of the tribe can only be fulfilled by devotion to what remains, and her energies must go to preservation of the past, to intercourse with nature, to disguising and delaying the inevitable dissolution." The narrator expounds people like Mrs. Todd, Mrs. Blackett, Joanna, Elijah Tilley, and Mrs. Martin as examples of those who have coped successfully. Her purpose is to understand, reassure, and console.

Pointed Firs explores an adequate authorial role for the narrator out of the variety of characters she encounters. A negative model is the minister who visited poor Joanna. Mr. Dimmick, Mrs. Fosdick says, "seemed to know no remedies, but he had a great use of words." He "put on his authority" and spoke cant rather than from the heart to the heart in his futile attempt to win Joanna back to society from her hermitage. The problem is to suit words to occasions, a skill that comes only from lively human sympathies. Dimmick possesses neither apt words nor deep sympathies. He is as useless in Joanna's home as he is in the boat going to see her. Without an intimate understanding of human nature, mere words are useless.

The narrator finds positive models for her healing art in three distinct types of her Dunnet neighbors: the herbalist, the spiritualist, and the solitary. They possess the traits necessary to the writer who also would heal the spirit. . . . Jewett's characters are fragments of the narrative self that tells their story in order to adapt them to her purposes. As Captain Tilley says, explaining how a fisherman's knowledge has helped him as a farmer, "one trade helps another." The narrator traces the analogic uses that others' professions and preoccupations have for the writer's art. As she records the lives of the inhabitants of Dunnet Landing, she is simultaneously recounting the resolution of her own status as a writer, one who begins as an outsider uneasy in her relation to her subject. Other characters, always engrossing in themselves, are doubly so for the narrator because their stories illumine her soulmaking.

Chief among the models for the narrator is Mrs. Todd, that "learned herbalist" whose garden is a "rustic pharmacopoeia," and who gathers and dispenses herbal medicine. Mrs. Todd makes her living by providing medical services to those in the neighborhood. Herbalism and folk healing generally had an important function in a young nation that required medical practitioners in remote areas. Women gained access to the medical profession only gradually during the century. Midwifery and herbalism provided outlets for women with healing missions and medical services for a widespread rural population. . . . Not surprisingly, Mrs. Todd is on good terms with the local physician and complements rather than competes with him.

Another of Jewett's healers is Mrs. Goodsoe, in many ways the prototype for Mrs. Todd, in **"The Courting of Sister Wisby"** (1888). In this story the narrator meets Mrs. Goodsoe gathering herbs. Mrs. Goodsoe remarks that Adam and Eve must have gathered herbs and defends herbalism against scientific medicine practiced by "win' rows of young doctors, bilin' over with book-larin', that is truly ignorant of what to do for the sick." **"Sister Wisby"** celebrates woman's healing powers as they derive from herbal knowledge that is part of a female healing tradition. The healer gets close to nature and "take[s] just what Nature is pleased to give." Herbalism represents woman's wisdom ("Wisby" = "be wise") passed down through the ages. Healing is woman's strength and this story, as in *Pointed Firs,* portrays the narrator's initiation into that healing tradition.

During the apprenticeship, Mrs. Todd at one point compliments the narrator on her knowledge of herbalism, saying to her, "all you lack is a few qualities, but with time you'd gain judgement an' experience, an' be very able in the business." The narrator later modestly endorses this estimate: "I was not incompetent at herb-gathering." Mrs. Todd sponsors the narrator, introducing her around the neighborhood, sharing her insights into nature and human nature. In a striking passage, Mrs. Todd is described as standing at the center of a mandala-like braided rug, "its rings of black and gray seemed to circle about her feet in the dim light." This description succinctly expresses the psychic function that Mrs. Todd has for the narrator. In this yantra image, Mrs. Todd is the focal point of her meditation. She appears as a perfectly integrated personality, as much at ease with herself as with the world. She is one who both supervises the initiation of the writer into the subtleties of the spiritual life around her and serves as an ego goal, one who has become whole by incorporating ancient wisdom and by trusting to the life of the instincts. [In his *Mandala Symbolism* (1972)], Jung says of such mandala images, "they serve to produce an inner order—which is why, when they appear in a series, they often follow chaotic, disordered states marked by conflict and anxiety. They express the idea of a safe refuge, or inner reconciliation and wholeness."

It is through the narrator's imitation of this normative, integrated personality that many of the central concerns of the book are filtered. Thus, the herbalist-healer's profession helps her formulate her artistic vocation as one that will search out the hidden, secret strengths of the region. The healer's visits around the community, her sociability as well as her independence and solitary ramblings all affirm the poles of the narrator's own inclinations. In addition, Mrs. Todd helps her establish an intimate relationship with human nature and define her social role as building community, healing, reassuring, and consoling. She too will heal, by offering accounts of those who successfully withstand adversity.

Captain Littlepage is one of several liminal, ecstatic, and visionary figures in *Pointed Firs* who inhabit the fringes of society and consciousness, "strayaway folks" who used to be even more prevalent. They represent the possibility of expanded consciousness, of shared consciousness, and of communication with the dead. He recounts visions of another polar explorer, Old Gaffett, who, "always brooding and brooding, and talking to himself," told him of seeing spirits in a ghost city. (Littlepage himself is subject to deep reverie and ecstatic excitement during his narrative.) According to Littlepage, this city is a spirit world, described variously as "the next world to this . . . a place where there was neither living nor dead . . . a kind of waiting-place between this world and the next." Mrs. Todd is frankly skeptical: she suspects Littlepage of "flighty spells" and believes that by reading too much "he overdid, and affected his head." Nevertheless, she compliments him as "amazin' now when he's at his best," and she admits that "some o' them tales hangs together toler'ble well."

The narrator's attitude towards Littlepage is at best ambivalent. She is too this-worldly to subscribe to his theories. At one point she finds his story "a little dull" but listens "respectfully" and regrets that Littlepage sees her "thoughts unkindly wandering." She underwrites the touching seriousness of the believer rather than endorses his beliefs. Mostly, the old Captain seems a diminished version of Romanticism, a little page in the book of Coleridgean supernaturalism, American transcendentalism, or, more recently, parapsychologism. On the other hand Littlepage's story succeeds in so touching the narrator that after it, when she looks off to the harbor, she imagines its shore as "all covered by the great army of the pointed firs, darkly cloaked and standing as if they waited to embark." . . . Though her intimate, sympathetic conversations with Littlepage, and later Elijah Tilley and Mrs. Martin, do not lead to unqualified assent to an other world, they do contribute a larger frame of reference. It is enough that others give serious credence to beliefs in a spirit world for the narrator to use them to enlarge the spiritual resonances of her narrative. (pp. 39-44)

The narrator comes to Dunnet Landing and leaves it as a solitary, gaining confidence from the many exceptional versions of solitude. Often in compensation for age, grief, or personal loss, the solitary turns inward to the strengths that the solitary life offers. Indeed, almost all of the characters pursue some solitary interest, with their self-exclusiveness often emphasized by remote residence on places like Green Island or Shell-heap Island, by time spent alone in fishing boats, or at refuges in polar regions or tending sheep in upcountry pastures. The herbalist and spiritualist are two instances of the solitary, the most general category of Jewett's Dunnet characters. The narrator finds solitude characteristic of human nature: "In the life of each of us . . . there is a place remote and islanded, and given to endless regret or secret happiness; we are each the uncompanioned hermit and recluse of an hour or a day; we understand our fellows of the cell to whatever age of history they may belong." Solitude offers the concentration and distillation of individuality, an absolute self-possession that allows a singleness of pursuit that makes a person truly remarkable, either in "endless regret or secret happiness." Elijah Tilley is one solitary who elicits the narrator's admiration: "I often wondered a great deal about the inner life and thought of these self-contained old fishermen; their minds seemed to be fixed upon nature and the elements rather than upon any contrivances of man." Lives of consequence are lived alone, often with great spiritual intensity, sometimes with monastic devotion.

Yet the narrator is often intent on exploring how solitude contains its contraries. What looks restrictive in solitary lives may in fact be liberating. She can, for instance, find in Joanna Todd a model of spiritual independence: "I had been reflecting upon a state of society which admitted such personal freedom and a voluntary hermitage." And, paradoxically, what looks like asociality from one perspective turns out to be an exemplary life, such as that lived by Mrs. Todd or Joanna Todd, to which the world comes for guidance or out of respect. The choices open to a strong woman bent on defining herself are indicated by the two islands she visits. Green Island, the home of Mrs. Todd's mother, Mrs. Blackett, represents a voluntary, fulfilling solitude that replenishes the world. Mrs. Blackett, with her unmarried son, William, lives a reclusive but eminently active and social life. She is as willing to receive visitors as she is to make visits. On her island she continually reestablishes bonds with the outside world: "Mrs. Blackett was of those who do not live to themselves, and who have long since passed the line that divides mere self-concern from a valued share in whatever Society can give and take." The other, Shell-heap Island, a shrine to self-abnegation and penance, continues to draw people from the region long after Joanna's death. The narrator's final glimpse of Mrs. Todd retains the special aura of one whose life takes its social value from a distillation of its singleness: "Her distant figure looked mateless and appealing, with something about it that was strangely self-possessed and mysterious. Now and then she stooped to pick something,—it might have been her favorite pennyroyal," and as her steamer moves away from Dunnet Landing, the narrator gives a farewell salute to Elijah Tilley in recognition of the shared, secret strength of the world's solitaries.

Solitude thus paradoxically underlines the tendency of individuals, even the most solitary ones, to affiliate, a tendency that the narrator formulates during the Bowden family reunion: "Clannishness is an instinct of the heart." Her characters, in their own particular ways, find some means of bonding, of creating social ties out of their radical solitude or "differentness." Sant Bowden, who Mrs. Todd says "ain't a sound man" since his mind is continually preoccupied with things military, finds a useful place in the reunion as the marshall of the grand march. Some, like Captain Littlepage, actively search out and detain auditors with their tales; others, like Joanna Todd, are themselves a center of society's interest, through whatever motives of solicitude, respect, or simple curiosity. Solitude invites visits and tea, themselves the first links in a chain that leads to reunions, connecting New Englanders with even more formal, inclusive communal acts, festivals and rites dating from medieval Europe or ancient Greece. The need to remedy solitude dictates the architecture of the American home with its formal parlor as well as the custom of gift-giving that leaves the narrator possessor of the coral pin given by Nathan Todd to Joanna, who in turn gave Mrs. Todd the pin, a touching emblem of both solitude and social obligation. Throughout ***Pointed Firs***, the narrator has been rewarded for her interest in the solitaries of the world by admission to the houses of remote or reclusive people and then to the inner sanctums of those houses—Joanna's hermitage, Elijah's "best room," Mrs. Martin's shrine to the Queen—in token of her sympathetic appreciation of lives lived alone.

The discovery the narrator has made is of the absolute human necessity of solitude concomitant with its inevitable vector towards community. If these tendencies, solitude and clannishness, are basal elements of human nature, then she is justified in preserving her simultaneous enjoyment of company with her desire for seclusion to write. In fact, the writer who would tell the truth in effective ways must pursue both and reconcile each. Mrs. Todd especially has come to represent the combination of a public, humanitarian office with a wise solitariness. Mrs. Todd brings the healing gifts of nature collected on her solitary walks back into the community. The herbalist especially is the exemplar of one who combines solitary and socially productive impulses.

The narrator makes several other claims for her art. She is, first of all, justifying her writing by giving herself the role of spiritual healer, just as earlier Jewett had explored parallels between a woman physician and her own career as a professional writer in the quasi-autobiographical novel *A Country Doctor*. She insists that the status of spiritual healer be granted to strong women living independent lives. She is also justifying writing on pragmatic grounds in an era that, tiring of romantic optimism, demanded realistic accounts and practical solutions. Jewett offers an eminently utilitarian text, one that nonetheless draws on optimistic and idealistic visions of human nature while advancing a gospel of amelioration.

Moreover, Jewett implies the advisability of a making a return to coastal Maine for worthy literary materials, thereby educating her narrator and reader in a high status for those on the edges of a society, those who explore marginal states of consciousness, those subject to "fits" and "spells," those dreamers and visionaries, those rural poor who possess a rich inner life and are sometimes possessed by it. Nina Baym has argued that a narrowly-conceived perspective in American literary criticism pits an individualized hero (nearly always young and male) against a restraining, civilizing society (usually female) in narratives of flights from society towards solitary self-definition. Women write, according to this strain of received criticism, only to substantiate the dominant culture and to prepare for the inevitable male literary revolt against it. And Jewett helps give the lie to such narrow stereotyping. By searching out a rural population, folk experience, and reclusive people—not one individual but many quietly independent personalities—she expands the provenance of the American heroic type. *Pointed Firs* asserts the heroic proportions of individualism, radical to the point of eccentricity, almost madness, while simultaneously maintaining the primacy of community. Jewett celebrates American individualism and American communality, for the salvation of society lies in the unique inner life. By affirming America's proximity to a primordial nature and a basic human nature that bestows strength on those who patiently gather, distill, and dispense hidden resources, she taps the wellsprings of health and spiritual comfort that are the heritage of the region and offers them to the world. (pp. 46-8)

> *Michael Holstein, "Writing as a Healing Art in Sarah Orne Jewett's 'The Country of the Pointed Firs'," in* Studies in American Fiction, *Vol. 16, No. 1, Spring, 1988, pp. 39-49.*

SARAH WAY SHERMAN (essay date 1989)

[*In the following excerpt, Sherman discusses methods used by Jewett to invite her readers to participate in the narrative of* The Country of the Pointed Firs.]

In *Pointed Firs* the narrator introduces the reader to a succession of Dunnet Landing's citizens. The sketches form a kind of portrait gallery through which we move at a leisurely pace. However, these portraits are not fixed or objective. We see the writer's "material" but always in the context of her coming to know it. Her portraits are of individuals in relation. Each is present not as an "other" but as a "thou." There are always two perceiving subjects: the narrator and the person with whom she is engaged. What the narrator knows, or can know, is determined by that dialogue. Thus, there are always two subjects in another sense: the story of each character and the story of how she came to know that story. The first is always embedded in the second.

The creation of the sketches depends fundamentally on the narrator's ability to enter into these dialogues. Faced with each person, she must bring herself into connection through an imaginative leap. Her ability to make this leap comes from her own history. That history is kept from us by the narrator's resolute anonymity. But this anonymity does not mean that she is a kind of "transparent eyeball," purged of subjectivity, perfectly void of identity. No, the narrator's life before and beyond Dunnet Landing is more like the submerged seven-eighths of the iceberg that Hemingway said gave a story its substance. It is the thing left out. She comes to these people with a history, just as we do. Her capacity to interpret them has been developed through living a human life.

But what of our capacity? In the midst of **"William's Wedding,"** the last in the *Pointed Firs* series, the narrator turns aside from her story and addresses the reader directly on the problems of her art: "It is difficult to report the great events of New England; expression is so slight, and those few words which escape us in moments of deep feeling look but meagre on the printed page." As a participant in these scenes she has had to read between the lines of New England speech. Her interpretive skills are considerable, but she herself is a New Englander, as she admits when she uses the first person plural, "those few words which escape *us*." The reader must come to her text prepared with the same skills she has brought to Dunnet Landing, and perhaps that is asking more than is fair: "One has to assume too much of the dramatic fervor as one reads." Finally, the success of these sketches depends on that assumption. To see what she would show us, we must reenact her process of interpretation. We must read these human texts as she has read them, with a sympathy of the mind as well as the heart.

The interdependence of love and knowledge appears in the portrait of Joanna Todd. As Josephine Donovan points out, Joanna's story is placed after the Green Island sketches and before the Bowden Reunion, thus reinforcing the theme of isolation versus community seen in the juxtaposition of Captain Littlepage and Green Island.

On Green Island the narrator is taken into the heart of Mrs. Todd's family. When she returns to Dunnet Landing with Mrs. Todd, they are so comfortable with each other that they live in the little white cottage "with as much comfort and unconsciousness, as if it were a larger body, or a double shell . . . until some wandering hermit crab of a visitor marked the little spare room for her own." A wandering hermit crab *is* due to arrive, however, and the narrator hears "of Mrs. Fosdick for the first time with a selfish sense of objection." Accepted by Mrs. Todd's family, the narrator now is challenged to be accepted by Mrs. Todd's friends, to become a part of the feminine community.

Mrs. Fosdick's prestige within this community is large. A visit from her is an honor, and she seems as grand a personage as Queen Elizabeth traveling through her dominions. The narrator describes her own apprehensions with amusement. She "inconsiderately" worries about sharing her supper, and after being formally presented, she sits alone in the front room while the two friends proceed to the warmer kitchen.

Looking out the front window, she has "an unreasonable feeling of being left, like the child who stood at the gate in Hans Andersen's story." She is lonely and jealous of Mrs. Todd's attentions. Perhaps after all she is only a visitor, a foreigner.

But then Mrs. Todd comes to the rescue. She gives a "ceremonious knock" on the door, then "reached behind her and took Mrs. Fosdick's hand as if she were young and bashful, and gave her a gentle pull forward." Mrs. Fosdick may seem as grand as a queen, but she too has a child's vulnerability. In her essay "For Country Girls" Jewett advised her shy readers that the enemy is as afraid of you as you are of him. Mrs. Todd, who takes friendships seriously, brings the two women together carefully, knowing the risks of failure. She gives them something to talk about and "a refuge in case of incompatibility." When Mrs. Fosdick and the narrator rejoin their hostess, they are "sincere friends."

Now commences the telling of stories. As the narrator notes, "the gathering of herbs was nearly over, but the time of syrups and cordials had begun." These tales, which distill the healing powers of experience, bring the women together. Mrs. Fosdick comments that " 'conversation's got to have some root in the past, or else you've got to explain every remark you make, an' it wears a person out.' " This analysis seems to foreclose the possibility of new bonds, but "Mrs. Todd gave a funny little laugh. 'Yes'm, old friends is always best, 'less you can catch a new one that's fit to make an old one out of.' " Although the narrator does not share the same past, her powers of sympathy are such that she can reconstruct the history that binds these women together. One story in particular heals old differences and reaffirms their friendship. This is the story of Joanna, the woman who could not find solace in such friendship, who chose to live on "Shell-heap Island," outside the warmth of home and community.

Joanna's story highlights a major theme of *Pointed Firs,* the humanizing of the grotesque through sympathy. She is first introduced in a conversation about the "strange, strayin' creatur's that used to rove the country." Mrs. Fosdick says that they don't see such characters much anymore. The narrator, however, cannot help thinking of Captain Littlepage and William Blackett, although she has the tact not to mention them. When Joanna, Mrs. Todd's cousin by marriage, is described as one of these "peculiar people," a kind of "nun or hermit person," Mrs. Todd is "confused by sudden affectionate feeling and unmistakeable desire for reticence." Anxiously, she says, "I never want to hear Joanna laughed about." In the give-and-take that follows we see them comparing their interpretation of this text, comparing their judgment and experience of life. At one point, the narrator senses that the two women had once disagreed. Now, through their double narrative, they discover that time has brought a "happy harmony." With this reassurance, Mrs. Todd's speech gains a "new openness and freedom." The origins of this tale were bitter, but the tale itself is healing.

Like Captain Littlepage, Joanna is associated with patriarchal Protestantism. Deserted by her lover, she believed that she had committed the unpardonable sin by cursing God. In her reminiscences Mrs. Todd recalls her visit to Shell-heap Island to visit Joanna—her husband's cousin—who had voluntarily retreated from human society. When Mrs. Todd entreated her to come to Green Island to live with Mrs. Blackett, "she looked the same way, sad an' remote through it all. . . . 'I haven't got no right to live with folks no more,' she said. 'I feel a great comfort in your kindness, but I don't

deserve it. I have committed the unpardonable sin. . . . I was in great wrath and trouble, and my thoughts was so wicked toward God that I can't expect ever to be forgiven.' "

While there is no true accounting for Joanna, Mrs. Todd and Mrs. Fosdick reflect on the lonely woman's character. Mrs. Todd remembers how the first sight of the simple cabin brought tears to her eyes: "I said to myself, I must get mother to come over an' see Joanna; the love in mother's heart would warm her, an' she might be able to advise." But Mrs. Fosdick, hearing the story afresh, interjects, "Oh no, Joanna was dreadful stern." Although Joanna told Mrs. Todd that in time of sickness she wished Mrs. Blackett to come for her, she would not turn to maternal sympathy for consolation, perhaps because her own mother was as stern as she was. Joanna is presented as attached to her father. As Mrs. Todd remembers, Joanna had spent the best of her girlhood on Shell-heap Island with him: "He was one o' the pleasantest men in the world, but Joanna's mother had the grim streak, and never knew what 't was to be happy. The first minute my eyes fell upon Joanna's face that day I saw how she had grown to look like Mis' Todd. 'Twas the mother right over again." Betrayed by one man, Joanna returns to where she was happiest with her father on Shell-heap Island: " 'T was the same little house her father had built him when he was a bachelor, with one livin' room, and a little mite of a bedroom out of it where she slept, but 't was as neat as a ship's cabin."

In a curious way Joanna, like Miss Chauncey, has retreated to the mansion of the Father. However, Miss Chauncey dealt with her suffering and injustice not by turning against her Father in the sky but by denying the reality of her life. Madness is the result. Caught in the same agonizing position, Joanna turns on God in wrath and denounces him. But having rejected the heavenly father, she cannot find forgiveness within herself: "I have come to know what it is to have patience, but I have lost my hope." The comfort of human sympathy is alien to her, and the sentiment of tears seems to threaten her integrity. Mrs. Fosdick explains that Joanna retreated not because she felt too little but because she felt too much: "No, I never went to work to blame Joanna, as some did. She was full o' feeling, and her troubles hurt her more than she could bear."

As a solitary sinner Joanna has a forbidding strength, a powerful independence: "I've done the only thing I could do, and I've made my choice." When Mrs. Todd sees Joanna, she is moved to tears and runs to embrace her, but consolation is not for Joanna, who prefers loneliness to vulnerability. Even Mrs. Blackett could not warm her heart. Joanna's resistance is a kind of blindness. As Mrs. Todd says, " 'T is like bad eyesight, the mind of such a person: if your eyes don't see right there may be a remedy, but there's no kind of glasses to remedy the mind." The link between poor Joanna's failure of vision and the Calvinism that she believed condemned her is seen in the Reverend Dimmick, whose very name suggests his own "bad eyesight."

Dimmick is a living illustration of the faults Jewett had condemned in her essay "The Decay of Churches." Mrs. Fosdick comments that another minister "would have been a great help to [Joanna],—one that preached self-forgetfulness and doin' for others to cure our own ills; but Parson Dimmick was a vague person, well meanin', but very numb in his feelin's." The vagueness of abstract theology and the numbness of the man's human sympathies are scathingly revealed in Mrs. Todd's tale of their visit to Joanna.

Reverend Dimmick's failure is prefigured on their sail out. He is afraid to cut his hand on the rope and insists on tying it, against Mrs. Todd's better judgment. Then, as he sits "talking rather high flown," "all of a sudden there come up a gust, and he give a screech and stood right up and called for help, way out there to sea." Never at a loss, Mrs. Todd knocks him down and sets things right. "He wasn't but a little man."

Confronted with Joanna's forbidding if gentle resistance, the minister prefers to avoid direct contact and pain. He again puts his behavior on a kind of automatic pilot and assumes his "high flown" speech. . . . Instead of giving forgiveness and comfort, Reverend Dimmick joins with the accusations of Joanna's own rigid conscience. He fails to see the depth of Joanna's pain, just as he does not understand the significance of the Bible lying right in front of him. Instead of mercy he offers a prayer, "all about hearin' the voice o' God out o' the whirlwind; and I thought while he was goin' on that anybody that had spent the long winter all alone out on Shell-heap Island knew a good deal more about those things than he did. I got so provoked I opened my eyes and stared right at him."

However, Joanna herself does not seem to hear; nothing could be louder than her own wrathful deity. She calmly brushes the ineffectual minister aside, just as Mrs. Todd had done "way out to sea." When he finishes his harangue, Joanna takes some Indian relics from her shelves and "showed them to him same's as if he was a boy." Quietly put in his place once more, Reverend Dimmick is unusually silent on the way home. Mrs. Todd remembers: "He preached next Sabbath as usual, somethin' high soundin' about the creation, and I couldn't help thinkin' he might never get no further; he seemed to know no remedies, but he had a great use of words." The characteristic word associated with Reverend Dimmick is "high": "high flown" and "high soundin'." But the way to wisdom is down, not up. He has not got past the creation: experience has not touched him nor sorrow educated him. He has a "great use of words," but he is spiritually undeveloped: "numb" and "dim."

While Mrs. Todd and Mrs. Fosdick agree that Joanna's retreat grew out of her overwhelming sorrow and her fright at her feelings, they also feel that "self-forgetfulness" might have been the remedy. The nurture of others can help heal one's own pain, as they themselves have discovered. Grief can deepen character and educate the heart, as we saw in *Pearl of Orr's Island*. In Francis Fike's fine essay on **Pointed Firs** he comments that "Mrs. Todd's own grief-stricken life is the living testimony of the resourcefulness of human nature." He draws attention to the scene on Green Island when Mrs. Todd tells the narrator of her own lost love. Her sorrow "is revealed precisely while she is standing in a patch of pennyroyal, as if to emphasize those healing resources which come from within the very source of grief."

Mrs. Todd's compassion for Joanna comes from her own experience: she shares in the other woman's pain. With trembling voice, Mrs. Todd recalls that as soon as she saw the minister's "stupid back" leave the cabin that long ago day,

> . . . I just ran to her an' caught her in my arms. I wasn't so big as I be now, and she was older than me, but I hugged her tight, just as if she was a child. "Oh, Joanna dear," I says, "won't you come ashore an' live 'long o' me at the Landin', or go over to Green Island to mother's when winter comes? Nobody shall trouble you, an' mother finds it hard

bein' alone. I can't bear to leave you here"—and I burst right out crying. I'd had my own trials, young as I was, an' she knew it. Oh, I did entreat her; yes, I entreated Joanna.

Mrs. Todd offers Joanna the remedy of women's love and community. She need not feel her pain alone; others will help her bear it. But this renewal Joanna cannot accept. She puts Mrs. Todd from her gently. Rather than become a child in Mrs. Todd's arms, she takes Mrs. Todd's hand "as if she turned round an' made a child of me." The reversal parallels the earlier scene with the minister, whom Joanna treats "same's if he was a boy." She has found identity in despair; hers is a separate and lonely knowledge, bereft of a child's hope. In parting Mrs. Todd gives Joanna a coral pin, a present from Nathan, Mrs. Todd's husband and Joanna's cousin. For the first time Joanna "lights up." But then she returns the pin to Mrs. Todd as a token of the deep love she feels but to which she cannot yield.

While this sketch clearly reveals the limits of Joanna's vision, it also underlines her dignity and strength. When the narrator makes her own visit to the now deserted island, she finds it "touching . . . that this lonely spot was not without its pilgrims." She reflects that "there are paths trodden to the shrines of solitude the world over,—the world cannot forget them, try as it may." These pilgrims are drawn through their own sense of solitude; their own awareness of that inner self, bounded and alone: "In the life of each of us, I said to myself, there is a place remote and islanded, and given to endless regret or secret happiness; we are each the uncompanioned hermit or recluse of an hour or a day; we understand our fellow of the cell to whatever age of history they may belong."

The writer alone in her schoolhouse watching the funeral procession below has much in common with Joanna, who watched the summer boating parties pass by her lonely island. The moment she spent lonely and jealous in the front room, while Mrs. Fosdick and Mrs. Todd talked cheerfully in the kitchen, is fresh in her memory. The narrator's own solitude teaches her to sympathize with Joanna's experience. As she hears voices from a pleasure boat sailing by, she "knew as if she had told me, that poor Joanna must have heard the like on many a summer afternoon, and must have welcomed the good cheer in spite of hopelessness and winter weather, and all the sorrow and disappointment in the world." Although the narrator originally had no root in the same past as Joanna, never knew or even saw her, nevertheless she can imaginatively reconstruct the other's experience. She stands in Joanna's place just as she sat in Mrs. Blackett's rocking chair, and she gazes out at the world through the other woman's eyes. This loneliness is human, as is this loss. Here too there is communion. (pp. 225-31)

Sarah Way Sherman, in her Sarah Orne Jewett, an American Persephone, *University Press of New England, 1989, 333 p.*

FURTHER READING

Bender, Bert. "To Calm and Uplift 'Against the Dark': Sarah Orne

Jewett's Lyric Narratives." *Colby Library Quarterly* XI, No. 4 (December 1975): 219-29.

> Calls for a critical reappraisal of Jewett's narrative style and analyzes the lyrical organization of "The Foreigner."

Cary, Richard. *Sarah Orne Jewett.* New York: Twayne Publishers, 1962, 175 p.

> Important critical biography by a prominent Jewett scholar.

Cather, Willa. "Miss Jewett." In her *Not under Forty,* pp. 76-95. New York: Alfred A. Knopf, 1936.

> Character sketch in which Cather praises Jewett's literary style, noting that Jewett's writing contains a "very personal quality of perception, a vivid and intensely personal experience of life."

Commager, Henry Steele. "Transition Years in Literature and Journalism." In his *The American Mind: An Interpretation of American Thought and Character since the 1880s,* pp. 55-81. New Haven: Yale University Press, 1950.

> Discussion of New England local colorists that includes Jewett and her collection *Deephaven.*

Cross, Olive. "From *Deephaven* to *The Country of the Pointed Firs.*" *Florida State University Studies,* No. 5 (1952): 113-21.

> Traces Jewett's stylistic development from *Deephaven* to *The Country of the Pointed Firs.*

Donovan, Josephine. "Silence or Capitulation: Prepatriarchal 'Mothers' Gardens' in Jewett and Freeman." *Studies in Short Fiction* 23, No. 1 (Winter 1986): 43-8.

> Offers a contemporary feminist reading of Jewett's "A White Heron" and Mary E. Wilkins Freeman's "Evalina's Garden."

Frost, John Eldridge. *Sarah Orne Jewett.* Kittery Point, Maine: Gundalow Club, 1960, 174 p.

> Comprehensive, largely biographical study.

James, Henry. "Mr. and Mrs. James T. Fields." *Atlantic Monthly* 116, No. 1 (July 1915): 21-31.

> Reminiscence of Boston's celebrated literary couple and of their friendship with Jewett. James calls Jewett the "mistress of an art of fiction all her own . . . surpassed only by Hawthorne as producer of the most finished and penetrating of the numerous 'short stories' that have the domestic life of New England for their . . . subject."

Jobes, Katharine T. "From Stowe's Eagle Island to Jewett's 'A White Heron'." *Colby Library Quarterly* X, No. 8 (December 1974): 515-21.

> Assesses Jewett's reworking of the Eagle Island episode from Harriet Beecher Stowe's novel *The Pearl of Orr's Island.*

Levy, Babette May. "Mutations in New England Local Color." *The New England Quarterly* XIX, No. 3 (September 1946): 338-58.

> Compares Jewett's stories about New England with those by her contemporaries Harriet Beecher Stowe, Rose Terry Cooke, and Mary E. Wilkins Freeman.

Martin, Jay. "New England Regional Literature: Sarah Orne Jewett." In his *Harvests of Change: American Literature, 1865-1914,* pp. 142-48. Englewood Cliffs, N.J.: Prentice-Hall, 1967.

> Examines Jewett's version of the New England idyll in stories from *A White Heron, and Other Stories* and *The Country of the Pointed Firs.*

Matthiessen, Francis Otto. *Sarah Orne Jewett.* Boston: Houghton Mifflin Co., 1929, 159 p.

> The first critical biography of Jewett.

Mobley, Marilyn E. "Rituals of Flight and Return: The Ironic Journeys of Sarah Orne Jewett's Female Characters." *Colby Library Quarterly* 21, No. 1 (March 1985): 36-42.

> Traces patterns in Jewett's repeated references to birds, travel, and returning home in her stories. Mobley determines that these images reflect an "heroic expression of the desire to remain connected to one's cultural roots."

Piacentino, Edward J. "Local Color and Beyond: The Artistic Dimension of Sarah Orne Jewett's 'The Foreigner'." *Colby Library Quarterly* XXI, No. 2 (June 1985): 92-8.

> Suggests that Jewett's "The Foreigner" is a "well-designed work of art whose carefully crafted texture and suggestiveness have been enhanced by mood-inducing and character-delineating motifs."

Renza, Louis A. *"A White Heron" and the Question of Minor Literature.* Madison: University of Wisconsin Press, 1984, 221 p.

> Explores Jewett's story "A White Heron" from various critical perspectives.

Stevenson, Catherine Barnes. "The Double Consciousness of the Narrator in Sarah Orne Jewett's Fiction." *Colby Library Quarterly* XI, No. 1 (March 1975): 1-12.

> Analyzes the perceptions of Jewett's narrators in *Deephaven,* "A White Heron," and *The Country of the Pointed Firs.*

Doris (May) Lessing

1919-

(Has also written under the pseudonym Jane Somers) Persian-born English novelist, short story writer, essayist, dramatist, poet, nonfiction writer, journalist, and travel writer.

Considered a powerful contemporary writer primarily in the realist tradition, Lessing has explored many of the most important social, political, psychological, and spiritual issues of the twentieth century. Her works display a broad range of interests and focus on such specific topics as racism, communism, feminism, and mysticism. In her fiction Lessing often delineates characters in routine activities through their interactions with daily objects. Adept at manipulating both the physical and psychological orientation of people and things in her stories, Lessing employs environment as a thematic motif, relating individuals to others, themselves, and, particularly in her African stories, to the land. While Lessing is perhaps best known for her acclaimed and controversial novel *The Golden Notebook,* many critics find the short story form more suited to her temperament and concerns. Judith Kegan Gardiner remarked: "Whereas [Lessing's] novels sometimes appear didactic, disproportioned, or flat, her short stories are often more finely crafted and broader ranging, achieving a forceful emotional impact or evoking a character, situation, or idea with a grace and concision achieved only rarely in her novels." Among Lessing's most acclaimed volumes of short fiction, *Five: Short Novels, The Habit of Loving,* and *African Stories* contain tales concerning racial problems in African settings, the dynamics of married life, and the emancipation of modern women.

Lessing was born in Persia (modern-day Iran) of English parents. At an early age she moved with her family to Rhodesia, in southern Africa, where her father struggled as a farmer. She attended public schools until her teenage years, when chronic eye problems forced her to return home, thus ending her formal education. As a young woman, Lessing relocated to Salisbury, the capital of Southern Rhodesia, where she supported herself through various secretarial jobs. During World War II, she was active in pro-communist organizations, and in 1949 she emigrated to London, England. In London, Lessing established herself as a fiction writer, critic, journalist, and political activitist. She joined the English Communist Party in 1952 and resigned about five years later. In 1956 she was banned from returning to Rhodesia, presumably for anti-apartheid sentiments expressed in her writings, and she continues to live in England. Although details of Lessing's personal life are sketchy, critics agree that in her fiction, Lessing draws significantly from her own experiences.

When Lessing began her literary career in the 1950s, she was promptly recognized as an accomplished short fiction writer in the realist mode. The tales collected in her first short story volume, *This Was the Old Chief's Country,* introduce the theme of alienation, which Lessing delineates chiefly through protagonists of English descent living as colonialists in Africa. Isolated from each other, the native people, and African landscape by class, age, gender, and racial barriers, these characters suffer the fragmentation that Lessing views as a direct consequence of apartheid. In *African Stories* Lessing fur-

ther chronicles racial issues from a variety of social perspectives. In "The Pig," for example, considered a prototype of Lessing's early short fiction, a white landowner assigns Jonas, an elderly black man, to guard his crops, which are being pilfered at night. Although the landowner infers that the culprits are his own farmhands, he remarks to Jonas that they are probably "pigs." Jonas, however, takes advantage of the situation and shoots his wife's lover under the pretense that he believed the man was one of the thieves. Jonas's comment that the dying man squealed like a pig aligns him with the landowner and provides insight into the dehumanizing effects of sexual and racial tension in human relations. In these and many other of her African stories, including *The Antheap, Eldorado,* and "Flavours of Exile," Lessing accentuates the estrangement of her characters by portraying the vapid nature of their lives against lush African landscapes.

Much of Lessing's fiction has definite political intentions; her involvement with communism is evident in many of her early works. In the novella *Hunger,* a straightforward social commentary in the manner of Charles Dickens's *Oliver Twist,* Lessing relates the experiences of Jabavu, an impoverished African boy from a small village who comes to a large modern city to better his condition, only to be assaulted by the town's depravity and inequities. Although some critics feel Jabavu's ultimate victory over his own cultural inadequacies and the evil forces operating in such an urban white environment strains believeability, *Hunger* remains one of Lessing's more popular novellas. The pieces in Lessing's later collection *The Temptation of Jack Orkney, and Other Stories,* contain analyses of the volatile international political situation during the 1960s. Young people in these stories search for social and political "truth" yet are ignorant of the lessons of history and apathetic about their own fate, an endless cycle that Lessing contends must cease if humanity is to avoid catostrope and flourish. In other stories, Lessing examines the nature of marriage and childbearing, focusing on how the roles of wife and mother affect her characters' creative lives. In these works, Lessing often presents strong-willed, independent heroines whose needs for love do not counteract their desires for self-sufficiency—a recurrent theme that anticipated many feminist concerns. Such stories in this vein as "To Room Nineteen" and "Our Friend Judith" were especially praised by critics for their complex narrative techniques and convincing characterizations.

Throughout Lessing's fiction, a major unifying element has been her characters' needs to confront many of their basic beliefs and assumptions about life in order to overcome preconditioned thinking and attain psychic and emotional wholeness. Using detailed, realistic descriptions, symbolism, and imagery to evoke environments and moods, Lessing achieves what Edward J. Fitzgerald termed "tension and immediacy" in her stories. Her enlightened portrayal of marriage and motherhood, her anti-apartheid stance, and her experimentation with genre and form has earned her a reputation as an exciting, and sometimes controversial, literary figure.

(For further information on Lessing's life and career, see *Contemporary Literary Criticism,* Vols. 1, 2, 3, 6, 10, 15, 22, 40; *Contemporary Authors,* Vols. 9-12, rev. ed.; *Dictionary of Literary Biography,* Vol. 15; and *Dictionary of Literary Biography Yearbook: 1985.*)

PRINCIPAL WORKS

SHORT FICTION

This Was the Old Chief's Country   1951; reprinted in *Collected African Stories,* 1973
Five: Short Novels   1953
No Witchcraft for Sale   1956
The Habit of Loving   1957
A Man and Two Women   1963
African Stories   1964
Winter in July   1966
Nine African Stories   1968
The Temptation of Jack Orkney, and Other Stories   1972; also published as *The Story of a Non-Marrying Man, and Other Stories,*   1972; reprinted in *Collected Stories,* 1978
Collected African Stories. 2 vols.   1973
The Sun between Their Feet   1973; published in *Collected African Stories,* 1973
Collected Stories. 2 vols.   1978
To Room Nineteen   1978; published in *Collected Stories,* 1978
The Fifth Child   1988

OTHER MAJOR WORKS

The Grass Is Singing   (novel)   1950
Children of Violence. 5 vols.   (novels)
    Martha Quest   1952
    A Proper Marriage   1954
    A Ripple from the Storm   1958
    Landlocked   1965
    The Four-Gated City   1969
Before the Deluge   (drama)   1953
Retreat to Innocence   (novel)   1953
Going Home   (essays)   1957
Each His Own Wilderness   (drama)   1958
Mr. Dolinger   (drama)   1958
Fourteen Poems   (poetry)   1959
In Pursuit of the English: A Documentary   (documentary)   1960
The Truth about Billy Newton   (drama)   1960
The Golden Notebook   (novel)   1962
Play with a Tiger   (drama)   1962
The Storm   (drama)   [adaptation]   1966
Particularly Cats   (autobiographical essay)   1967
Briefing for a Descent into Hell   (novel)   1971
Shikasta: re, Colonised Planet 5: Personal, Psychological, Historical Documents Relating to Visit by Johor (George Sherban) Emissary (Grade 9) 87th of the Period of the Last Days   (novel)   1971
The Singing Door   (drama); published in *Second Playbill 2,* 1973
The Summer before the Dark   (novel)   1973
The Memoirs of a Survivor   (novel)   1974
A Small Personal Voice   (essays, reviews, and interviews)   1974
The Marriages between Zones Three, Four, and Five (as Narrated by the Chroniclers of Zone Three)   (novel)   1980
The Sirian Experiments: The Report by Ambien II, of the Five   (novel)   1981
The Making of the Representative for Planet 8   (novel)   1982
The Diary of a Good Neighbour   [as Jane Somers]   (novel)   1983
Documents Relating to the Sentimental Agents in the Volyen Empire   (novel)   1983
If the Old Could . . .   [as Jane Somers]   (novel)   1984
The Diary of Jane Somers   (novel)   1984
The Good Terrorist   (novel)   1985
Prisons We Choose to Live Inside   (essays)   1987
The Wind Blows Away Our Words: and Other Documents Relating to the Afghan Resistance   (non-fiction)   1987

*This work comprises two earlier novels, *The Diary of a Good Neighbour* and *If the Old Could . . .,* that Lessing published under the pseudonym Jane Somers.

EDWARD J. FITZGERALD (essay date 1952)

[*In the following review, Fitzgerald discusses central themes in Lessing's first collection,* This Was the Old Chief's Country.]

Doris Lessing, whose first novel, *The Grass is Singing,* merited and received considerable critical acclaim, has now come forth with a collection of short stories which confirms her position as a writer of solid worth who works with consummate craft within a narrow emotional range. There are ten stories in *This Was the Old Chief's Country.* In all of them the setting is Africa, but it is an Africa not of those whose rightful home it is but one perceived through the sensibilities of an alien colonist.

The feeling of alienation, of not-belonging, is Mrs. Lessing's central concern. Here, she says in effect, are the people who, by force of empire, control but do not understand a vast territory and a subtly hostile population. This perverse situation sets up in even the kindliest of them a complex of unresolved conflict and inevitable frustration which infects their every act. Five of her stories deal directly with the chasm which separates the rulers from the ruled, the colonist from the native. Of these the most moving is the first person narrative **"The Old Chief Mshlanga"** which recounts the discovery by a child of the fact that, as a daughter of a colonist, she is an alien and an intruder upon the land which is her only home, among the people with whom she must live. More conventional in form, **"Leopard George"** reveals the gradual brutalization of a sensitive man in flight from the responsibilities of any personal relationship. **"The Nuisance"** and **"No Witchcraft for Sale"** are slighter vignettes, variations on the central theme of an enforced failure of communication between master and man.

In her other stories Mrs. Lessing enlarges her view of alienation. **"The Second Hut"** and **"The De Wets Come to Kloof Grange"** treat of the separation of the entrenched landholder (English) from the hired Afrikaaner, **"Old John's Place"** deals with the intruder who is such mostly by virtue of being a newcomer to a settled community. **"Winter in July"**—the most ambitious and least successful story in the volume—discovers to us the psychological roots of a *menage à trois.*

These notes have stressed the thematic elements of Mrs. Lessing's stories. It should be emphasized that Mrs. Lessing is no polemicist. She is a storyteller and a good one. There is tension and immediacy in all of her tales. She is entangled with a major theme. This volume is a brilliant statement of variations upon it. Its further development in future writing should be watched for. (pp. 19, 35)

Edward J. Fitzgerald, "Retreat from Home," in The Saturday Review, *New York, Vol. XXXV, No. 31, August 2, 1952, pp. 19, 35.*

F. BRUCE OLSEN (essay date 1965)

[*Olsen is an American academic and essayist. In the following excerpt from* Insight II: Analysis of Modern British Literature *(1965), he suggests ways in which Lessing's psychological portrayal of the main character, her use of narrative perspective, and her own persona contribute to the unfolding and conclusion of "A Sunrise on the Veld."*]

Because **"A Sunrise on the Veld"** has the barest of plots—almost "nothing happens" outside the boy's contemplation—, a consideration of it may help us to see more clearly some other kinds of elements which go into the artistic experience of a story. For it is simply untrue that "nothing happens" in this story; it is, in fact, fairly complex, and the reader who fails to see this is perceiving only surface actions. The boy's insight into himself is couched in symbols and images that establish an implicit pattern of conflict and movement. The story, in other words, is not merely a statement about a boy's discovery or about man's conflict with nature, but a controlled process which allows us to feel through the actions

of the boy on an imagistic level and to accept his personal resolution as more or less inevitable. The experience is not stated, but rendered. We need to be concerned with the way in which the process operates, that is, with the way in which various elements function in its form.

The story, first of all, concerns a boy's initiation into cruelty and human limitations, the ever-serviceable "discovery of evil" theme about which so much fiction is centred. (Hemingway's "The Killers", a much different story in most respects, may serve as a thematic comparison.) Mrs. Lessing's problem as a writer is to represent the psychology of this discovery so that the reader can feel its force and universal significance. And to do so she places details which suggest a range of feelings and values beyond the boy's conscious elaboration of his problems. If the story is to be successful, then the reader must have the experience of wide and stimulating ramifications of its implicit material—a suggestiveness far beyond what the boy could tell us.

Let us therefore address ourselves to two questions: In what ways can the process of the story be expressed? In what way is this process resolved, or brought to a satisfactory conclusion, so that the story ends in a way which makes it seem complete in itself ? These questions are designed to keep us on the problem of regarding the story as a process, in which different parts function in the whole effect, and to block consideration of it as a philosophic statement.

In locating the elements of the process, it is helpful to distinguish between the point of view and the author's persona. Although told in the third person, the story is regulated by the intelligence, vocabulary, and perceptual opportunities of the boy. We see what he sees, and according to his frame of reference. The selection of details is determined not only by his physical location—the author will not report events which the boy cannot observe—but also by his interests and general orientation. The boy, for instance, cannot actually see the way his parents are reacting to the yelping of the dogs; he can only imagine it, and does so, naturally enough, according to his own preoccupations. The point of view, in other words, represents a discrete "value system", reflecting the boy's personality with all the variousness that the word "personality" implies. This use of a point of view is often called an *interior monologue.*

The point of view, however, is not the only orientation operating in the story. Surrounding it, and including it, is what we may call the *persona.* This may be understood as a unified set of attitudes implicit in the author's total control and selection of material. It is a value-system not only discrete from the boy's point of view, but also in constant conflict with it. The author, after all, has final control of what goes into the story and can create a critical scheme about the boy which goes beyond the boy's comprehension of himself. The resolution, however, depends upon bringing these two orientations closer together in a convincing manner—specifically, in having the boy realize some of the implicit attitudes that have been developed about him by the persona. In the following passage, for instance, the reader is directed toward considerations which the boy cannot formulate and yet which affect his subsequent discovery.

> It was half-past four to the minute, every morning. Triumphantly pressing down the alarm knob of the clock, which the dark half of his mind had outwitted, remaining vigilant all night and counting the hours as he lay relaxed in sleep, he huddled down

for a last warm moment under the clothes, playing with the idea of laying abed for this once only. But he played with it for the fun of knowing that it was a weakness that he could defeat without effort; just as he set the alarm each night for the delight of the moment when he woke and stretched his limbs, feeling the muscles tighten, and thought: Even my brain—even that! I can control every part of myself.

The persona here—and everywhere—directs us toward implicit matters which run counter to the boy's estimate of himself. His belief that the "dark half" of his mind is such a willing servant of his conscious self makes the reader aware of how easily he may be fooled by unconscious forces deeply buried within him. The victory over the alarm clock is indeed a triumph of the will, but it is a common sort of triumph and not worth the value he places upon it. We are led to feel that the boy's confident declaration that he controls all of himself is an instance of pride before the fall, as it turns out to be. His playing with the temptation of staying in bed indicates another source of conflict—that of wanting and yet rejecting the protection of his parents and home against the hostility of the world—and subsequently this conflict is developed. The persona's attitudes, more patient, knowing, and cynical, are of course not explicitly stated. We have "read them between the lines". But it is not an arbitrary act of "reading things into" the story; the implicit meanings have been controlled for our perception.

The turning point of the story has been elaborately prepared by this conflict between an implicit persona and an explicit point of view. The first part of the story, up to the boy's discovery of the dying animal, is not merely a narrative and scenic introduction but a psychological seeding-ground as well. The images and symbols largely bear upon the boy's denial of unconscious forces beyond his control. We find, for instance, that he regards his arms and legs and fingers as "waiting like soldiers for a word of command"; yet, at the end of the story, "He walked heavily, not looking where he put his feet." There are, in addition, many other references to the uncertain footing in the veld, "the uselessly convulsing muscles of his empty stomach", the dying buck fighting with "a mechanical protest of the nerves", and so on. The process of his realization turns upon these images of self-control (or the lack of it), among others.

The first half of the story, in other words, shows the boy regarding himself as a kind of Nietzschean *Übermensch* while the validity of the idea itself is being undermined. He associates himself, for instance, with the dogs in which consciousness and instinct are one; he feels more alive than his parents whom he scornfully imagines "turning in their beds and muttering: Those dogs again! before they were dragged back in sleep". Important here also is the reversal of traditional associations in the boy's mind which indicate his distance from conventional wisdom. He feels that it is imperative to reach the uncultivated part of the farm (the vlei symbolizing his desire to break away from his parents) by daybreak (the new day standing for his aware entrance into life). In metaphorical terms, he intends to carry his wild impulses into the daylight and wilderness and face them down. He will be afraid of nothing: "He was clean crazy, yelling mad with the joy of living and a superfluity of youth." But before this moment of spontaneous exuberance he had already noted—"jerkily"— that the fields were covered with spiderwebs, prefiguring the death that lies in wait.

The latter half of the story details the downfall of the boy's exaggerated confidence and the development of new insight. No fewer than twenty-one distinct stages in the boy's awareness can be discerned. If the author is to show a major change in attitude in so short a time, then she must involve us in considerable psychological complexity. The stages show successive breakdowns and retreat of his defences. At first he becomes aware of the buck's cry of pain as a discordant quality in the all-embracing sounds of nature with which he totally identifies himself. His heart beating fast, and suddenly "clean sober, all the madness gone", he goes toward a belt of trees to begin his cautious investigation. The quickness with which his exuberance leaves him indicates its fragility. Faltering in the middle of a step, he is stunned by the sight of the buck as if it were "a figure from a dream"—and the nightmare has struck through his repressions. But his detailed interest in seeing the buck being eaten alive by the ants reveals that he is fascinated as well as repelled; we find him in a balanced state between flight and engagement.

Then he is described as seized by pity and terror. These designated emotions suggest the Aristotelian formula for tragedy and point up some major themes of the story. Having wilfully denied human limitations and the role of fate, he is then being initiated into what might be called a tragic view of life. His indecision about shooting the buck shows his refusal to admit his pity. He rationalizes his failure to shoot in two different ways, first by thinking that the buck could no longer feel; secondly, by asserting that this was the way that life was in the bush and that he had no right to interfere. The quickness with which this tough philosophy comes to his mind indicates perhaps that he had thought of it before to explain the contradiction between his joy of life and the horror with which he was familiar. But the "survival of the fittest" view must, by implication, apply to him as well.

After the buck has become unconscious and he is relieved of his decision about whether or not to kill it, the boy's rationalizations become rigidified into *It was right and nothing could alter it*—a strange contradiction to his claims of omnipotence some moments before. Though suffering, sick, and angry, and with tears streaming down his face, he is nevertheless "grimly satisfied" with his new stoicism. It was, after all, only a buck that had been killed, not himself. "The ants must eat too!" The horror recedes somewhat as the ants finish their job. But he swears, "using the words he had heard his father say", at the impressively short time it took to pick the bones clean.

As he thus takes into himself some part of his father's attitude and protection, he becomes bold enough to examine the bones thoughtfully and realistically. "Go away!" he says to the ants, "I am not for you—not just yet, at any rate. Go away." In this manner he indirectly admits his own mortality. While examining the bones, he imagines the buck's proud and graceful movements, its joy in being, so much like his own. How could such a swift surefooted thing be trapped by a swarm of ants? He then notices its broken thigh. But how could such a graceful animal break its leg? He decides that it was probably injured by natives throwing stones at it. But his very choice of this arbitrary reason is significant in foreshadowing the image which comes to his mind immediately after: he sees himself taking a quick shot at a buck and then not tracking it down to see if it were injured or not. Now he cannot avoid acknowledging his own guilt and responsibility in the scheme of things; he both injures and is injurable. He cannot escape the consequences of his own limitations. His anger gone, filled with dismay, he then rationalizes his desire to return home—he is now hungry and tired, in sharp contrast to his original enthusiasm. But he will return to the bush the next morning to "think about it".

Thus the boy's conscious thought is brought close to the persona's implicit view, providing a kind of resolution. Why is it that we don't demand that the story go on? Possibly it is because the terms of the conflict, the "universe of discourse" by means of which the process has been rendered, has been brought into balance. (pp. 234-38)

> *F. Bruce Olsen, "A Sunrise on the Veld," in* Insight II: Analyses of Modern British Literature, *edited by John V. Hagopian and Martin Dolch, Hirschgraben-Verlag, 1965, pp. 233-38.*

JOYCE CAROL OATES (essay date 1972)

[*A prolific and versatile American fiction writer and critic, Oates is perhaps best known for her novel* them (*1969*). *Her critical canon is diverse and includes scholarly studies on such writers as Shakespeare, Herman Melville, and Samuel Beckett. In the following excerpt, Oates briefly explicates stories from Lessing's collection* The Temptation of Jack Orkney, and Other Stories.]

The range of Doris Lessing's imagination is nothing short of remarkable. (p. 4)

[The] collection of excellent stories [*The Temptation of Jack Orkney, and Other Stories*]—Miss Lessing's nineteenth book—touches upon nearly all of the concerns of the novels. It concludes with the moving novella, **"The Temptation of Jack Orkney,"** which reads like a semi-autobiographical confession. Here Miss Lessing's energy and inventiveness transpose ordinary life into something quite "other"—for while we keep thinking we have come to know Jack Orkney, he finally eludes us as he eludes himself, never quite concentrating into a convenient metaphor for "modern, alienated, confused Man," and yet not surrendering to the temptation of either despair or religious mysticism. Orkney is victimized by a terrible sense of depression after his father's death. He doubts the worth and even the good motives of his years of work (he is an author, an intellectual Leftist), and sees in himself and his altruistic friends a self-defeating complacency and love of power that undercut their commitment to humanity.

But beyond Orkney's personal dissatisfaction is Miss Lessing's great theme: that the world cannot any longer afford the luxury of each individual's and each individual's generation's discovering for the first time all the "truths" about life; that our time is limited, our catastrophe too horribly imminent, to allow this "endless cycle, of young people able to come to maturity only in making themselves into a caste which had to despise and dismiss their parents, insisting pointlessly on making their own discoveries. . . ." Orkney's son, Joseph, is a radical who, with his friends, is doomed to repeat "the old story of socialist recrimination and division"; Orkney is helpless to instruct them, for they will not or cannot listen, believing that history begins with their generation—just as Orkney and his friends believed history began with them.

Miss Lessing's sympathies are with the young—and yet she seems to despair of their being able to transcend the mechani-

cal, time-wasting process of self-discovery, now that the events of history have so accelerated and the actual survival of the earth is a matter of doubt. In spite of their freshness and good will, these liberated young with their multiplicity of interests (political, Jesus, Eastern religions) seem at times like "laboratory animals unable to behave in any other way than that to which they had been trained." It is evident in *The Four-Gated City* as well as in several of the stories in this volume that Miss Lessing's vision of our future is not exactly an optimistic one; surely her troubled, self-divided hero, Jack Orkney, speaks for the author herself in speculating that

> a new kind of despair had entered into the consciousness of mankind: things were too desperate, the future of humanity depended on humanity being able to achieve new forms of intelligence, of being able to learn from experience . . .

"Report on the Threatened City" is matter-of-fact, and chilling: a certain West Coast city, famous for its beautiful shoreline and pleasant climate, is doomed to destruction in a few years (earthquake, followed by fire, is inevitable), and yet its inhabitants prefer not to think about it. Rather than move to another location, they attempt to "live with" the knowledge of their doom; they are tied to the city because of economic interests, mainly, and anyone who warns them of the impending disaster may run the risk of being considered a "communist." The young people are curiously passive, even inert; they realize what the situation is, but simply translate their despair into melancholy folksongs or occasional orgies of suicide. What an extraordinary species is man!—visitors from another planet on a mission to warn the city's inhabitants of their fate retreat, frustrated by the mental structure of Man which allows him to be so indifferent to his own impending extinction.

Part of the problem has to do with an "infinitely sub-divided" society, and so it is necessary to go beyond or beneath society to locate genuine human beings. Several stories of a near-mystical calm and beauty deal with a London park in various seasons. The narrator seems to enter another world in which "leaves, words, people, shadows whirl together toward autumn and the solstice." **"The Story of a Non-Marrying Man"** and **"An Old Woman and Her Cat"** are about isolated people who make no conscious choice but who come to reject ordinary society, in one case "going native" in Africa and making a final, satisfying marriage there, in the other "going savage" in the midst of London, and dying in an abandoned wreck of a house. Miss Lessing's instincts are always with the individual, whether the complex Jack Orkney or the relatively simple—natural—un-"white" Johnny Blakeworthy who turns away in disgust from the white African homesteaders and is drawn to to harmony of tribal existence.

"Not a Very Nice Story" is a kind of scaled-down, more believable *Couples,* whose four protagonists are driven emotionally by "hungers of all kinds . . . for security, affection, warmth." They drift into a form of "group marriage" after having survived a stormy early adulthood in which emotions were over-valued: "after all, emotion is the thing, we can none of us get enough of it." In the end, however, emotions fail and the pattern of a new conventionality asserts itself.

Where happiness is achieved, it is usually temporary because it has no foundation. Jack Orkney senses this, but fails to pursue his own despair far enough. In turning away from a transcendent vision and attempting to reassert the old values he has always had, he knows he "had missed an opportunity of some sort"—but in spite of his conscious decision, his dreams lead him into another country and he realizes that "behind the face of the skeptical world was another, which no . . . decision of his could stop him exploring." (pp. 4, 13)

Joyce Carol Oates, "So Much for the Search for Truth," in Book World—The Washington Post, *October 22, 1972, pp. 4, 13.*

PATRICIA CHAFFEE   (essay date 1978)

[*In the following essay, Chaffee examines cultural, psychological, and racial factors that distinguish and define African societies in Lessing's* African Stories. *Chaffee pays particular attention to specific forms of non-verbal communication employed by various characters to establish strict social boundaries and to emphasize racial and socioeconomic differences between groups.*]

Doris Lessing's **African Stories** is an exploration of conflicts and misunderstandings arising from a network of closed groups, a world of occasionally overlapping circles of individuals, in which the members of each circle share certain understandings and attitudes deemed superior to, or at least isolated from, those of other circles. In the most obvious example the colonists, assuming a superiority based on color and political power, establish physical and psychological boundaries between themselves and the Africans. Africans, however, assuming a superiority based on prior claim to the land and intimate knowledge of it, maintain their identification as a closed group by secretly mocking or openly defying their masters and by denying them the ultimate surrender of trust. Cast off by black and white alike, the circle of half-castes share their unique experience of physical and psychological isolation. But color is not the only criterion for inclusive/exclusive grouping in this collection of stories. Nationality separates English from Afrikaaner; vocation separates farmer from civil servant; financial status separates the comfortable from the poor and the rich from the comfortable; conscience separates oppressor from reformer; age separates child from adult; and sex separates man from woman.

Consciously or unconsciously, each of these groups communicates its closed nature to an outsider both verbally and nonverbally. Verbally, an outsider encounters not only the blatantly hostile tags "dirty kaffir" or "white boy," but also more subtle indications of simple alien status or outright unwelcome. As a Civil Service wife newly arrived from England, Marina Giles in *A Home for the Highland Cattle* finds herself on the outside of three groups: non-Civil Service employees, long-time colonials, and Africans. She becomes aware of her status through attempts at verbal communication. When, in response to a supposedly sincere inquiry by Mrs. Pond, her new neighbor, she says that her husband is in the Civil Service, she does not understand the "sceptical smile" she receives, nor does she fully understand the class-conscious resentment in Mrs. Pond's remark: "You have to be in the Service to get what's going." She discovers her alien position as a liberal when she sees that Mrs. Skinner, a long-time colonial, expects her to agree that "They're all born thieves and liars." But the story grows from her gradual realization that she will probably understand the Mrs. Ponds and the Mrs. Skinners sooner than she will understand the Charlies, the black servants, for whom her reference to "this country" suggests only the image of a "flat piece of paper, tinted pink and green and blue" and to whom the word "police" can never mean justice and protection.

In **"The De Wets Come to Kloof Grange"** verbal non-communication in the form of a written note aggravates the hostility between two mutually intolerant groups. Mrs. Gale, deliberately being the proper Englishwoman, sends a formal invitation to the young Afrikaaner wife of her husband's new assistant. The more casual Afrikaaner reports the incident "scornfully to her husband: 'She's nuts. She writes me letters with stuck-down envelopes when I'm only five minutes away. . . .' "

An especially chilling and recurrent non-verbal signal of a closed group is laughter. The narrator of **"Old Chief Mshlanga,"** recalling the sense of danger that bound white children together against Africans, observes: "It was this instilled consciousness of danger, of something unpleasant, that made it so easy to laugh out loud, crudely, if a servant made a mistake in his English, or if he failed to understand an order—there is a certain kind of laughter that is fear, afraid of itself." In **"The De Wets Come to Kloof Grange"** English-Afrikaaner prejudices fade as Major Gale and his assistant join in conspiratorial laughter over the male "joke" of Mrs. De Wet's disappearance. She is, after all, a woman "being upset, you know." Tommy Clarke in *The Antheap* has learned from Dirk, his half-caste friend, the "bitter ironical laugh" that excludes the circle of tyrants from the circle of the exploited. And Jabavu, the young innocent of *Hunger,* begins to learn, but never masters, the protean laugh of his mentor Jerry, which separates the world of cynical con-artists from the world of their victims.

The most pervasive mark of group separation, however, is spatial patterning. Almost all of the mutually closed groups in these stories observe explicit or implicit spatial rules. Ethnic prejudices, for instance, require a distancing between individuals of different backgrounds. Michele Piselli in **"The Black Madonna"** may be mildly dissolute, but it is more his Italian blood than his character that prompts the English Captain Stocker to stand "at ten paces from the disreputable fellow" as he addresses him. The English feelings of superiority over the Afrikaaners is likewise expressed in terms of distancing or violation of distance. Curiously, though, the isolation implicit in these English-Afrikaaner encounters is isolation of the English person rather than of the Afrikaaner, though of course separation is by definition a mutual experience. When Major Carruthers, in **"The Second Hut,"** lodges his Afrikaaner assistant in a thatched hut behind his house, he admits to himself that "if his new assistant had been an Englishman, with the same upbringing, he would have found a corner in his house and a welcome as a friend." Caroline Gale, of **"The De Wets Come to Kloof Grange,"** feeds her loneliness on yearning, unrealistic memories of her English woman friend, but when confronted with the imminent arrival of an Afrikaaner companion, she resents "the Dutch woman who was going to invade her life with impertinent personal claims."

Many of the stories, of course, include major or minor conflicts developing from spatial patterns separating blacks, coloreds and whites. Both city and country have undesirable areas of isolation for non-whites. In the city the section for Colored People is as neglected as the Native Township; in the country the compounds are crowded and generally unsanitary, while the "proper Native Reserve" seems to resemble an American Indian reservation in quality of land, for it is to such a reserve that Old Chief Mshlanga and his people were moved because their rich land "was going to be opened up for white settlement soon." Poor as they may be, however, these places are seen by both black and white as black territory, and a white person in them is considered a trespasser. A white man like Mr. Macintosh in **The Antheap,** presuming on his powerful position, may enter the compound to visit his mistress, but his presence is tolerated rather than welcomed. Even a visit to the blacks' territory by well-meaning whites or a sincere request for useful knowledge held by the closed African group is seen as intrusion. Thus, when Marina and Philip Giles, in **A Home for the Highland Cattle,** drive to a shack in the location in order to bring Charlie, his sweetheart Theresa, and the picture of the cattle as lobola for Theresa's father, the old man "did not want to see them, so the two white people fell back a little." Again, the Nkosikaas Jordan, the young white girl, pays a "friendly visit" to Chief Mshlanga in his kraal, but she can see that "he was not pleased." And when, in **"No Witchcraft for Sale,"** the pious white family, the Farquars, ask Gideon to show their scientist guest the plant that healed their son's eyes, Gideon acts "as if he could not believe his old friends could so betray him."

The Africans cannot risk open expression of displeasure at this violation of their space. They can no more drive out the white man or woman than they could repel the major invasions of their land, against which old Chief Mshlanga's only revenge is the helpless statement translated by his son: "My father says: All this land, this land you call yours, is his land, and belongs to our people." But the white man or woman can punish violations of his/her territorial boundaries. When, in **"Leopard George,"** George Chester's black mistress dares to leave the compound during the day and reveal her status to her master's white guests, she is sent to the mission school fifty miles away, at George's expense, but against the pleadings of Old Smoke, the faithful family servant. In **Hunger** Jabavu learns through bitter humiliation that his place is at the back of the white person's house. A more developed conflict in **The Antheap** involves the violation of personal spatial barriers, whose existence is made clear to everyone concerned when a boy or girl passes from babyhood to childhood. Tommy and Dirk, through their persistent defiance of these taboos, know that they win a victory when they force Mr. Macintosh to treat them as equals, but "now they had to begin again, in the long and difficult struggle to understand what they had won and how they would use it."

In two of the finest stories in the collection, spatial boundaries between the world of children and the world of adults both reflect the security of an adolescent girl's past, with its unequivocal definitions of place, and create her present confusion about where she belongs. When parents in the rural districts of these stories take children to parties, mothers put them to sleep in rooms provided as nurseries and then join their husbands in the living room or on the verandah. Each group is comfortably located in its appointed place. On other social occasions, when adults are seated together on the verandah to gossip, children know they belong out of the circle. But Kate Cope, in **"Old John's Place,"** is "too old to be put to bed with the infants, and too young to join the party"; and the narrator in **"Getting off the Altitude"** is, until the end of the story, "still in a short dress," yet she, like Kate, is old enough to visit adult neighbors alone. Because they no longer identify with children, they feel uncomfortable in the places assigned by custom to children. Because they are not accepted as adults, they feel uncomfortable in places assumed by that group. Thus at the parties given first by the Sinclairs and then by the Laceys, Kate drifts from the kitchen to the bed-

room to her parents' car. As she wanders between adult rooms and nurseries, she overhears enough and sees enough to understand two disturbing facts that carry her out of childhood into adolescence. She discovers that despite their staid external lives, few of the farmers of her district really share her father's rigid sexual morality and that further, even with these abberations, their lives are still dull and provincial compared to the glittering vitality of people like the Laceys, the new couple in the district. Her physical no-man's land reflects her psychological and emotional no-man's land. She feels herself drifting in and out of four groups, or two pairs of groups: child-adult, conservative-adventurous. It is again through a spatial pattern that she recognizes clearly the utter incompatibility between the latter groups. When she sees that Rosalind Lacey is pointedly excluded from the circle of women at her mother's Sunday lunch, she knows finally that she must direct her loyalty either to the mores of her own district or to those of Mrs. Lacey.

The narrator in **"Getting off the Altitude"** also suffers embarrassment and gains insight because, in her "between-group" status, she lacks both a child's access to a boys' play environment and an adult's poise in an adult environment. Thus, when she found herself in the presence of an ugly argument between Mr. and Mrs. Slatter, she awkwardly "made fast for the door" of the room and "ran down the passage away from it." Had she been younger, she might have been with the young Slatter sons, secure in their play rooms. As an adult she could have exited gracefully or, if close enough to the family, remained in the room. On another occasion, during a dance at the Slatters, she feels out of place on the verandah, for she considers herself too old for the younger boys, and the older boys consider her too young for them. She feels equally out of place in the living-room with the married people. Like Kate Cope, she seeks refuge in a bedroom. From this vantage point she discovers the relationship between Mrs. Slatter and the young assistant. With this knowledge she continues her growth out of childhood. A year later, in a similar scene she again seeks the refuge of isolation from groups she is not yet comfortable with, and this time sees the depth of Mrs. Slatter's frustration.

Perhaps the most significant spatial definition in **African Stories** is that which creates the mutually exclusive circles of men and women. The circles, of course, overlap superficially as husband and wife or lovers share a room, a table, or a bed. The separateness of the groups is, again superficially, indicated in the seating patterns that arise naturally at different gatherings: "But there was always a stage [at parties] when the women sat at one end of the verandah and the men at the other"; "When lunch was over, things arranged themselves as usual with the men on one side of the room and the women on the other." But the real difference between these two groups, that which underlies much of the tension in the stories, is profoundly spatial. It arises from categorically opposite responses to the very experience of pioneering, of colonizing a land that is repeatedly described as endlessly expansive. Story after story emphasizes this expansiveness. The "bigness and silence of Africa" includes, in a child's perspective, "thousands and thousands of miles of unused Government land" as well as actual three-thousand-acre farms "with the sky blue and brilliant halls of air and the bright green fields and hollows of country beneath and the mountains lying sharp and bare twenty miles off across the rivers." It is "this rich soil, this slow-moving water, and air that smelt like a challenge . . ."; it is "Four Winds, lifted high into the sky among the great windswept sun-quivering mountains, tumbled all over with boulders, offering itself to storms and exposure and invasion by baboons and leopards. . . . " Finally, it is a country so limitless that a "pocket" of land can mean an area "hundreds of miles in depth."

This country is a wedge that cleaves ever more deeply into whatever originally bound the married couple who settle in it. The man, having chosen a country life because he felt enclosed in an office and cramped in town, feels himself expand as he surveys his land, organizes his laborers, and gradually tames the wild space, seeing it take the shape he plans for it, thus filling it with himself. His farm or his mine becomes more and more solidly his world; he occupies it from sunup to sundown, and it occupies him always. His consciousness, fixed on outward space, becomes alien to small spaces or to inner space. A man is judged on the degree to which he measures himself against his land. Major Carruthers in **"The Second Hut"** feels that he announces failure when he tells his wife "I've written for a job at Home." And in *Eldorado* Alec Barnes's survival depends upon his being allowed to live in the illusion that he can command the gold under his land, since he has failed to control the soil on it.

But only these two white men fail in the stories; the rest identify with their particular interest in the land, growing so far beyond the space occupied by their wives or mistresses that they can no longer enter it. When, after listening to her husband and his assistant discuss farming for two hours, Mrs. Gale ventures a comment, "De Wet looked around absently as if to say she should mind her own business, and her husband remarked absently, 'Yes, dear,' when a Yes dear did not fit her remark at all. . . . " During one of Tom's absences in **"Winter in July,"** Kenneth enjoys sharing his bed with Tom's wife Julia, but he is not willing to share her world: " 'What do you want then?' he enquired briefly, giving what small amount of attention he could spare from the farm to the problem of Julia, the woman." Even when the men are "cheque-book farmers" like Mr. Hackett and Mr. Lacey, they cannot enter a woman's space. They "came in to meals and did not so much as glance at the work that had been done. . . . They were so clearly making preparations for when the restless thing in them that had already driven them from continent to continent spoke again. . . . " And as Margaret in **"A Mild Attack of Locusts"** contemplates the devastation wrought by the locusts, "She felt like a survivor after war." To her this was ruin. "But the men ate their supper with good appetites." They were planning the replanting and hoping for rain.

While the man's spatial consciousness expands outward in ever broadening and deepening swathes, the woman's world shrinks to a point within herself. Her outer limits may extend to the garden near the house, where she can feel that she plays at the grown-up work of planting and harvesting. Or they may correspond to the walls of the house, as in **"Lucy Grange"**: "Even on the verandah there were sacks of grain and bundles of hoes. The life of the farm, her husband's life, washed around the house. . . . " Managing the house, however, soon becomes as much non-work as maintaining the garden. Any necessary role is filled by black servants. If the woman is a Mrs. Black (*A Home for the Highland Cattle*), a Mrs. Farquar (**"No Witchcraft for Sale"**), or a Mrs. Grant (**"The New Man"**), she enjoys her "freedom" and fills it with gossip, complaints, sleep, some sewing, and whatever part of mothering she does not trust to the African servants.

If a woman is sensitive and vital, she rebels against her confinement. In the exceptional case her rebellion may prove to be fulfilling, as when Jane McCluster, in **"Little Tembi,"** assumes the role of public health nurse to her husband's laborers and their families. More often the rebellion is a futile gesture of defiance, like Lucy Grange's gloves, Van Gogh print, and salesman lover or like Rosalind Lacey's glass wall and white carpet. When the woman is sensitive but submissive, she responds to her useless allowance of space by withdrawing even from that limited area. Though she may occupy a room in the house and stroll through the garden, her living room is within herself, where she buries herself either in stoic resignation or in reverie. For these women and the land that their husbands see as challenge and potential is alien and hostile. Maggie Barnes, in *Eldorado,* succumbs to a "kind of fatalism" as she begins to realize that "the very country was against her." Annie Clarke, in *The Antheap,* finds herself finally desiccated: "Living here, in this destroying heat, year after year, did not make her ill, it sapped her slowly, leaving her rather numbed and silent." Mrs. Carruthers, whom "chance had wrenched . . . on to this isolated African farm into a life which she submitted herself to, as if it had nothing to do with her," retreats completely into herself: "she turned her face to the wall and lay there, hour after hour, inert and uncomplaining, in a stoicism of defeat nothing could penetrate."

Other women, like Caroline Gale, Julia, and the mother in **"Flavours of Exile"** fill their inner space with fantasies of bringing genteel English style and friendship into their farms or of buying an inviolable security by their acceptance of confinement. But the illusion is less safe even than cold resignation, for when its explosion forces the women to confront the reality of their "place," they re-discover the pain of its emptiness. For both women reality enters in the form of a new bride whose arrival into the country they watch or anticipate. Mrs. Gale, torn from her fantasy world by the desperate loneliness of the assistant's wife, and forced to acknowledge the false defenses she has built over the years, becomes "furious with that foolish couple who had succeeded in upsetting her and destroying her peace." Julia contemplates the future confinement that Kenneth, oblivious of any injustice, plans for his bride, and says: "I know what evil is."

Space, then, functions in *African Stories* as a thematic image. Conflicts flare up or smolder not so much between individuals as between "insiders" and "outsiders." The conflicts are expressed in terms of physical and psychological boundaries; that is, in terms of inner space and outer space, whether that space is an area of land or an area of consciousness. Furthermore, Lessing portrays this fragmentation, with its arid, sterile inbreeding, against the vastness and lush fertility of the African landscape. The final effect is more than pathetic irony; it is prophecy. The unresolved endings of most of the stories acknowledge the continuance of a society of closed systems, which must remind the reader of Thomas Pynchon's vision of entropy at work in human society. In her novels Lessing offers hope through various kinds of openness, but in these short stories, her statement is grim indeed. (pp. 45-52)

Patricia Chaffee, "Spatial Patterns and Closed Groups in Lessing's 'African Stories'," in South Atlantic Bulletin, *Vol. XLIII, No. 2, May, 1978, pp. 45-52.*

As a writer I am concerned first of all with novels and stories, though I believe that the arts continuously influence each other, and that what is true of one art in any given epoch is likely to be true of the others. I am concerned that the novel and the story should not decline as art-forms any further than they have from the high peak of literature; that they should possibly regain their greatness. For me the highest point of literature was the novel of the nineteenth century, the work of Tolstoy, Stendhal, Dostoevsky, Balzac, Turgenev, Chekhov; the work of the great realists. I define realism as art which springs so vigorously and naturally from a strongly-held, though not necessarily intellectually-defined, view of life that it absorbs symbolism. I hold the view that the realist novel, the realist story, is the highest form of prose writing; higher than and out of the reach of any comparison with expressionism, impressionism, symbolism, naturalism, or any other ism. . . .

Once a writer has a feeling of responsibility, as a human being, for the other human beings he influences, it seems to me he must become a humanist, and must feel himself as an instrument of change for good or for bad. That image of the pretty singer in the ivory tower has always seemed to me a dishonest one. Logically he should be content to sing to his image in the mirror. The act of getting a story or a novel published is an act of communication, an attempt to impose one's personality and beliefs on other people. If a writer accepts this responsibility, he must see himself, to use the socialist phrase, as an architect of the soul, and it is a phrase which none of the old nineteenth-century novelists would have shied away from.

But if one is going to be an architect, one must have a vision to build towards, and that vision must spring from the nature of the world we live in.

Doris Lessing, from her A Small Personal Voice.

MICHAEL THORPE (essay date 1978)

[*Thorpe is a British editor, poet, and critic living in Canada. In the following excerpt from his* Doris Lessing's Africa, *he compares and explicates four novellas from* Five: Short Novels, *focusing on Lessing's portrayal of various social, familial, and interracial relationships.*]

Of the four African novels first published in the collection entitled *Five* in 1953, three are among her finest works, while the fourth, *Hunger,* is her weakest and least characteristic. Nevertheless, the collection was awarded the Somerset Maugham prize, for the best work of the year by an English author under thirty-five, in 1954.

These short novels fall between short story length and that even of the usual short novel. They can best be distinguished from the short stories proper in Lessing's own words: 'There is space in them to take one's time, to think aloud, to follow, for a paragraph or two, on a side-trail—none of which is possible in a real short story.' There are risks as well as advantages in this looser method, which the failure of *Hunger* illustrates; the risks are greater when the story's message is uppermost in the author's mind, as she has admitted it was:

It came to be written like this. I was in Moscow with a delegation of writers, back in 1952. It was striking that while the members of the British team differed very much politically, we agreed with each other on certain assumptions about literature—in brief, that writing had to be a product of the individual conscience, or soul. Whereas the Russians did not agree at all—not at all. Our debates, many and long, were on this theme.

Stalin was still alive. One day we were taken to see a building full of presents for Stalin, rooms full of every kind of object—pictures, photographs, carpets, clothes, etc., all gifts from his grateful subjects and exhibited by the State to show other subjects and visitors from abroad. It was a hot day. I left the others touring the stuffy building and sat outside to rest. I was thinking about what Russians were demanding in literature—greater simplicity, simple judgments of right and wrong. We, the British, had argued against it, and we felt we were *right* and the Russians *wrong*. But after all, there was Dickens, and such a short time ago, and his characters were all good or bad—unbelievably Good, monstrously Bad, but that didn't stop him from being a great writer. Well, there I was, with my years in Southern Africa behind me, a society as startlingly unjust as Dickens's England. Why, then, could I not write a story of simple good and bad, with clear-cut choices, set in Africa? The plot? Only one possible plot—that a poor black boy or girl should come from a village to the white man's rich town and . . . there he would encounter, as occurs in life, good and bad, and after much trouble and many tears he would follow the path of . . .

I tried, but it failed. It wasn't true. Sometimes one writes things that don't come off, and feels more affectionate towards them than towards those that worked.

Lessing's affection for *Hunger* is easy to understand, for its failure is one of good intentions, of an anxiety that the message be conveyed overmastering the story-telling function. Plot and viewpoint were inevitably major problems. *Hunger* has one of the 'basic plots' amongst those earliest established in South African writing and long before that, as her reference to Dickens indicates, in the early Victorian English novels intended to reveal the life of the underworld. Jabavu runs through a fairly predictable gamut of experiences; as Mr. Samu, the African politician who befriends him, is made to comment: 'His experiences are typical for young men coming to town.' Jabavu's very name is symbolic. White City Jabavu is the name of one of the suburbs of Soweto (South Western Township), the agglomeration of dormitory suburbs attached to Johannesburg. . . . The town of the story is of course not Johannesburg, but that most seductive of all traps for the 'bush' African is often mentioned in the story and supplies, as it were, the prototype of all 'Joe Comes to Jo'burg' stories.

To the reader unfamiliar with the pattern such stories had taken for some forty years *Hunger* will at least be fresh in subject matter. If he comes to it with a grounding in English literature he will notice rather, in Jabavu's initiation into the life of the 'skellums' ('wicked persons') in the city—his instruction in petty thievery, his urge to goodness though he does wrong—and in the characterization of the prostitute, Betty, and the gang-leader Jerry, strong resemblances to *Oliver Twist.* These are in plot and a tendency to enforce the theme with black and white oppositions. Beyond these, there are touches of characterization that have possibilities of depth for which the story allows no scope, as for example in the analysis of Betty whose 'nature' it is 'to love the indifference of man'.

The difficulty of striking an apt viewpoint is evident from the very beginning. Stopping short of adopting a completely 'inside' presentation of Jabavu, which might have seemed to claim too much, the narrator becomes a camera eye, seeing him from the outside, alternating with a recording voice that witnesses thoughts and feelings. The immediate effect is to give the reader a disturbingly objective view of character and situation, as of a documentary about a strange people. The explanatory comment, on the degradation of life in the kraal, the childlike 'hunger' of the young for 'the white man's town', the heavy despair of the old at the passing of the traditional way of life and its corruption by the new, increase the distancing effect of the narration in the present tense. In large part the author's problem is that she cannot assume in her reader enough vital knowledge, but the effect is more damaging when her characters become mere mouthpieces for representative attitudes than when the narrative smoothly supplies this kind of ironical touch on Jabavu's physical examination at the Pass Office:

> The doctor has said, too, that Jabavu has an enlarged spleen, which means he has had malaria and will have it again, that he probably has bilharzia, and there is a suspicion of hookworm. But these are too common for comment, and what the doctor is looking for are diseases which may infect the white people if he works in their houses.

Perhaps because there is so much ammunition in the story that may be used against white rule and for African solidarity it has been, as Lessing thinks, one of her 'most liked' despite, or because of, its artistic simplification. Morality tales have always had their appeal, and are in fact the stuff of officially approved 'literature' in modern Russia and China. We should remember that *Hunger* was written when Lessing had returned flushed with political purpose from Moscow: no other story from her Communist years has so markedly political a flavour. The last page, when the imprisoned Jabavu becomes fired with a revived sense of the old tribal solidarity after reading the letter from the African leader, Mr. Mizi, could with little difficulty be converted into a paean prophesying the ultimate victory of the workers: '*We,* says Jabavu over and over again, *We.* And it is as if in his empty hands are the warm hands of brothers.' It is surely no accident that the fact that it is Mr. Mizi's message which touches Jabavu, not Mr. Tennent's, 'the man of God'—to whom Mizi is 'an intemperate and godless agitator'—contrasts so sharply with the Christian answer that closes Alan Paton's *Cry, the Beloved Country.* Our belief in Jabavu's ability to absorb Mr. Mizi's message strains to the utmost the author's need throughout to make us accept him as an exceptionally clever, almost entirely self-taught literate. In order to convey the message Jabavu has to carry too large a burden of probability, as did the working-class heroes of the Victorian novel-with-a-purpose or of Communist proletarian literature today. It is as well that Lessing only had one such lapse, but valuable that we have it still as a cautionary tale.

Turning to *The Antheap,* we find the problems of articulating complex feeling and of avoiding excessive commentary admirably solved. All grows naturally out of close relationship between the three principal actors: old Mr. Macintosh, the millionaire goldminer, his unwanted half-caste son Dirk, and Dirk's white friend Tommy Clarke, Macintosh's engineer's son whom he loves as if he were his own. The problem of communication between these three, who are repeatedly barred from mutual understanding by conflicting emotions that run deep and strong, and by sheer incapacity to enter fully into the thoughts and feelings of the others, is solved (as in **"The Black Madonna"**) by the casting of Tommy as artist. His art expresses more than he can say or consciously know: it communicates this knowledge to the others who, like him, are locked in pride, hatred and distrust. This means of communication is, of course, one that comes most naturally to the author; it enables her to convey the deeper meaning with a rich suggestiveness.

As in some of the short stories, the adoption of the child's eye view allows freshness of vision and response to a situation the adult characters have come to regard with a stale, hardened acceptance. It is natural that Tommy Clarke, the solitary white boy, should turn to the nearest children for playmates even though they are 'kaffirs'. It is natural, too, that the one to whom he feels closest should be the half-caste Dirk, the boss's unacknowledged son; wanted by neither black nor white, the 'coloured' is the one against whom the barrier of 'silence' and segregation is strongest. This very difficulty naturally spurs Tommy's attempts to breach it, rather than any precocious instinct for equality—that comes later, after the personal relationship has been established. When he asks his parents, 'Why shouldn't I play with Mr. Macintosh's son?' he is using the system, not revolting against it. The story never drops, throughout the slow progress of the relationship and of Tommy's insight, into simple heroics. (pp. 35-9)

[The brotherhood between Dirk and Tommy], unlike that too easily invoked in *Hunger,* is literally fought for with what continues to the end to be an almost desperate urge toward fulfilment. When Macintosh gives in and concedes chances of education to both boys, making them as equal at least as their society will allow, a new phase in their lives inevitably begins, to surmount the barrier that may yet break them; it remains an open question whether they can or will:

> The victory was entirely theirs, but now they had to begin again, in the long and difficult struggle to understand what they had won and how they would use it.

Only in this last sentence does the novel take the clearer-cut form of a parable and do we suddenly see the boys as more than themselves, as the symbols of promise for the future—or failure. Thus, the method reverses the approach in *Hunger,* where the symbolic overtones are insistently present from the outset. The essential separateness of all, white and black, it is borne in upon us, is underlined by Dirk's special role of outcast: though he is the child of both races, he is accepted by neither.

Tommy Clarke, the sensitive white boy, could easily have become sentimentalized. Instead of *using* him for the facile purpose of demonstrating the superiority of his perceptions to adult prejudice, Lessing lets him be drawn to Dirk by a complex of motives: the desire for companionship, the need to assert his wishes against the prohibitions of his parents, a fascinated compulsion to play with his 'superiority', the little-understood urges of his artistic self. From the moment he moulds a rough clay image of Dirk he becomes the agent of intuitive meaning: that first image is also the first constructive use of that African earth which Mr. Macintosh has obsessively pillaged, his carving of Dirk's mother and child stirs in Mr. Macintosh inexpressible feelings of bafflement and loss, the frieze of the mine becomes the pit of hell. Tommy carves, not only what he sees, but what he half knows: this Mr. Macintosh acknowledges, struggling between his love for the boy and fear of his art, in the only way he and his kind have ever known. He buys the advice of the art expert Mr. Tomlinson, who tells him of Tommy's second carving of Dirk, in a moment of ironic comedy: 'It has a look of you' . . . The ironies accumulate: Macintosh's money, wrenched from the African earth, becomes the means of 'investing' in Tommy's talent, though that is itself both a reverent, creative use of that earth and a challenge to the social subjection the 'antheap' symbolizes:

> Dirk was looking at himself. 'Why do you make me like that?' he asked. The narrow, strong face expressed nothing but that familiar, sardonic antagonism, as if he said: 'You, too—just like the rest!'
>
> 'Why? Why don't you like it?' challenged Tommy at once.
>
> Dirk walked around it, then back. 'You're just like all the rest,' he said.
>
> 'Why? Why don't you like it?' Tommy was really distressed. Also, his feeling was: What's it got to do with him? Slowly he understood that his emotion was that belief in his right to freedom which Dirk always felt immediately, and he said in a different voice: 'Tell me what's wrong with it?'
>
> 'Why do I have to come out of the wood? Why haven't I any hands or feet?'
>
> 'You have, but don't you see . . . ' But Tommy looked at Dirk standing in front of him and suddenly gave an impatient movement: 'Well, it doesn't matter, it's only a statue.'
>
> He sat on the trunk and Dirk beside him. After a while he said: 'How should you be, then?'
>
> 'If you make yourself, would you be half wood?'
>
> Tommy made an effort to feel this, but failed. 'But it's not me, it's you.' He spoke with difficulty, and thought: But it's important, I shall have to think about it later. He almost groaned with the knowledge that here it was, the first debt, presented for payment.
>
> Dirk said suddenly: 'Surely it needn't be wood. You could do the same thing if you put handcuffs on my wrists.' Tommy lifted his head and gave a short, astonished laugh. 'Well, what's funny?' said Dirk, aggressively. 'You can't do it the easy way, you have to make me half wood, as if I was more a tree than a human being.'
>
> Tommy laughed again, but unhappily. 'Oh, I'll do it again,' he acknowledged at last. 'Don't fuss about that one, it's finished. I'll do another.'
>
> There was silence.

Both understand more than they can say: as at the beginning of their relationship, when the boy Tommy had troubled his parents by '[infringing] the rule of silence' linked with Dirk, so at the end. This 'silence' cannot be bridged by slogans or

wishful attitudes; it is an inescapable condition of their existence.

In *Eldorado,* as in *The Antheap,* the elusive private worlds of emotion and desire of a closely-knit trio who can never be at one are again held in uneasy relationship by a potent symbolic force. This is the lure of gold—a dream, 'gleam', vision or trap, destroyer of sanity even; it is like the compulsion of art, its own reward or damnation, depending on your point of view. Yet it is a symptom, not a cause. The old wandering prospector who comes to the Barnes' farm and who 'spoke of the search for gold as a scientist might of a discovery, or an artist of his art' is no devil, leading Alec Barnes astray from the straight, if unspectacular path of farming maize. He is one visionary speaking to another, soul to soul. The search for gold that draws Alec into neglect of his farm only gives a new impetus to that need for 'freedom', that instinct for 'distance', an unconfined world all his own making, which first brought Alec out to the colony. His wife recognizes it with dread, her love cannot reach it.

> That *something else*—how well Maggie knew it! And how she grieved for Paul, whose heart was beating (she could positively hear it) to the pulse of that dangerous *something else.* It was not the elephants and the lions and the narrow escapes; not the gold; not underground rivers; none of these things in themselves, and perhaps not even the pursuit of them. It was that oblique, unnamable quality in life which Maggie, trying to pin it down safely in homely words, finally dismissed in the sour and nagging phrase: Getting something for nothing.

She tries to warn her son Paul against this lure. Of course, he does not understand. Like so many of Lessing's children, he oscillates uneasily between his parents' two worlds, condemned by love, shame, antagonism and the sheer necessity of close relationship to seek his own standing point apart from both.

Eldorado is one of Lessing's most painful treatments of a family relationship. Of how the bonds of blood and natural dependence war against the 'free' self-realization that each desires. Opposed to the father's self-centred vision of 'freedom' is that which the mother desires for her son: 'Knowledge freed a man; and to that belief she clung, because it was her nature; and she was to grieve all her life because such a simple and obvious truth was not simple for Paul.' Knowing he hasn't the academic ability, and looking for a solid form of security in reaction from his father's failure and drift into a world of fantasy, Paul turns to James, the rough and ready 'small-worker' whose mine lies on the farm's boundary. James is a drunkard, sleeps with native women—a minor version of Macintosh—is grounded in a saving earthy realism. Throwing in his lot with James, Paul fulfils Maggie's worst fears, that he would 'grow up lax and happy-go-lucky, like a Colonial'. Her husband and son combine in this, that they bear out her conviction—felt by so many of Lessing's women but rarely voiced—that 'the very country was against her'. The woman, with her dreams of order, security, a civilized life, knows that her unbeatable antagonist is Africa: Africa rude, vital, capricious, is the 'Other Woman' she must fear; her men will loot it, love it, rape it or be seduced by it away from her. To it, in *Eldorado,* Maggie loses both her men: Paul, the son, will loot that earth; her husband Alec scarcely sane at the last, will be bound for the rest of his life to its charms. Faithful to the gold that eludes him (but gives itself, indifferently, to his son), it is enough for him that it exists:

' . . . all he said was, and in a proud, pleased voice: "Well, that proves it. I told you, didn't I? I always told you so." '

So human loves are lost to the seductive earth. These three can only talk with their feeling eyes, watchful, dark, evasive, full of pain. They tremble often upon the verge of loving connection, of pity given and accepted, but always their natures drive them apart. Mrs. Barnes blames the country, but she is as wrong as those characters of Hardy's who rail against adverse 'Nature'; only in countries of the mind is happiness attainable, and this ironically is Alec's one treasure—'safe in that orderly inner world he had built for himself'. (pp. 40-4)

Members of both races, whether it be Jabavu's father in **Hunger** or Maggie Barnes in **Eldorado**, fear and distrust the city, which is synonymous with social disorder and the confusion of values. (The irony remains, of course, that the orders and values of the 'country' are those imposed by the white man for his own convenience.) This contrast and conflict between a stable rural and a corrupt urban life is, of course, one of the oldest themes in literature. In the Rhodesian, or any similar Colonial situation, only in the very few major cities is there any possibility of access to the values of a more open society. Into such towns there has over the past thirty or forty years been a steady flow of potentially disruptive influences—whites who have no stake in the 'country', but come to work often only for a few years in the schools, universities, the Civil Service or the developing industrial concerns. (We shall see how a large part of the Martha Quest sequence turns to portraying such people.) However, it must be remembered that while these newer colonials may be the bearers of more enlightened ideas, they nevertheless have hardly less interest than the rural settler in maintaining their ascendancy over the blacks. A piquant irony is inherent in this contradiction, which Lessing exploits to the full in **A Home for the Highland Cattle,** a masterpiece of ironic comedy.

Ironies multiply from the outset. We are going to read of a new type of white emigrant:

> It seems, from books, that the colonizers and adventurers went sailing off to a new fine life, a new country, opportunities, and so forth. Now all they want is a roof over their heads.

This sets the deflating tone of the whole story. The town (Salisbury) to which the Gileses come was to have been the bold city of Cecil Rhodes' vision; actually, it is the mean suburban world of the 'Old Country' transplanted to an 'exotic' setting inhabited by ten thousand whites and serviced by 150,000 blacks who 'do not so much *live* here, as squeeze themselves in as they can'. It soon dawns upon Marina Giles, who had come out as 'that liberally-minded person produced so plentifully in England during the thirties', that her vision was no less fatuous than Rhodes's:

> . . . what is a British Colony but a sort of highly-flavoured suburb of England itself? Somewhere in the back of Marina's mind has been a vision of herself and Philip living in a group of amiable people, pleasantly interested in the arts, who read the *New Statesman* week by week, and held that discreditable phenomena like the colour bar and the black-white struggle could be solved by sufficient goodwill . . . a delightful picture.

Life's necessities bring Marina's concerns down to a depressingly humdrum level. Like countless colonial wives before her, she is confounded by the 'servant problem'—reviving that very problem of conscience and convenience which good liberals in the 'Old Country' had disposed of a generation earlier. Ironically, it is one which their modern descendants now go abroad to encounter all over again. Throughout the colonial period it was inevitably the woman's problem, so that in India the *'memsahib',* in Africa the 'madam' found herself at the most sensitive point of contact with the native. We have seen the tragic side of this in *The Grass is Singing: A Home for the Highland Cattle* exploits its more comic possibilities, though the effects are nonetheless serious.

While Philip, her agriculturist husband, devotes his energies to furthering the African's well-being in his practical, worthwhile way, Marina struggles in their semi-detached box, 138 Cecil Rhodes Vista (wicked name!) to realize her notions of human equality in her handling of her 'boy', Charlie. From the beginning Charlie gropes to comprehend this new variety of 'madam' and clearly it will not be long before, as most servants will, he takes advantage of her guilt-ridden weakness.

This story requires a comic symbol. Nothing could have been more apt than one of those Victorian pictures of highland cattle, which used to be endemic in 'Old Country' drawing rooms and parlours ('Really, why bother to emigrate?'). Mrs. Skinner, the landlady, leaves it to Marina's safe-keeping. Marina, naturally, abhors it: it is the persistent image of what she had intended to escape. Charlie, however, seems to admire it—an admiration dimly connected, she supposes, with the part played by cattle in tribal life 'that could only be described as religious'. This part is the use of cattle as *lobola* (the 'bride-price' paid by the suitor to his loved one's father), now in a sadly degenerated state. Gradually, Marina works herself into a false position: her attempts to treat Charlie more humanely 'spoil' him, as Little Tembi was spoiled by Jane MacCluster; she becomes so embroiled in his personal life that she falls ironically into the despised role of the white paternalist, handling her Africans as foolish children. Her attempt to get Charlie married to Theresa, his pregnant girl-friend, brings the picture into play. Thinking it valuable, Charlie has the bright idea of presenting it to Theresa's father in lieu of *lobola;* and Marina, compromising her white integrity, agrees to give it him. She and Philip drive the pair and the picture out to the wretched location where the father exists, only to receive from the broken old man a nostalgic homily on the degenerate state into which the old ritual and ceremonies have fallen. Nevertheless, he accepts the picture. Philip and Marina drive back, grim but little wiser, unknowingly leaving the couple to celebrate their union in an illicit liquor den. The sequel is no less sordid. When Mrs. Skinner gets an inkling upon her return of what those 'white kaffirs' (the Gileses) have done with her precious painting, she has no difficulty in getting Charlie arrested for carrying off a few worthless objects including 'a wooden door-knocker that said *'Welcome Friend'.*

The sequel is crisp and could stand as epitaph for a legion of good intentions, fatally unsupported by imagination, like Marina's. Marina, having at last graduated into the higher suburbs she had at first scorned and ignorant of Charlie's fate, passes a file of handcuffed prisoners in a street 'in this city of what used to be known as the Dark Continent', thinks momentarily that she recognizes Charlie among them but, intent on discovering that 'ideal table' at once dismisses the thought. Her well-intentioned but amateurish meddling has merely violated the accepted order of things, causing both Charlie's misfortune (though he endures it with a well-taught philosophy) and her tired indifference. By now the story could be sub-titled 'The Making of a Madam'. We should not overlook in these closing paragraphs the significance of the reference to the Dark Continent in juxtaposition with the file of handcuffed prisoners: it ironically suggests the slave caravans of the days before white enlightenment. . . . In *A Home for the Highland Cattle,* exercising a firm, ironic control as assured as Forster's in *A Passage to India,* Lessing has, like that pioneering ironist of the diseased heart of imperialism, subtly exposed the perils of liberal efforts at 'connexion', if unsupported by extraordinary character and intelligence. It is a cautionary tale whose meaning can be applied to many situations other than the one that directly inspired it: claims to enlightened attitudes are far more easily professed than lived up to. (pp. 45-8)

Michael Thorpe, in his Doris Lessing's Africa, *Evans Brothers Limited, 1978, 117 p.*

MARGARET K. BUTCHER   (essay date 1980)

[*In the following excerpt, Butcher examines stylistic and conceptual distinctions in stories from* African Stories *to determine whether they indicate divergent paths of development in Lessing's fiction.*]

In her preface to the first complete collection of her African stories, Doris Lessing remarks on the kinds of short story the volume comprises. She distinguishes between the "real" short story (stories which appeared in her first collection *This was the Old Chief's Country*) and the long stories, "almost short novels," such as *A Home for the highland cattle, The antheap,* and *Hunger,* which appeared in *Five* (1953) and express a personal predilection in favor of a form which allows "space . . . to take one's time, to think aloud, to follow, for a paragraph or two, on a side-trail. . . ." The contrast is between the story which reflects the process of thinking and the story which exists as the product of carefully polished thought, with the implicit suggestion that the "short" stories represent the latter form and the long ones the former.

That this neither corresponds to Lessing's intention nor conforms to her practice is revealed in her subsequent references to the long story *Hunger,* which fails, she suggests, because, despite its length, it was written to conform to a predetermined social principle: it did not allow her to "think ahead" or "follow . . . on a side-trail."

Lessing defines the principal distinction between her stories stylistically and locates that difference in two very early stories **"The Pig"** and **"The Trinket Box,"** both "short" stories, the former "straight, broad, direct," a "highway to the kind of writing that has the freedom to develop as it likes," the latter "intense, careful, self-conscious, mannered," that "*could have led to the kind of writing usually described as 'feminine' "* [my italics]. The suggestion here, which Lessing in no way qualifies or contradicts, is that **"The Trinket Box"** was one of a kind, an experiment that was not so much a detour off the main highway as a venture up a blind alley, a literary cul-de-sac, whereas **"The Pig"** represents the road consistently taken thereafter which is, by implication, "masculine."

That Lessing's understanding of the difference between these two stories, the "two forks," and their implication for her subsequent development is wrong is the argument of this paper. I shall examine four early stories, the two mentioned as well as **"The Black Madonna"** and **"Old Chief Mshlanga,"**

and trace a line of convergence rather than divergence through these which culminates in the ironic detachment achieved in the late story **"Homage to Isaac Babel."** I shall argue that **"The Pig"** and **"The Trinket Box,"** though differing markedly in mode and subject matter—their very titles are evidence enough of some kind of contrast—far from representing the way that was chosen and the way that was rejected, are polarized expressions of a single, complex viewpoint that took Lessing over a decade to define and come to terms with. My argument, to paraphrase Frost's well-known lines, is that Lessing's two forks appear to diverge at one point in her career and her achievement is the discovery that they were after all really only one road, "and that has made all the difference."

The study of Lessing's short stories seems to be dogged by artificial distinctions, **African Stories, Collected Stories,** the various overlapping earlier collections. Taken together, **"The Pig"** and **"The Trinket Box,"** which, interestingly enough, were "uncollected" until the 1964 *African Stories* collection, represent the "stuff " of Lessing's literary milieu, the material which as a writer she had to find some way of shaping into art. She herself describes the process in her preface to Michael Marland's edition of some of her stories: "the way to do it is to let yourself be attracted by an incident, an overheard remark, a face; and then allow this germ to grow, to accumulate around it memories, associations, things of a similar substance, until a whole is reached with a shape, a texture of its own, and very different from how it started off."

The difference between these two stories lies exactly here, in how they "started off." Analysis of their stylistic difference can only proceed once this central fact of Lessing's experience has been understood. The germ of all her "African" stories is found in her own experiences as a girl in Southern Rhodesia. Somewhat solitary and in manner tending towards what would in such a society be regarded as "tomboyish," she grew up bounded by her father's farm and her mother's house. The recurring motif in Lessing's fiction dealing with this period in her life is that of an adolescent girl hovering between these two self-contained but related worlds. **"The Pig"** has its origin in "an overheard remark" in the stuffy interior of her mother's house where gossip and conversation take the place of action and decision. (pp. 55-7)

At the core of Lessing's story [**"The Trinket Box"**] is the irony of what happens to an old woman of spirit and action who on her deathbed provides only a source of garrulous speculation for her female relatives, but the writer herself is trapped in the room, too, and can only get out by posing more questions. The story reveals her distrust of the confining and demeaning "feminine" world and the mode of writing it encourages. The description of **"The Trinket Box"** as "intense . . . self-conscious, mannered" is as much a moral judgment as an aesthetic one.

When she gives herself the freedom of the outdoors, as it were, when she takes her inspiration from her father's world, we get a very different kind of writing and a correspondingly different judgment. **"The Pig,"** in common with a number of Lessing's stories, begins with a paragraph of generalized description in which a character is etched in against a landscape:

> The farmer paid his labourers on a Saturday evening, when the sun went down. By the time he had finished it was always quite dark, and from the

kitchen door where the lantern hung, bars of yellow
light lay down the steps, across the path, and lit up
the trees and the dark faces under them.

Dialogue is introduced only when the mutual distrust that exists between employer and employee has been carefully delineated, and then the story bifurcates. The farmer, wanting to
put a stop to the thefts of his mealiecobs, deliberately refers
to pigs as likely culprits, knowing only too well that the pigs
are his own farm hands. Jonas, the native detailed to guard
the crop from the thieves, instead tracks down the man who
has been "thieving" his wife. The story concerns itself with
the "masculine" theme of the exercise of power and its frustrations. The structure of the story provides implicit moral
comment on the relationship of man with man when the divisions of color, race, and sex obtrude and shows the writer already beginning to realize that the most telling way of making
her point is through indirection and irony. There is nothing
particularly "broad," "straight," or "direct" about Jonas's
carefully rehearsing how he will fit word to action when he
recounts the murder of his rival to his employer:

> "A pig," said Jonas aloud to the listening moon, as
> he kicked the side gently with his foot, "nothing but
> a pig."
>
> He wanted to hear how it would sound when he
> said it again, telling how he had shot blind into the
> grunting, invisible herd.

Nevertheless, the stories are set in mutually exclusive male
and female worlds, a polarization acknowledged in **"The
Black Madonna"** which Lessing says is "full of the bile" she
feels for the "white" society in Rhodesia as she "knew and
hated it." (pp. 57-8)

The girl who grew up to be a writer in this society had to find
a way of dealing with these polarities. Her instinct to reject
the feminine out of scorn in favour of the masculine foundered in her recognition that neither provided a very congenial
ally. **"The Old Chief Mshlanga,"** which is essentially a fable
to demonstrate the process by which Lessing herself learnt
to cope with her intractable basic material, shows how she
managed to establish a framework of irony as a means of
achieving an accommodation of the two modes. Having done
so, she made the story the virtual title story of her first collection and excluded the three earlier stories so far discussed: an
acknowledgment that in it the divergent had begun to converge.

The situation presented at the beginning of **"The Old Chief "**
is a familiar one. Like Schreiner before her, Lessing describes
the problem faced by a writer in a colonial society, nourished
by legends of the metropolitan center and having to deal with
a landscape and society totally alien to the imagination
trained by that experience. At first, retreat, on the model of
the Lady of Shalott, is easier than confrontation:

> . . . . a jutting piece of rock which had been thrust
> up from the warm soil of Africa unimaginable eras
> of time ago . . . would hold the weight of a small
> girl whose eyes were sightless for anything but a
> pale willowed river, a pale gleaming castle. . . .

Growing up, she models herself on her father rather than her
mother (the source, presumably, of her literariness), accepting as her due the title "Nkosikaas" from the Old Chief,
whose ancestral lands, she begins to realize, are those farmed
by her father. Her awkward confrontation with the old man,

whose grace, dignity, and reserve provide a moving contrast
to the values of both her mother and her father, initiates a re-
valuation of the "white" ethic and confounds the sexual polarities inherent in it. The attitudes of a Jane and Willie Mc-
Cluster (**"Little Tembi"**) are condemned outright in her assertion:

> I had learned that if one cannot call a country to
> heel like a dog, neither can one dismiss the past
> with a smile in an easy gush of feeling, saying: I
> could not help it, I am also a victim.

From this point on, it seems to me, Lessing develops an ironic
stance towards herself as narrator which allows her to deal
with such antithetical attitudes without resorting to "bile,"
on the one hand (**"The Pig," "The Black Madonna"**) or a reluctant mannerism (**"The Trinket Box"**), on the other.

To turn from her African stories to those in the two collected
volumes is to see at once that Lessing, far from abandoning
mannerism, has pushed it as far as it will go, even to the point
of the grotesque in a story such as **"How I Finally Lost My
Heart."** What distinguishes stories such as **"Between Men"**
and **"One Off the Short List"** from **"The Trinket Box"** is a
controlled and mocking irony, a ruthless kind of authorial detachment which conveys implicit moral judgment: a technique which, as we have seen, began in **"The Pig."**

The collected stories share a cosmopolitan milieu and are all
studies of sophisticated urban manners. Lessing shares with
Katherine Mansfield a keen ear for the spoken word, the recording of which can be almost spiteful. Colonial "bile" becomes that much more bitter when refined and directed towards the metropolitan culture. Stories then such as **"Pleasure," "Not a Very Nice Story,"** and **"Each Other"** are developments from **"The Trinket Box"** in their structural emphasis on carefully arranged dialogue, but derive from **"The
Pig"** their coolly ironic stance. Lessing is deceiving herself
when she suggests her two early styles diverge; rather, all her
subsequent development represents a convergence or accommodation of the two.

The line from **"The Pig"** and **"The Trinket Box"** runs
through **"The Old Chief Mshlanga"** by way of **"The Black
Madonna"** and appears in fabular form in the neatest and
most accomplished of the stories in the collected volumes,
"Homage to Isaac Babel." The story, one of her shortest,
though not as short as some of Babel's own, is Lessing's mature comment on her own stylistic development, an ironic
recognition of the distance she has traveled, and an example
of how the two modes, in fact, converge. Perhaps because of
her earlier acknowledged failure with the "broad, direct"
and, by implication, "masculine" mode of *Hunger,* Lessing
became less distrustful of the "feminine." At any rate, by the
time of **"Homage"** (1961) Lessing is prepared to recognize
such polarizations on her own part as the product of naivety
and inexperience. Philip, of "pure stern tastes in everything,"
represents that part of herself which reacted to Zambesian insensitivity much as he does to the cinema doorman: "Some
people don't know right from wrong even when it's *demonstrated* to them." Towards Caroline, the thirteen year old aspiring writer, she shows an amused tolerance even when her
only literary production is a garbled and unintentionally
amusing piece of schoolgirl gush and adolescent highmind-
ness. Perhaps what Lessing admires and respects in her is her
willingness to learn. She too, like Lessing herself, may discover in Babel a way of dealing with the pettinesses and the hor-

rors of life that is more mature than the response: "I think it's all absolutely beastly, and I can't bear to think about it."

"Homage to Isaac Babel" provides a rebuttal—if one were needed—to the suggestion that in her later stories Lessing moves away from her earlier larger concerns with moral and political issues and retreats into a "feminine" world of social satire. Catherine cannot see that a description of a man's legs looking like girls has much to do with Babel's life as a Jew in Russia and his experience of war and revolution. Lessing, in her appreciation of Babel's detachment and control, has at last learned that mannerism and a directness in writing are neither mutually exclusive nor antithetical: they are the two forks that converge to produce a writer whose best qualities are, like her own, simplicity and strength. (pp. 58-61)

> Margaret K. Butcher, " 'Two Forks of a Road': Di-
> vergence and Convergence in the Short Stories of
> Doris Lessing," in Modern Fiction Studies, Vol. 26,
> No. 1, Spring, 1980, pp. 55-61.

ORPHIA JANE ALLEN (essay date 1980)

[*In the following excerpt, Allen explicates central themes in Lessing's collection* A Man and Two Women, *theorizing that in these stories Lessing portrays marriage and motherhood as destructive to the individuality and creativity of women.*]

In *A Man and Two Women* Lessing portrays the collective life as it emerges in motherhood and the family, in the church, and in other traditional institutions. Its apparent surface calm, she shows, often hides its damaging effect on the individual. Yet her characters often, to their detriment, seek out the collective because they desire its mindlessness and the escape it provides from their own responsibility to *be.*

The fact that Lessing's fiction often—as it does in *A Man and Two Women*—presents a woman's point of view has led some critics to label her a feminist writer. In a conversation with Florence Howe she concedes that she does write "from inside a woman's viewpoint" but that she is essentially writing about "the rights of the individual." In her Introduction to *The Golden Notebook* she writes that she has "assumed that that filter which is a woman's way of looking at life has the same validity as the filter which is a man's way." In this respect, Lynn Sukenick writes that it is because Lessing's heroines "like men so much . . . that they must be so careful," that it is "woman's vulnerability rather than man's culpability" that she stresses.

Certainly it is woman's vulnerability, sometimes even her culpability, that Lessing stresses as she exemplifies in her portrayal of motherhood the mindlessness of overindulgence in the collective experience. In **"The Story of Two Dogs"** a consuming mother love is contrasted with the more natural mothering experience that grows in the relationship between the mongrel Jock and the untrainable dog Bill. The human mother in this story gives Jock her heart when her son goes off to boarding school. She has a "pathetic need for something 'delicate' to nurse and protect," and it becomes necessary for husband and children to acquire a new dog and thereby "rescue a perfectly strong and healthy young dog from being forced into invalidism" as they all "at different times had been." In **"A Man and Two Women,"** the title story, the birth of a child threatens the marriage of Jack and Dorothy Bradford. Dorothy, whose closeness to Jack had been through their work—their art—says that "[h]aving a

baby's killed everything creative in me." She is lost in her unconscious meeting of the child's needs, and her relationship to the new baby is compared to being in love. Jack reacts by calling the baby a "little bleeder" and having sex with other women. His reaction contrasts with the mindlessly united reproductive effort of the dung beetles in **"The Sun Between Their Feet,"** who in their Sisyphean mothering effort hug between their legs and bellies the ball of dung enclosing their sons as they "cherish" it up the side of a boulder in order that it might roll back down again.

One of the most pernicious women in the stories is the mother of Maureen Watson of **"Notes for a Case History."** "Conceived by chance," Maureen senses the "fatality, of being helpless before great impersonal forces." This great impersonal force is Mrs. Watson, for whom Maureen is the "infant support." Mrs. Watson grooms Maureen to "gain her a glamorous future," to use her "capital" to get the most for the least from the men she meets. Shirley Banner, Maureen's foil, is less a thinking individual than Maureen, who at least has occasional glimpses of the reality that "the million streets of London blossomed with girls as pretty as she." Shirley, who "went further" with the boys than Maureen, marries to have babies, perhaps to be another Mrs. Watson. Maureen, her future determined by her mother's emphasis on her capital, finds herself at the end of the story doomed to marry Stanley, her self-seeking male counterpart. In contrast to the mother-daughter relationship of **"Notes for a Case History"** is the mother-daughter relationship of the story which follows, **"The New Man."** Here Mrs. Grant is seemingly unaware of her daughter's new development and sensitivity to Mr. Rooyen's fierce, lonely tenderness. The young protagonist holds herself aloof from Rooyen; yet she pities him. And she is sensitive to the fact that her mother "had let her new breasts down." The "new man" in this story is not so much Mr. Rooyen, who buys the Rich Mitchell acres, as it is the small girl's father, whose fatherly (or is it motherly?) concern makes him sensitive to her growing self-awareness. It is not without significance that the woman Mr. Rooyen longs for, whose name he calls as the small girl sits on his knee, is Maureen. And the small girl later supposes Maureen is "some silly woman in an office in town," an apt description of the Maureen of **"Notes for a Case Study."**

The motherhood motif reaches its peak in **"To Room Nineteen,"** the final story in the collection. Susan Rawlings gives up her job in an advertising firm and her talent for commercial drawing to assume the mindless task of motherhood. The Rawlings' marriage is "grounded in intelligence"; and their lives, reminiscent of the Sisyphean family round of the dung beetles in **"The Sun Between Their Feet,"** are like the uroboric snake biting its tail:

> Matthew's job for the sake of Susan, children,
> house, and garden—which caravanserai needed a
> well-paid job to maintain it. And Susan's practical
> intelligence for the sake of Matthew, the children,
> the house and the garden—which unit would have
> collapsed without her.

The intelligence of this marriage even makes allowances for Matthew's infidelity. Susan reasons that "it was inevitable that the handsome, blond, attractive, manly man, Matthew Rawlings, should be at times tempted . . . by the attractive girls at parties she could not attend because of the four children." But trying to rationalize away Matthew's sleeping with Myra Jenkins, Susan muses that

> either the ten years' fidelity was not important, or she isn't. . . . But if she isn't important, presumably it wasn't important either when Matthew and I first went to bed with each other that afternoon whose delight even now . . . lays a long wandlike finger over us.

The result of her confining motherhood is that life becomes a desert for Susan; her soul is not her own. As her resentment grows she rejects the prison of motherhood for the freedom of a room of her own—Room 19 in Fred's Hotel. Motherhood, like the Roman Catholic Mission of the first sentence of **"The Sun Between Their Feet"**—"The road from the back of the station went to the Roman Catholic Mission, which was a dead end, being in the middle of a Native Reserve"—becomes a dead end for Susan Rawlings.

This critical reference to the church which opens **"The Sun Between Their Feet"** is reiterated in **"A Letter from Home."** Here the fanaticism and God-fearing dominance of Esther bring the poet Johannes Potgieter to skewer his chronicle of Blagspruit on a thorn tree. Like the beetle he skewers on a thorn to keep the ants from eating it, his manuscript, which "gave off a stink of church and right-doing, with the sin and the evil underneath," is skewered to keep it from Esther and the society it depicts.

The motif of collective experience dominates **"England versus England," "Homage for Isaac Babel,"** and **"Outside the Ministry."** In **"England versus England"** Charlie Thornton, a miner's son who is reminiscent of Paul Morel of D. H. Lawrence's *Sons and Lovers,* is a victim of his family's collective effort to educate him. Dominated by his potato-peeling and coal-carrying mother, Charlie is torn between the "home he loved" and the middle-class mores he finds at Oxford. Charlie is a split human being. He has two languages—a brogue for his family and an educated English for his middle-class acquaintances. And he has two girls—Jenny, the bookish clergyman's daughter, a mother figure with whom he performs dutiful sex; and Sally, whom he dislikes, and with whom "[e]very act of sex . . . was a slow, cold subjugation of her by him." Charlie is victimized by his family's sacrificial effort to educate him. He despises his father's job as union secretary and the nature that suits him to the job, which Charlie realizes makes it possible for him to attend Oxford. Charlie hates the ugliness of the village and the collective life it represents with its "two thousand houses, exactly alike, with identical patches of carefully tended front garden, and busy back yards." His didactic voice sees the futility of the work of the women in the village who "can't stop working"—if they were organized they could have "half a day to themselves sometimes," but under such circumstances "they'd think they were being insulted."

The miner's union and the family are the institutions that represent the collective experience in **"England versus England"**; the legal system provides the focus in **"Homage for Isaac Babel."** Here the picture attended by Philip and Catherine shows a "good priest who helped criminals in New York." But his goodness could not save one of the criminals from the gas chamber. The persecution motif is repeated in the reference to the fact that Babel, a Jew in Russia, had been murdered, that "his experience was all revolution and civil war." That Catherine fails to apprehend the implications of Babel's murder and its connection with the picture she has seen about capital punishment is obvious in the contradiction of her affected letter in which she writes that the film about

the Hoodlum Priest "demonstrated to me beyond any shadow of a doubt that Capital Punishment is a Wicked Thing" and that the "conscious simplicity" of the style of "the famed Russian short story writer" is "what makes him, beyond the shadow of a doubt the great writer that he is."

"Outside the Ministry" also deals with social institutions, the collective life, showing the turbulence that often lies beneath the surface calm. Here the punctual Mr. Chickwe, with his accusing dignity, subtly engineers the eclipse of the suffering Devuli—a "leader acknowledged by all." Under the surface lies a surge of political rivalry that has lowered men to murder—a motif that reinforces the allusion to Isaac Babel's murder and juxtaposes the ideas of political rivalry and sincere patriotism.

The detachment of Mr. Chickwe and of young Catherine in **"Homage to Isaac Babel"** are instances of the alienation motif that Lessing contrasts with the motif of the collective experience. One of her most alienated characters is Graham Spence of **"One off the Short List,"** the lead story in the collection. Unsuccessful as an artist, he lives by his wits "on the fringes of the arts . . . an impressario of other people's talent." He is bored with his twenty-year marriage and had been disappointed to find after ten years that his marriage was not a unique experience. Among his experiences is a "serious love affair with the young girl for whose sake he had *almost* divorced his wife—yet at the last moment had changed his mind, letting the girl down so that he must have her for always (not unpleasurably) on his conscience." Spence's failure to apprehend himself is reflected ironically in his own musings on his life. Attempting to justify his failure as a writer or artist, he sees that "his real talents and flair . . . had turned out to be not artistic after all, but to do with emotional life, hard-earned experience. It expressed an ironical dignity, a proving to himself not only: I can be honest about myself, but also: I have earned the best in *that* field whenever I want it." Contrary to his image of himself, Spence's actions reveal little talent for the emotional life. His main concern at home is "something convincing" to tell his wife or having "an excuse not to be home that day." Even his extra-marital affairs fail to qualify him as emotionally talented. When he identifies Barbara Coles as the next item on his list and chants his "private erotic formula: *Yes, that one*" over her, he does it without emotional involvement. Imposing himself into her energetic, animated life—a life that bound her and her colleagues with "the democracy of respect for each other's work, a confidence in themselves and in each other"—he maneuvers to control her and to get into her bed. But his manipulation is absent, except in one or two brief moments, of any real desire for her. When she finally admits him to her bed, determined "to *get it all over with,*" he proves impotent; and hate for her is all that stands between him and his shame.

Spence's hatred is similar to that of Stanley and Tom in **"A Woman on a Roof,"** which concerns the reactions of three workers to a strange woman who sunbathes, indifferent to their presence, on a roof in view of the roof where they are changing guttering. Harry, older and wiser, accepts her presence with relative tolerance, but to the younger men she becomes an object that mirrors their own sexual preoccupations. In Stanley she evokes the fear that he might fail to possess his wife, whom he would not permit to "lay about like that." Tom, on the other hand, dreams of the woman at night and sees her, somewhat tenderly, as the object of his amorous advances. But when, deluded by his dreams, he does finally approach her and she tells him to go away, he gets drunk "in hatred of her."

But Lessing's alienated characters are not all men. Often they are women who escape the mindlessness of the collective in romantic love and overindulgent motherhood only to become preoccupied with themselves as objects. Perhaps this was the case with the woman on the roof, just as it is with Maureen Watson of **"Notes for a Case History."** Another of these alienated women is Maureen Jeffries of **"Between Men."** Maureen's situation is complex, for it is her failure to find the mindlessness of the collective experience that breeds her self-conscious preoccupation with her face and figure. What Maureen really wants is a man so she won't have to *be*. At thirty-nine she has been the mistress of eleven men, and "since she had never put her own talent, painting, first; but always the career of whichever man she was living with, . . . she could not earn a living." Hence she invites Peggy Bayley, who was fortunate enough to have married—albeit the marriage was brought about by a false alarm of pregnancy, to visit her, to "meet the new me!", in the hope that Peggy might influence her professor husband to "use his influence to get her a job of the kind that would enable her to meet the right sort of man."

This is the dilemma of many of the women in Lessing's *A Man and Two Women.* They seem unable to *be*. They become Maureens, alienated and self-conscious, grooming themselves as objects to snare men. Or they fall into an emotional trap and lose themselves in romantic love or mindless motherhood. To do otherwise requires a tenacity that many seem without. . . . For Lessing's women this inclination to "melt into loving acceptance" is often the fatal flaw. Such was the generosity of Maureen in **"Between Men."** But the flaw, whether it stems from "love" or from a need to dispense with the pain of one's own selfhood, leaves women prey to men such as Jack Boles. (pp. 63-9)

The complex dichotomies of self-abandon and alienation are reflected in the characters of **"Each Other,"** where a brother and sister use his girlfriend and her husband as a means to enhance their own incestuous relationship. The erotic scene of Freda and Fred, brother and sister, "become one person, abandoned against and in each other, silent and gone" contrasts with the troubled anxiety of Freda and her husband. The "magazine attitudes" of her body "disposed prettily in the bed . . . its two white forearms engaged in the movements obligatory for filing one's nails," her holding up of "a studied hand to inspect five pink arrows," her waving of her "hands in front of her eyes to dry nail varnish which . . . was three days old"—all reflect the anxiety in the husband-wife relationship. Yet, like Maureen Watson, Freda is aware of her predicament—she is unhappy with the charade of her marriage and reflects a sensitivity not shared by Fred, who leaves their morning rendezvous with the words, "Keep him happy, then. Ta-ta."

The Freudian implications of this brother-sister relationship and the self-abandon of the erotic scene between Fred and Freda reiterate similar motifs from **"How I Finally Lost My Heart."** In this story the fortyish narrator rationalizes:

> My . . . way of looking at it is that one must search for an A, or a B, or a C or a D with a certain combination of desirable or sympathetic qualities so that one may click, or spontaneously combust: or to put it differently, one needs a person who, like a saucer of water, allows one to float off on him/her, like a

transfer. But this wasn't so at all. Actually one carries with one a sort of burning spear stuck in one's side, that one waits for someone else to pull out; it is something painful, like a sore or wound, that one cannot wait to share with someone else.

But this woman does become one of Lessing's free people. After two *real* love affairs, or four if her father and brother are counted, and four days of self-contemplation, she comes to realize that "sitting and analyzing each movement or pulse or beat of my heart through forty years was a mistake." Consequently, she extracts from herself, along with her heart, the need for someone to pull the burning spear from her side. At the same time, in her empathy with another woman, she loses her heart in quite another way. Unlike the narrator of **"The Story of Two Dogs"** and Maureen of **"Between Men,"** this woman is free to be.

It is this state that Lessing's successful people achieve. Seeking a mean between self-abandon and the alienation that causes them to view themselves as objects, they achieve a creative tension that permits them to be. Such is the case of Barbara Coles of **"One off the Short List,"** who has a room of her own, a working room, that evokes from Graham Spence the observation, to himself, of course, that "I wouldn't like it if my wife had a room like this."

The room becomes more clearly symbolic in **"A Room,"** the seventh story of the collection. This story is about a bedroom in a flat, but the room takes on archetypal significance as the narrator reveals the long line of previous occupants and that there are identical rooms overhead, that in fact this room is one of eight identical rooms in eight identical flats. Yet the narrator has decorated the room to give it individuality, modifying it as it had been left by the two girls who had lived there previously. This room is the bedroom in a flat of four small boxlike rooms, a room where the narrator says, "I feel I live." Here she sleeps in the afternoon because "afternoon sleep is more interesting than night sleep"; it helps her with her work, telling her what to write or where she has gone wrong. In this story the margin between dream and reality, between conscious and unconscious, vanishes. The narrator's art and her dreams, her conscious and unconscious mind, her self and the selves of others, all separate rooms, merge, overlap, and become indistinguishable one from another.

The dream world and the world of art similarly merge in **"Two Potters."** The narrator dreams and imagines events which have parallels in the life and work of the potter Mary Tawnish. The room motif appears here in the narrator's dream of the old potter and the low rectangular structures that surround him. . . . The room motif emerges, too, in the mention of Mary's potting room. The rabbit she creates corresponds to the old potter's rabbit. And the margin between dream and actuality blurs in the child's imagination as he insists that his imagined burning of the farmer's house—after the farmer had mistaken his clay rabbit for a real one and shot it—was indeed a factual reality.

The room motif dominates still another of the stories—**"Dialogue."** Here the dialogue is both a realistic dialogue between a woman and a man and a symbolic dialogue between the two aspects of a woman's self. The archetypal implications of identical rooms that are contained in **"A Room"** are present here in the building the narrator visits, which is described as holding

the lives of 160 people at forty families of four each,

one family to a flat. Inside this building was an atmosphere both secretive and impersonal, for each time the lift stopped, there were four identical black doors, in the same positions exactly as the four doors on the nine other floors, and each door insisted on privacy.

This building of similar rooms, each containing its own secret, represents both the collective and the individual aspects of the human being. Each individual shares in the collective self, but carries a sense of self as individual. A balance between the collective life and alienation of the individual is what Lessing seeks, and such is the experience of the narrator of **"Dialogue."** She visits Bill in this tall building which towers with Freudian and phallic implications six or eight stories higher than the "small shallow litter of buildings" that surrounds it. This woman has managed to lose her heart and, unlike the narrator of the early pages of **"How I Finally Lost My Heart,"** is free. . . . This woman is free of the need for romantic love, someone to share her wound or to pull the "burning spear" from her side. Her love becomes an all-embracing love that extends beyond a compelling need for acceptance. She takes her periodic dark journeys into herself and meets her *animus* because the "tall building, like a black tower, stood over her. It was not possible to escape from it." But she does not stay. Looking back at her earlier self, from the perspective of her male companion, she reflects: "This little bundle of flesh, this creature who will respond and warm, lay its head on my shoulder, feel happiness—how unreal, how vulgar, and how meaningless!" Reclaiming herself from the collective, she aches for Bill and for her self. She feels the hurt of exile, and she *chooses* the hurt of exile and goes back out into the street where "[s]he was saved from deadness, she was herself again." With one hand she clutches the leaf that brings her life; with the other she touches the tower whose shadow will challenge her until she once again dares to climb it. The narrator of **"Dialogue"** has found a room of her own. She resists the advice of others—and that part of herself—that prescribes "the warmth of a family, marriage if possible, comfort, other people." In her dialogue with Bill she asks: "[H]ow many people do we know . . . enclosed in marriages, which are for safety only, or attached to other people's families, stealing (if you like) security?" Hence she justifies the creative tension that permits her to live as an individual outside society's prescribed institution—marriage, marriage that could entail the giving up of self in a mindless round of collective experience.

Another of Lessing's characters who defies society's prescription for her is Judith of **"Our Friend Judith."** Judith too has lost her heart and has no need to "melt into loving acceptance." She wants no husband. Hence she goes to Florence to escape marriage to her professor friend because "she enjoyed waking up in the morning alone and *her own person,"* and she leaves Florence expressing remorse because her involvement with Luigi had interfered with her responsibilities: "That's what happens when you submerge yourself in somebody else." Unlike the Maureens of the other stories, Judith refuses to adorn herself—she casts off the Dior dress in order that she might stay in character. Judith is a poet, a nonconsumer, distant, and intelligent; and she despises people who feel they need attention. Judith, in short, has found a room of her own.

In *A Man and Two Women,* then, the room becomes an important unifying symbol. It can represent the collective, archetypal aspect of human nature. It can represent the alienated person closed off from communication with others. Or it can represent the individual who has achieved a poise between mechanical alienation and the total involvement of the collective experience. Out of the tension created by having a room of one's own, which is at the same time dependent upon the collective—all of the identical rooms of humanity—evolves the creative act and the work of art, which likewise has as its symbol the room. It is no accident then that the final and nineteenth story in this collection is entitled **"To Room Nineteen."** Room 19 is the sterile room of alienation to which Susan Rawlings resorts when she finds her self dissipated in the Sisyphean round of motherhood. **"To Room Nineteen"** is a work of art, the nineteenth in Lessing's collection of stories. For each of the stories of her collection is a room that participates in the collective while it expresses another facet or room of human experience. This collection of short stories is, in the words Lessing uses to describe the environment of the old potter, a system of "low flat rooms . . . not separated . . . but linked. . . . They [are] roughly the same size, but set at all angles to each other so that, standing in one, it might have one, two, three doors, leading to a corresponding number of . . . rooms." Like the people in *The Golden Notebook,* these stories and their people reflect each other and aspects of each other—"are each other, form wholes."

Through her repetition and counterpointing of motifs, Lessing exposes the destructiveness, the dead ends, of some traditional institutions, particularly marriage, which often confines women to the collective experience of motherhood at the expense of their creative selves. And she exposes humanity's destructive weaknesses that permit human beings to settle into the snug nest of the collective. Her free people are individuals who escape this destruction. Judith, Barbara Coles, the narrators of **"How I Finally Lost My Heart," "A Room,"** and **"Dialogue,"** all achieve a creative tension, a tension reminiscent of William Blake's proverbial "without contraries is no progression." These people are individuals who voluntarily submit their "will to the collective, but never finally," who insist on making their "own personal and private judgments before every act of submission." Lessing's "wordless statement" is that human beings are responsible and they can be free: but the prerequisite for their freedom is the *choice* of a creative mean between alienation and the mindlessness of the collective. (pp. 69-74)

Orphia Jane Allen, "Structure and Motif in Doris Lessing's 'A Man and Two Women'," in Modern Fiction Studies, *Vol. 26, No. 1, Spring, 1980, pp. 63-74.*

VIRGINIA PRUITT (essay date 1981)

[*In the following excerpt, Pruitt identifies similar patterns in the self-destructive processes of the three main female characters in Lessing's stories "Our Friend Judith," "Dialogue," and "To Room Nineteen."*]

"Our Friend Judith," "Dialogue," and **"To Room 19"** . . . form a trilogy of sorts, each delineating a stage or stages in the process of self-destruction. To identify this shared theme and hence to analyze the stories as a unit rather than independently makes possible, I believe, a better understanding of the tales individually. More importantly, such an approach helps to clarify what Lessing meant when, in *A Small, Personal Voice,* she declared that the main theme of *The Golden Note-*

book—her most influential work—is "this theme of 'break-down.' "

Defining this theme, Lessing spoke of the "false dichotomies and divisions" existing within the self. Each of these stories dramatizes the plight of a character afflicted with internal disunity. And each character signals this split by displaying three patterns of behavior: an attempt to preserve self-control, a preference for detachment from others, and a commitment to asceticism.

The obsession of each character with maintaining self-control is most clearly conveyed through his/her explicit statements. In **"Our Friend Judith,"** Judith tells a friend: "No one can interfere with me if I don't let them." The face of the male protagonist of **"Dialogue"** is one in which "every feature strove to dominate." Furthermore, the last sentence of the story informs us that he was a man "held upright by the force of will." Finally, in **"To Room 19,"** Susan, throughout the account, is not only shown trying to arrange conditions in accord with her needs; at one point she remarks, with obvious relief, "Yes, things were under control."

The preference for detachment from others is expressed as a quest for solitude. Judith's uneasiness over her growing attachment to her Italian lover, Luigi, is first revealed when she professes to be staying in Italy only "because of the cat"—a creature with which she presumably can identify because of its age-old reputation for remaining aloof. Eventually Judith severs the relationship with Luigi by her precipitous departure from Italy. In **"Dialogue,"** the male protagonist proudly describes himself as one of the "disconnected" and is depicted at the story's beginning and end as sitting alone "staring at a cold sky in vertiginous movement." Moreover, Susan fulfills her desire to separate from husband and children through her repeated escapes to a room in a sleazy hotel.

Such rejection of companionship and affection is related to the preeminent response of Judith, "he" and Susan: self-denial for no evident reason. Each refuses proffered sensual pleasures in favor of an austere existence. Most apparently, each surrenders a wholesome sexual relationship. Judith flees from Luigi, who adores her. By his coldness the male protagonist of **"Dialogue"** has estranged the female narrator of the story, who loves him but is said to value the messages of her "healthy nerves" and rejoices in the "irrepressible good nature of the flesh." And Susan ultimately gives up sexual relations with her husband Matthew, who, in the past, "had driven the misery out of her with his big, solid body."

This repudiation of sexual pleasure is symptomatic of a much broader renunciation of sensual and aesthetic satisfactions. Judith, for instance, given the opportunity to accept a dress in which she looks stunning, decides instead to resume wearing her usual drab and sexless clothing. In addition, after her sojourn in Italy, we learn that "Judith's flat was chilly, and she wore a bunchy sage-green woolen dress. Her hair was still a soft gold helmet but she looked pale and rather pinched. She stood with her back to a single bar of electric fire—lit because I demanded it—with her legs apart and her arms folded." This self-punitive defiance also distinguishes the male protagonist in **"Dialogue."** He lives in a two-room flat and elects to retreat to the room which is "very small and always darkened by permanently drawn midnight blue curtains, so that the narrow bed with the books stacked up the wall beside it was in a suffocating shadow emphasized by a small yellow glow from the bed lamp" rather than to occupy the other

room which is "large, high," with "airy white walls." Similarly, Susan, who has access to an elegant home with handsome grounds and a garden, holes up in Room 19: "The room was hideous. It had a single window, with thin brocade curtains, a three-quarter bed that had a cheap satin bedspread on it, a fireplace with a gas fire and a shilling meter by it, a chest of drawers, and a green wicker armchair."

What is the explanation for such seemingly masochistic behavior? I think Lessing locates a major cause in the larger cultural environment when she implies that these people are inheritors of a post-Darwinian Western mentality which is contemptuous of "the savage old world" (see **"To Room 19"**) symbolized in religious concepts. The narrator of **"Our Friend Judith"** says that Judith is an atheist. An intimation of the psychological consequences such a position invites emerges in **"Dialogue"**: the female narrator, having been chided by the male protagonist for "living on the fat of your ancestors, the fat of their belief," holds back tears, for "tears were not allowed." Significantly, then, in disowning that savage old world these sceptics also disown the component of personality which nourishes religious belief. It is Susan in **"To Room 19"** who spells out the connection between the jettisoning of religious belief and the complementary dynamic, suppression of emotion. She says: "There was no need to use the dramatic words 'unfaithful,' 'forgive' and the rest: intelligence forbade them. Intelligence barred, too, quarreling, sulking, anger, silences of withdrawal, accusations and tears. Above all, intelligence forbids tears."

More precisely, such denial of feelings suggests the individual's perception of "a certain discordance of substance" within the personality, a discordance which results from the presence of two opposed and irreconcilable elements: an intellectual component which they revere and nurture and an emotional component which they despise and seek to repress. In fact, their disgust for the emotional component of the self is so radical that each regards this *innate* capacity as a profound *external* threat. Judith, having spurned Luigi, remarks that during their relationship she had felt "ill at ease with the whole business" and "not myself at all"; and earlier, when she turned down a chance at self-adornment, she had said "One is surely right to stay in character." The male protagonist of **"Dialogue"** is no more tolerant of his emotions. He distances himself from this part of his personality by dehumanizing it, viewing it as " 'a fly buzzing in the sun.' " Furthermore, he perceives the affectionate overtures of the female narrator as those "due from one kind of creature to another." The implications of Susan's equally restricted definition of self are present throughout the story and are more alarming. The story commences with the statement that it will deal with a "failure of intelligence." The conspicuous omission of "emotion" is instructive, for it is Susan's wrongheaded exaltation of intelligence which makes her susceptible to a fatal depression. When her feelings initially begin to demand recognition, she decides "I'm a different person. I'm simply not myself." She castigates herself for having become so "irrational" and "unreasonable" and alludes to her "rational" "reasonable" self as the one "she liked, she respected." The demon which she repeatedly hallucinates while in this frame of mind appears to be the objectificate of the irrational self she wishes to banish from awareness. The most unequivocal association between the demon and her emotional self is established late in the story, where she ponders her image in the mirror and muses: "A sensible face . . . Much more to the point if what looked back at me was the gingery green-eyed demon."

The crucial realization which eludes these three individuals is that pursuit of isolation to avoid stimulation of their emotions and their concomitant efforts to stifle awareness of feelings through vigilant self-control do not result in rational, self-preserving behavior. Instead, such behavior generates an ineradicable sense of guilt in Judith, the "delight of nihilism" in the male protagonist of **"Dialogue,"** and in Susan, the conclusion that "life had become a desert, and that nothing mattered," although "her intelligence continued to assert that all was well." In short, achievement of "freedom"—that state which all three characters apotheosize and are convinced they have secured—is a condition of tragic vulnerability: vulnerability not only to varying degrees of nervous disorder but also to bodily injury. Judith brings herself to the verge of physical illness: she is described as "pale and rather pinched." The male protagonist of **"Dialogue"** has already succumbed to disease. Moreover, we are told that, on the occasion of the narrator's visit, he was not experiencing "one of his good days." The intensity of Susan's inner struggle, however, has placed her life in the most serious jeopardy. If, as Karl Menninger has asserted, a "self-imposed sentence of deprivation is a kind of slow suicide," then Susan, by eventually choosing to embrace death, actualizes the metaphor. By her own logic, she thus purchases "freedom" from the otherwise implacable demons. Ironically, it is only after she has turned on the gas that, for the first time in her many expeditions to Room 19, she lies down on the bed that "smelled of sweat and sex." Those pungent odors, in other words, serve as a reminder of the erotic energy—the life—she has disavowed. This act of suicide becomes the seemingly inevitable sequel to the creation of "false dichotomies and divisions."

Yet to end on this note might be to foster the misconception that the predicament of these three people is rare. Lessing clearly indicates otherwise. She implies that their inner "fragmentation" is a prevalent modern problem, and that all of us, as participants in contemporary Western culture, are subjected to their dilemma: the dissociation between intellectual understanding and emotional needs—what Lessing might call the predestined "true" dichotomy. The female narrator of **"Dialogue,"** who is as close to a paradigm of health as we get in Lessing's short fiction, admits the validity of the cruel taunt delivered by her suffering former lover: " 'You are more split than I am, do you know that?' " The key to coping with the anguish such an insight engenders is to "contain" one's fragmentation (see **"Dialogue"**). I say this because the critical and life-serving distinction between the female narrator's inner fragmentation and its destructive counterpart in Judith, "he," and Susan is that the female narrator of **"Dialogue"** neither projects emotions nor seeks to annihilate consciousness of them. Rather, she acknowledges them and cherishes their vitality, for it is that vitality which mitigates the perceptions of unalloyed intellect. And it is her words which express best the nature of the fundamental paradox created by this reconciliation: "All right, it's all meaningless, with my mind I know it, it's an accident, it's a freak, but all the same, everything gives me pleasure all the time. Why should it be a contradiction, why should it?' " (pp. 281-85)

Virginia Pruitt, "The Crucial Balance: A Theme in Lessing's Short Fiction," in Studies in Short Fiction, *Vol. 18, No. 3, Summer, 1981, pp. 281-85.*

MARGARET ATACK　　(essay date 1982)

[*In the following excerpt, Atack offers an intricate analysis of the characters, events, actions, and recurring language patterns in Lessing's short stories to determine the importance of narrative structure in her fiction.*]

> When he had first seen Barbara Coles, some years before, he only noticed her because someone said: 'That's Johnson's new girl.' He certainly had not used of her the private erotic formula: *Yes, that one.* He even wondered what Johnson saw in her. 'She won't last long,' he remembered thinking, as he watched Johnson, a handsome man, but rather flushed with drink, flirting with some unknown girl while Barbara stood by a wall looking on. He thought she had a sullen expression.

To see, to notice, to watch, to look on: in this, the opening paragraph of **"One off the Short List"**, the first story in *A Man and Two Women,* the relations mediating the group are almost entirely visual. It is a shifting network, where subjects and objects of the verbs interchange in a visual chain, where he watches Barbara who watches Johnson whose attention is all for the unknown girl. The information about each is minimal—each element is there to hold its position in the chain, and the information given is just enough to elucidate the nature of the chain. It is a complex example of one of the basic units of Lessing's narrative structure, that of the unreturned look—a dual structure where reciprocity plays no part. It is a simple pattern allowing of many variations:

> In my tiny bedroom I looked out on to a space of flat white sand . . . and there hurtled a mad wild puppy, . . . snapping at its own black shadow and tripping over its own clumsy feet. Then they saw her, between chimneys, about fifty yards away. She lay face down on a brown blanket.

This is a remarkably consistent structure, ordering both the initial encounters and their subsequent developments. In each case, it is constructed upon the basis of a *difference*: A, partaking of and integrated within one order, directs attention towards B, an element within another order, and B in turn is drawn towards C, who is either an element of the first order (as in **"One off the Short List"**) or of the same order (**"The Sun between their Feet"**) or oscillating between the two, as for example in **"The Story of Two Dogs"**, where the third element is either the moon, equated with madness and wildness, or another dog held within the confines of social domesticity. In each case can be seen the attraction of and for the other, for the one who is different and apart.

At this point it might be useful to stress that the logic of any narrative operating within the discourse of realism (by which I mean, very loosely, any narrative which concerns itself with 're-presenting' the real) demands an oppositional structure, and uses the oppositions it creates in order to advance to its own conclusion. The two terms of an opposition might be unambiguously marked by either positive or negative value, and the narrative account be the struggle to eliminate the latter (the structure of the Western film would be a classic example here). Alternatively, the narrative may conclude without a definitive resolution in favour of one or other of the oppositional terms, in which case ambiguity enters the signifying circuit as an important factor mediating the relations of the opposition. It seems to me that the Lessing narratives partake of the latter structure—not necessarily when considering each individual story or novel, but across the *oeuvre* as a whole. The constants of the differential structure return time and again (man *v* woman, Africa *v* England, white *v* black, domestic *v* wild, dream *v* the real, self *v* the other) and yet the complex orchestration of these many elements seems either to defeat a definitive critical reading, or produces many contradictory ones, especially in relation to the notion of the self which has been variously judged to be the inner self of emotion released through breakdown, or the cool, critical intelligence which alone survives the experience. It cannot be denied there is ample evidence for both readings, and yet they cannot both be entirely accurate. To produce either interpretation demands that considerations of the narrative *context* take a second place, in the name of the search for the *truth* of Lessing's worldview. The novels and short stories are interrogated for the meanings they are deemed to contain, as if they were formal repositories for a meaningful substance to be released by critical exposition and interpretation. That this can result in such contradictory conclusions justifies, in my view, adopting a different approach, one that does not seek to liberate the 'truth' of the narrative, but, rather, seeks to elucidate the structures ordering the narrative vision and its conclusion, to examine, for example, the self of breakdown in terms of its place and function *within* the narrative; in other words, to switch the emphasis away from the narrative as embodiment of ready-constituted meaning towards the narrative as *production* of meaning, away from the identification of a product and towards the investigation of a process. It is the play of the signifying elements which constitutes a narrative, not the other way round.

In addressing myself to the question of the text as narrative order, I shall therefore be concentrating on an analysis of the language and an examination of the mechanisms constituting the actions, events and characters, in order to unravel some at least of the structures governing them. The recurring patterns and their variations are one key to reading the order in which they are inscribed, that of the logic of the narrative. This is why the function of the conclusion is crucial: summum and summation, ending and end, it inscribes the sequence of the narrative within a teleology. The coherence of its development is ordered by an oscillation between temporal and causal structures, whereby that which comes after is at the same time logically motivated by that which precedes: as the narrative now reaches the conclusion towards which it has already tended from the beginning, it irrevocably places all that has preceded it under the sign of a finality. We can therefore see that to look at any element of a narrative independently of the space and function it occupies within the narrative as a whole, is inevitably to impose a reading from elsewhere which that element is invoked to support. Isolated from the narrative structures which inform it and which it furthers, it quite literally cannot 'make' sense. Given the complexity of the process, I have restricted the most detailed analysis to just one of the stories, **"One off the Short List"**.

Two major problems remain. First, the danger of reproducing once more the assumptions that the truth of the text is about to be spoken, that to concentrate upon the text somehow renders the criticism innocent of any discursive intervention. I hope that by having made the critical framework clear, it will remain apparent that this is offered as a possible reading, and a deliberately restricted one, aiming, above all, at elucidating the mechanisms by which the narrative produces itself as significant, and the elements in that process. Second, the choice of text, and the delineation of the text as unit, is far from straightforward. No analysis of one collection of

short stories can claim to exhaust the narrative categories of an *oeuvre*. Moreover, as a unit it is already in some ways a factitious one, gathering together stories over several magazines, so that they become a 'text' ordered by the publishing industry, the popularity of the writer, and so on. This in turn probably explains why the 'text' should probably be seen as greater than just the sum of the individual stories, for the short introductory blurb, present in nearly all the paperback editions, not only makes these stories into a unit ordered by the one author, but also proposes which elements are to be read as significant (being in this case, woman novelist, emotions, Africa and England); the stories are already inscribed within a critical discourse—the dominant discourse on literature which privileges the author, as subjective source and site of knowledge and power over the text, and the biographical elements which will be seen to have narrative significance (even the blurb is subject to narrative finality) and which are unproblematically offered as relevant, placing the real of the text firmly outside it.

To pose these questions is hardly to solve them, merely to note the constraints and assumptions inherent in concentrating upon one set of short stories. In considering them here as a text, I am doing no more than use them as a working unit, as a convenient section ready-made within the body of work signed 'Lessing'. And there are virtues to the limitations: the very heterogeneity of the collection which predates the realignment of the stories into 'African and other' affords a fairly wide range of narrative and socio-cultural connotations. They are broadly contemporaneous. Finally, the structure of the short story is less complex than that of the novel. It is possible to define the short story as a narrative determined by the account, elucidation and resolution of one primary narrative conflict, however complex the range of oppositions, of narrative figures, of social and cultural connotations and discourses in play.

The frequency with which sight is used, on the level of both description and act, suggests that the complex structure of the observer and the observed and the multiplicity of variations which it displays, occupies a privileged position in these narratives, with many implications for the nature of the terms of the oppositions which it mediates. Seeing does not necessarily coincide with the singling out of the one observed as special, chosen or loved. It does in **"The Story of Two Dogs"**, where the vision of the mad puppy dancing to the moon leads the child observing the scene to conclude 'That, of course, was my puppy', but in **"One off the Short List"**, further developments are necessary before Graham Spence will confer his elective phrase *'Yes, that one'* upon Barbara Coles. In either case, what is privileged is *appearance:* what the appraisal of the indirect look calls into play is how the other appears, and at the moment of the initial meeting, this is what counts: that the other appear as other. The figures who embody the differential oppositions of the narrative are immediately placed within a specific relation of difference by the indirect look which both binds and separates them. There is no hint here, at the initial encounter, that appearances are deceptive—on the contrary, to appear 'other' is to *be* 'other'. Within the same structure, the first sight of Barbara Coles (see the first quotation above) suggests there is nothing to see *in* her. Even in **"Dialogue"**, about a meeting of two people who know each other well, appearance still exhausts being, there is just a different level of competence in play:

A single glance from a stranger (or from herself be-

fore she had known better) would have earned him:
big, strong, healthy, confident man. Now, however,
she knew the signs, could, after glancing around a
room say: Yes, you and you and you . . . Because
of the times she had been him, achieved his being.

The primacy of appearance and the modes of its articulation
can perhaps facilitate a reading of the self and the other in
Lessing's fiction. That appearance, sight, look are such important mechanisms in structuring the significant elements
may also be a reason for the cultural preponderance of the
visual arts in the coding of the work of many of the characters. They are designers, artists, potters, or working in television, journalism, advertising, film, sometimes famous, sometimes not. With the media and the arts predominating, they
are inscribed within a cultural code which permits the preoccupation with appearance to be duplicated at other narrative
levels and also to further its progress. For example, that Barbara Coles is a stage designer who wins a prize and achieves
success and a certain fame is one of the ways in which she
is differentiated from the Barbara Coles of the first appearance while still remaining within Spence's field of vision:
'Barbara Coles was one of the "names" in the theatre, and
her photograph was seen about.' Success in the arts, in design, is, through the media, a public success, and the distinction between the acclaimed artist and the brilliant but unknown one may occur as a pertinent distinction so often precisely because it is a question of being in the public eye: to
appear successful is to be successful. Yet the romantic code
in which the greatness of an artist is guaranteed by obscurity
is completely opposed to this. Genius can only exist in so far
as it is singular and different, and mass recognition (that is,
both seeing and understanding) would negate it. This is no
longer the only possible code of cultural practice, but the continuing dominance of the discourse on art as being a uniquely
individual creation feeds it still, so it is not surprising, given
the equivalence between appearance and being in this collection, that it should appear as a narrative function and counterpoint. The beginning of **"A Man and Two Women"** is almost entirely devoted to placing the four characters each in
their respective oppositional positions across these codes.

A similar complexity governs the figure of Graham Spence
in **"One off the Short List"**. Public success is essential to the
choices operating in his list of 'especial women', but he himself is positioned within the code devaluing the media. His
'unique talent', and his 'struggles as a writer' have resulted,
as for many others, in being dependent upon the creative
work of others: 'Yet here they were, running television pro-
grammes about which they were cynical . . . or writing reviews about other people's books. Yes, that's what he had become, an impresario of other people's talent'. Both his marriage and his work are inscribed within a movement from the
particular to the general: in each sphere he considers his experience unique, only to discover it as part of a sameness, a multiplicity of similar experiences:

> Just as that melodramatic marriage had turned out
> to be like everyone else's . . . so it had turned out
> that his unique talent, his struggles as a writer, had
> led him here, to this pub and the half-dozen pubs
> like it, where all the men in sight had the same his-
> tory.

To look at them is to see himself as one of them. It is on the
basis of this serial generality that the list of 'especial women'
takes its place, to acknowledge his talents as he saw them, in
the realm of emotion and experience: 'The formula: *Yes, that*

one . . . expressed an ironical dignity, a proving to himself
not only: I can be honest about myself, but also: I have earned
the best in *that* field whenever I want it'. The woman's function is to enable the narrator to be singled out among his
peers and for himself. In one sense, the long process of watching leads to the true object of observation, himself:

> He watched the field for the women who were well-
> known in the arts, or in politics; looked out for pho-
> tographs, listened for bits of gossip. He made a
> point of going to see them act, or dance, or orate.
> He built up a not unshrewd picture of them . . . He
> would be seen out with her a few times in
> public . . . He might have a brief affair with this
> woman, but more often than not it was the appear-
> ance of an affair. Not that he didn't get pleasure
> from other people envying him—he would make a
> point, for instance, of taking this woman into the
> pubs where his male colleagues went.

One of the elements creating the bitter affect of the conclusion is that Barbara Coles proves not to be a cipher for his
narcissistic self-appraisal.

It has already been noted that in **"One off the Short List"** the
choice of the desirable object does not coincide with the moment of seeing. It is staggered across three moments of the
narrative, thus proving singularly useful in elucidating the
process of the articulation of desire in the text. In the visual
chain of the opening paragraph quoted above, 'to see' is not
synonymous with 'to notice'. Barbara Coles is only noticed
because it is pointed out that she has already been noticed by
Johnson; the structures of sight and choice are in fact relay-
ing their opposite—a refusal. The notion of choice is posed
as a narrative element, only to be denied at this stage to a specific narrative figure. 'Barbara Coles' is mapping out the negative space of the absence of desire, is poised on the limits between sequences of male choice: about to be eliminated from
the one signed Johnson as the narrative points towards his
lack of interest in her, and refused admission to the sequence
of the unnamed 'he', who turns out to be Graham Spence.
Spence and Johnson are aligned in implicit agreement; Barbara Coles has nothing to retain the attention. For this to
change, 'Barbara Coles' has to change. In other words, the
constituent elements constructing this figure will be modified,
some added, some eliminated—though a repetition of some
of the same elements is essential to maintain the fiction that
this is a 'character', a person to whom the story refers or
whom the story creates, offering her existence to our belief.
This is one of the major narrative functions of the proper
name: a name which reappears must 'be' the same figure of
that name already mentioned, even though the demands of
the narrative logic have radically altered its constitution. The
continuity and importance of this figure are also inscribed
within temporal structures in the opening paragraph—'when
he had first seen Barbara Coles', ' "she won't last long," he
remembered thinking'—and from the outset, this encounter
in the past is entered into the narrative finality. It will have
a sequel (that which follows it, that which it motivates). In
conjunction with descriptive changes (her 'gauche' hairstyle
becomes 'sophisticated'), the important differences are that
her name and appearance enter the circuit of public success.
This cultural cachet is accompanied by a remarkable change
of positions in the observer/observed structure. Coles is now
the refuser, Spence the onlooker:

> soon she went off with a group of people she was
> inviting to her home for a drink. She did not invite

Graham. There was about her an assurance, a carelessness, that he recognized as the signature of success. It was then, watching her laugh as she went off with her friends that he used the formula: *'Yes, that one'*.

Equally importantly, this is the first time in the relating of a narrative event, that 'Graham' has been used instead of 'he'. Until this point, 'he' has read as both figure in the text and narrator—a confusion inherent in many a third-person narration. The use of the proper name separates the two levels, and places the named figure of Graham Spence on a par with the others. So the initial structure of the observer/observed is reproduced, with Spence in Coles's position (the narrator sees Graham watch Barbara Coles leave). And *this* is the moment of choice: desire is inextricably linked to a refusal, and the narrative strategy subtly negates Spence's project as subject of observation and choice.

The third moment in the sequence alters the motivation of the choice from calculation to emotional need. Once again, Coles is inscribed within another order, this time when Jack Kennaway boasts of being her lover: 'There was no doubt the two were pretty close . . . Graham Spence felt he had put his finger on the secret pulse of Barbara Coles; and it was intolerable that he must wait to meet her'. 'Secret pulse' is very much a key term; the narrative circuit of otherness traced in the semantic line of pulse—throb—(heart)beat recurs time and again in Lessing. It is essential to the elaboration of the ironic **"How I Finally Lost my Heart"**. Here, the secret pulse is Coles turned emotionally towards another, and the reaction is 'intolerable'. It will recur later, when Graham presumes an affair between Barbara and James, a man she works with.

This equivalence of desire and refusal, the refusal of the object of attention to return the attention, to accept the relation of dominance inherent to the structure, is equally present in **"A Woman on a Roof "**, and operates here at the repeated moment of sight:

> Next morning, as soon as they came up, they went to look. She was already there . . . Stanley let out a whistle. She lifted her head, startled, as if she'd been asleep, and looked straight over at them. The sun was in her eyes, she blinked and stared, then she dropped her head again. At this gesture of indifference, they all three, Stanley, Tom and old Harry, let out whistles and yells. Harry was doing it in parody of the younger men, making fun of them, but he was also angry. They were all angry because of her utter indifference to the three men watching her.

These meetings of the observer and the observed punctuate this story: the progression of the narrative lies in the reaction of the observer, split across three figures. Three men are working on a roof and see a near-naked woman sunbathing on a roof nearby. In terms of this narrative, she is the empty space on which are written male discourses on women. Harry, who has grown-up children, is fatherly and protective, though not immune to the feelings of rejection of them as men; Tom, the youngster, nurtures erotic fantasies about the tender older woman; Stanley, the young married man, is the most aggressive and the most threatened:

> 'I've got a good mind to report her to the police,' said Stanley, and Harry said:

> 'What's eating you? What harm's she doing?'

'I tell you, if she was my wife!'

'But she isn't, is she?'

The two codes of woman as private possession of the man, and woman's object of display for any man, conflict directly here, not as contradictory discourses on women, but as contradictory elements in male discourse: ' "Christ," said Stanley virtuously, "if my wife lay about like that, for everyone to see, I'd soon stop her" '. It is the refusal of the woman to participate which allows this to be elucidated—there is no similar tension in Stanley's flirtatious teasing with Mrs Pritchett downstairs. The married man is inscribed within a particular discourse on women which the woman as other specifically throws into relief. Stanley is remarkably similar to Graham Spence:

> He went into a long, very tidy white room, that had a narrow bed in one corner, a table covered with drawings, sketchings, pencils . . . He was thinking: I wouldn't like it if my wife had a room like this. I wonder what Barbara's husband . . . ?

Indifference causes each to become overtly aggressive and uncontrollable:

> 'Graham, let me go, do let me go, Graham.' She went on saying this; he went on squeezing, grinding, kissing and licking. It might go on all night: it was a sheer contest of wills, nothing else. He thought: It's only a really masculine woman who wouldn't have given in by now out of sheer decency of the flesh! (**"One off the Short List"**).

> Stanley whistled again. Then he began stamping with his feet, and whistled and yelled and screamed at the woman, his face getting scarlet. He seemed quite mad, as he stamped and whistled, while the woman did not move, she did not move a muscle (**"A Woman on a Roof "**).

However, the irremediable difference of the other is not restricted to these relations, inscribed within socio-cultural discourses of the sexes. In **"The Story of Two Dogs,"** set in Africa, the same narrative structure appears, articulated across the domestic/wild opposition. A similar structure is crucial to a reading of *The Grass is Singing*, across which is articulated the attraction of Dick, marked by the wild, the bush, the outdoors, and Mary, marked by the order and domesticity of urban society. Once on the farm, the same opposition structures the difference between the house, the closed space indoors, and the farm, the outside. As much as anything, Mary's subsequent breakdown could be read as the breakdown of that opposition, the impossibility of maintaining that distinct order. She is irremediably marked by her removal from the order in which she was inscribed, as is apparent in her fruitless attempt to return to it in her visit to the town and her place of work. The last narrative avenue of escape and positive renewal is closed, rendering the final disintegration inevitable. **"The Story of Two Dogs"** partakes of the same opposition, with its two distinct lineages, the male dogs of the wild and the female dogs of the white domestic settlements being immediately attracted to one another:

> Then he lifted his head and howled, like the howl dogs give to the full moon, long, terrible, lonely. but it was morning, the sun calm and clear, and the bush without mystery. He sat and howled his heart out, his muzzle pointed away towards where his mate was chained. We could hear the faint whim-

perings she made, and the clink of her metal dish as she moved about.

This is uncomplicated desire for the other, without any of the aggression of frustration, partly because the desire is reciprocated by the locked-up female dog, partly because in this story the aggression is located in the transgression of the spatial boundaries separating the social order from the wild as Bill the wild dog, like his father before him, and Jock, the dog partaking of both orders, harass the livestock, and at night break into the settlements to steal chickens. It is the same boundaries which impose the separation of the two orders on the dogs. But the social order is not just constituted by farming and cultivation. It is also a network of emotional and family relations spread over the male (husband and father seeing the dogs in relation to the economic unit of the farm) and the female (the mother and the obsessively emotional response to the dogs) with the children positioned in relation to these dual constraints, all of which the wild dog Bill refuses. So although the major opposition of the asocial and the social orders the attraction of the young girl for her puppy, and, coinciding with the male/female distinction, the wild dogs for the domestic dogs, the two sexes are still present as a differential structure, with echoes of the narcissistic dominance of the male:

> We set forth each morning, first, my brother, earnest with responsibility, his rifle swinging in his hand, at his heels the two dogs. Behind this time-honoured unit, myself, the girl, with no useful part to play in the serious masculine business, but necessary to provide admiration.

The same structure is underlying the relations in **"Between Men"**, about a meeting of two women who have virtually made professional careers of being useful reflective seconds to various successful men, as one of them drunkenly asserts: 'Maureen now sat up, earnest, trying to control her tongue: "But . . . what . . . we are both *good* at, itsh, it's bolshtring up some damned genus, genius" '.

So the indirect relations of the one and the other constitute an important part of the Lessing narrative. As can be seen in the above analysis, the precise narrative positions of the various figures within this structure admit many variations, within a gamut of possibilities ranging from complete refusal to acceptance. As a structure, however, it is far from defining completely the elements constituting these figures. Across the strict spatial divisions of the African landscape the attraction of the domestic and the wild dogs is a mutual one: this interplay of the direct and the indirect is equally present in those stories where the moment of attraction is articulated across the structures of the observer and the observed. The confrontation of the two orders in the direct look constitutes a real threat to the controlling position of the observer as subject, and has important implications for the narrative construction of the emotional self.

There are many ambiguities in the structure of the indirect look. It poses the observer as subject, implicitly dominant in the relations with the observed, yet demands these relations be acknowledged and confirmed by the acquiescent look in return. When Spence's impotence provokes Coles into making him come to get the whole thing over with, it is precisely this acquiescence she refuses: 'She squatted beside him, the light from the ceiling blooming on her brown shoulders, her flat, fair hair falling over her face. But she would not look at his face'. A failure on the part of the observed to comply in-

duces aggression and anger at the implied rejection of dominance. Yet a confrontation of the two orders in the direct look is equally charged, when the observed becomes observer in turn. The other is the focus of attraction and hatred, both wanted and repulsive at the same time: it is a permanent struggle, inherent in the irreconcilable demands placed on the other, that he or she as subject enter into their given position as object. Lessing is, in this particular area at least, very close to an Existentialist analysis where the look is also used as a privileged site of interpersonal struggle. As Graham Spence pursues his physical onslaught on Barbara Coles, we read: 'And he could not stop because he could not face the horror of the moment when he set her free and she looked at him. And he hated her more, every moment'. But in terms of the narrative context, it is the interplay between the direct and indirect looks which is important. (pp. 135-47)

Throughout **"One off the Short List"**, Graham Spence never loses sight of himself. To watch his companion is simultaneously to watch himself. He is as he appears to Barbara. The sight of other marriages, other media employees in the pub, allows him to see the nature of his own marriage, his own career. To be able to see what he considers his unique flair for emotional experience, he needs his list of 'especial women'. In this narrative, the self is both subject and object, observer and observed, self and other for itself. But this structure is often temporarily overridden by a sudden, immediate emotion, by jealousy or anger or something which drastically alters his vision of himself. In short, Graham Spence is constantly *surprised,* surprise is the mark of the moment of rupture in the continuous process of self-appraisal. He lived through his marriage with 'such surprise of the mind and the senses', he is 'surprised by his jealousy over James'. For a moment, observer and observed collapse together in a flux of emotions, which in this narrative is a measure of the unsuitability, to say the least, of Barbara Coles as choice. It is not usually Spence who is the victim of such confusion in his series of affairs: 'his real pleasure came when he saw her surprise at how well she was understood by him'.

It is clear that the duality constructing the relations of the self and the other, articulated through the narratives across the interplay of the direct and the indirect look, finds its counterpart in the structures of the self, experienced both directly and indirectly, either at the moment of direct, immediate experience, or at the term of a mediation. It is something of a truism of Lessing criticism, to state that the self is fragmented in her work, yet it seems to me that the nature of that fragmentation, and the manner of its production in the narratives which articulate it, could bear further examination, for, in terms of fictional structure, it would be difficult to say that one was any more true or real than the other: the position and function of immediate experience only makes sense in relation to the mediated self. Like the elements constructing the divisions between the self and the other, they are bound by their oppositional structure, their co-presence is mutually determinant. Together, they form a consistent vision which founds the self as irremediably conscious of itself, and yet to which all possible discourses of self-expression are inadequate. Mediated across the terms of a difference which articulates its relation to the other, and hence to itself, self-consciousness is its hallmark. (pp. 152-53)

Lessing's impact on her women readers is far from surprising. The didactic implications of an ironic mode of writing in which the mechanisms of both personal and interpersonal relationships are not taken for granted, but are on display, holding the 'characters', and indeed the narration, too, at a critical distance, place the reader in a position of insight and knowledge into processes which elsewhere were discursively structured as pregiven reality. The romantic discourse of love and marriage is a case in point here. Her fiction also easily enters the feminist analysis which refuses the various discourses on the nature of women in the name of an elucidation of the mechanisms by which they construct 'woman' as 'natural'. Nor is it surprising that her fiction concentrates so often on the figure of the woman, for the social discourse of the woman as other, as object of visual display, coincides perfectly with the narrative vision of the differential otherness of the self to the other and itself. But perhaps there is a fundamental ambiguity here; many of the female figures are 'givens', as is the social typology of the male and female. One has only to think of the woman lying on the roof, and the parents in **"A Story of Two Dogs"**, or **"Notes for a Case History"**, to realise the contrast with Maureen Watson or Susan Rawlings. But it is an ambiguity inherent in the structures of the self and the other, and of the self: this is what governs the positions of the various figures, that they bear the significance of the other or of the divided, self-reflective self. If to appear other is to be other, then there is no space in this immediate duality for the mediating factors—social, political or personal—to be displayed. Only if the self can appear to itself can the complex variety of the discursive structures orchestrating it become visible. (pp. 162-63)

> *Margaret Atack, "Towards a Narrative Analysis of 'A Man and Two Women',"* in Notebooks/Memoirs/Archives: Reading and Rereading Doris Lessing, *edited by Jenny Taylor, Routledge & Kegan Paul, 1982, pp. 135-63.*

MAURINE MAGLIOCCO (essay date 1983)

[*In the following excerpt, Magliocco appraises Lessing's presentation in "A Man and Two Women" of the evolving perceptions and relationships of two married couples after one has a baby.*]

Though titled **"A Man and Two Women,"** this story is really about Stella and her response to the changes the birth of the baby has brought about in the lives of her friends, Jack and Dorothy Bradford. Stella and her husband, Philip, had met the Bradfords the year before in Italy. The two English couples liked each other immediately, continued traveling around Europe together, and maintained their friendship after returning to London. Their friendship is satisfying to all of them because they are kindred spirits; they are all in one way or another artists. They also have in common the fact that one member of each couple has achieved critical success while the other has not. Though this has put a strain on both marriages, it has not been a significant one because all four agree that the art world is a "racket" and that being successful is not the same as being talented.

Despite this conviction, they are very concerned about their images as artists, so self-conscious in fact that when Jack is first "discovered" he and the others are paralyzed over the decision of whether he should buy a new car or a second-hand one. They examine the implications from every direction and Jack finally decides on a second-hand car because the press waits for artists who have made money to buy flashy cars. This tendency to evaluate their every move, to turn themselves into objects as they might be seen by others, causes

Newquist: *To work from* **A Man and Two Women** *for a bit. The almost surgical job you do in dissecting people, not bodily, but emotionally, has made me wonder if you choose your characters from real life, form composites or projections, or if they are so involved you can't really trace their origins.*

Lessing: I don't know. Some people I write about come out of my life. Some, well, I don't know where they come from. They just spring from my own consciousness, perhaps the subconscious, and I'm surprised as they emerge.

This is one of the excitements about writing. Someone says something, drops a phrase, and later you find that phrase turning into a character in a story, or a single, isolated, insignificant incident becomes the germ of a plot.

If you were going to give advice to the young writer, what would that advice be?

You should write, first of all, to please yourself. You shouldn't care a damn about anybody else at all. But writing can't be a way of life; the important part of writing is living. You have to live in such a way that your writing emerges from it. This is hard to describe. . . .

To return to **A Man and Two Women.** *Which stories in this collection would you choose as personal favorites? . . .*

That's very difficult. I like the first one, titled **"One Off the Short List"** because it's so extremely cold and detached—that one's a toughy. I'm pleased that I was able to bring it off the way I did. Then there were a couple of zany stories I'm attached to. The story about incest I liked very much—the one about the brother and the sister who are in love with each other. Not autobiographical at all, actually; perhaps I wish it were. And I like **"To Room 19,"** the depressing piece about people who have everything, who are intelligent and educated, who have a home and two or three or four beautiful children, and have few worries, and yet ask themselves "What for?" This is all too typical of so many Europeans—and, I gather, so many Americans.

> *Doris Lessing, in a 1963 interview conducted by Roy Newquist and published in his* Counterpoint (*1964*).

many of Dorothy's problems in dealing with her impending motherhood and reflects that paradox familiar to some artists—they who should be showing others the way to free themselves from the conventions of society's expectations become so self-conscious of their own positions that they too become trapped in certain expectations which, though different from those of the society at large, can be equally as imprisoning.

This self-consciousness infects every part of the lives of these four people, but since the narration is limited to Stella's point of view, it is she who becomes the intellectual center of the story, and it is her awareness of herself and the others that we focus on. Also, she is the one eventually faced with the real dilemma, and her response to that situation is the result of the objectification of self that characterizes all of them. Her moment of decision is carefully prepared in the story as Stella goes to visit her friends in their cottage in Essex about six weeks after their baby is born. Stella's husband, a journalist who occasionally makes a small film (an aspiring artist), has just wired that he will be delayed another month. These circumstances force Stella to think about her marriage as well as the Bradfords', to compare and contrast the two. What she sees most are the similarities. Both marriages, she concludes, are "those of strong, passionate, talented individuals" who "shared a battling quality that strengthened them, not weakened them"; in neither marriage was one partner victim to the other. Stella is happy to reach a conclusion that reasserts the kinship between the two couples and helps to explain their friendship, but this conclusion seems almost forced since before her attempt to evaluate her marriage, she was beginning to take it for granted and sometimes even found it exhausting. Her feelings about her marriage are much different from the conclusions she reaches when she analyzes and intellectualizes it by comparing it with the Bradfords'. Indeed, she seems surprised to find how lucky she is. This pattern of operating on one level of awareness until events call it into question and demand another level characterizes Stella throughout the story.

That Stella is a person who sees herself as others see her is apparent when she gets off the train in Essex. The narrator tells us that "she stood smiling, accustomed to men running to wait on her, enjoying them enjoying her." Jack, waiting, also appreciates the scene, but during the ride from the station says little to Stella except to comment obliquely about Dorothy and the baby. His remarks cause Stella to remember the time when the Bradfords had first discovered Dorothy's pregnancy. In a flashback, we see they were not ecstatic; instead, they reacted self-consciously, trying to separate themselves from those who might anticipate happily the birth of a baby. Because they defined themselves as artists, they felt obligated to analyze and examine the situation, explore and discuss the implications.

Stella remembers that the Bradfords had had many misgivings, even though they had deliberately chosen to have a baby. Dorothy, the narrator tells us, was "like most independent women" in having divided thoughts about her pregnancy. Over thirty, she feared she was set in her ways. She thought she might not be fit to be a mother or that she might not really want a baby at all. Whatever it was that made her decide to have the baby is not clear. The only explanation comes in her unfinished statement: "Until recently Jack and I were always with people who took it for granted that getting pregnant was a disaster, and now suddenly all the people we know have young children and baby sitters and . . . perhaps . . . if . . . ".

Her situation is probably familiar to many of us in our mid-thirties trying to decide about having children. Like Dorothy, when we think about the issue, we tend to think in negatives. Why do we even think we might want to have children? In practical terms it is very hard to imagine any good reasons, especially if our careers are rewarding. Lessing seems to invite these comparisons by having Dorothy represent independent women; her dilemma is their dilemma. When Dorothy talks about her pregnancy, she cannot explain why she wants a baby and does not mention any possible fulfillment that might come from having one. It is this inability to imagine

anything positive about having a child before it is born that causes the problems for her after it is born. Lessing seems to suggest that the imagination of the modern independent woman has failed her.

When the flashback ends, we return to Stella and Jack as they drive to the cottage. Jack's comments to Stella about Dorothy and the baby reinforce the idea that perhaps there is nothing positive about having a baby. Once an excellent cook who hated having anyone in her kitchen, Dorothy now has no energy for cooking. She is worn out. When Jack asks Stella if she was "like that," she is forced to go back in time, remembering herself at nineteen alone with a small baby. Just as her friendship with the Bradfords had caused her earlier to redefine her career and her marriage, so it causes her now to re-examine her motherhood. Because of Jack's question, Stella begins to remember the woman she once was. She replies only that she too was tired and irritable with her baby, but the process of remembering feelings she has forgotten has begun.

Now, however, Stella ignores those feelings, thinking instead of Dorothy when she had visited her in the hospital following the birth of her son. Stella remembers being surprised at the ease with which the two parents had handled the baby, adjusted to him, and enjoyed him. The scene made their earlier doubts seem foundless. Despite their sophistication, their worldliness, Dorothy and Jack had reacted like typical parents, though very self-conscious ones. Their dual response is apparent when Stella recalls Dorothy in the hospital "parodying the expected words but meaning them: 'He's the most beautiful baby ever born. I can't imagine why I didn't have him before'." It is significant that we see this scene through Stella's eyes because she is the detached observer. She responds to the warmth and loveliness of the scene between parents and child, but like Dorothy she cannot be sentimental. Both women are trapped by their self-image as modern women, distrustful if not cynical about motherhood and babies.

By the time Stella visits the cottage, however, Dorothy has spent several weeks alone with the baby and her husband, and is now giving herself fully to the pleasure of motherhood. But Stella realizes this only gradually. She is prepared for some alteration in Dorothy because of Jack's comments during the ride from the station, and as Jack shows her around the greenhouse-turned-studio, she sees that Dorothy has not returned to her drawing. Before the birth of the baby, Jack and Dorothy had always worked side by side, her neat space contrasting his cluttered one, and now Jack admits that he misses his wife's presence. Stella thus has more insight into the change that has occurred, beginning to see that the baby has affected the husband/wife relationship.

When Dorothy first appears, however, Stella notices only that she has "recovered her figure," and thinks of the pleasure that she and Dorothy have often had in contrasting their differences—Stella large, blonde, and soft; Dorothy dark and dramatic-looking. Immediately after greeting Stella, Dorothy says to her friend and to her husband, "You two look good together." We see in Stella's appraisal and in Dorothy's comment (repeated again later) that the two women, though friends, have recognized each other as potential rivals. Dorothy's comment, though innocent enough when first uttered, brings out in the open the sexual dimensions of the couples' friendship.

Only slowly does it become clear to Stella what shifts in the husband/wife relationship have resulted from the birth of the baby. At first all she sees is that Jack has continued to be artistically productive while Dorothy has not. In fact, Dorothy admits to her friend: "Having a baby's killed everything creative in me—quite different from being pregnant." She insists, however, that she does not care and seems surprised at her own indifference. When the three have tea together, Stella is aware that this indifference and a kind of languor are quite different from the vivacity that formerly characterized Dorothy. Again, Stella is asked to remember her own post-partum experience, but again she does so only vaguely.

The atmosphere is relaxed until Dorothy suddenly begins to ask about Philip. It is very important for her to know how Stella and Philip feel about being away from each other. Though Stella is surprised and somewhat irritated by Dorothy's insistence, she comes to a greater understanding of her feelings about her marriage as a result of it. For her part, Dorothy presses because she needs to have her new opinion confirmed: she has decided that she and Jack have been much too close in their relationship. She asks Stella: "Don't you think there's something awful in two grown people stuck together all the time like Siamese twins?" In trying to respond to Dorothy, Stella finds herself missing her husband, full of self-pity, crying. She begins to have some insights about Philip that are new to her. As she articulates them, she realizes that "she had never said this before because she had never thought about it." Thus, we see in Stella an intelligent woman, very aware of her own image, who is clearly out of touch with her feelings. Stella is unnerved but continues to listen to Dorothy who explains that she is being stifled constantly shut up with Jack.

Dorothy's changed feelings do not make much sense until the baby is brought into the room. Stella has been aware that throughout their visit, Dorothy has been listening for the baby. When it cries and Jack goes to get it, both husband and friend recognize the mother's need to have the child in her arms, to feel its body against hers. As Stella watches the "instinctive conversation" that causes the husband to be aware of his wife's needs and to respond by giving her the baby, she misses her own husband violently. At the same time, however, she watches the mother and child and remembers something she acknowledges to herself "she really had forgotten." She remembers the joy of being a mother with a new baby— "the close fierce physical tie between herself and her daughter when she had been a tiny baby." What she remembers most is that "it was like being in love, having a new baby." This memory is verified when Dorothy's words indicate that she has had the same response: "This is better than any man, isn't it Stell? Isn't it better than any man?" Stella, still aching for Philip, responds: "Well—no. . . . No, not for long." The contrast between the two women at this point in their lives is very important. Though watching the mother and child together has awakened "all kinds of forgotten or unused instincts" in Stella, she knows what Dorothy, enveloped in the warmth of mother love, cannot possibly know—that this euphoric state is temporary.

Because Stella has been forced to remember what it is like to be a new mother, however, she does understand how Dorothy can think of the baby as a lover and is not nearly as surprised as Jack when Dorothy asks if Philip has affairs while he is away and if Stella minds. Once again, Stella is "forced to remember." She thinks about "having minded, minding, coming to terms, and the ways in which she now did not

mind." Thus, because of Dorothy's new role as mother and her subsequent questions about her marriage and her friend's, Dorothy inadvertently leads Stella, the observer, to more insight about her feelings, to greater awareness of her emotional self. The birth of the baby has been the catalyst for both women to re-evaluate themselves and their marriages.

Dorothy's attempts to redefine her marriage are confused, however, because she had been so totally unable to anticipate the pleasure having a baby would bring. She is unprepared for what is happening to her and is reaching some conclusions that make sense only in terms of her present situation. Because of her love affair with the baby, she does not mind that everything creative in her has been killed, and she does not mind that Jack has for the first time in their married life been unfaithful to her. While Stella and Jack both assure her there is no reason she should care about his casual, drunken sexual encounter with a neighbor, she believes she should and is upset that she does not. She describes herself as indifferent to the two things that mattered most to her before the birth of the baby, her art and her husband.

In discussing this change with Stella and Jack, Dorothy again causes Stella to think about her own husband, and Stella tries to explain to Dorothy that she need not care about Jack's unfaithfulness because she and Jack are "so marvelous together." Her phrase reminds Stella of the conclusion she had reached earlier about the similarity between her marriage and the Bradfords'. Just as Jack and Dorothy are good together, so she and Philip are good together. She goes on to explain to Dorothy about Philip's affairs, their subsequent fights, their jealousy, their making up, and "the delightful battle of their day to day living." Her perception of her own marriage has deepened as a result of her attempt to reassure Dorothy.

When Jack takes Stella upstairs to show her the couple of hundred pencil drawings Dorothy had done while she was pregnant, Stella sees for herself the contrast between Dorothy's present indifference to her art and her intense involvement in it before the baby was born. Dorothy must have sensed instinctively that the baby would alter her relationship with her husband, because all of the drawings are a celebration of that relationship, of its closeness and harmony. The last few drawings show the trust and confidence of the woman, her body "swollen in pregnancy," toward her husband who is strong and protective, his body "commanding hers." In looking at them, Stella suddenly understands more clearly Dorothy's present attitudes. She tells Jack that Dorothy feels guilty about being unfaithful to him. When Jack is aghast, Stella explains that Dorothy has been unfaithful with the baby.

What Stella does not explain is why Dorothy worked in such a frenzy before the baby was born and has no creativity in her now. Dorothy herself cannot explain it. It is not very difficult to understand, however, when we remember all of Dorothy's negative thoughts about having a baby while she was pregnant. Just as she seemed to instinctively know that her relationship with Jack would change, so she must have felt, though unconsciously, that she had to fulfill the artistic side of her nature before the baby was born because she might have no opportunity to do so after it was born. Though her current situation has proven these fears to be well-grounded, it is also rewarding in a way Dorothy had not anticipated. She is not creative now because she has no need to be; her energies and her whole being are taken up with the baby. When she nurses it, she is totally involved in the experience: "a savage creature," as Stella describes her. Dorothy happily agrees with the description.

This complete giving of herself to the baby and the full enjoyment of that giving has led Dorothy to some strange conclusions—strange, that is, to anyone who has not had a baby or to anyone who has forgotten the intensity of caring for a newborn. Dorothy wants to abdicate all of her responsibilities to her career and to her husband. She wants only to be taken care of so that she can take care of the baby. Yet she still loves her husband and recognizes that he has needs also. Her solution is to suggest what Stella laughingly calls a *ménage à trois.* The sexual undercurrents of the couples' relationship come again to the surface as Dorothy forces Jack and Stella to admit their attraction for each other and confesses to her own for Philip. Her plan, though it excludes Stella's husband because he is away, explains all of Dorothy's earlier probing into Stella's feelings about her relationship with Philip. Since Dorothy knows that Stella and Philip have affairs while they are separated, she apparently feels free to suggest that her friend and her husband provide for each other's needs. This plan solves her own dilemma of being torn between husband and baby because it will allow Jack and Stella to take care of each other and will allow her to take care of the baby. She comments that *before* [my emphasis] she never understood polygamy, but now she does. She will be the senior wife, and assures Jack and Stella that she will be totally indifferent to what they do. When they fail to take her seriously, Dorothy bursts into tears. Jack does not understand her behavior at all, while Stella is resentful.

It is not clear until a little later why Stella is resentful. She suppresses this resentment while she and Jack put Dorothy and the baby to bed. As Stella holds the baby for the first time, she realizes "how much another woman's holding her child made Dorothy's fierce new possessiveness uneasy." When Stella takes her leave of Dorothy she reassures her by saying that she would feel different soon. Dorothy's reply shows that she is not convinced: "I suppose so, if you say so." Furthermore, her last words urge Stella and Jack to walk to the station together because it is such a lovely night. As Stella turns to go, the sight of the mother and baby in the bed together causes "the nerves of her memory" to fill with "sweet warmth." But her resentment returns as she thinks: "What right had this woman, who was in possession of such delight, to torment her husband, to torment her friend, as she had been doing—what right had she to rely on their decency as she did?"

As Stella and Jack walk to the garden, both try to joke about Dorothy's plan but both have already been aroused by it. They embrace, and Stella gives herself to the moment, responding passionately to Jack's overtures. Suddenly, however, her thoughts intrude. The self-consciousness of the artist, of one who analyzes, of one who sees herself as others see her, manifests itself. First she thinks that what she and Jack are about to do will destroy everything—the baby, two marriages, the friendship—and she takes almost uncontrollable pleasure in the thought. But as she begins to dissolve herself in the ecstasy of union with Jack, she sees the image of the baby and pulls back, damning Dorothy for putting her into such a situation. Jack responds by damning them both. At the moment of crisis, Stella chooses to do the honorable thing, but not because of any abstract principles of ethics or morality; rather, her decision is made because she is a woman, a mother, who knows what Dorothy in her present euphoria

cannot be convinced of—that the passionate intensity a mother feels for a child is only temporary, that a baby is not a lasting substitute for a man. Because she knows this, Stella denies her own pleasure. Like Dorothy, she turns from Jack because of the baby. The last line of the story seems to indicate Stella's acceptance of her decision as well as the narrator's approval: "It really is a lovely night." Because of the bonding between mother and child, the bonding between woman and woman triumphs over the attraction between woman and man. (pp. 30-8)

Maurine Magliocco, "Doris Lessing's 'A Man and Two Women': Is It Universal?" in The Denver Quarterly, *Vol. 17, No. 4, Winter, 1983, pp. 29-39.*

CLARE HANSON (essay date 1984)

[*In the following excerpt from an essay originally presented at a Modern Language Association meeting in 1984, Hanson explores conflicts in Lessing's handling of form and content in her African stories and identifies methods through which Lessing uses gender variations in her narratives to manipulate reader reaction to her stories.*]

Doris Lessing's African stories are valued highly by critics, perhaps because in them Lessing writes about a landscape and a culture which she knows as she could not know her later countries of exile. These fissured, disjointed, problematic texts should not be viewed as a discrete unit somehow separable from Lessing's other work but as consistent with the main body of her fiction. They must be approached as representing a decentered subject and object: an exiled woman writer's response to Africa. (p. 107)

[I] argue that there is a conflict in Lessing's African stories between the form (or the expectations created in us by the use of the free story genre) and the content, and that it is in exploring such a conflict that we may locate some of the major sources of energy and interest in the texts.

I would like to open up the question of gender before going on to talk about "Africa," for I think that for Lessing herself *as a writer* the question of gender choice precedes and shapes some of the experience of Africa which she presents. It is as though Lessing feels that in these short stories she has the option of writing either in a "masculine" or a "feminine" way: this implies a kind of detachment from form and content, or a gap between feeling and form, which it would be hasty to judge as necessarily disabling. (I use these terms because Lessing does—I do not take them to designate essential, but cultural differences. What is interesting is the fact that Lessing herself makes these assumptions about the possibility of choosing a masculine or feminine style. We as critics must reproduce, before questioning, such assumptions.)

Gender is signalled as problematic in the African stories on many levels, including language. First, one is struck by the uncertainty about the sex of the narrator in the opening stages of many of the stories—**"Old John's Place," "The Story of a Non-marrying Man," "Flavours of Exile,"** for example. For several paragraphs the sex of the narrator is left in doubt, while the text presents a detailed account of sex- or gender-less activities which baffles and frustrates the reader. We remain in a state of impatience and unease because we are unable to settle down to identify with our protagonist until the key pronoun is dropped. The effect is to foreground the issue of gender, making clear to the reader the extent to which he or she relies on gender differentiation as a means of coding, sorting, making sense of the world and experience, in ways which may be entirely arbitrary.

The second signal in the texts comes from the frequent use of a young boy or girl as the main protagonist or observer. These observer figures may—just—be pubescent, but they have not yet entered into their sexually differentiated adult roles, and so if gender is initially made problematic in these texts through our uncertainty over the sex of the narrator, the problematic continues through the texts' apparent reluctance to engage fully with adult, gendered experience. The adolescent perspective skews the texts, giving strength through the scope it offers for the observations of an innocent abroad, but also acting as a kind of negative filter, blotting out large areas of experience. The reader identifies with the adolescent perspective because the texts themselves offer so little other leverage: there are so few occasions on which the language generalises itself to the extent that we emerge from this narrow point of view.

Through most of Lessing's African stories there is a shrinking away from sexuality, from what Pound would call "direct treatment of the thing": the texts seem to refuse sexuality but leave the trace of their refusal as a second troubling question for the reader.

Thirdly, there are disquieting shifts of tone in the *African Stories,* to put it crudely, but in terms taken from Lessing herself, there are shifts between a direct, free "masculine" prose style and an indirect, intense "feminine" prose style: to extrapolate from Lessing's own terms, there are shifts between a style which is abstract, analytic, predominantly metonymic, and one which is concrete, sensuous, and predominantly metaphorical. Often the shifts in style or tone may occur within a single story, as these brief quotations from **"The Black Madonna,"** a story to which Lessing has said that she is "addicted," might show. First of all the wordy "masculine" prose:

> Zambesia is a tough, sunburnt, virile, positive country contemptuous of subtleties and sensibility: yet there have been States with these qualities which have produced art, though perhaps with the left hand. Zambesia is, to put it mildly, unsympathetic to those ideas so long taken for granted in other parts of the world, to do with liberty, fraternity and the rest.

Now the "feminine," informed with a tone of longing or regret:

> Yet he spoke of her now to Michele, and of his favourite bush-wife, Nadya. He told Michele the story of his life, until he realised that the shadows from the trees they sat under had stretched right across the parade-ground to the grandstand. He got unsteadily to his feet, and said: "There is work to be done. You are being paid to work."
>
> "I will show you my church when the light goes."

Lessing has discussed her use of masculine and feminine prose styles with specific reference to two of her "African" stories, **"The Trinket Box,"** and **"The Pig."** She has written:

> [**"The Trinket Box"**] . . . intense, careful, self-conscious, mannered—could have led to a style of writing usually described as "feminine." The style of **"The Pig"** is straight, broad, direct; is much less

beguiling, but is the highway to the kind of writing that has the freedom to develop as it likes.

"The Trinket Box" and **"The Pig"** are both stories about possession. **"The Pig"** is open, direct, and above all composed. The prose seems plain and unadorned, but if *we* analyse *it* we find that it is analytic and abstract to a degree. The sentence structure is simple, but the sentences accumulate in a relentlessly logical way—we have the feeling that all the different elements in the text have been well weighed and judged before the story ever came to be written, and that nothing can now divert or deflect the narrative from its willed and chosen course. Take this paragraph, for example:

> Jonas did not reply. He did not like being appointed official guardian against theft by his own people, but even that did not matter so much, for it never once occurred to him to take the order literally. This was only the last straw. He was getting on in years now, and he wanted to spend his nights in peace in his own hut, instead of roaming the bush. He had disliked it very much last year, but now it was even worse. A younger man visited his pretty young wife when he was away.

Lessing feels that such writing "is the highway to the kind of writing that has the freedom to develop as it likes," and her statement must be respected. Yet it is my impression that this writing does not have freedom on the level of text or language: its freedom exists, if it exists at all, in the public, historical domain. In stories like these Lessing by her own admission writes "like a man" and in so doing attempts to enter the field of male discourse, male history, and male power. **"The Pig"** is thus not only about male power on the most obvious level—the story is concerned with one man's possession of another man's wife—but also exhibits a kind of textual possessiveness, through its relentlessly analytic prose style, which it would seem fair to call "masculine."

In calling Lessing's style "analytic" I do not mean that it is necessarily either very cerebral or very complex—clearly the style of the African stories is not in the remotest sense Jamesian. But the style is very selective: it is as though perceptions and language have been sifted through so that only the *typical* rather than the particular event or perception comes through to us. The texts are thus in a curious way bodiless, even when they are directly concerned with physical or sensuous experience.

Lessing's "masculine" prose is a language of selection, excision, expropriation: the law of (masculine) language becomes the law of being: (masculine) syntax does not so much mimic as construct the experience of Africa which we take away from such texts as **"The Pig"** and **"The Sun Between Their Feet."**

In the context of contemporary feminist theory, and in particular the writings of Julia Kristeva, I think it legitimate to claim that in "masculine" stories—or in parts of stories—like **"The Pig"** Lessing attempts a takeover, a possession of Africa which is doomed to fail. Recent feminist theory has stressed the repression of female desire which takes place in conventional representation: in the Lacanian "symbolic order" (the phallocentric order of language), utterance is made possible precisely through the repression of the feminine, the heterogeneous, the other. Kristeva goes on to argue that in literature femininity can characteristically be located in the breaks and *pulsions* of a text, where desire as it were "bounds back," and she particularly associates the feminine with the kind of disruption and fissuring of the text which occurs in modernist and postmodernist writing (e.g. Joyce, Sollers). This of course raises a problem—how can it be that the feminine in this sense is expressed by men? Kristeva has in fact been taken to task by some writers for failing to acknowledge that the feminine as she presents it is not truly other: it is defined by difference from the masculine, not otherness. This brings us up against the perennial different/other question in feminist theory. I would like to offer a way out of this by suggesting that "masculine" and "feminine" as Kristeva's critics, for example Juliet Mitchell, use them are not stable terms and are not ultimately tied to sexual identity—they are to do with *qualities* which can shift. In a sense therefore the debate about otherness takes us far beyond the notion of a "real" feminine: the notion of the other in this sense can be seen as rather like the Derridean postulate of the "third term" which would ideally break the antithetical relations of the word/the world. I'd like to stress the link between this "ideal" pursuit of the feminine and Derridean theory, before going back to discuss Lessing's stories in the very contingent terms which she has given to us—masculine and feminine.

It is in those stories of Lessing which seem most fissured and disjointed that we come closest to the subject, Africa, that "inexplicable majestic silence" as she calls it, and I would argue that the question of exile and possession in the African stories (the question of their "Africanness") is intimately bound up with a choice of "masculine" and "feminine" modes of writing. The "feminine" writer Lessing makes closer contact with, effects some kind of rapprochement with Africa, just as the feminine characters do in the texts we've been considering. It's actually very striking that in these texts (white) male and female attitudes to Africa are absolutely polarized. The men characteristically feel that they own Africa in both the literal and the metaphorical sense: they organize it, partition it, drive roads and railroads through it, imposing European notions of order on it. Men are associated with the hunt, the chase, guns and dogs—the young girl in the famous story **"The Old Chief Mshlanga"** feels safe when walking about her father's farm only when she mimics her father, takes over his accoutrements ("I had my rifle in the curve of my arm, and the dogs were at my heels"). The women settlers are by contrast alienated from Africa in both cultural and physical terms. Some may make brief *sorties,* make initial attempts to impose their kind of order or civilization on Africa—Mrs. Lacey, for example, in **"Old John's Place"** creates a bedroom which is an organza fantasy in the midst of the "red dust" of Africa. But these baroque efforts soon dwindle and fail, as the women come to recognize the impassable gulf which exists between their assumptions and expectations and the physical reality of life in "Zambesia." So Julia muses in **"Winter in July"**:

> "That is my home," said Julia to herself, testing the word. She rejected it. In that house she had lived ten years—more. She turned away from it, walking lightly through the sifting pink dust of the roads like a stranger. There had always been times when Africa rejected her, when she felt like a critical ghost.

In **"Winter in July"** the contrast between male and female responses to Africa is described in terms which begin to suggest a certain wise passiveness on the part of the female:

> Her liking for the evening hour, before moving indoors to the brightly lit room, was the expression of her feeling for them [the two men]. The mingling

lights, half from the night sky, half from the lamp, softened their faces and subdued their voices, and she was free to feel what they were, rather than rouse herself by listening. This state was a continuation of her day, spent by herself (for the men were most of the time on the lands) in an almost trance-like condition where the soft flowing of the hours was marked by no necessities of action strong enough to wake her. As for them, she knew that returning to her was an entrance into that condition. Their day was hard and vigorous, full of practical details and planning. At sundown they entered *her country,* (my italics) and the evening meal, where the outlines of fact were blurred by her passivity no less than by the illusion of indistinctness created by sitting under a roof which projected shadowlike into the African night, was the gateway to it.

In this text, the men embody the so-called "masculine" mode of possession: they are hard, practical, vigorous, driven by an instinct for self-preservation which forces them to annihilate, or to refuse the separate quality of "their" land, Africa. The woman is soft (indistinct), passive, more than willing to annihilate, or perhaps suspend herself in order to "feel" what her two companions and the landscape "are." The woman recognizes that presence ("what they were") cannot be freed from absence ("the evening hour" "an almost trance-like" state): she recognises not only her points of contact with but far more crucially her alienation from Africa. "In order to possess what you do not possess/you must go by the way of dispossession."

What of Africa, then, in **"The Pig,"** the story written, in Lessing's own words, in the style leading to freedom? I would argue that "Africa" in **"The Pig"** is not free in that it is not fully nor openly recognized as an entity distinct from the consciousness of character or narrator—it isn't available to the reader as both subject and object. I can only support this charge by direct quotation from passages which purport to evoke the feeling of Africa:

> Hours passed, and he watched the leaping dancing people, and listened to the drums as the stars swung over his head and the night birds talked in the bush around him. He thought steadily now, as he had not previously allowed himself to think, of what was happening inside the small dark hut that gradually became invisible as the fires died and the dancers went to their blankets. When the moon was small and high and cold behind his back, and the trees threw sharp black windows on the path, and he could smell morning on the wind, he saw the young man coming towards him again.

It's striking that here Lessing uses images which point us back to mechanization and civilization (particularly notable is the phrase "the trees threw sharp black windows"): it is as though there is some kind of confusion between an intention of conveying Africa and an inability to do so save through images which are literally mechanical or metaphorically so in the sense that they verge on cliché ("he could smell morning on the wind").

By contrast in the more disjointed, elliptical story **"The Trinket Box"** a dialectical relationship is set up between the characters and/or the narrator, and Africa. It is clear that, in the main, we are being presented with Africa as it has been perceived and imaged by "Aunt Maud"—there is not that ambiguity which still exists in **"The Pig,"** where we are not at all sure through whose eyes we are viewing Africa—those of the farmer, Jonas, or an omniscient narrator. We see Africa in **"The Trinket Box"** through a series of "characteristic," quirky photographic images. A relation between subject and object exists and is made clear even in the largely picture-postcard view which we have of Africa in this story: though the perspective may be limited, it is only because we have a sense of tension between the object—Africa—and its neat presentation in white-settler language that we can perceive or acknowledge that such limitation exists. Africa is presented in similarly complex, mediated ways in other stories written in Lessing's avowedly "feminine" style—**"Winter in July,"** **"Getting off the Altitude," "Old John's Place,"** for example.

To conclude: I have been studying the implications of Lessing's apparent refusal, in some of the African stories, to take what Simone de Beauvoir has called the "negative way" of female knowledge. I would like to make one final suggestion about the relationship between the forms some of these stories take and their content. I don't want to tie too easily together concepts which should remain significantly juxtaposed, rather than merging and becoming confused. But it does seem to me that we should at least entertain the idea of a relationship between Lessing's "masculine" style and the theme of colonization. It could be argued that in writing about a colonial system she wholeheartedly deplores, Lessing nevertheless reproduces or perpetuates in the processes of some of these texts patriarchal, and by extension colonial, systems and values. One has perhaps to turn again to the all-pervasive thought of Derrida to explain the logic of the supplement whereby a liberal attitude proposed by the texts on the level of ostensible content is undone, shown to be incomplete through the workings of the text. It is perhaps not so much that Lessing is a recidivist colonial figure, as some critics of the Canopus in Argos series have suggested: rather we should recognize that the texts *as texts,* if Derrida is right, will almost certainly work to show that a good, a desideratum, is incomplete, because/if it is proposed too confidently as absolute. (pp. 107-13)

> Clare Hanson, "The Woman Writer as Exile: Gender and Possession in the African Stories of Doris Lessing," in Critical Essays on Doris Lessing, edited by Claire Sprague and Virginia Tiger, G. K. Hall & Co., 1986, pp. 107-14.

JUDITH KEGAN GARDINER   (essay date 1989)

[*In the following excerpt from her* Rhys, Stead, Lessing, and the Politics of Empathy, *Gardiner explores "masculine" and "feminine" narrative styles employed by Lessing in her short stories from the 1950s and 1960s, noting that the resolution of certain key issues in Lessing's fiction frequently depends upon her choice of narrative voice.*]

A cunning exile devoted to art, Lessing began writing short stories about her childhood Africa. She consolidated her career with a series of autobiographical novels, the *Children of Violence* quintet, and *The Golden Notebook,* a comprehensive novel of female subjectivity. Now she is compiling a many-volumed cosmological epic space fiction. However, this schema omits several novels and the stories set in Europe, and it underestimates the continuing importance of her short fiction, which many critics consider her finest writing. Whereas her novels sometimes appear didactic, disproportioned, or flat, her short stories are often more finely crafted and broader ranging, achieving a forceful emotional impact or evoking a character, situation, or idea with a grace and concision

achieved only rarely in her novels. These are the qualities she praises in her most overt tribute to another author, the short story entitled **"Homage to Isaac Babel."** Joyce Carol Oates pays tribute to "how beautifully the craftsmanship of her many short stories illuminated lives, the most secret and guarded of private lives, in a style that was never self-conscious or contrived." (p. 84)

In the preface to her ***African Stories,*** 1965, she described herself as an "addict" to the short story form who would write them "even if there really wasn't any home for them," even if they found "no market." She thus signalled her short stories as privileged forms of self-expression, freer, perhaps, than the novels and reflecting her identity as an exile, homeless and ambivalent about seeking commercial approval. On the other hand, one of the advantages of "home" is that one can behave there in ways not permitted outside. "Home" is the privileged site of the private emotions, like the adult sexual passions bemusedly observed by young characters in **"Old John's Place,"** 1951, or **"Getting Off the Altitude,"** 1957. But "home" is also the place where one can get away with flying into a temper. Lessing sometimes encourages us to empathize with her characters, sometimes incites our antagonism against them. She commends as her favorite stories several that provoke especially nasty emotions—the "cold and detached . . . toughy" **"One Off the Short List,"** 1963 or **"Black Madonna,"** 1964, which is full of "bile" against Southern Rhodesia as she "knew and hated it" (*African Stories*)—stories whose protagonists include a racist white African and a self-satisfied rapist. Although many of her stories appear autobiographical, she often insists on her stories' separation from herself, saying, for example, that **"Each Other,"** 1963, dealing with incest, is "not autobiographical at all" and **"To Room Nineteen,"** 1963, is "all too typical of so many Europeans and Americans." The stories provide an arena in which Lessing can enact the interplay between self and other, the individual and her or his circumstances, that can be more detached, playful, and experimental than the more committed long fiction. Lessing recently spoke of her stories as "something small crystallized out" of the long transformative writing process.

Like Rhys and Stead, Lessing alternates in her fiction between self-expression and attempting to capture the other, most simply at first by writing vignettes shaded with local color. These early works assume that a vivid mimesis will insure the reader's duplication of the author's attitudes—often attitudes of rejection toward her subjects. Domination and empathy, the values of "market" and of "home" or of empire and colony, of sophisticated city and of pastoral retreat—and often of men and women—struggle with each other throughout Lessing's work. Domination and empathy may work to cross purposes when the narrative dominates its subject matter in such a way as to break the empathic identification between reader and characters, often by turning the tables on a dominating person and so exposing the social order that person represents. Lessing's narratives, in turn, struggle against both domination and empathy, seeking the autonomy of an individual identity, which is also the desire for a story of one's own, a story within a meaningful history.

In the 1964 introduction to her ***African Stories,*** Lessing saw her first literary choices as gender-coded:

> **"The Pig"** and **"The Trinket Box"** are two of my earliest. I see them as two forks of a road. The second—intense, careful, self-conscious, mannered—

could have led to the kind of writing usually described as "feminine." The style of **"The Pig"** is straight, broad, direct; is much less beguiling, but is the highway to the kind of writing that has the freedom to develop as it likes.

Indeed, most of her early work takes the implicitly "masculine" road of **"The Pig"** toward social realism, a road along which masses could march to a better future, in contrast to the "beguiling," seductive, and apparently backward-looking "feminine" modernist path with its "self-conscious" insistence on female difference.

Her overt rejection of the "feminine" path in writing accords with her persistent denial that she is a feminist and with her tendency to describe "larger" issues than gender in her work. Unlike Rhys, race, not sex, is the primary category through which she begins to organize her experiences of otherness and of injustice, even of the inequities of class, which is the primary category for Stead. Yet, as we shall see in analyzing the "feminine" line in her short stories in relation to the "masculine" line over the four decades of her career to date, Lessing's two paths repeatedly intersect; both address interactions among empathy and domination, female identity and male authority, and both struggle to resolve the contradictions between opposed sets of psychological needs and the historical outlooks that they imply.

Lessing's earliest story in the rejected "feminine" category, **"The Trinket Box,"** written in Africa in the 1940s, was not printed in the earliest collections of her African stories and admitted later only with a disclaimer, not destroyed but defensively denied. Although Lessing chastises the story for its style, it may be its woman-centered content that is truly disturbing, the gender-specific existential dilemma: what does a woman's life mean? This early, rejected story confronts questions about female identity squarely and centrally. Does a woman who devotes herself to others have a self? How can a woman with no sexual life claim happiness? What or who does her autonomy threaten? Lessing carries the unease of these questions into the story's interrogative style, which asks ten questions on its first page, one of which echoes the child's question to her parents, "where did it all begin?" (*African*). Perhaps Lessing, who was developing her reputation as a writer in the early 1950s, rejected identification with these questions; Aunt Maud is her first portrait of a "free woman," that is, of a woman unattached to a man, but she is a doomed and diminished creature, and after writing about her, Lessing drops the subject for over a decade.

Little happens in the story. Aunt Maud, an unassuming old spinster who served her relatives as an unpaid companion and domestic help, dies leaving only a box of valueless trinkets, carefully labeled for their many recipients. Although Maud's name recalls those of Lessing's own mother and grandmother, it is Maud's apparent rejection of such familial roles that defines her. The story begins with a bland narrative tone, discussing the possibilities of other stories embedded within this one: "Yes, but it was only recently, when it became clear that Aunt Maud really could not last much longer, that people began to ask all those questions which should have been asked, it seems now, so long ago." The narrator's defensive "yes, but" turns its guilt about unasked questions onto us readers, and the time shifts from "only recently" to "now" to "long ago" implicate us in puzzling out a coherent story from Maud's life, the task the narrator sets herself as well. Maud has lived so long that she is a part of history, but

not a history the narrator can understand. Perhaps women's history deliberately avoids public events: when asked about Oscar Wilde, Maud refers vaguely to an "interesting book" in the library, not to a scandal she lived through. The narrator imagines that Maud sees herself, too, as a fiction rather than as a person, as a "character in a historical play" rather than as a participant in change.

Although a "character" both literary and historical, Maud won't take center stage; she declines attention, even in death. The narrator approves Maud's self-effacing autonomy, yet she surprisingly deduces from it that the old lady's stoic generosity incited others to sadism: "we are forced to know that the thought of her aches and pains put warmth" into those who hired her as a companion. This narrative "we" seems to be the collective of Maud's surviving, mostly female relatives, though it also ambiguously includes the author and us readers, and the "mannered" quality that Lessing disavows in the story comes largely from this plural narrative voice. The old relatives Maud serves feel their mortality less when they have her, frail and uncomplaining, at their sides, a permanent scapegoat for the indignities of living. After each extended visit in which she has acted as the unpaid servant, Maud sends her relatives presents which they resent: giving and taking are always difficult in Lessing's world, even though they are among the main ways people relate to one another. Typically, women give, and, although they resent men and other women who take from them, they prefer the covert dominance of giving to being takers themselves. In addition, Maud's gifts arouse antagonism because of their aptness, which seems sinister to the narrator: "how did she come to know our most secret wants?"

The narrator dislikes being understood by this peripheral woman as though understanding is a kind of domination. The old lady's ability to empathize without asking for a return threatens the narrator, who judges that "it is all intolerable" and harangues Maud: "how could you stand, year in and year out, pouring out your treasures of affection to people who hardly noticed you?" The narrator seems to regard it as "intolerable" for *her,* not for Maud, that Maud's generous understanding was not reciprocated. Throughout Lessing's work, people's needs for love battle with their longings for autonomy, and she describes herself as a girl as independent and critical but longing for love (**"Impertinent Daughters"**). In this story a woman who seems not to need love shames others by giving rather than needing. But Maud's threat may also be that she usurps the power of the author by understanding others without being available to be understood herself; she presents her heirs with posthumous evidence of her understanding and concern which they cannot reciprocate. Though refusing marriage and motherhood, she has acquired the frightening maternal power of understanding others who do not wish to be understood, and hence, implicitly, exposed. It is a relief to the narrator when Maud dies "as a leaf shrivels."

After Maud's death, her survivors describe her as a "casket of memories" who hoarded the reminiscenses they wanted, and they are affronted when the casket snaps shut on them: "it is monstrous that a human being who has survived miraculously and precariously so many decades of wars, illnesses, and accidents should die at last, leaving behind nothing." This is one of Lessing's first statements about the intractability of history, which goes on and on without our understanding it and without it adding up to anything. The fury here, directed against the woman, not the wars, illnesses, and accidents, might seem to be that evoked by a woman who has re-fused to mother. The narrator futilely awaits "that one thing, the perfect word of forgiveness that will leave us healed and whole" and interprets the old woman's death as an aggressive act, a deliberate withdrawal of parental support. But perhaps more fundamentally the fury attacks the obliquity of the rela-tion between history and women's lives. A staunch believer in the Victorian heresies that became Lessing's causes and then, according to her, the dominant ideas of the twentieth century, socialism and feminism, Maud did not preach her beliefs. Despite all she has lived through, despite being cast as a historical character, she refuses to tell stories, to answer questions, to frame herself within a public and historical nar-rative. A woman who has no story has no history. Endlessly and quietly involved in female services, Aunt Maud refuses to make anecdotes of herself or to place herself in terms of the public stage. Lessing's professed beliefs throughout her career all oppose the threatening idea that each life sums zero and that each generation can do no more than repeat the last. This desire for a progressive history is also, of course, a desire for narrative, for shapely and intelligible stories. By refusing either to tell or to make herself into a story, the old lady re-sists narrative, defining a female anti-story and anti-history in opposition to the stories the narrator wants, conventional stories about adventure or romance.

Perhaps Maud *does* reveal her truth though she does so co-vertly in "the order of the words" of her last sentence: "I put everything right when people became so kind and I knew I was ill." Her "terrible knowledge" is people's—and fate's—indifference to others, especially to unattached women: "pro-test, is that what we are feeling," "a dull and sorrowful rage" because "we all feel . . . 'No, no! It can't all be for nothing!'" The narrator shies away from this "feminine" "protest," sub-limating her rage into heroic posturing, a sort of female mim-icking of Churchillian patriotism in adversity. (pp. 84-8)

If Maud will not tell her own story, she will have stories told about her. If we cannot empathize with her, at least we can resist her understanding of us by making her an object lesson about women's lives. The narrator expects us to share, first, her bafflement at Maud's life, then her confidence that she has unlocked the box of Maud's secrets. This knowledge reverses Maud's maternal power over us; we become little Maud's big parents: "now it seems that we hold Aunt Maud in the hollow of our palms. That was what she was; now we know her," and now, presumably, we can write her, replacing her muted voice and story with our own. Understanding Maud at last means that we will feel as she felt, her "persistent but gently humorous anger." But the story in fact creates and incites this anger, directing it back at the female collective represent-ed by the narrative "we," including the reader, and at Maud herself for colluding with society's marginalization of women.

If Maud's death expresses women's fears of becoming our mothers, the end of the story insists that we must become her. A retroactive moral missionary, Maud saves us through self-less martyrdom: "we are grown proud and honest out of the knowledge of her honesty and pride." But is the "anger" we feel "measuring ourselves against her" an anger against her for making us feel "small"? Both angry at Maud and angry in her behalf, the collective narrative voice enacts ambiva-lences redolent of mother-daughter psychological dynamics.

Lessing deprecates the style of **"The Trinket Box,"** though it is not a more artificial style than that she employs in **"The**

Pig," 1948, which she favors over it. She may have been un-comfortable with Maud's "box" as too obvious a Freudian symbol, or with the story's exclusive concentration on female identity, untempered by the explicit racial context that dis-tances and justifies other early African stories. However, it is more likely that the collective female narrator troubled her, encapsulating as it does the central difficulty of the female child's development as described by object relations theorists and of Lessing's development by her own account, that is, the daughter's differentiation of an individual identity from the symbiotic "we" of herself and her dominating mother: "I can't remember a time when I wasn't fighting with my poor mother" **("My Mother's Life")**. Her late work repeatedly re-turns to this problem of individuality in collectivity, ultimate-ly finding virtue and bliss in a cosmic "substance of we feel-ing." In literary terms, too, this feminine "we" may have seemed dangerous to Lessing in linking her with Virginia Woolf's fluid and apparently plotless female modernism, a style that postwar leftist writers considered elitist and reac-tionary.

Responding to '50s misogyny, Lessing rejects her earliest "feminine" writing without explicitly gender-coding its op-posite, so that she accepts the implicitly "masculine" style of postwar realism as simply generic. She associates the appar-ently guileless masculine style of **"The Pig,"** the "road" she was glad to take when starting her career, with open adven-ture, quest, and freedom. Like a male infant, the young "mas-culine" story must separate from its mother to develop inde-pendently, and Lessing as a young artist first feels comfort-able with neat stories that conform to a "masculine" esthetic of realism, action, and male-defined serious issues.

Unlike **"The Trinket Box," "The Pig"** begins in a flat third person voice with no hint of interchange between author and reader: "the farmer paid his laborers on a Saturday evening when the sun went down." The story places an ordered social world before us, ranked by class and race; the farmer is white and arrogant; his laborers, black, retiring, and apparently subservient. Together they stand silhouetted against the night sky, as though in a timeless tableau, "for all this had hap-pened before, every year for years past." The nameless farmer genuinely loves the fertile land: "how good those fields of strong young plants looked." The landscape of the story evokes comfortably familiar colonial and mythological asso-ciations: the white, light world of the "civilized" farmer against the dark land and its mysterious people, and all this made eternal, rather than being seen as a fairly recent histori-cal development of European colonialism in Africa. The far-mer associates the natives with the land, and with sexuality, youth, virility, darkness, and the "theft" of taking the fruit of their labors, corn grown on land stolen from them. The story's moral landscape seems as simply contrasted as the sil-houetted scene, though in reverse: the farmer is an exploiter; the Africans, his victims. After setting this scene, the story drops the white farmer and moves to its black protagonist, a "tall elderly man with a mild face." Despite his dignity, Jonas cannot redress the power imbalance between the far-mer and himself; he is coerced into following the white man's orders to guard the corn "against theft by his own people" and to shoot anything that moves through the field at night," and if it turns out to be a human pig, then so much the worse."

As the narrative moves into the old black man's mind, its style simplifies to a Hemingway-like swagger. The old man has an unfaithful young wife: "once he had snatched up a stick, in despair, to beat her with; then he had thrown it down. He was old, and the other man was young, and beating her could not cure his heartache." This style is as intense, self-conscious, and mannered as that of **"The Trinket Box,"** but mannered according to the conventions of the masculine plain style: short phrases, paratactic syntax, monosyllabic diction, rhetorical repetitions. The old man remembers with pleasure a waterbuck he shot, and as he imagines the "blood, and the limp dead body of the buck," he thinks of "the young man laughing with his wife." We are hardly surprised, then, when after nights of jealous vigil, Jonas follows his wife's lover after a tryst and shoots him in the cornfields: " 'a pig,' said Jonas aloud to the listening moon. . . . /He wanted to hear how it would sound when he said it again, telling how he had shot blind into the grunting, invisible herd." Like a joke, the story ends on a pun, here a moral one. The white man commissions murder to retain control over his property, the food his blacks grow that they wish to eat though he will not. Instead of protecting his people, black Jonas follows the immoral white command in order to retain control over what he considers his property, the wife that the lover can enjoy as he no longer can. The dying lover grunts and thrashes, reduced to the physical level of a pig while the old man sinks to second-hand white swinishness.

Like Lessing's first novel, *The Grass Is Singing,* **"The Pig"** places a woman in a situation that would produce anger but expresses that anger through a murderous black man whose aggression is justified by racist oppression: the reader should blame black brutality on white colonial brutalization. However, despite the story's assertively masculine stance, it encodes a covert feminist protest at the cross-racial male solidarity and violence used to keep women in place. Critic Michael Thorpe inadvertently acknowledges this male solidarity when he praises **"The Pig"** for its "universally intelligible" treatment of jealousy. No women murder men in Lessing's works, but men of both races kill women, as in **"The Nuisance,"** 1951; **"Hunger,"** 1953; and **"Plants and Girls,"** 1957. However, to read these stories as attacks on sexism avoids recognizing that they participate in tacit sexist literary conventions that invite the reader to collude in the imaginary destruction of women.

Racial injustice provides Lessing with her first model for understanding oppression in general. Her earliest published works display a steady knowledge about what happens when some people treat other people as objects, projecting their own desires upon them and encouraging them to act out their own worst impulses. She also understands the degrading consequences for women of accommodating to a patriarchal society, but she treats this issue as secondary.

By taking the "masculine" road in writing short stories, Lessing joined the unmarked, paradigmatically male dominant tradition of the postwar decade. She also found a way to shape her short fiction, setting up stories in terms of conflicts between men, sometimes white and black men, about women who could be, and often were, destroyed. These simple plots seem controlled and well-crafted in comparison to the more amorphous and dangerous "feminine" stories. Lessing's early African stories in her "masculine" mode display explicit insights about racial injustice, but present sexual roles more covertly. A maternal metaphor about authorship implies a special affinity between a woman writer and her female characters, which Lessing flirts with and rejects in the narrative

"we" of **"The Trinket Box."** In the "masculine" stories she develops a related, though opposite technique, which might be called projective disidentification, the device of getting "inside" another person whose consciousness seems alien, then exposing that character while apparently sympathizing with it. This is a device that works toward domination rather than toward empathy with its object, and Lessing seems to find it a useful way to distance herself from her characters. She uses this technique first and least successfully to create black men; later, for white men and antipathetic white women.

As she saw it in the 1960s, Lessing charted two possibilities for herself as a beginning writer in the 1940s: one was female modernism with its sensitivity, fluid characters and narrators, and an interior focus; the other, male-dominant realism, a fiction of neat plot, clear beginnings and endings, and of discrete characters who deftly represent political positions. Death in the "feminine" stories raises questions about individual identity and the meaning of life, about the connections between maternity and mortality; in contrast, death in the "masculine" stories is a result of human will. Through most of the 1950s she stayed close to the second track, sustained by a Marxist ideology that upheld the social usefulness of a realist esthetic. However, despite her either/or rhetoric, her actual practice tends toward both/and; her fiction oscillates between positions that it declares "correct" and others that it disavows, and her oppositions covertly admit their excluded categories. The binary division between "masculine" and "feminine" oversimplifies the categories; the "masculine" stories might more accurately be called oedipal in their triangular rivalries, whereas her "feminine" line often explores preoedipal anxieties about identity and the dominating powers of empathy. The story **"Traitors,"** 1951, for example, graphically portrays children's conflicted familial loyalties as sisters move from a position behind their mother's chair to one behind their father's. Throughout Lessing's fiction, this oscillation continues, though the values of the male and female poles change in the course of her and the century's history, and the stories thus dramatize a daughter's development through a looping process that incorporates and rejects variously reimagined paternal and maternal models. (pp. 89-92)

While the daughter stands behind her father's chair, Lessing writes realistic, oedipal stories that treat chronological narrative unproblematically. The illusion of verisimilitude arises from using conventions that signal the complexity of people's inner lives. Typically, Lessing paints with a primary palette of a few intense emotions—anger and resentment predominate, but she also attributes to her characters fear, hunger, sexual jealousy, longing for affection, and ecstatic joy in communion with nature. (pp. 92-3)

Although the line of **"The Pig"** leads to [Lessing's] African morality tales, most of her other early stories in the "masculine" mode are less simplistic; several explore heterosexual tensions within a racist, multiethnic, and patriarchal culture, sometimes from the viewpoint of a naive child who judges adult sexuality against the preoedipal bond between mother and child. Adolescent Katy in **"Old John's Place,"** 1951, romanticizes her notion of the natural mother, "a plump smiling woman" who nurses in public **(African),** in contrast to the coldly adulterous Mrs. Lacey, a rejecting modern mother. Without the mediating child narrator, **"Winter in July,"** 1951, encloses its analysis of a woman's identity within another heterosexual triangle, but Julia's quandary is not which man to choose but what kind of a person to be. Having decided not to have children, she asks herself, "what am I?" (*African*). Her crises are not just ones of female self-esteem; she is herself an agent of "evil," her despair and self-hatred springing from her denial of responsibility for herself and from her fused absorption in her two men, a plight that recalls the particularly female developmental danger of inadequate individuation. Later, in **"Each Other,"** 1963, Lessing draws a happily incestuous brother and sister whose fusion leads to moral decay. The three bitter and self-hating people in **"Winter in July"** may represent capitalism and white exploitation in Africa, but they provoke the author not to the easy scorns and ironies she directs at her explicitly political subjects but rather to the uncanny dis-ease of her "feminine" stories.

Lessing's stories of the early 1950s gain coherence from their focus on Africa, their realist esthetic, Marxist politics, and often their framing from the viewpoint of a naive girl. Her stories of the later 1950s continue along the same road, adding English and European settings to African ones. Although she later said she had been "unsuccessful as a dramatist," in the period of the late '50s and early '60s when she was heavily involved with the London theater, she gives her short stories more dramatic structures and uses dialogue more freely than earlier. She also takes the theater as a metaphor for the roles people play in everyday life, an approach that renders her fiction more self-conscious and begins to separate it from the complacencies of "masculine" realistic representation. **"The Habit of Loving,"** 1957, for example, dramatizes a woman's pain at feeling that she has no self inside the shell secreted by her overlapping social and theatrical roles. She appears in a nightclub act that delivers a "potted history" of the twentieth century and its wars, "a parody of a parody," as emotionless as "a corpse singing" (*Stories*) and in its sequel, an act that parodies love: "we go through all the motions. . . . If it isn't all bloody funny, what is it?" As the two nightclub acts indicate, history and love both depend on a recognition of the other; without this faith in meaning and value, love evaporates, history becomes a jangle of random gestures, and individual identity disappears into posture and costume. Without empathy, based on the ability to see the other as other, history and identity vanish; the wife looks like a "twin" to her young lover dancing partner, and she breaks her old husband's heart by refusing to dress for the role of charming young bride. But if lack of empathy brings death, it doesn't thereby destroy art. (pp. 94-5)

The 1960s inaugurate a major shift in Lessing's short fiction, a shift in which "feminine" interiority supersedes "masculine" event. By this time Lessing was an established British writer linked with the "angry young men" on stage and in print. After the Russian invasion of Hungary and the revelations about Stalin, she had left the Communist Party but retained an affinity for the Left; the Suez crisis signalled the evils of Western imperialism, and Lessing marched against the hydrogen bomb. Stories like **"England versus England,"** 1963, about a self-divided working-class Oxford student, continue her earlier "masculine" mode of realistic stories with a clear political point. Even here, however, the focus is more psychological than earlier and more self-conscious about the uses of language. (pp. 95-6)

Issues of generation become more insistent in Lessing's stories of the 1960s, and children figure less as innocent observers of adult corruption than as stakes over whom history is fought. At the same time, these stories show a fear of corruption that may relate to Lessing's being a successful but still socialist writer; these stories do not expose evils like racism but temptations to power over others or despair within oneself, temptations to which the stories, as well as the characters, may succumb. For example, **"One Off the Short List,"** 1963, enjoys its fantasy of humiliating a successful man. The stories of this period also evince profound uneasiness about what Lessing sees as the greedy, security-hungry generation growing up after the war, like the spoiled, ambitious working-class girl in **"Notes for a Case History,"** 1963. Antagonism to the young, of course, produces a very different historical perspective from her earlier one of identification with the young, which implies that the corruption of the old ways can be thrown off by the coming generation. Lessing's stance in these fictions is ironic and unempathic; people's emotions are all the same; we're all a self-deluded and selfish little lot, and she praises herself most for the "toughy" assignments of writing about non-autobiographical, unsympathetic characters. But even when such unsympathetic characters can be understood from the inside—fascists like those in the African stories, or rapists like Charlie from **"One Off the Short List"**—understanding seems circumscribed by wondering what makes some products of corrupt systems stay as they are, others reject the system. This question, necessary for understanding and thereby hoping to influence the attitudes that lead to political and historical change, relates to the artistic issue of the limits of empathy, especially with unsympathetic characters whom the author wants us to reject. One solution that Lessing uses especially in stories focused on the "feminine" is to place decent, empathetic characters in situations where they become incomprehensible, so that we blame the institution for the character's failures, as we do in the case of the woman driven to suicide by her lost identity within marriage and the family in **"To Room Nineteen,"** 1963. (pp. 97-8)

Susan Rawlings, the protagonist of **"To Room Nineteen,"** quits her job to devote herself to rearing her four children and feels the "flatness" of the Lessing woman without a mission: "but there was no point about which either could say: 'For the sake of *this* is all the rest'." Children, pleasant in themselves, are none the less not a "wellspring to live from." This contradiction recurs in Lessing's work as she expands inquiries about female roles into larger, metaphysical questions about life's purpose and meaning. Insuring the continuity of humanity always seems valuable; perhaps it is the only ultimate moral justification, but any particular set of children are barely worth the effort of raising them, and simple continuity seems pointless. In her work after *The Four-Gated City,* 1969, Lessing resolves this dilemma by positing conscious evolution for coming generations who will thus achieve the otherwise discredited socialist goal of progressive improvement. Before this ideological shift, and indicating its emotional source, is the despair that drives Susan Rawlings to suicide.

The story of this period in which the "feminine" line of **"The Trinket Box"** flowers is **"Our Friend Judith,"** a positive portrait of the "free" woman that also shows her limitations and susceptibilities. Unobtrusively it delineates conflicts basic to the Lessing canon, conflicts between heterosexuality and female bonding and between empathy and integrity. If **"A Man and Two Women"** and **"To Room Nineteen"** showed women damaged by marriage and motherhood, **"Our Friend Judith"** appears to champion a woman who is not confined by marriage or motherhood. Orphia Jane Allen, for example, heralds Judith as a modern "hero," a woman who "has found a room of her own" [see excerpt dated 1980].

Published in 1960, the story questions dominant assumptions about gender roles. Its narrator introduces us to "our friend Judith," a middle-aged unmarried woman who lives alone, writes poetry, and adores cats. If these facts lead us to believe that Judith is a pitiable old maid, however, the story satirizes this deduction: "I stopped inviting Judith to meet people when a Canadian woman remarked, with the satisfied fervour of one who has at last pinned a label on a rare specimen: "She is, of course, one of your typical English spinsters" (*Stories*). This label-pinning, a satisfying "click" of recognition which the narrator here condemns, has been one of the special joys of Lessing's earlier short stories.

Judith is a "free" woman, to use *The Golden Notebook*'s term for a sexually active woman unattached to a man; she appears to be completely self-sufficient, content with her life as an English poet, yet still adventurous enough for a research assignment to Italy, where her sensual possibilities bloom in a love affair with an Italian barber that crosses class, national, and religious boundaries. Judith suddenly leaves her lover because he killed the unwanted kitten of a wounded mother cat. This incident reveals to her the "complete gulf in understanding" between them. "It's not a question of right or wrong. . . . It's a question of what one is," she says. But the story's question "of what one is," that is, of the nature of female identity, turns out to be less a critique of conventional female social roles than an exploration of the limits of empathy and therefore of the possibility of identifying with other people through fiction.

The title **"Our Friend Judith"** poses the question from which **"The Trinket Box"** shied away: who is this proprietary, apparently female, first person plural? As is often the case in Lessing's fiction, a "free woman" is attached to other women, even though women's loyalties to men undercut this female solidarity. In **"Our Friend Judith,"** Judith's character rests on a baseline that connects her with her female friends, Betty, a happily married woman, and the narrator, whose own circumstances are unremarked. The narrator won't let other people meet Judith because they won't appreciate her, hoarding her like a special wine only to be shared with the discerning, who presumably include us readers.

The narrator both warns us against judgment and invites us to judge others; people are unfathomable: "one will, of course, never know" the truth of others' lives and feelings, though the story will corroborate one set of judgements rather than another. The narrator's impersonal "one" generalizes our ignorance about other people, and it also foreshadows Judith's style. Like Aunt Maud, Judith sometimes speaks of herself in the self-abnegating third person, saying, "one surely ought to stay in character," and her few lines of dialogue thus conflate her style with that of the narrator whose own life, habits, age, and marital status are hidden from us.

The narrator treats Judith as a mysterious character she only partly understands, one whose actions friends brood over and discuss. Most of the incidents that illustrate Judith's integrity have to do with sexuality and its refusal. She refuses to wear a dress that reveals her beauty because she feels it is out of character for her. Next she refuses to geld her annoying tomcat, having it killed rather than compromising it. Then she refuses to marry a nice old professor, who has been her lover for some time, because it seems unfair to his wife, and finally

she rejects her Italian suitor because he killed a kitten. It might appear that the story reinforces traditional judgements after all: Judith is not a miserable "spinster," but she maintains her autonomy only at the cost of disengagement from deep and messy human emotions. However, the story is more complicated than this.

The narrator tells some of the incidents concerning Judith and reports other incidents observed by her friend Betty. Betty, a conventional married woman, seems to be Judith's opposite, so that the narrator appears as an implied middle between the other two women, who are defined by their relationships to men. Betty reports a conversation in which Judith prefers being a mistress to being a wife but regrets not having children, and this childlessness, unlike her spinsterhood, seems to provoke contradictions both in Judith's character and in the story. Supposedly in Italy on an assignment to research the violent Borgia family of the Renaissance, she can't figure out "what made these people tick" and has to abandon the project. She claims that she doesn't "understand human behaviour" and isn't "particularly interested" in doing so. Judith's integrity here seems defensive rather than heroic. Because she is unwilling to admit change in herself, she refuses to understand other people, and we may infer that this foreclosure of change means she can't understand history, which depends on assessing the similarities and differences between one's own culture and others. Judith's lack of interest in "human behaviour" implies that she can't empathize with other people because she is hiding from herself. She admits she doesn't understand her own reactions in the pivotal incident about the cat: "I must have had the wrong attitude to that cat," she says; "cats are supposed to be independent. . . . I blame myself very much. That's what happens when you submerge yourself in somebody else." Her integrity requires the suppression of intimacy, and her yielding response to the Italian barber violated her sense of herself.

However, the cat incident is not merely an aspect of Judith's reaction to the barber, and details about cats expand disproportionately to the laconic narration of the rest of the story. A ring of sympathetic cats mysteriously surround the birthing cat, then disappear. Without children herself, Judith becomes midwife to the cat, which is too young to have kittens properly, and delivers its breach birth kitten: "the kitten was the wrong way round. It was stuck. I held the cat down with one hand and I pulled the kitten out with the other. . . . It was a nice fat black kitten. It must have hurt her. But she suddenly bit out. . . . It died. . . . She was its mother, but she killed it." Judith phrases her participation in the kitten's birth as a manifestation of her integrity, not of her desire to nurture: "it's not a question of right or wrong. . . . It's a question of what one is." This stance apparently reduces her integrity to the issue of preserving her own style, almost a literary matter, like the scientific, impersonal imagery of the poetry she writes. Moreover, this inviolability implies that she is incapable of change, withdrawing from a situation where her identity would have to reformulate rather than simply reassert itself.

At first **"Our Friend Judith"** seems a simple rebuttal of sexist condescension to unmarried women, even if it makes concessions to the stereotype of the spinster's rigidity. However, the incidents about cats point to deeper relationships among a woman's identity, her capacity to mother, and her capacity to understand herself and others. Contemporary "mothering" theory emphasizes the permeability of female ego boundaries and women's difficulties with psychological individuation from mother-child symbiosis. The mother in **"A Man and Two Women"** who effaces her artistic talent and adult sexuality while psychologically fused with her infant presumably represents a benign, because temporary, exaggeration of this maternal symbiosis. Throughout her fiction, Lessing dramatizes this polarity between fusion and autonomy; Judith, with her exaggerated need for autonomy, apparently rebels against maternal symbiosis experienced as an adult through a dangerous regression related to mothering others. This capacity of women to blur their ego boundaries appears in the odd frame of the story, not just within Judith's psyche; the narrator of the story has no character of her own but sometimes identifies with Judith and sometimes blends into Betty, who exists solely to talk about Judith to the narrator. Implausibly, both Betty and the narrator follow Judith to Italy to find out what she did there. This vague, multiple female narrative persona recalls the "we" speaker of "Aunt Maud" and contrasts with the first person child narrators of the African stories who are autonomous characters, distinct if naive centers of perception.

"Our Friend Judith" does not devalue Judith for being unmarried; rather, it shows her as an admirable new woman. However, its attitudes to motherhood are deeply ambivalent. When asked about having children, Judith replies, "one couldn't have everything," but she sounds completely satisfied with her life as it stands. Then the incident of the kitten exposes Judith's thwarted maternity as the essence of her character. Only in attending the birthing cat does she experience empathy and vulnerability, and only in this episode does she evoke our sympathy. But the incident closes when Judith returns to lonely integrity. The story separates this austere autonomy from both empathy and history. Presumably motherly people like the narrator, her friend Betty, and implicitly, us readers, can understand people as Judith does not because we are willing to risk the boundaries of our selves, and also because we are willing to risk speech with one another. Judith doesn't "understand why people discuss other people": "when something happens that shows one there is really a complete gulf in understanding, what is there to say?" Aunt Maud frightened her nieces by understanding them too well. Judith rejects the threat to her autonomy of understanding others and so having to empathize with their needs and desires, and she rejects conversation that could lead to such understanding: she does not understand people because she does not wish to understand that they can be different from herself. She therefore cannot understand the Borgias: despite her research, she cannot understand history if she is unwilling to understand human differences. Thinking "one surely ought to stay in character," Judith dooms herself to remain static, without a history, a fictional character herself rather than a motherly creator capable of empathy and therefore of change.

"Our Friend Judith," like other Lessing stories about free women, hides both a subtext of female bonding and a feminine fear of closeness. As we have seen, **"The Trinket Box"** uses a first person plural narrative voice that speaks for Maud's female relatives. In *The Golden Notebook, The Four-Gated City,* 1969, and the play *Each His Own Wilderness,* 1959, pairs of women support one another in the face of their traumatic relationships with men. When they have this core solidarity with other women, "free" women can safely withdraw from entanglements with men. When they do not, like Mrs. Rawlings in **"To Room Nineteen,"** they may lose their selves and die. (pp. 98-102)

"Our Friend Judith" cautiously criticizes Judith's fear of entangling emotions. In **"How I Finally Lost My Heart,"** 1963, the female narrator is herself a victim of this fear in an extreme form. After counting up the men she has loved and scorning herself for wanting to attract another, she becomes heart-whole by rejecting emotion altogether, pushing her emotional overload off unto others, including us. She gives her wrapped-up heart to a woman on the subway who is enacting the gestures of "Tragedy. There was no emotion in it. She was like an actress doing Accusation, or betrayed Love, or Infidelity" (**Stories**). The slippery narrative voice of this story makes for uncomfortable reading. The narrator declares herself an everywoman, yet we may shrink from her self-hatred, against the apparent grain of the story, unwilling to share such self-rejection or the assessment of human nature on which it is based. She categorically rejects empathy, intimacy, and understanding, and hence rejects her readers while ostensibly appealing to us. The narrator implies that we are mechanical fools like the subway woman, deadened by our devotion to emotion for its own sake. We also resist identifying with the narrator because her self-hatred does not arise from any vice or folly we despise. We may acknowledge our capacities for evil, but this story asks us to believe that the search for love is fatuous and that a liberating indifference is the best we can hope for, perhaps something like Judith's British equanimity. This feeling that feeling itself is corrupt increases in Lessing's later prose, reaching an effectively unsettling apogee in **"Not a Very Nice Story,"** 1972, and permeating her political discourse of the mid-1980s; in the late 1960s and 1970s this distrust of emotion counterpoints a distrust of reason as well, the arid everyday faculties that close people off to new mental powers.

Passing her heart to a younger woman is not progress but repetition. No saving baby provides the species' justification for emotion in **"How I Finally Lost My Heart."** Here as in **"To Room Nineteen,"** the younger generation is no worthier than the current one, and the idea of history carrying on just as before seems to induce despair. Without the rationale that we build toward a better future, human emotion seems a dangerous delusion; history, a cruel joke. If love does not bind couples to build a better future together, it sinks into narcissistic self-stimulation, a perverse search for immediate sensation that menaces the future. The decent liberals and ex-leftists in Lessing's stories of the 1950s and 1960s suffer disillusionment, their Marxist faith in historical progress eroded, their reason dried to despair. After experimenting with dreams, drugs, and humanistic psychology in the late 1960s, her answer to this despair is spiritual transcendence leading to species transformation, as in the apocalyptic culmination of *The Four-Gated City,* a book that reflects the existential psychology and countercultural experimentation of the late 1960s and early 1970s. (pp. 103-04)

Judith Kegan Gardiner, "Gendered Choices: History and Empathy in the Short Fiction of Doris Lessing," in her Rhys, Stead, Lessing, and the Politics of Empathy, *Indiana University Press, 1989, pp. 83-120.*

FURTHER READING

Brewster, Dorothy. *Doris Lessing.* New York: Twayne Publishers, 1965, 173 p.

　　Biography that traces major plots and themes in Lessing's early fiction.

Brown, Edward Hickman. "The Eternal Moment." *Saturday Review* XLVIII, No. 43 (23 October 1965): 67-8.

　　Favorable review of Lessing's collection *African Stories.*

Dinnage, Rosemary. "Before Her Time." *The New York Review of Books* XXV, No. 14 (28 September 1978): 12, 14.

　　Chronicles Lessing's writing career and reviews her short story canon.

Duchêne, Anne. "The Steps to the Pulpit." *Times Literary Supplement,* No. 3977 (23 June 1978): 695.

　　Considers Lessing's collected stories important for the insight they provide into the author's thought processes.

Hardin, Nancy Shields. "Doris Lessing and the Sufi Way." *Contemporary Literature* 14, No. 4 (Autumn 1973): 565-81.

　　Asserts that Lessing's fiction from the 1970s is influenced by Sufism.

Lessing, Doris. *A Small Personal Voice: Essays, Reviews, Interviews.* New York: Alfred A. Knopf, 1974, 171 p.

　　Important collection of essays by Lessing on her life and writing.

Levine, Norman. "On the Veld." *Spectator,* No. 7086 (17 April 1964): 522.

Mixed review of Lessing's *African Stories* in which Levine deems the earlier, shorter pieces superior.

Perry, Ruth. "Doris Lessing Out of Africa." *New Boston Review* IV, No. 111 (December 1978): 21-2.

　　Discusses characteristic elements in Lessing's short stories.

Sale, Roger. "Playboys and a Working Woman." *The New York Review of Books* XIX, Nos. 11 and 12 (25 January 1973): 42-4.

　　Admires Lessing's ability to "make being dead serious seem so interesting."

Seligman, Dee. *Doris Lessing: An Annotated Bibliography of Criticism.* Westport, Conn.: Greenwood Press, 1981, 139 p.

　　Comprehensive bibliography of criticism on Lessing's canon through 1978.

Sprague, Claire. "The Politics of Sibling Incest in Doris Lessing's 'Each Other'." *San Jose Studies* XI, No. 2 (Spring 1985): 42-9.

　　Examines Lessing's treatment of sibling incest in her story "Each Other," and compares Lessing's work with Thomas Mann's story "The Blood of the Walsungs."

Stitzel, Judith. "Reading Doris Lessing." *College English* 40, No. 5 (January 1979): 498-504.

　　Assesses Lessing's story "Report on the Threatened City," admiring the author's ability to inspire readers to reexamine their initial responses to her writing.

Thorpe, Michael. "*The Grass is Singing* and Other African Stories," in his *Doris Lessing,* pp. 9-18. Essex: British Council for Longman Group, 1973.

　　Surveys themes found in Lessing's African stories.

Joyce Carol Oates

1938-

(Has also written under the pseudonym Rosamond Smith.) American novelist, short story writer, poet, dramatist, essayist, critic, and editor.

One of the most prolific and versatile contemporary American writers, Oates has published myriad novels, short stories, poems, and plays, as well as books and articles of criticism and nonfiction. In these works, Oates focuses upon what she views as the spiritual, sexual, and intellectual decline of modern American society. Employing a dense, elliptical prose style, she depicts such cruel and macabre actions as rape, incest, murder, child abuse, and suicide to delineate the forces of evil with which individuals must contend. The tales in Oates's short story collections are frequently unified through central themes and characters, and while she has written extensively in several genres, most critics contend that her short fiction best evokes the urgency and emotional power of her principal themes.

Oates was born into a working-class Catholic family outside Lockport, New York, and was raised amid a rural setting on her maternal grandparents' farm. She attended a one-room schoolhouse in Erie County, a parallel community to her fictitious Eden County where many of her short stories are set, and displayed an early interest in storytelling by drawing picture-tales before she could write. Oates has said that her childhood "was dull, ordinary, nothing people would be interested in," but has admitted that "a great deal frightened me." In 1953 at age fifteen, Oates wrote her first novel, though it was rejected by publishers who found its subject matter, which concerned the rehabilitation of a drug dealer, exceedingly depressing for adolescent audiences.

Oates began her academic career at Syracuse University and graduated from there as class valedictorian in 1960. In 1961 she received an M. A. in English from the University of Wisconsin, where she had met and married Raymond Joseph Smith, who was also an English educator. The following year, after beginning work on her Ph.D. in English, Oates inadvertently encountered one of her own stories in Margaret Foley's anthology *Best American Short Stories.* This discovery prompted Oates to write professionally, and in 1963 she published her first volume of short stories, *By the North Gate.* Oates taught at the University of Detroit between 1961 and 1967, drawing upon that city's turbulent social and political environment during those years to write her National Book Award-winning novel *them.* In 1967 she and her husband moved to Canada to teach at the University of Windsor, where together they founded *The Ontario Review.* Since leaving the University of Windsor in 1977, Oates has been writer-in-residence at Princeton University in New Jersey.

Oates's first two short story collections, *By the North Gate* and *Upon the Sweeping Flood, and Other Stories,* established her reputation as an innovative and commanding voice in contemporary literature. In *By the North Gate* Oates unleashes an uncompromising attack on the decay of modern morality through a series of stories depicting a nonchalant brutality that, according to Oates, thrives and is often fostered in

American society. In the story "By the North Gate," for instance, an old man is repeatedly taunted by a group of boys who set fire to his field and kill his dog. The stories in *Upon the Sweeping Flood* continue Oates's examination of violence by focusing on the emotional abuse that frequently pervades interpersonal relationships. In "Stigmata" Oates characterizes the dynamics of the Turner family when the father, an emotionally isolated and self-centered individual, bleeds from his hands, feet, and side on Good Friday. All his children, except his alienated son Walt, interpret the incident as a miraculous sign of sainthood. When the bleeding fails to stop, however, Walt is the only family member who understands that his father's suffering is punishment for his having led a life devoid of passion and purpose.

The Wheel of Love is frequently described as Oates's finest volume of short stories. In these pieces, Oates explores the complex and sometimes mystifying emotions of love and the crippling effects that result from a failure to fulfill the potential of human relationships. The female protagonist in the title story, for example, commits suicide when she feels overwhelmingly confined by her husband's love. Oates also examines human sexuality in the critically acclaimed allegorical story "Where Are You Going, Where Have You Been?" Connie, the naïve teenage protagonist, is eager to experiment with sex. Yet, when a young man, who Oates symbolically portrays as the devil, presents himself, Connie slowly realizes the terrifying possibilities of their liaison. In the end, she loses control of their relationship, and the tale concludes with a strong implication of rape. Critics have observed that Oates's use of disturbing images in this story offers poignant new perspectives on the theme of sexual initiation. *The Goddess and Other Women* is another of Oates's collections that is unified by themes of sexual tension—specifically, sexual oppression of women. According to Joanne V. Creighton, Oates avoids the standard literary representation of women as either good or evil, instead delineating women who are trapped in destructive roles and "unliberated into the totality of female selfhood."

Thematic unity among collected stories is especially evident in Oates's volumes *Crossing the Border* and *All the Good People I've Left Behind.* Seven of the fifteen tales in *Crossing the Border* concern an American couple, Renée and Evan Maynard, who move to Canada. These stories are linked by the central motif of borders, suggested by the actual boundary line between the United States and Canada, as well as the psychological barriers that characters in these tales build to isolate themselves from close personal relationships. Interspersed between the Maynard pieces are unrelated stories that adhere to the theme of detachment, thus reinforcing the significance of the Maynard tales. In *All the Good People I've Left Behind,* Oates constructs tales around her characters' egocentric quests for love. Five of the eight stories in this volume's thematic cycle center upon the character of Annie Quirt, a woman who moves from one love affair to the next before finally realizing that each lover is essentially the same, and that the only way to break her succession of failed affairs is to avoid relationships altogether. In two other stories from this collection, Oates depicts collapsed marriages and the resultant feelings of estrangement. Though superficially unrelated to the Annie tales, these two works complement those pieces through parallel themes and character developments. The title story of this volume encompasses and coalesces the themes from the seven previous tales. Further emphasizing the malaise of loneliness and vulnerability that arises from self-centeredness, "All the Good People I've Left Behind" chronicles unsatisfying relations and marriages within a circle of friends, among whom Annie is included. Although the technique of thematic unity in the short story genre is not Oates's invention (Sherwood Anderson and William Faulkner, for example, created homogeneous atmospheres in *Winesburg, Ohio* and *The Unvanquished,* respectively), Katherine Bastian posits that Oates's cycles "rejuvenate [the genre], rendering it new fictional relevance as a medium capable of persuasively expressing a comprehensive vision of our modern predicament."

Critics generally have been impressed with Oates's versatility and prolificness; her profuse output has drawn comparisons to the work of such nineteenth-century writers as Charles Dickens and Honoré de Balzac. Though some critics have condemned Oates for eschewing the contemporary literary trend of "less is more," many commentators applaud her copious efforts, suggesting that her work may ultimately constitute an entire world of fiction. Most critics maintain that Oates vividly represents the underlying tensions of modern American society in her explosive tales, and at the same time stretches the boundaries of the conventional short story.

(For further information on Oates's life and career, see *Con-*

temporary Literary Criticism, Vols. 1, 2, 3, 6, 9, 11, 15, 19, 33, 52; *Contemporary Authors,* Vols. 5-8, rev. ed.; *Contemporary Authors New Revision Series,* Vol. 25; *Dictionary of Literary Biography,* Vols. 2, 5; *Dictionary of Literary Biography Yearbook: 1981;* and *Concise Dictionary of American Literary Biography, 1968-1987.*)

PRINCIPAL WORKS

SHORT FICTION

By the North Gate   1963
Upon the Sweeping Flood, and Other Stories   1966
The Wheel of Love, and Other Stories   1970
Marriages and Infidelities   1972
The Goddess and Other Women   1974
The Hungry Ghosts: Seven Allusive Comedies   1974
Where Are You Going, Where Have You Been?: Stories of Young America   1974
The Poisoned Kiss, and Other Stories from the Portugese   1975
The Seduction, and Other Stories   1975
Crossing the Border: Fifteen Tales   1976
Night Side: Eighteen Tales   1976
All the Good People I've Left Behind   1978
The Lamb of Abyssalia   1980
A Sentimental Education: Stories   1981
Last Days: Stories   1984
Raven's Wing: Stories   1986

OTHER MAJOR WORKS

With Shuddering Fall   (novel)   1964
A Garden of Earthly Delights   (novel)   1967
Expensive People   (novel)   1968
Women in Love, and Other Poems   (poetry)   1968
them   (novel)   1969
Wonderland   (novel)   1971
Bellefleur   (novel)   1980
Invisible Woman: New and Selected Poems, 1970-1982   (poetry)   1982
You Must Remember This   (novel)   1987
American Appetites   (novel)   1989
SOUL/MATE   [as Rosamond Smith] (novel)   1989

MILLICENT BELL   (essay date 1966)

[*Bell is a literary scholar whose works include* The Jargon Idea (*1963*), Edith Wharton and Henry James: The Story of Their Friendship (*1965*), *and* Marquand: An American Life (*1979*). *In the following review, she comments on Oates's various styles and themes in stories from* Upon the Sweeping Flood.]

Three years ago, in a first collection, **By the North Gate,** Joyce Carol Oates laid out a row of stories with a tough, mineral brilliance that dazzled and baffled many readers. They were vivid, brief tales of moments when life suddenly flashes a diamond ray from hidden planes, gives a hint of giant forces locked in dullness, forces for which we have hardly any names, energies that cannot be recognized in terms of the ordinary crystallizations of moral experience.

[*Upon the Sweeping Flood, and Other Stories*] is a second and even superior set that exhibits Miss Oates as a storyteller with a unique viewpoint rooted in her sense of the explosive power and mystery in human beings. It was this same vision, missed by most critics, I think, that also animated her novel. *With Shuddering Fall* (1964) repelled some by its choice of crude and violent materials and by what seemed like incoherence in their combination. Yet Nietzsche's epigram, "What is done out of love always takes place beyond good and evil," which she chose for an epigraph, does help to explain why Miss Oates had refused to write illustrations of familiar moral truisms, choosing to mine instead her own rough truthfulness.

There is a Nietzschean quality in this new collection, even in a couple of stories which deal with received religion, as though perhaps Miss Oates would have us discover beneath the bland distinctions of conventional good and evil a more ambiguous, violent, primitive source of behavior. Visiting her brother, who is undergoing a "spiritual crisis," the sullen elder sister of a seminarian is moved to violent irritation against the spirituality of the gleaming modern seminary. A willful vulgarity, a deliberate ugliness seizes her as she realizes that she is "doomed to faith" by an impulse more primitive than civilized religion.

In **"Stigmata,"** a disbelieving black-sheep son visits his father, in whose hands, feet and side wounds have miraculously opened on Good Friday. The miracle is almost complete, is proclaimed by the church, almost, even, accepted by the son, who at the same time remembers the terrible self-centeredness of the saint he has hated since childhood. Then, when the miracle fails to complete itself, and the wounds become merely a source of pain without transfiguration, he has a more awful insight than ordinary faith could have provided: "You're being punished . . . now you're getting it! God's on the right track!"

Even these, like most of the stories, are difficult to summarize, to reduce to plot and theme, for their power lies in the complex realization of character out of which the paradoxes of feeling "beyond good and evil" seem to stir. In **"The Survival of Childhood"** we see the relation between two brothers, the "simple," wild boy, family favorite, and the sensitive intellectual son who has escaped the "deep country" and become a college teacher. But dreams, visions of anguish, finally suicide, engulf not the inward-looking man whose sensitivity is, it would seem, second-rate, only of the mind. It is the handsome roughneck whom the intellectual son has always envied who really pays the price of sensitivity after all.

That fatal depths of feeling may gush into terrible force out of the most meager and inexpressive personality is, indeed, a discovery that these stories make again and again. Murder, in the terrifying **"The Man Who Turned into a Statue"** or the grotesquely comic **"The Death of Mrs. Sheer,"** is the "unmotivated" manifestation of hidden forces. And in both the title story and **"Norman and the Killer"** we have two more instances of the eruption of violence in characters whose conscious self-mastery has seemed complete until a fatal moment. Indeed, **"Upon the Sweeping Flood,"** with its marvelous description of a traveler caught in a back country flood, is a remarkable metaphor of a man overtaken by unforeseen and resistless inner tides.

For her interest in violence and rural scenes, Miss Oates has been compared with Faulkner, but she has no particular concern with the pursuit of regional myths, no visible preoccupation with historical issues. Yet Sartre's description of Faulkner's concept of present time would fit her concept as well— both see it as "irrational in its essence; it is an event, monstrous and incomprehensible, which comes upon us like a thief." Her characters are sharply defined in an immediate world of present reality without visible past or foreseeable future. It is a world which finds expression in contemporary symbols—the motorcycle, for example, which in **"What Death With Love Should Have to Do"** embodies sex, hate and the desire for ecstasy, all fused into the loud roar, the controlled violence, the death-ride. I am also reminded of D. H. Lawrence, in whom an awareness, similar to Miss Oates's, of complex and unnamed vitalities gives an electric force to his fictional scenes beyond anything even his own theories about life might have accounted for. And young as she is, near the beginning of what she may finally accomplish, Miss Oates is not unworthy of such comparisons. (pp. 4-5)

> *Millicent Bell, "Her Own Rough Truth," in* The New York Times Book Review, *June 12, 1966, pp. 4-5.*

MICHAEL WOOD (essay date 1972)

[*Wood is an English author living in the United States whose writings include a critical study of Stendhal, several screenplays, and a regular column in the journal* New Society. *In the following review, he comments negatively on Oates's characterizations in* Marriages and Infidelities.]

The life people live in the fiction of Joyce Carol Oates is both drab and electric, full of melodrama and yet curiously dull. Life is mysterious, a character thinks in her novel *them* (1969), and then wonders why the mystery is cast in the forms of such diminished people. The suggestion is that melodrama is not nearly as unusual as we think, is hardly extraordinary at all. It is all too often merely a familiar instance of life's heavy hand as a scenarist. We live with it, lose our friends and children by it, but we acquire none of the glamour that seems our due, we are as diminished as ever.

Yet there is also the suggestion in much of Miss Oates's work that the glamour refused to us in reality can nevertheless come to us as an irrational promise, an exhilaration in the midst of mess and despair. We can tell large, important lies to ourselves even when we are at our most diminished, and they are not entirely lies, because they arise out of feelings we really have. Melodrama fuels these feelings, seems to confirm them, but stops short of making them come true, leaves us with a bright mood only, stranded this side of transfiguration.

Miss Oates's talent is for getting this complex perception across without excessive insistence on its significance, and without rigging her fiction too much for the purpose. But the perception has to be whole in order to work—the drabness and the electricity have to be seen simultaneously—and in *Marriages and Infidelities* it appears to have come unstuck, fallen apart into its components. These 24 stories display variously diminished people at various moments of crisis and crack-up, but the diminishments and the crack-ups don't go together as often or as well as they should. The despair in most of these lives is too flat and too clear; these are failed, dim, weary people lacking the energies which call up Miss Oates's best writing—or to put that another way, Miss Oates is not a writer who can make compassion pay off when the objects of her compassion are so incapable of doing anything for themselves.

The crack-ups take the form of melodrama, which is not quotidian fact but an unreal frenzy, the sign of a writer racking her brains for action, wanting to write even in the absence of anything to write about. The frenzy reaches the ludicrous in two or three of the stories, where the girl-friend of a rock singer who has died asks to be present at his autopsy, as his skull is peeled forward and his innards extracted; where an air-hostess held up by a skyjacker has an affair with the F.B.I. man who sighted the malefactor through his long-range lens and shot him; where a kindly, rural dad kills his daughter and dumps her in the river for sullying his secretly cherished, lifelong idea of family honor.

Miss Oates has technical worries too; she experiments with a split-page parallel narrative, keeps insisting on the element of invention in all writing. It is as if she had been reading too much John Barth, or had given a course in Borges and modern fiction once too often. She is groping, then, for themes and forms in far too much of this book. But even her groping is worth looking at, reveals returning preoccupations that will surely blossom into better work.

She inverts the characteristic American myth of love in death, of a love which becomes possible only in the shadow of death, source of the power of countless terrible movies and one or two good ones, and she makes it new, an exploration of the erotic nature of death itself: a man stares at the newspaper photograph of a mutilated and murdered girl, and his wife thinks, "He will never look at me as he has looked at her, at her photograph," a respectable businessman, digging back into his past, recovers the excitement he felt making love to a girl on the bed the girl's mother died in.

There is a concern for immortality, for continuity, for the passing on of personal identity in death, or across death: a girl sleeps with her dying fiancé's friend, thinking her love is immortal, a link in a chain, a last gift from her fiancé to the living world; a writer, in another story, is planning a series of works in honor of certain dead writers—"I want to honour the dead by re-imagining their works, by reimagining their obsessions . . . in a way marrying them, joining them as a woman joins a man . . . spiritually and erotically . . . "

The man who says this wonders whether it is all nonsense or not, but Miss Oates herself offers three of the stories here (**"The Metamorphosis," "The Turn of the Screw," "The Dead"**) as unmistakable allusions and homages to predecessors. There is a haunting anxiety about disappearance, the fear not of dying, not of going insane, but of simply vanishing, not being there. And there is the continuing sense, which gives rise to the rather leaden title, of marriage as both a major human adventure and an oddly automatic event, something that happens to us all and leaves us beached one day in a life that doesn't make any sense and yields no clues as to how we got there.

The writer who wants to marry dead writers thinks of herself as terrified of her ability to survive her fame and all the noise that went with it. There are five or six good stories in this book (**"Love and Death," "29 Inventions," "The Children," "Wednesday's Child," "The Metamorphosis," "Where I Lived, and What I Lived For"**) and one marvelous one (**"Problems of Adjustment in Survivors of Natural/Unnatural Disasters"**) and I have gone on too long about its failures perhaps. But the successes make the failures

seem self-indulgent, a refusal by the writer to know what she knows.

The successes are about survivals—the survival of excitement in the language of a narrative about death and despair, the survival of hysteria by apparently comfortable normal people—and, above all, about the prices of such survivals, about the quantities of reality you have to shut out in order to keep going afterwards. And it seems to me that the form Miss Oates writes in—and is perhaps trying to find her way out of—is itself a technique of survival, a closed, shaped form set up against a shapeless, leaking world. I think the form can probably still be made to work, in important minor ways if not in major ones. But, for that, the form would have to acknowledge its artifice, its estrangement from reality, the degree to which it represents a wish, and not a picture of the world. (pp. 6, 43)

> *Michael Wood, in a review of "Marriages and Infidelities," in* The New York Times Book Review, *October 1, 1972, pp. 6, 43.*

KARL KELLER   (essay date 1975)

[*Keller is an American bibliographer and critic whose works include* The Example of Edward Taylor (*1975*), *a study of the late-seventeenth-century American clergyman and poet, and* The Only Kangaroo among the Beasts: Emily Dickinson and America (*1979*). *In the following excerpt, Keller examines the thematic relationship between Oates's collection* Upon the Sweeping Flood *and the poem of the same title by Edward Taylor.*]

It is surprising to find the poetry of Edward Taylor put to use in creative writings in the twentieth century. He seems too remote and archaic to be of service to the contemporary imagination. Yet like Robert Lowell's poetic uses of the sermons and letters of Edwards (in three poems in *For the Union Dead*), John Barth's fictional use of the poetry of Ebenezer Cook (in *The Sot-Weed Factor*), and Tom Foster's theatrical use of the prose of Paine (in *Tom Paine*), the uses of the poetry of Taylor may now assist in bringing early American literature alive to our own time. (p. 321)

[The] fullest modern use of Taylor is Joyce Carol Oates' for her story **"Upon the Sweeping Flood,"** published in *Southwest Review* for Spring 1964 and subsequently in her collection of stories *Upon the Sweeping Flood*. (p. 322)

Taylor's poem "Upon the Sweeping Flood" serves Miss Oates as the epigraph to the entire collection of stories:

> Oh, that Id had a tear to've quencht that flame
>   Which did dissolve the Heavens above
>   Into those liquid drops that Came
>   To drown our Carnall love.
> Our cheeks were dry and eyes refusde to weep.
> Tears bursting out ran down the skies darke Cheek.
>
> Were th'Heavens sick? must wee their Doctors bee
>   And physick them with pills, our sin?
>   To make them purg and Vomit, see,
>   And Excrements out fling?
> We've griev'd them by such Physick that they shed
> Their Excrements upon our lofty heads.

All of the stories in the collection are related in one way or another to the general theme of Taylor's poem: the disparity between man's desires and his deserts, and his inability to bridge the gap between himself and anything ultimate. In the story **"Stigmata,"** for example, a family fails to understand why their suffering father fails to achieve sainthood. In **"Norman and the Killer"** a man tries to force a confession out of a man he thinks has killed his brother, only to achieve "the numbed, beatific emptiness of one who no longer doubts that he possesses the truth, and for whom life will have forever lost its joy." In **"What Death with Love Should Have to Do"** two wild young people lose their illusions about love and find out that delight and destruction are irrevocably intertwined.

For the title story of the collection, Taylor provides much more—the setting, imagery, tone, and theme. We are in Eden County but a hurricane (Taylor's "liquid drops that Came / To drown our Carnall love") has turned it into a muddy, flooded hell. The main character, Walter Stuart, a man who "had shifted his faith with little difficulty from the unreliable God of his family's tradition to the things and emotions of this world," is making his way home through the storm but insists, in spite of warnings, that he can help save some of those who need to be evacuated. "I know what I'm doing!" he exclaims; "I know what I'm doing!" His presumptuousness shows him to be what Taylor calls a self-appointed "Doctor" of the sick heavens, but his presumptuous efforts to save only serve to "physick" the heavens and provoke something worse. Stuart's intentions are especially presumptuous in view of the fact of the aridity and selfishness of his own life. Though he would presume to save others, there is no substance to his own life; he is less than those he would rescue. (Taylor describes such emptiness thus: "Our cheeks were dry and eyes refusde to weep.") Stuart nonetheless drives to a farm and tries to save an idiot boy and his insolent sister from the storm and flood but instead becomes stranded with them in the farmhouse. When the house breaks apart in the violence of the storm, they float on a rooftop to a muddy hill, together with (other) vermin, rats, and snakes.

Confronting the chaos of the storm, each of the characters relates his faith. The girl is spiritually blind ("I ain't scairt of what God can do!") and the boy spiritually innocent ("See we don't forget about Him"), while Stuart is presumptuous in his piety: "God loves you! . . . Loves the least of you! The least of you!" His monomaniacal self-righteousness makes their stupidity look superior. Stuart cannot accept the chaos of nature (the order of chaos that animates the world) as the natural order of things, but wants it to conform to the form of things in his mind: "He liked to think that his mind was a clear, sane circle of quiet carefully preserved inside the chaos of the storm—that the three of them were safe within the sanctity of this circle; this was how man always conquered nature, how he subdued things greater than himself." This presumptuousness on his part is what Taylor refers to in his poem as the sin that "physicks" the heavens. The danger lies in presuming to be a saint before one has become a man.

The boy and the girl, and especially the elements of nature, do not fit the pattern of things in Stuart's mind, however; the erratic, convulsive actions of the boy and the repulsive attitudes of the girl, like the unpredictable convulsions of nature, alarm him. He has thought that he could save the world from its own throes. He goes about killing snakes like an evangelist chasing evil and then he kills the boy and attacks the girl; they all represent to his mind "the order of chaos" of things in the fallen world, an order that man is helpless to change and will go mad trying to correct. This is a fact that comes as a revelation to Stuart: "In that instant Stuart saw every-

thing. He saw the conventional dawn that had mocked the night, had mocked his desire to help people in trouble . . . He realized that the God of these people had indeed arranged things, had breathed the order of chaos into forms, had animated them, had animated even Stuart himself forty years ago." With his mind shattered (the resulting "Excrements [that fall] upon our lofty heads"), a helpless, humbled Stuart cries out to a white boat approaching, "Save me! Save me!" He has been shocked into a recognition of the excremental condition of man's existence in the world ("the order of chaos") and the foolishness of his attempts to change it (the "mock[ery of] his desire to help people in trouble"). This distorted man has no means for dealing with a distorted world.

Like Taylor's poem, Miss Oates' story is an argument against man's presumptuousness, the lack of what she calls a "self" in the face of the need for "selflessness." Chaos is a fact of man's life, and any effort on his part to be its "doctor" is, because man is "sinful" and himself in need of help, self-destructive. Though Miss Oates misses Taylor's point in the poem about man's excremental existence being God's disciplining gift of grace to man to draw him to Him, and makes a point of her own about the need to gain a *human* sufficiency, no analysis of Taylor's poem comes as close to the heart of Taylor's thought in the poem as Miss Oates' imaginative use of it. (pp. 322-24)

Karl Keller, "A Modern Version of Edward Taylor," in Early American Literature, *Vol. IX, No. 3, Winter, 1975, pp. 321-24.*

ANNE TYLER   (essay date 1976)

[*Tyler is a prominent American novelist and short story writer best known for her novels* Morgan's Passing (*1980*) *and* Dinner at the Homesick Restaurant (*1982*). *In the following review, Tyler discusses thematic tensions in* Crossing the Border: Fifteen Tales.]

In Joyce Carol Oates's [*Crossing the Border: Fifteen Tales*], a strange, erratic man named Blaine writes prose poems that draw unusual conclusions from trivial events. "Housewives pushing carts around the local Kroger's supermarket were participating in evil, bloody, capitalistic acts of violence . . . people who broiled or roasted or otherwise prepared meat were 'disguising blood as gravy' . . . old men playing checkers in the air-polluted park near a nursing home were wrestling to see who would outlive the other. . . ."

It's hard to resist comparing Blaine with Joyce Carol Oates herself. Like Blaine, she sees possibilities for horror in the most innocent and sunlit scenes—even feels that the innocence and sunlight may somehow *constitute* the horror. Her stories tremble on the brink of breakdown, with their bursts of anguished phrases torn by dashes and elliptical dots; her characters (outwardly prim, controlled, well-groomed, remote) may hurtle into madness at any moment. Her scenery is landscaped, neatly pruned, but lunatics and dirty old men are lurking in the bushes.

The horror in *Crossing the Border* revolves around borders, fittingly enough, but the borders are only nominally geographical. Although most of the stories concern Americans in Canada—people whose private sense of disengagement is intensified by their life in a culture half foreign, half familiar—the real borders are personal: the boundaries by which each individual defines himself and, rightly or wrongly, fends off other individuals. Renée, the young American wife who appears in many of these stories, lives on the riverside in Ontario, with a view of American smokestacks in the distance. In a series of brief, shattering scenes, she finds her own boundaries tested, buffeted, and swaying. A would-be lover pursues her by telephone and she listens in bewilderment, staring out the window, "aware of one of the barges edging into the corner of her vision, aware of something happening, something mysterious and alarming. . . . "

What causes the tension in these stories is that the boundaries are not always clear to the characters themselves. Renée's unreasonable panic alerts us to her inner defenselessness, or lack of *will* to defend herself: hearing her lover's knock on the front door, she not only fails to answer but retreats to the bathroom and locks the bathroom door. When we don't share the confusion (as with Renée, who seems formed by some exaggerated notion of vulnerable, hysterical femininity) it can be irritating; we wish she would simply pull herself together. When we do share it, it's stunningly effective. **"Love, Friendship,"** for instance, describes a single man's intrusion on a marriage. The secret horror lies in the married couple's almost, but not quite, unjustified sense of guilt when they evict him from their midst. Although they are technically blameless, they are conscious of the fact that, at one point in their marriage, a third person was a shamefully welcome addition. It's not a clear-cut case of invasion, therefore (which would hardly be much of a story); it's a fascinating tale of blurred and shifting limits, half-truths, semi-complicities.

"The Tempter"—the solidest piece in this collection—is a numbed, bitter old woman's account of meeting the man who wronged her in the past. Seventeen years after his crime (something violent, irreparable, never specifically named) he travels 900 miles to tell her he is dying and to ask her forgiveness. But the woman stands fast: "Should I forget seventeen years of my life . . . should I erase it all, should I give in just because of some bastard telling me lies . . . telling me to go back on my own self ?" There is little confusion in *her* mind, but much in ours: we are tempted, even more than she, though equally repelled by his blue-lensed glasses and slick, checkered clothing. We waver, forced to question; we become, for a moment, characters in a Joyce Carol Oates short story.

The style of this collection is generally lean, rapid, much sparser than that of the earlier stories. Protagonists are stripped to the bare essentials, as if to imply that who they are matters less than what happens to them, or what they dread happening. Or *who* happens, for that matter: the best-defined characters here are those who constitute events—the Polish waitress with her "pale-blond hair braided and wound in two separate coils around the side of her head, exactly like earphones"; the young retarded man with baggy sleeves, his nails clipped neatly "by someone who loved him." These people are vivid, immediate. They stand out sharply in what appears to be a deliberately stark landscape, where the most ordinary event—a phone call from a friend, a boy wading in a river—looms and threatens, and calls for a doubling of the border patrol. (pp. 8, 10)

Anne Tyler, in a review of "Crossing the Border," in The New York Times Book Review, *July 18, 1976, pp. 8, 10.*

GREG JOHNSON   (essay date 1976)

[*In the following review, Johnson focuses on the border motif employed by Oates in her collection* Crossing the Border.]

The novels and stories of Joyce Carol Oates describe a world that is dense, threatening, rife with unexplained terrors; there is often an ominous, shimmering tension which can be "relieved" only through acts of violence, eliminating the accumulated pressures of social as well as inner, emotional conflicts. Her people tend to be of two kinds: those who remain defeated, inarticulate, whose shadowed lives yield up meaning only through the writer's compassion; and those who do perceive faint glimmerings of a world outside themselves, who attempt to learn from their perceptions, and who struggle—with varying degrees of failure—to define the "phantasmagoria of personality" in terms of a world threatened on one side by a crippling social order, and on the other by utter formlessness. In reading *Crossing the Border,* Oates's ninth volume of short fiction, one may note the compassion, intensity of perception, and instinctive sense of form that have been the hallmarks of her previous collections. And yet, as its title indicates, this volume breaks new ground, moving dramatically toward explicit confrontations between human perception and an ultimate existential terror.

Although most of the stories are set in Canada, and a few (including the title story, **"Customs,"** and **"River Rising"**) deal symbolically with an actual border between two countries, Oates's chief concern is with boundaries set up between people, those precarious interpersonal "borders" which her characters cross, courageously or recklessly, and through which they are transformed. What most unsettling about these stories is the inability of Oates's characters to shape their own transformations; even her most intelligent people remain essentially helpless (especially that "intelligent" group she treats with slightly less compassion: academics) and seem utterly at the mercy of unconscious motives, the violence of emotions which they often seem to understand quite clearly. Seven of the stories deal with a young married couple, Evan and Renée, whose flight to Canada—from the husband's failing career, from the stale, rather uninspired marriage itself—represents an escape, yet one which seems doomed even at the outset. As they are leaving America Renée sits "studying the map, folding and unfolding it," and she reflects uneasily upon the nature of their flight, seeming already to perceive its hopelessness:

> The border between two nations is indicated by broken but definite lines, to indicate that it is not quite real in any physical sense but very real in a metaphysical sense: so nature surrenders to politics, as mythology surrenders to physiology. Probably necessary. Better that way. How could love compete with nightmares?

This question, as well as the assertion of wavering metaphysical "borders," sounds the recurrent theme of this collection, and describes the conflict faced by Renée. Once in Canada, she does begin a love affair with a poet ("he had something to do with her loneliness"), yet this relationship seems doomed as well; "[Renée's] daydreams hinted at wonders, but she knew better." Unlike her cynical, rather obtuse husband, Renée at times painfully grasps her dilemma, sensing that she is trapped within the safety and complacency of her marriage, lacking any real will toward change or personal growth. By the final story in the volume, the strong, suspenseful, highly symbolic **"River Rising,"** both Renée and her husband have relaxed back into this complacency:

> [Evan's] voice fell into a rhythm, a sing-song, a lullaby. "No danger . . . never was any . . . I told you, didn't I? . . . should have had faith in me. Now it's safe, we're safe. You see? Never was any danger."
>
> Renée laughed. . . . She could not remember why she was disappointed or why she was relieved or what the danger had been.
>
> " . . . safe, in our own bed," Evan said sleepily. "You see . . . ?"

This assertion of their "safety," which seems comforting (though only temporarily, we may be sure) even to Renée, is a fine ironic closure to a book fraught with dangers, warnings—most of which, like Renée's, are largely ignored.

In all these stories, the protagonists receive continual intimations—usually unbidden and unwanted—from those dark turbulent areas of the psyche which Oates has always explored so effectively. In **"Through the Looking Glass,"** a self-confident Catholic priest—himself trapped within a life-denying complacency—becomes obsessed with one of his students: an aging, recently divorced woman whose desperate struggle against loneliness, whose irritable and uncompromising search for meaning in her existence touch a buried chord in him, forcing him to recognize his own emptiness. Finally he tells her, "Living like this you have no joy in your life," and deluded, "Christlike," he leaves the priesthood to marry her—to save her, of course—and his ultimate fate illustrates forcefully the extent of his self-deception, a quality shared to some degree by all Oates's characters. The finest story in the collection, **"Love. Friendship.,"** traces the relationship between a married couple, Judith and Larry, and their unusual friend Blaine, who is lonely, artistic, tormented, and through whom the couple tries to make contact, vicariously, with a dimension of life from which their marriage shelters them. They fail, of course—Blaine is at times hysterical, unreasonably demanding; the couple suspects him of having stolen money from them—yet their obsession with him illustrates their own circumscribed existence, their unconscious desire to be free, and the crucial sad disparity between "love" and "friendship." Like many of the book's characters, they remain poised at the border between a comfortable marriage and their intense unconscious drive toward this freedom. The story concludes forcefully as Judith muses upon the friendship with Blaine, which has finally reached an impasse:

> We would forget Blaine; we would wish him happiness in his life, if only he would forget us. But he will not surrender us. . . . The telephone may ring tonight. Or in six months. Or in a few weeks. He may telephone us as he did, not long ago, demanding that we arrange for him to get a Canadian visa . . . demanding that we forgive him . . . or he'd kill himself . . . we could enjoy his death agony from our secure smug despicable marriage and our hideout in a foreign country. . . . Traitors, we were. We betrayed him, didn't we? Traitors. Liars. Stepped on him as if he were an insect, cast him aside, tried to forget him. . . . Traitors to their country and to their closest friends.
>
> *Please let us go, Blaine,* I whisper. But he doesn't hear.

Oates's prose style in this book is particularly suited to her theme: at times the pace seems frenetic, almost breathless, yet the artistic control is always sure and firm, the command of naturalistic detail combining effectively with an inchoate, gradually mounting sense of nightmare. Each story moves swiftly, in the natural movement of its characters' perceptions and responses, so that each seems a series of deft illuminations. It is difficult to find fault with such a book as this: the collection as a whole is beautifully constructed—achieving an organic coherence beyond that of the individual stories—and the writing is always skillful, taut, compelling. If the characters are not always admirable, Oates's compassion for them makes their lives absorbing; if events are occasionally unsettling, even grotesque, they nevertheless express the darker aspects of human consciousness with precision, clarity, and truthfulness—and in such coherent expression resides their great value. *Crossing the Border* is one of the most powerful and extraordinary collections we have yet had from America's foremost master of the short story. (pp. 438-41)

> Greg Johnson, "Metaphysical Borders," in Southwest Review, *Vol. 61, No. 4, Autumn, 1976, pp. 438-41.*

SUZANNE HENNING UPHAUS   (essay date 1977)

[*In the following excerpt, Uphaus examines Oates's focus in* Crossing the Border *on cultural and psychological differences between Americans and Canadians.*]

Joyce Carol Oates is an author known for both the quality and the quantity of her work. More specifically, her many novels and short stories deal most frequently with violence, both physical and psychological, and they often feature lower class protagonists. Firmly rooted in the tangible and sordid details of American life, her fiction is typically set in the back streets or the suburbs of specific American cities or in the dreary shacks of the poor white in the South or the American Midwest. Indeed, the particularization of the oppressive details of lower class American life has become Oates' trademark.

It is with some curiosity, therefore, that we turn to *Crossing the Border,* a collection of fifteen short stories, twelve of which are set in Canada. What has this formerly uncompromisingly American writer to say of Canada? For those who know that Oates has long been teaching and living in Canada the volume assumes added importance, for the observations in it can be neither cursory nor superficial. Teaching, as she does at the University of Windsor, located on the U.S.-Canadian border, Oates would seem to be an ideal source of information concerning the cultural differences between the two countries.

This differentiation between the American and Canadian cultures is a topic of inexhaustible interest to contemporary Canadians. We need to have reaffirmed the belief that Canada is not totally Americanized and thus we are eager to learn how outsiders perceive us. We wish such perceptions to reinforce our belief that there are distinctions to be made between the two cultures, perhaps hoping that inherent in the differentiation will be an acknowledgement that the Canadian way of life is somehow superior.

Of course Oates is far too intelligent for such meaningless value judgments. Instead she deals with the individual, the individual American moving to Canada, the individual Canadian academic. Joined, these two themes reflect Oates' private and professional lives as an American who has moved to Canada to teach as a member of a Canadian academic community.

Several of the stories in *Crossing the Border* actually deal with the physical activity of crossing the American-Canadian border. Almost all of the stories, however, can be said to deal with a different "border," the thin and often indistinguishable boundary between the "Canadian" and the "American" cultures. That there are differences, psychological rather than physical boundaries, Oates repeatedly demonstrates. But to pinpoint the exact nature of these differences is far more difficult.

Half of the stories in *Crossing the Border* deal with an American couple, Evan and Renée Maynard who, in the first and title story, are "Crossing the Border" into Canada. The Maynards have emigrated because Evan, a brilliant young biologist, discovers that the U.S. government project for which he has been working, euphemistically called "defense biology," is in fact "manufactured death," disease warfare. Appalled, Evan and Renée emigrate to Canada; at the border they suddenly feel "released, free, blameless." Renée believes that "Crossing the border she will forget," and even her name reflects her hope for "A new life, a new country." And as Renée looks at the map in her lap, a few blocks from the Ambassador Bridge in Detroit, she realizes that the "border between two nations is always indicated by broken but definite lines, to indicate that it is not quite real in any physical sense but very real in a metaphysical sense."

The metaphysical border is what Renée shortly becomes aware of, a barrier which persists in all her contacts with Canadians.

> The Canadians of her acquaintance were always mocking their own city, their own university, their own music and galleries . . . Renée could not quite understand why. She wondered if they were deliberately testing her and other Americans? . . . but no, they were sincere enough. If she pointed out something that was genuinely good, they resented her intrusion; if she said nothing they resented her silence. When they were most fiercely and unreasonably nationalistic—insisting that *their* work, *their* art should supplant Chekhov, and Picasso, and Yeats, and Faulkner, and Stravinsky, and even Shakespeare—she halfway suspected that they were grimly joking and that they wished to be saved, somehow, from the grimness of their joking; but she could say nothing. Their wild, hopeless wishes for insularity, for a kind of cultural protective tariff that would banish competition from the outside world . . . was, in a way, deeply moving to her. But if she was sympathetic with them, they suddenly reversed their positions and said that the nationalistic movement was childish and grotesque and doomed, and they wanted no part of it, they had no intention of becoming involved, *their* art was international.

Cultural conditioning is a barrier to friendship in all of Renée's contacts with Canadians. Even the casual conversation of an ingenuous and cheerful retarded boy is spoiled by Renée's mother's conditioned response:

> "Renée, who on earth was that?" her mother whis-

pered. "He's dangerous. That creature is dangerous."

Renée, insisting that the boy is harmless, tells her mother " 'You're not in the United States'." But Renée herself cannot escape the conditioned expectation of violence which she (and perhaps Oates) associates with the United States. Although she keeps resisting "that ugly self-dramatization panic, that entire way of life" that she "had left behind," in the end she locks her door and spends whole days in the house, frightened. Yet at no point has the boy indicated any dangerous characteristics.

Her increasing loneliness prompts Renée to make a day trip to the United States, from Windsor to Detroit, in the search for friendship. Crossing back over the border to visit some American friends, Renée finds that it is far more difficult than she expected to go back. Her identity as an American has altered since her emigration to Canada; no longer just an American, she has become an expatriate, an American residing in Canada, an object of suspicion to the American government. Crossing the border to the United States, she is subjected to questions and searching by the American customs officers, a process which she finds humiliating, and which causes her to question her own identity. Certainly she lacks the paper identification needed to satisfy the customs officials, and as they question her she becomes increasingly disoriented: "She knew where she wanted to go, but how to get there?"

Even with her Canadian lover (her eventual antidote to the loneliness she feels) Renée senses a barrier caused by her American background:

> Karl, too, disliked her. He claimed to love her, but he also disliked her; she could sense it. He resented something he could not have named. Though he knew very well how poor the Maynards were . . . he evidently believed, unconsciously, stubbornly, that since they were "Americans" they had money. It made no sense of course. Yet it was there, an idea that could not be dislodged. And he believed, just as unconsciously, that they were naturally critical of Canada; that their presence here was a kind of adventure, an interim period in their lives, like camping out.

From the stories about her we see that "crossing the border" has caused Renée's identity to shift and divide: to the Canadians she meets she will always be an American, and her American heritage does create, in her own mind, barriers impossible to cross over. Yet to the American officials she is an object of suspicion, they tell her bluntly that her "Canadian identification was worthless over here." But for Evan, Renée's husband, crossing the border has resulted in an even more disorienting loss of identity. As a young American scientist "he'd had such promise, had earned advanced degrees and worked with famous men—Nobel Prize-winning men." But "What value has a talent without a context to nourish it?" He had rejected the American context, one of incipient violence waged through molecular creatures, but in the Canadian context he has a degrading post as assistant to a less qualified scientist, supplying the menial labor without opportunity for his own research. Even that job is in jeopardy since the budget at the Institute where Evan works is about to be cut and he, as an American, will be the first to go. He realizes that "Whatever identity Evan had possessed had been abandoned on the other side of the border . . . and he had never guessed, had never dared imagine, that the value of a human being might be irrevocably bound up with an entire culture."

The last story in the volume, **"River Rising,"** sees Evan and Renée reconciled by the flooding of the Detroit River, the border over which they had originally crossed. This natural boundary is at the back of their house in Windsor; under normal circumstances the house is well away from the river but during the flood the raging river comes within two or three feet of their home. The house is representative of their marriage, as Evan himself admits by his admonition that Renée, at the height of the flood, "wanted to abandon our house . . . our marriage." The physical reality of this border, which expands and threatens to engulf the couple's marriage and perhaps their very lives, is like the metaphysical boundary which has engulfed their lives, taking their accustomed identities. Thus we return to Renée, in the first story, thinking that "The border . . . is not quite real in any physical sense but very real in a metaphysical sense." Although, as Oates demonstrates, we can clearly "cross the border" in a physical sense, it may threaten to engulf us in the metaphysical sense.

The loss of identity, the loss of recognition afforded one in the United States, occurs to all the Americans who come to Canada in Oates' collection. A dislocation similar to that of Evan and Renee is experienced by Leslie Knox, the main character in **"Falling in Love in Ashton, British Columbia."** Knox is treated with some contempt by Oates, perhaps because he has come to Canada as a tourist with his wife, in an attempt to save their shaky marriage by exposing it to a new, a "foreign," environment. Leslie Knox is a famous novelist in the United States, but he finds he is not recognized in Ashton, British Columbia. While this anonymity is at first exhilarating, allowing him to have a covert affair with a waitress in the Ashton café, once the girl has been bedded he packs up his willing wife and flees South for the border, saying " 'I've seen all of Canada I care to see'."

I mention this minor story only to demonstrate the constancy of the theme in Oates' stories of the American's loss of recognition and identity when he goes to Canada. The same thing happens to the academics in the stories I am about to discuss. (pp. 236-39)

[When] Oates comes to deal with the Canadian academic scene she is writing about what she knows best—and it shows. The two most successful stories in the volume deal with the English Department of a "small, nearly unknown college in southeastern Ontario," Hilberry College. The resulting stories are as close to satire as Oates ever comes, but the satire seems to be aimed at academic communities in general, not specifically the Canadian academic scene.

The first of the two stories deserves to be considered at some length since it is, I think, the most effective story in the collection and it does pinpoint, among other concerns, a weakness within some Canadian academic communities. In **"The Transformation of Vincent Scoville"** a young man moves from Columbia University and New York City—where he has done his graduate work and taught introductory courses—to Hilberry College in Telford, Ontario. He was forced to move there or, as he thinks of it, to "humble himself " by the lack of job openings in his area, Edwardian literature.

Vincent discovers the Canadian faculty is cynically critical of each other, of the college, of the city and "even felt superior to the nation, to Canada itself." One of the department members gives Vincent offprints of his two published articles: "The Decline of the Enjambed Couplet in the Early Eighteenth Century," and "The Return of the Enjambed Couplet in the Late Eighteenth Century." Vincent suffers the usual loss of identity which Oates associates with crossing the border: "The essential Vincent Scoville, intelligent, playful, even at times a little theatrical and frivolous, in the New York style—would slowly die."

Vincent's new identity begins to emerge when the President of the college awards him, their only Edwardian scholar, the project of researching the "Kipling-Horne" papers: five letters written by a niece of Rudyard Kipling, which have been bequeathed to the college. The President of the college is "most eager for the letters to be studied, to be given the publicity in the scholarly and academic world they deserve, and of course Hilberry College will . . . necessarily come in for its fair share of the publicity."

At first Vincent recognizes that the letters, written by Kipling's niece to a lover from whom she eventually parted, are "utterly worthless," and he writes a report in which he states that they have "no value, literary or historical." But Vincent's department chairman intercepts this report before it reaches the college President, and demands that it be rewritten. Vincent's revision is vacuous but less blunt, and receives the approval of the President.

The President of Hilberry College envisions a "Kipling Center" where "scholars and distinguished academics from all over Canada" will gather to study Kipling. Vincent becomes increasingly close to the President, who confides to him that he foresees the end of Western Civilization in the deterioration of the Anglican Church. With his fascination for Kipling and his fondness for the Church of England, the President of Hilberry College is the epitome of those Canadians, often academics, who believe that Canada is still a British colony, and who pride themselves in all things British regardless of worth.

Vincent Scoville gradually comes to believe in the formerly "hidden" significance of the Kipling-Horne letters. He begins to see in them "essential intricacies . . . a certain repetition of key images, motifs . . . curiously enough rather similar to image clusters to be found in Kipling's "The Peacock's Tail." Vincent begins to hate the teaching he formerly enjoyed, and to immerse himself exclusively in the research surrounding the letters. As the story closes he is "working out the prospectus for a monograph of his own which would necessitate a year's leave of absence . . . work in the British Museum and in special collections in England."

It is risky to speculate whether Oates is specifically lampooning Canadian academics in this story. Certainly the phenomenon of irrelevant scholarship is far from being indigenous to Canada. Yet the other theme of this story, the Anglophilia of the college President and eventually of Vincent, seems to me to occur with more frequency in Canadian than American institutions.

The other story concerning Hilberry College would seem to be even less specifically national in its implications. **"The Liberation of Jake Hanley"** traces a process in which a recently divorced member of the English Department spends more and more time, later and later in the evenings, in his office on campus rather than his lonely room. As he does so he discovers more and more of his colleagues doing the same thing; they move hot plates and cots into their offices and meet in the washroom brushing their teeth before bedtime. It is a curiously satisfying monastic fraternity for them. It is obvious that this phenomenon is not peculiar to Canadian institutions. Far from it; what English Department does not have a high divorce rate and a few members who spend virtually all their time in their offices?

The academic stories are thus not as clearly connected as the other stories with the nuances of differences between Canada and the United States; rather, they serve to illuminate the academic scene in general. Yet the fact that they are set in Canada links them to the stories concerning Americans in Canada, and gives **Crossing the Border** a tenuous unity from which only the most general conclusions can be drawn. For example we can safely say that Oates perceives Canadians as having an insecure estimation of the value of their institutions, their art and their country, especially in the presence of Americans with whom they feel defensive. This defensiveness, and the realities of inferior employment opportunities for Americans in Canada, combine to create an identity readjustment for the Americans who come north. Beyond this, the most striking difference between the countries, according to Oates, is one which the reader familiar with her work senses only by implication. There is no violence in any of these short stories; it is impossible to find such a sustained absence of violence in any other volume by Oates. This fact must be connected to Oates' perception of Canada as a nonviolent society, in contrast to the United States where the government employs biologists, like Evan Maynard, to research germ warfare, and where no one, not even a retarded child, is free from the suspicion of violence. (pp. 240-42)

> *Suzanne Henning Uphaus, "Boundaries: Both Physical and Metaphysical," in* Canadian Review of American Studies, *Vol. VIII, No. 2, Fall, 1977, pp. 236-42.*

JOANNE V. CREIGHTON (essay date 1978)

[*Creighton is an American critic who has written several studies of Oates's fiction. In the following excerpt, which originally appeared in* World Literature Written in English, *she examines the sexual and emotional oppression of Oates's female characters in* The Goddess and Other Women.]

Joyce Carol Oates is not usually thought of as a feminist writer. Although women play an important role throughout her fiction, she does not call attention to herself as an articulate woman thinking and writing about women. Nor does she for the most part present women who can articulate their own distress. While often her subjects are intelligent women, intellect is inadequate as a vehicle of self-understanding and equilibrium. All of Oates's characters—men and women—are buffeted about on the vicissitudes of emotion, and liberation, if it is to come, must first be emotional release. Characteristically, her central male characters seek emotional release through violence and her central women characters seek protection from emotion in passive withdrawal. Potential liberation through healthy sexuality is a possibility. But very few of Oates's characters—especially very few women—achieve this liberation. The quote from John Donne which prefaces **The Goddess and Other Women,** "Things naturall to the Species are not always so for the individual," is fittingly descriptive of the unnatural adjustments that most of Oates's women make to their unliberated selves. (p. 148)

Although stories about women are prevalent throughout

Oates's canon, **The Goddess and Other Women** focuses exclusively upon them. Jointly these twenty-five stories offer a composite view of women that is probing but disturbing because nearly all are images of Kali, the dark half of female totality. Kali, the unnamed Hindu Goddess specified in the title, appears in the volume as the garish red-and-yellow statuette in the story **"The Goddess,"** "standing with her legs apart, pot-bellied, naked, her breasts long and pointed, her savage fat-cheeked face fixed in a grin, her many arms outspread, and around her neck what looked like a necklace of skulls." The skulls are symbolic of Kali's destructiveness; she is often depicted as feeding on the entralis of her lovers. But for all her terribleness, Kali is yet looked upon not as evil but as part of nature's totality: life feeds on life; destruction is an intrinsic part of nature's procreative process. So, rather than portraying women as our literary myths would have them, which, as Leslie Fiedler and others have pointed out, almost invariably depict women as either good or evil, Oates presents them as locked into the destructive form of Kali, unliberated into the totality of female selfhood.

Some of the stories in **Goddess** depict pre-teens toying exploitatively and dangerously with a sexuality which they don't really understand. Betsy of **"Blindfold"** and Nancy of **"Small Avalanches"** are young girls who sexually taunt considerably older men. To be sure, the men are culpable. Betsy's uncle has devised the perverse little game of blindfold, and sexual molestation is the aim of the pursuer in **"Small Avalanches."** But Betsy and Nancy adopt with facility the mask of feigned innocence and deliberate naïveté. Betsy accepts the private game of blindfold in exchange for her privileged position as favored niece until their game is discovered by a stranger. Then she totally abnegates all responsibility. She cruelly relishes her uncle's death and exposes his weakness to her mother. At a very young age Betsy is learning the exploitative possibilities of sexual attraction. Similarly, Nancy of **"Small Avalanches"** also enjoys her superior role in the sexual game she finds herself engaged in with the man who follows her in a car and then on foot. Interpreting his pursuit as a childlike game of chase, she giggles and pretends to be ignorant of his aim. When he is overcome by fatigue and heart palpitations, she, like Betsy, cruelly denies any responsibility: "This will teach you a lesson, I thought." She is a young girl learning that sex is an exciting and dangerous game where "winning" is leading on the male and then frustrating him.

A number of Oates's stories in **Goddess** and elsewhere depict a teenage girl on the brink of existential self-definition, as a "good" girl or "bad," as mother's and father's daughter or as an anonymous pick-up. Oates captures so well that point in adolescence when a girl begins to be aware of herself sexually, when she makes tentative gropings out to the world beyond childhood. **"The Voyage to Rosewood,"** for example, depicts a sixteen-year-old, Marsha, who, bored with high school, decides to take a bus ride to another town, anywhere different. Her adventure ends with a beating by a wierd young man, Ike, who had picked her up. At the end of the story her father comes to the police station to take her home. This time she is returned to the parents whom she loves and the world that is familiar, but life is experimental and identity fluid for a young girl like Marsha who out of boredom half-consciously wills her own molestation.

Resilient, daring, and increasingly self-sufficient, Betsy, Nancy, and Marsha approach life experimentally and men exploitatively. In some ways more distressing are the many portrayals in this volume of girls and women who are passive, frightened, withdrawn and unfree. In spite of their inhibition, they are yet capable of unpredictable, violent behavior. They are sometimes the perpetrators, more often the victims of brutal assault.

Sarah of **"In the Warehouse"** is a small, skinny, insecure twelve-year-old who is totally dominated by her taller, bigger, and extremely abrasive girlfriend, Ronnie. Here Oates is depicting one of those inseparable adolescent relationships, but Sarah is suffering in her unwilling bondage to Ronnie. She plans and executes a brutal escape: she pushes her friend down the stairs of an abandoned warehouse, closing off the cries for help of the dying Ronnie. In murdering Ronnie, Sarah is killing off the frightening and unwanted part of herself and the world. Twenty years later, married with two children, living in a colonial house in a comfortable suburban neighborhood, she tries but is unable to feel guilt for what she did. In destroying Ronnie, Sarah has destroyed her own emotional life. Through her desperate act she has secured a kind of liberation and security, but at a permanent cost to herself as a person. She has made a typical bargain of an Oatesian woman. Like Maureen Wendall of *them,* she has paid dearly for immunity.

Frequently, however, these vacuous Oatesian women become disenchanted with their emptiness and reach out for some confirmation of their being. The girl of **"The Girl"** is a case in point. Beautiful and bland, the girl eagerly plays The Girl in the makeshift movie of The Director. Even though the action includes a brutal and unannounced assault and rape and the girl is as a result hospitalized, she holds no resentment towards the sadistic director. Seeing him several months later, her only concern is to be assured that there was film in the camera. Pathetically she needs the film to confirm her identity as The Girl since she has no selfhood as a girl.

Oates is aware of the unlimited capacity for self-abnegation and dedication to men of some women. In **"A Premature Autobiography"** a young girl who is a gifted composer has a brief affair with her one-time mentor, the famous composer Bruer, and then settles for the unchallenging and mundane life of a piano teacher in a teacher's college. Yet when Bruer's autobiography comes out and she is mentioned in one paragraph as a now faceless and nameless girl who Bruer says was talented and devoted to him and to whom "in a way he owes all the work he accomplished at this time (and after this time)," she feels completed and confirmed as a person. Feeling no need now for any further living, she happily embraces her fixed identity as the anonymous woman-behind-the-man.

Often the frustration of women is turned inward in a conscious or unconscious quest for death. So often for Oates's women freedom seems to lie in the deadening of emotion, in the deliberate quest for nothingness. The woman of **"& Answers"** has such a low self-esteem and so completely disparages women as people that she has unwittingly attempted to kill her daughter and herself. The story consists entirely of answers to apparent questions put to her by a psychiatrist in therapy following her car accident in which her daughter Linda was killed. High school tests indicate that she is an extraordinarily intelligent individual, but she insists that she is perfectly ordinary, average, and uninteresting. Having mastered the art of female self-deprication, she is embarrassed by the psychiatrist's attention and theories. She has an exaggerated respect for men's opinions—all men: "I believe anything

men tell me and I always did." But she thinks that "men expect too much" of women, expect "something like God," and women are doomed to disappoint them because they simply are not equal to these expectations. Unknowingly, this mother tried to undo her motherhood because her daughter reminded her too much of herself and she could not bear the thought that her daughter would endure similar emptiness, fearfulness, and anxiety. Oates presents here an extraordinarily painful yet credible portrait of a woman whose wholehearted acceptance of male superiority carries with it a total denigration of herself as a woman.

Not all of Oates's women sit on the brink of suicide or madness, listlessly waiting for something to happen. Some of her most effective stories depict women with successful careers whose professional competence unfortunately is not matched by a similar facility to relate comfortably and wholesomely to men. For example, Jenny, the bright psychiatric intern of **"Psychiatric Services,"** manipulated by her clever patient, becomes entangled in various sexual roles and loses control of therapy. By taking away the gun of her patient she unwittingly plays the role of virgin castrator and confirms his suicidal tendencies, and by listening to his late-night telephone conversations she falls into a pattern of love-play detrimental to their professional relationship. Meanwhile, she plays the dependent daughter to the father-like authority of her superior, Dr. Culloch, who belittles her by sarcastically pointing out how Jenny's feminine responses undermine her role as a professional.

The professionalism of Katherine, the social worker of **"Waiting,"** increases as her emotional responsiveness wanes. She evolves from the eager, concerned girl who takes home the files of her welfare clients and cries over them at night to the efficient casework supervisor who noses out fraud and cold-bloodedly enforces welfare regulations. Katherine's personal life undergoes a corresponding change. Pleading that she must care for her invalid mother, she postpones her wedding until her engagement disintegrates and gradually her life settles into an empty routine. Oates incisively yet sympathetically portrays the encroaching narrowness of the life of this woman who closes off her emotions without ever consciously making a decision to do so. The climax of the story comes when Mr. Mott, a former welfare client, encounters her on the street and gives her a ride home. After she invites him in and makes an awkward attempt to play the role of a woman hosting a male visitor, he slaps and lambasts her for her castrating professionalism in her handling of clients and pours out all his resentment against the welfare system. After he leaves, Katherine cries for the first time in years and realizes "there was a lifetime of weeping before her but she did not know why." Oates understands, as Katherine does not, that she has let her professional self engulf her identity as a woman, that professional competence often extracts a high price in a woman's emotional health, that many men carry an inevitable resentment against any woman who has authority over them, and that many women are hopelessly dependent upon male approval to sanction their self-esteem.

Another professional woman who finds herself in a similar situation is Nora, the university professor of **"Magna Mater."** Nora is a highly respected scholar who is puritanically dedicated to the view that art grows not "out of ordinary, routine, emotional life" but "from a higher consciousness altogether" and who is most happy when emersed in her work: "When she spoke of her work she seemed to move into another dimension entirely—she was not the overweight, perspiring, rather too anxious hostess, but a consciousness entirely freed of the body, of all temporal limitations." But Nora's personal life intrudes upon her professional detachment. Plagued with disquieting relationships with all the males in her life, she yet needs male approval. Her husband has left her for a younger, more attractive woman, and her father, also a famous scholar, is ill and seems to have lost interest in Nora and her work. She finds her precocious, unstable son irrationally demanding and accusing, and his male psychiatrist disrespectfully probing and insinuating. To complete the medley of unhappy relationships, one of her colleagues, Mason Colebrook, nastily tells her of a poem written about her by a former male student entitled "How Leda Got the Swan." Later in a drunken release of inhibition, he pours out all his contempt for her as a scholar and woman. When his wife attempts to apologize for the scene, he yells: "Nora's the same ugly old selfish sadistic bitch she's always been, she won't give a damn, will you Nora?" But Nora feels "again betrayed by a man she had somehow believed . . . might admire her."

Mason's cruel accusation that Nora is an "ugly old selfish sadistic bitch" has some measure of truth. Nora is guilty of being "ugly" and "old"—or at least plain and middle-aged—and women are still most frequently valued or devalued as women on standards of youth and beauty. Indeed, Nora has been attempting to keep her feminine ego intact after her husband's desertion for a twenty-four-year-old woman. Secondly, Nora has been "selfishly" dedicated to her work throughout her life. The "decade of research, teaching, and motherhood madly combined" angered her husband, "not liking the hurried meals, her distraction when he spoke of his work." He is also annoyed that *she* should make the "name *Drexler* known in the Cambridge-Boston-New York area, as if it were truly her name and not his." It is also implied that her father lost interest in her when his daughter's success and fame threatened to outstrip his own. Her son resents her selfish appropriation of a part of her time for her work and for friends, whereas he demands the rights of a son, her undivided attention. Finally, Nora is a "sadistic bitch." In the name of standards of academic excellence, she writes devastating reviews: "she had truly *hated* to say such blunt, irrefutable things about the intelligence that had written it—but unfortunately 'Someone had to do it,' she said." Obviously, she is deceiving herself. She does not hate to do such work, but positively relishes it. She takes a delight akin to the sadistic in destroying her opponent and in the process affirming her own superiority as a brilliant thinker, graceful writer of "loving cadences," and undaunted protectress of excellence Nora's critical reviews are the sublimated expression of her resentment against men. Intellectually if not sexually she has the upper hand, and it wields the castrating knife.

Yet Nora cannot be so easily dismissed with a disparaging diagnosis. She exemplifies the dilemma of the professional woman in Oates's fictional world—if not, indeed, in life. The qualities which make for Nora's success as a scholar—her lucid intelligence, uncompromising standards, aggressive arguments and refutations, cool self-assurance, unstinting dedication to her work—all serve to undermine her image as a woman in the eyes of her family, friends, colleagues, and acquaintances. It is not only Mason Colebrook who accuses Nora of sadistic dominion over men. Her former student sees her as Leda getting the Swan. Her son fantasizes that Nora murdered his father, and he has a recurrent dream where she

deliberately drowns him. But Oates offers a balanced view of Nora. She is intellectually arrogant yet highly competent, sadistic in her reviews yet dedicated to her research and to the upholding of academic standards, self-deceived by others, dependent upon the acceptance and praise of others yet capable of carrying on alone. A "magna mater" she is not, however, except in the most destructive sense of the term. Deeply ambivalent about the messy and distracting role of mother, she is excessively impatient with her son, demanding from him a maturity and rationality which this severely unstable child is incapable of. One of Dennis's recurrent nightmares is that a devouring mouth is in the room with him, a fantasy which—along with his compulsive eating—seems to express his regression to the oral phase of libidinal development, a frequent Oatesian pattern. Overcome with separation anxiety, Dennis's infantile response is to fantasize being devoured, drowned, or abandoned, and he attempts to overcome his fears in part through oral gratification, stuffing his overweight body with Ritz crackers. He is a whiny, obnoxious, cruel child largely because Nora's unconscious rejection and her guilty compensations for it create out of their relationship a sick little society of two, increasingly cut off from other human beings.

Nora has juggled her various roles as daughter, woman, mother, wife, scholar, and professor with uneven success. Despite her professional stature, she will never be a liberated woman. Emotionally insecure, she is too entangled in unsatisfactory relationships with men and too vulnerable to their demands and taunts, praise and criticism, attention and inattention.

With Jenny, Katherine, and Nora, Oates is showing that women's professional successes compound their problems in dealing with female sexuality. There is no such thing as neuter ground in Oates's stories, no professional equality for men and women. Women are different biologically, emotionally, psychically, and socially, and their sexuality necessarily enters into all facets of their lives, complicating their relationships with colleagues, clients, and students. The tensions and adjustments demanded by their professional selves, in turn, rebound back on their personal relationships with lovers, husbands, and children. Women are intruders in the male world of professionalism. The violence and aggression which for men is often a healthy release of emotion, for women—when channeled into the competitive drive for success—effects an unhealthy inhibiting and hardening of emotion. Competent women are often seen by the men with whom they work as usurpers of the male role and by the men with whom they deal professionally as castrators of male sexuality. But the most damaging repercussions of a woman's professionalism exist not in the way that others view her, but in the way she feels about herself as a woman. Sexuality is the ultimate reality for men and women in Oates's world, and women pay for their professional success with precious coin, their stifled sexual identities, and in so doing, they assure their perpetual nonliberation.

But the vast majority of Oates's women do not have careers. Their problem is not in reconciling a variety of selves but in coping with selflessness. They are not desexed by their aggressive intrusion into the male world but devitalized by their acquiescence to female vacuousness. Women are victims of an inadequate model of female selfhood. Those very qualities which are considered to be prototypically feminine—passivity, fragility, beauty, sensitivity, and dependence—

make many women vulnerable to the harshness of modern life, insufficiently resilient to cope with life's unpredictability. The characteristic Oatesian woman sits around waiting for something to happen, or builds an impenetrable wall around the self so that nothing can happen, or consciously or unconsciously seeks her own death. Oates's work offers a disturbing view of women's incapacity as a group to deal successfully with their sexuality and as a result with experience. . . . Most of Oates's women are so emotionally withdrawn that they are incapable of any degree of healthy sexuality. Oates does not offer any ready solutions. Of course, she has not encompassed the full range of female possibility in her fiction. Instead, she is exploring, more intensively than any other writer, the sexual roots of female nonliberation. (pp. 150-56)

> Joanne V. Creighton, "Unliberated Women in Joyce Carol Oates's Fiction," in Critical Essays on Joyce Carol Oates, G. K. Hall & Co., 1979, pp. 148-56.

Any remarks about the short story made by a writer of short stories are bound to be autobiographical, if they are at all honest. For me the short story is an absolutely undecipherable fact. Years ago I believed that art was rational, at bottom, that it could be seen to "make sense," that it had a definite relationship with philosophical inquiry, though its aim was not necessarily to resolve philosophical doubt. Now I am not so sure: certain short stories, certain works of fiction, are obviously more rational than others, more reducible to an essence. But others are mysterious and fluid and unpossessible, like certain people. The short story is a dream verbalized, arranged in space and presented to the world, imagined as a sympathetic audience (and not, as the world really is, a busy and indifferent crowd): the dream is said to be some kind of manifestation of desire, so the short story must also represent a desire, perhaps only partly expressed, but the most interesting thing about it is its mystery. . . .

I am in favor of a kind of monastic seclusion for the writer, absurd as that may sound today—when everyone is urged to plunge into life, as into a communal bath at a "sensitivity session"—and though I believe that the basis of the writing of fiction is the unconscious, that oceanic, ungovernable, unfathomable reservoir of human energy, it is still my deepest certainty that art, if not life, requires intelligence and discretion and transcendence, that we must make the choice of living or telling if what we have to tell is worth anyone else's concern.

> Joyce Carol Oates, from her essay "The Short Story" in Southern Humanities Review, Summer 1971.

JOANNE V. CREIGHTON (essay date 1979)

[*In the following excerpt, Creighton discusses the merits of several of Oates's stories that were adapted from well-known short works by Anton Chekov, Franz Kafka, Henry David Thoreau, and James Joyce. She also interprets stories from* The Poisoned Kiss, *whose inspiration Oates attributes to a fictional Portuguese author.*]

Joyce Carol Oates insists that she is writing within a "strong tradition" of other writers; the most interesting acknowledgment of her debt to other writers is her "reimagining" of famous stories, several of which are collected in *Marriages and Infidelities.* Her "spiritual marriages," as she describes them, to these famous writers are part of the volume's thematic unity as "a book of marriages. Some are conventional marriages of men and women, others are marriages in another sense—with a phase of art, with something that transcends the limitations of the ego." Some stories, such as **"The Lady with the Pet Dog"** and **"The Metamorphosis,"** closely parallel the originals, while others, such as **"Where I Lived, and What I Lived For,"** bear no thematic or formal resemblance to the originals and could only have been envisioned as startling ironic contrasts. Some, like **"The Dead,"** fall somewhere in between these two extremes—stories unique and effective in their own right, which are further enriched by borrowings from and allusions to famous works by other authors.

Oates's **"The Lady with the Pet Dog"** closely resembles Anton Chekhov's similarly titled story. In terms of context and theme this story is similar to many of Oates's others. It focuses on an adulterous affair initiated at a beach resort, supposedly terminated at the end of the couple's holidays, and resumed clandestinely after an encounter at a concert. Chekhov's Yalta becomes Nantucket Island; nineteenth-century Russia becomes twentieth-century America; the man's perspective shifts to that of the woman; and many of the details such as the ownership of the pet dog that conveniently precipitates conversation between the two and the order of telling of the events are changed. Oates embellishes the lives of the characters and the details of the story. The husband now has a blind son with him on vacation; he casually sketches Anna when they first meet on the beach. But the two stories are nearly identical in theme and basic outline. Both record the guilt of Anna over the affair, the unsuccessful attempts to resume separate married lives, the emotional meeting in the concert hall, and the climactic, joyful moment of revelation later in a hotel room—preceded in both versions by the man's sight of himself in a mirror—that this allegedly sinful affair must go on, that it embodies a truth to feeling, a love, that their staid, conventional marriages lack.

Oates's story is less imagined than transposed, less an original creation than an exercise. Her story is effective, but in the same way that Chekhov's is. Her reinterpretation of Franz Kafka's "The Metamorphosis," while still closely paralleling the original, diverges in significant ways from it. Here, however, the result is a story which is undeniably inferior to Kafka's masterpiece.

Oates has attempted to transform the phantasmagoric into the realistically credible, but not without sacrificing the heart of Kafka's macabre fable, the horror and fascination generated by Gregor Samsa's metamorphosis into a gigantic insect. In Oates's **"The Metamorphosis"** exactly what happens to Matthew Brown is not specified. While at work, he feels himself to be the recipient of someone else's dream (the story was originally entitled **"Others' Dreams"**) in which he sees himself as a mummy wrapped in blankets in bed. He drives himself home, feels his legs to be weakening and his body to be emitting a foul odor, and locks himself in his bedroom. It is credible that a man could all of sudden be stricken with an odious illness. In this realistic context the theme is the same as in Kafka's version: the precariousness of a person's being, the inexplicable threat that can strike one unaware. Moreover, Oates again gives her story a contemporary, particularized setting. Kafka's traveling salesman becomes Matthew Brown, a successful, well-dressed, well-preserved, forty-six-year-old American salesman who has been selling new cars for twenty years at Overmeyer Ford. He knows how to handle customers and his mind is filled, even in his illness, with the jargon of his trade.

But what is gained in Oates's story in particularity and realism is lost in the fascinatingly macabre details of Gregor's attempts to cope with his unwieldy insect's body. In spite of his condition, he is pathetically bent on doing his duty; in spite of the ingratitude and selfishness which surface in his employer and family, he bears no malice. In contrast, Matthew is only semiconscious of his condition, his duty, and his responsibility to those around him. Oates employs italicized sections showing the responses of his children and wife; their bewildered, embarrassed, sometimes angry reactions to the illness do not carry with them the indictment often implicit in Kafka's incisive portraits of Gregor's father, mother, and sister. For although Oates adds more characters to her version, they are not vividly realized as separate individuals. The realistic details diffuse and obscure rather than enhance the original thematic statement and characterization. Kafka's story is powerful precisely because it boldly employs the phantasmagoric, which Oates fails to attempt here, although she occasionally does, as in her startling reimagining of a chapter from Henry David Thoreau's *Walden*.

Her **"Where I Lived, and What I Lived For"** is a strange tale which takes the form of alternating monologues of a bloodthirsty pursuer and his prey, a tired and terrified man. One assumes that the pursuer is a figment of the prey's imagination. He admits to making up other fictions to dramatize his life. The cannibalistic, tireless pursuer who obliterates the man's footsteps with his size-thirteen shoes is probably one of his fictions, part of his attempt to give shape to his terror and to his conception of life as an endless chase. What does this have to do with Thoreau? This man is Thoreau's antithesis, a man who does not view time as the "stream" to "go a-fishing in," but as a perpetual chase during which it is "in the nature of the pursued to outwit the millions of people pursuing him, all those people who want to take his place, his possessions, the food he has left uneaten, his wrist watch, his very skin." Oates's character is a man who does not "live deliberately," who does not seek "simplicity, simplicity, simplicity," and who does not "crave only reality" (as Thoreau does), but who only fabricates self-deluding fictions; a man who does not find joy in sucking "all the marrow of life," but who fears a sadistic pursuer who wants to suck the blood out of his life!: "Eating on the run is no good—I'm still hungry—I could seize him and sink my teeth into his throat, why not? Suck his blood so that it runs down my chin, my chest; why not?"

Oates's grotesque tale of the prey's fear of the pursuer's gleeful, bloodthirsty cannibalism is an effective way of dramatizing through phantasmagoria the terrifying, feverish chase that is contemporary life for modern man. To contrast this self-victimized man with nineteenth-century Thoreau highlights a shocking loss of independence, optimism, and joy. The parallel enhances Oates's own highly original story; it serves to broaden its thematic implications.

Her reworking of James Joyce's "The Dead" is also successful. Although the story parallels Joyce's in structure and theme and even duplicates its language and symbolism at times, the situation is quite different. The central character of Oates's story, Ilena Williams, is a college teacher and nov-

elist whose recent popular novel has turned her, somewhat uncomfortably, into a minor celebrity. Gabriel Conroy, her counterpart in Joyce's story, is a newspaper reviewer rather than artist but he, too, as master of ceremonies at his aunts' Christmas party, is temporarily in the public limelight. Both stories focus on the emotional sterility of the central character, which is matched by the stultifying "dead" environments in which they live.

Oates is devastating in her depiction of the staid academic environment of the small Catholic university in Detroit where Ilena is employed before she is dismissed for refusing to pass the master's oral exam of a student, a Brother, who could not define "Gothicism" or the "heroic couplet," could not discuss a Shakespearean sonnet or define the sonnet or give any examples of a sonnet, could not talk about any poem at all or name his favorite poem or name the title of any poem. (The other members of the committee, amusingly and predictably, want to give him a "B"!) Like Joyce's story, Oates's reverberates with references to dead people and things. Ilena's book is entitled *Death Dance*. At parties the assassination of President Kennedy, the waste of Vietnam, the death of the NAACP are mentioned. In the worst moments of Ilena's marriage, her husband urges her to die. She recognizes that the endless pills she takes to cope with life are a kind of "substitute death." As a teacher she preaches the right to birth control and death control, a right which she at times considers exercising. At the end of the story, she learns of the death of her former student, Emmett Norlan.

Ilena, who becomes involved in one sexual liaison after another, feels a progressive deadening of response: "with Lyle her body was dead, worn out, it could not respond to his most tender caresses. She felt how intellectualized she had become, her entire body passive and observant and cynical." Gabriel, in contrast, awakened sexually by the sight of his wife in a pensive mood at the party, desires to "forget the years of dull existence together and to remember only their moments of ecstasy." Gabriel's final epiphanic self-revelation is thus more shocking to him than Ilena's, because he has been until then totally unaware of his emotional sterility, yet Oates's story closely follows Joyce's in the final few pages. Where ill-fated Michael Furey and his pure love for Gretta cause Gabriel to realize that he has been incapable of love, news of the death of Ilena's former student, Emmett Norlan, similarly awakens in her a realization that she has been incapable of responding to the potential communion once offered to her by this student or by anyone else. Recognizing that she has had too many lovers, too much physical contact and too little spiritual communion, she feels that she is fading away, dissolving into death: "Ilena was conscious of something fading in her, in the pit of her belly. Fading. Dying. *The central sexual organ is the brain,* she had read, and now her brain was drawing away, fading, dissolving." The language echoes Joyce's famous description of Gabriel's movement toward death: "His own identity was fading out into a gray impalpable world: the solid world itself, which these dead had one time reared and lived in, was dissolving and dwindling." Similarly, the snow, emblematic of death, lies on Ilena's lover's coat as it does on Gabriel's. As it falls "upon all the living and the dead" in the magnificent ending of Joyce's story, so also does it in Oates's, and Ilena like Gabriel swoons toward death: "Her brain seemed to swoon backward into an elation of fatigue, and she heard beyond this man's hoarse, strained breathing the gentle breathing of the snow, falling shapelessly upon them all."

Of course, Oates's story does not achieve here or elsewhere the sheer eloquence of Joyce's. By using such closely parallel passages, she risks the discrediting of her own achievement, but I think the gamble is successful. Autonomous and well-realized in its own right, the story achieves through its literary parallel a breadth of generalization impossible without it. Ilena shares a sterility not only with the other inhabitants of her world, but also with the lost souls of Joyce's *Dubliners,* and indeed of the world. Oates invites the reader to reexperience the Joycean story, while she offers a contemporary re-creation of it.

Oates's reimaginings of famous short stories take several forms, some more successful than others. It is to her credit that she dares to invite comparison with the most exceptional masters of the short story and even more to her credit that this literary inspiration has so often led her to fashion unique and memorable stories. That she honors these literary precursors in her reworking of their stories is also apparent, since the effort includes a humble recognition that she is writing within a strong tradition which will unconsciously if not consciously shape her own writing. Her humility extends so far in another short-story collection, *The Poisoned Kiss,* that she disclaims authorship altogether!

Oates attributes *The Poisoned Kiss* to an imaginary author, "Ferandes de Briao." She claims to be merely the translator of tales from an imaginary Portuguese work, *Azulejos.* Attempting to explain this curious phenomenon both in a prefatory note and a two-and-one-half-page afterword to the volume, she claims to be as mystified by the inspiration of these stories as the reader is likely to be by her disclaimers of authorship. She explains that she first experienced this alien authorship in November 1970 while she was preoccupied with her "own" writing: "If I did not concentrate deliberately on my own work, or if I allowed myself to daydream or become overly exhausted, my mind would move—it would seem to swerve or leap—into 'Portugal.' There seemed to be a great pressure, a series of visions, that demanded a formal, aesthetic form; I was besieged by Ferandes—story after story, some no more than sketches or paragraphs that tended to crowd out my own writing." Although she claims to "prefer the synthesis of the 'existential' and the 'timeless' of my own fiction" and would like to comprehend and to explain rationally the creation of these stories as merely "metaphorical," she cannot: "But in truth none of it was metaphorical, any more than you and I are metaphorical." An exceptional ability to imagine and to create characters and experiences seemingly antithetical to herself has always been typical of Oates's method. Here she carries the process further; it is not just her characters but "herself" who is imagined as a dandified, middle-aged Portuguese man of culture and letters. Thematically these stories are not alien to Oates's canon.

Just as this volume apparently grew out of a mysterious, uninvited bond to an alien self, the stories explore in a variety of contexts the mysterious and uninvited bonds of various characters to people, places, behavior, and aspects of themselves alien and antithetical to their conscious personalities. Like Oates, her characters often cannot rationally explain or accept their compulsive bondage. The title of the volume effectively capsulizes its theme. It is about the "kiss"—an intimate bond between the self and an "other"—but a kiss which is "poisoned" because this union is so disquieting and inexplicable; it brings the individual so little joy. The title story, a page-and-a-half sketch, presents the theme as bald parable.

The first-person narrator, in his determined effort to unite himself with his loved one, whose kiss haunts his dreams, obliterates the obstacles standing in his way. He pushes one stranger, chokes another, and shoves another into an open tomb. He is angered by their insensitivity to his special destiny, his all-consuming passion, his dangerous and determined quest. Although the brevity and lack of specificity of this sketch (duplicated in a number of other similar vignettes in the volume) are indeed atypical of Oates's other stories, the central matter—a character in the grips of a powerful passion—is at the heart of her fiction. Most of the other stories are similarly portrayals of characters driven by compulsions beyond their intellectual control.

Those which are closest to Oates's other fiction—a group encompassing most of the stories—depict characters whose compulsive behavior is psychologically explainable. Another small group of stories straddles the fence between the "real" and the "spiritual." One could explain the happenings in psychological terms, but since a spiritual realm is posited, a non-rational explanation is also possible. Finally, a few of the stories, the most unusual and atypical, are in the realm of fantasy—illustrative tall tales depicting unrealistic characters and actions.

The first group of stories portrays the compulsive attraction of alien lives, selves, people, or experiences, an attraction which is often "poisonous" because it disrupts the life of the protagonist. A number of these stories show a character's need for a stranger or strangers to confirm his individual selfhood. For example, the young bride in **"Loss"** finds a man watching her regularly as she lounges on the balcony of her apartment building. He responds sensitively to her, creating graceful prose translations of her appearance and movement: *"a woman with a supple, full body, her skin gleaming, a woman absolutely at ease because she wants nothing."* The woman is pleased but disquieted by this attention. She deliberately provokes an angry scene with her husband on the balcony, an act which serves to stop forever the peeping Tomism of her neighbor. His disappearance shatters her self-esteem. Without this flattering reflection and imaginative re-creation she feels lost in her own anonymity: "There was no illumination, no picture of herself. She felt her body grow weak, as if emptying out. She wept because she was going to nothing, becoming nothing."

Some characters like the young man in **"Sunlight/Twilight"** gain identity through a bond to a victimizer. Brutally castrated, he is the recipient of his mother's pity and concern; but he dreams recurrently of his victimizer, to whom he feels bound in love as he does not to his mother. He is like the women in other Oates stories who gain some relief from an anonymous self through their brutalization by an assailant. Sometimes a character finds himself bound to a person whom he intellectually despises, who he feels is unworthy of his obsession, and who exposes a side of his nature that is difficult to accept. Such is Ferandes's obsession in **"The Letter"** with an illiterate, coarse, and slovenly young man to whom he has written a self-incriminating letter. He seeks to retrieve the letter and so to negate this "other" self and its compulsive need to communicate with this brutish young man.

The dictates of another self—an alien personality within the conscious self—are sometimes very strong indeed, as the man in **"Distance"** discovers. The story centers on the London sojourn of a meticulous, orderly, ambitious young Portuguese who works in his country's embassy. Having always lived a busy, complicated, ego-centered life, he is disgusted by the vagrants who reside in the park outside his dwelling. As he finds the anonymity of his life in a foreign country increasingly comfortable, his obsession with the vagrants intensifies. Consciously disapproving of their life-style, he is unconsciously drawn to their anonymity. By the end of the story, his obsession gets the best of him. He buys a bottle of dinner wine, puts it into a paper bag, and gradually approaches the men on the bench. The anonymous self of a vagrant—so alien to his conscious personality—takes over.

Some characters do not fight but welcome their metamorphoses into other selves, but they may be blocked from achieving them. Such is the plight of the "you" of **"The Secret Mirror,"** a man who wishes to be a woman. This transvestite dresses himself lovingly in front of a secret mirror in a bridal outfit, a wig with copper-colored curls, and carefully applied theatrical makeup. He imagines his emergence into the street and the angry, derisive unmasking his appearance would provoke. So, instead of going out, he stares at himself in his secret mirror and weeps as he removes the disguise: "You are . . . weeping for your lost selves, whom no one can return to you, but who have slipped out of the mirror now, untouched, unpursued."

Sometimes the unacknowledged, anonymous self within is capable of criminal and insane behavior. The "you" of **"In a Public Place"** exploits his own anonymity and that of the "public place" by gratuitously murdering an old man who sits on a bench. The boy of **"Patricide"** has murdered his father but has so suppressed the murderous self that he can only recollect disconnected, nonincriminating facts before and after the incident: a "stranger" gives him an ax; it accidentally falls from his hands and cuts his foot; his father lies bleeding on the ground.

All of the aforementioned stories are essentially realistic, even though often particulars are left vague. In some stories, however, a spiritual realm coexistent with empirical reality is at least a possibility. For example, Dr. Thomaz in **"The Cruel Master"** posits a Master who requires him repeatedly to reexperience a dream in which he helplessly observes a young boy being trampled to death by a horse. By the end of the story his repulsion has turned to intense enjoyment. This "cruel master" could merely be the sadistic side of his being which he has always suppressed, or it could be an inhuman spiritual being.

By far the most interesting of this group of stories is **"Plagiarized Material,"** a portrayal of Cabral, a poet and man of letters who gradually realizes that his literary selfhood is being taken over by other younger, more talented writers. He begins by discovering that an appreciative American critic has used language that directly echoes one of Cabral's own unfinished, unpublished stories, in fact employing his exact phrases and words. A short time later, after he works on some poetry, he runs across a poem by a young Polish poet which duplicates exactly the idea of his poem. The grim discoveries continue, all the more galling because his plagiarists "were much younger than he. They would outlive him. They bred shamelessly and multiplied, like the lowest forms of animal life." Finally he wills his own death in protest over the shameful appropriation of his unique selfhood, "cursing all the Plagiarists who sucked his life from him." Obviously, this "plagiarism" of his ideas, thoughts, and words cannot be explained away in rational and realistic terms. The story is either an explicit demonstration of the fluidity of the realm of "spirit," which makes possible the literal invasion and robbery of one's consciousness by other human beings, or it is a witty fantasy, a parable designed to demonstrate that writers indeed draw from the same vast communal consciousness and should be appropriately humbled by the fact, not infatuated with their own egos as is Cabral.

Two other stories in this volume are out-and-out fantasy parables, one depicting a wooden statue of the Virgin Mary with the infant Jesus who suffers a frozen empathy with her worshipers and the other depicting a son of God who rebels against his temperamental and tyrannical Father. **"Our Lady of the Easy Death of Alferce"** is told in the first person by the statue, who feels the intense love that is poured out by her worshipers. Her empathy is so great for the love and sorrow of one boy who fiercely stares at her that a tear forces itself out of her eye. She would like to hide it, but she is "fixed like stone." The boy is startled and then crazed by this miracle—"*For me? For me . . . ?*" It precipitates even greater, almost unbearable, adoration of the statue who cannot move from her frozen posture: "*Don't love me, don't love . . . my lips want to open in a shriek, Don't love me.*" One day the boy's mother pushes through the crowd, shouting at the statue: "*You are not Mary! You are a thief, a murderer!* she screams. *My son was poisoned by you—they have taken him away.*" She attacks the statue, breaking off and carrying away the Child. Although workmen repair it and replace the Child with a wooden doll, the statue suffers in empathy with the sorrowful and tormented motherhood of this woman. Here too is a "poisoned kiss," a tenacious bond of love, which brings only grief and sorrow to the beings it unites.

Similarly, in **"The Son of God and His Sorrow"** a son of God finds his godliness brings only grief and sorrow to the people he helplessly loves. One day while blessing a village and promising a fine crop, he is overcome with the wretchedness of the villagers and breaks down and weeps. This so angers God that he brings a vicious storm which destroys the crop. The son can do nothing to help the people, since his well-intentioned love stirs the vengeful wrath of his temperamental Father:

> I ran from them and my running caused wind to be sucked after me—whirlpools of air struck out at the countryside and devastated it up and down the coast for hundreds of miles.
>
> Where I wept, where I passed, there were floods and tornadoes. . . .
>
> For many days I lay in the dark. I prayed to God to forgive me, to allow me release and death, and in His spite He sent more torments upon me, for if I turned my head too sharply to one side—startled by a rat, perhaps—sudden storms would rush out in that direction, a hundred miles out into the countryside; if I turned my head too sharply to the other side, identical storms would rush out to sea.

Finally, overcome by the grief he is bringing to the world, he gets his mother to help nail him to a cross, and at the end of the story he awaits his own death. The perfect final touch is the hysterical shrieking of God: "*Always this happens! Always my sons disobey me!*"

"The Son of God and His Sorrow," and other stories from *The Poisoned Kiss* such as **"Distance"** and **"Plagiarized Material,"** stand with the finest of Oates's fiction. While the volume is an interesting technical departure from the existential realism of most of her fiction, she has often used the short story as the experimental laboratory for her fiction. Here she performs an experiment which is largely successful, however much she may disclaim authorship. (pp. 131-41)

> *Joanne V. Creighton, in her* Joyce Carol Oates, *Twayne Publishers, 1979, 173 p.*

JOAN D. WINSLOW (essay date 1980)

[*In the following excerpt, Winslow compares Oates's conception of a dual human nature of good and evil in "Where Are You Going, Where Have You Been?" with Nathaniel Hawthorne's treatment of the same theme in "Young Goodman Brown."*]

In her story **"Where Are You Going, Where Have You Been?",** Joyce Carol Oates describes her main character, Connie, in this way: "She wore a pull-over jersey blouse that looked one way when she was at home and another way when she was away from home. Everything about her had two sides to it, one for home and one for anywhere that was not home." This detail tells us that Connie's identity is split: one part of her displays her emerging sexuality; the other part conforms to what the authorities in her life consider proper. Many of Oates's characters have this two-sided quality: one side ordinary and respectable, the other side ruled by such forbidden impulses as lust, violence, and hate. Often in her stories this under-side of the human personality erupts and compels these characters toward obsessive love affairs, cruelty, brutality, and even murder.

Yet society, and its representation in the individual conscience, persistently try to ignore or deny these underground emotions that can lead to sin and crime. To Oates, such refusal to acknowledge that these feelings are a part of human existence is a greater evil than the expression of the forbidden impulses. (p. 263)

This concern with the human tendency to deny the evil inherent in human nature also informs the fiction of an earlier American writer, Nathaniel Hawthorne. It is my contention that these two writers conceive of human personality similarly, and that both show the need to accept its coloring of evil. When Hawthorne's Aylmer is compelled to erase the one blemish on his bride's perfection, the birthmark on her cheek, he causes her death; deprived of this imperfection, she can no longer exist as a human being. The minister Dimmesdale, like Connie, finds it necessary to split his identity: to outward eyes he is the perfect spiritual leader, but underneath his clerical garments the sign of his sin is embedded on his breast.

The respectable, daylight side of human personality differs in the two writers, for the cultures they write about are very different. Hawthorne's community has strong traditions and a vital religion, while Oates's characters live in a society valuing money and social status and define themselves according to media images. The dark side of human nature, though, is very much alike for the two writers: it is comprised of the impulses of sexual passion, violence, cruelty, and hate. Samuel F. Pickering, Jr., writing on Oates, terms these impulses "demons . . . rising from suppressed psychological urges within." Pickering is speaking metaphorically, but in Oates's story **"Where Are You Going, Where Have You Been?",** a demon or devil figure does literally confront the protagonist. Hawthorne's fiction too uses this archetypal figure, traditionally a symbol for the "evil" tendencies within human beings,

notably in "Young Goodman Brown." The convention of an encounter with the devil—really an encounter with a part of oneself—is especially revealing because once a character has projected his emotions outside himself, his attitude toward this subterranean self can be made much more concrete. This discussion will focus on these two tales of an encounter with the devil. They are strikingly similar in structure and meaning. The use of a traditional narrative pattern brings these two writers from different centuries, writing about very different cultures, much closer together and makes the resemblances in their visions easier to see.

In **"Where Are You Going, Where Have You Been?",** the fifteen-year-old protagonist, Connie, chooses to stay at home one Sunday while her parents and older sister go off to a family barbecue. As she is listening to the radio, a gold-painted jalopy drives into the yard with two occupants, a boy Connie has seen once before, who identifies himself as Arnold Friend, and his companion Ellie, who listens to a transistor radio all during the conversation between Arnold and Connie. Arnold invites Connie to go for a ride with him, but she feigns disinterest, uncertain whether she wants to go. As their dialogue progresses, Connie begins to see that Arnold is not what he appears to be: his hair, face, clothes, and talk are all a disguise. As her fear grows, Arnold becomes more and more insistent that she go with him and gradually reveals his power over her. At the end the terrified girl finds herself moving irresistibly toward him and the "vast sunlit" land behind him.

In "Young Goodman Brown," Brown leaves his wife one evening in order to meet a stranger in the forest, apparently to go with him to a witch-meeting. During their conversation Brown's reluctance to proceed onward is gradually overcome by the stranger's assertions and demonstrations that those people Brown has always believed virtuous are journeying toward the meeting in the forest. As Brown is about to be formally initiated into the fellowship of evil, along with his wife whom he finds there, he cries out to her to resist, and all signs of the assembly vanish. Brown returns home to a life of suspicion and gloom, and Hawthorne raises the question of whether the meeting was only a dream.

Although Connie and Goodman Brown at first seem utterly dissimilar characters, an examination of their lives and thoughts at the time of the encounters with these two devil figures reveals a number of meaningful resemblances suggesting that the writers' views of human personality are close. The most significant similarity seems to be the connection with a sexual initiation. The figures appear to the two protagonists at a time in their lives when both are entering into sexual experience. Brown is "three months married," and the marriage, we assume, has discovered in him a sexual passion he had been unaware of before and is having difficulty accepting. Although Hawthorne does not make the sexual level of his story explicit, it has regularly been interpreted in this way. The discovery of sin in the adults of the community whom Brown has always thought virtuous, the loss of respect for his father and grandfather through learning of their involvement with the figure of evil, the fact that Brown and his wife are to be initiated as a couple into this society and will then know of the sin in all other adults, and the phallic suggestions in the description of the setting of this ceremony—all give support to this interpretation. Brown's new participation in sex and his new awareness of his own sexual desire are moving him across the threshold between innocence and knowledge, childhood and adulthood, but this is a movement about which he feels guilty and fearful.

Connie, if we are to take as true Arnold's statement, "You don't know what that is but you will," has not yet experienced sexual intercourse, but she is moving toward it. She spends hours parked in dark alleys with boys she meets. So far these tentative experiments with sex seem to her "sweet, gentle, the way it was in movies and promised in songs." But she is conscious of another attitude about sex, which she rejects: "the way someone like June [her older sister] would suppose." These repressed negative feelings of revulsion, fear, and guilt appear to Connie in the projected figure of Arnold Friend. For Arnold proposes to become her lover and to initiate her fully into sexuality. Connie reacts to this articulation of where she is headed with terror: " 'Shut up! You're crazy!' . . . She backed away from the door. She put her hands against her ears as if she'd heard something terrible, something not meant for her." Her feelings cause her to associate Arnold with danger, nightmare, and death, just as Brown's guilt entangles sex with evil and loss of faith in virtuousness. Connie is moving tentatively toward an experience she—like Brown—will be unable to handle emotionally. Neither protagonist is able to accept the full reality of his/her sexual nature, but instead turns it into something evil and frightening and projects it into the form of a devil.

There are many parallels in the structure of the encounter with the devil in the two stories. For both protagonists, their involvement requires the deception of another person, someone close to them who is concerned about their welfare and who represents the values of society. Both deceive this person as to the truth of their moral and emotional situations and by doing so refuse help in their moral danger. Brown's wife Faith feels strangely anxious over his journey and asks him to stay with her that night. Brown's jocular answer, "What . . . dost thou doubt me already?" is a response which rejects Faith's concern and forces her to accept his departure. Immediately afterward, Brown acknowledges to himself his falseness: "What a wretch am I," and the moral distance he is placing between himself and his wife: " 't would kill her to think it." In Connie's case it is her mother, who, occasionally feeling a misgiving about her daughter's activities, asks at one point, "What's this about the Pettinger girl?" Connie's response, "Oh, her. That dope," deceptively separates herself from a girl we later discover is one of her close friends. Like Brown, she feels regret at this deception: "Her mother was so simple, Connie thought, that it was maybe cruel to fool her so much." By offering false reassurances, both protagonists cover up their true involvement and reject the help of someone who might guide or save them.

In a physical sense, too, both separate themselves from all ties in order to meet with the devil figures. Brown insists he must go on his errand despite Faith's anxiety, and Connie refuses to join her family's outing despite her mother's anger. Thus they isolate themselves from family and community. This isolation is both a necessary condition for the meeting with the devil and a result of previous involvement with evil, for they feel they cannot share this experience with their families. Because they already feel guilty, they cannot permit the openness that might save them.

Both characters seem to have made a preliminary commitment to the encounter. Brown has "kept covenant" in meeting the stranger in the forest. Connie's commitment is less conscious; it seems to have occurred at the moment Arnold first saw her, when, having just been picked up by Eddie, her face was "gleaming" with joy and pleasure. Although Connie believes she has made no engagement with Arnold, he insists that she is expecting him. Despite the commitment, though, when actually confronted with the strangers, both become doubtful and afraid. The ambivalence of their responses can be seen in the uncertain physical movements each displays. Connie hesitates, half inside and half outside the screen door, refusing to go with Arnold but not fully withdrawing herself either. Brown vacillates between a refusal to continue on and an almost unconscious progress deeper into the forest.

The devil figures themselves have both similarities and differences. They are semi-strangers, familiar and yet unknown. Both have supernatural powers and a remarkable knowledge of their victims' lives. They display various characteristics traditionally associated with the devil. Connie's devil is more clearly sexual, taking a form like that of her boyfriends and proposing to become her lover. The numbers of the "secret code" painted on his car also carry a sexual meaning, for they add up to 69. He is linked with death as well: his threats suggest more and more definitely that Connie is to die, and at one point he seems to be trying to reassure her by mentioning a neighbor who has died: "Don't you like her?" The inadequacy of his disguise—the slang just a little out of date, the makeup that covers his face but not his neck, the voice that suddenly sounds just like the announcer on the radio—these details are both comic and sinister, as is his name, Arnold Friend. The knowing reader can easily identify him as the devil, although it is uncertain whether Connie does; for example, his awkwardness in walking suggests to her that his boots are stuffed with something so that he will seem taller, but our imaginations penetrate further and recognize the cloven feet of the devil.

Brown's devil is more companion than antagonist, although he is that, too. He awakens and affirms Brown's doubt of others and his belief that he is irrevocably committed to evil. Much more than Brown, Connie is surprised at the manifestation of her devil. This difference reflects the degree of consciousness each character has of the guilt within him/her. Connie has repressed any doubt, transforming her feelings into the clichés of songs and movies, and is astonished at the consequences of her behavior. She belongs to the line of Oates characters who are overwhelmed by the discovery of the dark instincts within them; Arnold turns out to be more powerful and frightening than she could have expected. Brown, on the other hand, has been struggling with his doubts and feelings of sinfulness more consciously, and therefore is not so alarmed at their materialization in the form of a mysterious stranger.

The endings of the stories are quite different; that is because Oates's story ends at the crisis point whereas Hawthorne's continues beyond it to show the way Brown is affected by his experience in his later life. Once we see that it is the different ending points that make the stories seem to end so differently, similarities in the experiences become more apparent. Possibly, we are meant to understand that Connie dies at the end of her story. But if we do not take the death suggestions literally, they communicate a meaning something like the ending of "Young Goodman Brown": just as a part of Brown, his trust in the goodness of others, dies, so a part of Connie dies, perhaps her innocence or her ignorance of the darker side of sexual passion.

The stories share a dream-like atmosphere and make the suggestion that each protagonist's experience was a dream. Hawthorne raises the question explicitly: "Had Goodman Brown fallen asleep in the forest and only dreamed a wild dream of a witch-meeting?" Oates hints at a similar explanation: Connie has fallen asleep once outside in the sun; she is sitting on her bed "bathed in a glow of slow-pulsed joy" emanating from the music on her radio when she hears the car outside. The question of whether the encounter was dream or reality permits two levels of interpretation for the stories: each can be read as a fantasy about a supernatural encounter and as a psychological analysis of the emotional state which could create such a dream.

The similarities in narrative pattern pointed out here, I believe, reflect a similar theme. Both Connie and Goodman Brown encounter their devils because they have tried to avoid a recognition of the disturbing character of human nature. Connie's experiences with sex must arouse in her feelings of confusion and uneasiness, but she forces her real feelings to fit the stereotypes imposed by songs and movies. She is determined to maintain in her own mind her superiority to the judgment of her mother and sister. Yet the effort to force her experience to fit a false shape becomes too difficult, and her repressed fear, uncertainty, and guilt finally emerge in the shape of Arnold Friend.

Brown holds to an even stricter framework into which he fits his experience of the world: people are either completely virtuous or completely evil. Even the discovery in himself of what he considers sin does not destroy the framework he has erected, for instead of acknowledging that good and evil exist in all people, he merely shifts all those he thought virtuous into the evil category. He resists the allegorical lesson shown him at the meeting when he sees "grave, reputable, and pious people" "consorting" with "men of dissolute lives and women of spotted fame." His reaction reveals the strength of his categories: "It was strange to see that the good shrank not from the wicked, nor were the sinners abashed by the saints." Just as he cannot accept the mingling of these people at the meeting, so he does not accept the lesson of his experience: that human nature is a mixture of good and evil impulses.

Both stories show that when we hide the knowledge of these disturbing impulses from ourselves, their inevitable emergence—whether as devil figure or unexpected aberrant behavior—surprises and terrifies us. If these two encounters with the devil were intended to force the protagonists to move from two-sidedness into a full awareness of themselves, neither seems to succeed. However, by means of their stories Oates and Hawthorne are urging their readers to break free of such categorizing and recognize that violence, lust, hate and cruelty are a part of human nature. (pp. 263-68)

> *Joan D. Winslow, "The Stranger Within: Two Stories by Oates and Hawthorne," in* Studies in Short Fiction, *Vol. 17, No. 3, Summer, 1980, pp. 263-68.*

JOYCE CAROL OATES [INTERVIEW WITH SANFORD PINSKER] (interview date 1980)

[*Pinsker is an American critic, educator, and poet. In the following excerpt from an interview he conducted with Oates by mail over the course of several months during 1980, Oates comments on the short story genre in general and her short fiction in particular.*]

[Pinsker]: *I. B. Singer once told me that he thought some sub-*

jects were more appropriate to the short story than to longer forms. A dybbuk, for example, could not be the protagonist of a family novel. As far as I know, there are no dybbuks in your canon, but would you agree with Singer's general premise—namely, that some subjects are, by definition, appropriate or congenial to the short story?

[Oates]: I cannot agree that some subjects are by definition appropriate or inappropriate to the short story. The "short story" is a highly elastic term, after all. A brief enigmatic dream-tale by Kafka . . . a dense, meditative, slow-moving story by Henry James . . . a spare exchange of dialogue by Hemingway: all can be considered "stories" yet each differs radically from the others. Surely there is a novelist somewhere who *could* write a family novel with a dybbuk as the protagonist? (In fact I may have done this myself, in a manner of speaking, in my new novel *Bellefleur*.)

Not only has criticism of individual short stories or of writers who work principally in this genre been rather sparse, but one gets the feeling that theoretical speculation about short fiction has been almost completely dormant. Am I right about these suspicions? Or put another way: Is there anything new to say about the American short story that Edgar Allan Poe hasn't already said in his famous remarks about Hawthorne's short stories?

Poe's remarks are inappropriate to our time, and in fact to the marvelous modern tradition of the story that begins with Chekhov, Joyce, Conrad, and James. Speculation about short fiction should probably remain minimal since "speculation" about most works of art is usually a waste of time. Those of us who love the practice of an art often hate theorizing because it is always theorizing based upon past models: as such, it must inevitably incline toward the conservative, the reactionary, the exhortative, the school of *should* and *should not*. Genuine artists create their own modes of art and nothing interests them except the free play of the imagination. Poe's and Hawthorne's impulses in fiction were bound up with the allegorical, the static, and the highly romantic (which is to say, the impersonal). How can one draw a reasonably sober line between Hawthorne, James, Stephen Crane, Faulkner, and Hubert Selby, Jr. . . . ? Where would Beckett or Flannery O'Connor or Saul Bellow fit in? It isn't even true that short stories are necessarily *short*.

One of the continuing myths about you is that you write many of your short stories in a single, long burst of creative energy—often nearly all night—and that in the morning there is a manuscript of yet another Oates story. Is this a fact about how you often work, or, rather, yet another version of the romantic artist that simply isn't true?

I would be interested in seeing the story or interview that claimed I wrote all night long—since in fact I have never done so. While it is true that my first drafts are almost always written out—often in longhand—in a single long (and draining) burst of what might be called energy, it is always the case that the subsequent drafts are much longer and are often spread out over a period of time. There are always "first drafts" of stories among my worksheets, waiting for their formalization, their re-imagining. What prompts me to begin work on them at a certain time, on a certain day—I can't know. I have never in my life written anything straight out, not even a five-line poem. I have always revised and edited. (pp. 239-40)

Some of your stories strike me as thoroughly conventional in technique, some as dazzlingly experimental. Nonetheless, one doesn't normally associate your stories with the work of Barthelme, Sukenick, Sorrentio or others of the Post-Modernist school. Could you comment about the whole matter of "experimentation" with regard to short fiction?

"Experimentation" for its own sake has never interested me, but if a story's content—if its protagonist—is "postmodernist" in sensibility, then the style of the story will probably reflect this predilection. As time passes and I become more and more comfortable with telling a linear story and populating it with characters, I inevitably become more and more interested in the structures into which fiction can be put, and the kinds of language used to evoke them. But the degree of sophistication of my protagonist usually dictates the degree of sophistication of the story. I admit to a current fascination with the phenomenon of *time*—I seem to want to tell a story as if it were sheer lyric, all its components present simultaneously. The only "stories" that interest me at the present time are long ones—very long. I am fascinated too with the concept of a "novel" shaped out of a sequence of closely related and intertwined "short stories." (My use of quotation marks indicates my skepticism about literary terms.)

Let's pursue your fascination with "sheer lyric" just a bit. I often have the sense that your fiction begins with a powerful, haunting image (e.g. the pack of wild dogs in Son of the Morning*) that may have surfaced first in a poem (as I think was the case with the dogs) or a short story. Do you generally move from shorter units of the imagination to longer ones, or do other considerations bring an image into its proper structure? In this regard, do you work like a painter, going through a series of "studies" in a subject until you find the one that fulfills the image's potential?*

This is very difficult to answer. I think yes, yes I do begin with an image; then again I think—well, no, I obviously begin with an "idea" (the "idea" of trying to create in words a "religious consciousness" set in a recognizable United States, in the era of Born-Again politicians and other hazzards to one's mental health . . .) The haunting image of the walled garden in *Bellefleur* was one point of departure for that novel; then again, the hope to create a microcosm of America—imperialist, exploitative, yet tirelessly optimistic—was certainly another. I suppose in some queer way the two evolve together: the image, the idea: and create somehow an adequate structure which can do justice to them both.

Perhaps we can move our discussion of the creative process from the writing desk to the lectern. A good many people who teach poetry workshops grumble that their students are unacquainted with poetry generally, that they don't read enough. Indeed, that complaint might also be leveled at those who have more manuscripts of their own to submit than they do individual volumes of poetry on their bookshelves. Do short story writers face similar problems in the classroom? And if so, do they matter as much? At all?

Prose fiction is probably more generally, because more easily, read. In any case I require an anthology of short stories in my workshops, and we spend a fair amount of time analyzing and discussing other writers. This is not only enormously rewarding in itself—my Princeton students are avid readers, and quite enthusiastic—but, as one might imagine, instructive for all. (pp. 241-42)

Joyce Carol Oates and Sanford Pinsker, in an inter-

view in Studies in Short Fiction, *Vol. 18, No. 3, Summer, 1981, pp. 239-43.*

EILEEN T. BENDER   (essay date 1980)

[*In the following excerpt, Bender discusses Oates's treatment of artistic imagination in her collections* The Hungry Ghosts, The Poisoned Kiss, *and* The Goddess.]

Attempting to create "intermediary" art for a time "between the categories," Oates has explored a variety of styles in a prodigious outpouring of fiction, testing traditional forms not only for their continuing relevance but for their ability to serve as vehicles for the polymorphic, fluid human "personality"—for her, the only reality.

Thus, using the devices of both realist and fabulist, sifting through fragments and larger patterned structures drawn from Milton, Yeats, Kafka, Dreiser, Dostoevski, Lewis Carroll, working with ideas from philosophy, psychology, and popular culture, Oates has traced alternative survival routes for her seemingly autonomous characters.

In her recent short fiction, Oates continues to work out what she herself has called a "horizontal" flow of obsessions: her own impulse to experiment, to re-imagine and to redesign certain crucial artistic and social themes and approaches. One continuing concern in her work is the predicament of the artist, who, like herself, is caught between the categories, a medium for both the voiceless and the articulate, registering traditional contexts and an evolving "new" consciousness. Two of her later collections, *The Hungry Ghosts* and *The Poisoned Kiss,* focus dramatically upon this issue, and the related questions of artistic autonomy, originality, and influence.

Unified in theme and setting, both could be considered "fragmented" novels—short stories that, taken together, seem to offer a coherent vision. They also provide insight into the evolution of Oates' own central mythology. Both are at a far remove from the early locus of her short fiction, Eden County. Instead, they explore worlds of esoteric cultivation and decadence. The first, *The Hungry Ghosts* (1974), subtitled "Seven Allusive Comedies," is dedicated to "fictitious and ghostly colleagues whose souls haunt this book." In her version of Joyce's "The Dead," Oates has already indicated that the university has become the testing ground for cultural values; she also suggests how inadequate it is to fulfill its mission. *The Hungry Ghosts,* set at a mediocre, imaginary Canadian university, "Hilberry," exploits a heavily satiric perspective. The "ghostly" presences in these stories include DeTocqueville, Bunyan, Nietzsche, and Booker T. Washington. Unlike the authors who haunt her previous literary "marriages," these allusive influences serve *only* to minimize the pathetic personae: shams, drones, falsifiers, men and women whose only mode of identity is unwitting parody or desperate plagiarism, whose "art" is hackwork, whose "social conscience" is a fraudulent pose, whose criticism is reductive and pedantic. The collection is thus a punning, savage attack on the "influence" peddlers who masquerade as mentors and curators.

Several of these stories seem autobiographical, drawn from personal observation of academic life: the politics of faculty meetings, the egocentric display of professorial ambition, the ambiguities of a graduate student's existence. The final story in the collection, **"Angst,"** dramatizes the absurd and terrifying experience of an artist, Bernadine Donovan, who—under the cover of a pseudonym—attends a session of the Modern Language Association devoted to her own writing. After listening in great discomfort to a series of attempts to trace the influence of Woolf, Proust, and Swift in her work, she is shocked when a strange red-haired woman rises to scream out that the participants are all "telling nasty filthy lies"—about *her*. The real Donovan tries to identify herself as the participants file out in excited conversation, but one by one they look at her name tag, smile "fearfully," and elbow her aside. She must finally accept the imposture. Standing above the crowded Palmer House lobby, Donovan stares down at students, critics, the "angel-fluff of the giant Christmas tree," trying to make sense of the experience:

> Perhaps she was looking for the mad-woman, down there in the crowd. But no, really she was looking for no one. She leaned over the railing, in a kind of peace. After a while she roused herself, as if calling her soul back into her body. It was reluctant to come back: it resisted. But she roused herself, she woke, and called it back.

From the perspective of an artist-victim, Oates offers an ironic critique of the hubristic appropriation and falsification that frequently is mistaken for academic "scholarship." It is also a half-terrified, half-mocking vision of her own ontological insecurity in the face of an army of commentators.

The conception of "demonic" influence is not a gloss, but is at the very heart of another collection of Oates' short stories. *The Poisoned Kiss* (1975) is a collection of twenty-two tales and parables which Oates presents as "translations from the Portuguese." They seem so different from her other fiction in theme, in style, in shape, that some have been accepted and published as if they *were* translations by "Fernandes de Briao." Oates issues a paradoxical disclaimer of authority:

> To the best of my knowledge [Fernandes] has no existence and has never existed, though without his very real guidance I would not have had access to the mystical "Portugal" of the stories—nor would I have been compelled to recognize the authority of a world-view quite antithetical to my own.

The "Fernandes" stories indeed embody an "alien" vision: erotic, fantastic, Latin. Written in a style both controlled and formally elegant, they are rarely more than a few pages long; and although they treat the secret dreams of both men and women, the controlling perspective is that of a masculine fabulator.

"Plagiarized Material," near the end of this collection, is a story not only "by" but about such a fabulator. Named "Cabral," he is born "loving words. . . . miniature as the shrewd iris of the eye," and enjoys a corresponding "miniature fame" for his "intricate works defining themselves as works, words on pages." Forced by his father to study law, similarly programmed by his mother to be the family historian, Cabral is now his own man with a vengeance, writing "iconoclastic prose fiction" in accordance with his literary manifesto of Ortegan anti-art:

> All my writing, as it is written, cancels out the tradition in which it is written. It is not magic, but anti-magic. It has no meaning. It *is*. It is not even "mine." As you read it, it is not "yours"—and, in fact, as you read it, "you" cease to exist. . . . All my writing is designed to prove that "writing" (and reading) does not exist; "writers" (and readers) subsequently do not exist.

> The world releases a stench; the world is not equal to any subjective, specific, anti-magical assault upon it. That is why my writing reduces the world to words and, ultimately, words to silence.

It seems the extreme of artistic solipsism and the antithesis of Oates' own view: this artist is not sanctifying or transforming, but erasing the world. Writing both anti-art and self-serving self-criticism, Cabral preens himself on the purity of his achievement. But in his vanity, he is equally delighted when another literary critic seems to have grasped the essence of his work: "Cabral," an English critic writes, "cancels out morality itself, he obliterates it by the cerebral perfection of *words*."

Cabral wakens from an uneasy sleep the night after he has read and re-read the Englishman's essay, with a sudden insight: the phrases he had found so apt and appealing in the essay are phrases of his own. But this is no ordinary plagiarism, for the "original" phrases have never been published. Still, the critic has uncannily and exactly lifted concepts and language from Cabral's manuscripts; Cabral feels the tug of ontological insecurity. Gaining possession of himself, however, he rationalizes it as pure coincidence: "in fact, like everything, it was meaningless." He throws himself into a new project, a group of "metasonnets." Again, he feels autonomous, controlling and designing not only the poems, but the critical response in advance.

But before these new poems are published (although after they are in galley proof), Cabral runs across another "ugly coincidence"—a Polish poet has now "plagiarized" his images, his very thoughts. Such coincidences multiply:

> There was a single week in January during which Cabral discovered three future works of his, in quite separate journals, each with a title that resembled the titles in his notes . . . each with a clear, logical advancement of the work Cabral had outlined and each . . . superior to the work Cabral himself would probably have written.

Cabral is terrified: "I am/am not losing my mind," he thinks with a characteristic fabulist's ambiguity. But his ego reasserts itself. Madly, he plots revenge on the "plagiarist masters" who have somehow made it their business to anticipate his own writing. He composes a deliberately dreadful essay, "On Humility," using an archaic, forced, pedantic style, hoping to embarrass these "exploiters." But three days later, he reads that very essay, authored not by one of the international geniuses, but by a local writer and failed novelist, who has placed the essay in the feature section of his own newspaper. He realizes all is lost. Bitterly, he thinks, "he has learned humility" himself; his own work is now fit only for the hack-plagiarist.

He has only one more piece of anti-magic left to write: symmetrical, logical, the consummation of anti-art: his own obituary. "His last word was Amen," he writes, ending his "unassailable, perfect" final paragraph; and, indeed "Amen" is the final word of the story, "Plagiarized Material," and the last word of Cabral himself. He has ironically and literally fulfilled one of the premises of his own fiction, obliterating his own identity and ceasing at that moment to exist.

Thus, Oates/Fernandes offers a parable about the essence of fabulation, a series of deft and witty ironies. This meta-fiction is an exposure of the deathliness of meta-fiction itself, the ultimate art of annihilation. In her "Afterword," Oates articulates her own artistic credo as antidote. First, she dissociates herself from the fabulator's practice, insisting she has no wish ". . . to write parables to pierce through the density of existential life. . . . I much prefer the synthesis of the 'existential' and the 'timeless' in my own fiction. I believe that writing should create a world, sanctifying the real world by honoring its complexities." Although these stories are more than a little reminiscent of the parables of a "real" fabulator, Jorge Luis Borges, Oates insists they are not imitations or parodies. She presents them as evidence of the mysterious autonomy of art:

> There seemed to be a great pressure, a series of visions, that demanded a formal, esthetic form; I was besieged by Fernandes—story after story, some no more than sketches or paragraphs that tended to crowd out my own writing. . . . Fernandes retreated when his story seemed complete. A kind of harmony or resolution must have been established, and the manuscript came to an end.

Oates ends her "Afterword" with a series of questions about selfhood, questions also raised by her later novels concerning the powerful forces which, time and time again, she finds exercising their autonomy over the imagination. She returns to *Wonderland's* nagging questions about the nature of the personality:

> Does the brain contain the mind? Does the brain generate the mind? Is the brain a kind of organic mechanism, in each of us unique as a mechanism, through which a larger trans-human or trans-species consciousness is somehow filtered? But what would the nature of this consciousness be, and what human being could even delude himself into imagining he might deal with it, especially in words?

Her own artistic story, unlike the parable of Cabral, is not "perfectly opened and perfectly closed." Refusing the consolation of "metaphor," Oates submits to both gentle seducers and hungry ghosts, seeking to give shape to the mysteries of human character. As medium, as gnostic intermediary, she also continues to recreate and redefine her own vision.

The ironic tales in these two collections focus on the autonomist-artist and an egocentric and masculine self. In contrast, *The Goddess* (1974) is a group of stories centered in the feminine imagination. They are punctuated by violence, dramatizing the characteristic Oatesian awakening from careless passivity; "innocence" is exposed as wanton provocation. Many of the heroines in these stories shrink from a world of aggressive combat, seeking instead an eerie inhuman quietude, the stasis of the stone goddess.

But two stories from the collection seem especially significant in this discussion of Oates' evolving concept of selfhood: **"The Maniac"** and **"Assault."** In both, the heroine has a loss of ego, a mystical insight; in both, the resurgence of the self throws the central figure back into life and human society. Both stories, unlike the tales in *The Hungry Ghosts* and *The Poisoned Kiss*, appear to be realistic in tone, setting, and subject, "existential" narratives.

"The Maniac" is the story of Yvette, a seductive, promiscuous woman in her mid-twenties, seemingly enclosed in a series of fixed structures, defined by society, by her husband, by her apartment, by "state lines, city limits, streets, boulevards, and highways." But Oates reveals that the security of

this world is only a veneer. Yvette has been singled out in the opening scene by a mysterious yellow-shirted man, ostensibly the "maniac" of the title. In a touch reminiscent of Flannery O'Connor, the menacing presence of this anonymous assailant shadows the tale and all its characters.

Filled with foreboding, Yvette is also perennially dissatisfied with her safe confinement; she leaves her apartment and walks defiantly out into the city park, moving past the bounded, tamed, and shaped areas of playground, duckpond, and rose garden toward the wildest place she can find. At first, she feels herself an alien thing in nature:

> She stood in the grass and felt how there was a network of attractions here that somehow excluded her. Every motion of her body violated it. Her thoughts violated it. . . . Helplessly, she would have to think herself back into nothing: a droplet of fluid, a single tear-sized drop in which a universe swam. Yet even that was a disturbance here. . . . In this network of dense, soft, fragrant connections, her own moving mind was a mistake.

She tries to focus on the buzzing, teeming world around her; yet her reverie is disturbed by two young and noisy girls, and she is forced to give in to physical discomfort, a cramp in one hand. Thoughts of her husband invade her mind. The way out seems a pantheistic and erotic fantasy; abandoning herself to the imagined embrace of an anonymous lover, she feels the force of nature itself "coursing through her and using her up . . . an unrepeatable process. . . . In a flood the field seemed to rush in upon her, pushing her aside. In relief, she felt how her mind was snatched from her, torn away."

Now, free of distractions, she feels the blossoming of a beneficent power; what Oates in *New Heaven, New Earth* had called an "incontestably suprapersonal spirit":

> Something seemed to be happening to her . . . her personality was only now emerging . . . another self, her truest self, was only now rising in her . . . She felt that she might be translated into something else. . . . A pendulum seemed to have swung far to one side and was now pausing before swinging back: in that heartbeat of an instant an entire world might spring into creation. . . . And in that instant she felt her body go transparent, utterly weightless, a substance like air that had somehow been given a density through thought, as if someone or something were watching her, buoying her up.

Oates ironically punctures such elation and plunges Yvette back into reality. Only inches away, she suddenly notices the partially-decayed body of a bird. Worse, just beyond the corpse, "someone" is indeed watching her—the man in the yellow shirt. For a moment, she imagines herself a willing victim: "why not press herself into his embrace, was it important enough to struggle?—why, if he wanted her, if he wanted to slash and tear at her, should she hold herself from him?" Only at the last moment, when her mind begins to frame the *words* for such assault, does Yvette recover the power to save herself. As another reminder of reality, a boy on a bicycle, crosses the path. Yvette breaks out of her trance and escapes from an ego-less world she cannot accommodate to the safety of husband, apartment, the constructs of the human, rational intellect. Awakened from her half-absurd Nirvanic dream, the "real" world seems more desirable than "a shape in the air."

"Assault" is the story of an emotionally-crippled, intellectual heroine: a young psychologist, Charlotte Pecora, who moves into her father's deserted house, presumably to ready the property for sale but actually to unravel her own tangled biography. Her vanished parent, a biologist, has left the premises in disorder, scattering enigmatic notes: *"genesis as a spark in a quivering field of energy. . . . A positive correlation between vulnerability of stimulus (female) and potency of response (male). . . ."* He has also left behind a ruined, vandalized garden: "all the windows of the old greenhouse broken in, the frames edged with jagged glass like icicles. . . . Small weeds were growing in the spilled topsoil. Everything looked quiet, cunning, at rest." It is a vision of destructive man and malevolent nature, Eden inverted once more.

Alone, Charlotte reads her father's words, his Skinnerian theories, hearing his "cynical and desperate" voice recounting the unnatural history of man. Like the mechanistic Dr. Perrault in *Wonderland,* he believes "a human being is an inefficient process of animate nature, a means by which certain life-elements are replicated; a far less efficient process than bacteria." He observes that the *"only advantage after millions of years of evolution seems to be increased autonomy with respect to environment but the complicated structures required reduce efficiency."* Charlotte would prefer to maintain a "masculine," scientific, neutral detachment. But as she "efficiently" sorts through her father's possessions, attempting to control her rising terror, memories begin to crowd her mind. Even setting fire to the books and manuscripts cannot save her from her own "outlaw thoughts"; unwillingly, she relives in memory the terrible events surrounding her brutal rape years before. That night, she wakes from a dream of a rapist, certain she has heard someone in the wreckage of shrubbery and weeds outside. It is a dark phantom, assaulting and overpowering her intellectual resistance, drawing her toward a primordial realm:

> She began to sense the presence of another person, another personality, and something in her gravitated toward it, a tangle of dark earth-loving roots, the easeful silence of vegetation, the disconnected sounds of crickets that were all the same sound at differing intervals. Her blood surged darkly, warmly. . . . She seemed to be descending, sinking, into the languid earth-damp life of the wild garden itself. . . . rotted leaves, compost, organic matter of a sweet, foul, tart personality. . . .

She fears she is losing her mind; she feels she is under the sway of demonic influence. She calls out, "Father," but no one responds. Much later, at dawn, Charlotte walks outside to discover the unmistakeable traces of vagrant, "vegetative" lovers who had met in the overgrown garden the night before. A wave of empathic tenderness suddenly overcomes her automatic disgust, transforming her own memories of sexual assault and her self-loathing as well:

> Something flowed through all these lovers in their contortions, shaping their bodies and their straining faces, leaving them helpless and pure. It flowed through them and through her, leaving her pure. Dreamily she recalled the instant of her pain and it seemed to her now an empty pain, the memory of another person.

No longer parroting her father's reductivist masculine critique of humanity but somehow attuned to a beneficent maternal vision, Charlotte feels the force of collective sympathy. All at once she is awed by the power of the self—not only able to name, to analyze, to differentiate, but also able to absorb and transcend the "facts" of experience, able to transmute a woman's pain (the pain of sexual initiation, the agony of birth) into love:

> So her mother had endured pain: all her mothers, her ancestors. They had endured it and transformed it. . . . If she refused to remember the pain, if she chose instead to transform it into something else, who could overcome her? Love, hate, pleasure, pain: they were identical, descending into the firmest, most stubborn layer of life, a vegetative neutrality, and then rearing up again into human life, innocent even in consciousness.

Her vision is a triumph of the feminine imagination and of the artist: an ideal order, born out of the power of communion, which illuminates but does not violate the world. Around her, nature flows, harmonious, continuous, miraculous, and irreducible.

For all of their transforming power, such ego-less "peak" experiences can only be transitory. In an early essay on "The Art of Eudora Welty," Oates had suggested that the "permanence" of the ego poses the essential human paradox: "The tragedy of life is our permanence of self, of Ego: but this is also our hope, in Mess Welty's phrase our 'assault of hope,' throwing us back into life." In Oates' own story, **"Assault,"** the heroine moves beyond the realm of egoistic combat; relaxing intellectual control, she is cleansed of the self-hatred that characterizes so many of Oates' uneasy heroines. Ultimately, she is reborn, able not only to recreate "ordinary" reality, but to embrace it, becoming her own author. "Now," she thinks, "she would forget; she was restless to leave this place, to return to her own life."

In her visionary fiction, Oates affirms, not the necessity of flight, but the transforming powers of the human consciousness, able to accommodate the shocks of the world. **"Assault"** may seem an ironic title for a story that becomes a hymn of praise; but it is clearly akin to Welty's phrase, "the assault of hope." The story is a clue to Oates' larger intentions—her view of the possibilities of redemption of the human spirit in an imperfect and chaotic universe.

In order to clear imaginative space for such a vision of transformation and individuation, Oates has come to recognize that she must chart the self's re-entry into an indifferent or even inhospitable environment. Thus, the work of Joyce Carol Oates continues to dramatize the threat of ontological insecurity that hounds the most protean and resilient human quarry. Her recent short fiction indeed falls "between the categories": providing compelling evidence of conflicting and disparate perceptions of the self and of art in contemporary American literature. (pp. 415-23)

Eileen T. Bender, "Between the Categories: Recent Short Fiction by Joyce Carol Oates," in Studies in Short Fiction, *Vol. 17, No. 4, Fall, 1980, pp. 415-23.*

CHRISTINA MARSDEN GILLIS (essay date 1981)

[*In the following excerpt, Gillis examines thematic developments in "Where Are You Going, Where Have You Been?"*]

Joyce Carol Oates' **"Where Are You Going, Where Have You Been?"** is a story about beginnings and passage points; and it is a story about endings: the end of childhood, the end of innocence. The account of fifteen-year-old Connie's encounter with a mysterious stranger named Arnold Friend, a man who leads his victim not to a promising new world, but, rather, to a violent sexual assault, is a tale of initiation depicted in grotesque relief.

But **"Where Are You Going"** is also a story where spatial limitations are of crucial concern, and to this degree it provides a commentary on stories and story-telling. As Oates transforms elements of fairy tale and dream into a chilling description of temptation, seduction, and probable rape, we are forced to consider the distinctions between fairy tale and seduction narrative, to note particularly that in **"Where Are You Going"** seduction involves the invasion of personal, interior space: ". . . his words, replete with guile,/Into her heart too easy entrance won," Milton says of Satan's meeting with Eve. Women are vulnerable to seduction, and of course rape, Susan Brownmiller has reminded us, for what at first may be seen as purely physiological reasons; and there is little doubt of physical violence when Arnold Friend croons to Connie, "I'll come inside you where it's all secret"; but the seduction motif functions so successfully in **"Where Are You Going"** because the delineation of interior space figured in the female body analogizes invasion at several levels: the domestic space, the state of childhood associated with the home, and, of course, the individual consciousness. (p. 65)

At the outset we may identify **"Where Are You Going"** as an American "coming of age" tale, the main character Connie joining that cast of characters which includes Huckleberry Finn, Isabel Archer, and Jay Gatsby. But while the poles of Oates' story are innocence and experience, the focus of attention is the process of seduction, or the threshold between the two states. The lines are clear, the threshold visually realized. Connie belongs to a tradition of domesticated Eves; for them, Satan's entrance into the garden is replaced by the invasion of a rake like Lovelace (in Richardson's *Clarissa*) into one's private chamber—or ultimately, in the twentieth century, by the approach of the cowboy-booted Arnold Friend to the kitchen door of an asbestos-covered ranch house. The physical world shrinks in this fiction; unlike Eden, the perimeter of a private room, or body, lends itself to specific accounting. Within a described locus, space itself is at issue, the fiction setting up a tension whereby the private is open to both attack and transformation.

Spatial limits are increasingly important in **"Where Are You Going."** If the threshold of the kitchen door ultimately receives the burden of tension in the tale, Oates carefully prepares us for the climactic scene by setting up, at the outset, contrasting *loci*. The very title of the story calls attention to duality: a future (where you are going) and a past (where you have been). The tale catches its main character at a passage point where, it is implied, the future may depend precipitously on the past. More specifically, the two major locations of the tale are the home and family unit it signifies, and the outside world represented first in the drive-in hamburger joint, later in Arnold Friend himself. Connie herself lives in two worlds, even dressing appropriately for each: she "wore a pull over jersey blouse that looked one way when she was at home and another way when she was away from home. Everything about her had two sides to it, one for home and one for anywhere that was not home." Home is the daylight world, a known, established order where so-called parental wisdom would seem to negate the dreams and desires of youth. Connie is, then, constantly at odds with her family, ever looking forward to her excursions to the drive-in, the nighttime

world, the "bright-lit, fly-infested restaurant" which she and her friend approach, "their faces pleased and expectant as if they were entering a sacred building that loomed up out of the night to give them what haven and blessing they yearned for." A mood of expectation pervades Connie's night-time world. Like the light on Daisy Buchanan's pier that promised romance to Jay Gatsby, the bright-lit hamburger joint also holds out new worlds within its "sacred" precincts: cars, music, boys, experience.

Even when the initial meeting with a boy named Eddie—the experience "down the alley a mile or so away"—is over, when the clock has struck eleven and the Cinderella land fades back into the night, a "big empty parking lot [with] signs that were faded and ghostly," even then, the mood of expectation is only temporarily broken. There will be other nights in this midsummer dream-time. Eddie and his like, all the boys, Oates tells us, "fell back and dissolved into a single face that was not even a face but an idea, a feeling, mixed up with the urgent insistent pounding of the music and humid air of July." No wonder that Connie resists being "dragged back to the daylight" by her mother's too-insistent voice. The mother who had once been pretty ("but now her looks were gone and that was why she was always after Connie") sees in Connie a dim outline of her own former self; but the dream perception seems long faded, and Connie's sister June, the only other female family member, is a plain, stalwart sort who has clearly never had much to do with dreams.

But mother and sister are not the villains here, of course, Connie no Cinderella for whom a night-time dream becomes daylight reality. Rather, dream becomes nightmare when Connie first meets at the drive-in Arnold Friend, no Prince Charming, but a man with metallic, cold eyes, driving a bright gold jalopy. And Arnold Friend only pretends to be young. Later, with the discovery of Arnold's true age, Connie will feel her heart pound faster; the bizarre realization that Friend's companion has the face of a "forty year old baby" will cause the teenager to experience a "wave of dizziness." And we are shocked too: there is no fairy tale world here, no romance after all. Friend's first muttered threat, "Gonna get you, baby," is to be played out not in a dream, but in the daylight hours and within a domestic space.

Even before Arnold Friend's entrance into the driveway of Connie's home, reality and dream are beginning to clash dangerously. Connie sits in the sun "dreaming and dazed with the warmth about her as if this were a kind of love, the caresses of love;" but when she opens her eyes she sees only a "back yard that ran off into weeds" and a house that looked small. Arnold's appearance in Connie's driveway on the Sunday morning when her family have gone off to a barbecue only underlines the confused merging of two worlds Connie has always kept apart. She approaches the kitchen door slowly, hangs out the screen door, "her bare toes curling down off the step." Connie is not yet ready to make the step outside.

With Arnold's arrival the significance of separate locations in **"Where Are You Going"** acquires new intensity, and the delineation of space becomes a matter of crucial concern. Connie's refusal to move down off the step bespeaks her clinging to a notion that walls and exact locations offer the protection of the familial order. Now, with Friend's initial invitation to join him and his friend in the car, and with his assertion that he has placed his "sign" upon her, Connie moves further back into the kitchen: she "let the screen door close and stood perfectly still inside it." From the familiar kitchen space, she attempts to make sense of her experience. But the mirror sunglasses make it impossible for the girl to see what Friend is looking at; the enigmatic smile tells nothing; and even as she attempts to amass assorted physical data on her visitor, she finds that "all these things did not come together."

Then the familiar and the private begin to give way to the unexpected visitor. Having realized the true age of the two intruders and being told that they will not leave until she agrees to go along with them, Connie has the sense that Friend "had driven up the driveway all right but had come from nowhere before and belonged nowhere . . . everything that was so familiar to her was only half real." The drawing of the magical sign, a sign of ownership over her, suggests control over her own private consciousness. Connie wonders how Friend knows her name; but later, much more troubling, is his knowledge that her father is not coming back soon, that the family is at the picnic. Connie finds herself sharing a perhaps imaginary, perhaps real, view of the barbecue. Friend refers to a "fat woman" at the barbecue:

> "What fat woman?" Connie cried.
>
> "How do I know what fat woman. I don't know every goddamn fat woman in the world!" Arnold Friend laughed.
>
> "Oh, that's Mrs. Hornsby. . . . Who invited her?" Connie said. She felt a little lightheaded. Her breath was coming quickly.

And penetration of consciousness is only the preamble to penetration in a sexual sense: "And I'll come inside you where it's all secret and you'll give in to me and you'll love me—" says Friend. The disorder implied in Friend's knowing too much, more than can be rationally explained, is now to be played out in trespassing upon the body itself. A limit has been passed. Connie does not want to hear these words; she "backed away from the door. She put her hand up against her ears as if she'd heard something terrible."

Connie retreats further within the kitchen, but the space of the room also loses familiarity as interior worlds break down. Just as earlier in the morning the adolescent has begun to see her own home as small, now the kitchen looked "like a place she had never seen before, some room she had run inside but that wasn't good enough, wasn't going to help her." Doors too become meaningless. "But why lock [the door]?" Friend taunts; "it's just a screen door, It's just nothing." Friend is still articulating spatial limits—"[I] promise not to come in unless you touch the phone"—but such limits no longer have meaning. The statement, "I want you," the words of the teenager's love song, now connote a world where the limits around self are not viable. The breaking of a limitation and the opening of a door . . . destroy both individual innocence and the order of the innocent's world. "It's all over for you here," Friend tells Connie. Crying out for the mother that will not come, Connie feels not the protective parental embrace, but rather a feeling in her lungs as if Friend "was stabbing her . . . with no tenderness." And then the horrible statement muttered in a stage voice, the statement which spells the end of a world: "The place where you came from ain't there any more, and where you had in mind to go is cancelled out. This place you are now—inside your daddy's house—is nothing but a cardboard box I can knock down any time."

Obliteration through violent assault is multi-dimensional in **"Where Are You Going."** The domestic space, a house as the nurturing place of childhood, yields to attack from outside no less than the body, consciousness, even "heart" of the girl is forced to give way. Observing that the house looks solid, Friend tells Connie, "Now, put your hand on your heart, honey. . . . That feels solid too but we know better." And when Connie feels her own pounding heart, "she thought for the first time in her life that it was nothing that was hers, that belonged to her." If **"Where Are You Going"** is the story of the end of childhood, the end of romance, the invasion and probable destruction of private and self-contained space provide one important definition of the end of innocence. Friend's taking over the "heart" of the young girl so that "it was nothing that was hers" spells a conquest of both space and will: his intimation that he will wait for and then kill the family if Connie does not go with him is the more terrible because of Connie's own ambivalent feelings about her family, the breaking in the child's trust in her parents. Finally, the satanic visitor's incantation, "We'll go out to a nice field, out in the country where it smells so nice and it's sunny," represents not only a chilling perversion of pastoral—for the words of Satan can lead not toward, but only away from, Eden—but a ritualized statement that all of the walls defining an individual self have been destroyed. Connie's pushing open the screen door to go off with Arnold Friend, the ultimate yielding, signifies that indeed the place she came from "ain't there any more." (pp. 66-70)

> *Christina Marsden Gillis, " 'Where Are You Going, Where Have You Been?': Seduction, Space, and a Fictional Mode," in* Studies in Short Fiction, *Vol. 18, No. 1, Winter, 1981, pp. 65-70.*

SANFORD PINSKER (essay date 1982)

[*In the following excerpt from a review of* A Sentimental Education, *Pinsker comments on Oates's treatment of love and violence in her stories.*]

A Sentimental Education, Joyce Carol Oates' latest collection of short fiction, continues to explore that region where love and violence threaten to become synonymous, infinitely interchangeable terms. She has, of course, visited that strange land of the heart before. If William Faulkner staked out Yoknapataphna County as his congenial turf, Joyce Carol Oates seems bent on appropriating *disturbing passions* onto herself. Only the social structures and physical settings change; Miss Oates' deeper truths about desperate needs and tragic misunderstandings continue unabated. We begin reading her newest book knowing full well what we're in for.

A Sentimental Education adds six more installments to the record of human obsessions already in. But that said, I think it important to correct a misconception. Critics talk about the Oates canon as if it were a seamless whole, as if her latest stories differ only slightly from her earliest ones. That is not entirely true, although one hardly ever finishes an Oates story imagining that it might have been written by somebody else. Nonetheless, her latest fictions have grown increasingly longer, fueled by an energy that resists the compression that was a prominent feature of her first collections. This is true not only of **"A Sentimental Education"**—the collection's title story and one long enough (83 pp.) to qualify as a novella— but also of **"Queen of the Night"** and **"A Middle-Class Edu-**

cation" (both printed originally in respective, limited editions).

Some years ago Miss Oates said she would like to write a novel about every person living in the United States. One *hopes* she was being metaphorical, even playful, although given Miss Oates and her enormous capacity for work, one can't be certain. For some years now she has also been hard at work on "exercises" propped against classic texts, re-imagining the bookshelf by re-writing *her* version of James Joyce's "The Dead," *her* rendition of Henry James' *The Aspern Papers*. If Oates' imagination is both wide and deep enough to encompass America, her "reading" is even more boundless. **"A Sentimental Education"** announces its echoes to Flaubert, with important differences, ones that transmogrify Frederick Moreau into a high-strung Johns Hopkins student, and Mme. Arnoux into his younger, but sexually precocious cousin:

> . . . That he should discover her so delicate, so pretty: so much his own: and yet a nighttime secret no one else would ever know. His blood surged, pulse upon pulse, in waves of clarity . . . Smelling his cousin's lemony hair, smelling her warm, alarmed body, holding her dark shifty gaze firmly with his own, he knew that he had been assailed by one of his own dreams; and out of the secrecy of the dream the girl had come forth to claim him.

Few writers have captured "young love" with such immediacy of detail, and such powerful seriousness. She may insist that life winds itself toward tragic inevitability, but she does not condescend to or patronize about her star-crossed lovers.

In **"The Precipice,"** a philosophy professor with impeccable "liberal" credentials (he organizes demonstrations against the Vietnam War and is generally regarded as "some sort of quaint folksy blend of Quaker and agnostic and Marxist and Spinozist") has an obsessive—and clearly self-destructive—attraction to violence. After the latest episode in which an argument with a motorcycle gang ends with one member kicking the professor in the face, he finds himself sharing a hospital room with an elderly man who quarrels about Pascal with him:

> . . . *"Between us and heaven or hell* [the old man insisted] *there is only life, which is the frailest thing in the world."*
>
> Wesley [the philosophy professor] said at once, *"We run carelessly to the precipice, after we have put something before us to prevent us from seeing it."*
>
> The old man said, *"A maker of witticisms; a bad character."*
>
> Wesley said, *"By space the universe encompasses and swallows me up like an atom; by thought I comprehend the world."*

At times people *do* that in Oates stories; on other occasions they burn with what one character calls "inchoate rage."

In **A Sentimental Education,** fiction unwinds to its own clock. The result is to bring what most appeals in her longer work—that chilling, violent sense of destiny's arrangements—into the world of her shorter fictions. Perhaps the distinction is, by now, a meaningless one. What matters, I suppose, is that not since **The Wheel of Love** (1970) have Oates' stories launched themselves into our brains with such

sharply etched opening lines. Here, for example, is how **"In the Autumn of the Year"** begins:

> One of them was her lover's son. Her dead lover's son. He had turned out curiously: a balding young-old man with hairs in his nostrils, an annoying habit of picking at his fingernails, a quick strained meager smile.

Not surprisingly, the speaker of those lines is a poet; and not surprisingly Oates weaves her remarks into a remarkable story, one of the half-dozen lessons that comprise **A Sentimental Education.** (pp. 94-6)

> *Sanford Pinsker, in a review of "A Sentimental Education," in* Studies in Short Fiction, *Vol. 19, No. 1, Winter, 1982, pp. 94-6.*

As to the nature of short fiction? There is no nature to it, but only natures. Different natures. Just as we all have different personalities, so the dreams of our personalities will be different. There are no rules to help us. There used to be a rule—"Don't be boring!"—but that has been by-passed; today writers like Beckett and Albee and Pinter are deliberately boring (though perhaps they succeed more than they know) and anything goes. Outrageous exaggeration. Outrageous understatement. Very short scenes, very long scenes . . . cinematic flashes and impressions, long introspective passages in the manner of Thomas Mann: anything. There is no particular length, certainly, to the short story or to the novel. I believe that any short story can become a novel, and any novel can be converted back into a short story or into a poem. Reality is fluid and monstrous; let us package it in as many shapes as possible, put names on it, publish it in hard-cover. Let us make films of it. Let us declare that everything is sacred and therefore material for art—or, perhaps, nothing is sacred, nothing can be left alone.

> *Joyce Carol Oates, from "The Nature of Short Fiction; or, The Nature of My Short Fiction," her preface to the* Handbook of Short Story Writing *(1970).*

KATHERINE BASTIAN (essay date 1983)

[*In the following excerpt from her book-length study of Oates's short fiction, Bastian discusses the arrangement of stories in* Crossing the Border *and* All the Good People I've Left Behind, *suggesting that these two collections are constructed as components of a thematic cycle.*]

In *Crossing the Border* and *All the Good People I've Left Behind* Oates composes 'sequences' within thematic cycles. *Crossing the Border* is a sequence of seven stories which are intentionally interspersed throughout the fifteen stories of the collection. The other narratives are placed in between those of the sequence to disturb its flow. This construction is chosen by Oates to underscore the validity of each independent 'part.' Carol Pearson conceives the central unifying theme of the collection as that of "separation":

Over half these tales about exile center around Renee and Evan Maynard, expatriates from the U.S. to Canada. Each sketch describes a separation—from country, friendship, Evan's profession, Renee's lover, and finally Evan's and Renee's separation from each other. Interspersed tales dramatize events which move other similar characters from inadequate and frustrating relationships to total, hopeless isolation.

In the other narratives as well as in the sequence Oates underscores the similarity of situation through repetition of theme and character constellations.

All the Good People is also a sequence within a thematic cycle whereby eight of the ten stories intertwine to form an integral whole. As in *Crossing the Border,* the extraneous narratives handle similar conflicts, couples who have grown apart from one another. Both *Crossing the Border* and *All the Good People* may be interpreted as tentative attempts at sequences in the manner of Anderson, whereby Oates still desires to stress that the short story cycle is a genre distinct from the novel.

In discussing Oates's principles of organization as a means of expanding the boundaries of the short story it is revealing to examine more closely her use of the 'sequence' in comparison to the other cycles. The sequence in *Crossing the Border* focuses on the marital relationship of Renee and Evan Maynard. It consists of seven stories which progressively reveal the internal turmoil within both protagonists. The title story, **"Crossing the Border,"** shows Renee and Evan about to cross the Canadian border. While waiting for Evan to return from the washroom, Renee ruminates on their past life in Florida and her daydreams of "escape." The narrative introduces the subsurface tension between Renee and Evan.

After crossing the border Renee's and Evan's relationship gradually dissipates. **"Hello Fine Day Isn't It?"** illustrates Renee's isolation and her inability to rectify the situation. In town she repeatedly meets a twenty-five year old "boy" who is described as being moronic, an "ageless creature with good intentions." He tries to make conversation with Renee, to establish some form of contact with her. Despite her awareness of his need for communication and sympathy, and also of her own, she is unable to respond. In the crucial scene of the narrative the "boy" and the river attain symbolic import, which is augmented in the course of the succeeding stories. The "boy" is a counterpart to Renee, representing her own innate need for companionship and simultaneous apprehension of emotional exposure:

> The two of them [Renee and Evan] were happy here. The prospect of being "happy" and of leading a simple, uncomplicated life was so new to them, so remarkable, that it more than compensated for other things [i.e. their impassivity for one another . . .] For weeks you won't see him [the boy]; you forget him. Then you see him everywhere.

Although Renee tries to suppress her memory of the "boy," her sensation of alienation and loneliness emerges repeatedly without forewarning.

In **"Natural Boundaries"** Renee meets Karl, her lover-to-be. The story begins with her watching the "rescue maneuvers" on the river behind her house. In order to 'escape' Karl's phone calls and Evan's insensitivity she leaves for the library, were she reads articles on adultery. In spite of this, she attempts to deny her attraction to Karl and her desire to break away from her stiftling marriage. Through phone calls, a letter, and a visit to her house Karl repeatedly tries to approach Renee, yet she remains impervious. At the end of the narrative she walks by Karl on the street:

> "Karl Davies" and "Renee Maynard" had almost come into existence, had almost confronted each other, yet had not. For some reason they had not. They had not even met. So "Renee" [. . .] did not care at all about the flood warnings: let the river rise, let it flood [. . .] She was not going to leave her life. "Renee" thought of how Renee would always be safe, no matter what.

'Natural boundaries,' the boundaries projected between people are, however, no assurance of security, 'safety.'

"Customs" depicts Renee waiting at customs, intending to cross the border to meet with friends, to emerge from her seclusion. She is deterred by the customs official who demands proper identification. Renee is upset by the situation and the unfriendliness of the officials and the other people waiting:

> [. . .] something alarmed her [. . .] Possibly the lack of communication. No one was saying much [. . .] Renee was trembling now; she was very frightened. Something was wrong, something was terribly wrong. Couldn't quite articulate it [. . .] Couldn't free herself of the paralysis of the moment, the eerie knowledge that something was wrong, out of focus, out of control. Why didn't he speak to her?

After her car has been searched she is allowed to cross the border, but now she no longer knows the way to her friends. She is confused by her sudden recognition of the hostile barrier between individuals. Renee has apparently become involved in a liaison with Karl in the interval between **"Natural Boundaries"** and **"The Scream."** In **"The Scream,"** Renee is in an art gallery contemplating whether or not to keep her rendezvous with Karl: "She had hoped that falling in love would allow her to love herself, once again, or to halfway respect herself; but it had not worked out that way." An old man approaches her in the gallery and tries to start a conversation with her. She, however, "draws away" from him. She then scans the exhibition of photographs:

> Painful, it was painful to stare so closely into those eyes, into the souls of strangers. Many of them suffered, yes, but many of them were happy [. . .] Renee might lose herself in them, in humanity [. . .] An Indian woman holding a skeletal baby [. . .] her face distorted with rage or despair, her mouth opened in a wide, soundless shriek. My God, it was so painful [. . .] the woman's mouth was a gaping hole [. . .] Renee stared until her vision glazed over. The woman's scream was everywhere around her: it forced the other sounds [. . .] into silence [. . .] How could it matter if a young woman went to her lover . . . or if she denied herself to him.

The woman's scream of anguish becomes Renee's own. Her fear of loneliness impels her to go to her lover, thus suppressing her scream temporarily.

Evan is the main character of **"An Incident in the Park."** He is walking in the park after a quarrel with Renee in which she finally screamed at him. Their comprehension of one another has reached its acme:

The argument had been shapeless, dreamlike. A mystery. Somehow they were in it, plunged in it, and he was accusing her of finding fault with him [. . .] though of course she had never expressed these feelings, not overtly—and she had never screamed at him, a desparation he had never heard in her voice before [. . .] she screamed at him that he never cared for people she tried to be-friend—[. . . that] he wanted to destroy her, he couldn't see how she was being destroyed.

Evan is sitting in the park poundering over their dispute when he witnesses a man, who is apparently crazy, wade into the pond. Evan suddenly believes that the man needs him, that he is "important." While he tries to quiet the man down, the police come and push Evan aside. Evan is markedly un-settled by the man's agony and despondency, yet he is unable to decipher the connection between the man's 'insanity' and his wife's dolor.

"River Rising," the closing story of the sequence, presents the climax of the preceeding stories. The story opens with Renee's dream-letter to Karl in which she rationally tries to justify the termination of their affair. She is, however, awak-ened by a raging storm and the noise of the waves lapping in the backyard. Renee panics at the thought of the river flood-ing the house. Evan, too, panics but refuses to evacuate. Renee perceives the storm as a punishment for her adultery. In her frenzy she stares at Evan: "In that instant she did not know him at all, did not know if she loved him or hated him or feared him." At this point she can no longer distinguish between sanity and insanity. She loses all rational orientation, and therefore obliterates the 'boundaries' which she has in-flicted upon herself. In the end she realizes that all marriages are "workable in ways that can't be described." The hysteria of the scene has affected an emotional cartharsis. The river gradually recedes and Evan and Renee turn to one another.

" . . . you wanted to evacuate, wanted to abandon everything," Evan whispered.

"We were in danger. It was real. People died to-night [. . .] the storm was so real, so terrible . . . the river was so real . . . "

[. . .] "You wanted to abandon our house," Evan murmured. "Our marriage . . . "

[. . .] Renee laughed, pressing her face against his neck [. . .] she could not remember why she was disappointed or why she was relieved or what the danger had been.

Renee has again found safety in Evan. Her despair has, at least temporarily, been alleviated.

The structural elements of the seven narratives provide a sub-stantial means of unification. The narratives succeed one an-other in a strict chronological order. **"Crossing the Border"** takes place in the summer, then follow consecutively Septem-ber, autumn, April, summer, and November. Only **"Cus-toms"** is without a specific time reference. This concise tem-poral order proves Oates's intention of constructing a cohe-sive sequence. The fact that five of the stories are told from Renee's perspective provides an additional element of unifi-cation. In these narratives Renee is depicted as suffering under the alienation generated by her marriage. In **"An Inci-dent in the Park"** Evan's complementary position is pres-ented. The final **"River Rising,"** however, discloses both of their points of view and thus underlines their re-union.

The recurrence of the two central characters also aids formal-ly to link the stories. Renee is present in all of the stories ex-cept **"An Incident in the Park,"** whereas Evan is present in only three. Although one of the characters may be physically absent, the dilemma of their estrangement is illuminated in all of the stories. In addition to the recurrence of characters, the character development which occurs is instrumental in producing a whole. In the opening narrative, **"Crossing the Border,"** Renee wishes to become "released, free, blameless." It is indicated that she is emotionally discontent. Her thoughts are torn between her personal psychological emo-tional needs, as revealed in her dreams, and her conscious res-ervations. The second narrative, **"Hello Fine Day,"** discloses her apprehension of reciprocal relationships. She has become "mechanically" defensive against other people's attempts at communication. She retreats into her protective shell, deny-ing her own desires. Although she tries to forget her knowl-edge of the "boy," her deep-rooted despair surfaces again and again. She tries to delude herself, to believe in her 'happiness' and "simple, uncomplicated, unsoiled life." In **"Natural Boundaries"** she progresses to contemplation of adultery and in **"The Scream"** she is finally able to overcome her moral in-hibitions. In committing adultery she acknowledges her sti-fling isolation. Through her affair, which is rather a tempo-rary escape, she attempts to reach out to another individual. Yet, this endeavor proves futile due to Karl's psychological incapacity, his ingrained familial bond. Only through her mo-mentary hysterics, her loss of control, in **"River Rising"** is she able to break through the invisible barrier which impris-ons her, and thus to restore contact with Evan. It is, however, important to note that Evan has also undergone a parallel process of liberation between **"Crossing the Border," "An In-cident in the Park,"** and **"River Rising."** Both Renee and Evan become aware of the nature of their loneliness, its ef-fects on others, and ultimately cure their separation (tempo-rarily?) by re-establishing their bonds on an inuitive basis. Through their mutual maturing they are able to raze the 'boundaries' between them, to commune once again.

The central theme of the sequence, as of the entire cycle, is that of "separation," which is examined in its variations of impassivity, alienation, dislocation. The sequence presents Evan's and Renee's sensations of separation as well as that of the secondary characters. The theme is thus unfolded in the actions of all of the characters, relating them in this man-ner to one another. The customs officer is cold and unfriend-ly, the people in the park are hesitant to help, the other chil-dren tease the "boy," even Karl constantly talks about his wife instead of responding to Renee's petition for love. The dilemma of detachment is apparently not unique to Renee and Evan but is typical of the general social condition.

Setting, the 'border' and the 'river,' and secondary characters gain a broader significance as the sequence advances. The set-ting, in its imagery of being situated "across the border" pic-torializes Renee's and Evan's loss of "identity" and their de-tachment from one another. The elements of the border and the river become meaningful as expressions of their psycho-logical experience. Throughout the sequence the American-Canadian border is representative of the intangible border which separates people. Renee's and Evan's marriage is de-picted as intact before they cross the "metaphysical" border:

The border between two nations is always indicated by broken but indefinite lines [on the map], to indi-cate that it is not quite real in any physical sense but very real in a metaphysical sense.

The border between individuals is equally enigmatic. Once across the physical border Renee and Evan enter a state of limbo, unable to identify with themselves or others. In **"Customs"** Renee seeks to return to a world of interpersonal relationships. But after her experience of the officials' animosity she is so disoriented that crossing a mere physical border becomes senseless for her. In that she has at this point not yet mastered her own internal inhibitions, she is incapable of permeating the invisible border.

Complementary to Renee's alienation induced by the 'border' is Evan's loss of identity upon crossing the border into Canada. In his transition to impersonality he forfeits his sensitivity to Renee's inarticulated emotional needs. He becomes submerged in his own private professional problems, rejecting contact with others. Only through his perception of the tragedy of the man in the park, of the barrier between himself, the man and the onlookers, does Evan become conscious of the necessity of personal interaction and the delusion of his reclusion.

The image of the border is applicable to all the relationships portrayed in the sequence. A 'border' is existent between Renee and the 'boy,' her mother, Karl, the old man, between the man in the park and the onlookers, and between the custom officials and the people waiting there. The border hindering community is therefore characteristic not only of Renee's and Evan's relationship, but of the overall "deteriorating nature of relationships" in society. The motif of the border functions as a representation of the abstract concept of isolation.

Another motif which recurs throughout the narratives is that of the river. The river is described as "continually changing," perpetually in motion. It embodies the concepts of time, experience, and the uncontrollable flow of life. Renee often watches the "rescue maneuvers" on the river:

> How orderly and logical it was, the rescue procedure [. . .] It was an orderly, sane procedure, yet, watching it Renee sometimes felt an accumulation of tension that was almost painful.

Renee longs to be rescued from the undertow of life. Although she contemplates her ennui in **"Customs," "Hello Fine Day,"** and **"Natural Boundaries"** she does not achieve the necessary insight into her own psychological disarray. She searches for external salvation through her affair with Karl, yet does not reach emotional maturity, the ability to give and receive affections unconditionally. Her rescue must come from within, from awareness of her personal needs and of those of others. The 'river' thus takes her past Karl, confronting her in the closing of the story with herself. In **"River Rising"** the river floods endangering her supposed 'safety':

> They had taken the river for granted. At times they had forgotten it. Now it was here two or three feet from the house itself. Hypnotic, in spite of the noise. And there was a rhythm to it, beneath the cacophony of air and water [. . .] The river was so real.

The river represents the stream of life, its rationally imperceptible order. This order is exerted on the one hand by external factors (relationships, physical setting, etc.) and on the other by the obscure psychological forces governing the individual. At times Renee is able to forget about the influence of the 'river,' to believe in her guise of invulnerability, and at other times she is in danger of being swallowed in the river's maelstrom. The motif of the river provides a binding thread, a 'rhythm,' to the sequence, connecting the stories on an emblematic level.

These seven narratives in *Crossing the Border* are thus interlinked through their chronology, point of view, central characters, theme, and motifs. Through the inclusion of other unrelated stories in the cycle, Oates clearly denies the short story sequence pretensions of novelistic structure or character development. (pp. 137-43)

All the Good People I've Left Behind is a short story sequence constructed on a similar basis to *Crossing the Border.* The collection consists of ten stories, of which eight are formally interconnected. The stories **"The Hallucination"** and **"Blood-Swollen Landscape,"** although concerned with common themes, are not woven into the sequence. As in *Crossing the Border,* the narratives are an explication of the 'fate' of interpersonal relationships as depicted in diverse examples of foundered relationships. The stories represent a single continuous strain of argumentation, each giving evidence for the narrator's final conclusion in the concluding **"All the Good People I've Left Behind."**

The sequence itself is composed of two basic story strains which merge in the final narrative. The first story strain is centered around the figure of Annie Quirt, who in a series of five stories progresses from one lover to the next. The time scheme of these narratives is compelling in that each story builds on the failure of the last affair. The stories are linked in their accumulation of depression and distrust of relationships.

Four of these stories are related from Annie's perspective, thus granting insight into her psychological needs and apprehensions. Through the presentation of Annie's subjective experience, Oates ventures to analyze the motivations of the individual caught in the maze of deteriorating relationships. In this strain the constellation Annie-lover is common to four of the stories. There are also frequent references to lovers from the proceeding stories, which are an additional link. The lovers in their uniformity of behavior remain essentially a single figure with insignificant minor variations. Annie's development on the other hand constitutes the primary element of unification as a summary of this narrative strain will illustrate.

In the opening story, **"The Leap,"** Annie is presented contemplating death as a possible means of escaping loneliness. In a later scene she is with her lover watching a group of boys teasing a girl by pushing her off a rock into the river. At first Annie is frightened that they may injure the girl. She then perceives the girl's sensation of a "moment of savage freedom" as she leaps from the rocks:

> She could see again the girl struggling with the boys, there on the ledge [. . .] she could see the girl pushing free of them—jumping free—throwing her body out into space [. . .] what had it been for her, Annie wondered, at that moment of savage freedom?—a strained, glowing rather mad look to the girl's face, as if everything had vanished for her at that instant [. . .] The jump into space, into oblivion: a terrible ecstasy in it, beyond all emotion.

As a result of this epiphany Annie ends her affair with her lover. This moment of "freedom" is, however, only temporary for Annie. Like the girl, Annie returns again and again to a lover seeking the "terrible ecstasy" in the leap beyond emotion which is coupled with the termination of an affair.

Annie has a new lover in **"The Tryst."** He, however, is only able to view Annie as an object of his infatuation, not as a partner. It is evident that Annie is injured by his emotional distance, his inability to give love. Her reaction to her rejection is drastic this time. Through slitting her wrists she tries to free herself forcibly from her affection for him. Yet, her attempted suicide is unsuccessful and her lover sends her callously away.

In **"Eye-Witness"** Annie is in the hospital after having taken an overdose of sleeping-pills. Here she undertakes to "observe" her life. She perceives that she has been in persistent quest of love and sympathy, yet finds herself not worthy of such affection:

> Lying in a lover's arms, whispering of your disappointment and sorrows and befuddlement, expecting to be loved. But who will love you, once he knows your innermost self? [. . .] You have always loathed yourself. Yet you lived, didn't you, for twenty-six years, you enjoyed getting drunk occasionally and you certainly enjoyed eating [. . .] and you enjoyed, or pretended to enjoy, the company of other people. All along, however, you detested yourself. But you made no move to die, you were too lazy, too distracted and foolishly hopeful.

She believes that her self-detestation makes her unqualified to be the object of someone's affection. She, however, refuses to give up hope of someday finding love, proclaiming that she is an "incurable romantic."

Her naive, optimistic conception of life leads her again to suffering. In **"Sentimental Journey"** she writes an old college acquaintance, Warren, of her memories of their times together. This expression of mere friendship is an attempt to deny physical love: "She had vowed, in this new phase of her life, to transcend and to obliterate the merely physical." Warren, however, turns up personally in answer to her letter, supposedly because of some "mystical connection." Annie immediately becomes enamored in him. As a couple they are incapable of communicating with one another, seeing in each other only that which they desire to see. The relationship is delusive and perverted. Warren, who is later revealed to be psychopathic, clings desperately to Annie. At the end of the story Annie is in a playground, afraid to go home to Warren, sitting on the top of a slide about to slide down. She does not know why she has climbed it, why she has become involved in this disillusioning affair with Warren:

> Impulsively she climbed the slide, taking the steps two at a time. She was a big powerful handsome girl. Well-loved. Enviable [. . .] she could handle her life as she wished. She was capable of anything [. . .] Now she stood at the top of the slide, gripping the wet railings. She could not recall having climbed the slide, and she did not know why she had climbed it. But it seemed as good a place as any on this rainy afternoon.

Annie is governed by impulsivity. She will never be able to control her life because she is prey to her own instinctive need for affection. After a brief high, she is now about to fall.

In **"Walled City"** she has fled to Quebec where she endeavors to commence a life of seclusion. In her self-imposed solitude she does not

> care to drift into personal conversations, since such conversations invariably lead to self-explanation.

People felt the instinct to defend themselves [. . .] as if setting up boundaries. Annie had come to Quebec City to live without boundaries and without the need to erect them [. . .] at the age of thirty-four she had come to think of herself as morbidly dependent on other people. But she lived alone now [. . .] She would live alone without loneliness; she would contemplate her life [. . .] She had without knowing it, always subjected herself to others—eager for their praise, their admiration, their awe, even their jealousy and spite. Now she was in a part of the world where no one knew her [. . .] She would experiment with anonymity, with a kind of freedom that had always frightened her.

Despite her resolution she soon enters into another relationship. This time she does not become fully saturated in the affair. She sees Philip as an "artifice," a superficial creature, one of many. He represents for her a stereotype lover equivalent to her first lover, Judd:

> '[. . .] the most remarkable thing of all,' Philip said [. . .], 'is that Judd and I discovered we had been in love with the same woman . . . Not only that, but we'd been involved with one or two others, in different times of our lives, and it only gradually developed how our lives had run parallel, as if we'd been threaded together by other people, by strangers.

In meeting Philip, Annie has in essence come full circle. With this revelation of the uniformity of her lovers Annie dissolves her relationship with Philip and returns to her solitude.

> She kept to herself after that [. . .] She wondered how long, for how many years, she had been perfectly safe, perfectly alone, without knowing it.

Annie has learned that she cannot be emotionally injured if she does not subject herself to the imminent dangers of an affair.

Not only Annie, but also the secondary characters, her lovers, are entangled in this cycle of search and disappointment, as expounded in **"The Tryst."** This narrative is told from the perspective of Annie's current lover, John Reddinger. John is an adult who is supposedly "in charge of the world." He is a typical suburbanite living in a neighborhood of "baronial" houses, each a symbol of superficial protection. As was Renee, John is caught in the inertia of life and is denied emotional security. John is in search of some self-affirmative emotional reciprocation. He has had other affairs but feels more attached to Annie than to those before her. Annie represents the epitome of a woman for him: "she obliterated other woman." In his state of friendlessness and estrangement from his family, Annie provides him with needed affection. He is, however, incapable of fully giving himself to her because of his tribulation over his amoral behavior and his fear of being discovered. Annie herself is beyond such trivial moral obstacles:

> It excited him to imagine her haphazard, promiscuous life; he knew she was entirely without guilt or shame or self-consciousness, as if, born of a different generation, she were a different species as well.

John is, however, unable to overcome his self-imposed constriction. Although infatuated by Annie, he would rather hold fast to his suburban security than risk engaging himself in a true 'love' affair. Thus when Annie attempts suicide in his house he panics. His only reaction is to dispose of her as quickly as possible. He abandons her as a risk to his protection. **"The Tryst"** demonstrates John's 'artificiality,' the impossibility of his responding to Annie's needs due to ingrained psychological and moral barriers.

Through the spiral process of infatuation and dejection Annie gains knowledge of her own predicament. She sacrifices her naive optimism in the face of callous reality. The cyclic course of affairs, however, does not end in **"Walled City."** It is to be assumed that Annie will continually become enmeshed in affairs because of her vulnerable, affection-seeking nature. As her exlover Judd writes in a letter to Philip, Annie is "used and recycled." The basic situation throughout these five stories remains the same, only the faces change. Annie, however, does develop. In her repudiation of "merely physical," superficial companionship and her acceptance of loneliness, individuality, Annie masters her inner insecurity and finds recourse in herself. In **"Walled City"** she no longer detests herself, but rather those other people who are "artifices." The term "artifices" is introduced in relation to Philip's sculptures but is nevertheless a precise description of the unnatural people with whom Annie is confronted:

> His sculptures were small, peculiar, quirky things, rather ugly, rather striking. He called them "artifices." They were fashioned out of once-organic material, for the most part, things he found in fields or alleyways or trash heaps or in the gutter: the skulls of mice, rats, squirrels, even cats or dogs [. . .] In his hand they achieved a quasi-living appearance . . . though, Annie thought, staring at them, they were really a mockery of life, an ironic, cruel comment on the nature of organic life itself [. . .] "This one here, this is my 'domesticated monster,' [. . .] 'I don't think it's finished yet and I've been working on it for weeks [. . .] Sometimes it wants to become a legitimate, zoologically respectable beast, and at other times it strains towards the human, it seems to want to acquire a soul'."

Her lovers have all been "beasts" without souls, too impaired by some inhibition to respond from their innermost selves. Through her affairs Annie has learned to distance herself from others, from manipulative, egoistic people.

After the introductory repetition of situation in **"The Leap,"** **"The Tryst,"** and **"Sentimental Journey,"** Annie matures as is illustrated in her self-examination in **"Eye-Witness"** and conscious retreat in **"Walled City."** Annie's transcendence, her awareness, is exemplary for the whole of *All the Good People.* She has managed, at least temporarily, to break the cycle of deteriorating relationships, if only through non-contribution to its propagation. Annie's development and her age consequently tie these five stories together in an obligatory chronological pattern.

The other story strain unfolded in **"High"** and **"Intoxication"** merges with the Annie-strain in the culminating **"All the Good People."** Whereas the Annie-narratives are centered on a single woman's futile search for love, these narratives focus on marriages which have dissolved and the protagonists' resulting estrangement. In **"High"** Deanna (whose husband, Jerry Hecht, has divorced her) looks for companionship in her friend Max. Max, however, has recently discovered that without his glasses people and things appear "blurred and inconsequential, and he did not have to see them." He is so entranced in his macabre perception of the world that he does not register Deanna's pleas. Although together with Max, Deanna is thus subjected to isolation and depression. She is shut off, unable to extricate herself from the surrounding apathy. Under these circumstances she ultimately becomes hysterical and runs frantically through the streets fleeing everyone.

"Intoxication" depicts a couple, Cynthia and Dean, who are in the process of divorce. They are dividing their possessions when visited by a friend, Darrell. In their conversation with Darrell their true predicament, their attachment to one another through habituation and their fear of loneliness comes to light. Divorce inducts them to separation, which is the opposite of the freedom they desire. Out of apprehension of this impending isolation they both cling to Darrell as their last resort.

The temporal relation between these two narratives is not fixed. They are, however, complementary in their themes and character constellations. In **"Intoxication"** there are references to characters from **"High."** **"High"** is essentially a preface to **"Intoxication"** in that Deanna's fate is that which awaits Cynthia and Dean.

"All the Good People I've Left Behind," an eighty-two page story, intertwines both story strains in such a manner that they form an intergral whole. The characters from the previous stories are drawn together into a circle of friends which has gradually sundered over the years. The story opens in 1960 at a party in Ann Arbor at the Hecht's apartment. Alex and Fern Enright, Ted and Maxine Mandel, Cynthia and Dean, Darrell, and Annie, at this time students, are all in attendance. Alex, Fern, Ted and Maxine are close friends whose marriages and friendship dissolve in the course of the narrative. They leave the party together to go to the Enrights' where they discuss 'philosophical' topics, such as free will versus determinism, reason versus instinct, life, consciousness, change, and the nature of reality. These are the themes which are central to the narrative as well as the entire cycle.

The second section of the narrative is set three years later in Cleveland where the Mandels are visiting the Enrights. Fern is totally absorbed in her children, oblivious of her guests. Maxine is critical of Fern but subconsciously envious of her domestic happiness. Ted, at the moment, is undergoing a "spiritual crisis" as a result of professional failure. Alex, now a top executive, has begun to detach himself from his surroundings. All four are depicted as being self-centered and subject to depressions.

The third section illustrates a further step in their degeneration process. Five years later Fern is visiting Maxine. Maxine tries rationally to explain the necessity of her husband's infidelity. She says:

> Emotions have been legislated out of existence in our society: intense joy, rage, anger, terror. They've been banished, denied, because people are afraid of them. Our society is a linear one, a rationalist one.

Although she rationally accepts Ted's adultery, she suffers internally. Fern in her impassivity is unwilling to console Maxine. As a consequence of Ted's rebellion both Maxine and Fern are compelled to alter their beliefs in marriage and adopt a facade of dispassion.

In the fourth section, Chicago 1973, both of the marriages have fully disintegrated. Alex is suffering from a terminal ailment but will not tell Fern. Because of his inability to communicate with her he becomes completely reticent. He has become a different person, a dispersonalized stereotype. Ted has a quarrel with Maxine and accuses her of emotional frigidity. Only after his rejection of Maxine is he able to find some form of "freedom":

> Chilling this sudden sense of freedom, of isolation. He doesn't love anyone and never did . . . A befuddled, lust-maddened young man got married many years ago [. . .] and lost himself for a period of years, in that marriage [. . .] he lost himself in it a certain space of time. And then, slowly, he found himself again—came to the surface of himself, and was awakened. Once awakened he cannot drift into sleep once again. He loves no one.

Ted has found himself through detaching himself from his marriage. As a result of his departure Maxine suffers a nervous breakdown. She desperately clutches to Fern, who refuses to respond to her hysterics. Fern herself is overcome by ennui. In a daze she searches for some ideal "dream-lover" in order to escape her "daylight-self," her lethargy. Fern's dream-lover is

> [. . .] a creation of the imagination, a god of the unconscious: he is far more than merely physical. He has no "existence" and yet he means more to her, in a way, than husband and lover and children [. . .] When she thinks of her dream-lover she is not Fern Enright, she is no one's wife and no one's mistress: she is no one at all: utterly free. And yet she cannot resist searching for him, in the human world.

Both Ted and Fern have 'freed' themselves by denying their marital bonds. Yet both of them appear destined to move from lover to lover in search of a non-existent ideal lover. Their actual isolation is their only freedom and is not equivalent with emotional contentment.

Section five unfolds the outcome of this separation process. Alex has become submerged in his role as a businessman, unaware of any intimate bonds. Ted is in Vermont with a new girl. They, too, part: "He loved a woman; he ceased to love a woman; he loves another woman now; . . . the only constant seems to be the subject 'he'." Fern is reluctant to answer Maxine's persistent phone calls. She has saved Maxine once from an attempted suicide and has neither the strength nor the personal commitment to do so again. Friendship has become a thing of the past for her: "It was a phenomenon of her adolescence and young adulthood." Fern suspects that Maxine has again attempted suicide but does not go to rescue her. After Maxine's death Fern and Alex take a "second honeymoon" in Miami where Alex accidentally comes across a pamphlet on the beach entitled "Is There A God Who Cares?". As a result of the pamphlet's impact, of its promised "new order," Alex converts to Jehovah's Witnesses. Some years later Fern meets with Ted. They discuss Maxine's death as if exhibiting their "bravery." In assessing their feelings they come to the conclusion that Maxine should have learned to "love unselfishly," that she was solely to blame. During their conversation they both feel attracted to one another, but the moment passes and they too part.

Each of the protagonists hides his inner self behind a facade of impersonal marital formalities: "Formalities are protective devices, like personae or masks shielding one's deepest self." The protagonists are afraid of exposing their inner selves to others for fear of rejection and injury. All of these characters are ego-centric, insensitive to others.

Both story strains circumstantiate the oscillating nature of relationships. Relationships develop in young adulthood to their peak and then gradually fade until final deterioration. A perpetual series of attraction and ensuing disillusionment arises. Of all of the characters only Annie is willing to love selflessly. Yet, even she must cower under repeated injuries. Ted is portrayed as the potential ideal partner for Annie:

> He had loved Maxine very much of course, in the early days of their marriage; but he had nevertheless daydreamt of Annie Quirt and had been foolishly jealous of her lover [. . .] It occurs to Ted that Lisabeth had been only a version of Annie [. . .] Perhaps she, Annie, had been the woman meant for him all along.

Ted, through his consciousness-raising, has become emancipated to a state where he is capable of returning love. Yet, Annie and Ted only come in contact with unqualified partners and therefore remain caught in the cycle. In all eight stories of the sequence the characters are compelled to function as 'artifices' because of the prevalent de-personalized nature of relationships.

Through the employment of recurrent characters, and most importantly through the explication of a unified theme, the eight stories converge to form a composite whole. The sequence is a single process, which the time scheme and the character development of both Ted and Annie underscore. The theme of loneliness, search for affection, and the individual's vulnerability due to his own selfishness, are handled on various levels of both story strains. The concluding disunion at the end of the sequence ultimately ties the two strains together to form a unified statement. The final narrative, **"All the Good People,"** reaches back in time and accumulates themes and motifs which have been introduced in the preceeding stories. **"All the Good People"** begins in the student days before the other stories take place and ends after them. This narrative thus encompasses and assimilates the other stories of the sequence. The fate of each of the characters, of Annie, Deanna and Jerry, Cynthia and Dean, Ted and Maxine, and Alex and Fern, are brought into relation and presented in their similarities as characteristic of contemporary social conditions. The 'loose' form of the short story sequence allows Oates to depict "lives flowing past one another." Through the initial circle of friends and their common fates the characters of the two story strains are interrelated.

It is irrefutable that *Crossing the Border* and *All the Good People I've Left Behind* are designed by Oates as sequences within short story cycles. The stories of each sequence are interlinked with precision, relying not only on similarity of themes, but employing in addition recurrence of characters and motifs, a stringent time scheme, an overall 'rhythmic' pattern evoked by repetition of situation, and dynamic patterns of development. (pp. 143-50)

In the construction of short story cycles Oates seeks to overcome the inherent limitations of the short story through means of comprehensive 'effects.' The narratives themselves remain autonomous whereby the "significances of each story deepen and expand as the reader moves from story to story, in a particular order." The 'thematic' cycles are designed to reinforce the statements of the individual narratives, to underscore their symptomatic quality. The sequences progress a step further. The recurrence of characters, motifs, and settings adds a mythic dimension to the whole, an impression of the universality of the situations presented, of its basis in human nature. In the sequence Oates is able to follow the intricate chain of cause and effect leading to the ailments portrayed.

Although the 'thematic' cycles, and especially the 'sequences,' are clearly more than mere short story anthologies, Oates, on the other hand, carefully differentiates them from the novel. Sequential short story cycles, such as Anderson's *Winesburg, Ohio* and Faulkner's *The Unvanquished,* have often been criticized as poorly constructed novels. In order to avoid the possibility of her short story sequences being falsely mistaken for novels, Oates intersperses other 'unrelated' narratives to underline the autonomy of the individual parts. The narratives, even in the sequences, remain intact, independent. Character development and temporal progression are episodic, choppy, rather than continuous. Through her composition of short story cycles it is Oates's intention to "stretch" the expressive potential of the short story through interlinkage of external formal elements, while at the same time honoring the merits of its brevity.

Similar to her approach to the short story, the narrative techniques of her cycles remain readily intelligible for the reader. As in the majority of her short stories, Oates shies from the overly experimental. In her short story cycles Oates combines the "single effects" to achieve a comprehensive statement. She thus compensates for the limiting 'brevity' of the short story, granting the individual narrative a more inclusive radius.

Oates's cycles do not introduce any revolutionary revisions of the genre, but they do offer several new impulses, such as the dynamic characterization of two protagonists in their relation to each other and the intertwining of two distinct narrative strains, of two perspectives, namely those of an individual and a community. In both cases Oates finds a technique which in its very structure emphasizes the indivisible bond between the individual and society. Her devices of recurrent characters, themes, symbols, and motifs are not unprecedented. It is again her use of point of view and the "compactness" and "concentration" of the stories which distinguish these collections. *Crossing the Border* and *All the Good People I've Left Behind* have been praised for the poignant sense of anguish which permeate these works. *Marriages and Infidelities* has in turn been cited for its allusive construction, beginning with a story on the regenerative powers of love in **"The Sacred Marriage,"** followed by such stories as **"Love and Death,"** and closing with **"The Dead."** In all of these cycles Oates depicts through minute observation the innermost anxieties and inhibitions symptomatic of contemporary American life. Although they lack the mythic impact of Faulkner's cycle, they formulate an encompassing appraisal of the situation of both the individual and the society today and their inter-causality. Oates's cycles do not significantly re-align the genre, but rather rejuvenate it, rendering it new fictional relevance as a medium capable of persuasively expressing a comprehensive vision of our modern predicament. Oates draws in these cycles on her predecessors only for stimulus. Her construction and characterization are distinctly unique. She may have been influenced by Joyce's and Anderson's thematic cycles and Faulkner's and Hemingway's sequential cycles, but there is no evidence of 'borrowing' from one particular example. As in her stories Oates combines literary sensitivity

with her own narrative intuition to produce a strictly autonomous expression. (pp. 151-52)

Katherine Bastian, in her Joyce Carol Oates's Short Stories: Between Tradition and Innovation, *Verlag Peter Lang, 1983, 173 p.*

ERICA JONG (essay date 1984)

[*Jong is an American writer best known for her novel* Fear of Flying (1973). *In the following excerpted review, she comments on Oates's thematic focus in* Last Days.]

The short story has always been the most flexible of forms. In the hands of some writers—Isaac Bashevis Singer, for example—it can become as complex a parable of good and evil as a 500-page novel. In the hands of others—O. Henry and Guy de Maupassant come to mind—it can seem as compressed and paradoxical as an aphorism. Some writers use short stories as warm-ups for novels—Vladimir Nabokov often did this. Others intuitively seem to know that the short story is for a different type of material from the novel: a brief and dazzling plunge into another state of consciousness. Joyce Carol Oates is one of these.

In **Last Days,** a new collection of 11 stories, Miss Oates displays the uncanny ability to penetrate different states of consciousness, which has always been one of her trump cards as a writer. The title story is an astonishing portrait of a young Jewish psychotic who is convinced he is "G-d" and murders his rabbi, then himself in a mad attempt to show the congregation that he is indeed the Messiah. The thought processes of a schizophrenic young man and the reactions of those around him are commingled in this story, which is one of the most convincing, and therefore unpleasant, descriptions of schizophrenia I have ever read. It is so convincing, in fact, that it produces in the head a din of the kind I imagine accompanies schizophrenic delusion:

"Saul Morgenstern, the Scourge of G-d. His style is outrage tinged with irony and humor. . . . He is a marvelous talker, a tireless spinner of anecdotes, tall tales, moral parables. With enviable agility he climbs the steps to the 'sacred' space before the congregation. With a burst of extraordinary energy he hauls himself over a six-foot wall (littered with broken bottles, it is afterward claimed) while his friends stand gaping and staring. He risks death, he defies death, knowing himself immortal. The entire performance is being taped. Not a syllable, not a wince, will be lost. He has penciled in last-minute corrections in his fastidious hand, the manuscript awaits its public, he can hear beforehand the envious remarks of his friends and acquaintances and professors. Am I the Messiah, he wonders, with so many eyes upon me?—standing erect at the lectern, the pistol in one hand and the microphone in the other."

Miss Oates is preoccupied with painful states. In one story, a little girl witnesses a murder; in another, the fanatically religious stepmother of three little girls prepares to take them all back to God. In the past, Miss Oates has been our poet laureate of schizophrenia, of blasted childhoods, of random acts of violence. And this latest collection has many excellent examples of this Joyce Carol Oates, the first public one we came to know.

But in this volume there appears a new Joyce Carol Oates I like even better than the hallucinatory chronicler of madness and violence performed on and by children. She is beginning to chronicle experiences only a mature writer can have. One of the best of these stories, **"The Man Whom Women Adored,"** traces the rise and fall of a beautiful, aristocratic man through the eyes of a woman writer—his sometime lover—who will eventually tell his story. It compresses a novel into its pages, a short story reminiscent of John Cheever's best—the fall of the wellborn man, told by one of his intended victims.

Six stories grouped together in this collection under the title **"Our Wall"** show Miss Oates dealing with the sort of material available to writers traveling around the world in their masks as celebrated personages. Here Miss Oates covers some of the territory cleared by John Updike's Henry Bech stories. She explores Eastern Europe through the eyes of various alter egos, the most appealing of whom, Judith Horne, a fictional American woman writer, of Polish-Jewish ancestry, comes close to a breakdown while visiting Warsaw. The anxious atmosphere of Eastern Europe and the unique unpleasantness of travel there are conveyed with great power in **"My Warszawa: 1980"** and its companion pieces about Berlin, about a Russian-American literary conference, Hungary, Africa and finally the wall that separates East from West, illusion from reality, life from death:

"Long lines in Centrum and in the other downtown stores. Futile for Judith to shop there, simply to spend her zlotys, and in any case the goods look second-rate, shoddy. Long queues at fruit stands: withered lemons, small shriveled apples in outdoor bins. . . . Red trolley cars, red buses, hurtling along the streets, emitting their poisonous exhaust. Crowds, noise, rain in the morning and sunshine at noon, a pervasive chill. Cobblestone streets. Monuments. The elegant Park Lazienkowski. The Palace Marszatkowska.—How many Jews live in Warsaw at the present time? Judith asks, and her guide Tadeusz replies, There are no statistics."

What Miss Oates makes of Eastern Europe in this last sequence of stories, which are ostensibly about Communism and capitalism, is quite different from what Mr. Updike made of it in his Bech stories, where Eastern Europe is a relatively jovial place, a target for delicious satire about political and diplomatic pretension, a treasure trove of insights about the absurdities of being a famous writer. Miss Oates's Eastern Europe is a state of mind familiar to us from Kafka's stories—that of "a sensitivity acute beyond usefulness," which Updike in his introduction to Kafka's complete stories has characterized as the quintessence of modernism. Miss Oates's is an Eastern Europe, in short, that is not far from the landscape of hysteria and violence that marks the first group of stories in this book. But in the last story, also called **"Our Wall,"** Miss Oates reaches beyond realism to create, in metaphorical terms, the philosophical underpinnings of all walls. This story rather reminds me of D. M. Thomas's hallucinatory conclusion to his novel *The White Hotel.* History here transcends itself and becomes poetry: "Come closer, have no fear, long before you were born The Wall was, and forever will The Wall endure."

Miss Oates is one of our most audaciously talented writers. Her gift is so large, her fluency in different genres—poems, short stories; novels, essays—so great, that at times she seems to challenge the ability of readers to keep up with her. In an age of specialization she is that rarest of generalists, a woman of letters. She gives her gifts with such abundance and generosity that we may pick and choose, preferring this Oates to

that, quibbling about which of her many talents we like best. I for one am happy to see her exploring the curious worlds of diplomacy, détente and literary vagabondage to which a much traveled, much translated writer is exposed.

Erica Jong, "Uncanny States of East and West," in The New York Times Book Review, *August 5, 1984, p. 7.*

SHARON DEAN   (essay date 1988)

[*In the following essay, Dean discusses Oates's analogy of womanhood and religious vocation in her story "At the Seminary."*]

Joyce Carol Oates's **"At the Seminary"** examines the conflict between religious vocation embodied in novice priest Peter Downey and the power of womanhood embodied in his sister, Sally. By exploring what it means to be a woman in the context of what it means to have a religious vocation, Oates may be suggesting that women in the twentieth century have a potential for upheaval often associated with spiritual crises or with powerful religious movements. Oates establishes the connection between vocation and womanhood through Sally's menstruation, which is both a curse and a cleansing. At the sudden, uncontrolled flow of her blood, Sally feels "an expression of awe that might have been religious, so total and commanding was it." The onset of the "faithful blood" is something she resists and embraces: "I never asked for it, I never asked God to make me a woman! She could not stop grinning. What beauty! What immeasurable beauty!" Menstruation is like a "centuries old" religious experience, "a sensation of overwhelming light or sound, something dazzling and roaring at once, that seemed to [Sally] to make her existence suddenly beautiful: complete: ended."

Just as vocation represents the inescapable pull of religion, Sally's menstruation represents the inescapable pull of womanhood. Vocation transforms; it is something one resists and then something one loses oneself in and gains power from. Thus Peter Downey recognizes in Sally's menstruation the beauty, power, and dread of the priestly vocation he finally accepts, and menstruation transforms Sally from one who resists to one who accepts her womanhood.

Oates stresses Sally's transformation and the power she gains through it by framing the story with an account of her journey with her mother and father to and from the seminary. Looking at a road map, Sally acts as "if she feared moving it would precipitate them into the wilderness." Shortly after this, the Downeys drive past a billboard image of a woman in a bathing suit diving into a pool, an image that suggests the upheaval accepting one's femaleness could create. Mother and daughter draw together. Mrs. Downey protects herself from this image of the threat of womanhood by pulling out a rosary; Sally protects herself by cultivating an arrogant ugliness.

In the journey away from the seminary, Oates shows Sally no longer struggling against the wilderness of her blood-nourished vocation. She has attained a new kind of power and through Mr. Downey's reaction to his daughter, we see the potential for upheaval this power holds. Mr. Downey believes he no longer needs the guidance of Sally's map, that he faces no challenge now, "fortified as he was by the knowledge of precisely where he was going." But Mr. Downey does not know where he is going; it is now he who drives toward a "wild darkness." While he has finally accepted Peter's vocation and believes Peter "would be safe, there was nothing to worry about," he does not yet realize that he can no longer ignore Sally, but will soon have to reckon with her transformation into a force as important as her brother.

"At the Seminary" ends on a moon image, the female principle Mr. Downey has to fear: "Out of the corner of Mr. Downey's eye [Sally's] face loomed blank and milky, like a threatening moon he dared not look upon." If sex is Sally's destiny, it is a destiny she shares with other women and one that contains within itself a power as awesome and as disturbing as the power traditionally associated with religious vocation. (pp. 51-2)

> *Sharon Dean, "Oates's 'At the Seminary',," in* The Explicator, *Vol. 46, No. 2, Winter, 1988, pp. 51-2.*

FURTHER READING

Barza, Stephen. "Joyce Carol Oates: Naturalism and the Aberrant Response." *Studies in American Fiction* 7, No. 2 (Autumn 1979): 141-51.
　　Suggests that Oates draws on the traditions of naturalism in her fiction, while still conveying a modern sensibility.

Bellamy, Joe David. "Joyce Carol Oates." In his *The New Fiction: Interviews with Innovative American Writers,* pp. 19-31. Chicago: University of Illinois Press, 1972.

Includes comments by Oates on her writing style and several of her stories.

Bender, Eileen T. "Autonomy and Influence: Joyce Carol Oates' *Marriages and Infidelities.*" *Soundings* LVIII, No. 3 (Fall 1975): 390-406.
　　Discusses perspective in Oates's fiction and examines her "reworkings" of stories by James Joyce, Franz Kafka, and Henry James.

———. "Conclusion: Missing Views, 'Last Days'." In her *Joyce Carol Oates, Artist in Residence,* pp. 165-78. Bloomington: Indiana University Press, 1987.
　　Examines "In a Region of Ice" and "Last Days" to reveal Oates's concerns as an artist and an academic.

Giles, James R. "Oates' *The Poisoned Kiss.*" *Canadian Literature,* No. 80 (Spring 1979): 138-47.
　　Discusses Oates's comments in the "Afterword" to *The Poisoned Kiss* and examines several stories from this collection.

Grant, Mary Kathryn. *The Tragic Vision of Joyce Carol Oates.* Durham, N.C.: Duke University Press, 1978, 167 p.
　　Discusses Oates's focus on violence and tragedy in her fiction.

Martin, Carol A. "Art and Myth in Joyce Carol Oates's 'The Sacred Marriage'." *The Midwest Quarterly* XXVIII, No. 4 (Summer 1987): 540-52.
　　Relates themes of "The Sacred Marriage" to ancient myths and rituals as presented in James G. Frazer's influential *The Golden Bough* (1890).

Phillips, Robert. "Joyce Carol Oates." *The Paris Review* 20, No. 73 (Spring 1978): 198-226.
　　Oates comments on her literary interests and personal experiences, and responds to criticism of her work.

Liam O'Flaherty

1896-1984

Irish short story writer, novelist, dramatist, autobiographer, biographer.

O'Flaherty is considered a preeminent modern Irish writer for his imaginative and energetic depictions of Irish life. He has been described as one of the last figures in the Irish literary renaissance of the twentieth century, a tradition that includes such seminal writers as William Butler Yeats, A. E. (George Russell), Sean O'Casey, and Frank O'Connor. Although he is best known for his novel *The Informer* and the subsequent Academy Award-winning film of the same title, critics characterize O'Flaherty's work in the short fiction genre as his highest literary achievement. An observer of the harsh and often violent conditions of life on his native Aran Islands, O'Flaherty produced a prodigious number of tales describing nature, animals, and the struggles of peasants existing in a rugged environment. His stories, which display elements of both romanticism and realism, are well regarded for their stark narratives that are drawn from the Gaelic oral storytelling tradition and exhibit an apparent artlessness, as well as a detached, objective point of view.

O'Flaherty was born on Gort na gCapall, Inishmore, the largest of the Aran Islands off the West coast of Ireland. The ninth of ten children in a Gaelic-speaking family, O'Flaherty demonstrated an early interest in storytelling and was influenced by his mother and neighbors, who would gather around his family's hearth to tell Gaelic tales. Although educated for the priesthood as a youth, O'Flaherty abandoned this vocation and in 1915 volunteered for the Irish Guards unit of the British Army. He was injured during World War I and discharged in 1918. Commentators maintain that O'Flaherty's war experiences left an indelible impression on his personal life and contributed to the presence of violence and brutality in much of his fiction. After finishing his university education in 1918, O'Flaherty traveled for several years, recounting his journeys in his first autobiography, *Two Years.* Long concerned with the plight of the poor and working classes, O'Flaherty strengthened his sympathy for these people during his travels, serving for a time as an active member of the Communist Party.

In 1921 O'Flaherty returned to Ireland, where he joined the Republicans fighting against the Free Staters in the Irish Civil War and wrote for the Republican paper *The Plain People.* O'Flaherty later became infamous in Ireland when he appointed himself "Chairman of the Council of the Unemployed" and seized a public building in Dublin for several days with other unemployed citizens. Although the protest ended peacefully, it prompted O'Flaherty's exile, and in 1922 he fled to England, where he began to write seriously. In 1923 he published his first short story, "The Sniper," in the *New Leader,* a British socialist weekly. This story attracted the attention of publisher Edward Garnett, who later helped publish several of O'Flaherty's books, including his first novel, *Thy Neighbour's Wife.* During the rest of the 1920s and 1930s, O'Flaherty wrote prolifically. Although his literary career was beginning to flourish during this time, O'Flaherty experienced two nervous breakdowns as a result of financial

difficulties and neurotic disorders. In addition, a great deal of O'Flaherty's writing was banned in Ireland during the 1930s because several of his characters, including Fergus O'Connor, the war-wounded protagonist of his semi-autobiographical novel *The Black Soul,* were thought shocking. In 1937, despite these setbacks, O'Flaherty published *Famine,* which many critics regard as his greatest novel. During World War II, O'Flaherty visited the Caribbean, South America, and eventually the United States, where he settled in Connecticut. Upon his return to Europe after the war, he lived at intervals in Ireland, England, and France. By this time, O'Flaherty's literary output had begun to decline, and between 1946 and the early 1960s, he published only two novels and one major story collection. He spent the remainder of his life in Dublin until his death at the age of eighty-eight.

O'Flaherty is noted for both his Gaelic- and English-language short stories. Although critics generally concur that O'Flaherty's style is more suited to Gaelic, the majority of his short fiction was written in English, and criticism has focused on his four principal English-language volumes: *Spring Sowing, The Tent, The Mountain Tavern,* and *Two Lovely Beasts.* O'Flaherty's first three collections, all published within five years, constitute the corpus of his early period. Stories in these early volumes are characterized by O'Flaherty's keen sense of observation, through which he realistically portrays events with little or no authorial intrusion. Most of O'Flaherty's stories take place in wild outdoor settings—bleak fields, rocky precipices, stormy seas—similar to those of the Aran Islands of his youth. These settings contribute to what is regarded as O'Flaherty's objective view of the often chaotic, random violence of nature. For example, in "The Wave," a brief yet dense tale, O'Flaherty vividly describes the great force of a wave crashing into and destroying the stony cliff upon which it breaks.

In O'Flaherty's early volumes, animals and their elemental beauty comprise his main subject matter. Critics note his dramatic portrayals of nature and evolutionary processes in stories in which animals face conflicts and restore balance through instinctual reactions. Although O'Flaherty's animal stories often include violence, critics perceive an important purpose in the severity of his depictions. For instance, in "The Wounded Cormorant," an injured bird is tormented to death by other cormorants so that the strength of the flock is not compromised. Critics note in this and other tales an austere tone and detached stance through which O'Flaherty eschews interpretation. Irish poet A. E. stated: "When O'Flaherty thinks, he's a goose, when he feels, he's a genius." In addition to animals, O'Flaherty's early works often focus on peasants and their relationships to nature. O'Flaherty claimed to have disdained what he viewed as the corrupted progress of society, but when he wrote of people living close to the elements, he celebrated the evolutionary processes of life and death. In "Spring Sowing," an oft-cited example of this theme, O'Flaherty lyrically presents a young couple planting seeds for their first crop. Focusing on the wife's point of view, O'Flaherty conveys her understanding of their role in the natural cycle of life, as she realizes that this first sowing will be followed by others until their death.

Many stories in *Two Lovely Beasts* feature subjects similar to those in O'Flaherty's earlier volumes. Critics maintain, however, that O'Flaherty's prose reveals more maturity and depth in this later collection. In the title piece, protagonist Colm Derrane raises two calves, an unprecedented act in his poor village. Eventually, through usury, Derrane attains wealth. However, he is ostracized by the villagers, both out of jealousy and because of his untraditional ways. Although Derrane is perceived by critics both as a hero and a villain, his character exemplifies O'Flaherty's delineation of an individual acting alone outside the laws of civilization that recurs in many of his later stories. James F. Kilroy contends that O'Flaherty's unpolished prose style and commonplace subject matter remain evident in these later stories yet his vision has matured enough to become "balanced and complex . . . , vivid and vehement." In "Post Office," another story from *Two Lovely Beasts*, O'Flaherty deviates from his characteristic terse, direct tone to write a story that, as Paul A. Doyle states, is "genial and good-humored."

In his works, O'Flaherty draws upon the forms and styles of oral Gaelic storytelling to create narratives that are distinctive for their poetic energy. Some critics, however, consider O'Flaherty's virtues the very substance of his faults, contending that his powerful imagination, in addition to attracting a reader's interest, may also lead to overwrought symbolism and melodrama. In commenting on O'Flaherty's artistic achievement, John Zneimer has asserted that O'Flaherty captures the essence of instinctual life by writing very structured tales that give the appearance of random order. He con-

cludes: "O'Flaherty's short stories are an attempt to express pure *being*. This is why they elude conventional analysis which, bringing mind to the scene, attempts to extract meaning. O'Flaherty's stories mean as nature means, and the meaning of nature is so inaccessible to man that all attempts to plumb its depths must be futile."

(For further information on O'Flaherty's life and career, see *Contemporary Literary Criticism*, Vols. 5, 34; *Contemporary Authors*, Vols. 101, 113 [obituary]; *Dictionary of Literary Biography*, Vol. 36; and *Dictionary of Literary Biography Yearbook: 1984*.)

PRINCIPAL WORKS

SHORT FICTION

Spring Sowing   1924
The Tent   1926
The Mountain Tavern, and Other Stories   1929
The Wild Swan, and Other Stories   1932
The Short Stories of Liam O'Flaherty   1937
Two Lovely Beasts, and Other Stories   1948
Dúil   1953
The Stories of Liam O'Flaherty   1956
Liam O'Flaherty: Selected Stories   1958
Irish Portraits: Fourteen Short Stories by Liam O'Flaherty   1970
Selected Stories of Liam O'Flaherty   1970
More Short Stories of Liam O'Flaherty   1971
The Pedlar's Revenge, and Other Stories   1976

OTHER MAJOR WORKS

Thy Neighbour's Wife   (novel)   1923
The Black Soul   (novel)   1924
The Informer   (novel)   1925
Darkness: A Tragedy in Three Acts   (drama)   1926
Mr. Gilhooley   (novel)   1926
The Life of Tim Healy   (biography)   1927
The Wilderness   (serialized novel)   1927; book edition, 1978
The Assassin   (novel)   1928
The House of Gold   (novel)   1929
The Return of the Brute   (novel)   1929
A Tourist's Guide to Ireland   (satire)   1929
Two Years   (autobiography)   1930
I Went to Russia   (autobiography)   1931
The Puritan   (novel)   1931
Skerrett   (novel)   1932
The Martyr   (novel)   1933
Shame the Devil   (autobiography)   1934
Hollywood Cemetery   (novel)   1935
Famine   (novel)   1937
Land   (novel)   1946
Insurrection   (novel)   1950

RHYS DAVIES   (essay date 1932)

[*Davies was a Welsh novelist, short story writer, editor, and dramatist. In his foreword to* The Wild Swan, and Other Stories *that appears below, Davies identifies rural settings and a* simple, direct prose style as characteristics of O'Flaherty's best writing.]

Mr. O'Flaherty is always refreshing, and the three stories published here are fair examples of his varied work. The immediate appeal of *The Wild Swan,* with all its fine perception of unhuman life and its fresh gleaming beauty, needs nothing said of it except an expression of gratitude. **"It was the Devil's Work"** has Mr. O'Flaherty's usual bucolic vigour and hard laugh: he knows his peasants and he knows his priests, and the satire is effective. **"Unclean"** is sour and sordid: like all Mr. O'Flaherty's work in this genre it is too bald and definite in its squalor to become literature: it has too much *story,* in the sense that the *News of the World* on Sundays has too much story. Here the flood of poetry, the sense of wonder and delight, that is in Mr. O'Flaherty is withheld: his mind has seen a story, he must get it down quickly on paper. But his blood has not been touched.

The variety of his work has lately been a little confusing to his admirers. We always look for drama from Mr. O'Flaherty: he will have drama at all costs (sometimes at the cost of truth, as I well know—though this is an aside not concerning his books). Frequently that elemental sense of drama has evoked wonderful, passionate books like *The House of Gold, The Black Soul* and many short stories. But sometimes it has led him sadly astray, as in the bold but frivolous autobiographical books and such shockers as *The Return of the Brute.* One notices that immediately his characters enter a city or become town-dwellers a wearisome binge with all its attendant flourishes ensues. Cities drive his characters desperate, and though we too are borne along by the wealth of incidents which befall them, upheld, if protestingly, by their energy, with what a sigh of relief we open another book of O'Flaherty and find ourselves back with the peasants among the farms and along that sea-coast where he is most sensitive.

There he is rich and vital. We lose the sense of printed words and smell the keen spray-cool air of wild spaces that open magically before us. We clearly see the anchored curraghs bobbing over the heavy moonlit silence of the sea, and know there is going to be a bit of real drama presently. We are more than in love with Red Barbara. The blackbirds are revealed to us for ever.

We must be grateful to him too that he has never prettified the country. With him we never take a stroll from the library to the village inn and, after buying a round, encourage the rustic company to talk in rich dialect. He doesn't weave eternal daisy-chains in a meadow that is also delicious with buttercups, sentimentally aware—in a careful style—how tranquil and beautiful is nature. His sheep and goats and cows are alive, suffering and pitiable in travail, observant and critical in well-being: they *are* sheep and goats, not things about which one can become literary. Neither do we have the feeling that his pieces of scenery have been let down from above or wheeled in from the wings, as one does in the stories of, say, Katherine Mansfield and those that run after her.

But the town is forever Babylon to him. Only disaster can come out of it. He is attuned to the roar of the waves, the sweep of the winds in remote villages, the pointed and humorous chattering of peasant voices (when they speak to each other and not to visitors). He has the kind of subtlety and wit that does not depend on sophistication and elegance. He is not profound except in the sense that man's conflict with elemental things is profound. He has no philosophy except that

of a simple man's enjoyment of what comes to his hand: a good drink, a Red Barbara of a woman, a pot of money. His books do not shatter us with their spiritual experiences or move us to fury at the baseness of civilization. But he tells a tale of a wild swan startled into flight from death, or a miser who swallows his money as he lies dying, or a sturdy young man who takes to his bed because of the howling sickness that has come with love, and his exhibitions of life's primal forces, though they may lack the development of sophisticated passion, become memorable in their simple directness.

And perhaps, even in these days of Proust and Joyce and Mrs. Woolf, his way is the more eternal. (pp. 7-10)

Rhys Davies, in a foreword to The Wild Swan and Other Stories *by Liam O'Flaherty, Joiner & Steele, Ltd., 1932, pp. 7-10.*

VIVIAN MERCIER (essay date 1956)

[*Mercier is an advisory editor of the* James Joyce Quarterly *and has written extensively on Irish and French literature. Below, in his introduction to* The Stories of Liam O'Flaherty, *Mercier extols O'Flaherty's treatment of the relationship between nature and humanity.*]

The Irish have always excelled at the short story, if we can judge by what survives of the old sagas. While all but one or two of the longer tales seem to the modern reader formless and quite unworthy of comparison with the *Iliad* and the *Odyssey,* many of the briefer prose narratives pack a whole gamut of emotions into two or three thousand words. Cross and Slover's *Ancient Irish Tales* includes many effective short stories, among which I would single out "The Story of Mac Datho's Pig" and "How Ronan Slew His Son" as exceptionally powerful.

Liam O'Flaherty, who has written short stories in Gaelic and in English, is a worthy successor to the anonymous storytellers of the past. He began to write just after the establishment of the Irish Free State in 1922, but his closest affinities are with two rather older writers, the Irishman John M. Synge and the Englishman D. H. Lawrence. If the author of *Riders to the Sea* had written short stories, they would have been very like O'Flaherty's, I believe. Lawrence, of course, wrote many short stories, but it is in his poems that we find the closest parallels with the short stories of O'Flaherty.

Misled by *The Informer* and similar but weaker novels like *Insurrection,* many readers and critics regard Liam O'Flaherty as the novelist *par excellence* of the Irish Revolution and Civil War. They do him an injustice.

His two best novels, *Skerrett* and *Famine,* are not set in the twentieth century at all. *Famine,* while containing many precise historical and political references, deals with a period of Irish history in which men struggled against forces of Nature rather than against their fellowmen—though admittedly human stupidity and greed had done much to strengthen those pitiless forces. Skerrett, in the book which bears his name, battles the Church and civil society, and is defeated—only to become a legend after his death. Not until we have closed the book do we realize that Skerrett symbolizes Nature rather than Man—perhaps it would be most accurate to say that he is the Natural Man—and that once again Nature has triumphed, as she does in almost every work by O'Flaherty.

It is to his short stories we must turn—or to his second novel,

The Black Soul—if we wish to see O'Flaherty nakedly at grips with his true subject, the relationship between Man and Nature. Take **"Spring Sowing,"** the title story in his first collection. This picture of a newly-married Aran Islands couple sowing their first crop of potatoes together is both realistic and symbolic. We are given sufficient detail to be able to visualize the young pair at what will be their annual task. At the same time, few tasks could better symbolize O'Flaherty's conception of the relationship between Man and Nature. The sowing is a triumph, but a short-lived one. Man can only triumph over Nature by co-operating with her; in the end he becomes her victim.

> They had done it together. They had planted seeds in the earth. The next day and the next and all their lives, when spring came they would have to bend their backs and do it until their hands and bones got twisted with rheumatism.

Even the solace which Nature offers to Man is unflattering because it leaves him helpless:

> But night would always bring sleep and forgetfulness.

Often enough an O'Flaherty short story is no more than a wild cry of protest against "the human condition," like the old man's cry in **"Life"**:

> Aie! Aie! . . . Everything is more lasting than man. Aie! The Virgin Mary have pity on me! Look at me now and I only the wreck of a man. Yet there was a day . . .

"Yet there was a day . . . Liam O'Flaherty has never pretended to believe that it is not good to be alive, nor does the old man in the story. If life and the prime of life were not so glorious, there would be no need to lament their passing. Wordlessly, the child in the same story expresses his delight in being alive:

> The infant hopped up and down, shouting merrily as he struggled to touch the bright feathers of the rushing birds with his outstretched hands.

Over and over again in these stories the point is made that Nature is both friend and enemy. She destroys us, but our greatest happiness, O'Flaherty implies, comes from yielding to her. The young girl in **"The Mirror,"** terrified of maturity and the perils of motherhood, becomes the bride of the sun and learns the lesson of that acceptance of Nature which brings joy and disarms fear.

The thwarting of Nature by Man entails its own punishment, but since Man is a part of Nature, she often defeats herself. Joseph's sterility in **"Red Barbara"** is "natural" in a sense, though we are led to believe that it is in part due to his being educated, overcivilized, "priestly." In **"The Wedding"** Nuala's madness is attributed to natural causes, but that does not make her spinsterhood any the less painful and frustrating.

In O'Flaherty's animal stories, too, Nature is at war with herself. Sometimes the sheer vitality of the creature preserves it, as in **"The Rockfish,"** but more often death ends the story, as in **"The Wounded Cormorant."** In **"The Wild Goat's Kid,"** life for the goat and her kid means death for the greedy dog. These and all O'Flaherty's stories sing a hymn to Life—while Death supplies the ground-bass to their defiant melody.

Sometimes, as in **"The Blow,"** Nature asserts herself with as-tonishing tenderness. The sow's concern for her brood finds a parallel in the almost animal love that wells up in the father's heart after he has struck his son.

To the treatment of this subject matter O'Flaherty brings an eye rather than an ear. Though he sometimes mars the objectivity of his narrative by an unnecessary comment, he always makes the reader see before urging him to judge. Even occasional repetitions and clichés fail to blur the moving picture which O'Flaherty's writing projects within the reader's mind.

If Liam O'Flaherty's work survives, posterity will not regard him as the novelist-historian of a turbulent era but as the celebrant of timeless mysteries—mysteries rooted in Nature and in that portion of Nature embodied in the life of Man. (pp. v-viii)

> *Vivian Mercier, in an introduction to* The Stories of Liam O'Flaherty *by Liam O'Flaherty, The Devin-Adair Company, 1956, pp. v-viii.*

FRANK O'CONNOR   (essay date 1956)

[*O'Connor was an Irish short story writer noted for his realistic and humorous depictions of Irish life; the poet William Butler Yeats once remarked that "O'Connor is doing for Ireland what Chekhov did for Russia." His* The Lonely Voice: A Study of the Short Story (1962) *is considered among the most distinguished analyses of the genre. In the following excerpt from a review of* The Stories of Liam O'Flaherty, *O'Connor lauds O'Flaherty's narratives as powerful delineations of instinctual life and distinguishes his prose as an art form derived yet different from the oral folktale.*]

"By the hokies, there was a man in this place one time by the name of Ned Sullivan, and he had a queer thing happen him late one night and he coming up the Valley Road from Durlas."

That is how a folk story begins, or should begin, and woe betide the storyteller whoever he may be who forgets that his story is first and foremost "news," that there is a listener he must grip by the lapel and shout at if necessary till he has attracted his attention. Yet that is how no printed short story should begin, because such a story seems tame when you remove it from its warm nest by the cottage fire, from the sense of an audience with its interjections, and the feeling of terror at what may lurk in the darkness outside. This is a tale, and even when handled by a master like Kipling, it looks and is contrived.

No such charge can be brought against Liam O'Flaherty. . . . (p. 1)

O'Flaherty never forgets that his stories are news. . . . Mr. Mercier's introduction [to **The Stories of Liam O'Flaherty** (see excerpt dated 1956)] compares O'Flaherty with Synge: I find it difficult to see a single point of comparison. He is on much safer ground when comparing him with D. H. Lawrence. My own tendency being to run hard whenever I see an animal, I can only offer as an act of faith the belief that O'Flaherty's animal stories are masterly presentations of instinctual life, but when he describes the instinctual life of human beings—of children, women and men from his own wild countryside—there is no question in my mind that he writes as a master. He has all Lawrence's power of conveying the enchantment of the senses which is part of the instinctual life and, unlike Lawrence, does not romanticize or rationalize it. He begins to go false only when he has to deal with people who are compelled to live by their judgment rather than their instincts, and this, and not any theological dispute, seems to me the real basis of his quarrel with Catholicism in Ireland.

Whatever O'Flaherty stories may lack, it is not the narrative impulse, because he comes from the Aran Islands, one of the last outposts of folk culture, and his native language is Irish. And since, like a Munsterwoman I once spoke to about him, "I do be lighting candles to Liam O'Flaherty," let me state my only complaints against his work, which are that his English lacks the distinction and beauty of his Gaelic, and his form is occasionally very dull indeed.

In spite of the powerful narrative line, O'Flaherty's form is an art form, not a folk one; but it is the convenient, ready-to-wear magazine form of the Twenties in England—two to three thousand words describing a single episode—and while, like the ready-to-wear suit it is a great convenience, the pattern is also in quantity very monotonous. (pp. 1, 20)

Yet, as the work of Tolstoy shows, the instincts account for a great part of human character, and O'Flaherty's range is remarkable. If I had to choose one story of his to stand . . . as one of the great masterpieces of storytelling, I should, I think, choose **"The Fairy Goose."** It is the story of a feeble little goose whom the superstition of her owner turns into the divinity of an Irish village. She makes the fortune and turns the head of her owner until the parish priest comes to break up the cult and the youths of the village stone the poor goose to death. In essence, the story tells the whole history of religion. The absurdity of the cult seems to call for satire, for an Anatole France or a Norman Douglas, but by a miracle of taste and feeling O'Flaherty never permits the shadow of a sneer to disturb the gravity of the theme. We laugh—laugh louder indeed than we would laugh at France or Douglas—but at the same time we are moved, and eventually the impression left on our mind is that of Turgenev's "Byezhin Meadow"—itself one of the great masterpieces of storytelling—of a vast sense of life's mystery and beauty. (p. 20)

> *Frank O'Connor, "A Good Short Story Must Be News," in* The New York Times Book Review, *June 10, 1956, pp. 1, 20.*

GEORGE BRANDON SAUL (essay date 1963)

[*Saul is an American writer and critic. In the excerpt below, he provides an overview of stories in O'Flaherty's collections* Spring Sowing, The Tent, The Mountain Tavern, *and* Two Lovely Beasts.]

Spring Sowing is a markedly lyrical collection; its reflections of Aran are fresh and those of revolutionary Dublin lively, especially since O'Flaherty has had by choice a vast personal experience of war and revolution. Its thirty-two mostly very brief tales include about a dozen of its author's better pieces, the most memorable being the title-story, **"The Sniper"**, a rooftop tragedy of Irish Republican Army-Free State feuding, and **"Going into Exile"**, which is concerned with a brother and sister's leaving the family cabin for Boston. **"Spring Sowing"** itself tells of a young peasant couple of the island of Inverara doing their first spring sowing together: this is an event of both practical and symbolical significance to them, though one also prophetic of weary years ahead. Here is the O'Flaherty who is sensitive to the gentleness that can set a glow even on life that is cruelly primitive and poverty-wounded.

In the early hours of the morning we left the factory, had breakfast at an eating-house, and went to bed. We spent most of the day in our room, as the town consisted entirely of factories and it hurt one's soul to walk through its streets. Sometimes, however, my brother insisted on bringing me for a tour, in order to explain the capitalist system in action. But I had lost all interest in socialism as soon as I had left Boston.

Generally, my brother wrote letters indoors. I found a complete set of Guy de Maupassant in English, bought for bawdy reasons by our landlord, who had been in Europe with the American army. Reading Maupassant became the only bright thing in my life while we stayed in that most horrifying town. When I had read him right through and was not inspired to re-read him because the translation was odious, I began to write stories in the same vein. I made four or five attempts, and then gave up the effort. I was dumbfounded by the fact that my stories were unreadable, even though I copied the material and motive, and merely transposed the scene. I came to the conclusion that the art of writing was incomprehensible.

> *Liam O'Flaherty, in his autobiographical work* Two Years (*1930*).

These stories certainly are various enough in both subject matter and appeal, and are suggestive of work to follow: a cow, seeing her dead calf in the tides, commits suicide from a cliff; a little boy is exhilarated by a lambing; a peasant sells a pig, gets drunk, and makes a fool of himself; a bullock and a wild sow are cruelly abused; two drunken young men quarrel in a curragh and are drowned; three fishermen land their curragh safely against dangerous odds; a cowardly young sea gull is tricked into flying by his mother; etc. The best tales are generally those which are closest to the soil and also to the beasts and human beings (the implied distinction is not always convincing) most nearly akin to it. Sometimes, however, the author's characteristic "psychological" analyses of the behaviour and assumed mental processes of brute animals are more imaginative than persuasive, however accurate his reports of physical responses, which seem based on sensitive and minute observation. A blackbird, for instance, is pictured as singing with self-conscious vanity and is ascribed motivations of a human sort. And of course there is O'Flaherty's interest—a recurrent concern—in detailed descriptions of sadistic, and sometimes nauseating, brutality: hence **"Sport: The Kill"** and **"Blood Lust"**, though there is happily nothing to match the horrifying crucifixion contained in the author's almost pathological novel *The Martyr* (1933).

Some of the pieces (**"The Wave"** and **"The Rockfish"**, for example) contain little more than description: this is characteristic of the later O'Flaherty. A further forecast is apparent in **"Wolf Lonigan's Death"**, in which a lurid miasma prophetic of *The Informer* (1925) appears. Here one must remember O'Flaherty's reported liking for Hemingway and Dreiser, as well as his belief that good writing 'must come out of reality' and 'the only true mysticism comes through reality'. His 'mysticism' is, however, sometimes confused with the kind of sentimentality that leads to theatricalism, poor taste, clichés: I am thinking of such work as **"Beauty"**, in which the sight of two trees stirs symbolical religious sentimentality in a man, with revulsion against a seductive woman just in time to prevent his being unfaithful to his fiancée; he staggers and groans—the rejected woman *hisses* 'you cur'—and he even ends by hugging and kissing one of the trees!

The twenty-nine stories of *The Tent*—O'Flaherty's titles are as literal as they are simple in designation—include three of striking quality: the title-piece, **"Milking Time"**, and **"The Wild Goat's Kid"**. Of these, **"The Tent"** concerns an ex-sergeant major who has taken to the roads. A tinker [an Irish gypsy] admits him to his tent during a storm; but when he tries to become intimate with a girl, one of the tinker's two wives, who responds to his advances, he is beaten and ejected, horrified, as the tinker carries the girl screaming back into the tent. This episode of brutal life is raw enough to appeal to O'Flaherty. The other two stories, in contrast, are wholly charming. Indeed they are almost perfect idylls which represent a precisely opposite type of appeal to this man of extremes. **"Milking Time"**, in which a young couple share the subject experience for the first time, parallels **"Spring Sowing"**; but **"The Wild Goat's Kid"** is less easily compared. It is a tale of an animal born above the sea-cliffs (a common locale for action in O'Flaherty's short stories and novels) and defended by its mother against a ferocious dog, before being taken eastward to safety. Nothing could be simpler; little in all O'Flaherty is more lyrically moving.

For the rest, there is the assortment which might have been predicted from *Spring Sowing*, with much description of the physical characteristics and responses of animals, constant concern with 'the short and simple annals of the poor', some sardonic handling of callous priests in **"The Outcasts"** and **"Offerings"**. O'Flaherty has a special scalpel for certain types of priest, especially the revolting specimen in *The House of Gold* (1929), conceivably his most powerful novel. There are also the unpalatable figures of **"The Strange Disease"** and **"The Child of God"** in *The Mountain Tavern*. O'Flaherty exhibits a sensitivity to seasonal change as acute as that of a lyric poet, and is deeply concerned with horror in such stories as **"Civil War"** and **"The Terrorist"**, and even with non-human cruelty in **"The Wounded Cormorant"** and **"The Jealous Hens."** But his range is now richer and wider than that he explored in *Spring Sowing*, though equally sparse in humorous content. One story—**"Poor People"**—is a picture of poverty and suffering so rending as to be at once story and almost-unendurable social document. **"Mother and Son"** comes as a relief after this; it is a story which is suspiciously suggestive of the whoppers O'Flaherty (see *Shame the Devil*, 1934, an autobiographical volume) used to tell his mother when he was a child. There are the technical slips which are not unusual in this author ('Her cheeks had a rosy flush like a young girl'); but these are less impressive than the unflagging drive of vitality and the freshness of observation ('a slight snapping sound like the end of a dog's yawn'). Ultimately this is a book that counts.

A similar judgement must be accorded *The Mountain Tavern and Other Stories.* But such rating does not depend on the longest of these twenty stories, **"The Painted Woman"**, whose forty pages, marred by the clichés O'Flaherty never hesitates to use ('The wind howled', 'the naked crags', etc.), present the author once more exploiting horror. In this story the elder of two middle-aged brothers marries, against the

judgement of the younger, a painted supposed widow back from America with an unhealthy-looking child. Bitterness finally leads to an effort by the elder brother to kill the younger in a curragh, the two ending up in each other's arms with the sharks, but somehow, in the rushed end, leaving an impression of theatricalism rather than tragedy. Horror, too, is the effect of **"The Alien Skull"**, the tale of a senseless army 'killer' which recalls *The Return of the Brute* (1929), O'Flaherty's novel of the fate of a bombing group of nine men in World War I (in which the author was himself blown up and shell-shocked). Indeed, horror and violence, as well as nature—including human nature—'red of tooth and claw', begin here to suggest a stereotype; and there are also ancillary efforts at voluptuous imagery, stimulated perhaps by a certain preoccupation with spring, for even the 'naked trees' have 'glossy bellies'. But happily there is less sentimentality in the concern with animals than usual in O'Flaherty. There is **"The Fairy Goose"**, a charming thing with the qualities appropriate to the suggestion of its title; **"Birth"**, concerned with the birth of a calf and with country tenderness; **"Red Barbara"**, the tale of a sensual, earthy, indolent widow wed to a gentle weaver whose impotence leads to a sort of madness before death; **"The Oar"**, a masterpiece of eerie and wild description of the struggle of two fishing curraghs to get to shore in a storm, and of Red Bartly's haunting by a helplessly passed face and upraised oar in the sea; and there is the touching, and wholly unsentimental, **"The Letter"**, in which a twenty-pound cheque from a daughter long silent in America is accompanied by a heartbroken letter revealing that she is a prostitute. And for ironic amusement, there is **"The Fall of Joseph Timmins"**, in which the husband of an arid, over-sanctimonious woman is caught by his disapproved-of nephew while trying to seduce a maid—and has got to become obliging.

Two Lovely Beasts and Other Stories represents a somewhat milder brew. Of the twenty tales, seven or eight are up to O'Flaherty's normal standard; but only one—**"Grey Seagull"**, reflecting its author's preoccupation with horse-racing—seems superlative. Here the reader's pulse runs with the champion. But there is nothing else to put beside the more memorable earlier tales, and such a piece of descriptive triviality as **"The Tide"** (with waters invading a messed-up beach with a desire 'to remould the beauty that had been torn"!) suggests a sentimentality beyond its author's earlier guilt.

As usual in O'Flaherty, the writing is almost bare of mere literary ornament—sparse even in figures of speech; his writing primarily depends for its effectiveness on sheer impact of his material. Plot counts for little; but O'Flaherty previously used a minimum of plot in his short stories, as also occasionally in his novels. Nor does *Two Lovely Beasts* contain much of the wildness common to his earlier work. Indeed, it has less emotion than emotion recollected in tranquillity—a circumstance which, despite the sainted Wordsworth, does not usually make for the keenest poetry. O'Flaherty seems mainly interested in offering a group of characters without much special significance in themselves. They are largely oddities—but without great claim to interest except for that fact in itself. And their presentation is curiously casual, for the narrative rarely carries the reader to any point of particular significance.

On the other hand, the prose is muscular, so nearly completely free of clichés that it is almost startling to come on 'foam-laced' and 'eyes . . . as blue as the sea'. Luckily this prose preserves hints of the O'Flaherty who is sensitive to the pathos of fierce age, affectionately observant of beast as well as man, and capable of poetry in individual dry-point in his response to nature. All this compensates for some apparent weakening in vitality.

O'Flaherty is an author whose miscellaneous achievement is critically somewhat disturbing. The dark tides sweeping through his best novels and short stories—the tumult and sometimes the uncouthness—can be very exciting; the O'Flaherty who counts is both gripping and panoramic; he is never a man to say nay to life. On the other hand, he generally lacks any impressive degree of real divination; his apparent lyricism is sometimes suggestive of the bogus—is too often merely a rush, rather than a grace, of wings; he is frequently tautological; and his minute descriptions and psychological meanderings can become very tedious, as can his seeming obsession with cruelty. Nor does he induce the unfaltering conviction that he is an artist who is never satisfied with anything but the precisely right word. Probably the *Times Literary Supplement* (19 April 1934) was correct to suggest that 'it is not unreasonable to surmise that his powerful and primitive imagination has been forced too rapidly, and therefore thwarted, by the modern cult of literary violence and exaggeration'. Yet, despite his failing, he remains well worth reading. (pp. 108-13)

> *George Brandon Saul, "A Wild Sowing: The Short Stories of Liam O'Flaherty," in* A Review of English Literature, *Vol. 4, No. 3, July, 1963, pp. 108-13.*

MICHAEL H. MURRAY (essay date 1968)

[In the essay excerpted below, Murray refutes the commonly held critical conception that the quality of O'Flaherty's short fiction depends upon his subject matter. Murray ascribes O'Flaherty's shortcomings to a tendency to overstate themes and symbolism regardless of subject.]

Before the publication of *Skerrett* and *Famine,* before Liam O'Flaherty had collected any of the stories that appear as parts of *A Mountain Tavern* or *Two Lovely Beasts,* William Troy [see Further Reading list] welcomed the new writer warmly to the Irish literary scene. This journeyman taleteller, according to his early critic, created in *Spring Sowing* and *The Tent,* his first two volumes of short fiction, "an impression of the profound solidarity of nature." Troy was the first of an unbroken line of commentators who have emphasized O'Flaherty's success as an interpreter of both the literal and symbolic aspects of nature. His contemporary Sean O'Faolain calls his brother in the craft an "introverted romantic [who] tilts too much at windmills" but hastens to add that in his animal stories the crusading O'Flaherty is at rest, his prose "the distillation of pure genius." John Kelleher, deploring the absence of a serious reading public in Ireland and the dearth of literary journals and unchecked powers of Irish censorship, notes that O'Flaherty lifted his stories out of "the rut of despair" that characterizes the work of so many Irish artists by his "power of describing natural phenomena." More recently, in *Modern Irish Fiction,* Benedict Kiely [see Further Reading list] has likened O'Flaherty to [Paul] Claudel. Both men, he asserts, have their roots in the earth; and "it is understanding of the earth, of animals worthy and human beings not always so worthy of the earth, that makes O'Flaherty's work important."

If commentators have been consistent in their agreement that

the best tales are those closest to the soil, another of Mr. Troy's contentions has failed to enjoy such enduring unanimity. Commenting on O'Flaherty's narrative art in 1929, he had praised the "trained intensity of style, the economy of detail, the exact sharpness of perception," characteristic, in his opinion, of the first two books of short stories. George Brandon Saul, of the more populous opposition camp, has argued in a recent critical survey [see excerpt dated 1963] that the Aran Islander's "apparent lyricism is sometimes suggestive of the bogus, [that] he is frequently tautological," and that he does not qualify as "an artist who is never satisfied with anything but precisely the right word."

Dispassionate readers must, alas, agree that Professor Saul's remarks are in many instances all too true; but at his best, Liam O'Flaherty nonetheless remains one of the finest craftsmen of the short narrative. Why this unevenness? Is he, as critics have contended, extraordinarily competent at peasant yarns and animal tales, but hopelessly inept when he turns his attention from the pasture?

A close reading of his short fiction does indeed reveal strained, disjointed writing in some selections, balanced elsewhere by indisputable narrative grace. I wish to establish, however, that inclusion in the "nature canon" has little bearing on the merit of an O'Flaherty story. In point of fact, though the majority of the animal pieces are excellent, many contain stylistic horrors every bit as jarring as those in his notoriously unsuccessful attempts to deal with the Anglo-Irish aristocracy.

The success or failure of Liam O'Flaherty's short fiction actually depends on quite a different phenomenon, one to which Vivian Mercier has made passing reference in a discussion of the stories of Corkery, Lavin, O'Connor, O'Faolain, and O'Flaherty [see Further Reading list]. Although he is a native speaker of Gaelic and "therefore born into the oral tradition," O'Flaherty is the "least oral in his approach to narrative of all five writers." Mercier refers here to the conception of so many of the stories in what he calls "cinematic terms," but the statement has other far-reaching implications. By extension he faults O'Flaherty for failing to remember that the relationship between story teller and audience is the indispensable component of the oral tradition. Liam O'Flaherty's style does not falter *only* when he leaves the barnyard; his imagery, his dialogue—in fact, the entire fabric of his narrative—disintegrates completely whenever he abandons his primary function as story teller in favor of self-conscious commentary on life; when, refusing to let his art suggest, he must speak *through* literature, only to pull down his tale under the weight of contrived symbolism or overstated theme.

Disparities in O'Flaherty's prose style bear out this argument. Whenever he rejects the straight narrative told for its own sake for the short story of philosophical statement, artless grace gives way to inappropriate imagery, careless structure, and tedious repetition. Selections from the first collection, *Spring Sowing,* will serve to illustrate this consistent stylistic problem in O'Flaherty's short fiction.

In choosing Liam O'Flaherty's finest stories, Mercier singled out the title piece of his first group for special praise [see excerpt dated 1956]. Here the writer deals with the central theme of nature and man's relations with the natural environment, but most important, according to Professor Mercier, is that "[t]his picture of a newly married Aran Islands couple sowing their first crop of potatoes together is both realistic and symbolic." This observation is entirely correct. The seeds in Mary's apron, Martin's cheeks on fire with a "primeval desire . . . to assert manhood and subjugate earth," his wife's deep sigh as he cleaves the ground to the accompaniment of his stooped grandfather's encouraging shrieks—all are symbolic of man's renewal in and through the regenerative earth mother. And, in this first story in Liam O'Flaherty's first collection of stories, the reader discovers in microcosm both the essence of his narrative strength and his potential for failure. The symbolism comes dangerously close to shouting the writer's theme, and both threaten to overwhelm the narrative straining to support them. The oral qualities of this story prove to be its salvation; but when the configuration of a symbolic structure or the statement of a theme becomes more important than the narrative in which it should inhere, O'Flaherty's style breaks down, consistently, and often horribly.

There are, for example, several stories in this first series in which, naturally enough for an Aran Islander, Liam O'Flaherty has chosen to deal with the sea. **"The Wave,"** a vignette without characters, would perhaps have been successful as purely descriptive prose. Yet O'Flaherty attempts to force from the landscape a symbolic evocation of mindless violence. The stress is painfully obvious; the story disintegrates into a series of grotesque images of which one contorted simile is sufficient example: "The trough of the sea was convulsing like water in a shaken glass." **"The Landing"** promises at first to be more successful. Thematically reminiscent of Synge's starkly beautiful "Riders to the Sea," the tale projects a powerful image of barren Ireland in the grieving Aran mother watching on the cliff, "wisps of grey hair flying about her face." Unfortunately O'Flaherty cannot permit the narrative to suggest its own multi-level meaning to his audience. Over and over he circles his theme, more and more explicitly *stating* the paradox of sea as simultaneous nourisher and destroyer. Finally, inevitably, he loses control and tells his reader that the raging ocean resembles "eau de cologne or something." Faulty parallelism and repetition mar this potentially fine story at its close.

O'Flaherty's attempts to deal with romantic love in *Spring Sowing* are also singularly unsuccessful. Critics have often remarked that he knew well the simple emotions of the peasant and should have limited himself to their depiction. This might explain the failure of **"Josephine,"** which is riddled with such narrative lapses as "Josephine laughed, not mirthlessly, but mirthfully." . . . (pp. 154-57)

On the other hand, one finds scattered through *Spring Sowing* several excellent tales in which O'Flaherty never permits overstatement, inflated symbolism, or outright authorial intrusion to separate the storyteller and his audience. In **"The Struggle,"** a curragh upended by the flailings of O'Halloran and O'Toole "begins to drift slowly westwards," inhering naturally in the story as a low-keyed harbinger of death. The tale of the trapped gull in **"The Hook"** is straight economic narrative, unblemished by incongruous imagery; and **"Three Lambs"** captures the lyric beauty of a farm boy witnessing the miracle of birth. In none of these stories does O'Flaherty become so obsessed by what he is saying *through the narration* that he neglects the telling of his tale.

Perhaps the most enjoyable story in this entire collection is the one closest in style to Frank O'Connor: the ear, not the eye, is O'Flaherty's main target in the atypical first-person narrative, **"The Black Mare."** "What," his persona queries

rhetorically, "is nearer to God than a beautiful horse? Tell me that, stranger, who have been in many lands across the sea." And later he denounces his arch-rival in the crucial race: "[H]e came crooked from his mother's womb and his father too was the same dishonest son of a horse-stealing tinker." But this foe rides the priest's horse, and "there [is] nobody in Inverara . . . willing to risk being turned into a goat by making a priest obey the rules of a race." Here the story and the manner of its telling are the focus throughout; no symbolic or thematic heavy-handedness intrudes to blur that focus.

Parallel examples of this ambivalence are ready to hand in each of the other major collections. The second, entitled *The Tent,* prompted Louis Dubois in 1934 to remark that Irish letters were moving away from the tradition of idealistic symbolism. . . . . Eleven of the pieces in this series deal specifically with politico-religious issues, and one could not term any of these stories optimistic in tone. Though this group does not suffer so much from forced symbolism undermining the writer's expression, they tend to bog down in the solemnity of overstated themes.

"Offerings," **"Charity,"** **"The Inquisition,"** and **"The Outcasts"** are all explicitly drawn diatribes against the Irish Catholic clergy; **"Poor People"** and **"The Tyrant"** sociopolitical tracts. O'Flaherty's aim in all these pieces is an exposition of "truth," and he relegates his narrative to a mere vehicle designed to deliver the message.

The animal stories in this second collection lend additional support to our basic premise. Stark understatement and fast-paced narration make **"The Wild Goat's Kid"** an almost perfect story of its type. **"The Foolish Butterfly,"** however, verges on moralizing parable; and as O'Flaherty begins to *draw* the lesson in wandering too far from shore, his style sinks as quickly as does his drowning butterfly: "The wings fluttered once and then the sea-water filtered through them, like ink through blotting paper."

Again, those pieces that best display the author's talents as storyteller are the ones closest to the oral tradition. **"The Reaping Race"** is structurally little more than a parable on the order of "The Tortoise and the Hare," but narrative strength and detailed characterization give the tale a warm dimension of reality. (pp. 157-59)

"The Old Hunter," like **"The Black Mare,"** is highly ironic first-person narrative. Here one does not find the same fidelity to speech rhythms as in the earlier story, but there are glorious moments of comic splendor. In one sequence Morrissey rides his rejuvenated nag to hounds only to have him stop dead at the workhouse drain. "Undoubtedly," muses the wry persona, "the animal was too well-bred to face it." The rider sails over his drooping mane and lands up to his ears in ooze and excrement, whereupon the blueblooded old hunter simply turns up his nose and trots off. This is a side of the oral narrative O'Flaherty has too seldom shown us.

Several of the longer stories in the third collection, *The Mountain Tavern,* suffer—though to a lesser degree—from the same inclination to overstatement discernible in parts of *Spring Sowing* and *The Tent.* **"The Painted Woman"** begins with a powerful image of evening—"The dying light of the hidden sun lay brown upon the earth's back like the shroud upon a corpse"—in perfect accord with the symbolic sensual death chronicled in the narrative. Unfortunately, voluptuous images soon proliferate as in **"Spring Sowing"**; phallic cornfields out of Sherwood Anderson loom on every horizon; a resurrection motif becomes hopelessly entangled in mixed metaphors of a three-day storm and a Freudian log, "snout upwards." The story is ultimately wrecked by runaway symbolism.

"**The Oar**" shows much of the same straining after symbolic-thematic effect, and the effort culminates in several disappointing paragraphs constructed of repetitive sentence patterns. (pp. 159-60)

In several of the selections, nonetheless, O'Flaherty is in full control of his material, subordinating all parts of the story to total narrative effect. Often given to careless repetition, in "**The Ditch**" O'Flaherty fashions a somber cadence skillfully attuned to his subject: "His name was Michael Cassidy. He was thirty years old. He was a farm laborer." This faltering, brutal Cassidy, whose personality is so subtly suggested in the modulations of prose rhythm, destroys his own child, only to be ruined in turn by the monstrous wife who has goaded him to kill.

In *Spring Sowing* and *The Tent,* Liam O'Flaherty achieved success most often in his more optimistic stories. Much of this third collection is mired in the pessimism and violence typified by "**The Ditch**." But one also discovers stories here that afford evidence of ability to coordinate his oral gifts in a starker narrative; there are, moreover, pieces in which he draws from the most somber material a note of genuine optimism.

The brief "**The Letter**" is of the first sort—a "darkly" successful narrative. In this story an entire peasant family labor in the lush natural beauty of their farmland home; larks sing gaily in the forest beyond. In a marvelously structured sequence, the father opens mail from his daughter in America. He is at first elated to find the money he had been hoping for. Suddenly, though neither letter nor father state the horrible truth, the reader knows that the girl has become a prostitute. Almost imperceptibly the details of setting and the elements of prose rhythm are realigned to mirror the grief of a simple family.

After the fragmentation of so many earlier tales through forced symbolism, O'Flaherty creates in "**The Stream**" a fully articulated narrative in which the story *is* the symbol. Beside the flowing fountain, a young woman and her daughter are frightened by a gray old hag. Ironically, the witch-like creature has come to the pond because the bones of her long dead lover are buried there. Her apostrophe to the spring echoes all the strident passion of a keening. "Ancient and withered . . . a sapless thing without fertility," the crone reviles the gurgling brook: "You crooning witch, you have seen them all die. They all died and you flow on." The young woman who sits beside the stream will someday *be* the hag, as will her young daughter; that which terrifies them so completely is a fate in which they share. Mother and daughter leave the witch with a new awareness of the common predicament of humanity, of the eternal nature to which all belong. The prose is Syngean, the imagery cyclic; and the stream ramifies from a simple symbol of creativity into a type of timelessness.

Many of the selections in the fourth volume of stories, *Two Lovely Beasts,* are markedly free of tautology and cliché. "**The Parting**" is in many ways finely reminiscent of Joyce's "Eveline" in *Dubliners;* "**The Wedding**" a stark sketch of barren Irish country life; and "**Galway Bay,**" the powerful tale

of an old Aran Islander's rejection of modern sham, a crystallization of restrained, rhythmic prose.

Yet side by side with this compelling evidence of growth, old problems continue to plague the maturing stylist. "**The Touch**" is a self-conscious paean to sexual spontaneity, and the lyric joy of fulfillment is painfully absent from the stiff, ineffectual prose of the embrace: "Their faces were aflame. They dropped the rope and grasped one another fiercely by both hands. They rushed together and stood bosom to bosom. They were trembling from head to foot."

In "**Light**" O'Flaherty strives for an idyllic portrait of two totally uninhibited nude lovers in a tropical paradise. His diatribe against repressive civilization is unfortunately overdrawn. Straining for the symbolic in his depiction of the lush setting, O'Flaherty loses control of his prose; and the overdone alliteration becomes a virtual cacophony: "The pointed leaves of the palm trees trembled on either side of their spear-shaped blades like a myriad oars feathering in frenzied haste about a fleet of galleys."

A few of the pieces selected by Vivian Mercier for *The Stories of Liam O'Flaherty* had not appeared in any of the major collections discussed in this paper. These tales, typified by "**The Mirror**" (a remarkably lyric picture of a young girl's first awareness of her great beauty), were written after O'Flaherty had begun to work in Gaelic; and the graceful style is, in many instances, consequently closer to the tradition of the oral narrative.

But the main body of his work—certainly all that goes to make up *Spring Sowing, The Tent, A Mountain Tavern,* and *Two Lovely Beasts*—reflects the peculiar stylistic dichotomy that I have tried to document. The real issue is clouded if we simply ascribe the two levels of writing in O'Flaherty's short fiction to a greater facility with "Nature themes [see David H. Greene in Further Reading list]." And, though there is much to Benedict Kiely's assertion that O'Flaherty is best when he is hopeful, some of his most impressive triumphs grew, as we have seen, out of essentially "pessimistic" material. It is crucial that the storyteller in Liam O'Flaherty be heard; this is the condition on which his short fiction rises or falls. When the storyteller speaks, when O'Flaherty dons the mantle of the *sgelai,* the Aran taleteller of old, artificial symbolism and aggressive preachment yield to the graceful narrative of a speaking voice. (pp. 160-62)

> *Michael H. Murray, "Liam O'Flaherty and the Speaking Voice," in* Studies in Short Fiction, *Vol. V, No. 2, Winter, 1968, pp. 154-62.*

JOHN ZNEIMER (essay date 1970)

[*In the following excerpt, Zneimer provides an in-depth analysis of differences between O'Flaherty's novels and stories, noting a profound transformation in the author's point of view. According to Zneimer, O'Flaherty's best stories employ a detached, cold narrative voice that presents, without moralization, the "wonder and awe" of nature.*]

To turn from O'Flaherty's novels to his short stories seems to be a move into another world. The violence of the novels "suggests the scream of a safety valve," as O'Faolain says in "Don Quixote O'Flaherty." The characters are hounded and tortured. Some mysterious relentless force drives them, torments them, sometimes even taking on a vague intense physical form like Gilhooley's man with a club and the brutes that pursue Private Gunn in *The Return of the Brute.* There seems to be no peace for these characters in the world, no resting place. (p. 146)

But the short stories are another world, and to move from one to the other is to pass through the looking glass. Some marvelous transformation has taken place. It is not just that the setting has changed, although indeed it has. The novels tend to be set in town, in the cities, or, more important, among people who aspire and interact. The short stories turn to the country, to animals, and to nature. The society that appears is a part of nature. The characters are rough-hewn from Aran rock. The whole tone has changed. The same vocabulary does not seem to apply. The novels can be described by a vocabulary of heat. The short stories can be described by light. Their surface is cold and shimmering. If the novels are marked by violence and melodrama and fury, O'Flaherty's short stories are best marked by their qualities of calmness, simplicity, and detachment. Or that is the impression so strong that it takes an effort of mind in retrospect to see that the violence is still there. A cow plunges over a cliff. A man crushes a fish to a pulp to relieve his blood lust. A water hen awaits the outcome of a furious struggle to see who will be her mate. Everywhere there is the conflict of nature and the anguish of those who are a part of nature. Yet all *is* changed. And this change must be explored. (pp. 146-47)

Although it is evident that a change has taken place, the stories themselves would seem to offer little clue to what this change has been. There is an air of inevitability, an austerity and simplicity that seem to defy analysis. The stories do not appear to be constructions, that is, arrangements of details to achieve an esthetic effect. Nor is there any meaning in the sense that the details are the garb of any systematic intellectual arrangement. The stories cannot be called symbolic as the term has come to be used in criticism, with a *this* representing *that* relationship of details and events. Indeed, the contemporary scholar who has become accustomed to approaching short stories as an intellectual challenge or problem in need of scholarly interpretation or explication will find no rich mine in O'Flaherty.

Simplicity is the keynote. The short stories do not *mean;* they *are.* And the essence of this simplicity is that O'Flaherty brings no outside furniture—theories, philosophies, or other impediments—to bear upon his material to cause that interrelationship of subject and author which results in complexity. That which is most usually the material for analysis is not there. What is left can be described as a quality of vision focused on a pattern of simple events tremendously significant but only half-understood.

The change that has taken place is not a change of mind or of ideas that can be discerned by analysis and explained in intellectual terms. And the change is one that cannot be explained as merely a change in technique. Something more profound takes place, the explanation of which lies beyond the bounds of conventional literary analysis. William James's *Varieties of Religious Experience* describes many such changes, and his account of the phenomenon of conversion and mystical experience describes O'Flaherty's change. In studying the phenomenon of religious experience James sees a classic pattern. Some healthy-minded "once born" individuals can shrug off the evil in life as an unhealthy aberration. But for the sick souls this evil is too deeply ingrained in the essence of things to be so easily dismissed. The precariousness of human existence weighs too heavily upon them. Regard-

less of life's pleasures "the spectre of death always sits at the banquet." Sometimes the effect is numbing, but for those individuals inclined to melancholy in its more acute forms, there is a profound disaffection. Life loses all meaning and this loss is the cause of positive anguish. (pp. 147-48)

One common characteristic of these disenchanted souls who must be "twice-born" to come into any sense of harmony is a divided self, what James calls "a certain discordancy or heterogeneity in the native temperament of the subject, an incompletely unified moral and intellectual constitution." (p. 148)

Conversion is the process, gradual or sudden, by which this discordancy is reconciled. Sometimes conversion is achieved by an effort of will, but more often by a process of self-surrender. For one whose spiritual turmoil is greatest, no deliberate process seems possible. The evil and absurdity that appear to be the warp and woof of the very nature of things cause a disenchantment so profound that no effort is possible that could make a soul so afflicted believe that any other view could exist. "So long as the egoistic worry of the sick soul guards the door, the expansive confidence of the soul of faith gains no presence." The only cause is exhaustion and despair; for as James goes on to explain, as long as one "center of consciousness" holds the fore, there is room for no other, but let this lapse, even for an instant, and that dramatic process of conversion may take place. It is the yielding and giving up, the surrender of self and will, that is at the center of the case histories of conversion that he then gives. James's explanation is psychological, but it is not important whether these experiences be explained in psychological or religious terms. What is important is that there has been a change, "the man *is* born anew." (pp. 148-49)

Whether or not the pattern of experiences that James discusses is indeed religious is of no concern here. Nor is there any concern as to how or why this phenomenon takes place or to what its value might be. It is the *fact* of this experience and not its meaning that relates to O'Flaherty, because it lends perspective to and points the direction through which his work can be understood.

It is the change of character that O'Flaherty seems to undergo between the novels and the short stories that this excursion into the psychology of religion is to illuminate. Changes of centers of consciousness do occur and with them profound transformations. That is evident from James's case histories. And these changes present the world in an entirely different perspective to those who have undergone the change. Although conversion may, it need not be a distinct event in time, before which a man is one thing and ever after another. The nature of the conversion is dependent upon the complexity of the psychological makeup of the individual. Infinite variations are possible. The fundamental mechanism is the shift from one center of consciousness to another. Everything about O'Flaherty indicates he would be most susceptible to this kind of experience: his discharge from the army with *melancholia acuta,* his acute consciousness of being a divided self (discussed previously in connection with his role as an artist), and the record of spiritual turmoil that permeates his autobiographical works. But probably *The Black Soul* presents this pattern of crisis and resolution most vividly. . . . (p. 150)

The Black Soul presents a classic account of the sick soul, the divided self, conversion, and mystical experience. Life has lost all meaning for Fergus O'Connor, the black soul, when he flees to Inverara after a futile effort to find answers "burrowing in the bowels of philosophy, trying to find consolation one day in religion, next day in anarchism, next day in Communism, and rejecting everything as empty, false and valueless . . . at last, despairing of life, flying from it as from an ogre that was torturing him." Fantastic visions crowd into his mind, "cries of the wounded, shrieks of the damned, corpses piled mountain-high, races wandering across deserts, chasms opening everywhere, devils grinning, wild animals with gory jaws rushing hither and thither in dark forests, myriads of men talking in strange languages . . . the wails of women, the bodies of children transfixed on spears." The vision of death haunts him: "He could see his own corpse lying stiff and naked." The cormorants croak from the rocks that all ends "in ashes and oblivion." He is aware of distinct contending forces within him: "Two personalities grew within him side by side. One embraced Little Mary and loved her bodily with the love of nature. The other hated her and kept hidden behind a gloomy silence." "The thought of suicide came to him now seriously, as a result of the hopelessness of thought."

Then, after numerous struggles, he experiences conversion. When he is poised at the edge of the sea, ready to plunge, something in him clutches onto life. The sea takes on new meaning: " 'Ah, beautiful fierce sea', he cried aloud, as if he were speaking to a mistress, 'you are immortal. You have real life, unchanging life.' And just as one morning in Canada when he had seen the reflection of a vast pine forest at dawn in the eastern sky, he had stood in awe, his imagination staggered, thinking that a new world had suddenly been born before his eyes, so now, looking at the sea, the meaning of life suddenly flickered across his mind. It flashed and vanished, leaving wonder and awe behind it." Although his black soul still grows on him, it loses its grip. Nature now can transport him into ecstasies of contemplation. He sits in the solitude of nature "for hours at a time thinking, without moving a muscle." He feels possessed of great and inexpressible knowledge: "He felt he knew something nobody else knew," but when he tries to say it "there was a pain in his heart as if something moved within him trying to come out and yet nothing came out. It was impossible to write anything about the sea. It was too immense."

The pattern here is unmistakable. There has been a profound change, and call it religious, spiritual, or psychological, it is the same kind of change that marks the difference between O'Flaherty's novels and short stories. The importance of this change is that the novels and short stories are not merely different in form and technique. They emanate from entirely different viewpoints. The shift is not just from the city to the country, from society to nature, but from one center of consciousness to another. When O'Flaherty writes about nature in his short stories something entirely new is involved. (pp. 150-52)

For O'Flaherty nature, creativity, and spiritual experience are all wound almost inextricably together. He sees his genius as something within him that separates him from his fellows, that makes him a spectator and not a participant in life. But this genius is also his black soul which cuts him off from everything in terrible aloneness, which shows him the world as terrifying, fantastic, and absurd. In nature this sense of self-division reaches a crisis. The awesome motion without purpose of nature drives his black soul to exhaustion and despair,

and in this bleak moment, when all seems hopeless and lost, the black soul ceases to struggle. Then, as if by miracle, a new consciousness floods his being. All seems one and harmonious and marvelous. Nature is both the cause and cure of his anguish. But this new awareness cries out for expression, and as an artist O'Flaherty must heed this cry. In the harmony of the new vision all is one, but now the artist must detach himself from the scene not to participate but to observe. Again the divided self and the apartness, and the cycle begins anew.

What is it that O'Flaherty sees when he emerges from his spiritual chaos and desolation into his new vision, the expression of which is both his gift and his curse? But that question assumes that he has seen some new truth which his stories are an attempt to communicate. What he sees is just what he has seen before; what is changed is the relationship. Before the vision the I, the black soul, the Dark Daniel side of O'Flaherty is wrenched into the most extreme separation from life and nature. And then the arrogance, pride, and selfhood which have been brought to an unbearable intensity scream out a No! of despair. From this storm there is a moment of emptiness. And then life flows back, simply, symbolized, and embodied in a sand insect that persistently, without reflection, removes the barrier placed before it. It is unquestioning life in nature, and O'Flaherty feels as one with this ongoing life. The world becomes new again in him.

To express this, the I or the creator does not stand off aloof and apart, shaping, manipulating, or analyzing. The I has almost ceased to exist. The vision, then, is nature expressed, *in its own voice*. It is not what O'Flaherty sees, for this subject-object relationship has ceased to exist. The writer is not standing apart, describing. Yet the detachment is greater because the writer is not selecting from nature and shaping nature to satisfy his own esthetic ends. He has become a part of nature. He feels within himself the rhythm of creation, as O'Flaherty said about writing **"The Caress."** He becomes the speaking part of nature. As a part of the oneness of nature he is detached from every part, severally, including himself. All is one, and the one is the vision. (pp. 156-57)

The story [**"The Rockfish"**] is short—not 1,500 words. And it is simple—a fish is almost caught. That is really all there is to it. Someone is fishing. The bait drops into a group of smaller fish who nibble and snatch the bait away. The hook is rebaited and a large rockfish emerges from his lair and gulps the hook. He is hauled nearly to the fisherman's hand when the hook tears out of his mouth and he escapes. It is almost easier to describe what the story is not than what it is. There are no characters in any common sense in which the term is used. The fisherman is merely there. Except that he is large, there is no special quality about the fish. The story is not a vehicle for the author's descriptions of nature. What little happens is not important as far as any sense of plot is concerned. Nothing is symbolic of anything. There are no hidden meanings, no allegory. The author makes no observations about the meaning of the experience. (pp. 157-58)

What is expressed is the vision, the kinship and oneness of the author with the natural scene in the most direct expression possible. The order of events is natural, inevitable. "Flop. The cone-shaped bar of lead tied to the end of the fishing-line dropped into the sea without causing a ripple." For some reason the equilibrium has been disturbed. There is an action, and a set of events follows. The fisherman never emerges as a person. His function is to fish as it is the function of stars to fall or clouds to rain. The bait stirs up other action. The little rockfish churn around and draw the attention of the large fish. He acts, struggles against the line and the fisherman, and tears himself loose. "He was free." The story ends, as the original equilibrium is restored. Apparently, the author does not arrange the parts. Each event occurs after every other. The connective is *then,* not *while* or *meanwhile.* Each sentence either depicts a static scene or advances the action. Nothing is described as being contemporaneous, for this would require the presence of an author holding one set of actions in abeyance while another took place. There is no backward or simultaneous flow. From the moment the lead hits the water until the fish is free all motion is forward and relentless, like the ticking of a clock.

As the special relationship of the author to his material must eliminate the complexities of time (and with it those words used to denote these complexities) so the careful elimination of author intervention in any form must eliminate intellectual and logical complexities. No relationships are stated through the use of logical words like *though* or *because.* No such words appear, for these are intellectual "author" words not a part of the natural scene which contains no intellect probing beneath the surface. That depicted is pure vision. No author is there explaining relationships, standing outside the material and seeing the parts relate to each other temporally or causally.

The intellect, the black soul, fixed outside the scene would see motion without purpose. But the author, driven to despair and to vision by his black soul, is not outside the scene. He is submerged, absorbed in it. A word like *purpose* has no meaning from this view. This is what man attempts to impose upon or extract from nature with his intellect. But it cannot be understood in these terms. There is a significance far beyond purpose, a significance in the very being of the scene, the import of which envelops but which cannot be understood. No part is more important than any other, no relationship need be pointed out or explained. All is important. All is wondrous. All is holy. So the details emerge, not significant because of some complex arrangement that the author is building, but because they are a part of the whole. They are not understood but are important because they are there. Their importance is felt as the import of the whole story is felt. All is significant. Nothing must be overlooked. (pp. 158-59)

The scene, the story, embodies the secret of life, which the author must express as felt, not understood, for the secret of life is not accessible to the understanding. Each detail is a part of this secret: The baited hooks show white against the broad strands of red seaweed. The man rests the fishing-rod in the crutch of his right arm. Excited, the man breathes through his nose. The large rockfish's belly is dun color. The man braces himself with his right foot. The top hook catches in the seaweed. The function of these specific details is not description, in the sense of an author describing. The vividness of the scene is incidental. The author apparently is not there observing, selecting, constructing this or that segment to be in harmony with his total design. The details appear not to have been chosen but to exist, and to exist as some significant manifestation of the marvelous incomprehensible vision which constitutes the whole of the story.

There is no reason to believe that O'Flaherty's spiritual experiences were not real, that from his spiritual turmoil did not arise a new sense of wonder and awe and significance. We can accept as true his sense of oneness, of peace, of marvelous insight. But to express the ineffable he had to create an illusion, and that is his art. For if O'Flaherty the man escapes from his black soul's torments by obliterating himself and merging into the life force of nature, O'Flaherty the artist must deliberately try to recreate this experience. Of course he is not one with what he represents. Of course he must choose and arrange. What appears in **"The Rockfish"** is a most deliberate arrangement according to a most rigid plan, and the most deliberate part of the arrangement is that it not appear as an arrangement at all. (pp. 159-60)

Not all O'Flaherty short stories are as rigorously patterned as **"The Rockfish,"** but those demands imposed by the peculiar nature of his vision which controlled form in **"The Rockfish"** continue to operate in the majority of his other stories. His fundamental concern is *seeing,* not *making.* And always it is the quality of the seeing which is his concern. (p. 160)

In a letter to [Edward] Garnett (July 16, 1915) about style he tells of striving for "a feeling of coldness." This is the coldness of extreme detachment, pure artistry, where the artist's warm human qualities represent a blot or an imperfection if they are allowed to intrude. For as these qualities intrude, the subject-object relationship is reestablished, and the essential quality of the oneness of the vision is imperiled or destroyed.

One way of classifying O'Flaherty's short stories is through the diversity and complexity of materials to which he is able to bring this coldness of vision, remembering that the coldness represents the detachment which his expression of intense personal experience requires. It is as if O'Flaherty tests how much experience the artist can encompass before the man breaks through and shatters the illusion. Those stories without human participants are at the simplest level; the most extreme of these is **"The Wave"** in which no living character, animal or human appears. Here at its bleakest and grandest is a natural process—motion without purpose in its barest essentials. It is the "poem about the cliffs and the sea" that Fergus O'Connor, the black soul, wanted to write to express the marvelous understanding wrought from his despair. If the material is the simplest, it also represents the greatest leap, for the impersonal inexorable sea *is* the motion without purpose that the intellect-black soul sees as intolerable, that renders all human life and activity meaningless, that motion of the waves from "Dover Beach" which

Begin, and cease; and then again begin,
With tremulous cadence slow; and bring
The eternal note of sadness in.

(pp. 161-62)

Stories like **"The Wild Goat's Kid," "The Blackbird," "The Wounded Cormorant," "The Water Hen,"** and **"The Wild Swan"** contain animals only. The patterns are the inevitable patterns of nature like **"The Wave"** and **"The Rockfish"**: something disturbs the equilibrium and a new equilibrium emerges. The wild goat gives birth to a kid, defends the kid in a fierce encounter with a dog, flees from the dog's gored body to other pastures. A cormorant, its leg broken by a falling rock, is pecked to death by the flock. A cat patiently stalks a blackbird which flies safely off at the cat's last leap. The water hen mates with the victor of a savage battle. The wild swan leaves its dead mate to migrate south and return the next season with a new one. The author does not intrude to judge or moralize. The stories have no meaning other than what they are. The subject is nature expressed. Fierce battles rage, intense dramas are enacted, great cruelty is perpetrated, but all is one to the artist's impassive eye.

But in **"The Wild Goat's Kid"** there is a break in the technique, a flaw, and this is most revealing in relation to the artist's problem. The wild goat emerges too much as a character, engaging sympathies, becoming a heroine. As a result, detachment and nonparticipation are lost; and though the story may be more personally gripping, it is artistically less successful. It tends to be just another animal story. O'Flaherty's magic is not there.

Up the scale of complexity are stories like **"The Rockfish," "The Hawk," "The Hook,"** and **"The Conger Eel"** in which human beings enter, but as agents or forces, not as characters. They retain the impersonality of the rock that fell to break the cormorant's leg. In **"The Conger Eel"** it is of no moment whether the eel escapes the men and regains its freedom or whether the men kill the eel that has destroyed their nets. As in **"The Rockfish"** the fish escapes, but this has no special significance. To have either of them caught would tend to shift the emphasis from the fish to the men and introduce an unnecessary complexity to restoring the equilibrium. The hawk is killed in an unsuccessful attempt to save its mate from human capture. The problem is not with the human characters but with the human characteristics of the animals that they engage sympathies. In **"The Hook"** a seagull falls into a trap laid by some boys and snatches a piece of liver in which a hook tied to a string is hidden. The string breaks, but the hook imbeds itself in the seagull's beak. The seagull flies back to his nest where his mate snips the string and tears the hook loose. In many respects this is like the other nature stories—the simplicity, the natural order, the restored equilibrium. But the detachment and objectivity are lacking. The author intrudes, interpreting. The seagull would swoop down and get the liver "but he wanted to bring a share to his mate that was sitting on the eggs." The other seagulls make a tremendous noise "blinking their eyes in amazement at the hook sticking from the trapped one's bill." His mate on seeing the string cackles shrilly "like a virago of a woman reviling a neighbour." When the hook is removed, his mate "smoothed her feathers with a shrug and closed her eyes in a bored fashion." Successful expression of his vision demands that the objects or creatures of nature behave according to their own laws, speak in their own voices. Here the animals behave like human beings, are described in human terms. The author observes and imposes his humanity upon the scene. A subject-object relationship is established, the coldness is lost, and with it the wonder and awe of the vision. (pp. 163-65)

In any collection of O'Flaherty stories, whether by chance or design, one cannot help noticing the mixture of stories about animals with stories about people. The effect is to show the similarities, of course, but not primarily in an intellectual sense or in any sense that judges animals or people. The main effect is to put them into the same perspective. They are all manifestations of life and nature as the stories are expressions of life and nature. A common coldness covers all. In man and animal nature behaves according to her own laws.

O'Flaherty's vision turned to the human scene is shown at its simplest in stories like **"Blood Lust," "The Struggle,"** and **"The Fight."** The participants are all human beings, but their expressions of passion are viewed not as they are characteristically human but as they are a part of nature. The most elemental forces operate. . . . In each of these stories the interest is not in the characters, in who they are, or what character

traits they illustrate. Nor is the interest in what, in particular, they do. Their relationship is not with society. They are manifestations of nature, in some of the elemental ways that nature is manifest through human beings. And O'Flaherty brings to this aspect of nature the same cold view that he brought to the inanimate and animal aspects of nature.

Complexity increases as the subject becomes not man as passion flames and dies in him in the restoration of natural equilibrium, but people in fundamental, elemental relationships. This too is a manifestation of nature. Stories of this kind include **"Spring Sowing," "The Landing," "Life," "Going Into Exile,"** and **"Galway Bay."** In **"Spring Sowing"** a young couple together sow their first potato crop and become a part of the land that will claim them. In **"Landing"** peasant women on the shore are exhilarated in the wild terror that accompanies the landing of their men's frail boat in the raging waves. Infancy and old age are depicted in **"Life,"** in which an old man withers as an infant develops. Their lives cross when the infant is weaned and the mash made for one is also the food of the other. As the lusty infant takes hold in the world the old man fades from it. **"Going into Exile"** is about the separation of a family as two young people leave their poor home for America. The unquenchable fires in doughty old age are the subject in **"Galway Bay,"** as an irascible old man takes his old cow to the market in Galway. He will have sport in Galway and then return with enough money for his funeral and for a mass to be said over his grave. But a loneliness unto death seizes him as he and the old cow walk slowly down the pier.

It is only when the spell has been broken that one can be aware that a spell has been cast in these stories. Frank O'Connor notes about **"Going Into Exile"** that O'Flaherty "with his own natural innocence . . . could ignore everything except the nature of exile itself—a state of things like love and death that we must all endure" [see Further Reading list]. But if the subject is exile itself—and surely it is this: there is no concern for the why of the exile or for individual psychological reactions to it—it is exile viewed under the aspect of eternity, in the cold view of O'Flaherty's vision. It is exile as a manifestation of nature somehow beyond individual human concern. That is the spell that O'Flaherty casts as his art controls and enforces this view. When a human relationship or a human reference point intrudes, the spell breaks . . . . (pp. 166-67)

The most complex relationships that O'Flaherty attempts in his stories are the relationships between man and society. If in the stories involving elemental human relationships and emotions the artist must avoid sympathetic participation to keep his cold view, in these stories he must avoid intellectual participation. The opportunity for polemic is great, for man's social institutions are involved. But these too must be seen as a manifestation of nature, under the aspect of eternity. There is no better or worse. As the wave crashes against the cliff, so man attempts economic success, or the religious spirit is expressed, or the artist is estranged from his society. In **"Two Lovely Beasts," "The Fairy Goose,"** and **"The Child of God"** the subjects are these three aspects of human life.

Against the wishes of his wife and family, against the traditions of his society, Colm Derrane takes the risk and attempts to raise a second calf on his barren twenty acres. This act and its consequences are the materials of **"Two Lovely Beasts."** What he did was unheard of. It violated every principle of the community tradition. It appeared to be against the will of

God. But with this initial leap made, Colm's resolve to rise up in the world was not to be daunted. He beats his wife into submission, and the whole family undergoes extreme privation as Colm makes every effort to gather capital. He is a shunned outcast from society. He now risks holding the two calves a second winter and uses his money to begin trade and open a shop. Success is almost immediate. His neighbors now accept him and consider him a wise man. Now his family has everything and more that it had been denied. Colm's ambition presses on. He decides to hire help and open a shop in town. Now his neighbors turn against him again. He is indifferent to their jeers. As the story ends, "His pale blue eyes stared fixedly straight ahead, cold and resolute and ruthless."

The objectivity seems complete. There is no judgment of Colm or of society. This is what happens. There is no commentary, no interpretation. But this is not a perfect example of cold vision, because the story seems to mean something. It appears to have a significance beyond that of its surface. Interpretation seems necessary. This is because O'Flaherty's technique here is primarily dramatic. He achieves objectivity by refraining from comment and using dialogue to advance and explain the action. Drama has depth because what the characters say requires interpretation. Their words relate to them. The sequence of speeches seems to be an arrangement. A whole series of cross-currents of meaning and consequence is set up, and in the resulting complexity the wonder and awe of O'Flaherty's vision is lost. The vision is expressed by a cold surface. The eye, not the ear governs. **"Two Lovely Beasts"** achieves a technical objectivity through dramatic technique, but this is not the absolute detachment and coldness achieved by the artist expressing an intense subjective relationship. The materials of nature are merely handled at a distance. They have not been put through the intense process which relates them to the oneness of O'Flaherty's vision. (pp. 168-69)

"The Fairy Goose" is about a scraggy little gosling hatched in Mary Wiggins' kitchen behind the stove. Although it was runted and deformed, she and her husband believe it would be wrong to kill it. It grows slowly into a most ungooselike goose. It ignores other geese, is afraid of water, cleans itself by rolling in the grass, makes tweeky ungooselike noises. The woman begins to think it is a fairy and adorns it with ribbons and blesses it with holy water. She begins to believe that the goose has given her supernatural powers. She gains some reputation for her powers and this report reaches the priest. He gallops out to end this pagan practice. He routs out the pampered delicate goose, strips it of ribbons, scatters its strange nest, and strikes Mary Wiggins a sharp blow as she attempts to stop him. Warning the village about the evil of this, he leaves. Now Mary Wiggins and her goose are no longer considered sacred. Boys stone the goose to death. Mary curses the village, and though the curse has no immediate effect, it is believed that the village has been quarrelsome ever since. O'Flaherty brings his cold vision to that which would be most likely to stir O'Flaherty the man to polemic—peasant superstition and priestcraft. In **"The Fairy Goose"** there is no trace of polemic. All is accepted and inevitable. The priest cannot be other than he is, nor can the peasants. All behave according to their own laws, and the law governing all is the inexplicable law of nature. **"The Fairy Goose"** is not the expression of social criticism and satire, but of the wonder and awe of human beings as manifestations of nature.

"The Child of God" depicts the relationship of the artist to society, in this case closely paralleling O'Flaherty's own relationship to the peasant community of his native Aran Islands. (p. 170)

Peter O'Toole, the Child of God, like O'Flaherty is a bright boy who tells his mother marvelous stories. At ten he decides he wants to be a priest, and the proud family gathers all its resources to finance his education. But after some time a letter comes from the seminary telling that Peter has been expelled. A year later Peter returns home. He had been expelled because he had ceased to believe in God. Now he is an artist. Like O'Flaherty he had worked a year in London as a laborer, waiter, and porter—in Peter's case to finance his art education. Their son's remoteness somehow terrifies his parents. "It is impossible to explain the instinct of peasants, their aversion for anything unlike themselves." And Peter too feels a strangeness and hostility in the land and the people. But this alienation melts for Peter as the beauty of the land and people is impressed upon him. The peasants gather one day in their kitchen, and Peter is moved by the "strange, beautiful faces, all sombre and dignified; mysterious faces of people who live by the sea away from civilization; age-old people, inarticulate, pitiless, yet as gentle as children." He shows them his pictures, "sketches of fierce, terrible men, everything done with a tremendous, almost uncouth power, the work of a raw, turbulent, half-developed genius." They are horrified. His family is shocked and disappointed. After that Peter is left alone and reverts to peasant dress. He takes up with the wild young people of the island; and between bouts of frenzied creative energy he carouses. An old man dies and the wild gang to which Peter belongs perpetrate a fantastic drunken wake. At the height of the debauch Peter hurries to get his paints and canvas and to everyone's horror begins to sketch the appalling scene: "the corpse, the carpenter lying drunk in the coffin, the stupefied men lying on the floor in gruesome attitudes, the dark kitchen, with sagging, black earthen roof and the silence of death." This is the final atrocity. Peter's house is stoned. The priest is called and Peter is banished from the parish.

This story is worth looking at in some detail, not as an example of O'Flaherty's most characteristic achievement but because it shows him as he sees himself in the role of an artist. It is noteworthy that Peter is a painter, for it is the visual with which O'Flaherty's art is most concerned. The artist is attracted by the natural beauty of the land and people but also alienated from it by the fact of his being an artist. When this "unexplainable gulf" which separates him even from his mother is bridged by "the force of their natural love," Peter feels reconciled and gay and delights freely in the joys of the natural life. But regardless of his personal feelings as a man, the absolute separation of the artist from society is revealed by that to which he brings his artistic vision. As an artist he is cold and detached, and to that scene which in the normal man would evoke terror and horror he feels impelled to bring his vision. The others are either drunk or appalled, but Peter is sober and detached. He has been a part of the scene as a man, a leading participant in all the debauchery. But always the second self—the artist—is watching, and when the scene reaches the stage when no normal man can watch unaffected, the artist detaches himself and makes the scene the material for his art. He wishes to express not the horror of a shocked observer—a subject-object relationship in which the artist's real subject is his personal feelings—but the absolute quality of the scene, the wonder and awe that lie beyond personal expression. (pp. 171-72)

The pattern of alienation in these last three stories is apparent. In each the central figure is set apart from society—Colm by his decision to raise two calves and improve his lot, the fairy goose by its strangeness, the Child of God by his art. After partial reconciliations in which society attempts to come to terms with and even to admire the central figure, the ultimate fact of strangeness and difference is the determining factor. In the end his neighbors jeer Colm's success, but he is unaware of their jeers, "cold and resolute and ruthless." The fairy goose, once pampered and admired, in the end is interdicted by the priest and stoned to death by the mob. So too the Child of God is showered with stones and banished by the priest.

Each of these stories bears the unmistakable imprint of O'Flaherty's personality in an archetypal pattern. In each he recreates the relationship to society which his genius forces upon him. This is the ultimate in the increasing scale of complexity by which his stories have been classed, for in these stories O'Flaherty must bring his cold goat's eye or snake's eye or weasel's eye to view that which is most himself, as the wave was most not himself. This is the limit of his art, and his success depends upon the extent to which he can scrutinize himself under the aspect of eternity, transcend all that most deeply concerns him, see himself as a manifestation of nature, and express through his cold vision the wonder and awe of the fact of his own existence.

This scheme of classification does not include one whole group of stories tangentially related to it, those stories involving a prank or trick where intellect is used for deception. Stories typical of this group are **"Colic," "The Shilling," "The Pot of Gold,"** and **"The Red Petticoat."** (pp. 172-73)

As has been said, these stories are tangentially related to those stories in the main current where O'Flaherty brings his cold vision to bear on scenes of great emotional impact. In the "trick" stories he employs the same objective technique. Only now the subject is the intellect in its elemental form in the lives of simple people. This too is nature, or ought to be. But for O'Flaherty this nature exists as an intellectual concept. It is not nature as felt—awesome and wonderful—to be expressed, where the art is in the tension between the subject and the telling. In the "trick" stories there is no tension. Nature speaking in her own voice does not evoke laughter. O'Flaherty brings the wrong formula to the subject, for the essence of his art is based in feeling. "When O'Flaherty thinks, he's a goose, when he feels, he's a genius," O'Connor quotes George Russell as saying. But feeling is the tragic quality—tragedy for those who feel, comedy for those who think. Comedy plays intellect over the subject. In the "trick" stories nothing plays over the subject nor is any deep feeling transcended. Nothing happens. (pp. 173-74)

Critical opinion is almost unanimous in its conclusion that O'Flaherty's short stories contain his most enduring achievement. And few would disagree with Vivian Mercier's final judgment in his Introduction to the 1956 edition of O'Flaherty's stories: "If Liam O'Flaherty's work survives, posterity will not regard him as the novelist historian of a turbulent era but as the celebrant of timeless mysteries—mysteries rooted in Nature and in that portion of Nature embodied in the life of Man" [see excerpt dated 1956]. The effect of the stories is direct and immediate. Rhys Davies in his Introduction to **The Wild Swan and Other Stories,** notes that these "exhibitions of life's primal forces, though they may lack the development of sophisticated passion become memo-

rable in their simple directness" [see excerpt dated 1932]. Francis Hackett believes that it was O'Flaherty's "deep folk quality" akin to the Russian that made Garnett take hold of him and that the short stories suited O'Flaherty's gift admirably. The stories are "charged with nervous force and the life of his people. . . . Aran is alive in them." Benedict Kiely parallels Mercier in believing that the most important aspect of O'Flaherty's work is not found in novels like *The Informer* or *The Assassin,* nor in connection with Irish-Ireland ideals or the revolution. "It is the understanding of the earth, of animals worthy and human beings not always worthy of the earth, that makes O'Flaherty's work important" [see Further Reading list]. O'Flaherty as a novelist, H. E. Bates observes in *The Modern Short Story,* is "scrappy, sensational, and often cheap." But in his stories about nature "O'Flaherty extracted a wild, tender, and sometimes violently nervous beauty" [see Further Reading list]. Sean O'Faolain in the course of his discussion of the violence of O'Flaherty's novels also concludes that the short stories are best.

Most critics stop here, yet always the question remains: What is the cause of the visual quality of the short stories, which have the "freshness of new paint," as Bates says. What does it hide? What does it represent? The reader of the short stories is aware of the turbulence of the novelist. L. Paul Dubois cannot but see the ferocity of the novels as a mask. . . . And this is the view that Benedict Kiely takes in *Modern Irish Fiction.* He believes that O'Flaherty's effort to protect himself from the softness of genuine love produces the Dark Daniel side of his genius. The simple life of nature in the short stories is a contrast and a retreat. The birds and beasts of the early short stories are "perfect children of the earth" existing in "absolute and undisturbed harmony." They are a safe haven and an ideal, the "ecstatic acceptance" of which produces the animal stories. Kiely believes that O'Flaherty creates his human characters in contrast to this natural harmony, but occasionally *"raises* them to the level of animals, making them worthy of the earth." It is to this earth that O'Flaherty flees in his short stories.

Mercier stresses in his Preface that O'Flaherty's true subject, and this is found almost entirely in his short stories, is "the relationship between Man and Nature." But Mercier makes this an intellectual relationship. He has O'Flaherty looking at Nature and its relationship to man, judging it, moralizing upon it. From this view **"Spring Sowing"** excellently symbolizes O'Flaherty's conception of the relationship between man and nature. Man can only triumph over nature by cooperating with her; in the end he becomes her victim. **"Life,"** that story of the crossing of young life with old, becomes "a wild cry of protest against 'the human condition.' " Mercier believes O'Flaherty's nature stories are full of lessons: "Over and over again . . . the point is made that Nature is both friend and enemy. She destroys us, but our greatest happiness . . . comes from yielding to her." **"Red Barbara"** is given as an example to show that "the thwarting of Nature by Man entails its own punishment." And though O'Flaherty sometimes mars the objectivity, "he always makes the reader see before urging him to judge."

In *The Lonely Voice,* Frank O'Connor points out two important hallmarks that he believes characterize and govern this strict form. The short story does not have a hero. Instead it has a "submerged population group." And the mood is akin to Pascal's saying: "The eternal silence of those infinite spaces terrifies me." These are his touchstones, and from one comes the other. O'Flaherty's short stories are marked clearly as conforming to this standard. O'Connor points to **"The Fairy Goose"** as one of the great Irish short stories because the author does not intrude. What O'Connor says surely lies near the heart of the matter. O'Flaherty is aware of giving voice to a "submerged population group." In a letter to Garnett he writes: "I don't think I exert any judgment whatsoever in my writing at the moment of writing but seem to be impelled by the Aran Islanders themselves who cry out dumbly to me to give expression to them." And this expression could be extended to the cliffs, the birds, the wild animals, and the sea of his native land with which he began his communion at the end of *Two Years* [O'Flaherty's first autobiography]. Moreover the effect of this expression is not a comfortable intimacy, but wonder and awe. It is not familiarity but coldness that O'Flaherty strives for in his art. (pp. 176-78)

In a sense this described what Kiely called "ecstatic acceptance," but it is in no way a retreat. O'Flaherty does not view nature as a warm, understanding mother. In *I Went to Russia* [O'Flaherty's second autobiography] he describes taking a trip up into the mountains when the ship docks at a Norwegian port: "Here brutal nature, by her sinister silence, brought vividly to my mind the realization that human life is governed by the same ruthless competition and brazen anarchy which governs the growth of nature. Plant wars with plant. . . . All is in continual movement, ever changing, blindly moving, being born, flowering, dying, from a miraculous beginning to an unexplainable end, beautiful only in movement, incomprehensible in purpose." This is O'Flaherty's nature, viewed with his reason, his black soul which makes all appear equally futile. His "ecstatic acceptance" does indeed accept this nature but only after profound spiritual agonies in the classical pattern of religious-mystical experience. Nature is not ideal, or comfortable; it is awesome and wonderful in a way that transcends all that man is. Expressing this is the aim of his art.

"All things appear equally futile when examined by reason," O'Flaherty concludes. And this is especially true of nature whose whole lesson, viewed intellectually, is futility. If O'Flaherty's true subject is the relationship between man and nature, as Mercier says, it is not a reasonable relationship. Reason has no place in nature, because nature has no reasons. Stories about man's relationship to nature can have no lessons to teach because nature is incomprehensible. If man brings reason to nature, or to O'Flaherty's stories about nature, his only lesson will be futility. O'Flaherty does not urge us to judge, as Mercier suggests, because judging is a process of reason, and no judgment is possible. O'Flaherty celebrates nature's timeless mysteries, but he does not in any way moralize on nature. His subject is not the relationship between man and nature as if these are separate and in conflict, but man *as* nature, as a manifestation of nature that cannot be thought about except in despair but whose wonder and awe can be celebrated in O'Flaherty's art.

It is in the light of the kinds of experiences that William James describes that O'Flaherty's art is best understood. At its root is a profound conflict. And whether this conflict and its resolution are explained in naturalistic or theological terms, it is an experience that is significant, because it causes change and transformation—the sort of radically altered points of view that exist between O'Flaherty's novels and his short stories. When O'Flaherty shifts to nature in his short stories, it is this new point of view that is most important and not the change in subject. For though in one sense nature could be said to be the cause of the new point of view, it is not a simple relationship.

Nature represents not a solace, but essentials. Nature is that which must be faced. Nature and O'Flaherty's relationship to it are the source of the conflict on the most elemental level. When O'Flaherty turns to nature, it is the apartness that he feels, nature's indifference. The extreme of separation is at the heart of his experience, for the intensity of this separation causes the exhaustion and emptiness from which a new consciousness can emerge. The new consciousness is a sense of oneness with nature commensurate with the sense of apartness that had previously existed. This is O'Flaherty's subject—not the oneness, which is an intellectual concept, but the *sense* of oneness, which is wonder and awe. Because O'Flaherty has chosen perfection of the work and not the life, his spiritual experience results not in saintliness, but art. (pp. 179-80)

For O'Flaherty the short story is not the development of an idea but the expression of an experience. The story is not an arrangement of details, events, or symbols to produce an epiphany. The epiphany has already taken place before the story begins. For O'Flaherty the story is *all* epiphany. Stories that are developments are in the realm of *becoming;* O'Flaherty's short stories are an attempt to express pure *being.* This is why they elude conventional analysis which, bringing mind to the scene, attempts to extract meaning. O'Flaherty's stories mean as nature means, and the meaning of nature is so inaccessible to man that all attempts to plumb its depths must be futile. (p. 180)

> *John Zneimer, in his* The Literary Vision of Liam O'Flaherty, *Syracuse University Press, 1970, 207 p.*

JAMES H. O'BRIEN (essay date 1973)

[*In the excerpt below taken from a chapter of his book* Liam O'Flaherty, *O'Brien focuses on two groups of O'Flaherty's short stories—what he terms "lyric sketches" and "comprehensive fables"—and provides commentary concerning influences and inspiration behind O'Flaherty's "search for an accurate rendering of man's instinctive life" in his fiction.*]

O'Flaherty builds in deceptively simple stories vivid images of the basic instincts of man. Somehow by stripping away the covering of civilization and the superstructures of reason, he penetrated to a bedrock of experience. It is indeed a complex critical problem to account for the simplicity and directness of his best short stories. To O'Flaherty these stories were secondary to the larger themes and characters of his novels; in fact, the stories sometimes resemble vignettes that could be extracted from his novels on the Aran Islands and the west of Ireland.

O'Flaherty's choice of peasants and animals as subject matter for his stories remains something of a mystery, despite Edward Garnett's instruction that he return to Ireland and write about cows, eels, and country matters instead of sensational stories about London. O'Flaherty's first stories, rejected by editors, were written in response to his reading de Maupassant while working in Connecticut. The Frenchman's bold exposure of peasant life may have stimulated O'Flaherty to write about peasants in a manner different from that of Yeats, A. E. [pseudonym of George Russell], and [John Millington] Synge. Besides, O'Flaherty's traumatic experience in

O'Flaherty in 1952.

the war and his years of wandering as seaman and miscellaneous worker may have sent him back, in imagination, to the certainties of his childhood on Inishmore. One suspects too that O'Flaherty's sympathy with Communistic causes helped him to discern a stability and permanence in peasant life in contrast to the flux and degradation of the proletariat. Through contemplating simple people and animals and the relatively uncomplicated forces of nature O'Flaherty may have hoped to present an instinctive response to a life that had been mangled or smothered by industrialization, cities, and wars.

This search for an accurate rendering of man's instinctive life marks both his short stories and his novels. In the novels, oversized Dostoevskian figures dominate the work; their dreams of perfection, twisted and fanatic as they generally are, represent man's upward movement to a perfection implicit in the evolutionary process. In the short stories O'Flaherty falls back on peasants, animals, and children; the setting is that of farm, sea, or village. As early as 1929, William Troy [see Further Reading list] speculated on the Gaelic qualities in O'Flaherty's work: "He is closer to the unknown writers of the early Gaelic folk literature than to any of his contemporaries. He is less the product of any modern school than of that period when European culture had not yet entirely lost its innocence." In both novels and short stories, a Gaelic influence is manifest in the directness of narrative, the simplicity of language, and an elemental concern with primary emotions. One of the most noticeable differences between novels and short stories, however, lies in the use of melodra-

ma, which is employed in the novels mainly in the interest of psychological realism. Melodrama seems to be his technique for showing the explosive emotions of his protagonists; for O'Flaherty it is a means to express a heightened level of intensity. The short stories, however, seem to be born in a different literary climate. Sean O'Faolain noted this difference in 1937 when a collected edition of O'Flaherty's stories was published. He questions the melodrama in the novels but praises the composure of the short stories. (pp. 93-5)

By far the greatest number of O'Flaherty's stories are lyric sketches, with a simple narrative, a limited plot, and with scene and characterization governed by what is immediate and readily observable. O'Flaherty does not neglect the narrative, but the effect of the narrative in his shortest works is similar to that of a lyric poem; in fact, as John Zneimer observes [see excerpt dated 1970], in these sketches the entire story is an epiphany. The uncomplicated plot discloses the inevitable working out of an emotion or a rhythm of nature. There is little attention to any causal arrangement of events; O'Flaherty holds tightly to the present tense; people speak and act; storms arise and fall without analysis. In the short stories, as in the novels, he does not experiment with point of view; he utilizes a reliable narrator who is clear-eyed, sane, and shrewdly alert to the forces in man, society, and nature, that maim or crush the individual. Neither does he psychoanalyze his characters; he has little use for flashbacks or the probings of memory. Similarly, O'Flaherty limits his language to ordinary words; at times he lapses into pedestrian phrases or clichés; he disdains style. In his theory the raw urgency of action and reaction should not be impeded by fastidious diction. Yet in the best of his lyric sketches, O'Flaherty places his men and women close to the earth or sea in narrative that is stark, unsophisticated, and accurate for evoking a sense of the relentless working out of man's instincts.

O'Flaherty's stories lack the breadth and complexity of those of Joyce, O'Faolain, or O'Connor, and he deals with an external world foreign to men in an industrial, urban society. Yet his simple world is perfectly attuned to the passions and instincts that he wishes to stress. Like Yeats and Lawrence, he selects his material to rediscover the wellsprings of man's emotional life. Although he does not explore as widely as these writers, he acquires, as Yeats would say, an intensity through simplification. His setting, characters, and language cling to the physical order in which all men must live, despite their attachment to cities and the demands of reason. Frequently O'Flaherty writes of man's bond with the earth as a source of life and wisdom. In **"Spring Sowing,"** for example, he describes a young couple's first day of work in the fields. . . . The course of their lives, their ultimate fate, is expressed in miniature in their first day of work together.

O'Flaherty sometimes uses the lyric sketch to dramatize a peasant's encounter with death, generally with an appreciation for the awesome beauty to be found in incidents of mortal danger. In **"Trapped,"** a young man gathering birds' eggs on a cliff is stranded because of crumbling rock; his path to the top of a cliff is cut off. Rigid with fear, he descends a steep-edged rock that no one had been on before. As he starts to swim in water infested with sharks, he regains his pride, praying and thinking of what the villagers will say of his feat. For the fishermen of Aran, death was imminent in the sudden storms at sea, whose importance in their lives is described by a woman in **"Landing"**: "Sure we only live by the Grace of God, sure enough. With the sea always watching to devour

273

us. And yet only for it we would starve." The convergence of life and death in the sea also dominates **"The Oar."** Two curraghs, with three men each, are fishing by moonlight. A school of bream sweeps by them, and so intent are the fishermen on filling their boats that they ignore a storm. When it breaks they row feverishly but they become engrossed with their skill as well as with their fear: "Now the men did not pull fiercely but cautiously. They measured out half and quarter strokes, saving their boats from the foamcapped monstrous waves that jumped at them from out the lightning flashes." But then Red Bartly, the leader of one boat, sees water like a falling cliff filling the other boat; through lightning flashes he and his men see an upraised oar, held by a man in great pain. Refusing to risk pursuit of the other curragh, Red Bartly explains, "Three widows are enough." Despite their skill and courage, one crew is destroyed, the other saved. Red Bartly and his men cannot forget the upraised oar: "It followed us and no hand was grasping it."

In O'Flaherty's lyric sketches, children often reveal parts of man's instinctive life. Through children he adds to the simplicity of peasants the quality of innocence, an un-self-conscious immersion in desires and fears. In **"The Wren's Nest,"** for instance, the unthinking cruelty of boys is as remorseless as that of men in trenches. In this story, two boys dare each other to climb a cliff. As they climb they see a wren with her little ones. In fighting over possession of the nest, the boys knock it down; the wrens fly away, and a small egg falls to the ground without breaking. Later the boys walk by the wrens without noticing the birds; but if they had, the author comments, they would have thrown stones. For O'Flaherty, the youngsters also retain a sense of awe and wonder at the great commonplaces of life, like the birth of animals. In **"Three Lambs,"** a country boy eagerly runs through the morning grass to be present at a lambing. When he sees three lambs born from one sheep, he shares the simple joy of the girl in Browning's "Pippa Passes."

In the lyric sketches, O'Flaherty sometimes brings his exploration of man's instincts to a sharp focus by using animals, which permits him to strip away the distorting colors of civilization. In his best stories of animals he is seldom pedantic or moralistic, although he occasionally adds a philosophical statement to press home a theme. In stories like **"The Conger Eel,"** he concentrates on a single eel, its wildness and strength, its insatiable appetite, and its desire for freedom of movement. . . . In the story the eel becomes something of a demonic force, scattering the mackerel, endangering the fishermen, and rousing all his strength to find his home in obscure depths beyond the reach of man.

The lyric sketches of animals are not always related to the demonic or the destructive aspect of nature. Any of the primary emotions may be emphasized. For instance, in **"The Cow's Death,"** O'Flaherty renders through his account of a cow and a stillborn calf the pathos of mother love. (pp. 103-08)

In such works as this, O'Flaherty exposes instincts outside of Victorian pieties or the longings of the Celtic Twilight. Yet he does not adhere to the naturalistic practice of using animals to show that man is trapped by his surroundings; he is not a strict determinist. Because his milieu is the field and sea rather than the slum, the factory, or the mine, he readily allows for acts arising from the strength, courage, or desperation of man or animal. In addition, O'Flaherty, as we have seen, is committed to an evolutionary view in which every being has a core of energy, an entelechy, that must be fulfilled

even if that fulfillment brings about injury or death. In **"The Hawk,"** for instance, a hawk attacks a lark and stuns it. On the second rush the hawk kills the lark instantly and takes the carcass to his mate on the edge of a cliff, after carefully luring away other birds from the ledge. At this point, O'Flaherty interprets, "His brute soul was exalted by the consciousness that he had achieved the fullness of the purpose for which nature had endowed him." This rather ponderous sentence intrudes upon the narrative, but O'Flaherty seems determined to stress the brute soul in man by the complications that he adds to the story. Three men climb near the ledge; the hawk attacks the eyes of one of the men who beats off the bird and captures the female, putting the female and her egg into his sack. Thus the instinctive rapacity of the hawk is complemented by the casual wantonness of man. The narrator does not comment on the action of the man, but with the addition of men to the story he suggests that animal and man are closely related in the process of destroying life. (pp. 109-10)

O'Flaherty's lyric sketches sometimes expand to embrace a cycle of experience with distinct parts, a shift that makes these stories close to conventionally plotted stories. In the few stories in this group, he often crowds the story toward allegory, but affinities with the lyric sketch remain strong. For instance, in **"The Black Rabbit,"** he embodies part of his thesis on the evolutionary nature of life processes. In this view, the intellect of man moves toward perfection. Men's concepts and images of the deity reflect their grasp of this ultimate perfection; and such positions as skepticism, cynicism, and agnosticism are self-defeating because they restrict a vigorous pursuit of perfection. These insights lead O'Flaherty to censure individuals and tendencies in society that block a gifted man's quest for perfection. In **"The Black Rabbit,"** the rabbit grows large and aggressive, "a sport of nature, a sudden upward curve in the direction of perfection and divine intellect; indeed, he was like that first monkey that became inspired with the vision of humanity." Yet the black rabbit inspires a hatred and fear among ignorant people as he grows more daring and complex. He frightens a housekeeper who determines to destroy him. First she has a fierce cat come into the back garden; later a group of wild cats manage to destroy the black rabbit. As in his earlier story, **"The Civil War,"** O'Flaherty demonstrates the capacity of the timid and mediocre to halt the upward movement of man. But in this story the thesis has carried the narrative too far from the inevitable, natural events that mark his best stories.

In O'Flaherty's comprehensive fables or parables, a series of simple episodes acquire coherence and vitality from rather extensive substructures. Surprisingly, in view of the simplicity and directness of the lyric sketches, O'Flaherty uses large substructures such as the origins of capitalism, the development of a religious belief, or the refusal of men to barter spontaneity and freedom for security. He has written only a few stories that might be called comprehensive fables or parables, but these few make up some of his best work and are frequently anthologized.

Perhaps the best known of the comprehensive fables is **"Two Lovely Beasts,"** which demonstrates the effect of greed on a peasant community and at the same time might be interpreted as a fable on the origins of capitalism. In a rural setting, traditional regulations enforcing cooperation dissolve because an individual flouts custom, allows an insatiable greed to grow within himself, and, in a way, introduces the community to a simple form of capitalism. The changes in the individual, the family, and the community have the implications that one associates with the best modern short stories. Colm Derrane is a simple peasant with a strong will, living in an impoverished part of the west of Ireland. Here neighbor helps neighbor no matter how little there is to share. Colm is importuned by Kate Higgins, a penniless widow, to buy her two calves because the cow has died; no one in the village has the money to buy the calves, nor has anyone enough milk to feed them. Attracted by the sleekness of the animals, Colm gives in to the widow's pleas. A chorus character, Old Gorum, warns Colm that he is breaking the law by depriving his neighbors and his family of milk in order to feed the two calves. According to Old Gorum, whoever stands alone to work for his own profit becomes the enemy of all the rest. Colm Derrane is then ostracized even though he has helped the widow Higgins; he no longer has a voice in the informal council of the landowners. Colm forces his family to eat limpets and periwinkles so that he may buy grass for the calves. Once started on his enterprise, Colm cannot be restrained. Up to the time of buying the calves, he had been governed by his wife, and she begins to complain about the undernourished children. One day she attacks Colm with tongs, a favorite weapon in marital disputes in O'Flaherty. But Colm subdues her and beats her severely, and wife and children thereafter are subservient to him.

Colm's prosperity now attracts the villagers and they readmit him to their circle. Encouraged by his rise in station among his neighbors, Colm next determines to open a shop. Again he stints his family on food and clothes. Because of the war, he finds a ready market for the foodstuffs that he accumulates. But the shop succeeds so well that the villagers again become envious; Colm has risen too far above them for neighborly conversation. The change in Colm is marked by a hardness, a withering of the affections: "His gaunt face looked completely unaware of their jeers. His pale blue eyes stared fixedly straight ahead, cold and resolute and ruthless." Within a peasant setting, O'Flaherty shows the effect of an initial act of greed and charity that leads to a momentous change for individual and community.

Another comprehensive fable, **"The Fairy Goose,"** may not compress all the history of religion as Frank O'Connor once said [see excerpt dated 1956], but it again utilizes the simple, permanent world of peasants to dramatize a cycle of a religious belief. O'Flaherty follows the rise and fall of a myth in a community, similar to the rise and fall of Christy Mahon's myth of killing his father in *The Playboy of the Western World*. In its brief compass, **"The Fairy Goose"** shows the perverse ingenuity of man, his gullibility, a cruelty in suppressing opposition under the guise of righteousness, a degeneration once a myth has been removed, and a nostalgia for a happiness never possessed. (pp. 111-14)

In his stories, O'Flaherty's approach is that of the storyteller consumed with his narrative; he has significant or amusing people and events to talk about; he seems driven to move forward rapidly. He weaves in the briefest description, characterization, or comment; he eschews a piling up of detail. He reveres the present; his characters do not look forward or backward, nor do they indulge in reverie. This omnipotent present demands all of the narrator's energies, and so, despite his Communistic leanings, O'Flaherty avoids propaganda, a lesson apparently derived from his early training from Edward Garnett. Even when the situation might tempt him, as

in **"The Tramp,"** one of his best stories, he stresses the opposition between educated men who cling to the wretched routine of the workhouse instead of accepting the invitation of a tramp to revel in the freedom of the roads. In this story the grimness of the workhouse stands out as a natural event, not as a result of capitalism.

O'Flaherty's accomplishment in the short story lies in the immediacy with which his lyric sketches and comprehensive fables present uncomplicated emotions and instincts. In these stories O'Flaherty foregoes the intricate craft of modern fiction as he searches for an elemental form to convey his experience. He searches, often with admirable success, for an accurate expression of these instincts and emotions. Only by attending passionately to raw experience can O'Flaherty produce a literary effect. By relying on an ancient and simple narrative form, O'Flaherty reveals again the adaptability of man's love for direct narrative.

O'Flaherty records in his short stories vignettes of peasants, children, and animals; he fashions images of a life that seems timeless; men and nature function under laws that cannot be altered by legislatures or technology. In his novels, O'Flaherty examines peasant life not from a timeless perspective but in its historical setting, showing the peasant in transition to a society in which money, government, and Church play determining roles. In *Thy Neighbour's Wife, Skerrett,* and other novels he portrays people caught in changes that they cannot comprehend. Yet this historical study, valuable as it may be, provides a background for enlarged characters who wrestle with distorted dreams of perfection that are often obsessions that betray and destroy them. (pp. 115-16)

Like Lawrence and other modern writers, O'Flaherty tries to reconstruct images that recall man's instinctual life. He pursues his task energetically, as he must if he is to avoid the paralysis arising from passivity, violence, or sentimentality. As an artist, O'Flaherty is engaged, then, in the creation of cultural images, temporary though they may be, to supply what the civilization does not furnish—cultural images that lead to an integration of personality or, in Yeats's terms, to a unity of being. Beneath O'Flaherty's absorption in the physical, external world lies a belief in the evolutionary process, of men, especially artists, finding fulfillment in the struggle for perfection. This perfection may be elusive, even nonexistent, but nevertheless it is still the highest goal for man. (pp. 116-17)

> *James H. O'Brien, in his* Liam O'Flaherty, *Bucknell University Press, 1973, 124 p.*

ANGELINE A. HAMPTON (essay date 1974)

[*Hampton is an English critic who, under the name A. A. Kelly, has edited several works by O'Flaherty and has written the critical study* Liam O'Flaherty, the Storyteller (1976). *In the excerpt below from an essay that she expanded in her book, Hampton focuses on visual and aural elements in O'Flaherty's stories, noting their relation to oral storytelling traditions.*]

Between 1922 and 1956 Liam O'Flaherty wrote some one hundred and fifty short stories, about a third of which remain uncollected. The present paper examines how O'Flaherty's strong visual imagination as evidenced in these stories, and his use of colour, sound, punctuation and repetition may be related to the author's oral heritage.

Many writers share with painters the gift of visual imagination; it helps them to remember and 'fix' scenes and faces, or to recreate a scene visually, drawing upon a vivid visual memory. There are numerous passages of description in O'Flaherty's peasant stories which testify to his powerful visual imagination. This is particularly evident in his nature descriptions as:

> When the foam bubbles are flying in the wind above the cliff-tops on an April day and the gay sun, shining through the rain is mirrored in their watering globes, they are more beautiful than rare pearls.

Sometimes his descriptions of characters are so clearly visualised that one suspects they are based on memories of people he has known in his youth. Here is the old carpenter from **"A Tin Can"**—

> his reddish beard thick with white shavings, his pale face puffed, his loose grey frieze trousers, with the large, black, square patch on the seat, bundled about his waist like a sack.

That the visual is important to O'Flaherty is also shown in his deliberate use of colour, as in **"The Oar"** where the bream have 'gauzy red lips', 'the enchanted light' is described as red over a black sea. 'The hairy yellow anchor rope' refers back to the 'clustering yellow weed' of the previous page. White, black, red and yellow make up the lurid colour scheme of the story. (p. 440)

The vivid description of small actions, of gestures, often serves as a pointer to the characters' inner state of mind, especially in the earlier stories where O'Flaherty uses little dialogue (but also in such a late story as **"The Fanatic"**). A good example is provided by **"Going into Exile"**, in which neither parent can quite comprehend the reality of their children's departure. Their inability to express themselves verbally creates an effect of mute suffering. Unspoken feelings which pass between the father and his son and daughter are suggested by physical gestures. Father and son walk about outside and 'yawn without need pretending to be taking the air'. The daughter crushes a handkerchief between her hands, then she finds her father's eyes upon her, his thumbs stuck in his belt.

In many stories O'Flaherty demonstrates his strong visual inclination by the variation of camera angle and distance in his descriptive writing. **"Wolf Lonigan's Death"** opens with a long shot of the horse-drawn barge coming slowly down the canal. When Wolf Lonigan leaps ashore and runs up the alleyway we are given a close-up of what he finds in the shed seen by the light of his torch. After crossing a maze of dark streets he then arrives at the corner of a street and we get a perspective view: 'at the end of the street a blaze of light struck him, running low to the ground in parallel lines until it ended in a dark lane at the far end'. (pp. 440-41)

In his early stories and in the animal stories, sound plays an important part and often, like colour, it is used to create atmosphere. In O'Flaherty's later work much of this aural description is replaced by dialogue. An example of the use of sound in O'Flaherty's early genre can be found in **"The Letter"**. The story opens with a lyrical passage of description in which the words have been carefully chosen to create both a visual and aural response:

> It was a summer afternoon. The clear blue sky was dotted with fluttering larks. The wind was still, as if it listened to their gentle singing. From the shining earth a faint smoke arose, like incense, shaken from invisible thuribles in a rhapsody of joy by

hosts of unseen spirits . . . Everything listened to the singing larks in brooding thoughtlessness. Yea, even the horned snails lay stretched out on grey stones with their houses on their backs.

The passage breathes an air of peacefully rapturous indolence, yet by the end of the story the family, instead of being in harmony with their surroundings, are estranged from them. The continued triumphant singing of larks as the story ends is contrasted with the frenzied despair and harsh wail of the broken human beings.

In another story **"Trapped"**, sound—it being night—plays a more important part than sight. When the cliff collapses 'the silence was broken by a slight snapping sound like the end of a dog's yawn'. The wings and screams of the birds provide a musical accompaniment to the situation. When in the end Hernon utters a wild yell of relief the sound re-echoes in the sea caves so that the birds rush out and 'the air was full of terrifying sound'.

The importance given to sound in O'Flaherty's early work indicates that he often intends his stories to be heard with the inner ear, but sometimes he also wishes to appeal to the outer ear and some of his work begs to be read aloud. This impression was confirmed when in conversation with the author I asked why he had not written more poetry and he replied 'What is poetry?' and recited the opening paragraph of **"The Oar"** as follows:

> Beneath tall cliffs,
> two anchored curraghs swung,
> their light prows bobbing on the gentle waves.
> Their tarred sides shone in the moonlight,
> In each, three stooping figures sat on narrow seats,
> their arms resting on the frail sides,
> their red-backed hands fingering long lines,
> that swam, white, through the deep dark water.

This is a visual passage written not only to impress the inner ear, but with oral intent, as the heavy punctuation shows. (pp. 441-42)

In the same way that O'Flaherty creates visual effects by means of varied devices such as the use of colour, description of physical action, control of camera angle and distance, and visual imagery, so, to create sound effects, he uses the appeal to the inner ear by means of imagery, vocabulary, punctuation and the description of sounds. By writing a passage of lyric description such as the opening lines of **"The Oar"** he is organising the language as a poet does, and thus drawing attention to its sound, an effect which is heightened when the passage is read aloud.

In his later stories O'Flaherty passed from the method of telling to the method of showing, and the musical or 'sung' narrative present in some of his early work is replaced by the dramatised spoken word. A look through the stories in the volume *Two Lovely Beasts* shows that, subtle though the characterisation often is, there is nothing here to compare in restrained emotional intensity with early stories such as **"The Oar"** and **"The Landing"**. If the opening paragraph of **"The Oar"** is read alongside the opening paragraph of **"The Lament"** or **"The Mirror"** it will be seen that, though in both of these later stories O'Flaherty is also setting the scene for the story which follows, the prose pales by comparison. On the other hand the lyrical impulse still occasionally emerges in the later stories; either in dialogue as when the blind man of **"The Beggars"** listens to the music and hilarious shouts on the race-course and murmurs: 'Black, hungry winter is no more and the son of man is dancing on the grass'; or more often in a descriptive story such as **"The Mirror"**.

This brings us to the consideration of another characteristic of O'Flaherty's style, his use of repetition. It should be said at once that some of O'Flaherty's repetition is unconscious and due to carelessness. In **"The Sinner"** for example, evidence of stylistic weakness occurs not only in the use of clichés (such as 'sorely tempted', 'boon companion', 'a transport of passion' or 'wreathed with smiles'), but there is also a threefold repetition of 'because' just before Julia jumps out of bed and rings for Sally. In **"The Landing"** carelessness manifests itself in the weak image: 'It was a spring evening and the air was warm and fresh as if it had just been sprinkled with eau de cologne or something', and the word 'something' is repeated a line farther on.

In general, however, it is easy to distinguish between haphazard repetition which contributes nothing and may sound clumsy, and the deliberate repetition used for emphasis, for its euphonic value, or to reproduce speech patterns.

Deliberate repetition to create emphasis, when it is used in a passage of narrative, can take the form of a keyword as with the word 'crooning' at the beginning of **"Milking Time"**, used in connection with the woman herself, her voice, her lips, her words and her dreaming thoughts. This is not only an associative word symbolic of the woman's future state as a mother, but it also acts as a musical refrain to colour the mood at the beginning of the story.

Repetition may sometimes take the form of linked associative words which carry the emotive content. This is illustrated in **"Blood Lust"**, towards the end of the story: 'His lower lip began to tremble. His right knee began to tremble. Then the trembling spread all over his body. He felt a desire to yell but he repressed the desire'. Later in the same paragraph other repetitive word pairs occur such as 'forward', 'idea' and 'fear' as the climax is built up by a chain of sensations associated with movements.

In **"The Oar"** we find this striking passage:

> Suddenly it became more silent. As when lead melts and flows in a silver stream, all smooth, so the wavelets melted into the sea's bosom. Now a motionless black floor supported the motionless coracles. Now there was no moon. Now a black mass filled the sky. From afar a bellowing noise came and then a wave shimmered over a smooth rock quite near. Tchee . . . ee . . . ee, it said.

It is obvious that O'Flaherty is here again drawing attention to the sound effects of the words and that he uses punctuation, repetition and alliteration to do so. (pp. 442-44)

Repetition under stress of excitement will often be found, with the natural repetitiveness of everyday speech. This is an example taken from **"The Eviction"** when Lynch is looking at Colonel Newell's portrait:

> 'I wanted above all', he shouted passionately, 'to get that grinning, bloody face into my power. I'll soon take that grin off it. We'll soon see who will be the last to grin. I'll soon fix that face. It won't be grinning long. Upon my oath, that face will soon look different'. . . .

The other form of repetition used by O'Flaherty is contained in the form of phrases sometimes identical and sometimes repeated with variation, which have the effect of a refrain, either uttered by the same voice, by different single voices or in the form of a chorus. Although in general it is a rhetorical device for inducing or suggesting emotion, it often acts also as a leitmotif pointing to the underlying archetypal theme of a story. Repetition is then being used to illustrate the traditional or collective significance behind the story.

Repetition of this type will be found in five of O'Flaherty's earlier stories, **"The Landing"**, **"Going into Exile"**, **"The Stream"**, **"The Mountain Tavern"** and **"Red Barbara"**; and in six later stories, **"Life"**, **"The Challenge"**, **"The Wedding"**, **"The Old Woman"**, **"The Beggars"** and **"The Mirror"**. (p. 444)

In **"Red Barbara"** the repetitive phrases suggest a chorus which is voiced by the narrator in comments about the villagers' reactions, using phrases such as: 'the people also grumbled', 'the people marvelled', 'the people learned', 'the people began to whisper', 'the people laughed', and so on. The people's behaviour shows the traditional reactions to an outsider who has come into their peasant community, and this is the theme of the story. Unvoiced and impersonal, 'the people' stands for exclusive tribal man.

In **"The Mountain Tavern"** the repetition is contained in recurring symbolic references to the falling snow. O'Flaherty here uses the traditional symbol of snow to represent abstract purity; as a double motif to point the contrast between enduring Nature versus transitory man, and the essential purity of man which he vitiates by doing evil. The falling snow creates a frame round the story, poignant in its contrast to the unpleasant plot outlined within. The word 'snow' occurs twenty-eight times, repetitively associated in various phrases in which words such as 'flat', 'fenceless', 'flakes', 'fading', 'flower', alliterate with derivatives of the verb 'to fall'. **"The Mountain Tavern"** and **"Red Barbara"** are, however, the only short stories in which O'Flaherty contains the repetition within descriptive narrative.

In **"The Mirror"** the repetition takes the form of a series of ejaculations which occur seven times: 'Great God!', 'Good Lord!' (twice), and 'Aie! Aie!' (four times), reflecting the emotions or physical sensations felt by the girl. But the presence of the narrator is so strong in this story that the ejaculations, which purport to come from the girl, become inconsistent, the last two being particularly intrusive. No simple peasant girl thinks of herself in terms of a 'Miraculous chalice of life' or 'a radiant virgin wantoning . . . ' (this is the author describing her naked body mirrored in the pool).

The spoken repetitions in the remaining eight stories carry a traditional or collective connotation. In **"The Landing"** Mary Mullen starts with 'Drowned, drowned they will be', as she works herself into a frenzy of fear and lamentation. Twice she will shriek the same phrase later in the story. The description of her outlined against the sea typifies the situation of so many other Aran women before and after her, widowed and rendered childless by the sea.

In **"Going into Exile"** the keening begins towards the end of the story: 'A dismal cry arose from the women gathered in the kitchen, "Far over the sea they will be carried", began woman after woman and they all rocked themselves and hid their heads in their aprons'. Here again these women are not lamenting these exiles only, but all exiles—in fact, the state of being exiled.

This kind of repetition amounting to an archetypal refrain connected with birth, marriage and death also occurs in **"Life"**, **"The Wedding"** and **"The Old Woman"**. (pp. 444-45)

The repetitive phrases of these stories emerge in the form of a keen, an expression of faith, a denial or a wish, as in **"The Beggars"** where the blind man repeats 'I wish you all a happy death. None of you know the hour . . . '. Repetition occurs in **"The Stream"** in the form of the hag's incantation, 'Flow on, white water . . . Let nothing that is young be merry, while you flow . . . '. While in his story **"The Challenge"**, which is the parody of a flyting match, O'Flaherty deliberately uses a refrain following the Irish oral pattern.

All these refrain-like repetitions vindicate the positive forces of life in reaction to the fear of death or weakness, sadness or evil, but they also express an elemental sorrow, a struggle against disillusionment and disbelief in a life which man can, at best, enjoy for so short a time. It is interesting in this connection to recall Synge's comments when describing a burying and wake in Inishmaan where, he says, one is forced to believe in a sympathy between man and nature:

> this grief of the keen is no personal complaint for the death of one woman . . . but seems to contain the whole passionate rage that lurks somewhere in every native of the island. In this cry of pain the inner consciousness of the people seems to lay itself bare for an instant, and to reveal the mood of beings who feel their isolation in the face of a universe that wars on them with winds and seas.

Were all O'Flaherty's repetitive refrains to voice the feelings, or describe the behaviour, of his peasant characters, we might presume that by using them he is merely being faithful to the traditional habits of life and speech of his people. But the fact that he also uses descriptive narrative repetition in **"Red Barbara"** and **"The Mountain Tavern"** points, I believe, to a subconscious as well as a deliberate reason for his using this literary device. O'Flaherty came from a community with a strong oral tradition and his liking for repetition, which he shows at all stages of his literary development, may have been subconsciously affected by the Gaelic story-telling he heard as a child, for a characteristic of the folktale is to use formulaic repeated phrases to create a special rhetorical effect. Liam's brother Tom mentions that in his youth the Aran islanders had stories for each season, and describes how the villagers used to gather every evening in the O'Flaherty home and pass the time telling stories and discussing various subjects, often well into the night.

In his discussion of the relationship between the Irish short story and oral tradition Vivian Mercier [see Further Reading list] favours the view that oral literature has had a direct influence, but he does not find O'Flaherty to be, on the whole, a very 'oral' writer. (pp. 446-47)

It is true that O'Flaherty's stories are an art form intended for the printed page, but his frequent descriptive aural as well as visual effects, his use of punctuation, repetition of words and phrases, all point to the fact that, in some of his stories at least, he expects his reader to listen and not only to visualise his stories, and that his aural and visual imagination were both active when he wrote them. It is probable that O'Flaherty's attention to the aural has been affected by, and perhaps also inherited from, the oral culture into which he was born. (p. 447)

Angeline A. Hampton, "Liam O'Flaherty's Short

Stories—Visual and Aural Effects," in English Studies, *Netherlands, Vol. 55, No. 5, October, 1974, pp. 440-47.*

RICHARD J. THOMPSON   (essay date 1983)

[*In the following excerpt, Thompson traces themes in stories from* Spring Sowing, The Tent, The Mountain Tavern, *and* Two Lovely Beasts, *focusing on ways in which O'Flaherty presents nature as "a teacher and guide that will recall human behavior from the excesses of intellectualization."*]

As a story writer, Liam O'Flaherty comes after Sean O'Faolain and Frank O'Connor in order of artistic worth, but he well preceded them as an established figure in the field. Four years older than O'Faolain and seven than O'Connor, O'Flaherty loosed a flood of prose work in the 1920s: he composed the main share of his fifteen novels and of his approximately 160 short stories in just one decade. (p. 80)

In the novel, his best work would not come until after the 1920s, beginning with *Skerrett* (1932); but in shorter fiction, the 73 stories in **Spring Sowing** (1924), **The Tent** (1925), and **The Mountain Tavern** (1929) stand out as O'Flaherty's best work in the form, along with the twenty new stories collected under the title **Two Lovely Beasts** in 1948.

These four volumes considered together at once figure among the most and least "Irish" of the notable work produced in the Irish short story between its originators, [George] Moore and [James] Joyce, and its major living practitioners, O'Faolain and [Mary] Lavin. They are among the most "Irish" stories because of their remarkably specific rendering of the folkways and social customs of Ireland's peasant population, the country's dominating population until the end of World War II. And, yet, in several dozen cases these stories lack any suggestion whatever of place, time, or social environment. O'Flaherty's "Irish" stories have a native purity, an authority in dealing with the feel and smell and essence of peasant life that O'Faolain and O'Connor, for all their insight, cannot match. At the same time, many of his tales of birds and animals resemble notes from some eternal beast-book of prehensile creation, outside time, beyond the temporary egotisms of place.

At their most obvious, O'Flaherty's nature stories are celebrations of the workings of instinct and appetite, of the biological chain, and of the struggle of natural selection which often brings random death to living creatures but never dishonor. The only "bad" death comes from any effort to sidestep the power of nature. Of birds and fish, and animals and human beings, only the latter strive to thwart natural process because only they aspire to exploit other creatures in order to amass wealth. O'Flaherty's biological and genetic conservatism followed from his espousal of Marxist dialecticism in the 1920s. In their simplest form, his stories uphold the ethical merit of things as they are and authenticate D. H. Lawrence's vision of natural impulses as the Holy Ghost speaking in us and to us. Thus, the two-and-a-half-page story, **"The Foolish Butterfly,"** might be regarded as a typical O'Flaherty nature story: the little butterfly, exulting in its young vigor and riding the wind as hungrily as Icarus, is blown out to sea. "Rejoicing once more in the wind and the heat and the light of the sun, it forgot its terror." When its strength wanes, the frail creature falls into the water and drowns. There is no implied regret in O'Flaherty's description of the way nature works; the story ends non-committally: "There were a few little movements of the round head. Then the butterfly lay still." But there is more to the story than an affirmation of nature, for in **"The Foolish Butterfly,"** as in the preponderance of his nature and peasant stories, O'Flaherty dowers his creature with the Promethean attributes that constantly shine through in his work—courage and rebelliousness. Even as it falters, the butterfly is determined to strive, to seek, to find, and not to yield:

> Again it skimmed the surface of the sea with the curved ends of its trunk. Again it rose. It performed a frenzied series of little jumps, tossing itself restlessly on the heated air, exhausting the last reserves of its strength in a mad flutter of its beautiful white wings. Then it sank slowly despite fierce flopping. The wings dropped, swaying as they had done at the moment of birth when they had come from the chrysalis. The trunk touched the crest of the sea. It sank into the water. The wings fluttered once and then the sea-water filtered through them, like ink through blotting-paper.

What aggrandizes the seemingly insignificant butterfly is his resistance and struggle within the overwhelming hugeness of a benign but indifferent nature. The quality admired throughout O'Flaherty's work is energy—the opposite of giving in to life. The highest good is to act, to take a chance, to "follow one's nature," as the saying goes. (pp. 80-2)

Although man may attain the heights through action, O'Flaherty's early stories maintain a preference for the world of nature over the world of culture; only gradually does his compassion for the foibles of humanity come to rival his regard for nonhuman life. The well-known early story, **"The Wren's Nest,"** is typical. The two boys, human marauders, smash the lovely nest and go on to other mindless destruction: "The inside [of the nest] was coated wonderfully with feathers and down, interlaced an art that could not be rivalled by human beings. The boys tore it into shreds and scattered the shreds." More beautiful even than the wren's nest is the black mare in the story of that title. As Dan of the Fury describes her, "Her tail swept to the ground, and when the sun shone on her sides you could see them shimmering like the jewels on a priest's vestments; may the good God forgive me, a sinner, for the comparison. But what is nearer to God than a beautiful horse?" Certainly not a human being.

O'Flaherty's stories are studded with this same preference for the natural over the human. . . . Over and over, O'Flaherty reworks this theme of the superiority of instinctual bird and beast to human meanness and calculation in what might be called his "S.P.C.A. stories." Only nature is instructive: from the fecundity of the soil and the dumb beasts, man gains sustenance and the softening of his greed and blood-lust. (pp. 82-3)

These stories are not epistles to the animals and fishes. Surely they are intended to chasten and subdue, by holding up to scorn, the less agreeable tendencies of those who read them. Despite his very evident disdain for formal education, for priestcraft, for politicians and businessmen—in short, for the signs and figureheads of "civilization"—O'Flaherty finally proves neither amoral nor misanthropic. He tries, rather, to shame the devil in mankind and to hold up nature as a teacher and guide that will recall human behavior from the excesses of intellectualization. **"Trapped,"** one of the best stories in the early volume *The Tent* (1926), aptly illustrates this attitude. Bartly Hernon escapes from the mountain fissure in

which he is trapped by becoming first like a goat—"He had done a mighty thing. He had descended where no man ever had descended."—and then like a fish as he makes his way through a shark-infested part of the ocean—"He began to swim with all his strength, swimming on his side, heaving through the water with a rushing sound like a swan." Conversion to animalness produces his salvation, but human vanity reasserts itself in the last sentence of the story as the saved Bartly offers thanksgiving: " . . . while he prayed he kept thinking of what the village people would say of his heroic feat."

Human motives are most often mendacious in O'Flaherty's stories. When, in **"The Hawk,"** the predatory bird catches a lark and takes it back to his nursing mate, we have a sense of nature fulfilled, but when the predatory egg-gatherer kills the hawk and makes off with his mate and her eggs, our anger rises at man's imbecile ruthlessness. The hawk acted against its own kind out of natural appetite and necessity, the man out of needless cruelty in the name of "sport." The poignancy of the story derives from our viewing it from the hawk's viewpoint. Nature, in tracing out its huge diurnal course, constantly gives man back good for bad. This is the theme of **"The Tide"** which simply describes the ocean's ecological reclamation of a beach after it is befouled by every sort of human litter. Perhaps O'Flaherty's most mystical story on nature as human benefactor is to be found in **"The Mirror,"** which first appeared in 1953. Here a young girl becomes accidentally wet and strips to dry her clothes. Seeing herself naked for the first time in a mountain pool, she sensually awakens to an anticipation of her biological mission in a florid passage that evokes the worst of Lawrence:

> Aie! Aie! Miraculous chalice of life! Now she brooded in proud delight over the beauty she had seen in the strangeness of the deep dark water. She felt pleased in her heart's deepest core at the loveliness that had been bestowed on her, in order that she might be able to fulfill the mystery of her womb.

> Aie! Aie! A radiant virgin wantoning naked in the sunlight on silken moss and no longer afraid in the least of love's awe-inspiring fruit, the labour of pregnancy.

It is as if the myth of sea-born Venus Aphrodite had been taken up by some social-realist choreographer for a revolutionary ballet, right down to the bird screams. Yet, O'Flaherty's point is clear: the beauty of the world is in nature; human beauty finds its true correspondence and biological model there.

O'Flaherty's distinctive strengths and weaknesses are clear enough. Among the former we may list his skill at distilling stories to their essences, his ability to convey important emotions affectingly, and his power of identifying the hidden communion between human beings and other living creatures. Among his shortcomings number imprecisions of eye and ear, a tendency to oversimplify plots, a persistent exaggeration of the line between human and animal behavior, and a habit of directing at adult audiences some stories better fitted for juvenile readers.

The strengths are hardly insignificant achievements. O'Flaherty's gifts of restraint and economy in storytelling often defy comparison among short story writers right back to his chief progenitor, Maupassant. His stories practically all focus either on life, on death, or on rebirth. His subjects are eternal and elemental. . . . Not only does O'Flaherty concentrate on the extreme moments of life and death, but he also writes largely about the extreme age groups, old people and children, flung off to the antipode of Europe and gripped by basic and extreme impulses such as hunger, hatred, greed, and sexual passion. His cameo art is the farthest thing from the warm social expansiveness of O'Connor and O'Faolain, as two stories of the 1940s demonstrate: **"Life,"** in which a child is born while the grandfather of the family is dying, and **"Light,"** in which the sun comes up and birds and animals stir, while a naked couple run from their tent, swim, and copulate beneath the blazing sun.

The price paid for O'Flaherty's less-is-more art lies mainly in character development, which is sometimes disastrously foreshortened, but, then, his characters are usually emanations of Everyman, and Everyman cannot bear much individuation. Rather than character, O'Flaherty's forte is action and the emotion that produces an action and is in turn colored by it. Hemingway is famous for his precise ordering of action and emotion; O'Flaherty, who admired him, is as good at it. In . . . **"The Rockfish,"** the hunger, curiosity, courage, and sense of danger of the fish are suggested, along with the suppressed anticipation and excitement of the fisherman. . . . The poised moment of silent communion between the hungry and wary fish below and the excited and waiting man above gives the scene its suspense and truth. This same kind of communion became O'Flaherty's stock-in-trade. Very few writers can match his power to transmit the way that the simultaneous strangeness and familiarity of animals frighten and delight humans. (pp. 83-6)

Occasionally O'Flaherty goes too far: his animals become too human or his humans too animal-like to be altogether credible. Thus, the title character of **"The Blackbird"** comes to "the sudden realization that he was making a fool of himself singing out there in complete darkness when all the other birds were gone to bed"—a becoming but unlikely self-awareness. The same sort of anthropomorphic breach occurs in **"The Jealous Hens"**—"The six little hens went off their food completely and spent the whole evening planning something or other, with their heads close together, standing on one leg"—and **"The Black Bird's Mate"**—"But the hen bird on the eggs still sat with the same look of drowsy happiness in her half-closed eyes"—as well as elsewhere. Concomitantly, **"Wolf Lonigan's Death"**—an ancestor of *The Informer*, which O'Flaherty published a year later in 1925—features a title character so unbelievably savage—no doubt based on Jack London's Wolf Larson—that one wonders why no one has killed him before.

That O'Flaherty should succumb occasionally to such extremeness is understandable when he is working so close to the horns of the bull, so to speak. Far more damaging can be problems with plotting, specifically O'Flaherty's habit of imposing an oversimplified, chockablock plot upon some of his stories before forcing home a melodramatic conclusion, and of making his plots so cryptic and thin as to be ineffable. The first tendency is exemplified by a story like **"The Sniper,"** identified by A. A. Kelly as O'Flaherty's first story to arouse public notice. In this tale, a Republican marksman atop a building near O'Connell Bridge during the Civil War callously picks off three people, the third of whom turns out unsurprisingly to be the sniper's own Free Stater brother. . . . Many stories suffer from severe plot anemia, such as **"Poor People," "The Alien Skull," "The Sinner," "The Little**

White Dog," and **"The Letter."** To sample just one, in **"The Letter,"** a poor family's daughter who has gone to America sends home twenty pounds, money that has, however, been earned by prostitution. At the end, the father of the family reads her tear-soaked letter: "His back was towards them but they knew he was crying. He had stood that way, apart, the year before, on the day their horse died." Stories like these seem juvenile and jejune, but then the stories of many writers composed in the heyday of literary naturalism now strike us as strained and mechanical. Mainly, O'Flaherty's stories of the period of the Troubles are overadorned with dated naturalistic *impedimenta*. There are only about half a dozen of these. They always lack the sort of easy grace and worldliness that O'Faolain and O'Connor demonstrate in their early stories of the Troubles—"Guests of the Nation" and "Midsummer Night Madness." On the other hand, other stories of O'Flaherty's that stand outside the naturalist inclination compare quite favorably with those written in the manner of which O'Faolain and O'Connor were acknowledged masters. **"The Eviction,"** for instance, has the same bittersweet wryness, while dealing with the same subject matter, as "Midsummer Night Madness." **"The Old Woman,"** about a buoyant old woman who carries her burial shroud about her neck, approaches O'Connor's "The Long Road to Ummera" in expressing nobility of spirit. Read end-to-end, O'Flaherty's stories offer frequent flourishes of adaptability and range which his singlemindedness in pursuing an overall theme of survival would seem to limit.

One delightful example of O'Flaherty's adaptability may be found in his humor, which occurs mainly in his stories about the conniving of country people to win some small test over those just above them in the social order and, so, win a victory over the harsh conditions of their life. Such a formulation is identical, of course, with the way that much of the humor in Irish literature—or any literature that deals with a submerged population striking back in covert political retaliation at a master class—works. If art is a weapon, as Lenin said, humorous art is the perfect weapon, because it defies reprisal—the upper-caste victim must accept his lot or lose face. O'Flaherty's humor sometimes is gentle and redemptive. In **"The Old Hunter,"** an eccentric horse, purchased for thirty shillings and unloaded on an unsuspecting rich man for thirty pounds, in fact helps the rich man recover his health. A much more acrimonious type of folk humor typifies the tale of Michael Feeney, called **"Stoney Batter"** by his fellow villagers in the story of that title. Stoney strikes back at his brother Peter, the gombeen man of the village, after Peter connives successfully to get his miserable cottage, his only possession, away from him. But the easygoing Stoney talks his housekeeper into naming Peter as the father of her child, and it is Peter that the parish priest makes "pay the bastardy." Peter has one arrow left: he evicts Stoney from the cottage, but this is still another miscalculation by Peter, for the town turns its contempt on him for hard-heartedness to his brother. The gombeen man has violated the ancient order of the village by acquiring property that was his brother's by right of primogeniture. Peter lives on under a cloud of contumely, known to the villagers as "the old ram," while he lets the victimized Stoney expire in the workhouse. They both endure a perverse, mocking fate. (pp. 87-9)

In **"The Post Office,"** three sophisticated travellers enter a tiny country post office in Connemara and demand to send a telegram, in Spanish, to Los Angeles. Many of the people of the town happen to be assembled in the post office, for it is pension day, and they delight in observing the patent exasperation of the postmaster, Martin Conlon, who is devastated by any request at any time to send a telegram: "They would rather listen to him than to a fiddler while he was engaged in that work." Various strident characters of the town have amusing walk-on parts while Conlon fumes, and one of the travellers ends up transmitting the message in his stead. This story first appeared in *The Bell* in 1954; all of the townspeople bask in O'Flaherty's affectionate regard, especially his comic butt, Conlon, and the story well reflects its author's mellowing in the second half of his writing career. As happens with many writers, humor came to O'Flaherty with age.

While humor constitutes one of O'Flaherty's special gifts, it is a sidelight to his main line of endeavor, which is to display men and beasts maintaining their independent natures in the face of collective pressures to regiment them. The outsider practicing his individualism courageously and at whatever cost is his constant subject, as courage is his chief theme. Although this subject and theme become predictable in O'Flaherty's stories, they do not fall into triteness. Almost any cross section of his stories offer evidence of these elements, from **"The Reaping Race"** of 1924, in which Michael Gill ignores ridicule from all sides to win a tortoise-and-hare contest in his own way, to **"The Test of Courage"** and **"Two Lovely Beasts"** of the 1940s. In the first of these latter two, a boy finds himself in a curragh helplessly drifting away from the Irish coast, tired, thirsty, and very possibly beyond the chance of rescue:

> Yet he experienced an exaltation that made him impervious to this torture. Ever since his imagination had begun to develop, he had been plagued by the fear that he would not be able to meet danger with courage. . . . Now the big test had come, [and] he experienced the first dark rapture of manhood instead of fear.

In **"Two Lovely Beasts,"** Colm Derrane starves himself and his family in order to rise in the world; in doing so, he ignores the town's obloquy. However, Derrane's gradual rise is admirable not because of its material accomplishment but, rather, as an acting out of a man's isolated and lofty determination. The townsmen turn their back on Derrane for a second time, at the end, when his prosperity again increases. Derrane disregards their taunts and simply moves away from them, as he has been doing in another sense for years:

> As Colm drove away in his new green jaunting car, quite a number of people whistled after him in hostility and derision. . . . His gaunt blue eyes looked completely unaware of their jeers. His pale blue eyes stared fixedly straight ahead, cold and resolute and ruthless.

O'Flaherty reiterates the same theme of indominance in animal stories like **"Prey," "The Fairy Goose,"** and **"The Black Rabbit."** In **"The Stone,"** only the hero "alone of all these strong men raised [the stone] to his throat and kissed it with his lips three times," an action that marks him off from the rest of the villagers for the rest of his life and assures him of his own specialness. In **"The Child of God"** and **"The Flute Player,"** a painter and a musician willingly give up everything for their artistic ideals. Throughout his work, the code of self-testing and obstinate courage is as omnipresent in O'Flaherty as in Hemingway.

Probably O'Flaherty's major benefaction to the Irish short story is the plentitude of closely considered social detail that

one finds in his work: details of western and island life that complement in fiction the documentary accounts of Maurice O'Sullivan and Peig Sayers, or the sociological studies of Arensberg and Kimball. Who has portrayed the ritual of emigration more authentically than O'Flaherty has done in two stories written twenty-two years apart, **"Going Into Exile"** and **"The Parting"**? Each facet of the first story comes into view with the inevitability of a pathetic ceremony: the father's need to sponsor a last-night social no matter how meager; the group of Mary Feeney's friends sitting with her on her bed in an "uncomfortable position just to show how much they liked her"; the father sprinkling the departing children with holy water; Michael taking a piece of loose whitewash from the wall and putting it in his pocket. **"The Parting"** tells of Michael Joyce's separation from his impoverished family in order to study for the priesthood. His brother Martin will inherit their father's farm when he marries the following spring, while Michael is fated to help "rear and educate the children Martin would beget." The poignancy of O'Flaherty's own boyhood separation from his poor family surely finds voice in the story's ending where Michael's "bitterness [is] terrible because his young heart knew that dark vows would make his parting final, forever and forever."

O'Flaherty catches the ethical values of island life emphatically in **"The Black Mare."** Here we are shown the special privileges of the priest and the sense of resentment that these cause, the feelings of inferiority of the proud islandmen in relation to people on the mainland, the special importance of horsemanship in making marriages and fortunes. O'Flaherty outlines death customs in **"Offerings"** in which "Life does not end with . . . death. . . . There are others who live on and they have customs and a common code of conduct that must be observed." In **"Stoney Batter,"** the plot devolves on Stoney's need to see that his house gets "a thorough cleansing and renovating," for "twice a year the priests visit each village in the parish," and "Mass is said in one house in each village and all the villagers gather into that house to hear Mass and confess their sins." Over and over, O'Flaherty has as his subject matter the social phenomena of western life, from the viewpoint of the ordinary peasant living it, rather than from that of the outsider looking in from above or beyond. **"The Mountain Tavern,"** which presents the devastation of an area caught between two uncaring armies during the Troubles, is a good example of where O'Flaherty's populist sympathies lie. As the best of the portrayers in English of ordinary Irish life on the land, O'Flaherty is more understandable to non-Irish readers than Daniel Corkery and Standish O'Grady, and more sheerly interesting than Brinsley MacNamara and Bryan MacMahon. Specifically, his skill in rendering country matters won O'Flaherty the admiration of both O'Connor [see excerpt dated 1956] and O'Faolain. (pp. 89-92)

O'Flaherty's wide use of folk elements constitutes yet another aspect of the romantic nature of his short stories, an aspect that honors Yeats's and AE's often expressed desire for the imminent return of the Celtic gods.

From *Spring Sowing* (1924) through *Two Lovely Beasts* (1946) and after, the best of O'Flaherty's stories prove to be also the most representative. **"Spring Sowing"** equates the energy and promise of a newly married couple with the immemorial forces set stirring by the fecundation of the earth in the spring. As in Stravinsky's *Rite of Spring*, everything strains: the sky looks "as if it were going to burst in order to give birth to the sun." Poised against the exultant rhythms of promise in the foreground is Mary's discordant knowledge that this backbreaking labor will be exacted from her and her husband right to the mouth of the grave, that she and Martin are now integral with the sidereal flow of life and death. A sort of hymn to the dignifying process of human effort and depletion, the story bespeaks the emergence of a young writer of unusual maturity and power. This same maturity informs **"Going Into Exile"** (1924), in which, for the departing children, the hurt and fear of emigrating are balanced by the excitement of new prospects. The main virtues of the story are its controlled yet emotional writing and its sensitivity to the mélange of feelings experienced by the parents and their children. In the final lines, the mother needs the stoical strength of Synge's Maurya in *Riders to the Sea* to absorb the realization that her loving Mary and Michael have been exchanged for the abstractions of time and patience. . . . (p. 93)

"The Tent" (1925) takes up the subject of hospitality abused, abused by ex-Sergeant-Major Carney who insults his tinker hosts when he mentions that he feels demeaned by having to walk the roads. Carney is an intruder in the tinker camp from the officious world; the tinker and his two women are "cut off from the mass of society," outsiders living still in a state of nature. After Carney commits the supercilious man's error of treating the tinkers as if they were social inferiors, he ends up pitched out into the night by the infuriated tinker for trifling with one of his women. "Fair play," pleads the retreating Carney, invoking one of the shibboleths of his recent imperial employers. The earmark of this story is subtlety. O'Flaherty leaves the tinker's inner reactions and sense of honor for the reader to infer. The story remains understated until Carney tramps off toward Roundwood crying out righteously, "God Almighty!" and crossing himself. The unorthodox and appealing code by which the taciturn tinker lives is indicated by his actions. O'Flaherty's sympathy for his sleazy and defiant way of life looks forward to Brian Moore's in *The Feast of Lupercal*. Even in their dirt and dissipation, the tinker and his women have more real dignity than the wretched Carney.

"Two Lovely Beasts" (1946) is an example of the man-of-independence story, and one of O'Flaherty's longest. After recounting the ups and downs of Colm Derrane's struggle to achieve fortune and status, during which Derrane climbs from farmer to bourgeois. O'Flaherty slyly questions the cost to Derrane and his wife of their "rise." The people of the village envy them, and the town scourge, Gorum, whips up a tirade about new exploiters who "are taking all our lovely beasts across the sea to fill the bellies of pagans." The word "our" in the mouth of the feckless Gorum drips with irony. Ultimately, we detect that the two lovely beasts of the title are not really the calves that Colm Derrane and his wife have sacrificed so much to raise; rather, they are themselves who have grown "cold and resolute and ruthless" in spiting the villagers. The observation that idealism takes a toll on one's humanity, may even make one a fanatic, introduces a viewpoint that continues through *Two Lovely Beasts* to **"Galway Bay"** at the very end. **"Galway Bay"** (1939) tells of a snappish eighty-year-old man, disappointed with life and recovering from an argument with his modern-minded daughter, who travels by steamer to Galway with his cow, which he intends to sell in order to purchase his coffin and to order some Masses said after his death. It is a beautiful, bittersweet story of old age, of Tom O'Donnell's will and senses in decline, of the last of the old breed of Aran men. Tom is puzzled and

disappointed by the new things he sees: women in trousers, an ocean-going liner, islandmen domesticated by life in the town city. Regretting having quarreled with his daughter, he marches off of the steamer and up the lonely road with the cow, which is as decrepit as himself: "He walked beside her with downcast head, one hand on her high hip-bone, the other leaning heavily on his stick." For this touching old man who still treasures his "spunk," everything is gone or going, and he can no longer apprehend the beauty of the bay he once knew so well. All of the sadness of aging is here, the ghostly sense of glories past. With **"Lovers,"** it is O'Flaherty's best story of the old.

"The Blow" (1954) contrasts two generations as a father and son go to purchase a litter of pigs from a large farm. The father has become a greedy hotel-keeper, "Almost . . . a complete savage," to whom the pigs are simply more chattels to be acquired. To his son Neiden they are creatures of vital beauty: "There was far more depth of understanding in [his eyes] already than in those of his father; understanding and wonder and suffering." Three blows in the course of the story attest to the insensitivity of Neidin's father. The first blow is that given by the boar to a pen door that separates him from the sow: "Oh, you devil," says Neidin, "there was a blow for you." He dislikes confining the animals, unlike his father, who believes in commercial mating. The second blow comes when the sow accidentally strikes her weakling piglet. To the father, the sow is correcting and rebuking the piglet's unaggressiveness by this action; to Neidin, she is showing her regret that the weakling cannot find a place at her teats. The father shouts that the sow hit the piglet on purpose, because that is "how it is in the world. There is neither pity nor mercy, among people as well as among animals, bad or good, for the weak or the cowardly." To veteran readers of O'Flaherty, the father merely voices truths reflected in his work since **"The Seal"** and **"The Wounded Cormorant."** But the third blow, administered to Neidin by his father in retribution for Neidin's siding with the weakling piglet, "banishes from his consciousness everything that pertained to the divinity of his nature." Neidin's godly love of life "is knocked out of him" and "pride and contempt" enter in, until the sow overtly summons its weakling to nurse. Then "love . . . returned to the world," and Neidin can decently cry and feel affection for his boorish father. Chastened in turn by his son's display of feeling, the father, for once, softens toward him. Clearly, the story marks a softening in O'Flaherty himself, a willingness to acknowledge in human animals the existence of transforming virtues, such as mercy and pity, which can alter behavior for the better. This appealing point of view indicates O'Flaherty's mellowing in later life. At the same time, **"The Blow"** retains his life-long attitude that earthly good resides mainly in animals and old people and children. (pp. 95-7)

Richard J. Thompson, "The Sage Who Deep in Central Nature Delves: Liam O'Flaherty's Short Stories," in Eire-Ireland, Vol. XVIII, No. 1, Spring, 1983, pp. 80-97.

JAMES F. KILROY (essay date 1984)

[*In the following excerpt, Kilroy links O'Flaherty with Seán O'Faoláin and Frank O'Connor as the three preeminent modern Irish short story writers, characterizing O'Flaherty as a naturalist whose "single-minded, bleak vision" is expressed most forcefully in his short stories.*]

Three masterful short story writers, Liam O'Flaherty, Frank O'Connor, and Sean O'Faolain, set the standards, the high water markings of artistic achievement, although they are so dissimilar in their techniques and favored themes that the common linkage of them as "the three O's" is not fair to any. Their dominant tones, the thematic equivalents of ruling passions, are widely varied: O'Flaherty's social commitment and natural vehemence contrasts sharply with O'Faolain's cool intelligence and with O'Connor's ironic but warm humaneness. But in at least one important respect they are properly linked as the conscious molders of the genre, three who transformed the traditional forms of short fiction and even reshaped the short story as developed by [George] Moore and [James] Joyce. (p. 95)

But perhaps there was something indigenous to Ireland in the troubled period of the 1920s and 1930s that nurtured the growth of this form, or some experience or attitude shared by the three as Irishmen that accounts for their eminence. They came from the provinces and wrote frequently of their native areas: O'Flaherty's Connaught, particularly the Aran Islands, and O'Connor and O'Faolain's Cork. All three quarreled with their native religion and occasionally expressed anticlerical sentiments. Although they all took part in military actions, they grew to mistrust the fervid nationalism they had felt as young men. But the greater common quality of the three, and of the best of their contemporaries as well, was an acute self-consciousness, a tendency to examine their own national identities, religious affiliations, and vocational choices that is parallel to Ireland's own self-scrutiny in this period. (pp. 95-6)

Of "the three O's," Liam O'Flaherty is the most forceful and bold. His stories treat violent and painful subjects, and their ethical implications are more profound than those of O'Connor or O'Faolain. Like [Emile] Zola and [Theodore] Dreiser, he is a naturalist who views man's attempts to counteract natural forces as futile, and who regards social institutions as essentially corrupting. Expressing such forceful convictions, his stories are less subtle than those of his two well-known Irish contemporaries, for they aim at an immediate impact.

Growing up on the Aran Islands, O'Flaherty knew nature at its most violent; in his stories it is most often an oppressive force. He observes and describes the sea, winds, and seasonal changes fastidiously but warily, acknowledging their destructive power. A farmer's efforts to work the recalcitrant soil or a fisherman's attempts to escape from a stormy sea appear as no more than animal responses, in which distinguishing human characteristics are ignored. Because man's innate powers are regarded as far inferior to antagonistic natural forces, plots tend to be lopsided when man is pitted against nature. Likewise, if reason is feeble in such conflict, human communication is largely futile, or merely self-deceptive, making the stories rely less on dialogue than on gestures and action. Sophisticated narrative techniques are absent, inappropriate as they are to the elemental subjects of the stories, and the structures tend to be simple, focusing attention directly on a single or a few incidents.

Although most of his publications are novels, the short story is the form in which O'Flaherty's harsh vision is most forcefully conveyed. . . . The constraints of the short story are consonant with O'Flaherty's single-minded, bleak vision.

He has published four major collections of short stories, plus several smaller gatherings and some selected editions. They fall into two periods: the first three collections, published in the first five years of his literary career (*Spring Sowing,* 1924; *The Tent,* 1926; *The Mountain Tavern and Other Stories,* 1929), and then, nearly twenty years later, *Two Lovely Beasts and Other Stories* (1948). Because he regarded the short story as less challenging than the longer fictional form, he neglected it for much of his writing career. Yet since he returned to it, the stories have expanded in scope and even employ more ambitious narrative techniques. (pp. 96-7)

"Spring Sowing," the title story of his first collection, reveals the dominant thematic concern of the early stories: the subjection of man to nature. Young newlyweds set forth on their first day of working the land. . . . The physical effort is not glossed over as being ennobling: they complete the day's tasks, ending only with the anticipation of "sleep and forgetfulness." In such a barren context the characters are little more than animals, slaves to the cycles of nature, hoping merely to stay alive. Only there seems to be no alternative to submission to a cruel natural order. In **"Poor People,"** a later stage in such a married life is presented, as a couple desperately seek food to keep themselves and their four-year-old son alive; at the story's end they are left, the son having died, sitting together and weeping. The naturalistic theme dominates such stories. Action is minimal, setting as stripped of appeal as to seem preternatural, and the conflict for survival is sharply, relentlessly focused. Individualizing characteristics are omitted, so that the people sometimes even lack names; background information is irrelevant to the immediate concern; distracting literary techniques are eschewed. Yet such stories have great force, for with so few details included, the stark natural images acquire great suggestiveness. In **"Spring Sowing"** the young couple's work suggests fruition and reproduction ("they were to open up the earth together and plant seeds in it"), and the husband's contention with the wife reveals his desire to achieve a dominant role as master, just as her ultimate submission reveals her willing acceptance of an inferior position. In this short, unrelieved story, the last sentence achieves special power: "Cows were lowing at a distance," reflecting the couple's animal state, their inevitable suffering, and yet their participation in natural processes.

Such animal behavior and primitive instincts tend to dominate rational concerns or civilized behavior. In **"Blood Lust,"** a man in a fishing boat with the handsome brother he envies struggles with a growing, nearly irrepressible desire to murder him. Eventually he crushes a fish to a shapeless mass, and when he has done so, he sighs; "his blood lust was satisfied." The most basic of instincts, the will to survive, is vividly conveyed in **"Trapped,"** in which a man escapes after being stranded on a mountain. The intense psychological frenzy of such characters is well conveyed, but their actions, extreme as they may be, are made to seem spontaneous and inevitable.

Man is depicted as so small and insignificant a creature in a cruel and indifferent universe that it is not really surprising that in several of O'Flaherty's best stories animals replace humans as characters. A cow jumps to death after losing her calf; a conger eel is captured and wrestles with a pair of cruel sailors, but heroically escapes back to the sea; a sea bird struggles, not only against wind and sea, but against the other birds, which reject a wounded animal. In the last of these stories, **"The Wounded Cormorant,"** the rejection and even attack by the healthy birds is horrifying, but it does not seem morally reprehensible, for human moral codes are irrelevant to a conflict with nature. The bird resists as long as it can and then falls off a ledge to the sea below, where "it disappeared, sucked down among the seaweed strands." That closing statement reveals how dispassionate the narration is, for the other cormorants are portrayed as no more cruel than the waves and weeds. (pp. 97-8)

Consistent with his naturalist intentions are O'Flaherty's unambiguous endings, the generally direct narrative techniques, and his rejection of stylistic elaboration. Stories tend to begin abruptly, with no historical background or topical commentary, and to end sharply, often with accounts of death or separation, or with some other full closure. Between those poles only essential action is described—perceptions, episodes, events, but little commentary. Yet even in such unadorned, skeletal accounts, a strong impression of the writer's authority is conveyed; the abrupt turns of plot, the selectivity of detail and incident, and the strength of the endings all give the impression of a sure-handed, controlling sensibility. Paradoxically, the more restricted the narrative, the greater the sense of such authority; for defying conventions of storytelling, an author, such as O'Flaherty, who presents only the least ambiguous actions, makes a statement that is so strong as to be distinctive.

O'Flaherty's implied criticism of Catholicism is consonant with his naturalist convictions; to him the institution of religion is unnatural in that it enforces conformity, weakness, and slavery. Cruel, uncharitable, and even perverse priests appear, but O'Flaherty's exposure of them is not much more vigorous than what is found in many pieces of Irish fiction or drama. What O'Flaherty most consistently denounces is the tyranny exercised by the clergy rather than the priests themselves. In **"The Inquisition,"** for instance, a young postulant is denounced by an old priest for buying cigarettes for his friends. When the postulant rebels, within his mind at least, he becomes free, but he has also become as deceitful as his oppressor, showing the poisonous effects of institutional victimization. Human tyranny in this and other forms is the target of some of O'Flaherty's most forceful stories. (pp. 98-9)

At times the force of O'Flaherty's denunciation of such tyrants is so strong that the stories become melodramatic. . . . But in those stories that are most pared down, in which the satiric target is clearly established and the responses sufficient, O'Flaherty's strong voice and conviction elevate the stories to true artistry. In **"The Outcasts"** a young woman confesses to a priest that she has given birth to an illegitimate child. When he drives her away, she walks to a lake, says some prayers, and goes to jump off the brink. But when she hears her baby cry, she returns to him "joyfully," picks him up, and then . . . jumps headlong into the lake. As the story's inscription, "I am the Good Shepherd," is applied to the insensitive priest, it is ironic; but in refraining from abandoning her child, the mother herself becomes such a model. Kitty's realizations that she will not be forgiven and that her child will be similarly abandoned are not articulated, nor does a narrator comment upon them. But clearly the tyranny of the priest is set in contrast to her human concern for her child.

Other forms of social control beyond those imposed by the church are likewise vigorously exposed. The stratification of society into classes is one such satiric target. In **"The Terrorist,"** a story that reveals O'Flaherty's early Marxist sympathies, a theater audience into which a bomb is thrown is neatly divided into three classes, corresponding to the orchestra and two balconies. In **"The Fireman's Death,"** the men tending the engines utter "curses on the sea, the fires, God, and the rich men who make slaves toil in the bowels of ships." In such stories, the exposure of injustice often determines the shape of the narrative, with plot and character development sacrificed to theme.

However, such social reactions and political convictions, striking as they may be, are not the elements that distinguish O'Flaherty's art. Naturalist tendencies are common in the literature of the period, and O'Flaherty's criticism of institutions and human tyranny are no more vehement than those of many other writers of the early twentieth century. Rather, what dignify the best stories are strange and powerful contrasts: between moral outrage and an irrepressible lyric impulse in some stories, between a conviction of men's subservience to nature and a celebration of life in others.

"The Mountain Tavern" includes some strong statements spoken by characters denouncing the Civil War which had occurred only a few years earlier. In particular, the family members whose home and place of business have been burned to the ground are victims of both the Republicans and Free State soldiers. The tavern owner's wife, Mrs. Galligan, is explicit in her denunciation: after the years of the Troubles, the two forces have turned on one another "like dogs after a bitch," she cries. Even the two exhausted soldiers who survive give up their will to fight. But such comments and conclusions do not determine the story's shape, for the narrative is more concerned with natural description than the people who traverse this desolate setting. It opens with a long, detailed description of falling snow which smooths, silences and obliterates all vestiges of humanity: "Up above was the sky and God perhaps, though it was hard to believe it; hard to believe that there was anything in the whole universe but a flat white stretch of virgin land between squat mountain peaks and a ceaseless shower of falling snow-flakes." Human beings impinge on the scene: three soldiers looking for shelter and food at a public house they know to be safe. But they find it burned to the ground, and when one of the three Republican soldiers dies, the people show their hatred, looking steadily and pitilessly, "with the serene cruelty of children watching an insect being tortured." The story moves to its conclusion when a lorry of Free State soldiers arrives, and the two Republicans surrender. Both groups are denounced by the old woman as robbers who have taken the possessions and even the lives of the common people. At the story's conclusion, the human characters disappear from the scene and nature reclaims the land, erasing the traces of man, a ruined tavern, and a bloodstained piece of ground where the soldier had died: "Night fell and snow fell, fell like soft soothing white flower petals on the black ruin and on the black spot where the corpse had lain."

O'Flaherty's expression, even when rough and imprecise, suits the combination of pessimism and lyric enthusiasm which appears in such stories. He favors similes over metaphors, thus suggesting that any proposed comparison is not quite adequate. He repeats words, not so much to expand meaning incrementally but to reveal the urgency and recognition that his intended statements are just beyond his power of expression. The impression of struggling to express one's self is particularly appropriate to the stories in which the characters themselves find verbal expression difficult. The parents in **"Going into Exile"** speak only in platitudes when they try to articulate their feelings of grief at the approaching emigration of their two children. In fact, the moments of strained silence are the most evocative: "They stood in silence fully five minutes. Each hungered to embrace the other, to cry, to beat the air, to scream with excess of sorrow. But they stood silent and sombre, like nature about them, hugging their woe." When the child departs, the mother can do no more than cry. But given the skeptical view of language the characters have expressed and the sparse use of dialogue in the story, the last comments of the neighbors—"There is nothing that time will not cure . . . Time and patience"—is painfully ironic, for such consolation does not relieve the suffering; in fact, this is a grief that neither time nor patience may alleviate.

O'Flaherty's insistence that men have only very limited power to control their lives or to combat natural forces severely limits possible modes of action in his early stories. Very few stories center on conflict between humans; more often, men struggle with the insurmountable forces outside, or with ungovernable impulses within themselves, the outcomes being predictable from the story's start. Thus the narrative form is determined by the explication of a conflict or the presentation of a theme, rather than by action. In **"The Tramp,"** for example, the title character tries to persuade inmates of a workhouse to join him in the freedom of wandering through the natural world; the inmates refuse to do so, so bound are they to social notions of propriety and respectability. Animals, in other stories, free from social restraints, can reconcile their own desire for freedom with nature's laws. The conger eel, in the story of that title, clearly escapes human bonds for the sea's depths, where it can enjoy unlimited freedom. In such animal fables, the narrative line is slight, serving aims of social criticism and moral instruction.

In stories about human beings, similar elements of fable are abundant; moral instruction is so predominant that detailed depiction of characters or complicated narrative lines are often sacrificed. **"The Fairy Goose,"** built upon a patently contrived plot, presents a forceful comment on folk superstition and religious belief. Such moral tales can have great force, as does **"Red Barbara,"** a celebration of natural vitality and even violence. But that story of a vivacious woman's marriage to a saintly, disciplined man is narrated with such strong moral implications that it becomes a kind of pagan sermon. In this regard, O'Flaherty's resemblance to D. H. Lawrence is striking: both authors occasionally abandon their considerable descriptive powers and their challenging theories of the integrity of human instincts in order to preach in a simplistic manner. In one of O'Flaherty's weakest early stories, **"Beauty,"** a man, having rejected the woman with whom he had fled into the wilds, turns from her and kisses a tree, which is supposed to symbolize an absolute, independent, life-affirming spirit. (pp. 99-102)

[In] 1948, a collection of new stories, *Two Lovely Beasts and Other Stories,* was published, most of which had appeared in periodicals in the ten years preceding. O'Flaherty's interests had evidently broadened, and his analytical powers sharpened, so that in these stories he recognizes more complex motives for human actions and subdues his anger at social institutions. The narrative forms are looser, accommodating varied incidents.

The title story, **"Two Lovely Beasts,"** is his longest, most complex and yet most balanced short story. The main character, Colin Derrane, succumbs to material ambition as he acquires a second calf, one more than he can easily support, and

more than the community regards as permissible, since he will have to use his cow's milk to nurture the two calves and will have none left for his poor neighbors. O'Flaherty's criticism of him is never directly stated, but the implications are clear and forceful. Derrane claims God's providence on his side, but he is clearly brutalized by his success; at the story's end, as he drives away from the fair after selling the two beasts for top prices, "his pale blue eyes stared fixedly straight ahead, cold and resolute and ruthless." By allowing the villagers to present the direct condemnation of him as a "bloodsucker" who has taken the food from the country to sell to foreigners, O'Flaherty can deflate their condemnation as well, for guilty as Derrane is of greed, his neighbors are driven by envy more than justice in accusing him of such crimes. This detailed presentation of Derrane's ambitions, their slow growth and destructive consequences, is made possible by the more ample form of the story. The efficacy of human actions is neither denied nor is it contrasted to the superior power of nature as insistently as in earlier stories, thus allowing wider narrative interests and thematic variety.

The author's more extensive treatment of the varieties of human responses in the later stories is seen in **"The Wedding,"** in which a celebration in a house only two hundred yards away is observed and commented upon by a mad, crippled woman and her alcoholic cousin. Their distorted, bitter view is contrasted to the vitality of three young girls who are excited about the event. By the story's end, the older women have revealed their frustration at being unwed; they are left hugging each other, the one weeping but the other pealing in "idiotic laughter." The story avoids both sentimentality and cynicism by such careful balance, yet presents a forceful contrast of youth with age, and sanity with madness.

Several of the stories in other volumes were written in Irish as well as English, and ten of these were published in 1953 as *Duil (Desire).* A comparison of versions in both languages reveals how conscious O'Flaherty was of achieving such balance and avoiding facile moral implications. In the earlier, Irish version of **"The Touch,"** for example, the young man who is in love with the vivacious daughter of a spiteful man for whom he works as a day laborer is much weaker than in the later English version of this story. The effect of the final version is to balance the young man's cowardice against the father's cruelty, so as to give prominence to the girl, who is symbolically identified with the spirited horse she rides. She is being sold like livestock, doomed to marriage with a man she does not love and separation from the man she does love, but who is too weak to carry her away.

The balance O'Flaherty achieves in his late stories is not gained by compromising his convictions or decreasing the intensity of the emotions expressed. In fact, the late stories return to many of the subjects of the early works: animal tales, accounts of man's contention with nature, and stories of death and violence. They are less vehement and provocative, so that some critics regard them as inferior to his earlier stories, but they treat subjects and attitudes that are more complex and subtle than such favored early themes as brute struggle and resentment. **"The Tide,"** a late story, deserves comparison with his earlier **"The Wave,"** in that both describe a natural phenomenon of water's motion. The early story is undoubtedly forceful in its vivid description of a wave acquiring enormous force and then breaking against the shore; but the later story, although quieter indeed, is more comprehensive in surveying the curative effects of the regressing and progressing tide. The humans who invade the beach are gross and voluptuous, attacking it selfishly; but the tide that drives them away at the story's end restores all to its original beauty. Critical as the story is of human rapacity, nature is seen as a positive force, not a destroyer, and the tone is austere, yet reassuring rather than angry.

"The Parting" represents the considerable achievement of his last collection of stories. Its main character, a thirteen-year-old boy leaving for the seminary in compliance with his family's plan, sees himself as one of the livestock being hoisted aboard the steamer to be sold for profit. His desire to remain home on the island, his need for his family's affection, and his inability to understand what is happening in this strange setting all turn at the end to an awful recognition of finality and the irreversibility of his fate. Criticism of the practice of taking such a young boy away from home is not disguised, yet it does not displace or prevent the reader's sympathy for the victim. For all their lack of perception, the characters are complex, affected by contrary motives and desires. When the boy, for instance, speaks "gruffly" to his mother, the narrator explains, "Indeed it was the intensity of his love that forced him to be gruff and almost brutal when he spoke to her. If he allowed any tenderness to creep into his voice, it would mean the collapse of his resistance." The boy's awareness of conflict within the family and his embarrassment are no stronger than his fear of leaving them. Yet the story's conclusion is as forceful as any of O'Flaherty's, as the boy realizes the "dark vows" he is about to take will make this parting "final, forever and forever."

O'Flaherty's expression in the late stories is no more polished or graceful than his early ones. But the rough style, the spare dialogue and the brutal commentary are well adapted to his mature outlook, one that is balanced and complex, but vivid and vehement. Like the rough landscapes of Jack Yeats, O'Flaherty's stories rely on violent contrasts and bold strokes to convey their energetic visions. They are striking, sometimes disturbing, but never pallid. (pp. 102-04)

> *James F. Kilroy, "Setting the Standards: Writers of the 1920s and 1930s," in* The Irish Short Story: A Critical History, *edited by James F. Kilroy, Twayne Publishers, 1984, pp. 95-144.*

WILLIAM DANIELS (essay date 1988)

[*In the following excerpt, Daniels provides a summary of criticism of both the Irish- and English-language versions of stories collected in* Dúil.]

Among critics who have written about O'Flaherty's Irish stories, [Tomás] de Bhaldraithe [see Further Reading list] compares passages from some of them to their English counterparts and objectively demonstrates O'Flaherty's fine adaptation of language to audience. But critics like [Maureen O'Rourke] Murphy too spiritedly adapts Frank O'Connor's belief that O'Flaherty's English "lacks the distinction and beauty of his Gaelic" [see O'Connor excerpt dated 1956]. Even though O'Flaherty was not an Irish speaker until after he started school and had left the island only when he was barely past puberty, she finds that "the excesses, the offensive intrusions, the tedious repetitions, the faulty diction, and the structural slack are present in the English versions and missing in the Irish. . . O'Flaherty filters his world to his English reader through the prism of his prose, but it is an Irish sensibility in a borrowed language."

Like [Máirtín] Ó Cadhain, [Sean] O'Faolain has high praise for *Dúil.* "I know of very few instances in Irish writing, in either language, that welds the tender and the tough as consistently as O'Flaherty does." His stories, "for all their pervasive hardness and occasional wildness, [are] shot through and through with as much elemental tenderness . . . This in sum is all I want to say about his stories." Critics writing in Irish like [Pádraic] Breatnach, [Breandán] Ó Buachalla, and [Fiachra] Ó Dubhthaigh tend to call tough 'energy' and tender 'poetry.' Breatnach, among many others, points out some of the tender/tough parallels in the deaths of lark and hawk in "An Seabhac." O'Flaherty himself was humble about this gift; in his review of *An Braon Broghach,* short stories by Máirtín Ó Cadhain, he claimed that Ó Cadhain was the first writer in Irish to have described nature as it is, 'the torments and the beauty that are together in life.' Every sensitive reader of *Dúil* must surely also notice that part of the joy in reading the stories comes from finding the tough and tender juxtaposed not only in one story but, through O'Flaherty's word repetitions, finding both tough and tender associated with each other across the stories. The 'rattle in the throat' (*"glothar ina scornach"*) of the excited child in "Dúil," for example, is heard also in the throat of the dying old man of "An Beo." And nearly every critic of the stories seems aware of O'Flaherty's animal and human parallels in the same stories, certainly in "Teangabháil" and "An Buille," but none of them has done more than to give one or two illustrations of this.

Breatnach and, also, [Vivian] Mercier find *Dúil* demonstrates O'Flaherty's growing powers as he grew older, that his later stories were breaking new ground, and that he "might have begun a new and greater career in fiction after 1950." John Kelleher agrees with [James F.] Kilroy [see excerpt dated 1984] and [A. A.] Kelly [see Further Reading list] that unfortunately O'Flaherty was "writing his best stories just when he stopped writing." Kelly believes this is so because she finds situations nearly always dominating character in his early work while in his later stories what "counts is how a man conducts himself." Because his later work is "less vehement and provocative," claims Kilroy, "some critics regard them as inferior to his earlier stories, but they treat subjects and attitudes that are more complex and subtle than such favored themes as brute struggle and resentment."

None of the stories in *Dúil,* however, has received anything even approaching the sort of explication deserved by a writer of O'Flaherty's stature. (pp. 124-26)

The general criticism of *Dúil* itself is seldom directed to the plots of the tales, but some of the criticism of O'Flaherty's English versions often sheds light on their Irish counterparts. Although [Richard J.] Thompson [see excerpt dated 1983] claims that O'Flaherty's "tendency to oversimplify plots" results in a "habit of directing at adult audiences some stories better fitted for juvenile readers," I find that the *Dúil* stories present a problem for adult readers that has nothing to do with O'Flaherty's intended audience. O'Flaherty was certainly not aware that his Irish readers would usually be given this book so early on in school that they would later assume it a young person's book; even the two books in Irish about *Dúil* clearly address an audience of critical first-readers. O'Connor, on the other hand, finds that "in spite of the powerful narrative line, O'Flaherty's form . . . is the convenient, ready-to-wear magazine form of the Twenties in England—two to three thousand words describing a single episode and while, like the ready-to-wear suit it is a great convenience, the pattern is also in quality very monotonous." Yet if we apply O'Connor's description to *Dúil,* we find that while only three of its eighteen stories—**"An Seabhac," "An Chulaith Nua,"** and **"Uisce faoi Dhraíocht"**—fall into this "suit" category, even they so differ from each other that they can hardly be called "monotonous."

Thompson's further claim that O'Flaherty's plots are sometimes "so cryptic and thin as to be ineffable" is counteracted by [John] Zneimer's suggestion that O'Flaherty often gives us a "quality of vision focused on a pattern of simple events tremendously significant but only half-understood" [see excerpt dated 1970] and by Kelly's recognition that his "better stories suggest more than they state." Although Irish critics have worked with the volume as a whole, only Pádraic Breatnach recognizes that the 'thinnest' stories in the volume gain in resonance when read as part of the volume as a whole. But critics of the stories in both languages have been attracted by their sudden beginnings and swift endings. [Brendan] Kennelly [see Further Reading list] admires their "crisp, definite" endings, yet Ó Dubhthaigh alone calls attention to the symbolic beginning of **"Daoine Bochta."** [James H.] O'Brien [see excerpt dated 1973] probably comes closest to suggesting the sort of explication that O'Flaherty's stories deserve when he says that "the effect of the narrative" in his shorter pieces "is similar to that of a lyric poem."

From its title, of course, one expects *dúil* to be the volume's main theme; and O'Flaherty's use of the word centers around such definite words as *"dúil," "fonn"* ('feeling'), and *"tnúthán"* ('longing'). [Proinsias] Ó Cuagáin, the most disciplined and sensitive of O'Flaherty's critics writing in Irish, finds *Dúil* ('desire') running through both human and animal characters in the stories, whether that of a girl for motherhood or of a dog to kill a rabbit. Ó Dubhthaigh wisely suggests that we not forget to look for 'desire without fulfillment.' Kelly shows herself aware of this latter aspect when she finds that the intense obsessions of O'Flaherty's characters are "usually the result of thwarted desire" which "often take[s] the form of a mental violence which is either directed against others or turns back against itself resulting in derangement and hallucination."

Among the early *Dúil* stories, mental frustration is found in both parents of **"Daoine Bochta,"** for they can find nothing physical to fight against, while in the 1946 **"Teangabháil,"** part of the tragedy for the young couple is that the boy cannot marry the girl without completely abandoning his dependent mother. The frustration of the two main characters in **"Díoltas"** is only relieved by death and/or revenge, while **"Mearbhall"** is possibly *Dúil*'s most powerful recreation of frustration.

In O'Flaherty's animal stories, Kelly finds violence "always related to animal's instinct to preserve the race," while the "cathartic effect on the reader of violence is best shown when man [and I'd add animal] is threatened . . . and rises through violent action or sacrifice to selflessness." But she is obviously overgeneralizing when she claims that "physical violence appears in no story written after 1932," for among O'Flaherty's later Irish stories, **"An Seabhac,"** the hawk of the title, after killing the lark, gives his life trying to protect his mate; the little cock is badly mauled while unsuccessfully fighting to gain a mate (**"An Chearc Uisce"**); lightning, smashing **"An Charraig Dhubh,"** kills most of the animal life around it; **"An Luchóg"** is tossed and tumbled by both cat and kitten before

its escape; Paddy is killed by his fall in **"Díoltas,"** and both piglet and boy are knocked about by their parents before the happy ending in **"An Buille."**

While most of O'Flaherty's early critics recognized his penchant for violence, all found him lacking in humor. With the publication of *Dúil,* however, this immediately changed; unfortunately, however, the humor in such stories as **"Oifig an Phoist"** was often seen as an end in itself. Kelly's usually solid thinking is refreshing after reading such obtuse criticism, especially when she points out the interrelationship between violence and humor: "violence does not create emotional relaxation but anxiety in the reader, from which he may later obtain release; whereas the comic usually causes an instantaneous impulse of relaxation."

Indeed, Kelly finds many of the stories contain simple humor, even the serious stories like **"The Blow"** treating "the child-parent relationship" or stories like **"The New Suit"** "revealing the emotional responses of the child. . . . in which the amusement arises out of the child's fearful helplessness." And she claims that satire like that in **"Oifig an Phoist"** "can also release tension when the ridiculous element of satire, which contains pity and some tolerance is predominant." In light of this, even the early **"An tAonach"** exhibits a bitter irony as we share the people's joy in selling their cattle until we are reminded that they will end up in English bellies.

None of O'Flaherty's critics explores the settings of his stories in anything like detail. Breatnach notices that O'Flaherty's little one-sentence pictures in his 'inside' stories give the reader the feel of the natural world 'outside,' while Ó Dubhthaigh sensitively recognizes that no matter which of the Irish stories you may be reading, islands always seem near. What [George Brandon] Saul [see excerpt dated 1963] finds true of the English stories is surely true for most of *Dúil:* the sea cliffs are a "common locale for action." (pp. 126-28)

In nine of the other stories, we find island-like settings: the sea cliffs in **"Bás na Bó,"** the field near the cliffs where sheep are shorn in **"An Chulaith Nua,"** the rabbit's hole at the cliff edge in **"An Fiach,"** lakes near the cliffs in **"An Chearc Uisce"** and **"Uisce faoi Dhraíocht,"** a terrain of ledges like those on the Aran Islands in **"Díoltas,"** strands where peasants gather seaweed in **"Daoine Bochta"** and **"Teangabháil,"** and a home from which the family goes out to gather carrageen in **"An Beo."** Of the four other stories, **"Oifig an Phoist"** is on the coast road west of Galway, while the other three, **"An Buille," "An tAonach,"** and **"Mearbhall"** seem set in or near *Cois Fharraige* towns.

As we would expect from the settings, most of the characters in *Dúil* are peasants. The only exceptions among the major characters are the little boy (and we could make a case for him) of the title story, the hotel-owner not far removed from the peasantry in **"An Buille,"** the shop-tavern keeper in the little village of **"Mearbhall,"** and, of course, the three tourists, one mysteriously native in speech and accent, who come to **"Oifig an Phoist."** (p. 128)

Eleven of the remaining eighteen stories in *Dúil* touch on or feature peasants exclusively, while the main characters of the other three stories are animals and a rock. [John] Broderick well describes the Irish peasant:

> Now, the Irish are not a sentimental people, like the Americans and the English. They are clear-eyed, realistic, and hard as nails, in spite of a certain su-

perficial sweetness and an elaborate code of manners. But they have never lacked courage: above all the ability to survive.

Kelly, contrasting the English "sentimental approach to animals" to the Irish, mistakes the underside of any bored rural population for the typical Irish peasant's attitude towards animals, "creatures to be preyed upon in order to sustain life, to be used for what they may produce, or to provide sport which may take a cruel form."

The typical islanders' attitude towards their animals is rather one of sympathy, like Neidin's for the pigs, big and little, in **"An Buille,"** the pedlar's love for his ass (**"Díoltas"**), the child's delight in the chickens (**"An Beo"**), the couple's for their cow in **"Bás na Bó,"** Cáit's for her mare in **"Teangabháil,"** and the narrator's and his wife's for the wild drake in **"Uisce faoi Dhraíocht."** Trying not to confuse my own criticism with "applied nostalgia," I think of O'Flaherty's English **"Parting"** when I remember a grandmother on the middle island unable to bring herself to see her family's fourteen-year-old cow off at the quay after selling her. And island dogs are not abused by their owners unless when pulling them from the trouser legs of careless strangers.

O'Brien finds that critical admiration for O'Flaherty's simple animal and peasant stories comes from the almost "total surrender of the author's personality to the nature of things outside of himself." Zneimer agrees; the mixing of human and animal stories has the effect of putting them "into the same perspective . . . A common coldness covers all." However, because she believes that the awareness of death "sets man apart from animal," Kelly holds that the only animal-like people in O'Flaherty's stories about the old are "either insane, drunk, senile, or infants." While this is true of the infants in **"Dúil"** and **"An Beo"** and for the old, senile, and near-mad in **"An Beo"** and **"Mearbhall,"** we must pull back when we remember that **"An Seabhac"** has a 'barbarous soul.'

Critics of the Irish stories rarely address themselves to O'Flaherty's handling of point of view; when they do, they usually echo the critics of his English stories who blame him for his authorial intrusions. Even so, neither group investigates the stories themselves closely enough for their generalizations to do more than lure students into their own explorations. Kelly tries to find a middle road by suggesting that O'Flaherty's early use of authorial intrusion seems justified by "Gaelic speech, and by the story-telling he heard as a child," yet she still believes that his "lack of detachment" hurts his control over "narrative point of view." Murray, as always, overstresses his academic approach towards "storytelling": "the entire fabric of his narrative—disintegrates completely whenever he abandons his primary function as story teller in favor of self-conscious commentary on life" [see excerpt dated 1968].

Kilroy and Kelly are kinder, Kilroy comparing him to D. H. Lawrence: "both authors occasionally abandon their considerable descriptive powers and their challenging theories of the integrity of human instincts in order to preach in a simplistic manner." Kelly simply states: "O'Flaherty is often himself more involved with his characters than he should be—hence, the occasionally intrusive author." While this may reflect O'Faolain's idea that O'Flaherty both loves and hates his characters, I have found that a close explication of his Irish stories usually reveals that, just because the narra-

tive voice is in the first person, it should not be identified as O'Flaherty's.

O'Flaherty's skill in description, of course, has merited universal praise. Mercier [see Further Reading list] finds him writing "as naturally for the eye as the mature Joyce does for the ear." Kelly believes that his descriptions—his "showing"—keeps him from intruding, from "telling." "In many stories O'Flaherty shows his strong visual inclination by the variation of camera angle and distance in his descriptive writing." But aren't his critics inconsistent in wishing to keep O'Flaherty from "intruding" in his story while allowing him to change camera angles, lenses, and filters at will? As Kelly notes, his camera is selective in focussing upon his characters' gestures: "The small actions of O'Flaherty's characters are often important as a pointer to their inner states of mind, especially in his early work . . . but also in a late story such as **'The Fanatic'.**" Mercier, however, turns our attention back from the camera to the storyteller: "gestures are an essential part of his communication with his audience," for "drama and the speaking voice" are essentials of most good storytellers.

Looking at O'Flaherty's descriptions in English, Kelly believes that "some of his work begs to be read aloud," but Irish-language readers seem to select passages of dialogue when reading **Dúil** aloud. . . . Dialogue seems to be in favor with O'Flaherty's more recent critics, too, yet they praise it as they do his camera-like descriptions as one of his best tools for satisfying their own academically oriented love for "objectivity." Zneimer, for example, finds that O'Flaherty "achieves objectivity by refraining from comment and using dialogue to advance and explain the action." Kelly, too, uses dialogue as her touchstone for distinguishing between O'Flaherty showing [good] and O'Flaherty telling [bad]. She finds that dialogue helps the "characters themselves to become more important than the action; something which points to a greater sense of humanity in O'Flaherty himself."

Surveying O'Flaherty's early (1925), middle (1946), and late (1953) **Dúil** stories, I have found that, although he uses dialogue in none of his early stories, he does employ it in half of his middle group and in four of his ten late stories. Because he uses dialogue earlier than some critics think, not only should his "late" use of dialogue be studied more carefully but his use of the spoken word in stories not so obviously built upon dialogue demand critical scrutiny. In his early, near documentary **"An tAonach,"** one entire paragraph, set in a pub, is constructed largely of a mosaic of sentences and phrases picked out of the air without identifying any of the speakers.

> Drink. I will not drink. Drink. Every single person was drinking. I don't touch it. Drink wine. There is no harm in wine. The priest drinks it. I won't drink, I took a promise. There is not any harm in wine. The priest drinks it. I will not drink. I took a promise. Yes. Juice of the vine. Cold juice bubbling from the bottle, seven thousand bubbles boiling in a foam. I prefer ale. Dark ale. Yellow foam. A pot of it. Whiskey. Whiskey without water. A cry. A hand is shaken. May we live to see this time next year.

Thompson finds that "over and over, O'Flaherty has as his subject matter the social phenomena of western life, from the viewpoint of the ordinary peasant living it, rather than from that of the outsider looking in from above or beyond." In

Dúil, certainly, this helps us to understand O'Faolain's claim: "From the very start of his career O'Flaherty developed an inspired technique for handling his tribal past—that of simultaneously rejecting and accepting it." This is true, right from the early **"Daoine Bochta"** through the middle **"Teangabháil"** to the late **"Oifig an Phoist."** While "in some of the later stories," Kelly finds "a confrontation . . . between traditional and new ways of life—rural and urban meet," surely O'Faolain is right, for the confrontation has been there throughout, with or without the urban man's presence, because O'Flaherty himself, both rejecting and accepting, both hating and loving their ways of life, makes us feel his involvement in his characters.

In concluding this introduction to the present state of the general criticism of Liam O'Flaherty's *Dúil,* I have found that, although only the critics of stories in Irish are qualified to discuss the author's figurative use of that language, they have usually only echoed critics of his English stories like Murray, claiming that he frequently violates decorum in using certain similes and metaphors, or, more originally but without exploring their discovery, they have found that he sometimes repeats them from story to story. Among the Irish-language critics, only Fiachra Ó Dubhthaigh touches on O'Flaherty's imagery as he notices that eyes, especially blue eyes, seem important in story after story, but he does not explore this insight. And while Kelly observes that he uses nature not only as a setting in his stories in English but often as "a symbolic framework within which the action takes place, as a metaphor for the expression of character or incident, or even personified as part of the action," O'Flaherty's handling of symbolism in individual stories has only been slightly touched on in **"Dúil,"** **"An Seabhac,"** **"An Scáthán,"** **"Mearbhall,"** and **"An Buille."**

O'Flaherty's *Dúil* deserves much better than it has received from critics in both Irish and English; each story needs to be explicated and related to the other stories in the volume. And I would suggest that scholars of modern Irish literature who do not know modern Irish itself should not wait around until their fifties as I did, but should begin that study now. After sifting and resifting the scholarship on [William Butler] Yeats and [James] Joyce, to read *Dúil* and to realize how much work needs to be done with it should rekindle that joy we once found as young graduate students on coming into a relatively unexplored field. Especially when we recognize that in learning Irish we create a solid foundation on which to rebuild our understanding even of those writers from Ireland who have used English, in whole or in part, as their medium. (pp. 129-32)

> *William Daniels, "Introduction to the Present State of Criticism of Liam O'Flaherty's Collection of Short Stories: 'Dúil'," in Eire-Ireland, Vol. XXIII, No. 2, Summer, 1988, pp. 122-34.*

FURTHER READING

Bates, H. E. "The Irish School." In his *The Modern Short Story: A Critical Survey,* pp. 148-62. Boston: Writer, 1941.
    Overview of Irish short fiction writers in which Bates briefly discusses O'Flaherty. Bates associates O'Flaherty's fiction with "the more lurid shades" of Guy de Maupassant's writing and describes O'Flaherty's prose style as "brutal, sensuous, and elemental."

De Bhaldraithe, Tomás. "Liam O'Flaherty—Translator(?)" *Eire-Ireland* III, No. 2 (Summer 1968): 149-53.
    Discusses differences in style and theme between Irish- and English-language versions of O'Flaherty's stories. De Bhaldraithe purports that O'Flaherty may have purposefully altered the English versions to appeal to an established English reading audience.

Doyle, Paul A. *Liam O'Flaherty.* New York: Twayne Publishers, 1971, 154 p.
    Critical biography. Sections devoted to O'Flaherty's short fiction emphasize his animal sketches and his stories about humanity's relation to nature. Doyle posits that in his fiction O'Flaherty combines elements of Naturalism and Romanticism without reconciling conflicts between the two.

——. *Liam O'Flaherty: An Annotated Bibliography.* Troy, N. Y.: Whitston Publishing Co., 1972, 68 p.
    Comprehensive annotated bibliography that includes material up to 1971.

Eglinton, John. "Irish Letter." *The Dial* 82 (May 1927): 407-10.
    Brief discussion of the direction of modern Irish literature, focusing on the Celtic Renaissance of the early twentieth century. While Eglinton recognizes O'Flaherty as a "pure Gael with literary genius," he accuses him of abandoning his Celtic birthright by seeking material for his fiction amid urban slum life.

Greene, David H. "New Heights." *The Commonweal* LXIV, No. 13 (29 June 1956): 328.
    Review of *The Stories of Liam O'Flaherty* in which Greene hails O'Flaherty's renewed interest in Irish peasants and the Irish language and praises the "poetic intensity" and evocative imagery of "The Post Office" and "The Mirror."

Kelly, A. A. *Liam O'Flaherty the Storyteller.* New York: Barnes and Noble, 1976, 154 p.
    Well-received critical biography in which Kelly analyzes technique in individual stories and studies how these stories as a whole reflect and define O'Flaherty's personal views. Includes useful bibliography.

Kennelly, Brendan. "Liam O'Flaherty: The Unchained Storm. A View of His Short Stories." In *The Irish Short Story,* edited by Patrick Rafroidi and Terence Brown, pp. 175-87. Atlantic Highlands, N.J.: Humanities Press, 1979.
    Considers O'Flaherty's short stories "poems in prose" written in an explosive style that reflects a thematic concern with energy.

Kiely, Benedict. *Modern Irish Fiction—A Critique.* Dublin: Golden Eagle Books, 1950, 179 p.
    A study of Irish society through works of Irish fiction. In passages concerning O'Flaherty, Kiely notes a sense of "brutal romanticism" in the author's fiction, contending that O'Flaherty adopted the pose of a harsh realist to protect his romantic character.

Mercier, Vivian. "The Irish Short Story and Oral Tradition." In *The Celtic Cross: Studies in Irish Culture and Literature,* edited by Ray B. Browne, William John Roscelli, and Richard Loftus, pp. 98-116. West Lafayette, Ind.: Purdue University Studies, 1964.
    Explores characteristics of traditional Irish storytelling and notes affinities with the folktale and oral traditions among Irish fiction writers. Mercier argues, however, that O'Flaherty's stories appeal to the visual rather than oral senses.

O'Connor, Frank. *The Lonely Voice: A Study of the Short Story.* Cleveland: World Publishing Co., 1962, 220 p.

Highly-regarded critical study of the short story that contains passing references to O'Flaherty. In the introduction, O'Connor stresses the instinctive nature of O'Flaherty's writing and contends that his most moving stories were written out of feeling rather than thought.

O'Connor, Helene. "Liam O'Flaherty: Literary Ecologist." *Eire-Ireland* VII, No. 2 (Summer 1972): 47-54.
    Praises O'Flaherty's stories for their authenticity in depicting ecological life cycles.

O'Faolain, Sean. "Liam O'Flaherty." In *Writers of To-Day: 2,* edited by Denys Val Baker, pp. 167-76. London: Sidgwick and Jackson, 1948.
    Discusses differences between O'Flaherty's novels and stories, citing that the excited and wild quality of the novels is replaced by quieter, more lyrical characteristics in his stories.

Troy, William. "The Position of Liam O'Flaherty." *The Bookman* LXIX, No. 1 (March 1929): 7-11.
    Appreciative early criticism of O'Flaherty's stories and novels.

Mark Twain

1835-1910

(Pseudonym of Samuel Langhorne Clemens. Also wrote under the pseudonyms Thomas Jefferson Snodgrass, Josh, Muggins, Soleather, Grumbler, and Sieur Louis de Conte) American novelist, short story writer, journalist, essayist, travel writer, memoirist, autobiographer, and dramatist.

Regarded by many as the father of modern American literature, Twain is often credited with freeing American fiction from the staid literary conventions of the nineteenth century. One of the best-known and most frequently read authors in the English language, Twain is most famous for his novels *The Adventures of Tom Sawyer* and *Adventures of Huckleberry Finn*. However, throughout his career, Twain wrote countless works of short fiction; Charles Neider observed: "One might even say that Twain felt most at home in the story, that it was the form most congenial to him, lover as he was of the yarn." Typical of Twain's disregard of formalism, his stories, sketches, anecdotes, and fables often obscure the boundaries separating journalism and literature, recollection and invention, and were published in a hodgepodge of places during his lifetime. Only some fifty years after Twain's death was his short fiction collected and thereby exposed to serious critical scrutiny. Among his most highly regarded short works, "The Celebrated Jumping Frog of Calaveras County," "The Man That Corrupted Hadleyburg," and *The Mysterious Stranger* exemplify Twain's diverse narrative and thematic scope.

Clemens grew up in the Mississippi River town of Hannibal, Missouri, whose landmarks and people served as models for the settings and characters of many of his writings, particularly his early sketches and stories, and his novel *The Adventures of Tom Sawyer*. At age twelve Clemens quit school and became a journeyman printer; by the time he was seventeen his first sketches were appearing in the newspapers he typeset. During the late 1850s Clemens piloted steamboats on the Mississippi River, a livelihood he enjoyed until the Civil War closed the river to commercial traffic. After brief service in the Confederate militia, Clemens traveled west, working as a silver miner and reporter in Nevada and California. During this period he began writing under the byline "Mark Twain," a navigational term indicating two fathoms of water and signifying safe passage for vessels. In 1865 Twain published his first important sketch, "Jim Smiley and His Jumping Frog," in a New York periodical. This story was widely popular and appeared two years later with some editorial changes as the title story in Twain's first book, *The Celebrated Jumping Frog of Calaveras County, and Other Sketches*. Shortly thereafter, Twain set out on a cruise to southern Europe and the Middle East. The letters he wrote to two American newspapers during his trip, detailing the clash of New and Old World cultures, also proved immensely popular and were later collected as *The Innocents Abroad; or, The New Pilgrim's Progress*. Although some readers considered Twain's rustic wit uncouth, the success of this book and Twain's growing fame as a comic lecturer established him as America's leading humorist.

In 1870 Twain married Olivia Langdon and, after settling in Hartford, Connecticut, published his first novel, *The Gilded Age*, written in collaboration with Charles Dudley Warner. The novel's title became a commonly used term to describe America's post-Civil War industrial boom. Twain's novel *The Adventures of Tom Sawyer* appeared in 1876, and immediately afterward he began work on a sequel, *Adventures of Huckleberry Finn*, which concerns Tom's friend Huck and his encounters with the adult world. Twain wrote this novel in three intermittent bursts of inspiration during the next eight years, and though it was critically misunderstood and banned from public libraries upon its appearance in the United States in 1885, *Adventures of Huckleberry Finn* came to be recognized by later critics as a masterpiece of American literature.

During the 1890s, several bad financial ventures plunged Twain into bankruptcy. The failure of the Paige typesetting machine, in which Twain had heavily invested, and the insolvency of his Webster Publishing Company culminated these ill-fated endeavors and forced Twain to return to the lucrative but grueling lecture circuit at the age of seventy. In the early 1900s, Twain suffered the death of his wife and two of his three daughters. Most biographers agree that these devastating events embittered Twain and turned his natural sarcasm into fatalistic despair over the nature of God and humanity. As a result, his work became increasingly introspective and polemical, focusing on such topics as mental telepathy, the relationship between dreams and reality, spiritualism, and diabolism. Although Twain's growing pessimism had been evident as early as his novel *A Connecticut Yankee in King Arthur's Court* and had dominated his short story "The Man That Corrupted Hadleyburg," in the years just before his death, Twain composed his darkest writings, including his "gospel" of determinism, *What Is Man?,* and the fragments assembled posthumously as *The Mysterious Stranger.*

Twain's earliest works evince characteristics that brought him fame as America's foremost humorist writer. Typical of the journalistic sketches prevalent in the mining town newspapers of the Western United States during the latter nineteenth century, these tales and comic sketches often feature deadpan humor and vernacular language and caustically satirize human frivolity. In his best-known early tale, "The Celebrated Jumping Frog of Calaveras County," Twain combines characteristics of nineteenth-century Western American folk literature with irony, satire, and allegory, creating what S. J. Krause termed "a fairly unsophisticated brand of fiction that rises above its genre." In the frame story to this work, an unnamed genteel Easterner, traveling west in search of a Reverend Leonidas Smiley, enounters Simon Wheeler, a storytelling frontiersman who sidetracks the inquiry, to the annoyance of the narrator, with a colorful yarn about the foibles of an incessant gambler named Jim Smiley. Wheeler's tale—the story within the frame story—relates an incident when Jim Smiley is goaded into challenging a stranger to a frog-jumping contest that Smiley is confident his trained frog will win. While Smiley searches a nearby swamp for a frog at the stranger's behest, the stranger fills Smiley's frog with buckshot so that he is unable to jump. The stranger wins the contest and the wager. Several essays have been written concerning the origins of this tale, whose basic plot was not created by Twain. Yet, critics concur that the literary value of the story resides with Twain's contribution of irony, satire, and a deadpan narrative style. Twain himself stated: "I only claim to know how a story ought to be told." Many critics regard "The Jumping Frog" as a complex work, illustrating cultural antagonisms between the Eastern and Western United States.

Although Twain continued to publish stories and narratives during the 1870s and 1880s, most were brief anecdotes or sketches, and few have received substantial critical attention. Instead, commentators have overwhelmingly focused on tales Twain wrote during the last two decades of his life, when his philosophical position, as described by E. S. Fussell, was "a grotesque medley of fatalism, misanthropy, and cynicism." Several stories, including "Which Was the Dream?," "Which Was It?," "The Great Dark," and "Three Thousand Years among the Microbes," focus on the ambiguous relationship between dream and reality and the various levels of conscious and unconscious experience. A principle theme recurs in these works, concerning a man of great fortune who experiences a nightmarish time of failure when his luck deserts him. However, a saving thought crosses his mind: perhaps he is in fact living a nightmare from which he will soon awaken. But there is also the possibility that what seems a disastrous dream may be reality.

Another set of Twain's stories from this period, including "The Man That Corrupted Hadleyburg," "The £1,000,000 Bank-Note," "The $30,000 Bequest," and *The Mysterious Stranger,* feature satanic figures that visit complacent towns to subvert the social order and reveal the townspeople's moral frailties. The widely-anthologized "The Man That Corrupted Hadleyburg," for instance, has been compared to both the biblical account of the Fall of humanity in Genesis for its study of what George Pierce Clark termed "Satan in his commerce with mankind" and Milton's "Areopagitica" for its treatment of the moral, as Twain's satanic character pronounces it: "[The] weakest of all weak things is a virtue which has not been tested in the fire." Twain's most often-analyzed work of short fiction, however, is *The Mysterious Stranger,* an episodically structured narrative fraught with allegory and symbolism in which a character named Satan functions as the communicator of knowledge and truth, revealing to his two young disciples that humanity has been corrupted by what he terms its "Moral Sense" and that all of life is a dream: "[There] is no God, no universe, no human race, no earthly life, no heaven, no hell. It is all a dream—a grotesque and foolish dream. Nothing exists but you. And you are but a *thought*—a vagrant thought, a useless thought, a homeless thought, wandering forlorn among the empty eternities!" Much of the criticism surrounding *The Mysterious Stranger* focuses on problems associated with its text. Although it had been known for some time that Twain composed three separate drafts of this story, not until 1963 when John S. Tuckey in his *Mark Twain and Little Satan* meticulously documented the composition and publication history of this work did the extent of the variance between Twain's original drafts and the published version become known. Perhaps the most startling revelation was Tuckey's discovery that editors Albert Bigelow Paine and Frederick A. Duneka added to one of Twain's drafts a vagrant final chapter, smoothing transitions between the two apparently unrelated manuscripts by changing characters' names and introducing a new character never conceived by Twain. Although Tuckey concluded that in light of his findings "much that has been supposed about *The Mysterious Stranger,* and indeed about Twain's later period, may have to be reconsidered," James M. Cox wrote in 1966 that "Tuckey's findings do not invalidate so much as they define [the originally published] text of *The Mysterious Stranger.* "

Scholars recognize in Twain a man divided in outlook between comic and tragic perceptions of existence. Throughout his career Twain looked back yearningly to his happy, youthful days on the Mississippi, finding in his memories spiritual rejuvenation and inspiration. At the same time he was often deeply pessimistic about the future, particularly near the end of his life. His longing for an idealized past as a haven from an increasingly hostile present is evident in most of his major works of fiction and is nowhere more pronounced than in the short fiction of his later years. Critics have sought to explain this division in Twain's outlook, and two major theories have risen from the debate. The first, expounded by Van Wyck Brooks in *The Ordeal of Mark Twain,* sees in Twain a genius beset from childhood with a deep guilt complex and stifled by America's crude frontier atmosphere, his writings edited into prettified respectability through the efforts of his wife and his friend William Dean Howells. The influence of Olivia Clemens and Howells has been greatly discounted by Bernard DeVoto, whose *Mark Twain's America* and *Mark Twain at Work* demonstrate the positive effects of frontier life on Twain's development and attribute his pessimism to the many personal tragedies he suffered during the last decades of his life. In his short fiction, Twain fully embodied these extremes. Commenting on Twain's later short works, Kathleen Walsh concluded: "Early and late we see Mark Twain's receptivity to important currents of his age and his experimentation with techniques in search of a form appropriate to this vision. Many of his readers have wished for a succession of *Tom Sawyers*, but Mark Twain left that formula before it became fixed as one and moved on to new modes. Wishing for "the old Mark Twain" and seeing these [late] works as mere "shards" of a particular moment in his genesis is a bit like wishing for the good old days, something that Mark Twain himself was not content with doing."

(For further information on Twain's life and career, see *Twentieth-Century Literary Criticism*, Vols. 6, 12, 19, 27; *Contemporary Authors*, Vol. 104; *Dictionary of Literary Biography*, Vols. 11, 12; and *Yesterday's Authors of Books for Children*, Vol. 2.)

PRINCIPAL WORKS

SHORT FICTION

The Celebrated Jumping Frog of Calaveras County, and Other Sketches 1867
Mark Twain's Sketches, New and Old 1875
The Stolen White Elephant Etc. 1882
The £1,000,000 Bank-Note, and Other New Stories 1893
Tom Sawyer Abroad, Tom Sawyer, Detective, and Other Stories, Etc. Etc. 1896
The Man That Corrupted Hadleyburg, and Other Stories and Essays 1900
A Double-Barreled Detective Story 1902
The $30,000 Bequest, and Other Stories 1906
Extracts from Captain Stormfield's Visit to Heaven 1909
The Mysterious Stranger: A Romance 1916; expanded as *The Mysterious Stranger, and Other Stories*, 1922
The Complete Short Stories of Mark Twain 1957
Letters from the Earth (stories, sketches, and prose fragments) 1962
Mark Twain's "Which Was the Dream?" and Other Symbolic Writings of the Later Years 1966
Mark Twain's "Mysterious Stranger" Manuscripts 1969
Mark Twain's Fables of Man 1972
"The Devil's Race-Track": Mark Twain's Great Dark Writings 1979
Early Tales & Sketches, 1851-1864. 2 Vols. 1979-81

OTHER MAJOR WORKS

The Innocents Abroad; or, The New Pilgrim's Progress (travel sketches) 1869
Roughing It (travel sketches) 1872
The Gilded Age [with Charles Dudley Warner] (novel) 1874
The Adventures of Tom Sawyer (novel) 1876
A Tramp Abroad (travel sketches) 1880
The Prince and the Pauper (novel) 1882
Life on the Mississippi (autobiographical novel) 1883
Adventures of Huckelberry Finn (novel) 1884
A Connecticut Yankee in King Arthur's Court (novel) 1889
The Tragedy of Pudd'nhead Wilson, and the Comedy of Those Extraordinary Twins (novel and sketch) 1894
Personal Recollections of Joan of Arc [as Sieur Louis de Conte] (biographical novel) 1896
Following the Equator (travel sketches) 1897
How to Tell a Story, and Other Essays (essays) 1905
King Leopold's Soliloquy (novel) 1905
What Is Man? (essay) 1906

Christian Science, with Notes Containing Corrections to Date (nonfiction) 1907
Mark Twain's Letters. 2 Vols. (letters) 1917
Mark Twain's Autobiography. 2 Vols. (autobiography) 1924
The Autobiography of Mark Twain (autobiography) 1959

WILLIAM ARCHER (essay date 1900)

[*A Scottish dramatist and critic, Archer is best known as an early and important translator of Henrik Ibsen's plays and as a drama critic in London during the late nineteenth and early twentieth centuries. In the following excerpt, Archer characterizes "The Man That Corrupted Hadleyburg" as a fable, stating that if the story were taken as a piece of representational fiction, "its cynicism would be intolerable."*]

It is no negligeable matter, the appearance of a new parable in literature. A parable is a sort of magic finger-post which has the power of popping up whenever we arrive at one of the countless moral cross-roads of life. Sometimes we follow its guidance—and as likely as not it lands us in a slough. More often, perhaps, we disregard it and take the other path; but it has marred our serenity, and we are haunted by a sense of its silently menacing presence in our rear. This property of appearing at the cross-roads renders the parable the most dynamic of literary forms. To vary the metaphor, it is a sermon that sticks. Most sermons are like gumless postage stamps; but the element of drama in the parable is powerfully adhesive, and glues it to the mind. Therefore all the great teachers—all, at any rate, whose teaching has come directly home to the mass of mankind—have dealt largely in parables. So avid are we, indeed, of instruction by apologue, that people have gone about again and again to force a moral scheme into literature which has, in fact, only the unconscious morality of life itself—to reduce Homer and Shakespeare to the level of Æsop. Mistaken though this effort be, it is none the less true that parable is the point at which the extremes of literary merit and demerit meet. Whatever the art-for-art's-sake theorists may tell us, it is quite possible to build great literature around hard-and-fast moral ideas—else where were Æschylus and Dante? As a rule, however, it is its dynamic rather than its literary quality that gives a parable its importance. Where it achieves literary greatness, it is apt to be at the cost of its dynamic virtue. We forget that it *is* a parable. The finger-post loses its terrestrial orientation, and points upward to the silent immensities.

Parables have their fates, like other forms of literature. Not every parable is found to possess the adhesive quality above adverted to. For one *Pilgrim's Progress* or *Candide* that "catches on" to the mind of the world, there are scores that drop off and are swept into the waste-paper bin. I shall be greatly surprised if this is the fate that awaits **"The Man That Corrupted Hadleyburg."** Mark Twain has before now shown himself a shrewd, penetrating, and even subtle psychologist. His new apologue reveals no new aspect of his genius. It is, moreover, a parable pure and simple, with no suspicion of art-for-art's-sake about it. Were we to take it as a story, as a representation of life, its cynicism would be intolerable. It would leave Maupassant nowhere. But taken simply for what it is—a fable designed to drive home an ethical lesson—it seems to me to possess such constructive skill and literary vigor as may well give it a place among the parables that stick tight to the popular imagination.

Perhaps you wonder to find Mark Twain among the moralists at all? If so, you have read his previous books to little purpose. They are full of ethical suggestion. Sometimes, it is true, his moral decisions are a little summary. Often, nay, generally, his serious meaning is lightly veiled in paradox, exaggeration, irony. But his humor is seldom entirely irresponsible for many pages together, and it often goes very deep into human nature. (pp. 413-14)

I am not going to discount ["**The Man That Corrupted Hadleyburg**"] by attempting to tell its story. Indeed, I could not if I would, even in six times the space that remains to me; for though it runs to only sixty pages, its construction is so ingeniously complex that it would take something like half that space to make even a comprehensible sketch-plan of its mechanism. A more tight-packed piece of narrative art it would be hard to conceive. . . . The thing it most nearly resembles in recent literature is Stevenson's delightful "Bottle-Imp"; but there is this difference, that Stevenson did not invent his fable, whereas Mark Twain did. And with all its earnestness of purpose and bitterness of tone, it is full of humor. The great meeting of the citizens of Hadleyburg is a scene of sustained and delectable comedy, not without a vein of real human pathos in the futile struggles of poor Richards and his wife to drag themselves out of the quicksand in which they are floundering.

And what is the moral of the apologue? In essence it is simple and even commonplace; in form it is somewhat daring. Mark Twain suggests an emendation in the text of the Lord's Prayer: the dropping of the negative particle in the petition, "Lead us not into temptation." We ought to pray, he says, to be led into temptation, for virtue that has never stood the test is a mere baseless opinion of self-righteousness. "You had an old and lofty reputation for honesty," writes the malign Mephistopheles to the Hadleyburgers, "and naturally you were proud of it—it was your treasure of treasures, the very apple of your eye. As soon as I found that you carefully and vigilantly kept yourselves and your children *out of temptation* I knew how to proceed. Why, you simple creatures, the weakest of all weak things is a virtue which has not been tested in the fire." Not otherwise did Mephistopheles argue in the first chapter of another and older apologue—the Book of Job, to wit. Mark Twain's message, you see, can scarcely lay claim to novelty. Another American philosopher has told us that "they didn't know everything down to Judee." But they knew one or two things that the world has but imperfectly learnt during all these centuries; and this thing Mark Twain has translated into modern terms of almost Swiftian sternness. (pp. 414-15)

William Archer, " 'The Man That Corrupted Hadleyburg'—A New Parable," in The Critic, *New York, Vol. XXXVII, No. 5, November, 1900, pp. 413-15.*

THEODORE DREISER (essay date 1935)

[*Considered among the foremost novelists in American literature, Dreiser was one of the principal American exponents of literary Naturalism. He is known primarily for his novels* Sister Carrie *(1901),* An American Tragedy *(1926), and the Frank Cowperwood trilogy (1912-47); in each Dreiser combines his vision of life as a meaningless series of chemical reactions and animal impulses with a sense of sentimentality and pity for humanity's lot. Deeply concerned with the human condition but contemptuous of traditional social, political, and religious remedies, Dreiser associated for many years with the American socialist and communist movements, an interest reflected in much of his writing after 1925. In the following excerpt, Dreiser decries the persistence of Twain's public reputation as a humorist and the denial of his tendencies as a "gloomy and wholly mechanistic thinker," asserting that Twain would have published his darker musings during his lifetime "had it not been, I think, for the noisy and quite vacuous applause accorded him as Genius Jester to the American booboisie."*]

A psychologic as well as literary enigma that has much troubled me, as it has many another who has surveyed American literature, is Mark Twain. Middle West American of quite humble Tennessee and Missouri village and farm backgrounds—with a few parent- and relative-owned slaves to complicate the picture—he remains to this hour, in the minds of most Americans, not the powerful and original and amazingly pessimistic thinker that he really was, and that several of his most distinguished contributions to American letters prove—but rather, and to this hour, the incorrigible and prolific joker and, at best, humorist who, up to the time of his death and since, has kept the world chuckling so continuously that it has not even now sobered sufficiently to detect in him the gloomy and wholly mechanistic thinker.

If, by chance, he had encountered Jacques Loeb!

If he had sensed the direction of scientific thought in the last twenty years!

As it is, for most, he remains the laughing, hoaxing biographer of Tom Sawyer and Huckleberry Finn, of Puddin' Head Wilson, and the American Claimant, rarely the critical and massive creator of *The Mysterious Stranger* (still sold as a Christmas book for children), and of *What Is Man?* which Loeb would have welcomed as an addition to his mechanistic biologic conclusions.

But how came this to be? Were there two Twains from the beginning, as one and another critic has asked since reading *What Is Man* and *The Mysterious Stranger?* I recall that so early as 1910, and in the editorial office of no less an institution than Harper and Brothers, then still his publishers, I discovered that there were really two Twains writing—one who possessed great fame and acclaim for the body of work which everyone knew and approved of as wholesomely humorous, exposing little more than the minor or more forgivable flaws of American character—and another, the really not-at-all-known Twain who brought the most amazing and Rabelaisian stories of his own composition to the then publishing intermediaries of Harper and Brothers, F. A. Duneka, and Major F. G. Leigh, both of whom had, as they felt, to employ to the utmost their arts of discreet and yet firm diplomacy, in order, as they said, to "protect Mark" from the violent and fateful public conservatism of Americans, if not the world in general, should any of the things he was writing and bringing in ever reach them. In substantiation of which, I have in my possession a copy of *1601—Conversation as It Was by the Social Fireside in the Time of the Tudors,* with an Introduction by Albert Bigelow Paine, and quoted comments by David Gray, John Hay, and others. I do not need to say more than that. The initiated will understand. All others must inquire.

However, it is not this particular Rabelaisian extension of Twain's classic gift for paradox and exaggeration and horseplay in the field of humor, quite rampant in his day (Bill Nye, Petroleum V. Nasby, Josh Billings), but rather his much more publicly subdued—and I may add, frustrated—gift as well as mood for dark and devastating, and at the same time quite tender and sorrowing, meditation on the meaning or absence of it in life, plus a force and clarity of realistic presentation and criticism which has arrested me as it has many another. And not only in such published works as *Joan of Arc,* **"The Man Who Corrupted Hadleyburg,"** *The Mysterious Stranger,* and *What Is Man?* but in various paragraphs and critical summaries which are to be found in his later letters and his still unpublished autobiography, which, now that the twenty-five years stipulated by him before his death as the length of time which must elapse before it could be issued has elapsed, might well be given to the world. (pp. 615-16)

The financial interest or investment in his earlier conventional works and their reputation is still very great.

In the meantime, however, we have had *Joan of Arc,* which when published anonymously in 1895 was so different from the accepted work of Twain himself at the time that it was suggested by Twain that it be published under a nom de plume. As it was, he feared an unfavorable reaction, and before signing it wished to know what the result was to be. Had it proved unfavorable, it might have remained under a nom de plume until after his death. Yet, as different as it was, the general opinion was favorable, and so he acknowledged it. Only it never sold as did *Innocents Abroad,* or *Huckleberry Finn,* or *Tom Sawyer.*

Just the same, shortly thereafter (1898) he wrote, although he withheld from publication until 1916—six years after his death—two works entirely out of harmony with anything he had previously written: *The Mysterious Stranger* and *What Is Man?* In the meantime, that is between 1898 and 1911, when he died, while these other works were on the shelf, he published such volumes as *A Double-barrelled Detective Story,* *King Leopold's Soliloquy,* **"Eve's Diary"**, *Christian Science,* plus the much more daring, although much more humorous and therefore much safer, **"The Man Who Corrupted Hadleyburg"**—the first real break in his public humor, salving of a naughty, naughty world. Also, *Captain Stormfield's Visit to Heaven,* equally laughable. But with *What Is Man?* and *The Mysterious Stranger* out, although ignored, there still remain other things which will see the light—when? In this reactionary day? I doubt it. (p. 617)

What I am earnestly seeking to convey is that by no means has Mark Twain been properly evaluated. In America, as it is intellectually running even at this time, I doubt if he can be. There is, as I have said, a financial interest in his reputation *as is,* which has to be and will be (never fear) taken into consideration.

Next, for all the labors of Hollywood and the young anarchists of sex in literature and art, compositions such as *1601* and his yet unpublished short stories will await a secret and a numbered issue—if so much. And for all the revelation of the laboratories that point to a mechanistic universe and the entire determinist philosophy, never fear that *What Is Man?* or *The Mysterious Stranger* will be given either wide publicity or achieve serious mental consideration in America if elsewhere. And there are several reasons for that: dogmatic religion, as well as social and moral convictions on every hand—these latter lying entombed or enwombed in the first—and next, the never ending benightedness of the mass—schools or

no schools, universities or no universities, biological and physical laboratories, or no biological and physical laboratories. I suspect that not only the Millikans but the Haldanes, and even the Julian Huxleys, would rise in revolt. And, as I say, you have only to consider the fate of Jacques Loeb, the most distinguished mental figure since Darwin, or rather his mechanistic data, to grasp what I mean. Do you know aught of his dozen volumes describing the mechanistic processes of life, as he unraveled them? I truly believe our present "Watch and Ward" guarded libraries will even shut their doors before they will distribute them.

What interests me, however, is this seeming duality of Twain, for, of course, there were not any two Mark Twains, just one. From the beginning, there was only the conventionally environed Twain who did not arrive, for instance, at the reading of Pepys's *Diary* until he was forty, and whose amazed curiosity as to Spencer, Darwin, Huxley, following his first trip abroad (*Innocents Abroad* [1869]), led naturally, if interruptedly—that is by way of fame—to introduction to the literary pundits of the East, marriage into a conservative and well-to-do family, the Langdons of Elmira, New York, the undying friendship and guidance of the conservative and even moralistic William Dean Howells, Charles Dudley Warner, Thomas Bailey Aldrich, and, naturally, Harper and Brothers, to name but a few. Also to such modified social protests (with brakes) as *The Prince and the Pauper, A Connecticut Yankee in King Arthur's Court,* etc. But not to the *Personal Recollections of Joan of Arc* or at long last to **"The Man Who Corrupted Hadleyberg,"** *The Mysterious Stranger,* or *What Is Man?* As I have said, these last two, though written in 1898, were not published in his lifetime. And his old-time contemporaries never lived to see them.

But of what was Twain so terrified? For contemporary with him was Zola—of equal fame—and D'Annunzio, and Chekhov, and Dostoevski, and De Maupassant, and Strindberg, and Ibsen. And he must have heard of Whitman and Herman Melville, ostracized for so wild a thing as *Typee.* He most certainly did hear of Maxim Gorky, for when, in 1905, he and his Russian actress sweetheart arrived in America, neither he nor Howells—their reputations as well as their social connections prohibiting—would attend a reception in his honor. And yet Twain could write not only *1601* but the stories that his publishers think should never be published! And his daughter Jean, writing of him that, "at home, he talked largely of serious things, with only an occasional humorous remark thrown in."

His letters to his Eastern friends, the pundits and powers, were different.

My suspicion is that it was the secondary social and conventional forces enveloping him after his early success and marriage, and playing on this sympathetic, and, at times, seemingly weak humanist, that succeeded for a time in diverting him almost completely from a serious, realistic, and I might say Dostoevskian, presentation of the anachronisms, the cruelties, as well as the sufferings, of the individual and the world which, at bottom, seem most genuinely to have concerned him. For, to a study of these he would have turned, had it not been, I think, for the noisy and quite vacuous applause accorded him as Genius Jester to the American booboisie. And by that I mean almost the entire American world of his time. He was too warm-hearted—among the tenderest of the humanists—and, as such, almost refuting his own worst charges. More, he was born (1835) into a scene that included slavery in the South, and wage slavery in New England, plus the struggling pioneers of the West. To be sure—and this must have proved a factor in his mental orientation—the American scene was still softened, and even quite gaily colored in spots, by its fabulous resources, as well as the economic optimism generated by said resources and the then still slowly receding frontier. Yet, even so, he could not have been unaware of the degradations, the deprivations, the inequalities, and the sufferings of the majority of the men and women about him or in the world. (pp. 619-22)

For most certainly in addition to, and in spite of, his humorous bent, he was a realist at heart, and a most extraordinary one. One need only thumb through the *Innocents Abroad,* or *Roughing It,* or *Tom Sawyer,* or *Huckleberry Finn,* or *The Gilded Age,* to find page after page, character after character, scene after scene, drawn movingly as well as brilliantly enough, and this, in spite of his Brobdignagian humor, from the life about him. (p. 622)

Inquiry and reflection have caused me to assume as follows: To begin with, he was as a child, and in so far as a liberal—yes, even a conventional—education was concerned, but poorly dealt with. No public schooling after his eleventh year. Next, swirling about him were those western and middle-western Americans of his day, semilunatic with bonanza religious as well as financial and "moral" dreams. Ah, the twisted sociologic, as well as psychologic, forces playing upon a nature at once sensitive, kindly, and at the same time exaggeratedly humorous! The jest! The jest! And about him—in the American newspaper and upon the American platform—those reigning American models of his day: Artemus Ward, Josh Billings, Bill Nye, Petroleum V. Nasby. And all so stupendously successful. America could afford to laugh. As yet it was sufficiently free and happy to permit it so to do. And not only these, but consider the crudities and nonsensicalities of his own Missouri smalltown world, Florida, Missouri! Hannibal, Missouri! Read of them in *Huckleberry Finn.* And related to him, even nondescript farmers, some of them owners of ill-kept and ill-trained slaves with whom, and with the children of whom, he, as a schoolboy and small-town loafer, played. And after that, the youthful life of a Mississippi pilot's apprentice, with all the crude midwestern river life that registered on the quivering, if jest-loving, sensibilities of a world genius of twenty—a stripling Falstaff as well as Dickens combined. Yet, never a novelist—never. He could not write a novel. Consider only *The Gilded Age!* Rather, your humanist annalist, but without the complete and tragic life of any single defeated mortal burned deep in his heart. Why? He who could write of the Mysterious Stranger? And the sorrows of Joan of Arc? Why?

But after these early days, swift success, stupendous, worldwide fame! The laughter of England, America, Germany, France. Our simple and almost boobish genius thrust willynilly into the company of wealth, reputation, title, conventional and mental assumption and punditry, in its most aggravated forms. And with handclapping and backslapping everywhere. Oh, our darling Mark—the great American World Genius!

Consider his first journey abroad. And then, *Innocents Abroad.* And then all of the foregoing. And more: his meeting up with, and on the boat that carried him abroad—first the photo of the girl who was to be his wife, and then the girl herself, Miss Olivia Langdon, of Elmira, whom, on February 2, 1870, and in the full flare of his sudden and most unexpected

Sam Clemens at age fifteen, in the earliest known photograph of him. During this time, young Sam was working as an apprentice printer.

acclaim, he married. And receiving at once, and along with fame and love, a completely furnished house, and even an interest in a Buffalo newspaper, as a wedding present! So you see fame, love, money tumbling in upon a hobbledehoy genius; and more and more fame and money, plus, and quite as swiftly, the companionship and applause of the acknowledged cognoscenti and literati of the ultra-snobbish literary East: Warner, Aldrich, Howells, Cable, Hay! And the cautious guidance of inlaws who were proud of, if slightly condescending toward, the upstart Genius who needed, of course—and of all things—polishing. Indeed, Charles Dudley Warner, critical poohbah of his hour, and so early as 1873 (!) already collaborating with Twain in the writing of that amazingly bad novel, *The Gilded Age.* And Howells hailing him as "Dear Mark!" in his book. Yet, with one deathless character at that, Twain's own maternal uncle—James Lampton—disguised as Colonel Mulberry Sellers.

And then after that, other successful books, of course: *Tom Sawyer, Life on the Mississippi, Huckleberry Finn, The Prince and the Pauper,* etc. And because of these, the this and the that of the European and American world of that day, doing all that they could to formalize and perpetuate this genius, as he was to them—not as he was to himself—in his deepest self. And so, letters and conversations indicating as much. His wife editing his books and cutting out the danger spots. Howells acclaiming him for his morality—he of *1601.* Yet, in spite of all the glamour, here was the other Twain thinking betimes of *What Is Man?* and *The Mysterious Stranger,* and, in his heart, hating his limitations. (pp. 623-25)

But because it was so glamorous and so grand, and he hated to hurt people, and there was his publisher's investment in his books, and what his good friends thought of him, he did not dare to revolt! He feared what they would say. That ostracism awaited him, as it awaits every man who will not march with the crowd. And so, eventually—pain and morbidity. He could not do this, and he could not do that—write, for instance, a towering indictment of anything American. Ah no! For that, to those about him, would have been corrupting his art, falling from his high place as a moral, laughing genius! Hence, all that was really going on in America—its corrupt and shameless politics (only laughingly indicated in *The Gilded Age*); its robber finance such as ended in the monopoly of the railroads, the telegraph, the oil, the coal, the silver and gold of the nation; its lunatic snobbery in the form of the "Four Hundred," with its Fifth Avenues, Newports, Southamptons, and its yachts and gold harnesses and pet-dog dinners, and its most fantastic heirs and assigns of the second and third generation, all going untouched. At that time they were sacred. Too sacred for him, or his art.

Not that I am calling on Twain to be anything that he was not. It is he, himself, who has indicated in all that he feared to publish in life that he was really calling on himself to do differently and to be different. But convention—convention, the dross of a worthless and meaningless current opinion—this was the thing that restrained him. Because of Howells and Rogers and Hay, and the Aldriches and Warners and Langdons, he did not, even though he could have. And he, himself, has proved it. Why, from his grave he fairly yells: "I was restrained. I was defeated. I hate the lying, cowardly world that circumvented me. Man is not good. He is not honest. Life is a lie! Life is a lie!"

Read *What Is Man?*

Read *The Mysterious Stranger.*

The truth is, as you see, that Twain was *not* two people, but one—a gifted but partially dissuaded Genius who, in time, and by degrees changed into his natural self. This second Twain was observing the world as it truly is; but alas! as I have shown, he had already been inducted into the social world of which, temperamentally, he was not truly a part, and which, at bottom, he resented. In short, the raw genius of the river raft and the mining camp, and the western newspaper of that day, was confused and, for a time, hypnotized by this audacious and insistent authoritarian world of convention, into which, thoughtlessly, he had drifted. And it led him astray. For at the time, not later, it seemed to represent and verify to this raw, gay youth all the accepted claims and distinctions of a world that he did not clearly grasp—fame, love, marriage. But later, of course, came the warning finger of convention. Naughty, naughty! Must behave! Must be good! Otherwise Grandma Grundy will slap. And how!

I often think of this: In Twain's day lived Whitman. Did he ever hear of him? Herman Melville was his contemporary. Did he ever hear or speak of him? There is no evidence. Poe had gone but a little while before. Was Poe taboo? To Howells—yes. To Aldrich—yes. To Twain—???

Yet below all this, and that on which his feet were resting, was the solid rock of his own temperament and understanding. And with this as his point of vantage and departure, and despite the impact of the meretricious life that was spinning about him, came the final conviction that most of what he saw and was so busy with was mere sound and fury, signifying nothing—tinsel and tawdry make-believe which could only detract from his true stature. The truth of it is apparent,

and not only that, but confessed, in his *Autobiography,* and in those really deathless works which his tinsel contemporaries never knew. I refer again to *The Mysterious Stranger* still sold, if you will believe it, as a Christmas book for children, and *What Is Man?* read by a corporal's guard of the initiated, in the course of, let us say, a year, if so often. (pp. 625-27)

Theodore Dreiser, "Mark the Double Twain," in English Journal, *Vol. XXIV, No. 8, October, 1935, pp. 615-27.*

E. S. FUSSELL   (essay date 1952)

[*In the following excerpt, Fussell discerns a "basic confusion" in* The Mysterious Stranger *that he views as stemming from Twain's inability to reconcile conflicts between the solipsistic philosophy he constructs in this work and his own responses to reality.*]

The Mysterious Stranger is Twain's most audacious fictional venture, and an analysis of its workings ought to tell us something about Twain as an artist, and, finally and peripherally, something about Twain as a man.

Twain struggled inordinately with this story; it was the last of several abortive attempts to get his late philosophic obsessions into fictional form, and even *The Mysterious Stranger,* in which Twain appeared at first to have solved his artistic problem, was started and laid aside several times before it was finally abandoned. What is undoubtedly the final chapter was found in Twain's papers by Albert B. Paine, and attached to the uncompleted story when it was posthumously published in 1916. Because the tale was never formally completed, one cannot properly speak of Twain's formal achievement; but the very fact that Twain, even though he left the story unfinished, was able to construct the conclusion corroborates our impression that *The Mysterious Stranger* is somewhat unique in Twain's writings in its degree of coherence of theme and in its adjustment of technique to the realization of that theme. Twain, briefly, must have had rather definite objectives clearly in mind as he wrote; what these goals were is revealed in the final chapter, and supported by evidence in the rest of the book. (p. 95)

Twain's philosophic position during his late years can be described as a grotesque medley of fatalism, misanthropy, and cynicism. In general, he reflects the post-Darwinian pessimism of the late nineteenth century; the use of an inverted "Great Chain of Being" concept, his attacks on the "Moral Sense," and his contempt for human reason and dignity might all be considered part of Twain's undifferentiated response to the impact of evolutionary ideas. Twain seems to have been, temperamentally, both romantic and idealistic, and it is not surprising, then, that as he was increasingly tortured by his ideas, he should finally have toyed with the possibilities of solipsism, the last refuge of the romantic subjectivist. The final chapter of *The Mysterious Stranger* outlines a general theory of solipsism, and if this is accepted as the ultimate framework of the story, meaningful analysis becomes possible.

The solipsistic position is expounded with force and some lucidity by Twain, and there is little reason to refuse him serious audience. His interests in mental telepathy, spiritualism and dreams indicate that he had been moving toward such a position for several years. The notebooks and manuscripts of these years are crowded with references to dream and the nature of reality; the apparent reality and duration of the dream state is a topic that constantly recurs. The solipsistic conclusion towards which Twain was apparently working is a theme imbedded in the whole story, and Twain has liberally posted signs to indicate its presence. (pp. 96-7)

A first reading of *The Mysterious Stranger* is likely to give an impression of meaningless disorder and frustrated purpose. The existence of allegory and symbolism is indisputable, but it is extraordinarily difficult to relate the action and the extra-literal significances in any very satisfactory manner. In various places, the story operates on several levels, either consecutively or simultaneously, and there often appears to be insufficient cohesion among these levels. The values of objects, characters, and events are constantly shifting: now the significances are sharply focussed, easily read, while a few pages later they will blur and then fade from sight. It may be taken for granted that Twain's architectonic powers were not of the first order in the full-length novel, but this is a short piece, and one might expect a more unified impression from a work on which so much devotion and care were lavished. Twain has open to him, of course, an aesthetic rationale for this apparent lack of integration, for logical patterns and clear vision are hardly to be demanded from a world that is "a grotesque and foolish dream"; the "imitation," as well as the thing imitated, may have been deliberately given "dream-marks."

But the basic confusion in *The Mysterious Stranger* arises from the nature of the peculiar philosophy which Twain tried to load onto "this vessel of abuse." The fictional problem approaches the threshold of desperation with the assumption that objective reality is totally non-existent. To meet this challenge, Twain is compelled to accept certain phenomenal levels as real in order to get on with the story, though he eventually will destroy the whole fabric. And this compromise indicates a tortured conflict in Twain's soul between the philosophy he believed he had worked out so carefully on the ratiocinative level, and his total reaction to experience which denied the truth of this philosophy and continually rejected it as it came into perspective during composition. It is the perennial conflict between "thought" and "emotion," the perpetual agony of the faulty hypothesis: failure satisfactorily to arbitrate the claims of objective and subjective phenomena ultimately explains the basic confusion in *The Mysterious Stranger.*

In order to illustrate the fluidity of Twain's method, one might consider briefly the shifting symbolic values attributable to Satan. He is first presented on the literal level as an unexceptionable and ordinarily attractive young man; his initial impression on Twain's boys is simply that of a pleasant stranger. Through his performance of a series of suggestive tricks, he is gradually given more extensive significance, though most of his legerdemain seems to have no further function than the establishment of his supernatural status. A characteristically Twain detail, and one that sends us back into biography, is Satan's capacity in mental telegraphy.

Suddenly Satan assumes additional stature, as he commences the creation of microcosmic units for the pleasure and edification of his young friends (and the reader). Although he announces himself as an angel he is, at this point, a symbol of deity, and his actions imitate in little the creation of the world. With this technique, Twain is enabled to hold forth simultaneously on the paltry and debased nature of man and the indifference or malignity of the deity—two chief items in the "abuse" he was most anxious to load onto this fictional vehicle. The microcosm is, of course, the type of the macrocosm, and the boys, curiously detached from normal involvement by what can only be called "internal philosophic distance," are enabled to comprehend in one vision both Creator and Creation. Meanwhile, action on the superficial level continues: the Lilliputian inhabitants of the tiny world fall to blows and Satan indifferently snuffs them out. This action, of course, arouses, as Twain was determined that it should, the boys' "moral" and "Humanitarian" feelings, feelings which Twain was eager to discredit. Satan now assumes more explicitly his role of "angel," as he tries to explain how angels differ from men on these matters. This whole scene is realized with a surprising degree of imaginative integrity somewhat reminiescent of Voltaire; the use of suggestive detail is delicate, charming, and mordant, and the little world has all the appearance of reality. Both spectators and reader know otherwise, and this gives Twain an early opportunity to question the nature of reality; it also gives the skillful artist a complex ironic situation, obviously dependent upon different planes of experience and divergent points of view. And by a nearly inevitable logical extension, the empty and meaningless illusion of Satan's creation is transferred to the universe at large. In one sense, we are already arrived at the solipsistic conclusion, though epistemological difficulties remain. How, in other words, given Twain's general framework, can this episode (and others) be assumed to confer valid information? There is only one possible reconciliation, shoddy as it is, and it is in fact the one that seems to be imbedded in the structure of *The Mysterious Stranger:* for just as the microcosm is unreal, so is the whole event, Satan and all, equally unreal; what Twain has presented is not final truth, but simply preliminary approximation. Through a series of such apparent but only proximate truths, Satan conducts the narrator, as Twain conducts the reader, to the final revelation. In the last view, deity can hardly be either malignant or indifferent, for it is totally non-existent; nonetheless, the view of diety as evil is, one is supposed to believe, more consonant with the phenomena which the "thought" (or individual) is able to apprehend than are traditional theological notions of God's attributes, and this level of illumination may then be taken as a partial "enlightenment," a limited intellectual progress.

Satan functions in a variety of ways in the implementation of Twain's theories. He is a detached satiric observer, a good mouth-piece for Twain's misanthropy; additionally, his supra-human status renders somewhat more palatable Twain's tortured assault on the rational and ethical pretensions of the "damned human race." But this role is more expository than functional, and of less importance than his utility as an artificer and explicator of mechanisms illustrative of Twain's sophomoric fatalism. Here Satan, omniscient and presumably omnipotent as well, demonstrates the excessive concentration on causation (without any very clear comprehension of the problems involved) that so overwhelmed Twain, simply by altering apparently insignificant links in the lives of the villagers, and thereby sending them to unsuspected disasters (according to human terms). Initially, this action is hardly motivated at all, and philosophically considered it is absurd, but once in operation and purely on the level of fantasy, it is surprisingly convincing, one of Twain's most aesthetically satisfying performances. One might notice, finally, Satan's intoxicating effect on the villagers, an effect which might be characterized as that of a low-voltage mystic experience. In his presence, feelings of ecstasy and enchantment gradually operate to overcome preconceptions and to pave the way for acceptance of startling new orientations. Considering Twain's views about the determinism of ideas, it would hardly have done for the narrator to accept at once the full implications of his world-view (nor could there have been any story, in such a case); his mind had to be prepared step by step, since the mind can only accept that for which it is prepared by previous experience. And in this progressive illumination resides, one finally sees, both the content and the form of *The Mysterious Stranger*. Abstracted, ideational determinism is plot; extended, it is also Twain's content, subject, and material.

Through an examination of these various roles emerges one constant factor. Satan is at all times the instructor, and every speech and action finally tends towards the communication of knowledge and "truth." Very little that Satan reveals (and this is the bulk of the tale) is ultimately true, yet he continually provides partial illumination, relative to the particular plateau of enlightenment that has been reached at that juncture in the story. And when he finally leads the narrator to the concluding vision, he says of himself:

> I myself have no existence; I am but a dream—your dream, creature of your imagination. In a moment you will have realized this, then you will banish me from your visions and I shall dissolve into the nothingness out of which you made me . . .
>
> I am perishing already—I am failing—I am passing away. . . . But I, your poor servant, have revealed you to your self and set you free.

Perhaps one ought not to press the issue, but in general function, if not in every detail, Satan has represented intuition all along. Gradually he has suggested the truth to the narrator, through a long series of lessons he has prepared the will for acceptance; one overpowering flash of insight, represented dramatically by Satan's last speech, is terminal:

> He vanished, and left me appalled; for I knew, and realized, that all he had said was true.

By putting his figures through these various progressive phases from unreality (literal materiality) to reality (solipsistic ideality), Twain has forced a certain degree of unity on his episodic structure; by treating each phase provisionally as if it were the only reality, he has eaten his cake all along and still has it at the end. He has denounced with abandon and with gusto, passed moral sentence on man's activities, and he concludes by wildly controverting all injustice, pain, and evil whatsoever. Philosophically, *The Mysterious Stranger* is bunkum, but through the technique of gradual revelation, Twain has laid out his basic conceptions in an artistic pattern that demonstrates a surprising direction and continuity. (One very serious flaw in the general pattern of functional development ought to be noticed: Twain occasionally allows Satan to become a purely humorous character, temporarily obscuring his organic utility. At one point, for instance, the mysterious stranger is said to be the nephew of the more conventional Satan, the original fallen angel. The temptation to employ this uncle-nephew relationship for comic irony was apparently irresistible, and Twain was never one to pass up a good thing. But the comedy has no integral relation with the narrative progress, and is surely inconsistent with the larger effect. Such a lapse of decorum suggests a certain lack of control and vagueness of aim, and it points, once again, to the serious indecision underlying the whole work.)

And yet striking contradictions remain, despite Twain's potential achievement of a certain degree of formal unity, and they cannot easily be dismissed. The presence of a strong satiric intention, for example, demands some examination. One of Satan's most significant speeches concerns the social efficacy of laughter, perhaps the most eloquent statement on the function of satire that Twain ever made. The speech in question is preceded by a bitter attempt to strip man of his illusory virtues; Satan proceeds to make a single concession to human dignity:

> You have a mongrel perception of humor, nothing more; a multitude of you possess that. This multitude see the comic side of a thousand low-grade and trivial things—broad incongruities, mainly; grotesqueries, absurdities, evokers of the horse-laugh. The ten thousand high-grade comicalities which exist in the world are sealed from their dull vision. Will a day come when the race will detect the funniness of these juvenilities and laugh at them—and by laughing at them destroy them? For your race, in its poverty, has unquestionably one really effective weapon—laughter. Power, money, persuasion, supplication, persecution—these can lift at a colossal humbug—push it a little—weaken it a little, century by century; but only laughter can blow it to rags and atoms at a blast. Against the assault of laughter nothing can stand. You are always fussing and fighting with your other weapons. Do you ever use that one? No; you leave it lying rusting. As a race, do you ever use it at all? No; you lack sense and the courage.

Twain is here considering satire as a positive social force, not as the cynical and futile railing one might expect from a mechanistic and misanthropic philosopher in a "closed" universe. Correlated either with Twain's solipsism or with his fatalism, this satiric weapon could have no possible meaning. A satisfactory resolution of this confusion is manifestly impossible, but one may return to one of the structural qualities of *The Mysterious Stranger,* apply it here as a tentative hypothesis, and carry deep into the heart of the peculiar tensions of this tale. Twain was apparently compelled (and here the personal motivation reinforces the artistic), as he explored his fictive problem, to accept "reality" as a relative term, fashioning his attack to the level of reality then under consideration. Although the ultimate truth may be quite otherwise, the apparent reality (and here one is carried back to biography again, into the notebook entries on dream) is sufficiently vivid to force certain limited values. For, in spite of his more volatile outbursts, Twain's cynicism and misanthropy were sorrowfully inexpressive of his total orientation to life. Constantly, in reading *The Mysterious Stranger,* one observes Twain's emotional reactions in serious conflict with his theoretical formulations. His sympathies are deeply involved in the human predicament, his heart continues to ache, as it always had, over injustice, misery, oppression, or sorrow. Life in the abstract may be paltry, meaningless, finally unreal; but in direct experience, in passion and suffering, certain values and a limited dignity emerge. In one suggestive passage, Twain illustrates what is happening:

> He [Satan] had never felt a pain or a sorrow, and did not know what they were, in any really informing way. He had no knowledge of them except theoretically—that is to say, intellectually. And of course that is no good. One can never get any but a loose and ignorant notion of such things except by experience.

And with this statement, one must juxtapose another, chronologically the latest comment in the tale. The narrator is now an old man, recapturing in memory the essence of the past; he has long since accepted the belief that he is only a random thought, fictitiously creating and peopling a mechanistic and meaningless dream-universe, a world whose unreality is proved by its evil and insanity. Yet in recollection, reality and virtue furtively take on significance:

> It was an awful eleven days; and yet, with a lifetime stretching back between to-day and then, they are still a grateful memory to me, and beautiful. In effect, they were days of companionship with one's sacred dead, and I have known no comradeship that was so close or so precious.

This is probably the final tension that Twain could never organize. Form, to a certain extent, he might have achieved, and in the face of such obstacles, his very attempt seems heroic. But Twain's failure as artist meant a partial personal salvation, for a total artistic integration could only have been purchased by a total destruction of the artist's humanity. (pp. 98-104)

> *E. S. Fussell, "The Structural Problem of 'The Mysterious Stranger',"* in Studies in Philology, *Vol. LXIX, No. 1, January, 1952, pp. 95-104.*

FRANKLIN J. MEINE (essay date 1952)

[*In the following excerpt from his foreword to a small press edition of Twain's first published story, "The Dandy Frightening the Squatter," Meine cites this work as an important early example of Twain's humor and style.*]

Sam Clemens wrote his first humorous story when he was only a youngster—little older than Tom Sawyer—at the age of 16. It was a colorful Huck Finn yarn, a rough river sketch localized in Hannibal, featuring river characters and steamboat life on the Mississippi. It revealed a youthful Mark Twain born to American frontier story-telling, and it pointed the direction of his great masterpiece, *The Adventures of Huckleberry Finn.*

Imagine Mark's thrill when, not yet seventeen, he saw his first story, **"The Dandy Frightening the Squatter"** in black newsprint. It appeared in the *Carpet-Bag* of May 1, 1852, a humorous family weekly published in Boston, under the initials "S. L. C." (p. 3)

Whether B. P. Shillaber, editor of the *Carpet-Bag,* polished off Sam's story for appearance in his paper, whether he pruned it or "smoothed" it we shall probably never know. Mark may have written in a style he regarded as suitable for publication in the genteel *Carpet-Bag* in far-off Boston, or he may simply have adopted some of the "literary standards" of thousands of stories that were floating around in newspapers and weeklies that circulated freely along western waterways. At sixteen one hardly expects a flair for literary style, and the **"Dandy"** may have been Sam's best effort at the time. One important value of the piece, Walter Blair reminds me, is that it shows where Mark Twain started and it makes one appreciate all the more how far he went later.

"The Dandy Frightening the Squatter" is not hilariously funny, nor does it seem to have been uniquely original. Some years after my discovery, Professor Fred Lorch of Iowa State College found the suggestion of a somewhat similar plot in an anecdote called "Scene on the Ohio" in the Bloomington (Muscatine, Iowa) *Herald* in 1849, reprinted from an earlier comic, *The Elephant,* in 1848, and Professor Prentice Miller of Emory University discovered an even earlier analogue, "A Georgia Cracker," in the New York *Spirit of the Times* in 1847. Professor Walter Blair has cited some similar themes in earlier tales, as has Professor Minnie Brashear of the University of Missouri. Professor Stith Thompson could undoubtedly stick a pin into this story and pin it down, like a butterfly, somewhere in his myriad of motifs in folk tales.

But the fact remains—after twenty-five years—that this is still Mark Twain's first story, "four months earlier than the earliest items extant in the Hannibal papers," notes Professor Gladys Bellamy of the University of Oklahoma. Whether the plot, or the theme, or the motif of the story was original with Mark is not critically important. The important fact is that it was typical of the humorous frontier tale that existed as part of an autochthonous American folk literature, and that consciously patterned or not it foreshadowed the genius of Mark Twain. For the secret lay not so much in the originality of the tale as in the art of telling the story. As in the case of the **"Celebrated Jumping Frog"** story, Mark did not claim originality. "I only claim," he said in later years, "to know how a story ought to be told." Most of us will agree that Mark Twain knew how to tell a story, and his first literary effort reveals him as a "natural born" story-teller in this tradition. This tremendously significant fact seems to have been overlooked.

The publication of **"The Dandy"** in a popular American weekly clearly tied Clemens into the tradition of frontier story-telling in which he had grown up and of which he so naturally became a part. It was an art of story-telling and a humor "instinct with the life of the frontier, wild and robust and male," observed Bernard DeVoto. "It was this humor—the humor of the South and the Southwest—to which Mark Twain was born. From his boyhood he heard it from the mouths of rivermen and wherever the villagers talked together in the leisurely water-side town of Hannibal. Through the printing shop where he was apprenticed and the office of his brother's newspaper passed the flood of 'exchanges' from all over the country." It was this humor that "gave to young Sam Clemens the interesting example of material immediately at hand . . . The life here pictured had been his; the characters were men and women whose counterparts he saw every day. These people, then, could be written about! When young Sam Clemens took to writing, he had to look for a model no farther than the boiler deck."

"The Dandy" early brought to a focus forces that later played tremendously important roles in Mark Twain's life and writings: the vast meandering Mississippi and its steamboat age replete with violence and fantasy. Young Sam's use of these materials and themes anticipated his epic uses of them later in *Tom Sawyer* and in *Huckleberry Finn.* Perhaps one can never know what that powerful kaleidoscopic river life may have meant to the youthful Sam Clemens, but in *Life on the Mississippi* Twain has himself accented certain memories of it that hark back neatly to his first story. (pp. 8-12)

The significance of **"The Dandy Frightening the Squatter"** in the Mark Twain canon has been aptly summarized by DeVoto in his *Mark Twain's America:*

> Sam Clemens' first literary effort is a humorous sketch contributed to a humorous newspaper. Its

material is the characteristic frontier life of Hannibal. It is typical of the newspaper humor of the
South and Southwest that was the first vigorous realism in American literature. It was the sort of
thing that Sam Clemens, printer's devil and journeyman printer, had seen flourishing in the little
weeklies that came to the exchange desk. Its *genre*
was the native expression of the frontier. He began
writing it in his first experiment and he continued
writing it all his life.

(pp. 13-14)

Franklin J. Meine, in his Mark Twain's First Story,
Prairie Press, 1952, 19 p.

GEORGE PEIRCE CLARK   (essay date 1956)

[*In the following excerpt, Clark characterizes "The Man That
Corrupted Hadleyburg" as a study in diabolism that is related
to* The Mysterious Stranger *and reminiscent of Milton's* Paradise Lost.]

Mark Twain's preoccupation with Satan is revealed in a number of his works, and has been frequently commented upon.
" . . . of all of the figures in the Christian mythology," observes Edward Wagenknecht, "Satan was the one that interested him most" [see Further Reading list]. . . .

Mark Twain's feeling of sympathy with Satan, together with
his cynicism regarding the human race, is clearly set forth in
his pessimistic story *The Mysterious Stranger,* the work
most often commented upon in connection with his interest
in diabolism. This account of the appearance of Satan's nephew in a small German village, with its uncomplimentary observations upon mankind, is regarded by Bellamy as Mark
Twain's *"most artistic use of Satan"* [see Further Reading
list]. But Mark Twain wrote another story, considerably better known than *The Mysterious Stranger,* which uses Satan
fully as artistically, and much more subtly. That story is **"The
Man That Corrupted Hadleyburg."** It is my purpose in this
essay to develop the basis for a reading of **"Hadleyburg"** as
another of Mark Twain's studies of Satan in his commerce
with mankind, and to indicate how added insight into the
story may be gained from such a reading.

The strongly deterministic *What Is Man?,* **The Mysterious
Stranger,** and **"The Man That Corrupted Hadleyburg"** were
written at that desperate period in Mark Twain's life when
the bankruptcy of his publishing venture, the failure of the
Paige typesetting machine and, above all, the death of his
daughter Susy had reduced him to the most uncompromising
cynicism. (p. 1)

"The Man That Corrupted Hadleyburg," then, belongs to
those years when Mark Twain increasingly was turning his
mind to the problem of the demonic in the nature of things.
It would be surprising if the Satanic theme had not insinuated
itself into its pages.

The suggestion of Satan may be found in three aspects of
"Hadleyburg": in the rather striking number of similarities
to be observed between it and *The Mysterious Stranger;* in
the number of places in which Mark Twain associates the
corrupter of the town specifically with Satan; and in the instances of Miltonic influence in the story, expressing itself
more or less directly through the author's "deep well of unconscious cerebration" (for, after all, **"Hadleyburg"** too is a
story of a paradise lost).

Most important of the similarities between **"Hadleyburg"**
and *The Mysterious Stranger* is a central situation shared by
both stories. In *The Mysterious Stranger* a wallet full of gold
coins (later transferred to a bag) is found by an honest priest,
Father Peter, who needs the money and is tempted by it. He
is almost immediately charged by an astrologer with having
stolen the money, and a trial of the priest ensues. At the trial,
Satan, ostensibly acting as the *advocatus dei,* succeeds in dis-
proving the astrologer's statement that the priest had entered
his room by stealth and made off with the money. Satan
pleads effectively for Father Peter, for he knows very well it
was he himself who placed the money—the devil's money—
in the priest's wallet.

This action is paralleled by the central situation in **"Hadleyburg."** A bag of "gold" comes into the possession of a poor
but reputable man. He is tempted to keep it for himself but
does not give in to the temptation. The money is left by a
"mysterious big stranger," who later comes forward to advance the poor man's claim to it. But, as in *The Mysterious
Stranger,* the money has the devil's curse upon it, and so destroys the finder. The accusation in *The Mysterious Stranger*
that the priest stole into the astrologer's room to purloin the
gold is paralleled in **"Hadleyburg"** by Wilson's accusation
that Billson stole into his office to learn the text of the secret
message.

In each of the stories the principal scene is dominated by a
mysterious stranger who manipulates the villagers as he wills.
And the villagers of the two communities are of the same undistinguished sort. Barclay Goodson, in Hadleyburg, calls his
fellow citizens "narrow, self-righteous and stingy." But
"Heaven took Goodson," and the one really honest person
was lost to the community. In *The Mysterious Stranger,* it
is Frau Brandt who stands in contrast to the hypocrisy of the
villagers, and who goes to heaven after her martyrdom. The
people of Eseldorf are "dull and ignorant and trivial and conceited," according to Satan; those of Hadleyburg "feeble and
foolish," according to the stranger. When, in *The Mysterious
Stranger,* old Ursula threatens to take a stick to Satan, the
young narrator is frightened for her safety. . . . (pp. 1-2)

The same complete indifference to human life is exhibited by
the stranger in **"Hadleyburg"**:

> I passed through your town at a certain time (he ex-
> plains), and received a deep offense which I had not
> earned. Any other man would have been content to
> kill one or two of you and call it square, but to me
> that would have been a trivial revenge . . . .

The phrase "kill one or two" is notably stark, coming as it
does in the midst of the rather humorous description of the
dismay of the nineteen. . . .

Mark Twain does not specifically associate the stranger with
Satan here, to be sure. But he does so in a number of places
in **"Hadleyburg."** (p. 2)

When, finally, Richards reads the stranger's last note to him,
the words seem "written with fire." And as for the checks of
large denomination which the stranger sent to him, Richards
recognized:

> You will never see them again—they are destroyed.
> They came from Satan. I saw the hell-brand on
> them, and I knew they were sent to betray me to
> sin.

Significantly, Mark Twain adds: "Richards was right; the checks were never seen again." Richards, clearly, had correctly divined their source.

Mark Twain was surely not unmindful of Milton as he wrote his story. It contains certain reminiscences of *Paradise Lost,* and one of the most familiar phrases in Milton's prose—the assertion in *Areopagitica.* "I cannot praise a fugitive and cloistered virtue, unexercised and unbreathed . . . "—serves as its basic theme. (pp. 2-3)

Hadleyburg, we are told, had had "the ill luck to offend a passing stranger—possibly without knowing it." And, as might be said of Milton's Satan, the passing stranger "kept his injury in mind, and gave all his leisure moments to trying to invent a compensating satisfaction for it." (p. 3)

Similarly, the stranger in Hadleyburg forms a plan, exclaiming, "That is the thing to do—I will corrupt the town."

The stranger has selected as his principal targets in the town Edward and Mary Richards, who serve in a sense as the Adam and Eve of the story. Upon arriving in Hadleyburg, he finds Mary Richards alone, and approaches her with something of the polite deference shown by the serpent when he came upon Eve in the Garden. And, like Eve, Mary Richards finds her curiosity aroused by "The mysterious big stranger." When Edward Richards returns home he becomes as excited as Mary regarding the riches that lie in the sack, and his excitement is conveyed to Cox, the editor of the town paper, with whom Richards shares the story of the stranger's visit. Once their greed has been aroused, they walk, says Twain, "with the gait of mortally stricken men." We recall the "mortal taste" of the forbidden tree in the second line of Milton's poem. And like Milton's Adam and Eve after the commission of their sin, Mary and Edward fall to quarreling and blaming one another.

Meanwhile, with diabolical cunning, the mysterious stranger had written a letter to each of the town's nineteen leading citizens suggesting that the recipient was the one who had the best claim to the sack of gold. When Richards receives this note, his mood of despair gives way to one of elation, and he and his wife, forgetting their bickering, enjoy a happy moment reminiscent of the old days "—days that had begun with their courtship and lasted without a break till the stranger brought the deadly money." "Deadly" in anticipation of the early death that comes to Mary and Edward Richards, and perhaps also in reminiscence of the fruit in the garden, of which God had said: "Ye shall not eat / Thereof, nor shall ye touch it, lest ye die." (*Paradise Lost* IX)

After the stranger has succeeded in his plan to corrupt Hadleyburg, apparently all but one of the nineteen leading citizens having been shown to be dishonest when faced with real temptation, a final communication from the tempter remains to be read. In it he further discomfits the nineteen by revealing how completely he had taken them in, and, in words reminiscent of *Areopagitica,* continues:

> As soon as I found out that you carefully and vigilantly kept yourselves and your children *out of temptation,* I knew how to proceed. Why, you simple creatures, the weakest of all weak things is a virtue which had not been tested in the fire.

In its final paragraphs, the story returns to this theme:

> By act of the Legislature—upon prayer and peti-

tion—Hadleyburg was allowed to change its name to (never mind what—I will not give it away), and leave one word out of the motto that for many generations had graced the town's official seal.

At this point, according to a note which Mark Twain penciled at the close of his manuscript, were to be printed two seals, one bearing the motto "Lead Us Not Into Temptation," the other the revised motto "Lead Us Into Temptation." Unfortunately, these instructions were never carried out, and the forcefulness of the conclusion is diminished by the placing of the mottoes—essential to the continuity of the story—as though they were merely an appended exhibit. (Indeed, one very popular anthology of American literature omits them altogether.)

Bernard DeVoto has shown how obsessed Mark Twain became in the late nineties (Susy died in August, 1896) with the thought of "man's complete helplessness in the grip of the inexorable forces of the universe, and man's essential cowardice, pettiness and evil" [see Further Reading list]. To this period belong **"Hadleyburg,"** published in *Harper's Magazine* for December, 1899, and *The Mysterious Stranger,* begun (after a number of false starts) early in the same year. It is hardly surprising, then, to discover Mark Twain dealing in **"Hadleyburg"** and *The Mysterious Stranger* with fundamentally the same ideas. Hadleyburg, Eseldorf, St. Petersburg, Hannibal—all these, as Mark Twain scholars have shown us, are the same village; and to them, in one or another of his guises, came the same mysterious big stranger. **"The Man That Corrupted Hadleyburg"** surely belongs with *The Mysterious Stranger* as a piece of Twainian diabolism, produced under Miltonic—and perhaps Satanic—inspiration. (pp. 3-4)

> *George Peirce Clark, "The Devil That Corrupted Hadleyburg," in* Mark Twain Journal, *Vol. X, No. 2, Winter, 1956, pp. 1-4.*

CHARLES NEIDER (essay date 1957)

[*Neider is a Russian-born American critic and editor who has written extensively on the works of Mark Twain and Franz Kafka. In the following excerpt from his introduction to* The Complete Short Stories of Mark Twain, *Neider characterizes Twain as a writer who achieves more "economy of effect" in his stories than in his long works.*]

During [Mark Twain's] lifetime his stories appeared in volumes which I can only call hodgepodge, containing as they did anecdotes, jokes, letters, essays—all sorts of serious and humorous nonfiction along with the fiction. Twain was a man who was easygoing about borderlines. Some of his short pieces fluctuate between fiction and fact. And he was a fellow who had very definite notions about the appeal of the grab bag. When he was a publisher himself he got William Dean Howells, his friend, to edit a collection of accounts of true adventure. Howells put the pieces together according to a scheme, and after Twain had looked at it he gently advised Howells to mix the things up, give them variety, so that the reader might be surprised. A formal scheme was about as appealing to him as a tight collar. Perhaps it was his unconventionality, his insistence on formlessness, which had left his stories in the lurch. (p. x)

In almost any other writer's work it is easy to say, "This is a short story, whereas that is not." Take the cases of Joyce, Mann, James, Hemingway, Kafka, Lawrence. There is no hesitation about it: a short story belongs to a particular genre and has a relation to the whole of fictional writing in the same way that a watercolor has to the whole of painting, or a song to the whole of composition. Even in Chekhov it is easy to say what is a short story and what isn't. I say "even" because his stories are so gentle in their shading, so clearly lacking in formalism (although not in form), that he of all the writers mentioned might cause some trouble in this respect. In Twain's case it is quite another matter. I have the sense that Twain wrote primarily to satisfy an audience rather than the requirements of a genre. Whatever came to mind that aided his cause was grist for his mill. This is why we find sketches in which it is not possible to distinguish between fiction and fact.

He rarely bothered about the niceties of fiction. Fiction has a tone all its own, which the literary artist reveres. For him it is in a special sense greater than reality. It shapes reality, controls it. It is hard to imagine a James or a Flaubert inserting raw material, untransmuted, unmodulated, into his fictions. For Mark Twain such problems were beside the point. He simply disregarded them, although he was quite aware of them, more aware than he was accustomed to admit. Twain had enough of the frontier spirit to dislike "form." Form was likely to be something eastern. Or if not eastern then something worse: European. Henry James went to Europe to seek form, to saturate himself in it, the form of old societies, old art, old manners and buildings. Twain went to Europe to poke fun at it and to make us laugh. The product of the frontier thought he could see where form was growing hollow and becoming a fraud. (p. xi)

Twain had the artistic temperament without much of the artistic conscience. His genius was essentially western, its strength the land, the people, their language, and their humor. What he lacked was a studied eastern conscience to refine the great ore he mined. Perhaps such a conscience would have inhibited and eventually ruined him. Probably he knew best what was necessary for him. What he had, he had in great measure: the naked power of the man with the gift of gab. He knew what a yarn was, and what it was for, and what to do with it. He did not think that a good yarn needs prettifying, and he told it straight, without trimmings. His high jinks are remarkable—his love of mugging, of monologue, dialect, caricature. He is a great proponent of the tall story, piling details on until the story comes crashing down. At his best he is uproarious, and he is often at his best in his stories, as you will see.

It has been said that his stories are an important part of our literary heritage. It would be difficult, if not impossible, to dispute this statement successfully, presuming one cared to try. They are also part of our folklore. Twain is our writer closest to folklore, our teller of fairy tales. The Jumping Frog story is a living American fairy tale, acted out annually in Calaveras County. Whatever may be its dim origins (it has been claimed to be close kin to an old Greek tale; but the latter probably descended from a Hindu one, and so on), it is now our story, mirroring something in us. **"The Man That Corrupted Hadleyburg"** is part of our moral heritage. These tales, together with several others, among them **"The $30,000 Bequest"** and **"The £1,000,000 Bank-Note,"** have been anthologized many times. Others—tales of moral indignation such as **"A Horse's Tale,"** and tales meant to shock, for example, *Captain Stormfield's Visit to Heaven,* are no less powerful and important for being less popular.

Twain during his days as a steamship pilot, 1859-60.

Twain is a dangerous man to write about. Unless you approach him with a sense of humor you are lost. You cannot dissect a humorist upon a table. Your first stroke will kill him and make him a tragedian. You must come to Twain with a smile. That is his prerogative: that he can make you do so or fail. In Twain it is not the line-by-line detail which is great, nor the day-by-day life—it is the mass, the contour, and the fragrance of a personality. Who would want, here in this place, to try to dissect that? I shall just pursue a few thoughts briefly, and if I seem to be critical at times, let the reader remember I love the man this side of honesty.

Twain poured his writing out in a stream, showering upon it all his gifts. Sometimes it carried everything before it but at others it failed naively. He was not the kind of versatile writer who is equally good at everything he puts his hand to. It is difficult to believe he could have written fastidious travel essays like Hawthorne's or the delicate, subtle criticism of James; yet at times he appeared to be attempting both. He carried a broadsword which he sometimes tried to use on butterflies. He wrote very rapidly and was as proud as a boy of his daily output. He didn't strive for the polished effect—or rather he strove for it too seldom. When his mood changed he pigeonholed a manuscript, sometimes for years. He wasn't a good judge of his work. Being essentially a man of humor, he was rarely humorless regarding himself in relation to his work. He was unlike Flaubert and Proust and James in this respect. To be humorless regarding oneself—or at least regarding one's work—can sometimes be a great advantage. To be well balanced doesn't guarantee better-grade work.

There is, in a good deal of Twain's writing—in the Hadleyburg story, for example—a kind of naïveté which one feels is literary, a sort of refusal to infuse prose with the sophistication of the mature man. This no doubt reflects in some measure an attitude Twain had to the act of writing and to the nature of his audience. Writing was not the whole man. It may have even been at times the lesser man. And the audience, one seems to perceive, like his family, was largely composed of women: naive women, sheltered from the painful realities of a man's world. The moral pressure in Twain's work is generally considerable but the purely literary, the aesthetic pressure is occasionally so low as to form only a trickle. This aesthetic pressure, impossible to define, is what is necessary to the creation of a work of art. In some cases it stems from moments of transcendent well-being, in others from the depths of frustration or despair. But whatever the causes, the pressure must be there, inside one, for the effect to be achieved. Too great a pressure may be as devastating to a work as too little. Writers like Twain are more likely to suffer from too little.

In Twain's case there is often something pleasant in even the lesser pages, precisely because of the low pressure: he is relaxed and his mood is infectious. Twain rarely tries to overreach himself, to strain after an effect of greatness. This lesson of being relaxed while writing, although a dangerous one for young writers, is an invaluable one for the mature ones. The right balance of pressure when one is about to sit down to work—one's health, one's relation to the material, one's linguistic resilience, the play of one's mind—is really what is called inspiration; the balance is everything: the container, which is one's own complex state, must exactly suit the thing contained, which is the raw material about to be transfigured into art. It is a pity that Twain did not often take the pains to find the just balance for himself. But if he didn't, he at least substituted another virtue. He says somewhere, wryly, that he had the habit of doing, and of reflecting afterward. One contrasts this habit with an opposite one, the habit of reflecting to the point of disease, often found in the later works of Melville and James, as well as in portions of the works of Thomas Mann and Marcel Proust.

Twain doesn't strive to be an artist—*artiste,* he probably would have called it with a grin. He would have felt more comfortable wearing the term "journalist." He grew up a journalist, like Dickens, and was one of those hearty nineteenth-century scribblers who strayed into literature almost without realizing it. He had the journalist's instinct, in the way Defoe had, and in the way Hawthorne and James did not. This is not necessarily a handicap in the creation of literature. Insofar as it stimulates a sense of audience, a sense of common scene, and the use of native speech and lore—insofar, that is, as it inspires one to attempt a colloquy in common terms but with uncommon genius, it is a definite and rare gift. Its limitations are likely to be great also, the limitations of the known, and especially what is known to the particular group. Twain's writing was almost always a means to an end. He had few impersonal objectives in mind in the way of form, experiment, texture, design. He had the common touch and knew it was a blessing. He was enriched by it and made world-famous.

He possessed in a limited degree the craft discipline of the writer who sees his prose, who carefully examines it, watching for design and effect, while at the same time listening to its music. Flaubert and Joyce were writers who intensely saw,

and it is by no accident that we find in their work a brilliance of visual images. (pp. xii-xv)

It is a large part of Twain's greatness that he heard so well. His dialogue is extraordinary. One sometimes wonders if he had a phonographic memory. His ability to imitate styles of speech, with a vast array of accurate detail, is remarkable. His biographer, Albert Bigelow Paine, has written: "At dinner, too, it was his habit, between the courses, to rise from the table and walk up and down the room, waving his napkin and talking—talking in a strain and with a charm that he could never quite equal with his pen. It is the opinion of most people who knew Mark Twain personally that his impromptu utterances, delivered with that ineffable quality of speech, manifested the culmination of his genius." Twain and the oral tradition: both are related to the frontier. Yet some of his chief faults stem directly from this side of his genius—an occasional looseness of texture, a kind of stage or vaudeville timing for effect, an overindulgence in burlesque, a sense as if he were lecturing from a platform. Early in his public career he achieved success as a lecturer and as a maker of speeches, and no doubt this success, this practice, this buttressed confidence in a talent he long must have known he possessed had a crucial influence upon his work.

There is a certain transparency in Twain's work, like that to be found in fairy tales. One senses the machinery behind the silken screen. But in this very transparency there is a kind of potency also found in the fairy tales, a foreknowledge of events, a delight in repetition, in the spelling out of the known, a sort of tribal incantation. There is also something abstract in certain of his fictions, some sort of geometric approach to the art of narrative which, to the modern reader, is not quite satisfying. I refer to pieces like *The American Claimant* and *The Tragedy of Pudd'nhead Wilson.* The latter is a very imperfect work whose imperfections are traceable to its conception, or rather misconception, a fact which Twain himself has revealed at some length. But when he speaks out of his own mouth, with the drawl and idiom and dialect, as he does in so many of his stories, he is unique, inspired, zany, wonderful. (pp. xv-xvi)

Twain, like many other nineteenth-century novelists, is sometimes guilty of padding. This is often due to the economics of book production of his day. The two-volume work, sold by subscription, sometimes serialized, was as much the thing in those days as it isn't now. If a man had only a book and a half in him, that was too bad. He had to get up the half somehow or throw in the towel. (p. xvi)

It is almost needless to add that in the story the impulse or the need to pad was at a minimum, and that consequently there is more economy of effect in Twain's stories than in most of his book-size works. One might even say that Twain felt most at home in the story, that it was the form most congenial to him, lover as he was of the yarn. It was the form which most effectively brought out his particular "voice." Some of his full-size books are more like a series of yarns strung together than works with an indigenous structure. (p. xvii)

His best books, with the exception of his travel books, are those with a western scene. And his travel books largely owe their humor, their geniality, and their wisdom to his western orientation. The sentimentality of the frontier, which ranged all the way from an exaggerated regard for females to the most deadly sort of sadism; the lack of form in social behavior, together with certain codes of behavior which smack of juvenile delinquents; the relative contempt for the written as against the spoken word, the racy language; the attitudes toward dudes and the East, the two being almost synonymous; the impatience with the ways and principles of law—all these characteristics of the American frontier are to be found in Twain's best work, and they are the motor of that work. They are also to be found, in more disguised form, in the work of his star descendant, Ernest Hemingway. (pp. xvii-xviii)

Twain has a wonderful wisdom. He is so essentially sane that it is exhilarating to be in his company. By his way of life he seemed to say, "I am of the tribe of writers but I am saner than they. I know how to savor life." You expect a man like that to live a long life. Twain did. . . . (p. xviii)

> *Charles Neider, in an introduction to* The Complete Short Stories of Mark Twain, *edited by Charles Neider, 1957. Reprint by Doubleday & Company, Inc., 1985, pp. ix-xix.*

GEORGE KNOT   (essay date 1959)

[*In the following excerpt, Knot interprets* The Mysterious Stranger *as "a kind of intellectual practical joke" that turns on a conflict between Twain's "theoretical formulations" and "emotional reactions."*]

The Mysterious Stranger is commonly described, and dismissed, as an unfunny, pessimistic, and illogically got up vehicle of Twain's darker moods and deterministic "philosophy." Critics have pointed out the conflict in the story between the author's emotional reactions and his theoretical formulations. But they have overlooked an interpretation that rests precisely on this conflict. That is, might the story not be a kind of intellectual practical joke to which this conflict is fundamental, even granting that Twain wrote the story in an atrabilious "humor"?

The tale is similar to **"The Man that Corrupted Hadleyburg,"** except that it goes far beyond exposing a community to derision and scornful laughter. In the later story "the mysterious stranger" of Hadleyburg has become a god named Satan, Twain's agent of entrapping all mankind, or so much of it as might read the tale. In both stories people are punished for accepting what they have no right to keep: unearned money, bogus respectability, false position, etc. In *The Mysterious Stranger* the boys entertain cold fears of Satan's unreality, yet they hold on to him because they enjoy a delicious, undeserved, and forbidden power, the sinful detachment from the suffering mass of men. Hence, Theodor-humanity-reader must be punished because he is completely taken in.

The humor is double-edged, in this light, because Twain is not only castigating the reader who swallows the "philosophy" of the story but is lashing himself for being intellectually committed against his emotional sympathies. E. S. Fussell states the usual dilemma of the reader [see excerpt dated 1952]. He finds the humorous role of Satan to be a serious flaw "in the general pattern of functional development," and Satan's laugh-pep-talk, or sermon, to be an unresolvable paradox: "Correlated whether with Twain's solipsism or with his fatalism, this satiric weapon could have no possible meaning. A satisfactory resolution of this confusion is manifestly impossible. . . ." Yet we know that Twain thought a good deal about making the story turn out to be "the right kind of vessel to contain all the abuse I am planning to dump into

it." That is, he must have been thinking in terms of tactics, of strategies for throwing the reader off balance. In fact, we are teased into laughing with Satan in order that our consternation and pain be intensified at the end, at that time when we are called on to laugh at the rather dismal prospect contrived for us.

Maybe I can open a perspective into the story's humor by relating an abbreviated version of an old frontier-type joke. A settler's home is attacked by Indians. His family is slaughtered and the home burned. He, partly scalped and otherwise mutilated, and with several arrows in his back, escapes and crawls through miles of snow before coming to the cabin of a woodsman who takes him in and administers to his wounds. After a time the woodsman asks the victim whether he now hurts. He replies, "Only when I laugh." At the point of writing the story this must have been Twain's state of mind, so he builds a story which makes us sacrificial victims to share his pain. We must adopt a theory of humor which forces us to say, "We must laugh only when it hurts." This is, simply put, the gist of Twain-Satan's laugh doctrine. Unfortunately, Twain did not foresee our indifference to the logic of his interplanetary Robert Ingersoll.

But, throughout, the story is full of upside-down relationships, ironic reversals, and inverted hierarchies. Philip Traum is a symbolic name in which we find prefigured the illusion-reality antinomy and Satan's philipics. And the many attraction-repulsion contrivances, stock responses played against the Twainian incongruous perspectives—these are the barbs on the ironic arrows. Throughout Twain-author intrudes his personal belief, often previously announced, that there is no humor in heaven, and offers us some aside-hints on how to get out of his trap without being hurt. Twain the empiricist in morals rejects the "pure" and detached intellectualism of Satan (and of all "angelic" creatures, for that matter) along with the theologically tainted "Moral Sense." His sympathies are strongly with the poor, weak, and suffering mankind as represented in the story.

We "fall for" his humorous bait but he gives us a chance to laugh it off. Just as he toys with the "fall" in contriving the nephew-uncle relationship between Philip Traum and the traditional Satan, so he makes the boys exemplify, in their ecstatic fascination with Satan's beauty, another kind of fall. Having vicariously tasted Satan's ambiguous good-evil power and prescience, they long to be taken up. They want a "heaven." Twain must have felt the pangs of his own "enlightenment" paralleled here. So he gets at us from above, tilting the planes of perception, disturbing our notions of illusion and reality, playing cat-like with us. From the dream-vision level or dimension he can "con" us into disbelieving what he tells us *must* be our only hold on reality. Man's low-level humor may be contemptible on occasion, Twain openly tells us, but the humor of a Satan is dangerous because god-like. Twain thus vents his splenetic vapors against himself as well as his readers for believing or having believed momentarily in Satanic angels and inhumane, so to speak, gods.

So then, it has been popular to point out the paradox of Twain's position, his desire to punish man for his misdeeds at the same time that he is reluctant to hold him responsible for his actions. Perhaps if we adopt the thesis that the story is a practical joke, we can see a delicate balance on the contradiction. If we reject Satan and our false deistic conceptions, the whole fabric vanishes into nothingness. That is, we must reject the Satan-god fiction while accepting him as a mouthpiece of Twain's laughter doctrine. Through Satan he tells us that laughter can blow any falsity "to rags and atoms at a blast." At least, man remains a thought, "the only existent thought . . . inextinguishable, indestructible." If thought is a poor kind of reality, it is nevertheless the primary impulse of laughter, the open-secret-weapon, the clean bomb that blows gloomy metaphysics to nothingness. It is the key to man's sense of sympathy with his poor deluded, suffering fellows.

Twain had decided on such a plea for laughter, even if it brought him a cold comfort; but his own ineradicable resentments and darker "humors" forced him to contrive a tale which would depress and discourage his readers. Then he tells the reader that he must laugh in order to dispel the carefully implanted gloom and disillusion. Enjoying the perplexing dilemma he created, Twain enjoyed the last laugh and succeeded in making his story the right kind of vessel. It hurt when he laughed, so he wanted to make us all hurt. The notion of laughter as it develops in the story is the weapon he would have liked to use in combatting sorrows and injustices, for he had to fight the proposal of his own satanic angel that life was a meaningless fiction.

Have we not been able to laugh at *The Mysterious Stranger* because we have missed Twain's intention; or because we have been too much preyed upon by the same obfuscations and misgivings; or because we persist in trying to square Twain's humor-psychology with "logic"; or because it hurts "only when we laugh": Which is it? (pp. 11-12)

> George Knot, " 'The Mysterious Stranger': Mark Twain's Last Laugh?" in Mark Twain Journal, *Vol. XI, No. 1, Summer, 1959, pp. 11-12.*

CLINTON S. BURHANS, JR. (essay date 1962)

[*In the following excerpt, Burhans argues that the often-noted conflict in "The Man That Corrupted Hadleyburg" between determinism and moralism is actually central to the story's meaning. He continues by refuting the commonly held view of this story as essentially pessimistic, concluding that "Twain's divergent moral and ethical ideas merge in a view of Man which places Twain within a great and a positive tradition."*]

Praising [**"The Man That Corrupted Hadleyburg"**] A. B. Paine [in his *Mark Twain: A Biography* (see Further Reading list)] calls it "a tale that in its own way takes its place with the half-dozen great English short stories of the world," and DeLancey Ferguson [in his *Mark Twain: Man and Legend* (see Further Reading list)] declares that while "the short story, as an art form, was not Mark's metier . . . in **'The Man That Corrupted Hadleyburg'** he came near to perfection." In contrast, Gladys Bellamy [in her *Mark Twain as a Literary Artist* (see Further Reading list)], though recognizing the story's power, feels that "for the thoughtful reader there is a mischief in it that keeps it from being altogether satisfying." She considers the story marred by inconsistencies stemming from two conflicting characteristics of Twain's mind—his determinism and his moralism. Twain, she says, establishes a deterministic framework to explain the motivation and behavior of his characters and then violates it illogically with "an implied theme of divine justice—the great theme of the judgment of God as it operates through the consciences of Mr. and Mrs. Richards. . . . There is no continuity of motivation, no steadiness of emotional effect, no philosophical unity to the story. In it the moralist gives an out-of-bounds

blow to the determinist, and Hadleyburg settles itself on a philosophic quicksand."

It seems to me, however, that Miss Bellamy's usually brilliant insight fails her here, for in this story Twain is consistent both logically and aesthetically. On the surface, the story is an attack on human greed and hypocrisy, but at its deeper levels it reflects Twain's return to the unresolved problems which had perplexed him in Huck Finn's moral conflict and an exploration of the possibility that experience can unify man's moral perceptions and his motivating emotions. In this context, Twain's concept of determinism, especially environmental determinism, or training, does not conflict with his moralism; on the contrary, his moralism functions here in terms of his determinism. Moreover, his view of conscience in this story is not, as Miss Bellamy implies, that of the conventional religious moralist; it is far more complicated than this, synthesizing as it does the principal elements in his earlier concepts of conscience.

Twain's determinism in **"The Man That Corrupted Hadleyburg,"** far from being inconsistent with his moralism, is the source of its real values. In his concern in this story with the relations between conscience and the heart, he views the moral values of conscience as determined by environment, by training; and one of his major aims is to show that such training in moral values must be empirical, not merely prescriptive. The people of Hadleyburg try to preserve the honesty which has made them famous by training it into their young. They forget, however, that originally this honesty was not just an abstract ideal, but a principle developed and maintained empirically in constant action against the forces and temptations of dishonesty and therefore rooted by experience firmly among the motivating impulses of the heart. "It was many years ago," Twain writes. "Hadleyburg was the most honest and upright town in all the region around about. It had kept that reputation unsmirched during three generations, and was prouder of it than of any other of its possessions."

So proud are the people of Hadleyburg of their reputation and so fearful of the slightest threat to it that they try to safeguard it not by the continued practice of honesty but rather by an attempt to exclude all temptations to dishonesty. . . . Hadleyburg has tried to create an environment in which the principles of honesty can be trained into the young without the dangers involved in practicing them against inimical temptations. The fame of the town, the people feel, will thereby be secure.

But Hadleyburg's training is defective and artificial on at least two counts: in the first place, it is impossible to shield men forever from all temptations to dishonesty, and when inexorably they do arise, men unpracticed in recognizing and resisting them will succumb, as Richards does in failing to clear Burgess—a failure which foreshadows the fall of Hadleyburg. And in the second place, Hadleyburg forgets that man is determined by heredity as well as by environment, that human nature is potentially petty and selfish as well as noble and kind. Thus, when the town becomes obsessed with vanity over its empty and now unearned reputation, its preoccupation with preserving that reputation by excluding the temptations to dishonesty not only fails but also leaves other vices free to develop unchecked. When Richards tells his wife that " 'we have been trained all our lives long, like the whole village, till it is absolutely second nature to us to stop not a single moment to think when there's an honest thing to be done,' " she refutes him prophetically:

> Oh, I know it, I know it—it's been one everlasting training and training and training in honesty— honesty shielded, from the very cradle, against every possible temptation, and so it's *artificial* honesty, and weak as water when temptation comes, as we have seen this night. God knows I never had shade nor shadow of a doubt of my petrified and indestructible honesty until now—and now, under the very first big and real temptation, I—Edward, it is my belief that this town's honesty is as rotten as mine is; as rotten as yours is. It is a mean town, a hard, stingy town, and hasn't a virtue in the world but this honesty it is so celebrated for and so conceited about; and so help me, I do believe that if ever the day comes that its honesty falls under great temptation, its grand reputation will go to ruin like a house of cards. There, now, I've made confession, and I feel better; I am a humbug, and I've been one all my life, without knowing it.

Obsessive vanity and insulated disuse, then, have made Hadleyburg's honesty artificial and hypocritical: much like Huck Finn's attitude toward slavery, it is largely an untested abstraction; it is almost entirely divorced from the townspeople's hearts. In short, the training of the people of Hadleyburg has shaped their consciences to an awareness of the moral ideal of honesty, but it has given them no experience in following the directions of conscience and therefore no true knowledge of its values.

Seeing in the people of Hadleyburg what they cannot see in themselves or, like the Richardses, see too late, the vindictive stranger directs his ingenious revenge at their most vulnerable spot—the greed for wealth and social position in hearts whose inexperience in resisting temptations to dishonesty has left them no answering passion for true honesty. That Hadleyburg falls, that all of the Nineteen succumb, is therefore not surprising. Nor is their subsequent sense of guilt, as reflected in the Richardses, at all inconsistent. Both are corollaries of Twain's concept of determinism; ironically, paradoxically, Hadleyburg's fall is determined by the abstract training which the people had counted on to keep them forever incorruptible; and their consciences, whose moral perceptions also stem from that training, cause them to feel guilt and shame.

In the end, of course, Hadleyburg learns the meaning of its mistakes: that only through experience can the moral perceptions of conscience be united with the emotions which motivate man. Moreover, this is also the significance of the story's central conflict as Twain develops it through the Richardses. From the beginning he defines this conflict largely in terms of the relationship between the Richardses' consciences and their hearts, an evolving relationship synthesizing most of his earlier concepts of conscience.

At times, Richards's conscience operates like Tom Sawyer's; that is, it makes moral distinctions and influences him to commensurate action. Learning that the town is planning to punish the Rev. Burgess for something which only Richards knows he did not do, Richards warns him. " 'When the thing was new and hot,' " he tells his wife, " 'and the town made a plan to ride him on a rail, my conscience hurt me so that I couldn't stand it, and I went privately and gave him notice, and he got out of the town and staid out till it was safe to come back.' " But Richards's training in honesty has been only prescriptive, and his conscience affects his actions only to the point at which they conflict with the desire for the good opinion of the town, which is the principal element in his basic emotion of self-approval. He warns Burgess privately, and almost at once regrets having saved him; he fears the town will find out and turn its dislike of Burgess against him. For, as Twain points out in the contemporaneous *What Is Man?*, "Corn-Pone Opinions," and "The United States of Lyncherdom," "the Sole Impulse which dictates and compels a man's every act: the imperious necessity of securing his own approval, in every emergency and at all costs," usually involves not only the disposition to do whatever will gain public approval but also "man's commonest weakness, his aversion to being unpleasantly conspicuous, pointed at, shunned, as being on the unpopular side."

Reflecting Hadleyburg's defective training in honesty, Richards's moral ideals are in this crisis almost entirely separated from his motivating emotion of self-approval. In addition to making him regret having saved Burgess, this basic emotion violates his conscience and prevents him from clearing the clergyman of the unjust accusation against him. " 'I am ashamed,' " Richards admits. " 'I was the only man who knew he was innocent. I could have saved him, and—and— well, you know how the town was wrought up—I hadn't the pluck to do it. It would have turned everybody against me. I felt mean, ever so mean; but I didn't dare; I hadn't the manliness to face that.' " Here, then, though its moral values and demands as well as the emotions it contends with are the reverse of Huck Finn's, Richards's conscience functions much like Huck's in that it exerts almost no influence on his actions but does punish him with a sense of guilt when he fails to obey it.

The stranger's bag of gold evokes in the Richardses and in the rest of the Nineteen the same conflict between the moral guidance and the demands of their consciences and the urgings of their emotions. Despite the warnings of his conscience, each is driven by his desires for wealth, security, and social position to rationalize and then to lie about his right to the gold. "All night long," Twain writes, "eighteen principal citizens did what their caste-brother Richards was doing at the same time—they put in their energies trying to remember what notable service it was that they had unconsciously done Barclay Goodson. In no case was it a holiday job; still they succeeded." Like Adam and Eve in Twain's version of their temptation and fall [in his *Europe and Elsewhere*], the Nineteen "could not understand untried things and verbal abstractions which stood for matters outside of their little world and their narrow experience."

The town meeting reveals the dishonesty of the rest of the Nineteen, but for the Richardses it means only more temptation and further conflict between the values and entreaties of their consciences and their passion for public favor. Twice again they are tempted and twice again they fall. When they think their dishonesty is going to be disclosed, they rise to confess and to plead for the town's forgiveness; but when the generous Burgess silences them and then fails to read Richards's note, they are "faint with joy and surprise" and no longer disposed to confess. " 'Oh, bless God,' " whispers Mary Richards, " 'we are saved!—he has lost ours—I wouldn't give this for a hundred of those sacks!' " Their desire for public approval completely overcomes the demands of their consciences that they confess and justly "suffer with the rest," and once more they succumb to the temptation to dishonesty.

Nor is this all, for they compound their dishonesty when the town proposes to auction off the stranger's bag of gold and give the proceeds to them. Again, their consciences point out the Richardses' deceitfulness and urge them to confess: "at the beginning of the auction," Twain writes, "Richards whispered in distress to his wife: 'O Mary, can we allow it? It—it—you see, it is an honor-reward, a testimonial to purity of character, and—and—can we allow it? Hadn't I better get up and—O Mary, what ought we to do?—'" She, too, understands the moral implications and requirements of their position and replies, "'it is another temptation, Edward—I'm all in a tremble—but, oh, we've escaped *one* temptation, and that ought to warn us to—. . . O Edward . . . we are *so* poor!—but—but—do as you think best—do as you think best.'" This, however, is precisely what he does not do; "Edward fell," Twain declares, "—that is, he sat still; sat with a conscience which was not satisfied, but which was overpowered by circumstances," circumstances of wealth and an intoxicating public admiration.

As the incitements to dishonesty become more tempting, then, conscience in the Richardses, as in the Hadleyburg they reflect, diminishes as an effective moral and ethical force; and finally, much as Twain defines it in *What Is Man?*, it has no moral and ethical function at all. For a while the consciences they have violated cause the Richardses to feel some last glimmerings of guilt and shame and regret: Richards decides to resign his position at the bank, feeling that he can no longer trust himself with other people's money; and both he and his wife are made profoundly miserable by Stephenson's note praising their honesty. But these feelings soon die, and the Richardses' sense of guilt becomes a matter not of morality but of exposure; "within twenty-four hours after the Richardses had received their checks," Twain writes, "their consciences were quieting down, discouraged; the old couple were learning to reconcile themselves to the sin which they had committed. But they were to learn, now, that a sin takes on new and real terrors when there seems a chance that it is going to be found out. This gives it a fresh and most substantial and important aspect."

Fearing the exposure of their dishonesty, the Richardses are no longer concerned with the moral values and responsibilities of their situation. The separation between their ideal of honesty and their motivating emotions is now complete, and their consciences lose all moral and ethical function and become in effect identical with the Richardses' self-approval in its passion for public approval. Conscience now moves the Richardses only to a suspicion that others know about their dishonesty and to fear that someone will disclose it, particularly the suspicion that Burgess knows of Richards's failure long ago to reveal his innocence and the fear that he intends to revenge himself by exposing them.

Tortured beyond endurance, the Richardses sicken and die, but not from any Divine punishment reflected in the agonies of a guilty conscience. They die because they cannot abide the knowledge that their good name may be destroyed and that they may be held up to an even greater obloquy than the rest of the Nineteen. In short, they are no longer aware of sin and guilt as matters of moral principle and individual responsibility; self-approval is their conscience, and its demand for public favor renders them obsessed, like the town they mirror, with the name of honesty at the cost of its essence, which would mean, as Richards realizes in the town meeting, confessing publicly that they have been as dishonest as the others.

Before the Richardses die, however, Twain reveals that they have not suffered barrenly. Their racking fear that their dishonesty will be exposed has rooted the knowledge of that dishonesty deeply in their hearts; through experience, the self-approval which is their conscience has learned moral and ethical responsibility and now makes moral distinctions which result in commensurate action. In Richards, as Twain in Huck Finn implies they must, conscience and the heart, moral perception and motivating emotion, at last function together. Richards's ideal of honesty is rooted in his heart, in the self-approval which governs his actions, and he dies an honest man.

Concerned anew with moral values, he destroys the checks which have cost him so dearly; "'they came from Satan,'" he tells the nurse. "'I saw the hell-brand on them, and I knew they were sent to betray me to sin.'" His self-approval now demands behavior consistent with moral rectitude, and he wants the essence of honesty, not its mere reputation. With his last breath, he admits his guilt—not privately, as in what he had told his wife about Burgess, but openly in a public avowal. "'I want witnesses,'" he declares. "'I want you all to hear my confession, so that I may die a man, and not a dog. I was clean—artificially—like the rest; and like the rest I fell when temptation came. I signed a lie, and claimed the miserable sack.'" Moreover, though he thinks Burgess has exposed him, Richards admits his cowardly failure to save the clergyman from undeserved disgrace.

Experience has made Richards's conscience a highly complex faculty in which moral perception and direction and the motivating emotion of self-approval work together to produce real honesty—honesty which is not simply allegiance to an abstract principle, but honesty expressed in practice against the temptations of dishonesty. Nor is this lesson lost upon Hadleyburg, which learns fully and well what the Nineteen and particularly the Richardses exemplify: the town's new motto, "Lead Us Into Temptation," is not an invitation to sin, but a means to grapple with it empirically. Whatever its new name may be, Hadleyburg is truly "an honest town once more, and the man will have to rise early that catches it napping again."

"The Man That Corrupted Hadleyburg" is therefore neither as inconsistent nor as pessimistic as it is usually considered. In it are reflected the major aspects of Twain's conflicting moral thought—moral values as abstract, moral values as empirical; conscience as the reflector of moral values, conscience as the amoral emotion of self-approval—but these conflicting ideas are reconciled by Twain's determinism into a formal and thematic unity which generates substantial beauty and power. Moreover, the story is in fact less pessimistic than soberly optimistic; it ends, after all, not with the greed, hypocrisy, and cynicism of the town meeting, but with the development of a significant conscience in Richards and in the affirmation of Hadleyburg's new motto. And if Twain shows man as a deterministic creature driven by vanity and greed, he also shows that this is neither the complete nor the final answer to the question of man, that the experience of living can determine man to his salvation as well as to his perdition.

In **"The Man That Corrupted Hadleyburg,"** then, Twain declares with Milton that

I cannot praise a fugitive and cloistered virtue, un-exercised and unbreathed, that never sallies out and sees her adversary, but slinks out of the race where that immortal garland is to be run for, not without dust and heat. Assuredly we bring not innocence into the world, we bring impurity much rather: that which purifies us is trial, and trial is by what is contrary. That virtue therefore which is but a youngling in the contemplation of evil, and knows not the utmost that vice promises to her followers, and rejects it, is but a blank virtue, not a pure; her whiteness is but an excremental whiteness. . . .

Again, Twain argues with [Joseph] Conrad's Stein [in *Lord Jim*] that " 'the way is to the destructive element submit yourself, and with the exertions of your hands and feet in the water make the deep, deep sea keep you up. . . . In the destructive element immerse. . . .' " In **"The Man That Corrupted Hadleyburg,"** Twain's divergent moral and ethical ideas merge in a view of man which places Twain within a great and a positive tradition. (pp. 375-84)

> Clinton S. Burhans, Jr., *"The Sober Affirmation of Mark Twain's Hadleyburg,"* in American Literature, *Vol. XXXIV, No. 3, November, 1962, pp. 375-84.*

I used to tell the story of the Jumping Frog in San Francisco, and presently Artemus Ward came along and wanted it to help fill out a little book which he was about to publish; so I wrote it out and sent it to his publisher, Carleton; but Carleton thought the book had enough matter in it, so he gave the story to Henry Clapp as a present, and Clapp put it in his *Saturday Press,* and it killed that paper with a suddenness that was beyond praise. At least the paper died with that issue, and none but envious people have ever tried to rob me of the honor and credit of killing it. The **"Jumping Frog"** was the first piece of writing of mine that spread itself through the newspapers and brought me into public notice. Consequently, the *Saturday Press* was a cocoon and I the worm in it; also, I was the gay-colored literary moth which its death set free. This simile has been used before.

Early in '66 the **"Jumping Frog"** was issued in book form, with other sketches of mine. A year or two later Madame Blanc translated it into French and published it in the *Revue des Deux Mondes,* but the result was not what should have been expected, for the *Revue* struggled along and pulled through, and is alive yet. I think the fault must have been in the translation. I ought to have translated it myself. I think so because I examined into the matter and finally retranslated the sketch from the French back into English, to see what the trouble was; that is, to see just what sort of a focus the French people got upon it. Then the mystery was explained. In French the story is too confused, and chaotic, and unreposeful, and ungrammatical, and insane; consequently it could only cause grief and sickness—it could not kill.

> *Mark Twain, from his "Private History of the 'Jumping Frog' Story," in his* How to Tell a Story, and Other Essays *(1905).*

PAUL BAENDER (essay date 1963)

[*In the following excerpt, Baender disputes the common interpretation of "The Celebrated Jumping Frog of Calaveras County" as a Southwestern frame-story, presenting it instead as a humorous regional sketch that is artfully modified.*]

"The humor of the **'Jumping Frog,'** " wrote Archibald Henderson [in his *Mark Twain* (1911)], " . . . is the savage and naïve humor of the mining camp, not the sophisticated humor of civilization" [see Further Reading list]. This merging of the sketch with a geographical area and a social group is typical, and even critics who defend Twain as a conscious artist do not question it. It follows from a principle well known to readers of Frederick Jackson Turner, that a man on the frontier enters into a relationship with the environment so close as to make him a symbol of its qualities, a realization of its latencies for politics and character. His works and acts contain cultural implications which may have nothing to do with his will or deliberate consciousness but which these cannot deny. Thus two recent critics, Paul Schmidt and Kenneth S. Lynn [see Further Reading list for both], regard the **"Jumping Frog"** as a parable illustrating cultural antagonisms between the East and the Frontier. The frame narrator and Simon Wheeler engage in a contest of innuendo and insult, the narrator standing for eastern gentility and Simon Wheeler representing a western "vernacular community" (Schmidt), like the author himself. "The basis of [Wheeler's] and Clemens's values," Schmidt says,

> is community established in common work and play. . . . Wheeler polarizes the values generated by community, as against the inept and grotesque isolation of individualism. . . . Clemens's story ultimately asserts the superiority of vernacular brotherhood over the competitive individualism which animates genteel attitudes.

The frame narrator, on the other hand, stands for the "competitive and hostile individualism of the genteel." He holds the assumptions of "an eastern traveler in the West, the assumptions which make up the complicated Enlightenment case of Civilization versus Nature, England and the Continent versus America, Boston versus the West." Thus Simon Wheeler's tale about the defeat of Jim Smiley, whose assumptions are much the same as the narrator's, is a subtle rebuke by a cunning frontiersman only pretending to be fatuous, a rebuke so subtle as to make the narrator miss the point when he retells the story.

The chief support for such an interpretation is the southwestern frame-story tradition. During the thirty-five years before the **"Jumping Frog"** southwestern humorists commonly wrote sketches purporting to be travelers' accounts of their adventures among rustics and poor whites. One of the stereotypes they developed was the frame story. After giving necessary background information the traveler introduced the rustic, who would proceed to deliver a short and usually humorous narrative. Writers often capitalized on the juxtaposition of literate traveler and colloquial rustic, exaggerating their differences of manners and speech to suggest cultural absurdities in one or the other or both. Some writers also contrived little contests between the traveler and the rustic in which the rustic deceived the traveler with a tall tale, thereby showing him up as a naïve gull. At first sight the **"Jumping Frog"** seems to fit neatly in this tradition, and Lynn, who accepts Schmidt's interpretation for the most part, quite explicitly makes the connection. A literate traveler has been asked by a "friend . . . in the East" to look up Simon Wheeler in Angel's Camp to discover the whereabouts of a certain Rev. Leonidas W. Smiley. He finds Simon Wheeler in a saloon, puts his question, and then stands by impatiently while Simon delivers a long series of anecdotes about a gambler named *Jim* Smiley. The traveler finally escapes by breaking off Simon Wheeler's tale with an interjection and suddenly walking away. Everything appears conventional so far as the summary goes. Speaking in dialect, a rustic tells a traveler a tall tale, and their differing attitudes toward it seem to indicate cultural divergences. Simon Wheeler talks with "impressive earnestness and sincerity," out of respect for Jim Smiley, while the traveler despises the old man's "monotonous narrative." The next step, one might think, is to infer a deliberate deadpan for Simon Wheeler and an effete gentility for the traveler-narrator. Thus eventually one might come out with an opposition between the East and the Frontier according to a common bias of southwestern humor and of local color sketches from the middle and far west.

But by the time Twain wrote the **"Jumping Frog"** the vogue of the southwestern frame story had declined, and his reason for using it in 1865 had more to do with his observation of literary comedians than with his southwestern heritage. In 1864, speaking of an inept tragic actor, Twain said ironically that he possessed "the first virtue of a comedian, which is to do funny things with grave decorum and without seeming to know that they are funny." Years later he was to elaborate upon this criterion in his well-known manifesto, "How To Tell a Story." Stating once again that the "humorous story is told gravely" and that the teller should "conceal the fact that he even dimly suspects . . . there is anything funny," Twain would prize the manner still more: "The humorous story is strictly a work of art—high and delicate art—and only an artist can tell it." Not long before this pronouncement he also described the man he heard tell the frog story at Angel's Camp early in 1865: "He was a dull person, and ignorant; he had no gift as a story-teller, and no invention . . . he was entirely serious, for he was dealing with what to him were austere facts . . . he saw no humor in his tale . . . none of the party was aware that a first-rate story had been told in a first-rate way." Twain already knew in 1864 and 1865 how effective humorous gravity could be, for it was basic to Artemus Ward's expertise on the lecture platform, and it was precisely this oral effect that Twain tried to get through the southwestern frame story. Unfortunately he never fully explained his taste or said what cultural significance, if any, he associated with the deadpan manner. But we can tell from his silence in this regard what things not to look for, and one of them is deliberateness in Simon Wheeler and the narrator of the **"Jumping Frog,"** on the assumption that they possess the psychology or class consciousness of the more familiar sorts of characters in fiction.

The relevance of the southwestern frame story to Twain's interest is clear. It gave him, in the narrator, a conventional and unobtrusive means to emphasize at the outset Simon Wheeler's "impressive earnestness and sincerity," and thus to suggest the mode of delivery readers should imagine when Wheeler starts talking. In 1865 Twain was in fact too eager to exploit this advantage. He had the narrator say, after mentioning Wheeler's gravity, that "the spectacle of a man drifting serenely along through such a queer yarn without ever smiling was exquisitely absurd." This was to insist on the humorous criterion too explicitly, and Twain later deleted the statement, recognizing that it was more important to maintain the

The "Jumping Frog" poster, advertising a Mark Twain lecture in Brooklyn, New York, February 7, 1869.

narrator's own seriousness and thereby to exploit another natural advantage of the frame story, the advantage of double deadpan. The only real problem in adapting the southwestern convention concerned Simon Wheeler's story of Jim Smiley. Twain could not have his narrator introduce the tale as "monotonous" and then proceed with something like the **"Bluejay Yarn"** or even **"Jim Blaine and His Grandfather's Old Ram,"** which take their hyperbolic courses at a comparative gallop. Nor on the other hand could he verge too close on actual monotony. His problem was to create an innocuous bore, so to speak, to devise a sketch that might seem the tedious talk of an old man, boring to the narrator yet amusing to us.

It will help show how Twain solved his problem to describe first the closest analogues of the **"Jumping Frog."** These were two brief sketches published in newspapers near Angel's Camp which Twain almost certainly never saw. The first appeared in the Sonora *Herald,* south of Angel's Camp, in 1853. A Yankee bets on a toad against a gambler's frog, and the gambler wins. Next morning the Yankee is back, offering a larger bet. This time he wins twice in a row because for some reason the gambler's frog can't jump far. " 'My frog is darn heavy this morning,' says the gambler. 'I reckoned it would be, stranger,' says the Yankee, 'for I rolled a pound of shot into him last night.' " The second sketch, longer but hardly more complicated, came out in the San Andreas *Independent,* north of Angel's Camp, in 1858. Its hero is a chronic but knuckleheaded gambler who is usually broke because he falls for con games like thimblerig and French monte. He catches a frog and bets him against an innkeeper's frog. He wins this bet but next morning, with the bet doubled, the innkeeper wins because the gambler's frog won't jump. The crowd is puzzled until a shrewd spectator called "Old Weasle-eye" picks up the frog and squeezes out a load of buckshot. The sketch ends with the roars and yells of the crowd as the gambler's coat tails disappear behind the next hill. These two sketches are what Twain would call comic stories. They count upon the matter of the ironic frog race for their effect, not upon the manner of the telling. They pretend to no gravity, and the first sketch as well as the second stresses its comic point through a chorus of onlookers who roar and laugh. While the humorous story typically rambles on at some length, these are quite short and would be shorter except that they must prepare for the buckshot trick. They are the barest embodiments of the reversal of fortune, a commonplace of folklore.

These sketches are important partly because they add to the evidence that most of Simon Wheeler's anecdotes about Jim Smiley were Twain's invention, from which we may infer a motive. The analogues show that in the five years between them, over the thirty or so miles from Sonora through Angel's Camp to San Andreas, the frog story did not develop much and hardly became one example among others in an expanded career of the gambler. It does not seem likely, therefore, that the considerable expansion in Wheeler's yarn occurred before Twain arrived in the Sierra foothills six years after the San Andreas version. The analogues also point us to the special quality of the gambler's career in Twain's sketch. While they try for irony, Twain plays it down as far as possible. In addition to the frog episode he had Simon Wheeler mention cat fights, chicken fights, birds on a fence, Parson Walker's powers as a preacher, the wandering straddlebug, the health of Parson Walker's wife, the asthmatic horse, the bull pup and the "yaller one-eyed cow that didn't have no tail, only just a short stump like a bannanner"—examples, like the frog, of Jim Smiley's gambling addiction. An obvious point of so many examples, all preceding the frog except the last, is to avoid ordinary narrative patterns of climax or of rise and fall. To this end Twain took the precaution of ordering Smiley's victories and defeats in a fairly hodgepodge way. His defeat in the frog episode follows a defeat which follows a victory, and we do not know the upshot of the "one-eyed cow" because the narrator leaves before Wheeler can do more than mention her.

The sequence implies Simon Wheeler's earnest strain, so tedious to the narrator. When Simon begins his irrelevant account in response to the question about Rev. Leonidas W. Smiley, it is only Jim Smiley's eccentric habit and his luck that interest him. But as he moves along, this interest matures into a respectful concern for Jim, his animals, and the circumstances of their contests. With each example the concern increases, consummating itself through the evocation of increasingly minute detail which in turn becomes the object for still further respect. When we reach the bull pup and the frog, Simon is bestowing heroism everywhere with homeric abandon. The animals are geniuses with elevating names, Andrew Jackson for the pup and Dan'l Webster for the frog, and their most poignant contests must be described not because they illustrate Smiley's habit but because they are dramatic and astonishing. These creatures even deserve simile: the pup's "underjaw'd begin to stick out like the fo'castle of a steamboat

and his teeth would uncover and shine like the furnaces"; the frog whirled in the air "like a doughnut" and landed "like a cat" or "solid as a gob of mud"; and when weighted down with the buckshot, he heaves his shoulders "so—like a Frenchman." In his example of the frog Simon Wheeler recreates the dialogue between Smiley and the stranger—full of "he says" and then "Smiley says"—and at this point his account is like that of the "long, lanky man" in *Huckleberry Finn* who recreates Sherburn's killing of Boggs by going through the motions himself—aiming his cane like Sherburn aiming his pistol, shouting "Bang!" and falling backward the way Boggs did.

The sequence also imitates a sober and mindless infatuation. The end of each example is a natural pause, where Simon might snap out of his indulgence and remember the narrator's question about Rev. Smiley, yet each time he moves up to a plateau of more systematic irrelevance. But the pattern of his yarn does not devastate our interest as the real thing would because the monologue is at the same time a brilliant comic invention. Its structure is in fact a condition of its brilliance as well as an image of tediousness. For though we recognize the kind of discourse and can guess that example will follow example, we cannot predict their nature or detail. Each example is wilder and more exact than the previous, it turns out, and thus the yarn amounts to a series of toppers. Meanwhile, according to the narrator's opening statement, he is rigidly impatient at Simon Wheeler, who has "never changed his voice from the gentle-flowing key [and] never betrayed the slightest suspicion of enthusiasm." We, however, are led only to suppose his boredom. We may regard the serial structure and Wheeler's manner as tedious under ordinary circumstances, and so far the narrator's response is understandable. But the circumstances are far from ordinary; what the narrator claims to be dull turns out amusing, and the discrepancy of responses is so thorough as to suggest an opposition of tempers, not just of moods. The narrator and Simon Wheeler represent the sober and the rigid, we say (recalling our Bergson), while we are the volatile and sensitive, for whom the humorous sketch is an exclusive reward of perception. If any contest is to be associated with the **"Jumping Frog,"** the winner is not frontier democracy or eastern gentility but the reader, not Wheeler or the narrator but ourselves.

In this respect also the **"Jumping Frog"** reveals its artificiality with regard to the southwestern tradition. The reader's superiority to characters had always been a common option of southwestern sketches, yet it was more definitely a class superiority—or a superiority to classes—than is our response to the **"Jumping Frog."** Take "The Big Bear of Arkansas" (1841) [by Thomas Bangs Thorpe], for example. Several men from various regions are relaxing in the lounge of a Mississippi steamboat when Jim Doggett, an Arkansas frontiersman, suddenly enters, disarms the group with his pleasant manner, and eases himself into a tall-tale account of the tremendous flora and fauna of Arkansas. Some of the men are doubters, particularly a "cynical-looking Hoosier" and a " ' live Sucker' from Illinois"; only a "gentlemanly foreigner . . . suspected to be an Englishman on some hunting expedition" is credulous from the start. But Doggett wins all of them over with his anecdote of the "Big Bar" hunt, after which everyone sits in "grave silence," sharing a spooky uncertainty as to whether Doggett actually killed the bear or he " *died when his time come.* '" In this way Thorpe brings the conventional interplay of regional characters to a rather subtle conclusion. At first, like so many other frame-story rustics, Doggett exaggerates his matter and manner to confuse the outsiders and indulge in the regional brag their presence calls for. Yet he loses himself in his own fantasy: his account of the "Big Bar" is so agonistic and so successful among the outsiders that, given a comic credulousness of his own, he too becomes absorbed in its hyperbolic issue. Thus regional and class lines have apparently been crossed by the very style through which Doggett meant to stress them. The irony is only apparent, however, for the common mood of gravity is a function of the regional differences, which are as strict at the end as at the beginning. This *plus-ça-change* maneuver is part of Thorpe's humorous substance, and a full appreciation of his humor therefore requires us to rise above regional limitations and be wise in their ways.

But the **"Jumping Frog"** lacks the regional concern that leads to such a relation between reader and sketch. Twain's adaptation of the southwestern frame story demanded at least an appearance of this concern, and the appearance is all he bothered to put forth, by giving the narrator and Simon Wheeler different forms of speech and by placing their meeting in Angel's Camp. The narrator does not claim a cultural identity from his impatience, and we cannot claim it for him since his impatience is not a response to an opposite claim or to a gambit like Jim Doggett's invasion of the steamboat lounge. It is the response of a vaguely middle-class figure to an old man's tediousness, inspired also by the discovery that his "friend . . . from the East" tricked him into the encounter. Simon Wheeler sees no class or regional pretensions in the narrator and has none of his own; he hears the name "Smiley" and the tale follows of course, not as a regional outgrowth but as a fabulous history even for the region. And though Twain distinguished forms of speech, his distinction is the obvious one between dialect per se and standard speech. The narrator is merely literate; Simon Wheeler uses the "Pike County" speech Twain was already developing for the comic urchins and rustics of various regions, San Francisco as well as Angel's Camp. Thus the sobriety of Wheeler and the narrator has no foundation comparable to Thorpe's. Posed at the beginning rather than developed in Thorpe's manner, the narrator's boredom and Wheeler's earnestness are syncopational failures of taste which direct us to the humor that follows. As such these attitudes are rightly gratuitous, for their truly instrumental bearing is toward the contest with our sense of humor, and it might be blocked if they were allowed the implicit apology of a sufficient cause. This bearing is all to the good. Sobriety and deadpan are everywhere around us, and we are more likely to attribute general and lasting relevance to the sketch that presents them absolutely. This is one reason why the **"Jumping Frog"** is still intelligible while many frame stories not much older are as dense as the cartoons in *Harper's Weekly.* (pp. 192-98)

The historical qualifications that apply to the **"Jumping Frog"** apply less strictly to Twain's humorous theory. Many years ago Constance Rourke wrote that it expressed the "tradition for the mask, and for the long procession of dull-looking, unlikely oracles [in the history of American humor]." But though this statement is true, we must be careful once again not to confuse exploitation with simple derivation. Twain never defined the humorous tale as indigenous to a region, nor did he associate a cluster of regional motives with his principle that the humorous story should be told gravely. And when he developed his theory most elaborately in "How To Tell a Story," he said that the "humorous story is American"—not western or southwestern but American.

His very abstraction of the principle, not to mention his silence as to its cultural significance, suggests that he had cut it free from wherever it may have been a customary mannerism and that he considered it important primarily in his professional dealings with a general American taste. This process is familiar, for Twain characteristically moved from the local to the national, from the old to the new, and he was always forced to adapt his heritage when it was relevant at all, answering the demands of the new sometimes by rejecting the past, yet also by saving it in the ways he could. (p. 200)

Paul Baender, "The 'Jumping Frog' as a Comedian's First Virtue," in Modern Philology, *Vol. LX, No. 3, February, 1963, pp. 192-200.*

JOHN S. TUCKEY (essay date 1963)

[*Tuckey is an American scholar and editor who has worked extensively with Mark Twain's papers and has served as editor of several authorized editions of Twain's writings. Tuckey is also the author of* Mark Twain and Little Satan, *an influential study of the composition and publication history of Twain's unfinished and posthumously published work* The Mysterious Stranger. *In the following excerpt from both the first and final chapters of* Mark Twain and Little Satan, *Tuckey introduces circumstances surrounding the publication of the initial, Paine-Duneka version of Twain's story, capsules the research of Bernard DeVoto in this area, and then summarizes the findings of his own study, which differ substantially from previous assumptions.*]

The Mysterious Stranger has become recognized as the most important of Mark Twain's later writings. Two decades have passed since Bernard DeVoto, having studied the unpublished drafts of the tale and also many related manuscripts, termed the work a highly "important key to Mark Twain's books" and announced that he hoped some day to tell the story of Mark Twain's writing of **The Mysterious Stranger** [see Further Reading list]. He was planning such a book-length study—one that would throw some light "into many areas of Mark Twain's personality that have so far been dark." But he did not live to write such a book and to share with his readers the fascination of "working on a mystery story" and discovering clues to "the unconscious workings" of the author's mind. Although **The Mysterious Stranger** has in recent years received much critical attention, the times and circumstances of its composition have nevertheless remained largely unknown.

The story exists in three quite different drafts, all in Twain's own handwriting, which were left unfinished when he died in 1910. These are, as named and catalogued by DeVoto, the "Hannibal" manuscript of about 15,300 words; the "Eseldorf" of 55,000 words; and the "Print Shop" of 65,000 words. All of these manuscripts are in the Mark Twain Papers, which are stored at the General Library of the University of California, Berkeley. There has been much uncertainty concerning the direction and tendency of the creative efforts that produced these several drafts; in particular, it has remained doubtful whether the posthumously published tale represents the initial, the intermediate, or the latest version.

Six years after Mark Twain's death, **The Mysterious Stranger** was published as edited by Albert Bigelow Paine, the author's biographer and literary executor, and Frederick A. Duneka, then general manager of Harper & Brothers. For the text, the editors used the "Eseldorf" version, completing the story with a chapter that Paine had found, separate from any of the versions, among the many manuscripts and fragments in the Papers. The setting for the story is the village of Eseldorf, in Austria; the time is 1590, "still the Middle Ages" in a remote and sleep-rounded region. Twain's naive narrator, young Theodor Fischer, explains, "Austria was far from the world, and asleep, and our village was in the middle of that sleep, being in the middle of Austria. It drowsed in peace in the deep privacy of a hilly and woodsy solitude where news from the world hardly ever came to disturb its dreams, and was infinitely content." The place "was a paradise for us boys. We were not overmuch pestered with schooling." But Theodor is destined to discover that Eseldorf (i.e., Ass-ville) is only a fool's paradise. Into the deceptively idyllic setting comes a mysterious stranger, appearing to Theodor and his friends Nikolaus Bauman and Seppi Wohlmeyer as a young angel, unfallen but nephew to the fallen Satan, and bearing the same name. The young Satan has unlimited powers of mind. He discloses that he knows the entire chain of future consequences that will result from any action. He is also able to read anyone's thoughts. Moreover, his thoughts are equivalent to actions; he has, for example, but to think of a journey and it is at once accomplished. Even this power is not the most wonderful of his abilities. "My mind creates," he tells the startled youngsters. "Do you get the force of that? . . . Creates fluids, solids, colors—anything, everything—out of the airy nothing which is called Thought." Before the eyes of his astonished comrades, he makes a group of tiny people, who promptly go to work and build a miniature castle; thereafter, he sets the castle on fire and, when the little people run out, brushes them back into the flames, saying that "they were of no value." And it soon becomes apparent that he regards all men as equally worthless.

Sitting in judgment upon the human race, Satan finds it contemptible: "Man's limited mind clumsily and tediously and laboriously patches little trivialities together"—for a paltry result. Also, the Moral Sense has corrupted man: knowing good and evil, he has the opportunity to choose to do evil. And, besides being mentally and morally of no value, man is physically of negligible worth, "a museum of disease, a home of impurities; he comes to-day and is gone tomorrow; he begins as dirt and departs as stench." Satan takes the boys on instantaneous journeys about the globe, exhibiting to them the frailties and depravities of their species. So wretched is the human condition that, by his calculation, not one life in a billion is worth living; he can do a person no greater kindness than granting him an early death. However, he does have one way of making people happy while they are in life. When Father Peter, the good priest of the village, is falsely accused of theft, tried, and acquitted, Satan makes him believe that he has been "forever disgraced as a thief—by verdict of the court!" The old man's reason is unseated by the shock of this false news; he becomes insane, fancies himself the Emperor of Austria, and is "the one utterly happy person in this empire." When the boys of Eseldorf regret that this contentment has been purchased at such a cost, the mysterious stranger admonishes them, "Are you so unobservant as not to have found out that sanity and happiness are an impossible combination? No sane man can be happy, for to him life is real, and he sees what a fearful thing it is." Illusion is shown to be man's only refuge. Finally, in the closing chapter—the one found and added by Paine—Satan reveals that illusion is, indeed, the basis of existence: *Life itself is only a vision, a dream.*" He tells the narrator, "I am but a dream—your dream, creature of your imagination. In a moment you will have realized this, then you will banish me from your visions and I shall dissolve into the nothingness out of which you made me." And Satan vanishes, after this valediction: "It is true, that which I have revealed to you; there is no God, no universe, no human race, no earthly life, no heaven, no hell. It is all a dream—a grotesque and foolish dream. Nothing exists but you. And you are but a *thought*—a vagrant thought, a useless thought, a homeless thought, wandering forlorn among the empty eternities!"

DeVoto thought that Mark Twain had, in writing the "Eseldorf" version and the "dream ending," arrived at a saving solution of an overwhelming personal problem. He believed that a series of misfortunes—financial reverses, loss of health, the death of his daughter Susy, and the discovery that another daughter, Jean, was an epileptic—had induced a sense of failure and guilt; had impaired Twain's "secret image of himself" and withered his talent. For a period of seven or eight years, he found, the despairing author had tried desperately to regain his creative abilities but had found his "compulsive need to write . . . constantly blocked, displaced, and distorted." He considered the period of lowest ebb of Twain's literary talent to be "the two and a half years following . . . May 18, 1897," when his prose had become "dead" in a "time of impotence and failure." And he believed that "Eseldorf" had been written about 1905, as the latest version of *The Mysterious Stranger* and as the final outcome of Twain's many earlier attempts to create in terms of his "symbols of despair": it was the work "that came through to triumph at the last . . . to achieve the completion denied its many predecessors, the book which we know as *The Mysterious Stranger*." By writing it, DeVoto theorized, Twain had "saved himself in the end" and had come "back from the edge of insanity." "The dream" had been "the answer and the proof":

> Or, if I may so phrase it, we see the psychic block removed, the dilemma solved, the inhibition broken, the accusation stilled, and Mark Twain's mind given peace at last and his talent restored. The miracles, which at first are just an idle game for the amusement of the boys and the astonishment of the villagers, become finally a spectacle of human life in miniature, with the suffering diminished to the vanishing point since these are just puppets, unreal creatures moving in a shadow-play, and they are seen with the detachment of an immortal spirit, passionless and untouched. And so from a spectacle they become a dream—the symbolic dream of human experience that Mark had been trying to write in such travail for so many years.

The thesis of DeVoto as here stated has gained very general acceptance and has been used as a basis for explaining what happened to Mark Twain and to his work during his later years. Nevertheless, the conclusions that have been drawn rest upon assumptions about an unknown chronology. DeVoto attempted to follow Twain's themes "rather by idea than by manuscript," acknowledging, "I cannot be sure that my arrangement is chronological." However, he did perforce make assumptions regarding the times of composition of the writings that he considered, as when he stated that "the themes come together in the end," that "Eseldorf" "came through to triumph at the last," and that Twain, by writing it, "saved himself in the end." It is fair to add that DeVoto stressed that he was making "a report only" concerning materials he planned to examine more fully; it has already been mentioned that his death prevented his completion of such a study.

His preliminary survey had led him to suppose that, in composing the drafts of *The Mysterious Stranger,* Twain had written first the "Hannibal" version as a "fumbling and tentative" account of "marvelous works done by the young angel for the admiration and stupefaction of the village"; later the "Print Shop" version, including a shop "such as young Sam Clemens worked in," but with the scene laid in Austria during the Middle Ages; and finally the "Eseldorf" version, using again the Austrian setting but this time bringing the story to a successful completion, "after it had been painfully written over and changed and adjusted and transformed." Actually, DeVoto's thesis—that Twain, after a long period of literary impotence, had restored his talent in writing "Eseldorf"—*required* the assumption that this version had been written quite late in Mark Twain's lifetime. This assumption ran counter to what Paine had recorded relative to the dating of *The Mysterious Stranger.* In discussing the writing that Twain had been doing at the beginning of 1898, much of which did not then "find its way into print," Paine mentioned in his *Biography* [see Further Reading list] the existence of "three bulky manuscripts" in which the author had "attempted to set down some episodes in the life of one 'Young Satan,' a nephew, who appears to have visited among the planets and promoted some astonishing adventures in Austria several centuries ago." Paine had perhaps not yet examined these materials closely (he did not undertake the editing and publication of *The Mysterious Stranger* until several years later). In only one of the existing versions—the "Eseldorf"—is Satan a nephew. Paine does not in the *Biography* attempt any specific dating of these manuscripts, but his reference to them at this point indicates his belief that Twain had worked upon a story of "Young Satan"—or, more particularly, "Eseldorf"—early in 1898. Later, in an introduction that he wrote for the Definitive Edition, Paine said flatly that *The Mysterious Stranger* "was written at Vienna, during the early part of 1898." He further stated that Twain "made three extended attempts at this story, and one of them—the first, and by far the best—he brought very nearly to conclusion. Then he put these various beginnings away and did not examine them again for many years." Paine also recalled that Twain had on one occasion at Stormfield (his home at Redding from June, 1908, until his death) told him, "I always had a good deal of fancy for that story of mine, *The Mysterious Stranger.* I could finish it, I suppose, any time, and I should like it some day to be published." Then, Paine related, "a considerable time after his death—after the publication of my biography of him . . . I found among a confusion of papers that tremendous final chapter, which must have been written about the time of our conversation. It may even have been written prior to that time, laid aside, and forgotten." Finally, in editing *Mark Twain's Notebook,* which was published in 1935, Paine partly contradicted his earlier statements. He spoke of Twain's entry regarding a "little Satan Jr. who came to Hannibal," which had been noted late in the fall of 1898, as a "hint of the story of *The Mysterious Stranger* which he presently began and partly finished, in three different forms." This account of the matter is, of course, incompatible with the previous assertion that the published story, and thus "Eseldorf," had been written in "the early part of 1898."

DeVoto readily discounted or disregarded Paine's remarks, for he considered that Paine had not understood the significance of the later manuscripts and had not adequately dealt with them. Yet DeVoto regarded his own conclusions as only tentative. No doubt, had the time been given to him, he would have proved or disproved his own theory that the "Eseldorf"

version was the last draft of *The Mysterious Stranger* and the work by which, after repeated literary failures, "the fallen angel of our literature, the mysterious stranger who seemed only a sojourner in the cramped spaces of our mortal world, saved himself in the end." Since the publication of those preliminary findings, no one has confirmed or refuted them by determining the actual chronology of Twain's writing of *The Mysterious Stranger* and showing the personal and literary significance of his work upon the story.

The present book is the product of an intensive study of the three holographic versions and of other manuscripts and fragments written by Twain after 1895. His working notes, marginalia, notebooks, autobiographical dictations, correspondence, and published works have also been considered, as well as relevant critical and biographical studies. The findings differ from what has heretofore been supposed, indicating a chronology that is substantially the reverse of the one assumed by DeVoto. Mark Twain, it will be seen, began "Eseldorf" not as the last but as the first of the existing versions. Indeed, he wrote the greater part of it during the two-and-one-half-year period that DeVoto believed had been most of all the "time of impotence and failure," the "time of desolation whose symbol he was not yet able to forge," and thus, according to DeVoto's theory, at a time when he should have lacked the talent to write it. (pp. 9-15)

• • • • •

The findings of this study are here summarized, showing the order and approximate times of composition of the existing versions of *The Mysterious Stranger:*

"Pre-Eseldorf" pages (included in "Eseldorf" as pages 53, 56-72, 74)*	October, 1897
"Eseldorf," pages 1-52, 54-55, 73, 75-85, 377-386	November, 1897—January, 1898
"Hannibal"	November—December, 1898
"Eseldorf," continued	
Pages 86-228	May—October, 1899
Pages 229-376, 387-423	June—August, 1900
"Print Shop"	
Pages 23-110	November, 1902—October, 1903
Pages 111-432	January—June, 1904
Six-page fragment ("Conclusion of the book")	February—June, 1904
Pages 433-587	June—July, 1905
Eight-page fragment ("added" chapter)	September, 1908

*Page 58½, inserted by Mark Twain in the sequence of pages 56-72, was not a part of the "pre-Eseldorf" draft.

These findings show that Mark Twain was intermittently engaged in writing the several manuscripts over a period of nearly eleven years. *The Mysterious Stranger* was the story that he most persistently worked on during this time; he returned to it repeatedly, almost as often changing the plot and the locale in his attempts to find the right form for the tale.

It is clear, however, that *The Mysterious Stranger* as published does not represent Mark Twain's intention. In view of the extensive editorial omissions and additions, the published text cannot even be regarded as his intended form of "Eseldorf." Furthermore, he abandoned that version after doing his last work upon it in 1900; thereafter he used the first chapter as the beginning of "Print Shop." He composed the latter story as the latest and also the longest of the versions, and the only one which he carried to a conclusion. Moreover, "Print Shop" is the manuscript that Twain himself called "The Mysterious Stranger." He so named it when he began writing it and so identified it when he did his last work upon it.

It is also evident that the actual order of composition of the versions is very nearly the reverse of the one that was assumed by DeVoto, who supposed that Twain had written first "Hannibal," then "Print Shop," and finally "Eseldorf." "Eseldorf" was actually written, not as the final draft of the story by which the author "saved himself in the end," but as the first of the existing versions; it was written during the years 1897-1900 and thus during the period that DeVoto believed had been a "time of desolation whose symbol he was not yet able to forge."

The "dream ending" chapter, it is clear, was not intended for "Eseldorf," to which it was joined in the published version. Composed in 1904, some three and one-half years after Mark Twain had abandoned "Eseldorf," it was written as an anticipated conclusion for "Print Shop," while he was in the middle of his work on that version. It is not surprising, therefore, that E. S. Fussell has found in *The Mysterious Stranger* "striking contradictions" which "cannot easily be dismissed" [see excerpt dated 1952].

It appears that much that has been supposed about *The Mysterious Stranger,* and indeed about Twain's later period, may have to be reconsidered. The theory that he "saved himself in the end" by writing the story that has been published (actually the "Eseldorf" version and the "Print Shop" conclusion) has been widely accepted as a basis for explaining what happened to him and to his literary work. The findings do not support that theory, and there seems to be a need for reappraisal and reinterpretation. It is hoped that this study of Mark Twain's writing of the several versions of *The Mysterious Stranger* will to some degree contribute toward a better understanding of the direction and tendency of his later writings.

Possibly it will be found that an important problem of his art during his later period was one of finding new material—a usual concern of the functioning literary artist but perhaps a crucial one for Mark Twain. The recollections of Hannibal which had served as the base of much of his writing had become temporally, geographically, and psychologically remote from the aging global traveler and unofficial ambassador to world capitals. Significantly, his attempts to use these remembrances in the story of little Satan did not succeed very well. It was when he made use of more recent experiences that the tale went forward strongly. Contemporary events in Austria in 1897 furnished an impetus for the beginning of "Eseldorf"; current military actions in China and in South Africa prompted him to continue that version in 1900 and to "dump" into it other topical material—the diatribe on "The Lowest Animal" which he had written at the time of the Cretan Revolt. News events that followed the death of King Humbert of Italy moved Twain to write the last part of "Eseldorf." And it has been seen that his very work upon his latest version of *The Mysterious Stranger* was evidently prompted by recent news of a children's theater movement. These are but a few instances of his use of current events for story material in "Eseldorf" and "Print Shop"; he used little, if any, of such material when he attempted the "Hannibal" version.

He had long ago taken physical leave of Hannibal—in 1853, or roughly half a century before the writing of *The Mysteri-*

ous Stranger—and had made only a few brief return visits at long intervals thereafter. He had not maintained any really vital connection with the one place in the world most important to his art. The Hannibal memories, once so vivid and compelling, must have "thinned away and thinned away" like the disappearing Philip Traum, until many of them had become ghostlike in their vagueness, their insubstantiality. It is remarkable that Mark Twain should have been able to draw upon his diminishing supply as long as he did. That he tried so persistently to base his fiction upon such memories even when they had aged fifty years and had grown dim and stale suggests that he had perhaps never found any other sustaining basis for literary creation—that is, for his "serious" work of the more deeply and personally meaningful sort.

During much of his adult life he was an illustrious vagabond; once he left his home town, he never put down strong roots in any other locality. Even after his marriage to Olivia Langdon, he remained somewhat a drifter, and the periods of residence in the Hartford mansion might be considered extended sojourns of the Clemens family, who lived a semi-nomadic existence. One of the many paradoxes of Mark Twain's life is that he became a citizen of the world and was in a way at home everywhere, but that he was in a deeper sense homeless. And it seems likely that in the later years his life and consequently his art had become so nearly rootless that he had to depend upon the news handouts of the latest day and hour for literary sustenance. If so, his problem was that of a maker with no adequate supply of material for making anything; it might even be said that his art required the unlimited powers of a creator who could make something out of nothing. It has been seen that these were, indeed, the powers claimed by Satan, the mysterious stranger:

> My mind creates! Do you get the force of that? Creates anything it desires—and in a moment. Creates without material. Creates fluids, solids, colors—anything, everything—out of the airy nothing which is called Thought.

In the final chapter of *The Mysterious Stranger,* after revealing that he is himself a dream-creation of the narrator, Satan informs the latter, "I shall dissolve into the nothingness out of which you made me." His statement indicates that the teller of this tale enjoys a lordly independence of the physical world, of all material.

Pascal Covici, Jr. [see Further Reading list], is no doubt right in feeling that in this concluding chapter "one can still sense . . . an integrated commitment to the artist's autonomy as maker." It might be added that there is an insistence upon an autonomy so absolute as to deny that art must have access to nature, must nourish itself on reality, must have a matter as well as a form. The revealing remarks that Mark Twain made upon returning to America in 1900 deserve further consideration here. When asked if he would be writing an American story, he replied, "You see, I write the story and then fill in the place, like blanks in a railway form. The places don't count so much. The story is the thing." He was then asked,

> But you will give your people some of their own types, with characteristic dialect, will you not? And won't that require you to select your scenes first?

He replied:

> No, not entirely. Even that can be filled in. It is astonishing how much can be filled in. I rewrote one

Olivia Langdon, whom Twain married in 1870.

of my books three times, and each time it was a different book. I had filled in, and filled in, until the original book wasn't there. It had evaporated through the blanks, and I had an entirely new book. I shall write my story, and then lay the scene where I want it, and, if necessary, change other things to suit the places.

It appears that he really did think that he could create with an almost complete independence of places and circumstances. It is hardly surprising that his "original book" (it has been shown that he had lately been working on *The Mysterious Stranger*) had "evaporated through the blanks." What is surprising is that he should have been so confident of his ability to create good literature in a void, apart from any essential background. How could he have so strangely mistaken the weakness of his art for its strength?

Albert Paine, who had every opportunity to know the later Mark Twain, wrote that he "lived curiously apart from the actualities of life. Dwelling mainly among his philosophies and speculations, he observed vaguely, or minutely, what went on about him; but in either case the fact took a place, not in the actual world, but in a world within." Paine also made this perceptive comment:

> Insubstantial and deceptive as was this inner world of his, to him it must have been much more real than the world of flitting physical shapes about him. . . . [Y]ou realized, at last, that he was placing you and seeing you not as a part of the material landscape, but as an item of his own inner world.

Given such a freedom from the "world of flitting physical

shapes," perhaps Mark Twain's art could not have failed to arrive at something like the solipsism that it reaches in the "dream ending." There it is disclosed that the only world is the story-teller's "world within." And what role is possible for an artist who has no use for the outer reality, "the material landscape"? He may be "but a *thought*—a vagrant thought, a useless thought, a homeless thought, wandering forlorn among the empty eternities!"

The same vacuity provides the base, or rather the *baselessness,* of events in the "Print Shop" chapter that Mark Twain wrote at Stormfield as his latest work on the story. The famous dead of many centuries flit by as dim and shadowy apparitions; there is little description, and there is no scenery at all in the "empty & soundless world" that remains as a vacant realm after a fade-away from the last lingering traces of reality.

Yet such an interpretation—that Twain's art lost contact with reality—must not be pushed too far. It has been noted that he could speak of a solipsistic view of life as someone's "foible." And he was probably more at home in the real world than his own words would sometimes suggest. Certainly he recognized the existence of other persons in the world. And it is greatly to his credit that he desired for them the same freedom that he claimed for himself. Dorothy Quick, who as a little girl enjoyed Mark Twain's friendship, has related that once in 1908 when he took her to a circus, Mark Twain became somewhat melancholy after seeing an elephant perform upon cues from its trainer. He remarked that he always felt "sad to see anything brought down from its high estate—or something meant to be great that doesn't know its own power." The elephant, he said, could probably have stampeded all the people who were present; however, it did not know its possibilities and so did tricks at the crack of a whip. And he was further saddened to think how many men were, like the elephant, unaware of their great powers. They toiled at low tasks, as they were ordered, although they had within them, all along, "the driving power of the universe." But he told Dorothy that she needn't worry; that he knew *his* powers—and he would see to it that she knew hers. He was thus proposing to play, in actual life, the role of the mysterious stranger, revealing to a young person the limitless power of the creative mind. One of the things he told her was "No matter what happens, you must write," an injunction that eventually led to the writing of her book about Mark Twain.

Mark Twain was the mysterious stranger. And he played his role wonderfully to the last. (pp. 76-81)

> *John S. Tuckey, in his* Mark Twain and Little Satan: The Writing of "The Mysterious Stranger," *Purdue University Studies, 1963, 101 p.*

S. J. KRAUSE (essay date 1964)

[*Krause is an American educator, critic, and editor who has written* Mark Twain as Critic *(1967). In the following excerpt, Krause presents "The Celebrated Jumping Frog of Calaveras County" as a combination of Eastern political satire and traditional folk humor.*]

Recent analyses of Mark Twain's **"Notorious Jumping Frog of Calaveras County"** tend to stress its projection of the traditional conflict between eastern and western values—or, more precisely, between the values of a gentle, civilized class and those of the frontier. Taking in its broadest potential reference, Paul Schmidt [see Further Reading list] has seen the **"Jumping Frog"** as dramatizing those assumptions which, as he has it, "make up the complicated Enlightenment case of Civilization versus the West." Moreover, construing the tale as "an attack on the genteel tradition," Schmidt holds that it "ultimately asserts the superiority of vernacular brotherhood over the competitive individualism which animates genteel attitudes"; while in Wheeler's story, the tale within the tale, he sees an attack on Rousseauesque romanticism.

Schmidt's analysis seems to involve some high-powered assumptions for a fairly unsophisticated brand of fiction. Yet at least two reasons why the **"Jumping Frog"** rises above its genre are that its simplicity—like Simon Wheeler's—is ironic and its social symbolism—like Wheeler's story—implies more than it asserts. A major artistic consideration is, therefore, the matter of how the inward moving structure of the tale accommodates its outward moving symbolic reference. An aspect of the symbolism that has remained relatively untouched is the extensive satire suggested by Jim Smiley's naming his bull-pup "Andrew Jackson" and his frog "Dan'l Webster." With this in mind, I wish to consider three questions: the degree to which there is a complexity of form in the story to sustain its social implications; the degree to which there is a secondary satire in the story to justify the inclusion of those implications; and the degree to which the satire implies a judgment of the East and West. To explore these questions is to see what Twain accomplished in bringing together the cream of the humor that preceded him. For his **"Jumping Frog"** blends the political satire perfected in Down East humor with the framework and oral techniques perfected in Old Southwestern humor.

Complex as the story is, the question of form—which has never been thoroughly described—is rather easily handled. To begin with, Twain has more than just a tale within a tale. He has in fact at least eight levels of story interest, each of which has several sides to it, so that the design better resembles a nest of boxes than it does a frame. There is 1) the story of the narrator's spoken and unspoken attitudes toward a) the friend who wrote him from the East and lured him into a trap, toward b) Simon Wheeler whom he regards as a garrulous simpleton, toward c) Jim Smiley, the fabulous gambler, toward d) the animals that Wheeler personalizes, and toward e) the stranger who pulled a western trick on a Westerner and got away with it. Then there is 2) the story of Simon Wheeler's attitudes toward a) the narrator and through him and his friend, toward b) Easterners at large, toward c) Jim Smiley, toward d) the animals and toward e) the stranger. Wheeler, moreover, represents 3) the western community at large that is continuously entertained by Smiley's antics. Also there are the attitudes of 4) the stranger, and of 5) Sam Clemens toward the various parties in his tale. Finally, we have the more restricted attitudes of 6) Smiley himself, which are confined to his animals and such persons as he can get to bet on them; and not the least significant attitudes are those of the animals themselves, particularly 7) the bull-pup and 8) the jumping frog.

At the level of story movement, the **"Jumping Frog"** has the same complexity as that of its multiple points of view. Twain employs an order of increasing detail and of ascending absurdity and fantasy. For example, after summary references to Smiley's willingness to bet "on anything that turned up" (a horse-race, dog-fight, cat-fight or chicken-fight), Wheeler tosses in two eccentric types of wager, one on which of "two

birds setting on a fence . . . would fly first" and the second on Parson Walker's being the "best exhorter." These are paired with two other situations, each of which is given in greater detail, and the first of which (number three in the sequence) is absurd and fantastic—Smiley's willingness to follow a straddle bug to Mexico, if necessary, to find out its goal. The last member of the group is crashingly absurd, figuratively fantastic and practically insane, though, based on past performance, completely understandable, as Smiley, on hearing that the Parson's sick wife seems to be recovering, blurts out, "Well, I'll resk two-and-a-half she don't anyway."

In the grouping of mare, pup and frog, one proceeds from lesser to greater detail, complexity and surprise, but mainly from a lesser to a greater infusion of personality, one source of which is Smiley's hanging Jackson's name on the pup (which is connotatively apt) and Webster's on the frog (which is both connotatively *and* physically apt). Therein lies a considerable tale, for when such magisterial names are paired with the descriptions given these creatures, the reader has two of Twain's liveliest and most carefully developed burlesques. More of them in a moment. What should be noted here is the matter-of-factness of the impending satire, which deals with familiar history and can be called forth or not as the reader wishes, since, concurrently, there is so much else going on in the story.

The meshing of structure and satire in the interplay of eastern and western character traits may be seen not only in the sectional names given the animals, but, more obviously, in the various points of view, which polarize specifically eastern and western attitudes, in much the way that Webster and Jackson do. We rather guess that the stranger at the end is an Easterner, and this is borne out by Twain's subsequently having specifically labeled him a "Yankee." He is therefore an Easterner who plays the game of the Westerner and is specifically induced to play it on Smiley's terms, those, as Twain described Smiley, of a "wily Californian." Smiley is taken in by one of his own kind, and by a weakness—his avidity for gaming—induced by the wit which puts him into a class with the stranger. Moreover, as Twain recalled the original telling of the story (that is, original for him), he noted that the Westerners' major interest in it was in "the smartness of the stranger in taking in Smiley" and in his deep knowledge of a frog's nature for knowing that "a frog *likes* shot and is always ready to eat it." The stranger whets Smiley's appetite first by his curiosity (What's in the box? What's the frog good for?), then by his smugness ("I don't see no p'ints about that frog that's any better'n any other frog"), and further by the helpless innocence of his appeal for western hospitality ("the feller . . . says, kinder sadlike, 'Well, I'm only a stranger here, and I ain't got no frog. . . . ' "). At the moment when the stranger is filling the frog, Twain gives us a glimpse of Smiley, out in the swamp, where he "slogged around in the mud for a long time." Being a humor character in the Jonsonian sense, Smiley was duped by his own single-mindedness.

In essence, then, the structure of the Jim Smiley story is that of a moral satire in the classical mold: Smiley's gambling fever led him to relinquish the normal protective xenophobia that guilefully motivated Simon Wheeler in the instructive tales he told about the guile that strangers might practice on simple Westerners.

To this exposure of simplicity in Smiley, Wheeler was an excellent foil. Furthermore, the relation of Wheeler to our narrator, "Mark Twain," recapitulates the structure of moral satire given in the relation of Smiley to the stranger and, with an even subtler grade of irony and one that renders the Smiley story itself ironic. Again the mounting complexity is based on characterization. This in part may be observed from what Twain did with Ben Coon of Angel's Camp, who inspired his sphinx-like Wheeler. Coon, according to Twain, was

> a dull person, and ignorant; he had no gift as a storyteller, and no invention; in his mouth this episode was merely history . . . he was entirely serious, for he was dealing with what to him were austere facts, and they interested him solely because they *were* facts; he was drawing on his memory, not his mind; he saw no humor in his tale, neither did his listeners; neither he nor they ever smiled or laughed; in my time I have not attended a more solemn conference.

If the tiresome earnestness of Coon was what first made the story "amusing" for Twain, in his retelling it, his own storyteller's earnestness is all ironic and "Mark Twain's" comments upon that earnestness make him a butt of the irony. We see more than our outside narrator, Twain, does in the fact that Wheeler "backed" him into a corner and "blockaded" him there with his chair, and *then* reeled off "the monotonous narrative." Wheeler is always several steps ahead of the narrator and never so many as when the narrator thinks him oblivious to the importance of what he relates.

> He never smiled, he never frowned, he never changed his voice from the gentle-flowing key to which he tuned his initial sentence, he never betrayed the slightest suspicion of enthusiasm; but all through the interminable narrative there ran a vein of impressive earnestness and sincerity, which showed me plainly that, so far from his imagining that there was anything ridiculous or funny about his story, he regarded it as a really important matter, and admired its two heroes as men of transcendent genius in *finesse.*

Here is Ben Coon, but with a world of difference in the meaning attached to his seemingly obtuse incomprehension.

The moral satire comes clearly into focus when we see that Wheeler is to some extent the West getting its revenge for the trick of an Easterner, at the same time that he plays an instructive joke on the fastidious Mark Twain, a Westerner trying to outgrow his background in exchange for eastern respectability. His pretensions can be immediately ascertained from his looking down upon Wheeler, from the difference between his language and Wheeler's, and from his failure to see Wheeler's story as anything but long, tedious and useless. The fictive Twain thus stands somewhat in the relation to Wheeler that Smiley does to the stranger.

Twain so completely maintains perspective on his characters that no single attitude can be strictly assigned to him as author. Yet that very condition reflects something of the final complexity of his own personal point of view on the interrelation of eastern and western attitudes. He had shown in the story that neither was morally sufficient unto itself, but that one could strengthen the other attitude, which was the view he would come to both in his life and subsequent writing. The fact that for several years after writing it he could, on and off, approve and disapprove of the **"Jumping Frog"** indicates that he was at first uncertain of where he really stood on the sectional aspects of his story. Not only had he been embarrassed that a "villainous backwoods sketch" should represent him

in the East; he was also disturbed that his wife-to-be might judge him by "that Jumping Frog book," with its distinctively western contents. However, when oral readings began to bring out the richness of his story, Twain recanted and told Livy he thought it "the best humorous sketch in America." The national reference signifies a triumph over sectionalism in his own attitudes, and a recognition that his tale contains both a criticism and a union of eastern and western values. That Twain was fully aware of the complexities of structure and attitude in his story is intimated by his remark to Livy that "a man might tell that Jumping Frog story fifty times without knowing *how* to tell it." For this reason, he went on, "I must read it in public some day, in order that people may know what there is in it."

The **"Jumping Frog"** assuredly does have a good deal more in it than usually meets the eye. Twain said that during one reading, "without altering a single word, it shortly [became] so absurd" that he had to laugh himself. Capital instances of the absurd were the sizable caricatures he had drawn of Andrew Jackson and Daniel Webster.

Twain did not name irrelevantly. Simon Wheeler was a free-wheeling yarn-spinner. Smiley, who was "uncommon lucky," had the perennial optimism of the gambler, which was the optimism of the West itself, and which also accounts for the superstitious naming of the pup and frog. In the pairing of the two animals, we get a western name pitted against an eastern one, a frontier democrat (supposedly) and National Republican against a Whig and spokesman for eastern capital. Added to this is the free and easy irreverence of the West indulging in one of its favorite democratic sports. Thus, Smiley's naming assumes a composite sectional and structural reference. On the one hand, actual correspondences between the animals and well-known traits of Jackson and Webster open up a considerable range of secondary meanings which are related to the basic story by their development of the East-West motif. On the other hand, the satire is functional. For while Twain seems to have been unacquainted with the earlier versions of his tale, he clearly had the imagination to recognize and exploit the vestigial ethos of its times, which Wheeler dates in the opening line of the internal story as "the winter of '49—or . . . spring of '50." In that context Smiley has the mood of a self-sufficient forty-niner; and as a means of dramatizing the assumptions of that mood, Twain endowed Smiley with the "Territory's" compensatory indifference to the values of the "States," specifically to the exalted associations of two high-ranking names in national politics. Indeed, Jackson and Webster were household gods for Smiley's generation, and for "old" Simon Wheeler's too. What better way for the western Adam to declare his worth than by smashing a few idols?

The events of the tale bring to mind some of the leading facts associated with the names of Jackson and Webster. Specifically, the bull-pup evokes the ironies of Jackson's reputation as a frontiersman, while the frog evokes the various flip-flops that characterized Webster's career. As the ironies surrounding Jackson are naturally different from those surrounding Webster, there are differences in the points Twain makes about them. However, with both men the central irony is that neither was what he seemed to have been.

Let us first consider Jackson and the bull-pup. For Wheeler to have had Jim Smiley casually compare his bull-pup with so stern a man as Jackson was to adopt the technique of insult used by the Whigs in Jackson's day when they associated him with the jackass. The technique was one of calculated insidiousness. Not only did the General not have the broad plebeian features of such animals as bulldogs and jackasses; he rather had the thinness, erect bearing and fine features of the true aristocrat that he prided himself on being. The nub of Twain's satire was that regardless of looks, it was how he acted and how he was thought of that counted; and Jackson, of course, had become identified with political democracy despite himself, and even with frontier ruffianism and the devious opportunism of Simon Suggs.

In the pup's pugnacity, his combination of nonchalant confidence with tenacity in battle, his ferocity, his dependence on sheer will, his gambling spirit, his single-mindedness and iron nerve, as well as his having been "self-made," Twain's descriptions directly follow major aspects of Jackson's career. Like Smiley's dog, Old Hickory was the very image of toughness—to use the western idiom, he was just nothing but fight. But much of his actual fighting record was somewhat at variance with the idolatrous view of it. For example, his pointless victory at New Orleans was more the result of British mistakes than of his own military genius; while, staunch friend that he was of Aaron Burr's, Jackson the duelist had gained himself a name for rashness, brutality and peremptoriness, which was corroborated by his campaigns against the Creek and Seminole Indians, and his highhanded tactics in the Florida campaign of 1818, in which he had exceeded his orders. As for his famed truculence, outright brawling, frontier style, as in a dog-fight, was something the aristocratic Jackson—quite unlike Lincoln, for example—would not stoop to. In fact, one of the ironies of Jackson's association with frontiersmen was that while they had made him a celebrated commander, and while there was mutual affection between him and them, in his personal dealings, Jackson disdained to fight anyone of lower station. Nor was Jackson's "indomitable perseverance"—so perfectly symbolized by the bulldog's grip—an unmixed blessing. His tenacity in battle was often in reality a euphemism for his equally well-known "inflexity of purpose," which netted him a hollow victory in his biggest political battle, that with Nicholas Biddle over the United States Bank.

Twain's description of the pup touches on several aspects of Jackson's relationship to the frontier. Take the opening statement about the pup: "And he had a little small bull-pup, that to look at him you'd think he warn't worth a cent but to set around and look ornery and lay for a chance to steal something." With such a look as that, this pup might be Simon Suggs, Sut Lovingood, Thomas Jefferson Snodgrass or even Davy Crockett. However, his look is also an analogue of the legendary flashes of temper with which Jackson was known to have frightened opponents into submission. At the same time, the broad descriptive touches make this dog a caricature of the Jackson whom Whig cartoonists had ominously portrayed as an embodiment of the western frontier—and that is just what the pup was meant to be.

Twain's second sentence about the bull-pup neatly captures the images in which the East and entrenched Whiggery at large viewed the specific threat of Jacksonism: "But as soon as the money was up on him he was a different dog; his underjaw'd begin to stick out like the fo'castle of a steamboat, and his teeth would uncover and shine like the furnaces." In addition to its suggesting the fearful union of savagery with avarice, the idea that Smiley's pup has caught the gambling fever also carries a lurking reference to the stories of Jackson's fabulous exploits in gaming. Over and above other traits he shared with frontier gamblers, Jackson was exceedingly lucky, and in one well-known instance he helped his luck by adopting a special relationship with an animal he owned and bet on.

Twain's most incisive reflection on Jackson involves the manner of his having become a self-made man—a legend Twain explicitly satirized several years after writing the **"Jumping Frog."** Many of the eulogies on Jackson pictured him as a man who had been "born . . . of poor, but respectable parents" and had achieved greatness "by no other means than the energy of his character." *Character,* in Jackson's case, invariably meant "obduracy and vehemence of will." In eulogizing the bull-pup, Wheeler gave a more meaningful account of character. He lamented that despite the inner quality of the dog ("it was a good pup"; "the stuff was in him"; he had "genius"), this Andrew Jackson had not had the chance to make a name for himself. In his last fight, seeing "how he'd been imposed on" by Smiley's mania for garish betting situations, the dog

> give Smiley a look, as much as to say his heart was broke, and it was *his* fault . . . and then he limped off a piece and laid down and died. It was a good pup, was that Andrew Jackson, and would have made a name for himself if he'd lived, for the stuff was in him and he had genius—I know it, because he hadn't no opportunities to speak of, and it don't stand to reason that a dog could make such a fight as he could under them circumstances if he hadn't no talent.

The crucial, and often repeated, question about Jackson's rise to eminence had been raised rather early in his career when Samuel Putnam Waldo inquired, "If he had not talents and virtues, would he not have remained in obscurity?" Twain gave that question an ironic treatment, when, using the same terminology and reasoning, he had Wheeler emphasize opportunity as the instrument of success for persons naturally endowed with talent and goodness.

If ferocity and iron will had made a bulldog of Jackson, the political turnabouts, the desire for pacification and harmony, plus an overall jelly-like softness were even more impressively the Websterian qualities suggested by Smiley's frog. While Jackson in no wise looked like the pup, Webster did resemble the frog. He had the protuberant belly, the length of nose, the black eyes, the high cheek bones and downward sloping face; and, of course, as a speaker, he had both the mouth and the wind of a frog as well as his deep intonation of voice. As politician, he could also display the frog's inscrutable placidity of mien. By such references as those to the frog's flopping down on the floor "solid as a gob of mud," to his being "solid as an anvil" (which in revision became a "church"), to his being "anchored out," and to his looking "mighty baggy" with the shot in him, Twain underscored the staunch Whiggery and solidity of character that had gilded Webster's reputation, while each reference equally implies stodginess and like pejoratives. The frog's jumping was everything, though, for through it Twain illustrated the combination of lumpish conservatism with the hectic, often slippery, politicking that were in reality the alpha and omega of Webster's accomplishment.

Closely allied to jumping are the matters of education and worth, which are its aims. On catching his frog, Smiley "cal'lated to educate him," and he did nothing for three months but "learn that frog to jump." This was more than a superfluous improvement on nature; for with the frog as much as with Webster, jumping was the triumph of an education that brought out what each was most gifted at. A ready learner, Webster developed the highest facility for moving from less to more convenient political positions. Still, for all his education, Webster was five times unsuccessful in capturing his party's presidential nomination, losing to some very ordinary, and, as he thought, unqualified candidates like Generals William Henry Harrison in 1840 and Winfield Scott in 1852. It was really as if the party had looked him over and found no points about Webster that made him any better than any other candidate.

But, fortunately for a man who had made a career of jumping, disappointments came as a challenge to his mobility. In fact, the politician's sense of numerous alternatives parallels the Westerner's sense of the vast opportunities afforded by the frontier. Since Webster's one unwavering motive had been to protect the New England business community, no small part of his role was to make the difficult jump or straddle, and, with froglike complacency, not let on that he had overly exerted himself. Additionally, Webster had an intense desire to enrich himself and to seem a man of moral worth.

Keeping in mind, then, the relevance to Webster of such matters as appearance, conservatism, education, jumping, complacency, cupidity and worth, one needs only to re-read the first paragraph about Smiley's frog to see how completely Twain had *done* Webster in almost every characterizing detail. . . . (pp. 562-73)

To know the extent to which the frog's vaunted jumps—as well as his crucial failure to jump—form a compound satire on Webster's favorite maneuver, one need only refamiliarize oneself with the salient points in his record.

One gets a fairly good sample of his dexterity in a few of the jumps inspired by Jackson, whose name alone gave the arch Whig more than one punch from behind. For example, when he heard that Jackson was prepared to use force if necessary to prevent southern states from nullifying disagreeable aspects of the Tariff of 1828, Webster at first objected, and then went over to Jackson's side. Just prior to this, Webster had bitterly opposed Jackson's veto of the bill for rechartering the United States Bank. But that position had not been completely firm, for when Jackson took action against the Bank, Webster was hesitant as to how he should react. He had every reason to support the Bank, but was reluctant to join Clay and Calhoun in its defense because he had been exposing them too recently as enemies of the Republic, and would have to condemn Executive interference with the Bank, after he had just approved Executive interference with the interests of South Carolina.

What was true of Webster's relationship to Jackson was true of his career as a whole. Richard C. Current probably understated his facility when he indicated that Webster "was to spend the better part of his long career in defending principles he had attacked and condemning others he had opposed during his apprentice years." The frequency of Webster's tergiversation placed him on both sides of every major issue of his time—free trade, protectionism, monopolies, nullification, states' rights, the sale of public lands, executive authority, Unionism, the nonexpansion of slavery and the enforcement of the Fugitive Slave Law. As with Smiley's frog, the very breadth of Webster's straddles gave promise of an ability that

would be belied by his performance in crucial tests. When a combination of northern businessmen and southern planters envisioned the possibility of running him on a bipartisan Unionist ticket in 1852, Webster responded by refusing to jump when pressed by friends not to desert the Whigs, and then by jumping in his very refusal to do so by stating that he knew the people would not elect General Scott, and that he himself would vote for his New Hampshire neighbor Franklin Pierce.

From all that one can tell, Twain's private opinions of Jackson and Webster were in some respects similar to those that emerge from the story and in others significantly different from them. He growled about Jackson's responsibility for the practice of using civil service for patronage, and he wished that the Battle of New Orleans had not been fought, so that the nation might have been spared the "harms" of Jackson's presidency. On the other hand, Twain did not let his affinity for Whiggish ideas interfere with his dislike of Webster, whose love letters struck him as "diffuse, conceited, 'eloquent,' [and] bathotic" and who was identified in his mind with the moralizing and empty rhetoric he burlesqued in schoolgirl compositions. With respect to the **"Jumping Frog,"** though Twain's political antipathy toward Jackson exceeded his literary antipathy toward Webster, the character and actions of the bull-pup have much more to recommend them than do the comparable aspects of the frog. Clearly, one reason why the story favors Jackson over Webster, despite the satire on *both* men, is the predominance of Simon Wheeler's point of view over others in the story. What happens, therefore, is that Wheeler's point of view permits Twain to eat his cake and have it: to vent his prejudices in the subsidiary satire and to maintain an artistic objectivity in the primary context of his story.

Twain's use of sectional values likewise reflects a coalescence of external comment (satire) with internal necessity (art). If he seems to favor the West over the East, sectional values are obviously mixed in the un-eastern credulity of the gentleman narrator and in the wryly un-western moral (beware of a stranger) of the frog anecdote. Ultimately, the ideal suggested by Twain's modification of eastern and western attitudes, seems to require a blending of the Whiggish paragon of the self-made man with the realization of it achieved by an Andrew Jackson in the unfettered conditions of the frontier. (pp. 574-76)

S. J. Krause, "The Art and Satire of Twain's 'Jumping Frog' Story," in *American Quarterly, Vol. XVI, No. 4,* Winter, 1964, pp. 562-76.

PAUL SMITH (essay date 1964)

[*In the following excerpt, Smith offers an interpretation of "The Celebrated Jumping Frog of Calaveras County" as "a dark and nearly tragic story" that betrays the first intimations of Twain's pessimistic view of humanity.*]

Much critical effort has been spent on fixing the original date of Mark Twain's darker view of humanity; and as the years have progressed, inevitably, the *terminus ad quem* of his pessimism has regressed, ineluctably: first it was placed in the early 1900's, later in the 1880's with *Adventures of Huckleberry Finn,* still later (or rather earlier) with *The Gilded Age* and the 1870's when the age was, indeed, gilded. However valid some of this critical work has been, to this writer's mind, it has overlooked the true turning point in Mark

Twain's conception of man, one that rests in the hitherto misread and misunderstood tale, **"The Celebrated Jumping Frog of Calaveras County,"** first published in November of 1865.

In this dark and nearly tragic story, most frequently dismissed as a folk-tale with a dash of Western humor, Mark Twain seems to have first become aware of the archetypal and mythic, the deeply autochthonic qualities of his fictional material. In this tale Mark Twain first grasped the great theme of the tragic decline of American culture from its originally noble ideals, associated that theme with the great archetypes and myths of our culture, and reinvested it with a contemporary meaning, a social, political, religious, and ethnic habitation and name.

To read **"The Jumping Frog"** as a simple humorous tale is to ignore utterly the very subtle yet resonant clues which Mark Twain has scattered through his work to guide the perceptive reader to his theme—to say nothing of the very obvious date of this work, November 18, 1865, just seven short months after Appomattox. At the very outset of the story the narrator notes that he has "a lurking suspicion that *Leonidas W.* [author's italics] Smiley is a myth. . . ." And lest our suspicion be not aroused, the narrator tells us of his ineluctable impression, which simply will not down, that what we are about to experience is some "infernal reminiscence," some recorded memory, that is, of an experience in the underworld of punishment and damnation, which calls to mind that later infernal reminiscence of J. Alfred Prufrock (a character not altogether unlike what the Rev. Smiley must have been like) to which T. S. Eliot gave the epigraph:

> S'io credesse che mia risposta fosse
> A persona che mai tornasse al mondo . . . etc.

Finally, it is trenchantly consonant with Twain's penchant for the literary hoax that he should cloak a meaning of terrifying import in this seemingly guileless story of a garrulous raconteur.

The major events of the plot are familiar and need no summary. Briefly the narrator from the East, ostensibly at the request of a friend, is seeking the Reverend Leonidas W. Smiley by calling upon one Simon Wheeler at the tavern in Angel's Camp. The narrator is obliged to listen to a story obsessively narrated by the unsmiling Simon Wheeler which concerns one *Jim* [italics mine] Smiley. This "tale within a tale" begins with an exposition of the latter Smiley's habit of gambling on any thing or event, describes the titular symbol, the frog Dan[ie]l Webster, and concludes with the central incident in which a "stranger" challenges Smiley to a jumping contest, i.e., with frogs, fills Dan[ie]l Webster with quail-shot and wins the contest. In an abrupt return to the frame story, Wheeler is called away, then returns and offers to tell another story and is rebuked.

It is not long, however, before the perceptive reader becomes aware of elements in this tale which are evocative of deeper and deeper levels of meaning and archetypal associations, suggesting that beneath this simple folk-tale, as in most folk literature, there is a theme of tragic proportions. Indeed, even *before* we begin to read, we note the date (1865) which calls to mind now as it did then the issue of sectionalism, that traumatic split in the national consciousness. Later we will see that the issue of the North pitted against the South, often brother against brother, was sublimated in Mark Twain's subconscious; he could not, although strongly Unionist, put down his Secessionist heritage. The historical North-South struggle becomes in this tale a symbolic conflict between the East and the West (which, in fact, was a fact), reified in the struggle between the narrator in his quest for truth and Simon Wheeler in his attempts to conceal the truth from that narrator—the truth of the fate of Leonidas Smiley. One need not labor the point that beneath the contemporary social conflict lie deeper associations with a cultural and mythological conflict: the East, traditional cradle of civilization and fountainhead of Christianity, is here in conflict with the West, traditional direction and place of discovery, the source of mystery, the locus of giants and wizards, the very mystery of the Source, to mention but a few.

Read on this level, of course, we have re-enacted here the old legend of the innocent hero (the unidentified narrator who has yet to win his name and personal identity) on a quest which takes him from the known to the unknown, beyond the pale of civilization (the East) to the enchanted wilderness (the West). Using his wits he cleverly conceals his true mission by saying that he is looking for Leonidas Smiley as a favor to a friend. His quest takes him to the "old, dilapidated" (n.b., perilous) tavern of Angel's Camp (n.b., chapel), i.e., the Perilous Chapel (cf., Weston, *From Ritual to Romance*). Here he undergoes the spiritual trials conventional in the *pathos* of the quest-myth and necessary for the revivification of the Fisher-King figure, impotent, enthralled and lost. That figure is represented by the Reverend Leonidas W. Smiley. A "minister of the gospel," he is a revered Fisher of Men, and like Leonidas, the Spartan hero at Thermopylae, a King of men. His riant surname suggests that in him the hopes of the land are invested and in his rejuvenation rests the chance to turn the waste land into the smiling land it once was.

The climax of the quest comes at the Chapel Perilous when the narrator seeks information from that strangely suggestive figure, Simon Wheeler. Like the Ancient Mariner archetype, Simon Wheeler is compelled to narrate his strange story; but he is a more inimical figure than Coleridge's character. Like the folkloristic *eiron* character, Simple Simon, he feigns simplicity in his unsmiling narration of the tale; yet he is a "wheeler," a "turner," a "changer"; and we have in him the traditional enchanter who works evil through magic spells. It will be remembered that the Tenth Tarot (The *Wheel* of Fortune) pictures Anubis, the escort of the dead, and Typhon, the spirit of evil; who, other than Simon Wheeler, could more appropriately narrate this "infernal reminiscence"?

The tale that Wheeler tells, although apparently irrelevant to our quest theme, in fact indicates its denouement. For all its enigmatic elements, the story of *Jim* Smiley and his jumping frog Dan[ie]l Webster holds the answer to the riddle of *Leonidas* Smiley's disappearance and thus the end of the narrator's quest. The lost Fisher-King was overwhelmed by the all-powerful enchanter in the Waste Land of the West and, as in other folk-tales of fabulous metamorphoses, was changed into a frog. The evidence lies in the artfully chosen names of the two figures; for just as there was a physical transformation of the minister into a frog, so there is a similar anagramic transformation of the letters of their names:

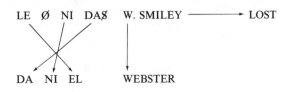

"Daniel" is an anagram for "Leonidas" (veiled slightly by the incongruity of the O and the S) and the W (middle initial) of the minister's name undergoes an expansion into Webster. The surname is "lost" or, more tragically, usurped by the obsessive gambler, Jim.

Here Twain touched upon a responsive chord in American literature, for we have here a declension from the religious (Rev. Smiley) to the political (Daniel Webster) which reflects that great cultural declension in the American Experience from the 17th century to the 18th, a declension from the grail-like vision of the Puritans' "Citie Upon the Hill" to the comparatively bestial concerns of man as a political (Daniel Webster) animal (the frog). Nor can we ignore the irony of this tragic transformation. For the reverend man of God who once, no doubt, preached the doctrine of transformation that was witnessed in the Ascension of Christ at Calvary, there is nothing left now but the cruel parody in *his* transformation and *de*-scension into the living hell of bestiality at *Calaveras*, with its diabolically mocking "ahh" sounds. That the questing narrator is aware of this irony is evident when, no longer able to bear the agony of the Reverend Smiley's degradation, he begs of Simon Wheeler to release his victim by affording him, at the very least, the dignity of a symbolic crucifixion (cf. the Hanged Man) and cries out, "Oh, hang Smiley. . . ." And lest we too easily grasp the burden of this tale, Mark Twain—humorist to the end—adds " . . . and his afflicted cow!'

Yet nevertheless however much a humorist Mark Twain was, he was aware of this tale's tragic significance and would have us share it with him. We need only note that he translated this tale into French and then retranslated it into English. Here then is a clear directive to the perceptive reader of this translation and retranslation of a physical "translation." Mark Twain could give us no more explicit instruction to suggest that we too translate this translation back into its original and mythic language. (pp. 41-4)

> *Paul Smith, "The Infernal Reminiscence: Mythic Patterns in Mark Twain's 'The Celebrated Jumping Frog of Calaveras County'," in* Satire Newsletter, *Vol. 1, No. 2, Spring, 1964, pp. 41-4.*

COLIN WILSON   (essay date 1965)

[*Wilson is an English novelist, critic, and philosopher. With his first book,* The Outsider *(1956), he began a series of works, both fiction and nonfiction, whose central purpose has been to investigate mental and spiritual faculties of an exceptional kind that are latent in certain individuals. These faculties, which Wilson considers visionary, have as their basis the capacity and need to experience a sense of meaning and purpose in human life. The frustration of this need, according to Wilson, is observable in the predominantly negative tone of such modern authors and philosophers as Samuel Beckett and Jean-Paul Sartre. Whereas Sartre's philosophy of existentialism demands a recognition of the basic absurdity and futility of human existence, Wilson's "new existentialism" proposes that "Man should possess an infinite appetite for life. It should be self-evident to him, all the time, that life is superb, glorious, endlessly rich, infinitely desirable." In the following excerpt from an essay in his collection* Eagle and Earwig *(1965), Wilson asserts that Twain's dim view of humanity in* The Mysterious Stranger *casts a shadow over the humor of his earlier works, making it clear "that Mark Twain did not find the world as funny as he pretended."*]

Mark Twain's *Mysterious Stranger* is one of his last works . . . and it seems to confirm the view advanced by Van

---

With the pen in one's hand, narrative is a difficult art; narrative should flow as flows the brook down through the hills and the leafy woodlands, its course changed by every boulder it comes across and by every grass-clad gravelly spur that projects into its path; its surface broken, but its course not stayed by rocks and gravel on the bottom in the shoal places; a brook that never goes straight for a minute, but goes, and goes briskly, sometimes ungrammatically, and sometimes fetching a horseshoe three quarters of a mile around, and at the end of the circuit flowing within a yard of the path it traversed an hour before; but always going, and always following at least one law, always loyal to that law, the law of narrative, which has no law. Nothing to do but make the trip; the how of it is not important, so that the trip is made.

With a pen in the hand the narrative stream is a canal; it moves slowly, smoothly, decorously, sleepily; it has no blemish except that it is all blemish. It is too literary, too prim, too nice; the gait and style and movement are not suited to narrative. That canal stream is always reflecting; it is its nature, it can't help it. Its slick shiny surface is interested in everything it passes along the banks—cows, foliage, flowers, everything. And so it wastes a lot of time in reflections.

> *Mark Twain, as quoted in Charles Neider's introduction to* The Complete Short Stories of Mark Twain.

Wyck Brooks in *The Ordeal of Mark Twain* [see Further Reading list], that Twain the humorist was a mask covering an altogether different personality. The serious American writer of the nineteenth century tended to be a failure: this holds true, from Charles Brockden Brown, whose *Wieland* is the cornerstone of American literature, to Hermann Melville. Even Hawthorne and Whitman could hardly be regarded as successes in any worldly sense. From the beginning, Twain found himself highly popular; he became the symbol of nineteenth-century 'go-getting' America. Everyone loved him; as he walked through the streets, he was saluted with the same affection and admiration that Norwegians of that period showed to Henrik Ibsen. (As Ibsen entered his favourite restaurant, all the diners used to stand up as a mark of respect; Americans are too informal for any such display, but it often came close to it.) In some ways, Twain's natural affinities were with Poe or Melville; but with the example of their failure constantly before his eyes, he never dared to risk alienating his great public. This, at all events, is Mr Brooks's theory, and he makes it sound plausible. When Twain set off on one of his lecture tours, he was preceded by sandwich men carrying boards that read: 'Mark Twain, Ha Ha'. This is enough to sour the sunniest nature.

To some extent *The Mysterious Stranger* seems to us a little too determinedly Swiftian; but its final pages certainly strike a note that would have alarmed even Swift. The story takes place in sixteenth-century Austria. Three boys are playing when they are approached by an angel called Satan—the nephew of the Prince of Darkness, he explains—who proceeds to perform miracles for them like conjuring tricks, creating a castle full of tiny people. He talks to them and they are enthralled—he seems altogether a great and noble being; yet when some of the tiny people fall to quarrelling, he squashes them between his fingers, then when the others begin to wail, crushes dozens of them by hitting them with a plank. But, as Satan points out, he created them, and he can make plenty more; life is cheap; so is death. Then he causes a storm and an earthquake for the boys' amusement, but only so that it affects the castle; and the boys are horrified as tiny men, women, and children are crushed and burnt to death. But Satan does good as indifferently as he does evil, and helps the village priest, who is having trouble with a money-lender and an envious astrologer.

The point of the story begins to emerge when one of the boys mentions the village loafer, who is always beating his dog, and calls him a brute; Satan tells him sternly that this is to libel the animals; they are never gratuitously cruel like human beings. He even objects when the boy says that the loafer's conduct is inhuman. 'No, it is distinctly human', and he explains that men act in this way because they are tainted with a disease called the Moral Sense. By way of driving home his indictment, Twain juggles with time, and makes Satan show the boys a factory in which half-starved women and children work fourteen hours a day.

The boys want Satan to change people's lives for the better; he proves to them that things are best as they are; a boy and girl who are drowned are only saved from lives of misery and sickness. He promises that the old priest shall be made happy for life, and accomplishes this by driving him insane so that he believes himself to be an emperor. 'Sanity and happiness are an impossible combination', Satan explains. In the closing pages Satan comes to take his leave, and reveals the final truth to the narrator: life is an illusion. 'There is no God, no universe, no human race, no earthly life, no heaven, no hell. It is all a dream. . . . Nothing exists but you, and you are but a *thought*—a vagrant thought, a useless thought, a homeless thought, wandering forlorn among the empty eternities.' Satan himself is only a figment of the narrator's brain. The narrator created the universe to avoid the horror of being alone, nothing. But the universe is always revealing that it is an illusion because it is 'so frankly and hysterically insane—like all dreams'. And Mark Twain finishes: 'He vanished, and left me appalled; for I knew, and realized, that all he had said was true.' (pp. 167-69)

[Twain] is repeating much that Shaw said in the third act of *Man and Superman* on the subject of man's stupidity and cruelty and dependence on illusions, but Shaw also took the trouble to answer his own indictment—most of which is placed in the mouth of the devil. The whole tone of the story is Swiftian; having shown that Satan creates and destroys life without giving it a second thought, Twain then shows that human beings themselves can easily outdo Satan. The story is a collection of episodes indicting human folly and cruelty. But one gets the feeling that the author has chosen a sitting duck for his target, and is often scoring rather cheaply. Much of the satire is reminiscent of Shaw at his worst; for example, Mark Twain writes about a woman who is hanged as a witch because 'she was known to have a habit of curing people by devilish arts, such as bathing them, washing them, and nourishing them, instead of bleeding them and purging them . . . in the proper way'. The woman's daughter looks on as she is hanged, and Theodor, the narrator, joins the crowd in flinging a stone at her because he is afraid to appear unlike the rest of the crowd. Afterwards, Satan tells him that sixty-

two of the sixty-eight people were as unwilling to throw a stone as Theodor, but stoned the woman for the same reason. He goes on to draw the moral: human beings are sheep and cowards.

There is obviously much truth here, but still, it is all a little too facile. Satirists have a habit of growing complacent and denouncing human folly with a self-satisfied smile on their faces; this is what happens to Shaw at his worst, and it happens to Twain here. The satire misses its mark because it is not accurate enough, not subtle enough; at times, it is little better than abuse. One then feels that Twain has worked himself into such a mood of violent raging nihilism that he carries the story to its life-denying conclusion without really intending to go that far; he is swept away by his own rhetoric.

The final effect of *The Mysterious Stranger* is not quite what the author intended. Clearly, one of his ideas in writing it was to prove that he was not 'merely a humorist'. In this he succeeds; it is certainly the finest of Mark Twain's stories. But it also makes one aware that the humorous works are not what they pretend to be. From this point of view, the story is a mistake—like a man who pretends to be the soul of tolerance and good humour giving way to a public tantrum. Many English readers find the humour of *Huckleberry Finn* rather hard to take, in spite of the exaggerated esteem in which that book is held by most Americans; there seems to be something forced about it; all its funny situations are taken just a little too far, and its satire is heavy handed. But the reader may be inclined to blame himself for his failure to recognize it as the great American masterpiece that Hemingway claims it is; *The Mysterious Stranger* destroys this doubt, for it makes very plain what one had always suspected: that Mark Twain did not find the world as funny as he pretended. True humour should spring out of exuberance; it should be a part of the genuine character of the humorist; otherwise it makes an impression of bad faith. One also feels that Van Wyck Brooks is right; if Twain had had the courage to write *The Mysterious Stranger* at the beginning of his career instead of at the end, he might have become a truly great writer. (pp. 169-70)

        Colin Wilson, "Madach's 'Tragedy of Man' and Mark Twain's 'Mysterious Stranger'," in his Eagle and Earwig, *John Baker, 1965, pp. 162-70.*

RUTH MILLER (essay date 1970)

[*Miller is an American critic and poet. In the following excerpt, she views* The Mysterious Stranger *as an allegory of Twain's experiences as a writer in which laughter is presented as the saving grace of humanity.*]

The Mysterious Stranger depicts Satan (Philip Traum), who arrives at a small village in Austria and stays on to initiate two youths into a truer awareness of the realities of life. Without any organic plot, the story is a display of episodes to verify Philip Traum's description of the damnable human race. For his amusement he demonstrates to the boys (a Tom and Huck out-pranked at last) the essential human qualities of man: his selfishness, cruelty, impurity, hypocrisy, and worst of all his mediocrity, his dullness. The reason for such damnation is the Moral Sense, man's especial creation, his own insistence upon the distinction between good and evil, his own conviction, born of reason, that evil does exist. This is the indictment. But no final sentence is passed, for Philip Traum says even now there is a way, but only one way, for man to save himself. He may unload his Moral Sense; he does not need to submit. This is stated in the guise of prophecy:

> Someday a handful will rise up on the other side and make the most noise—perhaps even a single daring man with a big voice and a determined front will do it—and in a week all the sheep will wheel and follow him, and witch-hunting will come to a sudden end.

Mark Twain's tale is like a medieval tapestry, or better still a stained-glass window, with its many panels illuminating episodes in the life of Man, all suffering as they oppose the Moral Sense (Marget, Adolph, Peter, the Astrologer, Lisa Brandt), some even experiencing the passion of refusal to live in conventional human terms: the eleven schoolgirls, Frau Brandt, Narr's grandmother and a nameless "lady" are burned at the stake. These disconnected episodes are events documenting the truth of a new Gospel, Satan's Gospel, that the history of civilization is a history of warfare, that the ideas of monarchy, aristocracy, religion and imperialism are all disasters that arise out of a belief in Morality. And finally, the Prophet Satan reveals a metaphysical truth to his two Adams—there is no afterlife, no heaven or hell, no present reality either—life itself is a dream.

Before Philip Traum departs he declares himself to be a dream and exhorts young Fischer to dream other dreams and better. And he gives Theodor a new Grail: laughter.

> Will a day come when the race will detect the funniness of these juvenilities and laugh at them—and by laughing at them destroy them? For your race, in its poverty, has unquestionably one really effective weapon—laughter. Power, money, persuasion, supplication, persecution—these can lift at a colossal humbug—push it a little—weaken it a little, century by century; but only laughter can blow it to rags and atoms at a blast. Against the assault of laughter nothing can stand. You are always fussing and fighting with your other weapons. Do you ever use that one? no; you leave it lying rusting. As a race, do you ever use it at all? No; you lack sense and the courage.

There is vitality in this writing. The conceptions are like the widening ripples in a pool: the stone is the Moral Sense and the ripples are private and social and economic and political and religious and metaphysical realities. The hollows are prisons and factory, dwellings and public squares, towns and cities, France, India, China, hell and heaven. Such expansiveness comes of a toughened conscience, railing and roaring, yes, but not conceding. Injustice and human degradation, yes, but the outcry is virile. For the mood generated by these truths is ironic and one laughs wryly at the satire, and experiences wrath, not despair. True pessimism is limp.

> He (Satan) said he was an orphan. . . . He said he had never known his mama; she passed away while he was a young thing; and said his papa was in shattered health, and he had no property to speak of—in fact, none of any earthly value—but he had an uncle in business down in the tropics, and he was very well off and had a monopoly, and it was from this uncle that he drew his support.
>
> (pp. 25-7)

If we submit *The Mysterious Stranger* to interpretation as allegory we can think of the tale as a myth of Mark Twain's experience as a writer. For "Philip Traum" or "Satan" we can read "Mark Twain"; for all the tricks and theatrical revelations we can substitute his stories; and for the weapon, laughter, a plea to the world to accept the comic writer. This is irony. We are led to contemplate a career and a testament. (p. 29)

Ruth Miller, "But Laugh or Die: A Comparison of 'The Mysterious Stranger' and 'Billy Budd'," in The Literary Half-Yearly, *Vol. XI, No. 1, 1970, pp. 25-9.*

RONALD J. GERVAIS   (essay date 1970)

[*In the following excerpt, Gervais proposes a reading of* The Mysterious Stranger *as an ironic tale in which Satan offers humanity salvation through complete knowledge.*]

(Any critical reading of *The Mysterious Stranger* must take into account John S. Tuckey's findings, "that *The Mysterious Stranger* as published does not represent Mark Twain's intention." *Mark Twain and Little Satan: The Writing of the Mysterious Stranger* [see excerpt dated 1963]. Tuckey distinguishes three separate manuscript versions of the story, the so-called "Eseldorf," "Hannibal," and "Printshop" versions. Tuckey then relates a hair-raising tale of how Albert Bigelow Paine, Twain's literary executor, and F. A. Duneka of Harper Brothers "edited" these manuscripts in the most free-handed fashion, even inventing another character—the old astrologer.

It might then be asked, given these conditions, how can a critical reading be undertaken, since we have a corrupt text. The answer is that there will never be a pure text—none exists. If any study is to be made of the tale, this is the version we must study, taking account of the textual abberrations pointed out by Tuckey and others. James M. Cox [in his *Mark Twain: The Fate of Humor* (see Further Reading list)] has taken what will probably be the definitive stand on the issue of *The Mysterious Stranger* text:

> Tuckey's findings do not invalidate so much as they define Paine's text of *The Mysterious Stranger.* Though clearly 'edited' by Paine, that text just as clearly is not going to be superseded by any future text. In one sense, Tuckey is right in concluding that Paine's version 'does not represent Mark Twain's intention,' since Paine played fast and loose with the versions of the story. Yet the point remains that there is *no* text of the story—that, far from finding his intention as he proceeded from version to version of his story (as DeVoto wished to believe), Mark Twain clearly lost it. . . . Considered from the point of view of 'principle,' Paine took outrageous freedoms. But given the state of the three versions which lay before him, Paine's edition was clearly a brilliant performance.

For the purpose of this analysis, the most important of Paine's editorial crimes to take note of is his tacking of the "Printshop" ending onto the conclusion of the "Eseldorf" manuscript. The "Eseldorf" manuscript ends with Satan's uplifting injunction to Theodore: ". . . I, your poor servant, have revealed you to yourself and set you free. Dream other dreams, and better!" A slight hiatus or "hitch" will then be felt, and Satan begins a curiously anti-climactic tirade against God. He then returns to the idea that everything is a dream, vanishes, and leaves Theodore "appalled; for I knew, and realized, that all he had said was true." But Theodore was not "appalled by Satan's revelations at the conclusion of the "Eseldorf'" manuscript. He felt "a gust of thankfulness," "a great hope," a "blessed and hopeful feeling that the incredible words might be true—even *must* be true." Theodore's being "appalled" simply does not fit in with the tale as we have it. Not only at the conclusion, but all the way through the story, Theodore is filled with ecstasy by Satan's teachings, once he has gotten over the initial shock and grief at feeling his illusions being stripped away. For a discussion of this textual question, see not only Tuckey's previously mentioned book, but his article, " 'The Mysterious Stranger': Mark Twain's Texts and the Paine-Duneka Edition," in his collection, *Mark Twain's 'The Mysterious Stranger' and the Critics* [see Further Reading list].)

As Henry Nash Smith has pointed out [in his "Mark Twain's Images of Hannibal: From St. Petersburg to Eseldorf," *Texas Studies in English* XXXVI (1958)], "the basic situation of an outsider of superior endowments who intervenes in the life of a small, isolated town" occurs frequently in Twain's fiction of the later 1880's and 1890's. But *The Mysterious Stranger* represents an ironic reversal of the underlying themes in *A Connecticut Yankee* or **"The Man that Corrupted Hadleyburg."** In those works, as in the earlier *Tom Sawyer,* innocents fall into the Moral Sense, introduced to them by a demonic stranger. This time it is the stranger who is innocent, and he comes to mock those who have already fallen, comes to mock the very Moral Sense which they now cherish in place of their lost innocence. The basic irony of the story is that the seemingly innocent children represent fallen mankind, while little Satan, who appears to be diabolic, is actually an unfallen angel who can do no wrong. The numerous critics who have interpreted *The Mysterious Stranger* as an educational tale, with Theodore Fischer and his companions as pupils, Philip Traum as instructor, and the absurdity and futility of human existence as the lesson, have not taken adequate account of this ironic relationship between Satan and the boys. For the knowledge that Satan brings does more than sear away their illusions. It also gives them a foretaste of paradise, and alleviates the pain and suffering brought about by the first fall into knowledge. This second fall into knowledge brings salvation, the bitter salvation of death and insanity, but also the salvation of solipsism—for anything can be endured in a dream, if we know it is only a dream.

The portrayal of little Satan as ultimately angelic rather than diabolical can be traced back to the earliest hint of the story, in a "Mr. Brown" letter of June 2, 1867. There Mark Twain reports on an Apocryphal New Testament, seen in a New York library.

> In one of the libraries I have found an edition of 1621 of the Apocryphal New Testament. It is rather a curious book, as one may judge by the titles of some of the chapters: . . . Chapter 15. 'Jesus and other boys play together and make clay figures of animals. Jesus causes them to walk; also makes clay birds which he causes to fly, and eat and drink.'
>
> The children's parents are alarmed and take Jesus for a sorcerer, and order them to seek better company. . . .' 'Sent to a schoolmaster, refuses to tell his letters and the schoolmaster going to whip him, his hand withers and he dies.' 'Kills a boy; causes blindness to fall upon his accusers, for which Joseph pulls him by the ear.' 'The young Savior's resentments were so frequent, and always of so exceedingly prompt and practical a turn, that Joseph finally grew concerned about the matter and gave

> it his personal attention.' 'Then said Joseph unto Mary, henceforth we will not allow him to go out of the house, for every one who displeases him is killed.' His society was pleasant, but attended by serious drawbacks.

Again in *The Innocents Abroad,* Twain also tells of reading about the boyhood of Jesus "from an edition of 1621 of the Apocryphal New Testament," and wonders about the "brothers" of Jesus, "what passed in their minds when they saw this brother (who was *only* a brother to them, however much he might be to others a mysterious stranger who was a god and had stood face to face with God above the clouds) doing strange miracles with crowds of astonished people for witnesses?" For more than thirty years Twain carried in his mind these pictures of the boy Jesus, "mysterious stranger," and when he finally made use of them, the portrait had become that of young Satan.

Twain's devil acts and thinks like a god. In the miracles he performs for the boys, he specifically takes over the functions of God the Creator, making fire and ice, then squirrels and dogs, and progressing finally to the creation of "a crowd of little men and women the size of your finger." Soon he has set a miniature world in motion, with "five hundred of these toy people swarming briskly about and working diligently and wiping the sweat off their faces as natural as in life." But by creating this spectacle of the human race in miniature, little Satan is also acting like a devil; for it is an educational exhibit, and the devil's function is to bring knowledge to man. By diminishing human suffering to the status of a Punch and Judy show, Satan provides the detached viewpoint from which the boys can begin to endure and ultimately transcend this suffering. From this beginning, suffering is reduced to the vanishing point, then passes over into a sense of dream and release from this life.

The object of Satan's terrestrial extension course is to expose and destroy the Moral Sense, which epitomizes the absurdity and futility of human existence. But Satan's purpose is not just to cruelly strip the children of their life-sustaining illusions. Evidence of the ultimately salvationist and messianic character with which Twain has imbued Satan can be found in the so-called "Hannibal" version of *The Mysterious Stranger* manuscripts. In that version, little Satan, called by the strange name of "44," was to rid man of the Moral Sense, so that the race might be guiltless and happy. He was to start his own Anti-Moral Sense Church and to have his little devil brothers print his "bible" for him—proclaiming such ideas as Mark Twain expressed in *What is Man?* (which in his later years he often termed his "gospel").

Unlike his uncle, the old Satan who had come earlier, little Satan comes not to flatter humans and to cajole them into the Moral Sense but to mock them for this acquisition. From the heights of his angelic innocence, he looks down scornfully on man's fallen condition, and his ridiculous Moral Sense. "And when he talked like that about" the Moral Sense, says Theodore Fischer, "it wounded me, and I felt as a girl feels who thinks her dearest finery is being admired and then overhears strangers making fun of it." The stranger continues to make fun of the Moral Sense, and in one of his finest moments, he upbraids Theodore for referring to a sadistic torture as "brutal."

> No brute ever does a cruel thing—that is the monopoly of those with the Moral Sense. When a brute inflicts pain he does it innocently; it is not

Twain's daughters—Clara, Jean, and Susy (from left)—with the family dog, Flash, on the steamboat-deck porch of their home in Hartford, Connecticut.

wrong; for him there is no such thing as wrong. And he does not inflict pain for the pleasure of inflicting it—only man does that. Inspired by that mongrel Moral Sense of his! A sense whose function is to distinguish between right and wrong, with liberty to choose which of them he will do. Now what advantage can he get out of that? He is always choosing, and in nine cases out of ten he prefers the wrong. There shouldn't be any wrong; and without the Moral Sense there couldn't be any. And yet he is such an unreasoning creature that he is not able to perceive that the Moral Sense degrades him to the bottom layer of animated beings and is a shameful possession.

In a similar spirit, Satan later says of a bullock that "he wouldn't drive children mad with hunger and fright and loneliness, and then burn them," as the witch-hunters of Eseldorf have done. "For he is not be-smirched with the Moral Sense, but is as the angels are, and knows no wrong, and never does it." Even when the Moral Sense is not manifesting itself in such direct brutalities as inquisitions and witch-hunts, it is still evident in such refined forms as the profit-system. Viewing the horrors of a French factory, Satan simply comments: "It is some more Moral Sense."

> The proprietors are rich, and very holy; but the wages they pay to these poor brothers and sisters of theirs is only enough to keep them from dropping dead with hunger. It is the Moral Sense which teaches the factory owners the difference between right and wrong—you perceive the result. They think themselves better than dogs. Ah, you are such an illogical, unreasoning race! And paltry—oh, unspeakably!

In Twain's earlier works, Satan's charge would probably have been directed only toward the adult world. But Twain can no longer depend upon his boys for the saving grace, and now they too share the curse of the Moral Sense. Theodore tells how Eseldorf had tried to extirpate witches, "but the more of them we burned the more of the breed rose up in their places." And Theodore himself then watches eleven little girls "burned at the stake all together." Even though he is disturbed by the sufferings of "a bonny, sweet girl I used to play with," he still concludes that it was "just and right." When Marget and Ursula begin to be suspected of witchcraft, Theo-

dore says that, "we boys wanted to warn them, but we backed down when it came to the pinch." This oft-recurring episode of Twain's fiction, that of a boy helping others in defiance of the community, comes to its sad conclusion here—such a boy no longer exists. In the name of the Moral Sense, the children commit the same cruelties committed by the adults. Theodore admits that he threw a stone at a woman hanged for witchcraft, "because all were throwing stones and each was watching his neighbor, and if I had not done as the others did it would have been noticed and spoken of." When Satan hears this admission from Theodore, he only bursts out laughing, the same contemptuous laugh he directs against adults.

The contrast, then, is not the usual one of Twain's fiction, between innocent children and corrupted adults. The contrast is between the entire human race, both adults and children, corrupted by the Moral Sense, and the unfallen little Satan free from the Moral Sense. Asked why he makes so much difference between humans and himself, Satan replies that, "man has the Moral Sense. You understand? He has the *Moral Sense.* That would seem to be difference enough between us, all by itself," Like his uncle before the Fall, little Satan is blameless and without sin, and he assures the boys that "the Fall did not affect me nor the rest of the relationship. It was only he that I was named for who ate of the fruit of the tree and then beguiled the man and the woman with it. We others are still ignorant of sin; we are not able to commit it; we are without blemish, and shall abide in that estate always."

Thus, in the consummate irony of the tale, it is Satan who is the Adamic figure, with the fallen children trying to tempt him into the Moral Sense. "I had the idea," Theodore says, "of trying to reform Satan, and persuade him to lead a better life." But the attempt to instill the sense of right and wrong into Satan is futile, and the boys later admit defeat. . . . Twain had commented a few years earlier in *Following the Equator* on the pious missionary who shuts up "poor natives in the unimaginable perdition of his civilization," and had commiserated with those natives who, "too late . . . repented that they had traded their heaven for this hell." This sixteen-thousand year old boy angel will be one of the few figures of innocence in Twain's fiction who does not fall into that hell of the Moral Sense. He has the innocence of youth and the knowledge of age, a double perspective which protects him from the boys' missionary work. He has complete knowledge of the Moral Sense, and so is not tempted to experience it.

In this tale where things are the reverse of what they are called, where a devil is innocent, it is only logical that the fallen world should be called "paradise." But although Theodore Fischer speaks of Eseldorf as being "a paradise for boys," it is not a paradise of innocence but one maintained through the Moral Sense that was gained in the fall from innocence.

> We were not over much pestered with schooling. Mainly we were trained to be good Christians; to revere the Virgin, the Church, and the saints above everything. Beyond these matters we were not required to know much; and, in fact, not allowed to. Knowledge was not good for the common people, and could make them discontented with the lot which God had appointed for them, and God would not endure discontentment with His plans.

Gaining the knowledge of good and evil was the gravest of sins. Yet once that knowledge was gained, it was revered and enshrined by the Church and by mankind, and set up as the limit of knowledge. To go beyond it would be another grave sin. With impeccable logic, the tale suggests that if we gained so much that was valuable at the first fall, why not try again. For man can exist in bliss only if he has complete innocence or complete knowledge. He cannot be happy with the partial knowledge which he gained when he lost his innocence. And since that lost innocence is irrecoverable, a continual fall into more and more knowledge is the only salvation. That is what Satan does for Theodore and the boys. "Satan was accustomed to say that our race lived a life of continuous and uninterrupted self-delusion. It duped itself from cradle to grave with shams and delusions which it mistook for realities, and this made its entire life a sham." Thus, Eseldorf, the microcosm of all human existence, is a paradise based not on innocence but on self-delusion; it is a paradise of partial knowledge, with the Moral Sense as its boundary gate, which Satan will destroy by means of complete knowledge.

But while the Moral Sense is of no value in itself, it has one important adjunct which would at first seem to diminish very seriously the value of Satan's educational campaign against it. Besides his lack of a Moral Sense, the most significant trait of Satan in his lack of sympathy for the suffering of others. He crushes the life from two of his mannikins, wipes the blood from his fingers, and goes on talking where he had left off: "We cannot do wrong; neither have we any disposition to do it, for we do not know what it is." He then smashes a crowd of the little people, "just as if they had been flies," and continues extolling his lack of Moral Sense. He finally creates a lightning storm that sets fire to the miniature castle, and when the tiny people come flying out, shrieking, "Satan brushed them back, paying no attention to our begging and crying and imploring." The boys, because they have the Moral Sense, also have sympathy for human suffering even though that same Moral Sense gives them the propensity to *make* people suffer. Later, when Satan takes him to an inquisitional torture chamber to watch a heretic having splinters driven under his fingernails, Theodore "could not endure it, and had to be whisked out of there," but "Satan was not disturbed." Finally, at the educational pageant which strips man of his last pretense of value and purpose, the "history of the progress of the human race," Satan watches "wars, and more wars, and still other wars," and begins "to laugh in the most unfeeling way. No one but an angel could have acted so; for suffering is nothing to them; they do not know what it is, except by hearsay." Like Hawthorne's Pearl in *The Scarlet Letter*, he "had not the disease of sadness," and like her, "It was certainly a doubtful charm, imparting a hard, metallic luster to the child's character. She wanted—what some people want throughout life—a grief that should touch her, and thus humanize and make her capable of sympathy."

This gap between Satan's knowledge and his experience is clearly and deeply felt by Theodore Fischer, and it is less Satan's lack of the Moral Sense than his lack of sympathy that inspires Theodore's missionary efforts. He wants to make Satan experience the human suffering which he only knows theoretically. (pp. 24-8)

But even though he does not show sympathy in the face of the terrible visions which he has revealed to the boys, he does tell them that he can "free" people from the terrible chain of circumstances that make up their lives, can grant them favors by changing single links in the chain. His first "kindness" is to arrange for Nikolaus Baumann to drown while trying to save a little girl friend. Nicky's two friends are shocked and implore Satan not to let it happen, but Satan explains:

> 'If I had not done this, Nickolaus would save Lisa, then he would catch cold from his drenching; one of your race's fantastic and desolating scarlet fevers would follow, with pathetic after-effects; for forty-six years he would lie in his bed a paralytic log, deaf, dumb, blind, and praying for the blessed relief of death. Shall I change his life back?'
>
> 'Oh no! Oh, no not for the world! In charity and pity leave it as it is.'

Satan's substitute for sympathy, which is cheap and hypocritical, is the kindness of severance from the source of that suffering. He grants the severance of death to Nicky, and then to Father Peter he grants the "kindness" of insanity, an equally effective means of cutting off the painfully direct relationship between the self and the world. And again he defends his action to the boys.

> 'I have taken from this man that trumpery thing which the race regards as a mind; I have replaced his tin life with a silver-gilt fiction; you see the result—and you criticize! I said I would make him permanently happy, and I have done it. I have made him happy by the only means possible to his race—and you are not satisfied!'

As Theodore says of Satan, "he didn't seem to know any way to do a person a favor except by killing him or making a lunatic out of him. He had such strange notions of kindness!"

Having initiated the children into the knowledge that life is not worth living, and that therefore death and insanity are the blessings and not the curses of man, Satan then offers a third "kindness." The alternative to death or insanity is to destroy the world while leaving the body and mind intact. If the world is known finally to be only a dream, then man is saved from its grief and pain. And so, Satan's final revelation to Theodore is that, "Nothing exists; all is a dream. God—man—the world—the sun, the moon, the wilderness of stars—a dream, all a dream; they have no existence. Nothing exists save empty space—and you!" This revelation hardly comes as a surprise, for it has been prepared for all along. "The dream-marks are all present," as Satan says; "you should have recognized them earlier." (pp. 29-30)

After performing his miracles for the boys, Satan dissolves away like a soap-bubble, "and presently exploded—puff! and in his place was vacancy." The boys sit "wondering and dreaming," then sigh and "suppose none of it has happened." "Dear, dear," exclaim the villagers when they see Satan, "but he is beautiful—what is his name? Philip Traum. Ah, it fits him! (You see, 'Traum' is German for 'dream')." After Satan has entered the body of the old astrologer, and made him perform fantastic acrobatic stunts, the crowd asks, "Was it real? Did you see it, or was it only I—and I was dreaming?" After the miracle of the ever-full wine vessel at Marget's house, an episode suggestive, of course, of Christ's miracle at Cana, the guests "walked like persons in a dream, their eyes open but seeing nothing." When Satan takes Theodore to a mountain top and shows him all the kingdoms of the earth, Theodore calls it, "A tranquil and dreamy picture." And so, when Satan finally tells Theodore that "life itself is only a vision, a dream," the education, the second fall into knowledge, the salvation is complete.

That the fall has also been a salvation can be seen in Theodore's continual reaction to Satan's lessons. "I should not be able to make any one understand how exciting it all was," he says. (p. 30)

And so the education ends with the master having revealed the student to himself and set him free. In the double irony of the tale, an innocent devil has come to an already fallen world, and offered it the salvation of complete knowledge, a second fall which alleviates the suffering and guilt caused by the partial knowledge acquired in the first fall. If man falls far enough, he reaches salvation. (p. 31)

Ronald J. Gervais, " 'The Mysterious Stranger': The Fall as Salvation," in Pacific Coast Philology, *Vol. V, April, 1970, pp. 24-33.*

RICKI MORGAN (essay date 1977-78)

[*In the following excerpt, Morgan examines thematic developments in Twain's stories "The £1,000,000 Bank-Note" and "The $30,000 Bequest."*]

Samuel Clemens, in an attempt to achieve vast returns quickly, invested in all sorts of inventions which brought him to financial ruin. In the ten year period (1893-1903) after he fell into indebtedness, he wrote to earn money to extricate himself from his creditors. It does not appear surprising that the central concern of two of the stories he wrote during that time is the sudden acquisition of vast sums of money which turn out to be chimerical or unspendable. **"The £1,000,000 Bank-Note"** (1893) is about a pauper suddenly given a bank-note for that amount which cannot be cashed, and **"The $30,000 Bequest"** (1903) is about an inheritance which never existed. Yet the endings of the stories are diametrically opposed to each other. In **"Bank-Note,"** the ending is that of a fairy-tale romance. In **"Bequest,"** it is total annihilation and death. Are these differences due to a thematic inconsistency or changing philosophy on Twain's part? I hope to show they are not.

In both stories it appears that money is depicted as "The great tempter." After the fall from Eden, Adam's curse was his necessity to work by the sweat of his brow. For Mark Twain, I feel, to try to circumvent this, and come into large fortunes of "easy money," is to try to defy man's fate, and is an enterprise doomed to failure. The man who engages in such enterprises is guilty of the sin of avarice. If man is morally weak, and values money more than his soul, he is guilty of a moral failing for which, in Twain's works, it appears that he will fall grievously. However, if the temptation of "easy money" is successfully withstood, if man has the moral fiber to value true wealth of character over monetary gains, it is then, I believe, that Twain's providence rewards him.

"£1,000,000 Bank-Note" appears to be a story of temptation successfully withstood and ultimately rewarded. **"$30,000 Bequest,"** on the other hand deals with a couple who worship money instead of God, fall sorely, and are completely destroyed by their greed.

There is strong evidence that the £1,000,000 bank-note is meant to offer a powerful temptation to a ruinous fate. It is furnished by two men who coldly gamble on whether or not Henry Adams will manage to last a month with it. The temptation of money as "original sin," the root of all evil, is hinted at in Twain's naming the protagonist Adams. (pp. 6-7)

The linking of money with the fall of man seems to be further hinted at in the imagery which surrounds Adams' receipt of the bank-note. He stands hungrily in front of the house of his future "benefactors" watching a piece of fruit; "a luscious big pear—*minus one bite,*" which is tolled before him. It would be too shameful for him to be seen picking up the fruit and eating it, but "I was just getting desperate enough to brave all the shame, and to seize it, when a window behind me was raised, and a gentleman spoke out of it, saying:

'Step in here please.' "

Once he has received the envelope with the bank-note, and returns out into the street, Adams says, "I would have picked up the pear now and eaten it before all the world, but it was gone." Adams receives the bank-note when he is about to eat the forbidden fruit, and after he has accepted it, the fruit is gone.

In the beginning of the story we are told that this descendant of Adam is ideally equipped to withstand the temptation of "easy money," and is prepared to work hard and honestly for a living. . . . We learn that he has withstood such temptation in the past. (p. 7)

Adams' bank-note begins propelling him into his startling position of prominence not through his own greed and money worship, but through the greed and money worship of the society surrounding him. Thinking he was given a gift of a pound note, he goes into "the nearest cheap eating house" and eats his fill. Adams takes out the note to pay his bill and discovers its denomination. After getting over his initial shock, "the first thing I noticed was the landlord. His eye was on the note . . . He was worshipping, with all his body and soul." Adams does the only "rational thing to do," and offers the note in payment, asking for change. The proprietor "Wanted to look at it and keep on looking at it; he couldn't seem to get enough of it to quench the thirst of his eye, but he shrank from touching it as if it had been something too sacred to handle." It is this worship of money by the people who surround Adams, and not any dishonesty on Adams' part that propels him to prominence. Adams is frank about his situation, but the landlord is over-whelmed by the sight of the bill and pays him no heed. Adams asks for change, telling him he hasn't anything else,

> But he said that wasn't any matter; he was quite willing to let the trifle stand over till another time. I said I might not be in his neighborhood again for a good while; but he said it was of no consequence, he could wait, and, moreover, I could have anything I wanted, any time I chose, and let the account run as long as I pleased.

Adams' first real temptation is the extended credit on a million pounds that doesn't belong to him. But at this point he pays it no heed and runs off to act with honesty, to return the note to its proprietors. He regards the note as "the monster," rather than an object of reverential worship, and goes off to return it post haste.

After Adams discovers that he is being made a loan "for thirty days without interest" and will receive any situation that he is able to prove himself "familiar with and competent to fill," he is not tempted to get credit against the loan. What leads him into temptation is the confidence that he can prove himself capable of deserving a good position and earning his bread by his work: "I got to thinking a good deal about that situation. My hopes began to rise high. Without doubt the salary would be large. It would begin in a month; after that

I should be all right. He then passes a tailor shop, and is seized by

> a sharp longing to shed my rags, and to clothe myself decently once more . . . The temptation persecuted me cruelly. I must have passed that shop back and forth six times during that manful struggle. At last I gave in; I had to.

But even this temptation is of the most modest kind; he only banks on being able to afford "a misfit suit."

He goes into the store, asks for the misfit suit and is treated with commensurate disdain. After being kept waiting, the salesman, "took me into a back room, and overhauled a pile of rejected suits, and selected the rattiest one for me." Once again, Adams' bank-note shows up the money worshipping values of the others around him. He asks for the suit on credit; is treated with contempt. As soon as he mentions he can pay for the suit but didn't want to put the salesman to the trouble of changing a large bill, the salesman "modified his style a little at that." After the production of the bank-note, the proprietor comes in, and the treatment given Adams is completely reversed:

> Please get those things off, sir, and throw them in the fire. Do me the favor to put on this shirt and this suit; . . . made to order for a foreign prince—you may know him, sir, his Serene Highness the Hospodar of Halifax.

Once again, Adams is honest about his inability to pay, but the sight of the bank-note makes the proprietor again disregard him. The credit he was previously denied is extended to him "indefinitely."

Adams accepts the loan, but is filled with trepidation:

> I judged there was going to be a crash by and by . . . You see there was just the element of impending disaster to give a serious, a sober side, yes, a tragic side to this state of things which would otherwise have been purely ridiculous.

Adams' bank-note makes him a celebrity. In the gossip columns of the newspaper, "I reached the highest altitude possible . . . taking precedence over all dukes not royal." However, although he takes loans and credit, he is careful not to incur any debts which he won't be able to work off. He takes nothing which he does not contemplate paying back. . . . (pp. 7-8)

Adams' nature is perhaps most clearly displayed in, and reaps its greatest reward for, his wooing of Portia Langdon. Like Shakespeare's Portia, the way to win this girl is by choosing the "lead casket"; realizing that true wealth resides in her person. Adams immediately makes a clean breast to her of his true financial straights. He never inquires into her fortune or family, and tells her she will have to expect to live in poverty for a while, and it will be a couple of years before they can get married. When Portia laughs after hearing the story of his adversity, Adams finds that

> I loved her all the more, seeing she could be so cheerful when there wasn't anything to be cheerful about; for I might soon need that kind of wife, you know, the way things looked.

Adams is rewarded for his uprightness but we see God helping those who help themselves. He earns his money not from any gift given him, but by using his intellect—honestly, and

generously. He devises a scheme to help his friend Hastings (whose predicament is a result of his attempt to make "easy money" with his mining stock deal). When Hastings asks Adams to help him by buying the stock,

> a white-hot idea came flaming through my head, and I gripped my jaws together, and calmed myself down till I was as cold as a capitalist. Then I said, in a commercial and self-possessed way,

> "I will save you Lloyd . . . I know all about that mine, of course; I know its immense value, and can swear to it if anybody wishes it. You shall sell out inside of the fortnight for three millions cash, using my name freely, and we'll divide, share and share alike."

So Adams gets wealth by his own efforts, and not through any gifts bolting out of the blue. This is made clear at the end of the story where it is also indicated that although he has money, this is not where he considers his true wealth to lie:

> My Portia's papa took that friendly and hospitable bill back to the Bank of England and cashed it; then the Bank canceled it . . . and he gave it to us at our wedding, and it has always hung in its frame in the sacredest place in our home ever since. For it gave me my Portia . . . And so I always say, "Yes, it's a million pounder, as you see; but it never made but one purchase in its life, and **then** got the article for only about a tenth part of its value."

So huge sums of unspendable money can make vast purchases, but only when its receiver is aware of where true wealth lies.

In **"Bank-Note"** Adams was given a vast sum of real but unspendable money; his strong moral fiber kept him from real ruination, and gave him a concrete reward. In **"Bequest"** the situation is curiously reversed. The Fosters are given a vast sum of imaginary money which they are free to imaginarily spend and invest. Their real life and real situation are not changed. The only thing in jeopardy is their imaginary life, their souls. So powerful is the force of greed, so dangerous is the placing of material wealth over spiritual wealth, that the loss of money they never possessed, and the return to a life that they never left, destroys them.

One of the most prominent themes in this story, and one that seems central to the story's meaning, is the religious attitudes of the Fosters. Saladin or Mr. Foster's nature appears to be greedy and impious, a dangerous personality in Twain's universe. Electra, his wife's outlook appears more dangerous still. She has a cash-nexus view of God and of religion. She is unable to distinguish between spiritual "investments" and monetary ones. While Saladin is capable of recognizing his irreverence and greed, even though he chooses not to reform, Mrs. Foster is incapable of even seeing her sins, of telling right from wrong. Consequently, any sort of repentance or reformation is even beyond her imagining. As Saladin says to her, when discussing her piety,

> I didn't mean so bad as that Aleck; I didn't really mean immoral piety. I only meant—meant—well, conventional piety, you know; er—shop piety; the—the why, you know what I mean, Aleck—the—well, where you put up the plated article and play it for solid, you know, without intending anything improper, but just out of trade habit, ancient policy, petrified custom, loyalty to—to—hang it, I

can't find the right words but **you** know what I mean.

The ironic part is that Mrs. Foster, by her self-righteous indignation during these frequent religious discussions with her husband, indicates that she does not know. She has been "playing the plated article for genuine" for so long that she has convinced herself of its solidity. Unfortunately, her husband will never convince her to the contrary. As their nicknames indicate, (Saladin's is Sally, and Electra's is Aleck) she is the dominant figure, her mercantile morality governs. Any such conversation with her husband always ends with his apologizing to her.

The "money" is left to the Fosters with their dying uncle's curse. The only provision for the inheritance is that the Fosters act totally ungrateful,

> That Sally should be able to prove to the executors that *he had taken no notice of the gift by spoken word or by letter, had made no inquiries concerning the moribund's progress toward the everlasting tropics, and had not attended the funeral.*

If there were true Christian sentiment among the couple, the money, of course, would pose no more threat to them than the possession of the bank-note did for Adams. They would immediately have done what was honorable, and their duty. They would have gone to Uncle Tilbury's death-bed and asked for his dying blessing, instead of his curse. But their behavior is quite the opposite:

> Man and wife entered into a solemn compact, now, to never mention the great news to anyone while the relative lived, lest some ignorant person carry the fact to the death-bed and distort it and make it appear that they were disobediently thankful for the bequest, and just the same as confessing it and publishing it, right in the face of the prohibition.

If the disposal of the "wealth" were left in the hands of Sally's simple greed, it would pose little threat to the Fosters' well being; he would have squandered it on imaginary purchases the first evening. The bubble would have burst at the outset, leaving no more than a passing pang of disappointment. But Aleck's acquisitive greed extends far beyond her husband's. She must invest the imaginary windfall into a vast imaginary fortune before she will allow Sally to "touch a penny" of the wealth.

After five weeks, Sally's simple greed is conquered by natural curiosity. Were he able to assert himself now, the situation would have ceased after five weeks instead of five years. But Aleck's cold, cautious acquisitiveness will not let this happen:

> Sally now resolved to brace up and risk a frontal attack. So he squarely proposed to disguise himself and go to Tilbury's village and surreptitiously find out as to the prospects. Aleck put her foot on the dangerous project with energy and decision.

Due to Aleck's "speculations" the imaginary wealth increases to a vast sum. They are completely overwhelmed by their greed which grows in like proportion. First they "fell,— and broke the sabbath" to count their imaginary money. Then Sally starts stealing candles from the shop he works in so they can stay up at night figuring their investments. Aleck's greed even corrupts her imaginary investments. She has "holdings" in "Tammany Graft and Shady Priviliges in the Post-office Department." From this point on, Twain punctuates his story with homilies like the following: "Vast wealth has temptations which fatally and surely undermine the moral structure of persons not habituated to its possession." I feel such interspersions most likely are meant to be interpreted as ironic, since the Fosters aren't corrupted by "vast wealth"—they do not have a penny more than they did at the beginning of the story; rather, it appears that their corrupt natures in the form of snowballing greed has brought them to their present state.

Aleck has lost herself in their greed to the point, where, when she loses her imaginary money in an imaginary investment, her despair and ruination are quite real. Sally has almost, but not quite, reached her stage. He has the presence of mind to realize that the money lost is imaginary. However, it is this last accurate observation that rekindles the spark of greed back to its height, so that they are totally annihilated when they learn that the bequest is nonexistent:

> You really never invested a penny of my uncle's bequest, but only its unmaterialized future; what we have lost was only the increment harvested from that future . . . Cheer up . . . we still have the thirty thousand untouched; and with the experience which you have acquired, think what you will be able to do with it in a couple of years!

Once they find out that there will never be any money forthcoming their *raison d'etre* is gone, and they succumb to death. If they had learned where true spiritual wealth lies, they could never have been robbed of existence by the chimerical kind. On Sally's death-bed, he appears to come to a partial realization of the truth:

> Vast wealth acquired by sudden and unwholesome means, is a snare. It did us no good, transient were its feverish pleasures; yet for its sake we threw away our sweet and simple and happy life—let others take warning by us.

But Sally's spiritual insight is as weak and as fluctuating as his imaginary fortune. Instead of repenting his moral frailty with his dying breath, and resolving that if he had his life to live over, he would place spiritual wealth over temporal, he curses his uncle for not leaving them a larger imaginary fortune, so that they wouldn't have been tempted to lose it in an imaginary speculation.

It appears that "vast wealth acquired by sudden and unwholesome means" is a snare and brings ruination. However, ruination is not brought about by the "vast wealth" itself, but by the "sudden and unwholesome means" of acquisition. Vast wealth alone poses no threat to the uncorruptable Adams, but the "sudden and unwholesome means" without real wealth is sufficient to destroy the morally deficient Fosters. (pp. 8-10)

> *Ricki Morgan, "Mark Twain's Money Imagery in 'The £1,000,000 Bank-Note' and 'The $30,000 Bequest',"* in *Mark Twain Journal, Vol. XIX, No. 1, Winter, 1977-78, pp. 6-10.*

RICHARD TUERK (essay date 1978)

[*In the following excerpt, Tuerk discusses Twain's exploration of the nature of dream and reality in his late pieces "Which Was the Dream?," "The Great Dark," "Which Was It?," and* The Mysterious Stranger.]

During his last 15 years Mark Twain wrote a number of basically ontological works that explore the relation between dream and reality. Especially in four unfinished novels—**"Which Was the Dream?"** (1897), **"The Great Dark"** (1898), **"Which Was It?"** (1899-1902), and the version of *The Mysterious Stranger* entitled **"No. 44, The Mysterious Stranger"** (1902-08)—he explores the possibility that the dream world is as real as or even more real than the waking world. Three of these titles are Twain's: **"Which Was the Dream?"**, **"Which Was It?"**, and **"No. 44, The Mysterious Stranger"**; as the first two indicate, in these works Twain rejects the facile distinction that people usually make between dream and reality. In fact, the three earlier fragments point toward No. 44's speech in the projected ending of **"No. 44, The Mysterious Stranger"** in which he tells August Feldner that dream and reality are ultimately indistinguishable, for *"Nothing* exists; all is a dream. God—man—the world,—the sun, the moon, the wilderness of stars; a dream, all a dream they have no existence. *Nothing exists save empty space—and you!"* In this solipsistic statement the only true reality is the subjective observer himself, and the only thing that can be perceived is the dream.

In the three of these works that lead to **"No. 44, The Mysterious Stranger,"** both chronologically and thematically, Twain does not make the clear distinctions between dream and reality that he makes in earlier works such as *The Adventures of Tom Sawyer* and *Adventures of Huckleberry Finn.* In *Tom Sawyer,* for example, Tom momentarily confuses dream and reality shortly after he and Huck discover Injun Joe's stolen

Twain in New York, around 1880.

treasure. But when Huck lets him know that the money is real, Tom declares: " 'Tain't a dream, then, 'tain't a dream!" Similarly, in *Huckleberry Finn,* when Huck tries to convince Jim that his adventures in the fog were all a dream, Jim quickly discovers that Huck is trying to "make a fool uv ole Jim wid a lie." Even Huck's explanation of Tom's getting shot—"He had a dream . . . and it shot him"—is a transparent lie through which the doctor easily sees. In *A Connecticut Yankee in King Arthur's Court,* whether Hank Morgan really goes to sixth-century England or just dreams he does also seems of little ultimate importance.

In the three earlier late fragments Twain does not assert that no distinction between dream and reality ultimately exists, as he does in the projected ending for **"No. 44, The Mysterious Stranger."** Rather, as two of Twain's titles imply, these unfinished novels demand that the reader try to distinguish between dream and reality for himself.

The few critics who treat these three works fail to take seriously the questions asked in the two titles. Either they blithely assume that the waking world is indeed real and the dream world is false, or they mention the questions the titles pose without exploring them in relation to the stories. If the distinctions are so simple or if they are not worth exploring, then the titles must be misleading. I feel that Twain, however, so constructed these fragments that in them the world that appears to be real more closely resembles the illusory world of sentimental romance than it does the real world Twain felt he inhabited during his last decade and a half. And the world that appears to be a dream more closely resembles the nightmarish real world that Twain became convinced he inhabited. Consequently, his inability—or perhaps refusal—to finish these works may reflect his conviction that in them the waking world is an illusion and the nightmare world is the real one from which there is no final escape except death.

In his introduction to *Mark Twain's Which Was the Dream? and Other Symbolic Writings of the Later Years,* John Tuckey treats Twain's interest in dream psychology and his feeling that parts of his own life are a dream [see Further Reading list]. As early as 1897, moreover, Twain became interested in the possibility that dream experiences are at least as real—even in an objective sense—as waking experiences, a possibility that is, of course, central to **"No. 44, The Mysterious Stranger"** in which dream selves have as much objective reality as waking selves. In **"Which Was the Dream?"** **"The Great Dark,"** and **"Which Was It?"** however, evidence indicates that the dream worlds are *more real* than the waking worlds.

In these three stories the waking life of each protagonist is, in a sense, too good to be true. In the shortest of these fragments, **"Which Was the Dream?"** Tom X makes it clear that he cannot be sure that his waking life is not a dream. He is, in fact, distinctly aware of the difficulty of distinguishing between dreams and reality. About his life with Alison, his wife, he writes: "Our days were a dream, we lived in a world of enchantment." He then writes about the "memorable . . . marvelous days" after his successes in the Mexican War:

> More than ever we seemed to be living in a world of enchantment. It all seemed so strange, indeed so splendidly impossible, that these bounties [that they enjoyed], usually reserved for age, should actually be ours, and we so young; for she was but 22 and I but 28.

And he adds: "Every morning one or the other of us laughed and said, 'Another day gone, and it isn't a dream *yet!*' For we had the same thought, and it was a natural one: that the night might rob us, some time or other, and we should wake bereaved." These words about their happiness, of course, describe the kinds of lives found in what Tom X calls "the golden land of Romance, where all things are beautiful, and existence is a splendid dream, and care cannot come." They do not ring true to real life as Twain knows and describes it in works such as *Pudd'nhead Wilson* (1893-94) and *King Leopold's Soliloquy* (1905). Tom's comment about himself and Alison—"We are happy, we are satisfied"—runs counter to the truths about human nature Twain depicts in his other works during this period. More and more he was coming to feel that it is contrary to the nature of what he calls "the damned human race" to be either happy or satisfied.

The X's two children, Jessie and Bessie, also are too good to be true; their descriptions are a sort of parody of what one can expect from children their age. Five-year-old Jessie is

> a practical, decisive, courageous, adventurous little soldier. . . . She is the embodied spirit of cheerfulness; everything that happens to her is somehow convertible into entertainment. . . . She bears pain with a rare fortitude, for a child—or for an adult. . . . She always had a thoughtful business head from the beginning.

On the other hand, eight-year-old

> Bessie is a thinker—a poet—a dreamer; a creature made up of intellect, imagination, feeling . . . an exquisite little sensitive plant, shrinking and timorous in the matter of pain . . . [She] is a sort of little woman, now. . . . To start with, she was a dear little baby, with a temper made all of alternating bursts of storm and sunshine. . . . She was a most sudden creature; always brimming with life, always boiling with enthusiasm. . . . Fortunately . . . her exaltations of joy were much more common than her ecstasies of anger, [but] It took both to make her thoroughly interesting; and she was that . . . ." From her babyhood she has made an idol of her mother. She and her mother are sweethearts, lovers, intimate comrades and confidants, and prodigal of endearments and caresses for each other. Nobody but the mother can govern her. She does it by love, by inalterable firmness, by perfect fairness, by perfect justice.

Certainly, the creator of the precocious and vexatious Little Bessie and her mother in "Little Bessie" (1908-09) knew that real children are not this way and that real mothers are not capable of "perfect" fairness and justice. In fact, Twain has Tom characterize himself and his family as being "limitlessly happy," words that more accurately describe families of sentimental romance than breathing, fleshly families.

Similarly, in **"The Great Dark,"** in their waking life the Edwardses resemble nothing so much as the "happy" families of sentimental romance. In her statement, in fact, Mrs. Edwards writes: "We were a happy family, we had been happy from the beginning; we did not know what trouble was, we were not thinking of it nor expecting it." And Mr. Edwards says about what he believes to have been his waking life: "It had been an ideal life." Even though Twain may be using "ideal" in a double sense—at this point in his narrative, Edwards can no longer determine with certainty which of his lives is real and which a dream—except in externals the wak-

ing life of the Edwardses does not resemble that of the Clemenses during the last few years of the 19th Century, the time of composition of this fragment.

In **"Which Was It?"** the longest of these fragments, in Book I of "The Wife's Narrative" Alison Harrison describes her two children in terms that clearly align them with figures from sentimental romance. About her older daughter, also named Alison, she writes:

> That is the blonde—6 years old, the dearest little fairy! All sweetness and sunshine and affection; and the deepest and wisest and cunningest little mind, that's always thinking and thinking, and putting this and that together, and dropping her small dredge into the awful depths of the mystery of life and bringing up the most astonishing results!

About her other child she writes:

> Margery is the brunette—5 years old, dear and sweet and loving, like her sister, but oh dear, what a steam-engine, what a tireless volcanic eruption of fun and frolic and gladness! and what an unutterable blessing they both are to this house! And how useful they are to me! When I can't persuade George, I send him those little rascals—he is their slave.

The trite platitudes ("all sweetness and sunshine," "dear and sweet and loving," and "fun and frolic and gladness"), the string of superlatives, and the abundance of exclamation points all give the descriptions of the children an air of unreality. That Twain during his last 15 years could believe that an otherwise sane, intelligent woman could really have such shallow, one-sided feelings about her children is difficult to accept. After all, by the time he wrote these fragments, Twain had created Roxy in *Pudd'nhead Wilson*. Thus, in all three of these dream tales, the apparently real world, the waking world, has elements in it that make us question its reality.

In these fragments reality is probably to be found—if anywhere—in the nightmarish dream world. In **"Which Was the Dream?"** Tom X's words quoted above—"the night might rob us, some time or other, and we should wake bereaved"— prove highly ironic, for in apparently falling asleep while inhaling the smoke from his cigar, he enters a nightmare world that robs him of a large portion of his happiness. Yet the irony is even greater, for the nightmare world more accurately reflects the real world as Twain knew it than does the waking world. In his narrative Tom himself is aware of the difficulty of distinguishing between dream and reality, for, he explains, "while you are *in* a dream it *isn't* a dream—it is reality, and the bear-bite hurts; hurts in a perfectly real way." Here he refers in particular to one of Bessie's recurrent dreams, but simultaneously he warns against any facile attempt to decide which is the dream and which the reality in his own narrative.

In **"The Great Dark"** man's inability to distinguish between dream and reality is a central theme. According to Tuckey, Twain made a note concerning page 74 of the holograph in which "The Superintendent of Dreams 'says his proper title is S [uperintendent] of R [ealities], and he is so-called in other planets, but here we reverse the meanings of many words, and we wouldn't understand him'" (Tuckey's brackets). This note indicates that at least at one time while composing the story, Twain consciously intended the dream world not just to seem but actually to be more real than the waking one. The

Superintendent of Dreams himself is an interesting figure. He may be viewed as a part of Henry Edwards, a sort of alter ego, or as a character with an objective reality of his own. At any rate, he is a highly capricious figure who controls the nightmare world into which Henry enters. Thus, the captain's statement toward the end of the manuscript—"*I* don't know where this ship is, but she's in the hands of God, and that's enough for me"—is highly ironic, for the only god that rules over the world in which the ship sails is the Superintendent who delights in tricking and confusing people.

The note indicating that the Superintendent of Dreams is really the Superintendent of Realities appears opposite one of many sections in the story in which Henry discusses with his wife, named Alice, which of their two sets of lives is the real one. One of the first indications of his dilemma in distinguishing between dream and reality comes during an early conversation he has with the Superintendent of Dreams. As they talk, Henry loses his temper, and he gets even angrier when the Superintendent tells him to "moderate" his "manner," for he is "not pleased with it." Henry responds: "You may like it or not, just as you choose. And moreover, if my style doesn't suit you, you can end the dream as soon as you please—right now, if you like." Then Henry writes:

> He looked me steadily in the eye for a moment, then said, with deliberation—
>
> "The dream? *Are you quite sure it is a dream?*"
>
> It took my breath away.
>
> "What do you mean? *Isn't* it a dream?"
>
> He looked at me in that same way again; and it made my blood chilly, this time. Then he said—
>
> "You have spent your whole life in this ship. And this is *real* life. Your other life was the dream!"

Thus, Henry finds himself face to face with Tom X's idea that in a dream the dream "is reality," an idea that points to man's ultimate inability to distinguish between dream and reality. At the same time Henry discovers that his waking life, which he assumes to be reality, may be a dream. As often happens, ontological problems produce epistemological problems, for if one cannot clearly distinguish between appearance and reality, one cannot be sure of the grounds of one's knowledge. Henry admits both his ontological and epistemological problems when he comments on the effect the Superintendent's words have on him: "So little a time before," he says, "I *knew* that this voyage was a dream, and nothing more; a wee little puff or two of doubt had been blown against that certainty, unhelped by fact or argument, and already it was dissolving away."

On page after page Henry records discussions in which he tries to determine which is the real world and which the dream one. When he asks Alice whether their life on land is a dream, she replies: "I know it; I know it positively." And her assurance makes Henry doubt himself. "The conviction stole through me," he writes, "that she must be right, since she felt so sure. Indeed I almost knew she was." And he adds: "I was privately becoming ashamed of myself now, for mistaking a clever illusion for a fact. So I gave it up, then, and said I would let it stand as a dream." But he cannot give it up. Instead, he wonders: "are we real creatures in a real world, all of a sudden, and have we been feeding on dreams in an imaginary one since nobody knows when—or how *is*

it?", a question he ultimately cannot answer. Moreover, about the ship's saloon he thinks: "Everything seemed substantial and genuine, there was nothing to suggest that it might be a work of the imagination"; and finally, after trying to piece together both of his "lives," he decides that he is indeed awake while on board the ship:

> The main incidents of both my lives were now recovered, but only those of one of them persistently gathered strength and vividness—our life in the ship! Those of our land-life were good enough, plain enough, but in minuteness of detail they fell perceptibly short of those others; and in matters of feeling—joy, grief, physical pain, physical pleasure—immeasurably short!

For Henry, dream and reality thus reverse. Significantly, Twain also does not take this story to its projected ending: as the manuscript now stands, Henry never awakens from his "dream"; it constitutes his final reality.

Among those parts of **"The Great Dark"** that Twain canceled in the manuscript is a section in which Henry discusses the relation between dream and reality with a person called the Mad Passenger. Perhaps Twain deleted this part of the manuscript because it treats material he covers elsewhere more subtly and without the artificial intrusion of the Mad Passenger. Nonetheless, the Mad Passenger confides to Henry that the captain and officers of the ship have "a chart of Dreamland, and they are navigating this ship by it!" After the Mad Passenger says that he has visited a part of Dreamland called "the World," Henry asks: "are you *sure* it is a part of Dreamland?" a question which the Mad Passenger answers with another question: "are you mad, too?" Henry then admits to himself:

> It seems manifest, from all sorts of evidences, that I have been under a delusion since I don't know when. Years, no doubt. I think I have lived in dreams so long that now that I have at last got back to realities I have lost the sense of them and they seem dreams, too.

Nonetheless, the Mad Passenger's question implies that he has been laboring under the same "delusion" as Henry. For Henry, then, the waking world becomes "Dreamland," and the nightmare world of **"The Great Dark"** with its horrible monsters and its tragedies becomes the only real world. In another late fragment entitled **"Three Thousand Years Among the Microbes"** (1905) Huck, the human-turned-microbe who narrates the story, learns "that it isn't safe to sit in judgment upon another person's illusion when you are not on the inside. While you are thinking it is a dream, he may be knowing it is a planet." Henry learns that it is not even safe to sit in judgment of one's own illusion, for it may indeed be not a dream but a planet.

Although explicit discussion of ontological and epistemological questions is not central to **"Which Was It?"** several passages in this long, unfinished novel also cast doubt on the unreality of the dream world. In his narrative of his dream, George Harrison comments: "It's a cursed world we live in, and a person's got to stand it." This world is the one cursed by Adam, to whose fall George traces his own troubles. Moreover, commenting to Frances Osgood about her children as well as his own wife and children, all of whom are dead in the dream but alive in the waking part of the story, George says: "They were all young, they saw all of life that was worth the living. In their innocence they took it for a boon and a reality, and never suspected it for what it is, a treachery and a sham." In this world, then, happiness is connected with innocence born of ignorance, and such innocence, as the author of **"The Man That Corrupted Hadleyburg"** (1899) knew, cannot survive in the real world in which human life is conditioned by Adam's fall or by some similar misfortune or misfortunes that have turned mankind into "the damned human race." As these few examples thus indicate, in **"Which Was It?"** the dream world resembles the world of duplicity in which, according to Twain, people live.

Thus, in **"Which Was the Dream?" "The Great Dark,"** and **"Which Was It?"** Twain consistently refuses to make facile distinctions between dream and reality. The waking world appears dreamlike, and the dream world appears real. Twain's reader must seriously ask himself which world is the dream one. Ultimately, of course, one cannot answer with absolute certainty, probably because in these late fragments Twain's conception of man's ability to perceive reality involves an inability to distinguish between it and illusion. But in each of these unfinished works Twain makes the real seem dreamlike and the dream seem real as he probes the very nature of existence. That he arrives at no conclusions and that he produces no consistent ontology in these tales should, of course, not surprise us; for although he dabbled in philosophy, Twain is ultimately no philosopher. Instead, he is a creator of fictions that often have serious philosophical implications. In some of these fictions he explores the region DeVoto calls the great dark [see Further Reading list]—which may ultimately be nothing more or less than the underside of human consciousness which, according to Twain, turns the world into a nightmarish place. In these fragments the nightmare never ends, possibly because Twain cannot find a way ultimately to distinguish between appearance and reality. The reader as well as the dreamer must continue to wander in the dark. (pp. 23-33)

> *Richard Tuerk, "Appearance and Reality in Mark Twain's 'Which Was the Dream?', 'The Great Dark,' and 'Which Was It?',"* in Illinois Quarterly, *Vol. 40, No. 3, Spring, 1978, pp. 23-34.*

MARK KOSINSKI (essay date 1979)

[*In the following excerpt, Kosinski explores the "philosophic despair" of Twain's later years as expressed in the themes and imagery of "The Great Dark."*]

The striking lack of critical attention to Mark Twain's late fragment **"The Great Dark"** is surprising, and reveals a need to reconsider the doom and pessimism that plagued Twain's final years. Critics have generally focused on *The Mysterious Stranger* when discussing Twain's *fin-de-siècle* pessimism, which seems to have precluded an examination of many of his late unfinished writings. It is the purpose of this paper to suggest that **"The Great Dark"** is one such fragment that offers rich commentary in understanding Twain's philosophic despair which sees man facing a meaningless and absurd world.

Bernard DeVoto, who was first to edit and publish this fragment [in an appendix to his *Mark Twain at Work* (1942); see Further Reading list], states in his essay, "Symbols of Despair" [in *Mark Twain at Work*], that **"The Great Dark"** is "a strange, powerful, and moving story . . . which holds your fascination despite some crudities of construction." DeVoto mentions the score of manuscripts Twain began in his

late years but never finished, manuscripts that were symptomatic of a talent blasted by personal tragedy and misfortune. Yet it is too easy to take these assumptions into some of his later writings. It hardly needs repeating that these writings belong to the decade of the 1890's when Twain suffered a series of personal disasters: the bankruptcy of his Webster publishing house, the collapse of his nine-year struggle to get the Paige typesetter on the market, and as a final blow the death of his most cherished daughter, Susy. These events have particular relevance to some of the dream-sequences, especially such fragments as **"Which Was the Dream?"** and **"Which Was It?"** Both of these pieces, like Twain's life, depict the fall of a man of high fortune to economic ruin.

DeVoto analyzes the despair in these writings and concludes that their origin is with other intellectual crises that antedate the period of his personal misfortunes. Beside the personal disasters which obviously had a powerful effect on Twain, DeVoto suggests an early development of pessimistically twinned themes: "man's complete helplessness in the grip of the inexorable forces of the universe, and man's essential cowardice, pettiness, and evil." **"The Great Dark"** is concerned with both of these themes. Gathering together those gloomy, often unbearable, scenes of man's paltriness in an indifferent universe, **"The Great Dark"** posits a dream vision turned to racking nightmare.

As a vision bearing these characteristics then, **"The Great Dark"** must be evaluated not as a personal utterance of Twain-the-man's frustration, but as a metaphysical statement by an artist moving into a state of silence. It is a state with both aesthetic and philosophical undergirdings. As one commentator of *The Mysterious Stranger* notes, "Twain's philosophic position during his late years can be described as a grotesque medley of fatalism, misanthropy, and cynicism. In general he reflects the post-Darwinian pessimism of the late nineteenth century . . . " [see Fussell excerpt dated 1952]. In an aesthetic sense **"The Great Dark"** anticipates the despair found at the end of *The Mysterious Stranger:* " 'It is true, that which I have revealed to you; there is no God, no universe, no human race, no earthly life, no heaven, no hell. It is all a dream—a grotesque and foolish dream. Nothing exists but you. And you are but a thought—a thought, wandering forlorn among the empty eternities!' " **"The Great Dark"** likewise points to freedom from the conceptions of life and the limitations of selfhood; in the end there is neither man nor God, only the solipsistic thought of the artist.

"The Great Dark" was originally titled "Statement of the Edwardses." DeVoto changed the title to correspond to that region of perpetual darkness in the drop of water on a microscope slide, the area on the edge of the microscope's field. The narrator and protagonist of the story, Mr. Edwards, after examining a drop of water through a microscope he has bought his daughter, is amazed by the bizarre animal life it reveals. " 'An ocean in a drop of water—and unknown, uncharted, unexplored by man!' " After falling asleep he makes arrangements with the Superintendent of Dreams—a supernatural being in the tradition of the trickster god—to explore the unknown sea. He next finds himself miniaturized and aboard a storm-tossed ship with his wife and children; it is a starless and moonless setting, the ship being somewhere on the edge of the drop of water. And somewhere far off from this desolate area is the everpresent horror of the great "white glare," or that region where light is cast through the water by the microscope's reflector.

Mr. Edwards turns out to be the only person on the ship who believes that it is all a dream experience. His wife, on the other hand, believes that "land" experiences were in fact dreams, and that her shipboard life has always been reality: " 'The earliest thing I can call to mind was papa's death by the sun-heat and mamma's suicide the same day [when] we were in the edge of a great white glare once for a little while. . . .'" The Superintendent of Dreams adds to the psychic trauma by cultivating doubts of reality in Edwards' mind: " 'You have spent your whole life in this ship. And this is *real* life. Your other life was the dream.' " Mr. Edwards philosophically reflects "that we seldom really know the thing we think we know; that our best built certainties are but sand-houses and subject to damage from any wind of doubt that blows." And the winds of doubt blow harder as Edwards eventually believes that his shipboard experiences are real and those on land only imaginary.

After an attempted mutiny by the crew and an attack by a "spider-squid," the fragment ends with the boat stranded in a frozen waste where monsters roam in the darkness. According to Twain's notes, which have been summarized by DeVoto [in his Editor's Notes to *Letters from the Earth* (1962)], the ship meets with another ship that contains a fabulous treasure in gold. A mutiny occurs and the treasure ship, with Edwards' newly born son and the captain's daughter, is spirited away by the crew now maddened by their lust for the gold. Further misfortunes and tragedy follow. Edwards' wife goes insane with grief; the ship containing crew and children enters the region of the "white glare" where they are all seared to death by the tremendous heat. Edwards and the captain arrive too late in the other ship, and finally, the helpless narrator is the only one left in the end. Perhaps Edwards was to awake from a nightmare at this point, but Twain gives no indication of this in his notes.

In the end the reader experiences a similar sense of doom that is realized at the end of *The Mysterious Stranger,* the recognition that man, perhaps, inhabits only an illusory reality. As one observer concludes, the story "gives Twain an opportunity to question the nature of reality—and the imaginative creation of an empty and meaningless universe—in one sense, therefore, we arrive at a solipsistic conclusion" [see Fussell excerpt dated 1952]. Twain's narrator is like the victim in Poe's "The Facts in the Case of M. Valdemar" who has been suspended in a state of animation at the very moment of death and reports to the reader on the forbidden land between living and unliving.

While parallels may be illuminating, it is important not to go too far in trying to identify Twain's vision with any school of philosophy. Yet **"The Great Dark"** is open to some philosophical and psychological comment. In this story man is faced with a horror the metaphysical presents when faith in meaning and certainty have disintegrated. It presents a kind of solipsism that expresses the individual's horror at being confronted with the overpowering task of coping with an indifferent universe, and his solitude in the face of its monstrous size and duration.

"The Great Dark" also mirrors a special tradition of literary iconology and imagery. Presenting a "voyage of disaster," the universe is described in color imagery that reaches back to Melville's *Moby-Dick.* White and black become interchangeable symbols representing the mystery and terror of life. Like Ishmael exploring and reporting from another world, Edwards alone survives to tell the tale. His pursuit into nothing-

ness in the great "white glare" is reminiscent of the white whale in *Moby-Dick* or the nothingness Kurtz perceives in *Heart of Darkness.* The whiteness at the end represents a final and metaphysical apocalypse, a kind of "colorless all-color atheism from which we shrink."

Jay Martin records the evolution of Twain's image-patterns that culminate in his later works in a cluster of images fraught with frustration and anxiety. Martin concludes that the "dream of vagrant, morally free drift [in *Huckleberry Finn*] had dissolved into a nightmare of feverish wandering." This idea of drift carries with it strong connotations. The helplessness and purposelessness show man whiling away his time in a succession of desultory, and never-ending movements.

The feeling of drift in an absolute void is particularly noticeable as the ship Edwards is on approaches the "white glare." DeVoto, for that matter, might just as easily have titled the fragment "The Great White Glare," because it becomes a central symbol of dissolution at the end. In an American iconological tradition the "white glare" represents a state of mental terror and despair. The fact that the light from the microscope is responsible for the final deaths of the crew suggests an ironic invocation at the end. It presents an inversion of God's command "Let there be light," and anticipates the grotesque parody of creation by Satan in *The Mysterious Stranger.* Twain inverts the traditional Christian symbolic meaning of intense light. Rather than representing a communion with God it manifests an absurd world-view. The great "white glare" is not a symbol of creation but a very powerful expression of a sense of deadness, of leaden heaviness and hopelessness, that is experienced in states of deep depression.

The dilemma the reader faces with the marooned sailors on this waste of ice and darkness is absurd purposelessness. And this is not a belief in a determinism, which is found in so many other of Twain's writings. That would suggest there is some agent at the helm, a distant if not indifferent God. The universe in **"The Great Dark"** is not a series of mechanical processes. Instead, the story fatally contradicts the notion of determinism. The reader confronts an inverted world, a clock-ridden world gone beserk, a place where man's instruments have gone willy-nilly. Laws of nature are suspended so the possibility of making referential calculations is completely eliminated: " '. . . the world has come to an end. Look at it yourself. Just look at the facts. Put them together and add them up, and what have you got? No Sable island; no Greenland; no Gulfstream; no day, no proper night. . . .' " And so, the miserable moments are repeated *ad nauseam.*

Twain casts a world that is non-temporal and populated by mutated beasts like the spider-squid. Along with presenting a hostile universe where man is forever an alien, Twain deliberately creates a world where man is doomed to drift in indefinite and centerless space. Like Heisenberg's principle of uncertainty, space-time references become inaccurate further underminding a cosmogony that hangs together and can be comprehended by the achievements of human thought and science.

The microcosmos in **"The Great Dark"** reaches beyond fatalism to a kind of nihilism. The psychic effects of this are found in the balance between claustrophobic and agoraphobic helplessness. Although Edwards is cast into a microscopic setting, there is a sense of macrocosmic proportions. At times it seems a supermacrocosm, especially when the Superintendent of Dreams informs him that it is six thousand miles across the drop of water. When Edwards asks if it will take more than a month to cross, the Superintendent replies: " 'I am afraid so. Possibly two—possibly longer, even.' " By the second half of the story four years have elapsed, and the voyage still goes on.

This sense of spaciousness is further revealed by the Superintendent of Dreams: " 'You came from a small and very insignificant world. The one you are in now is proportioned according to microscopic standards—that is to say, it is inconceivably stupendous and imposing.' " What he really means is that this is an inverted world, a place where microscopic objects and dimensions lose all proportion and become uncomfortably indefinite, producing the agoraphobic fear of the vast expanses of space. The sense of spaciousness is balanced by a corresponding sense of stasis. Edwards is essentially recording a basically static situation, emphasizing the sameness of the situation. The second half of the story announces that four years have passed, yet the conditions remain the same. Thus, man's hopelessness is also a kind of claustrophobic fidgeting in a void.

Twain had abandoned the notion of progress as early as 1887, and in **"The Great Dark"** he abandons Western man's faith in a comprehensible and objective reality. Man's function in the universe becomes merely janitorial. With no plan or sense to the voyage and no hope that the agony will end, Twain metaphorically creates a voyage of the mind into absolute solitude. (pp. 335-40)

> *Mark Kosinski, "Mark Twain's Absurd Universe and 'The Great Dark',"* in Studies in Short Fiction, *Vol. 16, No. 4, Fall, 1979, pp. 335-40.*

JOHN S. TUCKEY (essay date 1980)

[*In the following excerpt from his introduction to* "The Devil's Race-Track": Mark Twain's Great Dark Writings *(1980), Tuckey provides a thematic overview of selected stories from Twain's later years.*]

"There is no such figure for the storm-beaten human drift as the derelict," Mark Twain once told his friend and biographer Albert Bigelow Paine. The seas in which he voyaged, in his life and in his writings, were not only the earthly ones with their alluring and forbidding vastnesses and remotenesses. His imagination reached out to the uncharted deeps of the universe in which the globe was but a drifting particle, and also inward to the equally unfathomable inner space of the human psyche immersed in the ocean of the unconscious.

It was after he had passed the age of sixty that Mark Twain wrote all of the pieces that appear in [**"The Devil's Race-Track": Mark Twain's Great Dark Writings**]. In their focus they range from intensely personal matters to the cosmic situation as he envisioned it. Some deal with the disasters of the mid-1890s that had included financial failure and bankruptcy and the death of his daughter Susy, and these writings are much concerned with sudden turns of fate by which an individual may find himself in calamitous circumstances. Others view the human situation more generally, and sometimes from perspectives remote in time or scale. In **"Three Thousand Years Among the Microbes,"** events are perceived from a micro-macrocosmic viewpoint: the leading character is a germ who inhabits the river-like veins of a living human being that is his "planet" and also his deity.

A number of the writings dealing with personal and family misfortunes represent successive stages of work upon a story of a disastrous sea voyage that he felt compelled to produce, but which gave him trouble in finding the right approach. These various drafts are interesting both in themselves and for what they reveal of the direction and tendency of his thought and work. There are recurring themes. A man long favored by good luck has been pursuing a dream of high success that seems about to become a reality. Suddenly he experiences a nightmarish time of failure. As his thoughts race around the vicious circle track of his predicament (which Mark Twain was to call the Devil's Race-Track), he becomes confused and disoriented, both as to the passage of time and as to what is dream and what is reality. In several of the drafts, the fallen hero was to have a long dream of a tragedy-laden voyage and then awaken to find that what had seemed the events of terrible years had been the dream of a moment.

The voyage motif partly reflects Mark Twain's extensive sea travels during the globe-circling lecture tour of 1895-96 that he made in order to pay his debts, and from which he returned only to face the loss of Susy. But he had already, when financial ruin had only been impending, used the ship as a symbol of fortune. At a time in 1894 when he believed that the impracticable typesetter in which he had over-invested was finally to succeed, he cabled to his wife Olivia, "A ship visible on the horizon coming down under a cloud of canvas." A few days later, thinking that success had in fact come, he cabled again, *"Our ship is safe in port."* But within another ten days he had to send the woeful message, "Ships that pass in the night." Later in the same year his business advisor Henry H. Rogers had forced him to recognize that the typesetter had almost no commercial value. He wrote to Rogers, "It hit me like a thunder-clap. . . . I went flying here and there . . . , only one clearly defined thought standing up visible and substantial out of the crazy storm-drift—that my dream of ten years was in desperate peril." At this time he also penned some verses that were represented to be the mutterings of a crazed almshouse inmate who considered himself a storm-beaten derelict vessel, "Friendless, forlorn, and forgotten."

Another intertwining theme is that of the loss of the family home, usually by fire, and of the goal of a subsequent return to the once happy home situation that must somehow be achieved, whether in reality or in dream. In 1895, forced to look toward taking the round-the-world tour, he had visited the great house that had been the family center during seventeen more prosperous years but had become too expensive to live in. In a letter headed "At Home, Hartford," he wrote to Olivia, who was then in Paris, of his impressions upon entering the place: "[I]t seemed as if I had burst awake out of a hellish dream, and had never been away, and that you would come drifting down out of those dainty upper regions with the little children tagging after you." He added, "I was seized with a furious desire to have us all in this house again and right away, and never go outside the grounds any more forever—certainly never again to Europe." The desire quickly became a resolve: "I have made up my mind to one thing: if we go around the world we will move into our house when we get back." "At Home" was, thereafter, the title he used for the platform address that he was soon delivering repeatedly; he carried the dream of homecoming around the world with him. But close to the end of the long trip he received word of the death of Susy, of meningitis, on August 18, 1896. She had died in the Hartford house. Susy and he had been especially close, and the loss was for him the worst possible catastrophe. Moreover, her death had blasted the homecoming dream, for now the grieving family could not bear to live in the place at Hartford, and it seemed that there was no longer any goal or purpose to give meaning to their lives. "We are restless and unsettled," Mark Twain wrote early in the following year. "We had a charted course; we have none now. We are derelicts—and derelicts are indifferent to what may happen." It was at about this time that he wrote two story fragments in which a burning ship is made to symbolize a loss of fortune and of family.

In **"The Passenger's Story"** a sailing vessel is becalmed in the Indian Ocean. At night a fire breaks out, and the sailors are aroused just in time by a splendid and almost humanly intelligent St. Bernard dog, "the pet of the whole crew." All hands quickly take to the lifeboat and are saved—but the dog is left to burn. The captain has tied him to the mast, saying, "He'd be more in the way than a family of *children*—and he can *eat* as much as a family of children, *too.*" In the other fragment, **"The Enchanted Sea-Wilderness,"** the incident is developed more fully. Again the wonderful dog rescues the ship's company but is left to burn; again, copied word for word from the earlier draft, there is the captain's observation that the dog would have been as much in the way and would have eaten as much as a family of children. Susy, who had died of a brain-fever during an August heatwave, had almost literally burned up in the Hartford house; it is evident that Mark Twain was blaming himself for having left her behind during his travels.

The action of **"The Enchanted Sea-Wilderness"** begins with the ship becalmed as "a judgment on the captain" for letting the dog perish. The captain has always considered himself born lucky and for a while he cannot believe that his luck has been reversed. But storm follows calm as his ship is drawn southward into "the whirl and suck of the Devil's Race-Track," an immense circular region "in the midst of the vast ocean solitudes" that is "lashed and tossed and torn by eternal storms, is smothered in clouds and fog, and swept by fierce concentric currents." The Devil's Race-Track involves its victims in endlessly driven motion that goes around and around, arrives nowhere, and achieves nothing—or nothing but destruction. Once caught in its maelstrom forces there is no escape, only the possibility of further and final entrapment into the "Everlasting Sunday," an area of eternal and deathly stillness that lies at the center of the region, inside the storm belt. It is a Sargasso of the Antarctic, a graveyard for derelicts. The relevance of events of Mark Twain's life to the forbidding situation of the Devil's Race-Track and the Everlasting Sunday can easily be seen.

"Which Was the Dream?" was, as he planned it in the spring of 1897, to be a story that would begin with the burning of the family home and continue through a seventeen-year sequence of disasters, including again the voyage of a ship that would get into the Devil's Race-Track and then into the Everlasting Sunday. The narrator was at the end to find that it had all been a fifteen-second dream; yet the dream was to have been so terribly real to him that he would actually have aged by seventeen years and would upon awakening be unable to recognize his own children. Mark Twain did not write the story as planned. After dealing at some length with the business failure and subsequent disgrace of a great public figure and with the impact of these misfortunes upon his family, he left the manuscript incomplete. But in the following year

he found a more promising approach. He wrote to William Dean Howells, "I feel sure that all of the first half of the story—and I hope three-fourths—will be comedy; but by the former plan the whole of it (except the first 3 chapters) would have been tragedy and unendurable, almost. I think I can carry the reader a long way before he suspects that I am laying a tragedy-trap." What he was then envisioning became **"The Great Dark."**

Following his new plan, he did postpone the tragic aspects of his tale and play for humorous effects. There is, for example, much comic sea language: his narrator refers to the "mizzen foretop halyards" (much like referring to a basement penthouse), describes one sailor as "asleep on the binnacle" and another as "bending on a scuttle-butt," confuses "Topsail haul" with "Topsails all," and makes other ludicrous mistakes. There is also the scene in which the mate Turner is a butt for practical jokes of the spectral Superintendent of Dreams, who, while remaining invisible, keeps drinking Turner's coffee. After he had written these and other comic episodes, Mark Twain next gave further attention to the dream aspects of his story. It may be seen that he was particularly interested in the relationship of the waking self and dream self, or conscious and unconscious levels of mind, and the possibility of confusing dream and reality. Finally, in Book II he began to move toward his planned ending. But although he had a giant squid, a terrible kraken-like monster, attack the ship and so alarm the crew that they became ready to mutiny, he never completed the writing of a tragic outcome. At the time that the mutineers try to take over the ship, the captain, who has so far played no prominent part in the story, suddenly discloses himself to be a forceful leader. After calming the rebellious sailors, he makes a moving speech that ends on a note of high courage:

> Are we rational men, manly men, men who can stand up and face hard luck and a big difficulty that has been brought about by nobody's fault, and say live or die, survive or perish, we are in for it, for good or bad, and we'll stand by the ship if she goes to hell! . . . If it is God's will that we pull through, we pull through—otherwise not. We haven't had an observation for four months, but we are going ahead, and do our best to fetch up somewhere.

With this strong speech (which may remind one of Huckleberry Finn's "All right, then, I'll *go* to hell!"), the manuscript stops. Thus, the very last part of **"The Great Dark,"** as written, expresses strength and resoluteness rather than futility and despair. The courageous words of the captain must have been, for an author supposedly bent upon showing the hopelessness of life, a difficult act to follow. In projecting a tragedy-trap Mark Twain had perhaps failed to reckon with his own capacity for rebound and affirmation. His inability to finish the story as planned was less a failure than a success: one senses the resurgence of latent strengths, just when these had seemed about to capitulate to despair. Having intended to lead his readers on and spring a tragic ending upon them, Mark Twain had himself been trapped by his own returning courage.

In the long story **"Which Was It?"** . . . there is a somewhat different but basically similar trapping of weakness by strength. The cowardly George Harrison, who has committed murder while attempting to rob his way out of financial ruin, finds himself overmastered and "taken over" by the suddenly powerful ex-slave Jasper, who has found proof of Harrison's guilt. Jasper and Harrison can perhaps be viewed as alter egos representing respectively the stronger and the weaker aspects of Mark Twain's own nature (though on the primary level of meaning Jasper is first of all to be taken as a wronged black who is a truly impressive figure and who bears himself with dignity and pride and a good deal of forbearance when the tables are turned on the arrogant white man). In any case, it is evident that strength has asserted itself again in a story intended to show the frailty of human character and the general hopelessness of the situation. And once again it is just at this point of the emergence of a strong character in the story that the manuscript breaks off.

Mark Twain seems in effect to have engaged in a continuing dialogue between his own affirming and negating viewpoints. He had much difficulty in reconciling these, and a sudden reversal would occur when the side that was at a particular time being opposed or suppressed reasserted itself. These alternations must have been most disconcerting, and it is understandable that when they occurred he would be likely to abandon his manuscript and go to work upon a new one—until much the same thing happened again. Such reversals and abandonments can also be disturbing to readers. But a more positive way of looking at it is that Mark Twain was unable to stay for very long in the company of one-sided views and half-truths, especially when they were his own. It is his insistent seeking for the genuinely twofold, the duplicitous view that keeps him so interesting.

The story **"Three Thousand Years Among the Microbes"** is indeed interesting. In taking up the writing of it in 1905, Mark Twain was returning to a view of the human situation that had been in his thoughts since the time of his work on *Huckleberry Finn*. In August 1884, when he was reading proof for that book, he had noted, "I think we are only the microscopic trichina concealed in the blood of some vast creature's veins, and it is that vast creature whom God concerns Himself about and not us." **"Three Thousand Years Among the Microbes"** is, as Paine described it, a "fantastic tale . . . , the autobiography of a microbe that had been once a man, and through a failure in a biological experiment transformed into a cholera germ when the experimenter was trying to turn him into a bird. His habitat was the person of a disreputable tramp named Blitzowski, a human continent of vast areas, with seething microbic nations." Curiously, this story appears to have been closely associated in Mark Twain's thought with his voyage-of-disaster writings. It relates especially to **"The Great Dark,"** in which the voyage is taken in a seemingly vast ocean that is actually a drop of water which is under the lens of a microscope. Isabel V. Lyon, his literary secretary, kept a personal diary in which she wrote:

> I asked Mr. Clemens how long he'd been turning those marvellous imaginings over in his mind, and he said that the idea had been there for many years—he tried to work it up from a drop of water and a scientist with a powerful microscope; but it wasn't right. He had to become the microbe.

This was to be another story of great personal significance to Mark Twain. It is most interesting to find that in this bizarre narrative he was still attempting to use his early recollections of Hannibal and the Mississippi that served as the matrix of his best creative work. These Hannibalesque aspects are, however, curiously disguised or transformed. For instance, the narrator, whose microbic name is "Bkshp," eventually becomes known by the nickname "Huck." This "buried"

A suggestion for the title page of a book in Twain's handwriting.

identification is made only after the tale is well in progress. . . . (pp. ix-xv)

There is a further, hidden tie between the names "Huck" and "Bkshp." The latter is represented as the narrator's former earthly name rendered into "microbic orthography." In the microbe nation, the commoners, of which Bkshp is one, are not allowed to include vowels in their names. Actually, Bkshp appears to be a coding of "Blankenship," the name of the Hannibal boy who was a childhood acquaintance of Samuel Clemens and who later served as the real-life model for Huckleberry Finn: "In *Huckleberry Finn* I have drawn Tom Blankenship exactly as he was," Mark Twain says in his *Autobiography*. Moreover, the drunken tramp who is the planet of the microbes contains "rivers (veins and arteries)" that "make the Mississippi . . . trifling . . . by comparison." Huck Bkshp, who exists within Blitzowski, is thus in circumstances like those described in the note of August 1884. He is a germ "concealed in the blood of some vast creature's veins." He is a Huckian germ adrift in the Mississippi-like veins of a cosmic Pap Finn!

Mark Twain, writing with great creative exuberance in producing this story, was identifying himself closely with his narrator Huck. On one page of his manuscript . . . it may be seen that he at first wrote, in a revealing slip of the pen, his own name in place of the appropriate one in a fantastic listing of heraldic crests for an aristocracy of germs. He wrote "Mark Twain" and then substituted "Huck." . . . (pp. xv-xvii)

It is hardly surprising that he should have become so deeply immersed in his story. At last he had found the narrative perspective for the micro-macrocosmic analogy that had for many years been in his thoughts. He was able to express and explore the most comprehensive, even if not the most reassuring, view of the human situation that he had entertained. The tramp-planet-deity of the microbes is infested by the germs that are decaying and devouring him; but he in turn is also the infester and parasite of the greater cosmos, the "vast creature" in whom he moves and has his being. Huck, whose remembered former human life gives him an awareness that his fellow microbes do not share, observes of one of them:

> He did not suspect that he, also, was engaged in gnawing, torturing, defiling, rotting and murdering a fellow-creature—he and all the swarming billions of his race. None of them suspects it. That is significant. It is suggestive. It hints at the possibility that the procession of known and listed devourers and persecutors is not complete. It suggests . . . that man is himself a microbe, and his globe a blood-corpuscle drifting with its shining brethren of the Milky Way down a vein of the Master and Maker of all things.

In another story of the same period (written in 1905 and 1906) that he called **"The Refuge of the Derelicts,"** Mark Twain was again concerned with those conditions of life which impose upon everyone the roles of the devoured and the devourers. Old Admiral Stormfield is, like the captain in **"The Great Dark"** and the better known one in *Captain Stormfield's Visit to Heaven,* profane, courageous, opinionated, and generous. Maintaining a home that is fitted out like a ship and run like one, he lets his place serve as a haven for human derelicts. These are persons who are no longer chasing after power and success and are not trying to exploit and victimize their fellow beings. They have refused the role of predator, or at least have tried to do so. But it is shown that even the derelicts, resigned and harmless as they seem to be, are ironically still among the predators. They are feeding upon the bounty of Admiral Stormfield. Fittingly enough, on the occasion of their Plum Duff, an entertainment night with "intellectual raisins in it," they are shown by an illustrated lecture how parasites must treat their host. A sequence of horrific motion-picture close-ups is projected for the derelicts while a sanctimonious lecturer enlarges upon the bounty and goodness of Nature. The pictures, which have been hastily provided, prove to be terribly at variance with the reassuring text of the speaker. A mother spider is shown trusting happily that food will be provided for her little spiderlings; she then learns that *she* is their food: they suddenly begin to devour her. The mother spider is then seized by a mother wasp to provide food for *her* young—and so on. The incident conveys the idea that any creature that survives does so by preying upon another; that no one can decline the grisly banquet—and live.

The same idea that life is so ordered that all must be victimizers and victims appears again in the latest-written selection, **"Little Bessie,"** which was composed in 1908 when Mark Twain was in his seventy-third year. The question that naturally arises when one dwells upon the more grim aspects of life is the old one, older no doubt than the Book of Job, that is ever renewed in the thoughts of living mortals afflicted with pain and sorrow: "What is it all for?" Mark Twain phrased it thus as the query of a precocious little girl, not yet three years old. The question may be naïve, but behind it there is the vision of the boldly speculative Mr. Hollister whose discussions with Bessie have so disturbed her convention-bound

mother. The Hollister viewpoint is a more whole-seeing, or *holistic,* one that does not blink at disquieting aspects of the human situation. Behind that viewpoint, moreover, there lies the multifaceted and comprehensive awareness, the sagely ironic awareness, of Mark Twain.

There is no need to pretend that everyone has by now become so sophisticated or enlightened that considerations of the darker aspects of life as explored by Mark Twain no longer can shock or distress any readers; even the more venturesomely philosophical reader could well find a few unsettling notions. Yet it would likewise be a mistake to take these later writings always seriously, or to think that Mark Twain was always taking them so. One notices that the tone of the **"Little Bessie"** dialogues is a felicitously bantering one, and that there are indications that he must have had an enjoyable time with the writing, in which he shows himself to be still a humorist as well as a satirist. (pp. xvii-xx)

> *John S. Tuckey, in* "The Devil's Race-Track": Mark Twain's Great Dark Writings, *edited by John S. Tuckey, University of California Press, 1980, 385 p.*

JAMES C. WILSON (essay date 1982)

[*An American educator, critic, and journalist, Wilson has described his perspective as "loosely" Marxist and has said his interests include "politics, history, and literature, and the relationship that exists among all three." In the following excerpt, Wilson explores the symbolism of "The Great Dark," comparing it with Edgar Allan Poe's* The Narrative of Arthur Gordon Pym *(1838) and Herman Melville's* Moby-Dick *(1851).*]

Twain created in **"The Great Dark"** one of the most remarkable works of symbolism in American literature. In fact, its strangely haunting symbolism recalls the fiction of Poe and Melville a half century earlier, as Justin Kaplan points out in his biography. According to Kaplan, Twain became at the end of his life "a traveler in the spectral world of Poe and Hawthorne and among the 'invisible spheres' that Melville said 'were formed in fright.' "

The symbolic journey in **"The Great Dark"** bears unmistakable resemblance to those in Poe's *The Narrative of Arthur Gordon Pym* and Melville's *Moby-Dick.* Pym, Ahab, and Henry Edwards all journey toward knowledge, journeys that lead them to annihilation as well as knowledge. On his chartless voyage, Pym proceeds through murder and cannibalism, finally drifting aimlessly toward the South Pole; along the way, as he retreats further into his own mind, external reality becomes increasingly formless and disordered, until he reaches the primal chaos, symbolized by the giant cataract, the sheet of white ice, that opens to receive him at the end of the story. Pym penetrates the "white curtain," but he finds only "the perfect whiteness of the snow"—whiteness, the absence of all color, symbolizing the absence of all value and/or meaning. Ahab, too, has the same passion for knowledge and annihilation that drives him through madness and carnage to his final encounter with the white whale, when he punches "through the wall" only to plunge down to a watery death on the back of the mysterious Moby-Dick. In "The Quarterdeck" chapter of *Moby-Dick* Ahab asks, "How can the prisoner reach outside except by thrusting through the wall? To me, the white whale is that wall, shoved near to me. Sometimes I think there's naught beyond. But 'tis enough." Ahab, like Pym, confronts and is finally consumed by that "white wall," that absence of meaning, again symbolized by the color white.

Indeed, this symbolic journey to the "white wall" endures as a kind of mythos in American literature. Either consciously or unconsciously, Twain drew from this American mythos when he wrote **"The Great Dark."** He began work on the manuscript in August, 1898. He might have come by the specific idea for the story on August 10, when he recorded his previous night's dream "of a whaling cruise in a drop of water." However, he had used the image of the derelict ship to describe the condition of his own family in letters written throughout the 1890's, since the time of his impending backruptcy. At any rate, on August 16, 1898, he indicated in a letter to William Dean Howells that he had discontinued work on **"Which Was The Dream?"** and had been at work on a new story for about a week. This new story, **"The Great Dark,"** Twain described to Howells as a "tragedy-trap". . . . (pp. 230-31)

Though hardly comedy, **"The Great Dark"** succeeds very well as a tragedy-trap. The manuscript consists of a short "Statement By Mrs. Edwards" and a much longer "Statement By Mr. Edwards," both recounting the events of the same day. In her statement, Mrs. Edwards describes the "dreadful thing" that happened to her "happy family," which includes her husband, Henry, and their two children, Jessie and Bessie, on March 19, Jessie's birthday. For her birthday Jessie has been given a microscope, and she and her father are examining a drop of water through its powerful lens. Mrs. Edwards takes the children away, in order to prepare them for the birthday party later in the evening, but Henry remains in the bedroom with the microscope and falls asleep on the sofa. When she returns, Mrs. Edwards finds him at his table writing.

The "Statement By Mr. Edwards" begins: "We were experimenting with the microscope. And pretty ignorantly." In his statement, Henry recounts how he falls asleep on the sofa, and how the Superintendent of Dreams soon appears to him and offers to provide a "crew of whalers" so that Henry can explore this "ocean in a drop of water—and unknown, uncharted, unexplored by man!" Then, quite suddenly, Henry finds (dreams?) himself aboard a ship somewhere on a dark sea: "the ship was heaving and wallowing in the heavy seas. . . . Everything was dimmed to obliteration . . . the only thing sharply defined was the foamy mane of white water, sprinkled with phosphorescent sparks, which broke away from the lee bow." This passage effectively completes the transition from reality to dream, or at least from what Henry thinks is reality to what he thinks is dream. The distinction will soon become blurred.

At first Twain plays for humorous effects, parodying the language of sailors as found in various romantic sea novels of the time. But not even these touches can lighten the oppressive tone, which increases in darkness throughout the remainder of Book One. Though supposedly morning, the ship sails in a "solid bank of darkness," and on deck Henry and the other men appear and disappear in the gloom: "I saw the glow of a match photograph a pipe and part of a face against a solid bank of darkness." Faces emerge out of the darkness, much as images materialize on photographic paper; snow and sleet slant across, then dissolve into the blackness. True to the nightmarish quality of the "haunted ship," every scene is rendered in images of white and black—primal opposites, silhouettes rather than color. Indeed, I count three references to

colors other than white or black (or gray) in the entire manuscript. Otherwise, it is "always night—and such dismal nights, too. It's like being up at the pole in the winter time."

The nightmarish quality of this scene is somewhat alleviated by Henry's curiosity; Henry is "not so much terrified by his situation as deeply interested in exploring its meaning," according to William Macnaughton [see Further Reading list]. "I am not of a worrying disposition, so I do not care," Henry says to the Superintendent of Dreams at one point. But Henry fails to understand his predicament; what allows him the luxury of courage is his faith that the entire voyage is nothing but a dream, chartered and presided over by the Superintendent of Dreams. However, Henry's "sand-edifice of certainty" begins to crumble as he encounters others, crew members and passengers, who do not share his faith.

Turner, the First Mate, tells Henry that neither he nor the captain know the location of the ship. Not only are they lost, but the ocean itself does not conform to any chart or known referent. Moreover, Turner tells of "a whale with hairy spider legs" and laments being "lost at sea among such strange, uncanny brutes." As they speak, the giant monster appears: "He was gone like a shot, and the night swallowed him up. Now all of a sudden, with the wind still blowing hard, the seas went down and the deck became as level as a billiard table." And on deck walks the Superintendent of Dreams, wearing "a broad slouch hat and a long cloak," a mysterious mythical figure that they "glimpse and lose in the dark."

Turner's revelations begin to unsettle Henry, especially when he discovers that the captain has attempted to suppress the bad news for fear of inciting the crew to mutiny. In a foreboding comment, Turner calls Henry "a landsman, and there's no telling what a landsman can't overlook if he tries." Turner sums up their precarious navigational position by speculating that:

> . . . the world has come to an end. Look at it yourself. Just look at the facts. Put them together and add them up, and what have you got? No Sable Island; no Greenland; no Gulf Stream; no day, no proper night; weather that don't jibe with any sample known to the Bureau; animals that would start a panic in any menagerie; chart no more use than a horse-blanket, and the heavenly bodies gone to hell!

Next Henry encounters the Superintendent of Dreams, whom he reproaches for playing "tricks" on Turner. A little uneasy, Henry asks the Superintendent how long the voyage will last, and the Superintendent replies that it "will be some time yet," "because the ship is chartered for a voyage of discovery. Ostensibly she goes to England, takes aboard some scientists, then sails for the South Pole." But the Superintendent does answer some of Henry's questions. For example, he explains why it is always night: "All the drop of water is outside the luminous circle of the microscope except one thin and delicate rim of it. We are in the shadow; consequently in the dark," *i.e.* the Great Dark. The drop of water, on which they sail, extends some 6,000 miles; and though the world has been reduced to microscopic proportions, the proportions are not "fictitious." For, as the Superintendent reveals, "nothing but the laws and conditions have undergone a change."

Henry becomes entranced by the Superintendent's revelations: "there was something overpowering in the situation, something sublime. It took me a while to shake off the spell and drag myself back to speech." Feeling "cornered," Henry pursues the conversation, pursues it to a conclusion that neither he nor the reader expects:

> ". . . if my style doesn't suit you, you can end the dream as soon as you please—right now, if you like."
>
> He looked at me steadily in the eye for a moment, then said, with deliberation—
>
> "The dream? *Are you quite sure it is a dream?*"
>
> "What do you mean? Isn't it a dream?"
>
> He looked at me in that same way again; and it made my blood chilly, this time. Then he said—
>
> "You have spent your whole life in this ship. And this is *real* life. Your other life was a dream."

"It was as if he had hit me," Henry says. And the Superintendent's lip "curled itself into a mocking smile, and he wasted away like a mist and disappeared." Like the Superintendent's corporeality, Henry's "sand-edifice of certainty" wastes away and disappears forever. In this, the central scene of Book One, Henry finds his sense of reality "dissolving" what he has always thought of as reality now begins to fade into dream, and what he has always thought of as dream now begins to seem terrifyingly real. The Superintendent of Dreams becomes the Superintendent of Realities "as he is so-called in the other planets, but here we reverse the meanings of many words, and we wouldn't understand him," Twain wrote.

Mrs. Edwards confirms what the Superintendent has told Henry. Their land-life, Mrs. Edwards says, has always been a dream; and she does not remember the birthday party for Jessie, the microscope, etc. Instead, she recalls their sea-life: "The earliest thing I can call to mind was Papa's death by the sun-heat and mama's suicide the same day. I was four years old, then." (The "sun-heat" that she refers to is the Great White Glare, which in the scheme of the story is the light shining from the microscope's reflector through the slide at which Henry was looking.) And Mrs. Edwards says that her land-life memories do not correspond to Henry's because "people can't be expected to remember each other's dreams, but only their own." Likewise, the Edwards children remember only "dream-houses" from their land-life; they "cared for no other home" than the ship. Finally alone, Henry broods on the "elusive mysteries of my bewitched memory" and begins to recall incidents from his sea-life, incidents that his wife had described to him. And much to his surprise, Henry finds that "the main incidents of both my lives were now recovered, but only those of one of them persistently gathered strength and vividness—our life in the ship!" Once a "landsman," Henry has become an outcast, an exile.

In effect, Book One establishes Henry's sea-life as reality and his land-life as dream. But even more importantly, just as Twain gradually dissolves the reality of Henry's land-life, he invalidates Henry's means of understanding the world—his rationality. Always the empiricist, first pictured experimenting with his microscope (itself a symbol of science and empiricism) and later eager to explore the "unknown, unchartered, unexplored" ocean in a drop of water, Henry now finds himself a prisoner in a universe that does not conform to empirical thought. The very "laws and conditions have undergone a change," the Superintendent of Dreams had told him, and now Henry understands what he had meant. In a powerful moment of insight, Henry articulates his sense of impotency in the face of this knowledge, the failure of reason to comprehend the universe:

> We are strangely made. We think we are wonderful creatures. Part of the time we think that, at any rate. And during that interval we consider with pride our mental equipment, with its penetration, its power of analysis, its ability to reason out clear conclusions from confused facts, and all the lordly rest of it; and then comes a rational interval and disenchants us. Disenchants us and lays us bare to ourselves, and we see that intellectually we are no great things; that we seldom really know the thing we know; that our best-built certainties are but sand-houses and subject to damage from any wind of doubt that blows.

Book Two explores the nature of Henry's new sea-life reality and defines that life in images of darkness and destruction. Several years have passed since the close of Book One, and much has happened in the intervening years, including the birth of a son (Harry) to the Edwards. Meanwhile, the ship has taken on a new crew that "still think we are bound for the South Pole." And a new spirit of unrest has become evident on board, as the crew has mutinied several times, led by its "master spirit" Stephen Bradshaw. Another mutiny is imminent.

When Henry resumes his narrative, the tone has changed dramatically. Instead of his former curiosity, his narrative projects a fatalism, a quiet despair at the prospects of their chartless voyage. "I have long ago lost Book I, but it is no matter. It served its purpose—writing it was an entertainment to me," he begins. Then he sets the scene: "For a month or two the ship's company had been glimpsing vast animals at intervals of a few days, and at first the general terror was so great that the men openly threatened, on two occasions, to seize the ship unless the captain turned back."

Suddenly the "still and solemn black day" explodes into a "riot" of cries, as the giant squid attacks the ship and Henry rushes on deck to see "two full-moons rising close over the stern of the ship and lighting the deck and rigging with a sickly yellow glow—the eyes of the colossal squid." The crew retaliates by firing more than 2,000 rounds from a gatling gun into the eyes of the squid, blinding and further enraging the monster. And now, in a blind frenzy, the creature stalks them somewhere out in the Great Dark.

In the confusion, the Edwards children become lost. Henry, panicking, searches frantically for the children in a scene rendered in images that create a sense of absolute horror. The images are of darkness:

> Not a lantern was twinkling anywhere, and every figure that emerged from the gloom moved upon tiptoe.

Of helplessness:

> We stood dead still, hardly breathing. Here and there at little distances the men were gathering silently together and watching and pointing. The deep hush lay like a weight upon one's spirit. Even the faintest quiver of air that went idling by gave out a ghost of sound. A couple of mellow notes floated lingering and fading down from forward: *Booooom—booooom.* [Two bells in the middle watch.]

And of the violence that threatens to erupt at any moment:

> For five minutes we could hear him trashing about,
> there in the dark, and lashing the sea with his giant
> tentacles in his pain; and now and then his moons
> showed, then vanished again; and all the while we
> were rocking and plunging in the booming seas he
> made.

In fact, the images become apocalyptic as the passengers and crew wait, expecting destruction. They "lay in a dead calm, and helpless" while the monster continues to pursue them. And to make matters worse, the crew finally mutinies, demanding that the ship turn back, not realizing that home no longer exists. But the captain manages to temporarily assuage the men's fears by delivering an exaggerated heroic speech, asking "Are we rational men, manly men, men who can stand up and face hard luck . . . ?" Though his words are rhetorically effective, the captain's appeal to them as "rational men" makes no sense in this context, because rationality does not matter in the Great Dark. Perhaps the captain realizes this, as he then changes his appeal from reason to "faith"—they must have faith, he says, that they are "in the hands of God." "If it is God's will that we pull through, we pull through— otherwise not. We haven't had an observation for four months, but we are going ahead, and do our best to fetch up somewhere," the captain declares—not a very hopeful statement, considering the circumstances.

Unfortunately, the manuscript ends there, but Twain's notes indicate how he planned to conclude the story. After various intrigues, most of them caused by the greed of certain members of the crew, Henry's infant son and the captain's daughter Lucy are separated from them on a second ship, called *The Two Darlings.* They pursue the ship for ten years, until they at last come to the region of the Great White Glare. Now the sea dries up under the intense heat, and the giant animals become crazed in a frenzy of death. Finally they spot *The Two Darlings,* so Henry and the captain walk across the rough terrain to the other stranded ship. But they arrive too late—everybody has long since died, their corpses mummified by the heat. And when they return, they find the same gruesome scene on their own ship; Henry's wife, his two daughters, everyone has died from the heat.

At this point, Henry was to wake up to be with his family as he had been in the beginning of his narrative, before his supposed dream: "It is midnight—Alice and the children come to say goodnight. I think them dreams. Think I am back home *in a dream.*" Twain's notes indicate that Henry's hair was to have turned white (one more white image in this story suffused with whiteness, written by the dandy old man with white hair and white suits; as Ishmael says in "The Whiteness of the Whale" chapter of *Moby-Dick:* "it was the whiteness of the whale that above all things appalled me.") In other words, Henry was to be irrevocably changed by his voyage, by his encounter with Pym's "the perfect whiteness of the snow," whether it be dream or reality.

Henry's quest needs to be mentioned here. Henry is the "innocent," the "naif, who must make a journey of discovery," as Larry Dennis points out in "Mark Twain and the Dark Angel" [see Further Reading list]. But Henry represents more than just innocence and naivete; he illustrates the plight of rational nineteenth century man lost in the irrational universe of the Great Dark. Henry journeys into a universe that does not conform to empirical thought; it does not matter whether Henry's journey is real or dream, actual or visionary.

Stanley Brodwin writes in "Mark Twain's Masks of Satan: The Final Phase" [see Further Reading list] that "For Twain, reality has no inner logic to make it believable as an objective-existent structure with a meaningful *telos.* The universe, therefore, comes closest to the nature of a dream-nightmare." Thus by destroying reason as a means of understanding the universe, Twain in effect creates a new formerly uncognized universe—a universe that he defines in symbols of nightmarish horror and death. The important point is that his new universe can only be understood symbolically, *i.e.* through the use of symbols.

Like the voyages of Pym and Ahab, Henry's journey itself becomes symbolic. The journey can be charted as a movement from reality to dream, from objectivity to subjectivity, from realism to symbolism. From an empirical world represented by the microscope, Henry gradually ascends into a symbolic world. Not through reason, but only through symbols does Henry come to comprehend his nightmarish world. As Charles Feidelson defines it, symbolism attempts to unify the dichotomy between subject and object, mind and matter, by the use of symbols, which "are not mere signs, proxy for their objects," but rather "vehicles for the conception of obejects." Thus the Ship of the Dead provides a symbol that enables Henry to understand the human community, menaced by mutiny and greed and discord; the Great Dark provides a symbol that enables Henry to understand reality, irrational and without *telos* or purpose; and the Great White Glare provides a symbol that enables Henry to understand death, the inevitable annihilation waiting for all men at the end of their chartless voyage. In the Great Dark, all voyages come to the same end.

Thus **"The Great Dark"** recreates the mythos of the "white wall." For Henry Edwards, like Pym and Ahab, finds himself on a derelict ship, adrift in the Great Dark. No shores exist in the Great Dark, only the Great White Glare and the inevitability of death. Henry's journey is to annihilation, and what he discovers is the absence of meaning. And the manuscript, as it was planned, would have concluded with the symbol of whiteness—the Great White Glare, the mummified corpses, Henry's white hair. Again, the utter absence of meaning: nihilism. (pp. 232-41)

"The Great Dark" should be seen as an important symbolic work, in that it returns to and reexpresses the American myth of the symbolic journey to the "white wall"—a myth that persists even into the literature of the twentieth century. And **"The Great Dark"** provides perhaps the boldest statement of Twain's growing nihilism, a nihilism that surfaced from time to time in his fiction and in the fiction of many of his fellow nineteenth century American writers. Like Poe and Melville before him, Twain had his own mythopoeic "symbols of despair," with which he created some of his greatest literature. (p. 242)

> *James C. Wilson, " 'The Great Dark': Invisible Spheres, Formed in Fright," in* The Midwest Quarterly, *Vol. XXIII, No. 2, Winter, 1982, pp. 229-43.*

ELIZABETH McMAHAN (essay date 1982)

[*McMahan is an American educator, editor, and critic who has published several articles on Twain and served as editor of* Critical Approaches to Mark Twain's Short Stories *(1981). In the following essay, she explicates Twain's story "The $30,000 Bequest."*]

Mark Twain in **"The $30,000 Bequest"** spells out in detail the deleterious effects of money-lust—even fantasied money-lust—on human happiness. The story presents a young, innocent, happy couple who slip into daydreaming of untold wealth. Twain documents with wry humor their resulting moral decline and records with more seriousness the deterioration of their personal relationships. The wages of their imaginative sin is death.

The lure of money depicted in this tale is similar to the snare that enticed Twain's father into illusive hopes for realizing a fortune from a vast tract of inherited land in Tennessee. Twain writes in the *Autobiography* about the family's frustrated dreams of wealth: "It [the Tennessee land] kept us hoping and hoping during forty years, and forsook us at last. It put our energies to sleep and made visionaries out of all of us—dreamers and indolent. . . . It is good to begin life poor; it is good to begin life rich—these are wholesome; but to begin it poor and *prospectively* rich! The man who has not experienced it cannot imagine the curse of it." **"The $30,000 Bequest"** is Twain's artistic delineation of this curse.

The entire story is presented in monetary terminology spiced with stock market imagery. Twain includes few details that are unrelated to finance. His opening description of the husband tells us nothing about Saladin Foster except his occupation (bookkeeper), his age (thirty-five), and his salary (four hundred dollars a year to start, climbing to eight hundred—"a handsome figure indeed"). If this introduction of a character seems unusually monetary in nature, the description of his

An engraving by Florian from October 1895 that appeared in Harper's New Monthly Magazine, *May 1896.*

wife is even more so. We are told that Saladin's wife, Electra, is a "capable helpmeet, although—like himself—a dreamer of dreams." Then the following two-hundred and fifty words deal entirely with Electra's financial transactions since her marriage. We hear that "two children had arrived and increased the expenses," but she has handled the financial affairs of the family shrewdly and now has "an independent income from safe investments of about a hundred dollars a year."

One more peculiarity stands out in the opening of this story: the expected roles of male and female in relation to money are reversed, and the couple's nicknames reflect the change. "Saladin's was a curious and unsexing one—Sally; and so was Electra's—Aleck." Sally, the husband, dreams of spending their imaginary inheritance—frittering it away on luxuries—while Aleck, the wife, calculates means of making the money become fruitful and multiply. Only after their fanciful stock investments crash at the end of the story and their envisioned riches disappear, does Aleck regain a womanly role: "Then, and not till then, the man in her was vanished, and the woman in her resumed sway." Twain sees the calculating mind and financial absorption of Aleck as distinctly unfeminine. It is, for Twain, a perversion of the natural social order to invest the female with a drive for wealth and power. This curious "unsexing" constitutes one element that undermines the couple's once happy marriage.

The damage to human relationships resulting from the Foster's fantasies about their "fictitious finances" begins almost at once. When Sally and Aleck become wrapped up in their visions of wealth, they neglect their young daughters: "The children took themselves away early, for the parents were silent, distraught, and strangely unentertaining. The goodnight kisses might as well have been impressed upon vacancy for all the response they got; the parents were not aware of the kisses, and the children had been gone an hour before their absence was noted."

After a few years the two begin speculating about marrying their girls advantageously—for money and social prestige. They realize that the "rising young journeyman tinner" and the "journeyman plasterer," whom they had previously been pleased to have interested in their daughters, will never do now: their imaginary wealth has "raised up a social bar." Sally's use of stock market jargon in these intimate domestic discussions lends the passage humor and a satirical edge. After five years of playing this monetary marriage market, Sally develops reservations and tells his wife, " 'You've continued the same policy from the start, with every rise, always holding on for five points higher. . . . First, we turned down the dentist and the lawyer. That was all right—it was sound. Next, we turned down the banker's son and the pork-butcher's heir—right again, and sound. Next, we turned down the Congressman's son and the Governor's—right as a trivet, I confess it. Next the Senator's son and the son of the Vice-President of the United States—perfectly right, there's no permanency about those little distinctions.' " (The irony of the Fosters seeing the distinction of high office as "impermanent" is considerable in the light of the ephemeral nature of their own imaginary wealth.) The fact that these honors are "little" distinctions makes clear that according to their value system, money tops the list. Aleck has turned down baronets, barons, viscounts, earls, marquises—even "a brace of dukes." Sally is growing impatient. " 'Now, Aleck, cash in!—you've played the limit.' " But Aleck has her sights set on royalty. She whispers to Sally "a princely name," and he pronounces it "a stunning catch . . . , all gilt-edged five-hundred per-cent stock . . , the tidiest little property in Europe." Yet He knows Aleck and queries in a moment of doubt, " 'You didn't take him on a margin?' " And Aleck reassures him, " 'No. Trust me for that. He's not a liability, he's an asset.' "

But trust, which the couple once had in abundance, erodes away under the influence of their fiscal fantasies. Sally's conscience begins to gnaw at him because Aleck is devoting her fantasies to good works while he is directing his largely to dissipation. Eventually he confesses all of these imaginary sins and weeps upon her breast, begging for forgiveness. Aleck is profoundly shocked by the revelation: "She felt that he could never again be quite to her what he had been before; she knew that he could only repent, and not reform." Since she loves him, since he is "her very own," she forgives: "She opened her yearning heart and took him in." Twain's language is elevated and serious, but because the sins are imaginary, the tone of the passage becomes sardonic. Genuine forgiveness requires more character than Aleck can muster. The debilitating effect of their fantasies has separated the couple emotionally: "Sally's terrible revelation had done its work . . . ; she could see now . . . that her husband was becoming a bloated and repulsive Thing." At the same time, however, she has herself begun "acting dishonorably toward him" by breaking their solemn agreement to retire from stock speculation and enjoy in imagination the fruits of their imaginary investments. Aleck has secretly succumbed to temptation and risked the entire fortune by purchasing "all the railway systems and coal and steel companies in the country on a margin." Before this breech of trust, she has felt herself to be her husband's moral superior in every way. But now their financial *fata morgana* has left both of the Fosters morally bankrupt.

The two are also spiritually bankrupt, but they are comfortably unaware of this deficiency. Aleck, Twain says, "was a Christian from the cradle, and duty and the force of habit required her to go through the motions." But her religion is entirely a sham. It becomes another part of her social-climbing. In her real life Aleck "stuck loyally to the little Presbyterian Church, and labored faithfully in its interests and stood by its high and tough doctrines with all their mental and spiritual energies." In her fantasy life, however, she becomes an Episcopalian, "on account of the candles and shows." Eventually she moves on to Catholicism "where there were cardinals and more candles." Sally enjoys even more variety than this: "He kept every part [of his dream life] fresh and sparkling by frequent changes, the religious part along with the rest. He worked his religions hard, and changed them with his shirt." When he is not busy changing his own religion, Sally never loses a chance to snipe away at Aleck's flimsy faith. She often indulges her fancy by erecting "a batch of churches; now and then a cathedral." And Sally wounds her feelings by saying, "It was a cold day when she didn't ship a cargo of missionaries to persuade unreflecting Chinamen to trade off twenty-four carat Confucianism for counterfeit Christianity."

Aleck's religion is nicely representative of a kind long popular in American society—the love-God-and-He-will-make-you-prosperous variety. Sally, if he has any religious impulses at all, clings to them only as a kind of fire insurance—protection against the eternal torments of hell. When the cou-

ple is just beginning to pile up their imaginary fortune, Sally gets impatient for his uncle to die so they can begin stacking up money in reality. Aleck cautions him to be patient and " 'be grateful for what God is doing for us, and stop worrying. You do not believe we could have achieved these prodigious results without His special help and guidance, do you?' " But Sally doubts that Divine Power deserves all the credit: " 'When it comes to judiciousness in watering a stock or putting up a hand to skin Wall Street, I don't give in that 'you need any outside amateur help. . . .' " Aleck shudders at this irreverence and begins to sob; even Sally takes pause after such balsphemy and erects a lightning rod. Twain's satire here is double-edged, as he ridicules the sophisticated chicanery of Aleck's investment practices as well as her concealment of her moral failings behind a facade of what Sally calls "conventional piety."

For Aleck is not a "professing Christian," but rather a "professional Christian." She has, for instance, begun studying "with an eye single to finance" the *Wall Street Pointer* and a Chicago daily paper "as diligently all the week as she studied her Bible Sundays." Sally admires Aleck's manipulation of her "wordly stocks" as much as her "conservative caution in working her spiritual deals." Finally, though, their imaginary fortune reaches such gigantic proportions that the stock must be inventoried, a task requiring a full day's work, and neither has any leisure time—except Sunday. In a scene humorously exaggerated to produce a mock tension comparable to that in the Garden of Eden, they succumb to temptation. They fall—and break the Sabbath. "It was but another step in the downward path," comments Twain sonorously. "Others would follow. Vast wealth has temptations which fatally and surely undermine the moral structure of persons not habituated to its possession."

The Fosters' moral decline has, indeed, been steady throughout the story. The outward manifestation begins on a small scale with the drinking of a glass of imaginary champagne to celebrate a financial coup. Since both have previously been active temperance workers, Twain observes that "the pride of riches was beginning its disintegrating work." The moral weakening progresses, spurred by their infatuation with money and rationalized through their fantasies. Sally now cherishes Aleck for her financial wizardry. But far from possessing the "immeasurable deeps" Sally credits her with, Aleck exhibits only a calculating shrewdness about stocks and bonds and a flair for social climbing.

Sally is in even worse shape. His fantasies of dissipation have grown to such proportion that he now sits up nights working on "inventions of ways to spend the money." He begins stealing candles from the store where he works to provide light for these nighttime fabrications, for in reality the Fosters are quite pinched for money. "It is ever thus," intones Twain: "Vast wealth, to the person unaccustomed to it, is a bane; it eats into the flesh and bone of his morals. When the Fosters were poor, they could have been trusted with untold candles. But now they—but let us not dwell upon it. From candles to apples is but a step: Sally got to taking apples; then soap; then maple-sugar; then canned-goods; then crockery."

The moral degeneration is thus complete, and the final blow falls when the couple discovers that the bequest was an illusion also. Old Tilbury Foster, for some perverse reason, left this damning fraudulent bequest to his nephew with full knowledge of the grief he was causing. The original letter stated that he was leaving the thirty-thousand dollars "not for love, but because money had given him most of his troubles and exasperations, and he wished to place it where there was good hope that it would continue its malignant work." But Tilbury Foster died a pauper: there never was any thirty-thousand dollars in reality. The story has much in common with **"The Man That Corrupted Hadleyburg"** in that a situation is deliberately set up to entrap an unsuspecting and previously upstanding pair into courting their doom. When the Fosters discover that the money never existed, they go into a decline similar to that suffered by the old couple in **"Hadleyburg."** Their minds are affected; they begin to "twaddle to each other in a wandering and childish way." But in some ways the loss of that imaginary fortune brings them back into human contact again. Aleck regains her forfeited womanhood, and they cling to each other "in mutual compassion and support; as if they would say: 'I am near you, I will not forsake you, we will bear it together.'"

But the reconciliation comes too late to provide salvation from the debilitating effect of their moral losses. They live two years "in mental night, always brooding, steeped in vague regrets and melancholy dreams, never speaking." They both die quietly on the same day, and Twain lapses into the same didacticism that keeps **"Hadleyburg"** from being a satisfying story. From Sally's "ruined mind," we receive this superfluous summary of the theme: "'Vast wealth, acquired by sudden and unwholesome means, is a snare. It did us no good, transient were its pleasures; yet for its sake we threw away our sweet and simple and happy life—let others take warning by us.'"

It is, of course, not money *per se* which undermines the Foster's happiness but the preoccupation with money which distorts its importance and makes it the corrupter of simplicity and warm relationships. Twain makes this clear in Sally's final words: "'With base and cunning calculation [Uncle Tilbury] left us but thirty thousand, knowing we would try to increase it, and ruin our life and break our hearts. Without added expense he could have left us far above the desire of increase, far above the temptation to speculate, and a kinder soul would have done it. . . .'" Ironically, Sally still deceives himself. At the time Aleck made her final, disastrous plunge buying railroads, coal, and steel on margin, she had amassed an imaginary "twenty-four hundred millions, and all safely planted in Good Things, gilt-edged and interest-bearing." Aleck could never have been left sufficient money to place her "far above desire of increase, far above temptation to speculate." She is like Twain's celebrated contemporary, Commodore Vanderbilt, about whom Twain wrote privately,

> Poor Vanderbilt! How I do pity you; and this is honest. You are an old man, and ought to have some rest, and yet you have to struggle and struggle, and deny yourself, and rob yourself of restful sleep and peace of mind because you need money so badly. I always feel for a man who is so poverty-ridden as you. Don't misunderstand me, Vanderbilt. I know you own seventy millions; but then you know and I know that it isn't what a man has that constitutes wealth. No—it is to be satisfied with what one has; that is wealth.

"The $30,000 Bequest" demonstrates how seeking wealth, even in dreams, destroys any possibility for a fruitful and satisfying existence. Twain was convinced that most of his fellow citizens were like the Fosters: unaware of the hollowness of their goals, unconscious even that money had become their

god. In 1871 he published "The Revised Catechism" in the New York *Tribune:*

> Q. What is the chief end of man?
>
> A. To get rich.
>
> Q. In what way?
>
> A. Dishonestly if we can, honestly if we must.
>
> Q. Who is God, the only one and true?
>
> A. Money is God. Gold and greenbacks and stocks—father, son, and ghost of the same. . . .

Twain sensed that a society which encourages money-making above all else stands to suffer losses, both spiritual and moral. **"The $30,000 Bequest"** sounds a stern warning against the insidious acquisitive values which were then—and still remain—embodied in the great American dream of upward mobility. (pp. 23-6)

> *Elizabeth McMahan, "Finance and Fantasy as Destroyers in Twain's 'The $30,000 Bequest',"* in Mark Twain Journal, *Vol. XXI, No. 2, Summer, 1982, pp. 23-6.*

TERENCE J. MATHESON (essay date 1982)

[*In the following excerpt, Matheson defends* The Mysterious Stranger *against critics who dismiss the story as a noble but ultimately flawed attempt at serious literature by a "tired mind," describing Twain's work as a "tale of considerable ironic and satiric complexity."*]

It is now generally known that the version of Mark Twain's ***The Mysterious Stranger*** familiar to most readers is the product of considerable editorial liberties taken by the author's literary executor, Albert Bigelow Paine, and his publisher Frederick A. Duneka, who worked extensively on Twain's unfinished manuscripts in order to create a marketable product. Paine and Duneka, it has been proved, were responsible for deleting large sections from the original, adding material of their own, and in general changing the text to produce a work wherein the author's original purposes have been somewhat obscured. Given this, it is not surprising that many critics have turned to events from Twain's later life to provide them with possible clues as to the work's meaning, to say nothing of Twain's purpose in writing it. Unfortunately, what has emerged from this approach is a generally-held but untenable assumption that, since Twain's final years were full of suffering and personal misfortune, his views and those of the totally pessimistic, bitter and cynical Philip Traum must be virtually identical, and that given this, neither Traum nor the boys he appears to befriend should be interpreted ironically. Wendell Glick is typical of most critics in "feeling that Twain is unabashedly using Satan as his *redacteur*" [see Further Reading list]. To Glick, Satan is obviously Twain's "mouthpiece," as he is his "spokesman" to Coleman Parsons [see Further Reading list], serving as a source of information the veracity of which we are not supposed to question. He is a "deity" to E. S. Fussell [see excerpt dated 1952], "a supernatural spectator" to Henry Nash Smith [see Tuckey, *Mark Twain's 'The Mysterious Stranger' and the Critics* in Further Reading list], "a force of spiritual . . . innocence charged with divine-like creative power" to Stanley Brodwin [see Further Reading list], a "Self-controlled Gentleman of the Southwestern tradition" to Kenneth Lynn [see Further

Reading list]: anything, it seems, other than simply the Devil himself.

Critics have not been blind to the many inconsistencies in the philosophy and arguments expressed by Twain's Satan, but when examined, they have been dismissed simply as proof of the author's declining powers. To Albert E. Stone Jr., such weaknesses in Satan's arguments say more about Twain's lack of skill than anything else, any contradictions within Satan's account of man merely mirroring "the contradictions of Twain's own tortured mind" [see further Reading list]. At one point, commenting on the arguments Satan presents on behalf of determinism, Stone shrewdly observes that his deterministic assertions contradict his earlier remarks about man's freedom to choose between right and wrong. However, even though Stone sees this as typical of "many such ambiguities," he can only conclude that this proves the work to be "the end-product of a tired mind grappling with ideas foreign or inaccessible to it."

It is surprising that critics such as Stone have been so disinclined to appreciate *The Mysterious Stranger* in a manner more flattering to Twain. Once we are prepared to regard it as something other than a confused piece by a confused man, and stop placing so much importance on our knowledge that Twain's final years were unhappy, it can be seen as a tale of considerable ironic and satiric complexity. Dismal though Twain's last decade undoubtedly was, it is presumptuous to assume that he himself was in a state of continuous despondency, or that even if he were, it would produce in him a pessimism as transparently simplistic as that voiced by one of his created characters. While a good deal of what Satan says regarding human nature is undeniably true—what sensitive person has not, on occasion, felt as much when confronted with examples of human cruelty and evil?—we must not make the mistake of taking Satan's observations out of their literary context, or of placing them in isolation. Unfinished though *The Mysterious Stranger* may have been, it was still conceived by its author as a literary work and must be appreciated as such. Once we look at it in this way, we immediately see there are other events in the work which lead us to a different and more complex vision of human nature, a vision which, when set against the pessimistic position taken by Satan, goes far toward nullifying its effectiveness and force.

In discussing the various ways we determine when irony is present, Wayne Booth in *A Rhetoric of Irony* has observed that "If a speaker betrays ignorance or foolishness that is 'simply incredible', the odds are comparatively high that the author, in contrast, knows what he is doing." Later, Booth adds that the likelihood irony is present is logically apt to increase in proportion to the number of suspected ironic situations encountered. Given this, it is indeed difficult not to regard the beginning of *The Mysterious Stranger* as heavily ironic, for the opening pages are especially rich in such clues. A plethora of sleep imagery is initially used to describe the setting. . . . Everywhere the atmosphere is soporific and sluggish, suggesting dullness, complacency, and smug, unused intellects. Though it is 1590 (or 1702, as originally conceived) Austria is still in the "Middle Ages" which Twain defines as the "Age of Faith" or, in this sense, credulity, at least a full century behind the times and promising "to remain so forever." In short, not only are the inhabitants of this region intellectually asleep, they are uneducable as well. Not surprisingly, the boys are "not overmuch pestered with school-

ing," but are encouraged to remain docile and respectful of their superiors.

Booth elsewhere comments that "we are alerted [to irony] whenever we notice an unmistakable conflict between the beliefs expressed" by a character or narrator "and the beliefs we hold *and suspect the author of holding*." Any look at Theodor Fischer, Twain's narrator, reveals him as a person whose naivete and gullibility are beyond dispute, and just as surely suggests his credibility is extremely suspect. By presenting us with a narrator who, it is immediately evident from his opening statements, is easily duped, Twain increases the likelihood that we will see the subsequent encounter between Theodor and Satan ironically, and not simply as a straightforward transfer of knowledge from a wise and benevolent being to an ignorant but responsive and sensitive one. For that matter, Theodor is so gullible it is hard to imagine how this credulous fool could be respected sufficiently by readers ever to have been taken seriously in the first place. Theodor, it will be recalled, accepted without hesitation the premise that "knowledge was not good for the common people," and in so doing reveals an uncritical readiness to subscribe to beliefs which our experience tells us are patently false. Elsewhere, when telling us of Father Adolf's self-professed, direct encounter with the Devil, Theodor offers as proof the fact that "on occasion [Adolf] quarreled with the enemy, and intrepidly threw his bottle at him; and there, upon the wall of his study, was the ruddy splotch where it struck and broke." The ruddiness of the splotch strongly suggests Adolf was quite likely drunk at the time, but this does not seem to occur to naive Theodor. (pp. 5-7)

These and other examples compel us to view Theodor ironically, and to observe the effect the Mysterious Stranger has on him with considerable suspicion. But what of the Stranger himself? First, in order that Satan be at all convincing as a tempter, Twain must present his arguments as specious; he cannot be simply a comic Devil, or the underlying purpose of the encounter would be lost on the reader. However, lest we take him too seriously, Twain inserts many clues (especially in the opening pages) to show us we are intended to view him ironically as well. For example, Satan initially creates fire for the boys, which might in itself liken him to Prometheus. However, immediately after, he turns water to ice. The combination of fire and ice cannot help but bring to mind Milton's Hell, to say nothing of Dante's Satan ensconced in ice, and suggests he may not be the benevolent angel he claims to be. But surely Twain's choice of name for his "superior" being is the most obvious indication of his true nature. Though he attempts to reassure the boys he is the Devil's nephew, and that his uncle is " 'the only member of [the family] that has ever sinned' "—which incidentally contradicts his later claim that angels are " 'not able to commit' " sin—we can neither remain oblivious to the traditional associations the name "Satan" carries with it, nor can we assume that Twain chose perversely to ignore these implications. Coleman Parsons has demonstrated convincingly that on many occasions Twain expressed both outrage at the arbitrariness of the Old Testament God and sympathy for "the insulted and injured Satan." But, though undoubtedly Twain used Satan sympathetically and more straightforwardly in a work such as "Letters from the Earth," this would in no way prevent him from using the character ironically in another. Had Twain *not* meant us to view his mysterious stranger ironically, it does not make sense that he would assign him a name that, from earliest times, has carried with it negative connotations—Satan is, after all, the Father of Lies—connotations with which Twain would have been perfectly familiar, and then go out of his way to present him in a dubious light. One must not forget that Twain was at perfect liberty to do whatever he liked with his characters and situations. Had he wished his readers to respect Satan as a character and accept his views without irony, he could easily have called him by any other name, or could have presented him to us sympathetically; instead, he chose the one name which he knew carried with it connotations of evil, deception and mendacity. Now, if Satan's name were his only dubious aspect, that is, if he were in all other respects a sympathetic character, we could perhaps agree that Twain had chosen the name simply to emphasize his character's freedom from arbitrary social convention. But Twain goes out of his way to present *this* Satan as also cruel and unfeeling, incapable of love or kindness in any easily recognizable form. Several undeniable examples of Satan's cruelty are presented. . . . Plainly, this Satan has been made hard to like. Indeed, throughout the work Satan's contact with others invariably causes sorrow, despair or destruction for those concerned. At no point do people ever genuinely benefit from their association with him, as far as we can see. But, though Theodor even seems to realize all this, however dimly—at one point he pleads with him to "stop making people unhappy"—he has from birth been taught never to question his superiors, or to criticize anyone in a position of authority. Appalled though he may be at Satan's cruelty, because Satan appears aristocratic, so, Theodor reasons, he must also be "superior"; as such, everything Satan says must be in turn true. Blinded by Satan's impressive displays of magic and wit, he fails to see that anyone so unfeeling should not be trusted implicitly. Twain's point, of course, is that Theodor has been won over by Satan's "new and good clothes," his "winning face," and the "fatal music of his voice"—that is, his polish—just those superficial qualities one would expect shallow and gullible peasants to be impressed by.

We readers are meant to see an entirely different Satan. There is ample evidence that Philip Traum *is* the Devil of popular mythology, out to "damn" the boys by causing them to despair. With no one present capable of challenging him, Satan launches easily into his attack on man, never failing to speak of the human race in a debasing way. . . . Twain, of course, did not seriously adhere to Satan's belief that " 'Man is [only] a museum of diseases, a home of impurities.' " There is much evidence that, while he may have agreed with Satan on certain points, his own vision of human nature was more complex. In short, both Theodor's ignorance *and* Satan's pessimism are satirized throughout *The Mysterious Stranger,* and it is only when we realize Twain's satiric attack is taking place on these two fronts does the full worth of the work emerge.

Satan's campaign to drive the boys to despair takes place in three stages. First, he tries to convince them of man's utter worthlessness by showing that nothing man does can be anything but vile; secondly, he shows them through sophisticated but inherently-flawed arguments that man's moral sense is ironically the principal cause of evil; and finally, he forces them to concede that man is powerless, due to the presence of inexorable deterministic forces, to meliorate his miserable condition.

But as Stone and others have seen, if we are at the mercy of a universe which is essentially fatalistic, then the contempt Satan earlier heaped upon us for our viciousness can hardly be justified, since morality, as Twain well knew, is not operational in a world where free choice is non-existent. That Twain simply could not have been blind to this—the very fact that it *is* so obvious—should lead us to see that for Twain Satan's arguments are not meant to be taken seriously in themselves. For that matter, that he can abandon logic virtually at will and still impress Theodor and his friends, says much about the limited intellects of his pliable pupils and shows us how easily the ignorant can be impressed and led into error.

For example, when Satan speaks so disparagingly of the "moral sense," the success of his argument rests almost entirely on the fact that Theodor "had but a dim idea of what the Moral Sense was." Only vaguely aware of what it is, Theodor is in no position to debate Satan, much less require that he define his terms when he himself is so unsure of his own understanding of them. It goes without saying that when Theodor confesses ignorance of a basic ethical term the average reader would have little trouble with, there can be no longer any doubt about the low level of his learning and intelligence. But Twain does not stop there. Not only is Theodor ignorant; even when told what the moral sense is, he has no idea *why* such a faculty is valuable to man, and must ask Father Peter.

Peter defines the term as we would expect, as " 'the faculty which enables us to distinguish good from evil.' " But even with Peter's help, Theodor is only slightly less befuddled. Though disappointed (because he dimly expected a definition that would make sense of Satan's odd use of the term) and embarrassed (with good reason, in his very need to ask Peter such a question), in his stupidity Peter's definition does "not remind [him] of anything further to say," as well it should. Where a more intelligent person might easily have gone on from there to discuss Satan's cryptic use of the term with Father Peter, Theodor, ever unused to asking critical questions, simply leaves.

That Twain was deeply concerned with the prevalence of such ignorance is evident from the fact that Theodor is far from being the only gullible person in Eseldorf. Seppi and Nikolaus, Ursula, even Marget, are all easily won over. Ursula is an especially easy prey to the cynical Satan. When shown that Agnes (the name means "sacred") the cat is lucky, Ursula quickly changes spiritual allegiance, begins to refer to Satan as her " 'dear master and benefactor' " and "kissed his hand, over and over again. . . . In her heart she probably believed it was a witch-cat and an agent of the Devil [which of course it is!]; but no matter." For his part, while listening to Satan impress Marget and Ursula, Theodor fails to see anything unusual in an angel telling "a good many lies," because after all, "They do not know right from wrong; I knew this," he adds with a straight face, "because I remembered what he had said about it." Why Satan would feel the necessity to lie in the first place never crosses his mind. Furthermore, that Satan could freely lie to others does not shake the gullible Theodor's belief that all Satan has told *him* is nevertheless true. Surely by this point in the work, though Theodor can see nothing wrong in accepting Satan's every utterance, the reader should be viewing him with considerable reservation. Lest there be any lingering doubt as regards Satan's true identity and purpose, Twain has him mention to Marget and Ursula, in the midst of a discussion of his "uncle," that "he

Twain in what was a familiar attitude during the last decade of his life. From his imported Venetian bed, he received callers, gave interviews, dictated memoirs, wrote, and pursued his reading.

hoped some day to bring [Ursula] and his uncle together," a comment that makes even Theodor shudder.

In spite of all this, Theodor's faith in man is quickly destroyed. Satan first shows him a torture chamber and a workhouse, to both of which he responds in horror. He then presents Theodor with an argument on behalf of the ubiquity of human depravity, based on the examples he has presented. Though Theodor finds Satan's conclusions irrefutable, the reader should have no trouble seeing them as specious and glib. First, if we agree that Father Peter's definition of the Moral Sense was basically correct—that the term refers to an individual's sensitivity to moral issues—then the examples Satan is presenting to Theodor are not demonstrations of man's moral sense at work at all, but precisely the reverse: the torturers and workhouse proprietors are plainly examples of human moral *insensitivity*. Obviously, these are people who lack the ability to make meaningful distinctions between right and wrong. Secondly, while such evil undeniably exists, to argue as Satan does, that the perpetration of such atrocities is the direct result of man's possession of a moral sense, is demonstrably absurd. That *we* do not condone the torture of individuals and the evils of the workhouse and are appalled by what we see—or, for that matter, that Theodor is appalled as well—is proof in itself that man is capable of responses that

point to a more complex definition of our moral nature than the one suggested by Theodor to Satan. Indeed, the very horror and outrage we feel as we read and reflect sadly that such behavior is, lamentably, all too common, become the proof that other, more humane responses are possible.

Thus, when Satan concludes that " 'It is the Moral Sense which teaches the factory proprietors the difference between right and wrong—you perceive the result,' " all he is really showing us is that in the above instances, the moral sense either is not operating at all, or it has manifested itself in a perverted form which others can see as such. To argue as he does that our possession of this faculty leads directly to such acts of cruelty is to ignore or gloss over—as Satan does intentionally, of course—that there can be other, proper ways of reacting in situations which call for a moral response. All Satan has shown Theodor is one of two such possible responses, and a perverse one at that. While it is certain that man's inhuman treatment of his fellows has always been an unfortunate part of the human condition, it does not follow that the presence of such evil precludes the possibility of good, as Satan cunningly implies. We still lay claim to those virtues, the existence of which Satan tries to deny, even when confronted with the spectacle of evil and perverted persons.

Theodor's own moral revulsion becomes the most obvious proof within the work of the existence of those very qualities Satan is trying to get the boy to deny. But in his gullibility, Theodor is powerless to see that he himself is arguably the strongest evidence that Satan's conclusions are less than fair. Though, strictly speaking, terms such as "brutal" or "inhuman" are misnomers as Satan says, the boys fail to see (and Satan is too cunning to remind them) that Theodor's anger over Hans Oppert's cruelty to his dog and his pity for the animal are also distinctly human traits. At any rate, it is ridiculous to argue that the dog has a greater " 'stock of morals and magnanimities' " and in fact possesses a more highly developed moral sense simply because it is not cruel. When Satan calls the bullock out of the pasture and observes it " 'wouldn't drive children mad with hunger and fright and loneliness, and then burn them for confessing to things invented for them which never happened' " he ignores that the bullock would do no *good* either. To argue thus would force us to conclude that rocks, stones and trees possess greater virtue, and are in a sense morally better than man, simply because they do no visible harm. Crucial to the success of Satan's argument, of course, is that he "never had a kind word for" the human race. (pp. 7-9)

Satan's unconvincing defense of determinism follows. Theodor, of course, is unable to challenge his mentor, and can only observe that "It seemed so dismal." But, lest we take this seriously, Twain presents Satan at his most inconsistent here: for, immediately after telling Theodor the future cannot be altered, he proceeds to alter it in several cases, thus rendering anything he has said about the all-powerful nature of the forces of fate null and void. For his part, Theodor is completely convinced, but can only conclude that such makes man " 'a prisoner for life,' " failing to see that if so, man need not bear any burden of guilt for his acts. If anything, Theodor should be breathing a sigh of relief at this point; instead, he lapses even more into a despair that the reader should have no trouble seeing is simply unwarranted.

Throughout this work, Twain inserts much evidence to confute Satan's purely negative assessment of man. Sleepy though Eseldorf may be, it is still sprinkled with kind and decent people. Seppi, for instance, appears as a genuinely sensitive figure, whose "voice trembled with pity and anger" when speaking of the cruel Hans Oppert. Father Peter is "good and truthful," Marget is "lovely," and William Meidling displays courageous loyalty to them in the face of adverse public opinion. Nicky's heroic act of self-sacrifice is, of course, the most dramatic example of such decency. When told Nikolaus will die, Theodor and Seppi are understandably grieved, but ironically fail to see that their capacity to feel such grief reveals another distinctly human characteristic, and one of which we can be proud. For that matter, in their grief they also fail to see in the very circumstances of his death—dying in the act of rescuing a drowning girl—positive proof that man is something other than the loathsome creature of Satan's definition.

The boys are similarly unable to see anything editorially-slanted in Satan's subsequent parade of history, which carefully shows man at his depraved worst. Plainly, there is more to the Roman Empire than Caesar's invasion of Britain, more to the entire Christian era than war alone. Concluding his history lesson with an "evil chuckle" the ironic significance of which is lost on the boys, Satan summarizes his "findings," claiming that history shows us we " 'gain nothing; you always come out where you went in. For a million years the race has gone on monotonously propagating itself and monotonously reperforming this dull nonsense—to what end? No wisdom can guess!' " Needless to say, the force of this argument is entirely dependent on our acceptance of the panorama of futility we have just seen.

The lesson over, the boys are offered and drink "heavenly" wine, in a perverse parody of the communion. As they drink, Seppi wonders if they will enjoy Paradise some day, but receives no answer from Satan, whose silence (given his knowledge of the future) understandably distresses them. Here, Twain is pointing out that in his opinion these well-intentioned but weak-willed boys are "damned" as a result of their uncritical adoration of Satan, their blind respect for authority, and in short, their total lack of self-reliance. It is surely no accident that, immediately after this scene, Theodor is observed at his most despicable, stoning a woman against his will simply out of fear of offending members of the community.

Finally, Satan proceeds to show the boys that happiness as they understand the term can never be realized, and that given this, only the dead or the insane can ever be "happy." As if to prove this point, he drives Father Peter mad, thus creating an insane but happy person. When questioned by Theodor on his methods, Satan simply replies by stating that " 'No sane man can be happy, for him life is real, and he sees what a fearful thing it is. Only the mad can be happy, and not many of those.' " That happiness in Theodor's puerile understanding of the term may be beyond man does not deny the likelihood that more mature forms of fulfillment are possible. In Father Peter's case, there is a third alternative cunningly ignored by Satan—Peter sane *and* free, with the money, acquitted of the charge, his good name intact—which would obviously constitute a happier state of affairs for all concerned. It would, however, tend to undermine the credibility of Satan's pessimistic position, and this he cannot allow. Furthermore, it is very much in Satan's best interests to render Father Peter insane. Peter, it will be recalled, was the one person in Eseldorf "not ignorant and dull" and as such able to challenge Satan intellectually. It is doubtless for this reason Satan took such pains to avoid Father Peter throughout his sojourn in Eseldorf. By destroying Peter's mind Satan effectively removes the arguments. It is easy, then, to see why Peter is rendered insane. But we must not forget that Peter only appears to prove Satan's contention that "sanity and happiness are an impossible combination' "; the insane hilarity of Father Peter is not meant to convince the reader as well.

We can certainly agree with Kenneth Lynn that the ending was "a brilliant choice" on Paine's part, even while acknowledging that it does not necessarily represent how Twain himself would have finished the tale. For, though written as a conclusion to a later version of the work, the Mysterious Stranger's final comments relate to so much of the "Eseldorf" material, and in fact make so much more sense when set against the manuscript than they do when read in connection with the rambling and unstructured "Print Shop" version, it is almost inconceivable that Twain did not also have Theodor Fischer and Philip Traum somewhere in the back of his mind when penning this particular exchange. In brief, the conclusion Paine tampered with so extensively (by, among other things, changing the names to make it fit the Eseldorf version) perfectly summarizes everything Satan has been teaching Theodor: life is utterly without meaning, and our only proper response to it can be one of despair. Nor, I think, need we take the narrator's agreement with Satan's solipsism too seriously. For, although Theodor's initial reaction to Satan's revelation is one of "thankfulness" and relief, Satan's subsequent description of the implications of living in a solipsistic universe is, as ever, calculated to induce despair: " 'In a little while you will be alone in shoreless space, to wander its limitless solitudes, without friend or comrade forever. . . . And you are but a *thought*—a vagrant thought, a useless thought, a homeless thought, wandering forlorn among the empty eternities.' " Though the naive Theodor sighs a desperate assent—"I knew, and realized, that all he had said was true"—and is left "appalled," there is no reason for us to share his despair, for we have Theodor's own account of life in Eseldorf to counter Satan's dismal philosophical conclusions. There, we saw loyalty, generosity, and numerous demonstrations of love and self-sacrifice, in short, all those characteristics commonly considered to raise the human condition from the purely vile and sordid. That these qualities are ironically overlooked by a narrator too obtuse to see their significance does not invalidate them or nullify their existence or importance. Rather, this more complex picture of human nature, coming to us as it does from Twain, far from being untrue, completes the satire by giving us a framework whereby both the uncritical gullibility of Theodor and the pure pessimism of Satan can together be weighed in the balance and be found wanting. (pp. 9-11)

Terence J. Matheson, "The Devil and Philip Traum: Twain's Satiric Purposes in 'The Mysterious Stranger', " in The Markham Review, Vol. 12, Fall, 1982, pp. 5-11.*

KATHLEEN WALSH   (essay date 1988)

[*In the following excerpt, Walsh acknowledges Twain's experimental impulses in "The Great Dark" and "Three Thousand Years among the Microbes."*]

Obviously, we can err just as much by overpraising Mark Twain's modernity [in his late symbolic writings] as we can be regretting the loss of his old comic pose. The "Great Dark Writings," in fact, exhibit great variety in outlook and technique. As critics have pointed out, a number of common concerns and situations do recur: "A preoccupation with purposeless voyages which end in horror"; sudden downward reversals of fortune; the loss of an objective standard for distinguishing dreams from reality; "Weird symbolism and psychological atmosphere." Though these elements are to some degree present in each of the lengthier manuscripts—"The Great Dark," "Which Was It?," "Which Was the Dream?" and "Three Thousand Years Among the Microbes"—these writings are not uniform in their intellectual concerns and aesthetic approaches. [In his *A Cheerful Nihilism: Confidence and "The Absurd" in American Fiction* (1971)], Richard Hauck finds a consistent expression of total "absurdism" in Mark Twain's late writings:

> By the time he came to write his darkest books, Twain was convinced that not only is what man sees absurd but the position from which he sees is also absurd, unfixed, and not definable. The man who had for years consciously equated absurdity with distortion was by now convinced that reality was absurd.

Though we can see Twain moving toward such an intellectual position in these late manuscripts, to say that he was "con-

vinced" of this outlook overstates the case and ignores the variety of his late projects, the ambivalence and variety in the symbolic writings themselves, and Twain's dissatisfaction with these writings. We should begin by marking the difference between those symbolic writings which tend to view the *past* as dream ("Which Was It?" and "Which Was the Dream?") and those which undermine a secure sense of *present* reality and knowability ("The Great Dark," "Microbes"). In the second type, the manipulation of perspective in the direction of undermining reality is greatest, and thus Mark Twain's responsiveness to a new species of doubt is most obvious.

The dreamers of "What Was It?" and "Which Was the Dream?" tend to perceive the lost, happy past of family life and success as "a dream . . . a world of enchantment," and to see present reality as nightmarish, though not precisely as nightmare. George Harrison, in "Which Was It?," is consistently unable to oppose the relentless and apparent reality of the nightmarish disaster in which he loses his family, commits murder, and is forced to trade roles with his former slave. At one point, he does wake relieved, "with a vague sense of having passed through a desolating dream." But his dream, if it is one, continues: "Then followed that ghastly sinking at the heart which comes when we realize that the horror which seemed a dream was not a dream but reality." In "Which Was the Dream?," Major General "X" meets with sudden financial disaster and loss of reputation and sees his happy past as dreamlike. But the disaster seems genuine to him, as does his awakening from a disaster-induced coma, after eighteen months, to find himself in a rustic cabin where he listens to his wife's tale of her efforts to save the family. Though the title may prompt the reader to wonder, "X" does not doubt the reality of this awakening in profoundly changed circumstances. In these two manuscripts, Mark Twain seems interested in confusions of reality, but his emphasis is on an unhappy person's desire for a happier reality. The shift in perspective in these tales reveals the irony, the infirmity, of our sense of happiness; in "The Great Dark" and "Microbes," that shift operates to reveal the ironies and infirmities of our sense of reality. Immediately directing attention to perspective, both of these works require not simply that we enter a dream, but that we enter our world in a new way, through a microscope.

The manuscript which Bernard DeVoto titled "The Great Dark" is both a continuation and a reworking of "Which Was the Dream?" Despite the parallels in character and situation, "The Great Dark" is both more fantastic and more comic than the previous manuscript. The two versions begin in much the same way—a happy father nods momentarily while preparing for his beloved daughter's birthday—but "The Great Dark" emphasizes the adventure to be gained by a new viewpoint more than the instability of the father's happiness. Henry Edwards, fascinated by "an ocean in a drop of water" seen through a microscope, requests from the "Superintendent of Dreams" a dream voyage through this new world for himself and his family. The microscope itself, revealing worlds previously unknown, undermines stable definitions of reality, but Edwards is at first secure about the relationship of the microscopic world to his own. Early in his adventure, the dislocations and oddities which frighten the sailors are but comic departures from his standard of normalcy. Secure in his superior knowledge, Edwards plays with a sailor who complains of queer weather, lost bearings, and monsters of the deep; Edwards appears to prolong the sailor's tale to savor the oddities of salty dialect and culture and to fully enjoy his privileged vision:

> "What should you think if you was to see a whale with hairy spider legs to it as long as the foretogallant backstay and as big around as the mainmast?"
>
> I recognized the creature; I had seen it in the microscope. But I didn't say so. I said—
>
> "I should think I had a little touch of the jimjams."

So far Twain appears to be weaving a fantasy-adventure made comic by such traditional elements as the tall tale and the interplay between gentleman and clown.

However, Edwards' security weakens during the next encounter with the Superintendent of Dreams, who possesses knowledge superior to his own and who begins to play with him as Edwards played with the sailor. The Superintendent's game is more frightening because his knowledge destroys the "real" world while Edwards' knowledge restored it. Though Edwards remembers having ordered this "dream," he finds he cannot terminate it at will. "Are you quite sure it is a dream?" the Superintendent counters. When the Superintendent declares, "Your other life was the dream!", Edwards, with his "blood chilly," experiences the radical uncertainty which Mark Twain and others were beginning to glimpse as the modern condition. His immediate response is shock: "It was as if he had hit me, it stunned me so." Edwards begins to question the power of rationality: "we see that intellectually we are really no great things; that we seldom really know the thing we think we know; that our best-built certainties are but sand-houses and subject to damage from any wind of doubt that blows."

However, Edwards rather soon moves beyond shock; plucky, resourceful, and adaptable, he seeks methods of coping with such uncertainty. At first, finding that his wife shares some of his memories of a life outside the ship but regards these as dreams, he decides that a "policy of recollecting whatever anybody required me to recollect seemed the safest course to pursue in my strange and trying circumstances." But he does not continue to find the confusion and uncertainty trying. Surrealistically, he begins to remember his past life on the ship at the same time that he doubts its truth, and eventually he and his wife come to find these opposed realities a source of shipboard amusement: "We now had the recollections of two lives to draw upon, and the result was a double measure of happiness for us." Edwards' acceptance of uncertainty and his increasing absorption in the fantastic adventures of this microscopic world convey a sense of intrigue rather than despair. This fascination with the possibilities of a new perspective remains the keynote of the manuscript as Mark Twain left it.

Tony Tanner remarks on the multiplication of "hideous surreal incidents" as "the story spirals to a pitch of phantasmagoric insanity"; he sees in **"The Great Dark"** "an unrelenting vision of life as chaos." In his emphasis on disaster, Tanner must surely be drawing on Mark Twain's plans for the story. Despite the title—which is DeVoto's—the mood of the unfinished piece is neither totally dark nor hopeless. The manuscript breaks off with a scene which might be taken as a paradigm of the modern absurdist response to uncertainty. The uneasy sailors mutiny in order to get secure bearings, but the "fact" they wring from the captain is, "I don't know where this ship is." Despite the uncertainty, the captain's final asser-

tion is vital and courageous: "We haven't had an observation for four months, but we're going ahead, and do our best to fetch up somewhere." Rather than railing against uncertainty, Mark Twain seems totally absorbed in demonstrating it in this manuscript.

In **"Three Thousand Years Among the Microbes,"** Mark Twain seems equally absorbed in his fantasy, though this manuscript is less unified in its world view than **"The Great Dark"**; **"Microbes"** juxtaposes a modern sense of relativism with Swiftian satire. The narrator, who eventually becomes known as "Huck," has been transformed into a cholera germ, perhaps by a magician's incompetence, perhaps by his own choice. He now resides in "the blood of a hoary and mouldering old bald-headed tramp" named Blitzowski, whose "body is a sewer, a reek of decay, a charnel house" swarming with "all the different kinds of germ-vermin that have been invented for the contentment of man."

One effect of the shift of perspective to this microscopic world is the deflation of human pretensions by the aptness of the invidious comparison: "Our world (the tramp) is as large and grand and awe-compelling to us microscopic creatures as is man's world to man." By stressing the parallels between the two worlds, Twain achieves much the same sort of satire that Swift does by viewing human failings from Lilliput. These insignificant germs are obsessed with forms and ceremony, with "ranks-grades-castes," and are convinced that their "souls" are immortal and that they are the centerpiece of creation. According to a proud Duke, "This mighty planet we inhabit . . . was created for a great and wise purpose. It was not chance-work, it proceeded, stage by stage, in accordance with an ordered and systematised plan. . . . What was that purpose? That We might have a home." Microbes, like men, gain a false sense of superiority by measuring themselves against lesser forms and not considering the possibility of their relative insignificance if a larger measure were employed. Thus a microbe compares himself to the "swinks":

> There are some strange resemblances between Our Grand Race and those wee creatures. For instance, We have upper classes—so have they. That is a parallel, as far as it goes, but it is not a perfect one, for the reason that Our aristocracy is useful and not often harmful, whereas their aristocracy are disease-germs, and propagate deadly maladies in Our bodies.

The microbes are blithely unaware that their function is to induce disease in a scruffy tramp.

Mark Twain refers explicitly to Swift in **"Microbes,"** reflecting his admiration for Swift as predecessor. One of the principal microbes is named Lemuel Gulliver; the name recurs strikingly throughout Twain's text. Another has the Brobdignagian name of Lurbrulgrud. In fact, it is likely that much of the microbe language is formed through analogy with Swift's exotic place names. Twain alludes to Swift's "A Modest Proposal" when describing a microbe "munching an SBE," a lesser creature, this one "an infant of four weeks and quite fat and tender and juicy." Huck is tempted by the morsel, commenting, "I think them quite choice when they are well nourished." At such points, Mark Twain appears to look back to a more rational age with a certain desire for its recreation. Albert Bigelow Paine, who published a portion of **"Microbes"** with his biography, waxed enthusiastic about Mark Twain's Swiftian parallels, but seemed to see such satire as

Twain's sole interest: "It was a satire, of course—Gulliver's Lilliput outdone" [see Further Reading list].

Before we note Mark Twain's departures from Swiftian satire, we should recognize that the manipulations of perspective in *Gulliver's Travels* are neither singular nor simple, reaching their greatest complication in Book IV with the discrediting of Gulliver. But the alterations of perspective in **"Microbes"** are complicated in a different way and cannot be wholly understood within the framework of Swiftian satire. Swift manipulates perspective in the direction of increasingly complex and bitter satire; Mark Twain uses the perspective of the microbe world at some points to enforce satiric standards, and at others to display the arbitrariness of any standards. Though Twain delights in invidious comparisons between microbes and men, as striking and as central in **"Microbes"** is his sense of the difficulty, the absurdity, of attempting to measure one world against another, one subjective perception of reality against another. Unlike Swift, Mark Twain is fascinated with the arbitrariness of time and with the potentiality of science to transform our world into one which we are no longer certain of comprehending.

Microbe life is smaller and hence "faster" than human life; thus Huck's three thousand years in Blitzowski have been only a few weeks of human time. Huck provides a chart for time conversions, noting, "As nearly as I could get at it, a microbe hour seemed to be the fiftieth part of human second." But Mark Twain's interest is only superficially mathematical; he emphasizes the observer's difficulty in truly comprehending such a conversion, since any observer will necessarily be experiencing only one sort of time. Huck comments, "I used to be the best mathematician in Yale . . . but I can do nothing with human mathematics now." Huck, like Henry Edwards, is intellectually aware of two opposed versions of reality: in this case, his human past and his microbe present. His current experience of microbe time lends to that "standard" a sense of reality which his memory tells him is only partial. He still believes in human time, but is increasingly unable to grasp its reality: "Since ever so long ago, microbe time has been *real* to me, and human time a dream—the one present and vivid, the other far away and dim, very dim, wavering, spectral, the substantiality all gone out of it." The opposed standards result in a sense of displacement not found in *Gulliver's Travels.*

Huck's acceptance of relativism undergoes expansion. He gets lessons in the subject, even from his dizzy secretary: "She said there was no such thing as substance—substance was a fiction of Mortal Mind, an illusion." His awareness deepens when his explanation to his microbe friends of the relative insignificance of both their world and the human one—"that little world—so unimaginably vast, compared with yours!—paddles about in a shoreless solitude of space"—is treated by his auditors as a magnificent fiction. They simply applaud his creative powers. "There stands the palace!" admires one; "There stands the supernatural lie!" says another. At this point, Huck does not simply doubt his own knowing; he suffers what he himself terms a sea change as he recognizes the subjectivism of knowing, the impossibility of verifying one's private truth: "I knew, now, that it isn't safe to sit in judgment upon another person's illusion when you are not on the inside. While you are thinking it is a dream, he may be knowing it is a planet." Noting the self-deception whereby "Each of us knows it all, and *knows* he knows it all," Huck concludes, "mind is plainly an ass." Richard Hauck compares the satiric shifts of Mark Twain's travel books, where "viewpoints are shifted to reveal sequences of new absurdities" exposing "the ludicrous follies of the human race," with the shifts in "the later books which have the ambiguity of vision as their main subject." This sort of displacement makes suspect the concept of "enlightenment."

One of the modern consequences of relativism is what Sartre has termed "nausea," the fear of non-being; it is that fear rather than personal despair which informs the darkest moment in **"Microbes."** Contemplating the possibility of the tramp's death, Huck questions,

> What would become of me if he should disintegrate? . . . at last I should be all distributed, and nothing left of what had once been Me. . . . I wish I knew what it was going to feel like, to lie helpless such a weary, weary time, and see my faculties decay and depart, one by one, like lights which burn low, and flicker, and perish.

Huck here envisions the oozing away of existence later treated in Samuel Beckett's *Molloy.* However, moments of such deep fear are infrequent in **"Microbes,"** just as they are in **"The Great Dark."** Once again, Mark Twain takes the character beyond the discovery of relativism to the experience of living with it.

Tony Tanner has noted parallels between *The Education of Henry Adams* and Mark Twain's late fantasies, but one parallel he does not mention is that both authors juxtapose nostalgia for the Enlightenment with a commitment to modernity

Portrait of Twain in his later years.

at whatever cost. The juxtaposition of these attitudes is less conscious in **"Microbes"** than it is in *The Education*. The dual perceptions of Twain's fantasy—on the one hand, that the microbe world is a measure of our own, and on the other hand, that the microbe world unmakes our own—remain disjunctive in this manuscript. We can see Mark Twain straining both forward and backward, with complicated feelings about either direction. But whether or not we regard this unfinished manuscript as successful, we should recognize that Mark Twain is experimenting with new outlooks and techniques and not simply railing against new times and his personal difficulties.

In **"The Great Dark"** and **"Microbes,"** Mark Twain gives imaginative expression to new ideas about time, space, and reality. Readers have found statements of uncertainty and even nihilism in *The Mysterious Stranger* and *A Connecticut Yankee in King Arthur's Court*. In **"The Great Dark"** and **"Microbes,"** Twain not only voices such ideas, but he begins to develop aesthetic techniques appropriate to them; in particular, he experiments with characters who are aware of and living with competing realities. We can see here an initiation of strategies which Paul Armstrong, in another context, mentions as appropriate to modern "bewilderment": "Aesthetically, bewilderment calls for representational strategies that make strange our sense of reality by showing that it has no more certainty or stability than an interpretive scheme." Mark Twain's ability to glimpse new artistic possibilities in modern relativism is overlooked by readers who emphasize failure and despair in these works. Comparing these late manuscripts to *The Education of Henry Adams*, Tony Tanner argues that both writers express a despair which is not merely personal but is "hatched by the growing discords, conflicts, and problems of the age." Tanner is right to emphasize the importance of a large contemporary framework for approaching these works, but his emphasis on a drift toward despair is questionable—in both cases. Such emphasis distorts *The Education*, most obviously by asking us to overlook the positive solution of the "Dynamic Theory of History"; similarly, the emphasis on despair distorts Mark Twain's fantasies. Just as Tanner fails to note that Henry Adams "drifts" toward an acceptance of chaos and multiplicity, so do readers of Twain's late manuscripts tend to ignore the positive implications of his attempt to grapple with new ideas in new ways.

That Mark Twain was not entirely resistant to change is evident as early as *Life on the Mississippi*, where Twain's imagery of the river makes clear that he values "color, snap, surprise" over timeless serenity, and that his attitudes toward stasis and change are complex. Mark Twain regrets the changes which have robbed the river of romance, but he does not long for permanence. It is well to remember that this author's typical reaction to change is often positive and that his career throughout is marked by experiment and variety. Early and late we see Mark Twain's receptivity to important currents of his age and his experimentation with techniques in search of a form appropriate to this vision. Many of his readers have wished for a succession of *Tom Sawyers*, but Mark Twain left that formula before it became fixed as one and moved on to new modes. Wishing for "the old Mark Twain" and seeing these works as mere "shards" of a particular moment in his genesis is a bit like wishing for the good old days, something that Mark Twain himself was not content with doing. (pp. 20-7)

Kathleen Walsh, "Rude Awakenings and Swift Re-

coveries: The Problem of Reality in Mark Twain's 'The Great Dark' and 'Three Thousand Years Among the Microbes'," *in* American Literary Realism 1870-1910, *Vol. 21, No. 1, Fall, 1988, pp. 19-28.*

FURTHER READING

Baetzhold, Howard G. "Of Detectives and Their Derring-Do: The Genesis of Mark Twain's 'The Stolen White Elephant'." *Studies in American Humor* II, No. 3 (January 1976): 183-95.
    Cites various newspaper events of Twain's time as sources for his story "The Stolen White Elephant."

Bellamy, Gladys Carmen. *Mark Twain as a Literary Artist*. Norman: University of Oklahoma Press, 1950, 396 p.
    Pioneer study of Twain's literary techniques that includes several references to and brief discussions of Twain's short fiction.

Bertolotti, D. S. "Structural Unity in 'The Man That Corrupted Hadleyburg'." *The Mark Twain Journal* XIV, No. 1 (Winter 1967-68): 19-21.
    Discusses Twain's use of letters written by the character Barclay Goodson as a structural device in "The Man That Corrupted Hadleyburg."

Blair, Walter. *Native American Humor, 1800-1900*. New York: American Book Co., 1937, 573 p.
    Places Twain in the tradition of Southwestern humorists.

Branch, Edgar M[arquess]. " 'My Voice is Still for Setchell': A Background Study of 'Jim Smiley and His Jumping Frog'." *PMLA* LXXXII, No. 7 (December 1967): 591-601.
    Discusses the influence of Twain's personal life on his best-known story.

Branch, Edgar Marquess. *The Literary Apprenticeship of Mark Twain, with Selections from His Apprentice Writing*. Urbana: University of Illinois Press, 1950, 325 p.
    Studies Twain's life and career, beginning in 1839, when he lived in Hannibal, Missouri, until he set sail for Europe on assignment for a New York newspaper in 1867, a period during which he published many sketches and short fiction pieces.

Brodwin, Stanley. "Mark Twain's Masks of Satan: The Final Phase." *American Literature* 45, No. 2 (May 1973): 206-27.
    Examines various roles Twain created for his Satan character in works of his later years.

Brooks, Van Wyck. *The Ordeal of Mark Twain*. New York: E. P. Dutton & Co., 1920, 267 p.
    Controversial study in which Brooks characterizes Twain as having possessed throughout his life "a frustrated spirit." Consequently, Brooks states, "the poet, the artist in him . . . had withered into the cynic and the whole man had become a spiritual valetudinarian."

Chard, Leslie F., II. "Mark Twain's 'Hadleyburg' and Fredonia, New York." *American Quarterly* XVI, No. 4 (Winter 1964): 595-601.
    Argues that Fredonia, New York, served as a model for the fictional town of Hadleyburg in Twain's story "The Man That Corrupted Hadleyburg."

Covici, Pascal, Jr. *Mark Twain's Humor: The Image of a World*. Dallas: Southern Methodist University Press, 1962, 266 p.
    Examines Twain's use of humor in his writings. According to Covici, his study endeavors to "show what Twain was attempting, to suggest its importance, and to re-examine a few of his

works in the light of the artistry organized and given meaning by the humor."

Cox, James M. *Mark Twain: The Fate of Humor.* Princeton, N. J.: Princeton University Press, 1966, 321 p.
Interprets Twain from a Freudian perspective, stating that "the heart of Mark Twain's humor" was "pervasively concerned with repression, censorship, dreams, the conscience, and self-approval." Includes a chapter on *The Mysterious Stranger.*

Cuff, Roger Penn. "Mark Twain's Use of California Folklore in His Jumping Frog Story." *Journal of American Folklore* 65 (April 1952): 155-59.
Traces Twain's debt to the folklore of the Gold Rush era in California for his story "The Celebrated Jumping Frog of Calaveras County."

Davis, John H. "The Dream as Reality: Structure and Meaning in Mark Twain's 'The Great Dark'." *Mississippi Quarterly* XXXV, No. 4 (Fall 1982): 407-26.
Interprets "The Great Dark" as a story that "sets forth most clearly and dramatically of all his attempts Mark Twain's theories about dreams and their connection to life (reality) and self (consciousness)" within "a structure of four frames that converge upon each other as the story progresses."

Delaney, Paul. "The Dissolving Self: The Narrators of Mark Twain's *Mysterious Stranger* Fragments." *The Journal of Narrative Technique* 6, No. 1 (Winter 1976): 51-65.
Discusses various narrative voices Twain employed in his three "Mysterious Stranger" manuscripts.

Dennis, Larry R. "Mark Twain and the Dark Angel." *The Midwest Quarterly* VII, No. 2 (Winter 1967): 181-97.
Explores various ways in which Twain treated death in his fiction.

DeVoto, Bernard. *"Mark Twain's America" and "Mark Twain at Work."* Boston: Houghton Mifflin Co., and Cambridge: Riverside Press, 1967, 351 & 140 p.
Comprises two of DeVoto's most important critical works on Twain. *Mark Twain's America* is a study of the social and cultural conditions surrounding Twain's life and work. *Mark Twain at Work,* a collection of three essays written after DeVoto had been appointed successor to Albert Paine as custodian of the Mark Twain papers, has often been interpreted as a confutation of Brook's *The Ordeal of Mark Twain* [see Further Reading list above]. *Mark Twain at Work* includes "The Symbols of Despair," a preliminary outline of DeVoto's theory that the "writing of *The Mysterious Stranger* casts some light, however weak and intermittent, into many areas of Mark Twain's personality that have so far been dark."

Duncan, Jeffrey L. "The Empirical and the Ideal in Mark Twain." *PMLA* 95, No. 2 (March 1980): 201-12.
Discusses literary realism and philosophical idealism as they exist in Twain's fiction. Includes a brief consideration of *The Mysterious Stranger.*

Eby, E. H. "Mark Twain's Testament." *Modern Language Quarterly* XXIII, No. 3 (September 1962): 254-62.
Concurs with the opinion expressed by Edgar Lee Masters in his *Mark Twain: A Portrait* (1938), that *The Mysterious Stranger* is "a tribute to the greatness of man's imagination."

Emerson, Everett. *The Authentic Mark Twain: A Literary Biography of Samuel L. Clemens.* Philadelphia: University of Pennsylvania Press, 1984.
Literary biography.

Ensor, Allison. *Mark Twain & the Bible.* Lexington: University of Kentucky Press, 1969, 130 p.
Examines Twain's knowledge and use of the Bible in his writings.

Ferguson, DeLancey. *Mark Twain: Man and Legend.* 1943. Reprint. Indianapolis: Bobbs-Merrill Co., 1963, 352 p.
Traces Twain's career as a writer.

Geismar, Maxwell. *Mark Twain: An American Prophet.* Boston: Houghton Mifflin Co., 1970, 564 p.
Critical study of Twain's literary life.

Gibson, William M. *The Art of Mark Twain.* New York: Oxford University Press, 1976, 230 p.
Perceptive study of Twain's writings. In his preface, Gibson asserts that "Twain was at his brilliant best in his shorter works."

Glick, Wendell. "The Epistemological Theme of *The Mysterious Stranger.*" In *Themes and Directions in American Literature: Essays in Honor of Leon Howard,* edited by Ray B. Browne and Donald Pizer, pp. 130-47. Lafayette, Ind.: Purdue University Studies, 1969.
Contends that the theme of *The Mysterious Stranger* is "the ubiquitous twentieth century idea of the breakdown of epistemological certainty."

Harrell, Don W. "A Chaser of Phantoms: Mark Twain and Romanticism." *The Midwest Quarterly* XIII, No. 2 (January 1972): 201-12.
Credits Van Wyck Brooks's contention in his *The Ordeal of Mark Twain* [see Further Reading list above] that Twain suffered throughout his life a "deep malady of the soul" and explores Twain's affinity in his writings with Romanticism.

Harris, Susan K. *Mark Twain's "Escape from Time": A Study of Patterns and Images.* Columbia: University of Missouri Press, 1982, 169 p.
According to Harris, this text is "a study of those recurring images that serve to *resolve* alienation in Mark Twain's writings."

———. " 'Hadleyburg': Mark Twain's Dual Attack on Banal Theology and Banal Literature." *American Literary Realism, 1870-1910* XVI, No. 2 (Autumn 1983): 240-52.
Argues that "far from being representative of the town, [protagonists] Mary and Edward Richards are its most corrupt characters, and that their story differs both thematically and formally from the story of the town. Moreover, Mark Twain uses the elderly couple's tale not only to attack contemporary liberal notions of the power of free will, but also to attack the way such ideas are embodied in current forms of short fiction."

Henderson, Archibald. *Mark Twain.* London: Duckworth & Co., 1911, 230 p.
Appreciative early biography.

Hill, Hamlin. *Mark Twain: God's Fool.* New York: Harper & Row, Publishers, 1973, 308 p.
Provocative and controversial evaluation of the last ten years of Twain's life (1900 through 1910) that relies substantially on the writings of Twain, his family, and his secretary, Isabel Lyon, and argues that Twain lost psychological control during these years.

Johnson, James L. *Mark Twain and the Limits of Power.* Knoxville: University of Tennessee Press, 1982, 206 p.
Investigates Twain's use of "power figures"—those capable of dominating the worlds in which they exist—in his fiction. Includes a chapter on *The Mysterious Stranger.*

Kahn, Sholom J. *Mark Twain's Mysterious Stranger: A Study of the Manuscript Texts.* Columbia: University of Missouri Press, 1978, 252 p.
Study designed, in Kahn's words, "to show some of the delights the [*Mysterious Stranger*] manuscripts offer, to facilitate understanding, and to highlight their fascinating problems."

Karnath, David. "*The Mysterious Stranger:* Its Mode of Thought." *The Mark Twain Journal* XIX, No. 4 (Summer 1979): 4-8.
Places *The Mysterious Stranger* within a tradition of nineteenth-century thought "which might be loosely gathered under the

name pluralism"; a tradition that moved "toward a synthesis that accepted ambivalence."

Laverty, Carroll D. "The Genesis of *The Mysterious Stranger*." *Mark Twain Quarterly* VIII, Nos. 3 & 4 (Spring-Summer 1947): 15-19.
    Speculates on various sources for Twain's *The Mysterious Stranger*.

Lewis, Oscar. *The Origin of "The Celebrated Jumping Frog of Calaveras County."* San Francisco: Book Club of California, 1931, 27 p.
    Traces the history of this story "from its origin in the mining-camps of the Sierra foothills during the early days of the Gold Rush to the time Mark Twain gave it world-wide fame." Includes an appendix of early printed versions of the tale that appeared in mining-town newspapers during the 1850s and 1860s.

Lowrey, Robert E. "Imagination and Redemption: 44 in the Third Version of *The Mysterious Stranger*." *The Southern Review* 18, No. 1 (Winter 1982): 100-10.
    Examines themes of determinism, temperament, imagination, and renewal in the third manuscript version of *The Mysterious Stranger*, emphasizing that in this version Twain endows humanity with a "complex tripartite self" comprising a "Workaday-Self," "Dream-Self," and "Immortal-Self."

Lynn, Kenneth S. *Mark Twain and Southwestern Humor*. 1960. Reprint. Westport, Conn.: Greenwood Press, Publishers, 1972, 300 p.
    Treatment of Twain as a humorist writer who consciously and deliberately practiced his art.

Macnaughton, William R. *Mark Twain's Last Years As a Writer*. Columbia: University of Missouri Press, 1979, 254 p.
    Traces Twain's career following the summer of 1897, when he completed his travel book *Following the Equator,* until his death in 1910.

Marshall, W. Gerald. "Mark Twain's 'The Man That Corrupted Hadleyburg' and the Myth of Baucis and Philemon." *The Mark Twain Journal* XX, No. 2 (Summer 1980): 4-7.
    Suggests Twain's ironic use of this classic myth "as a matrix for understanding Hadleyburg, his microcosmic America."

May, John R. "The Gospel According to Philip Traum: Structural Unity in 'The Mysterious Stranger'." *Studies in Short Fiction* VIII, No. 3 (Summer 1971): 411-22.
    Seeks coherence in the structures of the first ten sections of *The Mysterious Stranger* and its conclusion "to show, if possible, how the whole narrative contributes to the development of the discerned underlying theme."

McKeithan, D. M. "The Morgan Manuscript of 'The Man That Corrupted Hadleyburg'." *Texas Studies in Literature and Language* II, No. 4 (Winter 1961): 476-80.
    Documents revisions Twain made to a manuscript version of this story.

McMahan, Elizabeth. *Critical Approaches to Mark Twain's Short Stories*. Port Washington, N. Y.: National University Publications, Kennikat Press, 1981, 147 p.
    Collection of previously published criticism on Twain's short stories, designed by McMahan "to be of use to teachers and students." Includes two essays by Mark Twain: "Report to the Buffalo Female Academy" and "How to Tell a Story."

Meltzer, Milton, ed. *Mark Twain Himself: A Pictorial Biography*. New York: Bonanza Books, 1960, 303 p.
    Story of Twain's life in pictures.

Miller, Robert Keith. *Mark Twain*. pp. 161-95. New York: Frederick Ungar Publishing Co., 1983.
    Surveys a selection of Twain's short fiction.

Morrissey, Frank R. "The Ancestor of the 'Jumping Frog'." *The Bookman* (New York) LIII, No. 2 (April 1921): 143-45.

Recounts a tale about a man and his trained grasshopper, claiming it to be a prototype of Twain's "The Celebrated Jumping Frog of Calaveras County."

Neider, Charles. *Mark Twain*. New York: Horizon Press, 1967, 214 p.
    Collection of Neider's introductions to various volumes of Twain's works, including his introductions to *The Complete Humorous Sketches and Tales of Mark Twain* (1961) and *The Complete Short Stories of Mark Twain* (1957) [see excerpt dated 1957].

Paine, Albert Bigelow. *Mark Twain, a Biography: The Personal and Literary Life of Samuel Langhorne Clemens*. 4 Vols. New York: Harper & Brothers Publishers, 1912.
    Official biography by the first custodian of the Mark Twain papers.

Park, Martha M. "Mark Twain's Hadleyburg: A House Built on Sand." *CLA Journal* XVI, No. 4 (June 1973): 508-13.
    Cites similarities between Twain's "The Man That Corrupted Hadleyburg" and the biblical parable of the two houses—one built on rock, the other on sand.

Parsons, Coleman O. "The Devil and Samuel Clemens." *The Virginia Quarterly Review* 23, No. 4 (Autumn 1947): 582-606.
    Probes Twain's life "in an effort to discover the source and the mythology of his gloom."

————. "The Background of 'The Mysterious Stranger'." *American Literature* XXXII, No. 1 (March 1960): 55-74.
    Details sources and background materials of *The Mysterious Stranger*.

Requa, Kenneth A. "Counterfeit Currency and Character in Mark Twain's 'Which Was It?'." *The Mark Twain Journal* XVII, No. 3 (Winter 1974-75): 1-6.
    Establishes "Which Was It?" as a work in the tradition of Twain's other late writings and interprets its central theme as the questioning of "appearance and reality, counterfeit and truth."

Rucker, Mary E. "Moralism and Determinism in 'The Man That Corrupted Hadleyburg'." *Studies in Short Fiction* 14, No. 1 (Winter 1977): 49-54.
    Contends that the characters in "The Man That Corrupted Hadleyburg" enjoy free, though limited, choice and that their "failure to attain a moral regeneration" may be attributed to "their not making the morally correct choices."

Salomon, Roger B. *Twain and the Image of History,* pp. 191-210. New Haven, Conn.: Yale University Press, 1961.
    Appraises Twain's use of history in *The Mysterious Stranger*.

Scharnhorst, Gary. "Paradise Revisited: Twain's 'The Man That Corrupted Hadleyburg'." *Studies in Short Fiction* 18, No. 1 (Winter 1981): 59-64.
    Scharnhorst asserts that in "The Man That Corrupted Hadleyburg," "Twain recast major sections of *Paradise Lost,* not the third chapter of Genesis [as other critics have suggested], to fashion a modern, though no less paradoxical, parable of the Fortunate Fall."

Schmidt, Paul. "The Deadpan on Simon Wheeler." *Southwest Review* XLI, No. 3 (Summer 1956): 270-77.
    Investigates Twain's use of comic gravity in the character Simon Wheeler in "The Celebrated Jumping Frog of Calaveras County."

Smith, Lawrence R. "Mark Twain's 'Jumping Frog': Toward an American Heroic Ideal." *The Mark Twain Journal* XX, No. 1 (Winter 1979-80): 15-18.
    Contends that "it is Twain's main purpose [in 'The Celebrated Jumping Frog of Calaveras County'] to define and explore just

what is true and valuable about Simon Wheeler and the qualities he represents."

Spengemann, William C. *Mark Twain and the Backwoods Angel: The Matter of Innocence in the Works of Samuel L. Clemens,* pp. 120-34. Kent Studies in English, edited by Howard P. Vincent. Kent, Ohio: Kent State University Press, 1966.

Examines Twain's use of innocence in *The Mysterious Stranger.*

Stone, Albert E., Jr. *The Innocent Eye: Childhood in Mark Twain's Imagination.* New Haven: Yale University Press, 1961, 289 p.

Examines the theme of childhood in Twain's writing, devoting particular attention to *The Mysterious Stranger.*

Taylor, J. Golden. Introduction to "The Celebrated Jumping Frog of Calaveras County," by Mark Twain. *The American West* II, No. 4 (Fall 1965): 73-6.

Asserts that "the literary significance of the Jumping Frog lies in the authenticity and artistry with which a humorous incident in an early western mining camp is made to yield fable-like insights into certain universal traits in human nature."

Tenney, Thomas Asa. *Mark Twain: A Reference Guide.* Reference Guides in Literature, edited by Ronald Gottesman. Boston: G. K. Hall & Co., 1977, 443 p.

Exhaustive annotated bibliography of criticism on Twain with annual supplements appearing in the journal *American Literary Realism, 1870-1910.*

Tuckey, John S. Introduction to *Mark Twain's 'Which Was the Dream', and Other Symbolic Writings of the Later Years,* by Mark Twain, edited by John S. Tuckey, pp 1-29. The Mark Twain Papers, edited by Frederick Anderson. Berkeley and Los Angeles: University of California Press, 1967.

Biographical background to Twain's later tales, including brief textual and compositional histories of each piece.

———, ed. *Mark Twain's 'The Mysterious Stranger' and the Critics.* Belmont, Calif.: Wadsworth Publishing Co., 1968, 227 p.

Collection of previously published criticism on *The Mysterious Stranger.* Also includes a newly published article by Tuckey, "*The Mysterious Stranger:* Mark Twain's Texts and the Paine-Duneka Edition."

Wagenknecht, Edward. *Mark Twain: The Man and His Work.* 3rd edition. Norman: University of Oklahoma Press, 1967, 302 p.

Respected biographical study first published in 1935.

Wilson, James D. *A Reader's Guide to the Short Stories of Mark Twain.* Boston: G. K. Hall & Co., 1987, 297 p.

Critical evaluations of sixty-five of Twain's short fiction pieces from throughout his career. Each entry includes publication history; historical, biographical, and compositional information; thematic and stylistic analyses; a critical synopsis summarizing scholarly commentary; and a bibliography of relevant materials.

H(erbert) G(eorge) Wells

1866-1946

(Also wrote under the pseudonyms Sosthenes Smith, Walter Glockenhammer, and Reginald Bliss) English novelist, short story writer, historian, essayist, autobiographer, and critic.

Wells is best known as a major progenitor of modern science fiction who foretold the development of such present-day realities as atomic weaponry and chemical and global warfare. In addition to such novels as *The Time Machine, The Invisible Man, The War of the Worlds,* and *The Island of Doctor Moreau,* several of Wells's short stories are acknowledged as classics in the fields of science fiction and fantasy and have profoundly influenced the course of both genres. In such farcical works of science fantasy as "The Purple Pileus" and "The Stolen Bacillus," Wells chronicled the conflicts between the individual and society and between social and natural instincts. Other stories, including "The Country of the Blind" and "The Man Who Could Work Miracles: A Pantoum in Prose," reflect his perceptive criticism of both human limitations and possibilities. Critics generally concur that the appeal of his work stems from his ability to introduce exotic or fantastic elements into mundane situations, which often arise from institutional and social pressures.

Wells was born into a lower-middle-class Cockney family in Bromley, Kent, a suburb of London. He escaped a servile life by winning a scholarship to London University and the Royal College of Science, where he studied zoology under noted biologist T. H. Huxley, who instilled in him a belief in social as well as biological evolution. Wells considered this conviction the most important and influential aspect of his education. After graduating from London University, Wells published his first nonfiction work, *Text-Book of Biology,* and contributed short stories to several magazines. The serialization of his short novel *The Time Machine* launched his career as an author of fiction, and his subsequent science fiction and science fantasies proved extremely popular with audiences and critics alike. Enabled by his growing fame to meet such prominent authors as Arnold Bennett and Joseph Conrad, with whom he exchanged criticism and opinions on the art of writing, Wells developed his own prose style while serving under editor Frank Harris as a literary critic for *The Saturday Review.* A socialist, Wells joined the Fabian Society in 1903, but left the group after fighting a long, unsuccessful war of wit and rhetoric over some of the group's policies with his friend Bernard Shaw, a prominent Fabian and man of letters. Wells's socialist thought, coupled with a belief in the gradual advancement of humanity through evolution and scientific innovation, is expressed in his short fiction in the form of imaginative fantasies in which the innovative ideas of liberated individuals intrude upon conformistic society.

Most of Wells's short stories were published prior to World War I, a period when Wells was commonly regarded as an advocate of the new, the iconoclastic, and the daring. However, the war and its aftermath of widespread disillusionment upset his optimistic vision of humankind. Wells's postwar ideas on the perfectibility of humanity were modified to stress the necessity of education in bringing about progress. Throughout the 1920s and 1930s, Wells's fiction became pro-

gressively less optimistic about the future of humanity. The advent of World War II increased Wells's despondency about the future, and his last book, *Mind at the End of Its Tether,* predicts the destruction of civilization and the degeneration of humanity. Wells died in London in 1946.

Wells's canon of short fiction includes approximately seventy short stories and two novellas, most of which were originally published in five collections. Early in his career, Wells was hired by the editor of the *Pall Mall Budget* to produce what he termed "single sitting stories." Wells commented: "I found that, taking almost anything as a starting-point and letting my thoughts play about it, there would presently come out of the darkness, in a manner quite inexplicable, some absurd or vivid little incident more or less relevant to that initial nucleus. . . . I would discover I was peering into remote and mysterious worlds ruled by an order logical indeed but other than our common sanity." These early sketches, many of which appeared in Wells's first short fiction collection, *The Stolen Bacillus, and Other Incidents,* are considered indicative of the exceptional descriptive skills, narrative prowess, and striking imagination that characterize his later stories and novels.

Although the stories in *The Stolen Bacillus* are generally considered uneven in quality, many reviewers have praised

Wells's ability to imaginatively suspend reader disbelief by investing convincing realistic situations with ostensibly irrelevant detail and fantastic premises. In "The Flowering of the Strange Orchid," for example, a gentleman bored with suburban existence obtains the adventure he craves after purchasing an unclassified orchid that attempts to drain his blood through aerial roots resembling tentacles. In "The Remarkable Case of Davidson's Eyes," a young scientist conducting an experiment in a laboratory during a thunderstorm discovers that his vision has become disordered; while he remains physically in London, he lives visually on a drab, uninhabited south sea island. Although little dramatic action occurs, the story succeeds due to Wells's ability to fully exploit his strange premise by describing, for example, how the scientist begins to view an underwater panorama of colorful fish as he is led downhill in London. Other stories in this collection anticipate Wells's later works of "hard" science fiction in their focus upon feasible, as opposed to fantastic, aspects of science. The title story concerns an anarchist who steals a tube of bacteria hoping to infect London with cholera. Unaware that the bacteria is harmless to humans but causes blue patches on monkeys, he swallows its contents and is stained dark blue.

The pieces in Wells's next major collection, *The Plattner Story, and Others,* are generally considered indicative of the wide range of his talent and are often based upon seemingly absurd premises that have their basis in concrete theory. "The Argonauts of the Air," for example, may have seemed implausible at the time of its appearance but anticipated by eight years the achievement of the Wright brothers in its tale of humanity's first successful attempt at mechanical flight. In "The Plattner Story," a teacher disappears in an explosion during a chemistry lesson. He reappears nine days later with his anatomical organs reversed—his heart, for instance, is now on the left side of his body. According to Bernard Bergonzi, "The facts of the case concerning Plattner are a graphic illustration of the mathematical truism that, just as a two-dimensional or 'flat' object can be turned over by lifting it into three-dimensional space, so the internal relationships of a three-dimensional body might be altered by removing it for the purpose into four-dimensional space." Other stories in this collection introduce farcical devices into commonplace domestic settings. In "The Purple Pelius," a small shop owner eats an unidentified fungus, hoping to escape his shrewish wife through suicide, and regains her respect after returning home in a stuporous rage and offending her guests.

Tales of Space and Time, a volume of science fiction tales, contains "The Star," a critically acclaimed story that is regarded as exemplary of Wells's technique of building vivid imagery in poetic terms. "The Star" concerns the discovery of a bright planet that is eventually revealed to be a comet hotter and brighter than the sun. As the celestial body approaches the earth, Wells invests the narrative with detailed images of impending catastrophe such as tidal waves, escalating temperatures, and earthquakes. John Ower commented: "The story is a genuine pioneer work of science fiction because it imaginatively applies to human experience not only the discoveries in astronomy and physics . . . , but also the radically altered world-picture which those findings implied." The shortsightedness of human efforts at progress is the focus of "The Man Who Could Work Miracles," in which a man with the ability to wish miracles into existence requests that the globe stand still so that he can do more in less time. However, he and all other unrooted objects are launched into the air by the centrifugal force of the earth. The stories in Wells's next volume, *Twelve Stories and a Dream,* are generally regarded as less consistent in range and quality than his previous tales. This volume contains "The New Accelerator," in which a physiologist discovers a drug that stimulates the nervous system to function at several thousand times its normal rate. After taking a dose with a friend, he walks along Folkestone Leas in England, observing the world in a seeming state of suspended animation. As in many of Wells's works, the discovery raises serious, and in some ways, disturbing implications; yet, as J. R. Hammond commented, the story also "bears vivid testimony to Wells's abundant zest for life and his infectious delight at the sheer joy of existence."

Wells wrote successively fewer short stories after 1910, preferring to devote himself to longer works. According to Wells, his last major collection, *The Country of the Blind,* contains "all the short stories . . . that I care for any one to read again." Although primarily comprised of pieces that appeared in previous collections, this volume contains several new stories written in the mature style of his later works. The title piece has appeared in many anthologies and possibly remains his most frequently debated work of short fiction. In "The Country of the Blind," a mountaineer named Núñez risks traversing the Andes Mountains in South America to reach a valley where all native inhabitants are blind. Recalling the mythical proverb "In the country of the blind, the one-eyed man is king," Núñez believes he will attain power over the natives but is instead treated as an insane criminal and reduced to menial tasks. Presented with the chance to marry a woman with whom he has fallen in love if he will consent to have his eyes removed, Núñez returns to the mountains, preferring the remote possibility of escape or death. While some reviewers view Núñez as a selfish exploiter who seeks to force European values on a peaceful and content native people, others view him as a heroic individual who resists the blind conformity of an inward society. Richard Hauer Costa commented: "Of all his vast array of works, this story best states H. G. Wells's philosophical position in terms of the techniques of the literary artist."

Together with Jules Verne, Wells is regarded as one of the most prominent innovators in the fields of science fiction and fantasy. The continued popularity of his books, the tremendous body of criticism devoted to them, and the liberalizing effect that much of his work has had on Western thought combine to establish Wells as one of the major figures in twentieth-century literature. Although some critics contend that Wells's stories reflect the distinct influence of such diverse authors as Jules Verne, Edgar Allen Poe, Charles Dickens, Victor Hugo, and Rudyard Kipling, many concur with the opinion of J. R. Hammond: "[In] the last analysis his stories have a distinctive quality which gives them a flavor peculiar to himself; it lies in their ability to stimulate thought, to suggest new possibilities of action, to unfold novel horizons of human endeavor."

(For further information on Wells's life and career, see *Twentieth Century Literary Criticism,* Vols. 6, 12, 19; *Contemporary Authors,* Vols. 110, 121; *Dictionary of Literary Biography,* Vols. 34, 70; and *Something about the Author,* Vol. 20.)

PRINCIPAL WORKS

SHORT FICTION

*Select Conversations with an Uncle, Now Extinct, and Two
　　Other Reminiscences*　1895
The Stolen Bacillus, and Other Incidents　1895
The Plattner Story, and Others　1897
Thirty Strange Stories　1987
Tales of Space and Time　1899
Twelve Stories and a Dream　1903
The Country of the Blind, and Other Stories　1911
The Short Stories of H. G. Wells　1927; also published as *The
　　Complete Short Stories of H. G. Wells* [enlarged edition],
　　1966
The Croquet Player　1936
Best Science Fiction Stories of H. G. Wells　1966
*The Man with a Nose, and the Other Uncollected Stories of
　　H. G. Wells*　1984

OTHER MAJOR WORKS

Text-Book of Biology　(nonfiction)　1893
The Time Machine　(novel)　1895
The Wonderful Visit　(novel)　1895
The Island of Dr. Moreau　(novel)　1896
The Wheels of Chance　(novel)　1896
The Invisible Man　(novel)　1897
The War of the Worlds　(novel)　1898
When the Sleeper Wakes: A Story of the Years to Come
　　(novel)　1899; also published as *The Sleeper Awakes* [re-
　　vised edition],　1910
Love and Mr. Lewisham　(novel)　1900
*Anticipations of the Reaction of the Mechanical and Scientific
　　Progress upon Human Life and Thought*　(essay)　1901
The First Men in the Moon　(novel)　1901
Mankind in the Making　(essays)　1903
The Food of the Gods, and How It Came to Earth　(novel)
　　1904
Kipps: The Story of a Simple Soul　(novel)　1905
A Modern Utopia　(essay)　1905
The Future in America: A Search after Realities　(essays)
　　1906
In the Days of the Comet　(novel)　1906
First and Last Things: A Confession of Faith and Rule of Life
　　(essay)　1908
New Worlds for Old　(essay)　1908
*The War in the Air and Particularly How Mr. Bert Smallways
　　Fared While It Lasted*　(novel)　1908
Ann Veronica　(novel)　1909
Tono-Bungay　(novel)　1909
The History of Mr. Polly　(novel)　1910
The New Machiavelli　(novel)　1911
Marriage　(novel)　1912
The War That Will End War　(essays)　1914
The Wife of Sir Isaac Harmon　(novel)　1914
The World Set Free　(novel)　1914
Boon [as Reginald Bliss]　(sketches)　1915
The Research Magnificent　(novel)　1915
Mr. Britling Sees It Through　(novel)　1916
God the Invisible King　(essay)　1917
*The Soul of a Bishop: A Novel (with Just a Little Love in It)
　　about Conscience and Religion and the Real Troubles of
　　Life*　(novel)　1917
Joan and Peter: The Story of an Education　(novel)　1918
The Outline of History. 2 vols.　(history)　1919-20
The Undying Fire　(novel)　1919
Men Like Gods　(novel)　1923
The World of William Clissold　(novel)　1926
Mr. Blettsworthy on Rampole Island　(novel)　1928

The Open Conspiracy　(essay)　1928
*The Autocracy of Mr. Parham: His Remarkable Adventures
　　in This Changing World*　(novel)　1930
The Bulpington of Blup　(novel)　1932
The Shape of Things to Come　(essays)　1933
Experiment in Autobiography　(autobiography)　1934
The Holy Terror　(novel)　1939
All Aboard for Ararat　(novel)　1940
Guide to the New World　(essay)　1941
Mind at the End of Its Tether　(essay)　1945
*Arnold Bennett and H. G. Wells: A Record of a Personal and
　　a Literary Friendship*　(letters and criticism)　1960
*George Gissing and H. G. Wells: Their Friendship and Corre-
　　spondence*　(letters and criticism)　1961

BASIL WILLIAMS　(essay date 1897)

[*In the following essay, Williams briefly reviews Wells's collection* The Plattner Story, and Others.]

Mr. H. G. Wells has happily given up the exaggerated horrors of *The Island of Doctor Moreau* for stories quite in his
best vein. He has all Jules Verne's convincing *insouciance* in
telling the most wildly improbable stories. This result is
largely gained by a solemn precision in the preliminary and
unimportant details of the story. Thus in **"The Plattner
Story,"** as in **"The Apple," "The Argonauts of the Air,"** and,
in fact, all the stories dealing with the marvellous, the reader
is prepared to accept anything after the minute description
of the principal characters' commonplace vulgarity or the in-
glorious dulness of their surroundings. There is hardly any
mystery left in their adventures, for one feels that it is almost
impossible for anything out of the way to have happened to
such people. This effect is heightened by a rigid avoidance of
any attempt to dwell on the marvellous character of the prod-
igy described, be it a flying machine, or the fruit of the tree
of knowledge, or what not. Precision in the unessential and
vagueness in the essential are really the basis of Mr. Wells's
art, and convey admirably the just amount of conviction. In
his more possible stories he shows that his constant choice of
commonplace characters is no fortuitous matter; all his characters would in themselves be fearfully dull, but by catching
and crystallizing the point of reality which is to be found everywhere, in showing the individuality which underlies the
veneer of gross conventionality, he often makes such stories
of a most seizing interest.

> *Basil Williams, in an originally unsigned review of
> "The Plattner Story and Others," in* The Athenae-
> um, *June 26, 1897, p. 837.*

ALFRED C. WARD　(essay date 1924)

[*In the following excerpt from his* Aspects of the Modern
Short Story, *Ward groups Wells's stories from* The Country
of the Blind *under four headings: comedies, horrors, fantasies,
and parables, deeming this collection outstanding and praising
it for representing "in a really extraordinary degree, the free
play of the human imagination."*]

[In] the introductory essay to **The Country of the Blind,**
H. G. Wells throws light upon the days, almost three decades
since, when short-story writers were many and prolific. He

thought (at the time of writing that introduction in 1911) that the short-story phase of English literature was already dead and gone; and in that year such a view was defensible. Now, more than twelve years later, the art of the short story has revived, yet with differences sufficient to make a study of Wells's methods distinctly interesting and illuminating.

Whether the scene of these stories is set upon sunlit oceans or in suburban gardens, the events are invariably transacted according to a plan which cannot be measured by rules deducible from "our common sanity." And if we would take refuge from the difficulty of criticising his subject-matter by turning to principles of construction and style, the author is ready to discredit any such endeavour by proclaiming:

> Insistence upon rigid forms and austere unities seems to me the instinctive reaction of the sterile against the fecund. . . . I refuse altogether to recognize any hard-and-fast type for the Short Story, any more than I admit any limitation upon the liberties of the Small Picture.

Generally-received canons, whether of art or of conduct, are not negatived of course by any individual refusal to recognize them; but as a fact, in his short stories, H. G. Wells is not the revolutionary his proclamation suggests. His themes may be unique, but his forms do approach a roughly generalized type. The stories are all eminently readable, though in a specifically technical sense they are undistinguished. Affectations or conscious tricks of style are rare in them; and in his short-story period the mannerisms characteristic of the maturer Wells were still unstereotyped. That now most familiar Wellsian hero, the rising young statesman who strikes a moral and ethical attitude as he sings: "All for love and the world well lost" (*cf.* **"A Dream of Armageddon"**) was then still a *rara avis;* and the notorious outbreaks of "dots" were sporadic rather than endemic. . . .

The only definitely "mannered" story included in *The Country of the Blind* (which contains "all the short stories . . . that I care for any one to read again") is the artificial trifle **"A Vision of Judgment"**—a strange medley in which facetiousness mixes very ill with the pomposities of a prose-poem. Of the remaining thirty-two stories, **"A Slip under the Microscope"** and **"Jimmy Goggles the God"** are least meritable; leaving thirty stories which might be grouped under four headings: Comedies (including Farces); Horrors; Fantasies; Parables.

In a broad view, the outstanding characteristics of these thirty pieces are that they are packed full of matter, and that they represent, in a really extraordinary degree, the free play of the human imagination. Considered in this aspect, the absence of technical distinction becomes almost a positive merit, as representing the exercise of a workmanlike sense of adequacy, to the exclusion of all possibly obtrusive technical fashioning. The stories, as to their external form, are no doubt as plain as deal packing-cases; and for Wells's purpose that is a more fitting outside than any gracefully proportioned casket with austere line could be. The content, not the casing, is his concern; by which it is not at all intended to imply that beauty (or even fine writing!) has no place in these stories. More often than in his novels there is apparent a luminous eloquence, as the author flashes meteorically into passages of acutely visualized description. There is the vision of the spheres vouchsafed to the disembodied operation-patient in **"Under the Knife,"** where a sense of spellbound wonder is stirred in the reader not so much by the actual picturing (excellent though that is) as by the conveyed sense of an incredibly rapid passage to the outposts of the universe.

Loose and flabby writing has often been a blemish in Wells's later work, but in **"Under the Knife,"** in **"The Star,"** and in **"A Dream of Armageddon,"** there is evidence as to what a master of English he could consistently have been if he had chosen to write less in recent years. He was, in the beginning, an author who knew how to write surpassing well—and had surpassing much about which it was worth while to write. *That* Wells breaks through from time to time even in the sociological novels (*cf.* the description of the voyage down the Thames in *Tono Bungay;* the fall of the aeroplane in *Joan and Peter;* and the sinking of the submarine in *The Undying Fire*); but in the short stories he had not woven round about himself that cocoon of prolixity which has stifled many valuable faculties in him.

The Comedies and Farces group in *The Country of the Blind* includes **"The Jilting of Jane"** (the earliest Wells story)—being the adventures of a servant-girl who threw a boot at her rival on the wedding-day. This was not a promising beginning for the man who was to lay the whole universe under contribution for subject-matter; but it is at least interesting to think that Jane might have been sister to Arty Kipps or Mr. Polly. In Mr. Polly's world lives, also, Mr. Coombes **"The Purple Pileus,"** who was "sick not only of his own existence but of everybody else's"; and who eats a strange fungus in the hope that it will poison him and give release from a nagging and domineering and extravagant wife. The purple pileus does not kill Mr. Coombes; on the contrary, it makes him "fighting drunk" and enables him to become master in his own house. This story has a touch of the fantastic Wells who is now so familiar—as also has **"The Stolen Bacillus,"** in which an anarchist, thinking to infect London with cholera, mistakenly steals a tube of the bacteria which causes blue patches on monkeys!

The best and most characteristic story among the pseudo-scientific farces is certainly **"The Truth about Pyecraft."** An intolerable bore to all his acquaintances, Pyecraft was the fattest clubman in London. He begged Mr. Formalyn to give him a weight-reducing prescription, taken from a collection of recipes which originated in India. Formalyn, being one day summoned by telephone to Pyecraft's flat in Bloomsbury, finds the fat man "right up close to the cornice in the corner by the door, as though someone had glued him to the ceiling." Pyecraft had always spoken of his bulk as "weight" instead of "fat"; and the Hindu prescriptions employed words with literal precision! The patient lost weight but not size, and became like a lighter-than-air balloon—a condition impossible to rectify except by means of Mr. Formalyn's plan to sew leaden weights into Pyecraft's clothing. Uproariously fantastic though the whole idea is, a kind of March-Hare logic is consistently followed. Supposing that those fat people who are continually desiring to "lose weight," could have their wish literally fulfilled—what would happen? The plain answer to that question exists in **"The Truth about Pyecraft."** How he ate all the heavy food he could procure—"pork 'e's had, sooit puddin', sossiges, noo bread," said his landlady; how he had to be put under a solid mahogany table to keep him temporarily away from the ceiling; how he slept beneath his wire-mattress instead of on top; how he transferred his Turkey carpet from the floor to the ceiling: these and other entertaining matters are madly comic and comically mad, but they do represent a meticulous working-out of that "order logical indeed, but other than our common sanity" which H. G. Wells puts forward to explain the line pursued in his short stories.

Questions which have never ceased to run in H. G. Wells's brain are: "Why should the world always conform to pattern? Why should man's logic always be supreme? What reason, apart from use and wont, is there to suggest that the universe, the planets and their inhabitants, will always retain their present relative status? Suppose the order of things did change, fundamentally, in some sudden and inexplicable way. . . . Suppose!"

That "Why?" and that "Suppose!" are the basis of nearly all Wells's short stories.

Suppose ants evolved directive intelligence, and worked out a highly specialized social organization, welded themselves into a single nation, and became armed with a deadly poison. . . . What could the human race do against swarming millions of tiny enemies of this species? Such a course of "supposing" produced the story of **"The Empire of the Ants,"** an empire at first confined to the upper reaches of the Amazon:

> So far, their action has been a steady progressive settlement, involving the flight or slaughter of every human being in the new areas they invade. They are increasing rapidly in numbers, and Holroyd at least is firmly convinced that they will finally dispossess man over the whole of tropical South America.
>
> And why should they stop at tropical South America?

"The Empire of the Ants" is one in the group of stories here labelled "Horrors." It has seven companions in the collection, and among the disturbing things born of H. G. Wells's "supposing" are flying spiders (**"The Valley of Spiders"**), a blood-sucking orchid (**"The Flowering of the Strange Orchid"**), a mighty flying animal in Borneo which attacks an astronomer in the dark (**"In the Avu Observatory"**), and flesh-eating sea-pigs with tentacles many feet long, which kill bathers and boaters at English watering-places (**"The Sea Raiders"**).

These stories (and also some placed in the category of Fantasies) are the work of an author who has the gift to induce, in his readers, "that willing suspension of disbelief for the moment which constitutes poetic faith." We do not strain at the improbabilities involved; we enter into the spirit of his "supposing," because we, too, are continually asking "Why?" in connexion with many common and uncommon things in life. It is probably true to say that every man and woman contains somewhere hidden—either near the surface or deep down—the thwarted spirit of a child whose "Why? Why? Why?" was never fully answered and whose "Supposing . . . " was invariably nipped by the perishing frost of adult impatience. Now and again, that thwarted child once more bursts into utterance, through an adult mind—insisting upon answers to its questions, and revelling in untrammelled exercise of the imagination. Then it is that the world gets its original geniuses, producing works which—whether they be like *The Faerie Queene* or like *The Food of the Gods*—are a child's supposings translated into adult dialect. Moreover, the horrors imagined by H. G. Wells are horrors indeed, but they are, mostly, no more terrifying than those independently summoned up by many a child; and Wells's imaginative horrors are convincing because he presents them with an appearance

of faith in their authenticity. He is not merely inventing or "making-believe"; he is setting imagination free to create its own shapes about some germ of an idea, and the result is a reality more intensely powerful than actually existent objects.

When, on the other hand, Wells traffics in horrors that are certainly derived from actualities of the "grown-up" mind, he fails abysmally. **"The Cone"** has several features which should ensure its receiving good reviews in high-class periodicals; nevertheless, it is a repulsive and revolting story, which no prating of "literary merit" could possibly excuse; and only little less undesirable is **"The Lord of the Dynamos."**

More than a dozen stories in this volume may conveniently be listed as Fantasies, although the word lacks the pungency and astringency that should be suggested in connexion with these tales. **"The Story of the Late Mr. Elvesham"** tells of a young man who was induced to drink a glass of "doctored" liqueur by an elderly man who had promised to leave him a fortune. When the prospective "heir" starts to get out of bed next morning, he notices a remarkable physical change in himself and finds that he has become in all outward respects like the aged and withered Egbert Elvesham—who entirely disappears, having evidently possessed himself of the young man's strength and lease of life. This theme of transferred personality is one which seems to exercise an increasing fascination for writers, and it has provided, in particular, the plot for one of Walter de la Mare's novels, *The Return,* although that book has a mystical element such as does not enter into the Wells story.

The *chef d'œuvre* among the Fantasies is **"The Star."** (pp. 130-38)

This story offers something better than studied technical rendering; it offers a vision fused at white heat from a rich imagination, maintaining its own momentum and equilibrium.

Turning to the Parables in *The Country of the Blind,* we find three stories that can be thus designated: **"The Door in the Wall," "The Beautiful Suit,"** and **"The Country of the Blind."** The first describes how Lionel Wallace, when a little fellow between five and six years old, wandered through West Kensington streets one day, and came to a green door set in a white wall. The door attracted the child, as it were magnetically, so that he opened it and discovered a wonderful and beautiful garden stretching far and wide, with distant hills. He found delightful playmates there; and, afterwards, a grave and sombre woman who took him to a seat and showed him a book:

> The pages fell open. She pointed, and I looked, marvelling, for in the living pages of that book I saw myself; it was a story about myself, and in it were all the things that had happened to me since ever I was born.

In a while the grave woman stooped to kiss the boy's brow, and at that moment he found himself crying in a long grey street in Kensington. He thought he would be able to find that door again whenever he went to look for it; but he could not. He did see it again, several times in his life, but it was always in some different locality; and Wallace was always prevented by some immediately urgent worldly call from passing again through the door. A time came when he determined that nothing whatever should keep him away from the wonderful garden whenever next he should see the green door in the white wall; and one morning his body was found in a railway excavation near East Kensington Station, beyond a hoarding in which a small doorway was cut. . . . The advantage of both this story and **"The Beautiful Suit"** is that they may be interpreted according to the temper of the individual mind. Wallace's mysterious garden might be any one of those fine aspirations by which men are moved, and from which they are debarred by the fret and wear and tear of the workaday world. Men cry: "We have no time for the beauty that lies beyond the door in life's wall. We are too busy to-day; let our time for rest and the sweet things of life be to-morrow." And when that remote to-morrow dawns at last, the wonderful garden of which they had the freedom in childhood, eludes them after all, and in the hour of delusion they walk behind a hoarding—into the pit beyond. Yet that is not all, maybe. H. G. Wells says of Lionel Wallace:

> I am more than half convinced that he had, in truth, an abnormal gift, and in sense, something—I know not what—that in the guise of wall and door offered him an outlet, a secret and peculiar passage of escape into another and altogether more beautiful world. At any rate, you will say, it betrayed him in the end. But did it betray him? . . . By our daylight standard he walked out of security into darkness, danger, and death.

> But did he see like that?

J. D. Beresford interprets *The Invisible Man,* one of Wells's longer works, as a statement of "man's revolt against imprisonment in the flesh," and suggests that a similar idea is expressed in the story named **"The Country of the Blind."** But there are sensible differences which make it difficult to agree with that allocation. If, however, Beresford had chosen to classify **"The Door in the Wall"** as a parable of "man's revolt against imprisonment in the flesh," there would seem to be little opportunity for questioning the interpretation.

In regard to **"The Country of the Blind,"** would it not be a more nearly accurate exposition to say that it presents, figuratively, the man of genius (or the man of normal vision, or the man of imagination, or wisdom, or understanding) as in revolt against his social environment, and not against his own incarnation? In the heart of South America lies an imagined mountain valley, all the inhabitants of which have been blind for many generations. Into that Country of the Blind there stumbled a man, Nunez, possessed of full vision; and remembering an old proverb—"In the Country of the Blind the One-eyed Man is King"—he felt certain of attaining power among that people. Instead, they regarded him as a demented creature; and when Nunez rebelled against them he was whipped and imprisoned in darkness, and afterwards made a menial. He fell in love with Medina-saroté, his master's daughter, but his suit was acceptable to the Elders only on the one condition that he would submit to an operation prescribed as a certain cure for the criminal idiocy from which he was considered to suffer. The operation proposed the removal of his eyes—irritant bodies which affected his brain, said the doctors. After an agony of revolt against the plan, Nunez agreed, in order that he might not be separated from his lover; but on the evening preceding the operation-day he rebelled finally, and set forth to climb the great mountains which bounded the Country of the Blind:

> When sunset came he was no longer climbing, but he was very far and high. He had been higher, but he was still very high. His clothes were torn, his limbs were blood-stained, he was bruised in many places, but he lay as if he were at his ease, and there was a smile on his face. . . .

> The glow of the sunset passed, and the night came, and still he lay peacefully contented under the cold clear stars.

Thus Nunez chose the shining heights of death rather than the darkened ways as of a human mole.

H. G. Wells has told that story of Nunez and Medina-saroté in the Country of the Blind, many times. Once Nunez was called Dick Trafford, Medina-saroté was named Marjorie Pope, and instead of **"The Country of the Blind"** the story was called *Marriage.* (pp. 139-43)

Neither **"The Country of the Blind"** nor *Marriage* is a statement of "man's revolt against imprisonment in the flesh," but of the uncommon man's revolt against the tyranny of the common man and of the unimaginative woman. (p. 144)

> *Alfred C. Ward, "H. G. Wells: 'The Country of the Blind'," in his* Aspects of the Modern Short Story: English and American, *University of London Press, Ltd., 1924, pp. 129-44.*

H. E. BATES   (essay date 1941)

[*Bates was one of the masters of the twentieth-century English short story and the author of* The Modern Short Story, *an excellent introduction to the form. Bates was also a respected novelist and contributor of book reviews to the* Morning Post *and* The Spectator. *In the following excerpt from* The Modern Short Story, *which was originally published in 1941, Bates characterizes Wells as a fiction writer, comparing him to his popular rival Rudyard Kipling.*]

The short story has at this time no equal status with the novel; nor has it any marked affinity with poetry; novelists are novelists, poets are poets, and the time has not yet come when poets have been turned aside from idle lyricism by the impact of a series of world catastrophes, each of which disturbs the smooth surface of the personal world with waves of increasingly greater barbarity. Poets are still cultured men with long hair and velveteen jackets and a tendency towards nobility of thought; prose is, generally speaking, outside their trade.

But the turn of the short story is coming, and its influence and popularity are, from 1850 onwards, spreading from America and the continent. Writers of distinction begin to understand, and then exploit, its possibilities as a separate form. Among those writers, whose collective expression may be said to have been made in *The Yellow Book* of the 'nineties, several names stand out: Stevenson, George Moore, Wilde, Wells, Kipling, and the almost forgotten Hubert Crackanthorpe. Of these Kipling is the great untouchable; in spite of being perhaps the most execrable famous poet the language has ever produced he has become a kind of national mouthpiece; in times of national crisis, of great wars and expectant sacrifice, the zeal with which the English quote Shakespeare is only equalled by the ardour with which they cite Kipling. (p. 104)

One of the strong points of the 'nineties period to which its champions always point triumphantly is its masculinity. This seems to imply that the short story, in order to be good, must always be masculine. Its movement must be bold and forceful; its meaning must be expressed through a fluent series of physical actions; to these actions must be added a culminating point, in which action and emotion will crystallize, leaving the reader stimulated but satisfied. In such a story femininity, passivity, introspection, the subtle and oblique, will have little or no place.

Is it true that the 'nineties short story depended for its success on these things? Setting aside Kipling for the moment, Wells was probably its most successful exponent. On what does Wells mostly depend? Not masculinity it is certain. Not primarily action. Wells is a scientific inventor inoculated with a dream bacillus; he is the teller of fairy tales talking in the language of scientific power. However Wells is analysed, I think, it will be found that every characteristic of him is forcefully and diametrically opposed by something opposite. The story may be of the wildest improbability, perhaps, but its narrator, or the mind through which it is narrated, is that of the commonest earth-bound man. The story may be exceedingly subtle in complexity, but Wells's attitude is one of the greatest humility, as if to say, "This is all a bungling chap like me can make of it." The story may project a dream world, but is in reality a social criticism. It may deal with an astronomical miracle, but is related in almost liturgical terms with strong Biblical rhythms. These and other opposing forces make of Wells a powerful dynamo capable of a tireless generation of ideas scintillating with a capricious and furious fancy.

He has been well described as a sort of literary Edison, and like Edison he was born at the right time. At pretty well any preceding period of history Wells and Edison might have stood an excellent chance of being hanged. But the moment was made for Wells, and that moment has been well described by Mr. Frank Swinnerton:

> Picture to yourselves the shock to readers of those days of a rush of new inventions, simple to us now, but then so novel and startling. . . . Here was a man who put posers—scientific posers—with the facility and enjoyment of a child; who said "Why?" "What if—?" "How?" "I suppose"—about all sorts of things people found they wanted to know. It was prodigious . . . he bubbled with new notions, and they were notions to which other minds jumped an instant too late.

Poe . . . anticipated the nineteenth-century hunger for dream worlds and scientific fantasy, but satisfied it only partially. Wells satisfied it completely. In an age when naturalism was the most advanced of literary fashions Wells was not interested in naturalism; in the short stories, at any rate, he was not interested in life as it was. "It is always about life being altered that I write, or about people developing schemes for altering life," he himself says. "And I have never once 'presented' life. My apparently most objective books are criticisms and incitements to change." To this restless desire to invert life, to turn it inside out, Wells brought a kind of impishness; and it is significant that in the hands of good cartoonists he is often portrayed with something of the attitude of a small boy holding a pin behind his back. With that pin Wells caused, indeed, any amount of delicious and exciting havoc in the flat, complacent, three-dimensional world of his time. Wells was unwilling to exclude the wildest improbability about life on earth. Supposing it were ten-dimensional instead of three? Supposing men could be made invisible? Supposing a man walked through a door and disappeared? Supposing we were not the only human beings in the cosmic world? Supposing men could fly? It is first in the abundance of such ideas, rather than their startling newness, and then in his manipulation of them into credible narratives, that

Wells excels. For clearly other people before Wells must have wondered if a man could suddenly disappear, or if men could fly, or if there were living creatures on other stars. For the task of making such ideas credible Wells possessed no other apparatus than that possessed by every writer in the world: words. Ideas, as most writers know, are two a penny. It is only by the translation of these ideas into words of a certain credible order that they can be given even ephemeral value for another person.

This is a truism, of course; but Wells has been derided as a stylist, as a Cockney vulgarian with "no sense of or care for beauty of style." But Wells's style has, in fact, a special kind of beauty: the beauty of artfulness. Take **"The Story of the Late Mr. Elvesham."** "I set this story down," says Wells in the opening sentence, "not expecting it will be believed." The touch is apparently that of a simple bland innocence; in reality it is an opening of beautiful subtlety; for it is followed at once by the very thing which Wells is anxious that the reader should swallow: "but, if possible, to prepare a way of escape for the next victim. He perhaps may profit by my misfortune. My own case, I know, is hopeless, and I am now in some measure prepared to meet my fate." The mind of the reader, abruptly stimulated, is set into eager motions of inquiry. Escape? Victim? Misfortune? Hopeless? Fate? By these words he has been cajoled by Wells into a world of mysterious and incalculable promise. Perhaps a shade too far? Not to be believed perhaps, after all? But Wells holds him back from these speculations on improbability by a plain statement of the most commonplace kind of fact. "My name is George Edward Eden. I was born at Trentham, in Staffordshire, my father being employed in the gardens there."

Several points in this apparently artless business call for comment and absolve Wells from the charge of stylelessness. Two are points of fact, two are points of word-arrangement. In stating the narrator's two Christian names, George Edward, and in giving not only the place of his birth but the county, Wells gives the whole statement the authentic validity of a birth certificate. He holds it firm on earth. The two examples of word-arrangement are conceived with comparable subtlety. "I am now in some measure prepared," and "my father being employed" are both examples of the most deliberate stylelessness. For the voice here is not Wells's voice, but the voice of the narrator. This is not Wells's idea of good style but the narrator's idea of good style. It is the utterance of the common man who, making a public statement, drops his natural manner and speaks in what he feels is "proper English." It is the subtle key to character.

This artful use of apparently trivial items of fact and apparently commonplace touches of formal style is to be seen repeatedly in Wells, although it is by no means Wells's invention. Through Dickens Wells derived the technique of artful artlessness from Defoe, who used it to perfection to describe with captivating validity and realism places and events he had never seen. And in this, I think, lies much of Wells's charm as a writer—the sort of charm that will, at some future date, give Wells an attractive touch of period bloom—and almost all his power as a story-teller. For Wells possesses not only a highly compressed vitality but the great power of doing what he likes with the reader's curiosity. By coaxing it, teasing it, disturbing it, tickling it, holding it in check, shocking it, Wells succeeds in leading that curiosity to investigate the most improbable situations with a sense of anticipation and excitement. For that reason, even if someone should some day explode completely the Wells of scientific and social ideas, he will always remain a great story-teller—perhaps a great kidder would be better, a man who succeeded in telling more tall stories than any other writer of his generation and yet, by a genius for binding the commonplace to the most astronomical exploration of fancy, succeeded in getting them believed.

Wells, indeed, is a parabolist, but with a difference. For his are not earthly stories with a heavenly meaning, but heavenly stories with an earthly meaning—perhaps more accurately an earthly warning. For Wells, like a true parabolist, is also something of a prophet; the Wellsian flights of fancy become, within Wells's own lifetime, things of momentuous and terrible actuality. The dream-world in 1895 is the world of terror-reality in 1941. This is well known, of course, and I mention it only to enforce a point of contrast with Wells's greatest popular rival of the 'nineties, Kipling, born exactly one year earlier, in 1865. Wells is the prophet, the seer, the visionary who has the doubtful satisfaction of seeing his visions become all too terribly true; he is the social iconoclast who smashes one age to pieces in order to show how another, and better, may be built and then sees a worse one building. (pp. 105-11)

H. E. Bates, "Tolstoy, Wells, and Kipling," in his The Modern Short Story: A Critical Survey, *T. Nelson and Sons Ltd., 1941, pp. 95-121.*

JORGE LUIS BORGES   (essay date 1952)

[*Regarded as among the foremost figures in modern Latin American literature, Borges is acclaimed for his esoteric and intricate short stories in which he combines fantasy and realism to address complex philosophical questions. His works often defy classification, synthesizing elements of both fiction and the essay, while generally eschewing the use of complex characters and realistic settings. In his writings, Borges employs paradox and oxymoron to examine such metaphysical issues as the existence of a supreme being, the malleability of personal identity, and the impotency of human intelligence. In the following excerpt, he debates Oscar Wilde's assertion that Wells was "a scientific Jules Verne."*]

Harris relates that when Oscar Wilde was asked about Wells, he called him "a scientific Jules Verne." That was in 1899; it appears that Wilde thought less of defining Wells, or of annihilating him, than of changing the subject. Now the names H. G. Wells and Jules Verne have come to be incompatible. We all feel that this is true, but still it may be well to examine the intricate reasons on which our feeling is based.

The most obvious reason is a technical one. Before Wells resigned himself to the role of a sociological spectator, he was an admirable storyteller, an heir to the concise style of Swift and Edgar Allan Poe; Verne was a pleasant and industrious journeyman. Verne wrote for adolescents; Wells, for all ages. There is another difference, which Wells himself once indicated: Verne's stories deal with probable things (a submarine, a ship larger than those existing in 1872, the discovery of the South Pole, the talking picture, the crossing of Africa in a balloon, the craters of an extinguished volcano that lead to the center of the earth); the short stories Wells wrote concern mere possibilities, if not impossible things (an invisible man, a flower that devours a man, a crystal egg that reflects the events on Mars, a man who returns from the future with a flower of the future, a man who returns from the other life with his heart on the right side, because he has been com-

pletely inverted, as in a mirror). I have read that Verne, scandalized by the license permitted by *The First Men in the Moon,* exclaimed indignantly, "*Il invente!*" (pp. 86-7)

Like Quevedo, like Voltaire, like Goethe, like some others, Wells is less a man of letters than a literature. He wrote garrulous books in which the gigantic felicity of Charles Dickens somehow reappears; he bestowed sociological parables with a lavish hand; he constructed encyclopedias, enlarged the possibilities of the novel, rewrote the Book of Job—"that great Hebrew imitation of the Platonic dialogue"; for our time, he wrote a very delightful autobiography without pride and without humility; he combated communism, Nazism, and Christianity; he debated (politely and mortally) with Belloc; he chronicled the past, chronicled the future, recorded real and imaginary lives. Of the vast and diversified library he left us, nothing has pleased me more than his narration of some atrocious miracles: *The Time Machine, The Island of Dr. Moreau,* "The Plattner Story," *The First Men in the Moon.* They are the first books I read; perhaps they will be the last. I think they will be incorporated, like the fables of Theseus or Ahasuerus, into the general memory of the species and even transcend the fame of their creator or the extinction of the language in which they were written. (p. 88)

Jorge Luis Borges, "The First Wells," in his Other Inquiries: 1937-1952, *translated by Ruth L. C. Simms, University of Texas Press, 1964, pp. 86-8.*

BERNARD BERGONZI   (essay date 1961)

[*An English novelist, scholar, and essayist, Bergonzi has written extensively on the works of H. G. Wells, T. S. Eliot, and other major figures in twentieth-century literature. In the following excerpt from his* The Early H. G. Wells: A Study of the Scientific Romances, *Bergonzi surveys major themes in Wells's short story canon.*]

[The stories from *The Stolen Bacillus, and Other Incidents*] are predictably uneven: some are merely expansions of facetious or sensational incidents, which bear obvious signs of their journalistic origin, but others possess, on a small scale, something of the imaginative distinction which had marked *The Time Machine.* As we have seen, *The Time Machine* itself, certainly Wells's finest literary achievement, originated in a similar commission by W. E. Henley to contribute a series of articles to the *National Observer.* Wells himself was to remark of some of these early stories, 'I would discover I was peering into remote and mysterious worlds ruled by an order logical indeed but other than our common sanity.'

A representative story from *The Stolen Bacillus* is "The Remarkable Case of Davidson's Eyes". Here we find a recurring element in Wells's early imaginative writing, the apposition of contemporary reality with some wholly 'other' setting of a remote and exotic kind, a theme already made manifest in the encounter between the Time Traveller and the Eloi. Sidney Davidson, a rather ordinary young scientist, is conducting an experiment in a laboratory during a thunderstorm. As a result his vision becomes disordered in some mysterious way, so that whilst he continues to be physically present in North London he is living *visually* on an uninhabited island somewhere on the other side of the world. In his everyday surroundings he is quite helpless and has to be led about like a blind man. There is no specifically dramatic interest in this story, but Wells exploits to the full the weird potentialities inherent in the situation. When Davidson is taken downhill in

London his vision similarly descends on the island, so that at certain points he sees and describes a strange undersea world of luminous fishes, though he can still hear people passing in the London street and a newsboy selling papers. Very gradually he begins to recover his normal vision; a 'hole' appears in his phantom world, and he sees part of his friend's hand: 'It looks like the ghost of a bit of your hand sticking out of the darkling sky.' As his normal vision returns the 'other' world becomes fainter and in time disappears altogether. Some years later Davidson recognizes from a photograph a ship he had noticed off the coast of the island, and he discovers from an officer who had been on the ship that the island really exists: a remote rock in the Antipodes inhabited only by penguins.

Up to this point Wells, or rather his sceptical and hardheaded narrator, Bellows, has only been concerned with the facts of the case and has made no attempt to give an explanation. So far, the story could be taken as a kind of ghost-story, or at least a pure mystery without any hint of a rational explanation. Bellows is more concerned with presenting the facts than with speculating about their possible cause, but in the final paragraphs he rather reluctantly puts forward the views of his scientific superior, Professor Wade:

> That completes the remarkable story of Davidson's eyes. It's perhaps the best authenticated case in existence of real vision at a distance. Explanation there is none forthcoming, except what Prof. Wade has thrown out. But his explanation invokes the Fourth Dimension, and a dissertation on theoretical kinds of space. To talk of there being a 'kink' in space seems mere nonsense to me; it may be because I am no mathematician. When I said that nothing would alter the fact that the place is eight thousand miles away, he answered that two points might be a yard away on a sheet of paper, and yet be brought together by bending the paper round. The reader may grasp his argument, but I certainly do not. His idea seems to be that Davidson, stooping between the poles of the big electro-magnet, had some extraordinary twist given to his retinal elements through the sudden change in the field of force due to the lightning. He thinks, as a consequence of this, that it may be possible to live visually in one part of the world, while one lives bodily in another. He has even made some experiments in support of his views; but, so far, he has simply succeeded in blinding a few dogs. I believe that is the net result of his work, though I have not seen him for some weeks. . . . But the whole of his theory seems fantastic to me. The facts concerning Davidson stand on an altogether different footing, and I can testify personally to the accuracy of every detail I have given.

Bellows, in his positivistic devotion to facts and his dislike of the 'fantastic', attempts to discourage us from accepting Professor Wade's explanation. Paradoxically, if, like Bellows, we do not accept it we shall be forced to move into the realms of mystery and the occult for an explanation, for the bare facts themselves are unlikely to satisfy us for long. Yet Bellows—as Wells uses him to manipulate the argument—invites us by his very obtuseness to accept Wade's explanation: 'The reader may grasp his argument, but I certainly do not.' Wells is here returning to the preoccupation of his student days with the Fourth Dimension and multidimensional geometries, which recurs in various forms in *The Chronic Argonauts* and *The Time Machine*, as well as in *The Wonderful*

Visit and "**The Plattner Story**". It is a point of interest that the notion of a 'kink' in space has since become a commonplace to writers of science fiction. The explanation, so offhandedly presented by Bellows, seems unlikely enough, it is true, but at the same time, we are constrained to think that there might be something in it. It is in this area between the improbable and the impossible that Wells achieves many of his successes. (pp. 63-5)

Among the other stories in *The Stolen Bacillus* one that deserves special mention for its thematic significance is "**The Flowering of the Strange Orchid**". The central figure of this tale, which characteristically combines the light-hearted and the sinister, is Mr Winter-Wedderburn, a suburban gentleman who constantly complains of the emptiness of his life, and whose only passion is collecting orchids. At a sale he buys a new orchid of a completely unknown kind, which had been found in the Andaman Islands by a young collector who had died there. He plants the orchid in his hot-house and soon it starts putting out aerial rootlets that resemble tentacles and grow to a considerable length. One afternoon Mr Winter-Wedderburn does not come in for his tea; his housekeeper goes to the hot-house and finds him lying motionless on the floor:

> The tentacle-like aerial rootlets no longer swayed freely in the air, but were crowded together, a tangle of grey ropes, and stretched tight with their ends closely applied to his chin and neck and hands.

With some difficulty he is extricated. He has lost a good deal of blood, but has sustained no further injury, and he soon recovers. On the immediately anecdotal level, the point of the story is that Mr Winter-Wedderburn has at last had the adventure for which he craves. Yet reading it in the context of Wells's other early novels and stories, one observes the recurring encounter between the exotic and the everyday. In "**Davidson's Eyes**" the encounter was presented as a strange but passive superimposition of two worlds; here there is a violent collision: the quintessential bourgeois is the victim of the exotic flower that had already cost the life of a probably better man. It anticipates those later works which describe onslaughts made on contemporary bourgeois society by strange forces from outside its boundaries, or from outside the world itself: "**The Sea Raiders**", "**The Star**", "**The Empire of the Ants**", and, above all, *The War of the Worlds*.

Another story from *The Stolen Bacillus* treats this theme rather differently, and in a much grimmer fashion. In "**The Lord of the Dynamos**" Wells's capacity for myth-making is immediately apparent: this story has comparatively little of the careful realism that characterizes others in the collection, and its symbolic implications are more emphatic. (pp. 67-8)

"**The Lord of the Dynamos**", despite its brevity, is a powerful piece of work, and its implications are complex. As its dominant imagery shows, it is, on one level, a kind of meditation on religion. The secularized Holroyd and the heathen Azuma-zi share a common god in the dynamo; but whereas Holroyd's is very literally a religion of 'service', Azuma-zi's is of an older and more full-blooded kind, which is accustomed to appease its god with human sacrifices. The clash of the two modes of worship proves equally disastrous for both adherents. In somewhat broader terms, the story can be seen as an image of the encounter between east and west, between—to put the distinction in perhaps excessively schematic language—the European consciousness that expresses it-

Wells and friend, photographed while Wells was a science student, 1886.

self in imperialism, technology and capitalism; and the Afro-Asiatic unconscious, that is drawn to the things of Europe but is still involved with dark gods and superstitions. Wells's language and symbolism are patently of their age; they recall Kipling, and perhaps the early Conrad (by anticipation, for Conrad had not yet published his first novel when **"The Lord of the Dynamos"** originally appeared); but the situation that the story embodies and epitomizes is a central concern of the mid-twentieth century. In its purely mythical fashion **"The Lord of the Dynamos"** is a more disturbingly prophetic work than many of Wells's later systematic attempts to plot the course of future events. Reading it, one is reminded of the Conrad of *Heart of Darkness* rather than the author of *Anticipations*.

The Stolen Bacillus was followed by three more collections of short stories: *The Plattner Story and Others* (1897), *Tales of Space and Time* (1899) and *Twelve Stories and a Dream* (1903). In 1911 Wells published *The Country of the Blind and Other Stories,* a selection from his four previous volumes together with some uncollected work. Many of the stories in these books are in Wells's realistic or comic vein, and do not fall within the scope of the present study.

The Plattner Story shows Wells expanding certain of the themes that he had outlined in his first collection. In the title story, the young schoolmaster, Gottfried Plattner, mysteriously disappears in an explosion during a chemistry lesson; when he reappears nine days later, it is discovered that his whole anatomical structure has been reversed: his heart is on the right, the position of his liver is similarly altered, and he is now left-handed. To account for this state of affairs, Wells reverts to his favourite motif of the Fourth Dimension:

> To put the thing in technical language, the curious inversion of Plattner's right and left sides is proof that he has moved out of our space into what is called the Fourth Dimension, and that he has returned again to our world. Unless we choose to consider ourselves the victims of an elaborate and motiveless fabrication, we are almost bound to believe that this has occurred.

The facts of the case concerning Plattner are a graphic illustration of the mathematical truism that, just as a two-dimensional or 'flat' object can be turned over by lifting it into three-dimensional space, so the internal relationships of a three-dimensional body might be altered by removing it for the purpose into four-dimensional space. It is the kind of speculation that C. H. Hinton delighted to illustrate in his 'Scientific Romances' of the eighties.

However, this is no more than the intellectual basis for an ambitiously imaginative piece of work. Plattner's account of his time in the Other-World provides an elaborate example of the superimposition of the exotic and the mundane that Wells had previously sketched in **"Davidson's Eyes"**. Its connection with the puzzle about the Fourth Dimension is, in fact, somewhat tenuous; Plattner's experiences in the Other-World exist on a different literary level from the bizarre transposition of his internal organs. It is true that in this story Wells pushes the contrast between the everyday world and its exotic opposite to an extreme: we have on the one hand the rather comic and pathetic young Plattner in his seedy private school—suggesting a first draft of Mr Lewisham—and on the other the dim green-lit world of the spirits who are constantly watching the living, with its suggestions of the *Inferno* and *Purgatorio* of Dante. It is arguable that this story is too ambitious in its structure to be really coherent: Wells is still separating and balancing the scientific and occult elements, but the balance is somewhat precarious. In terms of Wells's later fictional development **"The Plattner Story"** has a special significance. In a few years he was to abandon romance for what he conceived of as his true vocation as a writer of realistic novels; in this story he was trying to combine the two elements within a single brief narrative.

I hope by now to have given an adequate account of the procedure of Wells's early stories. Among the other pieces in *The Plattner Story,* **"The Story of the Late Mr Elvesham"** deserves mention as an essay in the purely occult: its substance might well have been used by Machen, but Wells's treatment is very different. **"The Red Room"** is an attempt at a traditional ghost-story, though the presence in the reputedly haunted room is finally found to be not a malignant spirit, but fear itself.

In other stories the 'scientific' element popularly associated with Wells's romances is more pronounced. The apposition of the exotic and the mundane—or, more strictly, the scientific—is apparent in **"In the Abyss"**. A diving-bell descends into the depths of the ocean and its occupant finds a city of reptilian bipeds, of quasi-human intelligence, who worship him as a visitant from heaven. One sees here, in a new guise, the theme of apotheosis that Wells had previously introduced in **"The Lord of the Dynamos"**. **"The Argonauts of the Air"** is a rather diffuse and extended piece, describing the first successful—though fatal—attempt of men to fly. It is noteworthy that when Wells wrote this story in 1895 he was inclined to regard the aeroplane as a somewhat remote and apocalyptic possibility: as late as 1901 he could only suggest that 'long before the year A.D. 2000, and very probably before 1950, a successful aeroplane will have soared and come home safe and sound'.

I have already referred to **"The Sea Raiders"** as being one of a group of stories that describe various attacks upon modern civilization. This account of the ravages of an unknown type of sea-creature upon the coasts of England and France is one of the most effective and economically told pieces in *The Plattner Story;* its sensational details are the more telling for being played down, and Wells makes a brilliant use of a semi-documentary style, with a wealth of irrelevant but persuasive details:

> Until the extraordinary affair at Sidmouth, the peculiar species *Haploteuthis ferox* was known to science only generically, on the strength of a half-digested tentacle obtained near the Azores, and a decaying body pecked by birds and nibbled by fish, found early in 1896 by Mr Jennings, near Land's End.

"The Sea Raiders" is an important example of what I have described as the 'fin du globe' myth, a central preoccupation of the final years of the nineteenth century. It was first adumbrated by Wells in his important essay, "The Extinction of Man", which contains the germ of **"The Sea Raiders"**. . . . (pp. 70-4)

This preoccupation was expressed in specifically global terms in Wells's powerful short story, **"The Star"**, which was first published in 1897 and then collected in *Tales of Space and Time.* The theme of some cosmic catastrophe overwhelming the earth was by no means new (the story of the Flood can be taken as one of its archetypes), and Wells's treatment of it in **"The Star"** may have owed something to Camille Flammarion's *fin de siècle* extravaganza, *La Fin du Monde,* published in 1894. Nevertheless, in the brilliance of its narrative technique and the controlled profusion of its images, Wells's story can be considered as entirely original. Here his prose reaches a level of poetic intensity that had only been surpassed in the vision of the dying world in the final pages of *The Time Machine* (the extent to which Wells's imagination could be fired by the theme of cosmic dissolution underlines his *fin de siècle* affiliations). The strange new planet wandering through outer space towards the solar system announces its presence to astronomers by irregularities in the motion of the planet Neptune; it becomes visible, and each night shines a little more brightly. Soon it becomes brighter than the moon, and finally hotter and brighter than the sun itself. In the earlier part of the story we are shown the effect of the star on human society throughout the world, in a series of vivid discontinuous images, but as the narrative approaches its climax and the star gets steadily nearer, we leave the world of men to contemplate the series of terrestrial disasters that the approach of the star brings about:

> So the star, with the wan moon in its wake, marched across the Pacific, trailed the thunderstorms like the hem of a robe, and the growing tidal

wave that toiled behind it, frothing and eager, poured over island and island and swept them clear of men. Until that wave came at last—in a blinding light and with the breath of a furnace, swift and terrible it came—a wall of water, fifty feet high, roaring hungrily, upon the long coasts of Asia, and swept inland across the plains of China.

Even when he is writing on this cosmic scale, Wells's sense of detail does not fail him:

> The whole side of Cotopaxi slipped out in one vast convulsion, and a tumult of lava poured out so high and broad and swift and liquid that in one day it reached the sea.

And there is a similar effect when we are told that the snows of the Himalayas melted and poured down upon the plains of India. One might find fault with Wells's occasionally inflated use of language in **"The Star"**—there can be no doubt that he regarded it as something of a set-piece—but this should not blind one to the brilliance with which he selects and juxtaposes his images of mounting catastrophe. His technique here is suggestive of the characteristic methods of post-symbolist poetry, as well as those of the cinema. The end of the story, when the destruction of the earth is narrowly averted, and mankind gradually recovers from its disasters, is inevitably somewhat anti-climactic: Wells's imagination lost its intensity when it was dealing with recovery rather than dissolution. The suggestion, in particular, that 'a new brotherhood grew among men' is out of keeping with what had gone before, and looks forward to Wells's later and very inferior novel, *In The Days of the Comet* (1906), which treats of a similar theme. **"The Star"** may illustrate Nordau's complaint that for the *fin de siècle* mentality 'the prevalent feeling is that of imminent perdition and extinction'; it also shows what Wells was capable of when writing as a literary artist.

The theme of global dissolution is treated comically—and perhaps parodically—in another story in *Tales of Space and Time,* **"The Man Who Could Work Miracles"**. The humble clerk, Fotheringay, discovers that he has the power to work miracles, and effects a number of modest changes in his environment, until, in order to give himself more time to complete his tasks, he unwisely requests the earth to stop rotating. Whereupon every object upon the surface of the earth flies off into space, Fotheringay included. For a paragraph or so Wells presents an image of universal destruction that recalls **"The Star"**; then Fotheringay is able to collect himself sufficiently to wish that he could be restored—minus his miraculous gifts—to the point in time at which he found he possessed them. This is done, and the world is as it was before he commenced his miracle-working regime. This story—which is extremely entertaining—represents a new approach by Wells, since it combines seemingly occult elements with comedy or even sheer farce (already evident to some extent in *The Invisible Man*). The combination was to recur in several pieces in his next book. (pp. 74-6)

Those pieces in *Twelve Stories and a Dream* which might be classed as romances tend to show Wells's inventiveness rather than any profound power of imagination, though **"The New Accelerator"** contains one of his most ingenious notions. Otherwise, they are less interesting rhetorically and conceptually than the stories in his previous volumes, and so reflect the parallel slackening of imaginative quality in his novels. (pp. 76-7)

The final efflorescence of Wells's talent as a short story writer is seen in two stories that he contributed to periodicals in 1904 and 1906; these are respectively **"The Country of the Blind"** and **"The Door in the Wall"**. In both of them the mythical note of his earliest work is once more evident; though they also contain elements which ultimately relate to Wells's personal preoccupations.

Superficially, as its title implies, **"The Country of the Blind"** is a dramatization of the proverb, 'In the country of the blind, the one-eyed man is king'. The mountaineer Nunez stumbles by accident on a remote and inaccessible valley in the Andes, where all the inhabitants have been blind for centuries, and where the very concept of sight no longer exists. At first he arrogantly assumes that his possession of sight will enable him to become their master. However, he finds that the blind inhabitants' other faculties are so keenly developed that he is no match for them, and he has to make an act of abject submission. Finally they decide to remove his eyes, which they regard as anomalous growths on his face: at this he succeeds in escaping over the mountains, leaving behind the blind woman, Medina-saroté, with whom he had fallen in love. Yet the story is not concerned merely to refute one truism and substitute for it another, such as that pride goes before a fall, or that the seemingly weak may have more resources than the strong. It is more than a mere transmitter of proverbial wisdom. Some attention paid to the fairly obvious implications of its symbolism will reveal a much richer complex of meanings.

One must remark, initially, that of all Wells's essays in romance, **"The Country of the Blind"** most closely approaches realistic fiction in its substance; there are no scientific elements here, and no obvious indulgence in fantasy at all. At the same time, in few of Wells's stories is the symbolism so suggestive. It must be admitted, by way of adverse criticism, that the prose is at times slack, and less precise and economical than in Wells's best work of the nineties, and the somewhat portentous manner of the first few pages is unfortunate. Nevertheless, the narrative movement is as vigorous and as well controlled as in any of the earlier works. Nunez is described to the reader as 'a mountaineer from the country near Quito, a man who had been down to the sea and had seen the world, a reader of books in an original way, an acute and enterprising man. . . . ' There is no question that Nunez is to be regarded favourably; he is a free, active and intelligent spirit; a two-eyed rather than a one-eyed man. Wells stresses early on, before Nunez completes his descent to the valley, that his sense of sight is keenly developed: 'among the rocks he noted—for he was an observant man—an unfamiliar fern. . . . His first response to the windowless and particoloured houses of the blind inhabitants is visual and aesthetic: ' "The good man who did that," he thought, "must have been as blind as a bat." '

The village of the blind has been built in a way that accords functionally with their mode of existence, but to Nunez it presents a strangely urban and even bourgeois appearance, contrasting with the wildness of the mountains that surround the valley:

> The irrigation streams ran together into a main channel down the centre of the valley, and this was enclosed on either side by a wall breast high. This gave a singularly urban quality to this secluded place, a quality that was greatly enhanced by the fact that a number of paths paved with black and white stones, and each with a curious little kerb at the side, ran hither and thither in an orderly manner.

The emphasis is on enclosure and regularity: the blind inhabitants have in fact made in this remote Andean valley a miniature approximation to the normal urban life of the civilized world. The valley-dwellers lead, in every sense, an enclosed life, and they cannot even conceive of a world existing outside their valley. Their degree of mental enclosure is apparent in their initial exchange with Nunez, who expresses himself in the spacious and visual terms appropriate to his nature:

> 'And you have come into the world?' asked Pedro.

> '*Out* of the world. Over mountains and glaciers; right over above there, half-way to the sun. Out of the great big world that goes down, twelve days' journey to the sea.'

> They scarcely seemed to heed him. 'Our fathers have told us men may be made by the forces of Nature,' said Correa. 'It is the warmth of things and moisture, and rottenness—rottenness.'

The blind people live in every respect in a closed world; it is even reflected in their cosmology:

> They told him there were indeed no mountains at all, but that the end of the rocks where the llamas grazed was indeed the end of the world; thence sprang a cavernous roof of the universe, from which the dew and the avalanches fell; and when he maintained stoutly the world had neither end nor roof as they supposed, they said his thoughts were wicked.

The opposition between the blind and Nunez is absolute, for his visual delight in what they would deny is frequently stressed:

> Nunez had an eye for all beautiful things, and it seemed to him that the glow upon the snowfields and glaciers that rose about the valley on every side was the most beautiful thing he had ever seen.

The implication becomes inescapable that Nunez's sight and his captors' blindness are to be read metaphorically as well as literally. Only very superficially is Nunez the would-be king of the country of the blind. He is, rather, the man who sees among those who do not see, the open mind among the conformists, a free spirit in a bourgeois world. Wells makes it clear that the blind are perfectly happy in their ordered, predictable mode of life; he seems to have been influenced in his conception by Johnson's picture of the Happy Valley in *Rasselas* (a book which he had first read as a boy): an enclosed world from which one ought not want to escape. Nunez's exploration of the world of the blind becomes successively more disturbing: structurally the story recalls the heuristic progresses made by the Time Traveller, the Angel in *The Wonderful Visit* and Prendick in *The Island of Dr Moreau*. The extreme development of the blind people's other senses means that his possession of sight gives him very little advantage, and in fact he is treated by them as an inferior being and systematically ridiculed and humiliated. He is unable to retaliate physically, for 'he discovered a new thing about himself, and that was that it was impossible for him to hit a blind man in cold blood'. The defeat of the would-be independent spirit by a conformist social order is a theme that meant a good deal to Wells, and it appears unmistakably in **"The Country of the Blind"**. Wells's identification of social conformity with physical incapacity had been anticipated nearly ten years earlier in his novel, *The Wonderful Visit*, in which the Philosophical Tramp describes the villagers as 'pithed'. The passing of time and the advent of totalitarian states which overtly aim at the crushing of individual consciousness has given a new dimension to **"The Country of the Blind"**. It even hints at Orwell's *Nineteen Eighty-Four*. The scene in which Nunez is finally driven by hunger and sleeplessness and despair to conform to the accepted notions of the blind world is an alarmingly precise anticipation of the 'brainwashing' techniques of modern totalitarianism. . . . (pp. 77-81)

Yet **"The Country of the Blind"** is more than a sociological or political fable. It reveals another aspect when we recall that Nunez reconciles himself to staying in the valley, because of his love for Medina-saroté: 'There came a time when Nunez thought that, could he win her, he would be resigned to live in the valley for all the rest of his days.' It is noteworthy that in this story Wells makes persistent use of certain archetypal images, and at this point we see Nunez, the man of light and air, an embodiment of the aspiring mind, who is constantly associated with the masculine imagery of high mountains, surrendering through love to a lifetime in a womb-shaped world, where the inhabitants live in perpetual darkness (and indeed sleep by day, and do their work by night). Here we see what Jung would describe as the surrender of *animus* to *anima*, of the masculine to the feminine principle. The ultimate surrender, both to social conformity and the dark forces of love, comes when Nunez reluctantly agrees to his masters' condition that he must be blinded—or, as they put it, that they must remove by surgery 'these irritant bodies', his eyes—before he can marry Medina-saroté. When he appeals to her by describing the visual delights of his world she is quite unable to understand him, and almost rebukes him: 'I know it's pretty—it's your imagination. I love it, but *now—*'

The themes of this story obviously have a wide human relevance, but at the same time they were extremely personal to Wells: one frequently finds in his other works the contention, implicitly or explicitly stated, that the demands of society and sexual love are both dangers to the free spirit of man. (p. 82)

At the eleventh hour, just before he is to submit to his literal and metaphorical blinding, Nunez recovers his spirit, and turns his back on the valley, determined to escape to his own world. He sees the mountains, and 'It seemed to him that before this splendour he, and this blind world in the valley, and his love, and all, were no more than a pit of sin.' For a whole day he climbs the mountain barrier, and by nightfall he has surmounted it, though still very high up:

> From where he rested the valley seemed as if it were in a pit and nearly a mile below. Already it was dim with haze and shadow, though the mountain summits around him were things of light and fire.

From having been a metaphorical 'pit of sin', the valley, far below him, has become a mere physical pit. Wells uses imagery brilliantly in the concluding sentences of the story. Nunez is once more in his own world, among physically beautiful things, ranging from the splendour of the mountain peaks to the delicacy of the lichen. But there is no certainty that he is able to descend again to the world of men; the implication of the final sentence, with its hint of menace in 'cold stars', is rather that Nunez perishes of exhaustion, content to have saved his soul by escaping from the Country of the Blind;

death among the mountains is preferable to a living death among the blind. (p. 83)

The end of the story expresses Wells's personal conviction that the individual can and should remove himself from any situation which he finds insupportable; at the same time, it shows how the human spirit can assert its true freedom, even at the cost of physical extinction. **"The Country of the Blind"** is a magnificent example of Wells's mythopoeic genius.

The last of Wells's short stories which I shall discuss is **"The Door in the Wall"**, which first appeared in the *Daily Chronicle* in 1906. In this story there is no exotic setting as in **"The Country of the Blind"**; instead we are in the world of politics and affairs that Wells was to explore realistically a few years later in *The New Machiavelli*. The politician Lionel Wallace is, in the eyes of the world, a successful man; but, as he confides to the friend who tells the story, he has a 'preoccupation' that is gradually dominating his life and even affecting his efficiency. As a child of five he had wandered out of his home and through the streets of West Kensington, where he had noticed a green door set in a white wall. It was immensely attractive to him, and he had a very strong desire to open it and pass through (he somehow knew that it would be unfastened), but at the same time he felt an equally strong conviction that this would be wrong or unwise: in particular he felt his father would be very angry if he did so. Nevertheless, he yields to the temptation and finds himself in a beautiful garden. (One is reminded here of the garden which Alice sees through the little door in Chapter I of *Alice in Wonderland*.) Wells's account of the garden tries to give the sense of a child's paradise but is scarcely satisfactory; nevertheless, it can be accepted as shorthand for a type of *locus amoenus*. It has a rare and exhilarating atmosphere, its colours are clean and bright, and the child is filled with joy. There are rich flower-beds and shady trees, and various animals, including two splendid tame panthers. He meets a tall fair girl who 'came to meet me, smiling, and said "Well?" to me, and lifted me and kissed me, and put me down, and led me by the hand. . . .' He meets other children and they play games together, though he cannot remember the games (a fact which later causes him much distress). (pp. 84-5)

Throughout his later life he dreams of revisiting the garden, and at long intervals he has unexpected glimpses of the door in the wall, in different parts of London, but always when the exigencies of his immediate circumstances make it impossible—or at least, highly inconvenient—for him to stop and open the door. The child's vision, as Wells presents it, has all the marks of a return in fantasy to a prenatal state: the door is an obvious womb-symbol. This suggestion is emphasized when we recall that Wallace's mother had died when he was two: the tall fair girl who greets him when he arrives in the garden, and the sombre dark woman who initiates him into the events of his life after birth (and who is referred to as 'the grave mother') can both be taken as aspects of the mother he had scarcely known. Yet Wells's picture is not exclusively Freudian in its implications; it also has elements of an older mode of regarding prenatal existence—the Wordsworthian. This is apparent in the reference to the children with whom the little boy plays, and who call him back when the dark lady draws him aside:

> Hence in a season of calm weather
>   Though inland far we be,
> Our Souls have sight of that immortal sea
>   Which brought us hither,

Can in a moment travel thither,
And see the Children sport upon the shore . . .

After his mother died Wallace had been brought up by a governess; his father is described as 'a stern preoccupied lawyer, who gave him little attention and expected great things of him'. In the sphere of public life his father's expectations are fulfilled, for Wallace has an unusually successful career. Yet his constantly cherished secret desire to return to the garden represents a potential revolt against his father's authority; had he not, as a boy of five, felt that his father would be very angry if he went through the green door? We have here the elements of an Oedipus situation: ultimately Wallace destroys himself in daring to risk, for the second time, his father's displeasure, by opening the door and returning to the delectable world which he identified with his dead mother.

This fate is, in a sense, predictable, but on the narrative level the way in which Wells brings it about is extremely adroit. Wallace tells his friend that three times in the past year he has seen the door, and on each occasion he has passed it by: once because he was on his way to a vital division in the House of Commons, once, significantly, because he was hurrying to his father's death-bed, and once because he wished, for reasons of personal ambition, to continue a discussion with a colleague. And now his soul 'is full of unappeasable regrets', and he is barely capable of working.

A few months later he is dead. . . . (pp. 85-7)

On the next apparition of the door, we may assume, Wallace resolved, at whatever cost, to open it and rediscover his garden; this represented a virtual and perhaps an actual abandonment of his career (and so struck, symbolically, at his father). At this point Wallace's visions—or hallucinations, if we prefer it—and the physical world around him were in fatal conjunction. There is a certain grim irony in the fact that the deep pit into which Wallace fell can be seen as just as much of a womb-symbol as the enclosed garden he was seeking. (The conclusion of **"The Door in the Wall"** is, in a sense, antithetical to that of **"The Country of the Blind"**: Wallace dies in a pit; Nunez is at least able to escape from one.)

"The Door in the Wall" is not a systematic Freudian parable, and it would be a mistake to try to treat it as one, just as it would be a mistake to over-emphasize the Jungian implications of **"The Country of the Blind"**. With both stories I have merely tried to indicate ways of looking at their symbolism which seem to me illuminating. **"The Door in the Wall"** has also a further and more personal dimension: the beautiful garden behind the closed door, with its rich and varied delights, can be readily taken as a symbol of the imagination, and Wallace as a projection of Wells's literary personality. At the start of his career as a writer he possessed a unique imagination, which flowered in a number of brilliantly original romances; yet after a few years he turned to realistic fiction, and then to works in which he tried to dragoon his imaginative powers for specifically didactic or even pamphleteering purposes; at which the quality of his original imagination deserted him. Here, perhaps, we see the implication of the closed door, glimpsed from time to time, but never opened again. Admittedly, **"The Door in the Wall"** was published only in 1906, little more than ten years after Wells's early work appeared, but in such a volatile and changeable writer ten years of development is a long time. By then Wells was already becoming known as the author of *A Modern Utopia* and *Kipps* rather than of *The Time Machine*. The death of

Wallace, in vainly trying to recapture his original vision, may relate to Wells's realization of the death of his original talent. **"The Door in the Wall"** is one of Wells's finest stories; and it is almost the last he wrote. (pp. 87-8)

> *Bernard Bergonzi, in his* The Early H. G. Wells: A Study of the Scientific Romances, *University of Toronto Press, 1961, 226 p.*

HERMANN WEIAND (essay date 1965)

[*In the following excerpt, Weiand examines Wells's narrative technique and explicates central concepts presented in "The Country of the Blind."*]

This story, published in 1911, [**"The Country of the Blind"**] contains characteristic features of the novella: its subject is a sensational event, its setting is intrinsically connected with the story proper, it has a turning-point (though not very distinct) and a central symbol in which the meaning of the whole is condensed.

The title of the story is the name of its place of action. It is set as a 'leitmotif' right from the beginning; it is mentioned in the first sentence and subsequently repeated several times. Thus its meaning is stressed and constantly kept in the reader's mind. Setting and story are spun around it.

The setting is given in the manner of an objective report. Its pseudoscientific language (e.g. the exact geographic location of the main scene, the details of the catastrophic disturbance which sealed it off from the outer world etc.), the linking of the hero with Englishmen, the reference to presumably well-known reports on the crucial accident, all are meant to root the setting firmly in a familiar reality and to confer credibility on the phantastic story proper.

The author has handled the transition from the pseudo-realistic setting to the fancy-world of the story very carefully. Some of the exotic names used are borrowed from reality, others are allusions to existing names. They take us to foreign regions far from our familiar surroundings and pave the way for the acceptance of those strange events, of which admittedly no evidence reached the outer world. The enormous difficulties and risks of the ascent to that "remoteness" are repeatedly stressed.

The author makes the abrupt transition from one reality into another (a device frequently used in myths, fairy-tales, satirical and philosophical writings) appear perfectly natural. First he mentions that "thereabouts it chanced that a man came into this community from the outer world". Then the "accident" is incidentally referred to as a matter so well known that any attempt to prove its truth seems superfluous. Next we learn that Nunez' fellow mountaineers "found he had gone from them . . . and . . . as the morning broke they saw the traces of his fall". This parenthetic, almost casual manner of mentioning the "fall" is meant to divert our attention from its incredible nature and to make us swallow its most incredible part: "And the man who fell survived".

Nunez is "stunned and insensible" during his "tremendous flight" in a saving "cloud of snow". He loses all objects which would have been proof of the existence of the outer world, which looks "phantasmal and mysterious" from where he is now. When he realizes his desperate position he is "seized with a paroxysm of sobbing laughter". Then he lies for a "great interval of time", works himself free from the snow, drinks and *falls asleep* for a long while. Then we are gently led by the hand with him into accepting the phantastic reality he has fallen into.

The Blind Men long ago also came from the "outer world" and were perfectly normal beings. They still are almost like Nunez, but there is a crucial difference: they lack sight. That is the particular twist the author gives to their reality, and this twist produces all the symbolic meaning of the story. When that mysterious disease began to afflict their eyes, they ascribed it, primitive as they were, to their "sins", and not to "germs and infections". Owing to their superstitious fear they do not want drugs to cure them, but "relics and such-like potent things of faith, blessed objects and mysterious medals and prayers". Their messenger paid a "keen-eyed priest" to obtain them, but they could not reap the benefit of this transaction as he never returned.

The disease ran its full course, and "they forgot many things, and they devised many things". They forgot everything connected with sight, even the very word. What they devised is conditioned by their tremendous shortcoming, their new, incomplete perception of the world. Their picture of it goes exactly as far as their limited senses go: anything beyond them simply does not exist. "The story of the outer world was faded and changed to a child's story, and they had ceased to concern themselves with anything beyond the rocky slopes above their circling wall." "Chance and heredity" had "sent" two "among them" who had "original minds . . . who could talk and persuade". They voiced the fatally limited picture of their little world and fashioned it as a creed, discarding the scraps of tradition that had survived.

The Blind Men's eye-sight had waned so gradually that they had time to adapt "their methods and procedure . . . to fit their special needs". They have ordered their little world so smoothly that they can get food, clothing and shelter by means of a strict routine, and lead a simple and contented life. There is the stitching of their clothes by which they know each other, the marked paths, the fixed angle at which these meet, the irrigation system, the smoothed-out meadows etc. They "met and settled social and economic problems that arose". They not only have a faulty theory of what the world is like, but also ridiculous notions of what nature and all beings are and of how they were created. Thanks to special good fortune nature has no sting for them, "neither thorns nor briars, with no evil insects nor any beasts save the gentle breed of llamas". Thus the futility of their illusion is never brought home to them by their environment, nor do they ever realize how vulnerable they are, and how precarious their hold on existence is. The absurd limitation of their theory is most clearly demonstrated by the assumption that the world is covered by a vault, "the lid of smooth rock that covered their cosmic casserole".

Nunez is first opposed to the Blind Men in a literal sense. He has one sense more—the most important one—, and with it a whole dimension of experience, sensation and knowledge: the outer world. He feels confident that they will hail him as a superior being, as a "god-send" with incredible power and abilities. The proverb "In the Country of the Blind the One-eyed Man is King" keeps running through his mind, at first confidently, later with exasperation and finally with bitter scorn. He expects "wonder and reverence at his origin and his gifts", but he is considered a "new-made being" instead: a sort of Caspar Hauser "wild man" with a "mind hardly formed yet" and "only the beginnings of speech", an "idiot,

incompetent thing below the permissible level of a man". His experience of sight is non-existent for them, as they know neither sight nor blindness and consider his frantic efforts to make them understand ("to bring them to reason") the mad raving of "mental incoherency". They can judge him merely through the senses known to them, which "had become marvellously acute", much keener than his because of their loss of sight.

Far from converting those people, he evokes a missionary zeal in them. His doubt of their puny world-picture is "wicked levity" for which "blind philosophers . . . reproved him". He is, after vain struggles, subdued into accepting "instruction" from them. Their "elders" constantly sit in "darkness", also when he tries vainly to explain the "great world . . . the sky and mountains, sight and such-like marvels" to them, and they try to "explain to him life and philosophy and religion". He is so stunned and exasperated by his incredible failure to make himself understood that he is temporarily tempted to use brutal force to convince them, but he finds that he is too civilized to kill a helpless human being in cold blood or even in anger. Due to this weakness he is almost subdued into accepting part of their madness. For the sake of a woman he is almost prepared to resign all the marvels of sight by being blinded, and to submit to life in a dull, minute routine, within the narrowest range, in a comfortable, warm sensual darkness, like the rest of the "citizens". But at the very last moment he rebels and escapes, perhaps to find death, but loyal to the free great world to which he belongs.

The symbolic meaning of this story is hinged upon the fact that the "gift of sight", the most powerful human sense, is a symbol for the human mind, that the "light" of man is his reason, his urge and capacity to think and find the truth. To live in blindness or darkness, on the other hand, means to live in ignorance, to have a confused and weak intellect.

The Blind Men have forgotten how to use their reason; seduced by false prophets, they have replaced it by their inferior senses. All marks of their physical shortcoming are signs of their spiritual deficiency: the red, sunken hollows in their faces, their groping walk, their sniffing, their "listening to the path", their looking away from the object they want to perceive. They are relying on their 'blind' senses alone for information, and accordingly they have a tremendously shrunken picture of the world, of their origin and purpose. They only acknowledge what they can touch, hear and smell. What they cannot perceive with their senses simply does not exist despite all evidence to the contrary, as they have no sense to grasp this evidence. Consequently they do not pay any attention to things which would interest a 'seeing' man, which is Nunez' main difficulty when trying to convince them. "Glossy smoothness" e.g. is the only criterion of their "ideal of feminine beauty": a rain-worm's perspective, when compared with Nunez' range and variety of appreciation. Their manner of life is completely adapted to their blindness: their economic and social order, religion and philosophy. All theories are shaped to make life flow smoothly and easily. The impenetrable "roof of rock and stone and darkness", an "article of faith" with them, shuts them off safely from "the deep of deeps, in which the circling stars were floating": eternity, the abode of the eternal spirit. To them it seems but a "hideous void, a terrible blankness" when Nunez describes it.

Nunez, the man with the "gift of sight", with a bright restless spirit and great courage, falls into this tiny valley. It is conceived as earth, its inhabitants as mankind; he is a being gifted with extraordinary mental power, "sent" to blind mankind to bring it knowledge and insight. He is "a reader of books in an original way"; his going down to the sea and his seeing the world indicate his search in the world of the spirit, also his climbing of mountains, which often stand for remote and lofty ideals, or are seats of the gods. The beautiful light of sunrise and sunset on their snowy cliffs, when the rest of the world lies in twilight and darkness, stands for the purity of these ideals and their closeness to eternity. Nunez' "acute and enterprising" nature is his urge for knowledge, his "powerful aspiration to spiritual light" (the task Wells had set for himself in many of his writings). Nunez is constantly trying to tell the Blind Men of mountains, sky and sunrise, sunset, the stars, symbols of eternity, of celestial ideas, of the home of the spirit. When he is on the brink of subsiding to darkness, of giving up thought, it is the light of the morning sun that recalls him. He is drawn out of the darkness with "his eyes . . . always upon the sunlit ice and snow", an image of light as the strength and purity of the spirit. The sun as the source of light stands for the source of the spirit, perhaps for God (Nunez "saw the morning like an angel . . . marching down the steeps"). The outer world, where the light is, must be the world of the spirit from which man comes and to which he is meant to return. The wonders beyond the mountains are not earthly things but the marvels of the realm of the spirit. When Nunez decides to go back to the outer world, to climb out of the valley of darkness into the light of the mountains, driven by a powerful inner urge, he shows that it is man's destiny to strive for light, to follow the command of his reason. "My world is my sight", he states. When he is but half-way up, "far and high", it is still likely that he will have to pay for his attempt with his life. "His clothes were torn, his limbs were blood-stained, he was bruised in many places, but he lay as if he were at his ease, and *there was a smile on his face.*" "The mountain summits around him were things of light and fire" is a statement twice repeated, and he rejoices in their view despite the closeness of death.

Nunez' fate is meant to reflect the fate of the messenger of the spirit, of the bearer of the light of truth, who is trying to enlighten the darkened minds of mankind. Not only do they fail to acknowledge his mission and to accept and honour his insight, but they even try to draw him into their darkness, to humiliate him by servitude and even to blind him. Their powerful ally for this is woman with her power over the senses. Her seeming understanding of the spirit is sheer vanity and a potent lure. She may become instrumental for the blinding.

From the reaction of the Blind Men (as representatives of mankind) to the offering of spiritual light that has literally fallen from heaven we can draw conclusions as to the author's conception of the average, "admirable citizen".

He is caught up in his everyday routine, his business of getting food, shelter and warmth to such an extent that he resents any disturbance and does not look up any more to see the sun, moon, stars or the sky, literally and figuratively. He is a prisoner of habit and prejudice, of the comfort of his senses. Even the strongest reasons and arguments cannot move him from an opinion which he has acquired on completely insufficient grounds. He is incredibly conceited, despite his primitive mind. He likes the warm sensual fog of his conceit and his comfort above everything else. He has no sense for the unusual, the unexpected, the original, the unconventional, because it does not fit in with his routine, his

convention, his primitive ideas. Nothing can move him from his prescribed path.

From this picture we can draw a number of conclusions. Habit, prejudice, convention, imitation are darkness, the enemies of the spirit, depriving man of his spiritual appetite, his natural thirst for knowledge, his true destiny, making him vegetate in darkness instead. Habit and prejudice spring from fatally limited human minds, they are incredibly persistent and silly. Men who can "talk and persuade" can easily seduce man, but he is deaf and even vicious towards the true bearer of light. Mankind has shut itself out from the wonders of the universe, of eternity and of the spirit and is groping blindly in the darkness of its senses. A life of sensuality is the mortal enemy of the spirit.

This story is profoundly pessimistic in outlook. The messenger who literally fell from heaven in a cloud can only escape slavery and servitude in the warm sensual darkness of man's world by fleeing to where he came from. The spirit no longer has a home in man's world. It is ruled by ignorance. People do not want intelligence, it worries and annoys them. They have no use for wise men and do not want them to guide their fate, but they are easy prey for talkers and flatterers. The average "admirable citizen" does not want anybody to know more than himself and strongly resents being told that he is ignorant. He will assert his ignorance by the argument of the multitude: force.

The irony of the story lies above all in the reversal of the old proverb that "In the Country of the Blind the One-eyed Man is King"; he is the humblest serf. The ludicrous absurdity of this proverb is repeatedly and strongly emphasized; in fact, the whole story serves to prove its evident untruth.

This story is strongly didactic; it is meant to convey a distinct message, but it is good fiction all the same. If its symbolic impact is ignored, it still is a good piece of entertainment with real drama and suspense. Its meaning is not forced down the reader's throat. There are no separate explanations, no comments or abstract reflections. Single ironical remarks are rare (e.g. lid of cosmic casserole), although the whole abounds in sarcasm. And yet the author wants to teach the reader a lesson through his hero's fate. He shows what he thinks man to be: blind—, and what he should be: seeing—, but just as he ignores the improbability of the physical side of the story and innocently takes its credibility for granted, so he refrains from any comment on symbolic implications. Because it is entirely implied the meaning of the story is the more forcible. The blind doctor, e.g., states that when Nunez' eyes will be removed "he will be perfectly sane, and a quite admirable citizen". This is supreme satire because of the very lack of apparent irony. The major part of the story seems entirely literal in its meaning, although, despite all efforts of the author, we ultimately remain unconvinced of its reality. On its own terms we are willing to accept it as an entirely symbolical piece of fiction. The author never intrudes himself, he simply is not there; he only reports impassively and objectively, he does not seem to have feelings or opinions of his own, so well are they incorporated in the characters of the story. Although Nunez has to carry a heavy symbolic burden, he still is a round character in his own right, and even some of the generally 'flat' Blind Men at some point "ceased to be a generalized people and became individualities and familiar to him".

Owing to the symbolic intention of the story, strong emphasis is laid on the aspect of physical sight. In contrast to the Blind

Men the central character, with whom our consciousness is largely identified, is exceedingly aware of contour and colour of his surroundings, of the different shades of light and darkness, of many hues of colour, above all when he is on the point of losing his sight. Then he also becomes exceedingly aware of the vital importance of sight for man, and of its incomparable beauty. Through him the reader becomes aware of the simple, orderly shapes in the valley with their preponderantly dark hues, mostly green and brown, of its 'urban quality' as compared with the bright chaos of rock, ice and snow all round, and of the play of light on them. There is also, because of the great dependance of the Blind Men on touch, a strong contrasting feel of soft and hard, often connected with dark warmth and bluey white cold, representative of the vulnerability of the senses and of the strength of the spirit. There is insistence on hard objects (knife, ice-axe, and mainly the spade with which Nunez hits a blind man). The story has a strong sensory impact despite its entirely symbolic intention. Because the marvels of sight are physically impressive, they also serve the ulterior purpose of the tale very well.

A close scrutiny of the central conceptions of the story, based on the symbolic meaning of light and darkness in it, will yield the following conclusions:

Sight is the capacity to see light, to understand, to think. Light is truth, reason and knowledge. Blindness or lack of sight means lack of light, reason, knowledge, truth. Nunez is as superior to the Blind Men as a spirit would be to him. The Blind Men are mankind, and Nunez is meant to be as superior to them as a spirit from another world. The valley of the Blind is earth. The outer world, hitherto our world, becomes the realm of the spirit from which Nunez has come.

Of course it would be easy to point out flaws of thought and theory in Wells' parable. We happen to live in the "outer world", and we know that it is far from being an abode of pure spirits. It is above all the identification of a presumed spiritual world with our world, the combination of the common and the sublime, of the earthly and the heavenly which makes it a little hard to swallow all the implications of the parable.

The story can be considered as representing two human communities on the same level with only different degrees of civilization, the inferiority of the one being the outcome of a general deficiency of one physical sense. This view does however not do full justice to the author's intentions. Nunez falls from above, out of the sky. He comes from a world not only different in degree but also in kind, lying on a higher level. He is called a "man or spirit". With his fall he stops being simply man. The Blind are man now, and, by the ritual of his fall and the mystery of his survival, he is transformed into something different, and with him the world he came from. It looks "mysterious and phantasmal" from the valley of the Blind. The author plainly wants us to look at the whole story from this hypothesis, from the perspective of '*if*'.

If the Blind Men's world stands for our world, then both have moved a step up. *Literally* taken *our* world is human, and their world subhuman (it is part of the superb irony of the story that Nunez is considered "beneath the permissible level of man" by them). *Symbolically their* world is human, and ours superhuman or rather supernatural,—spiritualized, ethereal. It has a marvellous, glorious dimension completely beyond any conception of the Blind. It is beyond the sky and the clouds, and even for Nunez himself Bogota, his home-town, becomes something like heavenly Jerusalem.

If sight is the faculty of seeing light, if light is truth and the reflection of the spirit, then the sun as the source of light must logically be the source of truth and spirit.

If the morning (seen as light appearing on the flanks of mountains) is called "an angel marching down the steeps", then the sun as the source of light and spirit must also be the origin of the angel: God. Angel is a Christian term for a supernatural being, a spirit, a heavenly messenger who has his origin in God and has access to his presence.

If we accept the central conception light = spirit, then we must draw all the conclusions which stem from it to make the intentions of the author quite clear.

It would have been easy to show that Nunez should have been more intelligent about it all, that he should have developed a strategy; what should have been, however, is not really the point, but what the author intends to express through him. Like the Blind Men Nunez is lifted by one step. He is human and spiritual at the same time. The whole conception of the story hinges upon this fact. Nunez falls out of the sky in a cloud. But to be able to understand the Blind he had to be Peruvian, and to get to them a mountaineer (a little crude perhaps in our opinion). We are assured that he is a "reader of books" and also "had an eye for all beautiful things". His clumsiness is a little exasperating for the intelligent reader who can easily think of ways how to convince those people of the marvels of sight—, but where would the point of the story be then? Nunez *had* to fail in order to prove Wells' point. In order to fulfil his function in the story he had to be a little stupid and awkward despite Wells' assertion that he is clever. Did not Wells give his story a pessimistic outcome to shock and improve, to make his readers scared enough to look into themselves and get a little insight and be more openminded? Is not the theme of the story meant to shock: the flagrant reversal of the truth of an old saying which is generally taken for granted?

At first sight the Blind Men do not seem to be stupid at all, considering their deficiency, and it is admirable how they have managed to keep their little world running smoothly. But they are just like ants or bees with their seemingly intelligent instinctive labour, with their confident and easy movements in heap or hive, which is a marvel of order as well. The Blind are also tolerant to a certain extent, but all their achievement is as nothing compared with the beauty of the great big world. The fact that they look upon their modest and scanty life as the only possible mode of existence, and upon their termite world as the crown of creation makes them unspeakably grotesque and absurd. (pp. 345-53)

Hermann Weiand, "The Country of the Blind," in Insight II: Analyses of Modern British Literature, *edited by John V. Hagopian and Martin Dolch, Hirschgraben-Verlag, 1965, pp. 345-55.*

RICHARD HAUER COSTA (essay date 1967)

[*In the following excerpt from his biography of Wells, Costa traces major themes in Wells's stories and asserts that "the tales all have the same message: how much worldlings could do—how much might come to pass—if they just let their fancy take off a bit from ground-level."*]

H. E. Bates praises Wells as "a great Kidder . . . a man who succeeded in telling more tall stories than any writer of his generation yet, by a genius for binding the commonplace to the most astronomical exploration of fancy, succeeded in getting them believed" [see excerpt dated 1941]. . . . [Wells's best] scientific romances persuade by making the cannot-happen thing into the does-happen-but-shouldn't; the short stories use the same device. An inexperienced ghost forgets his formula; a Mittyesque Cockney eats a berry and turns into a termagant; a man undergoing an operation has, like Conrad Aiken's Mr. Arcularis, a dream in which he dies, and the earth bearing his deserted body spins away while his mind remains to span a thousand years in seconds; a diving-bell descends into the deep, and its occupant finds a city of reptiles who worship him.

The stories may well be, as Frank Swinnerton has said, the "most characteristic" of Wells's works. They—some seventy of them were published—are products of the storyteller's art, written at a time when Wells was struggling to become launched as a writer, and long before the teacher-propagandist silenced the teller of tales.

Wells, who seems always to have known a marketable literary commodity when he saw it, started writing short stories at a propitious time. In the 1890's, the golden age of the English short story had begun. Kipling's stories of Anglo-Indian life were opening a new and exotic dimension to readers in several continents, Poe and his theory of the well-made story had become a pattern for imitation, and a flourishing de Maupassant community had come into existence on the English side of the Channel. Wells's range is narrower than Kipling's, only rarely does Wells achieve effects anywhere near Poe's, and Wells is incapable of the irony underlying the deceptively simple studies of de Maupassant. But from these three masters H. G. Wells discovered the technique of the short story. "I was doing my best to write as the other writers wrote," he acknowledges in his autobiography; "and it was long before

I realized that my exceptional origins and training gave me an almost unavoidable freshness of approach."

Wells came to realize that his knowledge of science gave him a vantage point for writing a kind of story which was out of the reach of Kipling, Poe, and de Maupassant. He soon occupied himself writing tales of the strange, which frequently described and usually extended some innovation of science or technology. In a progressive age, his visioning in 1903 of tank warfare (**"The Land Ironclads"**) and of aerial flight as early as 1897 (**"The Argonauts of the Air"**) combined the topical with the novel in affairs. Only two months after the flying-machine story had been published, a flight similar to the one detailed in the story, also climaxed by an accident, took place over Berlin. Camille Flammarion was one of the first to describe modern types of aircraft in fiction, but Wells pioneered in making a mishap in a flying machine the object of treatment in a story.

Early readers of Wells's tales, then, had the impression that they were being let in on something that had just happened, was happening, or was about to happen. However, the best stories transcend the merely topical. These, like the scientific romances, have the power to imbue the reader with a sense of personal freedom. Spirits soar; inhibitions fade. And the mood is sustained as it is only rarely in Wells's Realistic novels. That mood is nearly always the same—one of exhilaration, of anything-is-possible, even of awe. The tales all have the same message: how much worldlings could do—how much might come to pass—if they just let their fancy take off a bit from ground-level. (pp. 51-2)

"The Stolen Bacillus," the title story of Wells's maiden collection, not only is representative but is also the first of his "single-sitting" stories. It contains seedlings of *The Invisible Man, The War of the Worlds,* and *The History of Mr. Polly.* A bacteriologist tells a romantically inclined anarchist that he has imprisoned cholera bacillus in a test-tube—enough, if introduced into the drinking supply, to bring pestilence to

Title page for "The Stolen Bacillus," the first of what Wells termed his "single setting stories," as published in Pearson's Magazine, *1905.*

London. The anarchist, intent on destruction, steals the bottled cholera. The scientist pursues him by horse-cab and a maid-servant, anxious that the scientist not catch his death, brings up the rear carrying his coat. The scene flares into comic disarray, not unlike Mr. Polly's burning of the Fishbourne Hotel, with the three-way race described by a group of Cockneys. In his haste, the anarchist cracks the tube and, bent on martyrdom, drinks the potion. The bacteriologist confesses to his maid that he had only tried to astonish his visitor; that, far from being cholera bacillus, it was the bacterium bringing out blue patches in monkeys.

The story bears the early hints of Wells's penchant for superimposing exotic material from the laboratory on the prosaic lives of the lower-middle-class Wells knew so well. **"The Stolen Bacillus"** also reveals a strain of jolly humor amidst the most serious of possibilities, one which Wells was to retain in his writings and in his life almost to the end. The anarchist and the scientist appear ludicrous to the spectators, the dire aspects of the chase notwithstanding. Griffin in *The Invisible Man,* with all his transparency, rampaged more picaresquely than formidably until he went berserk and had to be destroyed.

A famous story, **"The Man Who Could Work Miracles"** (1898), is archetypal of a vast literature about unprepossessing souls unexpectedly endowed with the power to upset their worlds. The clerk Fotheringay was an early model for Thorne Smith's Topper. Topper cavorted invisibly, but Fotheringay had real room for enterprise: his supreme windfall lay in conjuring up miracles. But, as with so many who lack the proper combination of élan and restraint for the proper use of divine powers, Fotheringay let his reach exceed his grasp. Requesting that the earth stop rotating, he precipitated a scene of comic confusion as every object about him fell off into space.

If Wells in those early stories gave dramatic and sometimes bizarre expression to his feelings about the infinite plasticity of things, he was also capable, within the confines of the short story form, of spinning parables to illustrate his distrust of perfected civilization. In a story like **"The Lord of the Dynamos,"** the symbolic implications become more emphatic than in the "trick" fantasies. The first paragraph dramatizes one of Wells's polemical positions—hatred of Empire. The reader is introduced to the uncivilized-civilized white man, the characteristically wooden product of technological society, and to his "burden" who will rise against oppression and destroy:

> The chief attendant of the three dynamos that buzzed and rattled at Camberwell and kept the electric railway going, came out of Yorkshire, and his name was James Holroyd. He was a practical electrician but fond of whisky, a heavy red-haired brute with irregular teeth. He doubted the existence of the Deity but accepted Carnot's cycle, and he had read Shakespeare and found him weak in chemistry. His helper came out of the mysterious East, and his name was Azuma-zi. But Holroyd called him Pooh-bah. Holroyd liked a nigger because he would stand kicking—a habit with Holroyd—and did not pry into the machinery and try to learn the ways of it. Certain odd possibilities of the negro mind brought into abrupt contact with the crown of our civilization Holroyd never fully realized, though just at the end he got some inkling of them.

Holroyd is pictured as a brute of the sort who, seventy-five years before the story saw print, had imposed an uncongenial

order on the aboriginal population of Tasmania and had concluded by forcing its extinction. Wells acknowledged that conversations with his brother Frank about Tasmania had led to *The War of the Worlds.* At about the same time, his mentor Huxley was citing the extinction of the natives of that country as a tragedy of evolution.

Holroyd and Azuma-zi, white man and "white man's burden," are opposed on all points: the positivism of the one contrasts with the superstitious nature of the other. Like Yank in O'Neill's *Hairy Ape,* Azuma-zi learns to worship the dynamo but for all the wrong reasons:

> Holroyd delivered a theological lecture on the test of his big machine soon after Azuma-zi came. He had to shout to be heard in the din. 'Look at that,' said Holroyd; 'where's your 'eathen idol to match 'im?' And Azuma-zi looked. For a moment Holroyd was inaudible, and then Azuma-zi heard: 'Kill a hundred men. Twelve per cent on the ordinary shares,' said Holroyd, 'and that's something like a Gord!'

Wells fastens the electrician's religious intimations to the dynamo: it is a god to him because of its "kill-a-hundred-men" power and of its importance to the capitalist enterprise Wells would soon deride at length, if symbolically, in *The Time Machine.*

The climax of **"The Lord of the Dynamos"** is approached with a kind of dread inevitability rarely seen in Wells's longer fiction, except for *The Island of Dr. Moreau* and *The Invisible Man.* No polemic holds up the narrative; one feels the tightening of suspense. The native, under Holroyd's sneering tutorship, becomes a worshipper of the dynamo; and, by tribal custom, he must ritualize it. Azuma-zi one night grasps the lever and sends the armature in reverse. There is a struggle, and Holroyd is electrocuted. His death is taken to have been accidental, and a substitute arrives. For Azuma-zi, the newcomer is to be a second sacrifice. This time the Asiatic is foiled; to avoid capture, he kills himself by grasping the naked terminals of the dynamo. The conclusion is fittingly phrased in myth of undeniable power: "So ended prematurely the worship of the Dynamo Deity, perhaps the most short-lived of all religions. Yet withal it could at least boast a Martyrdom and a Human Sacrifice."

Wells's "Dynamo Deity" metaphor is suggestive of Henry Adams, who in *The Education of Henry Adams* refers to the Virgin Mary as the "animated dynamo." Adams, like the H. G. Wells whom E. M. Forster parodied in "The Machine Stops," conceived of man as a unit of energy capable of being attracted by powerful forces like the Virgin or the dynamo. It may even be that Wells, in this story of a primitive who tried to make a god of a dynamo, gave dramatic dimension to Adams's idea that "the movement of . . . forces controls the progress of [man's] mind, since he can know nothing but the motions which impinge on his senses, whose sum makes education."

However, in a more seminal way, **"The Lord of the Dynamos"** is almost pure Kipling, and one feels a wave of sympathy for the misled Azuma-zi. Certainly, the story broadly conceives the meeting of the twain, East and West—the aboriginal Tasmanians and the British colonials. The work, writes Bernard Bergonzi in his brilliant book on Wells the mythmaker, recalls the early Joseph Conrad and *Heart of Darkness,* a novel not yet published when Wells wrote **"Lord** of the Dynamos" in 1894 [see excerpt dated 1961]. Whether more Conradian or Kiplingesque is less important than that the story, like others among the handful by Wells that are consistently anthologized, can be read simply as a good yarn as well as for profounder implications beneath the parable.

In another of his earliest stories, **"The Remarkable Case of Davidson's Eyes"** (1895), Wells turns for the first time to the theme of what Bergonzi calls "the rootlessness and mental and emotional fragmentation of the modern intellectual." More simply, Wells was preoccupied from the beginning of his career with the conflicting compulsions of art, which he saw as alienating the practitioner from the mainstream of life, and with the teaching of ideas, which increasingly he came to see as his proper business. The publication in 1886 of *Dr. Jekyll and Mr. Hyde,* Stevenson's vivid reiteration of Poe's "William Wilson," dramatized an emergent end-of-century myth: the discovery of the unconscious mind. In his later idea novels, Wells directly acknowledged a debt to Carl Jung and his conception of the struggle in men's minds between Consciousness and the Shadow, Jung's feeling of living simultaneously in two different ages and of being two different persons. (pp. 53-6)

By the time Wells stopped writing stories, the theme of self-alienation had flowered into a giant contempt for *ars pro arte.* Wells's last story, **"The Pearl of Love"** (1925), rejected that year by the editors of *The Saturday Evening Post* but subsequently published in England, dramatized the folly of projecting esthetic means for spiritual ends. Twenty years before **"The Pearl,"** however, Wells had practically stopped writing short stories. Two of his latter ones, among his best known, provide a poetic rendering of Wells's own personal obsessions as man and artist.

"The Beautiful Suit," first published in *Collier's* (April 1909) under the title **"A Moonlight Fable,"** superficially follows the manner of a fairy tale by Oscar Wilde. A boy is presented by his mother with a shining suit but is constrained from wearing it, except on special occasions, by the poor woman's innate caution—a reference perhaps to Wells's own mother and to her sense of Victorian propriety. But the boy dreams of the fuller life he believes wearing the suit will bring him. One moonlit night he unwraps the precious gift, dons it, and in an ecstasy of fulfillment, plunges into what was, by day, a duck-pond but which to his enchanted night-sense "was a great bowl of silver moonshine . . . amidst which the stars were netted in tangled reflections of the brooding trees upon the bank."

The scene is suggestive of a familiar imagery in Wells: a "darkling" forest (*darkling,* almost Wells's favorite word, occurs countless times in his books and finally in the title of his penultimate novel) is bent on consuming the wanderer but is capable of being cleared by dint of superior guidance. To the boy's starry eyes, his suit equips him for his journey; but next morning his body is found in the bottom of a stone pit, "with his beautiful clothes a little bloody, and foul and stained with the duckweed from the pond [but] his face . . . of such happiness . . . that you would have understood indeed . . . he had died happy. . . . "

W. Warren Wager, in the finest recent study of the ideas of Wells, sees in the fatal passion of a small boy for fine clothes and for moonlight a transparent parable of the perils of *ars pro arte.* Certainly it and its more famous sister story, **"The Door in the Wall,"** reflect unmistakably an ambivalence in Wells that fame and status never dispelled.

In **"The Door in the Wall,"** written in 1906, three years before **"The Beautiful Suit,"** Wells's little boy has grown up. He is Lionel Wallace, a cabinet minister and an early foreshadowing of the ill-fated politician Remington in *The New Machiavelli.* Wallace's misgivings are less realistic than Remington's. He is haunted by a childhood memory of a door that leads into a garden containing all the things success has denied him—peace, delight, beauty. Three times Wallace rejects the door before yielding to its promise and, at the end, falls to his death, like the boy in **"The Beautiful Suit,"** but in an excavation pit. (pp. 57-8)

"The Country of the Blind" . . . is more than Wells's finest achievement as a writer of short fiction. Of all his vast array of works, this story best states H. G. Wells's philosophical position in terms of the techniques of the literary artist. Wells's conception of the world was mystical and his hopes for it, as viewed in all his authentic novels and stories, dark. In 1904, when he wrote **"The Country of the Blind,"** Wells had already approached the divided trail. Perhaps there is not in the entire history of world literature a comparable instance of a major writer who in one year produced both an epic to the position that man is a glorious creature of whims and fallibility and a classical blueprint aimed at showing that what man *is* is secondary to what mystical faith can induce him to *become.* In that year—1905—a few months after writing **"The Country of the Blind,"** Wells erected huge literary signposts to mark both paths: for the humanist in him there was *Kipps;* for the visionary, *A Modern Utopia.*

What probably tipped the scales toward books like *Utopia* over books like *Kipps* was a destructive Fabian interlude . . . which led Wells to see humanity less and less in terms of the individual and more and more in collective terms. His first essay for the Fabian Socialists was written about the same time as **"The Country of the Blind."** The latter is the outcry of the artist to the demands of the propagandist.

More effectively than anywhere except in certain of the scientific romances and in the last pages of *Tono-Bungay,* **"The Country of the Blind"** blends the riches of the humanist storyteller and the mystic visionary. To the mythmaker at the heart of Wells, no imagery proved so obsessive as that of this story. From his student days under T. H. Huxley down to his deathbed conviction that mankind had played itself out, Wells viewed mankind darkly: as a giant struggling in an evolutionary whirl to achieve a millennium of happiness and beauty, but always forced back into some sealed-off country of the blind.

Essentially, the story is a pessimistic restatement of Plato's Allegory of the Cave. The mountaineer Núñez comes unawares on a fastness deep in the Andes, where for centuries the inhabitants have been sightless and where the idea of seeing has disappeared. At first, Núñez brazenly assumes the truth of the proverb, "In the country of the blind, the one-eyed man is king" and he confidently expects to become master. However, he finds that the blind inhabitants have developed other faculties; that in a land where no one sees, the sighted are actually handicapped. Eventually Núñez is forced to submit and his submission includes giving up his eyes, regarded by the blind as grievous and useless appendages. As Núñez rebels and endeavors to escape over the mountains, he is obliged to leave behind the woman, Medina-saroté, he has come to love.

Like the prisoners of the cave, the blind have made the remote valley a symbol of estrangement. They can no more conceive of a world outside their valley than the chained cave-dwellers of Plato could imagine anything beyond the flickering shadows on the wall. Their mental inertia—and Wells wrote in a score of novels that bondage to empty tradition is the earmark of the uneducated mind—becomes apparent in the first dialogue between the newcomer and the blind:

> "And you have come into the world?" asked Pedro.
>
> "*Out* of the world. Over the mountains and glaciers; right over above there, half-way to the sun. Out of the great big world that goes down, twelve days' journey to the sea."
>
> They scarcely seemed to heed him. "Our fathers have told us men may be made by the forces of nature," said Correa. "It is the warmth of things and moisture and rottenness—rottenness."

The opposition between light and darkness—truth and superstition—is nowhere more forcefully depicted than in the contrast between the sighted Núñez and the unseeing: "They told him there were indeed no mountains at all, but that the end of the rocks where the llamas grazed was indeed the end of the world; thence sprang a cavernous roof of the universe, from which the dew and the avalanches fell; and when he maintained stoutly the world had neither roof nor end as they supposed, they said his thoughts were wicked." And later: "Núñez had an eye for all beautiful things, and it seemed to him that the glow upon the snowfields and glaciers that rose about the valley on every side was the most beautiful thing he had ever seen."

The glow of the greater world that wreathed the narrow valley was, metaphorically, H. G. Wells's challenge to the unnameable hordes of humanity content to live in their determinist furrows. Even in *Kipps,* a triple-decker novel seemingly written by another part of the mind which produced **"The Country of the Blind,"** Wells is preoccupied by the imagery of sight and shadow: "As I think of [Kipps and Ann] lying unhappily there in the darkness, my vision pierces the night. See what I can see. Above them, brooding over them . . . there is a monster . . . like all that is darkening and heavy and obstructive. . . . It is matter and darkness, it is the anti-soul, it is the ruling power of this land, Stupidity. My Kippses live in its shadow."

However, it is not Núñez's fate, as it was Wells's lifelong dream, to save the country of the blind from its torpor of ignorance. Rather, he is subjugated by the sightless hordes; humiliated by them; and, though he escapes the valley, defeated. The vanquishing of the spirit of independence by a conformist social order was detailed fully in Wells's early landmark of anti-utopian fiction, *When the Sleeper Wakes* (1899). (pp. 59-61)

Professor Bergonzi finds in **"The Country of the Blind"** a mythical anticipation of the brainwashing techniques of modern totalitarianism. Núñez, driven by hunger and sleeplessness and despair, agrees to conform to the blind rationale. His final surrender comes when he reluctantly agrees to the condition of his blind overlords that allow "those irritant bodies"—his eyes—to be removed by surgery. Núñez, however, rebels at the prospect of blindness, begs his lover Medina-

saroté to flee the valley with him, is refused, and dies, a worthless outcast. Meanwhile the blind world goes on, self-satisfied.

A revealing postscript to **"The Country of the Blind"**—indeed, to Wells's brief phase as fulltime literary artist—was provided a third of a century after his original writing of the story. In 1939, the Golden Cockerell Press of London, for a limited and numbered edition (280 copies), asked Wells to update his famous story. But, to grasp the significance of what Wells did to his finest effort in short fiction, it is necessary to jump ahead briefly. By 1939 Wells's voice had grown shrill with warnings which the world, it appeared, had failed to heed. The same year that he revised **"The Country of the Blind,"** he had made his last voyage to the United States. His pleas for a world state were heard by thousands with the respect due an elder statesman of letters. W. Somerset Maugham recalled the twilight phase in a memoir which concludes: "[Wells] was mortified that people looked upon him as a has-been. . . . When they listened it was . . . with the indulgence you accord to an old man who has outlived his interest." The world in 1939, even as the Andean valley reincarnated by Wells, *was* cracking.

The revision of **"The Country of the Blind"** runs parallel to the original until the final page when Núñez, having made his escape, sees along the vast rock a fresh scar. As certain of coming doom as his creator in his own agonizing last years, Núñez contemplates risking his life by returning to the valley. He considers falling at the feet of the blind people; pleading "Believe in my vision. Sometimes such an idiot as I can *see.*" Only the sight of a moving crack of disaster spurs him to action. Wells describes the sound of destruction as "like the shot of a gun that starts a race." The metaphor is vintage of the man who described humanity's race between education and catastrophe.

In a tacked-on epilogue, Wells reveals that Núñez and his beloved Medina-saroté won the race. They lived to tell their tale—among Núñez's people. Wells concludes on an ironic though not surprising note for a writer who soon afterward, under sentence of death in a mortal illness, would view the seeing world as "going clean out of existence, leaving not a wrack behind. . . ." Wells switches focus to Medina-saroté, now the mother of four. Her life saved by her husband's vision, she expresses no desire to see. Her last words are also the revised version's last: "The loveliness of *your* world is a complicated and fearful loveliness and mine is simple and near. . . . It may be beautiful . . . but it must be terrible to *see.*" Wells appears to be saying that blindness is the only bearable antidote to the coming catastrophe. He has reversed Plato's allegory by letting one of the prisoners of the cave (or valley of the blind) return from the light—unchanged. While Medina-saroté may not have *seen,* she knows sight saved her life; yet she still prefers the illusions of the cave—blindness.

The contrast between the two versions of his most well-known short story tells more about the fatal ambivalence in Wells than can be learned from the millions of words of hack journalism that occupied him during the fallow half of an intensely productive literary life. That Wells should at the end of his life go back to one of the acknowledged minor classics of his golden period and rewrite it to conform to a growing misanthropy is one more index to the truth that he failed to resolve the conflicting claims of the artist and the public educator. Although he flawed his imperishable story, he also provided undeniable evidence at the eleventh hour that his dark conception of the world—the conception that pervaded *The Time Machine* and *The Island of Dr. Moreau*—could no longer sustain the optimism of his journalism and would, in the end, overwhelm him. (pp. 61-3)

Richard Hauer Costa, in his H. G. Wells, *Twayne Publishers, Inc.*, 1967, 181 p.

THEO STEINMANN (essay date 1972)

[*In the following excerpt, Steinmann theorizes that the story told by Nunez in "The Country of the Blind" was "actually an instance of post-mortem consciousness."*]

John Kenny Crane asserts that in English literature only three examples of post-mortem consciousness can be found, i.e. in Bierce, Hemingway, and Golding. Indeed, on a first reading one would not include in this particular category H. G. Wells's story **"The Country of the Blind."** And yet the structural parallels with "An Occurrence at Owl Creek Bridge" are so remarkable that it may well be another case of "crossing the bar twice."

In Bierce's short story ["An Occurrence at Owl Creek Bridge"] a man who is being hanged lives in his imagination the long adventure of escaping and returning to his wife between the moment the trap falls and that of his final strangulation. Wells's mountaineer Nunez accidentally falls down a precipice, apparently lives for some time in a fabulous valley, and then climbs up again in order to go back to Bogotá on the other side of the mountain. Eventually he lies motionless but smiling under the cold stars.

My contention is that he actually died during his first fall. The whole episode of the country of the blind races through his mind while he is rolling down the mountainside. This interpretation is born out by circumstantial and internal evidence, and by certain references to time.

Witnesses who saw its tracks in the snow described the first two phases of Nunez' fall. The author refers to Pointer's—fictitious—account of the accident and states that the man "had slipped eastward," and "far below he had struck a steep slope of snow." What follows was not known to the members of the expedition: "At the end of the slope he fell a thousand feet." Then he "came down . . . upon a snow slope even steeper than the one above . . . at last came to gentler slopes . . . rolled out and lay still." This long and irregular fall prompts Nunez' fancy to weave a drawn-out tale combining his anxieties and the familiar legend of the country of the blind: "All the old stories of the lost valley and the Country of the Blind had come back to his mind." But it seems quite impossible that he should survive the brutal shocks that shatter his body when he bounces from one rock to the next, in particular after a drop of a thousand feet.

We expect the natural result to be as follows: "His clothes were torn, his limbs were blood-stained, he was bruised in many places." And this is indeed how the author continues the story of Nunez' death after the interlude in the valley. But for the time being the instinct of self-preservation suggests to Nunez' mind the delusion of being saved by a protective avalanche of snow enveloping him, that he is "stunned and insensible, but without a bone broken in his body." Bierce makes the distinction between rational awareness and purely physical sensations more explicit: "These sensations were unaccompanied by thought. The intellectual part of his nature was

already effaced." This explains the fact that Nunez is "insensible" and yet knows that he has not broken any bones. The details of his getting down into the village and of his being saved are quite as elaborate and plausible as the analogous escape of Peyton Farquhar.

The transition from delusion to the reality of death is in one story as masterly as in the other. Farquhar sees his wife waiting for him. "He springs forward with extended arms. As he is about to clasp her, he feels a stunning blow upon the back of the neck; a blinding white light blazes all about him, with a sound like the shock of a cannon—then all is darkness and silence! Peyton Farquhar was dead; his body, with a broken neck, swung gently from side to side beneath the timbers of the Owl Creek bridge." His outstretched arms are the flawless link between the imaginary act of joy and the actual hanging. Nunez dreams of a double escape, first from the fatal solitude of snow and cold, and then from being blinded. He decides to get back to the spot where he lost hold. Thus Wells completes the circle and takes his hero to the scene of his death.

> Then very circumspectly he began to climb.
>
> When sunset came he was no longer climbing, but he was far and high. He had been higher, but he was still very high. His clothes were torn, his limbs were blood-stained, he was bruised in many places, but he lay as if he were at his ease, and there was a smile on his face. . . .
>
> The mountain summits around him were things of light and fire. . . .
>
> But he heeded these things no longer, but lay quite inactive there, smiling as if he were satisfied merely to have escaped from the valley of the Blind in which he had thought to be King.

There is an almost malicious ambiguity in the sentence "He had been higher, but he was still very high", which fits in, both with his delusion and with the accident. (pp. 157-59)

In the rendering of Farquhar's ultimate consciousness, Bierce goes right through to the final "darkness and silence." Wells stops just one step before: he follows Nunez' dream as far as the illusion of climbing again. Then he switches over to omniscient narration, adding, as Bierce does in his last paragraph, a short description of the corpse and the original surroundings. During their agony both protagonists have intermittences of unconsciousness which their subconscious interprets as falling asleep on their way to safety. In both stories "a blinding white light" illuminates the moment of death. (Cf. also "unbelievably white in the sun", Hemingway; and the "absolute lightning" in Golding.) Both symbolize the supreme joy of self-deception. Farquhar projects it on to the face of his wife: "she stands waiting, with a smile of ineffable joy." Wells twice repeats the fact that "there was a smile on his face" which death had not been able to wipe out.

Besides these external circumstances which may not convince every reader that **"The Country of the Blind"** is actually an instance of post-mortem consciousness, the element of time is important. Farquhar is hanged in the light of "the early sun" and reaches his home "in the morning sunshine." His "delirium" has invented a lapse of twenty-four hours. Nunez, on the other hand, had time to imagine a longer, but not precisely defined stay in the secluded valley. He slipped off the shelf of rock while his party were building their night shelter. It is evident that this would have to be done by daylight, presumably late in the afternoon. The time of his death is explicitly mentioned: "When sunset came he was no longer climbing." Thus the accident and his—second—death occur at the same time of day. This indication is corroborated by the stars that mark the beginning and the end of his delusion: "he saw the stars," and: "he lay peacefully contented under the cold stars." The apparent contradiction between "sunset" and stars is easily explained. The camp was pitched high up, near the top of the mountain. As soon as one descends more than one or two thousand feet, the sun is hidden, and from the darkness of the valley the stars become visible.

But it is not certain at all that he actually saw them: He "came down in the midst of a cloud of snow. . . . Down this he was whirled . . . buried amidst of a softening heap of the white masses . . . [he] worked himself loose and . . . out until he saw the stars. He rested flat upon his chest for a space . . . his coat turned over his head." Neither his position nor the coat over his head can allow him to see the stars. It is worth mentioning how closely parallel this progression is to Bierce's story: "Encompassed in a luminous cloud, of which he was now merely the fiery heart . . . he swung through unthinkable arcs of oscillation . . . [deep down in the water]. . . . He opened his eyes in the blackness and saw above him a gleam of light, but how distant, how inaccessible! . . . [Whilst Nunez works himself loose, Farquhar's hands] beat the water vigorously with quick, downward strokes, forcing him to the surface." When he got there, "his chest expanded convulsively, and with a supreme and crowning agony his lungs engulfed a great draught of air, which instantly he expelled in a shriek!" Nunez "was seized with a paroxysm of sobbing laughter" when he was well clear of the avalanche.

The stars Nunez sees may be nothing but a physiological reaction. During his fall his head and possibly his eyes are hurt. Indeed, the feeling of pressure on his head is emphasized by the frequent repetition of the word *wall* and, more obviously, by "the lid of rock that covered their cosmic casserole," a theme that is constantly contrasted with the vastness of the starlit sky. Besides, several episodes of his turbulent fall are transposed into the delusion: " 'Carefully,' he cried, with a finger in his eye, and found they thought that organ, with its fluttering lids, a queer thing in him. They went over it again." He was "stumbling" and then had "fallen headlong" in a "room as black as pitch." "His arm, outflung, struck the face of someone as he went down; he felt the soft impact of features." "He struggled against a number of hands that clutched him." And on similar lines: "an unfamiliar fern that seemed to clutch out of the crevices with intense green hands."

A concussion could easily cause an erroneous interpretation of impulses coming from his optic nerves. Nunez' subconscious mind is aware that his eyes are damaged or seem to be. This explains the great number and intensity of visional impressions and the episode of the blind. His instinct of self-preservation snatches at the legend of that mysterious valley and compensates his anxiety about his eyes in two ways: by the wish-dream that he is the only one in a secluded world who can see; and, at the same time, a series of reassuring examples that men who cannot see are not only happy but even superior to those who can. Nunez pretends to prove to the blind that they are inferior. But his subconscious contrives the tests in such a way that they produce the opposite result

and minimize the importance of sight. Another subtle suggestion is the inversion of day and night that makes sight virtually useless. There is even the idea that eyes may be a nuisance. A blind doctor comes to the conclusion that Nunez' "eyes . . . are diseased . . . in such a way as to affect his brain. They are greatly distended, he has eyelashes, and his eyelids move, and consequently his brain is in a state of constant irritation and destruction." Here he comes very near to admitting to his rational awareness that his head has suffered in the fall, that he is facing "destruction." His subconscious control can only just disguise the fact.

Several objections may be raised to this interpretation. The length of Nunez' stay in the valley of the blind is one of them. It seems, however, fairly irrelevant when compared with the length of Golding's *Pincher Martin*. Another point is the hypothetical possibility that Nunez was really saved by the avalanche that carried him down. Yet this is not very likely. If it was volumionus enough, it would probably have smothered him; if it was just a cloud of snow, it was not sufficient to mitigate the terrible crashes on the rocks. The most important doubt arises, of course, from the sentence "And the man who fell survived."

If we take it simply as a statement of the author, the present reading becomes unlikely. Let us first have a look at the analogous situation in Bierce: "As Peyton Farquhar fell straight downward through the bridge, he lost consciousness and was as one already dead. From this state he was awakened—ages later, it seemed to him. . . ." In Wells we read: "And the man who fell survived. . . . Down this he was whirled, stunned and insensible, but without a bone broken in his body; . . . He came to himself with a dim fancy that he was ill in bed." The parallel is again very remarkable. Whilst one says he "survived," the other suggests that his hero was "as one already dead." Bierce's formula is more subtle, more flexible. Wells's sentence stands isolated between the authorial report on Pointer's expedition and the description of the fall which is clearly to be attributed to Nunez' sensationary awareness. It could be considered as omniscient narration, but I feel that it is the triumphant self-deception of a dying brain, just as in Bierce: "The power of thought was restored; he knew that the rope had broken and he had fallen into the stream." Neither of the two authors suggests through indirect speech or modal auxiliaries etc. that these are only impressions of their characters.

The reader is taken into the unknown realm between life and death. Its verisimilitude, its realistic relevance to the cause of the hero's death, varies according to the emphasis the author gives it within his story. In Golding's novel it is the scene for the final self-examination and judgement. Hemingway uses it incidentally as a literary device to end his story. Bierce is primarily interested in the virtuosity of continually interweaving strands of real physical awareness and their deceptive interpretation by the urge of self-preservation. On this point, H. G. Wells is very similar to Bierce. But he adds a philosophical tinge: The episode of the valley of the blind alludes to the Book of Genesis, to Plato's parable of the cave, and to Christ's advent and crucifixion. These references distort, revert, ironize and, above all, remain ambiguous. The blind people illustrate the fact that our senses register only an exterior, materialistic sort of reality. Essential life is lived in the mind. The mind, too, is unreliable; it creates its own realities, but these are eventually more important because they make man happy or unhappy. (pp. 159-63)

Theo Steinmann, "The Second Death of Nunez in 'The Country of the Blind'," in Studies in Short Fiction, Vol. IX, No. 2, Spring, 1972, pp. 157-63.

ALFRED BORRELLO (essay date 1972)

[Borrello is an American essayist, editor, and bibliographer. In the following excerpt, he explores the fear and hope concurrently expressed by Wells in his stories concerning the future of civilization.]

Throughout his long career as a novelist, Wells's fertile imagination never ceased to conjure vision after vision of the hell which his god-men must resolutely confront, somewhat like Dante in *The Divine Comedy,* bravely and directly if they would be successful in the struggle for the ultimate victory of their race and the fulfillment of themselves. These visions are fraught with the dangers presented by a hostile nature bent upon their destruction and more intensely divisive horrors wrought by the perversities of the human species. Thus the Time Traveller witnesses the world in its final agony as the sun grows cooler and cooler. But this vision, disquieting as it may be, is fundamentally less shaking than that of a humanity degenerate and divided at war with itself. Far more crushing a horror than the cannibalism of the Morlocks is the picture of the Eloi—complacent, childlike, loveless, and deintellectualized descendants of ancestors who had fulfilled man's dream for an earthly paradise devoid of desire, war, pain, and sorrow.

The Time Traveller's angst is no less severe, no less frustrating than that of characters such as Dr. Moreau (*The Island of Dr. Moreau,* 1896), Griffin (*The Invisible Man,* 1897), and Cavor (*The First Men in the Moon,* 1901) who, though sobered by the obstacles offered by nature to the survival of themselves and their kind, are devastated by the insights into their species presented by such obstacles. Essentially Wells understood, and these characters come to learn, that man must conquer himself before he can hope to address himself properly to the problems of a hostile nature. This is the principle which shapes and directs his protagonists. Though their struggles with forces outside of humanity are monumental, their fiercest enemy is the very nature of mankind. But, in these early works at least, Wells does not despair. Wells believed that man could achieve a victory over himself. But the reservations which clouded his hope, which he fought to control, grew ever stronger as he advanced in years and as he witnessed the manmade conflicts he had predicted. This doubt is clearly reflected in the quality of his work and the attitudes of his characters. The early, youthful, almost joyful optimism expressed in his first novel, *The Time Machine* (1895), and projected through his first hero, the Time Traveller, decays to a trenchant pessimism in *You Can't Be Too Careful* (1941) and its protagonist, Albert Tewler. (pp. 54-5)

Wells did not limit his warnings of doom to his novels. He insinuated them into his short stories as well, some sixty-three all told, most of which were written in the early years of his career when the form was reaching the height of its popularity. His first collection, *The Stolen Bacillus and Other Incidents* (1895), was an immediate popular success. Its popularity has not declined since its first publication. Though not widely reviewed, it was noted, nevertheless, as the product of a very striking imagination which, it would seem, had "a great deal within its reach." The success of the first collection was followed and intensified by that of three

more: *The Plattner Story and Others* (1897), *Tales of Space and Time* (1899), and *Twelve Stories and a Dream* (1903). In 1911, a fourth collection appeared, *The Country of the Blind, and Other Stories,* essentially a selection from the four preceding volumes, with several previously uncollected stories.

With the subsiding of the first great wave of popular acclaim which had erupted over what was thought to be an "unrivalled" and "audacious" insight into the literary possibilities of the discoveries of science, critics began to reexamine the stories. They discovered that certain aspects of them were strikingly familiar. Several reviewers noted elements of Swift, Verne, Poe, de Maupassant, Hugo, Kipling, and others in them.

Wells never denied nor affirmed that he had been inspired by these and other authors, nor did he ever claim originality for his short stories or for any of the writing he had done. He was disinterested in such questions. Besides, though his critics were skeptical of his inventiveness, his audience never was. His stories were overwhelmingly popular. James and Conrad admired them, and his public clamored for more. His readers sensed in them qualities not present in the tales of those to whom he is indebted. There is a sense of urgency and immediacy in his stories, a sense of danger and a sense of awe of the unknown, but above all a sense of youth and vitality projected through his use of recent discoveries of science and advances in technology. With these elements he was able to capture the exciting sense of a dawning century.

He made a pact with his readers. And in that pact, essentially a suspension of disbelief, he promised them visions of what they and their children could expect as the twentieth century opened before them. Through his predictions, based always on known fact, the future was made as clear and as meaningful as the morning newspaper. Thus he was able to predict air travel in **"The Argonauts of the Air,"** shortly before the first test flights proved the truth of his prediction, and tank warfare in **"The Land Ironclads"** long before it was to come to pass in the first great war.

But his stories contain more than suggestions of technological advantages or disadvantages coming in the future. They reflect, in tightly written, hysterically intense fashion, man's innate ability to deceive himself into believing that he is safe and secure in a world and a universe that contains no safety or security for a being as fragile as he. Thus in **"The Lamias,"** five young men confess that they have discovered that the objects of their devotion and love are nothing but an alarm clock, a phonograph, a stone that changes gold into knick-knacks, a châtelaine with keys, a bottle of perfume and a handful of busks and pads. Like the young man in the poem of a somewhat similar name by Keats, they see only what they wish to see. In a sense, these objects in Wells's story are akin to the serpent in the poem whose true form is revealed to the young man only by the philosopher who is capable of seeing below the surface of things. In this tale and those which follow it, Wells attempts to place himself in the position taken by Keats's philosopher. He desperately wants to restore to the young of all ages that clarity of vision, of perception, stolen by a corrupt society.

Despite his serious intent, Wells does not always treat so solemnly man's ability to deceive himself. There is a good deal of humor in a story, **"The Triumphs of a Taxidermist,"** which treats of a practitioner of the fine art of taxidermy so expert that one day, filled with a monumental sense of his own worth, he boasts that he can fashion a creature so true to life that he can "beat nature." He proceeds to fulfill his boast and creates a monster that never existed but is in every way so perfect that it convinces scientists who examine it that they have discovered a new species of animal. In **"The Stolen Bacillus,"** Wells tells of an anarchist who foolishly believes that he has stolen a vial of deadly bacillus capable of destroying mankind. This is his aim. In actuality, he has seized a strain that is harmless to humans but raises nasty welts on monkeys.

Underlying the humor of these situations is a note of seriousness. In the craftiness of the taxidermist and the evil intent of the anarchist, lies danger for humanity. In "beating nature," the taxidermist has produced a fraud which misdirects scientific enquiry. Thus the deception limits to a greater extent man's knowledge of himself and the universe so vital to his survival as a species. The action of the anarchist, on the other hand, suggests the magnitude of the evil which might be man's fate were the discoveries of science directed toward his destruction by one of his own kind. Humanity, Wells tells us, is not safe while it harbors such individuals in its midst.

But danger for mankind lies not only in the aberrations of its members, but in its very aspirations. These can be the sources of self-delusion and ultimately doom if man understands them only as the means whereby he might escape from his duties to himself and to his race. Lionel Wallace in **"The Door in the Wall"** is a cabinet minister whose childhood memory of a door haunts him. The door leads to an Eden-like garden filled with all the good things he has yearned for for so long but have been denied him because of his position in the world. He manages, at first, to reject the allurements of the vision, but ultimately he succumbs. He opens the door, steps through, and plunges to his death.

Like Wallace, William Hill (**"A Slip Under the Microscope"**) is a victim of his aspirations. A passionate student of science and a product of a poverty-stricken childhood, he wishes to achieve a first in his examinations and thereby triumph over H. J. Somers Wedderburn, the scion of a noted eye specialist whose wealth has permitted his son to progress leisurely through his education. Hill is tense with excitement on the day of the examination. Part of his task is the identification of a specimen under a microscope. The students are honor bound not to move the slide, which could lead to an easier identification. When it is Hill's turn to approach the microscope, he inadvertantly moves the slide. No one, including the proctor, notices what he has done. He is torn on the horns of a dilemma: is he to use the knowledge he has gained, or is he to leave the answer blank and thereby run the risk of losing to Wedderburn? After agonizing deliberation, he takes the former course. When the results are posted, his name appears first. But the victory is barren of joy. He has betrayed himself. Wracked by a conscience which refuses to permit him to believe that he would have been capable of identifying the specimen even if he had not moved the slide, he confesses his fault to his professor, who cannot believe that the act was unintentional. Hill is dismissed from the school, but only after learning that he would have achieved the first even if he had not answered the question. Hill's quixotic behavior based on a false sense of right and wrong has destroyed an opportunity for the world to enlist within the ranks of science one eminently capable of helping humanity.

Azuma-zi (**"The Lord of the Dynamos"**) has also deluded himself. His delusion centers upon a firm belief that the dynamos which he cares for under the direction of James Holroyd

Wells's second wife, Amy Catherine (Jane).

are gods to be worshipped and placated with sacrifices. Holroyd purposely aids and abets this delusion. He is a brute whose love for whiskey is matched only by an inordinate desire to kick his "nigger help" and keep them in their proper place considerably below his own station as a white man. He resembles that segment of humanity who, throughout the nineteenth century, willingly and somewhat religiously shouldered the white man's burden, understanding that burden to mean educating and helping the less fortunate shades of mankind, but only to the point where they could prove helpful to their white masters. Ironically, Holroyd falls victim to the delusion he has fostered. Symbolically, he becomes the first human sacrifice.

But man is not merely threatened by self-delusion, as in Wallace's case, nor by the delusions imposed upon him by an unworkable and constricting traditional sense of morality, as Hill is, nor by those delusions forced upon him by other members of his species. As his knowledge of himself and the universe increases through exploration, man becomes increasingly aware that his very existence is endangered by forces beyond his ability to comprehend, no less control. Mindless though these forces may be, they seem to conspire toward one end—his destruction.

This is the lesson Besset and Vincey (**"The Stolen Body"**) learn when they conduct an investigation into the potentialities of the human brain. Like latter-day investigators of extrasensory perception, they are convinced that man can communicate with man telepathically across vast distances. (Mind you, this is 1896). Their experiment, however, produces a strange side effect. Besset, in leaving his body, is thrust into another dimension of time wherein lurk evil powers waiting impatiently to inhabit the body he has left. This concept of evil apparently held Wells's imagination for most of his life as a writer. In his last work, *Mind at the End of Its Tether* (1945) he talks of cosmic forces at work, like Besset's evil powers, to destroy mankind from within. Alone and almost despairing in that other world, Besset's struggle to regain his body and wrest it from the evil which has possessed it is terrifying, but no less terrifying is his discovery of countless humans like himself whose struggles to regain their bodies were unsuccessful. Fanciful as Wells's picture may be, Besset's experiences are allegories of those terrors man will of necessity confront as he moves resolutely to explore the darker side of his own nature.

That very nature, Wells suggests, has willed man terrors and fears he must come to understand and control if he is to save himself from destruction. He explores this inheritance in **"The Grisly Folk."** He traces mankind's irrational and uncontrollable fears to his encounter with and struggle for superiority over subhuman types in the dark past of man's history. Like Freud, Wells calls for a probing of these fears despite the danger of such exploration, just as Click courageously pursued the apelike Neanderthal to his lair despite the certain death that awaited him.

But conquering his shadow nature cannot save man from certain extinction if he stands in the path of the vast and unmeasurable powers of the universe. In **"The Star,"** Wells describes what might come to pass if he does. A star is sighted in the telescopes of astronomers who continuously search the heavens to uncover its secrets. The star has come out of the black and untrackable depths which lie beyond our solar system. In its path lies Neptune, which it destroys. Between it and its goal, the sun, stands one obstacle—the earth innocently spinning about unaware of its end. Just as innocent are its inhabitants. Men of science warn them of the coming danger but they are unheeded, just as Wells's warnings fall on deaf ears. Each evening, the star grows larger and larger in the sky. A mathematician has determined that the earth is in absolute peril. No one will listen to his pleas nor accept his computations. Only when the star turns night into day and forces the earthly elements on a wild rampage of destruction will mankind believe in its vulnerability. But it is too late. No provisions have been made for the safety of anyone. As violent storms ravage the earth and volcanic eruptions and earthquakes shake it to its core, mankind's stature diminishes to nothing in terms of the dimensions of the disaster which awaits the planet.

Man's extinction, Wells warns us, may not necessarily be wrought by cataclysmic upheavals in the universe, but by nature smiling upon another species. Such is the message in **"The Empire of the Ants."** Reports have reached civilization that a highly destructive species of ant has wrested control from man in the interior of Brazil. The Brazilian government dispatches a gunboat up the Amazon to explore and report upon the situation. Its captain discovers that the creatures are so highly developed and so orderly as to be capable of controlling the world while destroying man in the process. Humanity has no weapons effective against the vast army. Like the guns in *The War of the Worlds,* cannons are less than useless. Holroyd (not to be confused with the character of the same name in **"The Lord of the Dynamos"**), an Englishman

who has joined the expedition, predicts that the ants will be masters of the world by the 1960s.

If extinction from one source or another is the fate of the fragile creature man, where then are the means to prevent it? The answer cannot come from a single individual—witness the destruction of Moreau, Griffin, Cavor, and the defeat of the characters in the short stories. Though these individuals are capable of sensing and, in some instances, of reporting the dangers which lie ahead of the species, as individuals, Wells grew to believe, they can do little more. The answer to man's salvation, Wells determined, lies in another direction which, when he discovered it, ironically spelled the end of his life as an artist. (pp. 70-7)

Alfred Borrello, in his H. G. Wells: Author in Agony, *Southern Illinois University Press, 1972, 137 p.*

JACK WILLIAMSON (essay date 1973)

[*A prolific and widely anthologized author, Williamson is considered one of the most important pioneers of science fiction. In the following excerpt from his* H. G. Wells: Critic of Progress, *he discerns similarities between tragic and comic heroes in* The Country of the Blind *in their attempts to defy society by asserting progressive beliefs.*]

Wells seems more deeply concerned with the internal than the external limits to progress, perhaps for two reasons. As the literary artist, he finds the internal struggle more complex, more appealing than the conflict with the external cosmos. As the prophet of progress, he is more hopeful of doing something about the human limits. The probable life of the solar system cannot be extended by any predictable human exertion; and no competing species, Martian or terrestial, now seems more dangerous to future human progress than does man himself. But the human limits seem to merit more attention. Not only are they nearer, but they seem to offer tantalizing possibilities of being somehow widened or removed by human knowledge and intelligence.

The short stories, though of course not deliberately planned to develop any common theme, do reflect Wells' early preoccupation with these human limits. Most of them were written before his rebellion against literary form; they are amazingly inventive, fully imagined, lively in style. A bright kaleidoscope of comic and tragic and tragicomic moods, they offer such richly varied glimpses and interpretations of life that classification is difficult and generalization dangerous. Still the literary artist, not yet the high priest of social reform through rational enlightenment, Wells is a perceptive critic of mankind. The elemental conflict between animal man and social man appears again and again, not because he has any thematic axe to grind, but simply because this conflict is the inevitable root of character and drama, because it creates the basic irony of life.

Like the novels, the short stories show a maturing ability to see this conflict as comedy. In Wells' own evolution, the most striking change at this period is shift from the tragic to the comic mood. The process, however, is not quite that simple. A shift from emotional identification to intellectual detachment, it does not always mean a growth of optimism, for detachment lends itself to satire, which more than tragedy is the natural vehicle of pessimism. Nor was the change ever entirely definite or complete. **"The Stolen Bacillus,"** one of the very first short stories, is a comic farce. The lightly comic *Wheels of Chance* and the darkly tragic *Island of Dr. Moreau* were written at about the same time. Comedy and tragedy are mixed in *The Invisible Man*. Some of Wells' last stories, **"A Dream of Armageddon"** (1903), **"The Country of the Blind"** (1904), and **"The Door in the Wall"** (1906), are tragedies. Yet, in spite of such ambiguous evidence, the change seems real enough. Wells' talent for realistic comedy, visible from the beginning, developed steadily until it found its most mature expression in *The History of Mr. Polly* (1909). Griffin, however, is the last major hero of the classic tragic type. The later tragic heroes represent a different pattern.

In the tragic figures of Griffin's type, Wells is criticizing the individual. In the comedies, as in the later tragedies, he shifts his fire to society. The conflict is the same; the viewpoint and effects are different. In the old war between the individual and society, neither side is right or wrong; that is the basic human irony. It is only some excess that makes a tragic flaw, for all men are individuals, inheriting animal traits through the genes just as inevitably as they inherit social traits through the culture. And these animal traits are vital; sacrificing too many of them is just as suicidal as sacrificing too few.

The comic hero, like the tragic, is an individual in revolt against society—a total conformist would be no hero. The difference is that the selfish tragic hero is destroyed for yielding too little to the mandates of society, while the comic hero is ultimately rewarded for resisting the collective selfishness that would make him yield too much. The tragic hero is the aggressor against the group. The comic hero is the victim. With the conflict forced upon him, he must at last revolt to save his own vital spark of self. In such stories as **"The Purple Pileus"** and **"The Crystal Egg,"** we glimpse the germ of the same comic hero who is more fully developed in the figures of Kipps and Mr. Polly.

The later tragic heroes, Nuñez in **"The Country of the Blind"** and Hedon in **"A Dream of Armageddon"** and Wallace in **"The Door in the Wall,"** resemble the comic type more than they do Griffin. Although each of them displays ego enough to make him convincingly alive, they are the defenders, not the attackers, in the inevitable clash with the crowd. What each defends in his own way is an individual freedom more precious than survival through conformity. In each of them, the essential traits of individual selfishness are overshadowed by an overwhelming collective selfishness. In each case, the tragic ending results from a choice that proves the vital worth of self.

Wells' favorite fiction pattern brings everyday reality into collision with something exotic. The familiar element in this group of stories is usually provided by the institutions and pressures of society. The fantastic element is often some device which allows the hero at least a glimpse of individual freedom. In the comic versions of the pattern, the hero makes some kind of escape. In the tragic version, his excessive individualism results in his destruction.

"The Diamond Maker" illustrates the tragic pattern. The hero is another Griffin: a selfish and solitary individualist who finds a way of making artificial diamonds. Because of his self-centered greed, which he sees reflected in the competitive society in which he lives, he works in secret. Successful, he finds himself a social outcast, unable to benefit from his discovery. Carrying a fortune in diamonds around his neck, he can find neither food nor shelter.

Another tragedy, **"The Cone,"** shows Wells' early recognition of this human conflict as a barrier to progress, and also his early awareness of "the conflict of the two cultures." Written before the final revision of *The Time Machine,* it is "the last surviving relic . . . of what was to have been a vast melodrama, all at the same level of high sensation." Horrocks, the progressive ironmaster, is pitted against a philandering aesthete. Overcome by a primitive lust for individual revenge, he burns the poet alive upon the cone that caps a blast furnace.

"The Moth" might have been called "The Science Jungle." The scientist, the very agent of progress, is represented as a primitive predator. The satire on the ruthless egoism of scientific controversy anticipates the savage quarrels I have seen between contemporary linguists. **"The Story of the Late Mr. Elvesham"** is an equally striking indictment of the amorality of science; the senescent scientist steals the youthful hero's body. **"The Red Room,"** a ghost story, displays fear itself as the primal enemy of progressive rationalism. In **"The Argonauts of the Air,"** the progressive individual is destroyed by the pressures of conservative society: the builder of the first successful flying machine is ridiculed by the world, finally killed by his invention.

The comic version of this pattern is illustrated by **"The Purple Pileus,"** which Wells calls "perhaps the best and reallest" of his very early stories. Here he uses the method of comedy to make a pessimistic view of life endurable. The harsh facts of reality are feelingly observed and accurately reported. Mr. Coombes, the comic hero, is trapped in the institution of marriage. A small shopman, he finds his private scheme of progress thwarted by a disloyal wife, "the luxuries of divorce" out of his reach. Driven from his own home, he tries to kill himself by eating the Pileus, a poisonous-looking fungus. The ensuing episode, in which the effects of this dangerous meal restore him to the mastery of his fate, is not only successful comedy but also, because of the very improbability of this kind of escape from social compulsion, an ironic restatement of his predicament. Fighting to preserve his essential self, the comic hero is made sympathetic by the shadow of the greater collective selfishness that he must defy.

"The Stolen Bacillus," the first of the "single sitting stories" that Wells "ground out" for £5 each, is a cheerful burlesque upon the ironic limitations of a typical promoter of progress: an anarchist whose unchecked individualism betrays him into a fantastic attempt to infect the city water supply with cholera germs. **"The Apple"** follows the same comic pattern; the hero is a young student who sacrifices progress upon the altar of social conformity when he throws away a magic fruit from the Tree of Knowledge because it would make an unsightly bulge in his pockets.

"The Man Who Could Work Miracles," which Wells later rewrote as a film play, gives a comic twist to the theme of *The Island of Dr. Moreau*. A skeptical young clerk, George McWhirter Fotheringay, finding that he has an unexpected miraculous gift, calls upon his pastor to help him hasten progress. They reform drunkards, change beer and alcohol to water, improve railway service, drain a swamp, enrich the soil on One Tree Hill, and cure the vicar's wart. Seeking more time for progress, they stop the earth's rotation—with cataclysmic consequences. Thus, as in *The Island of Dr. Moreau,* the benevolent effort to aid progress ends in disaster. For all its good humor, the story is darkly pessimistic. Bad as the world may be, human enlightenment can only make it worse.

"A Dream of Armageddon" is a tragedy of self against society, more complex and intellectual than *The Invisible Man.* Hedon's refusal to sacrifice personal love to public duty is followed by a holocaust that he might have prevented, and by his own destruction. Yet he seems more like the comic heroes than like Griffin, because the Armageddon is not of his making. Sex in this story is an element of the essential self, not its enemy, as it becomes in the later marriage novels. Hedon's selfish passion is overshadowed by the destructive collective selfishness around him, and his death for love seems a sort of victory.

Between **"A Dream of Armageddon"** and **"The Country of the Blind,"** the role of love is neatly reversed. Love to Hedon is the vital expression of self, worth more than even the survival of society. Love to Nuñez is the enemy of self, the most powerful force crushing him toward conformity. **"The Country of the Blind"** is one of Wells' finest stories, and perhaps his most mature and sophisticated survey of the universal conflict of self against society.

The story must have grown out of Wells' simpler study of the same theme in *The Invisible Man.* In that novel, describing his early mood of selfish elation, Griffin says, "I felt as a seeing man might do, with padded feet and noiseless clothes, in a city of the blind." Later, becoming aware of the tragic consequences of his intellectual solitude, he says, "I saw . . . a blind man approach me, and fled limping, for I feared his subtle intuitions." Nuñez, the seeing man among the blind, is at the beginning somewhat like Griffin, planning to use his unique advantage selfishly, but the development of the story shows a significant change in Wells' attitudes toward both sex and self.

Nuñez is the romantic individualist, his sight the symbol of self and the agent of progress. He falls into an isolated Andean valley where a blind tribe has been isolated for fifteen generations. With a flash of Griffin's tragic ambition, he recalls an old proverb, "In the Country of the Blind the One-eyed Man is King." The blind folk, however, shatter all his selfish dreams. They are society. Their world is small, static, closed, comfortably urban. They adhere to a classic theory of the innate evil of man. "Our fathers have told us men may be made by the forces of Nature," Nuñez is informed. "It is the warmth of things and moisture, and rottenness—rottenness." Refusing to believe what he says he can see, they tell him that there are no mountains, that their universe, at first an empty hollow in the rocks, is now covered with a smooth stone roof from which the dew and the avalanches fall. Two original minds in the past, sent as Wells says by "the chance of birth and heredity" had been agents of progress among them, but now they are middle-class conservatives, their stable ways of life fixed by tradition, supported by learning, sanctioned by religion.

Nuñez's talk of sight is not only incomprehensible but blasphemous. His attempt to use force is a failure. He soon abandons his egoistic ambition to be king, but Wells has not yet finished this dramatic analysis of the worth of self. Reduced to slavery, Nuñez falls in love with a blind girl, Medinasaroté. The match is opposed because the blind regard him as "a being apart, an idiot, incompetent thing below the permissible level of a man." A blind doctor proposes at last to cure him of the disease of sight.

> Those queer things that are called the eyes, and which exist to make an agreeable soft depression in

the face, are diseased . . . in such a way as to affect his brain.

For the girl's sake, Nuñez consents at first to the surgical removal of these irritant bodies. When the day comes, however, he looks upward at the beauty of the morning, with the sun above upon the slopes of ice and snow, and begins "very circumspectly" to climb.

> When sunset came he was no longer climbing, but he was far and high. He had been higher, but he was still very high. His clothes were torn, his limbs were blood-stained, he was bruised in many places, but he lay there as if he were at ease, and there was a smile on his face.

As the symbol of self, Nuñez's sight, like Hedon's lady, is more precious than life. Even though Nuñez should die where he lies "peacefully contented under the cold stars," his death is not defeat but victory.

"The Country of the Blind" is by no means simply a tract on progress. It is a complex aesthetic creation, rich in significance, concretely imagined, more emotional than intellectual. The seeing man, not merely a symbol of self or intelligence or progress, is also an intricate human being, haughty at the beginning with his imagined superiority, quickly responsive to visual beauty, unable to strike a blind man, capable of love, yet ready to sacrifice everything for the sight that is the metaphor of self. The closed world of the blind is fully created, from the guiding curbs along their uncluttered paths to their myth of their own creation. The dramatic tension which shapes the story arises from the antagonism between two views of life, a collision too nearly universal to be contained in any neat set of labels. It is the enmity between permanence and change, the incongruity between the poet and the plowman, the chasm between reckless youth and prudent age, the contrast between the self-directed liberalism of Wells' own father and the rigidly conforming conservatism of his mother. The story is successful because it gives an objective resolution to Wells' own conflicting attitudes toward self and society— and toward sex as an agent of society. The idea of progress is involved because society is inherently regressive and the self is the only instrument of change. The closed world of the blind rejects the instrument of progress, as in fact our real world commonly does.

This same conflict appears in many more of Wells' stories: in the complex mythical and personal symbolism of **"The Door in the Wall,"** and even in the practical jokes played upon society by the uninhibited hero of **"The Triumphs of a Taxidermist."** The stories reflect the varied experiences of Wells' own life; the unlucky student whose moral fragility is revealed in **"A Slip Under the Microscope"** might almost have been Wells himself. Spontaneous as dreams, produced in a mood of exuberant invention to be read for light amusement, these tales seldom display explicit thematic intentions, but the criticism of progress reappears as a persistent reflection of that central human conflict. Taken as a group, they emphasize the realistic awareness of human limitations with which Wells approached the myth of progress. Comte and Marx and Spencer planned their vast systems of reform with a lofty disregard for the human atoms involved. Wells, however, always knew that the coming world, whatever its shape, must be put together by the efforts of individual men, whose private lives are more precious than society, and whose limiting stupidity and ignorance and greed are as old and stubborn as the drive to survive. (pp. 88-94)

Jack Williamson, in his H. G. Wells: Critic of Progress, *The Mirage Press, 1973, 162 p.*

JOHN OWER (essay date 1977)

[*Ower is a contemporary American poet and essayist. In the following excerpt, he offers a detailed interpretation of narrative technique and thematic development in Wells's "The Star," extolling the tale as an important science fiction story.*]

As Bernard Bergonzi has noted in his study of the early "scientific romances," **"The Star"** is one of the most finely wrought and powerful of H. G. Wells's creations [see excerpt dated 1961]. Bergonzi rightly praises **"The Star"** for "the brilliance of its narrative technique" and for the "controlled profusion of its images." He does not, however, subject the work to a detailed analysis on either count. This is a pity, because, both in its thematic development and in its narrative method, **"The Star"** displays considerable subtlety and complexity. Moreover, as Jack Williamson has recognised in his selection of Wells's story for Robert Silverberg's anthology, *The Mirror of Infinity,* the piece is a most useful item in a college teaching repertoire. Besides the vivid and dramatic storytelling which gives **"The Star"** a considerable appeal to college students, it provides a textbook illustration of a number of important matters in the history of literature and of ideas. The story is a genuine pioneer work of science fiction because it imaginatively applies to human experience not only the discoveries in astronomy and physics which had been accumulating since the Renaissance, but also the radically altered world-picture which those findings implied.

"The Star" strikingly renders that vision of the universe as a "huge, dead, immeasurable Steam-engine," which was the imaginative fruit of the new scientific knowledge, and which echoes in European literature from Pascal onwards. Moreover, in depicting man as the helpless victim of a cosmos which is at best indifferent and at worst inimical to his physical and spiritual needs, **"The Star"** is an early example of the literature of existential crisis and the absurd. Like Sartre in "The Wall," or Camus in *The Plague,* Wells employs the shock tactic of making a crisis situation the metaphor for the norm in order to drive home an ironic revelation of man's dereliction. In this way, he attacks the comfortable illusions by which the hard reality of a hostile universe is concealed, and yet at the same time suggests that ignorance of our tragic absurdity is bliss.

Thus, **"The Star"** reflects Wells's sense of man's precarious position in a mysterious and ever-changing cosmos, a vision which also lies behind *The Time Machine* and *The War of the Worlds.* In particular, the body which hurtles from the depths of outer space, collides with Neptune, and is then swung by the gravity of Jupiter so as to produce catastrophic changes upon the Earth, is the imaginative equivalent of the Martian invasion that very nearly destroys the human race. Man is threatened in both cases by an alien enormity which symbolizes a universe largely beyond his comprehension. He is saved in both instances by so small a margin that his very escape is ironic. In **"The Star,"** just as the rogue planet seems about to envelop the world in a cataclysm which will extinguish all life, the same blind forces which have produced the disaster bring about a reprieve. Man, chastened but perhaps wiser for his sufferings, is left to forge a new brotherhood upon a radically altered planet.

The thematic core of **"The Star,"** from which arises both the story's irony and its pathos, is a contrast of two conflicting "world-pictures." These correspond to two antithetical sides of man's nature, and to two historically superimposed yet distinct stages in his growth to racial maturity. The first of the opposing cosmologies stems from the emotions and the imagination. Despite their noble aesthetic achievements, these faculties are bound up with the blind animal instinct for survival and comfort, with its "hedonistic calculus" of hope and fear, anxiety, and security. They consequently trap humanity in a pathetic immaturity of outlook, which attempts to cope with reality not through rational insight and practical action, but rather by emotional "projections." The result is a naive mythopoeia, which superimposes upon the universe not only man's physical image, but also such spiritual and psychological attributes as feeling and volition. This humanizing is suggested by Wells's continuous reference to the heavens in terms of the zodiacal signs and the traditional constellations. It appears also in the attribution to astronomical bodies of sexual identities and desires. Thus, Neptune and the intruding planet are seen as locked after their collision in a "fiery embrace." Such anthropomorphizations create a universe which is "sympathetic" to man not only in sharing his nature, but also in feeling for him either positively or negatively and in responding to his needs, wishes and fears. For example, in those primitive areas where "science has not reached," the advent of the star is seen as a portent of war and pestilence. The extent to which even "civilized" societies share such ingenuous thought processes is indicated by Wells through an ironic juxtaposition of the outlook of two "savage" lovers, with the "official" flattery inspired by the wedding of a South African notable:

> In a South African city a great man had married, and the streets were alight to welcome his return with his bride. 'Even the skies have illuminated,' said the flatterer. Under Capricorn, two negro lovers, daring the wild beasts and evil spirits for love of one another, crouched together in a cane brake where the fire-flies hovered. 'That is our star,' they whispered, and felt strangely comforted by the sweet brilliance of its light.

Both the "primitive" African and the "cultured" European see in the star a projection both of their own erotic desires and of the romantic wish to "live happily ever after." The white man's fantasy, far from approaching the truth more closely, is less humanly valid and appealing because it is far less sincere.

Wells's attitude toward the naive myth-making which pervades man's cosmological outlook is a complex mixture of the perspectives of the scientist and the artist, of human sympathy and sardonic rejection. On the one hand, he would be in ironic agreement with Freud that the thought-processes which have produced the anthropomorphized universe represent an immature reaction to reality, which attempts to overcome or evade unpleasant truths through fantasy. What can be termed the "traditional" world-picture is a reflection of the mental anility of the race, which has created for itself a metaphysical security-blanket, a cosmology of wishful thinking. Even disaster is rendered relatively comprehensible and bearable by the attribution to its agencies of human characteristics and motives:

> So the star, with the wan moon in its wake, *marched* across the Pacific, trailed the thunderstorms *like the hem of a robe,* and the growing tidal wave that *toiled* behind it, frothing and *eager,*

poured over island and island and swept them clear of men (italics mine).

Wells's ironic use of a Shelleyan mythopoeia to describe the final catastrophe epitomizes his sardonic dismissal of the old world-picture as childish and unrealistic. The sweep of vast impersonal forces, which destroy men *en masse* like so many ants, should have dispelled any illusions about the humanity of the universe. However, even though it is fatuous and pathetic to a purely rational perspective, the mythic outlook does possess beauty and even sublimity. Thus, Wells uses anthropomorphic imagery not simply to attack human naiveté, but also to enhance his descriptions poetically. Whatever their limitations, the emotions and imagination at least confer the capacity for aesthetic appreciation and for wonder. Moreover, if the universe is unsympathetic and even inimical to humanity, some sort of psychological defence is excusable, even if immature. Wells's attitude towards the traditional cosmology is thus ambivalent, a complex dialectic in which a harshly tragic experience at once ironically qualifies innocence, and yet reinforces our sympathy for it.

This double perspective is no less apparent in Wells's treatment of the new cosmology of science than in his attitude towards the old world-picture. The two ambiguities are of course reciprocal. On the one hand, Wells is sympathetic enough with science to see "classical" physics and astronomy as the product of a detached, clear-sighted rationality which evinces man's emerging maturity of mind. However, as a sensitive and imaginative artist, the author is repelled by the chilling cosmology of Newtonian mechanics in exact proportion to his attraction to the traditional outlook. Or, to put the matter differently, Wells not only views man from the cosmic perspective provided by science, but also sees the new world-picture from the viewpoint of a humanity to which it is indifferent, alien, and even inimical. The latter outlook appears in Wells's presentation of the Newtonian universe as an intimidating and ultimately menacing enormity, by which man is both physically and imaginatively overwhelmed. His evocation of the vast extent and emptiness of the cosmos recalls Pascal's statement that "The eternal silence of these infinite spaces frightens me." Thus, the astronomical bodies which pygmify man are in their turn reduced to dust-motes in comparison with the enormous vacancy which they scarcely occupy:

> Few people without a training in science can realise the huge isolation of the solar system. The sun with its specks of planets, its dust of planetoids, and its impalpable comets, swims in a vacant immensity that almost defeats the imagination. Beyond the orbit of Neptune there is space, vacant so far as human observation has penetrated, without warmth or light or sound, blank emptiness, for twenty million times a million miles.

Within this vacuity, enormous dead masses move with complete impersonality according to the inflexible dictates of mathematical law. The catastrophe which very nearly destroys the human race is produced by a mechanical chain of cause and effect, arising from such blind forces as gravitational attraction. These make the "rogue" star "ricochet" through the solar system like a cosmic billiard-ball:

> But near its [i.e., the star's] destined path . . . spun the mighty planet Jupiter. . . . Every moment now the attraction between the fiery star and the greatest of the planets grew stronger. And the re-

sult of that attraction? Inevitably . . . the burning star, swung . . . wide of its sunward rush, would 'describe a curved path' and perhaps collide with, and certainly pass very close to, our earth.

Wells's presentation of the Newtonian universe is in part designed to induce the condition of existential horror which can be termed "cosmos shock," a numbing of the emotions and the imagination by an overwhelming awareness of the size and inhumanity of the physical world. This negative reaction is, however, mixed with a poetic wonder, verging on that religious awe at the extent and magnificence of creation which pervades the Old Testament. Whatever may be the final significance of these contradictory reactions, Wells does not explicitly advocate a surrender to either mysticism or the absurd. His ostensible ideal combines a clear-sighted, detached rationality, with a stoic fortitude in the face of man's tragic vanity.

The emergence of this maturity in the race is aptly symbolized by a scientifically-minded schoolboy. Transcending the narrow, mundane self-interest displayed by his elders in a series of sketches immediately preceding his own, he applies his scientific knowledge to make a rough but accurate prediction of the star's future progress. The full fruition of the schoolboy's outlook appears in the calm, independent, and disinterested lucidity of the "master mathematician" who exactly calculates the star's course. There is a tragic nobility about this latter-day prophet interested only in discovering and proclaiming the truth, whatever may be its painful implications. He displays a heroic moral integrity in maintaining his convictions not only in the face of derision, but also in the face of the terrible reality that "Man has lived in vain." At the same time, he suggests that, in its capacity to understand if not to control, the scientific intellect can stand on a footing of almost godlike equality with the universe it has discovered:

> [The mathematician looked at the star] as one might look into the eyes of a brave enemy. 'You may kill me,' he said after a silence. 'But I can hold you—and all the universe for that matter—in the grip of this little brain. I would not change. Even now.'

This passage suggests the ironic and tragic ambivalence which invests even Wells's celebration of man's mature powers of soul. On the one hand, the mathematician displays a magnificent existential courage which matches the cosmic capacities of his reason. On the other, even he is bound by the archaic world-picture and the human weaknesses to which it caters. To cope with the star he finds it necessary to anthropomorphize it as a conscious "enemy," and to engage in a primitive ritual of heroic challenge which is not a little ridiculous under the circumstances. The physical and the spiritual limitations of the mathematician are emphasized by other details in Wells's account of him. He is elderly and graying, and he requires a stimulant to stave off the need for sleep so that he can complete his calculations. A corresponding psychic weakness is suggested by the fact that he is unable to lecture without a "piece of chalk to fumble in his fingers," and has been "stricken to impotence" when student pranksters have hidden his supply. This sexual innuendo suggests that even man's mature intellectual accomplishments may be inextricably involved with his bodily needs and appetites.

The ambivalence which is apparent in Wells's treatment of man and the universe in **"The Star"** is built into the story's narrative technique. This is analogous to that of the film documentary, which, within its broad overall "scoping" of a scene or of a story, focuses upon particular details in a series of closeups. Wells achieves this dual perspective in fictional form through an omniscience that contains passages, such as the accounts of the African lovers or of the schoolboy's calculations, in which events are rendered in terms of the awareness of the participants themselves. The author's mixture of narrative modes enables him to convey his complex spiritual stance by repeatedly shifting his narrative distance from a point which is "above" man and his catastrophe, to one which is in the midst of the disaster. The former, corresponding to the detached cosmic perspective of the scientist, is reproduced in a narrative sweep involving the entire globe and even the solar system. This is balanced against the "engaged" outlook of individuals or of particular groups such as the "European watchers." In these smaller human vignettes, Wells "condescends" from his distant "eye of God" omniscience, to approach sympathetically the viewpoints of those caught up in the tragedy. However, at the same time, the restrictions of such earthbound perspectives are ironically underlined by their inclusion within a larger field of vision. Sometimes, the cosmic and the "involved" viewpoints are not juxtaposed, but superimposed:

> Men looking up, near blinded, at the star, saw that a black disc was creeping across the light. It was the moon, coming between the star and the earth. And even as men cried to God at this respite, out of the East with a strange inexplicable swiftness sprang the sun. And then star, sun, and moon rushed together across the heavens.

Here, the events are seen through the eyes of the human participants, but in such a way as to imply the "cosmic" omniscience which encompasses them. The result is an emotional and intellectual tension which generates both irony and pathos. Another sort of narrative superimposition occurs in **"The Star"** when Wells's own omniscience dramatizes the perspective of humanity. Examples are his description of the catastrophe in mythopoeic terms as well as his rendition of the Newtonian universe in such a way as to convey its spiritual shock-effect. The author's assumption of a "lower" point of view not only reflects ironically upon racial immaturity, but also reminds us that Wells himself is not writing from a purely scientific and cosmic perspective. He is also a man among other men, who shares the feelings and the limitations of the victims of the holocaust. Like that of Thackeray in *Vanity Fair,* Wells's omniscience includes a fellow-feeling for his characters as well as detachment from them. His perspective as narrator is not simply that of the Martian astronomers who observe the cataclysm with a cool, detached interest reflecting their spiritual and emotional distance from it:

> The Martian astronomers—for there are astronomers on Mars, although they are very different beings from men—were naturally profoundly interested by these things. They saw them from their own standpoint of course. 'Considering the mass and temperature of the missile that was flung through our solar system . . .' one wrote, 'it is astonishing what a little damage the earth . . . has sustained. . . .' Which only shows how small the vastest of human catastrophes may seem, at a distance of a few million miles.

Although this passage is strategically placed by Wells at the very end of his story, it does not represent his own "last word." Rather, it is qualified by a spiritual outlook which is paradoxically larger because it includes the "inferior" perspective of humanity, with its full tragic knowledge. As the author implies, the pure rationality of the Martians is a sort of innocence, a luxury rendered possible by their comfortable distance from the disaster. Moreover, like Vonnegut in *Slaughterhouse-Five,* Wells exploits the pejorative emotional connotations of an alien race in order to suggest that their apparently superior outlook is, in fact, monstrous and subhuman in its total lack of compassion.

The subtlety and complexity of Wells's narrative technique are matched by that of his star-symbolism, which is based upon a nexus of ironic references to the Bible. The most obvious of these connections is between the rogue planet and the luminary which, according to Matthew's gospel, heralded the birth of Christ. Both are of course celestial prodigies. Moreover, the first signs of the coming of Wells's star are publicly announced on "the first day of the new year," a date which is not only close to that of the Nativity, but also carries appropriate connotations of the beginning of a new era. The reference to Matthew is clinched by the fact that Wells's story was originally published in the Christmas *Graphic.* The full ironic implications of his allusions to the star of the Nativity appear in conjunction with a further echo of Chapters 8 and 9 of the Book of Revelation:

> And the third angel sounded, and there fell a great star from heaven, burning as it were a lamp, and it fell upon the third part of the . . . waters; and the name of the star is called Wormwood: and the third part of the waters became wormwood; and many men died of the waters. . . . And the fourth angel sounded, and the third part of the sun was smitten, and the third part of the moon. . . . And the fifth angel sounded, and I saw a star fall from heaven unto the earth. . . . And he opened the bottomless pit; and there arose a smoke out of the pit, as the smoke of a great furnace; and the sun and the air were darkened. . . .

This series of events corresponds closely to the tidal waves, the partial destruction of the moon, and the volcanic eruptions of **"The Star."** Wells's allusion to Revelation, when taken together with his reference to the Nativity, suggests a subtle, ironic attack upon the Christian doctrines of Redemption and Apocalypse. The star which acts as a revelation of the hostility of the Newtonian universe at the same time parodies the celestial signs of both the First and the Second Coming of Christ. The unmistakable inference is that the Biblical vision of a destruction of the world by God's anger and its ultimate restoration by His love are part and parcel of the naive myth-making to which humanity is addicted. Even the traditional conception of evil, symbolized in an appropriate form by the fallen Lucifer of Isaiah, is quite irrelevant to the universe of science.

Thus, the "new brotherhood . . . among men" which follows Wells's ironic Apocalypse, like the "new heaven and . . . new earth" which it has created, has nothing to do with the personal, moral, and loving Divinity of Christianity. If there is any suggestion of a God in "The Star," it is of the unfathomable Omnipotence of the Book of Job. The only justification which this Divinity offers for the disasters which He has visited upon His faithful servant is a reference to the power and the enormity and the mystery of His Creation. This conception of God is certainly in keeping with the note of religious awe which pervades Wells's story. Moreover, as William V. Spanos has pointed out in a recent study, the "negative mysticism" of Job has much in common with the absurd-ist vision of **"The Star."** Both viewpoints stress man's derelic-tion, his impotence, and his mental inadequacy in the face of an utterly alien Absolute. Both dismiss as "inauthentic" the conventional assumptions and responses by which the truth of the human condition is concealed. It is accordingly possi-ble that **"The Star,"** like *The Island of Dr. Moreau,* reflects the "crisis theology" of the nineteenth and twentieth centu-ries. Such a serious religious concern is certainly in keeping with Wells's complex and ambiguous vision. It is also conso-nant with the author's attack upon the complacent faith in a progress deriving from man's mastery of a totally intelligi-ble and predictable universe. (pp. 167-73)

> John Ower, "Theme and Technique in H. G. Wells's
> 'The Star'," in Extrapolation, Vol. 18, No. 2, May,
> 1977, pp. 167-75.

J. R. HAMMOND (essay date 1979)

[*In the following excerpt from his* An H. G. Wells Companion:
A Guide to the Novels, Romances and Short Stories, *Ham-mond surveys Wells's short fiction, emphasizing the narrative strengths responsible for the enduring appeal of Wells's works.*]

The Stolen Bacillus contains fifteen stories, uneven in quality but strongly marked by those characteristics which were to earn for Wells a world-wide reputation in the ensuing de-cade—vivid descriptive powers, convincing narrative skill and, above all, an uncanny ability to translate unusual and inexplicable happenings into a commonplace environment. The collection includes a number of slight tales of the calibre of **"The Triumphs of a Taxidermist",** which are little more than episodes, but it also contains several stories of undoubt-ed literary power, most notably **"Aepyornis Island"** and **"The Diamond Maker".** These contain clear intimations of Wells's powers as a storyteller.

"Aepyornis Island" is a variant on the desert island myth, of which *Robinson Crusoe* and *The Coral Island* are earlier ex-amples. Wells imagines an explorer cast away on a remote atoll in the Indian Ocean hatching out the egg of an extinct bird, the aepyornis. It is written in a terse, economical style with a wealth of conversational vividness which adds colour and credibility to the narrative. Verisimilitude is lent to the story by the skilful use of detail:

> Presently the sun got high in the sky and began to
> beat down upon me. Lord! it pretty near made my
> brains boil. I tried dipping my head in the sea, but
> after a while my eye fell on the Cape *Argus,* and I
> lay down flat in the canoe and spread this over me.
> Wonderful things these newspapers! I never read
> one through thoroughly before, but it's odd what
> you get up to when you're alone, as I was. I suppose
> I read that blessed Cape *Argus* twenty times. The
> pitch in the canoe simply reeked with the heat and
> rose up into big blisters.

The atoll itself and the narrator's experiences on the island are described with a convincing use of detail (although Wells himself had not travelled outside England and Wales at the time of writing) and the moment when the death of the bird is recounted is written with extraordinary intensity. **"Aepy-ornis Island"** can be read on several different levels—as a highly readable and entertaining yarn in the Kipling manner, as a parable on the theme of loneliness, or simply as another version of the desert island fable which has haunted English

literature for centuries. What distinguishes Wells's vision is an engaging sense of wonder which holds the reader's atten-tion and suspends disbelief.

"The Diamond Maker" begins with the assurance of a short story by Poe or Conan Doyle: 'Some business had detained me in Chancery Lane until nine in the evening, and thereaf-ter, having some inkling of a headache, I was disinclined for entertainment or further work.' Reading it today it is difficult to realise that its author was a young man at the very outset of his literary career, so assured and convincing is his man-ner. In its essentials the story itself is slight enough—the nar-rator encounters by chance a down-and-out who claims to be a scientist in possession of the secret of making artificial dia-monds. The interest of the tale lies partly in its technique—the account of how a chance meeting on the Thames Em-bankment led to a vision of unparalleled riches which haunt-ed the imagination of the narrator—and partly in its intro-duction of the diamond maker, the man of science obsessed by dreams of power. The technique of the story is deceptively simple: the narrator describes how he came to be drawn in conversation with a ragged man he encounters by Waterloo Bridge and how, listening to the account of the man's experi-ences, he feels himself becoming more and more interested in the stranger. It is a device frequently employed by short story writers before and since, but in Wells's hands it has the effect of lending substance and credibility to the rather wild narra-tive unfolded to him by the tramp. At the beginning of the conversation, for example, the diamond maker produces 'a brown pebble' from a canvas bag and asks the narrator what he thinks it is. 'I took out my penknife and tried to scratch it—vainly. Leaning forward towards the gas-lamp, I tried the thing on my watch-glass, and scored a white line across that with the greatest ease.' It is impossible for the reader to doubt that, for a moment at least, the storyteller held in his hands a real man-made diamond: just as it is impossible for the read-er to doubt that Mr. Thomas Marvel was pursued by an In-visible Man, or that the Time Machine really did travel through time. Wells's peculiar gift lay in his ability to make the improbable and fantastic seem believable in terms of ev-eryday experience. Again and again the diamond maker is questioned and probed, but at the end Wells has convinced both himself and his readers that his apparently incredible narrative is true. The scientist himself, the half-deranged fig-ure who is consumed with visions of domination over his fel-low men, is a familiar figure in Wells's work. Nebogipfel in **"The Chronic Argonauts",** Moreau in *The Island of Doctor Moreau* and Griffin in *The Invisible Man* are variants on a similar theme: each, in their different ways, testifies to his deep conviction that science has unlimited possibilities for both good and evil and that knowledge without moral re-sponsibility corrupts and ultimately destroys its possessor.

The Plattner Story, a collection of seventeen stories, is not only a much more balanced compilation than *The Stolen Ba-cillus* but, in its diversity of theme and treatment, illustrates much more effectively the full range of his talent. It includes two horror stories in the Poe manner, **"The Red Room"** and **"Pollock and the Porroh Man"**; a remarkable anticipation of aviation, **"The Argonauts of the Air",** written eight years be-fore the Wright brothers' first successful flight; and a classic tale of the uncanny, **"The Story of the Late Mr. Elvesham",** frequently included in subsequent anthologies. There are also, for good measure, a number of exercises in the genre he was beginning to make all his own, and which our century has termed 'science fiction': among these are such brilliant fantasies as **"In the Abyss," "Under the Knife"** and **"The Sea Raiders"**. Of more significance, perhaps, to the development of Wells as a novelist and romancer are two stories which are both concerned with the impact of unusual occurrences upon ordinary people, **"The Purple Pileus"** and **"A Catastrophe"**. Neither story attracted much critical attention at the time, yet each encapsulates in miniature form a theme which was to dominate Wells both in his fiction and his personal life—claustrophobia, and the urge to disentangle oneself from frustrating or limiting circumstances.

Mr. Coombes, the central character of **"The Purple Pileus"**, is a small shopman unhappily married to a loquacious and disloyal wife. 'Bricklayers kick their wives to death,' he reflects, 'and dukes betray theirs; but it is among the small clerks and shopkeepers nowadays that it comes most often to a cutting of throats.' He wanders out into the countryside to reflect upon his miserable existence and, in a mood of curiosity, tastes a fragment of purple fungi he sees growing by the wayside. He eats more until, intoxicated, he decides to head for home. There he wreaks havoc upon a staid Victorian musical evening and scandalises his wife and her guests by appearing drunk. The incident proves to be a turning point in Coombes's life. His wife has a renewed respect for him after this episode for, as he tells her: 'Now you know what I'm like when I'm roused.' She abandons her extravagant ways and begins to help Coombes more in the running of the business. No longer is he meek and ineffective, but a man who has a reputation for violence when goaded by intolerable pressures. Five years later he passes the same patch of fungus to which he owes his reputation but walks past with the simple comment: 'I dessay they're sent for some wise purpose.' The story concludes with the words 'And that was as much thanks as the purple pileus ever got for maddening this absurd little man to the pitch of decisive action, *and so altering the whole course of his life*' [my italics].

Winslow in **"A Catastrophe"** is also a struggling shopkeeper, faced with the prospect of almost immediate bankruptcy. His little drapery shop is not paying, and he is in debt to his wholesale dealers, Helter, Skelter & Grab. His situation is saved, not by his own resolute action but by an unexpected legacy which transforms his gloomy financial prospects and permits him, after days of despondency, to face the world with good cheer. It is a slight tale of only nine pages, yet it is marked by a restraint and shrewdness of observation worthy of a short story by Gissing. Wells vividly conveys a sense of Winslow's hopelessness:

> A shop assistant who has once set up for himself finds the utmost difficulty in getting into a situation again. He began to figure himself 'crib hunting' once more, going from this wholesale house to that, writing innumerable letters. How he hated writing letters! 'Sir,—Referring to your advertisement in the *Christian World*.' He beheld an infinite vista of discomfort and disappointment, ending—in a gulf.

Winslow regrets having married, 'with that infinite bitterness that only comes to the human heart in the small hours of the morning'. After a sleepless night he conveys the seriousness of the financial situation to his wife, who listens with sympathy and understanding. The news of the legacy comes in the form of a letter marked with a deep mourning edge. At once the shopkeeper has a mental image of what the bereavement will mean: 'The brutal cruelty of people dying! He saw it all in a flash—he always visualised his thoughts. Black trousers

to get, black crepe, black gloves—none in stock—the railway fares, the shop closed for the day.' In fact the letter contains the news not only of the bereavement but of his wife's inheritance of seven cottages. It is this which transforms their lives and alters the whole perspective of their expectations. Despair is replaced by a resurgence of hope:

> The blow was a sudden and terrible one—but it behoves us to face such things bravely in this sad, unaccountable world. It was quite midday before either of them mentioned the cottages.

Both these stories may be regarded as first sketches of a situation Wells was to depict in fuller depth in *Kipps* and *Mr. Polly*: that of the 'little man' who, in seeking to escape from an intolerable or cramping environment, succeeds in changing the tenor of his life and achieving happiness in place of despair. In later years this was to become one of his most characteristic themes.

In *Tales of Space and Time* Wells collected together five stories which were originally published in various magazines during 1897-8. These are **"The Crystal Egg"**, **"The Star"**, **"A Story of the Stone Age"**, **"A Story of the Days to Come"** and **"The Man Who Could Work Miracles"**.

Of this group of stories by far the most well known is **"The Star"**. It is frequently included in anthologies, and is by common consent an outstanding example of Wells's technique as a literary artist. Its theme—that of the narrowly averted collision between earth and a strange new planet from outside the solar system—is elaborated on a broader canvas in the novel *In the Days of the Comet* (1906), but in **"The Star"** Wells made brilliant use of language and metaphor to achieve an effect of controlled suspense. Reading the story today one is struck again and again by the vivid use of imagery:

> And everywhere the world was awake that night, and throughout Christendom a sombre murmur hung in the keen air over the countryside like the belling of bees in the heather, and this murmurous tumult grew to a clangour in the cities.

> So the star, with the wan moon in its wake, marched across the Pacific, trailed the thunderstorms like the hem of a robe, and the growing tidal wave that toiled behind it, frothing and eager, poured over island and island and swept them clear of men.

> Everywhere the waters were pouring off the land, leaving mud-silted ruins, and the earth littered like a storm-worn beach with all that had floated, and the dead bodies of the men and brutes, its children.

Wells attains the effect he desires, as in the opening pages of *The War of the Worlds* and *The Island of Doctor Moreau*, partly by a terse documentary style and partly by the deliberate manner in which he introduces recognisably ordinary human beings into the narrative. **"The Star"**, although concerned with events on a cosmic scale, is brought within the range of the reader's own experience by the skilful introduction of everyday characters—'lonely tramps faring through the wintry night', 'the schoolboy rising early for his examination work', 'pretty women, flushed and glittering', and so on. A similar technique is employed in **"The Man Who Could Work Miracles"**, a humorous story which Wells adapted for a film version in 1936. Here, as in *The Invisible Man*, an element of farcical comedy is added to the matter-of-fact description of extraordinary events. The whole story of George

Illustration by W. G. Stacey for the first publication of "The Story of the Inexperienced Ghost" in Strand *magazine, March 1902.*

McWhirter Fotheringay and his inexplicable gift of working miracles is told with a high-spirited zest which anticipates the comic vitality of *Kipps* and *The History of Mr. Polly*. There can be no mistaking the enthusiasm with which Fotheringay's adventures are described: 'The small hours found Mr. Maydig and Mr. Fotheringay careering across the chilly market square under the still moon, in a sort of ecstasy of thaumaturgy, Mr. Maydig all flap and gesture, Mr. Fotheringay short and bristling, and no longer abashed at his greatness.' Here, as in so many of Wells's novels and stories, the unbelievable is rendered commonplace by the extraordinarily effective use of detail and engaging facility of language. It is no accident that the story is sub-titled 'A Pantoum in Prose'.

"A Story of the Stone Age" and **"A Story of the Days to Come"** are less successful experiments in the novella form. Wells regarded them as 'two series of linked incidents', and the two are indeed linked in the sense that they contrast attitudes to loyalty and emotional affinity between the remote past and the twenty-second century. **"A Story of the Days to Come"**, which describes a society closely akin to that of *The Sleeper Wakes,* is a powerful story marred by a curious ambiguity in the narration. It is never clear whether Wells approves or disapproves of the rigidly organised civilisation he describes—a civilisation which strongly resembles Aldous Huxley's anti-utopia *Brave New World*—and this deliberate

ambiguity inevitably lessens the impact of his vision. Continually one has a sense of a number of vivid incidents—the roads constructed of Eadhamite, the exile of the young lovers in the open country, the description of the city ways, the labour serfs—which yet fail to gell into a coherent and consistent narrative. Wells was conscious of the defects in the story, for many years later he wrote that the society described within it

> was essentially an exaggeration of contemporary tendencies: higher buildings, bigger towns, wickeder capitalists and labour more downtrodden than ever and more desperate. . . . It was our contemporary world in a state of highly inflamed distension. . . . I suppose that is the natural line for an imaginative writer to take, in an age of material progress and political sterility. Until he thinks better of it.

Of far greater literary and imaginative power is the short story **"The Crystal Egg"**, one of Wells's most remarkable inventions. It begins in the restrained and careful manner he was beginning to make his own: 'There was, until a year ago, a little and very grimy-looking shop near Seven Dials, over which, in weather-worn yellow lettering, the name of "C. Cave, Naturalist and Dealer in Antiquities" was inscribed.' With considerable skill Wells builds up a picture of the Cave ménage—of Mr. Cave himself, the little old antique dealer, of his wife, 'a coarse-featured, corpulent woman', and of the intriguing discovery that the crystal egg, when viewed under certain light conditions, reveals details of the landscape of what can only be the planet Mars. The reader is given a vivid sense of Cave's loneliness, of his desire to confide the secret of the crystal to no one except his closest friend, and of his growing fascination with the perusal of the Martian terrain. It is with a real sense of loss and regret that one learns, at the conclusion of the story, of Cave's death and of the sale of the crystal to 'a tall, dark man in grey'. The reader has a tantalising glimpse of the crystal egg being, possibly, 'within a mile of me, decorating a drawing-room or serving as a paper-weight—its remarkable functions all unknown'. **"The Crystal Egg"** embodies within its brief compass all those qualities which made Wells among the foremost storytellers of his time: convincing narrative, skilful and assured characterisation, accomplished use of scientific detail, and careful pacing of incident and dénouement.

Twelve Stories and a Dream comprises, as its title suggests, twelve tales (published during the years 1898-1903) together with **"A Dream of Armageddon"**, a sombre story of love and death told against a backcloth of a world war. The stories differ markedly in range and quality; perhaps the most characteristic, though for widely differing reasons, are **"Mr. Skelmersdale in Fairyland","** **"The New Accelerator"** and **"Miss Winchelsea's Heart"**. Each illustrates different facets of Wells's strengths and weaknesses as a storyteller.

"Mr. Skelmersdale" is notable for its preoccupation with a theme which was to haunt his writings as a *leitmotiv* throughout his life—that of the man who is obsessed by a vision of a beautiful, elusive lady and who searches in vain for the promise the vision seems to embody. The theme recurs again in **"The Door in the Wall"**, in *The Sea Lady* and in numerous other writings; it underlies much of *Tono-Bungay* and *The New Machiavelli*; even as late as *Apropos of Dolores* (1938) the dream of the elusive, beckoning love goddess continued to haunt Wells's fiction. The Mr. Skelmersdale of the story, a village shopkeeper, falls asleep one night on Aldington Knoll and wakes to find himself in Fairyland. There he meets a beautiful Fairy Lady who talks to him of love. Realising too late his longing for her he becomes parted from her company, and at length loses sight of the fairy kingdom altogether. He returns to the world of everyday only to find that he is filled with an insatiable desire to return to the beautiful land within the Knoll. He tries on many subsequent occasions to fall asleep there and so return to Fairyland, but without success.

What distinguishes this story, apart from the obsessive quality of its theme, is the poetic beauty of its writing. The description of Aldington Knoll and of the summer night at the prelude of Skelmersdale's adventure is written with an intensity and clarity of vision which recalls the most memorable sequences in *The Time Machine* and *The First Men in the Moon*. Wells was exceptionally gifted at describing scenes of natural beauty; here he conveys to the reader a vivid sense of the Knoll and of the splendour of its setting. He conveys too a sense of Skelmersdale's unhappiness and his troubled mental state at the outset of the story. The account of Fairyland and of the elf kingdom in which the unhappy man was temporarily imprisoned is perhaps a little contrived, but there can be no doubting the feeling of wonder with which the fairy kingdom is described and the aura of unattainable beauty which surrounds the lady of his dream-like encounter. 'It is

hard, it is impossible, to give in print the effect of her radiant sweetness shining through the jungle of poor Skelmersdale's rough and broken sentences. To me, at least, she shone clear amidst the muddle of his story like a glow-worm in a tangle of weeds.' The reader shares with the little shopkeeper the emotion of irreparable loss, the sense of almost physical anguish, which overwhelms him on his return to the village and his realisation that he will see the fairy lady no more. By contrast with Fairyland the world of humanity seems coarse and flat and uninspiring.

"The New Accelerator" is in complete contrast both in substance and style. It lacks altogether the poetic qualities, the atmosphere of haunting beauty, which irradiates **"Mr. Skelmersdale"**; it belongs rather to the zestful, exuberant manner of the scientific romances. Professor Gibberne, a noted physiologist, discovers a drug which stimulates the nervous system many thousands of times faster than the normal pace. He and a friend (the narrator) both take a dose of the stimulant and, under its influence, walk along the Folkestone Leas to observe its remarkable effects. Since they are both moving 'a thousand times faster than the quickest conjuring trick that was ever done' the effect is to make it appear that all other people are moving in extreme slow motion. This provides the material for a novel and entertaining tale in which Wells delights in observing his fellows from an unfamiliar stance. There is a girl and a man smiling at one another, 'a leering smile that threatened to last for evermore'; a brass band playing incomprehensible music; a man struggling to refold his newspaper against the wind; an apparently immobile cyclist frozen in the act of overtaking a stationary charabanc; and so on. All are described with wry humour and a vivid sense of the absurd. The account of the sudden wearing off of the drug, of the abrupt return to the normal pace of everyday, is handled with assurance and conviction, as are the narrator's reflections on the ethical considerations arising from the experiment. The reader has a vivid sense of the novelty, of the extraordinary elation, of living for half an hour while the remainder of humanity lives through a second or so of normal time. The story is indeed a variant on the theme of time travelling: reflecting on Gibberne's discovery, the storyteller remarks that the Accelerator 'must necessarily work an entire revolution in civilised existence. It is the beginning of our escape from that Time Garment of which Carlyle speaks.' **"The New Accelerator"** is in fact a not wholly successful attempt to fuse together the rumbustious humour of (say) *The Wealth of Mr. Waddy* with the scientific framework of the romances; but the tale bears vivid testimony to Wells's abundant zest for life and his infectious delight at the sheer joy of existence. (pp. 62-70)

The Country of the Blind and Other Stories was Wells's final selection: it consisted, he wrote, of a collection under one cover 'of all the short stories by me that I care for any one to read again'. The compilation includes 28 of the finest stories from previously published collections, together with five reprinted for the first time: **"A Vision of Judgment"**, **"The Empire of the Ants"**, **"The Door in the Wall"**, **"The Country of the Blind"** and **"The Beautiful Suit"**.

"The Country of the Blind" (1904) is by common consent one of Wells's most memorable short stories. It shares with *The Wonderful Visit* and *The Invisible Man* a concern with the fate of the outcast; it is, with them, a parable on intolerance, but it goes beyond them in its eloquent assertion of the invincibility of the human spirit. (pp. 71-2)

That **"The Country of the Blind"** is satirical, even parabolic, in intent, there seems little doubt. There is also no question that the story can be read on a number of different levels, rich as it is in symbolisms and nuances—of some of which Wells himself may have been unaware. In common with *The Time Machine* and *The Island of Doctor Moreau* one is continually aware of allegorical elements: the story has a transparent quality which renders the experience of reading it extraordinarily unsettling. Each generation will read into it the undertones which have meaning to its own age.

On its simplest level it is a homily on the theme of inhumanity: the sighted man in a blind world becomes a social outcast and is persecuted. Wells neatly inverts the saying 'In the Country of the Blind, the one eyed man is King' and demonstrates the truth that in a sightless world the gift of sight can bring in its train ostracism and danger. Read from a different angle, the story is a parable on conformity: Nunez is the rebel who refuses to conform with a rigid and narrow-minded social order. He seeks to disentangle himself from a situation which he finds intolerable, a course of behaviour which Wells in his own person invariably adopted and urged others to follow. My own reading supports these two interpretations but would add a third: that Nunez symbolises the free independence of the human psyche, the indomitable will to survive of the spirit. Faced with a choice between losing his eyesight (and, by implication, his ability to imagine a larger and freer world) and the prospect of escape, even at the risk of physical death, he chooses the latter. There is no doubt that for Wells this dilemma had direct relevance to the problems of daily life. Throughout his career he advocated the utmost freedom of thought and expression, and it was entirely characteristic of him that in September 1939, when war clouds were ominously gathering, he planned to deliver an address to the Annual Congress of the International P.E.N. entitled 'The Honour and Dignity of the Free Mind'.

"The Door in the Wall" (which, together with **"The Country of the Blind"**, is deservedly counted among his finest stories) marks a return to the central theme of **"Mr. Skelmersdale in Fairyland"** and *The Sea Lady*—that of the man who is haunted by an elusive vision of lost beauty. Lionel Wallace, the central figure, is a much more substantial character than Skelmersdale; he is a prominent politician on the brink of a Cabinet appointment. But he is a man obsessed, haunted by the tormenting memory 'of a beauty and a happiness that filled his heart with insatiable longings, that made all the interests and spectacle of worldly life seem dull and tedious and vain to him.' As a boy of five, Wallace had first stumbled across the door—a green door against a plain white wall. The door held a considerable attraction for him and, after some hesitation, he opened it 'and so, in a trice, he came into the garden that has haunted all his life'. Many years later Wallace describes to his friend Redmond the peculiar effect the wonderful garden had upon him as a child—its beauty, its exhilarating atmosphere, its indefinable quality of paradise. There he met kindly people who talked to him and played delightful games with him. There too he met a sombre woman who showed him a book containing an account of his own life, including his entry into the beautiful world beyond the green door. When he finds himself suddenly outside the white wall he is distraught with unhappiness and pleads in vain to be allowed to return. During the ensuing years Wallace sees the door again on no less than six different occasions but each time he passes by without entering, always for some pressing reason. At last he realises that the door symbolises for him

escape from a life he has come to despise, and swears to himself that if ever he encounters it again he will enter without hesitation. He confesses to Redmond that his soul 'is full of inappeasable regrets'. At the end of the story Redmond explains that Wallace is now dead, having fallen through a door into a deep excavation near East Kensington Station. The narrative concludes with the reflection that Wallace 'had, in truth, an abnormal gift, and a sense, something—I know not what—that in the guise of wall and door offered him an outlet, a secret and peculiar passage of escape into another and altogether more beautiful world'.

"The Door in the Wall" is essentially a fantasia on a characteristically Wellsian theme—that of the man who believes he has found a way of escape from the commonplace world of everyday into a *different* life, a life of paradisal enchantment. Many of Wells's novels and romances touch upon this theme, which was clearly a powerfully recurring element in his imagination. . . . To anyone with any understanding of Wells's life and background **"The Door in the Wall"** is a fascinating, indeed moving, piece of writing—for behind the obvious literary skill of the narrative is revealed a deeply divided personality: a man who, despite all the outward appearance of material happiness and success, was haunted by a vision of loveliness which continually eluded him.

After the publication of **"The Door in the Wall"** in 1906 Wells's output of short stories virtually ceased: during the remaining 40 years of his life he wrote nine stories (the last to be written, **"Answer to Prayer"**, dates from 1937). Already by the time *The Country of the Blind and Other Stories* was published Wells had realised that

> I was once an industrious writer of short stories, and that I am no longer anything of the kind. . . . I find it a little difficult to disentangle the causes that have restricted the flow of these inventions. It has happened, I remark, to others as well as to myself, and in spite of the kindliest encouragement to continue from editors and readers. There was a time when life bubbled with short stories; they were always coming to the surface of my mind, and it is no deliberate change of will that has thus restricted my production. It is rather, I think, a diversion of attention to more sustained and more exacting forms.

As a short story writer Wells has been described as 'the product of a union between Dickens and Poe'. Certainly it is possible to detect the influence of both these writers upon his work, as also the influence of Kipling, Barrie and Gissing. Wells would have been the first to acknowledge his indebtedness to other writers, and as a novelist he made no secret of his lifelong admiration for Charles Dickens and Laurence Sterne. But in the last analysis his stories have a distinctive quality which gives them a flavour peculiar to himself: it lies in their ability to stimulate thought, to suggest new possibilities of action, to unfold novel horizons of human endeavour. Each story, he insisted, 'is intended to be a thing by itself; and if it is not too ungrateful to kindly and enterprising publishers, I would confess I would much prefer to see each printed expensively alone, and left in a little brown-paper cover to lie about a room against the needs of a quite casual curiosity'. Any reader browsing through these stories in such a mood of curiosity would find a range diverse enough to suit his every mood. He would smile at the comic observation of **"The Truth About Pyecraft"** or **"The Jilting of Jane"**, be enthralled by the horror of **"The Empire of the Ants"** or **"The

Sea Raiders", be diverted by the tension of **"A Slip Under the Microscope"** or **"Under the Knife".** Above all he (or she) would find release from the limitations of the everyday world in the immense fertility of Wells's imagination.

The short stories, for all their manifold diversity, have one overriding factor in common: that they are *disturbing.* In their capacity to stimulate and inspire, to suggest unsuspected possibilities of both terror and happiness, to illuminate a thousand dark corners of human ignorance, lies their greatest strength. The stories will 'live' because they bear witness to man's limitless curiosity and sense of wonder. (pp. 73-6)

> *J. R. Hammond, in his* An H. G. Wells Companion: A Guide to the Novels, Romances and Short Stories, *Macmillan Press Ltd., 1979, 288 p.*

DARKO SUVIN (essay date 1979)

[*A Yugoslavian literary critic, Suvin has edited and contributed to numerous studies of short fiction. In the following excerpt, he assesses "The Crystal Egg," "The Remarkable Case of Davidson's Eyes," and "The New Accelerator," concluding that Wells's contribution to the development of science fiction was crucial.*]

H. G. Wells's first and most significant SF cycle (roughly to 1904) is based on the vision of a horrible novum as the evolutionary sociobiological prospect for mankind. His basic situation is that of a destructive newness encroaching upon the tranquillity of the Victorian environment. Often this is managed as a contrast between an outer framework and a story within the story. The framework is set in surroundings as staid and familiarly Dickensian as possible, such as the cozy study of *The Time Machine,* the old antiquity shop of **"The Crystal Egg,"** or the small towns and villages of southern England in *The War of the Worlds* and *The First Men in the Moon.* With the exception of the protagonist, who also participates in the inner story, the characters in the outer frame, representing the almost invincible inertia and banality of prosperous bourgeois England, are reluctant to credit the strange newness. By contrast, the inner story details the observation of the gradual, hesitant coming to grips with an alien superindividual force that menaces such life and its certainties by behaving exactly as the bourgeois progress did in world history—as a quite ruthless but technologically superior mode of life. This Wellsian inversion exploits the uneasy conscience of an imperial civilization that did not wipe out only the bison and the dodo: "The Tasmanians, in spite of their human likeness, were entirely swept out of existence in a war of extermination waged by European immigrants. Are we such apostles of mercy as to complain if the Martians warred in the same spirit?" (p. 208)

As Wells observed, the "fantastic element" or novum is "the strange property or the strange world." The strange property can be the invention that renders Griffin invisible, or, obversely, a new way of seeing—literally, as in **"The Crystal Egg," "The Remarkable Case of Davidson's Eyes,"** and **"The New Accelerator,"** or indirectly, as the Time Machine or the Cavorite sphere. It is always cloaked in a pseudo-scientific explanation, the possibility of which turns out, upon closer inspection, to be no more than a conjuring trick by the deft writer, with "precision in the unessential and vagueness in the essential"—the best example being the Time Machine itself. The strange world is elsewhen or elsewhere. It is reached by means of a strange invention or it irrupts directly into the

Victorian world in the guise of the invading Martians or the Invisible Man. But even when Wells's own bourgeois world is not so explicitly assaulted, the strange novelty always reflects back on its illusions; an SF story by Wells is intended to be "the valid realization of some disregarded possibility in such a way as to comment on the false securities and fatuous self-satisfaction of everyday life."

The strange is menacing because it looms in the future of man. Wells masterfully translates some of man's oldest terrors—the fear of darkness, monstrous beasts, giants and ogres, creepy crawly insects, and Things outside the light of his campfire, outside tamed nature—into an evolutionary perspective that is supposed to be validated by Darwinian biology, evolutionary cosmology, and the fin-de-siècle sense of a historical epoch ending. (pp. 208-09)

Wells remains the central writer in the tradition of SF. His ideological impasses are fought out as memorable and rich contradictions tied to an inexorably developing future. He collected, as it were, all the main influences of earlier writers—from Lucian and Swift to Kepler, Verne, and Flammarion, from Plato and Morris to Mary Shelley, Poe, Bulwer, and the subliterature of planetary and subterranean voyages, future wars, and the like—and transformed them in his own image, whence they entered the treasury of subsequent SF. He invented a new thing under the sun in the time-travel story made plausible or verisimilar by physics. He codified, for better or worse, the notions of invasion from space and cosmic catastrophe (as in his story **"The Star"** . . .), of social and biological degeneration, of fourth dimension, of future megalopolis, of biological plasticity. Together with Verne's *roman scientifique,* Wells's "scientific romances" and short stories became the privileged form in which SF was admitted into an official culture that rejected socialist utopianism. True, of his twenty-odd books that can be considered SF, only perhaps eight or nine are still of living interest, but those contain unforgettable visions (all in the five "romances" and the short stories of the early sociobiological-cum-cosmic cycle): the solar eclipse at the end of time, the faded flowers from the future, the invincible obtuseness of southern England and the Country of the Blind confronted with the New, the Saying of the Law on Moreau's island, the wildfire spread of the red Martian weed and invasion panic toward London, the last Martian's lugubrious ululations in Regent's Park, the frozen world of **"The New Accelerator,"** the springing to life of the Moon vegetation, the lunar society. These summits of Wells's are a demonstration of what is possible in SF, of the cognitive shudder peculiar to it. Their poetry is based on a shocking transmutation of scientific into aesthetic cognition, and poets from Eliot to Borges have paid tribute to it. More harrowing than in the socialist utopians, more sustained than in Twain, embracing a whole dimension of radical doubt and questioning that makes Verne look bland, it is a grim caricature of bestial bondage and an explosive liberation achieved by means of knowledge. Wells was the first significant writer who started to write SF from within the world of science, and not merely facing it. Though his catastrophes are a retraction of Bellamy's and Morris's utopian optimism, even in the spatial disguises of a parallel present on Moreau's island or in southern England it is always a possible future evolving from the neglected horrors of today that is analyzed in its (as a rule) maleficent consequences, and his hero has "an epic and public . . . mission" intimately bound up with "the major cognitive challenge of the Darwinist age." For all his vacillations, Wells's basic historical lesson is that the stifling bourgeois society is but a short moment in an impredictable, menacing, but at least theoretically open-ended human evolution under the stars. He endowed later SF with a basically materialist look back at human life and a rebelliousness against its entropic closure. (pp. 219-21)

> Darko Suvin, *"Wells As the Turning Point of the SF Tradition," in his* Metamorphoses of Science Fiction: On the Poetics and History of a Literary Genre, *Yale University Press, 1979, pp. 208-21.*

JOHN HUNTINGTON (essay date 1981)

[*Huntington is an American critic and educator who has written studies of modern science fiction. In the following excerpt, he illuminates Wells's intricate perceptions of mankind, admiring the author's numerous, multifaceted approaches to resolving the problems of incongruous civilizations sharing the same space.*]

The co-existence of opposites is a fundamental structural element in all of Wells's early fiction. When at the beginning of *The Time Machine* he develops a theory of four dimensions that will allow for time travel, he is doing more than merely justifying the "science" of the story, he is invoking a structure that allows our world and the world of 802,701 to share the same space. That this "two-world" structure is important to Wells's imagination is shown by the comparatively large number of stories in which he develops no plot or moral, but in which he takes considerable pains simply to establish a juxtaposition of two incongruous worlds.

In a story like **"The Remarkable Case of Davidson's Eyes,"** Wells seems to have no other aim than to work out the ways the two worlds fit and don't fit. Davidson, an acquaintance of the narrator, is working in a laboratory with electromagnets when lightning strikes close by and suddenly he sees, instead of a laboratory in London late on a stormy afternoon, a semi-arid south-sea island early in the morning. Since his body resides in London, Davidson has a difficult time getting around, for what he sees has no relation to the physical world he actually inhabits. The story spends some time working out oppositions—it's day there when it's night here; at times he thinks he is going underground and gets claustrophobia; at other times he thinks he's suspended in mid air and gets vertigo. At the end of the story evidence is produced which strongly suggests that Davidson was not hallucinating but was seeing an actual antipodal island. Neither of the opposite worlds is of any particular interest: that is, nothing of narrative consequence is happening in London, and the island is drab—its filthy penguins could hardly interest even an ornithologist. There is no mystery to be solved, no plot to be worked out in either world. Davidson does not want to escape London, and the island is no paradise. Clearly the fascination of the story, for author and for reader, lies in the juxtaposition itself, the superimposition of one world on the other. Wells's imaginative energy has gone to bringing together two discrepant worlds.

A number of early tales work out variations on the two-world system that **"Davidson's Eyes"** gives us in a pure form. **"The Crystal Egg,"** though it hints at plots tangential to the central structure—Mr Cave's home life is very unhappy and the customers who want to buy the crystal egg have an air of intriguing mystery—is at its core exactly like **"Davidson's Eyes."** The crystal egg is the device, like the twist to Davidson's sight, that links drab London and a strange (in this case Martian) landscape. Nothing derives from the opposition; the juxtaposition is an end in itself and sufficient. **"The Plattner Story"** ornaments the two-world structure further by raising the issue of fraud (is Plattner merely perpetrating a hoax?), by making the other world a world of the dead, and, towards the end, by giving us a vignette of a dying husband and his greedy wife. But nothing develops from these suggestions of plot, and ultimately they are secondary to the central dichotomy of the two worlds and the odd links between them. **"Under the Knife"** similarly juxtaposes a living and a dead world, and again there is no consequence. The opposition is itself the pleasure.

What we have in these stories, then, is an imaginative structure that is central to Wells's art. We can see it in increasingly disguised form in many of his other stories and novels, and we can see how by a series of fairly simple transformations a number of other oppositions in Wells's early fiction derive from this basic two-world structure. Before we do that, however, we should consider what it is that makes this elemental structure important and distinctive. First, the structure itself is free from moral suggestions: the oppositions it sets up are purely physical and we cannot apply to them the moral terminology of good and bad. Thus, it is not a matter of showing that one world is to be preferred to the other. Second, the principle behind the opposition is narrative. The point of such stories is not to describe a change, but to set up a static antithesis and then to fill in the relation between the two elements. Third, in such a structure neither world in itself holds our interest; what is important is the two of them together and the linked opposition they establish. Wells himself draws our attention to these aspects of the two-world structure near the end of **"The Plattner Story"** when he has the narrator point to the absence of plot. In part this is a conventional device for asserting the "truth" of the story, but then the narrator adds that the real value of the story lies not in its truth so much as in a particular sensation that the bare opposition of the two worlds generates:

> But quite apart from the objectionableness of falsifying a most extraordinary true story, any such trite devices [of conventional plot] would spoil, to my mind, the peculiar effect of this dark world, with its livid green illumination and its drifting Watchers of the Living, which, unseen and unapproachable to us, is yet lying all about us.

We should note that the "peculiar effect" derives in part from the "greenness" of the other world, but that greenness is essentially interesting for being so near the ordinary light of our own world and yet unperceived. While the two-world structure lends itself to a number of possible developments, its main function is the pleasure it itself provides. (pp. 240-41)

In **"The Flowering of the Strange Orchid"** we can see . . . abstract and static oppositions translated into meaningful plot. Wells is here working on the problem, which Huxley also perceived, of civilization's developing into a decadent oversensitivity. The opposition set up at the beginning of the story is between the hot-house civilization of Mr Winter-Wedderburn, a collector of orchids to whom "nothing ever happens," and the primitive, violent, natural world of the Andaman Islands where the orchid collector, Batten, died. Wedderburn's world is comically tame. When he has a premonition "that something is going to happen to me to-day" he means he may buy a new type of orchid. His housekeeper, even more cautious than Wedderburn, finds all ideas of "something happening" threatening, "for 'something happening' was a euphemism that meant only one thing to her." The orchid is the link that allows Wedderburn to meditate on the opposite sort of life, that of Batten: "That orchid-collector was only thirty-six—twenty years younger than myself—when he died. And he had been married twice and divorced once; he had had malarial fever four times, and once broke his thigh. He killed a Malay once, and once he was wounded by a poisoned dart. And in the end he was killed by jungle leeches. It must have all been very troublesome, but then it must have been very interesting, you know—except, perhaps, the leeches." The housekeeper can only respond as she has before that she is "sure it was not good for him." This opposition between a passionate, active, but deadly life in the antipodal jungle and a quiet, secure, but dull life in London is a form of the two-world structure with which we are familiar.

But in this story there is a plot: an orchid Wedderburn buys turns out to be a beautiful but murderous blood-sucker that almost kills Wedderburn as it has previously killed Batten. Wedderburn is saved by his housekeeper, who smashes the greenhouse and destroys the plant. The plot of the story performs a set of inversions on the original opposition. Wedderburn becomes, in effect, Batten. The housekeeper's worst fears about the meaning of "something happening" prove true. The calm of the London suburb is broken by the smashing of the greenhouse. The world is so transformed that even the odd-job man, hearing the glass breaking and seeing the housekeeper with bloody hands hauling out the body, "thought impossible things." Adventure, violence, and passion have momentarily become possibilities again. Though in terms of degree the passion and energy of the end is trivial compared to Batten's, because the "cut" has been crossed that separates Wedderburn's world of complacent non-action from Batten's world of risk and adventure, we can see Wedderburn's passion and the housekeeper's violence as *like* Batten's and as a balanced opposition to Wedderburn's earlier domestic quiet. And it seems to be the story's purpose to perform this reversal and restoration, to link the two worlds which in a story like **"Davidson's Eyes"** remain in static opposition.

"The Flowering of the Strange Orchid" in its light way asks questions about protective moral civilization and its separation from predatory nature. It would be a mistake, however, to read the story as simply an exultation of the primitive over the civilized. The balance we see elsewhere in Wells is skillfully achieved here. The antithesis between the two worlds is mediated by the orchid which is both an image of a decadent and listless civilization and a creature of predatory and dangerous nature. When Wedderburn is overpowered by the orchid's scent, the contradictory elements come together; the language of pure nature is the same as that of an almost rococo decadence:

> And, behold! the trailing green spikes bore now three great splashes of blossom, from which this overpowering sweetness proceeded. He stopped before them in an ecstasy of admiration.

> The flowers were white, with streaks of golden orange upon the petals, the heavy labellum was coiled into an intricate projection, and a wonderful bluish purple mingled there with the gold. He could see at once that the genus was altogether a new one. And the insufferable scent! How hot the place was! The blossoms swam before his eyes.

At this moment aesthetic civilization ("ecstasy of admiration," "wonderful bluish purple,") and the jungle overlap. And once the orchid has transformed the civilized hot-house into a murderous tropical jungle, the housekeeper restores civilization by smashing the windows and letting in "the cold outer air." This is an exact inversion of her earlier role, for before she had insisted that Wedderburn carry an umbrella even though the weather was clear. She enforced caution and protection from nature; now she acts rashly and violently to let that nature in. What should be observed here is that the antithesis has gone full circle, that her act of passionate violence, so directly opposed to the world she enforces at the beginning, restores that world. The oppositions of the story maintain a constant and balanced reciprocity, and the one cannot exist without the other.

While **"The Flowering of the Strange Orchid"** plays symbolically with how a decadent civilization incorporates violent nature, that violence civilization controls is the explicit subject of the first story of Wells's first collection of stories. The central conflict of the **"The Stolen Bacillus"** is between an anarchist who steals a test tube of cholera bacteria with the intention of poisoning London's public water supply and a bacteriologist who at the beginning shows the anarchist the test tube and later pursues him to prevent his crime. This elegantly simple story is useful to us at this point for two reasons: it is an example of a story that has the potentiality for making a serious moral about order's conquest of disorder but declines to do so, and it is an example of the way Wells can introduce considerable complexity into a story by the simple device of setting up a dichotomy within one of the terms of the initial basic opposition. The two sources of our interest are related, for it is the complexity of the pattern Wells creates out of his simple elements that prevents a unified and reductive moral theme from asserting itself.

The central opposition between the anarchist and the bacteriologist develops ironies that undercut its potential moral simplicity. The end of the story inverts and trivializes the beginning: at the start we see the anarchist as a weak, incompetent, unscientific man, but his seeming harmlessness reveals itself to be deadly. At the end of the story the anarchist's deadly threat proves to be harmless, and his vision of planned destruction is foiled by an accident: the anarchist, the figure of disorder and imbalance, breaks the test tube while trying to maintain his balance in a lurching cab. Finally, by drinking what he thinks is cholera but which is really only a bacterium that will stain him blue, the anarchist fulfills the bacteriologist's wish at the beginning of the story: "I wish, for my own part, we could kill and stain every one of them [i.e., living cholera bacilli] in the universe." The anarchist, a kind of moral cholera, has been stained and has been rendered trivial.

If Wells has treated the moral opposition represented by the scientist and the anarchist ironically and comically, in a subplot he creates an even more telling reversal. At the moment when the bacteriologist discovers the test tube is missing and anarchy most threatens, instead of focusing on the moral issue, the story turns to comedy: the bacteriologist's wife, Minnie, offended at the sight of her husband "running about London—in the height of the season too—in his socks," grabs his street clothes and joins the chase. Just as the scientist does his duty by chasing the anarchist, she does hers by chasing "her vagrant husband." As the scientist tries to save civilization from physical catastrophe, his wife tries to save it from a more trivial disaster by enforcing a set of clothing conventions. Minnie sees her husband as an agent of disorder: " 'He has gone *mad*!' said Minnie; 'it's that horrid science of his.' " At the end of the story the conquest is Minnie's; she restores a civilized order, but one devoid of moral or physical function. She insists her husband dress properly, and in the story's closing lines he replies, "Put on my coat on this hot day! Why? Because we might meet Mrs. Jabber. My dear, Mrs. Jabber is not a draught. But why should I wear a coat on a hot day because of Mrs.—? Oh! *very* well." The opposition between civilization and anarchy as represented by the scientist and the anarchist is undermined by the presence of Minnie. She becomes a pole in a second opposition within the term civilization which repeats the major opposition of the story but reverses its values, for here our sympathies are on the side of the "disorder" represented by the bacteriologist against the petty and conventional order represented by Minnie. It is this deadening order's victory that more than anything else undercuts the sense of melodramatic triumph we might otherwise expect to feel at the story's end.

The scientist is the enigmatic center of the story's oppositions, a middle term linking comedy and melodrama, symbol and function. His cry, "Blue ruin!" at the moment he discovers the theft of the test tube coyly reveals that he already knows that civilization is not at stake, that what appears to be catastrophe is really trivial. His own moral status is also a problem, for if he is the agent who will rescue civilization, he is also the creator of the bacillus; and it is an irony not to be overlooked that it is not the anarchist but the scientist who fully imagines the reign of death the cholera might bring. In the final balance the anarchist is as trivial as Minnie: though he tries to be the agent of death, he is powerless without "horrid science's" techniques and imaginings, and his motive is not a vision of justice, but of fame. Like Minnie, he cares, in his own way, about what Mrs Jabber says. The scientist's middle position between these two "threats" to meaningful civilization is given as a visual emblem in the cab chase— Minnie chasing her husband chasing the anarchist. The scientist is pursued and pursuer, the salvation of civilization and the participant in a series of comic misconstructions. And the cabmen, as they cheer the chase on, reiterate this ambiguity by converting a serious, functional activity (catching an anarchist) into a symbolic game (a horse race). Thus, at every level, the story raises serious problems but insists that they be the subject of *play* rather than of resolution.

"The Flowering of the Strange Orchid" and **"The Stolen Bacillus"** reveal a common symmetrical opposition: anarchy is transformed into harmless order; harmless order is transformed into a kind of natural anarchy. The fact that both stories end up with a restoration of order, though it may seem to display commitment on Wells's part to civilization itself, actually does nothing of the sort. In both cases the restoration of order is deeply ironic and a further operation of the principle of opposition. In **"The Stolen Bacillus"** the anarchist's vision of success is upset by the accidental breaking of the test tube, and the threat of chaos becomes a threat of nonsensical order. In **"The Flowering of the Strange Orchid,"** after the placid, cautious life of Wedderburn and his housekeeper has been upset by the murderous orchid, order is restored by an act of violence. In both cases what we might see merely as a restoration of order is really an inversion of the activities of the first part of the story. This symmetry is important for our understanding of Wells's method in these stories, for it disqualifies a dependence on any kind of simple moral message. Neither the disruption nor the order can be seen as good in

itself, but each is expressive only insofar as it is part of a system that contains its complementary opposite. Both stories, though simple, give us structures that force us to acknowledge a civilized and an uncivilized element and to stay alert to the tension between them.

Just as each story sets up a symmetrical opposition within itself, the two stories together form a complementary pair. In both stories one aspect of civilization is represented by women who take care to see that their men are well-clothed, and in both stories there is a discontinuity between the weather and the apparel: "Mrs. Jabber is not a draught"; the sky is clear but Wedderburn's housekeeper insists he take his umbrella. But clothes represent different things in the two women's minds. In **"The Stolen Bacillus"** clothes are important as symbols of social convention and have no physical function. The housekeeper in **"The Flowering of the Strange Orchid"** is not at all concerned with social convention; for her clothing is a protection against any physical contingency. If Minnie is the defender of an overly symbolic civilization, the housekeeper stands for an overly protective one. The common imagery expresses contradictory excesses; civilization can be studied from many angles, and we understand an essential quality of Wells's method if we see that his images have a real logical function. They are not symbols whose meanings come from outside and persist from work to work. Each work develops its own inner logic.

The simple structure of opposition that shapes these two stories can be further complicated by very simple means. We have seen how by setting up a "subordinate opposition" in **"The Stolen Bacillus"** Wells severely modifies the already ironic primary opposition in the story. On the model of the sentence, we can think of such a structure as a "complex opposition." The other elementary structural complication available is, on the same model, the "compound opposition" in which two oppositions are set up without subordination, in tandem, and connected by the narrative equivalent of *and*. **"The Lord of the Dynamos"** illustrates this structure of opposition in its purest form.

The opening opposition of **"The Lord of the Dynamos"** is between chauvinistic, technological civilization and superstitious primitivism. The former is embodied in Holroyd, the chief attendant of the dynamo, a complacent bigot, a thorough materialist, and an ardent imperialist. "He doubted the existence of the Deity but accepted Carnot's cycle, and he had read Shakespeare and found him weak in chemistry." The latter is embodied in Azuma-zi, Holroyd's native assistant, whom he persecutes cruelly and whom he instructs in the worship of the "Lord" of the Dynamo. Though the difference between the two figures is striking, they also have a large area of similarity. Holroyd's materialism is as much an irrational worship as Azuma-zi's spiritualization of technology. Like the orchid in **"The Flowering of the Strange Orchid,"** the dynamo itself participates in civilized and primitive visions; as both a technological marvel and a source of pure, raw power it links Holroyd's skeptical materialism and Azuma-zi's religion. As in the other tales we have looked at, the stark basic opposition is founded on an identity.

In the first half of the story Azuma-zi resolves the opposition by electrocuting Holroyd as a sacrifice to the dynamo. We can see here a similarity to **"The Stolen Bacillus"**: Azuma-zi is like the anarchist, and Holroyd represents loosely the civilization he threatens. There are important differences between the two stories, however. **"The Lord of the Dynamos"** has little of the comic trivialization that prevents us from treating **"The Stolen Bacillus"** as a moral parable. Also, in **"The Lord of the Dynamos"** the values of the main opposition have been inverted: whereas we could not sympathize with the anarchist, we side with Azuma-zi. And fittingly Azuma-zi succeeds in his "crime" whereas the anarchist failed. But **"The Lord of the Dynamos"** is not simply a tale of third-world vengeance; Wells balances the implicit attack on imperialist civilization with a second opposition: after the successful murder of Holroyd, the event is re-enacted with a new figure, the "scientific manager," in Holroyd's place. This second murder attempt fails. Then Azuma-zi, like the anarchist in **"The Stolen Bacillus,"** tries to commit suicide by turning the tool of the intended murder on himself, and he succeeds. In this second unit of the story a reversal of values has taken place: the scientific manager, though hardly a vivid figure, is noticeably unlike Holroyd, and Azuma-zi's attempt to murder this innocuous man loses its justification. If in the first part of the story Azuma-zi is seen mainly as an innocent sufferer, a victim of white, technological imperialism, and his violence as a kind of heroic justice, in the second part his homicidal urge has lost the personal dimension and the aspect of justice and has become a generalized murderousness in the name of superstition. Azuma-zi in this second version is simply a native run amok. Thus the revolutionary implications of the first half of the story are neatly balanced by a conservative version.

The coda of the story plays on this balance. Azuma-zi's suicide is, in its way, a primitive heroic act that recalls the just nihilism of the first half of the story, but then the scientific manager restores civilization by recircuiting the current and getting the trains running again. Finally the narrator combines the two treatments of Azuma-zi's violence in the closing lines of the story: "So ended prematurely the worship of the Dynamo Deity, perhaps the most short-lived of all religions. Yet withal it could at least boast a Martyrdom and a Human sacrifice." These lines are doubly ironic. Azuma-zi's superstition and Holroyd's materialism are both parodied in the comparison to religion, but they are also elevated, and the primitive natural forces that civilization in the form of the scientific manager generally ignores are acknowledged even as they are mocked. We might also note that the link between Holroyd and Azuma-zi is again made strong here, for either one can fulfill either role, martyr or sacrifice.

The opposition between civilization and nature in these tales is not there to be settled; it is a perpetual tension inherent in the human condition. We can understand how the imperative of the dilemma could drive Wells to seek and discover new forms of mediation and thereby begin to write not just parables of civilization, but stories alert to new possibilities. **"The Flying Man"** is, in its way, an evolutionary link between the conventional short story and what would become Wellsian SF, for in it a mediation is discovered which works elegantly to bridge the story's opposition but which makes no claim, either explicitly or allegorically, to any solution outside the story itself. We have here the logical structure of Wells's great SF without the explicit meanings that make other longer works so important to Wells's thought about the future.

"The Flying Man" explores a two-world structure. Initially the opposition is expressed by the location of two settlements: the English camp is downstream and the Chin village is upstream in the wilderness. The English expedition's task is to go from one to the other and back. Since there is no road, to get to the Chin village the expedition must use the river:

> When we went up we had to wade in the river for a mile where the valley narrows, with a smart stream frothing round our knees and the stones as slippery as ice. There it was I dropped my rifle. Afterwards the Sappers blasted the cliff with dynamite and made the convenient way you came by. Then below, where those very high cliffs come, we had to keep on dodging across the river—I should say we crossed it a dozen times in a couple of miles.

The allegory here is clear: the Lieutenant narrator relinquishes an important symbol of British power, enters a world "slippery as ice," and is forced to dodge his way forward. The loss of the rifle is just the first movement away from civilized forms towards some more elemental, savage, natural being. When the expedition reaches the village it is attacked by the Chin and loses the mule that carries provisions and utensils. And as the English are deprived of their civilized tools, the Chin seem to gain them: they have guns, albeit not rifles, and the Lieutenant describes them not as figures of nature, but in terms of civilization: "We became aware of a number of gentlemen carrying matchlocks, and dressed in things like plaid dusters." Thus, what at first looked to be a somewhat unbalanced horizontal opposition between technological civilization and primitive nature gradually becomes a balanced vertical opposition. The expedition gets trapped on a high ledge, while down below runs the river patrolled by the Chin. The ledge is completely safe but lacks water and offers no way out. The river is dangerous, but is life-giving and a route back to camp. The Lieutenant resolves the dilemma by improvising a parachute and leaping from one world to the other and escaping.

The act of flying is the central unifying gesture in the story. In flying the Lieutenant finally moves from the English world to that of the Chin, both by bridging the physical gap, and, importantly, by unintentionally committing an act of elemental savagery:

> Then I looked down and saw in the darkness the river and the dead Sepoy rushing up towards me. But in the indistinct light I also saw three Chins, seemingly aghast at the sight of me, and that the Sepoy was decapitated. At that I wanted to go back again.

> Then my boot was in the mouth of one, and in a moment he and I were in a heap with the canvas fluttering down on the top of us. I fancy I dashed out his brains with my foot. I expected nothing more than to be brained myself by the other two, but the poor heathen had never heard of Baldwin, and incontinently bolted.

Just as the Chin have decapitated the Sepoy, the Lieutenant dashes out the brains of a Chin. Under the fluttering canvas the union of Englishman and native is complete, and when the Lieutenant arrives at the English camp to summon help he is mistaken for a Chin by the sentinel who fires on him. If flying, becoming "the gay lieutenant bird," means in part becoming a savage again, it also means transcending the human altogether by an act whose suicidal potential is strongly underlined in the story. Before he thinks of parachuting the Lieutenant contemplates simply jumping off the cliff: "It seemed a pleasant and desirable thing to go rushing down through the air with something to drink—or no more thirst at any rate—at the bottom." After he parachutes, two of the Sepoy jump, and it is unclear whether they intended suicide or hoped to fly. As in Greek myth, the Daedalian triumph entails Icarian tragedy. In giving over civilization (suicide) and entering nature (becoming a bird) the Lieutenant becomes one with the natives below and also becomes a myth.

The act of radical mediation, it should be noted, is then rejected, but not before it has transformed the world. The Lieutenant does not accompany the rescue squad: "I had too good a thirst to provoke it by going with them." The story closes with him reaffirming his bond with British civilization by drinking whiskey and soda. But the ethnologist, to whom the Lieutenant narrates the tale, complains that the Lieutenant's act has permanently upset the purity of the opposition he has come to study: "Here am I, come four hundred miles out of my way to get what is left of the folk-lore of these people, before they are utterly demoralised by missionaries and the military, and all I find are a lot of impossible legends about a sandy-haired scrub of an infantry lieutenant."

"The Flying Man" uses a familar structure of opposition. By the act of radical mediation, by focusing on the "cut," or midway point between opposites however, it goes beyond the other stories we have looked at and opens the way for thought about the connections and disjunctions within the universe of opposition. The imaginative exercise does not solve the puzzle of the relation of civilization to nature. It brings the opposites close together: it discovers an image in which the opposition is an identity. Such a story in its elegant and simple way is a model for Wells's more intricate meditations on the problems of civilization. (pp. 246-53)

> *John Huntington, "Thinking by Opposition: The 'Two World' Structure in H. G. Wells's Short Fiction," in* Science-Fiction Studies, *Vol. 8, No. 25, November, 1981, pp. 240-54.*

FRANK McCONNELL   (essay date 1981)

[*McConnell is an American literary and film critic. In the following excerpt, he examines major political influences on and tendencies within Wells's science fiction stories.*]

[Wells] was by both class and temperament a revolutionary soul. He was also a true nineteenth-century ideologue, at least to the extent of insisting on "finished ideas" as the only possible basis for social action or social planning. But he was also—as Lenin is reported to have called him—a petty bourgeois. He mistrusted the brute force and inarticulate aspirations of the laboring class—that "mass man" whose existence Marx had discovered and whose destiny he had hymned as world dominion. He mistrusted the figure of the bomb-toting, metaphysically inclined terrorist (or "anarchist" or "nihilist," to use the age's catchphrases), the man willing to commit the unspeakable for the sake of a theory. And, perhaps most of all, he mistrusted theory itself. A voracious assimilator of systems and abstractions, he was nevertheless skeptical of any system whose complexity appeared to overweigh its application to the observable and observed facts of the life around us. This pragmatism, or empiricism, has been often described as a particularly "English" as opposed to Continental trait of mind; or it may also be explained as the special genius for observation of the novelist, as opposed to the social scientist or philosopher. At any rate, it is one of the hallmarks of Wells's distinctive vision of social possibilites, and of the chance for utopia. From the beginning, he believed in the ne-

cessity and the reality of social change, or revolution. But to the end, he wanted his revolution to be both rational and sensible, both total and civilized.

It can be argued that Wells expressed his fears of revolutionaries most fully in his fiction of the 1890s, and his hopes for revolution most fully in his fiction of the Edwardian years and afterward. Just as the Eloi of *The Time Machine* are partly a vision of the aesthetes and decadents of the literary and artistic world, the cannibalistic Morlocks who prey upon the Eloi are a much more explicit projection of the proletariat, the "mass man" whose emergence Wells feared. His dislike and suspicion of the dedicated "scientific" anarchist are the basis of one of his early short stories, **"The Stolen Bacillus."** . . . And his suspicion of abstraction, of theory without humanity, may fairly be said to run through all his early fiction. Griffin, the anti-hero of *The Invisible Man,* and Dr. Moreau of *The Island of Doctor Moreau* are both ferociously intelligent men—the former a physicist, the latter a biologist—who erect upon their scientific discoveries plans for a new world empire, a new order of things, only to find their structures collapse on them in a suicidal rubble. In *The War of the Worlds* and *The First Men in the Moon* Wells shows us alternate societies—the octopuslike Martians and the insectlike Selenites—that have been built upon an absolutely efficient, rational collectivism, and which are equally anti-human (there is an important anticipation of both these books in his 1896 story, **"In the Abyss"**).

It is **"The Stolen Bacillus,"** though, that best catches his attitude toward social revolution. This very short story tells how a pale-faced anarchist steals a phial containing what he thinks is a deadly concentration of cholera bacteria. He intends to empty it into the London water system. But the phial breaks in the cab in which he is making his escape; undaunted, the anarchist greedily swallows the few drops of liquid in the bottom of the phial and charges off amidst the busy London crowds, himself now a living instrument of death and contagion, shouting "Vive l'Anarchie!" Only then do we learn that the phial did not really contain cholera bacteria, but rather a dose of a new compound whose only effect is to turn its recipient bright blue.

What began as a tale of terror ends as a joke: but a joke with a serious point. Men and women really did dread anarchy, and particularly the threat presented by the figure of the anarchist, that outwardly normal, rational man who might, unsuspected, be harboring thoughts and plans of the most unspeakable violence and hatred. If revolution, even in its maddest aspects, could now be "rational"—i.e., philosophically planned and supported—then it was, to all intents and purposes, invisible. Wells's invention of the Invisible Man had been an early, very resonant expression of this fear: the invisible minister of apocalypse, the hyperintelligent terrorist, part of whose terror is that you can't see him. Joseph Conrad, in his novel of 1907, *The Secret Agent,* and G. K. Chesterton in his novel of 1908, *The Man Who Was Thursday,* would both treat the theme of anarchy in ways perhaps suggested by *The Invisible Man:* in terms, that is, of its fundamentally frightening aspects of normality, its terrible quality of being unrecognizable until it is too late.

"The Stolen Bacillus" is a reassuring version of the same situation. The anarchist, for all his dedication and care, has made a stupid blunder; a blunder, moreover, that henceforth will render him immediately, unequivocally recognizable. He will be bright blue, an all too visible man.

We can see the difference between *The Invisible Man* and "The Stolen Bacillus" as part of the difference between the despairing and the optimistic halves of Wells's sensibility. But "The Stolen Bacillus" is also reassuring because it insists that anarchists and their like are not to be feared: their own excessive hatreds will lead them into comically excessive postures of impotent violence. But, the story insists, they will be led into these absurdities because of the workings of a slower, surer, and ultimately more total revolution, the revolution of scientific thought, which is changing the world daily by making the animosities and class hatreds of the past irrelevant. The scientist who prepares the "blue" solution does not know he is thwarting anarchy. But he is, and the single-minded blindness of his research is revealed to be also the wisdom of history (Hegelian theme), its comic judgment upon the impulse to mass murder.

Wells, then, heir to a century of metaphysical and social revolutionaries, was impelled to a version of revolution much quieter, much more explicitly middle class, than many which were abroad in his time. This can be thought of as a very *English* taste in revolution, though Wells was tumultuous enough in his personal life and far-ranging enough in his social vision to alienate or scandalize the more conservative of his revolutionary English friends. (pp. 47-9)

> *Frank McConnell, in his* The Science Fiction of
> H. G. Wells, *Oxford University Press, 1981, 235 p.*

JOHN HUNTINGTON   (essay date 1982)

[*In the following excerpt from his* The Logic of Fantasy: H. G. Wells and Science Fiction, *Huntington discusses Wells's sensitivity in "The Country of the Blind" to inherent conflicts between an exceptional individual and a rigidly structured society.*]

In **"The Country of the Blind"** Wells explores the contradictions posed by the exceptional individual in society. Like **"Æpyornis Island,"** this story defines the problem in terms of unmediated oppositions. Nunez, a mountaineer from Bogota, falls into the valley inhabited by a race of humans who have been blind for generations. His first thought is of the adage, "In the country of the blind the one-eyed man is king," and he sets out to claim his throne. He badly misjudges the competence of blind people working together, however, and finally, after almost allowing himself to be blinded so as to be "cured" of the "insanity" of sight, he escapes back into the desolation of the mountains and, perhaps, dies. In the process of the tale Wells explores the promise and the drawbacks of individual superiority and the solace and terror of social cohesiveness.

One set of truths in the story is critical of Nunez and approving of the static civilization of the blind. Why, after all, do the blind need a king at all? They originally came to their valley "fleeing the lust and tyranny of an evil Spanish ruler." What could Nunez offer them that they need? Their valley "had in it all that the heart of man could desire," and they carefully work with nature to achieve something like paradise:

> They led a simple, laborious life, these people with
> all the elements of virtue and happiness, as these
> things can be understood by men. They toiled, but
> not oppressively; they had food and clothing suffi-
> cient for their needs; they had days and seasons of

rest; they made much of music and singing, and there was love among them, and little children. It was marvellous with what confidence and precision they went about their ordered world. Everything, you see, had been made to fit their needs.

Nunez's dream of kingship is a selfish fantasy that both ignores the happiness the blind people enjoy and condescends to the adjustment they have made. In the tradition of European imperialism, he aims to exploit a culture he does not appreciate, and Wells takes a certain pleasure in thwarting him. The blind, working together, unawed by a sense which they cannot comprehend, subdue Nunez and force him to conform to their way to life.

The triumph of blind society over Nunez's individual superiority gives rise to a second theme which directly contradicts the first. The blind paradise becomes totalitarian, and Nunez's arrogance becomes imaginative openness and majesty. The blind rulers are not merely defending their idyll against Nunez's sophistication, they are closed-minded and are unable to conceive of the very possibility of a sense of sight. And precisely because they are "scientific" about the world, because they exercise a sane skepticism and doubt about the ancient folklore that tells of a world outside their own, they trust a firm view, an unshakable paradigm, which leaves no room for the exceptional. The story emphasizes the oppressiveness of such scientific narrowness:

> The story of the outer world was faded and
> changed to a child's story; and they had ceased to
> concern themselves with anything beyond the
> rocky slopes above their circling wall. Blind men of
> genius had arisen among them and questioned the
> shreds of belief and tradition they had brought with
> them from their seeing days, and had dismissed all
> these things as idle fancies and replaced them with
> new and saner explanations. Much of their imagi-
> nation had shrivelled with their eyes, and they had
> made for themselves new imaginations with their
> ever more sensitive ears and finger tips.

The inadequacy of such an empiricism is most graphically displayed for us by the blind people's incomprehension of birds, which they call angels. Their windowless rock houses, which at one level are symbols of the world to which they have successfully adapted and which baffles Nunez, are also symbols of dwarfed thought. When Nunez is contemplating being blinded—an operation the blind propose to make him a worthy husband for Medina-saroté, his beloved—he laments, "I must come under that roof of rock and stone and darkness, that horrible roof under which your imagination stoops." Even Medina-saroté's understanding of Nunez's claim to vision, though by far the most generous to be found among the blind, treats it as a trivial poetic fancy, and she is offended that he insists on it when he might so easily be "sane."

At the end of the tale Nunez reasserts the grandeur of the unfettered imagination. His ability to see the sun gives his experience a quality altogether different from that of the blind. Early in the tale we see the first of his epiphanies:

> Nunez had an eye for all beautiful things, and it
> seemed to him that the glow upon the snow fields
> and glaciers that rose about the valley on every side
> was the most beautiful thing he had ever seen. His
> eyes went from that inaccessible glory to the village
> and irrigated fields, fast sinking into the twilight,
> and suddenly a wave of emotion took him, and he

thanked God from the bottom of his heart that the power of sight had been given him.

Near the end Wells's imagery defines the difference in "scale" between the sighted and blind imaginations:

> He had fully meant to go to a lonely place where the meadows were beautiful with white narcissus, and there remain until the hour of his sacrifice should come, but as he went he lifted up his eyes and saw the morning, the morning like an angel in golden armour, marching down the steeps. . . .

Once again the ability to see the heights as well as the local, domesticated surroundings is a sign of imaginative power, and here, instead of the birdlike angels of the blind, Nunez can imagine a majestic Seraph. Inspired by this power of metaphoric vision, his "imagination soared." He realizes he has a depth of vision that makes the blind world merely a prison:

> He thought how for a day or so one might come down through passes, drawing ever nearer and nearer to its busy streets and ways. He thought of the river journey, day by day, from great Bogota to the still vaster world beyond, through towns and villages, forest and desert places, the rushing river day by day, until its banks receded and the big streamers came splashing by, and one had reached the sea—the limitless sea, with its thousand islands, its thousands of islands, and its ships seen dimly far away in their incessant journeyings round and about that greater world. And there, unpent by mountains, one saw the sky—the sky, not such a disk as one saw it here, but an arch of immeasurable blue, a deep of deeps in which the circling stars were floating. . . .

The expansions of this passage show how Nunez, because he can see, can imagine more than he can see and can thus transcend the closed empiricism that restricts the blind imagination. He exists, thanks to his sight, in a two world system. Though he is in a valley, he can imagine the vast expanse of the sky on the ocean, and in the blue he can imagine "a deep of deeps." In order to be true to this imaginative openness he flees the valley of the blind, and we last see him lying "peacefully contented under the cold stars."

The acuteness of the dilemma **"The Country of the Blind"** poses betrays Wells's sensitiveness to and difficulty with the issue. The alternatives the story offers—the cavelike house of society and the open mountainside of lonely individualism— are antithetical and unmediated. We find here none of the ambiguous structures that in earlier stories and novels allowed the outside and inside to interact. The story acknowledges conflicting imperatives: blind society survives happily by enforcing conformity, but for the sighted (gifted) individual to submit is to deny the integrity of his imagination; society's traditions and scientific expectations are oppressive, but to demand kingly freedoms is selfish and involves a misunderstanding of the adaptive virtues of social organization. Thus, **"The Country of the Blind"** sets up the conflict between the gifted individual and society and treats it from both sides, and yet it offers no possibility of reconcilliation. (pp. 126-29)

> *John Huntington, in his* The Logic of Fantasy: H. G. Wells and Science Fiction, *Columbia University Press, 1982, 191 p.*

WILLIAM J. SCHEICK   (essay date 1984)

[*Scheick is an American educator, author, and editor of* Texas Studies in Language and Literature. *His critical works include* The Will and the Word: The Poetry of Edward Taylor (*1974*) *and* The Slender Human Word: Emerson's Artistry in Prose (*1978*). *In the following excerpt from his* The Splintering Frame: The Later Fiction of H. G. Wells, *Scheick discusses Wells's modification of the conventional Victorian ghost story in* The Croquet Player, *noting the influence of Edgar Allan Poe upon Wells's ghost stories.*]

Similar to his life-long artistic interest in dreams, so maturely managed in *The Autocracy of Mr. Parham,* Wells's fascination with the ghost story surfaced during the earliest phase of his literary career. Then, in fact, Edwardian culture indulged in the genre, perhaps as an unconscious expression of its *fin-de-siècle* fear of insubstantiality. From the first, however, Wells characteristically criticised the practitioners and the conventions of the genre. This is evident in his well-crafted **"The Inexperienced Ghost"** (in *Twelve Stories and a Dream,* 1903) and his review of Sheridan LeFanu's *The Evil Guest* (1895). LeFanu, Wells complained, mastered little more than the method of "piling it on," which manner ultimately dissipated any sense of horror. Moreover, Wells observed, LeFanu, among others, failed to work within the tradition established by Edgar Allan Poe, that "consummate creator of strange effects." Poe figured importantly in Wells's artistic self-awareness during these early years, and Wells readily compared books by Edmund S. Gunn, George MacDonald and several other Scotch novelists to Poe's works. In turn, the earliest reviewers of Wells's romances and short tales consistently referred to similarities to Poe's manner, though in fact to date little of substance has been remarked concerning Poe's influence on Wells. Nor have critics noticed the extent to which interest in Poe was expressed even in the latest phases of Wells's career. In the early Thirties Wells alluded to Poe, as he did in the late Twenties in proposed advertisement copy he personally prepared for *Mr. Blettsworthy on Rampole Island:* "of the fantastic events . . . we can give no conception here. As soon might we summarize a romance by Edgar Allan Poe."

In fact Poe wrote few works which could properly be designated as ghost stories. Doubtless Wells, who also wrote very few ghost stories, admired Poe most for his precise "bearing of structural expedients upon design" and for his mastery of "the necessary trick of commonplace detail which renders horrors convincing." Anticipating his prefatory comments in *Scientific Romances* (1933), pertaining to the best method for writing science fiction, Wells's observation about commonplace detail and convincing horror describes perfectly the stylistic technique of *The Croquet Player* (1936), in which the narrator confesses to a boyhood addiction to Poe's writings.

The Croquet Player is a first person plotless narrative recounting the unnerving experiences and conversations of an upper class young man, who by the end of his account casually dismisses the urgency of the apparently apocalyptic implications of the emergence of various types of malevolence in Cainsmarsh. Georgie Frobisher, the idle narrator of *The Croquet Player,* refers to his tale as "a sort of ghost story," one "much more realistic and haunting and disturbing than any ordinary ghost story." Initially his account appears to conform to a fundamental pattern of the genre: the characters are victims who do not *seem* to deserve the problem which emerges and who experience displacement of their sense of life as rationally ordered by exposure to an agnostic world where explanations are impossible and values are unstable. But Frobisher's authorially-directed qualification "sort of" is critical, for in his narrative the sensationalism for its own sake typical of late Victorian and turn-of-the-century ghost stories like LeFanu's gives way to moral purposes well beyond those evident in the occult novels of, say, Margaret Oliphant and Edward Bulwer-Lytton.

Reminiscent of the depiction of human existence in Poe's works, life as presented in *The Croquet Player* includes a latent subterranean force threatening serene commonplace activity. "Below the surface" of average daily behavior, Frobisher observes retrospectively, lurks "an unhappy, wicked spirit," something "bestial" which theological thought attributes to the legacy of Cain or to the influence of devils and which post-Darwinian scientific thought designates as a repressed caveman disposition for "cruelty, suspicion and ape-like malice." In the modern world of the Thirties, however, this powerful, irrational force can no longer be repressed, a fact made manifest by the archaeological unearthing of the human past and by the psychological delving into the underground of the human mind. That both of these parallel activities reveal a disconcerting reality underlying humanity and its civilization is implied in Dr. Finchatton's nightmare, which also specifically depicts the rise of militarism in the mid-Thirties:

> More and more did the threat of that primordial Adamite dominate me. I could not banish that eyeless stare and that triumphant grin [of a Paleolithic skull] from my mind, sleeping or waking. Waking I saw it as it was in the museum, as if it was a living presence that had set us a riddle and was amused to hear our inadequate attempts at a solution. Sleeping I saw it released from all rational proportions. It became gigantic. It became as vast as a cliff, a mountainous skull in which the orbits and hollows of the jaw were huge caves. He had an effect—it is hard to convey these dream effects—as if he was continually rising and yet he was always towering there. In the foreground I saw his innumerable descendants, swarming like ants, swarms of human beings hurrying to and fro, making helpless gestures of submission or deference, resisting an overpowering impulse to throw themselves under his all devouring shadow. Presently these swarms began to fall into lines and columns, were clad in uniforms, formed up and began marching and trotting towards the black shadows under those worn and rust-stained teeth. From which darkness there presently oozed something—something winding and trickling, and something that manifestly tasted very agreeably to him. Blood.

By coalescing archaeological find and psychological disclosure Wells here provides an emblem for the human condition, a modern emblem equivalent in effect, say, to Poe's use of the skull as an underlying design in "The Gold Bug" and "The Fall of the House of Usher."

Unlike the typical ghost story, however, *The Croquet Player* does not completely obscure the issue of cause and effect, with the result that in a special sense possibilities are not blocked for its characters. The ancestral skull, now visible within the underground of human civilization "like something being lit up behind a transparency," provides "an explanation that [is] itself an enigma"; and however enigmatic its explanation, it intimates a cause-and-effect verity encouraging rather than denying the assertion of human will. Dr.

Norbert, an agitated and prophetic psychotherapist, makes this point when he speaks of a possible supra-rational cure for the "new Plague" evident "all over the world" in "*intellectual men . . . going mad*" because the "cave-man who is over us, who is in us, and who is indeed *us*, is going against [our] imaginary selves." "There will be no choice before a human being," Norbert continues, "but to be either a driven animal or a stern devotee to that civilization, that disciplined civilization, that has never yet been achieved," "such a mental effort as the stars have never witnessed yet. Arise, O mind of Man!" This emphasis on cause and effect, on possibility of resolution, and on primacy of human rationality and will is uncharacteristic of the conventional ghost story, including Poe's tales of horror.

In the traditional ghost story plot is weak, authorial stress given to a style designed to induce a particular sensation in the reader. Although the style of *The Croquet Player* is effectively managed, neither it nor the plot engage Wells as much as does the "bearing of structural expedients upon design." The structure of *The Croquet Player* recalls the Poesque devices Wells used in *The Time Machine*, especially the creation of a narrator who directly addresses/represents the reader and who relates the words and actions of another (who may signify, as in psychomachia, a mental part of the narrator/reader). When the narrator thinks he is "like that wedding guest who was gripped by the Ancient Mariner" and refers to his account as "apocalyptic," the author behind him hints at a revision of *The Time Machine*, to which both remarks are germane. Whereas pessimism pervades this earlier romance, the fear of a possible "new Plague" of atavism resulting from the principle of regression (as defined in Darwin's *The Descent of Man*, 1871) is balanced in *The Croquet Player* by a therapeutic hope in prescriptive evolutionary synthesis. Aesthetically this therapy finds principal embodiment in Wells's revision of the structuring narrative frame of the earlier work.

Speaking of himself as a "frame," Frobisher narrates an account which encloses or frames Dr. Finchatton's story. This Chinese-box technique of enclosing a story within a story includes intimations of a parallelism between the account as rendered to the reader and the framed narrative as rendered to the narrator. Frobisher and Finchatton share more than somewhat similar names; they give identical reasons for recounting their stories. Frobisher's explanation that he writes primarily in a therapeutic attempt to clear up matters and gain reassurance from his readers echoes Finchatton's need to speak in order to hear how the narrative sounds. This pattern likewise emerges in the report given to Finchatton by the archaeologist at Eastfolk Museum—a story enclosed within the narrative that is itself enclosed within the frame—"as if he was trying out his ideas." Again, just as Frobisher commences with "a few particulars about" himself, Finchatton begins with "a touch of autobiography." Such an elaborate framing apparatus in fiction sometimes hints at something ominous, even while it initially invites reader comfort; in *The Croquet Player* it functions in this manner in a muted way. Deftly managed, the framing technique of this novel initially seems to invite the reader to experience enclosure as insulation and security. In final effect, however, the framing device intimates the real menacing presence of an underground life in the human self, something covered over by, as it were, layers of egotism—self-enclosing layers similar to strata hiding humanity's primitive ancestry, skin concealing humanity's ape-like skull, and narrative frames encircling some obscure hidden truth.

This tendency of Frobisher and, by implication, of his readers to seek patterns of insularity (as an effect of egotism on the self) is, for Wells, a Victorian inheritance. Significantly, in his efforts to escape haunted Cainsmarsh, which (as Finchatton's nightmare of the skull suggests) is at once a physical and a mental landscape, Frobisher refuses to "open a book later than Dickens." Escape into fiction or art generally and the application of antiquated Victorian fictive models (the past) to modern life specifically come under attack in *The Croquet Player,* which Wells designed to reflect the rupture of old social attitudes during the Thirties. Indicting civilization as an "artistic, fictitious," pseudo-orderly "world of Gods and Providences, rainbow promises and so forth," Dr. Norbert hints that the popular novels people favor reinforce their delusions about progress. These delusions about progress and about a framing Providence or rainbow comprise as it were, a comforting and insulating layering characteristic of the human self 's egotistical self-enclosure; and it is artistically manifested, in Wells's opinion, in the patterns of Victorian fiction reinforcing that self and its civilization. Beneath or within this layering "nothing [is] secured"; in reality life inside and outside the self is as repetitive as it is progressive—a notion correlating the image of the ape in *The Croquet Player* to Wells's typology of characterization and of texts generally. This life yields an enigmatic explanation or an inexplicable pattern which includes irrationality in the self and asymmetry in the world.

For Wells, the patterns of conventional ghost stories conform to the illusion engendered by Victorian fiction generally. In the traditional ghost story framing, or narrative layering, usually tends toward an enclosure permitting the reader a wide margin of safe distance from the horror. In particular, the reader of the traditional ghost story often senses that the supernatural has no ready referents in the material world outside the fictional frame, an effect created in part by distancing the reader from the central event through multiple layers of narrative. In one sense, of course, this manner can make the central event more dramatic and it might impart an impression of some ineffable enigma (as it does in certain works by James and Conrad). In the typical Victorian ghost story, however, such effects are balanced by a more benign development, through *enchâssement,* of a protective distance between reader and event. Aware of the latter feature and critical of its reflection of how people delusively insulate themselves from reality, Wells revised the device of the framed narrative in *The Croquet Player* so that it could serve the structural purpose of eliciting and then violating the reader's comfortable, conventional expectations associated with the formulaic ghost story. Just as in the novel archaeologists are said to dig beneath layers of dirt to unearth humanity's buried past and just as in the novel psychotherapists are said to penetrate layers of egotism to reveal humanity's bestial self, Wells's "archaeological" and "therapeutic" artistry requires the breaking of the strata of Frobisher's narrative. The multiple story-within-a-story pattern of *The Croquet Player* does not finally yield an apocalyptic revelation at the center of its layered text; it avoids the decisive moment of the direct appearance of the horror, so characteristic of Poe's works. Rather, Wells's novel splinters its frame or opens outwardly, as does the new truth (so disturbing to Frobisher's acquaintances) revealed by modern archaeologists and psychotherapists; as Finchatton remarks concerning the "breaking [of]

the frame of our present" in 1936: "We lived in a magic sphere and we felt taken care of and safe. And now in the last century or so, we have broken that. We have poked into the past, unearthing age after age and we peer more and more forward into the future. And that's what's the matter with us"; "the frame of the present was shattered and could never be restored. I had to open out . . . and enlarge my mind to a vaster world where the cave-man was as present as the daily [news]paper and a thousand years ahead was on the doorstep." Similarly, *The Croquet Player* opens outwardly, does not enclose the horror but releases it upon the reader.

Consider the conclusion of Frobisher's narrative. Quite conventionally the ending of his story returns the reader to its opening, formally suggesting a sense of closure. Indeed, the reader is particularly reminded of the narrator's desire to gain perspective. Yet a crucial distortion occurs in the final words of the book:

> [Dr. Norbert] made a move almost as though he would impede my retreat. He just wanted to go on being apocalyptic. But I had had enough of this apocalyptic stuff.
>
> I looked him in the face, firmly but politely. I said, "I don't care. The world *may* be going to pieces. The Stone Age may be returning. This may, as you say, be the sunset of civilization. I am sorry, but I can't help it this morning. I have other engagements. All the same—laws of the Medes and Persians—I am going to play croquet with my aunt at half-past twelve today."

In contrast to countless narrators of conventional ghost stories, Frobisher concludes with disinterest, and in doing so he becomes, or should become, the horror for the reader. The narrator's final attitude of disinterest, implying his desire to insulate himself from reality by living only on the surface of life—he said he was the frame of his narrative—lingers beyond the end of the text to haunt the reader. The horror, then, is not where or what the reader of conventional ghost stories of the period would expect; the horror is the ghost of unreason and ineffective will in the narrator, in the very frame rather than at the center of the story. The horror lurks in the spirit of English civilization (suggested by the narrator's name George and by his fondness for croquet)—in short, in the typical English reader, who as the obvious audience of *The Croquet Player* comprises the outermost frame in the dynamics of reader and text.

The shattered frame of Wells's "journalistic" artistry opens out into the future, just as Finchatton's vision of the future is forecast in the newspaper on his doorstep. This future lies within the "haunted" reader, who perhaps may yet be aroused to assert will and participate in the collective "mind of Man." Herein lies the revision of the pessimism concerning "the sunset of civilization" reflected in *The Time Machine.* Still, in effect the optimism here remains very tentative, a mere question: how will you, the reader, respond to the horror buried within you, the horror of an ineffective will? This irresolved conclusion, this implied question comprises a final instance of the fragmentation of narrative frame in *The Croquet Player.* (pp. 71-7)

William J. Scheick, in his The Splintering Frame: The Later Fiction of H. G. Wells, *University of Victoria, 1984, 134 p.*

ROBERT CROSSLEY   (essay date 1986)

[In the following excerpt from his critical biography of Wells, Crossley explicates Wells's short fiction, concluding that Wells's canon is "a testament to both the excellence and the pertinence of science fiction as a literary form."]

In his *Experiment in Autobiography,* Wells deprecates his "single sitting stories" as work "ground out" to subsidize his early career and, in their later reincarnations in anthologies, as unlooked-for insurance against his declining years. In fact, the short fiction includes many sophisticated and powerful tales and two imperfect though fascinating novellas. Apart from its usefulness in turning a quick profit, the short story form furnished Wells a playground of the mind, a small, enclosed space in which he could try out issues and techniques that might be more fully employed in the longer scientific romances. The title of his first volume of stories, *The Stolen Bacillus and Other Incidents,* accurately names the priority of most of the tales; they are basically reports of exhilarating or disturbing incidents, natural or preternatural, fantastic or technological shocks to the accepted norms and givens of daily life. But, as in the longer fictions, a Wellsian incident is seldom treated merely incidentally but as an occasion for speculation and critical inquiry.

Perhaps the kind of speculative story most often associated with Wells is the predictive tale like **"The Argonauts of the Air"** (1895), a forecast of the invention of flying machines—a theme whose implications never ceased to intrigue Wells. . . . Wells himself took a grim satisfaction in his prediction of tank warfare, a dozen years before its actual occurrence during the first World War, in **"The Land Ironclads"** (1903). Generally, though, despite their interest as illustrations of Wells's technological imagination, the predictive stories are not among his most accomplished fictions. The best of them may be **"Filmer"** (1901), the biography of the putative inventor of the first workable heavier-than-air flying machine. It focuses not on the fact of mechanical innovation but on its psychological implications for the inventor, who commits suicide on his day of glory. As a tale that speculates about "that recurring wonder of the littleness of the scientific man in the face of the greatness of his science," **"Filmer"** belongs in the company of those Wellsian fictions that ponder the insecurity of human intelligence and the tentativeness of civilization.

In one of his finest stories, **"The Star"** (1897), Wells takes the issue of the vulnerability of human civilization to an apocalyptic conclusion. In this panorama of disaster and panic occasioned by the approach of a huge comet to the earth, millions die, the climate grows hot, the planet's surface is remade by earthquakes and tidal waves, the lunar cycle is lengthened to eighty days, and the remnant of the human population migrates to the cool poles. The earth is barely rescued from annihilation by the interposition of the moon between the earth and the onrushing comet. The human species survives, but the tale offers neither reassurance nor the satisfaction of a minimally happy ending. The final paragraph takes us to Mars where astronomers—relatives, presumably, of the unsuccessful adventurers in *The War of the Worlds*—are observing through telescopes the spectacle of the collision of the comet and the moon and are preparing scientific papers on what they take to be the minor damage done to the earth. Wells's narrator then neatly upends homocentrist pretensions: "Which only shows how small the vastest human catastrophes may seem, at a distance of a few million miles."

Wells's perspectives on the contingency of civilization are not always extraterrestrial. **"In the Abyss"** (1896), a description of a primitive civilization at the bottom of the sea, is challenging and frightening in its suggestion that even on our own planet we may not be alone. Even a lightweight tale like **"The Stolen Bacillus"** (1894), in spite of its snickering treatment of both biological warfare and the tactics of modern terrorism, demonstrates the perverse human capacity to destroy its own culture. **"The Empire of the Ants"** (1905), a story with ideological links to *The First Men in the Moon,* ends with a vision of the gradual recolonizing of the earth by a remarkably clever and swiftly breeding strain of ants moving steadily through the Brazilian interior: "By 1920 they will be halfway down the Amazon. I fix 1950 or '60 at the latest for the discovery of Europe." Because we know what ensued from the "discovery" of the Americas by European conquistadors, the closing sentence is ominous. It puts human culture in its place—and that place is not at the center of creation.

Wells inquires more extensively and mythically into the nature of civilization in a pair of novellas published in 1897. **"A Story of the Stone Age"** and **"A Story of the Days to Come"** are picaresque fictions, anthologies of episodes from the lives of a paleolithic man and woman and of a couple from twenty-second-century London. The novellas are symmetrical in design and ideologically complementary: in each the protagonists are malcontents, exiled from the dominant culture, whether tribal or industrial; each is a story of fitness and survival; each portrays the hopeful genesis of a new stage in civilization that will replace and transcend a dying culture. Both stories depict individuals tensed against the societies that produced them and both offer a disquieting vision of the price in blood, anguish, and brutalizing labor that is paid for the achievements and adornments of civilization.

In the closing pages of **"Days to Come,"** Wells explicitly connects the story of Ugh-lomi and Eudena, exiles from the tribe of Uya, with the story of Denton and Elizabeth, economic and social rebels in futuristic London; the four misfits all occupy the same physical space, and Denton broods on the future, "trying in obedience to his instinct to find his place and proportion in the scheme" of human and cosmic history, while standing in the very spot that once was "the squatting-place of the children of Uya." To be civilized in the paleolithic age is nearly to die in the efforts to secure food, to tame a horse, to kill a grizzly bear; to be civilized in the future metropolis is to be born wealthy enough to live in elegant and extravagant indolence while others, unlucky enough to be born without money or to lose their money, labor at the production of luxuries they cannot enjoy. In the Stone Age, the price of civilization, though high in bodily harm, seems justified by the aspirations; in the days to come the price—psychological, spiritual, and physical—seems disproportionate to the purchase.

But Wells's point is not to suggest a mere linear devolution from stone-age vigor to post-modern decadence. The parallel design of the novellas emphasizes the *persistence* of certain human behaviors and cultural patterns. Human history is a story of continuities and recrudescences. Ugh-lomi establishes his independence by beating up his rival, Uya; Denton, thrust from a secure middle-class life into menial work in the Labour Company, quickly learns that in the twenty-second century "the fist ruled . . . even as it was in the beginning." Futuristic man discovers how much he remains stone-age man: "After all we are just poor animals, rising out of the brute." The poignancy of the mock-fairy-tale ending of **"The Stone Age"** lies in its placement of the provisional success of individual, heroic struggle within a larger, impersonal, Darwinian pattern of struggle: "Thereafter for many moons Ughlomi was master and had his will in peace. And on the fulness of time he was killed and eaten even as Uya had been slain." The same bitter contrast between individual suffering and social progress emerges when the future hero and heroine reflect on the misery of life in the Labour Company. Denton: "It will pass." Elizabeth: "We shall pass first."

Wells revisited his twenty-second century twice in *When the Sleeper Wakes* and in **"A Dream of Armageddon"** (1901). The two novellas and the two later works represent a diffuse effort by Wells to work out a comprehensive explanation of human history, a myth which might explain why the distance between stone-age and future man is so slight and why civilization remains both the elusive goal and the nemesis of human activity. As in *The Time Machine,* the cosmos is indifferent to human effort, to the small risings and fallings and recoveries of the species. As Eudena listens rapt to Ugh-lomi narrate his gory murder of Uya, she is observed by silent, stellar witnesses—which also observe Denton and Elizabeth 50,000 fictional years later—which also observe the readers reading those fictions in "real" time. In their constancy and stability, those witnesses mock the splendor of Ugh-lomi and Eudena's small achievements and of ours: "It was a splendid time, and the stars that look down on us looked down on her, our ancestor—who has been dead now these fifty thousand years."

Both novellas suffer from failures in conception and execution. The language of **"The Stone Age"** is embarrassingly clumsy and stilted at times, while the plot of **"Days to Come"** dishonestly resolves Denton and Elizabeth's fall from social favor. Still, these short works are representative of Wells's ambivalence towards civilization in the great decade bounded by *The Time Machine* (1895) and *A Modern Utopia* (1905). **"A Story of the Days to Come"** is the richer of the two, its world exercised a greater hold on Wells's imagination, and along with *When the Sleeper Wakes,* it has influenced the history of the modern urban dystopia. But in its awkward effort to create an anthropologically authentic portrait of prehistoric humanity, **"A Story of the Stone Age"** is one of Wells's most daring experiments and his most interesting failure. Despite their deficiencies, the two novellas document the Wellsian notions that human history is but a small part of planetary history and that the story of civilization is itself a short story.

Wells is renowned for perfecting a pseudo-documentary technique in his speculative fictions—what the narrator of the little-known romance *The Sea Lady* calls "the true affidavit style." But the mythic novellas are reminders of his imaginative versatility and the breadth of his range. **"The Stolen Body"** (1898), one of his several exercises in the tale of the preternatural, displays Wells at the height of his powers. A story of body snatchers from a parallel world who are loosed on the primary world by scientific dilettantes toying with mental telepathy, it provokes typical Wellsian questions: What are the consequences of aimless experimentation? In what respects is curiosity contaminated by failures of intelligence or foresight or moral sensibility? Are there limits beyond which human beings trespass only at the peril of life and sanity? Similar questions underlie the preternatural phenomena in stories like **"The Flowering of the Strange Orchid"**

Painting by Dudley Tennant for Wells's short story "The Country of the Blind."

(1894), **"The Crystal Egg"** (1897), and **"The Door in the Wall"** (1906), the last of which is probably closer in spirit than anything Wells wrote to the luminous mysticism of George Macdonald's "The Golden Key" (1867) and *Lilith* (1895).

At the other end of Wells's spectrum are the comic stories concerning human manipulation of mysterious events or technological inventions for mundane ends. That group of tales includes **"The Purple Pileus"** (1896), **"The Man Who Could Work Miracles"** (1898), and **"The Truth About Pyecraft"** (1903). One of the funniest stories in this group, **"The New Accelerator"** (1901), is a prose cartoon about an unscrupulous professor who manufactures a kind of super-amphetamine that speeds up physical movement. Professor Gibberne combines the technical expertise of Cavor with the business sense of Bedford, and the gullible narrator is so impressed by the idea of a miracle drug that he is swept up unquestioningly into the "trip" Gibberne arranges for him. The drug allows the user to make mischief with impunity because he moves so quickly that his victims can't see him and, as he watches the rest of the world go by in slow motion, people appear as mechanisms and caricatures. The psychedelic vision afforded by the drug is inevitably inhumane. Promenaders look like dummies; a wink or a gesture becomes a grotesque thing; a suitor's innocent smile slows to a leer. For all its madcap charm, **"The New Accelerator"** is as pointed as any of Wells's soberer speculations. The professor and narrator plan to push the sale of the new drug as fast as possible despite any ethical reservations they might have about its use. The only problems they consider themselves competent to address are technical and marketing ones:

> Like all potent preparations it will be liable to abuse. We have, however, discussed this aspect of the question very thoroughly, and we have decided that this is purely a matter of medical jurisprudence and altogether outside our province. We shall manufacture and sell the Accelerator, and, as for the consequences—we shall see.

Several of the best stories are visionary in theme and method. In these tales the protagonists acquire, usually accidentally or involuntarily, some special angle or instrument of vision that enables them to see familiar reality freshly and unfamiliar reality with both wonder and terror. Often these tales are narrated not by the protagonist but by a skeptical rationalist, an outsider describing and assessing mysterious events to which he has been a (generally unwilling) witness. The narrator characteristically tells his story in a state of shell-shock, his comfortable and fundamental presuppositions about how reality works no longer secure.

In two of the visionary tales, **"The Remarkable Case of Davidson's Eyes"** (1895) and **"The Plattner Story"** (1896), the transformations of perception occur in laboratories, and the locale dramatizes the upsetting of scientific certitudes and mental habits by a sudden eruption of visionary experience. In Davidson's case a thunderstorm triggers a displacement of vision; while his body and other sensory experience remain rooted in England, visually he exists on a bleak Antarctic island. In **"The Plattner Story"** a green powder explodes in a school chemistry lab and causes the teacher to disappear for nine days. When Plattner abruptly returns as a literal nine-days' wonder, he tells of a numinous other world lit by a green sun, a limbo inhabited by souls who keep watch over the living in our world. Scientists eager to dismiss Plattner's story as hallucination are stymied by one incontrovertible fact: all his body organs and features have shifted position so that his anatomical structure is a mirror reversal of what it was before he disappeared. The investigators are mortified and disgruntled; although publicly skeptical about his claims, they are in fact embarrassed by the body that exists as a living refutation of scientific assurance and rational sufficiency.

Variants on the visionary mode can be found in **"Under the Knife"** (1896) in which the narrator, on a hospital operating table, inhales chloroform and goes on a mental journey whose satirical and spiritual texture recalls the conventions of medieval dream-visions. The narrator's dream of himself in the company of a host of "naked intelligences" moving through the cosmos may have given Olaf Stapledon the idea for the pilgrimage of disembodied minds in *Star Maker* (1937). In **"The Crystal Egg,"** another of Wells's Martian satires, a strange crystal allows an unhappy shopkeeper to escape the demands of his domestic life by providing a magic—or electronic—window on the arcadian world of Mars. (When the shopkeeper is startled by an immense pair of eyes peering at him from the other side of the crystal, the reader may be reminded of J. R. R. Tolkien's *palantir* in *The Lord of the Rings* in which the eye of Sauron appears to those seeking a glimpse of the land of Mordor.) Eventually the shopkeeper, a prototype of the television addict, abandons his work so that "he might comfort himself with what was fast becoming the most real thing in his existence." He is later found dead, clutching

the crystal. An often anthologized visionary tale, **"The Country of the Blind"** (1904), is a parable about an El Dorado-like region in the Andes inhabited by blind people and accidentally discovered by a sighted man. While coldly refuting the proverb about the one-eyed man being king among the blind, the tale asserts the necessity of spiritual vision; blindness is treated not as a clinical phenomenon but as a metaphor for atrophied imagination and rigid dogmatism. (pp. 58-63)

The distinctively Wellsian quality of Wells's fantastic fiction may be studied in the two final stories to be considered here, both of which are fantastic parables rather than Tolkienian subcreations. In **"The Story of the Late Mr. Elvesham"** (1896), an old philosopher clings to life by spiking a liqueur with a magic powder which causes him to exchange bodies with the young materialist Mr. Eden. The premise is unblinkingly fantastic, but the heart of the story is the brilliant rendering of the duality of body and personality in the transformed victim. The account of Eden's gradual realization that he has awakened trapped inside the body of Elvesham, that he has in the space of a single night become wrinkled, toothless, thin-voiced, cold-footed, sniffling, bleary-eyed, bony-fingered, loose-skinned, wracked with cough, persistently and disablingly weary and slow while retaining all the desires and sensibilities and the lively consciousness of youth is one of the triumphs of Wells's imagination, the equal of some of the other great metamorphoses in the longer romances. Narrated by Eden "under restraint" in an effort to prove he is not crazy, the tale is closer than any of Wells's to Poe's monologues by demented narrators ("The Black Cat," "Berenice," "The Tell-Tale Heart"). But it is also a typical Wellsian assault on the modern confidence in the explicability of all phenomena and a portrait of a man imprisoned inside a miracle no one can credit. As Eden despairingly comes to see, the explanation of last resort—the explanation modern people apply to make otherwise intractable events tractable—is psychiatric. Unable to persuade anyone of his true identity, he is left with the choice of suicide or the asylum.

"The Man Who Could Work Miracles: A Pantoum in Prose" bypasses the horror of **"Elvesham"** and combines fantasy with whimsy in the adventures of the garrulous rationalist and materialist, Mr. Fotheringay, who finds himself in astonished possession of miraculous powers of mind over matter. The story follows the brief career of a man of slender intellect gifted with absolute power. Much of that career is devoted to puckish mischief-making, as when Fotheringay irritably tells a constable to go to Hades and immediately finds himself alone. But when he tries to alter nature, his power, neither harnessed by a modest sense of human limits nor wielded by a vigilant presence of mind, becomes cataclysmic. Under the influence of the revivalist Rev. Mr. Maydig, he attempts to duplicate Joshua's feat of making the sun stand still. Phrasing the command in colloquial English and with accurate scientific awareness of which heavenly body is moving, Fotheringay addresses the earth: "Jest stop rotating, will you?" But when the natural rhythms of the planet are interrupted, every person and thing on earth, in obedience to the laws of inertia, is whirled forward into annihilation. In the midst of chaos casually wrought, Fotheringay conceives "a great disgust of miracles" and ends his career with two simultaneous and final wishes: to lose his thaumaturgical powers and to have everything revert to the way it was just before he discovered these powers. Thus the jinni is rebottled, the damage undone, and the story returned full circle (following the form of the "pantoum" of its subtitle) to its opening conversation. As a work of fantasy, this makes a thoroughly absorbing and satisfying retelling of the classic fairy tale of miraculous power, the story of Aladdin from the *Arabian Nights*. And (how Wells would have appreciated this unintended application of his tale!) later readers can hardly help but find in **"The Man Who Could Work Miracles"** a cautionary fable for the Nuclear Age.

While some of Wells's short fiction was written with the left hand while he worked on the longer romances, the two novellas and a dozen or more short stories belong to his major work. Readers have sometimes overlooked the stories because of the stature of the science-fiction novels and have assumed that the short fiction is inferior. But even many of the flawed tales help reveal the process of Wells's imagination. **"The Sea Raiders"** (1896), one of his lesser efforts, describes in a crisp you-are-there style the invasion of the English coast by deep-sea monsters; in both substance and method it is a dry run for *The War of the Worlds*. The failure of Fotheringay in handling absolute power is presented with the same mixture of fantasy and farce Wells perfected in the first half of *The Invisible Man*. He published **"The New Accelerator"** and *The First Men in the Moon* in the same year and they share issues, character types, and techniques; notably, the story anticipates the visual effects of the stop-action or slow-motion camera, as the lunar dawn in the longer work gives a foretaste of time-lapse photography.

But the greatest of Wells's stories do not have to be studied as tailpieces to the novels or patronized as the hackwork of a writer notorious for overproduction. Many can stand on their own as authentic achievements of Wells's resourceful imagination and technical ingenuity. In fact, **"A Story of the Days to Come"** is in many respects more convincing and coherent than its novelistic sequel, *When the Sleeper Wakes*. The issues of size and scale and of the management of technology Wells raises in **"Filmer"** are treated more diffusely and with less power in *The Food of the Gods*. In *The Days of the Comet* is a bloated version of **"The Star"** and of interest chiefly in those passages that imitate the panoramic techniques of the earlier story. And **"The Door in the Wall"** makes poignant and real the perilous lure of imagination treated so ludicrously in *The Sea Lady*.

Wells's self-criticism in the opening pages of his *Autobiography* is notable for its candor and scrupulousness: "It scarcely needs criticism to bring home to me that much of my work has been slovenly, haggard, and irritated, most of it hurried and inadequately revised." But the honest reader and critic will not simply take Wells at his word. His enduring work is the gift of a generous imagination, an exacting but evocative use of language, and passionate intellectual integrity. Wells's short stories and the great romances of 1895-1901 are a testament to both the excellence and the pertinence of science fiction as a literary form; they remain a repository of the exhilaration, reflection, and admonition that are the distinctive aesthetic and moral values of science fiction. (pp. 64-6)

> *Robert Crossley, in his* H. G. Wells, *Starmont House, Inc., 1986, 79 p.*

ROBERT M. PHILMUS (essay date 1987)

[*In the following essay, Philmus examines references made by Wells in "A Story of the Days to Come" to William Morris and his desire to return to an idealized fourteenth-century world in* News from Nowhere, *noting Wells's presentation and eventual refutation in "Days to Come" of Elizabeth and Denton's pastoral utopian vision.*]

"A Story of the Days to Come" lends itself to a number of generic configurations. At least three of these can be thought of as having authorial sanction inasmuch as they arise from connections that Wells is responsible for making with other works of fiction, including his own. Each of the three carries with it its own hermeneutic emphasis and bias; each also presides over, and inflects the meaning of, the romance element in Wells's fiction.

The following remarks concern only one of these configurations, the one which emerges, as it were, in the text of **"A Story of the Days to Come"** printed in the pages of the *Pall Mall Magazine* for 1899—i.e., in the text which does not *immediately* associate itself with any other by Wells. Its opening sentence begins to establish its generic context by instantly bringing to mind another "excellent Mr. Morris" who "lived in the days of Queen Victoria the Good." To be sure, what we are next told about the fictive Mr. Morris and his avatar, Mwres, does not properly fit the man to whom Wells had recently paid tribute in an obituary-cum-review of *The Well at the World's End*. William Morris, after all, was in no usual sense of the words "heedless and impatient of the Future"; nor could he be said to have "nothing imaginative" about him. Yet it is here, and not at the very outset, that **"Days to Come"** ironically misdirects us to the extent that it convinces us to give up any thought of the Morris from Hammersmith. Even so, it countenances such a persuasion only for a moment. Once we learn, as we presently do, that Mwres is "one of the officials of the Wind Vane and Waterfall Trust," the significance of the disparity between him and his real-life namesake becomes clear. Its purpose, like that of the entire introductory disquisition on a character quite marginal to the events of the ensuing story, is orientational: it specifies, rather than obliterates, the connection with William Morris. The reference, that is, has nothing to do with persons, actual or fictive, or even to Morris-the-writer generally. Instead, Wells points precisely to *News from Nowhere,* with its vision of a return to an idealized Fourteenth Century, a vision which latterly transpires through a leisurely voyage up a resuscitated Thames.

By its recollection of Morris, **"Days to Come"** appears as a type of anti-utopian fiction. That is to say, it defines itself against—which also means in relation to—*Nowhere*, particularly as it derives its own dystopian possibility from the pastoral world that Morris there envisions as ideal. This ideal it more or less explicitly evokes in Denton and Elizabeth's "dream" of escape from the mechanized ways of the London of the Twenty-Second Century; it even locates their utopian longing for a better life in the selfsame "valley of the Thames" that Nowhere occupies. But as their dream in the event turns into a nightmare, so the Nowhere re-presented in "The Vacant Country" proves to be very far from an Earthly Paradise.

In this regard, **"Days to Come"** extends the critique of Morris inherent in *The Time Machine*. The "ruinous" world of the Eloi, as mediated through the hypotheses of the Time Traveller, at first paradoxically recalls *Nowhere's* "Epoch of Rest." Nor is it by accident that the word epitomizing his early impressions of 802,701 occurs to him as he stands in "the warm glow of the setting sun" after having partaken, Guest-like, of a communal banquet in "the great hall"; for the "Communism" that he speaks of is certainly of Morris's pastoral-utopian variety. This moment of affectionate parody, however, lasts only as long as the Time Traveller perceives the Eloi as living "in ease and delight" that is, until he descends to the "underworld" of the Morlocks. There he discovers the technological infrastructure which had hitherto been for him—and remains for the reader of Morris—a matter of problematic inference. It is true that he observes nothing which would contradict a premise of Nowhere: that "this is not an age of inventions. The last epoch did that for us, and we are now content to use such of its inventions as we find handy" (NFN). But that congruence merely reinforces the criticism that *The Time Machine,* primarily by way of its topographical details, levels at *Nowhere. The Time Traveller, after catching sight of the machinery underlying the "upper-world" and coming face to face with the Morlocks, does not simply return with a conviction applicable solely within the confines of his tale: that his* previous idea of an Aesthete Utopia was superficial and illusory. Having penetrated the (up till then sunlit) surface of 802,701 and glimpsed beneath it the dark reality that (quite literally) undermines it, he also casts light on the reasons for pronouncing *the* very idea of such a utopia to be a delusion.

This is the point that Denton expatiates on in communicating to Elizabeth his sad conclusion that they had deceived themselves when they imagined that "the old-fashioned way of living on the countryside" would be idyllic. "To each generation," he says, "the life of its time. . . . In the city—that is the life to which we are born. . . . Coming here was a dream, and this—is the awakening." His "this" refers, of course, to the natural elements, the wild dogs, and the perpetual struggle for existence against them and their like. The "awakening," however, has to do with more than that reality about survival in a hostile natural environment. It includes as well the recognition that history has cooperated with biology to destroy Denton and Elizabeth's romantic idyll, that cultural conditioning has unfitted these refugees from the technological world for the hardships and dangers of (Darwinian) Nature—or, in other words, that their pastoral utopian vision is an anachronism.

In its demonstration of that point, **"Days to Come"** analytically refigures *The Time Machine.* The Morlocks against which the Time Traveller chivalrically tries to defend Weena reappear as the dogs that Denton battles for his life and Elizabeth's, but with this difference: that the dogs have no association with machinery. In this way, **"Days to Come"** isolates the biological threat which they incarnate from the other threat to the pastoral utopia, that posed by the ineluctable fact of an acquired dependence on technology. These two factors do not remain entirely separate, however. The anti-utopian possibility adumbrated in "The Vacant Country's" denial of Denton and Elizabeth's romantic "dream" follows them back to London, where it manifests itself again—and perhaps more unmistakably than hitherto—in the compulsion towards violence and consequent brutalization of the "under-world." This, in turn, marks the denizens of those lower depths—in particular, the man suggestively named Whitey—as what the Time Traveller putatively takes such laborers to be: the ancestors of the (albino) Morlocks.

Like *The Time Machine,* **"Days to Come"** thus equates differences in social class with evolutionary disparities and thereby confounds sociology with biology. On the other hand, it re-verses their priority in the degradational scheme that its connection with *The Time Machine* brings into prominence. The devolutionary pattern informing the Time Traveller's vision of the future entails the triumph of Darwinian "Necessity" over civilized order, the return of Darwinian Law as the sole arbiter of the (backward) course of life on Earth. The focus accordingly falls on the Morlocks as the agents for that reascendance, and especially on the brutality which from this perspective they owe to their (d)evolutionary status as a distinct species, not to their hypothetical Lamarckian (or more precisely, Gulickian) origin in the working classes. By contrast, the "degradation" of Denton and Elizabeth is primarily a matter of sociology; and only when they reach the lowest level of a social scale that is graphically hierarchical does the specter of Darwinian struggle obtrude itself. Furthermore, the "under-world" approached by way of their social decline (and most notably Denton's) is not *The Time Machine's* but its logical antecedent: a brutalizing and brutalized, rather than a thoroughly brutal, place.

This brutalization does not come across as the natural and inevitable concomitant of exactly the kind of instinct that the lovers had previously encountered in the wild dogs. Instead, it appears as a social effect induced by an oppressive class system, whose rigors have provoked an atavistic imitation of nature. None the less, it has its originary locus in the natural world, and this makes **"Days to Come"** somewhat problematic as a literary model for subsequent anti-utopian fiction. Insofar as it apparently sets up a countryside totally apart from and alternative to the City and what that technopolis represents, it clearly establishes the topological convention which most twentieth-century anti-utopias adopt; but as that alternative proves specious, it seems to anticipate only the likes of Aldous Huxley and the dilemma of Brave New World versus the Reservation. Even so, it is not difficult to imagine how Zamiatin, under the influence of Dostoyevsky and by a species of poetic misprision, might have arrived at the central antithesis in *We* from his reading of **"Days to Come."** After all, Denton and Elizabeth do invest their utopian hope in the "vacant country"; and while that site of instinct and irrationality by no means shares the positive valence of the world beyond the Green Wall, the hope first associated with it continues to attach itself to their "love story."

By the same token, **"Days to Come"** preserves in its romance element that discernible vestige of Utopian Desire characteristic of all anti-utopian fiction properly so called. In this case, however, its antagonist is not the Entropic Reason of the United, or One, State, with its mania for regularity. Instead, it is instinct energy of the sort figured by Zamiatin as a potentially subversive force, but by Wells as the symptom and index of something radically wrong with the social arrangement that encourages it and also as the motivating factor behind the revolutionarily-sterile internecine conflict endemic to "the underways."

To be sure, the happy ending appears to sterilize Denton and Elizabeth's Utopian Desire as the opponent of brutalizing primeval impulse and hence of the status quo that invites such. The *deus ex machina* operation that prevents their being separated does, after all, restore them to their former place in the social hierarchy. Yet the idea of their reintegration remains exactly that, a bare idea, and one at odds with what the closing tableau implicitly proposes.

That final scene discovers Denton and Elizabeth, just "returned . . . from the labour servitude to which they had fallen," on "a balcony" at "the very verge of the city." The image of their situation instantly suggests their marginality relative to the existing social order, and this fits in with the point of the spatio-temporal survey that follows. Looking at the world from the vantage of his balcony, Denton sees the "latter days," his present moment, as all-too-continuous with the prehistoric past. But the glance which thus compresses human history into a seemingly unaltered and unaltering temporal landscape also has the opposite effect: like running a film at incredibly high speed (or instantaneously traversing whole geological epochs in a time machine), it induces a sense of changeableness, a sense of how far humankind has come from the days of "darkness and ignorance"—and how far it yet has to go before it fully outdistances their shadow. That is the prospect in which **"Days to Come"** ultimately locates Utopian Desire; that is the Utopian Horizon which Denton indicates when he says, "we are in the making."

It is significant that Denton's deliverance to that prospect requires the demise of a Bindon who has become more than a merely titular representative of the status quo. Possessed by a Huysmanite "imagination" which inclines him towards sensuous self-indulgence, this personage exhibits in his own effete fashion "passions" cognate to those which make for the "nightmare" of the "underways." By a fictive given consequent upon his disease, he also serves to identify the Utopian Horizon inherent in the romance of **"Days to Come"** with Science. This he does not only because the bequest of his that rescues the lovers from their "degradation" takes effect in the nick of time thanks to "the Euthanasia," but also because in extending his hostility for Elizabeth to a certain Medical Man, he establishes himself as the common obstacle to their apparently diverse aspirations. He thus functions to connect the "love story" with the Medical Man's forecast of a time when he and his colleagues "will know enough . . . to take over the management" so that "men will live in a different way"—a forecast totally consonant both with Denton's "spacious vision" and with Wells's own "dream of an informal, unselfish, unauthorised body of workers, a real and conscious apparatus of education and moral suggestion, held together by a common faith and a common sentiment, and shaping the acts and minds and destinies of men."

Denton's vision, like Guest's, proposes itself as an awakening from history-as-nightmare. Yet the desire that it educes from that shared and fictively rendered sense of history is not at all the one the *Nowhere* expresses: for "a time of rest" which must mean an end to the restlessness that is history, for a change which will end historical change. In this regard, the detail about Denton's point of vantage being "wide open to the sun and wind" is telling, for it is at once reminiscent of Nowhere's pastoral stasis and critical of the impulse towards closure which generates it. This, however, is also to say that the "spacious vision" which **"Days to Come"** at last arrives at dialectically proceeds from *Nowhere* and that whatever precision of meaning attaches to "we are in the making" does so largely by way of Nowhere. (pp. 450-54)

Robert M. Philmus, " 'A Story of the Days to Come' and 'News from Nowhere': H. G. Wells as a Writer of Anti-Utopian Fiction," in English Literature in Transition: 1880-1920, *Vol. 30, No. 4, 1987, pp. 450-55.*

WILLIAM J. SCHEICK   (essay date 1987)

[*In the following excerpt, Scheick discovers a tripartite structure in "In the Abyss" that conveys allegorical messages concerning humanity's options for confronting society's impending instability at the turn of the century.*]

At the end of the nineteenth century and the beginning of the twentieth century, many thinkers and writers considered their time to be a "transition age," as H. G. Wells referred to it in a short story entitled **"The Diamond Maker"** (1905). During this turn-of-the-century period many of these authors sensed a new instability, a result of an uncertain future emerging from the apparent erosion of former religious, social, and scientific beliefs. Typically, for example, William James thought that "the vast slow-breathing unconscious Kosmos" is comprised of "dread abysses and . . . unknown tides," Arnold Bennett thought that "humanity treads ever on a thin crust over terrific abysses," and Friedrich Nietzsche thought that "man is a rope stretched between the animal and the Superman—a rope over an abyss." Wells used this same image in **"In the Abyss,"** a short story about the open-endedness of the universe and about the open-endedness of human experience of the realities of this universe.

"In the Abyss" is a tale with a message, but the perception of this instruction requires a sensitivity to the emergent structure of the story. Wells's narrative privileges structure over characterization, a recurrent pattern in his early and late writings. As is the case in fiction generally, this privileging of structure in Wells's story conveys whatever ethical concern he has embodied in the tale.

At first encounter **"In the Abyss"** does not seem to evince many structural features. On the surface it appears to be a roughly linear narrative recounting Elstead's five-mile descent into the ocean; his discovery of a half-human, half-reptilian civilization; his near death as a result of these creatures' worship of him; his accidental escape and return to the ship on the surface of the sea; and his second descent less than two months later, from which he never returns. But several times the reader is reminded that Elstead rendered his account "in disconnected fragments," a fact calling attention to the effort of the narrator to tell the story. Moreover, the reader is especially reminded that the narrator, who finds it "impossible to re-tell it in [Elstead's] words," is presenting his text as a transitional narrative: one by no means complete and one nonjudgmental concerning the "verif[ication of] his strange story" of a suboceanic civilization. The narrator certainly draws attention to himself when he refers to himself as "me," a "me" trying "to piece together the discrepant fragments of [Elstead's] story from the reminiscences of Commander Simmons, Weybridge, Steevens, Lindley, and the others." Indeed, given the fractional dialogue between two sailors at the opening of the story and the equally fractional discussion by other sailors while Elstead makes his first descent, and given in the account the abiding uncertainty concerning the veracity of Elstead's report, **"In the Abyss"** is, as a narrative, only *somewhat* more organized than are the many fragments of the testimony on which it is based. Whatever cohesiveness the story seems to evince derives from a self-conscious, tentative, negotiating narrative voice, which guides the reader as best it can in a narrative that serves as an act of transition between the abyssal uncertainties of Elstead's disclosure and the stable meanings desired by the reader. This tripartite pattern of a narrative voice negotiating between Elstead and the reader parallels Wells's sense of the turn-of-the-century period as a transitional age between a past of apparent order and a future of uncertainty.

This subtle tripartite structure is reinforced in the tale by Wells's emphatic references to the depths of the sea and of the sky, between which resides humanity on earth's land surfaces, as if in a transitional state between the immensities of sea and sky. To stress humanity's intermediate position akin to that of the narrative voice and the turn of the century, Wells carefully, consistently correlates sea and sky in the story. We are told that "the water above [Elstead's descending sphere] was as dark as the midnight sky," that "a hovering swarm of little fishes veered about and came towards him as a flight of starlings might do," and that shapes in the sea's depths were "as faint as the zodiacal light of an English summer evening." This correlation of sea and sky as abyssal immensities surrounding intermediate humanity is most pronounced in the narrator's explanation of how the suboceanic civilization would perceive our existence: "We should be known to them . . . as strange meteoric creatures, wont to fall catastrophically dead out of the mysterious blackness of their watery sky."

This quotation reveals an allegorical trace in the "watery sky" analogy; for through the correlation of the creature's watery sky and humanity's heavenly sky, the narrator of **"In the Abyss"** probes the question of how intermediary humanity, living in a transitional age between a nineteenth-century past and a twentieth-century future, will respond to the startling meteoric challenges likely to be encountered during the new century.

That the suboceanic creatures evince this allegorical trace is suggested not only by the association of their watery sky to our airy heavens and by the comparison of how their astonishment over something descending from above correlates with our similar surprise were something alien to descend from our heavens, but also by references to their human features: such remarks as, in motion they "suggest . . . a walking man," "the vertical pitch of [their] face gave it a most extraordinary resemblance to a human being," their forelimbs "caricatured the human hand," and these "man-like creatures" look like "quasi human forms." The connection between the creatures and humanity is hammered home when the narrator refers to the creatures as "descendents like ourselves of the great Theriomorpha of the New Red Sandstone age."

Because of this association, how these relatives of humanity react to Elstead's sudden appearance in their world is important to note. They respond by dragging Elstead's bathysphere to their undersea city, where they worship him as a god from above. They have, in short, responded to his presence by resorting to a conventional explanation; they have retreated into the past, with its protective superstitious beliefs, rather than confront the encounter with a mind open to the mysteries of creation.

This implicit tripartite scheme of past, present, and future, suggested in the creatures' reaction to Elstead, reinforces the narrator's effort to negotiate between Elstead and the reader in an age in transition. And from these developmental tripartite patterns emerges the instruction of **"In the Abyss."** The lesson of the story concerns humanity's transitional state during the turn-of-the-century period. Humanity can react to the future in a way similar to the manlike creatures, and like them live in an "everlasting night," a "perpetual night" of a

mental darkness comprised of superstition; or humanity can respond to the future by letting fresh encounters take "hold of [its] imagination," as Elstead's story affects Weybridge, and by discerning these experiences with "eyes turned up in round wonder," as suggested by the two windows of Elstead's descending bathysphere. Imagination and wonder characterized Elstead's pursuit of the unknown, the abyss of mystery underlying the universe. Elstead represents a response to the future in contrast to the reaction of the undersea creatures. His futuristic science opposes their past-oriented superstition.

"In the Abyss," then, is a transitional text with an emergent structure comprised of tripartite patterns. The story exists in a "present" situated between the past and the future, superstition and science, the nineteenth century and the twentieth century. It even exists in a "present" situated between delusion and truth; for the accuracy of Elstead's report is left uncertain, something to be resolved in the future. Most significant, as narrative, **"In the Abyss"** exists in a "present" situated between Elstead and the reader; it improves upon the fragments related by Elstead, but it provides a still incomplete, unsynthesized, and non-judgmental account, which ideally should be advanced and refined by the reader in the future. This ideal reader will not react to the account with close-minded fear, skepticism, or superstitious belief, but with open-minded wonder, imagination, and scientific curiosity. In this way the narrative in-structs: its tripartite structural components incrementally or processively take shape (they in-struct) by expanding to include the reader (Elstead-narrator-reader). This inclusion of the reader in a reiterated tripartite pattern conveys the message or instruction concerning humanity's options of frightened retreat into the past and of bold, even possibly life-threatening advancement into the future; these are the options, Wells thought, that confront the turn-of-the-century reader of **"In the Abyss."** (pp. 155-58)

"In the Abyss" is a transitional text emphasizing perspective. Specifically, it informs (and in-forms as) an emerging perspective in the ideal reader, who finds himself included in the incremental tripartite structure of the story and who thereby finds himself instructed; he is instructed, first, to abandon the superstitions of the past and the desire for stable meanings such a retreat to the past signifies; second, to join in a tripartite fellowship with Elstead and the narrator, to refine their perception, and like them approach boldly, with imagination and a sense of wonder, the open-ended, even abyssal uncertainties of the future in the new century. (pp. 158-59)

William J. Scheick, "The In-Struction of Wells's 'In the Abyss'," in Studies in Short Fiction, *Vol. 24, No. 2, Spring, 1987, pp. 155-59.*

FURTHER READING

Brome, Vincent. *H. G. Wells: A Biography.* London: Longmans, Green and Co., 1952, 255 p.

A biography containing interesting personal glimpses into Wells's life and including many examples of the critical reception of his works.

Brooks, Van Wyck. *The World of H. G. Wells.* New York: Mitchell Kennerley, 1915, 189 p.

Critical and biographical study focusing on the development of Wells's social and political thought as discernible in his fiction.

Hillegas, Mark R. *The Future as Nightmare: H. G. Wells and the Anti-utopians.* New York: Oxford University Press, 1967, 200 p.

Traces anti-utopianism from Wells's early work through similar efforts by other important science fiction writers of the twentieth century.

Hughes, David Y. "H. G. Wells: Ironic Romancer." *Extrapolation: A Science-Fiction Newsletter* VI, No. 2 (May 1965): 32-8.

Identifies three scientific sources used by Wells in "The Sea Raiders," "Aepyornis Island," and "The Empire of the Ants," utilizing the references in his explication of the stories.

Huntington, John. "Utopian and Anti-Utopian Logic: H. G. Wells and His Successors." *Science-Fiction Studies* 9, No. 27 (July 1982): 122-46.

Companion piece to Huntington's essay "Thinking by Opposition: The 'Two-World' Structure in H. G. Wells's Short Fiction" [see excerpt dated 1981].

Lawrence, T. E. "The Complete Short Stories of H. G. Wells." *The Spectator* CXL (25 February 1928): 268-69.

Balanced assessment of Wells's short story canon.

Mackenzie, Norman, and Mackenzie, Jean. *The Time Traveller: The Life of H. G. Wells.* London: Weidenfeld and Nicolson, 1973, 487 p.

A detailed biography of Wells.

Snow, C. P. "H. G. Wells." In his *Variety of Men,* pp. 63-85. New York: Charles Scribner's Sons, 1967.

Snow's reminiscences of conversations with Wells.

West, Anthony. *H. G. Wells: Aspects of a Life.* London: Hutchinson, 1984, 405 p.

Painstaking and unsparing biography of Wells by Wells's son.

Edith (Newbold Jones) Wharton

1862-1937

American short story writer, novelist, critic, autobiographer, travel writer, and poet.

Wharton is best known as a novelist of manners whose fiction exposes the cruel excesses of aristocratic society in the United States at the beginning of the twentieth century. Her carefully crafted, psychologically complex short stories and novellas reflect concern for the status of women in society as well as for the moral decay she observed underlying the outward propriety of the upper classes. While her subject matter, tone, and style have often been compared with those of her friend and mentor Henry James, Wharton has achieved critical recognition as an original chronicler of the conflict between the inner self and social convention. Margaret B. McDowell observed: "[Wharton's] best work reveals her accomplished artistry, her grasp of social reality, her realization that manners are a key to the outer life of a society and the expression of an inner reality that escapes casual observation, her moral subtlety and incisiveness, and her unwavering insight into human nature."

Born into a wealthy New York family, Wharton was privately educated by governesses and tutors both at home and abroad. At an early age she displayed a marked interest in writing and literature, a pursuit her socially ambitious mother attempted to discourage. Nevertheless, Wharton finished her first novella at the age of fourteen and published a collection of verse two years later. From the perspective of an upper-class initiate, she observed the shift of power and wealth from the hands of New York's established gentry to the nouveau riche of the Industrial Revolution. Wharton considered the newly wealthy to be cultural philistines and drew upon their lives to create many of her best-remembered fictional characters and situations. In 1885 she married Edward Wharton, a man with whom she shared few interests or opinions, and who never understood her affinity for literature. Dissatisfied with society life and disillusioned with marriage, Wharton sought fulfillment in writing. Many of her stories and poems originally appeared in *Scribner's Magazine,* and both her first short story collection, *The Greater Inclination,* and her novel *The House of Mirth* were well received by critics and readers. Suffering from ill health and forced to contend with her husband's growing mental instability, Wharton filed for, and was granted, a divorce in 1912. Soon after, she moved to France, never returning to the United States. During World War I, Wharton organized relief efforts in France and cared for Belgian orphans, for which she earned the French Legion of Honor. However, her war novella *The Marne,* generated little positive critical interest. In 1921 Wharton became the first female recipient of the Pulitzer Prize, for her novel *The Age of Innocence.* During the final years of her life, Wharton continued to write short stories and novels, many of which reflect her growing disillusionment with postwar America and the Jazz Age. Her final novel, *The Buccaneers,* remained unfinished when she died in St. Brice-sous-Forêt in 1937.

From the start of her professional career and for many years afterward, Wharton was advised and encouraged by her inti-

mate friend Walter Berry. Romantic allusions about them have been made by several biographers, and Wharton's few sympathetic male characters are said to be modelled after either Berry or, as scholars have recently claimed, her lover, Morton Fullerton. The friendship, intellectual stimulation, and sexual fulfillment Wharton enjoyed with these men are transcribed in her stories as a welcome, if temporary, refuge from the repressiveness of America's upper class. This "smothered life" of the aristocracy, one of Wharton's common themes, is often evidenced in the diminished role of women in courtship and marriage in many of her works. For example, in "The Letters," a wife painfully reevaluates her marriage after discovering her unopened love letters in her husband's desk, while in "The Last Asset," a mother sanctions her daughter's engagement to a wealthy Frenchmen as a means to restore her own social position. Wharton's story "The Bunner Sisters" is regarded by many critics as her most incisive treatment of society's subtle victimization of women. In this short piece, sisters Ann Eliza and Evalina Bunner compete for the attentions of Ramy, a boorish clock repairman. However, when Ramy proposes to Ann Eliza, she subdues her feelings and rejects him so that he may marry her beloved younger sister. Tragically, Ann Eliza's self-sacrifice collapses, as does her idealistic vision of marriage, when she later discovers that Ramy's abuse and neglect contributed to her sister's death. Judith P. Saunders commented: "Wharton allows us to infer that [Ann Eliza] is better off without her illusions than with them, but it is nonetheless sobering to watch her walk away with nothing when traditional values have failed her."

In other short stories, Wharton ironically presents the limitations of society upon personal freedom. Attempts to circumvent convention through adultery and divorce often prove futile in Wharton's fiction, and illuminate those social conditions which deny the possibility of meaningful human relationships. Wharton's treatment of these concerns ranges from the satirical humor of "The Other Two," a story of a twice-divorced woman, to the tragic implications of "Autres Temps. . . ." In the latter work, protagonist Mrs. Lidcote is an expatriate American who has been ostracized by her community for her divorce twenty years earlier. When she learns of her daughter Lydia's divorce and quick remarriage, she returns to her former neighborhood, where her daughter lives, believing that Lydia is facing similar derision. She arrives, however, to discover that it is still her past and not her daughter's actions that society, and later Lydia, cannot tolerate. In "Souls Belated," another story in this vein, a woman leaves her husband for another man only to have her hopes for a life unfettered by conventional mores destroyed when her lover proposes marriage and a return to their social set. R. W. B. Lewis observed: "The impossibility of founding a new ethic—of a man and woman arranging their life together on a new and socially unconventional basis—was one of Mrs. Wharton's most somber convictions, and a conviction all the stronger because . . . she tested it again and again in her stories."

In addition to her realistic short fiction, Wharton also published several supernatural tales that present the inner experiences of her characters in allegorical terms. Her story "Pomegranate Seed" takes its name from the Greek myth of the goddess Persephone, who, as a compromise for having been enticed by her captor and husband, Hades, to eat pomegranate seeds while in his custody, must leave her mother, Demeter, each year and spend winter with Hades in the underworld. In Wharton's story, the spectre of a dead wife undermines the second marriage of her living husband through the tangible letters she sends to him. Like the mythical Persephone, her husband cannot resist the persuasive force of the ghost, and, like Demeter, his living wife cannot compel him to remain with her. In "The Eyes," a vision of hideous, sunken eyes haunts the protagonist each time he attempts to change his self-absorbed existence. In the end, he learns that they are his own eyes in old age, mocking him for what he will become. The title "After Holbein" from one of Wharton's most successful and unsettling horror stories, is derived from a series of woodcuts by sixteenth-century artist Hans Holbein the Younger, which depict death as a skeleton insinuating itself into the lives of unsuspecting noblemen. In the story, Warley, an aging gentleman, becomes lost on a wintry evening and happens upon the mansion of Mrs. Jasper, a senile society matron who is in the midst of giving an imaginary dinner party for long-dead guests. Caught up in the surreal atmosphere of the house, Warley believes he has attended a dazzling social event, but, upon stepping out into the night, he collapses and dies. Margaret B. McDowell observed: "Edith Wharton's ghost stories represent, in general, the work of a mature and sophisticated artist. . . . Like the best of her other efforts in this genre, the short stories of the macabre and the supernatural, more often than not, manifest in concentrated fashion the careful technique, the evocative style,

and the concern for aesthetic order that she revealed in her best novels."

In addition to her short stories, Wharton is recognized for novellas that further explore her characteristic themes and concerns. Her first novella, *The Touchstone,* focuses upon a man who anonymously sells the intimate love letters written to him by an author before her death. Yet his guilt over publicly displaying her private thoughts motivates him to identify himself as their recipient, an act that realizes the potential for good the writer had once divined in him. In *Madame de Treymes,* Wharton contrasts the moral and cultural aspects of France and the United States through the experiences of families—one from each country—that become intertwined in complex romantic relationships. She later recreated the social history of her birthplace in *Old New York,* a collection of novellas comprising *False Dawn* (The 'Forties), *The Old Maid* (The 'Fifties), *The Spark* (The 'Sixties), and *New Year's Day* (The 'Seventies).

Wharton's most popular novella, *Ethan Frome,* marks a departure from her portrayals of the upper classes in its examination of the frustration and limitations imposed on individuals by poverty and adherence to strict social codes. Using the background of rural New England, Wharton explores the difficulties involved in male-female relationships, revealing a loathing of society's rigid standards of decency, propriety, and loyalty. As the novella opens, the narrator, Ethan Frome's employer, seeks information concerning the handsome yet crippled title character. He discovers that twenty-four years earlier, Frome had fallen in love with Mattie Silver, a young cousin of his wife, Zeena, after she came to live with them. Yet Frome, bound by a sense of duty to his jealous wife, had attempted to send Mattie away. Driving to the train station, the pair impulsively decided to go sledding, and Mattie, unable to accept their separation, suggested that they commit suicide by crashing their sled into an elm tree. As they traveled downhill, however, Ethan's attention was diverted by a vision of his wife, and he failed to steer directly into the tree, leaving both he and Mattie severely crippled. The narrative frame then resumes with a visit by the employer to Ethan's house where Mattie, now an ill-humored invalid, snaps at Zeena, who has acted as her nurse since the "accident." Because of their poverty and immobility, Ethan, Zeena, and Mattie are unable to improve their situation, spending interminable hours together in their decaying farmhouse. As in such of Wharton's short stories as "Atrophy" and "The Long Run," *Ethan Frome* depicts a world in which no satisfactory escape from a loveless marriage exists, and infidelity invariable leads to further unhappiness. Although some critics initially objected to the starkness of Wharton's vision in this work, most have lauded *Ethan Frome* as an intelligent, complex portrait of moral corruption.

Readers and critics have often failed to recognize essential concerns in Wharton's fiction and have mistakenly viewed her as an outdated novelist of manners whose settings, style, and slow-moving pace belong to the nineteenth century. Comparisons of Wharton's work to that of Henry James are frequent. Some commentators, however, notably Irving Howe, believe claims of James's influence to be exaggerated—the result of superficial readings of Wharton's work. With the rise of the women's movement in the 1970s, criticism has tended to focus on Wharton's expression of feminist issues, occasionally to the exclusion of the author's other concerns. Yet simultaneously, the feminist movement has spurred renewed interest in Wharton's portrayals of the position of women at the turn of the century. As Elizabeth Ammons has commented, Wharton's fiction "is both a record of one brilliant and intellectually independent woman's thinking about women and a map of feminism's ferment and failure in America in the decades surrounding the Great War." Furthermore, according to Margaret McDowell, Wharton provided an important "link between the morally and psychologically oriented works of Hawthorne and James, who preceded her, and the later realists like Sinclair Lewis or F. Scott Fitzgerald with their tendency toward the sardonic and iconoclastic."

(For further information on Wharton's life and career, see *Twentieth-Century Literary Criticism,* Vols. 3, 9, 27; *Contemporary Authors,* Vol. 104, and *Dictionary of Literary Biography,* Vols. 4, 9, 12.)

PRINCIPAL WORKS

SHORT FICTION

The Greater Inclination   1899
The Touchstone   1900; published in England as *A Gift from the Grave*
Crucial Instances   1901
The Descent of Man, and Other Stories   1904
Madame de Treymes   1907
The Hermit and the Wild Woman, and Other Stories   1908
Tales of Men and Ghosts   1910
Ethan Frome   1911
Xingu, and Other Stories   1916
The Marne   1918
Old New York: False Dawn (The 'Forties). The Old Maid (The 'Fifties). The Spark (The 'Sixties). New Year's Day (The 'Seventies).   1924
Here and Beyond   1926
Certain People   1930
Human Nature   1933
The World Over   1936
Ghosts   1937
The Collected Short Stories.   2 vols.   1968

OTHER MAJOR WORKS

The Decoration of Houses   [with Ogden Codman, Jr.] (nonfiction)   1897
The Valley of Decision   (novel)   1902
Sanctuary   (novel)   1903
Italian Villas and Their Gardens   (essays)   1904
The House of Mirth   (novel)   1905
Italian Backgrounds   (memoirs)   1905
The Fruit of the Tree   (novel)   1907
A Motor-Flight through France   (travel essay)   1908
The Reef   (novel)   1912
The Custom of the Country   (novel)   1913
Summer   (novel)   1917
French Ways and Their Meaning   (essays)   1919
The Age of Innocence   (novel)   1920
In Morocco   (travel essays)   1920
The Glimpses of the Moon   (novel)   1922
A Son at the Front   (novel)   1923
The Mother's Recompense   (novel)   1925
The Writing of Fiction   (criticism)   1925
Twilight Sleep   (novel)   1927
The Children   (novel)   1928

Hudson River Bracketed   (novel)   1929
The Gods Arrive   (novel)   1932
A Backward Glance   (autobiography)   1934
The Buccaneers   (unfinished novel)   1938

ANNA McCLURE SHOLL   (essay date 1903)

[*In the following excerpt, Sholl identifies strengths and weaknesses of what she terms Wharton's epigrammatic literary style.*]

Artificiality of style, while precluding literary greatness, may possess certain positive merits, if it be an intimate expression of the author's mode of thought, an honest artificiality, weighed, measured and beautified. (p. 426)

In this country Henry James has discredited artificiality by divorcing it—if the paradox be allowed—from the natural processes of his thought. On the other hand, the peculiar, if limited, merits of this style receive organic expression in the work of Edith Wharton. She illustrates effectively, and without loss of literary integrity, the uses to which such a style can be put; its fitness to express uncommon moods involved mental processes, curious psychological situations; to adumbrate beauty of the elusive order; to portray certain types of modern women, whose sensitiveness of fibre, the fruit of artificial conditions precludes a robuster setting.

Of one of her heroines she writes that she had the air of tacitly excluding the obvious and the unexceptional. It is the exclusion of the obvious and the unexceptional that gives to Mrs. Wharton's style at once its charm and that kind of artificiality which is just a trifle inhuman—except from hearty joys and hearty sorrows. She writes of tragic things epigrammatically, and tragedy and epigram are not mates. In comedy—her sense of humor is keen and delightful—she is nearer the human heart, but still unabandoned, keeping throughout her aristocrat detachment and self-possession. If in the majority of her tales neither gaiety nor high tragedy predominates, it is perhaps because the moderate emotions of life are apt to be more complex, more obscure in their workings than a strong, direct feeling of joy or sorrow, and with what is complex and concealed in the human spirit she is chiefly concerned. In her two collections of short stories, *The Greater Inclination* and *Crucial Instances,* things seen are as a rule ancillary to the hidden spiritual drama. The brilliant flashes of her wit emerge from mystery, as scarlet and green and purple from the matrix of the opal.

If Mrs. Wharton has justified her style in the choice of her subjects, she has shown also that the short story is adapted to the artificial manner at its best. Though in her longest work, *The Valley of Decision,* and in the novelette, *The Touchstone,* her peculiar virtues are evident, they flower in her short stories. In these her self-restraint, her remarkable sensitiveness to the uses of words, her gift of condensing a volume in an epigram, her fondness for fleeting moods, delicately balanced situations, her rare humor find agreeable setting. Such masterpieces as **"The Pelican"** and **"The Duchess at Prayer"** place her in the first rank of short-story tellers of whatever country.

Few writers understand with equal clarity and present with equal truth the masculine and the feminine natures, distinct in many ways despite the theory of one, undivided human nature. Mrs. Wharton's talent for complex psychological analysis finds its fittest exercise in the portrayal of high-bred modern women—souls requiring special study in this age of forced growths. She realizes that such women create curious situations by the very nature of their being.

In **"The Muse's Tragedy"** Sylvia Averton married to commonplaceness, but lifted out of the banality of her marriage and glorified by the famous poet Vincent Rendle, is enthroned, when the story opens, upon a lonely pinnacle of memories. The world, concretely represented by the young hero-worshiper, Danyers, believes her to have been the Laura of this Petrarch who has immortalized her in a sonnet cycle. Enshrined in Vincent Rendle's supposed love, her life after his death is paled by all the exclusions of such a distinction. Danyers's genuine and discriminating admiration of the great man enables him to penetrate the moral mausoleum where the woman entrapped by fame is hidden. Their talk at first is all of Rendle. A new book about him is projected. Later Venice holds a young lover, and a middle-aged woman pitifully glad to be loved, but running away at last, and, in the act of flight, lifting a weight of confession from her soul.

> You thought it was because Vincent Rendle loved me that there is so little hope for you. I had had what I wanted to the full, wasn't that what you said? It is just when a man begins to think he understands a woman that he may be sure he doesn't! It is because Vincent Rendle *didn't love me* that there is no hope for you. I never had what I wanted, and never, never, never, will I stoop to wanting anything else.

She writes of the years when she hoped against hope, then of the doubt and despair that settled upon her—doubt of her powers; despair lest she should be that anomaly of nature—an unlovable woman.

> Was I so ugly, so essentially unlovable that though a man might cherish me as his mind's comrade, he could not care for me as a woman? . . . I wanted you to like me; it was not a mere psychological experiment. And yet in a sense it was that, too—I must be honest, I had to have an answer to that question; it was a ghost that had to be laid.

In this characteristic story of Mrs. Wharton's, it is not only the Muse's tragedy that is presented, but a clear sketch of a certain type of a man of genius; childish, monstrously selfish, full of contradictions, incapable of love, but not of passion, achromatizing all lives that his own hues may be the more resplendent and throughout unconscious of egotism.

In **"The Recovery"** another type of a genius is shown, but the central character of the story is his clear-sighted, sensitive wife, who has discovered his artistic limitations, long before he himself awakens to them, in the accusing presence of the Old Masters.

> She had always imagined that the true artist must regard himself as the imperfect vehicle of the cosmic emotion—that beneath every difficulty overcome a new one lurked, the vision widening as the scope enlarged. To be initiated into these creative struggles, to shed on the toiler's path the consolatory ray of faith and encouragement, had seemed the chief privilege of her marriage. But there is something supererogatory in believing in a man obviously disposed to perform that service for himself; and

Claudia's ardor gradually spent itself against the dense surface of her husband's complacency.

Mrs. Wharton's delightful understanding of certain provincial foibles underlies the delicate satire of this tale.

> To the visiting stranger Hillbridge's first question was, "Have you seen Keniston's things?" Keniston took precedence of the colonial State House, the Gilbert Stuart Washington and the Ethnological Museum; nay, he ran neck and neck with the President of the University, a pre-historic relic who had known Emerson, and who was still sent about the country in cotton-wool to open educational institutions with a tooth less oration on Brook Farm.

The stranger psychology of humanity has for Mrs. Wharton the fascination it possessed for Hawthorne. A mystic element underlies the realism of **"The Angel at the Grave"** with its faint, echoing pathos like chance footsteps in a deserted house. Mystic also is the theme of **"The Moving Finger"**, a tale of the obscure processes of grief. **"The Coward"** portrays an unconscious hero, haunted forever by an inexplicable cowardice of his youth. The same remote pathos of **"The Angel at the Grave"** is in this curious little tale of an obliterated American husband. Mrs. Wharton's close observation and keen understanding of all things American are among her greatest merits. She discerns the child-likeness of the great, exuberant nation under its precocity of thought and feeling, its crude strength, its adoration of success, of "culture", its wistful resentment of the Old World and its standards. Thoroughly American is **"The Portrait"**, in which an eminent painter famed for his insight into the essential character of his sitters is called upon to paint the portrait of a noted "boss", Alonzo Vard, whose villainies are public property. Vard has an innocent and adoring daughter who idealizes him, knowing nothing of his history as a public man. The eminent painter for her sake "expurgates" a face whose spirit he has at once read, and what should have been his masterpiece becomes his biggest failure.

An unusual gift possessed by Mrs. Wharton, a lambent masculine humor, is embodied in the **"The Pelican"**, one of the best short stories ever written. Nothing could exceed in delicate satirical wit the presentation of the widowed Mrs. Amyot, lecturing "for the baby" on a ridiculous variety of undigested subjects. Like some members of women's clubs she knew less about more things than the ordinary imagination could compass. (pp. 426-30)

The climax of this masterpiece occurs when "the baby", grown into a bearded man with a family of his own, makes the appalling discovery that his mother—still lecturing—still claims to be tearing her breast to feed her young. The stormy scene which follows ends with the last plea of the Pelican.

"I sent his wife a seal-skin jacket last Christmas!" she said, with the tears running down her cheeks.

The humorous quality predominates in **"The Rembrandt"** also, but for the most part it only touches here and there in gleams of pure gold, tales of graver import.

Mrs. Wharton's delicate psychology finds fit expression in her epigrammatic style, in her admirable workmanship. Through her workmanship, indeed, she holds her reader. The plots of her tales, while always coherent, logical and well carried out, are, as a rule, of the simplest, but the clear, thin lines point the way to many enchantments of style, the reserve of a noble prose, combined with epigram brilliant yet organic. The clever things she says flower out of the story—are the story. So true is this that it is difficult to do her justice in quotation.

Her sensitiveness to the souls of words is unerring. Going back to their essential meaning, she re-creates them and leads them into fertile marriages, fully aware that not the uncommon words lend vividness to a style, but common words in unusual vital combination.

Her similies are vivid and true. Behind the door of a closed room in an Italian villa "the cold lurked like a knife" "A girl's motives in marrying are like a passport apt to get mislaid." "In this interpretative light Mrs. Graney acquired the charm which makes some women's faces like a book of which the last page is never turned."

It is just possible that in Mrs. Wharton's pre-occupation with words, with delicacies and beauties of style may be found one reason why her tales are pictures rather than warm human life itself. **"The Duchess at Prayer"** is like an unforgettable fresco on the wall of an Italian villa, bringing into the present the sinister tragedy of a highly colored past where both pain and joy are acuminated beyond modern experience. Yet this vivid tale, full of picturesque phrases, of dramatic simile, is still a fresco. The passion is pictured not real. Mrs. Wharton is perhaps too scholarly, too aloof, for strong dramatic feeling, but of the enchantments of the intellect she is mistress.

Into this story a certain quality enters which is found more or less throughout Mrs. Wharton's work, and in a high degree in *The Valley of Decision*—a fine and rare moral detachment from what she portrays. She has the natural talent of producing fiction as free from subjective comment as a chronicle. For a woman she is wonderfully impersonal, and in this consists her essential refreshment to many minds. She presents the moral problem, but does not unduly meddle with it. She tells the story of the sin, but does not judge. A delicate indifference pervades her work, the indifference of one always aware that the margin of mystery in the Universe may in the course of ages disprove not only accepted creeds but accepted moralities. This most modern of all forms of reverence is invaluable to her as an artist. (pp. 430-32)

> *Anna McClure Sholl, "The Work of Edith Wharton," in* Gunton's Magazine, *Vol. 25, November, 1903, pp. 426-32.*

EDWIN BJÖRKMAN   (essay date 1913)

[*Björkman was a Swedish-American novelist, translator, and critic who introduced American readers to the works of such major Scandinavian authors as August Strindberg and Georg Brandes. In the following excerpt from his* Voices of To-Morrow: Critical Studies of the New Spirit in Literature, *Björkman suggests alternate denouements for* Ethan Frome, *pondering Wharton's psychological exploration of her characters and their setting, and concluding that* Ethan Frome *is a social rather than a personal tragedy.*]

[The Berkshire region of Connecticut] is the country which Mrs. Wharton has chosen as setting for one of her recent novels, **Ethan Frome.** And as we look at it with the keen vision that is hers, the ancient spinners of fate become transformed into those modern Norns whom we have named Climate, Soil and Race. The thread of events used by Mrs. Wharton for her purpose is of the slimmest and simplest. Ethan Frome is the last sprout of a characteristic Berkshire family. At twenty-

eight he has been worn down to the resignation of an old man. He has seen first one and then the other of his parents yield up reason and life under the blows of a fate that must be held logical rather than unkind. He has seen the inherited hillside farm run dry as an old cow. Panic-stricken by the hemming solitude, he has clutched at the one human being that ever showed a willingness to share his fate; and thus he has become saddled with a wife seven years his senior—a dyspeptic, self-centred, unlovable being with a genius for imaginary invalidism and a passion for patent medicines. Into this blighted and blighting home comes a young girl with a pretty face and a soft heart—not an extraordinary girl, but one whose main charm lies in a desire to give and get sympathy not uncommon in youth when sundered from all its natural ties.

Love steals into the hearts of these two. And at the same time the older woman's heart grows increasingly heavy with a jealousy that is not rendered less bitter by its failure of open expression. Step by step, yet within a brief space and without introduction of a single useless detail, the author reveals love and jealousy growing apace, until at last the fatal moment of open clash can no longer be avoided. The girl is sent away by the wife. Ethan plans to go with his love toward a new life in the West. This plan is checked not by any conscientious scruples, but by poverty—by actual inability to raise the small sum needed for travelling expenses.

Spurred into undisguised defiance, he insists on driving the young girl down to the railroad station in person. At the moment of separation utter despair floods their hearts. They are standing at the top of the snow-carpeted hill down which they had hoped to go coasting together some moonlit evening. There is a sled left behind by departed merry-makers. The course is made dangerous by a big elm standing too close to its most difficult turn. Down the glassy smoothness of that hill the two lovers glide together in search not of pleasure but of a common death. And under the firm pressure of Ethan's heel, the sled speeds straight into the menacing tree trunk.

Few features of this remarkable book stand out more strikingly than its general design, by which the author has managed to satisfy at once our craving for surprise and our dislike of too much surprise. From the very start the shadow of that final "smash-up" lies over the pages of the book. We know that everything else must lead up to it. We know that Ethan himself is to come out of it as a man crippled and cursed forever afterward. And we know also that he must return to Zeena, the wife, and that the ruinous purchases of quack remedies will go on as before. But what of the second traveller on that sled speeding toward the consummation so often denied to the few that seek it? What of Matt? Not a word is said in advance as to her fate.

And so, when the teller of the story, the young engineer from the outside, having discovered and told all the rest, at last by a conspiracy of circumstances finds his way into Ethan's home—otherwise closed to all the world but the owner—the shock of what the visitor discovers there leaves an impression on the reader's mind rarely equalled in the annals of fiction. For there, in the bare, inhospitable kitchen, where Zeena once brooded over her jealousy and Matt huddled her love—there the visitor meets both of them alive. Matt as a peevish, helpless, narrow-featured invalid with a broken back, and Zeena as a resigned, dullhearted nurse. And there Ethan has to live the rest of his spoiled life between those two spectres of his lost hopes: the woman he needed and the woman he loved. All other tragedies that I can think of seem mild and bearable beside this one. What is death, or sorrowing for the dead, in comparison with a life chained to the dead remains of what might have been love?

Even to a mere reader such an outcome might seem unendurable—not to be born in mere print, as a tale told rather than an experienced fact—but for one consideration. And this one redeeming factor asserts itself subtly throughout the book, though Mrs. Wharton never refers to it in plain words. It is this: that, after all, the tragedy unveiled to us is social rather than personal. It is so overwhelming that the modern mind rebels against it as a typical specimen of human experience. And if it had no social side, if it implied only what it brought of suffering and sorrow to the partakers in it, then we could do little but cry out in self-protective impatience: "Sweep off the shambles and let us pass on!" As it is, and because that social aspect asserts itself so irresistibly, we are led into almost overlooking what those crushed lives must have meant to those living them.

Ethan and Matt and Zeena are, indeed, as real as men and women can become in a book. But just because we see them thus, and because their common fate is so insufferably pitiful, that process of mental cauterization by which life guards itself against too rude shocks sets in even while we are reading. Just as we could not live on if we were not mercifully permitted to forget certain pains that have shot across our own fields of consciousness, so we are here instinctively moved to "shake off" the thought of Ethan and Matt and Zeena as individual sufferers. They become instead embodiments of large groups and whole strata; and the dominant thought left behind by the book is not concerned with the awfulness of human existence, but with the social loss involved in such wasting of human lives.

Ethan Frome is to me above all else a judgment on that system which fails to redeem such villages as Mrs. Wharton's Starkfield. And I am not now preaching socialism in the narrower sense. I am talking it in a sense in which it is being more and more accepted by those most fervently bent on orderly progress. I am pleading merely for the extension of certain forms of social cooperation and coordination—or call it simply organization—that have already been found inevitable in many fields of human activity. If a little crew of wrecked sailors be cast up on some coral reef in midocean, we do not say that they deserve their fate, nor do we demand that they rely wholly on their own resources for escape. The moment we learn of their plight, we send a vessel to relieve them. And this we do not only for their sake but for our own—because we need those men to carry on the world's business, and because we do not want to discourage other men from engaging in their perilous trade.

Those who dwell in our thousand and one Starkfields are just such wrecked mariners, fallen into their hapless positions by no fault of their own. And though helpless now, they need by no means prove useless under different conditions. Vessels should be sent to take them off their barren hillsides—or social effort should be employed in making those hillsides fruitful once more. There is hardly an inch of ground that has not its use of some kind—its paying use. There is hardly a human being, either, who cannot be rendered socially paying if given a chance. This we must learn ere the new day can be hoped for.

Mrs. Wharton has wisely refrained from every attempt at pointing toward a solving way. All she has done—and all she

was called on to do—was to reveal the presence of Starkfield and its population of Fromes within a social body that should contain nothing but living and growing tissue. In doing this, and doing it with her usual exquisiteness of word and phrase and portraiture, Mrs. Wharton has passed from individual to social art; from the art that excites to that which incites.

Glancing over the all too brief volume in retrospect, I can find only one point where it suggests a certain degree of failure, of growth still unachieved. With the building of the tale as it now stands I can have no fault to find. It is against a certain lack of outlook, a certain onesidedness of conception, that I direct my adverse criticism. And to what I say along this line, the author may, of course, reply that what I am wishing for did not fall within the scope of her plan. And yet I wish it had!

Let me try to explain, though the task undoubtedly will prove hard—and let me be frankly personal in order to be wholly just. As I read the book now, I come away with an impression that, in the author's mind at least, the one thing needed to change Ethan's life from a hell to a heaven would have been the full and free expression of his love for Matt. Had Zeena died and Matt married him, then, I am made to feel, the barren farm of Ethan might have blossomed once more; the strangled dreams of his youth might have ceased to harass and haunt his soul; nay, life in its entirety might have changed its face.

This is the very thing which poets through the ages have been tempting man to believe. It is the very thing which I cannot accept as a true interpretation of life's reality. Love is not a cure-all capable of righting all wrongs in an ill-managed world. It is an appetite, if you please; or, if so it please you better, it is a spiritual force springing from one of life's most material aspects. But at any rate it is a necessity—one of several—and as such it is bound to work havoc when not filled. But if, on the other hand, it be properly satisfied, then it reveals itself promptly as no end in itself, but a means to other ends—a prerequisite to the filling of new and no less essential necessities. We need love to live properly, but we can no more live properly on love alone than we can do so on bread.

Romantic love, as idealized for us by our sentimental-minded forefathers, has long ago gone into bankruptcy. Henrik Ibsen sat as judge in the case, and George Bernard Shaw was appointed receiver with full power to reorganize the failing concern. And so it is becoming more evident with every passing day that the race of pale youths and slender-waisted maidens who took or lost their own lives because of "unrequited love" never really belonged to this world.

Of course, if you have no soul-dominating interest to focus your activities, and you happen to pick up such an interest in the shape of a love dream, however silly or commonplace, and fate wakes you prematurely out of your sweet dream, then you are very likely to sink back into something much worse than your previous state of comparatively harmless inanition. But if, on the other hand, all your faculties are normally employed; if each day brings you new problems to solve, and if life does not deny you every means of applying your solutions, then the same kind of love dream, ending in pretty much the same way, may change but not mar the rest of your life. It will then serve as an added impetus toward activities already dear to your heart. The law of compensation will assert itself—energy will be transmitted instead of wasted—and life will go on even more effectively, though perhaps less placidly than before.

Had Zeena died and Matt married Ethan—well, it is my private belief that inside of a few years life on that farm would have been practically what it was before Matt arrived, with Matt playing the part of a Zeena II—different, of course, and yet the same. For the life in our Starkfields is cursed or saved not by this or that single incident, not by the presence or absence of this or that individual. "Most smart ones get away," says the old stage driver in Mrs. Wharton's book. The curse lies in staying there, in breathing the crushing, choking atmosphere of Starkfieldian sterility.

Ethan was doomed when he did not get away as a boy. Having returned and stayed for a certain length of time, his life was no longer susceptible to more than momentary alleviation. And a forewarning of this fact I read out of Mrs. Wharton's repeated references to Matt's physical frailty—a state of mind and body certain to have made her an easy victim of the Starkfield atmosphere even if no "smash-up" had been the cause of her stay within it. A few weeks or months of complete surrender to love's bliss would have been what the grog is to the fainting stoker in the ocean steamer's boiler-room. That grog may bring temporary relief, it may save life, and it may even carry with it a quick sting of pleasure, but it cannot turn stoking into a wholesome or pleasurable task. And life in a place untouched by the onward sweep of the world, especially when lived by individuals soured and weakened by a too long and too hard struggle against conditions unfit for any human being, is nothing but another form of stoking. For saying which each present Starkfield inhabitant will probably rise up and curse the rash critic. (pp. 291-304)

Edwin Björkman, "The Greater Edith Wharton," in his Voices of To-Morrow: Critical Studies of the New Spirit in Literature, *Mitchell Kennerley, 1913, pp. 290-304.*

FRANCIS HACKETT   (essay date 1917)

[*Hackett was a respected Irish-American biographer, novelist, and literary critic during the first half of the twentieth century. His reviews appeared in the* New Republic, *the* Saturday Review of Literature, *and other prominent American periodicals. In the following excerpt from a review of* Xingu, and Other Stories, *Hackett faults Wharton's lack of humor but praises her excellence in portraying relations among the upper classes.*]

Mrs. Wharton comes very near affording complete gratification with this volume of short stories [*Xingu, and Other Stories*]. She takes her subjects as only an artist can take them, for the values, the resonances, they happen to have for her; and the fact that she writes mainly of a restricted class seems at the moment irrelevant. It would be really irrelevant if Mrs. Wharton didn't, in a subtle enough way, become condescending to persons who live on, and off, the fringe. Sometimes as between a perfectly initiated pet and a bounding newcomer one gets a whiff of sublimated sensibilities. Of such assaulted

The problem before me [in writing ***Ethan Frome***], as I saw in the first flash, was this: I had to deal with a subject of which the dramatic climax, or rather the anti-climax, occurs a generation later than the first acts of the tragedy. This enforced lapse of time would seem to anyone persuaded—as I have always been—that every subject (in the novelist's sense of the term) implicitly *contains its own form and dimensions,* to mark Ethan Frome as the subject for a novel. But I never thought this for a moment, for I had felt, at the same time, that the theme of my tale was not one on which many variations could be played. It must be treated as starkly and summarily as life had always presented itself to my protagonists; any attempt to elaborate and complicate their sentiments would necessarily have falsified the whole.

It appears to me, indeed, that, while an air of artificiality is lent to a tale of complex and sophisticated people which the novelist causes to be guessed at and interpreted by any mere looker-on, there need be no such drawback if the looker-on is sophisticated, and the people he interprets are simple. If he is capable of seeing all around them, no violence is done to probability in allowing him to exercise this faculty; it is natural enough that he should act as the sympathizing intermediary between his rudimentary characters and the more complicated minds to whom he is trying to present them.

The real merit of my construction seems to me to lie in a minor detail. I had to find means to bring my tragedy, in a way at once natural and picture-making, to the knowledge of its narrator. I might have sat him down before a village gossip who would have poured out the whole affair to him in a breath, but in doing this I should have been false to two essential elements of my picture: first, the deep-rooted reticence and inarticulateness of the people I was trying to draw, and secondly the effect of "roundness" (in the plastic sense) produced by letting their case be seen through eyes as different as those of Harmon Gow and Mrs. Ned Hale. Each of my chroniclers contributes to the narrative *just so much as he or she is capable of understanding* of what, to them, is a complicated and mysterious case; and only the narrator of the tale has scope enough to see it all, to resolve it back into simplicity, and to put it in its rightful place among his larger categories.

Edith Wharton, in her introduction to a 1922 edition of Ethan Frome.

class consciousness as this sort of thing implies, Mrs. Wharton occasionally gives signs. Among the petty bourgeoisie she moves with comparative sympathy. Among more formidable representatives of the same ilk she moves with something not unlike a sniff. She is difficult to please, but the difficulty is not always due to intrinsic considerations. For a person of such lancing intelligence she is strangely deficient in comedy. It is not that one wants her to have a richer palette or a more dashing line. It is not that one wishes her to burst on the world exuberantly, with a barbaric yawp. It is merely that with a higher sense of comedy other realities would emerge in her landscape which, under the light that is habitual with her, is somewhat acid, cold and bleak.

But astringent as one may deem Mrs. Wharton's mood, it would be absurd to miss her deep excellences on that account. There are many manifestations of America for which she has not the faculty, but those that peculiarly arrest her, those that depend on being of the feminine gender among well-off people in a given time and sphere, extract from her the sort of appreciation that amounts to genius. The fate that she has most absorbingly contemplated and most handsomely represented is perhaps that of persons whose lot is enhanced by money or family or taste, and whose impulses pay reluctant toll to an order in whose establishment their happiness and their honor are involved. It is, if you like, worldly wisdom that here occupies Mrs. Wharton; it happens, however, to be wisdom. Congruous as she is with *Scribner's Magazine,* incongruous with the Walt Whitmans, she is still the intent observer of nature adaptive and assertive, of pliancies and subjections, desertions and rebellions. In some respects she is a pharmacist in her handling of vital forces. She deals in essences and double distillations. She uses a delicate measure to weigh out what is precious or deadly. She dispenses little that she regards as lethal or valuable outside what would fit in an apothecary scales. She is grave, minute, scrupulous, analytic. She is dramatic hypodermically. But to such fine uses does she put the sympathies and perceptions with which she is endowed, that a reader would be strangely callous who was not lost in admiration among the merits of her art.

Take as perhaps the best example in this volume the tale called **"The Long Run."** It is a favorite theme of Mrs. Wharton's, the drama of a love that is not coincident with marriage. In this case, as indeed in most of the stories in *Xingu,* Mrs. Wharton is seeing these things in retrospect, not as matters of palpitation so much as matters of eventual chemistry. The man in this instance harks back to his hour of decision, the hour when everything depended on the driving force of his impulse as against her husband's preemption. She is willing to go out with her lover, she has no sense of having been preempted. She knows that to her husband she is furniture, that there are no "reasons—honest reasons—for staying there." This woman at the lift of the flashing sunny wave can invite her lover to it. "The first great anatomist was the man who stuck his knife in a heart that was beating; and the only way to find out what doing a thing will be like is to do it!" The male in the man, orthodox in possessiveness, refuses. She cannot swim, he sees it, except in the lifebelt of matrimony.

And what that decision came to, in the perspective of his own resignation and her later re-marriage, is the story Mrs. Wharton beautifully and sympathetically contrives. They are not people seen in the various successive attitudes of a morality, registering this and that. They are people whose morality is in solution, never labeled for that particular brand of interest by Mrs. Wharton herself. She has no intention for them save to reveal them, to give them in their own "flood of joy that comes of heightened emotion," their own persuasions as to life, and the price it cost them to have had him incapable of

crossing a stream that had no bridge. A story like this is the flower of a career.

Permeated with equal sympathy, rather a dejected and vengeful sympathy, is **"Bunner Sisters,"** a fascinating novelette of two middle-aged tradeswomen in old New York. The odor of condescension does not, for me, cling to this example of Mrs. Wharton's studies in a sphere not excitingly fashionable. There are inflections she catches with sharp exactness. There is no attempt to make Ann Eliza and Evelina seem less like morons than they really were. But the story has an almost affectionate completeness of detail and a totally affectionate occupation with both Ann Eliza and Evelina is the bitter-sweet of their intimacy with the fated Mr. Ramy. The Bunners do not come off very well, defenseless in a fight so manifold and so complicated as life; but they are not exceptional. In not one of Mrs. Wharton's eight stories does any one come off particularly well, except of course the potential murderer in **"Triumph of Night"** and the brute-husband in **"The Choice."**

"Xingu" is perhaps the cleverest of these stories. It is also the least valuably perceptive. A satire on the excessive seriousness, the pretentiousness, the false zealotry of a small American "culture" club, it goes rather too far in an acrimonious caricature of the women as human beings. Mrs. Wharton's acid bites fairly into their idiocy as the pursuers of culture, it scarifies them too deeply in their social character. The Laura Glyde and Mrs. Plinth and Mrs. Leveret of real life would be equally insufferable about books, but Mrs. Wharton's cold dislike for their natures is quite unjustified. It is in dealing with such women as these, women who if anything would err on the side of amiability and whose main mistake is to take too seriously the obligations imposed on them by a culture not native, that Mrs. Wharton becomes frigidly conventional. Her Mrs. Plinths and Mrs. Leverets are misjudged from the vantage point of Lenox or Tuxedo, or wherever it is that women do not allow even their illiteracy to detract from their self-confidence.

Despite **"Bunner Sisters,"** it would be egregious loyalty to Mrs. Wharton as an artist not to admit that she is primarily a person interested in a restricted world. She has an ear for the clash and chime of life outside Lenox and those other places where ministers of grace draw your bath and steal about, exaggerating your wardrobe, while you pretend to be asleep. Her story of wartime in the Vosges and the German intrusion on a château there indicates that. But it is not too much to say that she tends to start with men of means and women who use those means to their ends. One has only to glance at her personæ—Horace Pursh, Halston Merrick, Susy Suffern, Harriet Fresbie, Wilbour Barkley, Austin Wrayford, Cobham Stilling, Philip Trant, Mrs. Lidcote, Mrs. Lorin Boulger, H. Macy Greer, Franklin Ide, Jim Cumnor. These are not the kind of people with whom you share cracker-jack in a day-coach. . . . Mrs. Wharton holds these persons in preference—out of proportion to their constituency in society as a whole though not by any means out of proportion to their interest. For their interest, as Mrs. Wharton considers them, is not a fatuous fashionableness. It is the chance they offer for intensive human relations, those relations that include love, but also so often preclude it, and always pivoting on marriage. Marriage and love are the great factors in the drama Mrs. Wharton concentrates upon. Of these the greater, in the frankly middle-aged stories in *Xingu,* is neither one nor the other automatically; she is cool enough to say that the cost of love may be too heavy, and warm enough to have its balance sheet her main preoccupation. It is this absorption in the delicate processes, the feminized processes, which decide where the bemedaled warriors shall dine, and whom sit next to, and whom take to wife and whom to bed, that has kept her up-town and socially excited. The quality of that excitement is the principal charm of *Xingu,* an achievement that no other American is emulating. (pp. 50-2)

Francis Hackett, "Mrs. Wharton's Art," in The New Republic, *Vol. X, No. 119, February 10, 1917, pp. 50-2.*

J. D. THOMAS (essay date 1955)

[*In the following essay, Thomas discusses narrative inconsistencies in* Ethan Frome.]

Edith Wharton in *Ethan Frome* performed a real artistic service in imaging that isolated world of snowdrifts, sledges, and weary struggle for the mere survival of man and beast which until yesterday was the lot of over half the American people during nearly a half of their lives. It is regrettable that she felt obliged to narrate her story from a masculine point of view. To think of the contrived Mr. Lockwood against the infinitely human Nelly Dean is to take the measure of the ability of

Wharton in 1900.

even a highly intuitive authoress to fathom male psychology. Mrs. Wharton, of course, had vastly more experience of men than Emily Brontë, but it counted for little in a book like *Ethan Frome.* The men she knew intimately were men in society, where the established controls drive behavior and speech toward a feminine norm. Thus she was deluded into supposing that an engineer in the field would observe that "outcroppings of slate . . . *nuzzled up* through the snow like animals pushing out their noses to breathe." This figure could not possibly occur spontaneously to a man of action (one may as well say, to any man), though the phrase might be self-consciously employed in an effort to please a drawing room.

An evident uncertainty of the author about the occupational concerns of men leaves the "job connected with the big powerhouse at Corbury Junction," which accounts for her narrator's presence in Starkfield, the shadow of a wraith. But she cannot totally ignore the daily affairs of Ethan Frome; her efforts to describe them sometimes veer between the ludicrous and the pathetic, depending on the precise cast of the reader's sympathies. Ethan's main source of cash income is his sawmill, and during Zeena's "therapeutic excursion" to Bettsbridge he is engaged in hauling several loads of lumber to Starkfield. At least they begin as "lumber," but presently are termed "logs" and even "tree trunks . . . so slippery that it took twice as long as usual to lift them and get them in place on the sledge." Exactly what Andrew Hale, a carpenter and house builder, would want with logs, or in any event how sawed lumber could be reconverted to tree trunks, is not revealed. On this delivery of lumber (logs?), Ethan asks Hale for a "small advance" of fifty dollars. If from the word *small* we have a right to assume that he is now creditor to the builder for perhaps a few hundred dollars, we are bound to question the financial crisis two days later, when "he knew that without security no one at Starkfield would lend him ten dollars. . . . There was no way out—none." Probably Edith Wharton had never had occasion to hypothecate or discount a note, but the shift certainly would have occurred to the well-experienced Ethan—who "six months before . . . had given his only security to raise funds for necessary repairs to the mill"—as a natural alternative to catastrophe.

Mrs. Wharton's vagueness about the common affairs of life is not wholly limited to men, for she once attributes to her narrator's chief informant, Mrs. Ned Hale, a singular obtuseness. Following an account of Ethan's attempted suicide with Mattie, Mrs. Hale remarks that "the folks here could never rightly tell what she and Ethan were doing that night coasting, when they'd ought to have been on their way to the Flats to ketch the train." Now, any small-town woman would know that "the folks" have a sure instinct for scandal, and that there would be no doubt whatever in the collective mind of the village—especially in its female lobe—as to the general situation between Ethan and his wife's cousin. Here Mrs. Wharton is betrayed by a fundamental ignorance of rural life, which she thought she understood after watching it for a few seasons from the windows of a villa. What real country woman, in telling a story, would allow the moon to set and rise at approximately the same hour on successive nights?

The plot of *Ethan Frome* involves an interesting, if perhaps unimportant, problem of chronology. Ethan and Zeena have been man and wife for seven years. They were married following the death of his mother, who "got queer and dragged along *for years*" after the death of his father. These clear and coherent data are unreconcilable with a report at the beginning of the main action of the story that "*four or five years earlier* he had taken a year's course at a technological college at Worcester," especially when read in conjunction with an accompanying explicit statement: "His father's death, and the misfortune following it had put a premature end to Ethan's studies . . . ."

In all probability the inconsistency of dates is to be explained as a simple *lapsus calami aut memoriae,* and if so is inconsequential. However, the book raises a much more fundamental problem that cannot be so summarily dismissed. The principal moral crisis occurs on the day after Zeena's return from Bettsbridge. Faced with the certainty of his loss of Mattie, Ethan goes into Starkfield determined to find some way out of his difficulties: "He had made up his mind to do something, but he did not know what it would be. . . ."

> Suddenly it occurred to him that Andrew Hale, who was a kind-hearted man, might be induced to reconsider his refusal and advance a small sum on the lumber if he were told that Zeena's ill-health made it necessary to hire a servant. . . .

> The more he considered his plan the more hopeful it seemed. If he could get Mrs. Hale's ear he felt certain of success, and with fifty dollars in his pocket nothing could keep him from Mattie. . . .

The expected sympathy of Mrs. Hale is quickly forthcoming, and Ethan is hurrying on to present his request to her husband when suddenly scruples of the most remarkable character assail him. The ethical situation would seem clear enough. He had willingly married a relative older than himself, a woman with whose character he was more intimately acquainted than most bridegrooms with that of their brides, and whose only new faults revealed after marriage where chronic ill health (no doubt genuine enough) and chronic lamentation about it. On her side, she certainly had enough hardship to bear, and at least she showed some virtue of forbearance, for we learn that she had never once quarreled openly with her husband until the pretty face of Matt came between them. Such considerations might give him pause before the house of Andrew Hale, but his actual thoughts are very different:

> . . . he pulled up sharply, the blood in his face. For the first time, . . . he saw what he was about to do. *He was planning to take advantage of the Hale's sympathy to obtain money from them on false pretences.* That was a plain statement of the cloudy purpose which had driven him in headlong to Starkfield.

Only as an afterthought does the real ethical problem occur to him, and then obliquely and in relation to the forced issue of his dun of Mr. Hale for payment of a legitimate debt:

> With the sudden perception of the point to which his madness had carried him, the madness fell and he saw his life before him as it was. He was a poor man, the husband of a sickly woman, whom his desertion would leave alone and destitute; and *even if he had had the heart to desert her he could have done so only by deceiving two kindly people who had pitied him.*

> He turned and walked slowly back to the farm.

This extraordinary passage could be interpreted as an ironical revelation of the moral darkness into which a man can wander, but there is no indication that it is so intended. From the author's point of view, the fictional problem was to force the story at this point into a tragic resolution. If the genuine moral issue had been threshed out in Ethan's mind, it would have been necessary for him either to repent or to yield openly and knowingly to temptation. Repentance would have meant walking "back to the farm" for good and ever. Yielding could have led easily enough to the catastrophe of the sled, but it doubtless would have destroyed the empathy of most readers for the runaway lovers. To make illicit love attractive is simple enough, but to make it seem right is difficult. Mrs. Wharton solves the problem by a dodge that we must agree is clever, whatever we may think of the intention behind it. (pp. 405-09)

> *J. D. Thomas, "Marginalia on 'Ethan Frome'," in* American Literature, *Vol. 27, No. 3, November, 1955, pp. 405-09.*

PATRICIA R. PLANTE   (essay date 1963)

[*In the following excerpt, Plante traces early critical reception of Wharton's stories and defends the author against various literary detractors.*]

Edith Wharton's chief concern in **"The Recovery"** as well as in other stories is a vivid presentation of the subject, and this she accomplishes with a high degree of competence. First, her short stories are never mere sketches or breathless summaries. For example, in the story under discussion, the subject of Keniston's original blindness and eventual enlightenment is analyzed in detail. Enough time is taken so that the reader can see him respond to Mrs. Davant and his other home town admirers, share his bewilderment when faced with the works of genius at the National Gallery in London and experience his failure when his paintings are exhibited in Paris. Second, her openings are not only effective and colorful, but contain the germ of the story about to be developed. **"The Recovery"** begins with the sentence, "To the visiting stranger Hillbridge's first question was, 'Have you seen Keniston's things?'" And finally, her skillful use of dialogue contributes greatly to the vividness of her presentation of a situation. It is used sparingly and discriminately, and only at moments of crisis in the tale. For example, in **"The Recovery"** it is used four times, and each time one of the most important phases of the situation is made clear. The first time dialogue is used, Mrs. Davant's uncritical and valueless opinion of Keniston's work is contrasted to his wife's perceptive and sensitive view of the same. The second time, Keniston's blind acceptance of Mrs. Davant's encouragement is made clear to Mrs. Keniston. The third time, Mrs. Keniston is given hints as to an approaching change in her husband's attitude, and the reader is prepared for the ending. And the last time, Keniston shares his artistic awakening with his joyful wife. Thus, the situation in Edith Wharton's **"The Recovery"** had been very clearly and vividly presented, but a doubt persisted in the critics' minds as to whether it had been worth presenting at all.

The Descent of Man and *The Hermit and the Wild Woman* fared about the same. There was no denying their brilliancy, their skill, their cleverness, but without explaining what they meant by "elemental art" reviewers shouted that these collections of short stories were without it—and seemingly, nothing could replace "it." Readers of the volume were also beginning to accuse Edith Wharton of monotony and coldness. One found no lifting from minor to major, no relieving touch of cheerfulness. Agnes Repplier wrote in *The Outlook* that the latter collection had the chill of winter in its pages and that it would best appeal to an impartial reader who was prepared to accept the ironies of life as a substitute for its illusions. *The Spectator* argued that the invariable recurrence of failure and disillusionment as leading motives made for both depression and monotony. *The Nation* repeated the charge in slightly different words and hoped that the uniformity of key was only coincidence.

What is most striking in these two volumes, other than the similarity of tone discernible in all the tales, is Edith Wharton's preoccupation with the irony of things—especially in connection with man's failures. The best example of this ironic spirit in dealing with the weaknesses of man is probably found in the story entitled **"The Other Two"** from the collection *The Descent of Man.* Again, the situation is all. Waythorn marries a beautiful woman who has had two previous husbands, Haskett and Varick. For personal and business reasons, the three men and Mrs. Waythorn are continuously brought together. At first, Waythorn's sense of decorum is offended, but gradually he comes to accept the fact that his wife's great talent for anticipating and fulfilling all of his domestic needs had had to be acquired at some school. "He even began to reckon up the advantages which accrued from it, to ask himself if it were not better to own a third of a wife who knew how to make a man happy than a whole one who had lacked opportunity to acquire the art." The tale ends with all four parties involved happily taking tea together in the Waythorn parlor. Admittedly, Waythorn's concessions and his wife's pliability are not weaknesses which would suggest man's potential greatness. There is no hint of tragedy in Waythorn's final illumination concerning the disconcerting fact that his wife was "as easy as an old shoe—a shoe that too many feet had worn. Her elasticity was the result of tension in too many different directions."

If there is no tragedy in **"The Other Two,"** there is a great deal of humor which critics seemingly insisted on not discovering. Surely reviewers were right in drawing attention to Edith Wharton's vein of irony which ran through her tales, and they were also right in noticing that this ironic treatment of nearly all situations contributed to a nearly monotonous similarity of tone. However, when Agnes Repplier wrote in *The Outlook* that this irony is "remote from humor," one wonders whether Edith Wharton's spirit of fun was in reality too subtle or whether readers needed time to orient themselves to a writer whose humor was anything but obvious. At any rate, it seems fairly certain, in the light of her other works, that when Edith Wharton described the adaptability of a Mrs. Waythorn, who could diffuse about her a sense of ease and familiarity while offering her two former husbands and her present one a cup of tea, she was actually joining Waythorn himself who "took the third cup with a laugh." Edith Wharton's use of irony had always been the method best suited to both her purpose and talent in communicating humor. The ironic treatment of a situation always allowed her to juxtapose a character's view of himself and the circumstances in which he finds himself, with the author's own view of both revealed through description or dialogue. And this very juxtaposition is what makes for the Wharton variety of humor. For example, in **"The Other Two"** when Waythorn, watching his wife preparing his coffee, yields to feelings of possessorship, the author, through a sudden use of romantic

phrases, makes it clear that poor Waythorn's feelings are quite unwarranted. "They were his, those white hands with their flitting motions, his the light haze of hair, the lips and eyes. . . . " At that very moment, Mrs. Waythorn pours cognac in the coffee. Unfortunately, Varick (husband number two), was the one who liked the combination of cognac and coffee. Waythorn utters an exclamation, and his thoughts of possessorship are given a violent jolt—much to the amusement of the reader.

It was generally agreed that the stories in Edith Wharton's next collection, *Tales of Men and Ghosts,* were of strangely unequal merit, but what is a bit disconcerting is that they were accused of two rather contradictory defects. On the one hand we read the by now familiar complaint that while maintaining a high literary standard as to form, diction, and structure, the author is too subtle and inconclusive and too deficient in action to please the average reader; and on the other, a new note was sounded when *The Nation* found the tales too patent and trumped up. For the first time, Edith Wharton was accused of writing magazine fiction. An announcement had been made the year before that she would come out with this collection in 1910, and some felt that here they were—skillfully turned out according to contract.

Only the rare and discriminating magazine fiction reader, it seems to me, would experience any satisfaction in reading *Tales of Men and Ghosts,* a collection of psychological studies of abnormal or supernatural episodes. By "ghosts" most readers would certainly expect something quite different from the clever suggestions of the preternatural happenings found in these pages. In **"His Father's Son,"** for example, a young man, at the height of his romantic folly, imagines that he is the illegitimate son of a very famous pianist; and discovers, to his chagrin, that he is truly the son of the man who brought him up—Mason Grew, inventor of a suspender buckle. The story involves very little action, and is told in a very unexciting way. The first half describes Mason Grew's background and relationship to his son; the second half records the conversation between the two wherein the son discovers his mistake. This type of subtle, mild satire against "Wertherian" excess is apt to cause but a ripple on the surface of the average imagination. And the ordinary reader is not apt to understand or sympathize with a Mason Grew whose unattractive person clothed a rare and sensitive nature.

Nor are the other stories in this collection made for popular wholesale acceptance. In **"The Daunt Diana"** a man impoverishes himself in order to own a beautiful statue of Diana and speaks of it almost in mystical terms: "I always cared—always worshipped—always wanted her. But she wasn't mine then, and I knew it, and she knew it. . . . and now at last we understand each other." In **"The Debt"** a protégé of a famous biologist repays the latter for all his guidance and encouragement by developing a scientific theory that destroys the older man's thesis. Again, these two understand each other, but it is to be doubted that the reader does—the reader of fiction who expects and welcomes patent, trumped-up tales. Those critics who claimed that such stories were the run-of-the-mill magazine type might have been forced to change their minds had they tried to find others to match them in subtlety and quiet thoughtfulness. (pp. 365-70)

[In *Xingu, and Other Stories*], Edith Wharton is decidedly the lady of various moods and the author of many talents. One need but look at the first and last tales—both of which attracted a good deal of comment—to get an insight into the amazing "grande dame's" power in handling the setting and characters of two nearly completely different worlds. The collection opens with **"Xingu,"** a story about society ladies and their literary pretensions. With the very first, and by now quite famous line, the author treats the reader to great satire: "Mrs. Ballinger is one of the ladies who pursue culture in bands, as though it were dangerous to meet alone." After reading this sentence, anyone who knows Edith Wharton is prepared for great fun, and all expectations are fulfilled on a grand scale. Mrs. Ballinger's Lunch Club, composed of herself and "other indomitable huntresses of erudition," is led from one literary *faux pas* to another until all the members very plausibly admit having read about and having practiced "Xingu." That "Xingu" is a river in Brazil is the story's well guarded secret, climactically revealed to the club and the reader at the same time. Edith Wharton's spirit of humor and masterful use of irony in such a scene as the visit of Osric Dane, the writer, foreshadow some of the great satirical theater and dinner scenes in *The Age of Innocence.*

In contrast to **"Xingu,"** the volume ends with a sombre novelette, **"Bunner Sisters"** filled with pathos. In portraying the emotionally starved lives of Ann Eliza and Evelina, who run a small shop in a shabby basement on a New York side street, Edith Wharton employs the grim simplicity of *Ethan Frome* without attaining its power. Ethan and Mattie's sufferings are every bit as painful as those of these two sisters, but one accepts them because they are made to bear a great theme. In this novelette, however, the pain inflicted on the protagonists seems meaningless, and the reader can only recoil at the sight of it. But having said this, there is no denying Edith Wharton's outstanding skill in recording manners. Hers is not merely the ability to picture the ways of her restricted world; for the back parlor of Ann Eliza and Evelina Bunner is as clearly *seen* as the Marvell's dining-room in *The Custom of the Country* or Pauline Manford's sitting room in her country home in *Twilight Sleep.* Indeed, Mr. Ramy's visits in that pathetic back parlor would be less painful to observe were Edith Wharton's description of them less sharp and vivid. As it is, one can but witness Evelina taking his thread-bare overcoat and shabby hat and laying them "on a chair with the gesture she imagined the lady with the puffed sleeves [a society lady] might make use of on similar occasions," and praise the author's power to select the very details which will render a passage unforgettable. Whether Edith Wharton etches the ladies of the Lunch Club looking up the word "Xingu" in the encyclopedia, or the Bunner sisters nervously attempting to entertain a guest, she is able to create a mood almost instantaneously through clever use of description.

A decade later, Wharton published her seventh collection of tales, entitled *Here and Beyond,* and the consensus at the time of its appearance seemed to be that although the six tales therein would add nothing to the author's reputation, they certainly would not detract from it. In fact, one of the sketches, **"Bewitched,"** was praised as very deft and as containing within its narrow field a great deal of tragic power. Its setting is the bare and bleak New England of *Ethan Frome* and *Summer,* but its plot contains "supernatural" elements not found in either of these novelettes. The noncommunicative Mrs. Rutledge requests the advice of her minister and of two other citizens on how to deal with an unusual family problem: her husband Saul is betwitched; he meets a dead former sweetheart in an old deserted house. Edith Wharton creates an atmosphere of mystery and witchcraft with such skill that the

Wharton in 1905.

reader believes throughout the telling of the tale that the Deacon is right in claiming that an apparition is "sucking the life clean out of " Saul. The icy solitude, the tumble-down house of mystery, the spectral footsteps in the snow—all make for a most satisfying ghost story.

"The Seed of Faith," a story of religious fanaticism and martyrdom in a small Baptist mission under the blinding June sky of Africa, was also much admired. It is to the author's great credit to have been able to create the atmosphere of a small African town with every bit as much skill as she had that of a small New England one in **"Bewitched."** Edith Wharton may have been at her best when describing an aristocratic New York setting, but this volume should prove that she was not incapable of doing anything else. Admittedly, the collection was one which would appeal to those who had a penchant for their rather exotic and special qualities, and quite obviously, the old flame of conviction was probably burning less brightly; however, Edith Wharton's familiar grace of phrase, worldly wisdom, and urbane detachment were still happily present. Besides, the themes were made more poignant because the forms had an architectural quality for which contemporary magazine tales often substituted a flashy virtuosity. (pp. 371-73)

"After Holbein" really preserves in miniature all of Edith

Wharton's finest gifts. This dreadful yet fascinating variation on the Dance of Death has as its protagonists Anson Warley and Evelina Jaspar, two old and ailing members of the high society set. In their senility and mental decay, the latter imagines that guests are coming to dine, and the other that he has been invited. And in one of the most macabre scenes in any short story, these two vestiges of the age of innocence entertain each other while observing all the minutiae of the accepted amenities. Death is actually calling each of them in the guise of the other, for what they prized most in life were shallow appearances—symbolized here by Mrs. Jaspar's and Warley's perfect dress even at the point of death. Warley appears in fastidious evening clothes, fur-lined overcoat, and thin evening watch in proper pocket, while Mrs. Jaspar is truly a "petrifying apparition" in purple wig, evening gown, and weighty diamond necklaces. Coldness is not the basis of this caustic satire, but a realization that as a man lives, so he is apt to die. If the Jaspars and the Warleys have spent their days promoting vanity and superficiality, death-bed conversions are not to be expected. Those tempted to accuse Edith Wharton of blindness to the deficiencies of brownstone aristocracy, are amply refuted in **"After Holbein."** This is satire based on strong conviction, not on coldness or spleen. Edith Wharton's morality is based on taste, and Anson Warley and Evelina Jaspar's vanity is so grotesque that it violates all principles of taste—even if they did once serve ninety-five Perrier-Joust. (p. 375)

"Her Son" is certainly one of Edith Wharton's finest short stories. Like Henry James's tale, "Four Meetings," it is told from the point of view of the narrator who, at various intervals and in different countries, follows the adventures of an American woman deceived by conniving cosmopolitans. Mrs. Catherine Glenn, after the death of her husband, spends all her time and fortune looking for her illegitimate son, whom she has not seen since he was a baby, twenty-seven years ago. In Europe she meets Mr. and Mrs. Brown, who pass off a young man as Mrs. Glenn's son, Stephen. These three individuals proceed to ruin Mrs. Glenn financially, and in a malicious rage at her refusal to provide them with more money, Mrs. Brown tells her that Stephen is not her son. He is, in fact, Mrs. Brown's lover, who could conceive of no other means to support her and himself. Edith Wharton's contrast between the vulgar Browns with their incessant, arid talk and sophisticated Catherine Glenn with her desperate, fear-ridden meekness is excellent. The story's ending is probably one of the most skillful and compact in the canon of Wharton's tales. At the very moment when Mrs. Brown is convinced that she has dealt Mrs. Glenn the worst of blows by announcing that she and Stephen are lovers, the latter points to the speaker's disordered headgear and says, "My dear—your hat's crooked." For a moment the reader is bewildered, but he soon realizes that Mrs. Brown's blow never hit its intended mark. "A pitying fate had darkened Catherine Glenn's intelligence at the exact moment when to see clearly would have been the final anguish." Not only had Mrs. Glenn's intelligence mercifully clouded, but the shaft she had launched at her enemy had been in terms of her world—the world of good manners which placed such infinite importance on meticulously proper dress. A vulgar, conniving Mrs. Brown could be ruffled by such a remark, but she could never understand the depths of disapproval implied by it. Having uttered it, Mrs. Glenn could, indeed, lean back "with the satisfied sigh of a child." (pp. 376-77)

Whenever Edith Wharton is mentioned as a short story writ-

er today, she is praised for her cool detachment, her fine finish, and her structural brilliance. She is even credited, along with Henry James, for having contributed a great deal to the advancement of the form of the short story in this country. Yet these qualities are evidently not those by which modern readers are particularly moved, regardless of how much they admire them: there is no doubt whatever that Edith Wharton's popularity has declined and that many today would not question Robert Morss Lovett for calling her the last of the Victorians. It is difficult to state exactly to what depths her fame has plunged, for no graphs can be drawn where values are concerned. It is certainly significant, however, that her collections of short stories are now out of print and that editors such as Norman Foerster do not even mention her in their surveys. It is to be hoped that she will continue to be read by a discriminating audience because of her mastery of form and language and because of a few ideas which will always deserve universal attention: man's humanity or inhumanity to man, man's relation and responsibility to society, and the importance of such virtues as order, tradition, culture, and control. (p. 379)

Patricia R. Plante, "Edith Wharton as Short Story Writer," in The Midwest Quarterly, *Vol. IV, No. 4, Summer, 1963, pp. 363-79.*

R. W. B. LEWIS (essay date 1968)

[*Lewis is an American literary critic and editor. In the following excerpt from his introduction to a collection of Wharton's short stories, Lewis examines a representative selection of Wharton's short fiction, finding it reflective of the author's multi-faceted personality.*]

Edith Wharton began as a writer of short stories and, in a sense, she finished as one. Her first publications (apart from the poems that appeared anonymously in the New York *World* and the *Atlantic Monthly,* and were privately printed as *Verses* in 1878) were a series of stories brought out by *Scribner's,* starting with the issue of July, 1891, when Mrs. Wharton was in her thirtieth year. By the time she completed her first novel, *The Valley of Decision,* in 1902, two volumes of her shorter works had appeared, volumes which included such fine and remarkably varied stories as **"A Journey," "The Pelican," "Souls Belated"** and **"The Recovery."** And while she wrote no unquestionably first-rate full-length novel after *The Age of Innocence* in 1920—*The Buccaneers,* had she lived to finish and revise it, might have proved the gratifying exception—the four collections of stories in those later years contained items as distinguished as **"A Bottle of Perrier," "After Holbein," "Roman Fever"** and **"All Souls',"** the latter composed apparently within a year or so of her death in 1937. Mrs. Wharton produced eighty-six stories in all, leaving behind in addition several promising but tantalizingly fragmentary manuscripts; and of this impressive number, eighteen or twenty strike this reader as very good indeed, many more as displaying an at least occasional excellence (the description of an Italian garden, the disclosure of a moral quirk, a flash of wit), and no one of them as totally bereft of interest.

What does distinguish the best of them must be specified with some care. It cannot be said, for example, that Mrs. Wharton significantly modified the genre itself—as during her lifetime, James Joyce and D. H. Lawrence and Ernest Hemingway were so differently doing. On the formal side, she was, to borrow a phrase from Louis Auchincloss, "a caretaker." She was the dedicated preserver of classical form in narrative, of the orderly progression in time and the carefully managed emphasis which, she reminds us in "Telling a Short Story" the French writers of *contes* had derived from the Latin tradition and the English in turn had taken over from the French. In "Telling a Short Story" (the second chapter of her book, *The Writing of Fiction,* 1925), Mrs. Wharton says much that is engrossing and valid, but virtually nothing that is new, at least to a reader of late Victorian literature. Perhaps the one surprising element—I shall come back to this—is her special admiration for the ghost story, "the peculiar category of the eerie" to which she turns her attention at once, even before getting down to questions about subject matter, characterization and the proper degree of economy in the short story proper. Elsewhere, she talks sensibly about "unity of vision," the strategically chosen "register" or point of view by which the experience is to be seen and by which it is to be shaped, with due acknowledgment to Henry James for first establishing the primacy of this fictional resource. She observes that the development and exploration of character is not the business of the short story, but rather that of the novel. And she lays it down that "situation is the main concern of the short story," so that "the effect produced by the short story depends entirely on its form, or presentation."

Such critical language does not sound very demanding, and in story after story Mrs. Wharton remained faithful to the principles announced. An old lady's view of the grubby yards adjacent to her boardinghouse—her one consolation in life—is about to be cut off; a young woman returning from Colorado to New York with her desperately sick husband, finds that he is lying dead in his sleeping-car berth and that she may be put off the train, with his corpse, in the midst of nowhere; a married woman has fled to Italy with her lover; a young man who is about to be exposed as an embezzler prepares to escape to Canada—in each case, we are introduced at once to a "situation." And yet in practice, Edith Wharton was often subtler, and both her ambition and her imaginative achievement greater, than her common sense critical remarks might lead one to expect.

Early stories like **"That Good May Come"** and **"A Cup of Cold Water"** do in fact consist in the *working out* of a given situation, the active resolution, happily or unhappily, of some moral dilemma. But in the best of her stories—in **"Souls Belated," "The Other Two," "The Eyes," "Autres Temps . . . ," "A Bottle of Perrier"** and others—it is rather that the situation itself is gradually revealed in all its complexity and finality. What we know at the end, in these "crucial instances," is not so much how some problem got resolved, but the full nature, usually the insurmountable nature, of the problem itself. It is then that Mrs. Wharton's stories gain the stature she attributed to the finest stories everywhere—those, in her account, which combined French form with Russian profundity: they become "a shaft driven straight into the heart of experience." It is then too that they comprise what she felt all so rightly any work of fiction should seek to comprise: a judgment on life, an appraisal of its limits, an assessment of the options—if options there be—that life has to offer. The immediate human situation has, in short, become a paradigm of the human condition.

The situations she chose so to treat and to enlarge upon are not, at first glance, very original or unusual ones. In "Telling a Short Story," Mrs. Wharton quotes with approval Goethe's contention that "those who remain imprisoned in the false

notion of their own originality will always fall short of what they might have accomplished." Mrs. Wharton, who entertained no such false notion, was content with the received forms and conventions of the short story; and she did not attempt to apply the art of storytelling to any hitherto unheard-of subject. There was, however, one area of experience which she was perhaps the first *American* writer to make almost exclusively her own: even more, I dare say, than Henry James, who would in any event be her only rival in this respect. This is what, in the loose groupings of stories appended to this introduction, I call the marriage question. (pp. vii-ix)

[Wharton] made, one might say, almost everything of it. It is not only that she explored so many phases and dimensions of the question: the very grounds for marrying, and premarital maneuvering, in **"The Quicksand," "The Dilettante," "The Introducers"** and others; the stresses and strains, the withering hopes and forced adjustments of the marital relation in **"The Fullness of Life," "The Lamp of Psyche," "The Letters," "Diagnosis"** and elsewhere; the intricate issue of divorce in **"The Last Asset," "The Other Two," "Autres Temps . . . "**; the emotional and psychological challenge of adultery in **"Souls Belated," "Atrophy," "The Long Run,"** and so on; the phenomenon of illegitimacy in **"Her Son," "Roman Fever"** and with gentle mockery in **"His Father's Son"**; the ambiguous value of children in the piercingly satirical **"The Mission of Jane."** It is not only that her treatment of the question, in these multiple phases, displays so broad a range of tone and perspective, and so keen an eye for the dissolving and emergent structures of historical institutional and social life with which the question was enmeshed. It is that the question, as Mrs. Wharton reflected on it, dragged with it all the questions about human nature and conduct to which her generous imagination was responsive.

There are of course urgent biographical reasons for Edith Wharton's near obsession with the perplexities of marriage, though, as I shall suggest, her deeper and more private passions found covert expression in ghost stories and romances. The chief cluster of stories bearing upon marriage, divorce and adultery were written during the years (up to 1913) when her personal problems in those regards were most pressing: when, among other things, her own marriage was becoming unbearable to her, when her husband Edward Robbins ("Teddy") Wharton was succumbing to mental illness and given ever more frequently to bouts of disjointed irascibility, and when her relation to Walter Berry (the international lawyer who was her mentor and romantic idol) arrived at one peak of intensity. But whatever the immediate causes, the whole domain of the marriage question was the domain in which Edith Wharton sought the truth of human experience; it was where she tested the limits of human freedom and found the terms to define the human mystery.

"Souls Belated" is an excellent case in point. The situation there is that of Mrs. Lydia Tillotson, who has abandoned her husband and come to Europe with her lover Ralph Gannett to spend a year wandering through Italy and then to settle for a time, registered as man and wife, at a resort hotel on one of the Italian lakes. Her divorce decree is at this moment granted, and the lovers are free to marry; but Lydia, to Gannett's astonishment, is passionately opposed to remarrying. She is appalled at the thought of yielding to that conventional necessity, of returning to the social fold and eventually of being received by the very people she had hoped to escape. "You judge things too theoretically," Gannett tells her. "Life is made up of compromises." "The life we ran away from—yes!" she replies. To this Gannett remarks with a smile: "I didn't know that we ran away to found a new system of ethics. I supposed it was because we loved each other." One of the merits of **"Souls Belated"** is the author's delicate division of sympathy between Lydia's anguished impulse to escape and Gannett's readiness to compromise (just as one of this early story's minor flaws is a certain shiftiness in point of view); but it is evident that on this occasion Gannett speaks for Edith Wharton. The impossibility of founding a new ethic—of a man and woman arranging their life together on a new and socially unconventional basis—was one of Mrs. Wharton's most somber convictions, and a conviction all the stronger because (partly out of her own anguish) she tested it again and again in her stories. (pp. ix-xi)

The relation between man and woman—whether marital or extramarital—was, in Mrs. Wharton's sense of it, beset by the most painful contradictions. "I begin to see what marriage is for," Lydia Tillotson says in **"Souls Belated."** "It's to keep people away from each other. Sometimes I think that two people who love each other can be saved from madness only by the things that come between them—children, duties, visits, bores, relations. . . . Our sin," she ends up, is that "we've seen the nakedness of each other's souls." But such dire proximity, such exposed nakedness—which Mrs. Wharton seems to have ardently desired and fearfully shrunk from—could occur within marriage as well.

Her consciousness of the dilemma was made evident in the exchange that took place a good many years after the writing of **"Souls Belated"** between Mrs. Wharton and Charles Du Bos, the gifted French essayist and student of French and English literature, who had known her since 1905, when he undertook to translate *The House of Mirth.* On an afternoon in the summer of 1912, driving through the French countryside, the two of them had been comparing their favorite literary treatments of married life. In fiction, they agreed upon George Eliot's *Middlemarch,* and Du Bos quoted the words of the heroine, Dorothea Brooke, that "marriage is so unlike anything else—there is something even awful in the nearness it brings." But if Mrs. Wharton assented to that, she also—after an interval, during which they selected Browning's "By the Fireside" and his "Any Wife to Any Husband" as the best poetic examples—went on to exclaim, with a kind of desolation, "Ah, the poverty, the miserable poverty, of any love that lies outside of marriage, of any love that is not a living together, a sharing of all!"

It is because of some such principle that Halston Merrick, in **"The Long Run"** (a story written a few months before the exchange just quoted), sends away his mistress Paulina Trant, when the latter offers to abandon her dreary husband and run off with him. In the course of their dialogue about the risks and sacrifices that might be in store for them, Paulina had observed with sad irony that "one way of finding out whether a risk is worth taking is *not* to take it, and then to see what one becomes in the long run, and draw one's inferences." What becomes of Halston and Paulina, as they retreat into the conventional, is in its well-cushioned manner not much less dreadful than what becomes of Ethan Frome and Mattie Silver. (One notes in passing that more often than not Edith Wharton's destroyed characters survive to take the full measure of their destruction.) Halston, who once had serious inclinations to literature, turns into a joyless bachelor, the manager of his father's iron foundry. Paulina, after her husband's

death, marries "a large glossy man with . . . a red face," and is seen regularly at dinner parties, listening to the banal conversations with "a small unvarying smile which might have been pinned on with her ornaments," ready at the proper moment to respond with the proper sentiment. This superb and gruesome story adds to the impression that, for Edith Wharton, if the individual is offered any real choice in life, it is usually a choice between modes of defeat.

Of course, the human condition envisaged is not always so bleak in Edith Wharton's short stories, nor the alternatives so desperate; she was not so driven by a theory of life that she remained blind to variety both in experience and in narrative. In **"The Letters,"** when Lizzie Deering discovers that her husband had not even opened the tender letters she had written him years before during the time of their courtship, she does not yield to her first impulse—to take their child and to leave him. She is stricken by the deception and by all that it implies, but she slowly adjusts "to the new image of her husband as he was." He was not, she realizes, "the hero of her dreams, but he was the man she loved, and who had loved her." The situation she now takes in and accepts—in a "last wide flash of pity and initiation"—is that "out of mean mixed substances" there had, after all, been "fashioned a love that will bear the stress of life." And in an altogether different mood, there is **"The Mission of Jane,"** wherein Mrs. Lethbury (a woman "like a dried sponge put in water; she expanded, but she did not change her shape") and her elegant, helplessly embarrassed husband adopt a baby girl. This unspeakable child, as she grows up, assumes as her mission the relentless reform of the entire household. She fulfills that mission at last, and after hair-raising hesitation, by marrying and departing—thus allowing her parents to come together on the common ground of enormous relief, joining in fact and spirit as they had never done in two decades of marriage.

One of the seeming options for the domestically harried and entrapped, under the circumstances of modern American life, was, needless to say, the act of divorce; and it is not surprising that Mrs. Wharton (whose decree was granted in 1913) dealt with this alternative a number of times. For some years before Mrs. Wharton began writing, divorce had been "an enormous fact . . . in American life," as William Dean Howells had remarked when he was writing *A Modern Instance* (1882), a novel of which "the question of divorce" was to be "the moving principle." Howells complained that "it has never been treated seriously"; but following his lead, Edith Wharton did so in some of her most successful stories—among them, **"The Reckoning," "The Last Asset," "Autres Temps . . ."** and **"The Other Two."** She caught at the subject during the period when divorce was changing from the scandalous to the acceptable and even the commonplace; and it is just the shifting, uncertain *status* of the act on which Mrs. Wharton so knowingly concentrated. In her treatment, it was not so much the grounds for divorce that interested her (though she could be both amusing and bitter on this score), and much less the technicalities involved. It was the process by which an individual might be forced to confront the fact itself—especially in its psychological and social consequences—as something irreversible and yet sometimes wickedly paradoxical. (The contemporary reader, for whom, again, divorce may seem little more than tangential to the main business of the personal life, can enjoy a shock of recognition in reading the stories cited.) Divorce, thus considered, was also the source of a revelation: about manners and the stubborn attitudes they may equally express or conceal; about the essential nature of the sexual relation; about the lingering injuries to the psyche that divorce, given certain social pressures and prejudices, may inflict on all concerned.

It is all those things that Julia Westall is driven to understand in **"The Reckoning."** Julia had been a young woman with "her own views on the immorality of marriage"; she had been a leading practitioner, in New York Bohemia, of "the new dispensation . . . *Thou shalt not be unfaithful—to thyself.*" She had only acted on her own foolishly selfish ideas when she brusquely demanded release from her first husband; now she is reduced to hysteria and almost to madness when her second husband, who had been her disciple in these matters, makes the same demand of her. **"The Reckoning"** is somewhat overwritten, and it is uneven in tone; it is an anecdote, really, about the biter bit, though by no means unmoving. A richer and more convincingly terrible story is **"Autres Temps . . . "** the account of Mrs. Lidcote's forced return from a dream of freedom to "the grim edges of reality," a reality here constituted by the social mores, at once cheerfully relaxing and cruelly fixed, about divorce. Years before (the story was written in 1916), Mrs. Lidcote had suffered disgrace and exile because she had been divorced and remarried. Now it appears that times must have changed, for her daughter has done the very same thing without arousing the faintest social disapproval. Mrs. Lidcote dares to return to America; but after two experiences of profoundest humiliation, she learns that for her the times and the mores will never change. Few moments in Edith Wharton's short stories are as telling in their exquisite agony as those in which first Mrs. Lidcote's daughter and then her kindly would-be lover acknowledge by a slow, irrepressible and all-devouring blush the truth of *her* situation. Those moments have the more expansiveness of meaning, because few of Edith Wharton's heroines accept the grim reality with greater courage or compassion for their destroyers. And in few stories are the radical ironies of social change more powerfully handled.

"The Other Two" is a yet more brilliant dissection of the mannered life, and it is very likely the best story Mrs. Wharton ever wrote. It can stand as the measure of her achievement in the short story form; for it has scarcely any plot—it has no real arrangement of incidents, there being too few incidents to arrange—but consists almost entirely in the leisurely, coolly comic process by which a situation is revealed to those involved in it. It is revealed in particular to Waythorn, his wife's third husband, who discovers himself in mysterious but indissoluble league with "the other two," as exceedingly different in background or in style as all three are from one another. Waythorn comes by degrees to perceive that the wife he adores, and who had seemed to him so vivid and above all so unique a personality, is in fact (and in a disconcertingly appropriate figure) " 'as easy as an old shoe'—a shoe that too many feet had worn. . . . Alice Haskett—Alice Varick—Alice Waythorn—she had been each in turn, and had left hanging to each name a little of her privacy, a little of her personality, a little of the inmost self where the unknown god abides."

Those last echoing phrases add up to a splendid formulation, and they contain a good deal of Edith Wharton's basic psychology. But for the most part, the rhetoric of **"The Other Two"** does not need or attempt to rise to such overt and summary statement. Everything is communicated, rather, by the exact notation of manners—of dress and gesture and expression: of Haskett's "made-up tie attached with an elastic," and

Waythorn's uneasy distaste for it; of Varick sitting by Mrs. Waythorn at a ball and failing to rise when Waythorn strolls by; of Mrs. Waythorn absent-mindedly giving her husband cognac with his coffee. The story's last sentence brings an exemplary little comedy of manners (which could serve as a model in any effort to define the genre) to a perfect conclusion. The three husbands are together for the first time, in the Waythorn drawing room. Mrs. Waythorn enters and suggests brightly, easily, that everyone must want a cup of tea.

> The two visitors, as if drawn by her smile, advanced to receive the cups she held out.
>
> She glanced about for Waythorn, and he took the third cup with a laugh.

Edith Wharton declared her affection for the supernatural tale in both *The Writing of Fiction* and the preface to **Ghosts;** and though, like the historical romances, her ghost stories are a provocatively mixed lot, she displayed her skill in this category often enough to be ranked among its modern masters. For an addict like the present commentator, **"Kerfol," "Mr. Jones," "Pomegranate Seed,"** and **"All Souls' "** are thoroughly beguiling and rereadable; while **"The Eyes"** verges on the extraordinary and contains something of "the appalling moral significance" Mrs. Wharton discerned in *The Turn of the Screw,* that novella of Henry James for which she had a sort of absolute admiration.

Most of these stories deal, as I have said, with the marriage question, but they deal with it in an atmosphere which is a curious and artful blend of the passionate and violent with the muted and remote. In **"Kerfol,"** an American visitor to

Photograph of Morton Fullerton, Wharton's lover, circa 1908. In her diary, Wharton wrote that she longed to be to Fullerton "like a touch of wings brushing by you in the darkness, or like the scent of an invisible garden that one passes by on an unknown road."

Brittany encounters what turn out to be the ghosts of a pack of dogs, spectral survivors of a seventeenth century domestic drama of sadism, revenge and madness. In **"Mr. Jones,"** the ghost of a majordomo who a century earlier had served as jailer to an unfortunate lady, the deaf-and-dumb wife of his villainous master, endures to commit a contemporary murder. In **"Pomegranate Seed,"** Kenneth Ashby, widowed and remarried, vanishes after receiving a series of letters written in a hand so faint as to be almost illegible; his second wife is left with the belated and blood-chilling knowledge of their source. The genre of the supernatural, Mrs. Wharton conjectures in "Telling a Short Story," did not derive from French or Russian writing, but "seems to have come from mysterious Germanic and Armorican" (i.e. Breton) "forests, from lands of long twilight and wailing winds." She might have added that it seems to derive also from recesses of the imagination other and perhaps deeper than those which give rise to realistic fiction. But this may be one part of what she had in mind when, in the preface to *Ghosts,* she contended that "the teller" of ghost stories "should be well frightened in the telling."

With the ghostly tales of Mrs. Wharton, in any event, one is inevitably interested not only in what happens in the plot, but in what happens in the telling of it. **"Pomegranate Seed"** offers one kind of clue. In the preface to *Ghosts,* while lamenting a decline in the practice and enjoyment of ghost stories, Mrs. Wharton speaks of the many inquiries she had received about the title of **"Pomegranate Seed,"** and refers a bit cryptically to the deplorable contemporary ignorance of "classical fairy lore." The reference is no doubt to the legend of Persephone (in the Latin version), who was abducted by Pluto, god of the underworld, and who would have been entirely liberated by Jupiter if she had not broken her vow to Pluto—of total abstinence from food—by eating some pomegranate seeds; whereafter she was required to spend the dark winter months of each year in the underworld, returning to earth only with the arrival of spring.

The connection with Mrs. Wharton's tale is superficially slender, especially since the Persephone story is usually interpreted as a seasonal myth—the annual return of winter darkness and sterility, the annual rebirth of nature in the spring. But theorists of a Freudian or, alternately, a Jungian persuasion, have made out a strong sexual motif in most ancient mythology, and find the sources of myth as much in sexual struggles and yearnings as in the cycle of nature. The story of Persephone yields quickly to such an interpretation, and so obviously does **"Pomegranate Seed."** Edith Wharton, in this view, has taken a familiar story of sexual combat—two women battling over one man, and the man himself divided between conflicting erotic leanings—and turned it into a ghost story: which is then cast into a dimly mythic pattern, and carefully labeled for our guidance. It is thus the dead wife Elsie who has assumed the role of Pluto and has summoned her spouse to leave his earthly existence and cohabit with her in the land of the dead—Ashby having broken *his* vow of constancy by remarrying.

In this and other tales, in short, Mrs. Wharton's imagination was moving in the direction of the mythic, but arriving only at the way station of the ghostly and fantastic. This, for Mrs. Wharton, was far enough; for she was doing no more than adopting the Victorian habit (itself a gesture toward the mythic) of "distancing" the most intense and private sexual feelings by projecting them in the various forms of fantasy. It is notable, for example, that the ghostly context permits a

more direct acknowledgment of sexual experience than we normally find in the dramas of manners and the social life. In **"The Lady's Maid's Bell,"** the action turns on the brutish physical demands made by one Brympton upon his fastidious wife: "I turned sick," says the narrator, the English-born maid Hartley. "to think what some ladies have to endure and hold their tongues about." Nor is there much mystery about the nature of Farmer Rutledge's bewitchment by the ghost of Ora Brand in **"Bewitched,"** an artificial yarn which strives for effect by converting the figurative into the literal. But the expertly harrowing **"All Souls' "** indicates how erotic material could be transmuted into the terrifying without losing either its essential nature or its power.

On the last day of October, Sara Clayburn encounters a strange woman who has come to see one of the maidservants on the large staff of her Connecticut home. Later, Mrs. Clayburn sprains her ankle and is forced to her bed. The maidservant fails to appear next morning, and Mrs. Clayburn hobbles through the house in great pain, searching for help. The house is empty, the electricity cut off, the fire dead. She spends a day and night in panic-stricken solitude. When she awakens again, the servants are at their appointed tasks, all of them insisting that there had been no such passage of time, and the entire episode simply a bad dream. Exactly a year later, Mrs. Clayburn sees the same strange woman approaching the house, and she flees in hysterics to her cousin in New York. Together, they speculate that the woman must have been a "ketch," who had come to escort the maid and the other servants to a nearby "coven." The story is a fine and highly original narrative study of steadily increasing fear; and I am sure that what one remembers is Mrs. Clayburn's painful progress through the empty house. But the full force of **"All Souls' "** comes from the retrospective juxtaposition of Mrs. Clayburn's experience and the gathering which is the cause of it. Edith Wharton knew well enough that a coven was an exercise in witchcraft which usually led to the wildest erotic activities. And to put it in a ruinously oversimplified manner, Mrs. Clayburn's terrors—her sense of physically trapped solitude, the loss of her grip on reality, her later hysteria—are in fact her intuitive moral and psychological *reaction* to the coven.

To what extent, in the stories under discussion, was Edith Wharton's imagination working with her own private passions, impulses and fears? To what extent was she "distancing" elements in her personal life by converting them into the eerie or setting them in a far-gone age, or both (as in **"Kerfol"**)? To a very considerable extent, I should suppose. It is easy enough—so easy that I did not pause to say so—to find reflections of Mrs. Wharton's experience of marriage with Teddy Wharton in the stories examined earlier: for example, in **"The Letters"**; to which we could add **"The Lamp of Psyche,"** in which Delia Corbett's attitude to her husband, after she has detected his basic flaw, changes from "passionate worship" to "tolerant affection"; and the first of the little fables in **"The Valley of Childish Things,"** where the female figure matures after going out into the great world (i.e., Europe) and coming back home, but the male on his return simply reverts to the childish. With the ghostly tales, and with those of the historical romances which can be helpfully included here, the problem is usually more complex, and exactly because the elements being converted were so much more deeply rooted, so much a matter of obscure or wayward or almost inexpressible emotions—and perhaps so alien to Edith Wharton's temperament, as the latter has normally been understood. But even in **"Kerfol"** (to take an apparently extreme instance), one can, by making a number of substitutions, come upon a fantasy of savage personal revenge, a violent but purely imagined repayment for a series of psychological cruelties.

There the translation from life into story is complete; **"Kerfol"** needs no biographical interpretation to give it interest. Sometimes, however, Mrs. Wharton's imagination was overcome by her personal feeling, and she failed to make the full translation: which explains, I believe, the unevenness mentioned at the start of this section. **"The Hermit and the Wild Woman"**—which can stand for several of the romances (including **"The Duchess at Prayer"** and **"Dieu d'Amour"**)—is instructive, for it is just such a failure; *its* interest is almost entirely biographical. This story, which takes place in late medieval Italy, is told in a somewhat pretentious style founded on that of the lives of the saints. A so-called Wild Woman has escaped from a convent because she was forbidden to bathe herself; she wanders the mountains till she meets with a Hermit of singular austerity; she performs many miraculous cures, but she is constantly chided by the holy man for her continuing desire to clean and refresh her body in the mountain lake; finally she drowns in the water, and the Hermit realizes too late that her nature was yet more saintly and devout than his own. It is a tedious and contrived piece of work; and one is at a loss to understand why Mrs. Wharton wrote it—until it dawns on one that this is Mrs. Wharton's effort to make a story out of a deeply troubled period in her life, while retaining her privacy by placing the experience in the far temporal distance and the most remote possible atmosphere. It becomes uncomfortably clear that the relation between the Wild Woman and the Hermit is an elementary version, at several kinds of remove, of the relation between Edith Wharton and Walter Berry, during the period when she was escaping or trying to escape from her own convent, her marriage. (pp. xi-xix)

"The Eyes," written in 1910, springs from the same cluster of longings and resentments, but it is an immeasurably superior story; the author's personal feelings have here been perfectly translated into a nearly seamless work of art. Andrew Culwin's reminiscence of his two acts of seemingly spontaneous generosity—the proposal of marriage to his cousin Alice Nowell, his pretense of admiration for the literary talent of young Noyes—and of the two ugly red sneering eyes which appeared after both incidents to glare at him derisively through the night: this is all of a piece. Gilbert Noyes, the godlike youth who turns up suddenly in Rome, is also a cousin of Alice Nowell's, and Culwin's fear of wounding him by making plain his literary ineptness is confused by some vague sense of remorse over abandoning Alice three years before. But the turn of the screw in *this* story is the fact that Frenham, one of the two men listening to Culwin's hideous and shockingly unconscious self-disclosure, is another attractive young neophyte, Noyes's most recent successor. He is the latest proof of the "ogreish metaphor" of one of Culwin's friends, that the old man "liked 'em juicy." To the climax of Culwin's reminiscence, there is added the climax of the tale itself, when Frenham sits transfixed with horror. In the face of his mentor, the very shaper of his own life and personality, Frenham has seen what Culwin remembered seeing: eyes that reminded him "of vampires with a taste for young flesh."

It is not only that the eyes represent Culwin's real self, the egotistical and gradually evil self that (like that of Lavington

in **"The Triumph of Night"**) lies hidden behind his "cold and drafty" intelligence, his utter detachment, his occasional moral contentment. It is also that, on the two occasions of generosity, his good conscience—his "glow of self-righteousness"—*is* the glare of the eyes. For a character like Culwin's, the generous gesture is a necessary concession to the ego; it is a feeding of the ego on the tenderness of flesh and spirit; and a part of him knows it. Like Henry James, Edith Wharton was alert to the sinister impulses that can sometimes take the form of moral self-satisfaction. But the implications of this astonishing story go beyond that, and open up almost endlessly to thoughtful scrutiny.

Culwin's treatment of Alice Nowell is more than paralleled by his treatment of Noyes. It is explained by it; and all the carefully chosen (and as the manuscript shows, painstakingly revised) details about the old man, about his habits and tastes, his manner of speech and way of life, combine to give a chilling portrait of a dilettantish, devouringly selfish homosexual. The two victims coalesce; indeed, Miss Nowell's Christian name was originally Grace, before Mrs. Wharton (as it appears) decided that it would be too schematic to provide both victims with the same initials. Nevertheless, when we put together the young woman with her unreproachful grief (still unreproachful, one surmises, after Culwin had fled from her) and the aspiring young writer of fiction, we begin to identify a single and very real personality, and to identify **"The Eyes"** as the projection by Mrs. Wharton of her most buried feelings about Walter Berry. It is, as Louis Auchincloss has pointed out, the Walter Berry as seen in the resentful perspective of Percy Lubbock: "a dogmatic, snobbish egotist and the evil genius of Edith Wharton's life." But the perspective on this occasion at least was also Mrs. Wharton's—though her imagination was in such firm control of her materials that it is unlikely she ever quite knew what she had accomplished. Yet surely, as this beautifully composed story took shape, Mrs. Wharton must have been, however obscurely, more than a little frightened in the telling. (pp. xix-xxi)

[**"The Pelican," "The Descent of Man"** and **"Xingu"**] are the best of the many stories that touch upon the cultural scene. Among the others, little need be said about the stories of art and artists, since, as Blake Nevius has observed, they are not really about the artistic life as such, or the drama of the imaginative struggle, but about the human foibles and limitations and disappointments looked at, in these instances, within an artistic context. **"The House of the Dead Hand"** and **"The Daunt Diana,"** for example, deal with the melodramatic or bizarre obsessions here attributed to art lovers. Others focus on the purely *human* nature, usually the quite unsatisfactory nature, of the great artist or writer: as in **"The Muse's Tragedy,"** which, with its idealistic and frustrated married woman, her shadowy "ridiculous" husband, and the dryly intellectual and apparently sexless poet, seems to be one more reflection of the triangle composed of Edith and Teddy Wharton and Walter Berry. In the more complicated but also more light-spirited story, **"The Temperate Zone,"** Mrs. Wharton, through the eyes of a young American critic, inspects the improbable human sources of creative inspiration: the artlessly greedy and tasteless widow of a distinguished painter, and her present husband, the slack and ingenuous onetime lover of a lady poet of genius. **"The Recovery"** alone enacts a genuine and important aesthetic experience, and does so most effectively: the confrontation by the skilled but provincial American painter of the European masters, "the big fellows," as Keniston calls them in the story. It is a very real experience which (as one has had occasion to notice) continues to be re-enacted in the halls of the Louvre and the Uffizi. But even in **"The Recovery,"** for all its valid implications about American cultural history, the impact of the event is felt mainly from without, by the painter's worried and watchful wife, for whom the confrontation has as much to do with their happiness together as with the nature of artistic achievement.

Keniston's integrity is impressive; and so is that of Dodge in **"The Debt,"** and of Pellerin in **"The Legend."** But when dealing with integrity, Edith Wharton was not much more than competent. It was the opposite—the loss or total absence or the pretense of intellectual seriousness—that engaged Mrs. Wharton's larger talent: that summoned into play the virile wit, trenchant but falling just short of the merciless, characteristic of the stories set in the New England university town sometimes called Hillbridge (which seems to be Cambridge, Massachusetts, displaced a little way toward Amherst). These—in particular, **"The Pelican," "The Descent of Man"** and **"Xingu"**—are the finely wrought predecessors of the many recent fictional anatomies of cultural snobbery and the academic world, a genre which, among American writers, Edith Wharton collaborated with Henry James in inventing.

The language of these stories has the air of taking a rational delight in itself, as it cuts sharply into folly and hypocrisy, drawing blood which only increases the attacker's appetite. But there is an air of tolerance, too, if not always of compassion, and especially in **"The Pelican."** Here we meet the bemused and humorless but oddly touching Mrs. Amyot, who lectures on everything, everywhere, to pay the various needs of her "baby" son, and does so for a decade after he has grown up, graduated from college and paid his mother back in full. Despite himself, the narrator helps Mrs. Amyot work up a lecture on Plato: "If she wanted to lecture on Plato she should!—Plato must take his chance like the rest of us." Later, Mrs. Wharton sums up a whole range of spurious pedantry when she explains that Mrs. Amyot's lectures on literary "influences" (in the manner popularized by Matthew Arnold) were no longer successful, since "her too-sophisticated audiences . . . now demanded either that the influence or the influenced should be quite unknown, or that there should be no perceptible connection between the two." But with all her capacity for inexhaustible inanity, Mrs. Amyot remains appealing—to the narrator, to Mrs. Wharton and to us—because, as the narrator says, she was "full of those dear contradictions and irrelevancies that will always make flesh and blood prevail against a syllogism."

Mrs. Wharton is harder on Professor Lynyard, Hillbridge's eminent philosopher of science, in **"The Descent of Man,"** a story which begins as a satire on the massive gullibility of the reading public and the cultivated idiocy of publishers, and goes on to portray the corruption of the intellectual by enormous popular success. **"Xingu"** is an elaborate joke (the entity named in the title being in actual fact what, to the dazed consternation of the ladies involved, it is discovered to be in the story); but in the course of telling it, Mrs. Wharton's masculine wit flexes itself happily to expose the silly snobberies and the fuzzy puritanical idealism of literary clubs. Whether she was or was not a social snob, Edith Wharton (who was learned in the literatures and philosophies of several countries and epochs) was not a snob of the intellectual variety, and could not abide that quality in others. But as we listen to her dismantling it in a story like **"Xingu,"** we hear that

sound of full-throated laughter which her friends so well remember. (pp. xxi-xxiii)

R. W. B. Lewis, in an introduction to The Collected Short Stories of Edith Wharton, Vol. I, *edited by R. W. B. Lewis, Charles Scribner's Sons, 1968, pp. vii-xxv.*

A curious distinction between the successful tale and the successful novel at once presents itself. It is safe to say (since the surest way of measuring achievement in art is by survival) that the test of the novel is that its people should be *alive*. No subject in itself, however fruitful, appears to be able to keep a novel alive; only the characters in it can. Of the short story the same cannot be said. Some of the greatest short stories owe their vitality entirely to the dramatic rendering of a situation. Undoubtedly the characters engaged must be a little more than puppets; but apparently, also, they may be a little less than individual human beings. In this respect the short story, rather than the novel, might be called the direct descendant of the old epic or ballad—of those earlier forms of fiction in all of which action was the chief affair, and the characters, if they did not remain mere puppets, seldom or never became more than types—such as the people, for instance, in Molière. The reason of the difference is obvious. Type, general character, may be set forth in a few strokes, but the progression, the unfolding of personality, of which the reader instinctively feels the need if the actors in the tale are to retain their individuality for him through a succession of changing circumstances—this slow but continuous growth requires space, and therefore belongs by definition to a larger, a symphonic plan.

The chief technical difference between the short story and the novel may therefore be summed up by saying that situation is the main concern of the short story, character of the novel; and it follows that the effect produced by the short story depends almost entirely on its form, or presentation. Even more—yes, and much more—than in the construction of the novel, the impression of vividness, of *presentness*, in the affair narrated, has to be sought, and made sure of beforehand, by that careful artifice which is the real carelessness of art. The short-story writer must not only know from what angle to present his anecdote if it is to give out all its fires, but must understand just *why* that particular angle and no other is the right one. He must therefore have turned his subject over and over, walked around it, so to speak, and applied to it those laws of perspective which Paolo Uccello called "so beautiful," before it can be offered to the reader as a natural unembellished fragment of experience, detached like a ripe fruit from the tree.

Edith Wharton, from "Telling a Short Story" in her The Writing of Fiction.

MARGARET B. McDOWELL   (essay date 1970)

[*McDowell is an American biographer, essayist, and academic who has written a critical biography of Wharton. In the follow-*

ing excerpt, she finds Wharton's ghost stories indicative of an "extraordinary psychological and moral insight."]

Edith Wharton's ghost stories represent, in general, the work of a mature and sophisticated artist. These works form a well-defined group in subject and technique, and they provide a convenient focus for an inquiry into Mrs. Wharton's methods and achievements in short fiction. Like the best of her other efforts in this genre, the short stories of the macabre and the supernatural, more often than not, manifest in concentrated fashion the careful technique, the evocative style, and the concern for aesthetic order that she revealed in her best novels. In listing the six items that would endure from her work, E. K. Brown included, as one of these, a dozen ghost tales, and implied, accordingly the importance of these efforts to a consideration of her achievement. In his recent edition of Edith Wharton's short stories, R. W. B. Lewis judged her work in this category to be distinguished enough to rank her "among its modern masters," and he found in **"The Eyes,"** for example, "appalling moral significance" [see excerpt dated 1968], a phrase Edith Wharton had used to describe the effects engendered by James's *The Turn of the Screw.*

Just before her death Edith Wharton collected in *Ghosts* (1937) eleven of her best stories concerned with spectres, witches, and eerie happenings. Unlike her ten earlier collections of stories, *Ghosts* contains only one kind of story. It is also the only collection for which she provided a preface, although she had commented on the supernatural tale a dozen years before in *The Writing of Fiction.* All things considered, her ghost stories illustrate meticulous craftsmanship and imaginative power as they drive toward what she called "the thermometrical quality" of successful ghost tales, the sending of "a cold shiver down one's spine." Still, her finest efforts in this mode are notable precisely because they are more than adroit evocations of the otherworldly.

Edith Wharton maintains in the preface to *Ghosts* that the "moral issue" question is irrelevant in estimating the aesthetic excellence of a supernatural tale. Her immediate aim, which she implied was enough in itself, was to generate an atmosphere conducive to such psychic states in the reader as fear, dread, terror, and horror. In *The Writing of Fiction* she had asserted that for most ghost-story writers it is enough to invoke "simple shivering animal fear." But, like *The Turn of the Screw* which she praised so highly, her own stories go beyond her initial aim and reveal her extraordinary psychological and moral insight.

In fact, these stories achieve ultimate distinction, I think, to the degree that she explores in them, often symbolically, human situations of considerable complexity. In *The Writing of Fiction* she had contended that fiction is the art of disengaging "crucial moments from the welter of existence." These moments are crucial to the degree that they illuminate or question critically "a familiar social or moral standard." Superficially it seems that fantasy, involving spectres and other extraordinary phenomena, would have little bearing upon the realms of social experience and philosophical value. In Edith Wharton's best tales of the supernatural, however, fantasy provides, by an unusual angle of penetration, a new perspective from which to review the mundane and the perhaps unfamiliar problems of human beings.

In several of these stories Edith Wharton works, as did Henry James, in an American tradition of literary art that has its origins in Hawthorne. Like Hawthorne and James in many of their short stories, Mrs. Wharton possessed an acute sense of the immemorial conflict between the forces of good and evil. Whereas both James and Mrs. Wharton were less preoccupied with allegory than was Hawthorne, still the strength of their best supernatural tales lies partly in their analysis of those ethical issues and human relationships that possess, in their ultimate ramifications, a universal relevance. All three writers, as conscious or unconscious moralists, delve into the remoter reaches of the consciousness and all are haunted by the ineffable, the unfathomable, the preternatural, the super-human, the transcendent. (pp. 133-35)

Also like Hawthorne and James, Edith Wharton recognized the ambiguities in inner experience, in human behavior, and in all ethical and metaphysical formulations. Sensitive as she was to the complications inherent in human motives and values, she tended in her work, as James did in his, to illuminate rather than resolve the complex issues and situations that she subjected to her scrutiny.

Mrs. Wharton reveals such strength and subtlety of insight in one of her best tales, **"The Eyes,"** an acute analysis of the blindness of the aesthetic temperament. She is concerned in this tale with the ramifications of Andrew Culwin's moral deficiencies as they have undermined his own life and the lives of others. A gracious, wealthy, cultured man, Culwin surrounds himself with disciples and does help them to mature intellectually and to define their own ideas; and yet his interest in these young men is that of the amused spectator, not that of the deeply-concerned friend and mentor. Passively, he is also able to satisfy the homosexual bent of his emotional nature which he never frankly acknowledges.

Twice at times of self-satisfaction when he has judged that he has acted in a kindly and disinterested way, he has had a vision of leering red eyes at night in his bedroom. Whether they are the result of his own faulty vision, whether they are a hallucination, or whether they are "a projection of my inner consciousness," we are free to decide. We do not have to rule out entirely the first two explanations to accept more readily than for years Culwin does the fact that these eyes are indeed a symbol of his own corruption.

A master at self-deception, Culwin cannot see, until the final moment in the story, that the eyes are a symbol of his own hidden weaknesses. In recounting the decisions he had made both times just before the eyes appeared, he implies that he lied in order to be kind, whereas he obviously wanted only to save himself distress. The eyes first appear after he proposes to the rather plain Alice Nowell without loving her, and they disappear once he has acted without hypocrisy and left her. The eyes next appear every night for a month after he falsely reassures her handsome cousin, Gilbert Noyes, that he may become a successful writer. At their second appearance, Culwin has enough insight to sense their difference from what they had been three years before, but not enough to apply their changed aspect to a judgment of his own nature: "I saw now what I hadn't seen before; that they were eyes which had grown hideous gradually, which had built up their baseness coralwise, bit by bit, out of a series of small turpitudes slowly accumulated through the years."

At the completion of his narrative Culwin admits that he had never found the link between himself and the appearance of the eyes. He fails to see that it is just his own evasiveness that has cut off vital self-knowledge. He is amused, rather than disturbed, when Phil Frenham, who parallels Gilbert Noyes

A postcard from Wharton of herself to Morton Fullerton, circa 1907-10.

in his dependence on Culwin's encouragement and advice, recoils from him after he finishes talking. He has no way of knowing that his latest disciple has discerned the truth of his corruption. At last, as Culwin looks into the mirror and recognizes the lurid countenance with its horrible eyes as his own, he does make the connection between them and his own inner being. The supernatural has, in fact, become the natural; the fearful hallucination has become the even more terrifying actuality and emphasizes thereby the completeness of Culwin's degeneration. In contrast to James's more discursive supernatural narratives, Mrs. Wharton often made use of a single obsessive and obtrusive image to organize a given tale.

The lurid eyes are, furthermore, a compelling projection of the slightly decadent atmosphere surrounding Culwin and a comment on his continuing moral occlusion: his inability to realize that non-involvement in human relationships represents, in reality, the most despicable kind of involvement. One irony consists in his revulsion, when the eyes appear for the second time, from the "vicious security" which he senses in them, without perceiving that he himself is viciously secure because of his wealth, complacency, Olympian superiority, and moral insensitivity. Another irony derives from Culwin's assumption, before he relates his experience, that he is done now and forever with the apparition.

"Miss Mary Pask," an extraordinary *tour de force*, again ex-

poses moral weakness. The narrator is a hedonistic bachelor who, like Culwin, resists an individual needing sympathy and evades the injunction that we are to be our brother's keeper. When he visits Mary Pask in her desolate Brittany home, he feels drawn to her as a pleasant woman, until he remembers that she is, in reality, dead and that the being before him must be a wraith rather than a woman. He recoils from her as if she is indeed a vampire; and he resists her appeal to him to stay longer and to assuage her unendurable loneliness. Instead, he yields to his fear and becomes obsessed with the need to flee from her. Months later, he learns that she was, in fact, alive and that the report of her death had been a mistake. He feels no compunctions about his past unkindness to her, no satisfaction that she is still alive, and no wish ever again to hear of her. She has disturbed the even tenor of his life as if she had truly been a vampire; for this, he cannot forgive her, because it is really he who is the vampire, the one who, in his heedlessness, sucks the life from other people. He chooses to efface her memory rather than to recognize what his obligations to her as a fellow human being ought to have been. He chooses to efface her memory and extinguish his conscience rather than to let them disturb his comfort. His insensitivity is in sharp contrast with Miss Mary Pask's plaintive need for reassurance. This contrast gives rise to those intonations of poignancy which reverberate through our minds when, in retrospect, we review the story.

The story is also a triumph in tone and atmosphere. And indeed, it is Mrs. Wharton's ability to assimilate the very landscape into her art, to make of natural setting as it were an active agent in the unfolding psychic drama that distinguishes her work in this realm from James's and brings it, in this respect as in some others, closer to Hawthorne's. The fog-enshrouded loneliness of Mary Pask's Brittany residence, the absence there of all sound except the sea, and the narrator's nocturnal encounter with her spectral figure, dimly illumined by candlelight, intensify for us her unwilled isolation and the pathos informing her situation. The psychological insight and the intensity of mood present in the story compensate for the elements of contrivance: the narrator's forgetting, almost inexplicably, the news of Miss Mary Pask's death when he plans his visit, and the reversal at the end when the narrator learns that she is alive by virtue of a cataleptic trance that had been at first interpreted as death.

Other stories that impress by Mrs. Wharton's psychological and moral penetration and by her ability to domesticate the supernatural into the natural are **"Pomegranate Seed," "Kerfol,"** and **"The Triumph of Night."**

"Pomegranate Seed" is in part effective because the tangible acts of its spectral figure, Elsie Ashby, impinge so decisively on the personal and moral lives of her widowed husband, Kenneth, and his new wife, Charlotte, although Charlotte never actually confronts her ghostly rival. Elsie's authority is expressed through the actuality of the letters she sends to her living husband and through their disintegrative effects upon him and his new wife. The observable disasters attributable to these letters argue, in short, for the reality of their sender, who is otherwise almost excessively wraithlike even for a ghost. Suffice to say, Elsie resents her husband's happy second marriage and connives to possess him beyond the grave. The situation is similar to that explored by Henry James in "The Friends of the Friends": a jealous woman finds herself impotent in the struggle with a dead woman for the affections of a living man.

Outward suspense and inner psychic tension parallel each other in **"Pomegranate Seed,"** with the result that the tale is finally imposing for its moral and psychological significance, not simply for its convincing supernatural aspect. The first letter, because of Kenneth's furtive and preoccupied reaction to it, disturbs his bride; and succeeding missives undermine her absolute trust in him. If her husband is reticent, Charlotte is one of little faith, and bland New York can become a psychic hell for the woman who thinks she is being scorned and for those subjected to her quiet fury. In effect, her egotism and jealousy cause her to reject Kenneth's appeal to her for tacit support and loyalty. He is, however, too indecisive for his own good and too little considerate of Charlotte's well-being, as he casts lingering looks behind and keeps always visible before her his memories of Elsie and his happiness with her.

If Kenneth has not been altogether candid with her, Charlotte has helped him too little in his crisis. She loses him forever as much by her moral flaccidity as by her rival's malevolence. Neither Kenneth nor Charlotte is equal to the spiritual demands imposed upon them by extraordinary circumstances, and their differing weaknesses allow the sinister visitant from another world her opportunity to come between them, to triumph over them, and to reclaim Kenneth as her own. In classic mythology Persephone must return to the underworld once each year because, as a hungry captive there, she had eaten a pomegranate seed. The "seed" could be the letters which Kenneth kisses as if to consume them; he is unfaithful in thought to Charlotte and so is captive to the underworld. Or perhaps the "seed" is the seed of jealousy in Charlotte which she is not able—or even willing—to control; and by consuming this seed she may condemn her husband to the power of one who dwells in the spirit world. Or perhaps, as R. W. B. Lewis suggests, the "seed" may be Kenneth's own perfidy to his wife's memory, and Elsie is the Pluto figure who gathers to herself the man she loves to dwell forever with her in the spirit world. To carry Lewis's interpretation further, Kenneth would be compelled to renounce the forbidden food of which he has just partaken—to spit forth Charlotte, as it were, after he had consumed her. In any event, death and negation triumph in this marriage because of Charlotte's distrust, possessiveness, and cowardice; because of Kenneth's inertia, nostalgia, and resentment; and because of Elsie's craving for continued power over one whom she has supposedly cherished in the past for his own sake. Charlotte is at best a Demeter-figure manqué, lacking the force, vitality, and persuasive presence of the goddess and the imagination to save her captive husband from the demonic powers.

In **"Kerfol,"** an impressive story, the moral line is convincing and forceful. The ghosts here are animals, although human beings from the past also hover in the background as felt presences though not as apprehensible spirits. The ghostly dogs have a substantial reality since, from the first, they convince the narrator of their actuality before he comes to wonder at their strangeness. Only gradually do we, and the skeptical narrator, become aware that these animals are spectres when they retreat instead of accosting him, stand motionless for long periods of time, refrain from barking or growling, and cause no sound as they move. Solemn and sorrowful of mien, these animals, the narrator senses, are not only ghosts in the here and now but ghosts who now appear because they were in the past implicated in a tragedy. As such, these wraith-like creatures coalesce to form a compelling organizing image for this tale:

> I should have liked to rouse them for a minute, to coax them into a game or a scamper; but the longer I looked into their fixed and weary eyes the more preposterous the idea became. . . . The impression they produced was that of having in common one memory so deep and dark that nothing that had happened since was worth either a growl or a wag.

The dogs appear once each year to commemorate the death of a sadistic seventeenth-century aristocrat who had once owned Kerfol, in Brittany. The narrator learns this fact from his host who also provides him with a history of seventeenth-century court proceedings as they pertain to this nobleman, Yves de Cornault. He had been possessive, jealous, and cruel, whereas his wife, Anne, was beautiful, charitable, innocent, and long-suffering. In retaliation for her suspected infidelity, Yves had killed in succession all his wife's pet dogs, each time placing the body on her bed. Her beauty and her plight as a miserable and childless woman attract the attentions of a neighbor, Henri de Lanrivain; as a virtuous woman, she resists him when all her instincts would propel her toward him. The still youthful Henri, after several years, sends word he is returning; and in her attempt to warn him away, Anne discovers her husband dead on the darkened outer staircase.

Thereafter, she steadily maintains that her dogs, reincarnated, attacked Yves and mauled him to death. No one believes her, with the result that she is taken into custody as a madwoman until her death. Perhaps we discount her vision of the murder and of the apparition of her pets because of her supposed insanity, the remoteness in time of the action, and the narrator's pragmatic cast of mind. But these factors are more than offset by the plaintive aspect of the dogs as we see them in the early part of the story, and by the inevitable, compelling way in which their somber countenances project the muffled and pitiful life of their mistress. Mistress and animals both are the mute, uncomprehending victims of an evil that destroys those who challenge its supremacy. As perturbed, avenging forces, the dogs acquire a reality so strong as to convince us at times of their dual actuality as dogs and as spirits.

"The Triumph of Night" derives its power from the way in which the protagonist develops also an awareness of perfidy and evil when he visits a remote estate inadvertently. Mrs. Wharton in this tale powerfully evokes the New England mansion and rural scene in winter. She thus centers her moral and psychic drama in an American setting, something which her master Henry James apparently never did in a ghost tale except perhaps for the New York locales figuring in "The Jolly Corner." When Faxon's new employer fails to meet him, he accepts the invitation of a young stranger, Rainer, to spend the night at the nearby estate of his uncle. During the evening Faxon learns that John Lavington (the uncle), despite his wealth, his taste in painting, his love of flowers, his graciousness as a host, and his effusive concern for his nephew's welfare, is self-centered and vicious. Faxon, as the experiencing consciousness in the tale, is enlightened by a malevolent ghost, which only he sees as it stands behind Lavington. The apparition shocks him as intensively as the spectres of Miss Jessel and Peter Quint shock the governess in *The Turn of the Screw;* and Faxon, like the governess, is the only one who sees a ghost. The repulsive apparition in Mrs. Wharton's story is, in fact, an exact double for the "kindly" uncle and a symbolic projection of the actual evil in his soul, which Faxon only gradually perceives. The uncle, solicitous about his nephew's health, really wishes his death in order to control his money.

Mrs. Wharton's virtuosity in this story is masterly. The isolation of the uncle's house, the omnipresent cold, the compression of the action into a few hours, and the contrast between the uncle's gracious hospitality and the sinister threats emanating from his double—all intensify the inevitability of Rainer's doom. Mrs. Wharton establishes the reality of the ghostly-double, all the more forcibly perhaps, by implying that the apparition might have been a hallucination of Faxon's. Early in the story, we learn that Faxon's temperament is unsteady, "hung on lightly quivering nerves." In the epilogue the doctor, five months after the crucial evening in the story, tells him that he had been "bottling up for a bad breakdown" even before he had left for New Hampshire. Furthermore, we know that Rainer could have died without the intervention of Lavington's malignant spirit or double, since Rainer's illness is far advanced, his pursuit of Faxon occurred on a night of extreme cold, and his exertions to overtake him were exhausting. But we choose to believe that the sinister alter-ego did stand behind Faxon's host and that Rainer's fate might have been avoided had Faxon acted decisively after he saw the leering apparition. We accept these conclusions because we identify strongly with Faxon and his interest in Rainer. The pathos of the tale is increased by Rainer's being an archetype of the beautiful, gifted youth who will be cut down in his prime. His coughing of blood and his withered hands are symptomatic of his mortality and his doom, a symbolic intimation that the good and beautiful are aliens in our imperfect world. He is the innocent creature trapped in the web spun out by his insidious, hypocritical relative.

The chilling effect of the tale also derives from Faxon's gradual recognition of the fact that he might have saved Rainer. Faxon has been reluctant to face the evil that, as a responsible moral agent, he ought to have combatted strenuously, once he was apprized of it. Instead, his one action—fleeing through the snow-covered landscape—becomes the immediate cause of Rainer's death when the consumptive youth pursues him. The uncle's active malignancy is exactly balanced by Faxon's destructive passivity; and between the two of them, Rainer, a youth who possesses good will and courage in abundance, meets his death. The exact nature of Lavington's motives Faxon does not learn until months later; but he had been warned, by the appearance of the spectre, of the elder man's evil nature and had refused to struggle against it.

Again, as in **"The Eyes,"** non-involvement really represents an involvement on the side of the least acceptable alternative. Faxon's breakdown, we are convinced, results not from his having seen a ghost, but from his guilt at realizing the effects of his own cowardice and self-concern in the presence of a discerned evil force. His unstable temperament is unequal to the shock produced by Rainer's actual death: the lifeless youth becomes for him a symbol of his own guilt and, as such, overpowers him physically as well as spiritually. Most chilling in the tale (as in **"Afterward"** and **"The Eyes"**) is one range of psychic experience peculiar to Mrs. Wharton's tales of the supernatural as opposed to those of Henry James, the disintegrative effects of a strong-willed man upon a defenseless, but morally superior younger man. The destructiveness of latent, often unacknowledged, homosexual passion is powerfully, if reticently, depicted in these tales of Mrs. Wharton's, striking precursors as they are of such classics as D. H.

Lawrence's "The Prussian Officer" and Thomas Mann's "Death in Venice." (pp. 136-43)

Margaret B. McDowell, "Edith Wharton's Ghost Stories," in Criticism, *Vol. XII, Spring, 1970, pp. 133-52.*

JUDITH P. SAUNDERS   (essay date 1977)

[*In the following essay, Saunders deems Wharton's "Bunner Sisters" an ironic anti-*bildungsroman *in which the main character reassesses and ultimately rejects her principles and perceptions.*]

Edith Wharton's novella **"Bunner Sisters"** (1916) is a special kind of *Bildungsroman,* for it is the story of an educative process in reverse. The events of a tightly compressed time period force the heroine to discover the inadequacy of the principles she has hitherto learned to live by. Her optimistic assumptions about human nature prove false, as does her naive belief that right conduct will be rewarded by a higher power.

The process of discovery and reassessment which is the chief subject of the novella begins, significantly, with the appearance of a man on the scene. The story opens on the two Bunner sisters and their life of drab spinsterhood. Their struggles to preserve their dress shop on the harsh edge of poverty are rendered more dreary by the emotional lacklustre of their daily existence. Both sisters are galvanized into a state of pleasurable excitement and aliveness when Herman Ramy, the clock repairman, enters their lives. Wharton presents Ramy as a singularly unprepossessing specimen of manhood, not omitting such unappetizing details as his "row of yellowish teeth with one or two gaps in it" and his "fingertips rimmed with grime." Nor does he manifest any intellectual or spiritual qualities which might redeem his unappealing exterior. A faint aura of sinister possibilities surrounds him from the first, but even as a potential villain he fails to achieve stature: his predominant trait is dullness. His obvious inadequacy for the role of romantic bachelor—a role in which the spinster sisters immediately cast him—strikes the reader like a wrong note in a familiar tune.

It is clear that the women in the story do not respond to Ramy as an individual, but as the embodiment of a Platonic Idea of Maleness. Satirically Wharton describes the comfort they derive from deferring to his masculine wisdom: "There was something at once fortifying and pacific in the sense of that tranquil male presence in an atmosphere which had so long quivered with little feminine doubts and distresses; and the sisters fell into the habit of saying to each other, in moments of uncertainty: 'We'll ask Mr. Ramy when he comes,' and of accepting his verdict, whatever it might be, with a fatalistic readiness that relieved them of all responsibility." In his role as Male Incarnate, Ramy is in no way distinguishable from other men who appear briefly in the story; to a certain Mr. Hawkins, for example, Ann Eliza attributes "the mysterious masculine faculty of finding out people's addresses." Wharton creates the large discrepancy between our view of Ramy and the sisters' idealized conception of him in order to underline the risks they run in responding to a gender instead of a person.

Ann Eliza is not forced to revise her view of Ramy for some time, but his presence causes her to consider her sister Evalina in a new and disquieting light. As the elder of the two, Ann Eliza has sheltered and indulged her sister as much as possible. The first cup of tea, the largest slice of pie, are always for Evalina, just as all the more boring and confining tasks naturally fall to Ann Eliza. To Evalina her elder sister also assigns the right to protest against her poor and drudging life. "Ann Eliza . . . never dreamed of allowing herself the luxury of self-pity; it seemed as much a prerogative of Evalina's as her elaborately crinkled hair." But as Ann Eliza gradually perceives that everyone—especially Evalina herself—assumes as a matter of course that Mr. Ramy's visits are inspired by the younger and prettier sister, she rebels. She is dismayed to catch herself criticizing the sister whose "superior aspirations" she has hitherto fostered and admired. "It seemed to Ann Eliza that the coquettish tilt of her head regrettably emphasized the weakness of her receding chin. It was the first time that Ann Eliza had ever seen a flaw in her sister's beauty, and her involuntary criticism startled her like a secret disloyalty." The reader is only too happy to see Ann Eliza acknowledge Evalina's obvious shallowness, her self-important vanities and selfishnesses. Ann Eliza's budding feelings for Herman Ramy, in the face of her sister's nonchalant dismissal of her as a possible rival, cause her to question her life-long role of motherly selflessness. Desire for "a personal and inalienable tie, for pangs and problems of her own" wells up in her, and she can no longer deny her own demands on life: "now she began to transfer to herself a portion of the sympathy she had so long bestowed on Evalina."

In short, for Ann Eliza, Herman Ramy's arrival precipitates the recognition that her desire for life is not yet dead. Her years of self-effacement in favor of her sister now appear to have been a denial of her own nature and needs. Even as she continues to plot for Evalina's happiness, stepping into the background whenever Ramy comes to call, inner voices of jealousy and longing claim her attention. The "chill joy of renunciation" now is bitter cold indeed. Her shattered assumptions about herself and her sister suffer a final collapse when, against all her expectations, Ramy proposes to her rather than to Evalina. That she—older and plainer, resigned and renouncing—should be the one courted and chosen, is a triumphant reversal of her too humble self-appraisal. Her rejection of the proposal (in hopes that Ramy will marry Evalina after all) in no way lessens the perfect fulfillment of knowing she is his first choice.

Ann Eliza's feelings for Evalina verge on the maternal from the beginning, but after this act of supreme self-sacrifice her sense of identification with her sister grows even stronger. Sending off the man she loves to court her sister, she has in effect traded her life's happiness for Evalina's: "The elder sister's affection had so passionately projected itself into her junior's fate that at such moments she seemed to be living two lives, her own and Evalina's." Having purchased Evalina's happiness at so dear a price, Ann Eliza must watch with growing horror the rapid downward course of events. Certain baffling and unpleasant aspects of Ramy's character are explained in a series of painful revelations: he is a drug-addict; he is discharged from job after job; he loses all his money and Evalina's as well; he beats her when he learns she is pregnant; he sends her out to earn money scrubbing floors and waiting tables; he abandons her eventually and runs off with another woman. Ann Eliza hears the whole wretched story when Evalina staggers home one and a half years after her smug departure with Ramy. The final touch of grimness is added to her tale when we discover that her health has been destroyed by illness, abuse, and overwork: she is dying of con-

sumption. Ann Eliza's self-sacrifice has purchased death for her sister, not life.

This catastrophic reversal of Ann Eliza's expectations is the culmination of the increasingly disconcerting recognitions which have been forced upon her. With Ramy serving as emotional catalyst she has discovered that Evalina is not the perfect and all-deserving creature she had thought her; that her own approval and admiration of Evalina are tinged with criticism and jealousy; that she herself in fact possesses a strong, unacknowledged hunger for life. That series of unanticipated insights climaxes with the proposal, only to be disastrously followed up by the unmasking of Ramy. She had assumed that her renunciation would guarantee romantic bliss and domestic contentment for Evalina; instead it has brought her misery, starvation, illness, and death. The cruel irony of the situation is that Ann Eliza has apparently saved herself at her sister's expense. Her act of renunciation now looks like presumptuous meddling. With her perceptions of herself, her sister, and Ramy all turned upside down, she faces a grave moral uncertainty, for her notions about right conduct have proven as unreliable as her judgments about character:

> For the first time in her life she dimly faced the awful problem of the inutility of self-sacrifice. Hitherto she had never thought of questioning the inherited principles which had guided her life. Self-effacement for the good of others had always seemed to her both natural and necessary; but then she had taken it for granted that it implied the securing of that good. Now she perceived that to refuse the gifts of life does not ensure their transmission to those for whom they have been surrendered; and her familiar heaven was unpeopled.

Wharton has put her heroine through a brutally ironic experience which teaches her that reliance on the traditionally female principle of renunciation and self-sacrifice is dangerous. Admitting the moral inadequacy of the policy of self-abnegation "inherited" by her sex is the final step in Ann Eliza's re-education, and that admission plunges her into an existential void: "She felt she could no longer trust in the goodness of God, and that if he was not good he was not God, and there was only a black abyss above the roof of Bunner Sisters." Ann Eliza's story reverses the usual *Bildungsroman* formula, for her enlightenment depends upon *un*learning: her experience gives her nothing to replace what she has lost. Wharton allows us to infer that she is better off without her illusions than with them, but it is nonetheless sobering to watch her walk away with nothing when traditional values have failed her.

The story implicitly links the dangers of self-sacrifice to woman's chattel-like place on the marriage market. Both sisters see marriage as a vehicle to happiness and a measure of self-worth. Being chosen by Ramy causes Ann Eliza to feel that her value has increased; she thinks of her rivalry with Evalina and reflects that "at last . . . they were equals." And Evalina clearly believes her engagement to Ramy is proof of her superiority: "a married woman's the best judge." But the disparity between the sisters' high opinion of Ramy and our more cynical perception of him emphasizes the hazards inherent in their abdication of self-esteem.

The offer of marriage which sends Ann Eliza into a state of "dreamy ecstasy" reads almost like a parody of the traditional romantic declaration. Ramy "dispassionately catalogu[es] her charms" with all the sensitivity of a farmer purchasing a workhorse. Remarks such as "I guess you're healthier than your sister, even if you are less sizable," and "She eats heartier than you do; but that don't mean nothing" preface his announcement that he is tired of eating cold meals and doing his own dusting. He genially suggests that they are "suited to one another" because Ann Eliza is "not afraid of work." While the reader wonders if he will examine her teeth next and demand a certificate of health from a local physician, Ann Eliza is "floating on a summer sea" of joy. She receives the proposal uncritically. Ramy, for his part, is confident that she will accept him, and is dissuaded from his suit only when she pleads headaches and ill-health, hinting that her sister is "spryer" and more hard-working than she. That Ann Eliza should feel honored by such a proposal is as ludicrous as it is horrifying. (The horror increases when we recall that, as Ramy's wife, Evalina is quite literally worked to death.) The womanly virtue of self-deprecation proves doubly vicious here, for had Ann Eliza recognized Ramy's proposal for the insult that it is, she might not have been so eager to see Evalina in his clutches.

Over and over we observe that behind the crudely exaggerated events of the novella, Wharton is posing complicated questions about the morality of self-abnegation. The unexpected and disastrous reverses in the story's plotline summarily overturn the heroine's inherited social and moral assumptions. Ann Eliza's apparent selflessness discovers itself to be bound up with a fatal egotism, and events rebuke her god-like attempt to assume responsibility for the happiness of another human being. Her renunciation is based, moreover, upon a possessive projection of herself and her desires onto another person; but her parasitic need to identify with Evalina and live through her cannot be met. Evalina's last thoughts are all for her dead baby and her newly acquired Catholic faith, and the chastened Ann Eliza is effectively shut out from her sister's dearest ties, both in this world and the next. Her collapsed expectations are a harsh reminder that one cannot, after all, live through someone else. Self-sacrifice may be the ultimate presumption. Ann Eliza fails miserably at living second-hand through her sister; the final bitter irony of her story is that she might just as well have lived for herself. (pp. 241-45)

> *Judith P. Saunders, "Ironic Reversal in Edith Wharton's 'Bunner Sisters',"* in Studies in Short Fiction, *Vol. 14, No. 3, Summer, 1977, pp. 241-45.*

GEOFFREY WALTON (essay date 1982)

[*In the following excerpt from his* Edith Wharton: A Critical Interpretation, *Walton surveys and categorizes stories from Wharton's collections* The Hermit and the Wild Woman, Tales of Men and Ghosts, *and* Xingu, and Other Stories.]

The short stories that Mrs. Wharton collected in her volumes, ***The Hermit and the Wild Woman,*** 1908, ***Tales of Men and Ghosts,*** 1910, and ***Xingu,*** 1916 include some distinguished work. The title story of the first belongs with her other medievalizing sketches to a period fashion and the supernatural stories also are not very interesting contributions to a genre. On the other hand, the stories that dramatize, without adventitious aids, a psychological condition or a problem of moral choice have kept their interest even though particular situations may belong in some cases to out-of-date social custom. Here one appreciates the subtlety and delicacy of the handling and the fineness of the values involved. One

or two stories may be said to achieve a genuine artistic autonomy.

"The Verdict" and **"The Pot-Boiler"** are both concerned with the artistic conscience. One is reminded of [Henry] James's stories of novelists, though Edith Wharton's stories are much slighter work. Like James's writers, Mrs. Wharton's artists inhabit the edges of the fashionable world. **"The Pot-Boiler"** presents an elaborate, though formalized situation. We have a painter who is a real artist and a very "sincere" but mediocre sculptor, both unsuccessful financially. In changed circumstances the sister of the sculptor berates her brother's friend for sacrificing his convictions, but goes on ". . . you must see the distinction because you first made it clear to me. I can take money earned in good faith—I can let Caspar live on it. I can marry Mr. Mungold because, though his pictures are bad, he does not prostitute his art." One infers that the mere fashionable artist who paints as well as he is able does not deserve censure and that, though one may prostitute oneself for the sake of art, art is sacred. It is a clear moral and aesthetic judgment.

Edith Wharton's artist-heroes compel actuality to identify itself with the ideal whatever the human cost. Her stories of other problems are less ruthless in their upshot and more leisurely and deeper in treatment. Irony is pervasive in all of them, accentuating pathos and the tragic in the marriage and divorce stories but absurdity and the comic in the treatment of most other themes. **"His Father's Son"** and **"The Blond Beast"** deal with parental relationships. From the point of view of the characters they may be said to be based on conflict between the ideal and actuality—Mason Grew in the first talks about "the big view" and Orlando G. Spence in the second talks of "principle." Looked at from the outside by the reader through the author's eyes, the idealism seems more a matter of keeping up appearances; as social and moral criticism the comedy works in that way, but below this there is a layer of sympathetic psychological analysis. **"His Father's Son"** is a picture of absurd romanticism and vicarious living. Mason Grew is shown as living on his son's social success, which is a ridiculous situation, but the value of the story lies in the way we see the dependence of both characters on their illusions and, in the case of the father, see that he sees this too. The combination of sympathy and criticism that is Edith Wharton's final attitude is implied in Mason Grew's words on the last page,

> "Look at here, Ronald Grew—do you want me to tell you how you're feeling at this minute? Just a mite let down, after all, at the idea that you ain't the romantic figure you'd got to think yourself . . . Well, that's natural enough, too; but I'll tell you what it proves. It proves you're my son right enough, if any more proof was needed. For it's just the kind of fool nonsense I used to feel at your age—and if there's anybody here to laugh at it's myself, and not you. And you can laugh at me just as much as you like."

which by its simple forthrightness exposes both of them, but leaves us with a general sense of human frailty rather than foolishness.

"The Blond Beast" has a similar quality. It is brilliant satire and the central scene in which the millionaire philanthropist dictates his sentiments during luncheon and condoles with his secretary for missing the soufflé is one of Edith Wharton's funniest pieces of dramatization. The millionaire is a comparatively simple study of humbug—"it was one of Millner's discoveries that an extremely parsimonious use of the emotions underlay Mr. Spence's expansive manner and fraternal phraseology . . ." Draper Spence, his son, reflects his father's philanthropy on another plane by holding Bible classes in a poor district, but Millner, the secretary, is more complex. The story is told as it is registered by his consciousness; in his developing attitude lies the full effect. Millner begins by feeling that:

> The opportunity of a clever young man with a cool head and no prejudices (this again was drawn from life) lay rather in making himself indispensable to one of the beneficient rich, and in using the timidities and conformities of his patron as the means of his own advancement. Young Millner felt no scruples about formulating these principles to himself. It was not for nothing that, in his college days, he had hunted the hypothetical "moral sense" to its lair, and dragged from their concealment the various self-advancing sentiments dissembled under it. His strength lay in his precocious insight into the springs of action, and in his refusal to classify them according to the accepted moral and social sanctions. He had to the full the courage of his lack of convictions.

His critical detachment is gradually weakened until a complete reversal of situation is brought about; Millner discovers in himself impulses that he had not previously acknowledged and he sees the need for even Spence's vast structure of hollow idealism as a source for his son's very existence. Once again, underlying the satire of the whole and the absurdity of the details, there is the feeling for the interdependence of human needs and qualities.

The stories of matrimonial problems form a distinct group. It would be idle to deny that the subject had a special personal interest for Mrs. Wharton, though there is nothing unduly personal in the matter or the manner. They are poised and ironical like the rest, but there is a stronger feeling of pathos and even tragedy. It would be fair to say that, in terms of what James called "felt life," these stories merit the most attention of the work in this form up to date. **"The Letters"** is a curious and a noteworthy production, especially as it was written before *The Reef.* It is extraordinarily disillusioned and yet completely unembittered. Edith Wharton makes the worst of her chosen situation and yet makes happiness grow

Photograph of Wharton's close friend Walter Berry, Wharton, and a French officer in the forward area at Verdun, France, 1915.

out of it. A governess, who inherits a fortune, is married in peculiarly unpropitious circumstances by a former employer and made aware of descending degrees of casualness until the bottom is reached when, three years later, she finds all her pre-marital letters to him—unopened. The ending clearly implies the author's comment:

> As her husband advanced up the path she had a sudden vision of their three years together. Those years were her whole life; everything before them had been colourless and unconscious, like the blind life of the plant before it reaches the surface of the soil. The years had not been exactly what she had dreamed; but if they had taken away certain illusions they had left richer realities in their stead. She understood now that she had gradually adjusted herself to the new image of her husband as he was, as he would always be. He was not the hero of her dreams, but he was the man she loved, and who had loved her. For she saw now, in this last wide flash of pity and initiation, that, as a comely marble may be made out of worthless scraps of mortar, glass, and pebbles, so out of mean mixed substances may be fashioned a love that will bear the stress of life.

One almost feels that Edith Wharton is teaching a lesson in the meaning of mutual toleration and acceptance of the plain reality of ourselves, but once again it is all dramatized for us vividly to experience it. It is an individual relationship, not a mere type case. Sadness and absurdity are just about equally balanced.

"The Long Run" is near tragedy in that the hero fails, because he is what he is, to accept the great opportunity of his life when it comes to him. The story is distanced a little by the use of double narration, but this makes possible a preliminary sketch of the background in old New York with "exceedingly 'nice' " "unobtrusive" people and portraits of Merrick, the brilliant young man who has become "conventional and rather dull," and Paulina, the faded beauty and her rich, commonplace second husband. The rest of the story is a subtle self-portrait, in part ironical, in part directly self-critical, of a fundamentally timid man who resembles several of Edith Wharton's other old New-Yorkers and also suggests a male version of Anna Leath. Out of Merrick's own mouth we hear an account of his "robust passion" for Paulina during her first marriage, of her offer to give up everything for love and how he had prevaricated with all the arguments of conventional prudence. It is a most powerful scene and the mode of telling makes it devastating to the narrator, Merrick himself, however inevitable may be its conclusion; "life-as-it-is, in contrast to life-as-a-visiting-list" is what he has never faced except intellectually. The ending is tragic-comic; "the long run" shows that the risks would have been worth taking. Whereas the heroine of **"The Letters"** makes the best of an actuality that the author has begun by making the worst of, it is, in this case, the hero who deliberately makes the worst of life.

"Autres Temps" takes a long-term view of divorce in the social context of New York Society before the First World War. The title is ironical and the effect depends once again on balance, this time of two juxtaposed situations. The whole treatment is subtler and more restrained than in **"The Long Run,"** but nevertheless full of poignancy. On one plane it is a comedy of manners in the full sense, on another a pathetic personal tragedy. The two situations are those of a mother, Mrs. Lidcote, who left her husband long ago and had to go away and is used to being "cut," and her daughter, Leila, who has also divorced her husband and remarried. The gist of the story is that it is *"autres moeurs"* for Leila but not for her mother. After some quietly ominous scenes in New York, the full implications emerge at a country house party where Mrs. Lidcote is in fact kept out of her daughter's life by a mixture of guile, apparent solicitude for her fatigue, and, above all, her *own* tact:

> "Then won't they think it odd if I don't appear? . . . Will they think it odd if I *do?*"

By such typically conversational understatements, Leila's time-serving and her mother's moral triumph but social defeat are conveyed to us. It is a further irony that Leila and her mother really are fond of each other; probably only within the conventions of the time could this mutual affection have survived.

These stories are the product of mature and studied art and of a well-balanced and intelligent attitude to Society and its conventions; one could cite a number of observations such as: "Traditions that have lost their meaning are the hardest of all to destroy." Mrs. Wharton contemplates her problems in their individual and social implications. Her irony of so many kinds, from the straight satirical to the almost tragic, forms a continuous indication of her sense of complexity. She offers no final solutions but, in showing her characters' solutions, she makes us conscious of certain simple values of sincerity and understanding.

"Xingu," the title story of the 1916 volume, deals with the permanent rather than the changing in Society and the subject is a state of affairs rather than a problem. The material is the American cultural association; it had been the Uplift Club in "The Legend" and is the Lunch Club in "Xingu." In both these cases she uses it as the basis for satiric comedy of pretentious social appearances and discrepant reality. "Xingu" is an American *Précieuses Ridicules,* and its distinction as a story lies in the all-inclusive demolition of affectation that is contrived. The mode is farcical.

The ladies of Hillbridge claim "to centralize and focus its intellectual effort," and each is a beautifully sketched individual portrait of social and the most superficial kind of intellectual snobbery. The opening scene just suggests that Mrs. Roby may really be more cultivated than the others, who illustrate various forms of empty pretence, but one soon finds that she represents mere honest frivolousness combined with a certain quickness of wit. The central episode, in which Osric Dane, a celebrated woman novelist, is entertained, is brief and brilliant farce, from the scene in the drawing-room, with copies of books on which the members feel they ought to be "up" scattered on the table, to the crucial "discussion." In this Mrs. Roby is made to show up everyone, the pompously superior novelist and the fatuous pursuers of culture. She slips in the title word as their current interest and an earnest conversation is constructed as if they all knew what it meant:

> "It has done me worlds of good," Mrs. Leveret interjected, seeming to herself to remember that she had either taken it or read it the winter before.
>
> "Of course," Mrs. Roby admitted, "the difficulty is that one must give up so much time to it. It's very long."
>
> "I can't imagine," Miss Van Vluyck, "grudging the time given to such a subject."

"And deep in places," Mrs. Roby pursued; (so then it was a book!) "And it isn't easy to skip."

"I never skip," said Mrs. Plinth dogmatically.

"Ah, it's dangerous to, in Xingu. Even at the start there are places where one can't. One must just wade through."

"I should hardly call it *wading,*" said Mrs. Ballinger sarcastically.

Mrs. Roby sent her a look of interest. "Ah—you always found it went swimmingly?"

Mrs. Ballinger hesitated. "Of course there are difficult passages," she conceded.

"Yes; some are not at all clear—even," Mrs. Roby added, "if one is familiar with the original."

"As I suppose you are?" Osric Dane interposed, suddenly fixing her with a look of challenge.

Mrs. Roby met it by a deprecating gesture. "Oh, it's really not difficult up to a certain point; though some of the branches are very little known, and it's almost impossible to get at the source."

The absurdity rises to a climax as each asserts that it is something quite different and deflation is completed by the discovery that it is a river in Brazil and that everything Mrs. Roby has said could, as one can see, be applied to a river, as neatly and expressively as Sir John Denham once hoped that his description of the Thames could be applied to his poetry. Nothing has been left standing except this lady's honesty and mischief. Edith Wharton has avoided the obvious contrast of introducing a genuinely cultivated person and in this way given her satire more devastating implications. But it is as a *jeu d'esprit* that one values "Xingu"; it is both highly intelligent and very funny. (pp. 105-13)

> *Geoffrey Walton, in his* Edith Wharton: A Critical Interpretation, *revised edition, Fairleigh Dickinson University Press, 1982, 223 p.*

ALLEN F. STEIN (essay date 1984)

[*In the following excerpt, Stein discusses* Ethan Frome *as "Wharton's fullest treatment of the disasters that can occur when one attempts to leave even a repellent marriage."*]

In Edith Wharton's short story "The Introducers," Tilney, a supremely knowing fellow, asserts in his most knowing manner, "It takes a pretty varied experience of life to find out that there are worse states than marriage." As a paean to domesticity, this is hardly in the same league with old chestnuts of the "it takes a heap of living to make a house a home" variety, but it is as close to an impassioned defense of marriage as Wharton ever presents explicitly in her fiction. At least once in her conversation, though, she went well beyond Tilney's tepid affirmation. Percy Lubbock reports [see Further Reading list] that he was present one day when Wharton in the course of a discussion of *Middlemarch* "spoke out, 'Ah, the poverty, the miserable poverty, of any love that lies outside of marriage, of any love that is not a living together, a sharing of all!'" Such an outburst is, of course, more than a little surprising given the failure of Wharton's own marriage, the predominantly bleak tenor of her work generally, and the fact that the bleakness inheres most strongly in her marriage stories, which, as Geoffrey Walton notes aptly, convey "a stronger feeling of pathos and even tragedy" than do her other works [see excerpt dated 1982]. Clearly, a glance at most of the marriages Wharton presents, a group that includes such infelicitous matings as those of the Fromes, Dorsets, Marvells, and deChelleses, might lead one to find even Wharton's wry avowal of faith in matrimony in **"The Introducers"** a bit improbable. Yet neither Tilney's comment nor the emphatic assertion recorded by Lubbock is finally at odds with the overriding outlook on marriage that Wharton presents in her works. Though she knows that all too few marriages offer the perfect "living together" and "sharing of all" that she so passionately envisions—and, to be sure, presents no marriages of this sort—she also knows full well that there are indeed "worse states" outside marriage, states verging on the "miserable poverty" of emotional, moral, and spiritual chaos. And her defense of marriage is not merely negative, for she stresses throughout her career that even unfortunate marriages can have worth for the individual and society. Positive as it tends to be, though, her defense is almost invariably a somber one, as even her best marriages are successful usually only insofar as they lead married folk to see the bleakness of life and the depth of human folly. (pp. 209-10)

Wharton's fullest treatment of the disasters that can occur when one attempts to leave even a repellent marriage is *Ethan Frome.* Perhaps no other character in Wharton's work is tied to a more insensitive mate than is poor Ethan. Indeed, so unremitting is his pain throughout his long marriage that some have suggested that this work is not much more than a nasty little horror show. Lionel Trilling, for one, asserts that it "presents no moral issue at all" and merely reveals Wharton's limitation of heart [see Further Reading list]. Though Trilling's reading is admirably responsive to Ethan's suffering, it seems to miss the point when it implies that the loveless Frome marriage is only a means by which Wharton indulges virtually sadistic tendencies in herself by tormenting her protagonist. Actually, Wharton's tale does present a discernible counsel on how best to face life in a universe that apparently cares little for those who inhabit it.

In Ethan's small New England town, one sees a way of life with none of those genteel trappings that in polite society shelter people from a daily confrontation with the grimmer facts of existence. Perhaps the grimmest of these is that people are often victimized irremediably by forces over which they have no control. Gary H. Lindberg, in fact, sees Wharton as essentially deterministic in her outlook in that her characters generally seem to be caught up in a "flow of destiny" in which their private schemes "generated by personal lines of intention are simply dwarfed." It is not, he notes, a "scientific formulation of biological and environmental determinism but rather a configuration of moral inevitability posited by the conjunction of a given choice and the social world within which that choice is made." Lindberg's point about Wharton's determinism is well-taken, though in this particular case the crucial conjunction is not that of a "given choice" and the "social world" but of a choice (itself not quite freely made) and the very nature of things, of which the dense social world usually seen in Wharton's works is merely a manifestation. Though the context here is cosmic rather than social, the configuration of moral imperatives that inevitably takes shape is no different from that to be seen in Wharton's tales of marital entrapment that are set in circumstances less bereft of social relations.

That Ethan's marriage is an unhappy one for him is well known and needs no rehearsal here. What may be less obvious, though, in the narrator's account of things is that both his decision to marry Zenna and his subsequent attempt to escape the marriage through suicide with Mattie grow out of a deep, almost childish fear of loneliness, a fear instilled in him, in great measure, by the bleak landscape itself and all that it seems to symbolize about the bleakness of the universe. Ethan proposed to Zeena because he had an "unreasoning dread of being left alone on the farm." This dread evoked, substantially, by the wintry scene around him led him to overestimate Zeena's capacity for human feeling. Reflecting on his error, Ethan "often thought since that it would not have happened if his mother had died in spring instead of winter . . .". Showing more fully that Ethan was a good deal less than a free agent when he married are the references to the landscape about him as having been shaped by the huge, timeless pressures exerted on it, these references serving as an implicit reminder that those who people this landscape are similarly shaped by elements larger than themselves. Thus, the "ledge of granite thrusting up through the ferns," which seems to unroll the "huge panorama of the ice age and the long dim stretches of succeeding time," forces one to see Ethan's story in a larger context than the one in which one normally thinks Wharton's tales operative—forces one, in other words, to see Ethan in a universe of powerful and inevitably enigmatic forces that buffet people about uncaringly and probably unknowingly.

Positing implicitly this central vision, then, the narrator's account of the disaster of Ethan establishes as a central issue the problem of ascertaining how one is to confront life in a bleak, indifferent universe in which one's options are severely limited. The young Ethan's inability to cope with the pressures in his life in no way indicates that means of coping cannot be found; rather, it is an index to his own sentimentality and immaturity as he childishly sees Mattie as embodying virtues and as linked to a happiness that are, quite obviously, well removed from the world we all know. As Cynthia Griffin Wolff notes [in her *A Feast of Words: The Triumph of Edith Wharton* (1977)]; "It is always easier for Ethan to retreat from life into a 'vision' " than to face what must be faced. He is, Wolff goes on to say, invariably too receptive to the "appeal of passivity and a life of regression" [see Further Reading list]. The childishness of his attempt—typically bungled, of course—to regress to a state of ultimate passivity through suicide is brought out by the very form that the attempt takes: a downhill ride on a sled. One can imagine few others in Frome's village who would have chosen such a ride. The Powells, Hales, and their ilk, glimpsed briefly through the narrative, are there, in part, to offer an instructive contrast to the dreamy, dissatisfied Frome. They go quietly about their business and in the routine they establish create a little realm of order and responsibility in the midst of a stark wintry scene, an order that Ethan's crack-up crudely violates.

One possibility in this work that cannot, of course, be overlooked is that the facts as presented by the narrator may not accord with the events that occurred. The narrator's vision of Ethan's past is just that—a vision, and Joseph X. Brennan suggests, therefore, that *Ethan Frome* must be judged "in terms of the special character of the narrator's mind" and, further, that "since the narrator has had to imagine almost the whole of Ethan's history and the most important traits of his character as well, in many respects, inevitably, the sensibilities of the two are indistinguishable" [see Further Reading list]. So indistinguishable might they be that one cannot be sure that the real Ethan Frome ever felt anything akin to what the narrator attributes to him or did the things he did for the reasons the narrator either consciously or inadvertently offers. What *is* objectively verifiable does not necessarily reinforce one's sense of the narrator's accuracy. For example, the picture of Ethan, Mattie, and Zeena with which Wharton closes the work calls into question much of what has been offered previously as a probable version of the past. Though Mrs. Hale asserts that before the crash she "never knew a sweeter nature than Mattie's," whereas Zeena was, she says, "always cranky," in evidence nevertheless as the narrator enters the Frome farmhouse are Mattie's "querulous drone" and Zeena's quiet patience in ministering to this irritable invalid. Inevitably, this makes one wonder whether Mattie was ever quite so good or Zeena quite so bad as the narrator envisions them to have been. On this central question as elsewhere, the narrator may well be indulging his propensities for the exaggerated and the romantic that he reveals throughout the work. Indeed, were the narrator not an exceedingly romantic fellow, even something of a sentimentalist, he would not involve himself in an extensive reverie about thwarted dreams and longings in the first place, nor would he construct the monolithic (and perhaps reductive) image patterns he does in contrasting Mattie and Zeena before the sledding disaster. As Brennan notes, the narrator consistently links Mattie with lovely and delicate objects in nature, such as birds and field mice, whereas he characterizes Zeena throughout with stifling imagery of the indoors and the artificial and through ties to such predators as cats and owls (which, of course, have an innate yen for field mice and small birds). Moreover, the narrator's liking for such phrasing as "in a sky of iron the points of the Dipper hung like icicles and Orion flashed his cold fires" and Ethan "had found Mattie's lips at last and was drinking unconsciousness of everything but the joy they gave him" further reveals the presence here of an exceedingly romantic sensibility and, consequently, must lead one to question the accuracy of his vision of the past.

Whatever the case, however, whether the narrator's vision is a valid one or not, Wharton's allegiances are clear. An accurate telling implies, whether the perhaps too romantic narrator is aware of it or not, that Frome was, as I have noted, a sentimentalist who could not face up to the facts of his existence. If it is an inaccurate account, then it is the narrator who stands indicted as a mawkish sentimentalist (or, as Wolff puts it, one with a "ghastly" mind) who indirectly and inadvertently makes a powerful argument for living up to such commitments as those he envisions the young Ethan as trying to escape. Finally, if one concludes, as one well might, that **Ethan Frome** is irresolvably ambiguous, Wharton's position is no less clear. In a world in which the truth is nebulous, perhaps impossible to glean with certainty, one must, she teaches, strive for order, even self-imposed order; and this must be carried out even in the face of the determinism that she sees as operative, for, rightly or wrongly, she does not regard moral responsibility as incompatible with a restricted will. The establishment of routine, of order, by carrying out ordering responsibilities imposed by the severe demands of marriage is thus a goal to strive for, one that either Ethan or the narrator (or both) could not perceive as valuable. Without such order, Wharton believes, a difficult existence can only be made more difficult. (pp. 225-30)

Allen F. Stein, "Edith Wharton: The Marriage of Entrapment," in his After the Vows Were Spoken:

Marriage in American Literary Realism, *Ohio State University Press, 1984, pp. 209-30.*

ADELINE R. TINTNER   (essay date 1987)

[*In the following excerpt, Tintner explores Wharton's literary perspective and manipulation of narrative structure in the novella collection* Old New York, *comparing Wharton's technique and stories with those of Honoré de Balzac, Henry James, and F. Marion Crawford.*]

Old New York (1924), Edith Wharton's quartet of *novellas,* is her successful attempt to write a pocket Balzac's *Comédie Humaine* as well as a pocket New York Edition (in emulation of James's New York Edition and as a correction of its prolixity). James's four late New York stories, "Julia Bride" and "The Jolly Corner" (1908) followed by "Crapy Cornelia" and "A Round of Visits" in *The Finer Grain* (1910), as well as F. Marion Crawford's four New York novels, *The Three Fates, Marion Darche, Katherine Lauderdale* and *The Ralstons* (1894-95), have demonstrably significant roles as models for her narrative strategies and as spring-boards for her original transformations, which Wharton's close personal relations with these two authors facilitated. In all these sources the desire and need for money controls Society and determines the behavior of its members. It is the overall thrust in Wharton's quartet as well. (p. 76)

Many of Edith Wharton's names are reminders of names from F. Marion Crawford's interrelated families as well as from the relationships of cousins. Katherine and Charlotte Lauderdale, in his novel *Katherine Lauderdale,* appear to be models for the cousins Charlotte and Delia in Wharton's **The Old Maid.** The jealousy between Mrs. Lauderdale and her own daughter is transferred to Wharton's cousins. Charlotte Lauderdale is fair, and Katherine dark. Katherine wants a secret marriage with John Ralston; Charlotte is married to Benjamin Slaybrooke whom she hates, and Mrs. Lauderdale is jealous of her own daughter. Edith Wharton imitates this in **The Old Maid** where Delia is jealous of Charlotte's affair with Clem Spender and of their illegitimate child. She cares for her and becomes her surrogate mother. Whereas Crawford tells us too much, Wharton condenses and concentrates her material in her *novella.* Of the four books—**False Dawn** is concerned with men, **The Old Maid** with women, **The Spark** again with men, and **New Year's Day** with one woman against a band of women. There is added a young man who is involved with the woman.

In order to achieve a wider social panorama within her self-limited confines Wharton has to fashion what is virtually a new fictional genre. This is a complex of four *novellas* or double-decker short stories, which echo Balzac's groups of related tales within the *Comédie Humaine.* It also is a reminder of James's stories connected by the pressure of a coarse-grained woman on a man of "finer grain" in his book of tales, *The Finer Grain* (1910), in which the four New York stories of James appeared and which we infer were all built around Edith herself. Her emphasis on dialogue and on the New York of James's youth point to this influence, especially since around 1920, when preparing the letters with Lubbock, she revived and kept alive her feelings of loss for Henry James. She wrote to Gaillard Lapsley on Sept. 24, 1920: "My longing to talk with you about Henry James is getting *maladive.*"

Fiction for Wharton was "the disengaging of crucial moments

Fiction for Wharton was "the disengaging of crucial moments from the welter of existence," as she expressed it in *The Writing of Fiction,* written in 1925 just after her **New York Quartet** had been completed. Her new genre depends on the "disengagement" of crucial situations from the novel's grab-bag of detail—each item so arranged as to convey the essence of the situation through a concrete symbol. For her the requirements of a short story were determined by an incident "which a single retrospective flash sufficiently lights up." She fashioned for each *novella* in her quartet what are essentially two short stories linked by the passage of time with two incidents and two flashes, the second illuminating the first. In **The Old Maid,** the most popular of the quartet, the crucial situations occur when Delia Lovell Ralston takes over Tina, her lover's illegitimate child by her cousin Charlotte: once in Part One, where she brings the child into her own household and, again in Part Two, when she adopts her legally. She does this for the sake of the father of the child, Clement Spender, with whom she had been in love. Both actions are dramatically motivated and the last is a cooperative one between adoptive and biological mothers. Charlotte, the biological mother and "old maid," intercepts Tina and her own lover when they come back late to make love in the Gramercy Park house so that Tina will not repeat the error of her own life, and Delia adopts the girl so that her beau's family will recognize her as a socially fit daughter-in-law. The double plot underlines the ironical situation that in the first half of the *novella* an old maid is actually the biological mother, and that in the second half Delia, the cousin rejected by Clement, takes her unconscious vengeance by supplanting the real mother.

To order the structure of the quartet as a whole Wharton developed within it tactics of both unification and diversification. These elements include, first, a chronological sequence of separate decades covered by each *novella* (The **Forties** through the **Seventies**), determining the order of each tale in the boxed set, the crucial time-span dividing the episodes as well as the amount of elapsed time and the number of time-breaks which change in each tale.

Second in importance is the necessity of "a vivid opening" formulated in *The Writing of Fiction.*

> If his first stroke be vivid and telling the reader's attention will be instantly won. . . . The arrest of attention by a vivid opening should be something more than a trick . . . [for] the narrator can "situate" his tale in an opening passage which shall be a clue to all the detail eliminated.

The most striking example of this is in the fourth, climactic *novella,* **New Year's Day.** There the dramatic first sentence is repeated in the last part of the tale to emphasize the final irony of the judgment contained in it. ("She was *bad* . . . always. They used to meet at the Fifth Avenue Hotel.") What we have learned in the body of the *novella* is that Lizzie Hazeldean was completely justified in her self-imposed prostitution, since it was an act of heroic self-sacrifice to insure her husband's happiness in his final illness.

The third narrative device is the use of a recurrent first person narrator, the Harvard graduate who appears in three of the *novellas.* He is eliminated only in **The Old Maid** since the chronological action is "not naturally within his register," a regulation stressed by Edith Wharton in her *Writing of Fiction.* The tale also is restricted to three women and is told from the point of view of one of them, which facilitates the concision and tension of the plot.

The fourth device is that of recurrent family names and characters, the device so important to Balzac's narrative technique. Some, like Mrs. Manson Mingott, constitute a potent offstage presence, and some, like Sillerton Jackson, are active in several tales. These are all legatees from *The Age of Innocence* and constitute a dynasty, further amplified by the importation of the rich and powerful Ralstons. It is significant that this is a name recurrent not in Wharton's tales or novels but in Crawford's quartet of related New York novels.

The fifth device is the initial concealment and then gradual revelation of some crucial factor. This factor may be the unconscious drive displayed by Charlotte for control over Delia and her daughter in **The Old Maid** or may consist of the gradually revealed names of the great writers and artists—Poe, Ruskin and the pre-Raphaelites in **False Dawn** and of Whitman in **The Spark.** The extent to which the revelation is delayed is variable and the reader, by a flattering allusion to his cultivation, is invited to be an accomplice in solving the riddle for which the author's multiple clues are the key. This is a device inherited from Henry James, but Wharton is taking no chances that her reader may fail to follow the clues as James's readers often did; she finally always tells.

The sixth device is the accumulation of often multiplied ironies resulting from the above strategies. These become dense at the end of each tale for they demonstrate the effects of the action of the first part of the *novella* upon the second.

The seventh device is the use of indexical icons. The outstanding one is the French clock in **The Old Maid,** whose presence keeps her lost lover Clement before Delia all her life, and which emphasizes his role in the past. Its dozen citations build up to the revelation that it stands for the continued presence of the absent lover, as well as for the passage of time that replicates the first episode and repairs its damages. A second potent indexical icon is the steeplechase motif in **The Spark** with its unspoken but unmistakable reference to Tolstoy's *Anna Karenina,* a book which is featured in Wharton's *The Writing of Fiction* as combining situation, character and manners.

The last device is the focusing on a separate social sin in each tale. The precocious taste in art is vanquished by Philistinism in **False Dawn.** Illegitimacy is punished by the loss of intimacy between the biological mother and her child in **The Old Maid.** Revealed cuckoldry is punished, although concealed adultery is acceptable, in **The Spark,** and, finally, the nobly motivated intramural prostitution in **New Year's Day** is punished by social excommunication.

Wharton has learned from her literary heroes. The area occupied by the quartet is defined by Balzacian interest in *genius loci* and recurrent characters. It is dominated by Jamesian probing of not only psychological but also of linguistic puzzles. Crawford's interest in American dynasties, which he had placed in the form of a quartet, is reproduced in small in the four *novellas.* Proustian attention to both unconscious behavior and to morbid and abnormal relationships is repeated in **New Year's Day.** By the end of the quartet the Jamesian narrator has turned into a Proustian narrator, a kind of Marcel, echoing the latter's relations with Madame Swann in the pattern of his love for Mrs. Hazeldean. This is cleverly placed in the tale which includes the 1920s, a time contemporary with Proust's masterpiece.

The Old Maid is the real "first" of the quartet in terms of having been written first, although **False Dawn,** a report of soci-

Wharton in Paris, after World War I.

ety in the 1840s in New York, is the first to be read in the series. The unique technique of narration which develops as it goes along is established in this story. *The Old Maid* begins in typically Balzacian manner or even in the manner of *Washington Square* which is that novel among James's early books which most apes Balzac's complex technique of working in the background: geographical, architectural and sociological. Wharton's chief personal contribution here is her use of one word to allude to a whole social vista and a whole social complex. She lists things, including the names of the ruling families of New York of this period, that of 1850: The Ralstons, Lovells, Halseys, Vandergraves, the conservatives who rule and "who revered Hamilton." That one word "Hamilton" describes their ingrained attitudes, their reverence for established tradition and their worship of money. The Lannings, Dagonets and Spenders, on the other hand, are the risk-takers. Like Clem Spender, the natural father of Tina, Lanning Halsey in *The Old Maid* has a combination of both family traits which makes it possible for him to propose marriage to Tina, Charlotte's illegitimate daughter, although Spender could not have proposed to Charlotte. Delia makes it possible for them to marry by adopting Clementina Lovell and so making her Clementina Ralston.

The fusion of strategies adapted from those authors Wharton most admired, yet whom she basically criticized by making her own solutions of their social and formal problems, consti-

tutes a mode with implications for the future of the writing of fiction. The next time we are aware of a similar and successful experiment is fifty years later in *Zuckerman Bound* by Philip Roth, a set of three novels and an epilogue which are unified by a common hero and a common literary source in Henry James. Yet Roth too is as critical of his inherited model as Wharton has been, and like her, he reshapes his literary inheritance into new forms. (pp. 76-80)

Adeline R. Tintner, "The Narrative Structure of 'Old New York': Text and Pictures in Edith Wharton's Quartet of Linked Short Stories," in The Journal of Narrative Technique, *Vol. 17, No. 1, Winter, 1987, pp. 76-82.*

LESLIE FISHBEIN   (essay date 1987)

[In the following excerpt, Fishbein asserts that critics frequently fail to recognize the moral relativism implicit throughout Wharton's novella New Year's Day.]*

Edith Wharton's literary reputation rests securely on her skill as a chronicler of a narrow segment of New York society, a nostalgic exploration of a world of fixed conventions and rigid mores, a society that might victimize its wayward souls but which provided tradition and honor as guides to the perplexed. R. W. B. Lewis has argued that in the aftermath of the First World War, disillusioned by the isolationism, materialism, and ignorance of American civilization, Wharton engaged in an imaginative search for a usable past: "Looking across the vast abyss of the war, she located the lost America in the New York of her girlhood: the New York she had come back to in 1872, after six years in Europe; the world in which she had passed her adolescence and the first years of her womanhood—a safe, narrow, unintellectual, and hidebound world, but from the tremendous distance of time and history, an endearing and honorable one" [see Further Reading list].

While critics have devoted considerable attention to her major accounts of New York society, *The House of Mirth* (1905) and *The Age of Innocence* (1920), her four novellas that comprise **Old New York** (1924) have suffered nearly complete critical neglect. The fourth of these, **New Year's Day (The 'Seventies),** the most provocative thematically in its treatment of adultery and prostitution, has baffled the handful of critics, largely contemporaneous, who sought to plumb its deeper levels of meaning. While Edmund Wilson claimed that the tales offered little more than a mediocre effort at local color by "probably the only absolutely first-rate literary artist, occupying himself predominantly with New York, that New York has ever produced," most critics viewed the novellas as exquisite examples of Wharton's artistry in miniature. They emphasized the rigidity of the social universe of all the works—"The world thus revealed in Edith Wharton's novels and stories is a small closed circle of tight security wherein men and women behave like toys in the discipline of a heartless social mechanism."—and the essential impermeability to change of old New York, a society that punishes all deviation from its rigid decorum with harsh cruelty disproportionate to the erring act: "The old New York of the four stories is represented in four successive decades of its progress, yet its life reveals no qualitative expansion under the flow of time, and the social organism suffers no least modification." In particular, the critics tended to view **New Year's Day** as exemplifying the "helpless incapacity" society enforced on women like Lizzie Hazeldean, forced to be entirely ornamental and subservient to men even in an era of budding feminine independence, a woman whose sexual lapse can be excused by social constraints that offer no other viable means of attaining economic autonomy and personal control. And a few hostile critics damned the inauthenticity of **New Year's Day,** noting either the psychological impossibility of a loving and loyal wife like Lizzie Hazeldean choosing to become Henry Prest's mistress to provide comforts for her ailing husband and to secure for herself the luxuries he wished her to have, or the historical inaccuracy on which the opening of the novel turns, as Mrs. Hazeldean's clandestine affair is discovered as she and Henry Prest emerge from the notorious Fifth Avenue Hotel during a fire:

> The scandal on which the tale is founded rests on the very insecure foundation of a glimpse obtained by a New Year's party of a man and woman emerging from the Fifth Avenue Hotel. The pair might just as well have been caught in the act of leaving Central Park, for the lobby of that hotel was a thoroughfare and the house itself was respectable in the highest degree.

What all of the contemporary critics, whether hostile or friendly, seem to have missed is the moral relativism implicit in both the structure and content of **New Year's Day.** Rather than a nostalgic attempt to take refuge in the firmly established social patterns of her youth or a condemnation of the harshness and cruelty of a rigid social mechanism, the book instead can be viewed profitably as a product of the era in which it was written, an era critical of the pretensions of moral absolutism, an age whose ethics had been rendered increasingly situational.

The Twenties was an era of moral relativism. While there is evidence of substantial liberalization in attitudes toward sexuality, feminine autonomy, female dress, birth control, and film in the pre-World War I period, these gains were consolidated and popularized in the Twenties. Rouge, once the mark of the harlot, now adorned the respectable young; drinking and smoking came to be practiced by "nice" girls, not only by their fallen sisters; and petting came to be so essential to popularity on campus that its extent came to be governed by rules of seniority as strict, despite their *de facto* status, as any union might devise. The repeal of reticence, that startling new frankness in public discourse regarding sex, permitted women to articulate emotions that would have been steadfastly repressed a generation earlier. The sharp distinction that had differentiated true women and their fallen sisters blurred as the use of cosmetics, smoking, drinking, and nonmarital sexual activity no longer were confined largely to the prostitute class.

The Twenties also was marked by the popularization of Freudian doctrine, which was considerably simplified and distorted in the process. As Freudian theory was debased by its American popularizers, psychoanalysis came to be commonly conceived as a rationalization of sexual laxity, and the distinction between the normal and abnormal seemed to lose its validity. Psychoanalysis appealed to Twenties writers and intellectuals "because it was new, unorthodox, shockingly frank, and because it implied—though it certainly did not advise—a more liberal view of sex matters." A Freudian substructure in which ostensive meaning is revealed as inadequate because of irrational motives not available to the untutored observer came to characterize many novels of the period, and **New Year's Day (The 'Seventies)** is no exception.

The book's narrative strategy undermines any belief in moral absolutism because the opening of the work encourages the reader to assume a false view of events from which he subsequently will be disabused. In that sense the novel is Freudian in that its manifest content is betrayed by a more revealing latent substructure; in this world, appearances serve to belie reality. The work opens on a false note: " 'She was *bad . . .* always. They used to meet at the Fifth Avenue Hotel,' said my mother, as if the scene of the offense added to the guilt of the couple whose part she was revealing." The object of scorn is Lizzie Hazeldean, the charming, somewhat unconventional wife of an ailing lawyer, whose marriage had rescued her from a life of drab dependence. The narrator, a boy of twelve at the time of the New Year's party that saw Lizzie Hazeldean and Henry Prest emerge from the hotel fire, initially accepts his mother's account as the truth, focusing new light on "an unremarked incident of [his] boyhood."

The second chapter shifts to Lizzie Hazeldean's point of view, an authorial decision that implies the absence of any fixed absolute vantage point on the truth. The chapter emphasizes the young wife's efforts to conceal her illicit rendezvous, and the reader becomes increasingly confused as subsequent chapters offer evidence of genuine love and respect that Lizzie feels for her husband Charles. It is not until half a year later, when the widowed Mrs. Hazeldean receives Henry Prest, that we learn her true motivation in the affair: " 'You thought I was a lovelorn mistress; and I was only an expensive prostitute'." She informs Prest that she had become his mistress not out of passion or discontent with her own marriage, but out of a desire to provide comforts for her ailing husband and to acquire luxuries for herself that were crucial to the maintenance of her husband's self-esteem. Even when the point of view shifts back to that of the male narrator, now a young man thoroughly enamored of the middle-aged widow, it is Lizzie Hazeldean's interpretation of events that seems the most accurate since it best accounts for the actions that mark her final days: her "cold celibacy," her refusal of the renewed attentions of Henry Prest, and her creation of a shrine out of the books of Charles' library. Wharton's narrative strategy here resembles that of Charlotte Perkins Gilman's *The Yellow Wallpaper* (1899), a brief fictional account of a woman's descent into madness as a result of the very therapeutic idleness that has been forced upon her. Despite the fact that the narrator is progressively becoming madder as the story unfolds, Gilman succeeds in rendering her the only trustworthy witness of events. Thus, Wharton and Gilman force the reader to adopt the vantage point of the deviant, whether adulterous wife or madwoman, thereby undermining any belief in absolute morality and suggesting that those who betray convention may be the more honest for their rebellion.

Wharton also suggests moral relativism in her use of time. She makes it clear that morality is little more than codified folkways, that society condemns in one era what it will condone in another. Old New York had been shocked by the affair at the Fifth Avenue Hotel and felt compelled to denote the locale with a precision that a later era, more accustomed to sexual misbehavior, would scorn. As a result, it becomes difficult to treat the same offense in the later era with the same degree of high seriousness and moral obloquy. . . . Wharton indicates that the 'Seventies, the era in which her tale is set, had been more rigid regarding socially acceptable behavior than the periods preceding and following it. And Wharton notes a new ambivalence regarding the *déclassé* a mere decade after Mrs. Hazeldean's social ostracism. Mrs. Hazeldean sat alone in her box at the opera, still a pariah in the 'Eighties: "In the New York of my youth every one knew what to think of a woman who was seen 'alone at the opera'; if Mrs. Hazeldean was not openly classed with Fanny Ring, our one conspicuous 'professional,' it was because, out of respect for her social origin, New York preferred to avoid such juxtapositions." Nevertheless, the sanctions against her had weakened in practice as ladies, whetted by the excitement of her notoriety, joined her at supper or even called at her home, thereby subverting the moral code that demanded that true women eschew all contact with their fallen sisters. The ladies that the narrator meets at the widow's house were "mostly younger than their hostess, and still, though precariously, within the social pale: pretty trivial creatures, bored with a monotonous prosperity, and yearning for such unlawful joys as cigarettes, plain speaking, and a drive home in the small hours with the young man of the moment." While Wharton claimed that "such daring spirits were few in old New York," certainly her description of them amply fits the flappers, who existed in abundance during the Twenties when the novel appeared. What Wharton is suggesting is that society is arbitrary, chaotic, and randomized and that precisely that disorder which may unfairly penalize some wayward spirit in a given era also will afford the same creature refuge in another era less mindful of the social proprieties that had animated its predecessors. (pp. 399-403)

Wharton may well have had a personal interest in the moral relativism that suffuses *New Year's Day.* She was painfully aware of the social rigidities of Old New York, and she had inherited an aversion to scandal from her family. Wharton knew that the penalty for deviating from the strictest standards of probity in business or personal life was social ostracism of the most merciless kind. Her cousin George Alfred had been "vanished" from society and respectability on account of "some woman," who inevitably was blamed for his lapse. But her mother's disapproval and scorn failed to simply intimidate Wharton and exact social obedience. Her cousin's example also tempted her latent hostility against her parents' social code: "The vision of poor featureless unknown Alfred and his siren, lurking in some cranny of my imagination, hinted at regions perilous, dark and yet lit with mysterious fires, just outside the world of copy-book axioms, and the old obedience that were in my blood; and the hint was useful—for a novelist."

The novella imbues Lizzie Hazeldean's adultery with heroic qualities, justifying it on account of its altruistic motivation. The victim of a hapless marriage with Edward Robbins ("Teddy") Wharton in which there appears to have been little sexual activity or interest beyond the first few weeks although their union lasted twenty years, Mrs. Wharton remained ambiguous regarding any evasion of the marriage vow: "Divorce (though she was to come to it herself) she considered crude and antisocial, and the facile forming of new marital ties unspeakably vulgar. On the other hand, the dishonesties and evasions of concealed adultery struck her as offensive and degrading, while any open disregard of the conventions led to a slow, sordid end in those shabby European watering places with which the minds of her contemporaries seemed always to identify extramarital passion." Yet Wharton herself was guilty of adultery, and not merely of the retaliatory sort to repay her husband for his vulgar and boastful indiscretions. At age forty-four she preceded him in adultery and discovered hitherto unexplored dimensions of eroticism with the journalist Morton Fullerton, a man of bizarre and prodigious sexual attachments. Rigidly opposed to adultery in theory, Wharton practiced it in actuality. If adultery could be justified on altruistic grounds in the case of Lizzie Hazeldean, might not one look more charitably upon Wharton's own, less highminded, indiscretion? (p. 404)

Leslie Fishbein, "Prostitution, Morality, and Paradox: Moral Relativism in Edith Wharton's 'Old New York: New Year's Day (The 'Seventies)'," in Studies *in Short Fiction, Vol. 24, No. 4, Fall, 1987, pp. 399-406.*

FURTHER READING

Bewley, Marius. "Mrs. Wharton's Mask." *The New York Review of Books* 111, No. 3 (24 September 1964): 7-9.
    Discussion of Wharton's moral beliefs as revealed in her life and writing that includes a refutation of Lionel Trilling's critical interpretation of *Ethan Frome* [see Further Reading list].

Brennan, Joseph X. "*Ethan Frome*: Structure and Metaphor." *Modern Fiction Studies* VII, No. 4 (Winter 1961-62): 347-56.
    Detailed textual analysis of *Ethan Frome,* noting the impor-

tance of the work's narrative framework and elaborate meta-phorical patterns.

Burgess, Anthony. "Austere in Whalebone." *Spectator,* No. 7171 (3 December 1965): 745.
    Reviews *Ethan Frome, The Custom of the Country,* and *Summer.* According to Burgess: "The utter pessimism of *Ethan Frome*—the Immortals sporting in a frigid New England—is too bad to be true; it is Hardyesque self-indulgence; a tragic thesis takes over and manipulates chess-characters."

Clough, David. "Edith Wharton's War Novels: A Reappraisal." *Twentieth Century Literature* XIX, No. 1 (January 1973): 1-14.
    Examines Wharton's novella *The Marne* and novel *A Son at the Front,* illuminating American attitudes about World War I and the significance the war held for Wharton.

Iyengar, K. R. Srinivasa. "A Note on *Ethan Frome.*" *Literary Criterion* V, No. 3 (Winter 1962): 168-78.
    Praises the craftsmanship and psychological insight of Wharton's plot presentation in *Ethan Frome,* and compares the novella with Ford Madox Ford's *The Good Soldier* (1927) and Rabindranath Tagore's *The Garden* (1933).

Kronenberger, Louis. "Mrs. Wharton's Literary Museum." *The Atlantic Monthly* 222, No. 3 (September 1968): 98-100, 102.
    Critical overview of many of Wharton's short stories and novels. Kronenberger concludes that Wharton was a stronger novelist than short story writer.

Lewis, R. W. B. *Edith Wharton: A Biography.* New York: Harper & Row, Publishers, 1975, 592 p.
    Definitive biography.

Lubbock, Percy. *Portrait of Edith Wharton.* New York and London: D. Appleton-Century Co., 1947, 249 p.

Biography of Wharton that consists of reminiscences of her friends and excerpt from letters.

McDowell, Margaret B. "Viewing the Custom of Her Country: Edith Wharton's Feminism." *Contemporary Literature* XV, No. 4 (Autumn 1974): 521-38.
    Thoughtful study of Wharton's implicit feminist concerns and her changing attitudes toward women throughout her life.

———. *Edith Wharton.* Boston: Twayne Publishers, 1976, 158 p.
    Insightful biography and analysis of Wharton's literary canon.

Shuman, R. Baird. "The Continued Popularity of *Ethan Frome.*" *Revue des Langues Vivantes* XXXVII, No. 3 (1971): 257-63.
    Discusses symbolism in *Ethan Frome* as the novella's most pervasive element.

Trilling, Lionel. "The Morality of Inertia (Edith Wharton: *Ethan Frome*)." In *Great Moral Dilemmas in Literature, Past and Present,* edited by R. M. MacIver, pp. 37-46. New York: Cooper Square Publishers, 1964.
    Discussion of *Ethan Frome* and the morality imposed by social demand, circumstances, habit, and biology. Trilling maintains that *Ethan Frome* is a morally bankrupt work that fails to meet the precepts of Aristotelian tragedy.

Wolff, Cynthia Griffin. *A Feast of Words: The Triumph of Edith Wharton.* New York: Oxford University Press, 1977, 453 p.
    Biography of Wharton in which Wolff interprets Wharton's major works as reflective of her psychological development.

———. "Cold Ethan and 'Hot Ethan'." *College Literature* XIV, No. 3 (Fall 1987): 23-45.
    Relates Wharton's marital and romantic experiences to episodes from *Ethan Frome* and *Summer.*

Appendix:

Select Bibliography of General Sources on Short Fiction

BOOKS OF CRITICISM

Allen, Walter. *The Short Story in English.* New York: Oxford University Press, 1981, 413 p.

Bates, H. E. *The Modern Short Story: A Critical Survey.* Boston: Writer, 1941, 231 p.

Bennett, E. K. *A History of the German Novelle: From Goethe to Thomas Mann.* Cambridge: At the University Press, 1934, 296 p.

Bone, Robert. *Down Home: A History of Afro-American Short Fiction from Its Beginning to the End of the Harlem Renaissance.* Rev. ed. New York: Columbia University Press, 1988, 350 p.

Bruck, Peter. *The Black American Short Story in the Twentieth Century: A Collection of Critical Essays.* Amsterdam: B. R. Grüner Publishing Co., 1977, 209 p.

Burnett, Whit, and Burnett, Hallie. *The Modern Short Story in the Making.* New York: Hawthorn Books, 1964, 405 p.

Canby, Henry Seidel. *The Short Story in English.* New York: Henry Holt and Co., 1909, 386 p.

Current-García, Eugene. *The American Short Story before 1850: A Critical History.* Twayne's Critical History of the Short Story, edited by William Peden. Boston: Twayne Publishers, 1985, 168 p.

Flora, Joseph M., ed. *The English Short Story, 1880-1945: A Critical History.* Twayne's Critical History of the Short Story, edited by William Peden. Boston: Twayne Publishers, 1985, 215 p.

Foster, David William. *Studies in the Contemporary Spanish-American Short Story.* Columbia, Mo.: University of Missouri Press, 1979, 126 p.

George, Albert J. *Short Fiction in France, 1800-1850.* Syracuse, N. Y.: Syracuse University Press, 1964, 245 p.

Hankin, Cherry, ed. *Critical Essays on the New Zealand Short Story.* Auckland: Heinemann Publishers, 1982, 186 p.

Kilroy, James F., ed. *The Irish Short Story: A Critical History.* Twayne's Critical History of the Short Story, edited by William Peden. Boston: Twayne Publishers, 1984, 251 p.

Leibowitz, Judith. *Narrative Purpose in the Novella.* The Hague: Mouton, 1974, 137 p.

Lohafer, Susan. *Coming to Terms with the Short Story.* Baton Rouge: Louisiana State University Press, 1983, 171 p.

Lohafer, Susan, and Clarey, Jo Ellyn. *Short Story Theory at a Crossroads.* Baton Rouge: Louisiana State University Press, 1989, 352 p.

Matthews, Brander. *The Philosophy of the Short Story.* New York: Longmans, Green and Co., 1901, 83 p.

May, Charles E., ed. *Short Story Theories.* Athens, Oh.: Ohio University Press, 1976, 251 p.

Moser, Charles, ed. *The Russian Short Story: A Critical History*. Twayne's Critical History of the Short Story, edited by William Peden. Boston: Twayne Publishers, 1986, 232 p.

Newman, Frances. *The Short Story's Mutations: From Petronius to Paul Morand*. New York: B. W. Huebsch, 1925, 332 p.

O'Connor, Frank. The Lonely Voice: *A Study of the Short Story*. Cleveland: World Publishing Co., 1963, 220 p.

O'Faolain, Sean. *The Short Story*. New York: Devin-Adair Co., 1951, 370 p.

Pattee, Fred Lewis. *The Development of the American Short Story: An Historical Survey*. New York: Harper and Brothers Publishers, 1923, 388 p.

Peden, Margaret Sayers, ed. *The Latin American Short Story: A Critical History*. Twayne's Critical History of the Short Story, edited by William Peden. Boston: Twayne Publishers, 1983, 160 p.

Peden, William. *The American Short Story: Continuity and Change, 1940-1975*. Rev. ed. Boston: Houghton Mifflin Co., 1975, 215 p.

Reid, Ian. *The Short Story*. The Critical Idiom, edited by John D. Jump. London: Methuen and Co., 1977, 76 p.

Rohrberger, Mary. *Hawthorne and the Modern Short Story: A Study in Genre*. The Hague: Mouton and Co., 1966, 148 p.

Shaw, Valerie. *The Short Story: A Critical Introduction*. London: Longman, 1983, 294 p.

Stevick, Philip, ed. *The American Short Story, 1900-1945: A Critical History*. Twayne's Critical History of the Short Story, edited by William Peden. Boston: Twayne Publishers, 1984, 209 p.

Summers, Hollis, ed. *Discussions of the Short Story*. Boston: D. C. Heath and Co., 1963, 118 p.

Vannatta, Dennis, ed. *The English Short Story, 1945-1980: A Critical History*. Twayne's Critical History of the Short Story, edited by William Peden. Boston: Twayne Publishers, 1985, 206 p.

Voss, Arthur. *The American Short Story: A Critical Survey*. Norman, Okla.: University of Oklahoma Press, 1973, 399 p.

Ward, Alfred C. *Aspects of the Modern Short Story: English and American*. London: University of London Press, 1924, 307 p.

Weaver, Gordon, ed. *The American Short Story, 1945-1980: A Critical History*. Twayne's Critical History of the Short Story, edited by William Peden. Boston: Twayne Publishers, 1983, 150 p.

West, Ray B., Jr. *The Short Story in America, 1900-1950*. Chicago: Henry Regnery Co., 1952, 147 p.

Williams, Blanche Colton. *Our Short Story Writers*. New York: Moffat, Yard and Co., 1920, 357 p.

Wright, Austin McGiffert. *The American Short Story in the Twenties*. Chicago: University of Chicago Press, 1961, 425 p.

CRITICAL ANTHOLOGIES

Atkinson, W. Patterson, ed. *The Short-Story*. Boston: Allyn and Bacon, 1923, 317 p.

Baldwin, Charles Sears, ed. *American Short Stories*. New York: Longmans, Green and Co., 1904, 333 p.

Current-García, Eugene, and Patrick, Walton R., eds. *American Short Stories: 1820 to the Present*. Key Editions, edited by John C. Gerber. Chicago: Scott, Foresman and Co., 1952, 633 p.

Fagin, N. Bryllion, ed. *America through the Short Story*. Boston: Little, Brown, and Co., 1936, 508 p.

Frakes, James R., and Traschen, Isadore, eds. *Short Fiction: A Critical Collection.* Prentice-Hall English Literature Series, edited by Maynard Mack. Englewood Cliffs, N. J.: Prentice-Hall, 1959, 459 p.

Gordon, Caroline, and Tate, Allen, eds. *The House of Fiction: An Anthology of the Short Story with Commentary.* Rev. ed. New York: Charles Scribner's Sons, 1960, 469 p.

Gullason, Thomas A., and Caspar, Leonard, eds. *The World of Short Fiction: An International Collection.* New York: Harper and Row, 1962, 548 p.

Havighurst, Walter, ed. *Masters of the Modern Short Story.* New York: Harcourt, Brace and Co., 1945, 538 p.

Litz, A. Walton, ed. *Major American Short Stories.* New York: Oxford University Press, 1975, 823 p.

Matthews, Brander, ed. *The Short-Story: Specimens Illustrating Its Development.* New York: American Book Co., 1907, 399 p.

Menton, Seymour, ed. *The Spanish American Short Story: A Critical Anthology.* Berkeley and Los Angeles: University of California Press, 1980, 496 p.

Mzamane, Mbulelo Vizikhungo, ed. *Hungry Flames, and Other Black South African Short Stories.* Longman African Classics. Essex: Longman, 1986, 162 p.

Schorer, Mark, ed. *The Short Story: A Critical Anthology.* Rev. ed. Prentice-Hall English Literature Series, edited by Maynard Mack. Englewood Cliffs, N. J.: Prentice-Hall, 1967, 459 p.

Simpson, Claude M., ed. *The Local Colorists: American Short Stories, 1857-1900.* New York: Harper and Brothers Publishers, 1960, 340 p.

Stanton, Robert, ed. *The Short Story and the Reader.* New York: Henry Holt and Co., 1960, 557 p.

West, Ray B., Jr., ed. *American Short Stories.* New York: Thomas Y. Crowell Co., 1959, 267 p.

ISBN 0-8103-2555-1

9 780810 325555

90000>